NICHOLSON

→

COLOUR LONDON

KU-714-837

STREETFINDER

London Streetfinder
© Robert Nicholson Publications
1989
Based upon the Ordnance Survey Map
with the sanction of the Controller of Her
Majesty's Stationery Office. Crown
Copyright reserved.

London Information
© Robert Nicholson Publications
1989

All other maps
© Robert Nicholson Publications

London Underground map by kind
permission of London Transport.

Designed by Robert Nicholson and
Romek Marber

Published and distributed by
Robert Nicholson Publications
16 Golden Square
London W1R 4BN

Great care has been taken throughout
this book to be accurate but the
publishers cannot accept responsibility
for any errors which appear, or their
consequences.

Printed in Great Britain by
Cradley Print plc,
Wardley, West Midlands

ISBN 0 948576 27 8

85/3/690

Symbols

† Church

✚ Hospital

🚗 Car park

🏛 Historic buildings

🚌 Small buildings

🎒 Schools

🏟 Sports stadium

⊖ London Underground station

🢆 British Rail station

🚌 Coach station

✈ Air terminal

🢆 British Rail terminal

PO Post Office

Pol Police station

→ One ways (central area only)

::::: Footpath

▮ Park, Golf Course Sports Field
Recreation Ground Garden

▮ Cemetery Allotment Heath
Down Open Space

300 ▶
◀ 400 Figure indicating the direction
of street numbering and the
approximate position

Outer area

▭ ½ mile

▭ ½ km

Large scale Central area

▭ ½ mile

▭ ½ km

ROBERT NICHOLSON PUBLICATIONS

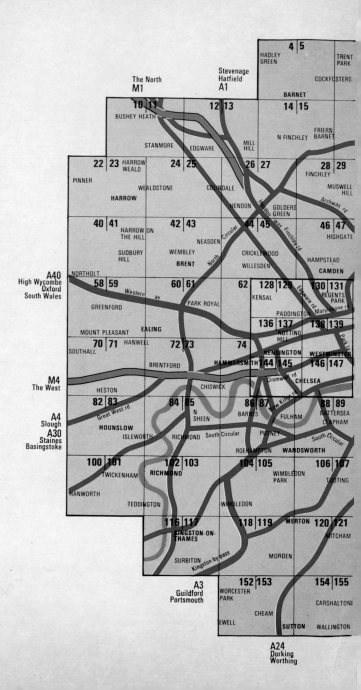

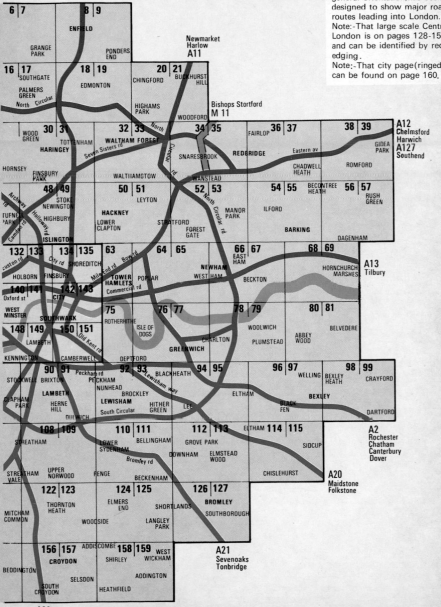

Key to map pages

This general map, apart from giving map numbers and general orientation, has been designed to show major road routes leading into London. Note:-That large scale Central London is on pages 128-151 and can be identified by red edging.
Note:-That city page (ringed on 1 can be found on page 160.

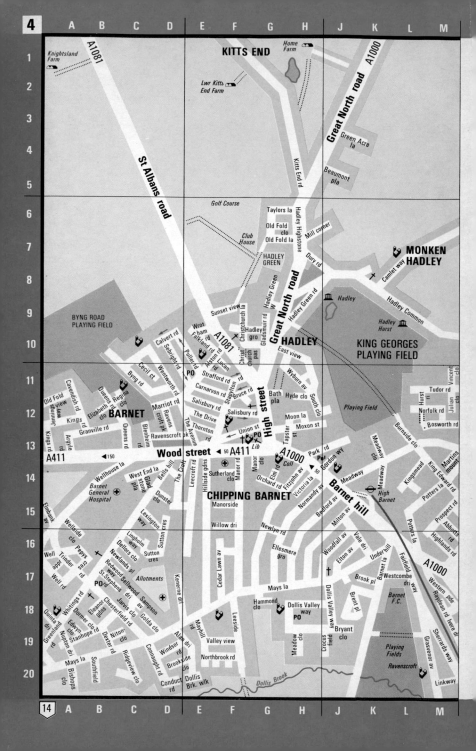

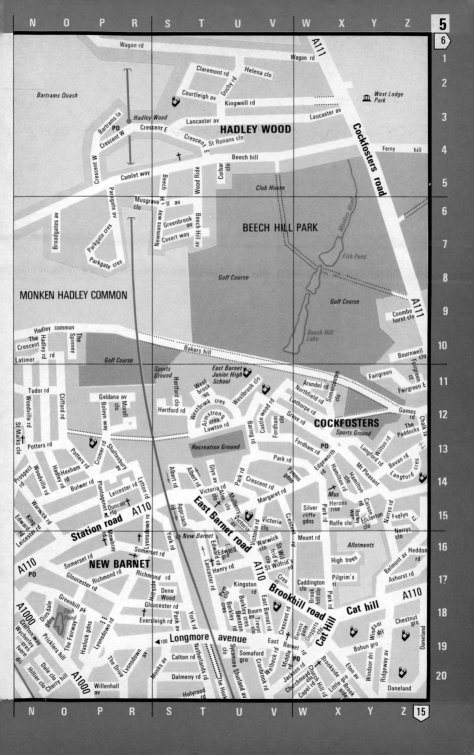

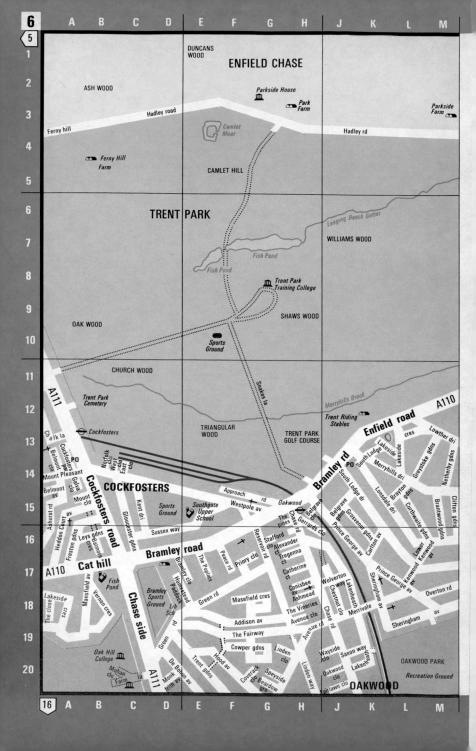

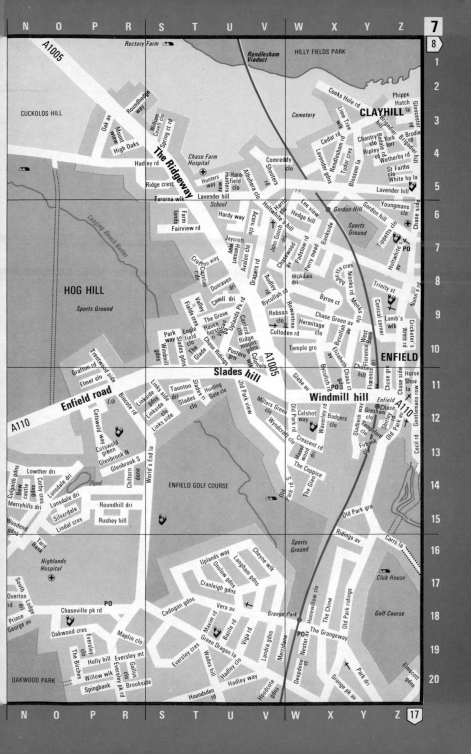

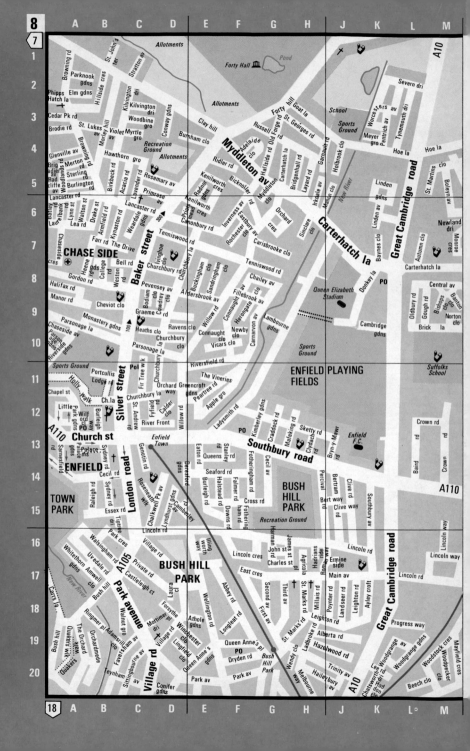

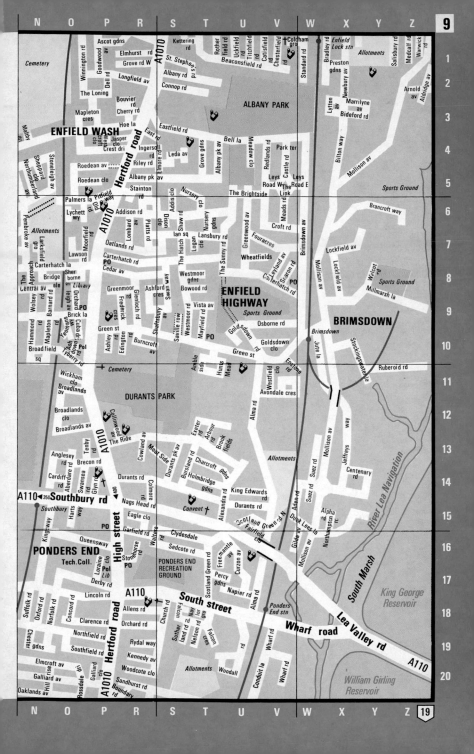

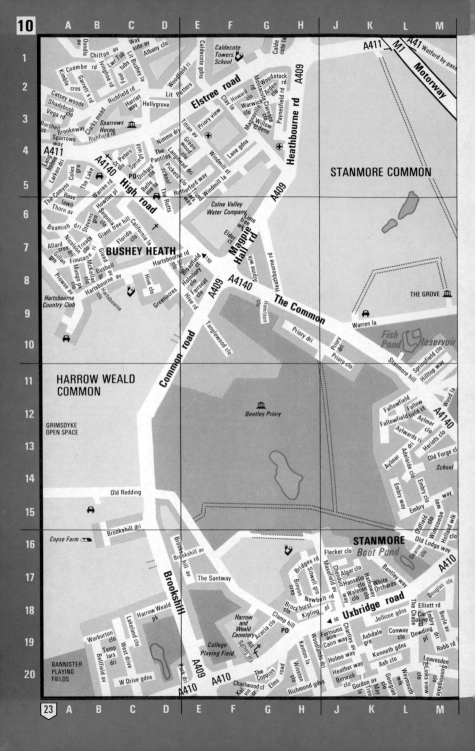

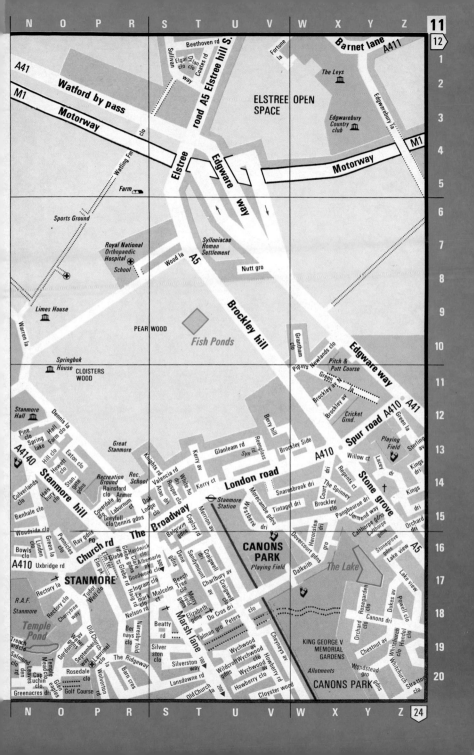

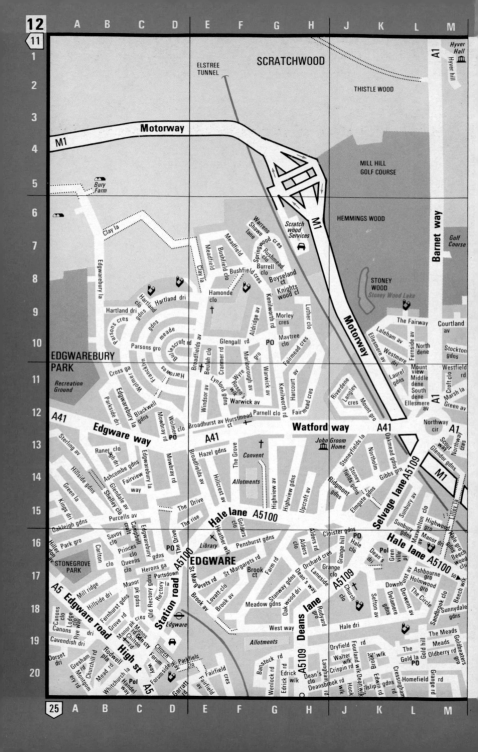

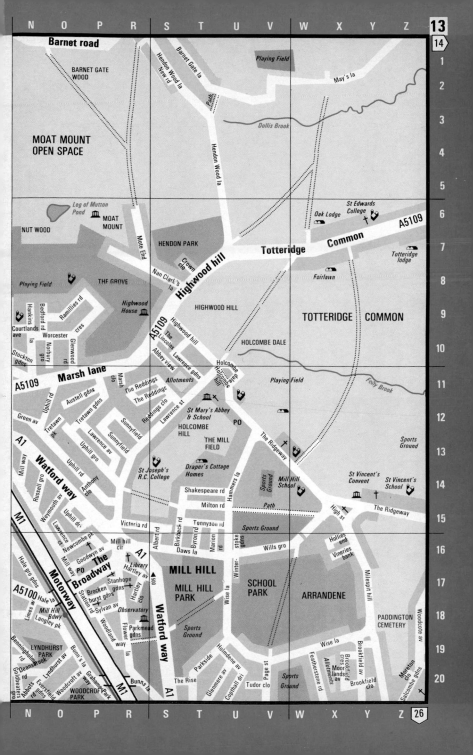

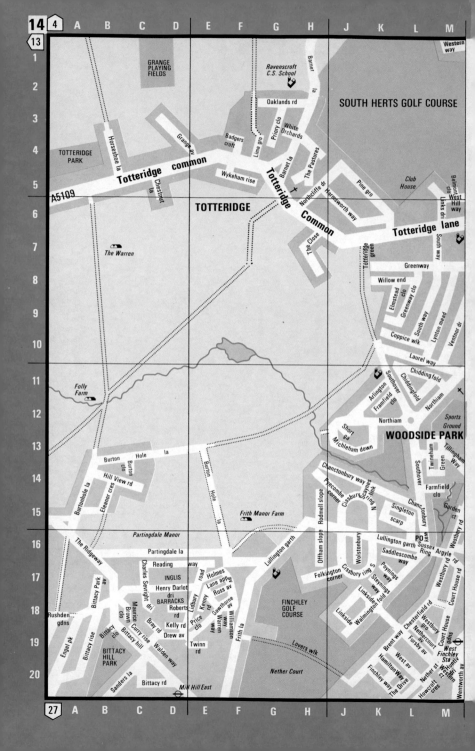

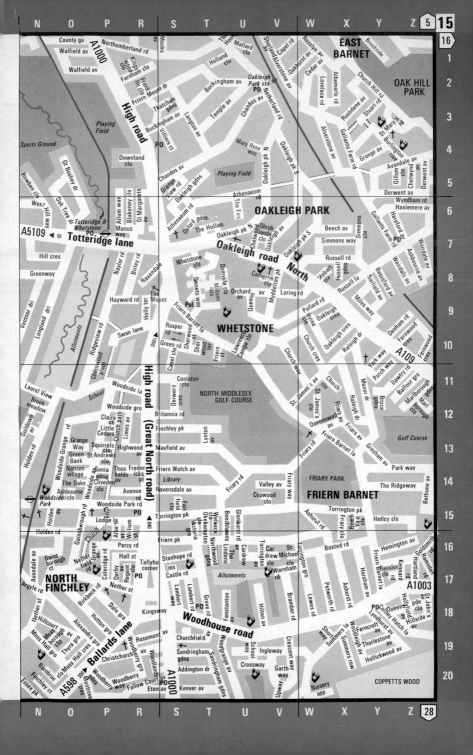

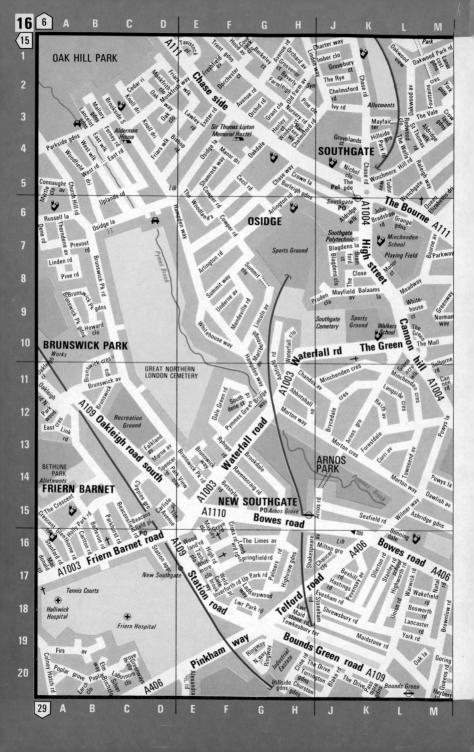

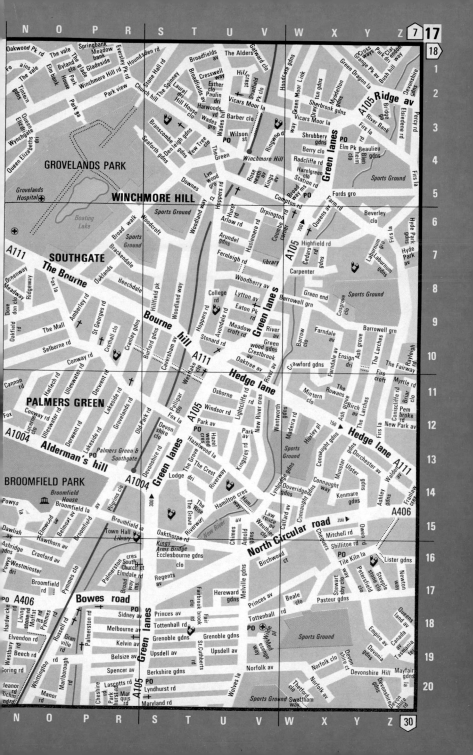

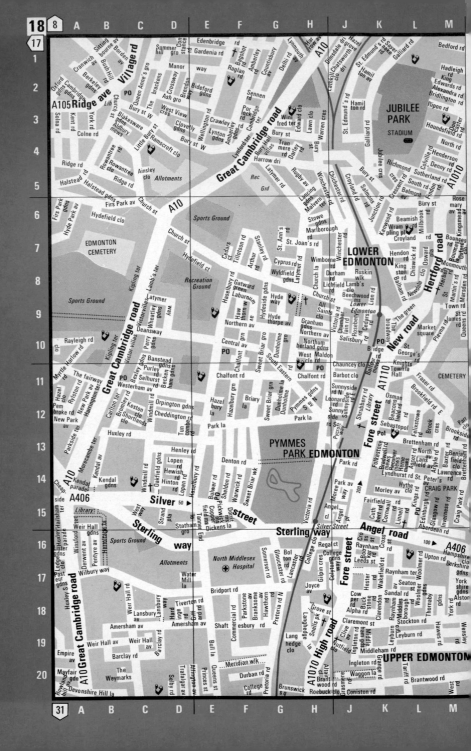

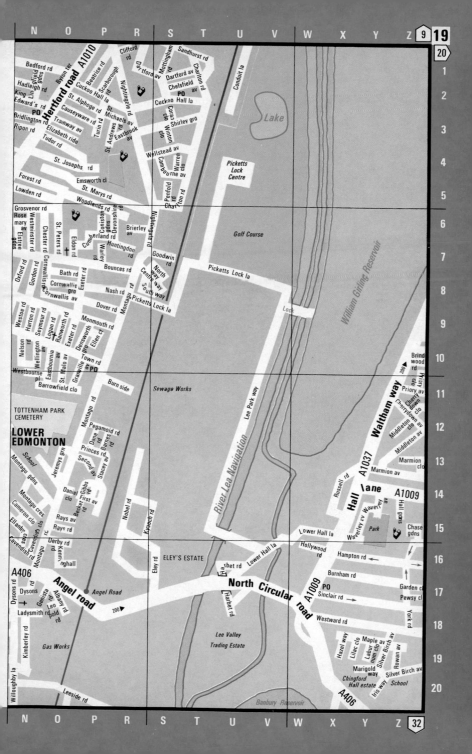

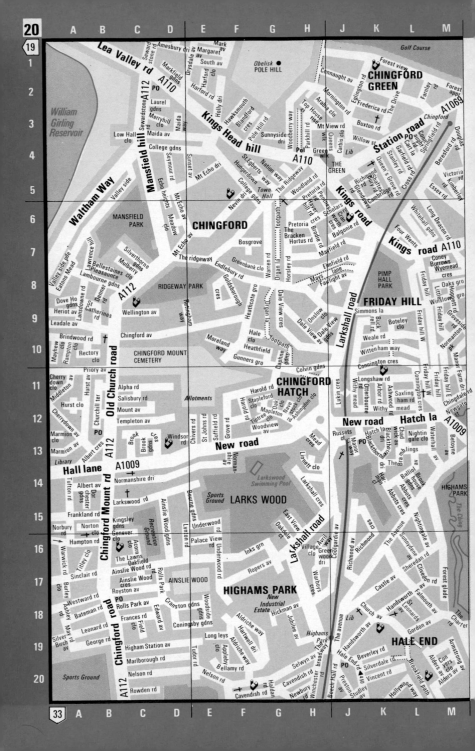

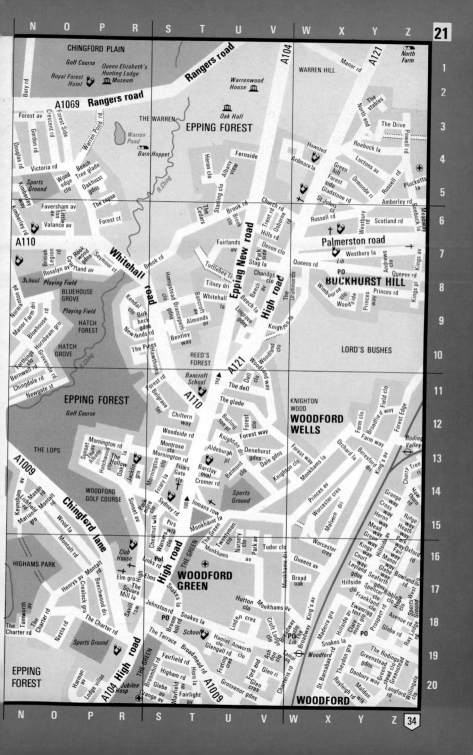

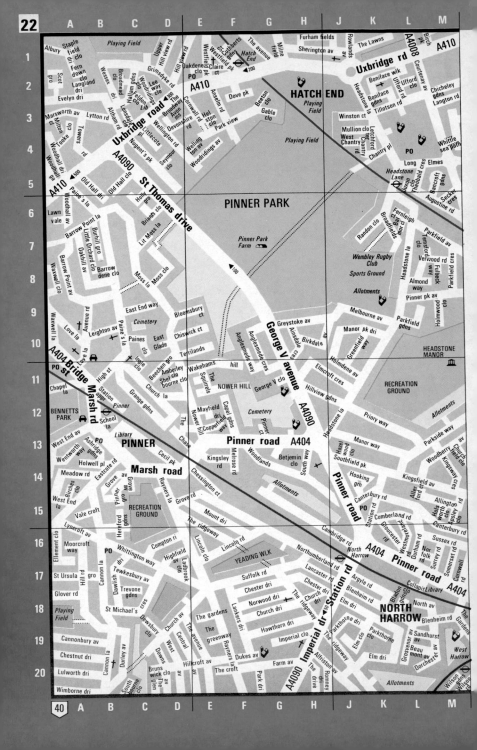

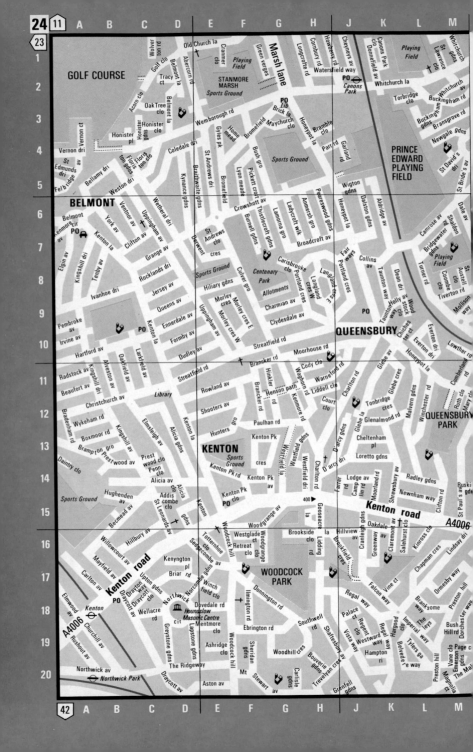

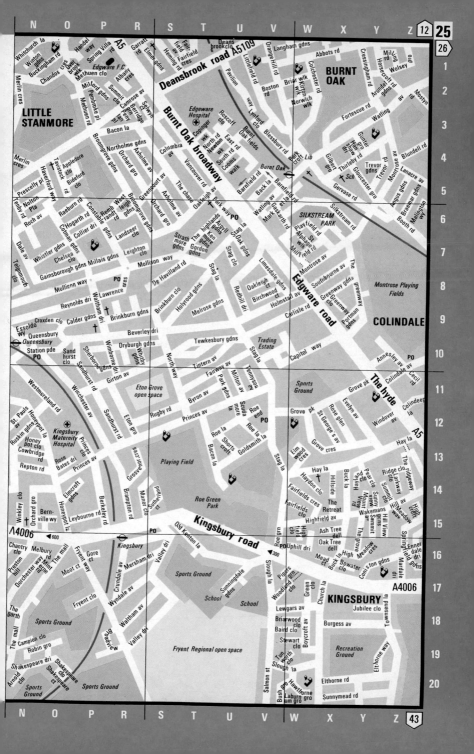

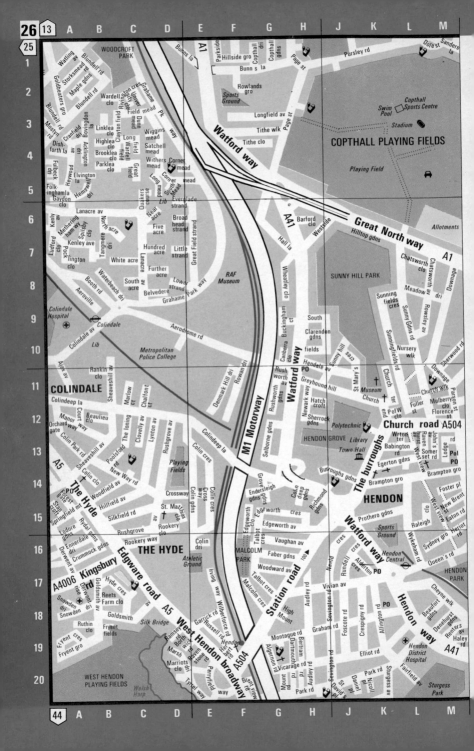

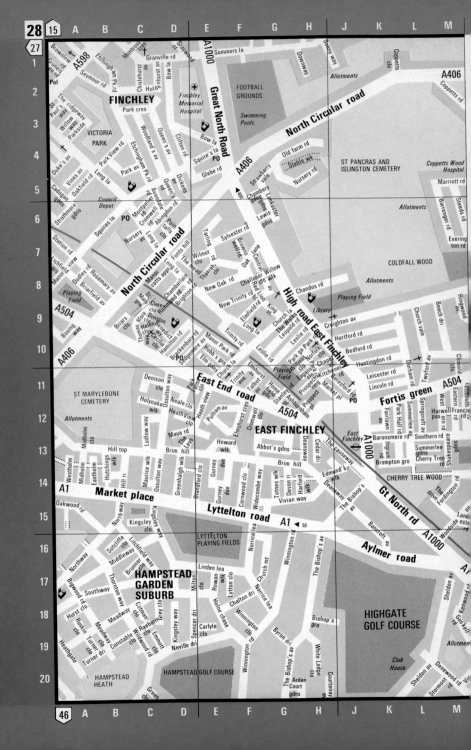

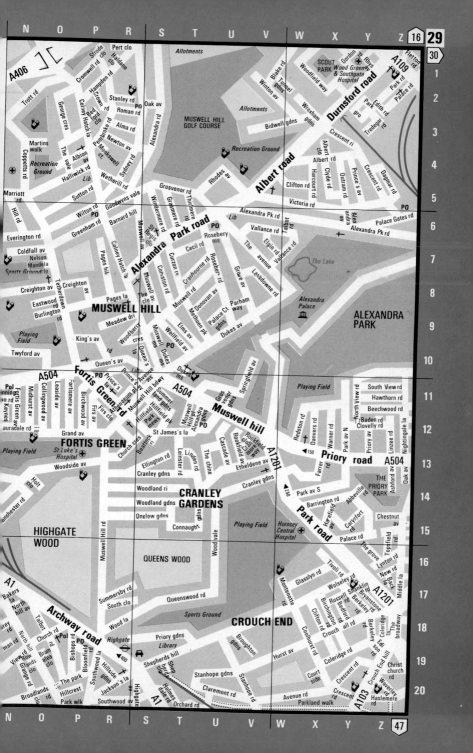

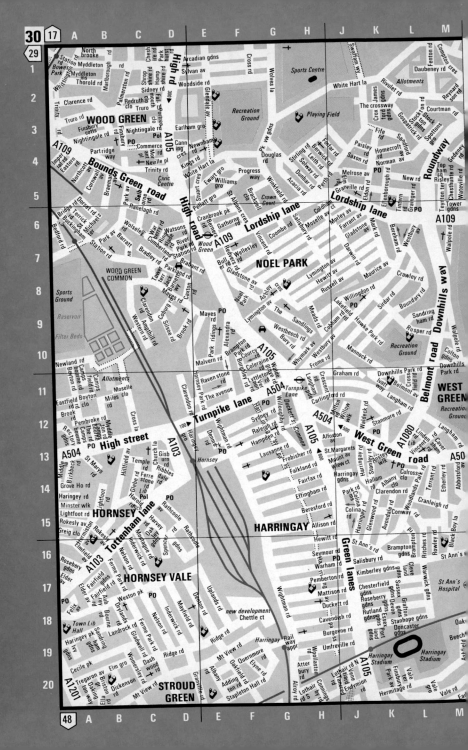

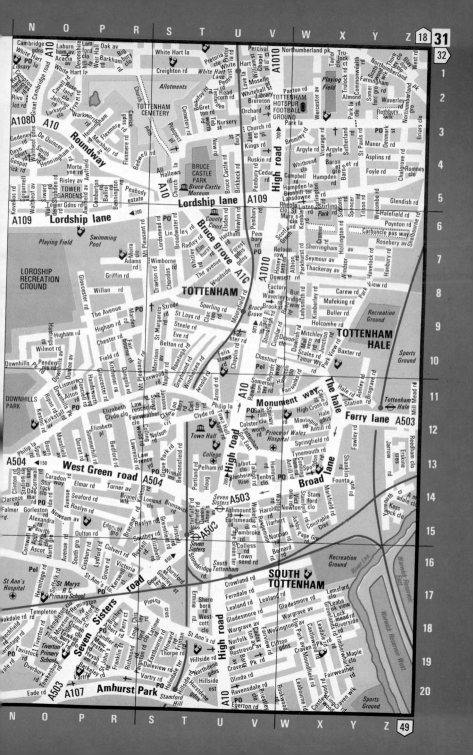

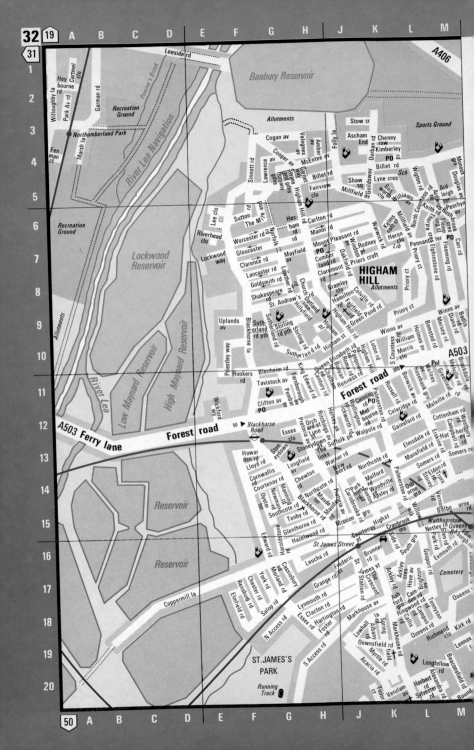

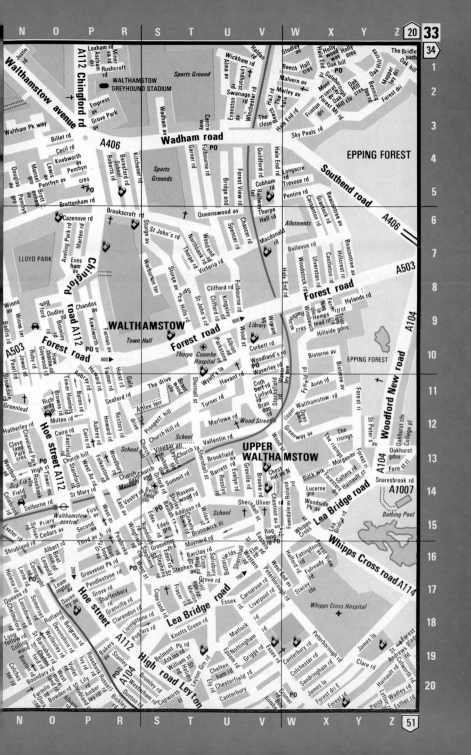

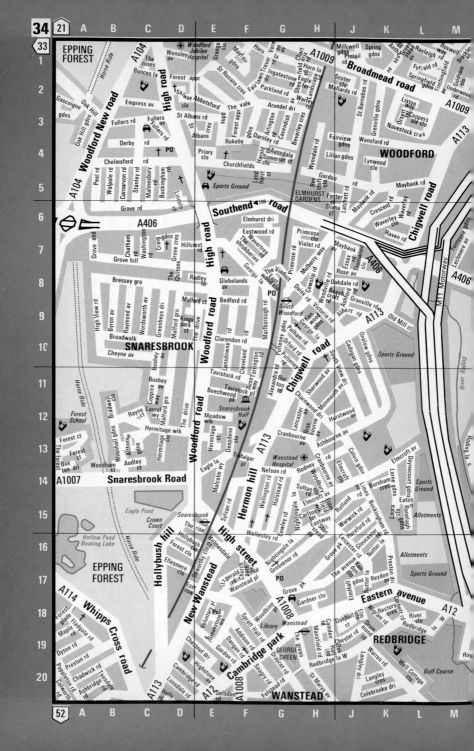

WOODFORD BRIDGE

Claybury Hospital
Tomswood rd

Gaynes Hill rd

Brackley sq
Beaumaris dri

Uplands end
Uplands rd
Canfield rd
Highfield rd
Crownhill rd
Gales way
Claybury rd
Woodbridge rd
Viscount rd

Claybury Hall

Forest House

Henkstones way
A113
Broadmead rd

Challond wik
M11 Motorway

HOSPITAL HILL WOOD

Sports Ground

Claybury Farm

Ravensbourne
Wadley
Waverley gdns
Caemarvon dri
Calne av

Hospital Farm

Cemetery

Roding la N
Playing Field

Repton
ct gro
Repton clo
Copper beech clo
Wiffin av
Moore av

Wyfields
Bysouth clo

SOUTH WOODFORD

Kensington dri
Marston rd
Wensleydale gdns
Naseby rd
The glade
Humphry clo
Fullwell av
Hurstleigh gdns
Barrington rd
Basildon av
Clifford av
Ryecroft av
Jerningham av

Westview dri
Rivington av
Summit av
Hillington gdns
Chalgrove cres
Wensleydale av
Roundway
Atherton rd
Harewood av
St Clair clo
Cheriton av
Caterham av
Kirkland av
Stratford av
Dovedale av
Dacre av
Kirkland av
Sheldon av
Berkeley av
Dunspring la
Purley clo
Belvedere av
Keiston rd
Ashie

Lambs mw
N View
dri
Portman dri
Bodly la N
Peel dri
Ewellhurst rd
Cruchmore av
Cottesmore av

A406 Southend road

Sports Ground
PO
Clayhall av
Stradbroke av
Brinkworth
Marlborough dri
Stradbroke gro
Marlands rd
Mellows rd
Lessingham av
Clayhall av

Anderson rd
School
Sports Ground
Clavbury bdwy
Gayfere rd
Heather
Maitlands cley
Cleudace av
Lord av
Werneth Hall rd
Dymchurch clo
Tiverton av
Tiptree
Cemetery
Beaminster gdns
Hatfield

Roding la S
Stoneleigh rd
Griel gdns
Herent dri
Stradbroke gro
Wray av
Evesham way
Rushden gdns
Longwood gdns
Greenleafe dri
Dakleafe gdns
Mapleleafe
Greenleafe dri

Woodford Bridge rd
School

Woodford Bridge Lodge rd
Borrondale clo
Coniston gdns
Lord View rd
Lord av
Abbotswood gdns
Dellwood gdns
Monkswood gdns
Earlswood gdns
Beattyville gdns
Glenthorne gdns
Gaysham hall
Woodville gdns
Greenleafe

REDBRIDGE
CLAYHALL PARK

Roding la s
Carswell gdns
Whitney rd
Rec Grd
Widecombe clo
Derwent gdns
Brantwood gdns
Hedgley
Longwood gdns
Wychwood gdns
Rosedene
Thorpedale gdns
Sunnymede dri
Georgeville gdns

Woodford avenue

Falmouth gdns
Lakeside av
Leigh av
Merrivale av
Peaketon av
Keswick gdns
Keswick gdns
Grasmere gdns
PO
Ambleside gdns
Ridgeway gdns
East
lane
Highwood
Beechwood
Collinwood
Hedgeman
gdns
Kenwood gdns
Bronte clo
Southwood gdns
Little Gearies

Mighell av
Fowey av
Bergholt av
College gdns
Grangeway gdns
Sotersby gdns
Bealve la
Gantshill cres
Kenwood gdns
Cranbrook road
A123

Mighell
av
Trylan clo
Highcliffe gdns
Falmouth gdns
Redbridge
Copsford gdns
Glenwood
Gantshill cres
Gantshill
Louisdown av
Pershore clo
Icknield av

Cobbetts
Vista dri
The Mews
Fairmead gdns
Edwina gdns
Wycombe rd
Avery gdns
Roll gdns
Shere rd
Gaysham av
Glenham dri

Avondale dri
Rosemary dri
Fenhall dri
Crombie cl
Radnor cres
Ethelbert gdns
A406
Roll gdns
Martley dr
Parham dri
Otley dri
Headley dri appr
Otley dri
Ashurst

Redbridge lane East
Margaret way
PO
Windermere
Inglehurst gdns
Essex rd
Beehive la
Lib
Head
PO
A12

A12
150
Evanston gdns
Castle dri
Castleview gdns
Preston gdns
Devonport gdns
Hill View cres
Clarence rd
The crescent
Panfield
Frinton
Bramley cres
ms
Lons dale cres
Perth rd
South View
Lynton cres
A12
500
Albemarle gdns
Middleton gdns

Eastern avenue

Studley
Wanstead la
Stoneha/ av
Cranbrook
St. Helens rd
Blenheim rd
St. Edmunds rd
Mornington av
GANTS HILL
Middleton gd
lefield gdns

Carlisle gdns
Wakefield
Canterbury gdns
Worcester gdns
Ely gdns
Hereford gdns
Fairholme
Emerson rd
VALENTINES PARK

Wanstead Pk rd
A406
Sydon rd
St. George's rise
PO
A123 Cranbrook rd
The Mansion

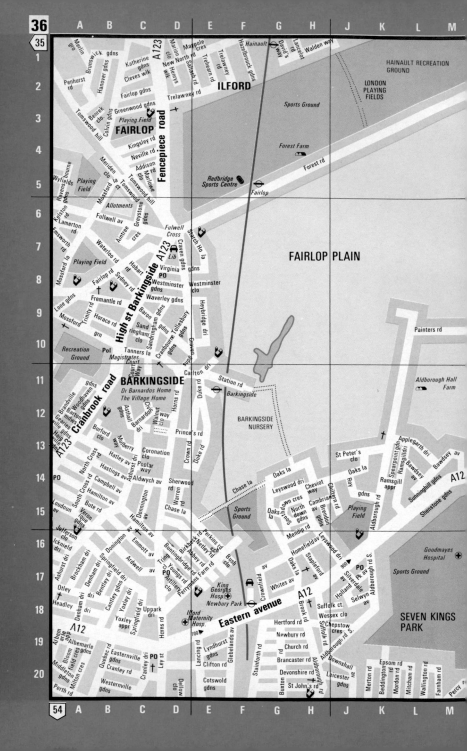

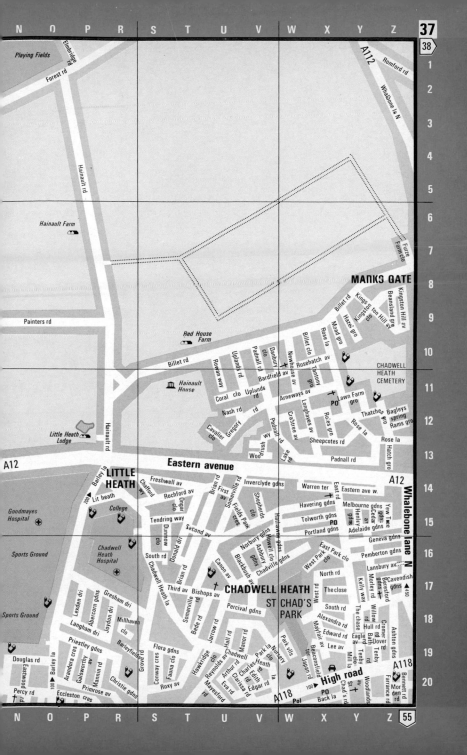

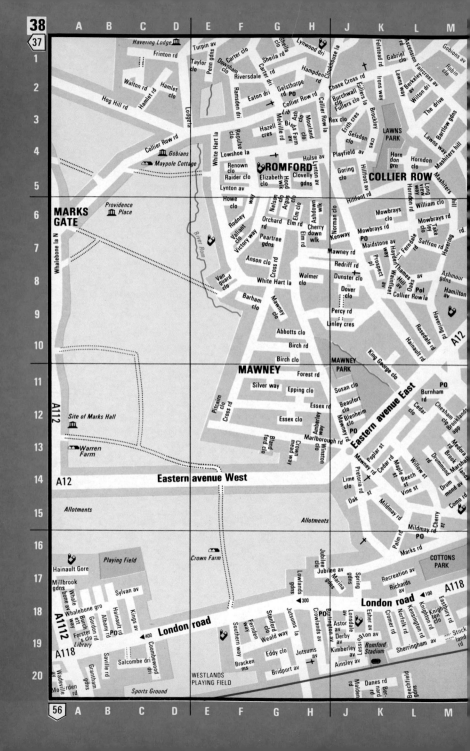

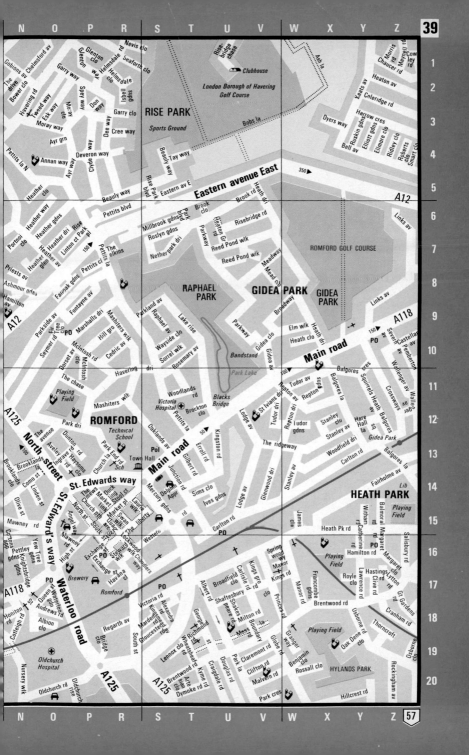

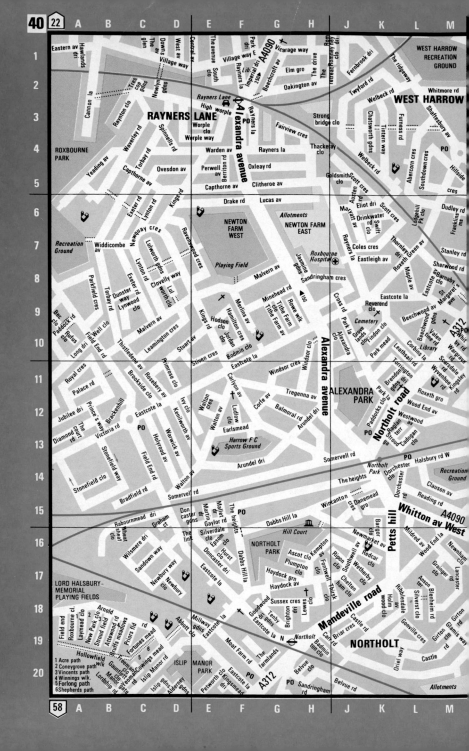

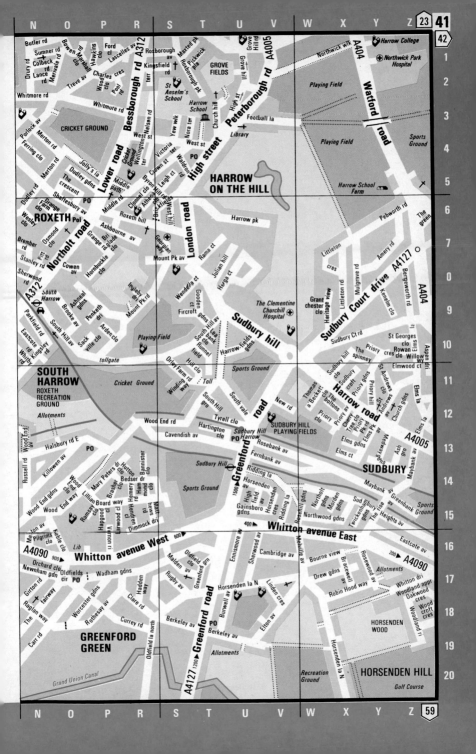

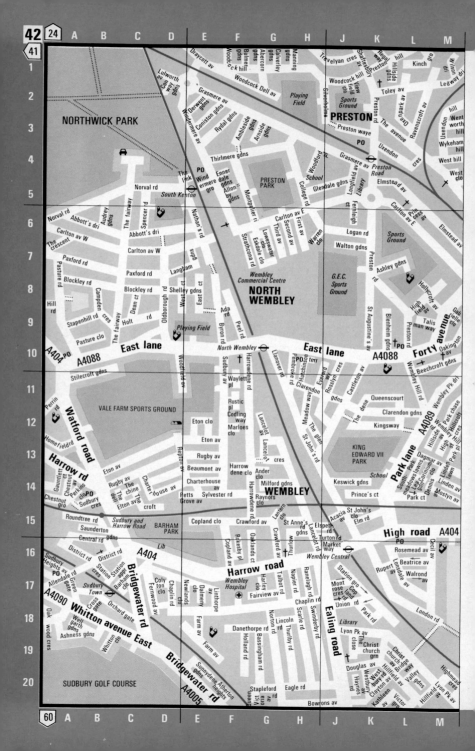

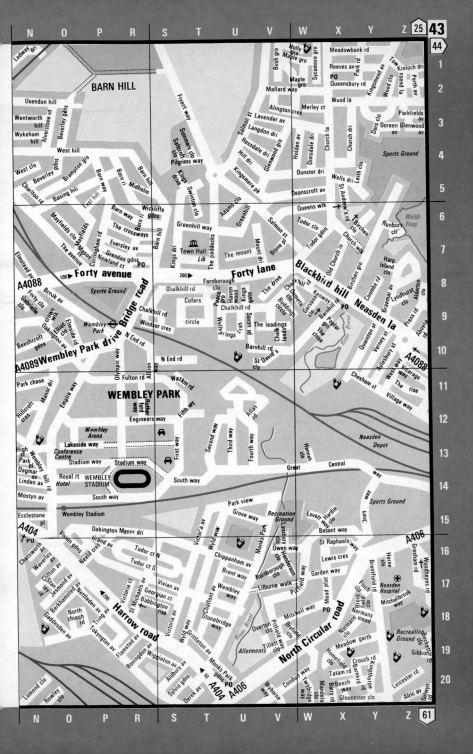

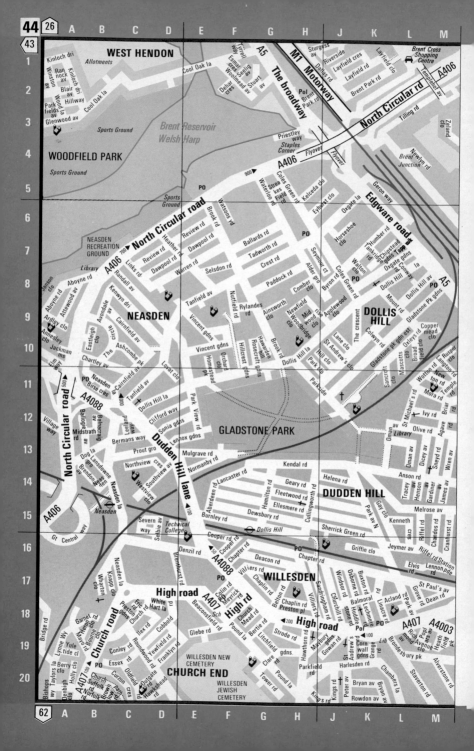

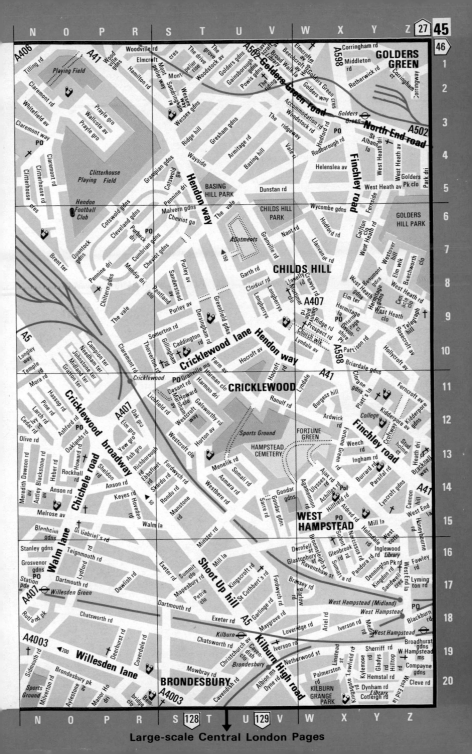

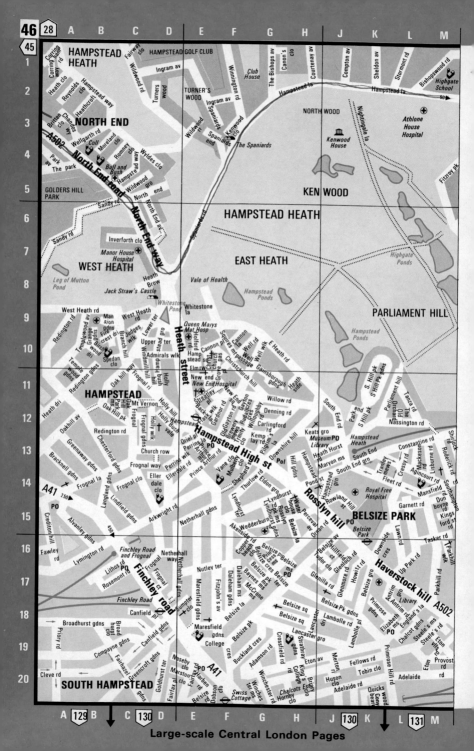

Large-scale Central London Pages

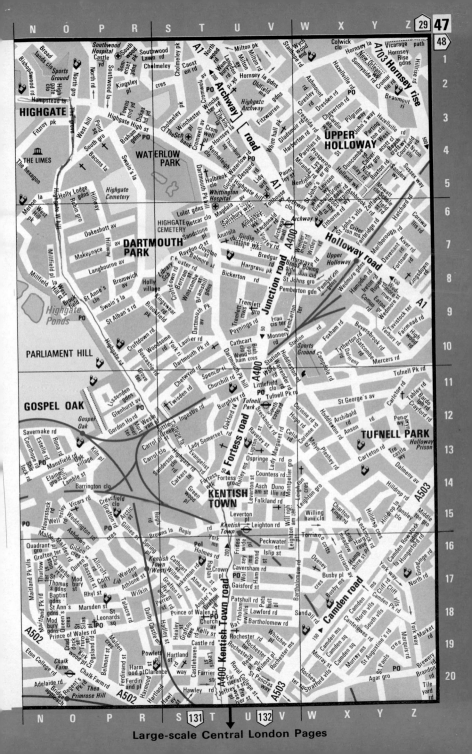

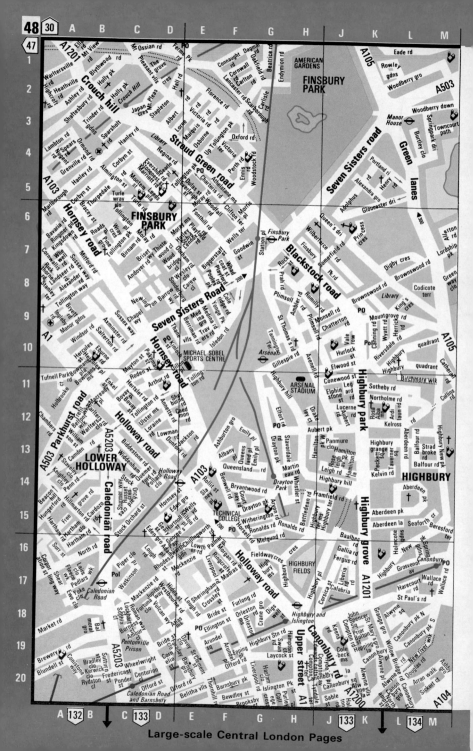
Large-scale Central London Pages

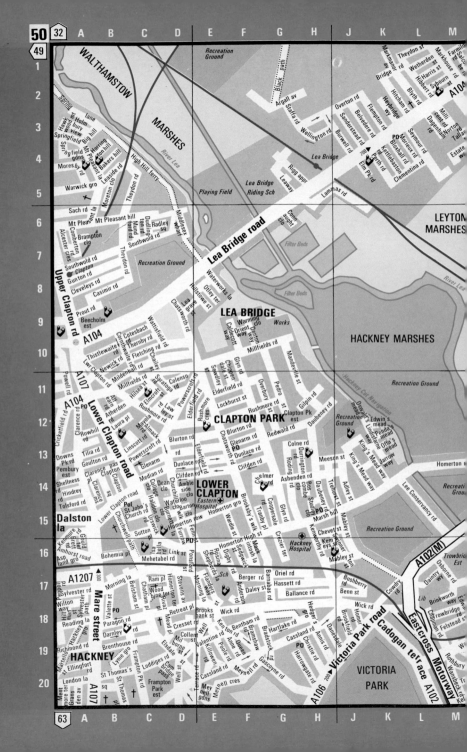

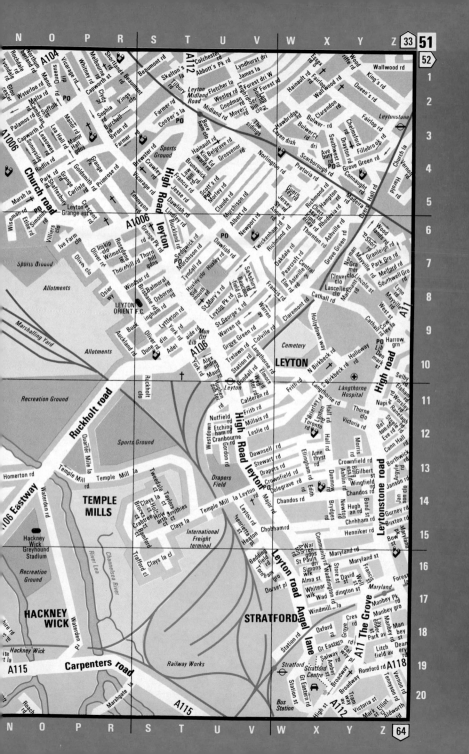

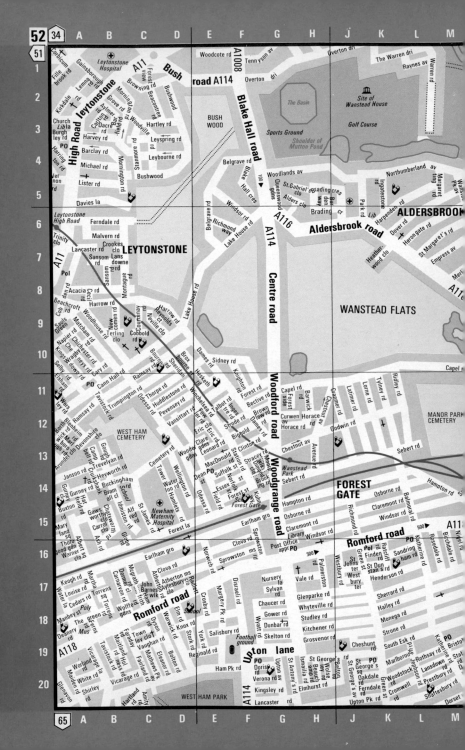

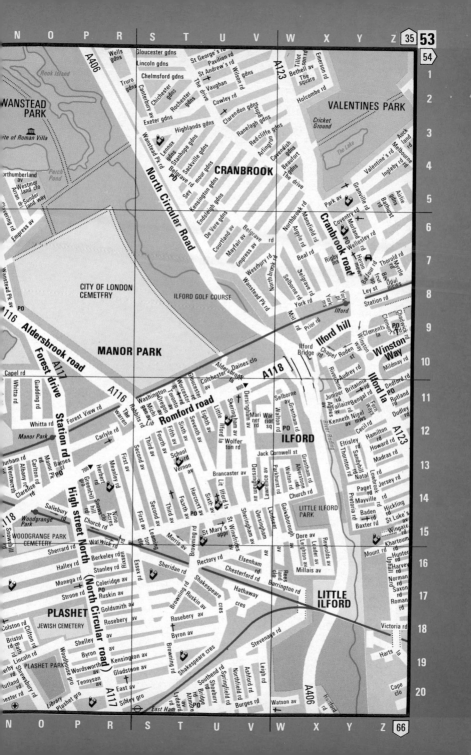

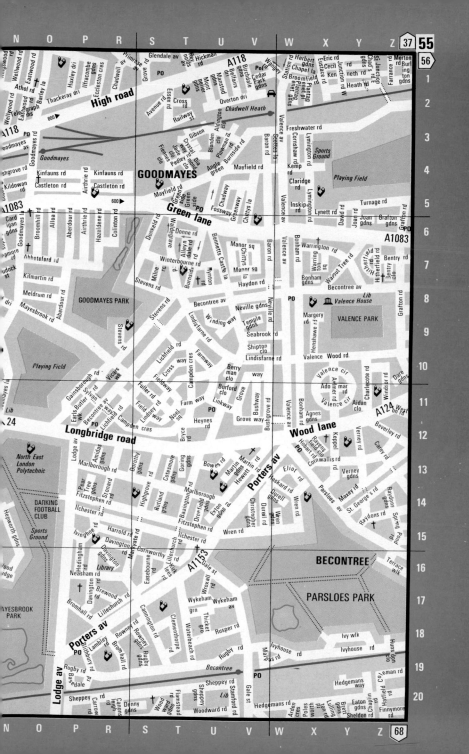

This is a map of the Goodmayes, Becontree, and Chadwell Heath area.

GOODMAYES

BECONTREE

PARSLOES PARK

High road

Green lane

Longbridge road

Wood lane

Porters av

Lodge av

Chadwell Heath

GOODMAYES PARK

VALENCE PARK

Valence House

Lib

North East London Polytechnic

DARKING FOOTBALL CLUB

Sports Ground

Playing Field

Sports Ground

AYESBROOK PARK

A118

A1083

A124 West

A1153

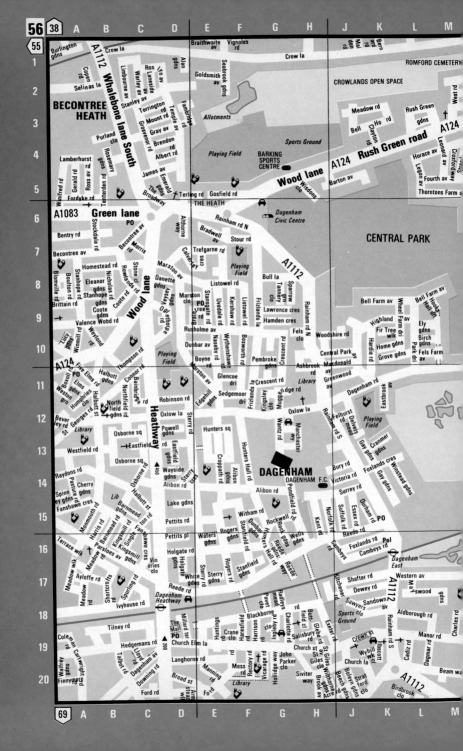

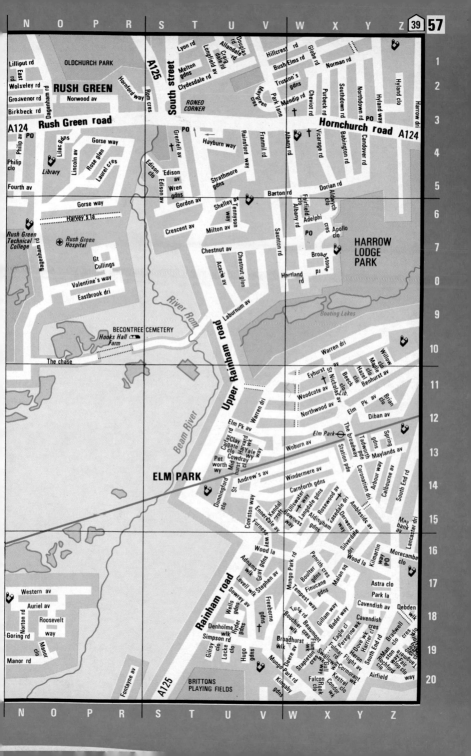

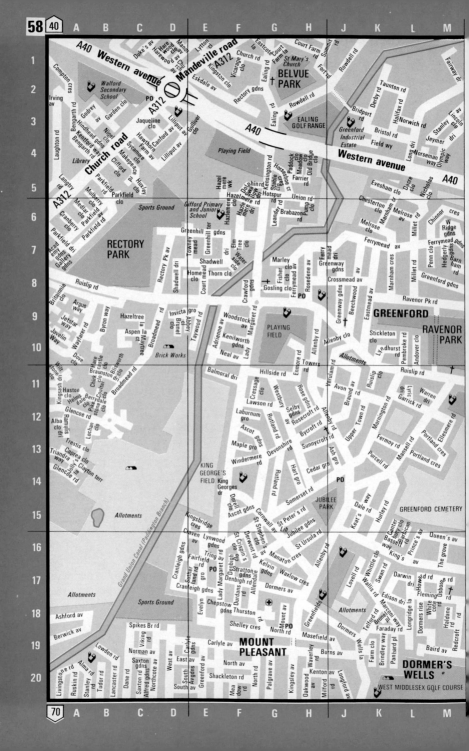

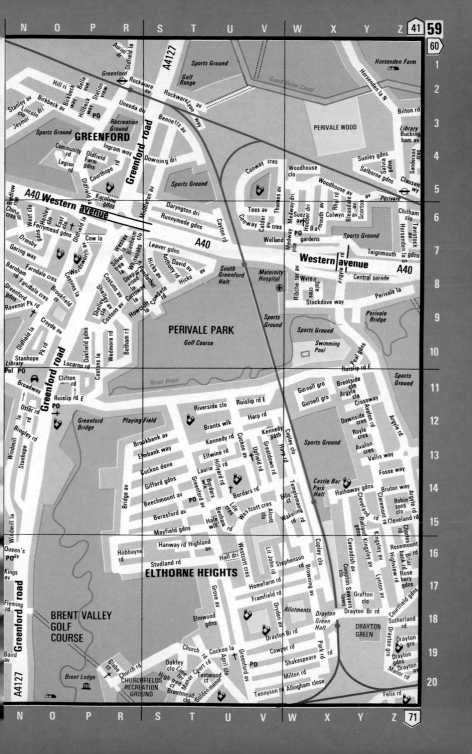

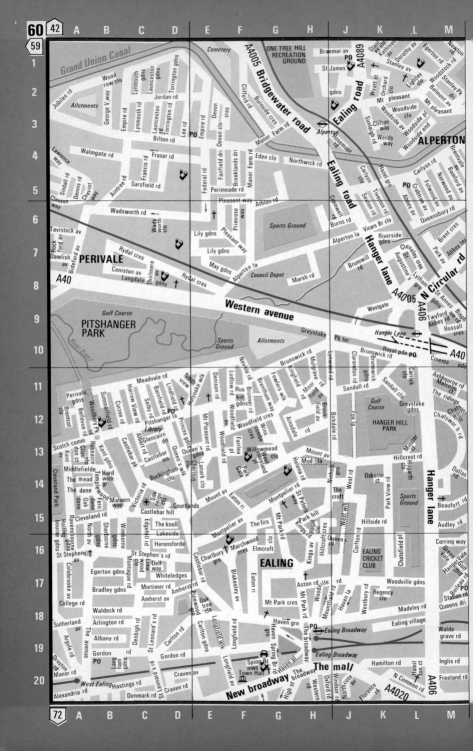

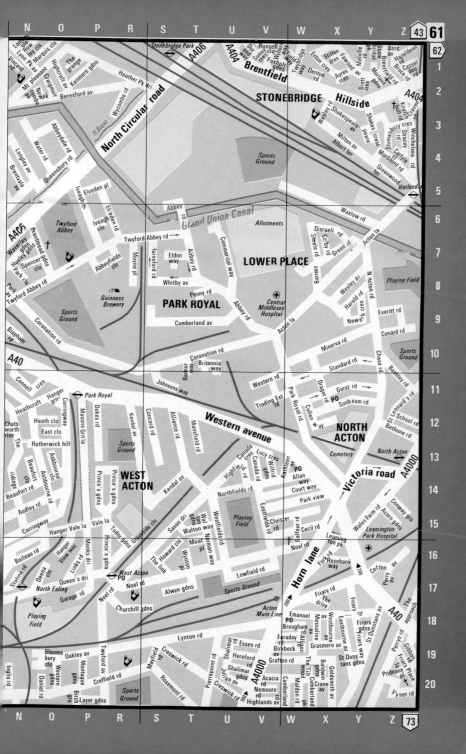

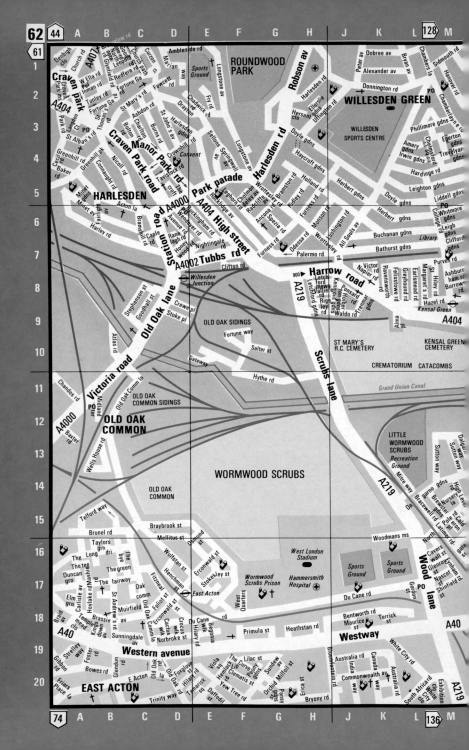

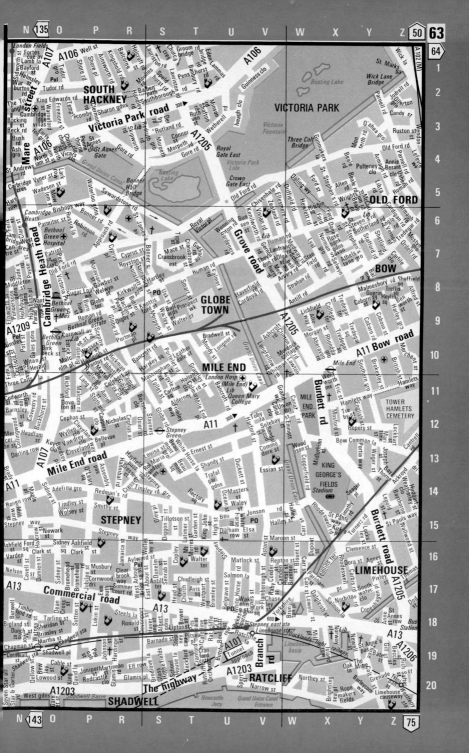

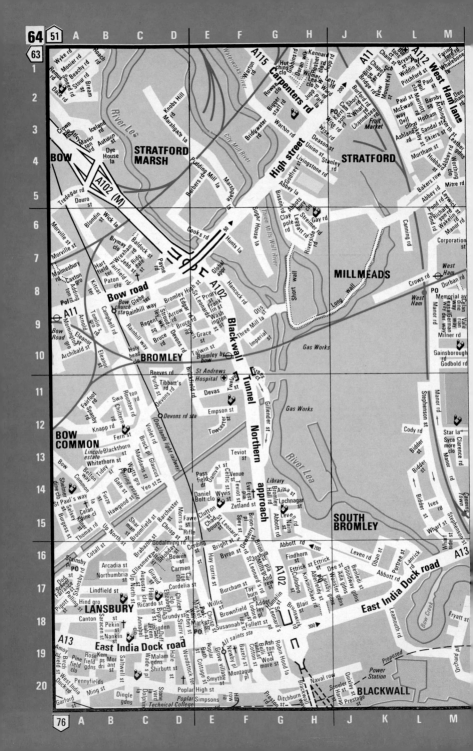

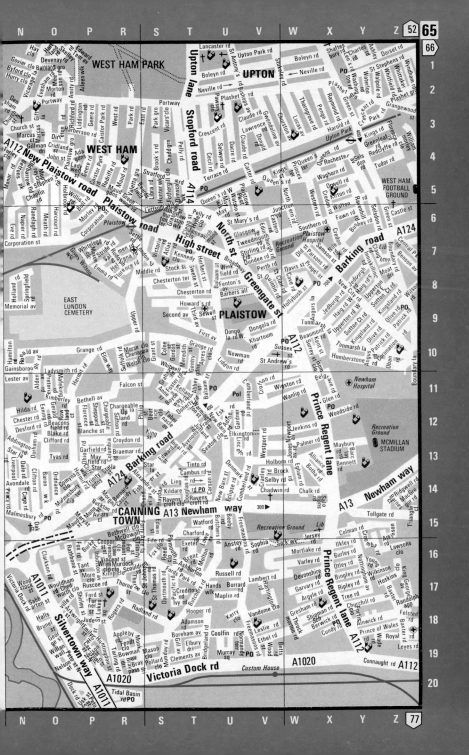

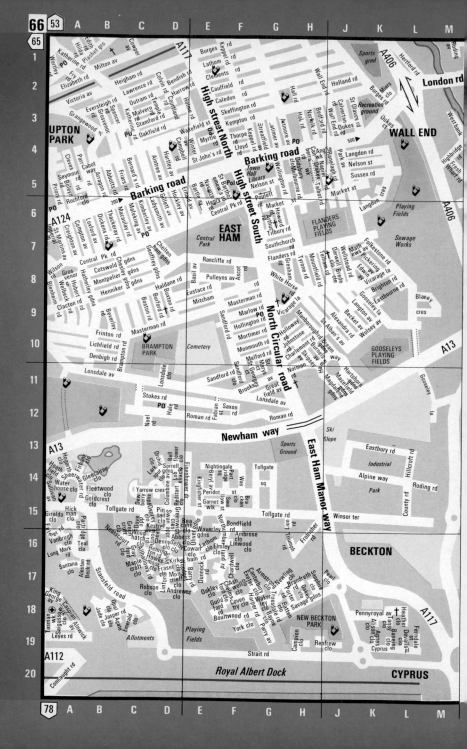

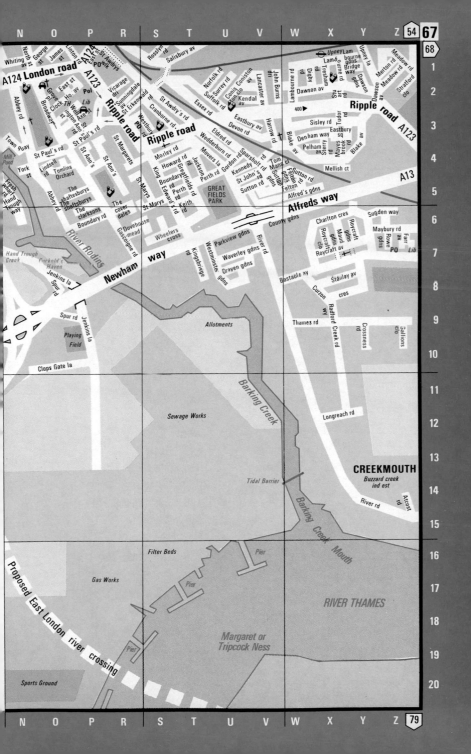

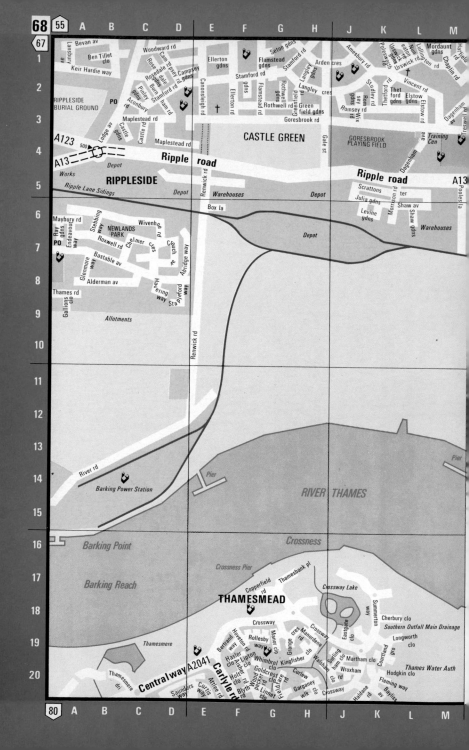

A B C D E F G H J K L M

1
2
3
4
5
6
7
8
9
10
11
12
13
14
15
16
17
18
19
20

Bevan av
Lansbury av
Ben Tillet clo
Keir Hardie way
Woodward rd
Crum rd
Rosedale
Campsey rd
Stamford rd
Ellerton gdns
Flamstead gdns
Seton gdns
Stamford rd
Arden cres
Amesbury rd
Poleswdth
Urswick
Nun eastrd
Mordaunt gdns
Hartshorne
Chaplin rd

RIPPLESIDE BURIAL GROUND
PO
Pinley
Bann
Stamford rd
Banham rd
Aconbury
Stamford rd
Canonsleigh rd
Ellerton rd
Flamstead rd
Rothwell rd
Rothwell rd
Green field gdns
Greenhill
Langley gdns
Langley cres
Studley rd
Romsey
Wix
Thetford gdns
Elstow gdns
Elstow rd
Dagenham

Maplestead rd
Lodge av
Castle gdns
Castle rd
CASTLE GREEN
Goresbrook rd
GORESBROOK PLAYING FIELD
Training Cen

A123
500
Maplestead rd
Ripple road
Gale st
Dagenham ave

A13
Depot
Works
RIPPLESIDE
Ripple Lane Sidings
Depot
Warehouses
Depot
Ripple road
Scrattons
A13
Poolesla

Box la
Julia gdns
Morrison rd
Shaw av
Shaw gdns

Maybury rd
Ray gdns
PO
Endeavour way
Stebbing way
Wivenhoe rd
NEWLANDS PARK
Roxwell rd
Chelmer cres
Couch rd
Abridge way
Depot
Levine gdns
Warehouses

Glenmore way
Bastable av
Alderman av
Havering way
Pleford
Sta

Thames rd
Gallions clo
Allotments
Renwick rd

River rd
Barking Power Station
Pier
RIVER THAMES
Pier

Barking Point
Crossness
Barking Reach
Crossness Pier
Thamesbank pl
Crossway Lake
Crossway
Summerton way
Cherbury clo
Southern Outfall Main Drainage

Copperfield rd
THAMESMEAD
Crossway
Manordene cres
Manordene
Crossway
Eastgate clo
Longworth clo

Thamesmere
Bertrand way
Hoveton way
Rollesby way
Manor clo
glang
Wolsham rd
Selling ham rd
Martham clo
Wroxham clo
Longworth
gro
Thames Water Auth
Hodgkin clo

Thamesmere dri
Hasler clo
Linton clo
Alsher rd
Whimbrel clo
Kingfisher clo
Curlew
Garganey
Safling rd
Courtland
Fleming way
Bayliss
Hodgkin clo

Centralway A2041
Carlyle rd
Saunders way
Corfis way
Attlee rd
Holt rd
Blyth rd
Wood
Goldcrest clo
Field
Linnet clo
wlk
Crossway
Haldane av

A B C D E F G H J K L M

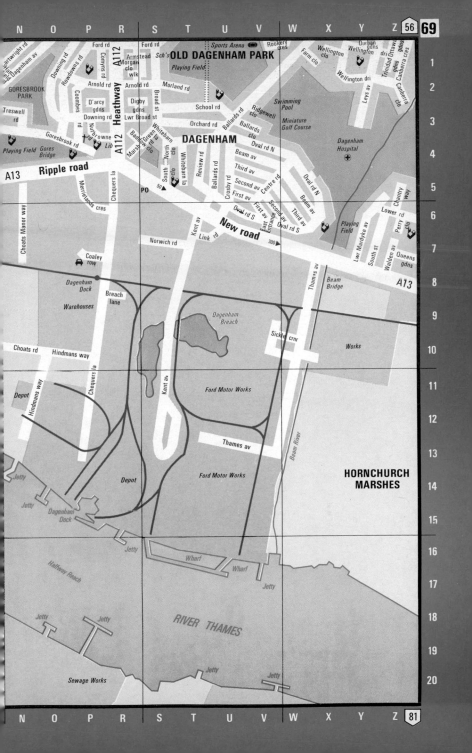

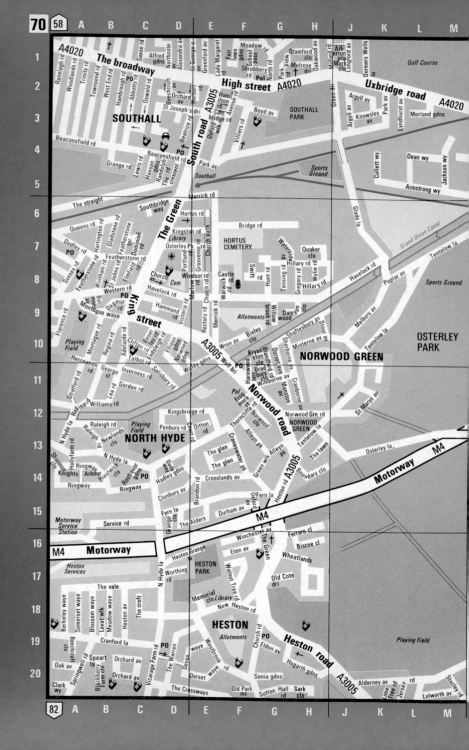

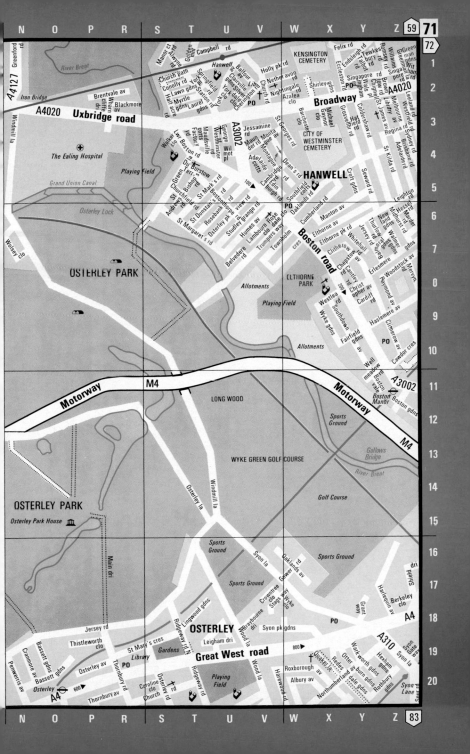

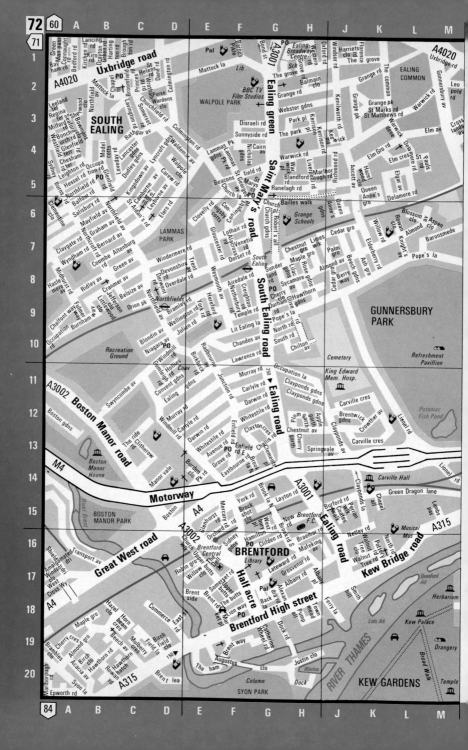

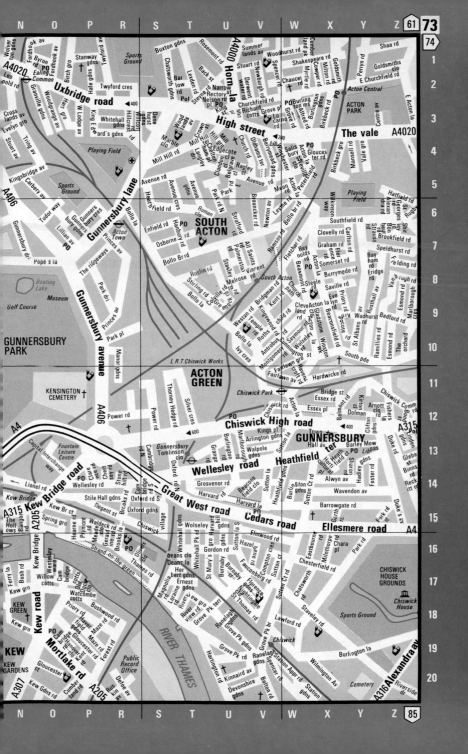

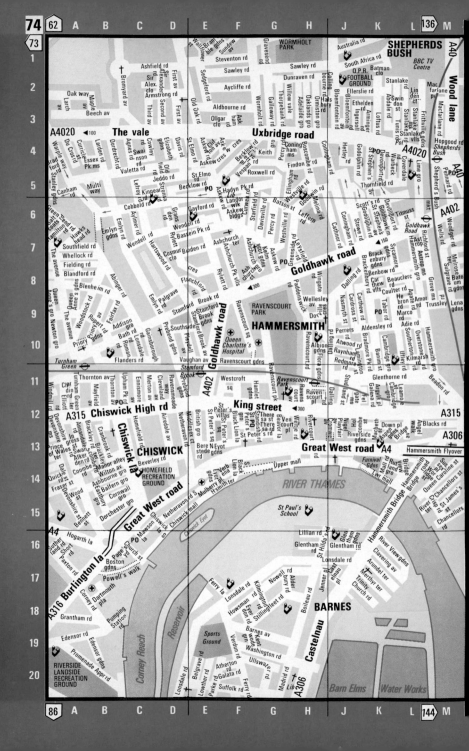

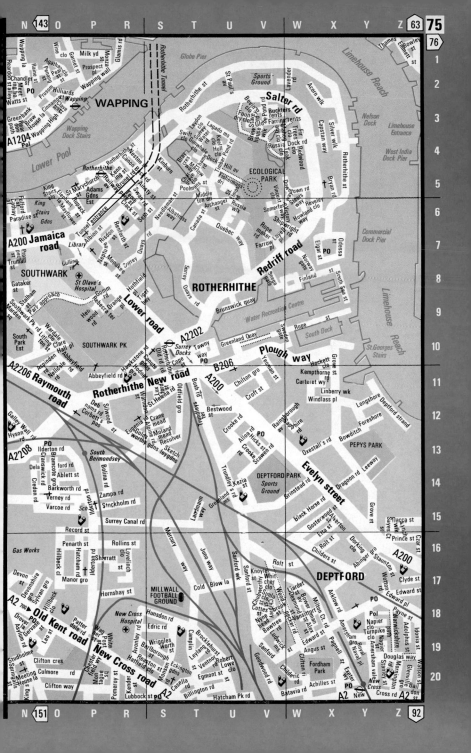

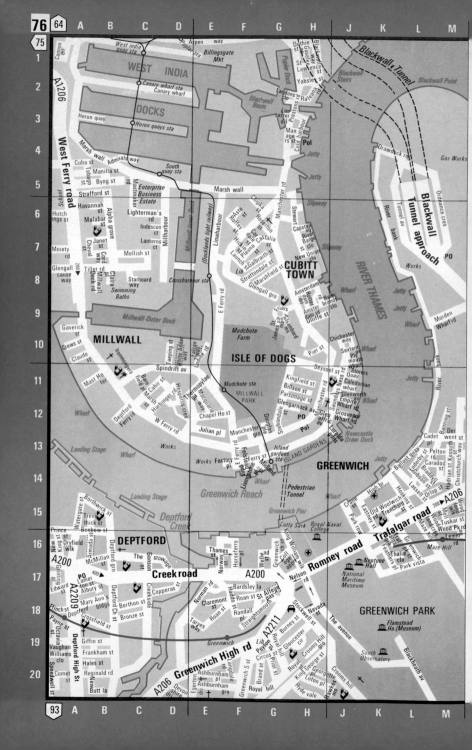

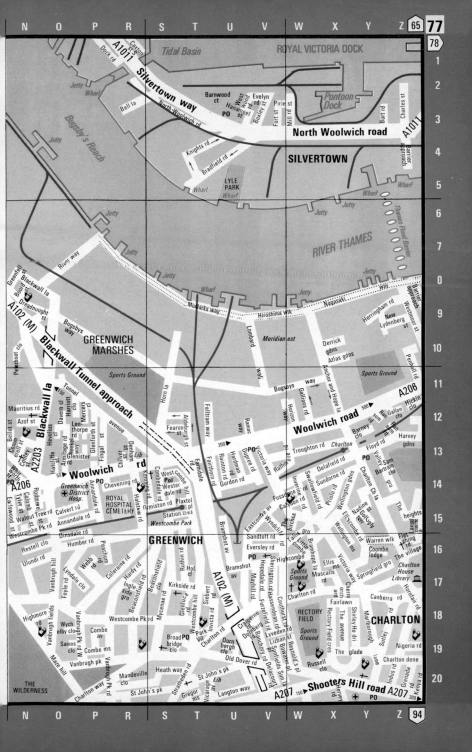

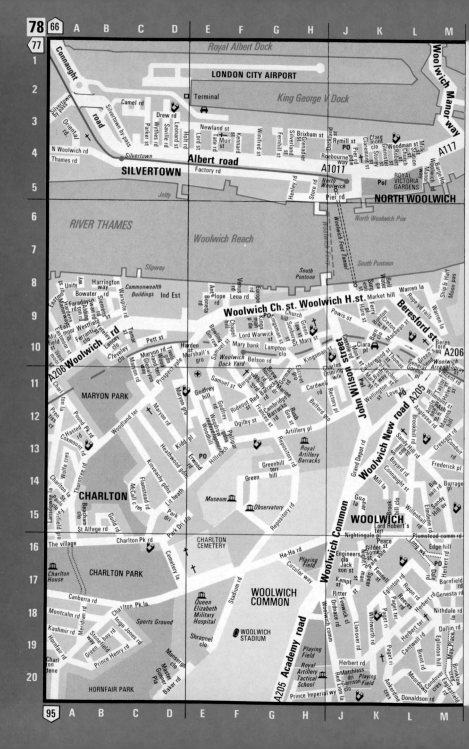

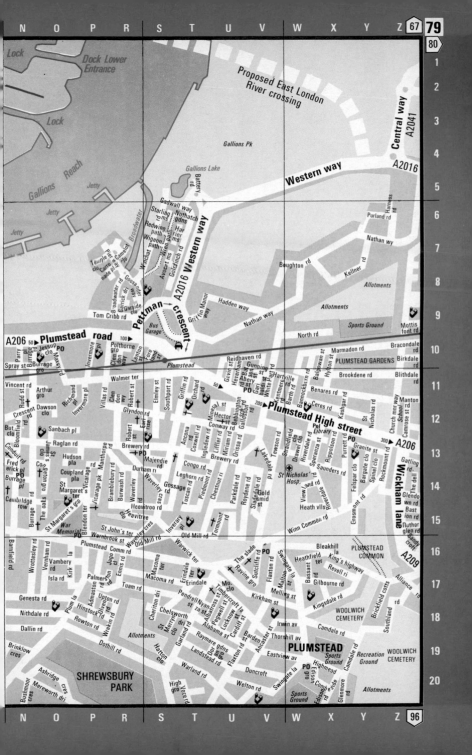

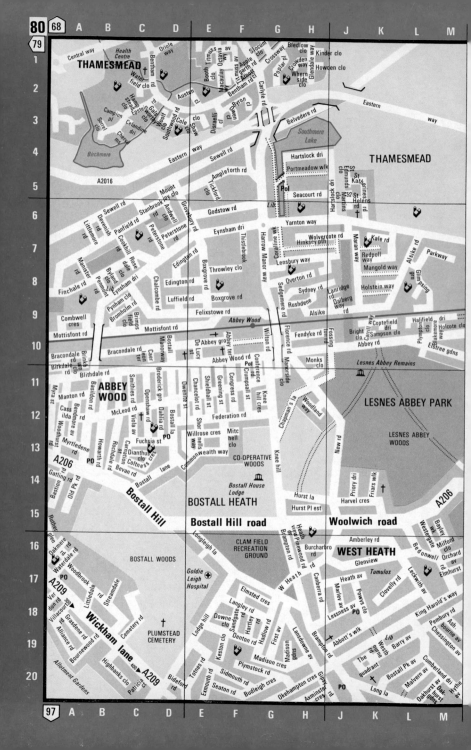

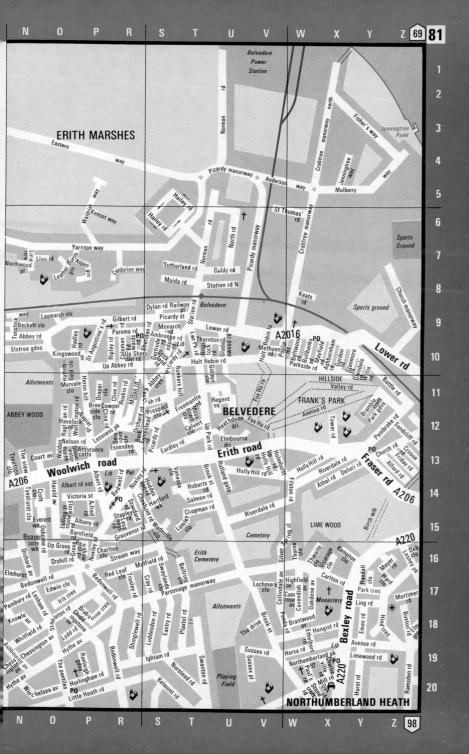

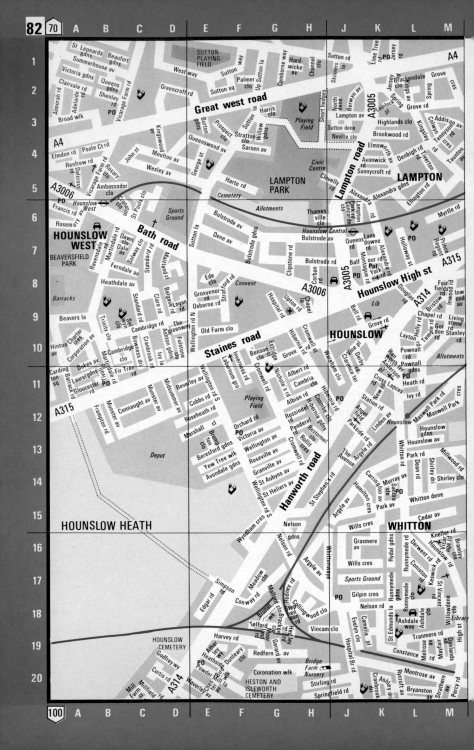

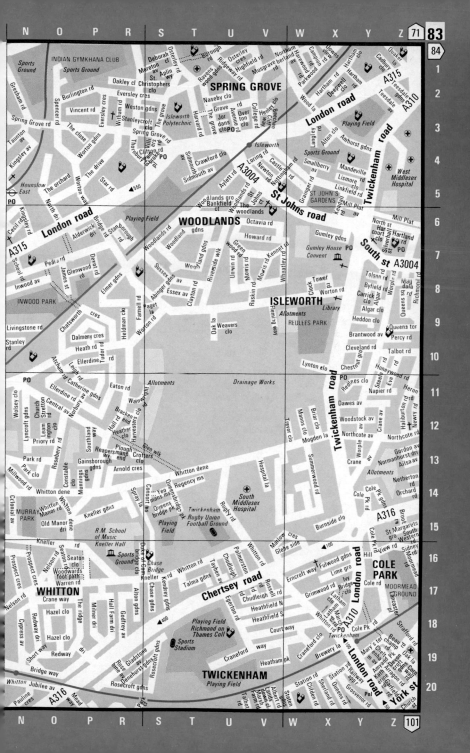

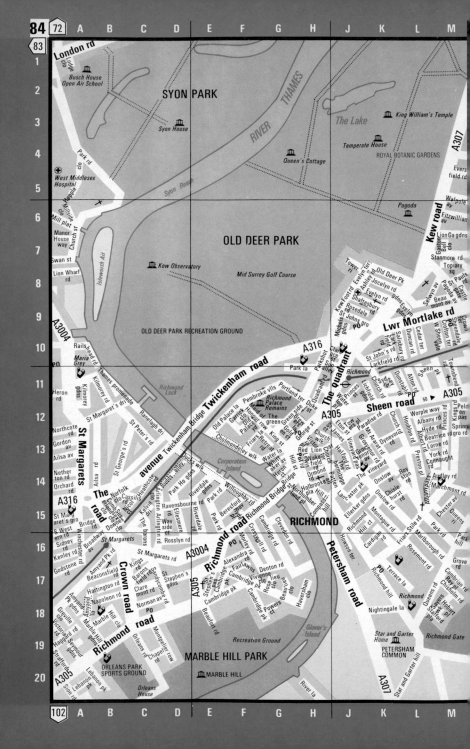

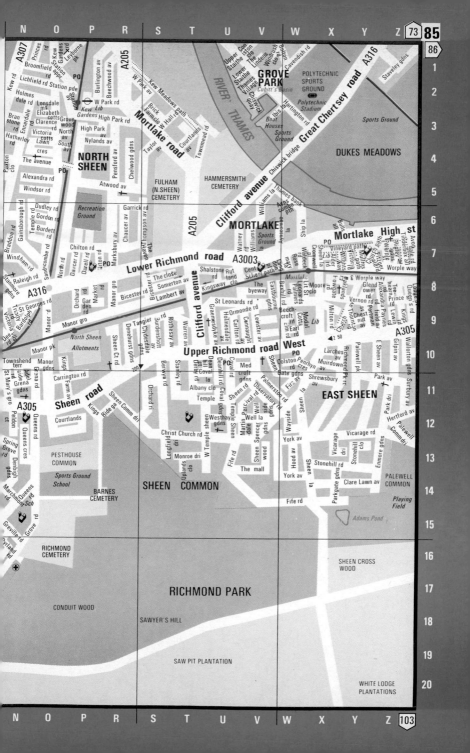

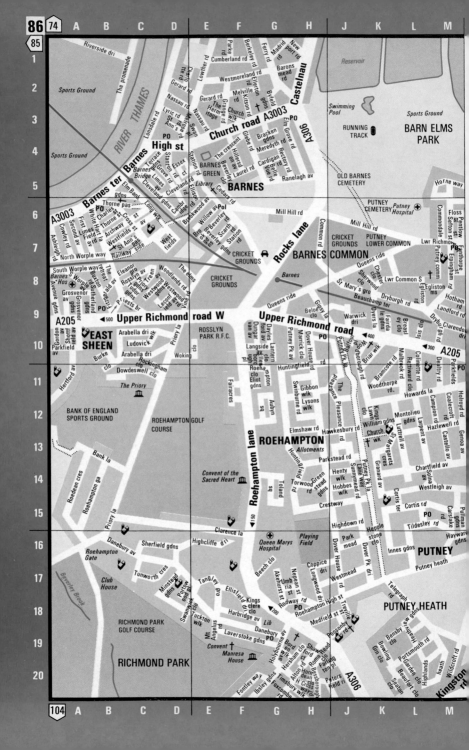

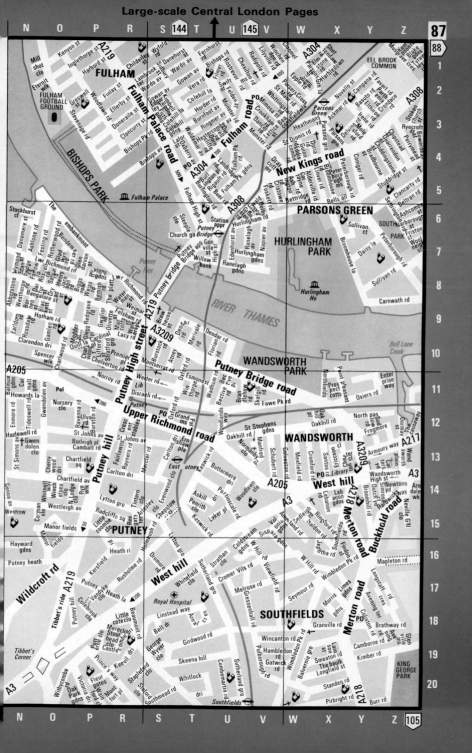

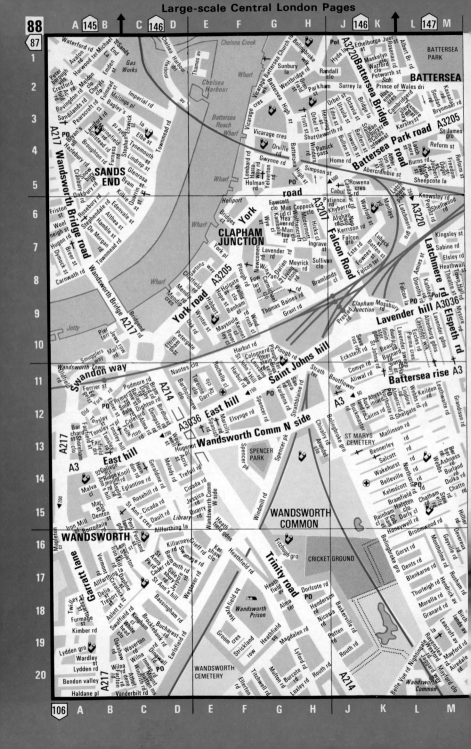

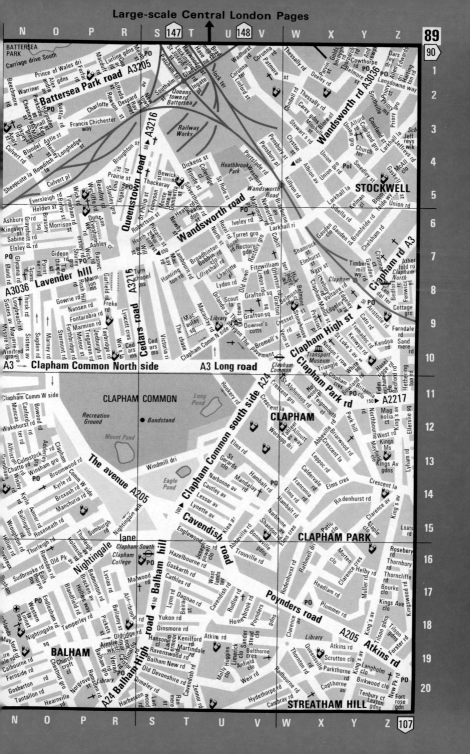

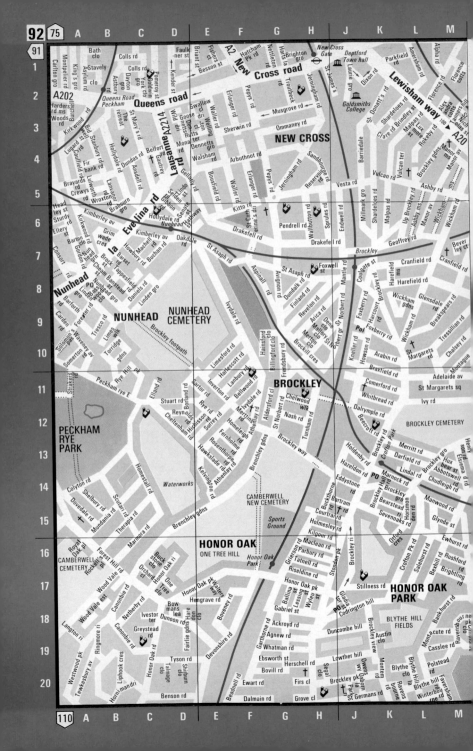

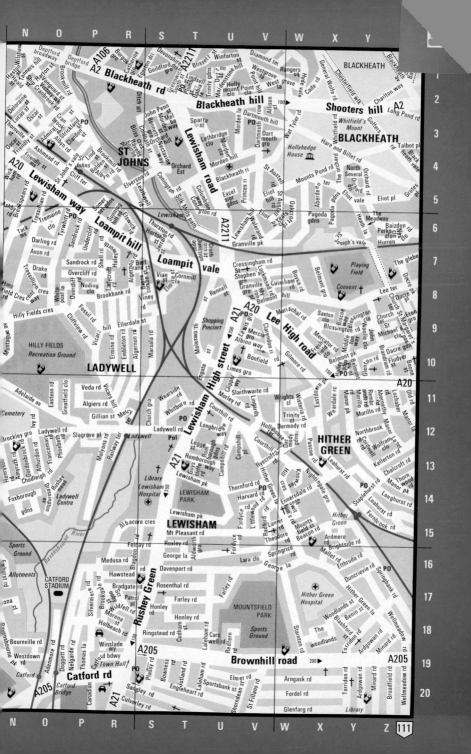

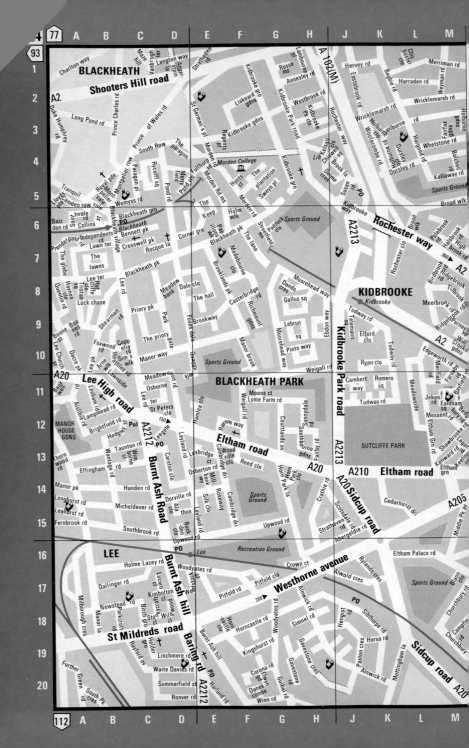

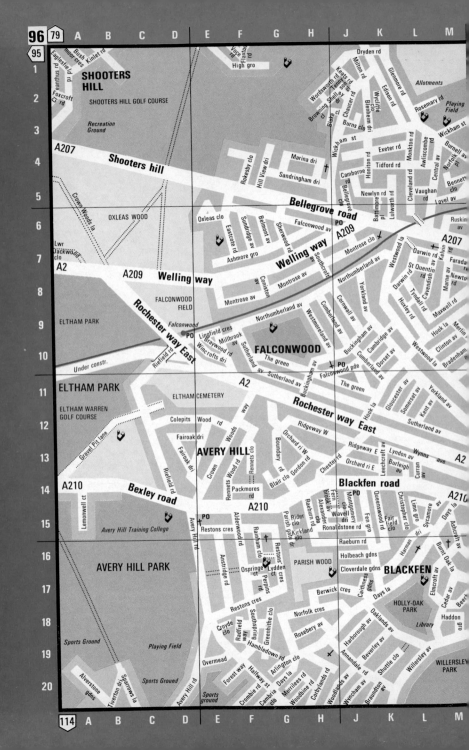

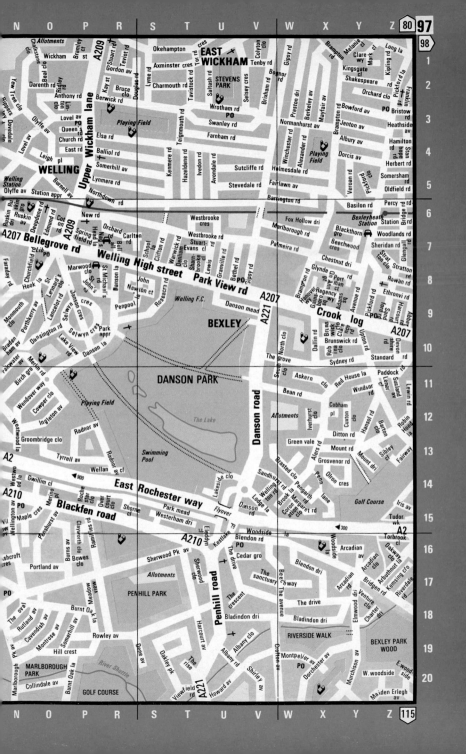

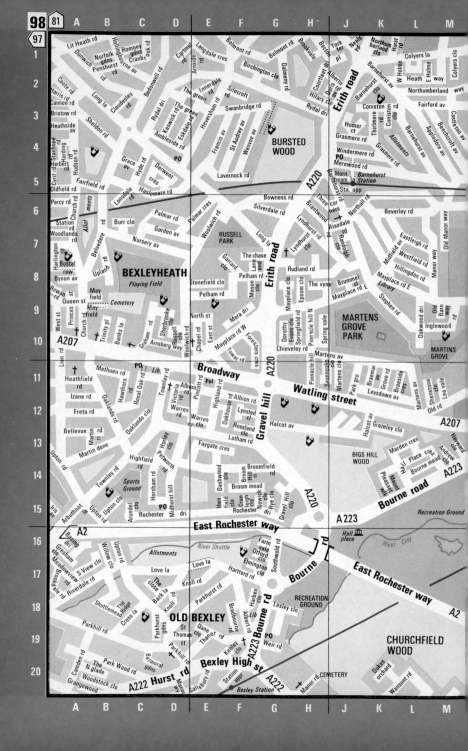

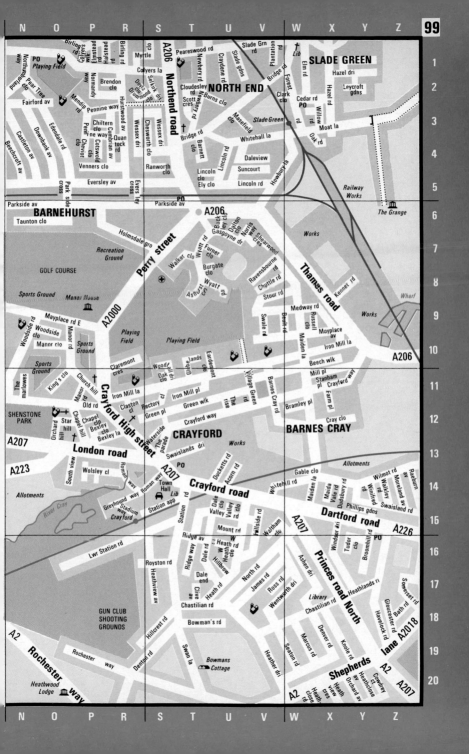

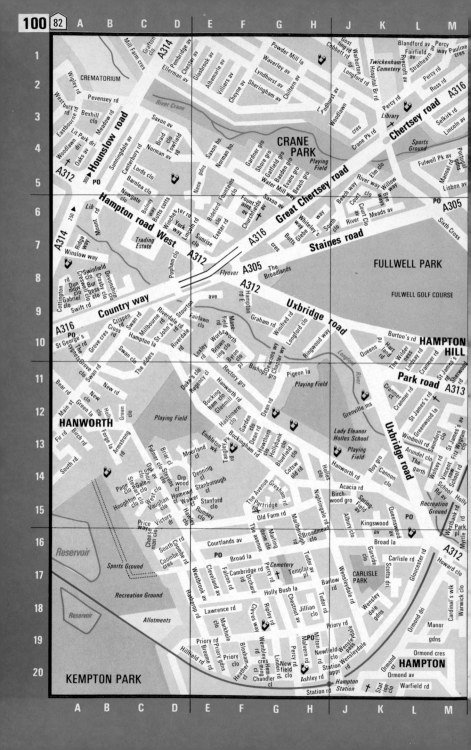

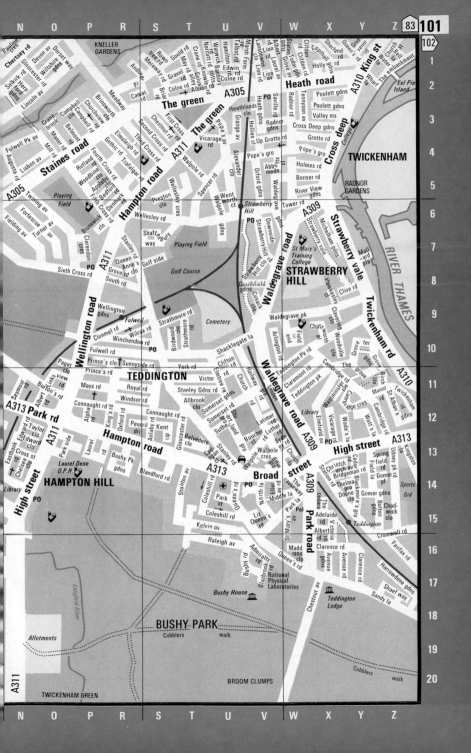

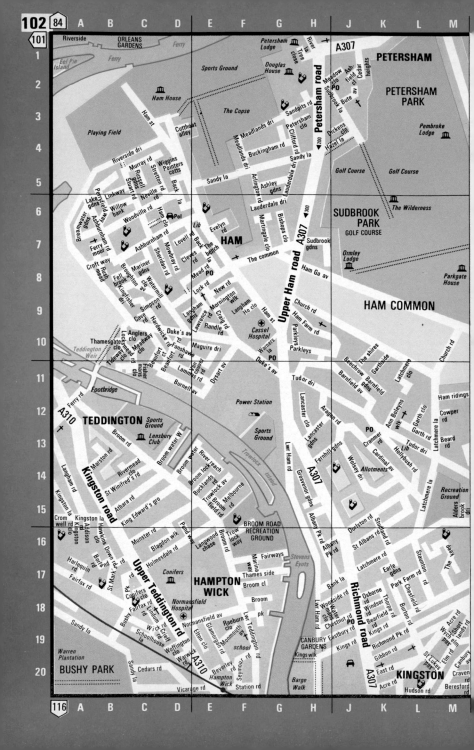

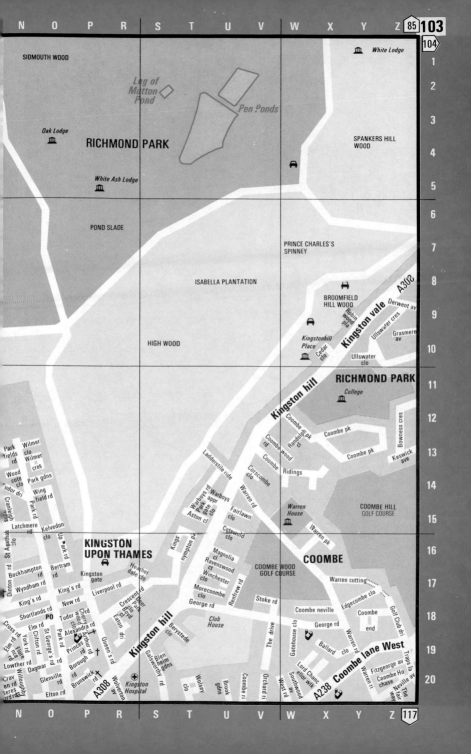

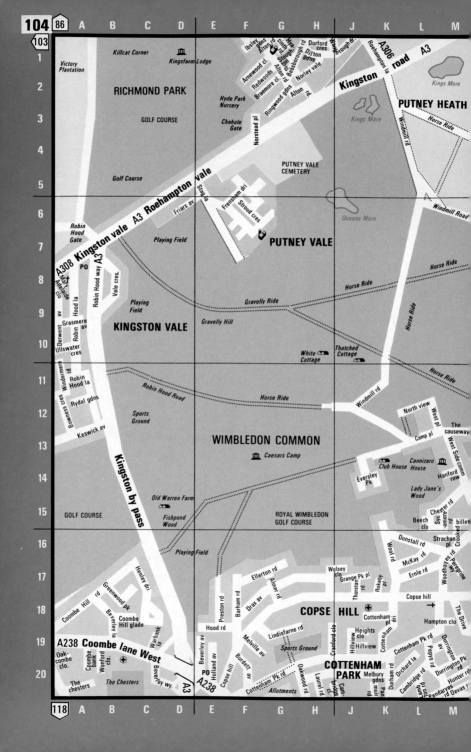

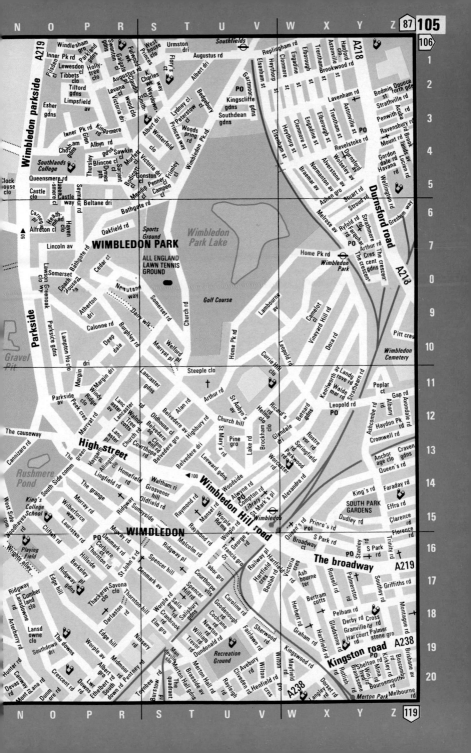

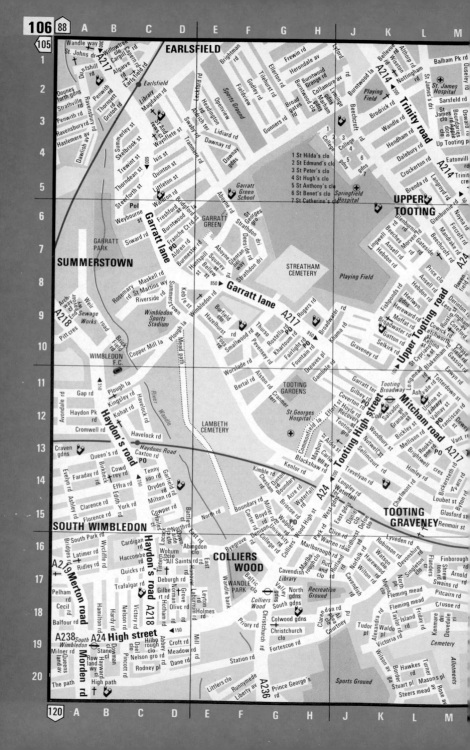

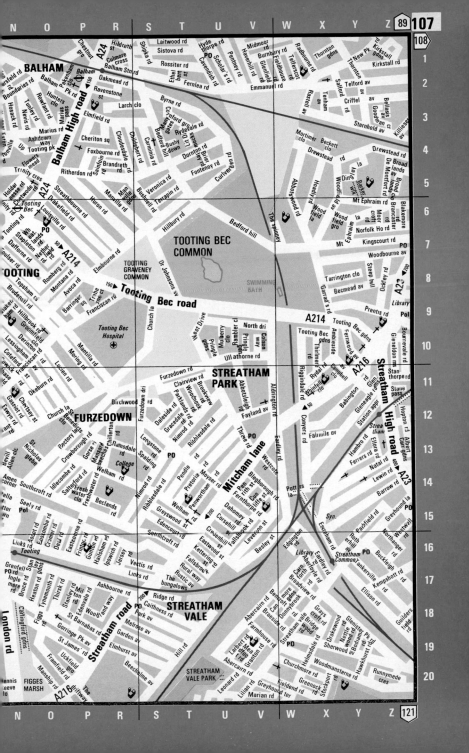

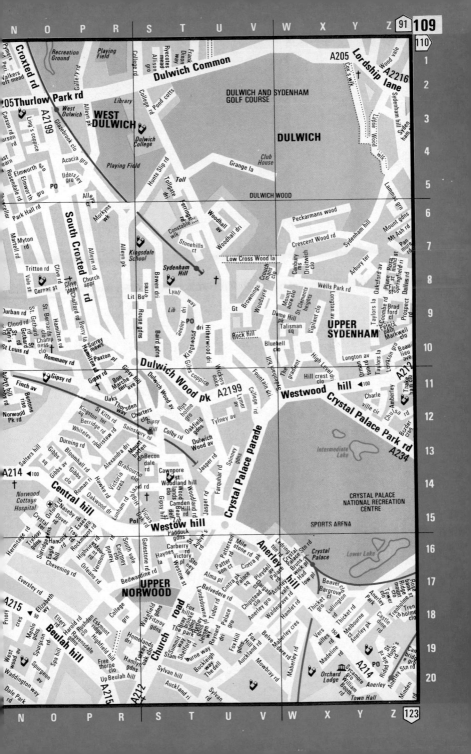

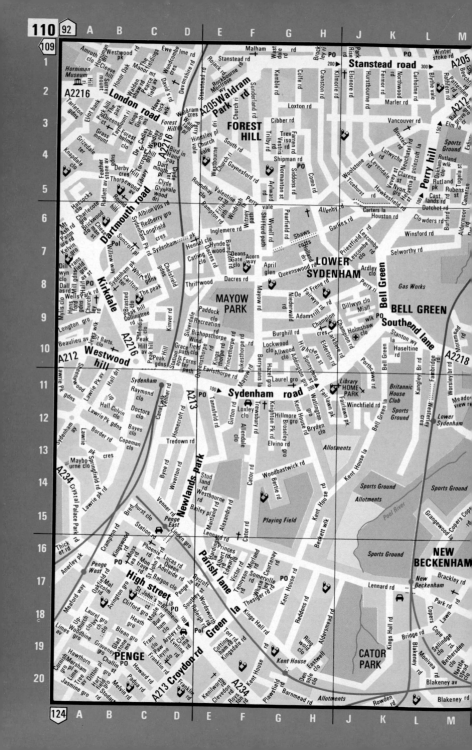

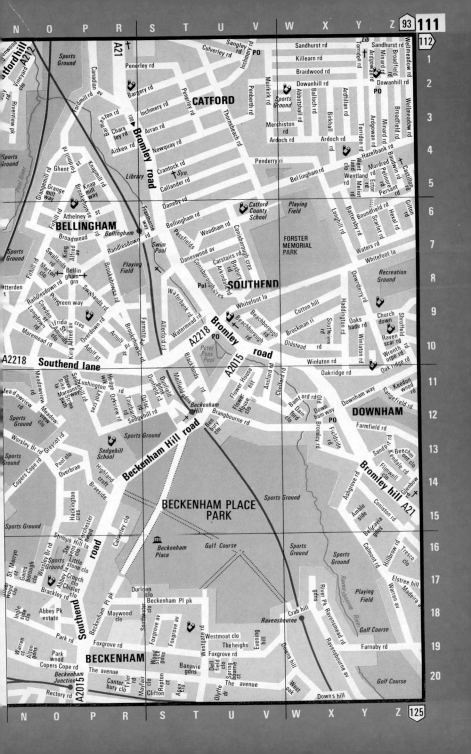

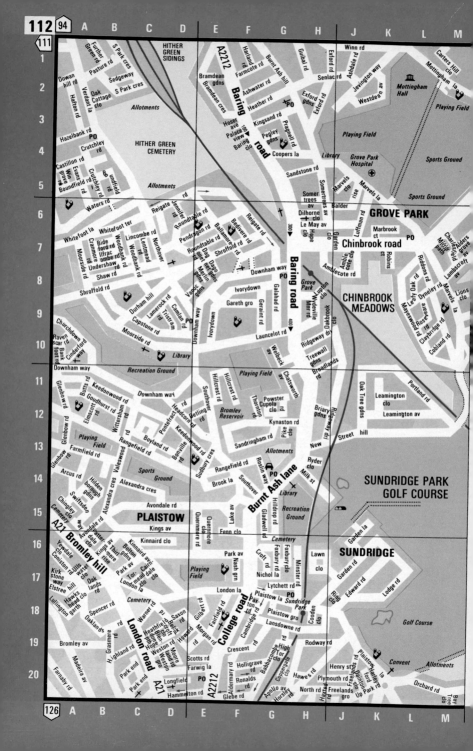

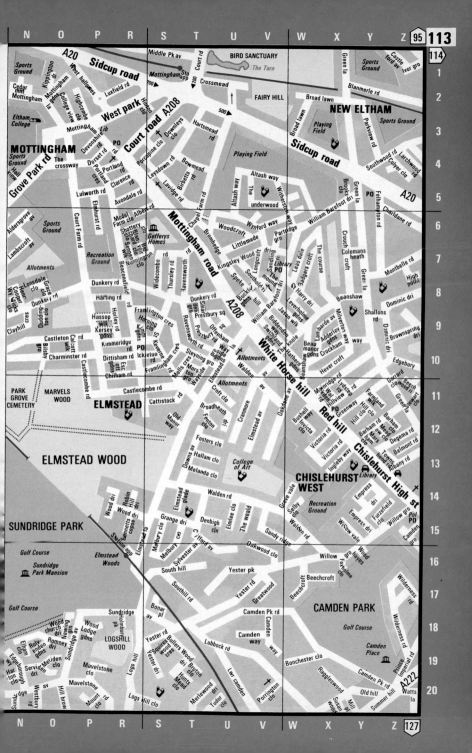

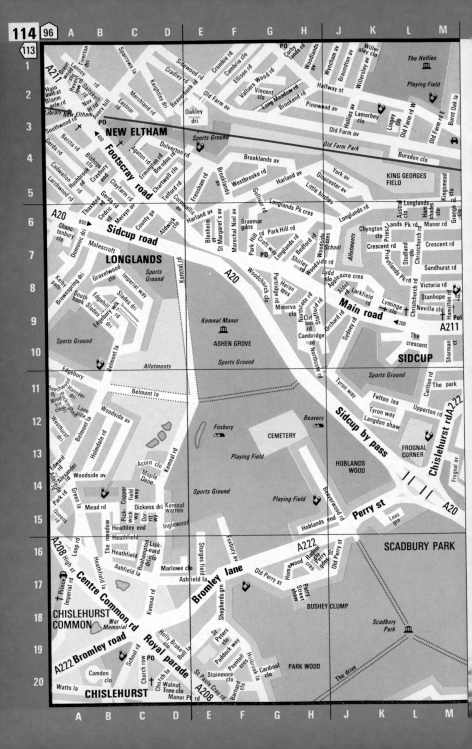

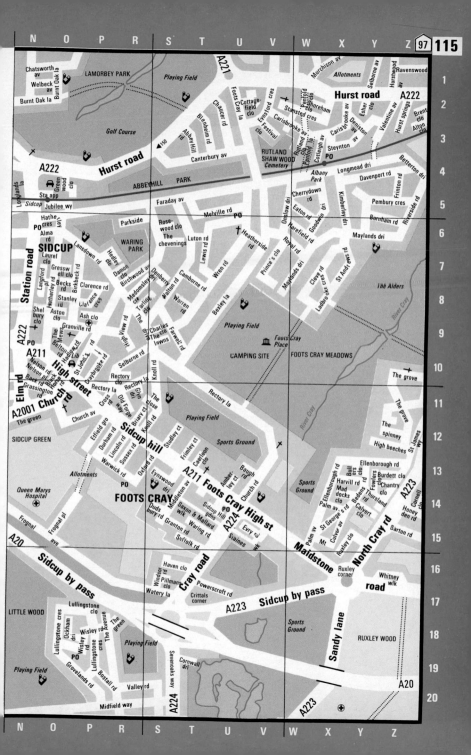

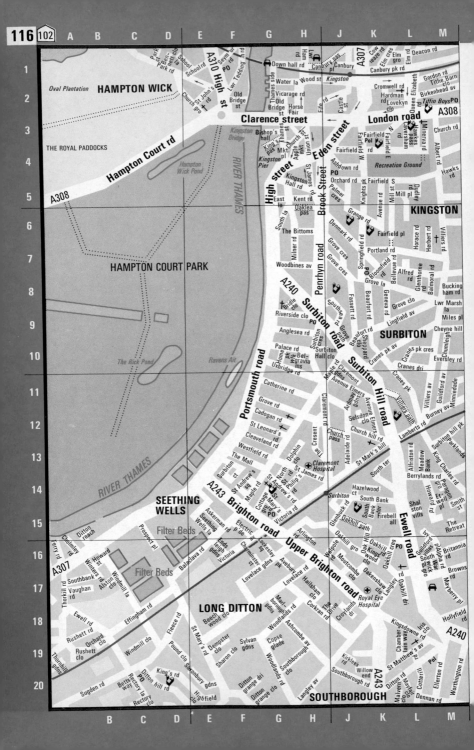

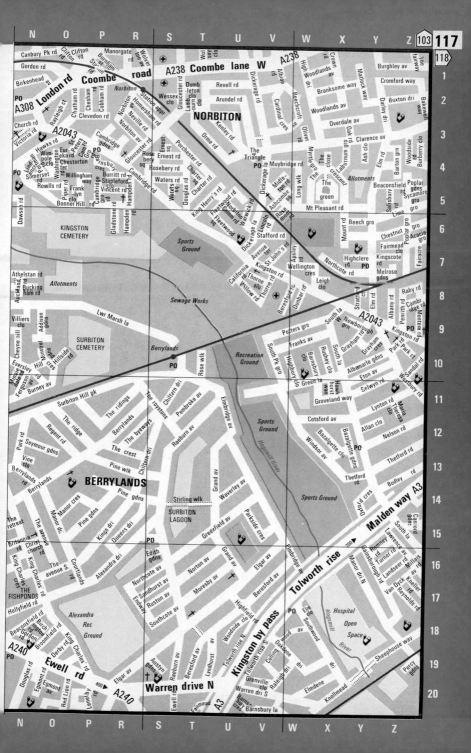

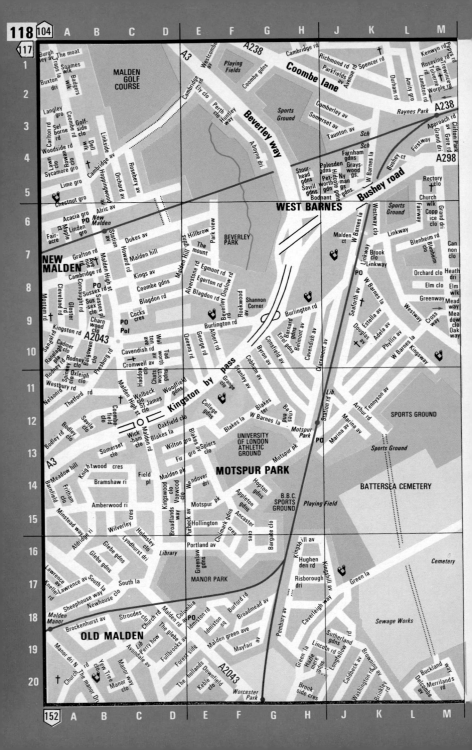

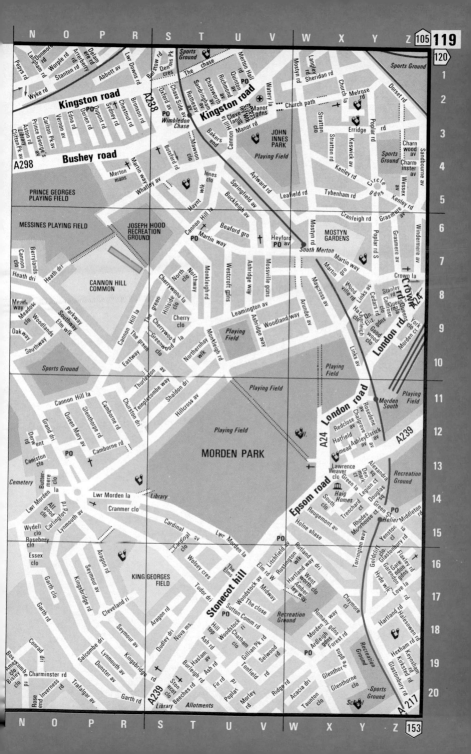

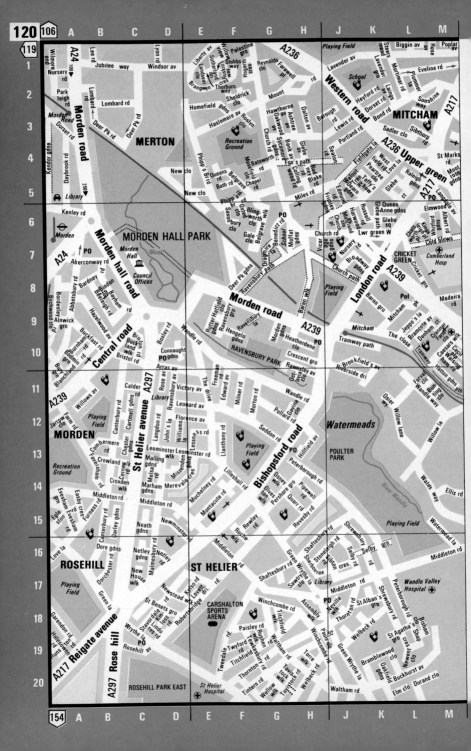

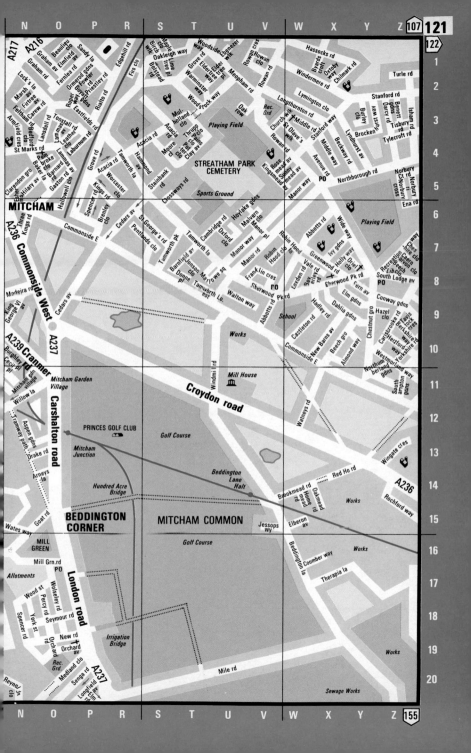

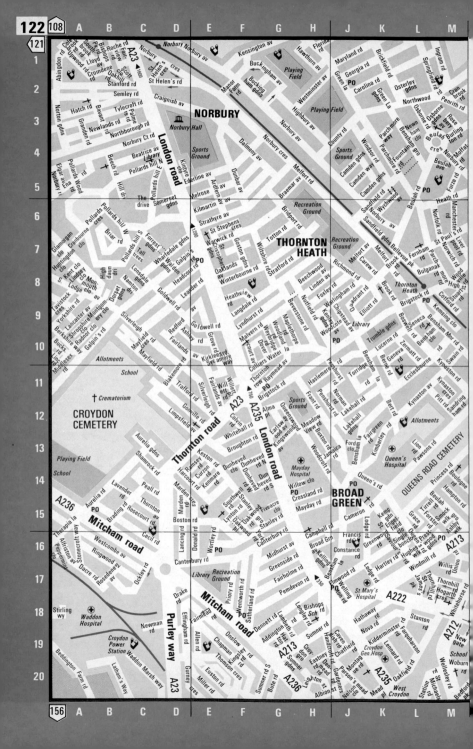

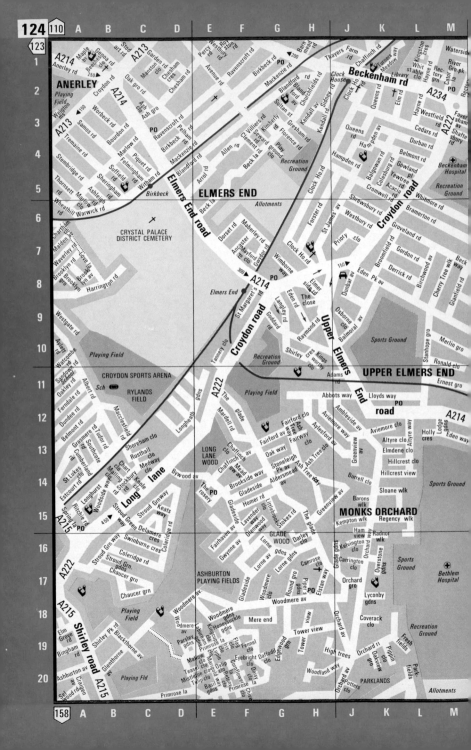

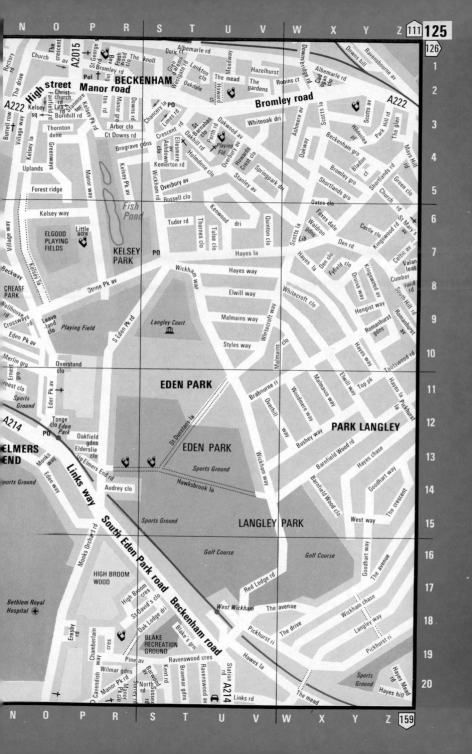

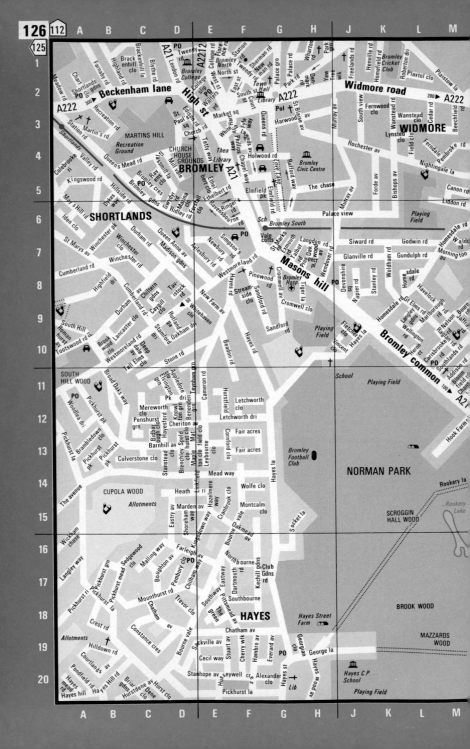

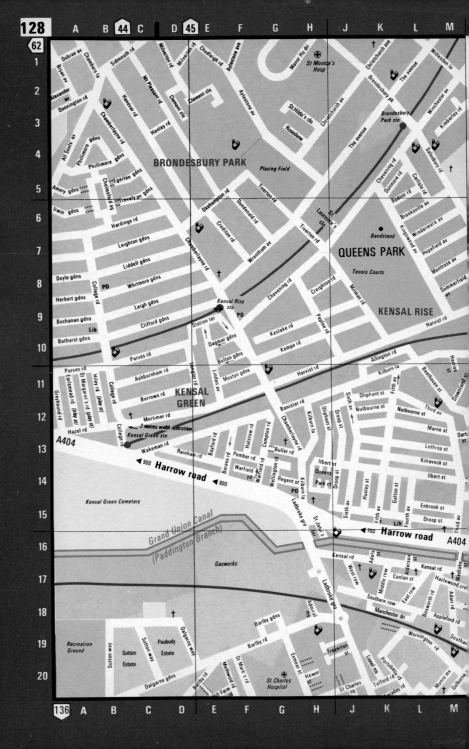

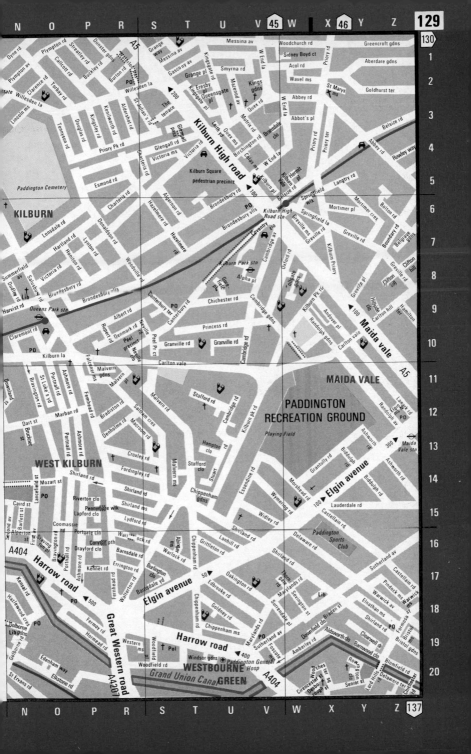

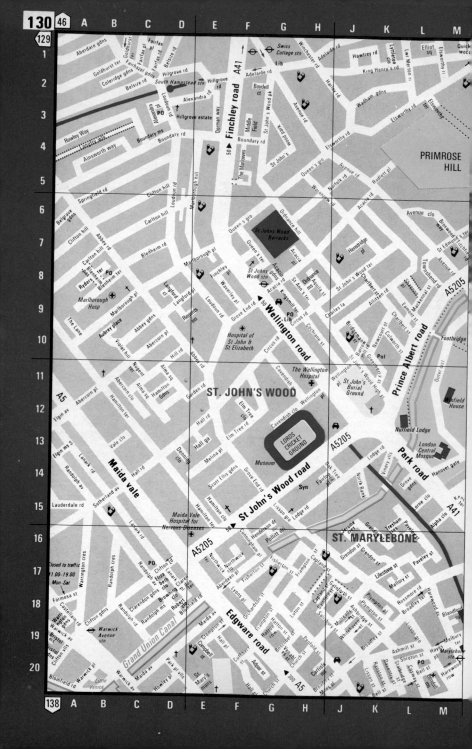

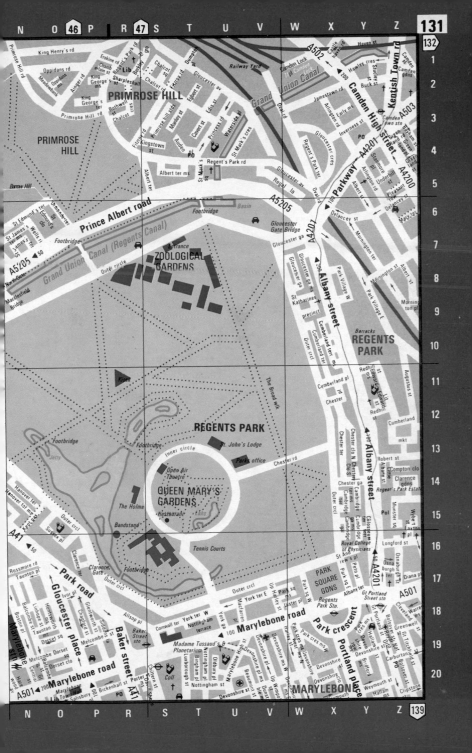

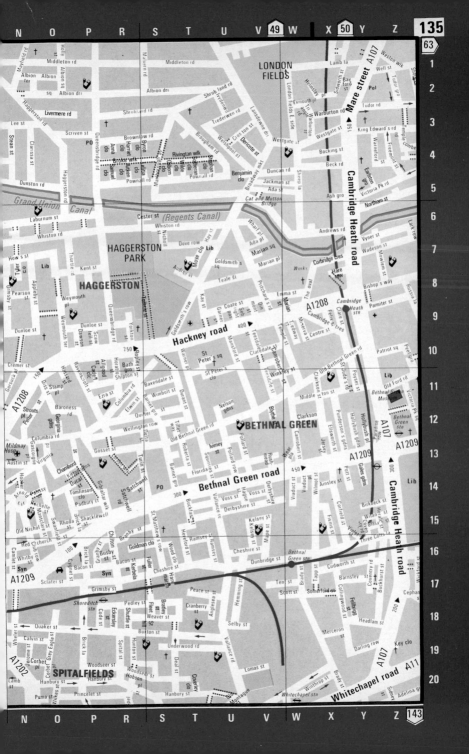

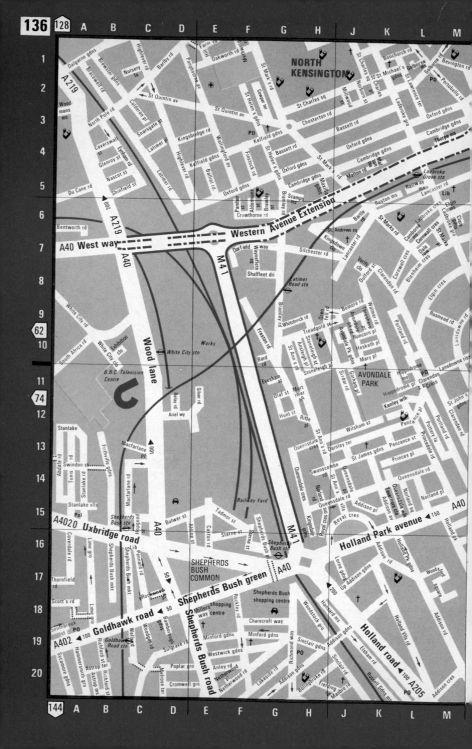

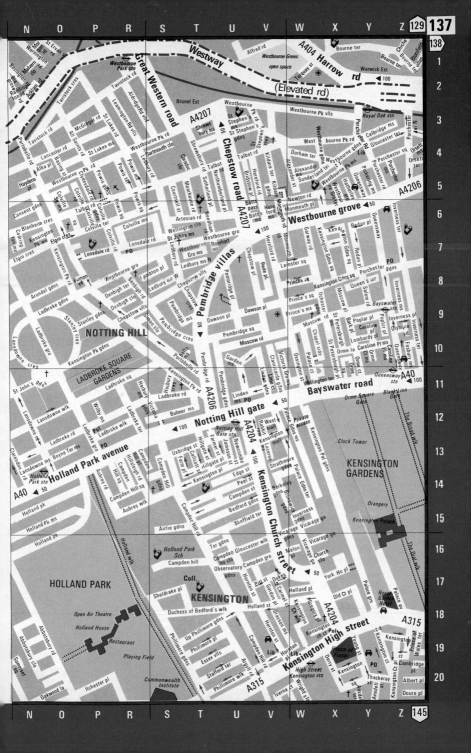

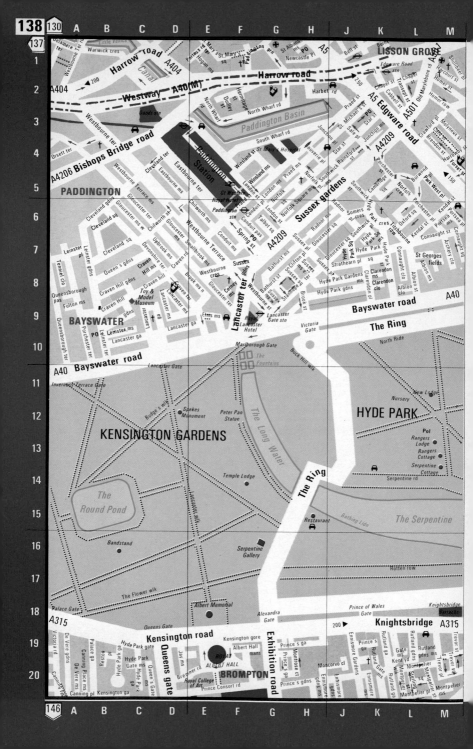

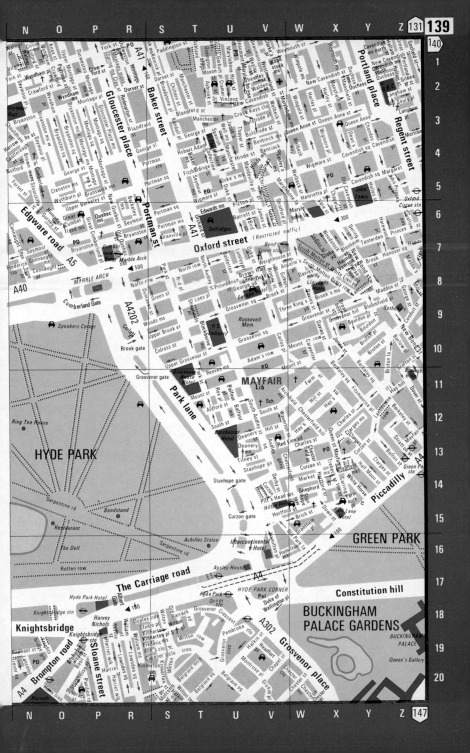

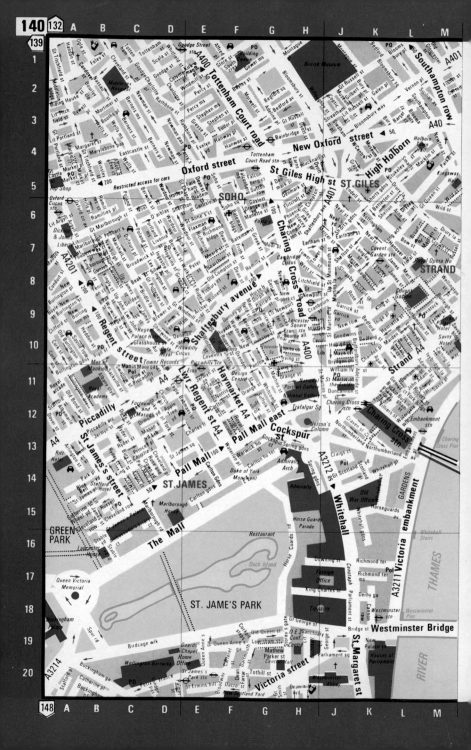

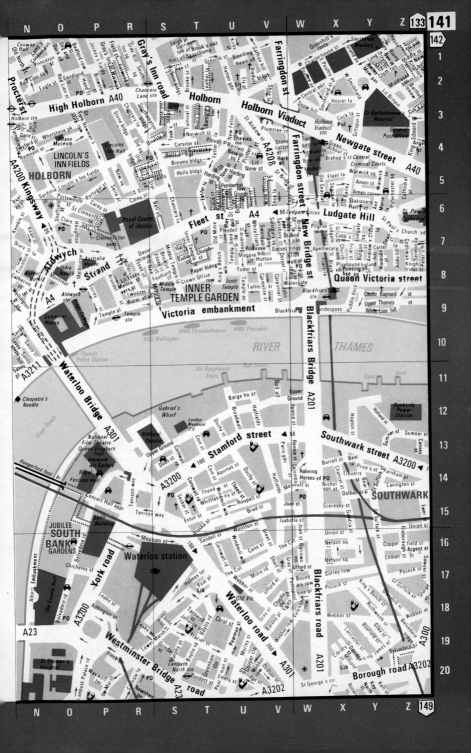

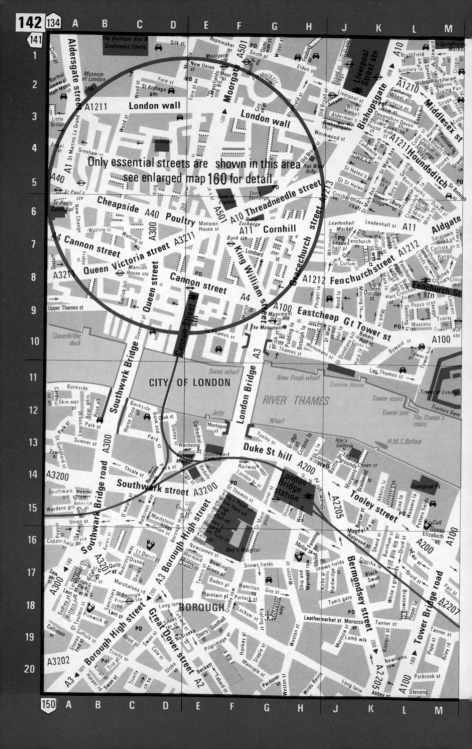

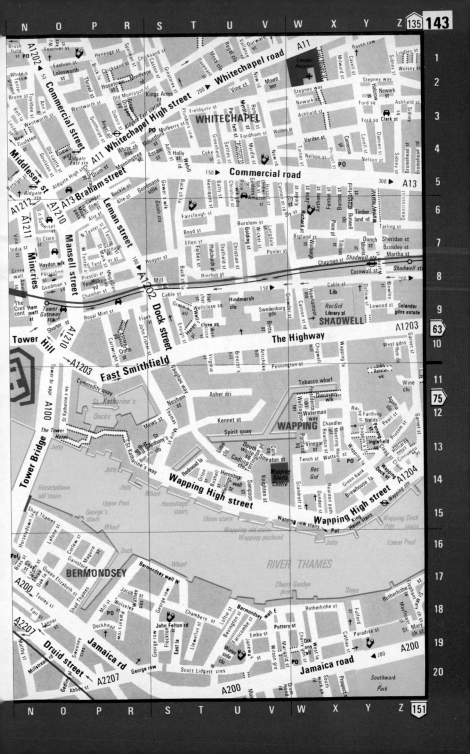

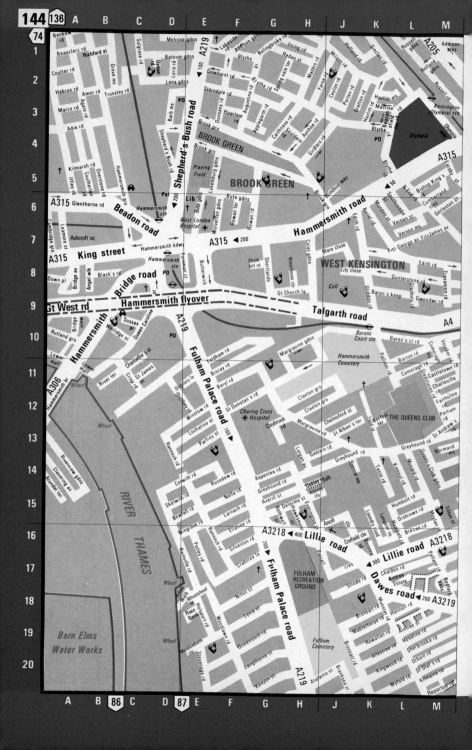

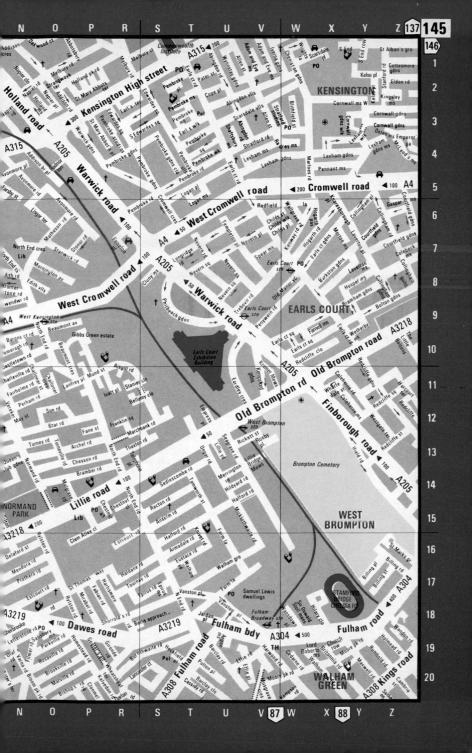

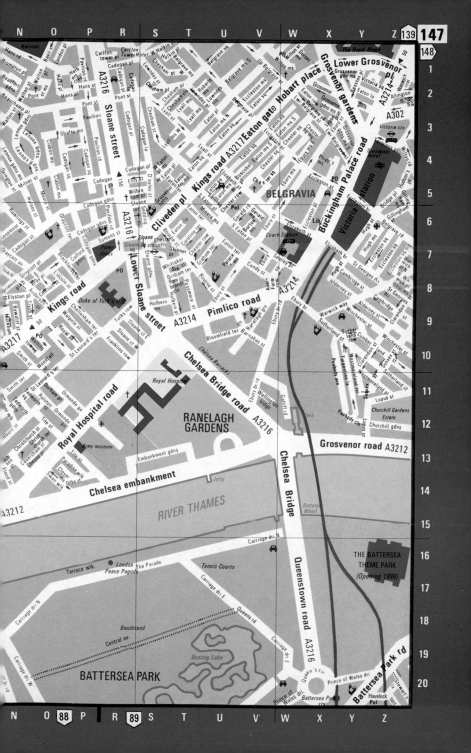

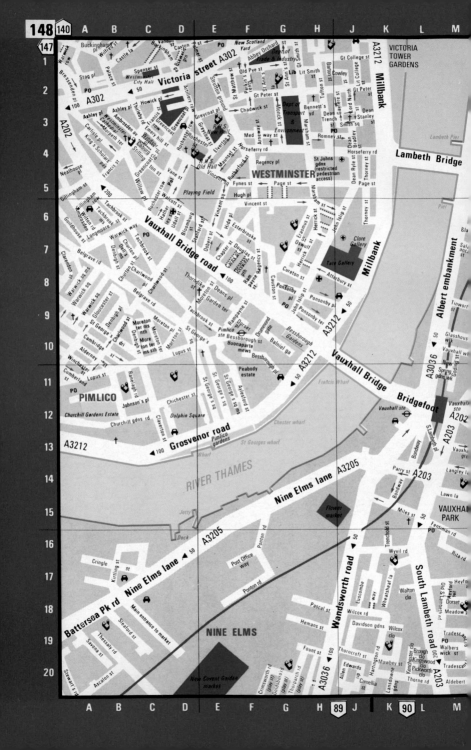

LAMBETH

ARCHBISHOPS PARK

GERALDINE MARY
HARMSWORTH PARK

St George's road

VAUXHALL

Kennington lane

Kennington lane

Harleyford road

THE OVAL
CRICKET GROUND

Kennington oval

KENNINGTON
PARK

NEWINGTON

KENNINGTON

Camberwell new road

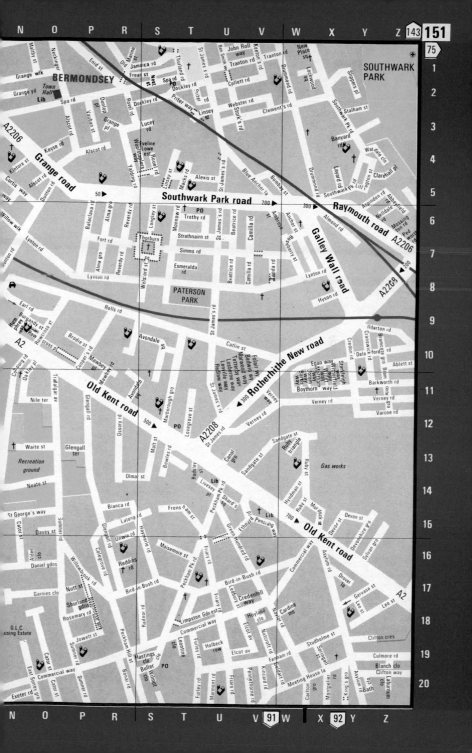

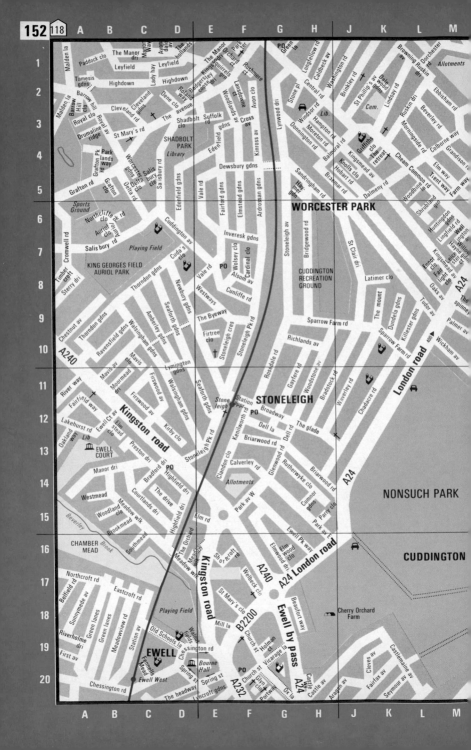

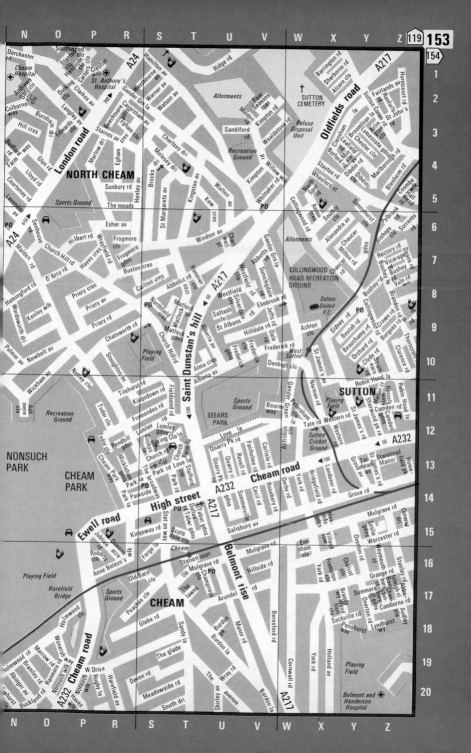

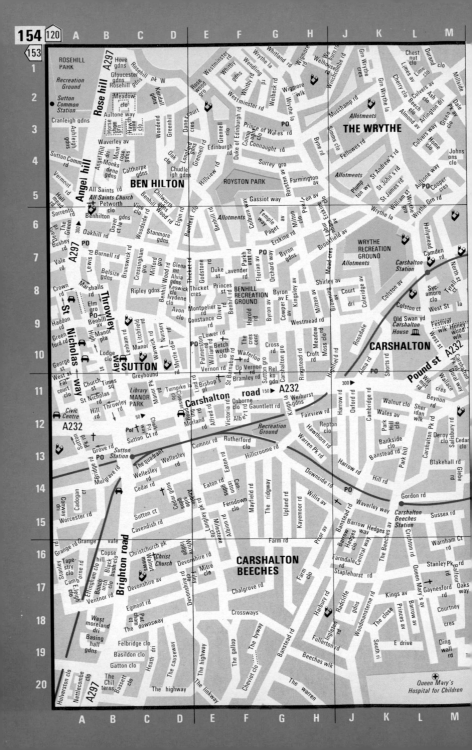

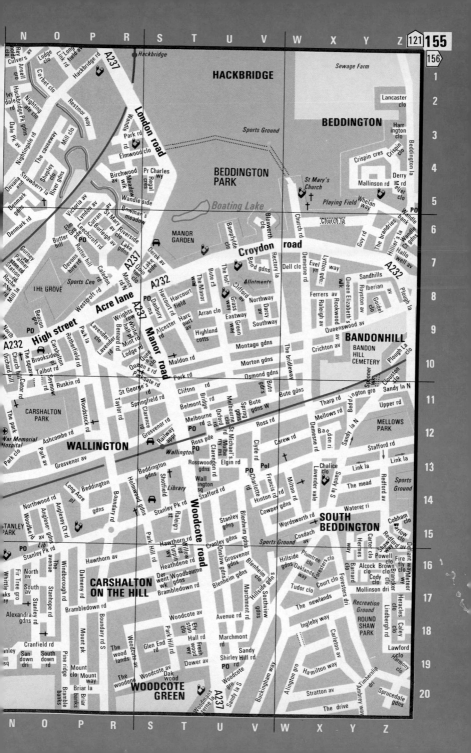

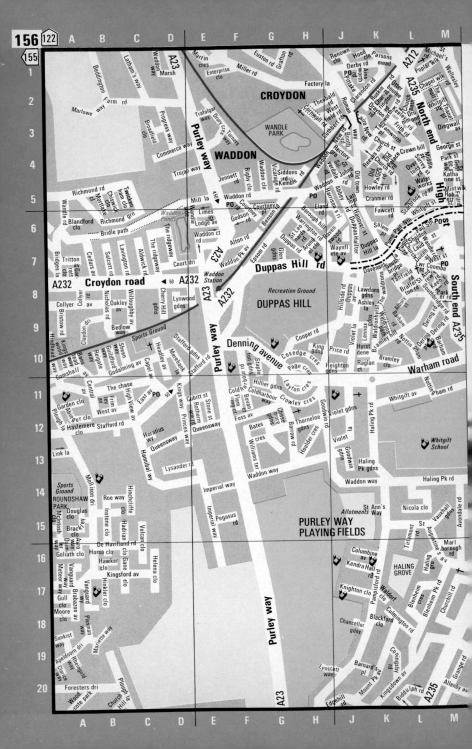

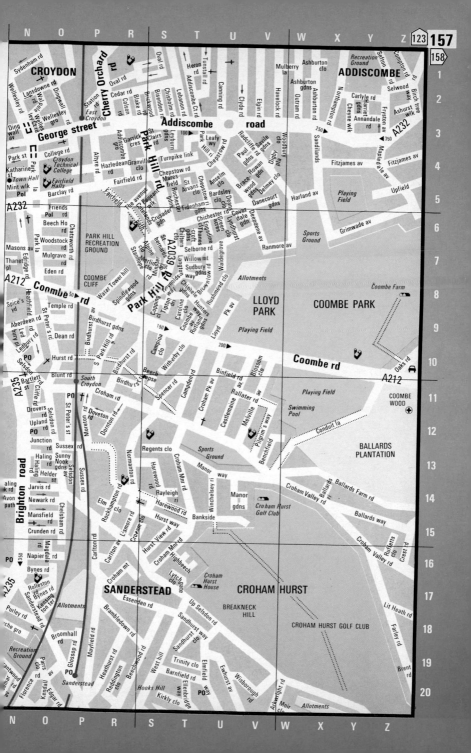

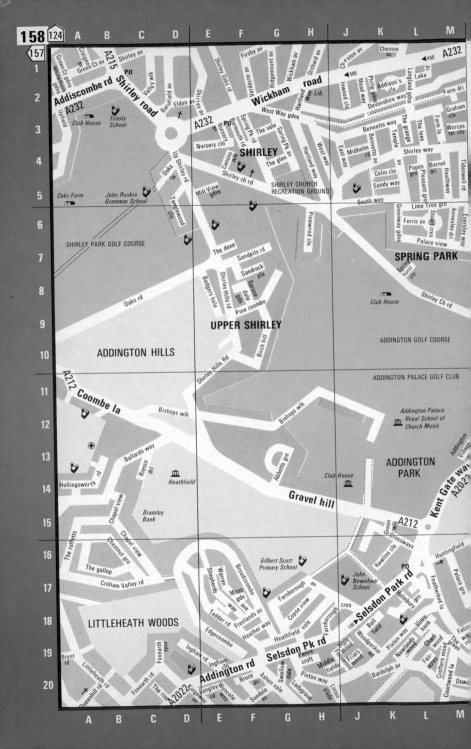

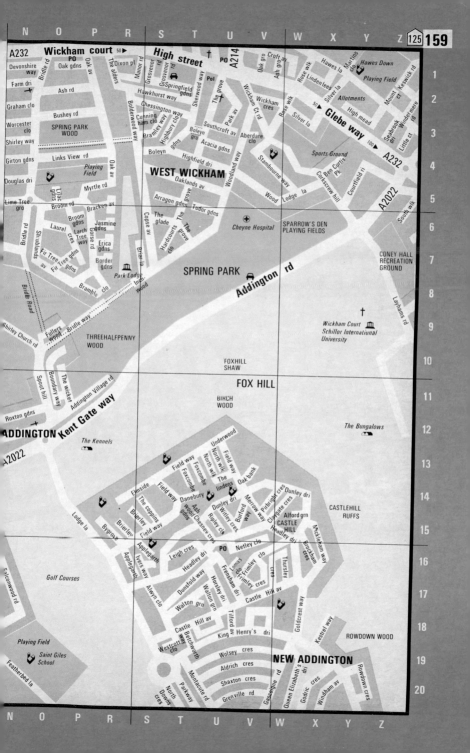

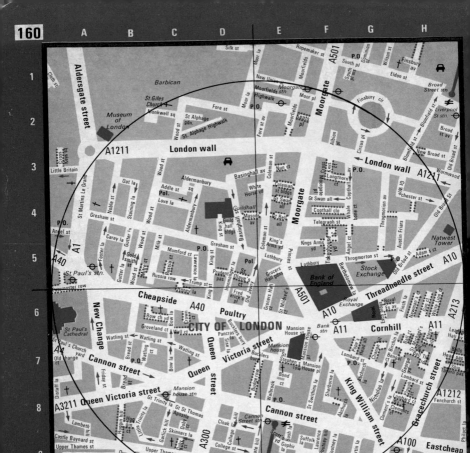

Enlargement of crowded city area for extra clarity

NOTES

The figures and letters before a street name indicate the page number and map square where the name will be found. The figures and letters following a street name indicate the postal district or locality of the entry.

For example **139 T 7 Oxford st W1** will be found on page **139** in square **T7** in the postal district of **W1**.

Abbreviations

Outer districts

Barking **Bark**
Barnet **Barnt**
Beckenham **Becknhm**
Belvedere **Blvdr**
Bexley Heath **Bxly Hth**
Bexley **Bxly**
Borehamwood **Borhm wd**
Brentford **Brentf**
Bromley **Brom**
Buckhurst Hill **Buck Hl**
Carshalton **Carsh**
Chislehurst **Chisl**
Croydon **Croy**
Dagenham **Dgnhm**
Dartford **Drtfrd**
East Molesey **E Molesey**
Edgware **Edg**
Enfield **Enf**
Feltham **Felt**
Greenford **Grnfd**
Hampton **Hampt**
Hornchurch **Hornch**
Hounslow **Hounsl**
Ilford **Ilf**
Isleworth **Islwth**
Kingston **Kingst**
Mitcham **Mitch**
Morden **Mrdn**
New Malden **New Mald**
Northolt **Nthlt**
Orpington **Orp**
Pinner **Pinn**
Rainham **Rainhm**
Richmond **Rich**
Romford **Rom**
Ruislip **Ruis**
Sidcup **Sidcp**
South Croydon **S Croy**
Southall **S'hall**
Stanmore **Stanm**
Surbiton **Surb**
Teddington **Tedd**
Thornton Heath **Thntn Hth**
Twickenham **Twick**
Wallington **Wallgtn**
Watford **Watf**
Wembley **Wemb**
West Wickham **W Wkhm**
Woodford Green **Wdfd Grn**
Worcester Park **Worc Pk**

Streets etc

Alley **all**
Approach **appr**
Arcade **arc**
Avenue **av**
Boulevard **blvd**
Bridge **br**
Broadway **bdwy**
Buildings **bldgs**
Church **ch**
Churchyard **chyd**
Circle **crcl**
Circus **cir**
Close **clo**
Common **comm**
Cottages **cotts**
Court **ct**
Crescent **cres**
Drive **dri**
Embankment **emb**
Estate **est**
Gardens **gdns**
Gate **ga**
Green **grn**
Grove **gro**
House **ho**
Junction **junc**
Lane **la**
Manor **mnr**
Mansions **mans**
Market **mkt**
Mews **ms**
Mount **mt**
Palace **pal**
Parade **pde**
Park **pk**
Passage **pas**
Path **pth**
Place **pl**
Rise **ri**
Road **rd**
Square **sq**
Station **sta**
Street **st**
Terrace **ter**
Villas **vlls**
Walk **wlk**
Yard **yd**

A

66 E 16 Abbess clo E6
108 G 1 Abbess clo SW2
29 Y 14 Abbeville rd N8
89 V 15 Abbeville rd SW4
60 L 5 Abbey av Wemb
58 D 9 Abbey clo SW 2
81 S 11 Abbey cres Erith
130 C 9 Abbey gdns NW8
80 E 10 Abbey gro SE2
115 T 3 Abbey Hill rd Sidcp
111 O 17 Abbey la Becknhm
64 G 5 Abbey la E15
148 F 1 Abbey Orchard st SW1
111 O 18 Abbey Park est Becknhm
67 N 2 Abbey rd Bark
80 K 10 Abbey rd Blvdr
81 N 9 Abbey rd Blvdr
97 Z 9 Abbey rd Bxly Hth
156 J 5 Abbey rd Croy
64 L 5 Abbey rd E15
8 F 17 Abbey rd Enf
36 E 16 Abbey rd Ilf
61 T 5 Abbey rd NW10
61 T 7 Abbey rd NW10
129 Y 4 Abbey rd NW6
130 B 7 Abbey rd NW8
106 D 19 Abbey rd SW19
65 T 11 Abbey st E13
150 L 1 Abbey st SE1
143 O 20 Abbey st SE1
80 F 10 Abbey ter SE2
60 M 7 Abbey ter Wemb
13 S 10 Abbey view NW7
80 F 10 Abbey Wood rd SE2
61 O 3 Abbeydale rd Wemb
75 P 11 Abbeyfield rd SE16
151 Z 5 Abbeyfield rd SE16
61 P 7 Abbeyfields clo NW10
61 P 7 Abbeyfields cres NW10
100 C 15 Abbot clo Hampt
40 D 19 Abbot clo Nthlt
49 T 17 Abbot st E8
129 W 3 Abbot's pl NW6
20 L 14 Abbots cres E4
28 G 13 Abbots gdns N2
142 K 14 Abbots la SE1
108 G 1 Abbots pk SW2
25 W 1 Abbots rd Edg
13 N 20 Abbots rd NW7
124 J 11 Abbots way Becknhm
64 G 5 Abbotsbury clo E15
137 N 19 Abbotsbury clo W14
120 A 8 Abbotsbury rd SW19
137 N 19 Abbotsbury rd W14
30 M 14 Abbotsford av N15
34 E 2 Abbotsford gdns Wdfd Grn
55 O 7 Abbotsford rd Ilf
16 H 12 Abbotshall av N14
111 W 3 Abbotshall rd SE6
153 Z 17 Abbotsleigh clo Sutton
107 V 11 Abbotsleigh rd SW16
87 N 8 Abbotswell rd SE4
92 M 13 Abbotswell rd SE4
35 V 11 Abbotswood gdns Ilf
107 W 5 Abbotswood rd SW16
119 P 1 Abbott av SW20
40 D 18 Abbott clo Grnfd
64 G 15 Abbott rd E14
64 K 16 Abbott rd E14
38 G 9 Abbotts clo Rom
7 X 8 Abbotts cres Enf
42 A 6 Abbotts dri Wemb
42 C 6 Abbotts dri Wemb
158 G 13 Abbotts grn Croy
51 U 1 Abbotts Park rd E10
4 M 16 Abbotts rd Barnt
66 B 5 Abbotts rd E15
25 X 1 Abbotts rd Edg
121 X 6 Abbotts rd Mitch
70 C 2 Abbotts rd S'hall
153 V 7 Abbotts rd Sutton
80 J 19 Abbotts wlk Bxly Hth
101 V 4 Abbottsmede clo Twick
160 F 8 Abchurch la EC4
136 A 14 Abdale rd W12
74 K 3 Abdale rd W12
150 J 4 Abedour st SE1

63 X 10 Aberavon rd E3
107 V 18 Abercairn rd SW16
120 A 7 Aberconway rd SW19
27 T 2 Abercorn clo NW7
130 C 11 Abercorn clo NW8
40 L 4 Abercorn cres Harrow
42 G 1 Abercorn gdns Harrow
37 P 18 Abercorn gdns Rom
130 C 10 Abercorn pl NW8
27 U 2 Abercorn rd NW7
124 D 2 Abercorn rd Stanm
88 K 5 Abercrombie st SW11
159 V 3 Aberdare clo W Wkhm
130 A 1 Aberdare gdns NW6
129 Z 1 Aberdare gdns NW6
27 O 3 Aberdare gdns NW7
9 O 14 Aberdare rd Enf
48 K 15 Aberdeen la N5
48 K 15 Aberdeen pk N5
130 F 17 Aberdeen rd Blvdr
157 N 9 Aberdeen rd Croy
23 V 8 Aberdeen rd Harrow
18 L 15 Aberdeen rd N18
48 L 13 Aberdeen rd N5
44 E 14 Aberdeen rd N10
120 F 2 Aberdeen rd SW19
93 X 5 Aberdeen ter SE3
55 P 8 Aberdour rd Ilf
64 H 17 Aberfeldy st E14
107 X 17 Aberfoyle rd SW16
94 J 15 Abergeldie rd SE12
93 Z 11 Abernethy rd SE13
49 V 15 Abersham rd E8
79 U 11 Abery st SE18
106 E 16 Abingdon clo SW19
28 D 6 Abingdon rd N3
122 A 1 Abingdon rd N9
145 U 1 Abingdon rd W8
148 K 2 Abingdon st SW1
145 U 2 Abingdon vlls W8
153 N 20 Abinger av Sutton
127 P 6 Abinger clo Brom
54 M 13 Abinger clo Ilf
156 A 12 Abinger clo Wallgtn
83 S 8 Abinger gdns Islwth
75 Y 16 Abinger gro SE8
129 S 16 Abinger ms W9
74 B 8 Abinger rd W4
75 O 14 Ablett st SE16
151 Z 10 Ablett st SE16
118 G 4 Aboyne dri SW20
44 B 8 Aboyne rd NW10
32 Y 9 Aboyne rd NW10
106 E 5 Aboyne rd SW17
68 O 7 Abridge way Bark
88 K 12 Abyssinia rd SW11
72 A 20 Acacia av Brentf
57 U 8 Acacia av Hornch
31 O 1 Acacia av N17
42 J 15 Acacia av Wemb
10 G 19 Acacia clo Harrow
119 W 20 Acacia dri Sutton
159 U 4 Acacia gdns W Wkhm
130 G 8 Acacia gdns NW8
118 A 6 Acacia gro New Mald
117 Z 6 Acacia gro New Mald
109 P 4 Acacia gro SE21
130 G 8 Acacia gro NW8
52 A 8 Acacia rd E11
32 J 19 Acacia rd E17
8 C 5 Acacia rd Enf
100 J 14 Acacia rd Hampt
121 R 4 Acacia rd Mitch
30 G 5 Acacia rd N22
130 G 8 Acacia rd NW8
108 B 20 Acacia rd SW16
61 V 20 Acacia rd W3
123 V 20 Academy gdns Croy
58 A 7 Academy gdns Nrthlt
95 U 2 Academy pl SE18
78 G 19 Academy pl SE18
95 U 1 Academy rd SE18
89 N 8 Acans rd SW11
45 W 3 Accommodation rd NW11
88 A 2 Acfold rd SW6
45 W 14 Achilles rd NW6
75 X 20 Achilles st SE14
137 O 1 Acklam rd W10
26 A 4 Acklington dri NW9
87 X 3 Ackmar rd SW6
63 Z 14 Ackroyd dri E3
92 G 18 Ackroyd rd SE23
91 N 8 Acland cres SE5
44 L 17 Acland rd NW2

129 W 1 Acol rd NW6
68 C 3 Aconbury rd Dgnhm
114 C 13 Acorn clo Chisl
20 C 16 Acorn clo E4
7 V 6 Acorn clo Enf
24 C 2 Acorn Clo Stanm
123 T 1 Acorn gdns SE19
61 Z 15 Acorn gdns W3
99 U 14 Acorn rd Drtfrd
75 W 2 Acorn wlk SE16
90 C 11 Acre la SW2
155 R 8 Acre la Wallgtn
56 H 20 Acre rd Dgnhm
102 K 20 Acre rd Kingst
106 G 14 Acre rd SW19
88 D 14 Acris st SW18
61 Z 6 Acton la N10
73 W 4 Acton la W3
73 W 5 Acton la W3
73 W 12 Acton la W4
134 M 3 Acton ms E8
134 M 4 Acton ms E8
133 O 13 Acton st WC1
105 Z 3 Acuba rd SW18
64 J 17 Ada gdns E14
64 J 18 Ada gdns E15
135 V 7 Ada pl E2
150 H 20 Ada rd SE5
42 F 9 Ada rd Wemb
135 V 5 Ada st E8
128 M 18 Adair rd W10
140 B 4 Adam & Eve ct W1
145 V 1 Adam & Eve ms W8
146 C 5 Adam ct SW7
140 L 10 Adam st WC2
144 E 18 adam wlk SW6
160 H 5 Adam's ct EC2
43 U 6 Adams clo NW9
75 P 5 Adams gdns SE16
48 D 16 Adams pl N7
124 H 11 Adams rd Becknhm
31 R 7 Adams rd N17
39 V 10 Adams row W1
97 Y 9 Adams sq Bxly Hth
65 T 18 Adamson rd E16
46 G 19 Adamson rd NW3
8 B 19 Adamsrill Clo Enf
110 H 9 Adamsrill rd SE26
108 B 5 Adare wlk SW16
113 X 9 Adderley gdns SE9
89 O 13 Adderley rd Harrow
23 V 5 Adderley rd Harrow
64 F 18 Adderley st E14
15 S 20 Addington dri N12
110 G 10 Addington gro SE26
158 K 12 Addington pal Croy
158 L 14 Addington rd Croy
159 W 7 Addington rd W Wkhm
122 G 19 Addington rd Croy
65 N 13 Addington rd E16
64 A 8 Addington rd E3
30 E 20 Addington rd N4
158 E 20 Addington rd S Croy
150 D 16 Addington sq SE5
141 P 18 Addington st SE1
158 M 13 Addington Village rd Croy
159 P 11 Addington Village rd Croy
9 S 6 Addis clo Enf
123 W 18 Addiscombe av Croy
24 D 15 Addiscombe clo Harrow
157 T 2 Addiscombe ct Croy
157 R 4 Addiscombe gro Croy
158 A 2 Addiscombe rd Croy
157 U 3 Addiscombe rd Croy
82 M 3 Addison av Hounsl
6 F 18 Addison av N14
136 K 15 Addison av W11
145 N 4 Addison Bridge pl W14
144 M 1 Addison cres W14
136 M 20 Addison cres W14
117 N 9 Addison gdns Surb
144 F 1 Addison gdns W14
136 G 20 Addison gdns W14
74 B 9 Addison gro W4
123 X 9 Addison pl SE25
136 J 15 Addison pl W11
126 M 10 Addison rd Brom
127 N 10 Addison rd Brom
34 F 19 Addison rd E11
33 T 15 Addison rd E17
9 R 6 Addison rd Enf
36 C 5 Addison rd Ilf

123 Y 9 Addison rd SE25
102 A 15 Addison rd Tedd
136 M 18 Addison rd W14
145 O 2 Addison rd W14
27 X 13 Addison way NW11
158 K 2 Addisons clo Croy
141 Y 7 Addle hill EC4
160 C 3 Addle st EC2
118 K 9 Adela av New Mald
128 K 17 Adela st W10
92 M 11 Adelaide av SE4
93 N 11 Adelaide av SE4
8 F 4 Adelaide clo Enf
10 K 13 Adelaide clo Stanm
71 V 4 Adelaide cotts W7
37 Y 15 Adelaide gdns Rom
74 H 3 Adelaide gro W12
114 A 14 Adelaide rd Chisl
51 T 3 Adelaide rd E10
82 A 2 Adelaide rd Hounsl
54 A 6 Adelaide rd Ilf
130 H 1 Adelaide rd NW3
46 M 20 Adelaide rd NW3
47 N 20 Adelaide rd NW3
85 N 11 Adelaide rd Rich
170 B 10 Adelaide rd S'hall
116 J 13 Adelaide rd Surb
101 X 15 Adelaide rd Tedd
71 Z 4 Adelaide rd W13
140 J 11 Adelaide st WC2
63 O 14 Adelina gro E1
135 Z 20 Adelina gro E1
140 G 3 Adelina pl WC1
57 W 6 Adelphi cres Hornch
140 L 11 Adelphi ter WC2
49 O 13 Aden gro N16
9 V 15 Aden rd Enf
54 A 2 Aden rd Ilf
49 N 12 Aden ter N16
144 H 15 Adeney clo W6
93 O 19 Adenmore rd SE6
144 A 3 Adie rd W6
74 L 9 Adie rd W6
65 U 12 Adine rd E13
143 S 4 Adler st E1
50 J 14 Adley st E5
79 P 18 Admaston rd SE18
128 H 18 Admiral ms W10
95 T 9 Admiral Seymour rd SE9
93 O 3 Admiral st SE4
76 B 4 Admirals way E14
46 D 16 Admirals wlk NW3
101 V 16 Admiralty rd Tedd
57 V 17 Adnams wlk
111 P 10 Adolf st SE6
48 J 5 Adolphus rd N4
75 Z 19 Adolphus st SE8
55 X 11 Adomar rd Dgnhm
130 G 20 Adpar st W2
58 E 10 Adrienne av S'hall
91 W 9 Adys rd SE15
26 D 9 Aerodrome rd NW4
26 B 8 Aeroville NW9
133 O 10 Affleck st N1
88 J 6 Afghan rd SW11
45 W 14 Agamemnon rd NW6
132 D 1 Agar gro NW1
47 Y 20 Agar gro NW1
140 K 10 Agar st WC2
66 C 18 Agate clo E16
144 A 3 Agate rd W6
74 L 8 Agate rd W6
75 O 2 Agatha clo E1
114 C 4 Agaton rd SE9
44 M 12 Agave rd NW2
133 W 15 Agdon st EC1
46 L 13 Agincourt rd NW3
53 X 11 Agnes av Ilf
66 K 19 Agnes clo E6
55 X 11 Agnes gdns Dgnhm
74 C 4 Agnes rd W3
63 Y 16 Agnes st E14
92 G 18 Agnew rd SE23
8 H 16 Agricola pl Enf
55 Y 11 Aidan clo Dgnhm
65 P 1 Aileen wlk E15
84 A 13 Ailsa av Twick
83 Z 13 Ailsa av Twick
84 B 13 Ailsa rd Twick
64 G 14 Ailsa st E14
131 P 2 Ainger rd NW3
22 H 10 Ainsdale cres Pinn
60 H 13 Ainsdale rd W5
38 J 19 Ainsley av Rom
63 N 9 Ainsley st E2
135 X 14 Ainsley st E2
89 R 19 Ainslie wk SW12
20 C 17 Ainslie Wood cres E4

20 D 15 Ainslie Wood gdns E4
20 C 17 Ainslie Wood rd E4
75 R 5 Ainsty st SE16
44 G 9 Ainsworth clo NW2
156 K 1 Ainsworth rd Croy
63 P 1 Ainsworth rd E9
130 A 4 Ainsworth way NW8
66 C 5 Aintree av E6
36 B 7 Aintree cres Ilf
60 B 5 Aintree rd Grnfd
144 L 18 Aintree st SW6
140 D 10 Air st W1
133 N 2 Airdrie clo N1
74 D 12 Airedale av W4
88 M 20 Airedale rd SW12
89 N 19 Airedale rd SW12
72 F 8 Airedale rd W5
57 Z 20 Airfield way Hornch
53 Z 5 Airlie gdns Ilf
137 S 15 Airlie gdns W8
55 P 5 Airthrie rd Ilf
68 F 20 Aisher rd SE28
94 A 12 Aislibie rd SE12
135 R 5 Aitken clo E8
111 R 4 Aitken rd SE6
26 A 10 Ajax av NW9
45 W 14 Ajax rd NW6
86 G 17 Akehurst st SW15
46 F 15 Akenside rd NW3
116 E 15 Akerman rd Surb
79 T 18 Alabama st SE18
72 F 7 Alacross rd W5
4 D 19 Alan dri Barnt
56 D 1 Alan gdns Rom
105 T 12 Alan rd SW19
94 D 15 Alanthus clo SE12
141 T 16 Alaska st SE1
58 A 12 Alba clo Hay
27 T 18 Alba gdns NW11
137 N 4 Alba pl W11
93 R 15 Albacore cres SE13
10 D 1 Albany clo Bushey
97 U 19 Albany clo Bxly
30 K 14 Albany clo N15
85 U 11 Albany clo SW14
140 B 11 Albany courtyard W1
25 R 2 Albany cres Edg
25 Z 4 Albany ct NW9
9 R 5 Albany Park av Enf
9 T 4 Albany Park rd Enf
102 H 16 Albany Park rd Kingst
84 L 14 Albany pass Rich
9 U 2 Albany pk Enf
72 H 17 Albany pl Brentf
48 F 13 Albany pl N7
81 P 15 Albany rd Blvdr
72 H 17 Albany rd Brentf
97 U 19 Albany rd Bxly
113 Z 13 Albany rd Chisl
33 O 20 Albany rd E10
53 O 13 Albany rd E12
32 J 18 Albany rd E17
9 S 2 Albany rd Enf
57 W 6 Albany rd Hornch
19 O 17 Albany rd N18
30 E 20 Albany rd N4
117 Y 8 Albany rd New Mald
84 L 12 Albany rd Rich
38 B 18 Albany rd Rom
150 M 10 Albany rd SE1
150 C 15 Albany rd SE17
150 H 13 Albany rd SE5
105 Z 12 Albany rd SW19
60 B 19 Albany rd W13
131 X 8 Albany st NW1
21 P 13 Albany the Wdfd Grn
21 U 4 Albany view Buck Hl
79 T 18 Albatross st SE18
75 S 6 Albatross way SE16
36 A 19 Albemarle appr Ilf
100 E 2 Albemarle av Twick
117 Y 10 Albemarle gdns New Mald
36 A 19 Albemarle gdns Ilf
35 Z 19 Albemarle gdns Ilf
11 R 17 Albemarle pk Stanm
125 X 1 Albemarle rd Becknhm
15 X 2 Albemarle rd Barnt
140 A 12 Albemarle st W1
27 V 14 Alberon gdns NW11
20 B 14 Albert av E4
146 M 16 Albert br SW11
88 L 1 Albert Bridge rd SW11
146 M 18 Albert Bridge rd SW11
147 N 20 Albert Bridge rd SW11
108 A 13 Albert Carr gdns SW16
107 Z 13 Albert Carr gdns SW16
29 X 3 Albert clo N22
20 A 13 Albert cres E4
105 T 2 Albert dri SW19
148 M 8 Albert emb SE1
141 N 17 Albert emb SE1
139 R 17 Albert ga SW1
63 S 18 Albert gdns E1
105 P 20 Albert gro SW20
138 F 19 Albert Hall mans SW7
146 A 1 Albert ms W8
31 U 9 Albert pl N17
27 Y 4 Albert pl N3
137 Z 20 Albert pl W8
5 T 14 Albert rd Barnt
81 P 13 Albert rd Blvdr
127 P 12 Albert rd Brom
98 F 18 Albert rd Bxly
56 D 4 Albert rd Dgnhm
51 U 6 Albert rd E10
78 E 4 Albert rd E16
33 O 16 Albert rd E17
34 J 9 Albert rd E18
101 O 12 Albert rd Hampt
23 N 11 Albert rd Harrow
82 H 11 Albert rd Hounsl
54 C 9 Albert rd Ilf
120 M 6 Albert rd Mitch
31 R 18 Albert rd N15
29 V 5 Albert rd N22
48 D 3 Albert rd N4
118 E 10 Albert rd New Mald
27 F 13 Albert rd NW4
129 R 9 Albert rd NW6
13 S 16 Albert rd NW7
84 L 13 Albert rd Rich
39 T 17 Albert rd Rom
110 E 16 Albert rd SE20
124 B 11 Albert rd SE25
123 Z 8 Albert rd SE25
113 R 6 Albert rd SE9
154 F 12 Albert rd Sutton
101 X 15 Albert rd Tedd
101 V 1 Albert rd Twick
83 V 20 Albert rd Twick
60 C 13 Albert rd W5
81 P 14 Albert Road est Blvdr
52 A 16 Albert sq E15
90 C 1 Albert sq SW8
149 N 20 Albert sq SW8
15 P 15 Albert st N12
131 Z 8 Albert st NW1
131 S 5 Albert ter NW1
61 X 4 Albert ter NW10
131 S 4 Albert Terrace ms NW1
153 U 9 Alberta av Sutton
8 J 19 Alberta rd Enf
98 J 2 Alberta rd Erith
149 X 9 Alberta st SE17
29 O 4 Albion av N10
89 W 4 Albion av SW8
39 O 18 Albion clo Rom
138 L 8 Albion clo W2
135 O 2 Albion dri E8
56 F 14 Albion gdns Dgnhm
74 H 10 Albion gdns W6
49 R 11 Albion gro N16
133 T 2 Albion ms N1
45 V 20 Albion ms NW6
138 L 7 Albion ms W2
133 X 19 Albion pl EC1
160 F 2 Albion pl EC2
123 W 7 Albion pl SE25
98 D 11 Albion rd Bxly Hth
33 U 9 Albion rd E17
82 G 12 Albion rd Hounsl
117 V 1 Albion rd Kingst
49 P 10 Albion rd N16
31 W 7 Albion rd N17
154 E 15 Albion rd Sutton
101 T 2 Albion rd Twick
135 O 1 Albion sq E8
122 H 20 Albion st Croy
75 P 7 Albion st SE16
138 L 8 Albion st W2
135 N 1 Albion ter E8
110 C 6 Albion Vlls rd SE26
93 V 9 Albion way SE13
43 R 10 Albion way Wemb
91 S 8 Albrighton rd SE22
7 U 5 Albuhera clo Enf
97 Y 4 Albury av Bxly Hth
71 W 20 Albury av Islwth
156 L 8 Albury ct CR0
22 A 1 Albury dri Pinn
76 A 17 Albury st SE8
127 V 7 Albyfield Brom
93 P 4 Albyn rd SE8
50 A 6 Alcester cres E5
155 S 9 Alcester rd Wallgtn
155 Y 16 Alcock clo Wallgtn
49 X 8 Alconbury rd E5
153 X 1 Alcorn clo Sutton
59 V 15 Alcott clo W7
56 K 18 Aldborough rd Dgnhm
54 H 1 Aldborough rd Ilf
36 K 15 Aldborough Road north Ilf
54 G 5 Aldborough Road south Ilf
36 K 17 Aldborough Road south Ilf
74 F 3 Aldbourne rd W12
150 J 9 Aldbridge st SE17
43 S 20 Aldbury av Wemb
18 B 3 Aldbury ms N9
148 M 20 Aldebert ter SW8
149 N 20 Aldebert ter SW8
21 T 13 Aldeburgh pl Wdfd Grn
77 T 12 Aldeburgh st SE10
65 N 11 Alden av E15
132 D 10 Aldenham st NW1
74 K 9 Aldensley rd W6
151 O 16 Alder clo SE15
44 H 8 Alder gro NW2
114 J 8 Alder rd Sidcp
85 X 7 Alder rd SW14
89 R 18 Alderbrook rd SW12
71 G 17 Alderbury rd SW13
68 B 8 Alderman av Bark
160 C 4 Aldermanbury EC2
160 C 3 Aldermanbury sq EC2
17 O 13 Aldermans hill N13
136 F 6 Aldermans st W10
142 J 3 Aldermans wlk EC2
112 F 20 Aldermary rd Brom
151 S 9 Alderminster rd SE1
110 M 6 Aldermoor rd SE6
70 K 20 Alderney av Hounsl
40 D 20 Alderney gdns Nthlt
63 T 11 Alderney rd E1
148 A 10 Alderney st SW1
147 X 8 Alderney st SW1
20 M 19 Alders av Wdfd Grn
52 G 6 Alders clo E11
12 H 16 Alders clo Edg
12 H 16 Alders rd Edg
100 C 11 Alders the Felt
70 E 15 Alders the Hounsl
17 U 1 Alders the N21
159 R 1 Alders the W Wkhm
8 E 8 Aldersbrook av Enf
102 M 15 Aldersbrook dri Kingst
53 U 10 Aldersbrook la E12
52 H 6 Aldersbrook rd E11
53 O 9 Aldersbrook rd E12
54 F 18 Aldersey gdns Bark
92 F 12 Aldersford clo SE4
142 A 1 Aldersgate st EC1
160 A 1 Aldersgate st EC1
112 M 7 Aldersgrove av SE9
113 N 6 Aldersgrove av SE9
129 R 3 Aldershot rd NW6
124 G 14 Aldersmead av Croy
110 H 18 Aldersmead rd Becknhm
128 L 16 Alderson st W10
43 Z 8 Alderton clo NW10
26 J 17 Alderton cres NW4
123 V 16 Alderton rd Croy
90 L 9 Alderton rd SE24
87 W 5 Alderville rd SW6
83 P 6 Alderwick dri Hounsl
96 F 15 Alderwood rd SE9
139 T 12 Aldford st W1
142 M 6 Aldgate EC3
143 O 5 Aldgate High st E1
136 E 16 Aldine st W12
57 X 15 Aldingham gdns Hornch
55 U 3 Aldington clo Dgnhm
78 A 9 Aldington rd SE18
106 H 13 Aldis st SW17
45 X 15 Aldred rd NW6
106 D 7 Aldren rd SW17
159 U 19 Aldrich cres Croy
106 E 3 Aldrich ter SW18
20 F 19 Aldriche way E4
12 F 9 Aldridge av Edg
9 Z 2 Aldridge av Enf
24 K 6 Aldridge av Stanm
137 R 3 Aldridge rd vlls W11
118 A 16 Aldridge ri New Mald
16 M 3 Aldridge wlk N14
107 V 11 Aldrington rd SW16
129 X 19 Aldsworth clo W9
114 D 6 Aldwick clo SE9
156 C 7 Aldwick rd Croy
93 T 16 Aldworth gro SE13
51 Z 20 Aldworth rd E15
36 C 14 Aldwych av Ilf
57 X 5 Aldwych clo Hornch
141 O 7 Aldwych WC2
97 X 13 Alers rd Bxly Hth
66 B 17 Alestan Beck rd E16
128 A 2 Alexander av NW10
62 K 1 Alexander av NW10
5 U 14 Alexander clo Barnt
126 F 20 Alexander clo Brom
96 H 15 Alexander clo Sidcp
101 U 4 Alexander clo Twick
6 G 16 Alexander ct N14
137 W 4 Alexander ms W2
146 J 4 Alexander pl SW7
97 W 4 Alexander rd Bxly Hth
114 A 14 Alexander rd Chisl
48 A 8 Alexander rd N7
146 J 4 Alexander sq SW7
137 W 4 Alexander st W2
40 F 4 Alexandra av Harrow
29 Y 6 Alexandra av N22
70 D 1 Alexandra av S'hall
153 X 6 Alexandra av Sutton
89 O 2 Alexandra av SW11
73 Z 20 Alexandra av W4
40 J 10 Alexandra clo Harrow
92 M 3 Alexandra cotts SE14
112 B 14 Alexandra cres Brom
112 C 14 Alexandra cres Brom
109 R 13 Alexandra dri SE19
117 R 16 Alexandra dri Surb
82 K 5 Alexandra gdns Hounsl
155 N 18 Alexandra gdns Carsh
29 T 12 Alexandra gdns N10
15 O 18 Alexandra gro N12
48 K 5 Alexandra gro N4
29 W9 Alexandra palace N22
40 J 11 Alexandra park Harrow
29 Z 9 Alexandra park N22
29 S 7 Alexandra Park rd N22
123 R 19 Alexandra pl Croy
130 C 3 Alexandra pl NW8
130 C 3 Alexandra pl NW8
123 P 11 Alexandra pl SE25
72 G 17 Alexandra rd Brentf
123 R 19 Alexandra rd Croy
51 U 10 Alexandra rd E10
32 L 20 Alexandra rd E17
34 G 11 Alexandra rd E18
66 J 9 Alexandra rd E6
9 T 15 Alexandra rd Enf
82 K 7 Alexandra rd Hounsl
103 P 18 Alexandra rd Kingst
106 K 19 Alexandra rd Mitch
29 S 3 Alexandra rd N10
16 E 20 Alexandra rd N11
31 O 15 Alexandra rd N15
30 F 9 Alexandra rd N8
27 P 13 Alexandra rd NW4
130 D 3 Alexandra rd NW8
85 N 5 Alexandra rd Rich
39 S 18 Alexandra rd Rom
37 X 18 Alexandra rd Rom
110 E 15 Alexandra rd SE26
85 Z 8 Alexandra rd SW14
105 W 14 Alexandra rd SW19
84 F 17 Alexandra rd Twick
73 Z 6 Alexandra rd W4
119 Y 13 Alexandra sq Mrdn
65 R 14 Alexandra st E16
75 W 18 Alexandra st SE14
60 A 20 Alexandria rd W13
151 T 5 Alexis st SE16
50 B 11 Alfearn rd E5
159 W 15 Alford grn Croy
134 C 10 Alford pl N1
81 Z 13 Alford rd Erith
89 Y 3 Alford rd SW8
30 H 13 Alfoxton av N15
70 C 1 Alfred gdns S'hall
58 C 20 Alfred gdns S'hall
132 E 20 Alfred ms W1
140 E 1 Alfred pl W1
81 P 14 Alfred rd Belvdr
52 C 15 Alfred rd E15
116 L 7 Alfred rd Kingst

123 Y 10	Alfred rd SE25
154 E 12	Alfred rd Sutton
71 Y 1	Alfred rd W13
137 U 1	Alfred rd W2
73 W 3	Alfred rd W3
63 Z 8	Alfred st E3
89 R 2	Alfreda st SW11
67 W 5	Alfreds gdns Bark
67 W 5	Alfreds way Bark
105 O 7	Alfreton clo SW19
122 A 16	Alfriston av Croy
22 H 20	Alfriston av Harrow
116 L 13	Alfriston rd Surb
89 N 13	Alfriston rd SW11
83 Y 9	Algar clo Islwth
10 J 17	Algar clo Stanm
83 Y 8	Algar rd Islwth
106 B 1	Algarve rd SW18
26 G 19	Algernon rd NW4
129 S 5	Algernon rd NW6
93 R 8	Algernon rd SE13
93 P 11	Algiers rd SE13
150 J 2	Alice st SE1
24 C 14	Alicia av Harrow
24 D 14	Alicia clo Harrow
24 D 13	Alicia gdns Harrow
143 R 6	Alie st E1
43 V 3	Alington cres NW9
155 W 20	Alington gro Wallgtn
66 K 18	Alison clo E6
88 J 11	Aliwal rd SW11
74 A 13	Alkerden rd W4
49 V 7	Alkham rd N16
31 S 4	All Hallows rd N17
18 H 9	All Saints clo N9
10 F 19	All Saints ms Stanm
154 B 5	All Saints rd Sutton
106 D 16	All Saints rd SW19
137 O 3	All Saints rd W11
73 V 7	All Saints rd W3
132 M 7	All Saints st N1
133 N 7	All Saints st N1
128 A 4	All Souls av NW10
62 J 6	All Souls av NW10
139 Z 2	All Souls pl W1
117 Y 12	Allan clo New Mald
61 W 13	Allan way W3
27 T 10	Allandale av N3
57 U 1	Allard cres Bushey
10 A 7	Allardyce st SW9
90 C 10	Allbrook clo Tedd
101 T 11	Allcroft rd NW5
47 P 16	Allcroft rd NW5
148 J 20	Allen Edwards dri SW8
89 Z 1	Allen Edwards dri SW8
124 E 4	Allen rd Becknhm
122 E 19	Allen rd Croy
63 X 5	Allen rd E3
49 R 12	Allen rd N16
145 U 1	Allen rd W8
156 M 20	Allenby av S Croy
58 J 10	Allenby clo Grnfd
58 H 10	Allenby rd S'hall
110 H 6	Allenby rd SE23
58 G 17	Allendale av S'hall
110 F 12	Allendale clo SE26
42 A 17	Allendale rd Grnfd
9 R 18	Allens rd Enf
95 S 6	Allenswood rd SE9
22 L 14	Allerford ct Harrow
111 S 10	Allerford rd SE6
48 N 6	Allerton rd N16
144 K 19	Allerton rd N16
109 P 5	Alleyn cres SE21
70 F 13	Alleyn pk S'hall
109 P 3	Alleyn pk SE21
109 P 7	Alleyn rd SE21
55 T 7	Alleyndale rd Dgnhm
88 B 17	Allfarthing la SW18
119 O 15	Allgood clo Mrdn
135 P 10	Allgood st E2
66 C 16	Allhallows rd E6
65 X 13	Alliance rd E13
80 A 19	Alliance rd SE18
79 Z 17	Alliance rd SE18
61 S 12	Alliance rd W3
59 W 20	Allingham clo W7
134 A 7	Allingham st N1
105 P 13	Allington clo SW19
22 M 15	Allington rd Harrow
26 K 18	Allington rd NW4
128 K 10	Allington rd W10
147 Z 2	Allington st SW1
93 V 2	Allison clo SE10
109 S 1	Allison gro SE21
30 H 15	Allison rd N8
61 W 19	Allison rd W3
130 K 8	Allitsen rd NW8
89 W 12	Allnutt way SW4
55 O 6	Alloa rd Ilf
75 U 13	Alloa rd SE8
42 E 5	Allonby gdns Wemb
63 W 9	Alloway rd E3
131 R 18	Allsop pl NW1
15 P 6	Allum way N20
110 G 10	Allwood clo SE26
33 U 1	Alma av E4
153 T 10	Alma cres Sutton
151 P 6	Alma gro SE1
62 K 9	Alma pl NW10
109 T 17	Alma pl SE19
122 G 12	Alma rd Carsh
154 K 10	Alma rd Carsh
9 U 12	Alma rd Enf
29 R 3	Alma rd N10
58 A 20	Alma rd S'hall
115 O 6	Alma rd Sidcp
88 C 12	Alma rd SW18
23 S 3	Alma row Har
130 D 11	Alma sq NW8
51 X 16	Alma st E15
47 T 17	Alma st NW5
88 G 18	Alma ter SW18
50 C 12	Almack rd E5
133 W 3	Almedia st N1
104 G 17	Almer rd SW20
88 K 12	Almer rd SW11
48 B 4	Almington st N4
154 L 3	Almond av Carsh
72 J 8	Almond av W5
72 L 6	Almond av W5
127 W 17	Almond clo Brom
72 A 19	Almond gro Brentf
31 X 2	Almond rd N17
151 X 6	Almond rd SE16
127 W 17	Almond way Brom
22 L 8	Almond way Harrow
121 Y 10	Almond way Mitch
21 T 9	Almonds av Buck Hl
82 A 2	Almorah rd Hounsl
134 F 1	Almorah st N1
66 A 18	Alnwick av Ilf
120 A 9	Alnwick gro Mrdn
65 Y 18	Alnwick rd E16
94 H 17	Alnwick rd SE12
60 F 7	Alperton la Wemb
129 N 16	Alperton st W10
130 L 15	Alpha clo NW1
76 B6	Alpha gro E14
129 U 8	Alpha pl NW6
146 M 13	Alpha pl SW3
123 R 20	Alpha rd Croy
20 C 11	Alpha rd E4
9 W 15	Alpha rd Enf
18 J 18	Alpha rd N18
92 M 1	Alpha rd SE14
116 M 16	Alpha rd Surb
101 P 12	Alpha rd Tedd
91 X 5	Alpha st SE15
157 S 7	Alpine clo Croy
127 V 4	Alpine copse Brom
75 S 12	Alpine rd SE16
66 K 14	Alpine rd E6
10 G 8	Alpine wlk Stanm
118 B 6	Alric av New Mald
61 Z 1	Alric av NW10
43 Z 20	Alrick av NW10
30 G 20	Alroy rd N4
150 H 10	Alsace rd SE17
151 O 5	Alscot rd SE1
80 H 9	Alsike rd Belvdr
152 E 8	Alsom av Worc Pk
116 B 17	Alston clo Surb
4 E 10	Alston rd Barnt
18 M 18	Alston rd N18
106 F 11	Alston rd SW17
105 U 17	Alt gro SW19
18 H 20	Altair clo N17
113 U 5	Altash way SE9
72 B 7	Altenburg av W13
88 L 10	Altenburgh gdns SW11
22 B 3	Altham rd Pinn
88 B 6	Althea st SW6
117 N 7	Althorne way Kingst
34 B 13	Althorne gdns E18
56 D 6	Althorne way Dgnhm
106 K 1	Althorp rd SW17
23 O 16	Althorpe rd Harrow
66 G 4	Altmore av E6
53 T 20	Altmore av E6
23 W 2	Alton av Stanm
115 Z 3	Alton clo Bxly
83 X 3	Alton clo Islwth
111 N 19	Alton gdns Becknhm
83 R 17	Alton gdns Twick
156 F 7	Alton rd Croy
31 O 11	Alton rd N17
84 L 11	Alton rd Rich
104 G 1	Alton rd SW15
86 H 19	Alton rd SW15
64 C 16	Alton st E14
124 K 13	Altyre clo Becknhm
157 P 4	Altyre rd Croy
124 L 12	Altyre way Becknhm
46 B 15	Alvanley gdns NW6
123 S 11	Alverston gdns SE25
15 V 2	Alverstone av Barnt
105 X 5	Alverstone av SW19
96 A 20	Alverstone gdns SE9
118 E 8	Alverstone rd E12
53 W 14	Alverstone rd E12
44 M 20	Alverstone rd NW2
43 N 3	Alverstone rd Wemb
75 X 15	Alverton st SE8
24 B 11	Alveston av Harrow
150 J 9	Alvey st SE17
154 D 8	Alvia gdns Sutton
49 U 15	Alvington cres E8
94 J 17	Alwald cres SE12
73 X 14	Alwyn av W4
159 S 17	Alwyn clo Croy
61 T 17	Alwyn gdns W3
48 K 19	Alwyne la N1
48 K 19	Alwyne pl N1
48 K 20	Alwyne rd N1
105 V 14	Alwyne rd SW19
71 S 1	Alwyne rd W7
48 L 18	Alwyne sq N1
48 K 20	Alwyne vlls N1
27 X 18	Alyth gdns NW11
72 A 17	Amalgamated dri Brentf
143 V 6	Amazon st E1
82 B 5	Ambassador clo Hounsl
140 B 16	Ambassadors ct SW1
32 H 4	Amber av E17
51 Z 19	Amber st E15
27 Z 10	Amberden av N3
149 X 10	Ambergate st SE17
22 D 11	Amberley clo Pinn
115 U 13	Amberley ct Sidcp
152 C 9	Amberley gdns Epsom
18 F 4	Amberley gdns Enf
123 U 18	Amberley gro Croy
109 Z 11	Amberley gro SE26
21 Z 5	Amberley rd Buck Hl
33 P 20	Amberley rd E10
18 F 1	Amberley rd Enf
17 P 9	Amberley rd N13
80 J 16	Amberley rd SE2
129 W 19	Amberley rd W9
119 W 17	Amberley way Mrdn
38 H 12	Amberley way Rom
118 B 15	Amberwood ri New Mald
112 J 7	Amblecote clo SE12
112 J 7	Amblecote rd SE12
48 H 9	Ambler rd N4
124 J 12	Ambleside av Becknhm
57 Y 15	Ambleside av Hornch
107 X 10	Ambleside av SW16
111 Y 15	Ambleside Brom
50 D 14	Ambleside clo E9
9 T 11	Ambleside cres Enf
154 D 14	Ambleside gdns Sutton
42 F 3	Ambleside gdns Wemb
35 S 14	Ambleside gdns Ilf
98 D 4	Ambleside rd Bxly Hth
62 D 1	Ambleside rd NW10
155 Y 20	Ambrey way Wallgtn
81 S 9	Ambrooke rd Belvdr
148 B 3	Ambrosden av SW1
27 U 20	Ambrose av NW11
66 F 16	Ambrose clo E6
151 V 6	Ambrose st SE16
150 A 8	Amelia st SE17
148 Z 8	Amelia st SE17
141 Y 5	Amen corner EC4
107 N 14	Amen corner SW17
141 Y 5	Amen ct EC4
143 N 8	America sq EC3
142 A 15	America st SE1
87 W 15	Amerland rd SW18
75 X 18	Amersham ga SE14
123 N 13	Amersham rd Croy
23 S 18	Amersham rd Harrow
18 B 18	Amersham rd N18
92 L 1	Amersham rd SE14
75 Y 19	Amersham vale SE14
128 A 5	Amery gdns NW10
62 L 3	Amery gdns NW10
41 Y 7	Amery rd Harrow
119 N 19	Ames clo Worc Pk
108 B 4	Amesbury av SW2
20 D 1	Amesbury dri E4
68 J 1	Amesbury rd Dgnhm
127 O 5	Amesbury rd Brom
51 X 13	Amethyst rd E15
60 C 17	Amherst av W13
60 D 17	Amherst av W13
83 V 4	Amhurst gdns Islwth
31 R 20	Amhurst pas E8
50 A 16	Amhurst rd E8
49 Z 15	Amhurst rd E8
49 U 11	Amhurst rd N16
49 W 12	Amhurst ter E8
55 P 13	Amidas gdns Dgnhm
63 P 11	Amiel st E1
88 L 8	Amies st SW11
118 L 2	Amity gro SW20
65 O 2	Amity rd E15
89 O 15	Amner rd SW11
144 A 2	Amor rd W6
74 L 8	Amor rd W6
91 W 8	Amott rd SE15
48 C 19	Amour clo N7
64 A 19	Amoy pl E14
80 F 5	Ampleforth rd SE2
53 N 13	Ampton pl WC1
133 N 14	Ampton st WC1
110 A 1	Amroth clo SE23
76 H 8	Amsterdam rd E14
8 B 17	Amwell clo Enf
133 S 12	Amwell st EC1
84 A 18	Amyand la Twick
84 A 18	Amyand Park gdns Twick
84 B 17	Amyand Park rd Twick
83 Z 19	Amyand Park rd Twick
93 N 13	Amyruth rd SE4
89 N 3	Anatis st SW11
47 U 7	Anatola rd N19
118 F 15	Ancaster cres New Mald
124 F 7	Ancaster rd Becknhm
79 V 19	Ancaster st SE18
77 X 11	Anchor & Hope la SE7
151 W 6	Anchor clo SE16
105 Z 13	Anchorage clo SW19
144 J 15	Ancill clo W6
62 G 6	Ancona rd NW10
79 T 12	Ancona rd SE18
90 A 8	Andalus rd SW9
42 G 13	Ander clo Wemb
82 K 11	Anderson clo Hounsl
50 F 17	Anderson clo W10
35 O 9	Anderson rd Ilf
147 N 8	Anderson st SW3
81 V 5	Anderson way Belvdr
91 P 8	Anderton clo SE5
58 L 10	Andover clo Grnfd
129 X 9	Andover pl NW6
101 R 2	Andover rd Twick
49 Y 14	Andre st E8
98 M 14	Andrew clo Bxly
89 Y 1	Andrew pl SW8
64 G 17	Andrew st E14
66 D 17	Andrewes clo E6
21 Y 7	Andrews clo Buck Hl
153 N 2	Andrews clo Worc Pk
135 X 6	Andrews rd E8
80 D 6	Andwell clo SE2
109 V 18	Anerley gro SE19
109 W 17	Anerley hill SE19
109 Y 17	Anerley Park rd SE20
110 A 17	Anerley pk SE20
109 Y 18	Anerley pk SE20
124 A 1	Anerley rd SE20
109 Y 20	Anerley rd SE20
109 Z 20	Anerley Station rd SE20
109 W 17	Anerley vale SE19
89 V 19	Anfield clo SW12
143 P 3	Angel all E1
18 H 15	Angel clo N18
160 A 4	Angel ct EC1
160 F 5	Angel ct EC2
140 C 14	Angel ct W1
154 B 4	Angel Hill dri Sutton
154 A 5	Angel Hill Sutton
51 X 18	Angel la E15
133 T 9	Angel ms N1
90 G 7	Angel Park gdns SW9
160 E 10	Angel pass EC4
18 J 15	Angel pl N18

9 O 14 Angel rd Enf
23 U 18 Angel rd Harrow
19 O 17 Angel rd N18
142 A 4 Angel st EC1
141 Z 4 Angel st EC1
39 O 15 Angel way Rom
144 B 8 Angel wlk W6
74 L 12 Angel wlk W6
82 K 12 Angelfield Hounsl
190 G 6 Angell rd SW9
94 D 1 Angerstein la SE3
55 U 4 Angle green Dgnhm
102 C 10 Anglers clo Rich
47 T 17 Anglers la NW5
108 B 9 Angles rd SW16
78 M 12 Anglesea av SE18
116 G 9 Anglesea rd Kingst
78 L 12 Anglesea rd SE18
135 U 18 Anglesea st E1
155 O 15 Anglesey Ct rd Carsh
155 O 15 Anglesey gdns Carsh
9 O 13 Anglesey rd Enf
22 G 10 Anglesmede cres Pinn
22 F 10 Anglesmede way Pinn
66 H 4 Anglia wk E6
63 Y 6 Anglo rd E3
25 Z 5 Angus gdns NW9
65 Y 10 Angus rd E13
75 W 19 Angus st SE14
146 L 19 Anhalt rd SW11
78 L 20 Ankerdine cres SE18
95 Y 1 Ankerdine cres SE18
101 S 12 Anlaby rd Tedd
136 F 20 Anley rd W14
11 R 14 Anmer lodge Stanm
24 H 6 Anmersh gro Stanm
146 F 16 Ann la SW10
88 C 17 Ann's Park rd SW18
135 R 4 Anna clo E8
64 C 18 Annabel clo E14
39 O 4 Annan way Rom
157 Y 3 Annandale rd Croy
77 P 14 Annandale rd SE10
96 J 19 Annandale rd Sidcp
74 A 13 Annandale rd W4
102 K 12 Anne Boleyns wlk Kingst
153 R 16 Anne Boleyns wlk Sutton
65 S 11 Anne st E13
25 Z 10 Annesley av NW9
44 A 10 Annesley clo NW10
158 M 6 Annesley dri Croy
94 G 2 Annesley rd SE3
47 U 6 Annesley wlk N19
23 T 7 Annette clo Harrow
48 D 12 Annette rd N7
63 Z 4 Annie Besant clo E3
29 N 11 Annington rd N2
50 H 19 Annis rd E9
139 S 19 Anns clo SW1
143 O 2 Anns pl E1
123 N 7 Annsworthy av Thntn Hth
123 P 4 Annsworthy cres Thntn Hth
92 C 5 Ansdell rd SE15
137 Y 20 Ansdell st W8
137 Y 20 Ansdell ter W8
155 N 1 Ansell gro Carsh
106 K 7 Ansell rd SW17
157 U 4 Anselm clo Croy
22 E 3 Anselm rd Pinn
145 S 15 Anselm rd SW6
111 V 11 Ansford rd Brom
136 H 10 Ansleigh pl W11
38 F 7 Anson clo Rom
47 X 12 Anson rd N7
44 L 14 Anson rd NW2
45 P 14 Anson rd NW2
40 L 17 Anson ter Nthlt
65 U 16 Anstey rd SE15
91 X 7 Anstey rd SE15
30 K 13 Anstey wlk N15
96 E 16 Anstridge rd SE9
78 E 8 Antelope rd SE18
13 P 14 Anthony clo NW7
59 S 7 Anthony rd Grnfd
123 X 15 Anthony rd SE25
97 O 2 Anthony rd Welling
143 X 5 Anthony st E1
63 W 8 Antill rd E3
31 W 13 Antill rd N15
63 S 17 Antill ter E1
153 W 6 Anton cres Sutton
49 Y 14 Anton st E8
46 L 17 Antrim gro NW3
46 L 18 Antrim rd NW3

153 W 13 Antrobus clo Sutton
73 V 10 Antrobus rd W4
21 U 19 Anworth clo Wdfd Grn
156 A 19 Apeldoorn dri SM6
111 S 20 Apex clo Becknhm
83 S 1 Aplin way Islwth
112 G 20 Apollo av Brom
57 X 6 Apollo clo Hornch
146 F 17 Apollo pl SW10
141 W 7 Apothecary st EC4
90 E 14 Appach rd SW2
8 E 12 Apple gro Enf
116 H 4 Apple mkt Kingst
140 D 12 Apple Tree yd SW1
20 E 19 Appleby clo E4
31 O 16 Appleby clo N15
101 P 5 Appleby clo Twick
65 R 18 Appleby rd E16
49 Y 20 Appleby rd E8
135 N 8 Appleby st E2
98 L 4 Appledore av Bxly Hth
126 D 11 Appledore clo Brom
25 O 4 Appledore clo Edg
106 L 3 Appledore clo SW17
114 J 8 Appledore cres Sidcp
128 M 18 Appleford rd W10
72 H 12 Applegarth Brentf
158 S 16 Applegarth Croy
36 L 13 Applegarth dri Ilf
80 F 1 Applegarth rd SE28
144 G 3 Applegarth rd W14
118 F 14 Appleton gdns New Mald
95 P 7 Appleton rd SE9
44 J 9 Applewood clo NW2
134 J 20 Appold st EC2
5 S 15 Approach rd Barnt
63 P 7 Approach rd E2
118 M 3 Approach rd SW20
9 N 8 Approach the Enf
27 O 15 Approach the NW4
61 Z 17 Approach the W3
27 N 13 Aprey gdns NW4
59 U 19 April clo W7
110 F 7 April glen SE23
49 V 13 April st E8
22 M 15 Apsley clo Harrow
32 K 14 Apsley rd E17
117 W 7 Apsley rd New Mald
123 Z 9 Apsley rd SE25
130 H 8 Aquila st NW8
141 T 14 Aquinas st SE1
86 C 10 Arabella dri SW15
20 H 2 Arabia clo E4
92 K 10 Arabin rd SE4
152 H 20 Aragon av Epsom
102 H 12 Aragon rd Kingst
119 P 16 Aragon rd Mrdn
11 S 14 Aran dri Stanm
37 O 19 Arandora cres Brom
63 V 7 Arbery rd E3
125 R 3 Arbor clo Becknhm
20 K 11 Arbor rd E4
9 T 12 Arbour rd Enf
63 R 17 Arbour sq E1
57 Y 14 Arbour way Hornch
95 S 7 Arbroath rd SE9
109 Y 8 Arbury ter SE26
98 A 15 Arbuthnot la Bxly
97 Z 16 Arbuthnot la Bxly
92 F 4 Arbuthnot rd SE14
134 M 2 Arbutus st E8
39 R 17 Arcade pl Rom
142 J 2 Arcade the EC2
27 X 6 Arcadia av N3
64 B 16 Arcadia st E14
97 Y 16 Arcadian av Bxly
97 Y 16 Arcadian av Bxly
30 E 1 Arcadian gdns N22
97 Y 17 Arcadian rd Bxly
150 A 3 Arch st SE1
75 U 6 Archangel st SE16
149 O 2 Archbishops pk SE11
90 D 17 Archbishops pl SW2
91 V 11 Archdale rd SE22
145 P 13 Archel rd W14
123 Z 8 Archer rd SE25
140 E 9 Archer st W1
23 W 9 Archery clo Harrow
138 M 7 Archery clo W2
95 U 12 Archery rd SE9
139 W 11 Archibald ms W1
64 A 10 Archibald rd N7
64 A 10 Archibald st E3
47 V 6 Archway clo N19
106 A 9 Archway clo SW19

47 V 6 Archway mall N19
29 O 18 Archway rd N6
47 U 3 Archway rd N6
86 B 7 Archway st SW13
49 U 14 Arcola st E8
47 R 15 Arctic st NW5
112 A 14 Arcus rd Brom
91 O 14 Ardbeg rd SE24
10 G 2 Arden clo Bushey
41 P 10 Arden clo Harrow
28 G 20 Arden Court gdns N2
68 H 1 Arden cres Dgnhm
55 W 20 Arden cres Dgnhm
27 V 9 Arden rd N3
122 E 5 Ardfern av SW16
111 Y 3 Ardfillan rd SE6
93 Y 19 Ardgowan rd SE6
111 Y 3 Ardgowan rd SE6
48 L 12 Ardilaun rd N5
119 X 19 Ardleigh gdns Sutton
32 L 5 Ardleigh rd E17
49 P 18 Ardleigh rd N1
32 M 5 Ardleigh ter E17
44 A 9 Ardley clo NW10
110 J 7 Ardley clo SE23
108 L 4 Ardlui rd SE27
116 J 12 Ardmay gdns Surb
93 X 15 Ardmere rd SE13
21 W 4 Ardmore la Buck Hl
111 W 4 Ardoch rd SE6
152 F 5 Ardrossan gdns Worc Pk
36 C 17 Ardwell av Ilf
108 A 3 Ardwell rd SW2
45 X 12 Ardwick rd NW2
50 G 2 Argall av E10
141 T 16 Argent st SE1
145 U 19 Argon ms SW6
38 G 6 Argus clo Rom
58 A 9 Argus way Nthlt
82 H 17 Argyle av Hounsl
82 J 15 Argyle av Hounsl
59 Y 11 Argyle clo W13
74 K 11 Argyle pl W6
4 A 13 Argyle rd Barnt
63 S 11 Argyle rd E1
51 Z 13 Argyle rd E15
59 X 8 Argyle rd Grnfd
22 J 17 Argyle rd Harrow
53 W 6 Argyle rd Ilf
14 M 16 Argyle rd N12
15 N 17 Argyle rd N12
31 W 4 Argyle rd N17
18 L 13 Argyle rd N18
60 A 19 Argyle rd W13
59 Z 12 Argyle rd W13
132 L 12 Argyle sq WC1
132 L 13 Argyle st WC1
70 J 2 Argyll av S'hall
25 T 7 Argyll gdns Edg
137 U 20 Argyll rd W8
140 A 6 Argyll st W1
92 H 9 Arica rd SE4
91 O 16 Ariel rd NW6
136 D 12 Ariel way W12
89 Y 9 Aristotle rd SW4
108 J 19 Arkell gro SE19
111 U 8 Arkindale rd SE6
32 K 17 Arkley cres E17
32 K 17 Arkley rd E17
75 X 17 Arklow rd SE14
46 D 15 Arkwright rd NW3
157 V 20 Arkwright rd S Croy
65 P 18 Arkwright st E16
90 A 7 Arlesford rd SW9
87 S 14 Arlesley clo SW15
90 F 15 Arlingford rd SW2
134 D 6 Arlington av N1
96 G 19 Arlington clo Sidcp
153 Y 3 Arlington clo Sutton
84 C 14 Arlington clo Twick
154 L 3 Arlington dri Carsh
53 V 3 Arlington gdns Ilf
73 V 13 Arlington gdns W4
14 K 11 Arlington N12
34 G 3 Arlington rd Wdfd Grn
16 G 6 Arlington rd N14
132 A 8 Arlington rd NW1
131 Y 5 Arlington rd NW1
102 F 5 Arlington rd Rich
116 H 15 Arlington rd Surb
101 V 10 Arlington rd Tedd
84 C 15 Arlington rd Twick
60 B 18 Arlington rd W13
134 C 6 Arlington sq N1
140 A 13 Arlington st SW1
133 U 12 Arlington way EC1
17 U 6 Arlow rd N21

31 Z 14 Armadale clo N15
145 T 16 Armadale rd SW6
63 Y 4 Armagh rd E3
121 N 3 Armfield cres Mitch
8 B 6 Armfield rd Enf
74 K 3 Arminger rd W12
45 U 4 Armitage rd NW11
77 O 13 Armitage rd SE10
87 Y 13 Armoury way SW18
56 D 20 Armstead wlk Dgnhm
69 R 1 Armstead wlk Dgnhm
20 M 19 Armstrong av Wdfd Grn
66 G 17 Armstrong clo E6
5 T 12 Armstrong cres Barnt
77 Y 12 Armstrong gdns SE7
100 B 13 Armstrong rd Felt
74 D 2 Armstrong rd W3
70 L 5 Armstrong wy S'hall
87 T 18 Arnal cres SW 18
87 Z 14 Arndale wlk SW18
140 L 6 Arne st WC2
94 B 10 Arne wlk SE3
148 F 3 Arneway st SW1
37 W 11 Arneways av Rom
104 F 2 Arnewood clo SW15
121 N 14 Arneys la Mitch
93 W 19 Arngask rd SE6
91 S 13 Arnham way SE22
4 Z 2 Arnold cir E2
135 N 14 Arnold cir E2
25 N 20 Arnold clo Harrow
83 R 13 Arnold cres Islwth
17 U 15 Arnold gdns N13
69 P 2 Arnold rd Dgnhm
68 R 2 Arnold rd Dgnhm
64 A 9 Arnold rd E3
31 T 11 Arnold rd N15
40 B 18 Arnold rd Nthlt
106 M 17 Arnold rd SW17
16 K 12 Arnos gro N14
16 J 15 Arnos rd N11
80 F 1 Arnott clo SE28
73 Y 12 Arnott clo W4
91 P 9 Arnould av SE5
98 D 10 Arnsberg way Bxly Hth
42 G 3 Arnside gdns Wemb
98 E 2 Arnside rd Bxly Hth
150 D 13 Arnside st SE17
111 R 10 Arnulf st SE6
108 H 15 Arnulls rd SW16
90 D 15 Arodene rd SW2
110 D 19 Arpley rd SE20
159 S 5 Arragon gdns W Wkhm
108 A 16 Arragon gdns SW16
66 B 5 Arragon rd E6
83 Z 20 Arragon rd Twick
155 T 8 Arran cl Wallgtn
53 N 5 Arran dri E12
111 S 3 Arran rd SE6
48 M 20 Arran wlk
120 D 10 Arras av Mrdn
124 E 5 Arrol rd Becknhm
64 D 9 Arrow rd E3
95 T 6 Arsenal rd SE9
105 N 18 Arterberry rd SW20
39 T 20 Artesian clo Hornch
137 T 6 Artesian rd W2
64 M 3 Arthingworth st E15
79 O 11 Arthur gro SE18
60 O G Arthur rd E6
103 P 19 Arthur rd Kingst
48 D 11 Arthur rd N7
18 F 7 Arthur rd N9
118 K 12 Arthur rd New Mald
37 U 19 Arthur rd Rom
105 Y 7 Arthur rd SW19
160 F 9 Arthur st EC4
122 K 14 Artichoke hill E1
91 O 2 Artichoke pl SE5
36 D 17 Artillery clo Ilf
142 L 1 Artillery la E1
142 M 2 Artillery pas E1
78 H 12 Artillery pl SE18
148 D 2 Artillery row SW1
119 W 9 Arundel av Mrdn
98 C 15 Arundel clo Bxly
156 H 7 Arundel clo Croy
52 A 13 Arundel clo E15
100 L 13 Arundel clo Hampt
88 H 13 Arundel clo SW18
34 G 2 Arundel ct Wdfd Grn
40 F 14 Arundel dri Harrow
25 Y 2 Arundel gdns Edg
55 N 6 Arundel gdns Ilf

17 U 7	Arundel gdns N21
137 N 8	Arundel gdns W11
49 R 15	Arundel gro N16
48 F 19	Arundel pl N1
5 X 12	Arundel rd Barnet
123 O 15	Arundel rd Croy
117 U 2	Arundel rd Kingst
153 U 17	Arundel rd Sutton
48 F 19	Arundel sq N1
141 P 8	Arundel st WC2
144 A 14	Arundel ter SW13
74 K 17	Arundel ter SW13
48 G 15	Arvon rd N5
148 B 20	Ascalon st SW8
38 L 1	Ascension rd Rom
33 P 1	Ascham dri E4
32 J 3	Ascham end E17
47 V 14	Ascham st NW5
40 G 16	Ascot clo Nthlt
9 P 1	Ascot gdns Enf
58 F 15	Ascot gdns S'hall
66 F 8	Ascot rd E6
31 O 16	Ascot rd N15
18 L 13	Ascot rd N18
107 N 15	Ascot rd SW17
72 J 5	Ascott av W5
154 L 2	Ash clo Carsh
117 Y 3	Ash clo New Mald
38 G 3	Ash clo Rom
124 C 3	Ash clo SE20
116 P 9	Ash clo Sidcp
10 K 20	Ash clo Stanm
135 X 5	Ash gro E8
18 D 2	Ash gro Enf
17 X 12	Ash gro N13
45 R 13	Ash gro NW2
58 J 13	Ash gro S'hall
124 C 3	Ash gro SE 20
159 V 1	Ash gro W Wckm
72 K 8	Ash gro W5
41 Y 13	Ash gro Wemb
39 W 1	Ash la Rom
159 O 2	Ash rd Croy
52 B 15	Ash rd E5
119 T 19	Ash rd Sutton
127 X 15	Ash row Brom
124 H 13	Ash Tree clo Croy
25 X 15	Ash Tree dell NW9
124 G 12	Ash Tree way Croy
124 H 14	Ash Tree way Croy
81 N 19	Ashbourne av Bxly Hth
41 R 7	Ashbourne av Harrow
34 H 13	Ashbourne av E18
107 R 17	Ashbourne av Mitch
15 Z 7	Ashbourne av N20
27 V 14	Ashbourne av NW11
15 O 14	Ashbourne clo N12
61 O 13	Ashbourne clo N17
12 L 17	Ashbourne gro NW7
91 U 12	Ashbourne gro SE22
74 B 14	Ashbourne gro W4
60 M 11	Ashbourne rd W5
61 O 14	Ashbourne rd W5
105 W 17	Ashbourne ter SW19
27 V 14	Ashbourne way NW11
24 E 19	Ashbridge clo Harrow
34 A 20	Ashbridge rd E11
130 K 18	Ashbridge st NW8
56 H 10	Ashbrook rd Dgnhm
47 X 5	Ashbrook rd N19
146 A 5	Ashburn gdns SW7
146 B 5	Ashburn ms SW7
146 A 5	Ashburn pl SW7
23 W 20	Ashburnham av Harrow
23 X 20	Ashburnham gdns Harrow
76 E 20	Ashburnham gro SE10
28 G 12	Ashburnham pl N2
76 E 20	Ashburnham pl SE10
128 C 11	Ashburnham rd NW10
146 D 19	Ashburnham rd SW10
62 M 8	Ashburnham rd NW10
81 X 10	Ashburnham rd Erith
102 C 7	Ashburnham rd
123 Z 20	Ashburton av Croy
54 H 14	Ashburton av IIf
157 W 1	Ashburton clo Croy
157 W 2	Ashburton gdns Croy
48 F 13	Ashburton gro N7
157 W 2	Ashburton rd Croy
123 W 20	Ashburton rd Croy
65 T 17	Ashburton rd E16
65 S 6	Ashburton ter E13
37 V 16	Ashbury gdns Rom
89 N 6	Ashbury rd SW11
48 M 20	Ashby gro N1
92 L 6	Ashby ms SE4
31 W 15	Ashby rd N15
92 L 5	Ashby rd SE4
93 N 5	Ashby rd SE4
133 X 13	Ashby st EC1
122 M 15	Ashby wlk Croy
74 F 8	Aschurch ct W12
74 F 7	Aschurch gro W12
74 F 8	Aschurch Park vlls W12
74 F 7	Aschurch ter W12
116 G 18	Ashcombe av Surb
12 B 14	Ashcombe gdns Edg
44 C 10	Ashcombe pk NW2
155 O 12	Ashcombe rd Carsh
105 Y 12	Ashcombe rd SW19
117 V 5	Ashcombe sq New Mald
87 Z 6	Ashcombe st SW6
96 M 15	Ashcroft av Sidcp
97 N 16	Ashcroft cres Sidcp
63 V 9	Ashcroft rd E3
144 A 7	Ashcroft sq W6
82 L 18	Ashdale clo Twick
10 K 19	Ashdale gro Stanm
112 J 1	Ashdale rd SE12
82 L 18	Ashdale way Twick
21 V 19	Ashdon clo Wdfd Grn
62 C 3	Ashdon rd NW10
125 S 4	Ashdown clo Becknhm
47 O 15	Ashdown cres NW5
9 O 10	Ashdown rd Enf
116 J 4	Ashdown rd Kingst
107 O 3	Ashdown way SW17
38 H 6	Ashdown wlk Rom
99 W 16	Ashen dri Drtfrd
105 X 5	Ashen gro SW19
158 G 20	Ashen vale S Croy
50 G 14	Ashenden rd E5
143 U 11	Asher dri E1
102 J 2	Ashfield clo Rich
114 C 17	Ashfield la Chisl
16 J 6	Ashfield pde N14
16 G 11	Ashfield rd N14
30 M 19	Ashfield rd W3
74 C 1	Ashfield st E1
63 N 16	Ashfield st E1
63 P 16	Ashfield st E1
143 W 3	Ashfield st E1
29 Z 14	Ashford av N8
58 A 18	Ashford clo Hay
9 R 8	Ashford cres Enf
32 K 18	Ashford gro E17
34 J 8	Ashford rd E18
53 V 20	Ashford rd E6
45 O 12	Ashford rd NW2
134 J 12	Ashford st N1
111 Y 14	Ashgrove rd Brom
54 L 5	Ashgrove rd IIf
55 N 4	Ashgrove rd IIf
87 W 5	Ashington rd SW6
108 A 10	Ashlake rd SW16
139 T 1	Ashland pl W1
64 L 3	Ashland rd E15
78 M 12	Ashlar pl SE18
154 A 3	Ashleigh gdns Sutton
124 B 5	Ashleigh rd SE20
86 A 7	Ashleigh rd SW14
35 Z 8	Ashley av IIf
119 Y 12	Ashley av Mrdn
27 N 7	Ashley clo NW4
30 G 8	Ashley cres N22
89 P 7	Ashley cres SW11
82 K 20	Ashley dri Twick
17 Z 14	Ashley gdns N13
102 G 5	Ashley gdns Rich
42 K 7	Ashley gdns Wemb
156 J 8	Ashley la Croy
27 N 7	Ashley la NW4
148 B 3	Ashley pl SW1
20 A 18	Ashley rd E4
65 Y 1	Ashley rd E7
9 P 10	Ashley rd Enf
100 H 20	Ashley rd Hampt
31 Y 11	Ashley rd N17
48 A 2	Ashley rd N19
84 K 8	Ashley rd Rich
106 A 15	Ashley rd SW19
122 D 10	Ashley rd Thntn Hth
27 N 2	Ashley wlk NW7
51 Y 13	Ashlin rd E15
123 X 20	Ashling rd Croy
87 N 6	Ashlone rd SW15
6 H 18	Ashmead N14
93 O 4	Ashmead rd SE8
125 W 3	Ashmere av Becknhm
153 N 12	Ashmere clo Sutton
90 A 11	Ashmere gro SW4
130 L 19	Ashmill st NW1
149 O 15	Ashmole est SW8
149 R 16	Ashmole pl SW8
149 R 16	Ashmole st SW8
96 F 7	Ashmore gro Welling
129 O 11	Ashmore rd W9
31 U 14	Ashmount rd N15
47 V 14	Ashmount rd N19
38 M 8	Ashmour gdns Rom
39 N 8	Ashmour gdns Rom
41 O 9	Ashneal gdns Harrow
42 A 19	Ashness gdns Grnfd
88 M 13	Ashness rd SW11
24 E 19	Ashridge clo Harrow
79 O 20	Ashridge cres SE18
16 M 15	Ashridge gdns N13
17 N 16	Ashridge gdns N13
22 B 13	Ashridge gdns Pinn
119 U 8	Ashridge way Mrdn
49 X 1	Anstead rd E5
153 W 9	Ashton clo Sutton
82 O 10	Ashton gdns Hounsl
37 Z 19	Ashton gdns Rom
51 X 16	Ashton rd E15
64 G 19	Ashton st E14
120 H 3	Ashtree av Mitch
123 V 17	Ashurch rd Croy
99 T 8	Ashurst clo Drtfrd
36 C 14	Ashurst dri IIf
35 Z 18	Ashurst dri IIf
6 A 15	Ashurst rd Barnet
5 Z 17	Ashurst rd Barnet
15 X 17	Ashurst rd N12
157 Z 2	Ashurst wlk Croy
106 L 11	Ashvale rd SW17
51 W 8	Ashville rd E11
112 F 2	Ashwater rd SE12
66 F 17	Ashwell clo E6
49 T 17	Ashwin st E8
159 T 15	Ashwood gdns Croy
20 K 11	Ashwood rd E4
91 N 4	Ashworth clo SE5
129 Y 13	Ashworth rd W9
97 X 11	Askern clo Bxly Hth
74 F 6	Askew bldgs W12
74 E 4	Askew cres W12
74 E 4	Askew rd W12
74 E 5	Askew rd W12
74 G 7	Askew rd W12
74 F 3	Askew rd W12
87 T 14	Askill dri SW15
88 B 18	Aslert st SW18
45 U 14	Asmara rd NW2
27 X 15	Asmuns hill NW11
27 W 15	Asmuns pl NW11
72 M 6	Aspen clo W5
127 U 3	Aspen copse Brom
41 Z 10	Aspen dri Harrow
121 N 12	Aspen gdns Mitch
74 K 13	Aspen gdns W6
81 P 7	Aspen grn Blvdr
58 C 10	Aspen la Nthlt
74 E 1	Aspen way E14
16 L 9	Aspenlea rd W6
92 F 8	Aspinall rd SE4
75 O 10	Aspinden rd SE16
151 Y 5	Aspinden rd SE16
50 A 16	Aspland gro E8
88 B 14	Aspley rd SW18
31 Y 4	Asplins rd N17
143 S 4	Assam st E1
63 P 13	Assembly pas E1
120 H 18	Assembly wlk Carsh
81 P 13	Assurance cotts Blvdr
23 R 5	Astall clo Harrow
92 B 1	Astbury rd SE15
76 F 6	Aste st E14
146 L 9	Astell st SW3
36 C 12	Asthall gdns IIf
89 O 3	Astle st SW11
45 N 14	Astley av NW2
133 Z 1	Astleys row N1
24 E 20	Aston av Harrow
103 T 15	Aston clo Kingst
115 O 9	Aston clo Sidcp
119 N 3	Aston rd SW20
60 H 17	Aston rd W5
63 V 16	Aston st E14
105 Y 3	Astonville st SW18
38 J 18	Astor av Rom
90 E 7	Astoria wlk SW9
57 Y 17	Astra clo Hornch
136 B 20	Astrop ms W6
74 L 7	Astrop ms W6
136 B 20	Astrop ter W6
74 L 7	Astrop ter W6
146 A 6	Astwood ms SW5
92 A 1	Asylum rd SE15
75 N 19	Asylum rd SE15
151 X 16	Asylum rd SE15
144 J 20	Atalanta st SW6
102 C 15	Atbara rd Tedd
83 O 10	Atcham rd Hounsl
67 Z 14	Atcost rd Bark
88 B 20	Atheldene rd SW18
111 P 6	Athelney st SE6
117 N 8	Athelstan rd Kingst
63 X 7	Athelstane gro E3
48 F 5	Athelstane ms N4
23 R 8	Athelstone rd Harrow
41 R 5	Athena clo Harrow
29 R 11	Athenaeum pl N10
15 S 6	Athenaeum rd N20
92 F 13	Athenlay rd SE15
50 B 12	Atherden rd E5
90 A 7	Atherfold rd SW9
89 Z 7	Atherfold rd SW9
146 C 4	Atherstone ms SW7
105 P 9	Atherton dri SW19
42 F 20	Atherton heights Wemb
52 D 17	Atherton ms E7
70 J 1	Atherton pl S'hall
52 C 17	Atherton pl E7
35 S 7	Atherton rd IIf
74 F 20	Atherton rd SW13
88 K 5	Atherton st SW11
60 E 8	Athlon rd Wemb
90 D 19	Athlone rd SW2
47 R 17	Athlone st NW5
81 X 14	Athol rd Erith
54 M 2	Athol rd IIf
55 N 1	Athol rd IIf
8 E 18	Athole gdns Enf
93 O 13	Athurdon rd SE4
33 S 19	Atkins rd E10
89 Z 19	Atkins rd SW12
65 Z 15	Atkinson rd E16
90 F 11	Atlantic rd SW9
77 X 10	Atlas gdns SE7
48 D 18	Atlas ms N7
65 S 7	Atlas rd E13
62 B 10	Atlas rd NW10
43 U 12	Atlas rd Wemb
64 A 3	Atley rd E3
87 S 10	Atney rd SW15
30 G 19	Atterbury rd N4
148 H 8	Atterbury st SW1
44 A 9	Attewood av NW10
40 B 19	Attewood rd Nthlt
68 F 20	Attlee rd SE28
33 S 11	Attlee ter E17
133 S 15	Attneave st WC1
90 E 20	Atwater clo SW2
91 Y 5	Atwell rd SE15
85 R 5	Atwood av Rich
74 J 10	Atwood rd W6
78 G 3	Auberon st E16
48 H 12	Aubert pk N5
48 J 12	Aubert rd N5
130 B 10	Aubrey rd NW8
33 P 11	Aubrey rd E17
30 B 18	Aubrey rd N8
137 P 14	Aubrey rd W8
137 R 15	Aubrey wlk W8
109 N 11	Auburn hill SE27
86 G 12	Aubyn sq SW15
123 U 1	Auckland clo SE19
123 T 1	Auckland gdns SE19
108 M 9	Auckland hill SE27
51 R 9	Auckland rd E10
54 A 2	Auckland rd IIf
53 Z 3	Auckland rd IIf
117 N 8	Auckland rd Kingst
123 T 3	Auckland rd SE19
109 V 19	Auckland rd SE19
88 J 12	Auckland st SW11
109 T 20	Auckland ri SE19
149 N 11	Auckland st SE11
131 T 3	Auden pl NW1
131 T 4	Auden pl NW1
125 R 14	Audley clo Becknhm
34 C 14	Audley ct E18
54 K 8	Audley gdns IIf
153 Z 18	Audley pl Sutton
7 V 8	Audley rd Enf
26 H 18	Audley rd NW4
84 M 14	Audley rd Rich
60 M 15	Audley rd W5
61 N 14	Audley rd W5
139 V 13	Audley sq W1
42 B 6	Audrey gdns Wemb
53 Y 10	Audrey rd IIf
135 T 8	Audrey st E2

65 X 9	Augurs la E13
101 N 4	Augusta rd Twick
64 C 17	Augusta st E14
22 M 6	Augustine rd Harrow
144 F 3	Augustine rd W14
72 F 20	Augustus clo Brentf
105 R 2	Augustus rd SW15
105 T 1	Augustus rd SW19
131 Z 11	Augustus st NW1
151 R 13	Aulay st SE1
149 U 12	Aulton pl SE11
154 L 5	Aultone way Carsh
154 B 2	Aultone way Sutton
122 C 13	Aurelia gdns Croy
122 A 15	Aurelia rd Croy
57 O 18	Auriel av Dgnhm
49 R 15	Auriga ms N1
152 B 6	Auriol clo Worc Pk
59 R 1	Auriol dri Grnfd
152 B 6	Auriol Park rd Worc Pk
144 K 6	Auriol rd W14
13 O 11	Austell gdns NW7
80 E 2	Austen clo SE28
40 J 6	Austen rd Harrow
127 S 13	Austin av Brom
92 K 19	Austin clo SE23
160 G 5	Austin friars EC2
89 O 3	Austin rd SW11
134 M 14	Austin st E2
114 L 6	Austral clo Sidcp
149 W 4	Austral st SE11
74 J 1	Australia rd W12
62 J 19	Australia rd W12
117 S 19	Austyn gdns Surb
8 L 7	Autumn clo Enf
64 R 3	Autumn st E3
7 U 7	Avalon clo Enf
59 Y 13	Avalon cres W13
88 A 1	Avalon rd SW6
59 Y 12	Avalon rd W13
106 M 14	Avarn rd SW17
141 Y 6	Ave Maria la EC4
116 G 16	Avebury pk Surb
51 X 3	Avebury rd E11
105 V 19	Avebury rd SW19
134 F 5	Avebury st N1
39 O 13	Aveline rd Rom
149 R 10	Aveline st SE11
33 O 7	Aveling Park rd E17
48 H 10	Avenell rd N5
87 Z 18	Avening rd SW18
87 Y 17	Avening ter SW18
65 T 12	Avenons rd E13
6 H 19	Avenue clo N14
44 M 19	Avenue clo NW2
130 L 6	Avenue clo NW8
73 S 5	Avenue cres W3
116 J 11	Avenue elmers Surb
116 K 12	Avenue elmers Surb
123 W 5	Avenue gdns SE25
86 A 8	Avenue gdns SW14
101 X 16	Avenue gdns Tedd
73 T 5	Avenue gdns W3
29 S 11	Avenue ms N10
108 J 3	Avenue Park rd SE27
81 W 11	Avenue rd Blvdr
72 E 13	Avenue rd Brentf
97 Y 9	Avenue rd Bxly Hth
52 H 13	Avenue rd E7
81 Y 19	Avenue rd Erith
83 U 3	Avenue rd Islwth
116 K 6	Avenue rd Kingst
15 R 14	Avenue rd N12
16 H 1	Avenue rd N14
6 H 19	Avenue rd N14
31 O 16	Avenue rd N15
29 W 20	Avenue rd N6
118 B 7	Avenue rd New Mald
62 D 6	Avenue rd NW10
130 J 4	Avenue rd NW8
22 A 9	Avenue rd Pinn
55 S 2	Avenue rd Rom
70 F 2	Avenue rd S'hall
110 D 20	Avenue rd SE20
124 E 2	Avenue rd SE20
123 V 4	Avenue rd SE25
121 X 4	Avenue rd SW16
118 J 2	Avenue rd SW20
101 X 16	Avenue rd Tedd
71 Y 1	Avenue rd W13
73 S 5	Avenue rd W3
155 U 18	Avenue rd Wallgtn
21 Z 18	Avenue rd Wdfd Grn
117 O 16	Avenue South the Surb
117 V 7	Avenue ter New Mald
4 E 13	Avenue the Barnt
111 U 20	Avenue the Becknhm
127 O 7	Avenue the Brom
97 W 18	Avenue the Bxly
155 O 16	Avenue the Carsh
157 R 5	Avenue the Croy
34 J 17	Avenue the E11
20 J 19	Avenue the E4
142 K 9	Avenue the EC3
100 F 14	Avenue the Hampt
23 V 4	Avenue the Harrow
82 J 13	Avenue the Hounsl
29 V 7	Avenue the N10
16 D 15	Avenue the N11
31 P 9	Avenue the N17
27 X 7	Avenue the N3
30 E 11	Avenue the N8
22 E 19	Avenue the NW6
22 G 1	Avenue the Pinn
85 N 4	Avenue the Rich
39 O 12	Avenue the Rom
76 J 19	Avenue the SE10
77 X 18	Avenue the SE7
95 U 14	Avenue the SE9
117 O 15	Avenue the Surb
153 U 20	Avenue the Sutton
89 P 13	Avenue the SW4
84 C 14	Avenue the Twick
126 A 14	Avenue the W Wkhm
125 W 18	Avenue the W Wkhm
60 A 19	Avenue the W13
74 A 9	Avenue the W4
42 K 3	Avenue the Wemb
43 O 7	Avenue the Wemb
152 D 3	Avenue the Worc Pk
108 H 16	Averil gro SW18
144 G 15	Averill st W6
147 V 8	Avery Farm row SW1
35 V 16	Avery gdns Ilf
96 B 16	Avery Hill pk SE9
96 D 20	Avery Hill rd SE9
114 B 2	Avery hill Sidcp
139 X 8	Avery row W1
65 P 15	Aviary clo E16
124 K 12	Aviemore clo Becknhm
124 J 12	Aviemore way Becknhm
92 G 8	Avignon rd SE4
110 B 17	Avington gro SE20
63 T 17	Avis sq E1
107 P 8	Avoca rd SW17
79 S 8	Avocet ms SE28
154 D 8	Avon clo Sutton
152 F 2	Avon clo Worc Pk
22 D 3	Avon mews Pinn
142 C 19	Avon pl SE1
157 N 14	Avon pth S Croy
33 X 11	Avon rd E17
58 J 11	Avon rd Grnfd
93 O 7	Avon rd SE4
34 F 11	Avon way E18
15 Y 4	Avondale av Barnt
15 N 17	Avondale av NW2
44 B 9	Avondale av NW2
118 C 19	Avondale av Worc Pk
9 V 11	Avondale cres Enf
35 O 17	Avondale cres Ilf
34 G 4	Avondale ct E18
82 E 14	Avondale gdns Hounsl
136 J 10	Avondale Park gdns W11
136 J 9	Avondale Park rd W11
136 K 11	Avondale pk W11
112 C 15	Avondale rd Brom
65 N 14	Avondale rd E16
51 N 1	Avondale rd E17
23 W 9	Avondale rd Harrow
17 U 9	Avondale rd N13
30 K 15	Avondale rd N15
28 C 5	Avondale rd N3
156 M 15	Avondale rd S Croy
113 R 5	Avondale rd SE9
85 Z 7	Avondale rd SW14
106 A 12	Avondale rd SW19
105 Z 12	Avondale rd SW19
97 U 5	Avondale rd Welling
91 U 7	Avondale rd WE15
151 S 10	Avondale sq SE1
151 S 11	Avondale sq SE1
75 R 19	Avonley rd SE14
145 N 4	Avonmore pl W14
145 N 5	Avonmore rd W14
150 A 1	Avonmouth st SE1
82 K 4	Avonwick rd Hounsl
20 H 16	Avril way E4
156 A 15	Avro way Wallgtn
31 P 5	Awfield av N17
96 L 4	Awliscombe rd Welling
67 P 3	Axe st Bark
25 R 4	Axholme av Edg
80 H 20	Axminster cres
97 S 1	Axminster cres Welling
48 B 9	Axminster rd N7
139 T 2	Aybrook st W1
127 V 8	Aycliffe clo Brom
74 F 2	Aycliffe rd W12
52 D 17	Aycliffe rd SE12
126 E 7	Aylesbury rd Brom
133 W 17	Aylesbury st EC1
43 Y 10	Aylesbury st NW10
124 H 13	Aylesford av Becknhm
148 F 11	Aylesford st SW1
128 F 2	Aylestone av NW6
45 O 20	Aylestone av NW6
83 U 5	Aylett rd Islwth
124 A 10	Aylett rd SE25
123 Z 10	Aylett rd SE25
8 K 18	Ayley croft Enf
10 L 12	Aylmer clo Stanm
10 K 13	Aylmer dri Stanm
55 X 11	Aylmer rd Dgnhm
52 B 2	Aylmer rd E11
28 K 16	Aylmer rd N2
74 C 6	Aylmer rd W12
56 A 17	Aylofe rd Dgnhm
119 V 5	Aylward rd SE23
119 V 6	Aylward rd SE23
63 H 16	Aylward st E1
10 L 13	Aylwards ri Stanm
144 H 3	Aynhoe rd W14
85 V 6	Ayncscombe la SW14
85 W 6	Ayncscombe pth SW14
39 O 4	Ayr grn Rom
39 O 4	Ayr way Rom
65 T 10	Ayres clo E13
61 X 1	Ayres cres NW10
142 B 16	Ayres st SE1
49 R 8	Ayrsome rd N16
91 P 17	Aysgarth rd SE21
90 D 5	Aytoun rd SW9
71 W 2	Azalea clo W7
91 U 4	Azenby rd SE15
77 N 12	Azof st SE10

B

48 J 15	Baalbec rd N5
35 P 12	Babbacombe gdns Ilf
112 G 19	Babbacombe rd Brom
43 R 18	Babbington ri Wemb
55 T 14	Babbington rd Dgnhm
57 X 4	Babington rd Hornch
26 K 13	Babington rd NW4
107 Y 11	Babington rd SW16
140 E 12	Babmaes st SW1
134 G 13	Baches st N1
143 T 5	Back Church la E1
133 T 18	Back hill EC1
72 G 18	Back la Brentf
98 C 18	Back la Bxly
25 V 5	Back la Edg
29 Z 17	Back la N8
46 E 12	Back la NW3
102 D 5	Back la Rich
37 X 20	Back la Rom
115 N 10	Back rd Sidcp
73 T 2	Back st W3
150 K 8	Backhouse pl SE17
150 M 3	Bacon gro SE1
25 P 3	Bacon la Edg
135 R 16	Bacon st E2
47 P 4	Bacons la N6
63 R 8	Bacton st E2
69 S 4	Baddow clo Dgnhm
142 F 17	Baden pl SE1
53 Y 14	Baden rd Ilf
29 Z 12	Baden rd N8
57 X 18	Bader way Rainhm
7 X 12	Badgers clo Enf
23 R 19	Badgers clo Harrow
152 E 2	Badgers copse Worc Pk
14 F 4	Badgers croft N20
113 W 7	Badgers croft SE9
158 E 8	Badgers hole Croy
118 A 2	Badgers wlk New Mald
33 N 9	Badlis rd E17
40 H 19	Badminton clo Nthlt
23 S 13	Badminton clo Har
89 P 17	Badminton rd SW12
150 B 20	Badsworth rd SE5
90 L 1	Badsworth rd SE5
88 B 3	Bagleys la SW6
37 Z 12	Bagleys spring Rom
95 W 1	Bagshot clo SE18
18 F 1	Bagshot rd Enf
150 K 10	Bagshot st SE17
75 Z 20	Bailden st SE8
110 E 15	Bailey pl SE26
72 H 5	Bailles wlk W5
56 C 11	Bainbridge rd Dgnhm
140 G 4	Bainbridge st WC1
58 M 19	Baird av S'hall
25 V 18	Baird clo NW9
109 S 10	Baird clo SE21
8 L 4	Baird rd Enf
94 A 6	Baizdon rd SE3
93 Z 6	Baizdon rd SE3
132 D 2	Baker dri NW1
121 N 4	Baker la Mitch
62 A 4	Baker rd NW10
78 D 20	Baker rd SE18
95 R 1	Baker rd SE18
8 D 6	Baker st Enf
131 R 19	Baker st NW1
139 S 2	Baker st W1
33 R 19	Bakers av E17
119 T 3	Bakers end SW20
50 B 4	Bakers hill E5
29 N 17	Bakers la N6
72 G 1	Bakers la W5
139 T 4	Bakers ms W1
64 L 5	Bakers row E15
133 T 17	Bakers row EC1
117 Z 2	Bakewell way New Mald
65 U 11	Balaam st E13
16 K 8	Balaams la N14
151 P 6	Balaclava rd SE1
116 D 16	Balaclava rd Surb
63 S 2	Balbenpath E9
95 V 12	Balcaskie rd SE9
94 M 4	Balchen rd SE3
91 Z 15	Balcombe st NW1
131 N 18	Balcombe st NW1
63 R 1	Balcorne st E9
112 J 5	Balder ri SE12
139 U 7	Balderton st W1
64 C 7	Baldock st E3
108 B 16	Baldry gdns SW16
90 K 2	Baldwin cres SE5
61 X 19	Baldwin gdns W3
134 A 8	Baldwin st EC1
133 S 20	Baldwins gdns EC1
132 L 9	Balfe st N1
74 B 14	Balfern gro W4
88 J 4	Balfern st SW11
53 Z 7	Balfour appr Ilf
71 V 2	Balfour gro N20
15 Z 11	Balfour gro N20
18 K 10	Balfour ms N9
139 U 12	Balfour pl SW15
86 J 10	Balfour pl SW15
139 U 11	Balfour pl W1
127 P 11	Balfour rd Brom
154 M 17	Balfour rd Carsh
23 R 16	Balfour rd Harrow
82 J 7	Balfour rd Hounsl
54 B 12	Balfour rd Ilf
53 Z 7	Balfour rd Ilf
48 M 13	Balfour rd N5
123 X 10	Balfour rd SE25
106 A 18	Balfour rd SW19
74 B 13	Balfour rd W13
61 W 15	Balfour rd W3
150 D 5	Balfour st SE17
20 J 6	Balgonie rd E4
39 Y 11	Balgores cres Rom
39 X 11	Balgores la Rom
39 Y 12	Balgores sq Rom
118 B 10	Balgowan clo New Mald
124 K 4	Balgowan rd Becknhm
79 X 11	Balgowan st SE18
89 R 19	Balham gro SW12
107 P 3	Balham High rd SW17
89 R 20	Balham High rd SW12
89 S 17	Balham hill SW12
89 S 19	Balham New rd SW12
106 M 1	Balham Park rd SW12

Ref	Name
107 O 2	Balham Park rd SW12
18 L 8	Balham rd N9
107 R 1	Balham Station rd SW12
160 H 7	Ball ct EC3
112 E 7	Ballamore rd Brom
50 G 17	Ballance rd E9
88 C 11	Ballantyne st SW18
103 X 19	Ballard clo Kingst
69 V 3	Ballards clo Dgnhm
157 Y 14	Ballards Farm rd Croy
27 Y 4	Ballards la N3
69 U 3	Ballards rd Dgnhm
44 G 7	Ballards rd NW2
157 X 14	Ballards ri S Croy
158 C 13	Ballards way Croy
157 Y 15	Ballards way S Croy
76 L 13	Ballast quay SE10
157 U 11	Ballater rd S Croy
90 B 11	Ballater rd SW2
92 G 17	Ballina st SE23
89 N 15	Ballingdon rd SW11
20 K 14	Balliol av E4
31 P 5	Balliol rd N17
136 E 5	Balliol rd W10
97 R 4	Balliol rd Welling
111 X 3	Balloch rd SE6
44 B 11	Ballogie av NW10
150 H 20	Ballow clo SE5
49 O 17	Balls Pond pl N1
49 R 17	Balls Pond rd N1
72 H 2	Balmain clo W5
63 Y 8	Balmer st E3
134 G 3	Balmes rd N1
124 J 9	Balmoral av Becknhm
98 C 20	Balmoral gdns Bxly
54 J 5	Balmoral gdns Ilf
71 Y 7	Balmoral gdns W13
48 B 18	Balmoral gro N7
51 S 8	Balmoral rd E10
52 L 14	Balmoral rd E7
40 G 12	Balmoral rd Harrow
116 L 8	Balmoral rd Kingst
44 K 17	Balmoral rd NW2
39 Y 15	Balmoral rd Rom
152 H 4	Balmoral rd Worc Pk
6 B 16	Balmore cres Barnt
47 T 7	Balmore st N19
87 N 11	Balmuir gdns SW15
44 B 12	Balnacraig av NW10
148 G 10	Balniel ga SW1
106 F 17	Baltic clo SW19
134 A 18	Baltic st EC1
96 K 5	Baltimore pl Welling
87 W 19	Balvernie gro SW18
136 D 18	Bamborough gdns W12
60 M 5	Bamford av Wemb
51 S 15	Bamford ct E15
54 B 19	Bamford rd Bark
111 W 12	Bamford rd Brom
155 U 6	Bamfylde clo Wallgtn
110 E 6	Bampton rd SE23
111 T 20	Banavie gdns Becknhm
101 U 2	Banbury cotts Twick
153 Z 17	Banbury ct Sutton
140 K 8	Banbury ct WC2
63 T 1	Banbury rd E9
88 K 4	Banbury st SW11
77 V 19	Banchory rd SE3
21 T 9	Bancroft av Buck Hl
28 K 15	Bancroft av N2
22 M 5	Bancroft gdns Harrow
63 U 11	Bancroft rd E1
23 N 6	Bancroft rd Har
155 X 12	Bandon ri Wallgtn
87 O 8	Bangalore st SW15
40 K 15	Bangor clo Nrthlt
73 N 15	Bangor rd Brentf
74 K 10	Banim st W6
128 G 12	Banister rd NW10
120 G 4	Bank av Mitch
142 D 12	Bank end SE1
102 J 17	Bank la Kingst
86 B 13	Bank la S SW15
47 S 3	Bank the N6
83 U 5	Bankfield ct Islwth
112 A 10	Bankfoot rd Brom
92 L 18	Bankhurst rd SE6
98 B 10	Banks la Bxly Hth
154 K 13	Bankside clo Carsh
7 X 7	Bankside Enf
157 T 15	Bankside S Croy
142 A 11	Bankside SE1
90 F 12	Bankton rd SW2
94 A 11	Bankwell rd SE13
134 B 18	Banner st EC1
76 M 12	Banning st SE10
41 R 13	Bannister clo Grnfd
90 F 20	Bannister clo SW2
79 W 11	Bannockburn rd SE18
18 C 10	Banstead gdns N9
154 K 13	Banstead rd Carsh
92 B 8	Banstead st SE15
156 A 10	Banstead way Wallgtn
12 G 20	Banstock rd Edg
8 M 9	Banton clo Enf
150 F 19	Bantry st SE5
150 X 3	Banyard rd SE16
47 O 17	Baptist gdns NW5
144 D 3	Barb ms W6
49 R 10	Barbauld rd N16
149 V 1	Barbel st SE1
17 U 3	Barber clo N21
65 U 8	Barbers all E13
64 E 5	Barbers rd E15
58 L 15	Barbican rd Grnfd
18 J 11	Barbot clo N9
88 A 13	Barchard st SW18
71 W 3	Barchester clo W7
23 R 6	Barchester rd Harrow
64 D 15	Barchester st E14
145 T 20	Barclay clo SW6
21 T 14	Barclay oval Wdfd Grn
157 O 5	Barclay rd Croy
52 B 4	Barclay rd E11
65 Y 13	Barclay rd E13
33 T 16	Barclay rd E17
18 B 19	Barclay rd N18
145 U 19	Barclay rd SW6
108 B 4	Barcombe av SW2
136 G 10	Bard rd W10
79 U 19	Barden st SE18
37 V 11	Bardfield av Rom
120 B 8	Bardney rd Mrdn
158 K 20	Bardolph av Croy
47 Z 12	Bardolph rd N7
85 N 9	Bardolph rd Rich
63 O 13	Bardsey pl E1
157 T 5	Bardsley clo Croy
76 F 17	Bardsley la SE10
129 N 15	Barfett st W10
15 Y 8	Barfield av N20
127 X 5	Barfield rd Brom
52 B 3	Barfield rd E11
136 F 7	Barfield way W10
26 H 6	Barford clo NW4
133 U 6	Barford st N1
92 A 8	Barforth rd SE15
118 G 16	Bargate clo New Mald
79 Y 13	Bargate clo SE18
78 M 4	Barge House rd E16
141 U 11	Barge House st SE1
111 S 2	Bargery rd SE6
109 X 17	Bargrove clo SE19
110 M 3	Bargrove cres SE6
127 S 20	Barham clo Brom
113 Z 12	Barham clo Chisl
38 F 9	Barham clo Rom
42 C 17	Barham clo Wemb
113 Y 12	Barham rd Chisl
156 L 9	Barham rd CR2
156 M 10	Barham rd S Croy
104 F 18	Barham rd SW20
112 F 4	Baring clo SE12
5 U 12	Baring rd Barnt
123 Y 19	Baring rd Croy
94 D 19	Baring rd SE12
112 F 2	Baring rd SE12
134 E 5	Baring st N1
146 B 14	Barker st SW10
31 P 1	Barkham rd N17
54 E 17	Barking pk Bark
65 R 13	Barking rd E16
66 F 4	Barking rd E6
151 W 11	Barkis way SE16
145 X 7	Barkston gdns SW5
75 O 14	Barkworth rd SE16
151 Y 11	Barkworth rd SE16
75 R 19	Barlborough st SE14
128 G 18	Barlby gdns W10
128 F 19	Barlby rd W10
55 O 2	Barley la Ilf
37 P 14	Barley la Rom
141 Y 2	Barley Mow pass EC1
73 Y 13	Barley Mow pass W4
63 Y 20	Barleycorn way E14
37 R 19	Barleyfields Rom
155 Z 15	Barlow clo Wallgtn
139 Z 10	Barlow pl W1
100 J 17	Barlow rd Hampt
45 V 17	Barlow rd NW6
73 T 2	Barlow rd W3
150 G 6	Barlow st SE17
111 R 3	Barmeston rd SE6
22 L 6	Barmor clo Harrow
59 X 6	Barmouth av Grnfd
158 F 3	Barmouth rd Croy
88 D 17	Barmouth rd SW18
78 K 9	Barn clo SE18
11 R 20	Barn cres Stanm
144 A 19	Barn Elms Water Works SW13
43 R 5	Barn hill Wemb
43 S 7	Barn hill Wemb
43 R 5	Barn ri Wemb
43 R 5	Barn ri Wemb
49 P 8	Barn st N16
43 P 5	Barn way Wemb
43 R 6	Barn way Wemb
50 G 17	Barnabas rd E9
40 M 8	Barnaby clo Harrow
114 F 20	Barnard clo Chisl
155 Y 16	Barnard clo Wallgtn
118 G 9	Barnard gdns New Mald
65 O 1	Barnard gro E15
29 R 6	Barnard hill N10
9 N 9	Barnard rd Enf
121 O 4	Barnard rd Mitch
88 K 10	Barnard rd SW11
156 J 19	Barnard's pl S Croy
36 C 12	Barnardo dri Ilf
63 S 19	Barnardo st E1
141 T 3	Barnards Inn EC4
64 L 2	Barnby sq E15
64 L 2	Barnby st E15
132 C 11	Barnby st NW1
98 K 2	Barnehurst av Bxly Hth
98 L 4	Barnehurst av Bxly Hth
98 K 2	Barnehurst clo Erith
98 J 5	Barnehurst rd Bxly Hth
74 F 19	Barnes av SW13
53 O 13	Barnes clo E12
99 V 11	Barnes Cray rd Drtfrd
65 Z 14	Barnes ct E16
118 H 12	Barnes end New Mald
86 C 4	Barnes High st SW13
72 F 1	Barnes pickle W5
54 C 14	Barnes rd Ilf
19 P 13	Barnes rd N18
63 V 18	Barnes st E14
86 B 5	Barnes ter SW13
13 T 1	Barnet Gate la
135 S 13	Barnet gro E2
4 J 14	Barnet hill Barnt
4 K 17	Barnet la Barnt
11 X 1	Barnet la Brhm Wd
14 G 5	Barnet la N20
12 L 7	Barnet way NW7
99 T 4	Barnett clo Erith
77 Y 12	Barney clo SE7
158 D 2	Barnfield av Croy
102 J 11	Barnfield av Kingst
121 T 7	Barnfield av Mitch
102 K 11	Barnfield gdns Rich
118 A 14	Barnfield New Mald
81 P 15	Barnfield pl E14
25 U 5	Barnfield rd Edg
157 T 20	Barnfield rd S Croy
79 N 16	Barnfield rd SE18
60 C 11	Barnfield rd W5
125 X 14	Barnfield Wood clo W Wkhm
125 X 13	Barnfield Wood rd Becknhm
58 M 7	Barnham rd Grnfd
59 N 8	Barnham rd Grnfd
142 K 16	Barnham st SE1
126 C 13	Barnhill av Brom
43 W 9	Barnhill rd Wemb
100 C 5	Barnlea clo Felt
56 C 15	Barnmead gdns Dgnhm
110 G 20	Barnmead rd Becknhm
56 B 15	Barnmead rd Dgnhm
43 X 20	Barns rd NW10
117 W 10	Barnsbury clo New Mald
117 U 20	Barnsbury cres Surb
48 E 19	Barnsbury gro N7
117 V 20	Barnsbury la Surb
48 F 20	Barnsbury pk N1
133 S 5	Barnsbury rd N1
133 S 1	Barnsbury sq N1
133 V 1	Barnsbury st N1
133 R 1	Barnsbury ter N1
129 R 16	Barnsdale av E14
129 S 17	Barnsdale yd W9
63 N 12	Barnsley st E1
135 X 17	Barnsley st E1
133 Z 4	Barnston wlk N1
90 G 13	Barnwell rd SW2
129 Y 19	Barnwood clo W9
77 U 3	Barnwood ct E16
133 T 9	Baron clo N1
36 C 9	Baron gdns Ilf
120 K 8	Baron gro Mitch
55 V 3	Baron rd Dgnhm
133 T 9	Baron st N1
65 O 14	Baron wlk E16
120 H 9	Baron wlk Mitch
135 O 12	Baroness rd E2
31 X 4	Baronet gro N17
31 X 4	Baronet rd N17
144 L 10	Barons Court W14
145 N 10	Barons Court rd W14
5 W 18	Barons ga Barnt
144 K 8	Barons keep W14
23 U 12	Barons mead Harrow
141 V 18	Barons pl SE1
84 C 15	Barons the Twick
124 J 14	Barons wlk Croy
84 C 17	Baronsfield rd Twick
86 G 2	Baronsmead rd SW13
72 M 7	Baronsmede W5
28 K 13	Baronsmere rd N2
76 G 13	Barque st E14
95 W 2	Barr vlls SE18
82 A 11	Barrack rd Hounsl
23 R 9	Barrat way Harrow
30 B 6	Barratt av N22
28 M 6	Barrenger rd N10
33 U 13	Barrett rd E17
139 U 6	Barrett st W1
61 X 7	Barretts Green rd NW10
49 T 13	Barretts gro N16
92 J 4	Barriedale SE14
77 Z 9	Barrier appr SE7
107 P 9	Barringer sq SW17
35 V 5	Barrington clo Ilf
47 O 14	Barrington clo NW5
97 W 6	Barrington rd Bxly Hth
53 W 17	Barrington rd E12
29 X 14	Barrington rd N8
153 X 1	Barrington rd Sutton
90 H 7	Barrington rd SW9
132 M 20	Barron clo WC1
154 L 18	Barrow av Carsh
17 W 10	Barrow clo N21
154 J 15	Barrow Hedges clo Carsh
154 J 15	Barrow Hedges way Carsh
152 A 2	Barrow Hill clo Worc Pk
130 J 10	Barrow Hill rd NW8
152 A 2	Barrow Hill Worc Pk
22 A 8	Barrow Point la Pinn
22 A 6	Barrow Point la Pinn
156 G 12	Barrow rd Croy
107 Z 14	Barrow rd SW16
22 B 8	Barrowdene clo Pinn
17 W 9	Barrowell grn N21
19 O 11	Barrowfield clo N9
73 X 15	Barrowgate rd W4
80 L 19	Barry av Bxly Hth
31 V 19	Barry av N15
66 E 17	Barry rd E6
43 X 20	Barry rd NW10
91 X 14	Barry rd SE22
92 B 7	Barset rd SE15
110 C 17	Barson clo SE20
108 M 6	Barston rd SE27
108 D 2	Barstow cres SW2
140 L 3	Barter st WC1
79 W 11	Barth rd SE18
88 D 12	Bartholomew clo SW18
141 Z 2	Bartholomew clo EC1
160 F 5	Bartholomew la EC2
142 A 2	Bartholomew pl EC1
47 V 18	Bartholomew rd NW5
134 C 15	Bartholomew sq EC1
150 F 3	Bartholomew st SE1
47 U 18	Bartholomew vlls NW5
66 E 5	Bartle av E6
136 J 6	Bartle rd W11

141 U 4 Bartlett ct EC4
157 N 11 Bartlett st Croy
38 M 3 Bartlow gdns Rom
56 J 5 Barton av Rom
97 Z 12 Barton clo Bxly Hth
92 A 6 Barton clo SE15
117 Z 4 Barton grn New Mald
36 A 12 Barton meadows Ilf
57 V 5 Barton rd Hornch
115 Z 15 Barton rd Sidcp
144 L 10 Barton rd W14
148 H 2 Barton st SW1
92 J 14 Bartram rd SE4
5 P 3 Bartrams la Barnt
52 H 11 Barwick rd E7
125 S 20 Barwood av
W Wkhm
100 G 5 Basden gro Felt
55 P 20 Basedale rd Dgnhm
66 K 19 Baseing clo E6
61 Z 10 Bashley rd NW10
66 E 8 Basil av E6
124 E 20 Basil gdns CR0
139 O 19 Basil st SW3
35 W 5 Basildon av Ilf
154 B 19 Basildon clo Sutton
97 Y 6 Basildon rd Bxly Hth
80 B 11 Basildon rd SE2
98 A 16 Basing dri Bxly
45 U 4 Basing hill NW11
43 O 5 Basing hill Wemb
134 L 12 Basing pl E2
137 O 4 Basing st W11
28 A 9 Basing way N3
27 Z 10 Basing way N3
91 O 10 Basingdon way SE5
154 A 19 Basinghall gdns
Sutton
160 D 4 Basinghall st EC2
134 C 3 Basire st N1
88 J 18 Baskerville rd SW18
95 R 13 Basket gdns SE9
23 R 5 Baslow clo Harrow
89 P 7 Basnett rd SW11
91 U 12 Bassano st SE22
79 W 17 Bassant rd SE18
74 E 7 Bassein Park rd W12
154 B 20 Bassett clo Sutton
71 O 19 Bassett gdns Islwth
136 J 3 Bassett rd W10
47 P 17 Bassett st NW5
58 K 16 Bassett way Grnfd
160 D 3 Bassinghall av EC2
88 D 18 Bassingham rd
SW18
42 G 19 Bassingham rd
Wemb
68 B 7 Bastable av Bark
67 W 8 Bastable av Bark
80 A 14 Bastion rd SE2
79 Z 15 Bastion rd SE2
134 A 16 Bastwick st EC1
133 Z 16 Bastwick st EC1
87 Y 2 Basuto rd SW6
75 W 20 Batavia rd SE14
133 T 6 Batchelor st N1
63 Y 19 Bate st E14
20 B 18 Bateman rd E4
140 F 6 Bateman st W1
140 F 6 Batemans bldgs W1
134 L 15 Batemans row EC2
156 F 12 Bates cres Croy
92 A 1 Bath clo SE15
151 Z 20 Bath clo SE15
135 R 10 Bath gro E2
121 U 11 Bath House rd Mitch
4 G 11 Bath pl Barnt
134 J 14 Bath pl EC2
99 Z 18 Bath rd Drtfrd
53 N 19 Bath rd E7
82 D 7 Bath rd Hounsl
19 O 8 Bath rd N9
37 Y 18 Bath rd Rom
120 E 5 Bath rd SW19
74 B 10 Bath rd W4
134 D 14 Bath st EC1
150 A 2 Bath ter SE1
105 P 7 Bathgate rd SW19
127 O 8 Baths rd Brom
128 A 10 Bathurst gdns NW10
62 K 7 Bathurst ms W2
138 G 8 Bathurst ms W2
53 Z 5 Bathurst rd Ilf
138 G 8 Bathurst st W2
78 K 11 Bathway SE18
49 U 10 Batley pl N16
8 A 6 Batley rd Enf
49 U 10 Batley rd N16
74 K 2 Batman clo W12
144 D 1 Batoum gdns W6

74 M 8 Batoum gdns W6
79 U 11 Batson st SE18
74 G 6 Batson st W12
120 F 5 Batsworth rd Mitch
66 G 18 Batten clo E6
88 K 7 Batten st SW11
111 Y 6 Battersby rd E5
146 H 18 Battersea br SW11
146 J 19 Battersea Bridge rd
SW11
88 K 2 Battersea Bridge rd
SW11
88 G 1 Battersea Church rd
SW11
146 J 20 Battersea Church rd
SW11
88 G 3 Battersea High st
SW11
88 K 4 Battersea Park rd
SW11
89 O 2 Battersea Park rd
SW11
147 Z 20 Battersea Park rd
SW11
148 A 18 Battersea Park rd SW8
88 M 1 Battersea pk
SW11
147 R 20 Battersea pk
SW11
88 L 11 Battersea ri SW11
79 T 5 Battery rd SE28
133 W 2 Battishill st N1
142 J 14 Battle Bridge la SE1
132 J 9 Battle Bridge rd
NW1
106 D 15 Battle clo SW19
81 Y 10 Battle rd Erith
48 H 15 Battledean rd N5
143 T 5 Batty st E1
111 Z 4 Baudwin rd SE6
115 U 13 Baugh rd Sidcp
87 X 19 Baulk the SW18
122 B 3 Bavant rd SW16
48 A 7 Bavaria rd N19
90 M 5 Bavent rd SE5
91 V 13 Bawdale rd SE22
36 L 14 Bawdsey av Ilf
75 V 18 Bawtree rd SE14
15 Y 11 Bawtry rd N20
15 R 8 Baxendale N20
135 S 11 Baxendale st E2
65 Z 17 Baxter rd E16
53 Y 15 Baxter rd Ilf
49 P 19 Baxter rd N1
31 X 10 Baxter rd N17
18 M 13 Baxter rd NW10
62 A 12 Bayfield rd SE9
94 M 11 Bayfield rd SW9
128 E 13 Bayford rd NW10
63 N 1 Bayford st E8
135 X 2 Bayford st E8
132 B 7 Bayham pl NW1
120 B 6 Bayham rd Mrdn
72 A 1 Bayham rd W13
73 Y 7 Bayham rd W4
132 A 4 Bayham st NW1
132 B 7 Bayham st NW1
131 Z 3 Bayham st NW1
140 F 2 Bayley st WC1
80 M 15 Bayley wlk Blvdr
141 T 19 Baylis rd SE1
68 K 20 Bayliss av SE28
66 G 18 Bayne clo E6
8 K 7 Baynes clo Enf
46 G 17 Baynes ms NW3
132 C 2 Baynes st NW1
144 K 16 Bayonne rd W6
49 V 10 Baystron rd N16
138 A 11 Bayswater rd W2
138 K 9 Bayswater rd W2
137 W 11 Bayswater rd W2
63 Z 14 Baythorne st E3
90 D 12 Baytree rd SW2
117 X 12 Bazalgette clo
New Mald
117 X 12 Bazalgette gdns
New Mald
64 F 19 Bazely st E14
7 U 19 Bazile rd N21
100 H 5 Beach gro Felt
78 B 15 Beacham clo SE7
111 V 10 Beachborough rd
Brom
52 A 8 Beachcroft rd E11
47 Y 4 Beachcroft way N19
64 A 1 Beachy rd E3
155 O 9 Beacon gro Carsh
48 A 15 Beacon hill N7
93 W 15 Beacon rd SE13
66 E 16 Beacons clo E6

77 S 17 Beaconsfield clo SE3
73 U 14 Beaconsfield clo SE3
84 B 17 Beaconsfield rd
Twick
70 D 4 Beaconsfield rd
S'hall
44 E 18 Beaconsfield rd
NW10
127 O 6 Beaconsfield rd
Brom
123 O 14 Beaconsfield rd Croy
51 U 8 Beaconsfield rd E10
65 O 12 Beaconsfield rd E16
32 M 20 Beaconsfield rd E17
9 U 1 Beaconsfield rd E17
16 C 15 Beaconsfield rd N11
31 T 14 Beaconsfield rd N15
18 K 12 Beaconsfield rd N9
117 Z 5 Beaconsfield rd New
Mald
150 H 12 Beaconsfield rd SE17
77 R 17 Beaconsfield rd SE3
113 R 8 Beaconsfield rd SE9
117 N 18 Beaconsfield rd Surb
73 X 9 Beaconsfield rd W4
72 F 5 Beaconsfield rd W5
66 K 18 Beaconsfield st E6
144 K 3 Beaconsfield Ter rd
W14
37 X 19 Beaconsfield ter Rom
87 V 3 Beaconsfield wlk
SW6
33 Y 7 Beacontree av E17
52 C 2 Beacontree rd E11
108 K 9 Beadman st SE27
92 F 20 Beadnell rd SE23
126 E 10 Beadon rd Brom
144 C 6 Beadon rd W6
74 M 11 Beadon rd W6
119 U 6 Beaford gro SW20
140 B 8 Beak st W1
140 C 8 Beak st W1
97 O 2 Beal clo Well
53 W 7 Beal rd Ilf
17 W 17 Beale clo N13
63 Y 5 Beale pl E3
63 X 4 Beale rd E3
65 S 5 Beale st E13
69 V 4 Beam av Dgnhm
56 M 20 Beam way Dgnhm
35 Y 9 Beaminster gdns Ilf
10 A 6 Beamish clo Bushey
18 L 6 Beamish rd N9
97 W 11 Bean rd Bxly Hth
113 W 10 Beanshaw SE9
37 Z 9 Beansland gro Rom
141 W 4 Bear all EC4
142 B 12 Bear gdns SE1
141 Y 14 Bear la SE1
100 A 11 Bear rd Felt
140 G 10 Bear st WC2
102 M 13 Beard rd Kingst
109 T 15 Beardell st SE19
6 G 20 Beardow gro N14
65 R 5 Beardsfield E13
102 K 18 Bearfield rd Kingst
92 K 14 Bearstead ri SE4
122 C 4 Beatrice av SW16
42 L 16 Beatrice av Wemb
33 O 16 Beatrice rd E17
48 G 1 Beatrice rd N4
19 P 2 Beatrice rd N9
84 L 13 Beatrice rd S'hall
70 D 3 Beatrice rd S'hall
151 U 6 Beatrice st SE1
65 S 12 Beatrice st E13
75 U 2 Beatrice st SE16
29 S 13 Beattock ri N10
49 T 11 Beatty rd N16
11 S 18 Beatty rd Stanm
132 A 7 Beatty st NW1
35 X 12 Beattyville gdns Ilf
146 M 2 Beauchamp pl SW3
88 K 10 Beauchamp rd
SW15
153 Y 9 Beauchamp rd
Sutton
52 H 20 Beauchamp rd E7
123 O 2 Beauchamp rd SE19
83 Z 19 Beauchamp rd Twick
141 T 1 Beauchamp st EC1
86 K 8 Beauchamp ter
SW15
144 A 1 Beauclerc rd W6
74 L 8 Beauclerc rd W6
24 A 11 Beaufort av Harrow
23 Z 11 Beaufort av Harrow
38 J 12 Beaufort clo Rom
86 K 20 Beaufort clo SW15
61 N 13 Beaufort clo W5

102 C 10 Beaufort ct Rich
27 V 12 Beaufort dri NW11
82 B 1 Beaufort gdns
Hounsl
53 W 4 Beaufort gdns Ilf
26 L 18 Beaufort gdns NW4
108 D 18 Beaufort gdns SW16
146 M 1 Beaufort gdns SW3
147 N 2 Beaufort gdns SW3
27 V 12 Beaufort pk NW11
116 J 10 Beaufort rd Kingst
102 D 10 Beaufort rd Rich
84 E 18 Beaufort rd Twick
60 M 15 Beaufort rd W5
61 N 13 Beaufort rd W5
146 E 12 Beaufort st SW3
146 G 15 Beaufort st SW3
152 G 18 Beaufort way Epsom
31 T 2 Beaufoy rd N17
89 P 5 Beaufoy rd SW11
149 P 8 Beaufoy wlk SE11
109 P 19 Beaulah hill SE19
110 A 10 Beaulieu av SE26
109 Z 10 Beaulieu av SE26
121 O 1 Beaulieu clo Mitch
26 B 12 Beaulieu clo NW9
91 P 7 Beaulieu clo SE5
84 G 17 Beaulieu clo Twick
17 V 4 Beaulieu gdns N21
39 R 5 Beauly way Rom
113 W 10 Beaumanor gdns
SE9
35 N 2 Beaumaris dri
Wdfd Grn
22 L 19 Beaumont av Harrow
84 M 9 Beaumont av Rich
145 O 9 Beaumont av W8
42 E 13 Beaumont av Wemb
57 X 18 Beaumont cres
Rainhm
145 O 10 Beaumont cres W14
45 Y 8 Beaumont gdns NW3
63 S 13 Beaumont gro E1
139 U 1 Beaumont ms W1
4 J 4 Beaumont pl Barnt
132 C 17 Beaumont pl WC1
51 R 2 Beaumont rd E10
108 L 15 Beaumont rd SE19
87 R 18 Beaumont rd SW19
73 W 8 Beaumont rd W4
47 Z 2 Beaumont ri N19
63 T 13 Beaumont sq E1
139 V 1 Beaumont st W1
131 V 20 Beaumont st W1
91 U 15 Beauval rd SE22
109 X 17 Beaver clo SE19
114 D 2 Beaverbank rd Sidcp
81 O 16 Beavercote wlk Blvdr
82 A 9 Beavers la Hounsl
114 H 14 Beaverwood rd Chisl
74 G 12 Beavor la W6
79 U 12 Bebbington rd SE18
40 A 9 Bec clo Ruislip
54 J 17 Beccles dri Bark
63 Z 19 Beccles st E14
124 E 6 Beck la Becknhm
135 X 4 Beck rd E8
18 C 11 Beckenham gdns N9
125 X 4 Beckenham gro
Brom
111 S 13 Beckenham Hill rd
Becknhm
126 B 2 Beckenham la Brom
111 S 16 Beckenham pl
Becknhm
111 P 18 Beckenham Place pk
Becknhm
111 T 15 Beckenham Place pk
Becknhm
124 K 2 Beckenham rd
Becknhm
125 T 18 Beckenham rd
W Wkhm
66 J 9 Becker av E6
123 X 14 Becket clo SE25
19 O 14 Becket rd N18
23 W 16 Becketfold Harrow
81 N 9 Beckett clo Blvdr
43 Z 19 Beckett rd NW10
110 H 15 Beckett wlk Becknhm
150 C 11 Beckford rd SE17
123 V 15 Beckford rd Croy
74 E 5 Becklow rd W12
115 O 8 Becks rd Sidcp
65 R 15 Beckton rd E16
124 M 7 Beckway Becknhm
125 N 8 Beckway rd Becknhm
121 X 4 Beckway rd SW16

150 H 7 Beckway st SE17
91 O 14 Beckwith rd SE24
107 R 14 Beclands rd SW17
24 B 15 Becmead av Harrow
107 Y 8 Becmead av SW16
109 S 13 Becondale rd SE19
56 A 7 Becontree av Dgnhm
55 T 8 Becontree av Dgnhm
87 U 11 Bective pl SW15
52 F 11 Bective rd E7
87 U 11 Bective rd SW15
98 H 1 Becton pl Erith
7 Y 4 Bedale rd Enf
142 E 14 Bedale st SE1
51 V 16 Beddingfield rd E15
122 A 19 Beddington Farm rd Croy
156 C 2 Beddington Farm rd Croy
155 P 14 Beddington gdns Carsh
155 Y 11 Beddington gro Wallgtn
155 Z 3 Beddington la Wallgtn
121 W 16 Beddington la Croy
155 U 4 Beddington pk Wallgtn
36 K 20 Beddington rd Ilf
37 T 18 Bede rd Rom
115 Y 14 Bedens rd Sidcp
4 J 15 Bedford av Barnt
140 G 2 Bedford av WC1
121 N 4 Bedford clo Mitch
29 P 3 Bedford clo N10
140 K10 Bedford ct WC2
137 U 15 Bedford gdns W8
107 V 6 Bedford hill SW16
144 M 17 Bedford pass SW6
122 M 20 Bedford pk Croy
123 O 20 Bedford pl WC1
140 K 1 Bedford pl WC1
132 K 20 Bedford pl WC1
33 O 8 Bedford rd E17
34 E 8 Bedford rd E18
66 H 3 Bedford rd E6
23 N 17 Bedford rd Harrow
54 A 10 Bedford rd Ilf
53 Z 10 Bedford rd Ilf
31 R 13 Bedford rd N15
28 J 10 Bedford rd N2
30 A 6 Bedford rd N22
29 Y 17 Bedford rd N8
18 M 1 Bedford rd N9
19 N 2 Bedford rd N9
13 N 9 Bedford rd NW7
114 H 7 Bedford rd Sidcp
89 Z 8 Bedford rd SW9
101 P 5 Bedford rd Twick
72 A 1 Bedford rd W13
73 Z 9 Bedford rd W4
153 N 4 Bedford rd Worc Pk
141 O 1 Bedford row WC1
140 G 2 Bedford sq WC1
140 K 9 Bedford st WC2
132 H 18 Bedford way WC1
140 J 10 Bedfordbury WC2
105 T 2 Bedgebury gdns SW19
94 M 11 Bedgebury rd SE9
112 F 6 Bedivere rd Brom
98 C 2 Bedonwell rd Bxly Hth
81 N 16 Bedonwell rd Blvdr
81 R 17 Bedonwell rd Blvdr
80 M 16 Bedonwell rd Blvdr
41 P 14 Bedser clo Grnfd
109 R 17 Bedwardine rd SE 19
81 R 14 Bedwell rd Blvdr
31 R 4 Bedwell rd N17
151 V 10 Bedwin way SE16
65 U 15 Beeby rd E16
72 B 19 Beech av Brentf
21 V 8 Beech av Buck Hl
15 X 6 Beech av N20
96 M 17 Beech av Sidcp
74 B 3 Beech av W3
154 L 2 Beech clo Carsh
8 L 20 Beech clo Enf
57 X 11 Beech clo Hornch
121 Z 8 Beech clo Mitch
86 G 17 Beech clo SW15
104 L 15 Beech clo SW19
127 T 2 Beech copse Brom
157 S 10 Beech copse S Croy
28 K 19 Beech dri N2
56 J 20 Beech gdns Dgnhm
72 J 8 Beech gdns W5
121 X 10 Beech gro Mitch
117 Y 6 Beech gro New Mald

33 W 1 Beech Hall cres E4
20 J 20 Beech Hall rd E4
33 V 3 Beech Hall rd E4
5 S 5 Beech Hall av Barnt
5 U 4 Beech hall Barnt
5 V 7 Beech Hill pk Barnt
157 O 6 Beech House rd Croy
21 U 9 Beech la Buck Hl
15 U 15 Beech lawns N12
17 N 19 Beech rd N11
122 B 4 Beech rd SW16
134 A 20 Beech st EC1
38 L 14 Beech Tree clo
11 S 17 Beech Tree clo Stanm
21 O 4 Beech Tree glade E4
15 X 15 Beech Vale clo N12
43 X 20 Beech way NW10
100 J 5 Beech way Twick
99 X 10 Beech wlk Drtfnd
12 M 18 Beech wlk NW7
40 G 2 Beechcroft av Harrow
98 M 4 Beechcroft av Bxly Hth
117 W 2 Beechcroft av New Mald
45 V 1 Beechcroft av NW11
70 D 2 Beechcroft av S'hall
113 W 17 Beechcroft Chisl
70 A 19 Beechcroft clo Hounsl
42 M 10 Beechcroft gdns Wemb
43 N 10 Beechcroft gdns Wemb
34 H 8 Beechcroft rd E18
85 W 9 Beechcroft rd SW14
106 J 3 Beechcroft rd SW17
17 R 8 Beechdale N21
90 D 16 Beechdale rd SW2
83 V 3 Beechen Cliff way Islwth
22 D 11 Beechen gro Pinn
154 K 16 Beeches Avenue the Carsh
124 B 1 Beeches clo SE20
119 T 20 Beeches rd Sutton
106 K 6 Beeches rd SW 17
154 H 19 Beeches wlk Carsh
38 L 20 Beechfield gdns Rom
126 M 3 Beechfield rd Brom
31 N 18 Beechfield rd N4
110 M 1 Beechfield rd SE6
95 V 12 Beechhill rd SE9
111 Z 13 Beechmont clo Brom
153 R 3 Beechmore gdns Sutton
89 N 2 Beechmore rd SW11
59 S 14 Beechmount av W7
107 R 19 Beecholme av Mitch
50 A 9 Beecholme est
102 J 11 Beechrow Rich
97 W 17 Beechway Bxly
122 H 8 Beechwood av Thntn Hth
40 L 9 Beechwood av Harrow
58 J 8 Beechwood av Grnfd
27 W 11 Beechwood av N3
85 P 2 Beechwood av Rich
12 M 16 Beechwood clo NW7
116 F 18 Beechwood clo Surb
97 Y 7 Beechwood cres Bxly Hth
21 P 17 Beechwood dri Wdfd Grn
40 L 9 Beechwood gdns Harrow
35 U 14 Beechwood gdns Ilf
34 E 11 Beechwood pk E18
157 R 19 Beechwood rd S Croy
49 U 18 Beechwood rd E8
29 Y 11 Beechwood rd N8
45 Z 8 Beechworth clo NW3
92 J 12 Beecroft rd SE4
35 T 15 Beehive la Ilf
90 F 9 Beehive pl SW9
120 B 8 Beeleigh rd Mrdn
147 Y 2 Beeston pl SW1
5 U 18 Beeston rd Barnt
11 T 1 Beethoven rd Borhm Wd
128 L 11 Beethoven st W10
22 G 3 Beeton clo Pinn
94 K 2 Begbie rd SE3
152 E 16 Beggars hill Epsom
62 E 18 Begonia wlk W12
89 T 17 Beira st SW12

63 U 18 Bekesbourne st E1
112 D 18 Belfast clo Brom
55 U 1 Belfairs dri Rom
49 U 6 Belfast rd N16
123 Z 10 Belfast rd SE25
48 B 12 Belfont wlk N7
78 H 12 Belford gro SE18
92 C 4 Belfort rd SE15
49 T 13 Belgrade rd N16
6 H 15 Belgrave clo N14
73 U 4 Belgrave clo NW4
6 J 15 Belgrave gdns N14
130 A 6 Belgrave gdns NW8
129 Z 7 Belgrave gdns NW8
11 S 15 Belgrave gdns Stanm
139 S 20 Belgrave Mews north SW1
147 U 1 Belgrave Mews south SW1
147 T 1 Belgrave Mews west SW1
147 U 3 Belgrave pl SW1
51 U 3 Belgrave rd E10
52 F 4 Belgrave rd E11
65 X 11 Belgrave rd E13
33 O 18 Belgrave rd E17
82 D 8 Belgrave rd Hounsl
53 T 4 Belgrave rd Ilf
120 F 5 Belgrave rd Mitch
123 V 8 Belgrave rd SE25
148 C 8 Belgrave rd SW1
147 Z 6 Belgrave rd SW1
74 E 20 Belgrave rd SW13
139 T 20 Belgrave sq SW1
147 U 1 Belgrave sq SW1
63 U 17 Belgrave st E1
21 S 11 Belgrave ter Wdfd Grn
120 G 6 Belgrave wlk Mitch
147 W 2 Belgrave sq SW1
111 Y 15 Belgravia gdns Brom
116 H 10 Belgravia ms Kingst
132 K 12 Belgrove st WC1
91 J 8 Belham st SE5
90 J 8 Belinda rd SW9
48 E 20 Belitha vlls N1
39 Y 4 Bell av Rom
87 S 18 Bell dri SW18
56 K 9 Bell Farm av Dgnhm
158 K 18 Bell field Croy
110 K 9 Bell Green la SE26
110 J 12 Bell grn SE26
110 K 8 Bell grn SE26
110 K 8 Bell grn SE26
56 K 3 Bell House rd Rom
160 H 7 Bell inn yd EC3
142 M 2 Bell la E1
143 N 3 Bell la E1
77 R 2 Bell la E16
9 U 4 Bell la Enf
27 N 14 Bell la Enf
101 Z 1 Bell la Twick
8 C 7 Bell rd Enf
82 J 9 Bell rd Hounsl
138 J 1 Bell st NW1
130 K 20 Bell st NW1
78 K 8 Bell Water ga SE18
160 D 10 Bell Wharf la EC4
141 S 6 Bell yd WC2
145 R 11 Bellamy clo SW5
24 B 5 Bellamy dri Stanm
20 E 20 Bellamy rd E4
89 R 18 Bellamy st SW12
107 Z 3 Bellasis av SW2
27 O 14 Belle View rd NW4
88 K 20 Belle Vue rd E17
90 D 8 Bellefields rd SW9
96 J 5 Bellegrove clo Welling
96 G 5 Bellegrove rd Welling
97 O 7 Bellegrove rd Welling
91 V 4 Bellenden rd SE15
20 B 7 Bellestaines E4
88 K 14 Belleville rd SW11
59 P 2 Bellevue Grnfd
10 C 5 Bellevue la Bushey
122 L 7 Bellevue pk Thntn Hth
63 P 13 Bellevue pl E1
98 A 13 Bellevue rd Bxly Hth
33 W 7 Bellevue rd E17
116 K 8 Bellevue rd Kingst
16 B 16 Bellevue rd N11
86 G 5 Bellevue rd SW13
106 K 1 Bellevue rd SW13
60 A 12 Bellevue rd W13
106 E 7 Bellevue rd SW17
10 B 20 Bellfield av Harrow
152 A 18 Bellfield rd Epsom
66 D 14 Bellflower clo E6

111 P 8 Bellingham grn SE6
111 S 6 Bellingham rd SE6
77 N 12 Bellot st SE10
81 T 16 Bellring clo Blvdr
87 X 5 Bells all SW6
4 D 14 Bells hill Barnt
108 E 12 Belltrees gro SE16
92 F 11 Bellwood rd SE15
118 H 10 Belmont av New Mald
6 A 14 Belmont av Barnt
5 Z 17 Belmont av Barnt
17 O 15 Belmont av N13
30 L 11 Belmont av N17
18 L 5 Belmont av N9
70 B 9 Belmont av S'hall
96 F 6 Belmont av Welling
60 M 2 Belmont av Wemb
24 A 6 Belmont cir Harrow
21 U 13 Belmont clo Wdfd Grn
6 A 14 Belmont clo Barnt
89 W 8 Belmont clo SW4
93 X 8 Belmont gro SE13
93 V 8 Belmont hill SE13
114 B 10 Belmont la Chisl
24 D 3 Belmont la Stanm
93 Y 10 Belmont Park clo SE13
33 S 19 Belmont Park rd E10
93 X 10 Belmont pk SE13
124 L 4 Belmont rd Becknhm
113 Z 12 Belmont rd Chisl
98 F 1 Belmont rd Erith
81 S 20 Belmont rd Erith
23 X 10 Belmont rd Harrow
54 C 9 Belmont rd Ilf
30 L 12 Belmont rd N17
124 A 13 Belmont rd SE25
89 W 8 Belmont rd SW4
101 P 3 Belmont rd Twick
73 X 12 Belmont rd W4
155 T 11 Belmont rd Wallgtn
153 U 16 Belmont rt Sutton
47 P 19 Belmont st NW1
89 Y 2 Belmore st SW8
86 H 9 Beloe clo SW15
50 C 17 Belsham st E9
17 R 19 Belsize av N13
46 J 16 Belsize av NW3
72 C 8 Belsize av W13
46 G 16 Belsize cres NW3
154 B 7 Belsize gdns Sutton
46 K 17 Belsize gdns NW3
46 K 16 Belsize la NW3
46 J 17 Belsize Park gdns NW3
46 G 17 Belsize Park ms NW3
46 J 17 Belsize pl NW3
23 P 1 Belsize rd Harrow
130 C 2 Belsize rd NW6
130 D 1 Belsize rd NW6
46 E 20 Belsize rd NW6
129 Z 3 Belsize rd NW6
46 H 18 Belsize sq NW3
46 G 17 Belsize ter NW3
78 F 10 Belson rd SE18
105 P 6 Beltane dri SW19
89 V 19 Belthorn cres SW12
51 Z 12 Belton rd E11
52 J 20 Belton rd E7
31 S 10 Belton rd N17
44 G 17 Belton rd NW2
115 O 9 Belton rd Sidcp
64 A 14 Belton way E3
87 Z 5 Beltran rd SW6
81 W 10 Beltwood rd Blvdr
35 Z 8 Belvedere av Ilf
105 T 12 Belvedere av SW19
141 T 19 Belvedere bldgs SE1
101 T 13 Belvedere clo Tedd
105 T 13 Belvedere dri SW19
105 S 13 Belvedere gro SW19
26 C 8 Belvedere NW9
141 Z 19 Belvedere pl SE1
98 B 7 Belvedere n Bxly Hth
50 J 3 Belvedere rd E10
141 O 18 Belvedere rd SE1
109 U 17 Belvedere rd SW19
80 H 3 Belvedere rd SE2
71 U 7 Belvedere rd W7
105 S 12 Belvedere sq SW19
24 K 19 Belvedere way Harrow
113 R 6 Belvoir clo SE9
91 Y 19 Belvoir rd SE22
40 H 20 Belvue clo Nthlt
58 H 2 Belvue pk Nthlt

40 J 20 Belvue rd Nthlt
45 R 20 Bembridge clo NW6
132 M 3 Bemerton st N1
87 P 8 Bemish rd SW15
32 L 9 Bemsted rd E17
159 X 4 Ben Curtis pk Wkhm
91 P 2 Ben Hill rd SE5
63 U 15 Ben Jonson rd E1
151 U 1 Ben Smith way SE16
68 B 1 Ben Tillet clo Bark
79 X 11 Benares rd SE18
144 A 1 Benbow rd W6
74 K 8 Benbow rd W6
76 B 15 Benbow st SE8
111 U 12 Benbury clo Brom
102 E 7 Bench the Rich
157 V 13 Benchfield S Croy
107 W 17 Bencroft rd SW16
130 M 20 Bendall ms NW1
87 O 7 Bendall rd SW15
66 D 2 Bendish rd E6
80 A 12 Bendmeer av SE2
88 A 20 Bendon valley SW18
120 G 7 Benedict rd Mitch
90 E 7 Benedict rd SW9
28 C 9 Benedict way N2
126 D 12 Benenden grn Brom
121 Z 3 Benett gdns SW16
154 D 8 Benfleet clo Sutton
160 G 7 Bengal st EC3
53 Y 11 Bengal rd Ilf
23 R 7 Bengarth dri Harrow
58 A 3 Bengarth rd Nthlt
41 Z 8 Bengeworth rd Harrow
90 L 7 Bengeworth rd SE5
11 N 1b Benhale clo Stanm
88 F 9 Benham clo SW11
59 U 15 Benham rd W7
154 B 19 Benhill av Sutton
150 G 20 Benhill rd SE5
154 E 6 Benhill rd Sutton
154 C 5 Benhill Wood rd Sutton
154 B 6 Benhilton gdns Sutton
57 Y 11 Benhurst av Hornch
108 E 12 Benhurst ct SW16
93 Y 18 Benin st SE13
18 M 13 Benjafield clo N18
135 V 4 Benjamin clo E8
39 W 19 Benjamin clo Hornch
133 W 20 Benjamin st EC1
64 J 16 Benledi st E14
50 J 17 Benn st E9
88 K 13 Bennerley rd SW11
140 A 13 Bennet st SW1
116 D 1 Bennett clo Kingst
96 M 5 Bennett clo Welling
93 S 3 Bennett gro SE13
94 C 6 Bennett pk SE3
65 X 13 Bennett rd E13
37 Z 20 Bennett rd Rom
74 A 15 Bennett st W4
158 K 4 Bennetts av Croy
59 S 3 Bennetts av Grnfd
55 U 7 Bennetts Castle la Dgnhm
113 R 15 Bennetts copse Chisl
158 K 3 Bennetts way Croy
148 H 3 Bennetts yd SW1
13 N 19 Benningholme rd Edg
33 Y 2 Bennington rd Wdfd Grn
31 P 5 Bennington rd N17
36 B 3 Benrek clo Ilf
86 K 19 Bensbry clo SW15
122 L 10 Bensham clo Thntn Hth
122 L 3 Bensham gro Thntn Hth
122 J 10 Bensham la Thntn Hth
122 M 9 Bensham Manor rd Thntn Hth
123 N 10 Bensham Manor rd Thntn Hth
15 Y 17 Bensley clo N11
65 Z 7 Benson av E6
82 G 10 Benson clo Hounsl
156 G 6 Benson rd Croy
92 D 20 Benson rd SE23
49 W 9 Benthal rd N16
50 F 18 Bentham rd E9
80 C 1 Bentham rd SE28
68 C 20 Bentham rd E9
139 V 3 Bentinck ms W1
139 V 4 Bentinck st W1
36 B 17 Bentley dri Ilf

10 G 12 Bentley priory Stanm
49 S 18 Bentley rd N1
21 S 9 Bentley way Wdfd Grn
10 K 17 Bentley way Stanm
54 D 3 Benton rd Ilf
108 M 11 Bentons la SE27
109 N 11 Bentons ri SE27
55 Z 7 Bentry clo Dgnhm
56 A 7 Bentry rd Dgnhm
55 Z 7 Bentry rd Dgnhm
136 A 6 Bentworth rd W12
62 J 18 Bentworth rd W12
48 E 14 Benwell rd N7
63 Z 8 Benworth st E3
134 G 3 Benyon rd N1
88 M 13 Berber rd SW11
114 A 4 Bercta rd SE9
128 F 13 Berens rd NW10
15 Y 8 Beresford av N20
117 T 19 Beresford av Surb
84 F 15 Beresford av Twick
59 S 15 Beresford av W7
61 P 2 Beresford av Wemb
127 P 6 Beresford dri BR1
21 Y 13 Beresford dri Buck Hl
82 E 13 Beresford gdns Hounsl
8 D 14 Beresford gdns Enf
37 Z 17 Beresford gdns Rom
117 V 8 Beresford rd New Mald
33 R 4 Beresford rd E17
20 M 4 Beresford rd E4
23 O 16 Beresford rd Harrow
102 M 20 Beresford rd Kingst
100 N 20 Beresford rd Kingst
28 J 11 Beresford rd N2
49 N 15 Beresford rd N5
30 H 15 Beresford rd N8
153 V 18 Beresford rd Sutton
78 M 10 Beresford sq SE18
78 L 9 Beresford st SE18
48 M 15 Beresford ter N5
74 E 13 Berestede rd W6
50 F 17 Berger rd E9
35 P 14 Bergholt av Ilf
49 R 1 Bergholt cres N16
132 D 2 Bergholt way NW1
97 X 2 Berkeley av Bxly Hth
41 S 18 Berkeley av Grnfd
35 Y 7 Berkeley av Ilf
38 L 2 Berkeley av Rom
71 Z 18 Berkeley clo Brentf
16 G 1 Berkeley ct N14
18 A 2 Berkeley gdns N21
137 V 14 Berkeley gdns W8
139 R 5 Berkeley ms W1
105 P 17 Berkeley pl SW19
53 R 16 Berkeley rd E12
31 P 19 Berkeley rd N15
29 Y 17 Berkeley rd N8
25 P 14 Berkeley rd NW9
86 F 1 Berkeley rd SW13
139 Y 11 Berkeley sq W1
139 Z 12 Berkeley st W1
70 A 18 Berkeley waye Hounsl
81 R 12 Berkhampstead rd Blvdr
43 O 18 Berkhamsted av Wemb
5 U 18 Berkley cres Barnt
131 S 1 Berkley grn NW1
131 R 1 Berkley rd NW1
17 S 20 Berkshire gdns N13
18 M 17 Berkshire gdns N18
51 N 17 Berkshire rd E9
122 A 10 Berkshire way Mitch
121 Z 10 Berkshire way Mitch
44 C 13 Bermans way NW10
150 K 1 Bermondsey sq SE1
142 J 17 Bermondsey st SE1
143 R 16 Bermondsey Wall west SE16
143 U 18 Bermondsey Wall east SE16
72 B 7 Bernard av W13
65 R 14 Bernard Cassidy st E16
105 W 12 Bernard gdns SW19
31 V 15 Bernard rd N15
56 K 1 Bernard rd Rom
38 K 20 Bernard rd Rom
155 R 9 Bernard rd Wallgtn
132 K 18 Bernard st WC1
11 R 19 Bernays clo Stanm
90 D 9 Bernays gro SW9
122 K 10 Berne rd Thntn Hth
158 M 4 Bernel dri Croy

140 C 2 Berners ms W1
140 D 4 Berners pl W1
133 V 6 Berners rd N1
30 E 6 Berners rd N22
140 C 3 Berners st W1
123 N 17 Berney rd Croy
25 O 15 Bernville way NW9
21 N 11 Bernwell rd E4
25 R 3 Berridge grn Edg
109 P 12 Berridge rd SE19
48 E 9 Berriman rd N7
40 E 5 Berriton rd Harrow
17 W 4 Berry clo N21
11 V 13 Berry hill Stanm
109 P 9 Berry la SE27
133 X 14 Berry pl EC1
133 X 16 Berry st EC1
72 J 8 Berry way W5
58 B 11 Berrydale SE12
127 R 2 Berryfield clo BR1
33 S 14 Berryfield clo E17
149 Y 10 Berryfield rd SE17
95 Y 10 Berryhill gdns SE9
95 Y 9 Berryhill SE9
116 L 13 Berrylands rd Surb
117 N 13 Berrylands rd Surb
117 R 12 Berrylands Surb
119 N 7 Berrylands SW20
55 V 10 Berrymans clo Dgnhm
110 F 10 Berrymans la SE26
73 V 4 Berrymead gdns W3
73 X 8 Berrymede rd W4
122 K 12 Bert rd Thntn Hth
8 J 14 Bert way Enf
106 F 11 Bertal rd SW17
76 C 18 Berthon st SE8
44 G 18 Bertie rd NW10
110 G 14 Bertie rd SE26
105 X 18 Bertram cotts SW19
8 J 14 Bertram rd Enf
103 O 17 Bertram rd Kingst
26 H 19 Bertram rd NW4
47 S 8 Bertram st N19
93 R 7 Bertrand st SE13
68 F 19 Bertrand way SE28
58 A 19 Berwick av Hay
10 J 20 Berwick clo Stanm
96 H 17 Berwick cres Sidcp
65 X 18 Berwick rd E16
30 H 4 Berwick rd N22
97 R 3 Berwick rd Welling
140 C 5 Berwick st W1
82 J 2 Berwyn av Hounsl
85 S 10 Berwyn rd Rich
108 J 1 Berwyn rd SE21
66 E 14 Beryl av E6
144 F 11 Beryl rd W6
103 T 18 Berystede clo Kingst
45 S 11 Besant rd NW2
43 W 15 Besant way NW10
107 V 16 Besley st SW16
148 G 10 Bessborough gdns SW1
148 F 9 Bessborough ms SW1
148 F 10 Bessborough pl SW1
104 G 1 Bessborough rd SW15
86 H 20 Bessborough rd SW15
41 R 3 Bessborough rd Harrow
148 F 10 Bessborough st SW1
148 G 10 Bessborough st SW1
90 M 6 Bessemer rd SE5
91 N 5 Bessemer rd SE5
92 E 1 Bessett st SE14
75 T 12 Bestwood st SE8
154 F 10 Betchworth clo Sutton
54 H 8 Betchworth rd Ilf
159 T 18 Betchworth way Croy
59 R 10 Betham rd Grnfd
23 T 14 Bethecar rd Harrow
97 U 8 Bethel rd Welling
65 P 11 Bethell av E16
53 W 1 Bethell av Ilf
110 M 19 Bethersden clo Becknhm
135 U 14 Bethnal Green rd E2
135 Z 11 Bethnal Green museum E2
15 Z 14 Bethune av N11
49 S 4 Bethune rd N16
61 Z 12 Bethune rd NW10
150 C 17 Bethwin rd SE5
149 Z 17 Bethwin rd SE5
22 G 13 Betjemin clo Harrow

124 E 20 Betony clo CRO
20 M 13 Betoyne av E4
16 F 14 Betstyle rd N11
125 Z 4 Betterton dri Sidcp
140 K 5 Betterton st WC2
65 N 4 Bettons pk E15
87 W 5 Bettridge rd SW6
65 V 19 Betts rd E16
143 V 9 Betts st E1
116 B 20 Betts way Surb
122 M 4 Beulah av Thntn Hth
12 E 10 Beulah clo Edg
122 M 4 Beulah cres Thntn Hth
122 L 14 Beulah gro Croy
108 K 16 Beulah hill SE19
33 T 14 Beulah rd E17
153 Y 9 Beulah rd Sutton
105 V 17 Beulah rd SW19
122 L 5 Beulah rd Thntn Hth
99 W 9 Beult rd Drtford
68 A 1 Bevan av Bark
156 F 11 Bevan ct Croy
5 Z 13 Bevan rd Barnt
80 C 14 Bevan rd SE2
134 B 6 Bevan st N1
134 G 12 Bevenden st N1
82 D 11 Beverley av Hounsl
104 E 19 Beverley av SW20
17 Y 6 Beverley clo N21
88 F 10 Beverley clo SW11
86 F 5 Beverley clo SW13
34 H 3 Beverley cres Wdfd Grn
16 H 2 Beverley ct N14
92 M 7 Beverley ct SE4
26 N O Beverley dri Edg
27 T 20 Beverley gdns NW11
23 Y 5 Beverley gdns Stanm
86 E 7 Beverley gdns SW13
43 O 3 Beverley gdns Wemb
104 B 18 Beverley la Kingst
118 F 7 Beverley pk New Mald
118 F 9 Beverley rd New Mald
98 K 6 Beverley rd Bxly Hth
86 A 12 Beverley rd Dgnhm
55 Z 12 Beverley rd Dgnhm
20 K 19 Beverley rd E4
66 B 9 Beverley rd E6
102 E 20 Beverley rd Kingst
121 W 8 Beverley rd Mitch
70 C 10 Beverley rd S'hall
123 Z 3 Beverley rd SE20
86 E 6 Beverley rd SW13
74 C 14 Beverley rd W4
152 L 3 Beverley rd Worc Pk
104 C 20 Beverley way New Mald
118 G 3 Beverley way SW20
47 Y 10 Beversbrook rd N19
122 H 9 Beverstone rd Thntn Hth
90 C 12 Beverstone rd SW2
107 N 13 Bevill Allen clo SW17
75 V 3 Bevin clo SE16
133 R 11 Bevin way WC1
125 P 7 Bevington rd Becknhm
136 M 1 Bevington rd W10
137 N 2 Bevington rd W10
143 U 18 Bevington st SE16
142 L 6 Bevis marks EC3
7 N 14 Bewcastle gdns Enf
49 F 20 Bewdley st N1
89 S 4 Bewick st SW8
63 O 19 Bewley st E1
143 Z 8 Bewley st E1
108 J 11 Bewleys rd SE27
100 A 3 Bexhill clo Felt
16 J 17 Bexhill rd N11
92 L 17 Bexhill rd SE4
85 W 8 Bexhill rd SW14
99 P 12 Bexley clo Dartford
18 B 11 Bexley gdns N9
98 E 20 Bexley High st Bxly
99 P 12 Bexley la Drtford
115 U 8 Bexley la Sidcp
96 C 14 Bexley rd SE9
154 L 11 Beynon rd Carsh
151 R 14 Bianca rd SE15
27 V 8 Bibsworth rd N3
85 S 8 Bicester rd Rich
131 P 20 Bickenhall st W1
106 M 14 Bickersteth rd SW17
47 U 8 Bickerton rd N19
127 R 8 Bickley cres Brom
127 U 5 Bickley Park rd Brom

127 P 4	Bickley rd Brom
33 R 20	Bickley rd E10
106 K 13	Bickley st SW17
90 M 8	Bicknell rd SE5
8 F 5	Bicknoller rd Enf
126 C 12	Bidborough clo Brom
132 H 13	Bidborough st WC1
113 V 9	Biddenden way SE9
64 L 14	Bidder st E16
48 C 13	Biddestone rd N7
156 L 20	Biddulph rd S Croy
129 Y 14	Biddulph rd W9
60 A 7	Bideford av Grnfd
25 O 5	Bideford clo Edg
100 E 6	Bideford clo Felt
18 E 2	Bideford gdns Enf
112 B 7	Bideford rd Brom
9 X 3	Bideford rd Enf
80 D 20	Bideford rd Welling
29 V 3	Bidwell gdns N11
92 A 3	Bidwell st SE15
50 A 3	Big hill E5
31 R 1	Bigbury clo N17
64 G 2	Biggerstaff rd E15
48 E 7	Biggerstaff st N4
120 L 1	Biggin av Mitch
108 K 17	Biggin hill SE19
108 K 19	Biggin way SE19
108 H 19	Bigginwood rd SW16
87 O 8	Biggs row SW15
63 N 18	Bigland st E1
78 M 14	Bignell rd SE18
52 F 13	Bignold rd E7
28 A 17	Bigwood rd NW11
37 W 10	Billet clo Rom
32 H 5	Billet rd E17
33 O 3	Billet rd E17
37 T 10	Billet rd Rom
145 Y 17	Billing pl SW10
145 Z 16	Billing st SW10
145 Y 17	Billing st SW10
92 G 10	Billingford clo SE4
76 G 16	Billingsgate st SE10
75 T 20	Billington rd SE14
142 K 7	Billiter sq EC3
142 K 7	Billiter st EC3
76 G 11	Billson st E14
113 O 10	Bilsby gro SE9
60 D 3	Bilton rd Grnfd
59 Z 3	Bilton rd Grnfd
9 X 4	Bilton way Enf
146 B 8	Bina gdns SW5
7 R 12	Bincote rd Enf
74 E 7	Binden rd W12
120 B 8	Bindon gdns Mrdn
157 U 10	Binfield rd S Croy
90 A 3	Binfield rd SW4
132 M 3	Bingfield st N1
133 N 3	Bingfield st N1
131 T 19	Bingham pl W1
123 Y 20	Bingham rd Croy
49 O 17	Bingham st N1
65 X 17	Bingley rd E16
59 N 12	Bingley rd Grnfd
139 V 8	Binney st W1
73 Z 13	Binns rd W4
10 H 17	Binyon cres Stanm
113 T 5	Birbetts rd SE9
17 Y 12	Birch av N13
72 B 19	Birch clo Brentf
38 G 10	Birch clo Rom
91 Y 5	Birch clo SE15
101 Y 11	Birch clo Tedd
56 L 10	Birch gdns Dgnhm
94 C 18	Birch gro SE12
73 O 2	Birch gro W3
61 P 20	Birch gro W3
97 N 11	Birch gro Welling
158 G 10	Birch hill Croy
22 L 1	Birch pk Harrow
100 A 13	Birch rd Felt
38 G 10	Birch rd Rom
127 X 16	Birch row Brom
157 Z 2	Birch Tree way Croy
81 Y 15	Birch wlk Erith
121 S 1	Birch wlk Mitch
123 X 12	Birchanger rd SE25
55 V 1	Birchdale gdns Rom
52 M 15	Birchdale rd E7
43 X 6	Birchen clo NW9
43 X 8	Birchen gro NW9
7 P 19	Birches the N21
77 W 15	Birches the SE7
72 D 19	Birchfield clo Brentf
64 A 19	Birchfield st E14
160 G 7	Birchin la EC3
98 F 1	Birchington clo Bxly Hth
29 X 17	Birchington rd N8
129 V 4	Birchington rd NW6
117 O 18	Birchington rd Surb
88 M 18	Birchlands av SW12
89 N 18	Birchlands av SW12
48 L 11	Birchmore wlk N5
124 L 8	Birchwood av Becknhm
155 R 4	Birchwood av Wallgtn
29 P 11	Birchwood av N10
115 R 7	Birchwood av Sidcp
25 V 8	Birchwood ct Edg
17 V 16	Birchwood ct N13
46 B 10	Birchwood dri NW3
100 J 15	Birchwood gro Hampt
107 R 11	Birchwood rd SW17
110 D 4	Bird in the Hand pass SE23
139 V 6	Bird st W1
82 E 20	Bird wlk Twick
151 R 17	Bird-in-Bush rd SE15
127 O 4	Bird-in-Hand la Brom
56 K 20	Birdbrook clo Dgnhm
81 R 1	Birdbrook clo Dgnhm
94 M 8	Birdbrook rd SE3
140 C 19	Birdcage wlk SW1
127 S 12	Birdham clo Brom
157 P 9	Birdhurst av S Croy
157 P 9	Birdhurst gdns S Croy
157 R 10	Birdhurst rd S Croy
88 C 12	Birdhurst rd SW18
106 J 16	Birdhurst rd SW19
157 R 11	Birdhurst ri S Croy
150 J 15	Birdlip clo SE15
38 G 3	Birds Farm av Rom
59 O 3	Birkbeck av Grnfd
61 W 19	Birkbeck av W3
21 R 9	Birkbeck gdns Wdfd Grn
73 X 4	Birkbeck gro W3
108 K 2	Birkbeck hill SE21
108 K 2	Birkbeck pl SE21
124 D 4	Birkbeck rd Becknhm
49 U 16	Birkbeck rd E8
8 B 5	Birkbeck rd Enf
36 D 16	Birkbeck rd Ilf
15 O 17	Birkbeck rd N12
31 U 5	Birkbeck rd N17
30 A 13	Birkbeck rd N8
13 S 16	Birkbeck rd NW7
57 N 3	Birkbeck rd Rom
115 O 8	Birkbeck rd Sidcp
106 B 14	Birkbeck rd SW19
73 X 3	Birkbeck rd W3
72 E 10	Birkbeck rd W5
63 O 10	Birkbeck st E2
135 Y 14	Birkbeck st E2
59 O 3	Birkbeck way Grnfd
22 H 10	Birkdale av Pinn
80 A 11	Birkdale rd SE2
79 Z 10	Birkdale rd SE2
60 J 12	Birkdale rd W5
116 M 2	Birkenhead av Kingst
117 N 2	Birkenhead av Kingst
111 X 3	Birkhall rd SE6
89 Y 20	Birkwood clo SW12
15 R 8	Birley rd N20
89 O 5	Birley st SW11
99 R 1	Birling rd Erith
48 C 7	Birnam rd N4
44 B 11	Birse cres NW10
31 T 15	Birstall rd N15
144 F 11	Biscay rd W6
70 H 16	Biscoe clo Hounsl
93 X 9	Biscoe way SE13
157 S 2	Bisenden rd Croy
120 L 18	Bisham clo Carsh
47 R 3	Bisham gdns N6
7 V 7	Bishop Craven clo Enf
23 W 6	Bishop Ken rd Harrow
144 L 5	Bishop Kings rd W14
16 D 4	Bishop rd N14
134 B 4	Bishop st N1
154 E 11	Bishop's pl Sutton
126 K 5	Bishops av Brom
65 U 2	Bishops av E13
37 T 17	Bishops av Rom
87 R 4	Bishops av SW6
46 G 2	Bishops av the N2
28 H 16	Bishops av the N2
138 B 4	Bishops Bridge rd W2
4 A 20	Bishops clo Barnt
33 S 13	Bishops clo E17
8 M 9	Bishops clo Enf
47 U 10	Bishops clo N19
102 G 6	Bishops clo Rich
114 B 4	Bishops clo SE9
153 Z 6	Bishops clo Sutton
141 X 4	Bishops ct EC4
141 R 4	Bishops ct WC2
100 G 11	Bishops gro Hampt
28 H 18	Bishops gro N2
116 G 3	Bishops hall Kingst
108 A 20	Bishops Park rd SW16
122 B 1	Bishops Park rd SW16
87 R 4	Bishops Park rd SW6
87 O 4	Bishops pk SW6
122 H 18	Bishops rd Croy
29 P 19	Bishops rd N6
145 O 20	Bishops rd SW6
87 U 1	Bishops rd SW6
71 T 5	Bishops rd W7
149 T 5	Bishops ter SE11
63 O 6	Bishops way E2
135 Y 8	Bishops way E2
44 A 20	Bishops way NW10
158 G 12	Bishops wlk Croy
120 G 13	Bishopsford rd Mrdn
142 J 3	Bishopsgate chyd EC2
142 K 3	Bishopsgate EC2
110 E 9	Bishopsthorpe rd SE26
46 M 1	Bishopswood rd N6
47 N 2	Bishopswood rd N6
119 N 20	Bisley clo Worc Pk
61 N 9	Bispham rd NW10
60 M 9	Bispham rd Wemb
64 G 5	Bisson rd E15
33 X 10	Bisterne av E17
14 B 18	Bittacy clo NW7
14 C 19	Bittacy hill NW7
27 S 2	Bittacy hill NW7
14 B 19	Bittacy Hill pk NW7
14 B 18	Bittacy Park av NW7
14 D 20	Bittacy rd NW7
14 A 19	Bittacy ri NW7
142 A 18	Bittern st SE1
116 H 6	Bittoms the Kingst
70 E 9	Bixley clo S'hall
30 M 16	Black Boy la N15
135 N 19	Black Eagle st E1
150 F 1	Black Horse ct SE1
75 W 15	Black Horse rd SE8
115 O 10	Black Horse rd Sidcp
74 F 12	Black Lion la W6
143 S 2	Black Lion yd E1
149 O 7	Black Prince rd SE11
50 G 2	Black pth E10
142 K 17	Black Swan yd SE1
90 G 9	Black Tree ms SW9
134 H 16	Blackall st EC2
70 B 20	Blackberry Farm clo Hounsl
43 W 8	Blackbird hill NW9
56 F 18	Blackborne rd Dgnhm
127 V 5	Blackbrook la Brom
45 Z 18	Blackburn rd NW6
139 T 10	Blackburns ms W1
37 V 17	Blackbush av Rom
154 B 16	Blackbush clo Sutton
87 O 8	Blackett st SW15
96 J 14	Blackfen rd Sidcp
97 P 15	Blackfen rd Sidcp
156 K 18	Blackford clo S Croy
141 W 10	Blackfriars br EC4
141 X 8	Blackfriars la EC4
141 W 17	Blackfriars rd SE1
141 V 9	Blackfriars underpass EC4
93 Z 1	Blackheath av SE10
94 C 6	Blackheath gro SE3
93 T 2	Blackheath hill SE10
94 E 7	Blackheath pk SE3
93 R 2	Blackheath rd SE10
93 U 4	Blackheath ri SE13
93 Z 4	Blackheath vale SE3
94 B 6	Blackheath village SE3
123 Y 17	Blackhorse la Croy
32 F 9	Blackhorse la E17
32 G 14	Blackhorse la E17
111 T 10	Blacklands rd SE6
147 O 7	Blacklands ter SW3
71 R 2	Blackmore av S'hall
101 Y 14	Blackmores gro Tedd
91 Z 5	Blackpool rd SE15
144 B 8	Blacks rd W6
74 M 12	Blacks rd W6
134 L 2	Blackshaw pl N1
106 H 13	Blackshaw rd SW17
157 H 7	Blackstock rd N4
45 N 14	Blackstone rd NW2
124 B 19	Blackthorn av Croy
97 Y 7	Blackthorn gro Bxly Hth
64 B 13	Blackthorn st E3
20 K 13	Blackthorne dri E4
77 N 8	Blackwall la SE10
77 O 12	Blackwall la SE10
64 F 9	Blackwall tunnel northern appr E14
76 K 1	Blackwall tunnel E14
77 P 1	Blackwall tunnel1 appr SE10
76 H 1	Blackwall way E14
64 H 20	Blackwall way E14
91 U 13	Blackwater st SE22
23 P 2	Blackwell clo Harrow
12 C 12	Blackwell gdns Edg
150 D 10	Blackwood st SE17
97 V 18	Bladindon dri Bxly
125 Y 4	Bladon ct Brom
22 K 18	Bladon gdns Harrow
14 A 14	Blagdens clo N14
15 N 14	Blagdens la N14
118 E 8	Blagdon ho New Mald
118 E 8	Blagdon rd Mald Mald
93 R 16	Blagdon rd SE13
102 D 16	Blagdon wlk Tedd
137 N 2	Blagrove rd W10
44 A 2	Blair av NW9
96 G 14	Blair clo Sidcp
64 H 18	Blair st E14
108 A 3	Blairderry rd SW2
67 W 4	Blake av Bark
87 Z 1	Blake gdns SW6
52 F 5	Blake Hall cres E11
52 F 3	Blake Hall rd E11
157 R 2	Blake rd Croy
65 O 12	Blake rd E16
120 H 5	Blake rd Mitch
16 J 20	Blake rd N11
29 V 2	Blake rd N11
154 M 13	Blakehall rd Carsh
122 D 11	Blakemore rd Thntn Hth
107 Z 6	Blakemore rd SW16
80 L 9	Blakemore way Blvdr
110 M 20	Blakeney av Becknhm
15 P 6	Blakeney clo N20
110 L 19	Blakeney rd Becknhm
106 L 10	Blakenham rd SW17
107 N 9	Blakenham rd SW17
118 E 13	Blakes av New Mald
125 T 19	Blakes grn W Wkhm
118 D 13	Blakes la New Mald
150 L 19	Blakes rd SE15
118 G 12	Blakes ter New Mald
60 F 17	Blakesley av W5
119 U 3	Blakesley wlk SW20
18 C 3	Blakesware gdns N9
151 Z 19	Blanch clo SE15
113 R 6	Blanchard clo SE9
49 Y 19	Blanchard way E8
65 P 12	Blanche st E16
91 O 8	Blanchedowne SE5
120 A 11	Blanchland rd Mrdn
89 P 17	Blandfield rd SW12
124 G 2	Blandford av Becknhm
100 L 1	Blandford av Twick
156 A 6	Blandford clo Croy
28 E 14	Blandford clo N2
38 G 13	Blandford clo Rom
20 F 3	Blandford cres E4
124 D 5	Blandford rd Becknhm
70 G 10	Blandford rd S'hall
101 S 14	Blandford rd Tedd
74 A 8	Blandford rd W4
72 H 5	Blandford rd W5
130 M 18	Blandford sq NW1
139 T 3	Blandford st W1
66 L 9	Blaney cres E6
114 A 2	Blanmerle rd SE9
113 Y 2	Blanmerle rd SE9
94 M 17	Blann clo SE9
146 E 18	Blantyre st SW10
93 Y 18	Blashford st SE13
23 U 14	Blawith rd Harrow
31 Z 1	Blaydon clo N17
79 X 16	Bleakhill la SE18
110 B 18	Blean gro SE20
59 X 6	Bleasdale av Grnfd
97 U 15	Bleddyn clo Bxly
80 H 1	Bledlow clo SE2
59 N 6	Bledlow ri Grnfd
141 U 1	Bleeding Heart yd EC1

107 V 14 Blegborough rd SW16
97 W 17 Blendon dri Bxly
112 D 19 Blendon pth Brom
97 V 16 Blendon rd Bxly
150 E 9 Blendon rd SE17
150 E 8 Blendon row SE17
79 P 15 Blendon ter SE18
35 V 19 Blenheim av Ilf
17 Y 4 Blenheim clo N21
59 R 7 Blenheim clo Nrthlt
38 J 12 Blenheim clo Rom
118 L 7 Blenheim clo SW20
155 V 16 Blenheim clo Wallgtn
156 L 17 Blenheim cres S Croy
136 L 7 Blenheim cres W11
137 N 6 Blenheim cres W11
114 E 6 Blenheim ct Sidcp
96 K 3 Blenheim dri Welling
103 S 19 Blenheim gdns Kingst
155 V 15 Blenheim gdns Wallgtn
45 N 15 Blenheim gdns NW2
90 B 15 Blenheim gdns SW2
42 K 9 Blenheim gdns Wemb
91 W 5 Blenheim gro SE15
156 L 17 Blenheim Park rd S Croy
130 B 8 Blenheim pas NW8
4 C 13 Blenheim rd Barnt
127 R 9 Blenheim rd Brom
52 A 12 Blenheim rd E15
32 G 10 Blenheim rd E17
66 A 8 Blenheim rd E6
40 L 10 Blenheim rd Grnfd
22 J 17 Blenheim rd Harrow
22 L 18 Blenheim rd Harrow
30 E 8 Blenheim rd N22
130 C 7 Blenheim rd NW8
110 C 18 Blenheim rd SE20
115 T 3 Blenheim rd Sidcp
153 Z 4 Blenheim rd Sutton
118 L 7 Blenheim rd SW20
74 B 8 Blenheim rd W4
31 V 14 Blenheim ri N15
139 X 7 Blenheim st W1
130 B 8 Blenheim ter NW8
88 L 17 Blenkarne rd SW11
25 V 4 Blessbury rd Edg
93 X 9 Blessington clo SE13
93 X 9 Blessington rd SE13
134 C 10 Bletchely st N1
134 D 10 Bletchley st N1
105 P 4 Blincoe clo SW19
93 R 3 Bliss cres SE13
93 T 1 Blissett st SE10
58 B 10 Blisworth clo Grnfd
55 P 19 Blithbury rd Dgnhm
80 B 11 Blithdale rd SE2
79 Z 11 Blithdale rd SE2
145 W 3 Blithfield st W8
42 A 8 Blockley rd Wemb
74 J 3 Bloemfontein av W12
62 H 19 Bloemfontein rd W12
74 J 3 Bloemfontein rd W12
130 E 18 Blomfield rd W9
129 Z 20 Blomfield rd W9
160 H 2 Blomfield st EC2
142 H 3 Blomfield ct EC2
137 Z 1 Blomfield vlls W2
56 A 8 Blomville rd Dgnhm
89 N 4 Blondel st SW11
72 C 10 Blondin av W5
64 B 6 Blondin st E3
108 J 7 Bloom gro SE27
145 N 20 Bloom Park rd SW6
148 D 6 Bloomburg st SW1
36 A 19 Bloomfield cres Ilf
139 Y 8 Bloomfield pl W1
126 M 11 Bloomfield rd Brom
127 N 10 Bloomfield rd Brom
116 K 8 Bloomfield rd Kingst
29 P 19 Bloomfield rd N6
79 N 13 Bloomfield rd SE18
147 U 9 Bloomfield ter SW1
109 P 13 Bloomhall rd SE19
61 O 19 Bloomsbury clo W5
22 E 9 Bloomsbury ct Pinn
140 L 3 Bloomsbury ct WC1
140 L 1 Bloomsbury pl WC1
140 K 1 Bloomsbury sq WC1
140 H 2 Bloomsbury st WC1
140 K 3 Bloomsbury way WC1
89 X 3 Blore clo SW8

157 V 10 Blossom clo S Croy
72 L 6 Blossom clo W5
7 X 5 Blossom la Enf
134 M 19 Blossom st E1
70 B 18 Blossom waye Hounsl
63 W 16 Blount st E14
50 K 4 Bloxhall rd E10
100 F 19 Bloxham cres Hampt
95 R 13 Bloxham gdns SE9
155 V 6 Bloxworth clo Wallgtn
150 B 20 Blucher rd SE5
91 X 1 Blue Anchor la SE15
151 V 5 Blue Anchor la SE16
143 R 10 Blue Anchor yd E1
140 B 14 Blue Bell yd SW1
109 V 10 Bluebell clo SE26
100 G 13 Bluefield clo Hampt
21 N 9 Bluehouse rd E4
26 A 3 Blundell rd Edg
25 Z 4 Blundell rd Edg
48 A 20 Blundell st N7
55 U 3 Blunden clo Dgnhm
157 O 11 Blunt rd S Croy
95 W 14 Blunts rd SE9
50 D 13 Blurton rd E5
50 L 2 Blyth rd E17
68 F 20 Blyth rd SE28
92 K 19 Blythe clo SE6
92 L 19 Blythe Hill la SE6
92 L 20 Blythe hill SE6
126 C 1 Blythe rd Brom
144 F 1 Blythe rd W14
144 K 3 Blythe rd W14
135 V 12 Blythe st E2
110 L 2 Blythe vale SE6
64 M 2 Blythwood rd Ilf
48 B 1 Blythwood rd N4
133 N 6 Boadicea st N1
80 M 9 Boarers Manor way Blvdr
151 P 18 Boathouse wlk SE15
89 U 7 Bobbin clo SW4
39 U 3 Bobs la Rom
103 N 17 Bockhampton rd Kingst
135 X 4 Bocking st E8
63 N 3 Bocking st E9
8 C 9 Bodiam clo Enf
57 Y 19 Bodiam rd SW16
105 R 5 Bodicott clo SW19
118 A 13 Bodley clo New Mald
117 Z 13 Bodley rd New Mald
40 E 10 Bodmin clo Harrow
120 A 10 Bodmin gro Mrdn
105 Z 2 Bodmin st SW18
118 H 5 Bodnant gdns New Mald
49 Z 14 Bodney rd E5
97 V 2 Bognor rd Welling
50 B 16 Bohemia pl E8
5 Y 19 Bohun gro Barnt
74 H 18 Boileau rd SW13
60 M 17 Boileau rd W5
61 N 16 Boileau rd W5
93 P 4 Bolden st SE8
159 R 3 Bolderwood way W Wckm
8 M 5 Boleyn av Enf
159 S 4 Boleyn gdns W Wckm
56 J 20 Boleyn gdns Dgnhm
159 T 3 Boleyn gro BR4
66 A 5 Boleyn rd E6
65 W 1 Boleyn rd E7
49 S 14 Boleyn rd N16
5 P 12 Boleyn way Barnt
75 P 14 Bolina rd SE16
88 K 16 Bolingbroke gro SW11
144 G 1 Bolingbroke rd W14
136 H 20 Bolingbroke rd W14
88 H 1 Bolingbroke wlk SW11
73 T 7 Bollo Br rd W3
73 R 6 Bollo la W3
73 V 10 Bollo la W4
149 N 18 Bolney st SW8
100 C 6 Bolney way Felt
131 Z 20 Bolsover st W1
121 S 2 Bolstead rd Mitch
141 U 6 Bolt ct EC4
27 P 11 Boltmore clo NW4
149 V 17 Bolton cres SE5
146 A 10 Bolton Gardens ms SW5
112 C 16 Bolton gdns Brom
128 F 10 Bolton gdns NW10
146 A 8 Bolton gdns SW5
101 Y 15 Bolton gdns Tedd

52 D 19 Bolton rd E15
18 G 16 Bolton rd N18
62 C 3 Bolton rd NW10
129 Z 6 Bolton rd NW8
73 V 20 Bolton rd W4
85 W 1 Bolton rd W4
138 Z 13 Bolton st W1
146 B 10 Boltons the SW10
41 X 12 Boltons the Wemb
151 V 5 Bombay st SE16
136 J 8 Bomore rd W11
109 R 11 Bon Marche ter SE27
113 S 18 Bonar pl Chisl
151 R 20 Bonar rd SE15
113 W 19 Bonchester clo Chisl
154 B 17 Bonchurch clo Sutton
136 K 1 Bonchurch rd W10
72 A 4 Bonchurch rd W13
160 E 7 Bond ct EC4
155 V 7 Bond gdns Wallgtn
120 K 3 Bond rd Mitch
51 Y 14 Bond st E15
Bond st W1
see under
New & Old Bond St
73 Z 12 Bond st W4
72 G 1 Bond st W5
66 F 15 Bondfield rd E6
148 K 14 Bondway SW8
78 E 8 Boneta rd SE18
93 V 10 Bonfield rd SE13
55 W 7 Bonham rd SW2
90 B 13 Bonham rd SW2
73 Y 7 Bonheur rd W4
134 G 18 Bonhill st EC2
22 K 3 Boniface gdns Harrow
22 K 2 Boniface wlk Harrow
117 O 5 Bonner Hill rd Kingst
63 P 6 Bonner rd E2
63 S 7 Bonner st E2
23 X 17 Bonnersfield clo Harrow
23 X 17 Bonnersfield la Harrow
89 V 15 Bonneville gdns SW4
149 N 14 Bonnington sq SW8
132 A 1 Bonny st NW1
101 W 5 Bonser rd Twick
150 J 18 Bonsor st SE5
112 D 13 Bonville rd Brom
18 K 16 Booker rd N18
94 A 9 Boone st SE13
93 Z 10 Boone st SE13
94 A 9 Boones rd SE13
77 N 8 Boord st SE10
134 H 14 Boot st N1
80 E 2 Booth clo SE28
156 J 3 Booth rd Croy
26 B 8 Booth rd NW9
25 Z 6 Booth rd NW9
47 X 6 Boothby rd N19
140 B 3 Booths pl W1
59 U 14 Bordars rd W7
59 T 14 Bordars wlk W7
18 B 1 Borden av Enf
86 G 19 Borden wlk SW15
109 Z 12 Border cres SE26
106 K 20 Border ga Mitch
159 P 7 Border gdns Croy
110 B 13 Border rd SE26
120 A 9 Bordesley rd Mrdn
65 T 18 Boreham av E16
51 T 3 Boreham clo E11
30 K 6 Boreham rd N22
78 F 11 Borgard rd SE18
92 D 11 Borland rd SE15
102 B 17 Borland rd Tedd
87 N 9 Borneo st SW15
142 B 19 Borough High st SE1
156 H 6 Borough hill Croy
83 T 1 Borough rd Islwth
103 P 19 Borough rd Kingst
120 J 3 Borough rd Mitch
142 A 19 Borough rd SE1
141 Y 20 Borough rd SE1
149 Z 10 Borrett clo SE17
88 B 15 Borrodaile rd SW18
23 Y 8 Borrowdale av Harrow
35 R 12 Borrowdale clo Ilf
52 A 12 Borthwick rd E15
51 Z 13 Borthwick rd E15
26 D 19 Borthwick rd NW9
76 B 15 Borthwick st SE8

32 K 11 Borwick av E17
111 U 8 Bosbury rd SE6
47 R 10 Boscastle rd NW5
147 V 4 Boscobel pl SW1
130 G 19 Boscobel st NW8
33 V 20 Boscombe av E10
50 H 14 Boscombe clo E5
108 B 16 Boscombe gdns SW16
119 N 19 Boscombe rd Worc Pk
107 O 15 Boscombe rd SW17
105 Z 19 Boscombe rd SW19
74 H 4 Boscombe rd W12
20 F 7 Bosgrove E4
143 N 16 Boss st SE1
98 A 8 Bostal row Bxly Hth
80 E 14 Bostall heath SE2
80 F 15 Bostall Hill rd SE2
80 C 15 Bostall hill SE2
80 E 14 Bostall House lodge SE2
80 D 12 Bostall la SE2
80 D 10 Bostall manorway SE2
80 L 20 Bostall Park av Bxly Hth
115 P 19 Bostall rd Orp
72 A 12 Boston gdns Brentf
71 Z 12 Boston gdns Brentf
74 B 16 Boston gdns W4
72 B 13 Boston Manor ho Brentf
72 B 12 Boston Manor rd Brentf
72 D 15 Boston Park rd Brentf
131 N 18 Boston pl NW1
122 D 15 Boston rd Croy
33 N 19 Boston rd E17
66 C 9 Boston rd E6
25 V 2 Boston rd Edg
71 X 7 Boston rd W7
135 S 9 Boston st E2
71 Y 11 Boston vale W7
71 U 5 Bostonthorpe rd W7
132 M 20 Boswell ct WC1
122 L 9 Boswell rd Thntn Hth
132 M 20 Boswell st WC1
32 K 5 Bosworth clo E17
4 M 12 Bosworth rd Barnt
56 F 10 Bosworth rd Dgnhm
16 L 18 Bosworth rd N11
128 L 18 Bosworth rd W10
20 K 9 Boteley clo E4
65 X 13 Botha rd E13
65 R 15 Bothwell clo E16
144 G 15 Bothwell st W6
160 H 9 Botolph all EC3
142 H 10 Botolph la EC3
119 S 4 Botsford rd SW20
137 V 6 Botts ms W2
137 U 6 Botts pass W2
101 V 13 Boucher clo Tedd
57 W 18 Bouchier wlk Rainhm
126 C 17 Boughton av Brom
79 W 7 Boughton rd SE18
63 U 18 Boulcott st E1
122 M 14 Boulogne rd Croy
123 N 14 Boulogne rd Croy
57 X 17 Boulter gdns Rainhm
56 A 8 Boulton rd Dgnhm
66 F 18 Boultwood rd E6
18 M 7 Bounces la N9
19 P 8 Bounces rd N9
106 M 3 Boundaries rd SW12
107 N 2 Boundaries rd SW12
117 S 5 Boundary clo Kingst
70 H 14 Boundary clo S'hall
65 Z 11 Boundary la E13
150 C 14 Boundary la SE17
130 C 4 Boundary ms NW8
67 P 6 Boundary rd Bark
67 S 5 Boundary rd Bark
65 Z 7 Boundary rd E13
33 O 19 Boundary rd E17
30 L 8 Boundary rd N22
9 P 20 Boundary rd N9
130 D 4 Boundary rd NW8
39 V 18 Boundary rd Rom
96 G 13 Boundary rd Sidcp
106 F 15 Boundary rd SW19
106 G 14 Boundary rd SW19
155 R 14 Boundary rd Wallgtn
155 R 18 Boundary Road south Wallgtn
141 W 17 Boundary row SE1
134 M 15 Boundary st E2
159 O 11 Boundary way Croy
112 A 5 Boundfield rd SE6
111 Y 6 Boundfield rd SE6

30 B 4 Bounds Green rd N22
16 J 19 Bounds Green rd N11
140 E 7 Bourchier st W1
139 X 9 Bourdon pl W1
124 B 3 Bourdon rd SE20
139 Y 9 Bourdon st W1
89 Z 17 Bourke clo SW2
140 B 2 Bourlet clo W1
5 U 18 Bourn av Barnt
31 O 13 Bourn av N15
95 O 7 Bournbrook rd SE3
16 M 7 Bourne av N14
44 B 19 Bourne clo NW10
20 E 15 Bourne gdns E4
17 S 9 Bourne hill N13
98 L 14 Bourne mead Bxly
126 M 9 Bourne rd Brom
127 N 8 Bourne rd Brom
98 K 15 Bourne rd Bxly
52 C 10 Bourne rd E7
30 B 18 Bourne rd N8
147 S 7 Bourne st SW1
137 X 1 Bourne ter W2
16 L 6 Bourne the N14
17 O 8 Bourne the N14
126 D 19 Bourne vale Brom
41 W 16 Bourne view Grnfd
153 V 12 Bourne way Sutton
91 X 4 Bournemouth rd SE15
105 Z 20 Bournemouth rd SW19
107 Z 10 Bournevale rd SW16
80 A 19 Bournewood rd SW2
93 N 18 Bournville rd SE6
5 Z 10 Bournwell clo Barnt
92 E 5 Bousfield rd SE14
88 J 11 Boutflower rd SW11
24 H 20 Bouverie gdns Harrow
49 S 7 Bouverie ms N16
138 H 4 Bouverie pl W2
23 O 20 Bouverie rd Harrow
49 R 6 Bouverie rd N16
141 U 7 Bouverie st EC4
9 R 3 Bouvier rd Enf
48 C 11 Bovay pl N7
48 C 11 Bovay st N7
92 E 18 Boveney rd SE23
92 G 20 Bovill rd SE23
43 R 19 Bovingdon av Wemb
47 W 8 Bovingdon la NW9
26 A 3 Bovingdon la NW9
88 A 3 Bovingdon rd SW6
160 B 6 Bow Church yd EC4
64 A 13 Bow Common la E3
63 Y 13 Bow Common la E3
160 C 7 Bow la EC4
28 D 1 Bow la N12
64 C 8 Bow rd E3
5 Y 10 Bow rd E3
51 Z 15 Bow st E15
140 L 7 Bow st WC2
25 X 16 Bowater clo NW9
77 W 19 Bowater pl SE3
78 B 8 Bowater rd SE18
33 O 20 Bowden st E17
149 T 10 Bowden st SE11
75 X 12 Bowditch SE8
109 S 8 Bowen dri SE21
41 O 1 Bowen rd Harrow
23 O 20 Bowen rd Harrow
64 D 16 Bowen st E14
93 Z 1 Bower av SE10
39 N 2 Bower clo Rom
63 T 18 Bower st E1
87 Z 3 Bowerdean st SW6
75 W 18 Bowerman av SE14
97 P 16 Bowes clo Sidcp
55 U 13 Bowes rd Dgnhm
16 G 15 Bowes rd N11
16 L 16 Bowes rd N13
17 P 17 Bowes rd N13
62 A 20 Bowes rd W3
144 E 15 Bowfell rd W6
97 Y 3 Bowford av Bxly Hth
89 Y 11 Bowland rd SW4
21 Z 17 Bowland rd Wdfd Grn
151 S 13 Bowles rd SE1
109 U 13 Bowley clo SE19
75 Z 1 Bowley st E1
86 K 19 Bowling Green clo SW15
133 U 17 Bowling Green la EC1
142 E 17 Bowling Green pl SE1
78 E 9 Bowling Green row SE 18

149 T 13 Bowling Green st SE11
134 H 12 Bowling Green wlk N1
11 N 16 Bowls clo Stanm
65 R 19 Bowman av E16
72 A 3 Bowmans clo W13
92 D 18 Bowmans lea SE23
155 R 6 Bowmans meadow Wallgtn
48 A 11 Bowmans ms N7
48 B 11 Bowmans ms N7
99 T 18 Bowmans rd Drtfrd
113 T 4 Bowmead SE9
104 A 12 Bowness cres SW15
103 Z 12 Bowness cres SW15
82 C 10 Bowness dri Hounsl
98 G 6 Bowness rd Bxly Hth
93 S 19 Bowness rd SE6
57 W 15 Bowness way Hornch
9 T 8 Bowood rd Enf
89 O 12 Bowood rd SW11
42 H 20 Bowrons av Wemb
150 D 18 Bowyer pl SE5
150 B 18 Bowyer st SE5
56 A 11 Boxall rd Dgnhm
91 R 17 Boxall rd SE21
80 F 8 Boxgrove rd SE2
120 D 10 Boxley rd Mrdn
77 V 3 Boxley st E16
24 A 13 Boxmoor rd Harrow
23 O 3 Boxtree la Harrow
133 R 4 Boxworth gr N1
78 L 13 Boyard rd SE18
65 T 12 Boyce way E13
25 W 18 Boycroft av NW9
70 G 3 Boyd av S'hall
103 R 18 Boyd clo Kingst
106 F 15 Boyd rd SW19
143 T 7 Boyd st E1
130 F 2 Boydell ct NW8
141 Y 19 Boyfield st SE1
112 C 13 Boyland rd Brom
10 M 18 Boyle av Stanm
140 A 9 Boyle st W1
27 R 13 Boyne av NW4
56 E 10 Boyne rd Dgnhm
93 W 8 Boyne rd SE13
137 O 13 Boyne Terrace ms W1
12 G 8 Boyseland ct Edg
150 D 14 Boyson rd SE17
151 X 11 Boythorn way SE16
63 R 12 Boyton clo E1
30 A 11 Boyton clo N8
30 A 11 Boyton rd N8
30 D 7 Brabant rd N22
156 A 17 Brabazon av Wallgtn
58 G 6 Brabazon rd Grnfd
64 C 16 Brabazon st E14
92 B 6 Brabourne gro SE15
109 R 14 Brabourne clo SE19
81 P 18 Brabourne cres Bxly Hth
125 V 11 Brabourne ri Becknhm
41 X 17 Bracewell av Grnfd
136 A 2 Bracewell rd W10
62 L 14 Bracewell rd W10
157 V 5 Bracewood gdns Croy
48 B 6 Bracey st N4
159 P 6 Bracken av Croy
89 O 7 Bracken av SW12
66 F 15 Bracken clo E6
83 R 11 Bracken end Islwth
86 G 4 Bracken gdns SW13
38 F 20 Bracken ms Rom
20 G 7 Bracken the E4
74 K 7 Brackenbury gdns W6
28 D 10 Brackenbury rd N2
74 K 8 Brackenbury rd W6
82 L 2 Brackendale clo Hounsl
17 R 7 Brackendale N21
126 C 1 Brackenhill clo Brom
126 C 1 Brackenhill la Brom
40 B 12 Brackenhill Ruis
26 C 2 Brackens the Enf
156 A 15 Brackley clo Croy
111 O 17 Brackley rd Becknhm
74 B 12 Brackley rd W4
35 N 1 Brackley sq Ilf
34 M 1 Brackley sq Wdfd Grn
134 B 19 Brackley st EC1
30 F 5 Brackley ter W4
46 A 13 Bracknell clo N22
45 Z 13 Bracknell gdns NW3
80 C 10 Bracondale rd SE2
79 Z 10 Bracondale rd SE2

141 U 15 Brad st SE1
98 F 18 Bradbourne rd Bxly
87 Y 4 Bradbourne st SW6
70 G 11 Bradbury clo S'hall
49 T 16 Bradbury st N16
85 N 7 Braddon rd Rich
76 L 13 Braddyll st SE10
129 X 18 Braden st W9
96 M 10 Bradenham av Welling
97 N 10 Bradenham av Welling
24 A 12 Bradenham rd Harrow
54 M 16 Bradfield dri Bark
77 T 4 Bradfield rd E16
40 C 15 Bradfield rd Ruis
152 C 14 Bradford av Epsom
54 F 4 Bradford rd Ilf
109 Z 9 Bradford rd SE26
74 A 4 Bradford rd W3
93 R 17 Bradford rd Twick
52 H 5 Brading cres E11
52 H 6 Brading cres E11
122 B 15 Brading rd Croy
90 D 18 Brading rd SW2
129 R 12 Bradiston rd W9
48 B 20 Bradley clo N7
60 B 17 Bradley gdns W13
9 X 1 Bradley rd Enf
30 C 7 Bradley rd N22
108 L 14 Bradley rd SE19
133 T 9 Bradleys clo N1
89 U 1 Bradmead SW8
74 K 10 Bradmore Park rd W6
50 G 19 Bradstock rd E9
152 H 11 Bradstock rd Epsom
56 E 6 Bradwell av Dgnhm
34 B 12 Bradwell clo E18
57 Z 19 Bradwell clo Hornch
18 K 14 Bradwell ms N18
63 U 9 Bradwell st E1
63 N 14 Brady st E1
135 X 20 Brady st E1
122 G 5 Braemar av Thntn Hth
98 K 11 Braemar av Bxly Hth
30 B 5 Braemar av NW10
43 Y 8 Braemar av NW10
157 N 20 Braemar av S Croy
105 X 5 Braemar av SW19
60 J 1 Braemar av Wemb
125 T 20 Braemar gdns W Wkhm
25 Z 6 Braemar gdns NW9
114 F 6 Braemar gdns Sidcp
72 H 16 Braemar rd Brentf
65 R 13 Braemar rd E13
31 R 15 Braemar rd N15
152 J 5 Braemar rd Worc Pk
104 F 2 Braemore clo SW15
54 K 8 Braemore rd Ilf
105 T 20 Braeside av SW19
111 P 14 Braeside Beckhm
81 P 11 Braeside clo Blvdr
98 L 11 Braeside cres Bxly Hth
107 V 18 Braeside rd SW16
156 L 8 Brafferton rd Croy
149 W 10 Braganza st SE17
143 P 5 Braham st E1
62 A 18 Braid av W3
100 C 4 Braid clo Felt
111 X 2 Braidwood rd SE6
142 K 14 Braidwood st SE1
90 G 15 Brailsford rd SW2
35 P 14 Braintree av Ilf
56 E 9 Braintree rd Dgnhm
63 P 10 Braintree st E2
56 E 1 Braithwaite av Rom
24 E 5 Braithwaite gdns Stanm
29 O 19 Bramalea clo N6
15 V 18 Bramber rd N12
145 P 14 Bramber rd W14
155 O 20 Bramble banks Carsh
159 P 8 Bramble clo Croy
24 H 4 Bramble clo Stanm
122 C 6 Brambledown SW16
174 E 1 Brambledown gdns W12
79 P 14 Bramblebury rd SE18
81 Y 11 Bramblecroft Erith
126 A 13 Brambledown clo Brom
155 P 17 Brambledown rd Carsh
157 R 18 Brambledown rd S Croy
72 A 19 Brambles clo Brentf

120 K 20 Bramblewood clo Carsh
20 L 14 Bramblings the E4
120 L 9 Bramcote av Mitch
75 O 13 Bramcote gro SE16
151 Z 10 Bramcote gro SE16
86 K 11 Bramcote rd SW15
112 E 2 Bramdean cres SE12
112 E 2 Bramdean gdns SE12
124 L 6 Bramerton rd Beck
146 J 13 Bramerton st SW3
88 L 15 Bramfield rd SW11
16 K 7 Bramford ct N14
88 C 11 Bramford rd SW18
145 Y 8 Bramham gdns SW5
77 W 16 Bramhope la SE7
88 H 8 Bramlands clo SW11
32 J 8 Bramley clo E17
6 D 17 Bramley clo N14
156 K 10 Bramley clo S Croy
82 M 16 Bramley clo Twick
35 X 18 Bramley cres Ilf
97 P 1 Bramley ct Welling
156 K 10 Bramley hill S Croy
99 W 12 Bramley pl Drtfrd
6 J 14 Bramley rd Enf
6 D 17 Bramley rd N14
154 F 11 Bramley rd Sutton
153 N 19 Bramley rd Sutton
136 G 9 Bramley rd W11
72 D 9 Bramley rd W5
136 G 6 Bramley st W10
159 S 3 Bramley way W Wkhm
52 B 14 Brammel clo E15
50 A 6 Brampton clo E5
30 K 16 Brampton gdns N15
24 A 13 Brampton gro Harrow
23 Z 12 Brampton gro Harrow
26 K 14 Brampton gro NW4
43 O 4 Brampton gro Wemb
30 F 10 Brampton Park rd N8
80 H 19 Brampton rd Bxly Hth
97 X 1 Brampton rd Bxly Hth
123 T 16 Brampton rd Croy
66 C 10 Brampton rd E6
30 L 16 Brampton rd N15
25 R 15 Brampton rd NW9
80 G 16 Brampton rd SE2
50 F 19 Bramshaw rd E9
118 B 14 Bramshaw rd New Mald
47 T 8 Bramshill gdns NW5
62 C 6 Bramshill rd NW10
77 U 15 Bramshot av SE7
62 G 5 Bramston rd NW10
53 U 13 Brancaster dri E12
36 G 19 Brancaster rd Ilf
107 Z 6 Brancaster rd SW16
21 S 9 Brancepeth gdns Buck Hl
46 C 10 Branch hill NW3
134 N 3 Branch pl N1
63 V 19 Branch rd E14
155 S 16 Brancker clo Wallgtn
24 F 10 Brancker rd Harrow
76 G 20 Brand st SE10
87 V 11 Brandlehow rd SW15
33 V 12 Brandon rd E17
47 Z 20 Brandon rd N7
70 E 14 Brandon rd S'hall
153 Z 8 Brandon rd Sutton
150 B 6 Brandon st SE17
150 C 7 Brandon st SE17
93 Y 10 Brandram rd SE13
66 H 17 Brandreth rd E6
107 R 4 Brandreth rd SW17
155 Z 6 Brandries the Wallgtn
36 A 12 Brandville gdns Ilf
153 X 17 Brandy way Sutton
111 U 12 Brangbourne rd Brom
149 R 10 Brangton rd SE11
120 E 1 Brangwyn cres SW19
144 J 20 Branksea st SW6
18 F 18 Branksome av N18
105 Y 20 Branksome rd SW19
90 A 12 Branksome rd SW2
24 L 18 Branksome way Harrow
117 X 2 Branksome way New Mald

17 S 3	Branscombe gdns N21	
93 R 8	Branscombe st SE13	
129 V 3	Bransdale clo NW6	
24 M 3	Bransgrove rd Edg	
85 N 3	Branstone rd Rich	
59 U 12	Brants wlk W7	
81 W 18	Brantwood av Erith	
83 Y 9	Brantwood av Islwth	
33 S 11	Brantwood clo E17	
6 M 15	Brantwood gdns Enf	
35 S 14	Brantwood gdns Ilf	
98 H 6	Brantwood rd Bxly Hth	
18 L 20	Brantwood rd N17	
157 N 20	Brantwood rd S Croy	
90 L 12	Brantwood rd SE24	
41 P 14	Brasher clo Grnfd	
45 W 17	Brassey rd NW6	
89 O 6	Brassey sq SW11	
82 B 18	Brassie av W3	
97 W 13	Brasted clo Bxly Hth	
110 B 9	Brasted clo SE26	
87 Z 18	Brathway rd SW18	
135 S 18	Bratley st E1	
123 O 15	Bratten ct Croy	
58 J 11	Braund av Grnfd	
114 J 1	Braundton av Sidcp	
96 K 20	Braundton av Sidcp	
58 C 11	Braunston dri Grnfd	
129 O 16	Bravington pl W9	
129 O 11	Bravington rd W9	
129 O 16	Bravington rd W9	
92 K 11	Braxfield rd SE4	
108 C 15	Braxted pk SW16	
75 T 4	Bray cres SE16	
65 R 19	Bray dri E16	
65 R 19	Bray gdns E16	
147 O 8	Bray pl SW3	
14 C 18	Bray rd NW7	
92 A 5	Brayards rd SE15	
91 Z 5	Brayards rd SE15	
71 U 18	Braybourne dri Islwth	
62 D 15	Braybrook st W12	
109 T 18	Braybrooke gdns SE19	
89 V 5	Brayburne av SW4	
49 W 2	Braydon rd N16	
133 S 2	Brayfield ter N1	
6 L 14	Brayton gdns Enf	
96 E 10	Braywood rd SE9	
69 R 8	Breach la Dgnhm	
160 B 7	Bread st EC4	
92 M 9	Breakspears rd SE4	
93 N 6	Breakspears rd SE4	
66 J 10	Bream gdns E6	
64 A 2	Bream st E3	
104 G 2	Breamore clo SW15	
54 K 8	Breamore rd Ilf	
55 N 7	Breamore rd Ilf	
141 S 4	Breams bldgs EC4	
102 A 7	Breamwater gdns Rich	
86 L 9	Breasley clo SW15	
146 C 8	Brechin pl SW7	
47 Y 15	Brecknock rd N7	
9 O 13	Brecon rd Enf	
144 L 16	Brecon rd W6	
66 J 8	Brede clo E6	
47 V 7	Bredgar rd N19	
110 B 15	Bredhurst clo SE20	
123 U 17	Bredon rd Croy	
90 M 6	Bredon rd SE5	
88 A 7	Breer st SW6	
143 U 10	Breezers hill E1	
41 N 7	Brember rd Harrow	
138 D 20	Bremner rd SW7	
126 D 13	Brenchley clo Brom	
127 X 1	Brenchley clo Chisl	
92 D 15	Brenchley gdns SE23	
106 L 5	Brenda rd SW17	
44 A 14	Brendon av NW10	
99 P 2	Brendon clo Erith	
40 K 11	Brendon gdns Harrow	
36 H 15	Brendon gdns Ilf	
56 D 4	Brendon rd Dgnhm	
114 D 4	Brendon rd SE9	
138 M 4	Brendon st W1	
18 D 2	Brendon way Enf	
121 P 6	Brenley clo Mitch	
95 O 9	Brenley gdns SE9	
115 Z 2	Brent clo Bxly	
60 M 7	Brent cres NW10	
27 O 16	Brent grn NW4	
72 D 20	Brent Lea Brentf	
44 H 2	Brent Park rd NW4	
4 J 18	Brent pl Barnt	
72 E 18	Brent rd Brentf	
158 A 19	Brent rd CR2	
65 T 16	Brent rd E16	
157 Z 19	Brent rd S Croy	
78 L 19	Brent rd SE18	
72 E 17	Brent side Brentf	
27 O 16	Brent st NW4	
26 F 20	Brent View rd NW9	
72 G 19	Brent way Brentf	
14 K 19	Brent way N3	
43 U 17	Brent way Wemb	
60 A 12	Brentcot clo W13	
43 X 18	Brentfield clo NW10	
27 P 20	Brentfield gdns NW11	
61 V 1	Brentfield NW10	
61 Y 1	Brentfield rd NW10	
43 Y 17	Brentfield rd NW10	
72 G 18	Brentford High st Brentf	
60 F 11	Brentham way W5	
50 B 19	Brenthouse rd E9	
44 D 16	Brenthurst rd NW10	
59 T 20	Brentmead clo W7	
61 N 7	Brentmead gdns NW10	
27 P 18	Brentmead pl NW11	
63 W 17	Brenton st E14	
59 Y 11	Brentside clo W13	
71 P 2	Brentvale av S'hall	
60 M 4	Brentvale av Wemb	
61 N 5	Brentvale av Wemb	
72 J 12	Brentwick gdns Brentf	
114 A 1	Brentwood clo SE9	
39 X 18	Brentwood rd Rom	
31 V 2	Brereton rd N17	
140 A 2	Bressenden pl EW1	
34 B 8	Bressey gro E18	
49 R 7	Brett clo N16	
61 Y 2	Brett cres NW10	
55 Y 20	Brett gdns Dgnhm	
50 A 16	Brett rd E8	
150 F 10	Brettell st SE17	
33 O 5	Brettenham av E17	
33 O 5	Brettenham rd E17	
18 M 13	Brettenham rd N18	
18 L 13	Brettenham Road east N18	
140 D 9	Brewer st W1	
148 D 1	Brewers grn SW1	
84 G 12	Brewers la Rich	
83 X 19	Brewery la Twick	
127 S 19	Brewery rd Brom	
47 Z 19	Brewery rd N1	
48 A 19	Brewery rd N7	
79 R 13	Brewery rd SE18	
143 Y 14	Brewhouse la E1	
78 G 11	Brewhouse st SE18	
87 S 9	Brewhouse st SW15	
75 V 3	Brewhouse wlk SE16	
133 X 17	Brewhouse yd EC1	
55 R 17	Brewood rd Dgnhm	
136 A 1	Brewster gdns W10	
62 M 14	Brewster gdns W10	
51 S 4	Brewster rd E10	
57 Y 11	Brian clo Hornch	
37 U 14	Brian rd Rom	
92 E 1	Briant st SE14	
22 C 6	Briants clo Pinn	
108 D 17	Briar av SW16	
155 P 20	Briar banks Carsh	
100 D 14	Briar clo Hampt	
83 W 12	Briar clo Islwth	
17 Z 11	Briar clo N13	
40 J 19	Briar cres Nthlt	
126 B 20	Briar gdns Brom	
155 P 20	Briar la Carsh	
159 R 7	Briar la Croy	
24 D 17	Briar rd Harrow	
44 M 11	Briar rd NW2	
122 B 7	Briar rd SW16	
101 S 2	Briar rd Twick	
25 W 2	Briar wlk Edg	
86 K 10	Briar wlk SW15	
59 Z 16	Briarbank rd W13	
45 X 10	Briardale gdns NW3	
31 Z 3	Briars clo N17	
28 B 9	Briars clo N2	
25 W 18	Briarwood clo NW9	
152 F 13	Briarwood rd Epsom	
89 X 12	Briarwood rd SW4	
46 H 20	Briary clo NW3	
115 R 12	Briary ct Sidcp	
112 H 12	Briary gdns Brom	
18 F 12	Briary la N9	
141 S 8	Brick ct EC4	
85 S 3	Brick Farm clo Rich	
143 P 2	Brick la E1	
8 L 9	Brick la Enf	
9 O 9	Brick la Enf	
24 G 3	Brick la Stanm	
24 G 3	Brick la Stanm	
139 W 15	Brick st W1	
106 B 10	Brick-Field rd SW19	
79 Y 18	Brickfield cotts SE18	
122 K 1	Brickfield rd Thntn Hth	
64 D 10	Brickfield rd E3	
41 S 6	Brickfields Harrow	
157 S 2	Brickwood rd Croy	
141 W 6	Bride la EC4	
48 D 19	Bride st N7	
141 W 7	Bridewell pl EC4	
131 Y 19	Bridford ms W1	
47 N 20	Bridge appr NW3	
144 A 8	Bridge av W6	
74 L 14	Bridge av W6	
59 R 14	Bridge av W7	
9 N 8	Bridge clo Enf	
39 P 19	Bridge clo Rom	
88 F 6	Bridge ct SW11	
33 U 5	Bridge end E17	
17 Y 3	Bridge ga N21	
27 R 14	Bridge la NW11	
88 J 3	Bridge la SW11	
123 P 18	Bridge pl Croy	
147 Y 6	Bridge pl SW1	
110 L 18	Bridge rd Becknhm	
97 Z 6	Bridge rd Bxly Hth	
64 K 2	Bridge rd E15	
50 K 2	Bridge rd E17	
53 T 20	Bridge rd E6	
99 T 3	Bridge rd Erith	
99 V 1	Bridge rd Erith	
83 P 6	Bridge rd Hounsl	
30 A 6	Bridge rd N22	
18 K 10	Bridge rd N9	
44 A 19	Bridge rd NW10	
70 E 5	Bridge rd S'hall	
154 B 14	Bridge rd Sutton	
84 A 15	Bridge rd Twick	
155 T 11	Bridge rd Wallgtn	
43 R 9	Bridge rd Wemb	
123 P 19	Bridge row Croy	
22 A 11	Bridge st Pinn	
84 G 14	Bridge st Rich	
73 X 11	Bridge st W4	
64 K 1	Bridge ter E15	
23 U 11	Bridge the Harrow	
144 A 9	Bridge view W6	
16 G 12	Bridge way N11	
27 V 16	Bridge way NW11	
83 O 19	Bridge way Twick	
142 H 13	Bridge yd SE1	
153 X 14	Bridgefield rd Sutton	
148 L 12	Bridgefoot SE1	
65 T 18	Bridgeland rd E16	
133 O 2	Bridgeman rd N1	
101 X 14	Bridgeman rd Teddt	
130 J 9	Bridgeman st NW8	
97 Y 17	Bridgen rd Bxly	
88 C 9	Bridgend rd SW18	
8 H 5	Bridgenhall rd Enf	
156 A 7	Bridges la Croy	
87 W 2	Bridges pl SW6	
10 H 17	Bridges rd Stanm	
106 A 16	Bridges rd SW19	
105 Z 16	Bridges rd SW19	
74 L 13	Bridges rd SW19	
24 L 7	Bridges rd Edg	
42 D 19	Bridgewater rd Wemb	
42 C 17	Bridgewater rd Grnfd	
134 A 20	Bridgewater sq EC1	
67 Y 1	Bridgeway Bark	
132 D 9	Bridgeway st NW1	
42 L 19	Bridgway Wemb	
152 H 7	Bridgwood rd Worc Pk	
107 X 18	Bridgewood rd SW16	
106 D 6	Bridgford st SW18	
73 W 8	Bridgman rd W4	
64 F 3	Bridgwater rd E15	
140 C 9	Bridle la W1	
156 B 6	Bridle path Croy	
159 O 1	Bridle rd Croy	
159 P 9	Bridleway Croy	
155 W 10	Bridleway the Wallgtn	
18 M 2	Bridport rd N9	
19 N 3	Bridport rd N9	
38 G 20	Bridport av Rom	
134 F 6	Bridport pl N1	
134 F 8	Bridport pl N1	
58 K 3	Bridport rd Grnfd	
18 E 18	Bridport rd N18	
122 G 6	Bridport rd Thntn Hth	
75 O 18	Bridson st SE15	
137 U 5	Bridstow pl W2	
90 H 3	Brief st SE5	
19 R 6	Brierley av N12	
123 Y 9	Brierley clo SE25	
159 R 15	Brierley Croy	
51 Y 11	Brierley rd E11	
107 T 4	Brierley rd SW12	
76 H 12	Brig st E14	
8 A 5	Brigadier av Enf	
7 Y 3	Brigadier hill Enf	
49 X 7	Briggeford clo E5	
64 E 16	Bright st E14	
94 B 12	Brightfield rd SE12	
92 M 17	Brightling rd SE4	
63 X 20	Brightlingsea pl E14	
106 E 1	Brightman rd SW18	
32 L 17	Brighton av E17	
40 G 18	Brighton dri Nthlt	
92 H 1	Brighton gro SE14	
66 K 8	Brighton rd E6	
49 T 12	Brighton rd N16	
28 D 9	Brighton rd N2	
157 N 14	Brighton rd S Croy	
116 F 15	Brighton rd Surb	
154 B 17	Brighton rd Sutton	
90 D 10	Brighton ter SW9	
93 X 15	Brightside rd SE13	
9 U 5	Brightside the Enf	
106 L 13	Brightwell cres SW17	
41 P 7	Brigade clo Harrow	
122 L 9	Brigstock rd Thntn Hth	
81 T 10	Brigstock rd Blvdr	
132 G 10	Brill rd NW1	
28 D 13	Brim hill N2	
80 C 9	Brimpsfield clo SE2	
9 W 7	Brimsdown av Enf	
92 L 3	Brindley st SE14	
58 K 19	Brindley way S'hall	
20 A 10	Brindwood rd E4	
19 Z 10	Brindwood rd E4	
25 S 9	Brinkburn clo Edg	
80 A 10	Brinkburn clo SE2	
25 R 9	Brinkburn gdns Edg	
152 J 2	Brinkley rd Worc Pk	
78 M 20	Brinklow cres SE18	
79 N 19	Brinklow cres SE18	
35 R 9	Brinkworth rd Ilf	
50 M 17	Brinkworth way E9	
27 O 11	Brinsdale rd NW4	
23 P 7	Brinsley rd Harrow	
143 Z 7	Brinsley st E1	
101 P 2	Brinsworth clo Twick	
105 Z 20	Brisbane av SW19	
51 S 8	Brisbane rd E10	
54 A 2	Brisbane rd Ilf	
71 Z 4	Brisbane rd W13	
150 E 20	Brisbane st SE5	
106 G 15	Briscoe rd SW19	
95 N 8	Briset rd SE9	
133 W 19	Briset st EC1	
48 C 7	Briset way N7	
86 L 19	Bristol gdns SW15	
130 A 19	Bristol gdns W9	
129 Z 19	Bristol gdns W9	
130 A 19	Bristol ms W9	
129 Z 19	Bristol ms W9	
53 N 18	Bristol rd E12	
52 M 19	Bristol rd E7	
58 K 3	Bristol rd Grnfd	
120 C 10	Bristol rd Mrdn	
30 B 20	Briston gro N8	
98 A 3	Bristow rd Bxly Hth	
97 Z 3	Bristow rd Bxly Hth	
156 A 9	Bristow rd Croy	
82 M 9	Bristow rd Hounsl	
109 R 12	Bristow rd SW19	
58 A 8	Britannia clo Nthlt	
89 Y 11	Britannia clo SW4	
53 Y 11	Britannia rd Ilf	
15 S 12	Britannia rd N12	
116 M 16	Britannia rd Surb	
117 N 16	Britannia rd Surb	
145 X 19	Britannia rd SW6	
133 Z 4	Britannia row N1	
133 N 12	Britannia st WC1	
61 T 10	Britannia way NW10	
134 E 12	Britannia wlk N1	
74 E 12	British gro W4	
21 O 7	British Legion rd E4	
140 H 2	British Museum WC1	
63 Z 10	British st E3	
56 A 9	Brittain rd Dgnhm	
46 A 3	Britten clo NW11	
146 J 10	Britten st SW3	
133 W 19	Britton st EC1	

54 H 14 Brixham gdns Ilf
97 V 2 Brixham rd Welling
78 H 3 Brixham st E16
90 A 19 Brixton Hill pl SW2
90 C 16 Brixton hill SW2
90 F 5 Brixton rd SW9
149 T 18 Brixton rd SW9
90 F 9 Brixton Station rd SW9
90 E 14 Brixton Water la SW2
140 L 6 Broad ct WC2
122 H 16 Broad Green av Croy
100 F 17 Broad la Hampt
31 W 14 Broad la N15
113 W 2 Broad lawn SE9
126 B 11 Broad Oaks way Brom
160 H 2 Broad st av EC2
142 J 2 Broad st bldgs EC2
56 D 20 Broad st Dgnhm
69 S 2 Broad st Dgnhm
142 H 1 Broad st Stn
160 H 2 Broad st Stn
101 V 14 Broad st Tedd
45 V 1 Broad Walk la NW11
23 U 7 Broad Way the Harrow
82 A 3 Broad wlk Hounsl
17 R 6 Broad wlk N21
94 L 6 Broad wlk SE3
95 T 3 Broad wlk SE3
133 V 19 Broad yd EC1
139 X 9 Broadbent st W1
77 S 19 Broadbridge clo SE3
158 F 17 Broadcoombe S Croy
24 H 7 Broadcroft av Stanm
156 C 3 Broadfield clo CR0
44 L 10 Broadfield clo NW2
39 U 17 Broadfield clo Rom
10 E 8 Broadfield ct Bark
93 Z 20 Broadfield rd SE6
111 Z 3 Broadfield rd SE6
9 N 10 Broadfield sq Enf
21 Y 12 Broadfield way Buck Hl
12 E 14 Broadfields av Edg
17 T 1 Broadfields av N21
22 K 6 Broadfields Harrow
5 O 7 Broadgates av Barnt
106 G 3 Broadgates rd SW18
26 D 6 Broadhead strand NW9
113 U 11 Broadheath dri Chisl
89 T 7 Broadhinton rd SW4
12 E 12 Broadhurst av Edg
54 K 13 Broadhurst av Ilf
46 C 18 Broadhurst clo NW6
46 B 18 Broadhurst gdns NW6
45 Z 19 Broadhurst gdns NW6
57 W 19 Broadhurst wlk Rainhm
9 O 11 Broadlands av Enf
9 O 12 Broadlands av Enf
108 A 5 Broadlands av SW16
107 Z 4 Broadlands av SW16
107 Z 5 Broadlands clo SW16
9 O 12 Broadlands clo Enf
47 N 1 Broadlands clo N6
29 O 20 Broadlands clo N6
112 H 10 Broadlands rd Brom
29 O 20 Broadlands rd N6
100 G 8 Broadlands the Felt
118 D 15 Broadlands way New Mald
23 W 5 Broadlawns ct Harrow
130 H 20 Broadley st NW8
130 L 18 Broadley ter NW1
118 F 18 Broadmead av Worc Pk
100 H 16 Broadmead clo Hampt
22 C 2 Broadmead clo Pinn
34 K 2 Broadmead rd Wdfd Grn
35 N 3 Broadmead rd Wdfd Grn
21 T 19 Broadmead rd Wdfd Grn
58 B 11 Broadmead rd Grnfd
58 C 10 Broadmead rd Nthlt
111 O 7 Broadmead SE24
139 S 2 Broadstone pl W1
57 W 7 Broadstone the Hornch
25 P 19 Broadview NW9
107 W 17 Broadview rd SW16
34 B 10 Broadwalk E18

141 U 12 Broadwall SE1
31 S 6 Broadwater rd N17
79 P 9 Broadwater rd SE18
106 H 9 Broadwater rd SW17
123 O 12 Broadway av Croy
84 A 16 Broadway av Twick
67 O 3 Broadway Bark
98 E 11 Broadway Bxly Hth
21 W 18 Broadway clo Wdfd Grn
105 W 16 Broadway ct SW19
65 U 7 Broadway E13
51 Y 20 Broadway E13
152 G 12 Broadway Epsom
120 J 7 Broadway gdns Mitch
59 N 11 Broadway Grnfd
135 V 5 Broadway mkt E8
131 P 17 Broadway ms N13
49 U 1 Broadway ms N16
17 W 5 Broadway ms N21
39 V 9 Broadway Rom
140 F 20 Broadway SW1
56 C 6 Broadway the Dagnhm
21 W 18 Broadway the Wdfd Grn
57 Y 13 Broadway the Hornch
20 H 19 Broadway the E4
29 Z 18 Broadway the N8
18 K 9 Broadway the N9
13 P 17 Broadway the NW7
44 G 2 Broadway the NW9
22 D 3 Broadway the Pinn
70 B 1 Broadway the S'hall
11 S 15 Broadway the Sutton
153 S 14 Broadway the Sutton
105 X 16 Broadway the SW19
60 H 19 Broadway the W5
72 A 2 Broadway W13
71 X 2 Broadway W7
140 C 8 Broadwick st W1
64 C 13 Brock pl E3
65 W 14 Brock rd E13
92 B 7 Brock st SE15
54 J 16 Brockdish av Bark
118 A 18 Brockenhurst av Worc Pk
13 P 17 Brockenhurst gdns NW7
54 B 14 Brockenhurst gdns Ilf
123 Z 18 Brockenhurst rd Croy
121 Y 3 Brockenhurst way SW16
105 V 13 Brockham clo SW19
159 X 16 Brockham cres Croy
36 A 17 Brockham dri Ilf
90 C 19 Brockham dri SW2
150 C 1 Brockham st SE1
10 H 18 Brockhurst clo Stanm
92 H 10 Brockill cres SE4
88 C 19 Brocklebank rd SW18
75 T 19 Brocklehurst st SE14
123 Z 10 Brocklesby rd SE25
11 X 12 Brockley av Stanm
11 X 11 Brockley Avenue north Stanm
11 X 15 Brockley clo Stanm
38 K 3 Brockley cres Rom
92 C 9 Brockley footpath SE15
92 L 4 Brockley gdns SE4
92 K 14 Brockley gro SE4
92 L 14 Brockley gro SE4
93 N 12 Brockley gro SE4
92 K 14 Brockley Hall rd SE4
11 U 9 Brockley hill Stanm
92 J 20 Brockley pk SE23
92 K 13 Brockley rd SE4
92 K 8 Brockley rd SE4
110 H 1 Brockley ri SE23
92 J 16 Brockley ri SE23
11 W 13 Brockley side Stanm
92 K 18 Brockley view SE23
92 G 13 Brockley way SE4
111 W 9 Brockman ri Brom
153 S 4 Brocks dri Sutton
72 F 15 Brockshot clo Brentf
39 T 12 Brockton clo Rom
90 H 20 Brockwell Park gdns SE24
90 H 18 Brockwell park SE24
150 K 16 Brockworth clo SE15
80 D 11 Broderick gro SE2
49 T 8 Brodia rd N16
20 H 7 Brodie rd E4
8 A 3 Brodie rd Enf

7 Z 3 Brodie rd Enf
151 P 10 Brodie st SE1
63 S 19 Brodlove la E1
106 K 3 Brodrick rd SW17
125 R 4 Brograve gdns Becknhm
31 Y 11 Brograve rd N17
135 R 4 Broke wlk E8
63 Y 10 Brokesley st E3
91 T 7 Bromar rd SE5
95 U 8 Brome rd SE9
24 E 5 Bromefield Stanm
63 P 17 Bromehead rd E1
63 O 17 Bromehead st E1
89 V 10 Bromells rd SW4
89 Y 6 Bromfelde rd SW4
89 Z 5 Bromfelde way SW4
133 U 7 Bromfield st N1
55 P 18 Bromhall rd Dgnhm
113 T 7 Bromhedge SE9
80 B 9 Bromholm rd SE2
112 A 19 Bromley av Becknhm
126 K 10 Bromley comm Brom
127 P 16 Bromley comm Brom
126 C 5 Bromley cres Brom
126 C 5 Bromley gdns Brom
125 X 5 Bromley gro Brom
64 G 14 Bromley Hall rd E14
64 D 8 Bromley High st E3
112 A 16 Bromley hill Brom
111 Y 14 Bromley hill Brom
114 E 18 Bromley la Chisl
132 A 19 Bromley pl W1
125 V 2 Bromley rd Becknhm
114 B 19 Bromley rd Chisl
33 S 20 Bromley rd E10
33 O 9 Bromley rd E17
31 W 3 Bromley rd N17
18 B 12 Bromley rd N18
111 S 4 Bromley rd SE6
111 U 9 Bromley rd SE6
63 U 17 Bromley st E1
82 E 13 Brompton clo Hounsl
28 K 13 Brompton gro N2
147 N 1 Brompton pl SW3
146 K 3 Brompton rd SW3
139 O 19 Brompton rd SW3
146 K 2 Brompton sq SW3
47 R 8 Bromwich av N6
74 B 2 Bromyard av W3
128 K 2 Bromsbury pk NW6
44 L 19 Brondesbury pk NW2
45 O 20 Brondesbury pk NW2
129 U 6 Brondesbury rd NW6
129 U 7 Brondesbury vills NW6
31 W 5 Bronhill ter N17
144 J 19 Bronsart rd SW6
119 R 2 Bronson rd SW20
35 X 14 Bronté clo Ilf
150 C 10 Bronti clo SE17
76 C 18 Bronté st SE5
56 H 20 Brook av Dgnhm
12 E 18 Brook av Edg
43 O 8 Brook av Wemb
27 U 3 Brook clo NW7
39 T 6 Brook clo Rom
118 K 7 Brook clo SW20
20 C 13 Brook cres E4
18 L 13 Brook cres N9
12 F 17 Brook ct Edg
23 O 12 Brook dri Harrow
149 T 3 Brook dri SE11
149 X 5 Brook dri SE11
20 C 13 Brook gdns E4
103 U 20 Brook gdns Kingst
86 E 7 Brook gdns SW13
144 E 4 Brook grn W6
112 E 14 Brook la Brom
97 W 15 Brook la Bxly
94 J 4 Brook la SE3
72 G 14 Brook Lane north Brentf
138 E 8 Brook Mews north W2
4 K 17 Brook pl Barnt
21 U 6 Brook rd Buck Hl
36 H 18 Brook rd Ilf
30 D 9 Brook rd N22
30 A 12 Brook rd N8
44 E 6 Brook rd NW2
39 U 5 Brook rd Rom
122 K 7 Brook rd Thntn Hth
122 K 8 Brook rd Thntn Hth
83 Z 15 Brook rd Twick
72 G 15 Brook Road south Brentf
81 T 13 Brook st Erith

81 V 18 Brook st Erith
116 H 4 Brook st Kingst
31 V 9 Brook st N17
139 Y 7 Brook st W1
138 H 9 Brook st W2
12 K 20 Brook wlk Edg
141 T 1 Brook's mkt EC1
59 S 13 Brookbank av W7
93 P 8 Brookbank rd SE13
98 A 17 Brookdale rd Bxly
33 N 11 Brookdale rd E17
93 R 17 Brookdale rd SE6
79 Y 11 Brookdene rd SE18
41 O 9 Brooke av Harrow
33 V 14 Brooke rd E17
49 X 9 Brooke rd N16
141 T 2 Brooke st EC1
10 A 3 Brooke way Bushey
111 P 5 Brookehowse rd SE6
114 G 2 Brookend rd Sidcp
33 U 13 Brookfield av E17
154 H 7 Brookfield av Sutton
60 H 12 Brookfield av W5
13 Y 20 Brookfield clo NW7
24 J 16 Brookfield cres Harrow
13 X 20 Brookfield cres NW7
59 O 8 Brookfield ct Grnfd
47 O 8 Brookfield N6
47 R 9 Brookfield pk NW5
20 L 20 Brookfield pth Wdfd Grn
50 J 18 Brookfield rd E9
93 O 13 Brookfield rd W4
18 L 11 Brookfield Road east N9
120 J 10 Brookfields av Mitch
9 T 13 Brookfields Enf
5 W 17 Brookhill clo Barnt
78 T 15 Brookhill clo SE18
5 V 17 Brookhill rd Barnt
78 L 12 Brookhill rd SE18
20 L 14 Brookhouse gdns E4
52 G 14 Brooking rd E7
38 M 12 Brookland appr Rom
27 Z 13 Brookland clo NW11
27 Z 13 Brookland garth NW11
27 Z 13 Brookland hill NW11
27 Z 12 Brookland ri NW11
114 G 4 Brooklands av Sidcp
105 Z 4 Brooklands av SW19
39 N 14 Brooklands clo Rom
60 F 4 Brooklands dri Grnfd
39 N 13 Brooklands la Rom
94 E 7 Brooklands pk SE3
38 M 14 Brooklands rd Rom
26 B 4 Brooklea clo NW9
124 A 8 Brooklyn av SE25
124 A 8 Brooklyn gro SE25
127 P 10 Brooklyn rd Brom
124 A 8 Brooklyn rd SE25
127 U 11 Brookmead av Brom
152 B 15 Brookmead Epsom
121 W 14 Brookmead rd Croy
15 N 12 Brookmeadow N12
93 O 2 Brookmill rd SE8
66 F 11 Brooks av E6
113 X 5 Brooks clo SE9
51 S 14 Brooks ct E15
73 R 16 Brooks la W4
139 X 8 Brooks ms W1
65 S 4 Brooks rd E13
73 R 15 Brooks rd W4
50 E 18 Brooksbank st E9
48 G 20 Brooksby st N1
50 F 14 Brooksby's wlk E9
33 R 6 Brookscroft rd E17
10 D 16 Brookshill av Harrow
10 C 16 Brookshill dri Harrow
10 D 17 Brookshill Harrow
5 X 20 Brookside Barnt
124 F 14 Brookside way Croy
27 U 13 Brookside wlk NW11
128 L 6 Brooksville av NW6
98 H 1 Brookvale Erith
107 T 11 Brookview rd SW16

145 O 19	Brookville rd SW6
94 E 9	Brookway SE3
86 E 6	Brookwood av SW13
126 B 10	Brookwood clo BR2
82 K 4	Brookwood rd Hounsl
105 X 1	Brookwood rd SW18
127 S 14	Broom clo Brom
102 F 17	Broom clo Tedd
159 P 6	Broom gdns Croy
98 F 14	Broom Hill ri Bxly Hth
102 E 14	Broom lock Tedd
98 F 14	Broom mead Bxly Hth
102 F 18	Broom pk Tedd
159 O 6	Broom rd Croy
102 B 13	Broom rd Tedd
102 D 14	Broom water Tedd
102 D 13	Broom Water west Tedd
100 E 19	Broome rd Hampt
150 D 19	Broome way SE5
17 P 15	Broomfield av N13
32 L 20	Broomfield E17
17 O 14	Broomfield ho N13
17 R 15	Broomfield la N13
17 N 14	Broomfield pk N13
98 F 14	Broomfield rd Bxly Hth
124 K 7	Broomfield rd Beck
17 O 17	Broomfield rd N13
85 N 1	Broomfield rd Rich
55 W 1	Broomfield rd Rom
117 O 18	Broomfield rd Surb
102 E 15	Broomfield rd Tedd
72 C 2	Broomfield rd W13
64 C 15	Broomfield st E14
25 P 4	Broomgrove gdns Edg
90 D 6	Broomgrove rd SW9
157 O 18	Broomhall rd S Croy
21 S 18	Broomhill rd Wdfd Grn
21 S 20	Broomhill rd Wdfd Grn
99 Y 16	Broomhill rd Drtfrd
55 O 6	Broomhill rd Ilf
87 Y 14	Broomhill rd SW18
87 X 7	Broomhouse la SW6
87 X 5	Broomhouse rd SW6
153 Y 3	Broomloan la Sutton
45 W 16	Broomsleigh st NW6
88 L 16	Broomwood rd SW11
89 P 13	Broomwood rd SW6
110 G 12	Broseley gro SE26
148 L 19	Brough clo SW8
148 K 19	Brough st SW8
135 T 3	Brougham rd E8
61 W 18	Brougham rd W3
27 R 10	Broughton av N3
102 C 8	Broughton av Rich
90 G 11	Broughton dri SW9
29 V 18	Broughton gdns N6
122 F 13	Broughton rd Thntn Hth
88 B 4	Broughton rd SW6
72 C 1	Broughton rd W13
89 R 4	Broughton st SW8
73 V 6	Brouncker rd W3
155 Z 16	Brown clo Wallgtn
139 V 7	Brown Hart gdns W1
64 E 18	Brownfield ct E14
93 V 19	Brownhill rd SE6
118 K 19	Browning av Worc Pk
154 J 8	Browning av Sutton
59 W 17	Browning av W7
100 E 10	Browning clo Hampt
130 D 18	Browning clo W9
96 H 2	Browning clo Well
52 C 2	Browning rd E11
53 T 18	Browning rd E12
8 A 2	Browning rd Enf
150 B 8	Browning st SE17
54 M 8	Brownlea gdns Ilf
133 O 17	Brownlow ms SW1
157 T 8	Brownlow rd Croy
52 G 12	Brownlow rd E7
135 R 3	Brownlow rd E8
16 M 18	Brownlow rd N11
28 A 1	Brownlow rd N3
62 B 1	Brownlow rd NW10
44 B 20	Brownlow rd NW10
71 Y 2	Brownlow rd W13
141 P 2	Brownlow st WC1
142 K 5	Browns bldgs EC3
47 R 15	Browns la NW5
33 O 11	Browns rd E17
116 M 17	Browns rd Surb
139 N 4	Browns st W1
114 A 8	Brownspring dri SE9
113 Z 9	Brownspring dri SE9
28 F 7	Brownswell rd N2
48 K 8	Brownswood rd N4
89 P 14	Broxash rd SW11
34 H 12	Broxbourne av E18
52 D 10	Broxbourne st E7
108 F 7	Broxholm rd SE27
110 K 3	Broxted rd SE6
130 M 7	Broxwood way NW8
31 T 5	Bruce Castle museum N17
31 T 4	Bruce Castle pk N17
31 U 5	Bruce Castle rd N17
97 R 2	Bruce clo Welling
158 F 20	Bruce dri S Croy
15 Y 12	Bruce gdns N20
31 T 6	Bruce gro N17
4 F 12	Bruce rd Barnt
64 C 9	Bruce rd E3
64 D 9	Bruce rd E3
23 T 8	Bruce rd Harrow
107 N 17	Bruce rd Mitch
61 Z 1	Bruce rd NW10
123 O 8	Bruce rd SE25
129 N 13	Bruckner st W10
107 N 8	Brudenell rd SW17
40 B 19	Bruffs meadow Nthlt
98 J 8	Brummel clo Bxly Hth
60 J 7	Brumwill rd Wemb
143 N 2	Brune st E1
58 D 9	Brunel clo Nthlt
58 K 18	Brunel pl S'hall
78 R 6	Brunel rd SE16
62 B 15	Brunel rd W3
65 O 18	Brunel st E16
31 R 14	Brunel wlk N15
28 C 17	Brunner clo NW11
32 J 16	Brunner rd E17
60 F 11	Brunner rd W5
43 V 7	Bruno pl NW9
16 B 11	Brunswick av N11
97 X 9	Brunswick clo Bxly Hth
22 C 20	Brunswick clo Pinn
16 B 11	Brunswick cres N11
142 L 18	Brunswick ct SE1
36 B 1	Brunswick gdns Ilf
60 K 10	Brunswick gdns W5
137 W 15	Brunswick gdns W8
16 B 12	Brunswick gro N11
139 P 5	Brunswick ms W1
16 B 9	Brunswick Park gdns N11
16 B 8	Brunswick Park rd N11
91 P 1	Brunswick pk SE5
134 F 14	Brunswick pl N1
109 W 16	Brunswick pl SE19
75 V 9	Brunswick quay SE16
97 X 10	Brunswick rd Bxly Hth
51 T 4	Brunswick rd E10
103 P 20	Brunswick rd Kingst
31 S 14	Brunswick rd N15
154 C 7	Brunswick rd Sutton
60 K 10	Brunswick rd W5
8 G 20	Brunswick sq N17
132 L 17	Brunswick sq WC1
33 T 15	Brunswick st E17
91 R 1	Brunswick vils SE5
16 E 13	Brunswick way N11
63 W 18	Brunton pl E14
142 L 1	Brushfield st E1
143 N 1	Brushfield st E1
88 G 11	Brussels rd SW11
113 T 19	Bruton clo Chisl
139 Y 10	Bruton la W1
139 Y 9	Bruton pl W1
120 C 10	Bruton rd Mrdn
139 Y 10	Bruton st W1
139 Y 11	Bruton way W13
128 A 1	Bryan av NW10
44 K 20	Bryan av NW10
62 L 1	Bryan av NW10
75 X 5	Bryan rd SE16
88 A 4	Bryans all SW6
82 L 20	Bryanston av Twick
70 F 10	Bryanston clo S'hall
139 O 3	Bryanston Mews east W1
139 O 3	Bryanston Mews west W1
139 N 3	Bryanston pl W1
139 O 4	Bryanston sq W1
139 R 6	Bryanston st W1
29 Y 17	Bryanstone rd N8
4 J 19	Bryant clo Barnt
64 L 1	Bryant st E15
48 F 14	Bryantwood rd N7
55 T 12	Bryce rd Dgnhm
16 J 12	Brycedale cres N14
110 H 12	Bryden clo SE26
140 J 10	Brydges pl WC2
89 P 8	Brydges rd E15
132 L 4	Brydon wlk N1
48 A 9	Bryett rd N7
64 B 6	Brymay clo E3
8 J 13	Bryn-y-Mawr rd Enf
88 M 3	Brynmaer rd SW11
23 W 10	Bryn rd Harrow
62 H 20	Bryony rd W12
92 C 7	Buchan rd SE15
128 A 9	Buchanan gdns NW10
62 K 7	Buchanan gdns NW10
88 D 19	Bucharest rd SW18
138 H 10	Buck Hill wlk W2
25 X 16	Buck la NW9
131 Y 2	Buck st NW1
33 W 13	Buck wlk E17
94 D 15	Buckden clo SE12
120 B 10	Buckfast rd Mrdn
135 T 14	Buckfast st E2
87 Y 16	Buckhold rd SW18
120 L 20	Buckhurst av Carsh
63 O 12	Buckhurst st E1
135 Y 17	Buckhurst st E1
140 L 12	Buckingham arc WC2
122 G 1	Buckingham av Thntn Hth
96 H 11	Buckingham av Welling
59 Z 3	Buckingham av Grnfd
15 R 3	Buckingham av N20
100 E 12	Buckingham clo Hampt
8 E 8	Buckingham clo Enf
60 D 14	Buckingham clo W5
26 G 9	Buckingham ct NW4
148 C 1	Buckingham ga SW1
122 F 2	Buckingham gdns Thntn Hth
24 L 3	Buckingham gdns Edg
140 A 19	Buckingham pal SW1
139 Z 19	Buckingham pal SW1
139 X 18	Buckingham Palace gdns SW1
147 X 6	Buckingham Palace rd SW1
62 E 6	Buckingham rd NW10
100 F 13	Buckingham rd Hampt
116 M 8	Buckingham rd Kingst
117 N 8	Buckingham rd Kingst
23 R 15	Buckingham rd Harrow
51 R 9	Buckingham rd E10
34 K 15	Buckingham rd E11
52 B 14	Buckingham rd E18
34 C 5	Buckingham rd E18
24 M 2	Buckingham rd Edg
25 N 1	Buckingham rd Edg
54 E 7	Buckingham rd Ilf
122 A 10	Buckingham rd Mitch
49 S 19	Buckingham rd N1
30 A 6	Buckingham rd N22
102 F 4	Buckingham rd Rich
140 L 11	Buckingham st WC2
155 V 20	Buckingham way Wallgtn
46 F 19	Buckland cres NW3
51 T 6	Buckland rd E10
153 N 20	Buckland rd Sutton
134 G 9	Buckland st N1
118 M 20	Buckland way Worc Pk
120 C 10	Buckland wlk Mrdn
102 E 14	Bucklands rd Tedd
143 R 5	Buckle st E1
119 U 5	Buckleigh av SW20
107 Z 16	Buckleigh rd SW16
109 T 19	Buckleigh way SE19
113 U 8	Buckler gdns SE9
160 D 7	Bucklersbury EC4
99 U 6	Buckley clo Drtfrd
129 P 2	Buckley rd NW6
88 J 12	Buckmaster rd SW11
140 H 4	Bucknall st WC2
90 D 11	Bucknall st SW2
20 K 9	Buckrell rd E4
18 K 18	Buckstone rd N18
75 V 3	Buckters rents SE16
92 H 14	Buckthorne rd SE4
43 V 9	Buddings crcl Wemb
84 D 14	Budds all Twick
160 D 7	Budge row EC4
80 F 20	Budleigh cres Welling
55 N 7	Budoch ct Ilf
55 N 8	Budoch dri Ilf
87 U 5	Buer rd SW6
77 V 11	Bugsbys way SE7
122 L 7	Bulganak rd Thntn Hth
148 H 7	Bulinga st SW1
141 V 12	Bull all SE1
97 R 7	Bull all Welling
114 D 19	Bull la Chisl
56 G 8	Bull la Dgnhm
18 E 19	Bull la N18
65 P 5	Bull rd E15
160 B 9	Bull Wharf la EC4
63 S 9	Bullards pl E1
81 W 10	Bullbanks rd Blvdr
88 J 4	Bullen st SW11
151 S 19	Buller clo SE15
54 G 20	Buller rd Bark
31 X 9	Buller rd N17
30 E 7	Buller rd N22
128 G 13	Buller rd NW10
123 O 6	Buller rd Thntn Hth
115 X 13	Bullers clo Sidcp
113 S 18	Bullers Wood dri Chisl
12 D 10	Bullescroft rd Edg
64 G 19	Bullivant st E14
85 X 6	Bulls all SW14
146 L 5	Bulls gdns SW3
160 H 7	Bulls Head pas EC3
42 F 1	Bulmer gdns Harrow
137 S 12	Bulmer ms W1
82 F 6	Bulstrode av Hounsl
82 F 7	Bulstrode gdns Hounsl
139 V 3	Bulstrode pl W1
82 H 7	Bulstrode rd Hounsl
139 V 3	Bulstrode st W1
51 W 3	Bulwer Court rd E11
5 P 14	Bulwer gdns Barnt
5 O 14	Bulwer rd Barnt
51 X 3	Bulwer rd E11
18 E 15	Bulwer rd N18
136 D 15	Bulwer st W12
34 C 1	Bunces la Wdfd Grn
143 Y 7	Bunch st E1
123 S 9	Bungalow rd SE25
107 S 17	Bungalows the SW16
134 D 16	Bunhill row EC1
81 S 11	Bunkers hill Blvdr
26 O 1	Bunns la NW7
13 O 19	Bunns la NW7
63 U 6	Bunsen st E3
120 M 11	Bunting clo Mitch
36 D 16	Buntingbridge rd Ilf
78 K 9	Bunton st SE18
32 J 10	Bunyan rd E17
148 F 10	Buonaparte ms SW1
150 E 2	Burbage clo SE1
150 E 2	Burbage clo SE1
90 M 15	Burbage rd SE24
91 N 17	Burbage rd SE24
117 Z 4	Burberry clo New Mald
31 W 8	Burbridge way N17
64 F 17	Burban st E14
80 H 16	Burcharbro rd SE2
51 R 3	Burchell rd E10
92 A 3	Burchell rd SE15
38 A 18	Burchett way Rom
38 J 2	Burchwall clo Rom
88 G 20	Burcote rd SW18
72 E 14	Burden clo Brentf
52 H 5	Burden way E11
85 S 9	Burdenshott av Rich
49 S 17	Burder clo N1
104 F 20	Burdett av SW20
115 Y 13	Burdett clo Sidcp
123 P 15	Burdett rd Croy
63 Y 15	Burdett rd E14
85 O 6	Burdett rd Rich
141 T 20	Burdett st SE1
153 A 2	Burdon la Sutton
153 U 18	Burdon pk Sutton
106 E 9	Burfield clo SW17

55 U 11 Burford clo Dgnhm
36 B 12 Burford clo Ilf
17 S 10 Burford gdns N13
72 J 15 Burford rd Brentf
127 R 10 Burford rd Brom
64 J 2 Burford rd E15
66 C 9 Burford rd E6
110 M 6 Burford rd SE6
153 X 4 Burford rd Sutton
118 F 18 Burford rd Worc Pk
159 V 15 Burford way Croy
151 N 9 Burgandy st SE1
99 T 8 Burgate clo Drtfrd
150 E 2 Burge st SE1
150 F 3 Burge st SE1
66 E 1 Burges rd E6
66 K 2 Burges rd E6
53 V 20 Burges rd E6
25 X 18 Burgess av NW9
100 B 8 Burgess clo Felt
45 W 11 Burgess hill NW2
51 Y 13 Burgess rd E15
153 Z 9 Burgess rd Sutton
64 A 15 Burgess st E14
133 Z 8 Burgh st N1
110 G 9 Burghill rd SE26
118 A 1 Burghley av New Mald
117 Y 1 Burghley av New Mald
52 A 3 Burghley rd E11
30 F 10 Burghley rd N8
47 T 11 Burghley rd NW5
105 R 9 Burghley rd SW19
121 N 10 Burgley pl Mitch
141 Y 7 Burgon st EC4
93 R 1 Burgos gro SE10
30 H 19 Burgoyne rd N4
123 T 8 Burgoyne rd SE25
90 C 7 Burgoyne rd SW9
110 C 18 Burham clo SE20
22 B 7 Burhill gro Pinn
86 B 10 Burke st E16
65 P 16 Burke st E16
88 M 14 Burland rd SW11
96 K 13 Burleigh av Sidcp
155 P 6 Burleigh gdns Wallgtn
16 G 5 Burleigh gdns N14
87 P 13 Burleigh pl SW15
8 E 14 Burleigh rd Enf
119 T 19 Burleigh rd Sutton
140 M 8 Burleigh st WC2
8 B 12 Burleigh way Enf
20 A 17 Burley clo E4
121 Y 3 Burley clo SW16
65 X 16 Burley rd E16
140 A 11 Burlington arc W1
85 P 2 Burlington av Rich
38 H 18 Burlington av Rom
129 S 17 Burlington clo W9
56 A 1 Burlington gdns Rom
55 Z 1 Burlington gdns Rom
140 A 11 Burlington gdns W1
73 X 3 Burlington gdns W3
73 W 14 Burlington gdns W3
74 A 17 Burlington la W4
73 Y 19 Burlington la W4
73 W 3 Burlington ms W3
87 T 5 Burlington pl SW 6
118 E 9 Burlington rd New Mald
122 M 4 Burlington rd Thntn Hth
123 N 3 Burlington rd Thntn Hth
8 A 5 Burlington rd Enf
83 O 2 Burlington rd Islwth
29 O 9 Burlington rd N10
31 X 5 Burlington rd N17
87 T 5 Burlington rd SW6
73 U 13 Burlington rd W4
15 Y 4 Burlington ri Barnt
49 N 12 Burma rd N16
149 X 2 Burman st SE1
106 D 7 Burmester rd SW17
19 P 11 Burn side N9
73 U 17 Burnaby cres W4
73 U 16 Burnaby gdns W4
66 M 19 Burnaby st SW10
146 B 20 Burnaby st SW10
146 D 19 Burnaby st SW10
15 N 19 Burnbrae clo N12
107 V 1 Burnbury rd SW12
9 R 10 Burncroft av Enf
138 K 1 Burne st NW1
102 D 11 Burnell av Rich
96 M 4 Burnell av Well
97 O 5 Burnell av Welling
24 F 7 Burnell gdns Stanm
154 B 7 Burnell rd Sutton

66 H 10 Burnels av E6
48 C 19 Burness clo N7
50 D 15 Burnett clo E9
149 N 10 Burnett st SE11
116 L 12 Burney av Surb
117 N 11 Burney av Surb
76 G 19 Burney st SE10
87 T 3 Burnfoot av SW6
8 E 4 Burnham clo Enf
34 K 14 Burnham cres E11
27 N 13 Burnham ct NW4
153 O 3 Burnham dri Worc Pk
68 C 2 Burnham rd Dgnhm
19 X 17 Burnham rd E4
120 A 10 Burnham rd Mrdn
38 L 11 Burnham rd Rom
115 Y 5 Burnham rd Sidcp
63 P 8 Burnham st E2
117 P 1 Burnham st Kingst
72 A 9 Burnham way W13
125 O 3 Burnhill rd Becknhm
44 E 15 Burnley rd NW10
90 C 4 Burnley rd SW9
58 J 19 Burns av S'hall
97 O 16 Burns av Sidcp
99 T 2 Burns clo Erith
96 J 3 Burns clo Welling
62 C 3 Burns rd NW10
88 L 4 Burns rd SW11
72 A 5 Burns rd W13
60 J 6 Burns rd Wemb
146 L 10 Burnsall st SW3
4 L 13 Burnside clo Barnt
83 X 15 Burnside clo Twick
60 G 3 Burnside cres Wemb
55 U 3 Burnside rd Dgnhm
94 E 19 Burnt Ash hill SE12
112 G 1 Burnt Ash hill SE12
112 G 14 Burnt Ash la Brom
94 C 14 Burnt Ash st SE12
25 S 3 Burnt Oak bdwy Edg
25 U 3 Burnt Oak fields Edg
96 L 16 Burnt Oak la Sidcp
114 M 3 Burnt Oak la Sidcp
97 P 18 Burnt Oak la Sidcp
145 R 19 Burnthwaite rd SW6
106 H 2 Burntwood clo SW18
106 H 2 Burntwood Grange rd SW18
106 D 6 Burntwood la SW17
143 X 5 Buross st E1
98 B 6 Burr clo Bxly Hth
87 Y 20 Burr rd SW18
79 O 10 Burrage gro SE18
79 N 14 Burrage pl SE18
79 O 10 Burrage rd SE18
65 U 17 Burrard rd E16
45 Y 14 Burrard rd NW6
124 J 14 Burrell clo Becknhm
12 G 8 Burrell clo Edg
125 N 3 Burrell row Becknhm
141 X 13 Burrell st SE1
117 P 4 Burritt rd Kingst
26 J 13 Burroughs gdns NW4
26 J 13 Burroughs the NW4
141 W 16 Burrows ms SE1
128 C 12 Burrows rd NW10
62 M 8 Burrows rd NW10
142 K 15 Bursar st SE1
114 L 4 Bursdon clo Sidcp
9 S 13 Bursland rd Enf
143 U 6 Burslem st E1
87 S 10 Burstock rd SW15
87 P 12 Burston rd SW15
119 S 1 Burstow rd SW20
105 S 20 Burstow rd SW20
77 Y 3 Burt rd E16
48 L 3 Burtley clo N4
82 E 3 Burton gdns Hounsl
150 F 11 Burton gro SE17
147 V 6 Burton ms SW1
132 H 15 Burton pl WC1
34 G 11 Burton rd E18
102 L 18 Burton rd Kingst
129 R 2 Burton rd NW6
90 F 4 Burton rd SW9
90 H 4 Burton rd SW9
132 H 15 Burton st WC1
14 B 13 Burtonhole la NW7
64 L 1 Burtons ct E15
100 K 10 Burtons rd Hampt
101 O 11 Burtons rd Hampt
79 R 14 Burwash rd SE18
41 T 18 Burwell av Grnfd
63 N 18 Burwell clo E1
143 X 6 Burwell clo E1

50 J 3 Burwell rd E10
138 L 5 Burwood pl W2
142 K 5 Bury st EC3
120 A 10 Bury gro Mrdn
18 G 4 Bury Hall vlls N9
140 K 2 Bury pl WC1
56 J 14 Bury rd Dgnhm
21 N 2 Bury rd E4
30 G 10 Bury rd N22
142 K 5 Bury st EC3
18 K 5 Bury st E3
140 C 13 Bury st SW1
18 D 4 Bury st west N9
146 J 8 Bury wlk SW3
47 X 17 Busby ms NW5
47 X 17 Busby pl NW5
135 P 16 Busby st E2
36 F 16 Bush clo Ilf
57 V 1 Bush Elms rd Hornch
43 V 1 Bush gro NW9
25 V 20 Bush gro NW9
24 F 4 Bush gro Stanm
8 B 18 Bush hill Enf
17 Y 2 Bush hill N21
24 M 19 Bush Hill rd Harrow
18 B 2 Bush Hill rd N21
160 E 8 Bush la EC4
52 D 1 Bush rd E11
63 N 3 Bush rd E8
135 W 5 Bush rd E8
73 N 17 Bush rd Rich
75 T 11 Bush rd SE8
50 J 17 Bushberry rd E9
108 E 3 Bushell clo SW2
10 B 8 Bushell gro Bushey
143 T 14 Bushell st E1
113 W 12 Bushell way Chisl
34 C 10 Bushey av E18
118 L 4 Bushey av E7
91 T 2 Bushey Hill rd SE5
153 Z 7 Bushey la Sutton
101 S 18 Bushey pk Tedd
159 O 3 Bushey rd Croy
65 Y 6 Bushey rd E13
31 R 18 Bushey rd N15
154 A 7 Bushey rd Sutton
153 Y 8 Bushey rd Sutton
118 K 5 Bushey rd SW20
119 P 4 Bushey rd SW20
125 W 13 Bushey way Becknhm
12 E 8 Bushfield clo Edg
12 F 8 Bushfield cres Edg
55 V 11 Bushmoor cres SE18
96 A 1 Bushmoor cres SE18
79 N 10 Bushmoor cres SE18
107 S 5 Bushnell rd SW17
55 V 11 Bushway Dgnhm
52 D 2 Bushwood E11
73 P 18 Bushwood rd Rich
8 G 15 Bushy Hill pk Enf
101 U 17 Bushy House Tedd
101 R 13 Bushy Park gdns Tedd
102 B 18 Bushy Park rd Tedd
101 V 16 Bushy rd Tedd
63 U 19 Butcher row E14
65 T 17 Butchers rd E16
102 J 2 Bute av Rich
155 V 11 Bute Gardens west Wallgtn
144 F 6 Bute gdns W6
155 V 11 Bute gdns Wallgtn
122 G 20 Bute rd Croy
36 B 15 Bute rd Ilf
155 U 7 Bute rd Wallgtn
146 F 6 Bute st SW7
23 R 20 Butler av Harrow
55 P 11 Butler rd Dgnhm
41 N 1 Butler rd Harrow
23 P 20 Butler rd Harrow
63 R 8 Butler st E2
155 O 7 Butter hill Carsh
155 O 7 Butter hill Wallgtn
33 U 16 Butterfields E17
95 Z 15 Butterfly la SE9
119 N 14 Buttermere clo Mrdn
87 U 13 Buttermere dri SW15
144 E 8 Butterwick W6
134 G 12 Buttesland st N1
56 H 18 Buttfield clo Dgnhm
79 N 12 Buttmarsh clo SE18
100 C 6 Butts cotts Felt
100 G 7 Butts cres Felt
112 A 11 Butts rd Brom
72 F 18 Butts the Brentf
54 C 16 Buttsbury rd Ilf
49 U 20 Buxted clo E8
15 X 16 Buxted rd N12
92 C 16 Buxton clo SE23

153 R 7 Buxton cres Sutton
34 A 14 Buxton dri E11
118 A 2 Buxton dri New Mald
117 Z 2 Buxton dri New Mald
73 S 1 Buxton gdns W3
52 A 15 Buxton rd E15
51 Z 15 Buxton rd E15
32 J 14 Buxton rd E17
20 K 3 Buxton rd E4
66 D 9 Buxton rd E6
81 G 1 Buxton rd Erith
36 G 20 Buxton rd Ilf
47 Y 5 Buxton rd N19
44 K 17 Buxton rd NW2
86 B 8 Buxton rd SW13
122 H 13 Buxton rd Thntn Hth
135 R 18 Buxton st E1
88 C 5 Byam st SW6
121 X 1 Byards croft SW16
58 H 13 Bycroft rd S'hall
110 E 17 Bycroft st SE20
7 X 10 Bycullah av Enf
7 V 9 Bycullah rd Enf
62 B 16 Bye the W3
23 U 5 Bye Way the Harrow
100 K 5 Bye ways Twick
106 F 16 Byegrove rd SW19
152 E 9 Byeway the Epsom
85 V 8 Byeway the SW14
117 R 12 Byeways the Sutton
86 G 3 Byfeld gdns SW13
83 Y 8 Byfield rd Islwth
65 N 1 Byford clo E15
159 R 15 Bygrove Croy
64 C 18 Bygrove st E14
17 O 1 Byland clo N21
80 B 8 Byland clo SE2
154 H 4 Byne rd Carsh
110 D 14 Byne rd SE26
157 O 17 Bynes rd S Croy
132 F 18 Byng pl WC1
4 C 11 Byng rd Barnt
76 B 5 Byng st E14
98 A 8 Bynon av Bxly Hth
107 T 2 Byrne rd SW12
53 P 19 Byron av E12
34 B 9 Byron av E18
118 G 10 Byron av New Mald
25 T 11 Byron av NW9
154 G 9 Byron av Sutton
154 G 9 Byron Avenue east Sutton
135 S 4 Byron clo E8
100 F 10 Byron clo Hampt
80 F 3 Byron clo SE18
7 X 9 Byron ct Enf
28 G 19 Byron dri N2
154 G 7 Byron gdns Sutton
41 R 5 Byron Hill rd Harrow
51 R 3 Byron rd E10
33 P 11 Byron rd E17
23 T 18 Byron rd Harrow
44 J 8 Byron rd NW2
13 T 16 Byron rd NW7
73 O 1 Byron rd W5
42 F 9 Byron rd Wemb
64 F 16 Byron st E14
19 O 1 Byron terr N9
58 B 9 Byron way Nthlt
35 Z 5 Bysouth clo Ilf
106 M 14 Byton rd SW17
142 L 10 Byward st EC3
147 N 9 Bywater st SW3
154 F 19 Byway the Sutton
140 A 3 Bywell pl W1
124 D 14 Bywood av Croy

C

138 K 2 Cabbell st NW1
143 X 8 Cable st E1
66 B 5 Cabot way E6
88 J 5 Cabul rd SW11
62 D 18 Cactus wlk W12
5 W 17 Caddington clo Barnt
45 S 10 Caddington rd NW2
23 W 1 Caddis clo Stanm
93 W 2 Cade rd SE10
76 L 13 Cadeb pl SE10
135 P 11 Cadell clo E2
88 C 17 Cader rd SW18
56 L 19 Cadiz rd Dgnhm
150 C 11 Cadiz st SE17

110 C 3	Cadley ter SE23
118 A 10	Cadmer clo New Mald
125 X 2	Cadogan clo Becknhm
40 L 13	Cadogan clo Harrow
101 U 13	Cadogan clo Tedd
154 A 14	Cadogan ct Sutton
147 P 5	Cadogan ga SW3
34 J 10	Cadogan gdns E18
7 S 18	Cadogan gdns N21
28 A 5	Cadogan gdns N3
147 P 6	Cadogan gdns SW3
147 R 2	Cadogan la SW1
147 S 3	Cadogan la SW1
147 R 1	Cadogan pl SW1
116 G 12	Cadogan rd Surb
147 O 4	Cadogan sq SW1
147 N 7	Cadogan st SW3
50 K 18	Cadogan ter E9
31 V 18	Cadoxton av N15
114 A 4	Cadwallon rd SE9
48 E 12	Caedmon rd N7
115 T 13	Caerleon clo Sidcp
80 C 10	Caerleon ter SE2
121 Z 7	Caernarvon clo Mitch
35 W 4	Caernarvon dri Ilf
134 M 11	Caesar st E2
104 F 13	Caesars camp SW19
120 M 10	Caesars wlk Mitch
76 C 11	Cahir st E14
129 N 15	Caird st W10
72 G 4	Cairn av W5
10 J 19	Cairn way Stanm
112 C 17	Cairndale clo Brom
44 C 11	Cairnfield av NW2
88 K 12	Cairns rd SW11
150 J 0	Cairo New rd Croy
33 O 12	Cairo rd E17
65 P 3	Caistor Park rd E15
65 P 4	Caistor pk E15
89 R 19	Caistor rd SW12
96 J 17	Caithness gdns Sidcp
107 S 18	Caithness rd Mitch
144 G 3	Caithness rd W14
48 K 17	Calabria rd N5
90 J 1	Calais st SE5
57 Z 14	Calbourne av Hornch
89 N 19	Calbourne rd SW12
113 O 10	Calcott wlk SE9
118 J 19	Caldbeck av Worc Pk
91 N 4	Caldecot rd SE5
10 E 1	Caldecote gdns Bushey
10 G 1	Caldecote la Bushey
50 F 9	Caldecott way E5
59 V 6	Calder av Grnfd
8 D 12	Calder clo Enf
25 O 9	Calder gdns Edg
120 C 11	Calder rd Mrdn
136 C 3	Calderon pl W10
62 M 15	Calderon pl W10
51 V 11	Calderon rd E11
89 W 13	Caldervale rd SW4
78 K 10	Calderwood st SE18
150 E 16	Caldwell st SE5
149 R 20	Caldwell st SW9
81 U 7	Caldy rd Blvdr
146 J 9	Cale st SW3
142 B 17	Caleb st SE1
66 F 2	Caledon rd E6
155 P 7	Caledon rd Wallgtn
132 L 10	Caledonia st N1
132 M 9	Caledonian rd N1
133 N 4	Caledonian rd N1
48 C 15	Caledonian rd N7
76 J 11	Caledonian wharf E14
155 Z 18	Caley clo Wallgtn
10 C 7	California la Bushey
117 U 7	California rd New Mald
49 O 18	Callaby ter N1
111 S 5	Callander rd SE6
17 W 15	Callard av N13
129 O 1	Callcott rd NW6
137 T 13	Callcott st W8
32 L 18	Callis rd E17
146 E 13	Callow st SW3
150 K 13	Calmington rd SE5
111 Y 16	Calmont rd Brom
35 Y 4	Calne av Ilf
105 P 9	Calonne rd SW19
133 O 10	Calshot st N1
7 W 12	Calshot way Enf
154 C 4	Calthorpe gdns Sutton
11 Y 15	Calthorpe gdns Edg
133 P 16	Calthorpe st WC1
91 S 14	Calton av SE21
5 S 19	Calton rd Barnt
111 R 16	Calverley clo Becknhm
56 D 7	Calverley cres Dgnhm
42 G 1	Calverley gdns Harrow
152 F 14	Calverley rd Epsom
134 M 14	Calvert av E2
81 T 12	Calvert clo Blvdr
115 Y 14	Calvert clo Sidcp
4 D 10	Calvert rd Barnt
77 O 14	Calvert rd SE10
66 J 3	Calverton rd E6
135 N 18	Calvin st E1
77 W 14	Calydon rd SE7
64 J 3	Cam rd E15
101 R 2	Camac rd Twick
87 P 13	Cambalt rd SW15
118 J 3	Camberley av SW20
8 D 15	Camberley av Enf
8 D 15	Camberley clo Enf
94 J 11	Cambert way SE3
132 L 4	Cambert wlk N1
91 P 3	Camberwell Church st SE5
91 P 2	Camberwell glebe SE5
91 N 1	Camberwell grn SE5
91 P 2	Camberwell gro SE5
149 W 18	Camberwell New rd SE5
91 N 2	Camberwell pas SE5
150 C 17	Camberwell rd SE5
90 L 2	Camberwell Station rd SE5
56 K 16	Cambeys rd Dgnhm
72 C 5	Camborne av W10
136 L 6	Camborne ms W11
123 W 18	Camborne rd Croy
119 P 12	Camborne rd Mrdn
115 T 8	Camborne rd Sidcp
154 A 16	Camborne rd Sutton
153 Z 17	Camborne rd Sutton
87 Y 19	Camborne rd SW18
96 J 4	Camborne rd Welling
82 G 1	Camborne way Hounsl
19 S 4	Cambourne av N9
89 W 20	Cambria clo SW12
82 H 11	Cambria clo Hounsl
114 F 1	Cambria clo Sidcp
96 F 20	Cambria clo Sidcp
90 L 7	Cambria rd SE5
145 Z 20	Cambria st SW6
36 H 15	Cambrian av Ilf
108 H 6	Cambrian clo SE27
51 N 2	Cambrian rd E10
84 M 17	Cambrian rd Rich
118 B 4	Cambridge av New Mald
96 K 10	Cambridge av Welling
41 V 16	Cambridge av Grnfd
129 V 7	Cambridge av NW6
78 G 12	Cambridge Barracks rd SE18
140 G 7	Cambridge cir WC2
82 C 10	Cambridge clo Hounsl
104 J 20	Cambridge clo SW20
104 J 20	Cambridge clo SW20
73 O 17	Cambridge cotts Rich
63 N 7	Cambridge cres E2
135 W 9	Cambridge cres E2
101 X 11	Cambridge cres Tedd
94 E 13	Cambridge dri SE12
131 X 15	Cambridge ga NW1
131 Y 15	Cambridge Gate ms NW1
136 K 4	Cambridge gdns W10
117 P 3	Cambridge gdns Kingst
129 V 9	Cambridge gdns NW6
8 K 9	Cambridge gdns Enf
31 N 1	Cambridge gdns N17
18 A 2	Cambridge gdns N21
95 Y 20	Cambridge grn SE9
109 Z 19	Cambridge gro SE20
144 A 7	Cambridge gro W6
74 K 10	Cambridge gro W6
117 P 4	Cambridge Grove rd Kingst
117 P 5	Cambridge Grove rd Kingst
63 O 9	Cambridge Heath rd E2
135 Y 5	Cambridge Heath rd E2
63 N 3	Cambridge Lodge vlls E9
50 D 19	Cambridge pass E9
34 F 19	Cambridge pk E11
84 E 17	Cambridge pk Twick
137 Z 19	Cambridge pl W8
118 B 8	Cambridge rd New Mald
22 J 16	Cambridge rd Harrow
117 Z 8	Cambridge rd New Mald
54 B 20	Cambridge rd Bark
112 F 18	Cambridge rd Brom
154 K 11	Cambridge rd Carsh
34 D 20	Cambridge rd E11
20 K 5	Cambridge rd E4
100 F 17	Cambridge rd Hampt
82 C 9	Cambridge rd Hounsl
54 J 1	Cambridge rd Ilf
117 R 5	Cambridge rd Kingst
121 U 6	Cambridge rd Mitch
129 U 12	Cambridge rd NW6
129 V 10	Cambridge rd NW6
73 O 19	Cambridge rd Rich
70 E 3	Cambridge rd S'hall
123 Z 5	Cambridge rd SE20
114 H 10	Cambridge rd Sidcp
88 L 3	Cambridge rd SW11
86 D 6	Cambridge rd SW13
118 H 1	Cambridge rd SW20
104 L 20	Cambridge rd SW20
101 X 11	Cambridge rd Tedd
84 G 15	Cambridge rd Twick
71 V 5	Cambridge rd W7
70 O 10	Cambridge Road north W4
73 S 14	Cambridge Road south W4
79 N 14	Cambridge row SE18
138 K 5	Cambridge sq W2
148 A 10	Cambridge st SW1
147 Y 8	Cambridge st SW1
18 F 3	Cambridge ter Enf
131 X 14	Cambridge ter NW1
131 Y 14	Cambridge Terrace ms NW1
65 T 13	Cambus rd E16
79 X 19	Camdale rd SE18
91 U 1	Camden av S'hall
114 B 20	Camden clo Chisl
122 J 4	Camden gdns Thntn Hth
131 Z 1	Camden gdns NW1
153 Z 12	Camden gdns Sutton
113 Z 15	Camden gro Chisl
151 N 20	Camden gro SE15
132 A 6	Camden High st NW1
131 Y 2	Camden High st NW1
109 T 15	Camden Hill rd SE19
47 Z 16	Camden la N7
131 W 1	Camden Lock pl NW1
47 X 18	Camden ms NW1
113 Y 20	Camden Park rd Chisl
47 Y 18	Camden Park rd NW1
133 V 8	Camden pas N1
113 X 17	Camden pk Chisl
113 Y 19	Camden pl Chisl
98 A 20	Camden rd Bxly
154 L 7	Camden rd Carsh
34 H 18	Camden rd E11
32 K 18	Camden rd E17
48 B 13	Camden rd N7
47 X 18	Camden rd N7
132 A 2	Camden rd N1
153 Z 11	Camden rd Sutton
94 A 5	Camden row SE3
47 X 19	Camden sq NW1
132 A 2	Camden st NW1
131 Z 1	Camden st NW1
122 J 5	Camden way Thntn Hth
113 V 18	Camden way Chisl
133 X 7	Camden wlk N1
63 W 17	Camdenhurst st E14
78 B 2	Camel rd E16
82 J 18	Camelia pl Twick
148 J 20	Camellia st SW8
79 R 7	Camelot clo SE18
105 X 9	Camelot clo SW19
146 E 14	Camera pl SW10
19 N 15	Cameron clo N18
15 U 8	Cameron clo N20
15 V 8	Cameron clo N20
143 X 4	Cameron pl E1
126 E 11	Cameron rd Brom
122 J 15	Cameron rd Croy
54 H 4	Cameron rd Ilf
110 M 5	Cameron rd SE6
66 L 19	Cameron st E6
151 V 6	Camilla rd SE16
112 D 9	Camlan rd Brom
135 N 16	Camlet st E2
4 L 8	Camlet way Barnt
5 R 5	Camlet way Barnt
132 E 5	Camley st NW1
142 K 4	Camomile st EC3
104 L 13	Camp rd SW19
104 L 12	Camp view SW19
87 Y 2	Campana rd SW6
36 M 14	Campbell av Ilf
95 X 3	Campbell clo SE18
101 O 3	Campbell clo Twick
12 C 15	Campbell Croft Edg
122 H 15	Campbell rd Croy
52 A 13	Campbell rd E15
32 M 12	Campbell rd E17
64 B 9	Campbell rd E3
66 D 4	Campbell rd E6
31 W 4	Campbell rd N17
101 P 3	Campbell rd Twick
71 T 1	Campbell rd W7
130 E 19	Campbell st W2
47 W 10	Campdale rd N7
105 S 5	Campden clo SW19
42 B 8	Campden cres Wemb
55 T 10	Campden cres Dgnhm
137 V 16	Campden gro W8
137 S 14	Campden Hill gdns W8
137 V 13	Campden Hill pl W11
107 T 15	Campden Hill rd W0
137 R 14	Campden Hill sq W8
137 S 16	Campden hill W8
137 U 16	Campden House clo W8
157 T 11	Campden rd S Croy
137 U 14	Campden st W8
143 O 6	Campfield rd SE9
94 M 18	Campfield rd SE9
95 N 18	Campfield rd SE9
66 H 19	Campion clo E6
25 N 19	Campion clo Harrow
157 S 10	Campion clo S Croy
80 B 3	Campion pl SE28
83 W 1	Campion rd Islwrth
86 L 12	Campion rd SW15
45 P 10	Campion rd NW2
24 J 14	Camplin rd Harrow
75 T 19	Camplin st SE14
30 A 11	Campsbourne rd N8
30 B 12	Campsbourne the N8
68 D 2	Campsey gdns Dgnhm
68 D 1	Campsey rd Dgnhm
30 A 10	Campsfield rd N8
93 U 13	Campshill pl SE13
93 U 13	Campshill rd SE13
32 L 18	Campus rd E17
24 L 6	Camrose av Edg
25 R 2	Camrose av Edg
81 W 17	Camrose av Erith
119 Y 9	Camrose clo SW19
79 Z 12	Camrose clo SE2
17 Z 18	Canada av N18
61 U 13	Canada cres W3
61 U 13	Canada rd W3
75 T 6	Canada st SE16
62 K 20	Canada way W12
111 P 2	Canadian av SE6
93 P 20	Canadian av SE6
63 V 11	Canal clo E1
151 U 13	Canal gro SE15
91 W 1	Canal head SE15
63 W 12	Canal rd E3
150 E 15	Canal st SE5
134 G 3	Canal wlk N1
110 D 12	Canal wlk SE26
76 B 2	Canary wharf E14
69 Z 2	Canberra clo Dgnhm
26 G 10	Canberra clo NW9
69 Z 1	Canberra cres Dgnhm
80 H 17	Canberra rd Bxly Hth
66 H 4	Canberra rd E6
78 A 17	Canberra rd SE7
77 Y 18	Canberra rd SE7
102 M 19	Canberra av Kingst
109 W 8	Canbury ms SE26
116 K 1	Canbury Park rd Kingst
117 N 1	Canbury Park rd Kingst
116 H 1	Canbury pas Kingst

116 J 1	Canbury pl Kingst
90 G 1	Cancell rd SW9
88 J 5	Candahar rd SW11
31 P 18	Candler st N15
57 Y 4	Candover rd Hornch
140 A 1	Candover st W1
63 Z 3	Candy st E3
46 D 19	Canfield gdns NW6
46 C 18	Canfield pl NW6
35 P 2	Canfield rd Wdfd Grn
58 D 3	Canford av Nthlt
7 U 9	Canford clo Enf
117 Z 15	Canford gdns New Mald
89 N 12	Canford rd SW11
123 S 6	Canham rd SE25
74 A 5	Canham rd W3
107 W 18	Canmore gdns SW16
51 Z 12	Cann Hall rd E11
30 D 4	Canning cres N22
91 R 6	Canning cross SE5
138 A 20	Canning pas W8
138 B 20	Canning Place ms W8
157 U 2	Canning rd Croy
64 L 6	Canning rd E15
32 K 12	Canning rd E17
23 U 10	Canning rd Harrow
48 K 9	Canning rd N5
55 S 18	Cannington rd Dgnhm
104 M 13	Cannizaro ho SW19
105 N 13	Cannizaro rd SW19
100 K 14	Cannon clo Hampt
118 M 7	Cannon clo SW20
119 N 7	Cannon clo SW20
76 A 1	Cannon dri E14
119 R 8	Cannon Hill la SW20
16 L 9	Cannon hill N14
45 Z 14	Cannon hill NW6
46 F 9	Cannon la NW3
40 A 3	Cannon la Pinn
22 B 20	Cannon la Pinn
46 E 10	Cannon pl NW3
98 A 3	Cannon rd Bxly Hth
16 M 11	Cannon rd N14
17 N 11	Cannon rd N14
140 K 18	Cannon row SW1
142 A 7	Cannon st EC4
160 E 8	Cannon st EC4
143 W 9	Cannon St rd E1
142 D 10	Cannon street sta EC4
22 A 19	Cannonbury av Pinn
11 X 20	Cannons pk Stanm
37 V 17	Canon av Rom
75 R 4	Canon Beck rd SE16
126 M 5	Canon rd Brom
127 N 5	Canon rd Brom
134 B 5	Canon st N1
92 B 17	Canonbie rd SE23
48 L 20	Canonbury gro N1
48 J 20	Canonbury la N1
48 L 18	Canonbury Park north N1
48 L 19	Canonbury Park south N1
48 K 19	Canonbury pl N1
8 D 6	Canonbury rd Enf
48 J 19	Canonbury rd N1
48 J 20	Canonbury st N1
48 L 20	Canonbury st N1
133 Y 1	Canons vlls N1
12 A 18	Canons clo Edg
46 G 1	Canons clo N2
11 Y 18	Canons dr Edg
12 A 19	Canons dr Edg
24 K 1	Canons Park clo Edg
158 F 4	Canons wlk Croy
68 E 2	Canonsleigh rd Dgnhm
55 R 20	Canonsleigh rd Dgnhm
135 W 13	Canrobert st E2
47 X 18	Cantelowes rd NW1
35 R 20	Canterbury av Ilf
53 S 2	Canterbury av Ilf
115 T 3	Canterbury av Sidcp
111 P 20	Canterbury clo Bcknhm
66 G 17	Canterbury clo E6
58 K 15	Canterbury clo Grnfd
90 F 8	Canterbury ct Brix
108 G 8	Canterbury gro SE27
149 Y 8	Canterbury pl SE17
22 M 16	Canterbury rd Harrow
23 N 16	Canterbury rd Harrow
122 G 16	Canterbury rd Croy
33 U 20	Canterbury rd Enf
100 C 4	Canterbury rd Felt
120 B 12	Canterbury rd Mrdn
129 T 9	Canterbury rd NW6
129 S 10	Canterbury ter NW6
36 B 18	Cantley gdns Ilf
123 V 1	Cantley gdns SE19
71 X 8	Cantley rd W7
64 B 18	Canton st E14
63 Z 12	Cantrell rd E3
78 L 19	Cantwell rd SE18
75 R 10	Canute gdns SE16
141 Z 13	Canvey st SE1
53 Z 20	Cape clo Bark
31 W 11	Cape rd N17
156 C 10	Capel av Wallgtn
127 S 20	Capel clo Brom
15 S 10	Capel clo N20
54 K 12	Capel gdns Ilf
22 F 12	Capel gdns Pinn
15 V 1	Capel rd Barnt
5 W 20	Capel rd Barnt
53 N 10	Capel rd E12
52 M 10	Capel rd E7
106 B 1	Capern rd SW18
139 S 19	Caperners clo SW1
73 O 13	Capital Interchange way Brentf
25 W 10	Capitol way NW9
62 C 6	Caple rd NW10
132 D 19	Capper st WC1
58 A 13	Caprea clo Hay
123 V 18	Capri rd Croy
7 T 8	Capstan ride Enf
76 H 6	Capstan sq E14
75 X 3	Capstan way SE16
112 C 9	Capstone rd Brom
40 E 5	Capthorne av Harrow
11 N 20	Capuchin clo Stanm
51 R 1	Capworth st E10
33 S 20	Capworth st E10
137 S 4	Caradoc clo W2
76 M 13	Caradoc st SE10
3 I O 14	Caradon way N15
109 T 16	Carberry rd SE19
73 O 5	Carbery av W3
63 Y 17	Carbis rd E14
31 Y 6	Carbuncle Passage way N17
131 Z 19	Carburton st W1
76 F 7	Cardale st E14
92 A 9	Carden rd SE15
9 O 14	Cardiff rd Enf
71 Y 8	Cardiff rd W7
79 U 18	Cardiff st SE18
55 N 6	Cardigan gdns Ilf
63 Z 6	Cardigan rd E3
84 K 16	Cardigan rd Rich
86 G 4	Cardigan rd SW13
106 C 16	Cardigan rd SW19
149 S 10	Cardigan st SE11
119 S 15	Cardinal av Mrdn
102 K 14	Cardinal av Tedd
150 F 3	Cardinal Bourne st SE1
142 A 11	Cardinal Cap all SE1
114 G 20	Cardinal clo Chisl
119 S 15	Cardinal clo Mrdn
152 F 8	Cardinal clo Worc Pk
117 V 3	Cardinal cres New Mald
87 P 9	Cardinal pl SW15
100 M 18	Cardinal's wlk Hampt
47 X 3	Cardinals way N19
151 W 18	Cardine ms SE15
82 A 11	Cardington sq Hounsl
132 B 13	Cardington st NW1
48 B 15	Cardozo rd N7
15 U 16	Cardrew av N12
15 V 16	Cardrew clo N12
74 J 9	Cardross st W6
78 H 11	Cardwell rd SE18
48 D 8	Carew clo N7
121 N 3	Carew rd Mitch
31 X 8	Carew rd N17
122 J 7	Carew rd Thntn Hth
72 D 5	Carew rd W13
155 W 12	Carew rd Wallgtn
90 K 4	Carew st SE5
89 W 3	Carey gdns SW8
160 B 4	Carey la EC2
148 E 7	Carey pl SW1
55 Z 12	Carey rd Dgnhm
141 R 5	Carey st WC2
57 U 13	Carfax rd Hornch
106 B 1	Cargill rd SW18
123 V 9	Cargreen pl SE25
123 V 10	Cargreen rd SE25
110 L 2	Carholme rd SE23
115 V 2	Carisbrooke av Bxly
24 G 7	Carisbrooke clo Stanm
8 G 7	Carisbrooke clo Enf
126 L 10	Carisbrooke rd Brom
32 J 15	Carisbrooke rd E17
121 Z 9	Carisbrooke rd Mitch
47 S 14	Carkers la NW5
155 X 18	Carleton av Wallgtn
47 Z 11	Carleton rd N7
107 N 18	Carlingford gdns Mitch
119 O 15	Carlingford rd Mrdn
30 H 12	Carlingford rd N15
46 G 12	Carlingford rd NW3
142 M 7	Carlisle av EC3
62 A 18	Carlisle av W3
63 Z 7	Carlisle clo E3
24 G 20	Carlisle gdns Harrow
35 P 19	Carlisle gdns Ilf
141 R 20	Carlisle la SE1
149 P 1	Carlisle la SW1
130 H 20	Carlisle ms NW8
148 A 3	Carlisle pl SW1
51 P 5	Carlisle rd E10
100 K 17	Carlisle rd Hampt
48 G 2	Carlisle rd N4
128 L 5	Carlisle rd NW6
25 W 9	Carlisle rd NW9
39 U 17	Carlisle rd Rom
153 V 13	Carlisle rd Sutton
140 E 5	Carlisle st W1
139 V 9	Carlos pl W1
132 A 7	Carlow st NW1
24 A 17	Carlton av Harrow
6 K 16	Carlton av N14
157 R 16	Carlton av S Croy
42 G 6	Carlton Avenue east Wemb
42 C 7	Carlton Avenue west Wemb
12 B 16	Carlton clo Edg
47 N 7	Carlton clo NW3
153 S 8	Carlton cres Sutton
36 D 11	Carlton dri Ilf
87 N 14	Carlton dri SW15
140 E 14	Carlton gdns SW1
60 E 19	Carlton gdns W5
92 A 1	Carlton gro SE15
151 X 20	Carlton gro SE15
130 C 6	Carlton hill NW8
129 Z 9	Carlton hill NW8
140 G 13	Carlton House ter SW1
119 O 3	Carlton Park av SW20
52 B 3	Carlton rd E11
53 O 13	Carlton rd E12
32 H 6	Carlton rd E17
81 X 17	Carlton rd Erith
16 B 16	Carlton rd N11
31 T 12	Carlton rd N4
48 F 2	Carlton rd N4
118 A 3	Carlton rd New Mald
39 Y 13	Carlton rd Rom
157 P 16	Carlton rd S Croy
114 M 11	Carlton rd Sidcp
85 U 9	Carlton rd SW14
73 Y 7	Carlton rd W4
60 D 19	Carlton rd W5
93 T 7	Carlton rd Welling
53 T 11	Carlton sq E1
140 E 12	Carlton st SW1
34 H 15	Carlton ter E11
18 B 12	Carlton ter N18
110 B 8	Carlton ter SE26
147 R 1	Carlton Tower pl SW1
129 S 10	Carlton vale NW6
106 H 13	Carlwell st SW17
127 N 7	Carlyle av Dgnhm
58 F 19	Carlyle av S'hall
28 E 19	Carlyle clo N2
58 D 19	Carlyle gdns S'hall
157 Y 2	Carlyle rd Croy
53 R 12	Carlyle rd E12
68 F 20	Carlyle rd SE28
72 F 11	Carlyle rd W5
146 H 12	Carlyle sq SW3
40 F 11	Carlyon av Harrow
60 J 4	Carlyon clo Wemb
60 L 4	Carlyon rd Wemb
87 N 11	Carmalt gdns SW15
137 V 17	Carmel ct W8
23 N 5	Carmelite clo Harrow
23 O 8	Carmelite rd Harrow
141 V 8	Carmelite st EC4
23 O 7	Carmelite way Harrow
23 N 6	Carmelite wlk Harrow
64 D 11	Carmen st E14
88 G 9	Carmichael clo SW11
123 W 19	Carmichael rd SE25
107 S 4	Carminia rd SW17
140 B 8	Carnaby st W1
109 O 8	Carnac st SE27
33 X 5	Carnanton rd E17
8 F 10	Carnarvon av Enf
4 E 11	Carnarvon rd Barnt
33 U 17	Carnarvon rd E10
52 B 17	Carnarvon rd E15
34 B 5	Carnarvon rd E18
80 C 13	Carnation st SE2
95 S 14	Carnecke gdns SE9
105 N 6	Carnegie pl SW19
133 O 6	Carnegie st N1
57 W 14	Carnforth gdns Hornch
107 W 17	Carnforth rd SW16
133 N 1	Carnoustie dri N1
88 A 8	Carnworth rd SW6
87 Y 8	Carnworth rd SW6
132 A 4	Carol st NW1
122 K 2	Carolina rd Thntn Hth
157 S 9	Caroline clo Croy
71 S 20	Caroline clo Islwth
137 Y 10	Caroline clo W2
10 M 18	Caroline ct Stanm
134 L 12	Caroline gdns E2
137 Y 9	Caroline gdns W2
137 Y 10	Caroline Place ms W2
105 U 18	Caroline rd SW19
63 T 18	Caroline st E1
147 T 6	Caroline ter SW1
139 W 10	Carpenter st W1
64 G 2	Carpenters rd E15
61 G 19	Carpenters rd E15
32 M 7	Carr rd E17
41 N 18	Carr rd Grnfd
40 H 19	Carr rd Nthlt
63 W 15	Carr st E14
147 U 17	Carriage Drive east SW11
147 V 15	Carriage Drive west SW11
89 N 1	Carriage Drive south SW11
147 N 19	Carriage Drive west SW11
83 Y 8	Carrick clo Islwth
60 L 11	Carrick clo W5
31 P 3	Carrick gdns N17
31 R 3	Carrick gdns N17
80 K 10	Carrill way Blvdr
82 K 14	Carrington av Hounsl
85 P 11	Carrington st W1
139 X 14	Carrington st W1
52 B 15	Carrol clo E15
47 R 13	Carrol clo NW5
47 R 13	Carrol pl NW5
72 K 8	Carron clo E14
79 R 8	Carronade pl SE18
149 O 17	Carroun rd SW8
55 R 20	Carrow rd Dgnhm
59 R 8	Carroway la Grnfd
8 A 17	Carrs la Enf
7 Z 16	Carrs la N21
154 G 10	Carshalton gro Sutton
154 L 9	Carshalton ho Carsh
154 M 10	Carshalton Park rd Carsh
155 O 10	Carshalton pl Carsh
121 O 12	Carshalton rd Mitch
154 E 11	Carshalton rd Sutton
86 M 15	Carslake rd SW15
5 Y 15	Carson rd Barnt
65 T 14	Carson rd E16
109 N 3	Carson rd SE21
111 U 7	Carstairs rd SE6
94 D 13	Carston clo SE12
35 O 12	Carswell clo Ilf
93 U 18	Carswell rd SE6
20 L 4	Cart la E4
38 F 1	Carter clo Rom
155 Y 15	Carter clo Wallgtn
38 G 2	Carter dri Rom
141 Y 7	Carter la EC4
150 B 11	Carter pl SE17
65 U 4	Carter rd E13
116 F 15	Carter rd SW19
150 A 12	Carter st SE17
149 Z 12	Carter st SE17

140 F 19 Carteret st SW1
75 W 11 Carteret way SE8
8 L 7 Carterhatch la Enf
9 N 8 Carterhatch la Enf
9 P 8 Carterhatch rd Enf
153 P 2 Carters clo Worc Pk
112 M 1 Carters Hill clo SE9
110 J 5 Carters la SE23
87 Y 13 Carters yd SW18
74 J 8 Carthew rd W6
74 K 8 Carthew vlls W6
133 Z 20 Carthusian st EC1
140 M 10 Carting la WC2
32 A 1 Cartmel clo N17
98 D 1 Cartmel rd Bxly Hth
120 C 12 Cartmell gdns Mrdn
132 H 14 Cartwright gdns WC1
56 A 19 Cartwright rd Dgnhm
69 N 1 Cartwright rd Dgnhm
143 P 10 Cartwright st E1
90 L 15 Carver rd SE24
47 Y 4 Carverley gro N19
72 J 12 Carville cres Brentf
52 B 10 Cary rd E11
49 O 11 Carysfort rd N16
29 Y 15 Carysfort rd N8
29 U 12 Cascade av N10
75 T 20 Casella rd SE14
108 H 10 Casewick rd SE27
50 B 8 Casimir rd E5
91 O 12 Casino av SE24
135 Y 17 Caslon pl E1
150 E 18 Caspian st SE5
66 A 18 Caspian wlk E16
61 Z 1 Casselden rd NW10
145 U 20 Cassidy rd SW5
80 A 12 Cassilda rd SE2
84 C 14 Cassilis rd Twick
32 G 17 Cassiobury rd E17
123 N 9 Cassland rd Thntn Hth
50 H 19 Cassland rd E9
92 L 19 Casslee rd SE6
143 S 1 Casson st E1
76 G 7 Castalia st E14
130 A 18 Castellain rd W9
129 X 15 Castellain rd W9
39 Z 10 Castellane av Rom
23 W 1 Castellane clo Stanm
86 M 13 Castellane av SW15
74 J 17 Castelnau pl SW13
74 H 18 Castelnau SW13
86 H 2 Castelnau SW13
94 F 8 Casterbridge rd SE3
78 J 10 Castile rd SE18
112 A 4 Castillon rd SE6
111 Z 5 Castillon rd SE6
110 L 5 Castlands rd SE6
20 K 17 Castle av E4
152 H 20 Castle av Epsom
141 Z 9 Castle Baynard st EC4
125 Y 7 Castle clo BR2
115 O 5 Castle clo SW19
160 G 7 Castle ct EC3
35 R 18 Castle dri Ilf
68 B 3 Castle gdns Dgnhm
159 U 18 Castle Hill av Croy
148 B 1 Castle la SW1
47 R 19 Castle ms NW5
68 C 4 Castle rd Dgnhm
9 V 4 Castle rd Enf
83 V 4 Castle rd Islwth
15 S 17 Castle rd N12
40 J 19 Castle rd Nthlt
47 T 19 Castle rd NW1
70 E 8 Castle rd S'hall
65 Z 6 Castle st E6
116 J 2 Castle st Kingst
152 H 20 Castle way Epsom
105 O 5 Castle way SW19
47 P 1 Castle yd N6
60 C 15 Castlebar hill W5
60 C 13 Castlebar ms W5
60 B 13 Castlebar pk W5
60 E 16 Castlebar rd W5
87 R 19 Castlecombe dri SW19
113 P 11 Castlecombe rd SE9
109 Z 19 Castledine rd SE20
113 Z 1 Castleford av SE9
95 Z 20 Castleford av SE9
84 M 9 Castlegate SE9
47 S 19 Castlehaven rd NW1
131 X 1 Castlehaven rd NW1
8 C 17 Castleleigh ct Enf
152 K 18 Castlemaine av Epsom
157 U 11 Castlemaine S Croy

139 N 3 Castlereagh st W1
98 M 3 Castleton av Bxly Hth
99 N 4 Castleton av Bxly Hth
42 J 12 Castleton av Wemb
33 X 7 Castleton rd E17
55 O 4 Castleton rd Ilf
121 W 9 Castleton rd Mitch
113 O 10 Castleton rd SE9
144 M 11 Castletown rd W14
145 N 10 Castletown rd W14
35 S 18 Castleview gdns Ilf
95 V 4 Castlewood dri SE9
5 V 12 Castlewood rd Barnt
49 W 1 Castlewood rd E5
31 X 20 Castlewood rd N16
135 V 5 Cat & Mutton br E8
6 A 17 Cat hill Barnt
5 X 18 Cat hill Barnt
35 V 7 Caterham av Ilf
93 V 8 Caterham rd SE13
150 G 7 Catesby st SE17
93 P 19 Catford bdwy SE6
111 N 1 Catford hill SE6
93 P 19 Catford rd SE6
51 X 8 Cathall rd E11
51 Y 9 Cathall rd E11
75 N 6 Cathay st SE16
143 X 18 Cathay st SE16
47 U 10 Cathcart hill N19
146 A 13 Cathcart rd SW10
47 S 16 Cathcart st NW5
141 Z 5 Cathedral pl EC4
142 E 13 Cathedral st SE1
48 M 10 Catherall rd N5
6 H 17 Catherine ct N14
83 P 11 Catherine gdns Hounsl
93 R 1 Catherine gro SE10
140 B 20 Catherine pl SW1
39 Y 16 Catherine rd Rom
116 G 11 Catherine rd Surb
141 N 8 Catherine st WC2
142 K 2 Catherine Wheel all EC2
72 G 19 Catherine Wheel rd Brentf
140 B 15 Catherine Wheel yd SW1
89 T 17 Cathles rd SW12
74 J 7 Cathnor rd W12
9 V 1 Catistield rd Enf
151 U 10 Catlin st SE16
110 D 7 Catling clo SE23
89 Y 9 Cato rd SW4
138 M 3 Cato st W1
91 V 1 Caton st SE15
124 M 1 Cator la Becknhm
110 J 19 Cator pk Becknhm
155 N 11 Cator rd Carsh
110 F 15 Cator rd SE26
151 O 17 Cator st SE15
10 A 5 Catsey woods Bushey
113 S 11 Cattistock rd SE9
140 M 2 Catton st WC1
66 E 2 Caulfield rd E6
92 A 4 Caulfield rd SE15
155 O 4 Causeway the Carsh
28 H 13 Causeway the N2
154 D 19 Causeway the Sutton
87 Z 12 Causeway the SW18
104 M 12 Causeway the SW19
105 N 12 Causeway the SW19
101 W 14 Causeway the Tedd
19 O 3 Causeyware rd N9
47 T 1 Causton rd N6
148 G 8 Causton st SW1
89 T 14 Cautley av SW4
37 T 12 Cavalier clo Rom
146 O 12 Cavaye pl SW10
65 W 8 Cave rd E13
102 C 9 Cave rd Rich
7 U 8 Cavell dri Enf
31 O 2 Cavell rd N17
63 N 16 Cavell rd E13
143 Y 4 Cavell st E1
34 G 3 Cavendish av Wdfd Grn
118 H 10 Cavendish av New Mald
96 M 8 Cavendish av Welling
81 W 17 Cavendish av Erith
41 T 13 Cavendish av Harrow
57 Y 18 Cavendish av Hornch
27 X 8 Cavendish av N3
130 G 13 Cavendish av NW8
97 N 18 Cavendish av Sidcp
59 Y 16 Cavendish av W13
130 G 12 Cavendish clo NW8

45 U 19 Cavendish clo NW8
57 Y 18 Cavendish cres Hornchurch
142 K 3 Cavendish ct EC2
51 X 3 Cavendish dri E11
12 A 19 Cavendish dri Edg
54 L 15 Cavendish gdns Bark
53 W 3 Cavendish gdns Ilf
37 Z 17 Cavendish gdns Rom
139 Y 1 Cavendish mews north W1
139 Y 1 Cavendish mews south W1
139 Y 3 Cavendish pl W1
118 C 10 Cavendish rd New Mald
4 A 12 Cavendish rd Barnt
122 J 19 Cavendish rd Croy
20 H 20 Cavendish rd E4
19 N 16 Cavendish rd N18
30 H 18 Cavendish rd N4
45 U 19 Cavendish rd NW6
154 C 15 Cavendish rd Sutton
107 T 1 Cavendish rd SW12
89 T 17 Cavendish rd SW12
106 H 17 Cavendish rd SW19
106 J 17 Cavendish rd SW19
85 W 1 Cavendish rd W4
139 Y 4 Cavendish sq W1
134 E 9 Cavendish st N1
125 P 20 Cavendish way W Wkhm
54 E 10 Cavenham gdns Ilf
118 H 18 Caverleigh way Worc Pk
17 T 10 Cavershan av N13
162 R 2 Caversham av Sutton
30 L 13 Caversham rd N15
47 U 17 Caversham rd NW5
147 N 13 Caversham st SW3
136 B 4 Caverswall st W12
62 L 16 Caverswall rd SW19
31 T 3 Cavert st NW1
127 W 1 Caveside clo Chisl
71 Z 10 Cawdor cres W7
109 T 14 Cawnpore st SE19
64 A 7 Caxton gro E3
30 D 8 Caxton rd N22
106 C 13 Caxton rd SW19
136 E 16 Caxton rd W12
148 D 1 Caxton st SW1
65 P 19 Caxton Street north E16
77 R 1 Caxton Street south E16
126 C 9 Caygill clo Brom
134 D 13 Cayton pl EC1
59 U 7 Cayton rd Grnfd
134 D 13 Cayton st EC1
33 O 6 Cazenove rd E17
49 Y 5 Cazenove rd N16
54 D 20 Cecil av Enf
8 G 14 Cecil av Enf
42 M 16 Cecil av Wemb
4 C 10 Cecil ct Barnt
140 H 10 Cecil ct WC2
22 D 13 Cecil pk Pinn
120 M 9 Cecil pl Mitch
121 N 11 Cecil pl Mitch
122 C 16 Cecil rd Croy
52 A 8 Cecil rd E11
65 T 4 Cecil rd E13
33 O 3 Cecil rd E17
8 R 14 Cecil rd Enf
7 Z 13 Cecil rd Enf
23 S 10 Cecil rd Harrow
83 N 6 Cecil rd Hounsl
53 Y 12 Cecil rd Ilf
29 T 7 Cecil rd N10
16 F 5 Cecil rd N14
62 A 4 Cecil rd NW10
25 Z 11 Cecil rd NW9
55 X 1 Cecil rd Rom
153 V 14 Cecil rd Sutton
106 A 18 Cecil rd SW19
H W 15 Cecil rd W3
126 E 19 Cecil way Brom
30 A 19 Cecile pk N8
28 C 10 Cecilia clo N2
49 W 15 Cecilia rd E8
15 W 1 Cedar av Barnt
9 P 8 Cedar av Enf
37 Y 15 Cedar av Rom
96 M 17 Cedar av Sidcp
82 M 15 Cedar av Twick
127 T 2 Cedar clo Brom
38 L 12 Cedar clo Rom
154 M 12 Cedar clo SM5
103 X 10 Cedar clo SW15
127 T 3 Cedar copse Brom

105 P 8 Cedar ct SW19
28 H 13 Cedar dri Barnt
154 D 14 Cedar gdns Sutton
97 V 16 Cedar gro Bxly
58 H 14 Cedar gro S'hall
72 J 7 Cedar gro W5
102 J 1 Cedar heights Rich
14 F 17 Cedar Lawn av Barnt
113 N 2 Cedar mt SE9
55 V 1 Cedar Park gdns Rom
8 A 3 Cedar Park rd Enf
126 L 3 Cedar rd Brom
7 X 4 Cedar rd Enf
99 W 2 Cedar rd Erith
31 V 4 Cedar rd N17
45 N 12 Cedar rd NW2
38 K 14 Cedar rd Rom
154 C 14 Cedar rd Sutton
101 Y 13 Cedar rd Tedd
16 C 2 Cedar ri N14
84 L 10 Cedar ter Rich
108 J 12 Cedar Tree gro SE27
132 F 2 Cedar way NW1
89 R 10 Cedar's ms SW4
89 S 10 Cedar's rd SW4
94 K 14 Cedarhurst dri SE9
145 W 19 Cedarne rd SW6
156 B 7 Cedars av Croy
33 O 15 Cedars av E17
121 P 8 Cedars av Mitch
27 O 10 Cedars clo NW4
18 E 7 Cedars ct N9
124 L 3 Cedars rd Becknhm
156 B 7 Cedars rd Croy
52 A 18 Cedars rd E15
102 C 20 Cedars rd Kingst
119 Y 8 Cedars rd Mrdn
17 W 7 Cedars rd N21
18 K 9 Cedars rd N9
86 F 5 Cedars rd SW13
73 V 15 Cedars rd W4
21 T 6 Cedars the Buck Hl
101 X 15 Cedars the Tedd
108 D 16 Cedarville gdns SW16
39 R 10 Cedric av Rom
114 B 6 Cedric rd SE9
80 B 4 Celadine dri SE28
64 A 15 Celandine clo E14
80 C 3 Celandine dri SE28
64 M 9 Celandine way E15
137 Y 3 Celbridge ms W2
47 V 12 Celia rd N19
126 A 7 Celtic av Brom
125 Z 7 Celtic av Brom
64 F 13 Celtic st E14
78 D 17 Cemetery la SE7
52 D 13 Cemetery rd E7
31 T 3 Cemetery rd N17
80 C 19 Cemetery rd SE2
45 Z 8 Cenacle clo NW3
149 R 1 Centaur st SE1
9 X 13 Centenary rd Enf
51 X 7 Central av E11
8 M 8 Central av Enf
9 N 8 Central av Enf
83 O 12 Central av Hounsl
28 F 7 Central av N12
18 F 10 Central av N9
22 D 19 Central av Pinn
147 R 19 Central av SW1
156 B 11 Central av Wallgtn
96 M 4 Central av Welling
109 P 14 Central hill SE19
141 W 2 Central mkts EC1
56 H 10 Central Park av Dgnhm
66 F 6 Central Park rd E6
65 Z 7 Central Park rd E6
59 Y 8 Central pde Grnfd
56 L 7 Central pk Rom
120 B 10 Central rd Wemb
42 B 15 Central rd Wemb
152 H 2 Central rd Worc Pk
85 V 7 Central School pth SW14
27 Z 17 Central sq NW11
134 A 16 Central st EC1
133 Z 12 Central st EC1
154 J 16 Central way Carsh
80 A 1 Central way SE28
68 C 20 Central way SE28
79 Z 3 Central way SE28
73 Y 3 Centre av W3
114 B 17 Centre Common rd Chisl
69 V 5 Centre rd Dgnhm
78 H 13 Centre rd SE18
63 N 7 Centre st E2

135 W 9	Centre st E2	
33 T 3	Centre way E4	
54 B 7	Centre way Ilf	
19 S 8	Centre way N9	
48 C 20	Centurion clo N7	
81 R 7	Centurion way Blvdr	
32 H 11	Century rd E17	
63 R 12	Cephas av E1	
63 O 12	Cephas st E1	
135 Z 17	Cephas st E1	
79 X 12	Cerise rd SE18	
91 X 3	Cerise rd SE15	
120 C 14	Cerne rd Mrdn	
135 S 6	Cester st E2	
144 J 2	Ceylon rd W14	
35 U 9	Chadacre av Ilf	
152 J 12	Chadacre rd Epsom	
64 E 15	Chadbourn st E14	
127 S 7	Chadd dri Brom	
65 S 4	Chadd grn E13	
37 V 16	Chadville gdns Rom	
55 U 5	Chadway Dgnhm	
55 R 1	Chadwell av Rom	
37 S 17	Chadwell Heath la Rom	
133 U 11	Chadwell st EC1	
20 L 12	Chadwick av E4	
101 Z 15	Chadwick clo Tedd	
34 A 20	Chadwick rd E11	
53 Z 9	Chadwick rd Ilf	
62 E 2	Chadwick rd NW10	
91 U 5	Chadwick rd SE15	
148 F 3	Chadwick st SW1	
65 V 14	Chadwin rd E13	
124 F 13	Chaffinch av Croy	
124 F 13	Chaffinch clo Croy	
124 K 1	Chaffinch rd Becknhm	
37 S 14	Chafford way Rom	
131 P 18	Chagford st NW1	
8 F 8	Chailey av Enf	
50 C 10	Chailey st E5	
133 R 8	Chalbury wlk N1	
80 D 8	Chalcombe rd SE2	
153 X 16	Chalcot clo Sutton	
131 R 3	Chalcot cres NW1	
46 L 18	Chalcot gdns NW3	
131 S 2	Chalcot rd NW1	
131 S 1	Chalcot sq NW1	
93 Z 13	Chalcroft rd SE13	
144 L 17	Chaldon rd SW6	
90 A 17	Chale rd SW2	
43 T 18	Chalfont av Wemb	
26 C 11	Chalfont ct NW9	
18 F 10	Chalfont grn N9	
18 F 11	Chalfont rd N9	
123 V 6	Chalfont rd SE25	
72 A 9	Chalfont way W13	
109 P 8	Chalford rd SE21	
35 N 3	Chalford wlk Wdfd Grn	
119 Y 12	Chalgrove av Mrdn	
35 P 7	Chalgrove cres Ilf	
27 T 10	Chalgrove gdns N3	
31 Z 4	Chalgrove rd N17	
154 F 17	Chalgrove rd Sutton	
155 X 13	Chalice clo Wallgtn	
47 O 20	Chalk Farm rd NW1	
6 A 13	Chalk la Barnt	
5 Z 12	Chalk la Barnt	
154 C 12	Chalk Pit way SM1	
65 W 14	Chalk rd E13	
144 G 8	Chalkhill rd W6	
43 R 9	Chalkhill rd Wemb	
43 V 9	Chalklands Wemb	
97 N 1	Chalkstone clo Welling	
8 C 15	Chalkwell Park av Enf	
90 D 20	Challice way SW2	
110 B 19	Challin st SE20	
72 G 13	Challis rd Brentf	
28 F 8	Challoner clo N2	
145 O 11	Challoner cres W14	
145 O 11	Challoner st W14	
92 M 10	Chalsey rd SE4	
28 F 18	Chalton dri N2	
132 D 8	Chalton st NW1	
143 P 8	Chamber st E1	
125 P 19	Chamberlain cres W Wckm	
28 D 8	Chamberlain rd N2	
18 J 9	Chamberlain rd N9	
131 P 1	Chamberlain st NW1	
116 K 19	Chamberlain way Surb	
128 D 7	Chamberlayne rd NW10	
62 M 2	Chamberlayne rd NW10	
28 F 5	Chambers gdns N2	
128 B 1	Chambers la NW10	
62 L 1	Chambers la NW10	
44 L 20	Chambers la NW10	
48 A 12	Chambers rd N7	
143 T 18	Chambers st SE16	
135 O 13	Chambord st E2	
110 H 9	Champion gro SE26	
91 P 6	Champion gro SE5	
91 O 7	Champion hill SE5	
91 R 8	Champion hill SE5	
80 B 4	Champion la SE28	
110 J 9	Champion rd SE26	
109 O 10	Champness clo SE27	
153 T 17	Champneys clo Sutton	
141 X 14	Chancel st SE1	
156 J 18	Chancellor gdns CR2	
108 M 5	Chancellor gro SE21	
109 N 6	Chancellor gro SE21	
144 C 10	Chancellors rd W6	
144 D 11	Chancellors rd W6	
74 M 15	Chancellors rd W6	
144 C 11	Chancellors rd W6	
74 M 14	Chancellors rd W6	
80 E 11	Chancelot rd SE2	
125 S 3	Chancery la Becknhm	
141 R 3	Chancery la WC2	
114 A 6	Chanctonbury clo Chisl	
153 Z 17	Chanctonbury gdns Sutton	
14 J 14	Chanctonbury way N12	
65 S 14	Chandler av E16	
100 G 20	Chandler clo Hampt	
75 N 2	Chandler st E1	
143 X 12	Chandler st E1	
39 S 16	Chandlers way Rom	
33 P 8	Chandos av E17	
16 H 11	Chandos av N14	
15 S 5	Chandos av N20	
15 U 3	Chandos av N20	
72 F 10	Chandos av W5	
21 V 8	Chandos clo Buck Hl	
25 N 2	Chandos cres Edg	
140 K 10	Chandos pl WC2	
51 W 14	Chandos rd E15	
23 O 16	Chandos rd Harrow	
31 S 8	Chandos rd N17	
28 H 8	Chandos rd N2	
62 A 11	Chandos rd NW10	
44 M 15	Chandos rd NW2	
139 Y 3	Chandos st W1	
46 A 3	Chandos way NW11	
160 G 7	Change all EC3	
82 H 2	Channel clo Hounsl	
64 J 3	Channelsea rd E15	
64 K 1	Chant st E15	
90 D 8	Chantrey rd SW9	
7 Y 3	Chantry clo Enf	
115 Z 14	Chantry clo Sidcp	
126 M 11	Chantry la Brom	
127 N 11	Chantry la Brom	
22 K 4	Chantry pl Harrow	
22 K 4	Chantry rd Harrow	
133 Y 6	Chantry st N1	
69 Z 5	Chantry way Rainhm	
72 K 14	Chapel all Brent	
99 P 12	Chapel clo Drtfrd	
28 H 10	Chapel ct N2	
142 E 17	Chapel ct SE1	
113 T 6	Chapel Farm rd SE9	
99 P 12	Chapel hill Drtfrd	
78 F 9	Chapel hill SE18	
76 E 12	Chapel House st E14	
22 A 11	Chapel la Pinn	
55 W 1	Chapel la Rom	
133 S 8	Chapel mkt N1	
133 T 8	Chapel pl N1	
31 V 1	Chapel pl N17	
139 X 5	Chapel pl W1	
98 E 10	Chapel rd Bxly Hth	
82 M 9	Chapel rd Hounsl	
53 X 10	Chapel rd Ilf	
120 F 5	Chapel rd Mitch	
108 K 10	Chapel rd SE27	
84 C 19	Chapel rd Twick	
72 B 2	Chapel rd W13	
137 W 10	Chapel side W2	
64 K 1	Chapel st E15	
8 A 11	Chapel st Enf	
138 K 2	Chapel st NW1	
139 V 19	Chapel st SW1	
158 B 15	Chapel view S Croy	
126 F 4	Chapel way Brom	
48 C 9	Chapel way N7	
156 M 2	Chapel wlk Croy	
141 V 17	Chaplin clo SE1	
68 M 1	Chaplin rd Dgnhm	
55 Z 20	Chaplin rd Dgnhm	
65 O 5	Chaplin rd E15	
31 U 10	Chaplin rd N17	
44 H 18	Chaplin rd NW2	
42 H 18	Chaplin rd Wemb	
24 L 17	Chapman cres Harrow	
81 T 14	Chapman rd Blvdr	
122 E 19	Chapman rd Croy	
50 L 18	Chapman rd E9	
63 N 19	Chapman st E1	
143 X 8	Chapman st E1	
80 G 12	Chapman's la SE2	
44 F 16	Chapter rd NW2	
149 Y 12	Chapter rd SE17	
148 E 7	Chapter st SW1	
100 G 11	Chapter way Hampt	
73 X 16	Chara pl W4	
9 T 13	Charcroft gdns Eng	
74 A 11	Chardin rd W4	
49 X 4	Chardmore rd N16	
66 F 17	Chardwell clo E6	
136 G 18	Charecroft way W12	
65 T 15	Charford rd E16	
65 R 11	Chargeable la E13	
65 P 12	Chargeable st E16	
75 T 5	Chargrove clo SE16	
140 G 7	Charing Cross rd WC2	
130 K 9	Charlbert st NW8	
11 T 17	Charlbury av Stanm	
54 L 7	Charlbury gdns Ilf	
60 E 16	Charlbury gro W5	
113 Z 6	Charldane rd SE9	
110 A 6	Charlecote gro SE26	
55 Y 11	Charlecote rd Dgnhm	
66 H 10	Charlemont rd E6	
115 S 9	Charles clo Sidcp	
41 P 2	Charles cres Harrow	
78 J 10	Charles Grinling wlk SE18	
140 E 12	Charles II st SW11	
130 J 9	Charles la NW8	
56 M 19	Charles rd Dgnhm	
65 Y 1	Charles rd E7	
37 V 19	Charles rd Rom	
59 Z 15	Charles rd W13	
14 C 17	Charles Sevright dri NW7	
134 H 14	Charles sq N1	
77 Z 3	Charles st E16	
8 G 17	Charles st N19	
86 B 6	Charles st SE13	
139 W 12	Charles st W1	
112 M 7	Charlesfield SE9	
150 C 7	Charleston st SE17	
109 Y 12	Charleville cir SE26	
144 M 11	Charleville rd SE26	
145 N 10	Charleville rd W14	
81 X 19	Charleville rd Erith	
106 L 14	Charlmont rd SW17	
89 P 2	Charlotte Despard av SW11	
132 C 20	Charlotte ms W1	
89 U 7	Charlotte pl SW4	
140 D 2	Charlotte pl W1	
56 G 18	Charlotte rd Dgnhm	
134 K 14	Charlotte rd EC2	
86 D 2	Charlotte rd SW13	
155 V 14	Charlotte rd Wallgtn	
132 C 20	Charlotte st W1	
140 D 2	Charlotte st W1	
133 R 6	Charlotte ter N1	
77 Y 14	Charlton Church la SE7	
81 R 16	Charlton clo blvdr	
67 X 6	Charlton cres Bark	
78 A 20	Charlton dene SE7	
77 Z 19	Charlton dene SE7	
78 A 17	Charlton ho SE7	
47 X 15	Charlton Kings rd NW5	
78 C 18	Charlton Park la SE7	
78 B 17	Charlton Park SE7	
78 B 17	Charlton Park SE7	
133 W 7	Charlton pl N1	
24 J 11	Charlton rd Harrow	
19 T 1	Charlton rd N9	
62 C 3	Charlton rd NW10	
77 U 18	Charlton rd SE3	
77 W 17	Charlton rd SE7	
43 N 5	Charlton rd Wemb	
93 Y 2	Charlton way SE10	
94 A 1	Charlton way SE3	
77 P 20	Charlton way SE3	
10 G 20	Charlwood clo Harrow	
158 L 19	Charlwood Croy	
148 C 8	Charlwood pl SW1	
87 O 10	Charlwood rd SW15	
148 B 9	Charlwood st SW1	
24 G 9	Charmian av Stanm	
119 Z 4	Charminster av SW19	
113 O 10	Charminster rd SE9	
97 S 2	Charmouth rd Welling	
49 Z 11	Charnock rd E5	
119 Z 3	Charnwood av SW19	
118 B 9	Charnwood clo New Mald	
34 G 12	Charnwood dri E18	
15 P 11	Charnwood pl N20	
123 P 10	Charnwood rd SE25	
49 Y 7	Charnwood st E5	
156 K 2	Charrington rd Croy	
132 E 8	Charrington st NW1	
11 R 4	Charsley rd SE6	
126 A 2	Chart clo Brom	
124 B 13	Chart clo Croy	
134 G 13	Chart st N1	
54 E 3	Charter av Ilf	
82 A 10	Charter cres Hounsl	
97 Y 18	Charter dri Bxly	
117 T 5	Charter rd Kingst	
20 M 18	Charter Road the Wdfd Grn	
21 P 18	Charter Road the Wdfd Grn	
117 T 4	Charter sq Kingst	
16 J 1	Charter way N14	
27 V 11	Charter way N3	
42 C 14	Charterhouse av Wemb	
133 Y 19	Charterhouse sq EC1	
141 W 1	Charterhouse st EC1	
133 Y 20	Charterhouse st EC1	
34 H 1	Charteris rd Wdfd Grn	
21 W 19	Charteris rd Wdfd Grn	
48 E 5	Charteris rd N4	
129 R 5	Charteris rd NW6	
109 S 12	Charters clo SE19	
86 L 14	Chartfield av SW15	
87 P 14	Chartfield av SW15	
87 P 13	Chartfield sq SW15	
108 H 7	Chartham gro SE27	
123 Z 7	Chartham rd SE25	
44 B 10	Chartley av NW2	
10 J 19	Chartley av Stanm	
114 D 5	Chartwell pl Sutton	
153 U 7	Chartwell pl Sutton	
108 F 10	Charwood SE27	
87 P 10	Charwood ter SW15	
38 J 2	Chase Cross rd Rom	
7 X 11	Chase Court gdns Enf	
19 Z 15	Chase gdns E4	
83 S 17	Chase gdns Twick	
7 X 9	Chase Green av Enf	
7 Z 11	Chase grn Enf	
7 Y 10	Chase hill Enf	
36 D 15	Chase la Ilf	
6 H 15	Chase rd N14	
16 K 2	Chase rd N14	
61 Y 10	Chase rd NW10	
7 T 10	Chase Ridings Enf	
119 S 2	Chase Side av SW20	
7 Z 11	Chase side Enf	
126 H 5	Chase the Brom	
98 G 7	Chase the Bxly Hth	
53 N 11	Chase the E12	
25 S 5	Chase the Edg	
22 D 12	Chase the Pinn	
57 O 10	Chase the Rom	
39 O 11	Chase the Rom	
37 Y 18	Chase the Rom	
10 L 18	Chase the Stanm	
108 E 17	Chase the SW16	
119 T 1	Chase the SW20	
89 T 9	Chase the SW4	
156 B 11	Chase the Wallgtn	
16 G 5	Chase way N14	
106 M 10	Chasefield rd SW17	
107 N 11	Chasefield rd SW17	
63 V 17	Chaseley st E14	
156 G 12	Chasemore gdns Croy	
8 A 9	Chaseside av Enf	
8 A 7	Chaseside cres Enf	
7 O 18	Chaseville Park rd N21	
7 V 7	Chasewood av Enf	
99 X 17	Chastilian rd Dart	
47 N 16	Chaston st NW5	
122 J 19	Chatfield rd Croy	
88 E 8	Chatfield rd SW11	
126 D 18	Chatham av N1	
27 Z 16	Chatham clo NW11	

119 V 18 Chatham clo Sutton
50 C 17 Chatham pl E9
34 C 7 Chatham rd E17
32 H 11 Chatham rd E17
117 O 2 Chatham rd Kingst
88 L 15 Chatham rd SW11
150 F 5 Chatham st SE17
60 K 16 Chatsfield pl W5
112 G 11 Chatsworth av Brom
26 L 8 Chatsworth av NW4
115 N 1 Chatsworth av Sidcp
119 T 2 Chatsworth av SW20
43 N 16 Chatsworth av Wemb
26 L 8 Chatsworth clo NW4
83 P 9 Chatsworth cres Hounsl
18 J 1 Chatsworth dri Enf
8 K 20 Chatsworth dri Eng
118 D 11 Chatsworth dri New Mald
40 K 4 Chatsworth gdns Harrow
73 S 2 Chatsworth gdns W3
101 X 9 Chatsworth pl Tedd
157 O 7 Chatsworth rd Croy
52 B 15 Chatsworth rd E15
50 D 9 Chatsworth rd E5
45 O 18 Chatsworth rd NW2
153 R 9 Chatsworth rd Sutton
73 W 17 Chatsworth rd W4
60 M 12 Chatsworth rd W5
60 M 12 Chatsworth ri W5
108 K 6 Chatsworth way SE27
127 N 11 Chatterton rd Brom
48 J 9 Chatterton rd N4
88 M 14 Chatto rd SW11
89 N 13 Chatto rd SW11
85 R 6 Chaucer av Rich
16 J 16 Chaucer clo N11
153 Y 6 Chaucer dri Sutton
124 C 17 Chaucer grn Croy
34 E 18 Chaucer rd E11
33 U 7 Chaucer rd E17
52 G 18 Chaucer rd E7
39 Z 1 Chaucer rd Rom
90 G 14 Chaucer rd SE24
115 T 2 Chaucer rd Sidcp
153 X 7 Chaucer rd Sutton
73 W 2 Chaucer rd W3
96 J 2 Chaucer rd Welling
18 J 10 Chauncey clo N9
95 T 16 Chaundrye clo SE9
152 L 4 Cheam Common rd Worc Pk
153 P 14 Cheam Park Sutton
153 R 13 Cheam Park way Sutton
153 P 20 Cheam rd Sutton
92 B 7 Cheam st SE15
142 B 6 Cheapside EC2
160 B 6 Cheapside EC2
18 A 14 Cheapside N13
18 C 12 Cheddington rd N18
65 P 17 Chedworth clo E16
100 D 15 Cheeseman clo Hampt
111 W 11 Chelford rd Brom
68 C 7 Chelmer cres Bark
50 F 14 Chelmer rd E9
39 O 1 Chelmsford av Rom
66 F 18 Chelmsford clo E6
53 S 1 Chelmsford gdns Ilf
51 Y 3 Chelmsford rd E11
33 N 18 Chelmsford rd E17
34 B 4 Chelmsford rd E18
16 H 4 Chelmsford rd N14
128 B 5 Chelmsford sq NW10
62 L 4 Chelmsford sq NW10
144 J 12 Chelmsford st
147 W 13 Chelsea br SW1
147 U 11 Chelsea Bridge rd SW1
25 O 7 Chelsea clo Edg
101 N 13 Chelsea clo Hampt
147 R 14 Chelsea emb SW3
146 L 15 Chelsea Embankment gdns SW3
88 D 1 Chelsea Harbour dri SW10
146 K 12 Chelsea Manor gdns SW3
146 L 12 Chelsea Manor st SW3
146 F 14 Chelsea Park gdns SW3
146 H 10 Chelsea sq SW3
19 S 2 Chelsfield av N9

110 D 8 Chelsfield gdns SE26
157 O 15 Chelsham rd S Croy
89 Y 7 Chelsham rd SW4
79 S 18 Chelsworth dri SE18
83 Y 19 Cheltenham av Twick
40 J 17 Cheltenham clo Nthlt
66 D 7 Cheltenham gdns E6
24 J 13 Cheltenham pl Harrow
73 T 4 Cheltenham pl W3
33 U 19 Cheltenham rd E10
92 D 12 Cheltenham rd SE15
147 P 9 Cheltenham ter SW3
87 P 10 Chelverton rd SW15
85 R 4 Chelwood gdns Rich
15 U 7 Chelwood N20
92 G 11 Chelwood wlk SE4
65 R 10 Chenappa clo E13
10 J 17 Chenduit way Stanm
132 J 10 Cheney rd NW1
32 K 4 Cheney row E17
52 A 10 Cheney rd E11
132 E 18 Chenies ms WC1
132 F 8 Chenies pl NW1
132 E 20 Chenies st WC1
145 W 1 Cheniston gdns W8
145 X 1 Cheniston gdns W8
87 S 15 Chepstow clo SW15
36 J 19 Chepstow cres Ilf
137 T 8 Chepstow cres W11
58 F 18 Chepstow gdns S'hall
137 U 7 Chepstow pl W2
157 S 4 Chepstow rd Croy
137 U 4 Chepstow rd W2
71 X 7 Chepstow rd W7
167 T 6 Chepstow ri Croy
137 R 9 Chepstow vlls W11
134 D 18 Chequer st EC1
69 R 5 Chequers la Dgnhm
95 U 15 Chequers par SE9
17 X 15 Chequers way N13
68 K 18 Cherbury clo SE28
134 G 9 Cherbury st N1
71 V 2 Cherington rd W7
126 D 12 Cheriton av Brom
35 V 6 Cheriton av Ilf
60 E 14 Cheriton clo W5
79 S 18 Cheriton dri SE18
107 P 4 Cheriton sq SW17
154 L 2 Cherry clo Carsh
119 S 9 Cherry clo Mrdn
72 G 8 Cherry clo W5
72 A 19 Cherry cres Brentf
143 W 19 Cherry Garden st SE16
72 H 13 Cherry garth Brentf
56 A 14 Cherry gdns Dgnhm
5 O 20 Cherry hill Barnt
156 D 8 Cherry Hill gdns Croy
157 P 1 Cherry orchard Croy
123 R 20 Cherry Orchard rd Croy
77 X 17 Cherry orchard SE7
9 R 3 Cherry rd Enf
38 M 15 Cherry st Rom
41 X 12 Cherry Tree clo Wemb
28 L 13 Cherry Tree rd N2
21 Z 13 Cherry Tree ri Buck Hl
124 M 8 Cherry Tree wlk Becknhm
28 L 14 Cherry Tree wood N2
126 F 19 Cherry wlk Brom
20 A 12 Cherrydown av E4
19 Z 11 Cherrydown av E4
20 A 11 Cherrydown clo E4
19 Z 11 Cherrydown clo E4
115 W 5 Cherrydown rd Sidcp
38 H 7 Cherrydown wlk Rom
108 B 7 Cherrytree dri SW16
11 O 18 Cherrytree way Stanm
103 P 18 Cherrywood clo Kingst
87 O 13 Cherrywood dri SW15
119 S 8 Cherrywood la Mrdn
153 T 4 Chertsey dri Sutton
51 X 5 Chertsey rd E11
54 D 13 Chertsey rd Twick
100 L 3 Chertsey rd Twick
101 N 1 Chertsey rd Twick
83 U 17 Chertsey rd Twick
73 P 14 Chertsey rd W4
107 N 12 Chertsey st SW17
80 B 4 Chervil ms SE28
88 B 2 Cheryls clo SW6
110 A 6 Cheseman st SE26

102 L 18 Chesfield rd Kingst
127 Z 14 Chesham av NW7
38 M 12 Chesham clo Rom
147 S 2 Chesham clo SW1
124 D 1 Chesham cres SE20
147 S 2 Chesham pl SW1
117 P 2 Chesham rd Kingst
124 D 2 Chesham rd SE20
106 F 13 Chesham rd SW19
43 Y 11 Chesham st NW10
147 S 1 Chesham st SW1
147 S 3 Chesham st SW1
72 A 4 Chesham ter W13
121 Z 7 Cheshire clo Mitch
30 C 1 Cheshire rd N22
17 P 20 Cheshire rd N22
135 S 16 Cheshire st E2
49 S 9 Chesholm rd N16
81 R 14 Cheshunt rd Blvdr
52 J 19 Cheshunt rd E7
87 U 1 Chesilton rd SW6
66 C 8 Chesley gdns E6
159 U 15 Chesney cres Croy
89 N 2 Chesney st SW11
31 W 10 Chesnut rd N17
80 M 19 Chessington av Bxly Hth
81 N 19 Chessington av Bxly Hth
81 O 19 Chessington av Bxly Hth
27 V 11 Chessington av N3
22 E 14 Chessington ct Pinn
152 B 20 Chessington rd Epsom
159 S 3 Chessington way W Wckm
145 P 13 Chesson rd W14
82 E 20 Chester av Hounsl
84 M 15 Chester av Rich
100 D 1 Chester av Twick
153 Y 3 Chester clo Sutton
139 W 20 Chester clo SW1
86 K 8 Chester clo SW13
131 X 13 Chester Close north NW1
131 X 13 Chester Close south NW1
147 S 6 Chester cotts SW1
22 H 17 Chester dri Harrow
131 X 14 Chester ga NW1
9 N 19 Chester gdns Enf
120 C 13 Chester gdns Mrdn
139 W 20 Chester ms SW1
131 X 11 Chester pl NW1
65 N 12 Chester rd E16
32 F 17 Chester rd E17
53 N 20 Chester rd E7
54 L 2 Chester rd Ilf
31 P 9 Chester rd N17
47 S 7 Chester rd N19
19 N 7 Chester rd N9
131 V 13 Chester rd NW1
96 H 13 Chester rd Sidcp
104 M 15 Chester rd SW19
147 T 7 Chester row SW1
147 U 5 Chester row SW1
147 V 4 Chester sq SW1
147 W 3 Chester Square ms SW1
139 W 20 Chester st SW1
131 X 13 Chester ter NW1
149 T 7 Chester way SE11
148 G 12 Chester wharf SW1
139 W 13 Chesterfield gdns W1
30 K 17 Chesterfield gdns N4
91 U 12 Chesterfield gro SE22
139 W 12 Chesterfield hill W1
4 B 18 Chesterfield rd Barnt
33 U 20 Chesterfield rd E10
9 V 1 Chesterfield rd Enf
14 L 18 Chesterfield rd N3
73 W 17 Chesterfield rd W4
139 W 13 Chesterfield st W1
75 P 20 Chesterfield way SE15
93 X 1 Chesterfield wlk SE10
46 B 13 Chesterford gdns NW3
53 U 17 Chesterford rd E12
104 A 20 Chesters the New Mald
58 K 6 Chesterton clo Grnfd
87 X 13 Chesterton clo SW18
65 T 8 Chesterton rd E13
136 H 3 Chesterton rd W10
65 S 8 Chesterton ter E13
117 O 4 Chesterton ter Kingst

30 M 5 Chesthunte rd N17
145 R 15 Chestnut all SW6
72 H 12 Chestnut av Brentf
52 G 13 Chestnut av E7
11 Y 19 Chestnut av Edg
152 A 9 Chestnut av Epsom
100 G 18 Chestnut av Hampt
57 U 7 Chestnut av Hornch
29 Z 15 Chestnut av N8
33 V 14 Chestnut av SE17
85 Y 9 Chestnut av SW14
101 W 18 Chestnut av Tedd
42 A 14 Chestnut av Wemb
33 V 13 Chestnut Avenue north E17
154 L 1 Chestnut clo Carsh
6 J 18 Chestnut clo N14
49 O 6 Chestnut clo N16
97 X 8 Chestnut dri Bxly Hth
34 E 19 Chestnut dri E11
23 V 3 Chestnut dri Harrow
22 A 19 Chestnut dri Pinn
57 U 8 Chestnut glen Hornch
118 A 5 Chestnut gro New Mald
117 Z 6 Chestnut gro New Mald
5 Z 18 Chestnut gro Barnt
83 Y 10 Chestnut gro Islwth
121 Y 9 Chestnut gro Mitch
158 B 16 Chestnut gro S Croy
107 P 1 Chestnut gro SW12
72 G 7 Chestnut gro W5
89 O 19 Chestnut gro W5
42 A 14 Chestnut gro Wemb
14 C 5 Chestnut la N20
102 J 18 Chestnut rd Kingst
108 K 6 Chestnut rd SE27
119 R 3 Chestnut rd SW20
101 S 3 Chestnut rd Twick
79 U 14 Chestnut ri SE18
21 S 16 Chestnut wlk Wdfd Grn
158 K 1 Cheston av CR0
158 J 1 Cheston av Croy
99 S 3 Chesworth clo Croy
150 E 2 Chettle clo SE1
30 E 18 Chettle ct N8
107 N 5 Chetwode rd SW17
15 Z 5 Chetwode rd SW17
47 S 11 Chetwynd rd NW5
146 L 1 Cheval pl SW7
76 A 7 Cheval st E14
128 G 9 Chevening rd NW6
77 R 14 Chevening rd SE10
109 O 16 Chevening rd SE19
115 S 6 Chevenings the Sidcp
47 X 3 Cheverton rd N19
50 H 15 Chevet st E9
99 P 4 Cheviot clo Bxly Hth
8 B 9 Cheviot clo Enf
154 F 20 Cheviot clo Sutton
45 S 6 Cheviot ga NW2
45 R 7 Cheviot gdns NW2
57 W 2 Cheviot rd Hornch
108 J 10 Cheviot rd SE27
60 B 5 Cheviot way Grnfd
36 H 14 Cheviot way Ilf
32 H 14 Chewton rd E17
34 B 10 Cheyne av E18
100 F 2 Cheyne av Twick
146 M 14 Cheyne gdns SW3
116 M 9 Cheyne hill Surb
117 N 10 Cheyne hill Surb
146 L 14 Cheyne ms SW3
147 O 13 Cheyne pl SW3
146 K 15 Cheyne row SW3
157 X 3 Cheyne wlk Croy
7 V 16 Cheyne wlk N21
26 M 18 Cheyne wlk NW4
146 F 17 Cheyne wlk SW10
146 K 16 Cheyne wlk SW10
146 L 15 Cheyne wlk SW3
24 J 1 Cheyneys av Edg
11 V 19 Cheyneys av Edg
157 T 8 Chichele gdns Croy
45 P 13 Chichele rd NW2
22 M 2 Chicheley gdns Harrow
23 N 3 Chicheley rd Harrow
141 O 16 Chicheley st SE1
94 L 1 Chichester clo SE3
24 L 10 Chichester ct Stanm
53 S 2 Chichester gdns Ilf
157 U 6 Chichester rd Croy
52 A 10 Chichester rd E11
18 J 5 Chichester rd N9
129 U 9 Chichester rd NW6

129 Z 20 Chichester rd W9
141 R 5 Chichester rents WC2
148 D 11 Chichester st SW1
76 J 10 Chichester way E14
143 R 1 Chicksand st E1
14 L 11 Chiddingfold N12
81 P 18 Chiddingstone av Bxly Hth
87 Y 4 Chiddingstone st SW6
98 G 10 Chieveley rd Bxly Hth
71 Y 2 Chignell pl W13
143 X 10 Chigwell hill E1
34 H 10 Chigwell rd E18
64 D 18 Chilcot clo E14
145 V 6 Child's pl SW5
145 V 6 Child's st SW5
27 W 15 Child's way NW11
145 V 6 Child's wlk SW5
107 S 4 Childebert rd SW17
75 W 20 Childeric rd SE14
87 R 1 Childerley st SW6
75 X 16 Childers st SE8
59 Z 6 Chilham clo Grnfd
113 R 10 Chilham rd SE9
126 D 17 Chilham way Brom
107 P 13 Chillerton rd SW17
48 E 16 Chillingworth rd N7
118 F 15 Chilmark gdns New Mald
121 X 2 Chilmark rd SW16
100 G 2 Chiltern av Twick
99 P 3 Chiltern av Bxly Hth
157 T 6 Chiltern clo Croy
7 R 14 Chiltern dene Enf
117 R 13 Chiltern dri Surb
126 C 8 Chiltern gdns Brom
45 P 8 Chiltern gdns NW2
64 B 12 Chiltern rd E3
36 J 14 Chiltern rd Ilf
135 R 15 Chiltern st W1
131 S 19 Chiltern st W1
139 S 2 Chiltern st W1
21 T 12 Chiltern way Wdfd Grn
154 B 20 Chilterns, the Sutton
92 M 18 Chilthorne clo SE6
10 B 1 Chilton av Bushey
72 G 10 Chilton av W5
75 U 11 Chilton gro SE8
12 C 19 Chilton rd Edg
85 P 7 Chilton rd Rich
135 R 15 Chilton st E2
34 D 8 Chiltons The E18
77 R 13 Chilver st SE10
154 D 5 Chilworth av Sutton
138 E 6 Chilworth ms W2
138 C 6 Chilworth st W2
17 U 15 Chimes av N13
112 J 7 Chinbrook rd SE12
29 U 13 Chine the N10
7 X 18 Chine the N21
42 C 14 Chine the Wemb
20 M 11 Chingdale rd E4
21 N 11 Chingdale rd E4
20 C 9 Chingford av E4
21 O 14 Chingford la Wdfd Grn
20 B 16 Chingford Mount rd E4
20 B 19 Chingford rd E4
33 P 2 Chingford rd E4
112 A 15 Chingley clo Brom
58 M 6 Chinnor cres Grnfd
59 N 6 Chinnor cres Grnfd
76 F 6 Chipka st E14
75 V 18 Chipley st SE14
50 F 10 Chippendale st E5
43 U 16 Chippenham av Wemb
129 U 15 Chippenham gdns W9
129 U 19 Chippenham ms W9
129 T 18 Chippenham rd W9
122 J 9 Chipstead av Thntn Hth
109 V 18 Chipstead clo SE19
44 L 7 Chipstead gdns NW2
87 Y 3 Chipstead st SW6
58 B 11 Chirk clo Grnfd
63 V 5 Chisenhale rd E3
157 S 2 Chisholm rd Croy
84 M 17 Chisholm rd Rich
28 C 2 Chislehurst av N12
113 Z 14 Chislehurst High st Chisl
127 S 1 Chislehurst rd Chisl
84 K 14 Chislehurst rd Rich
114 M 13 Chislehurst rd Sidcp
31 R 18 Chisley rd N15

94 H 4 Chiswell sq SE3
134 E 20 Chiswell st EC1
85 V 4 Chiswick br W4
156 B 5 Chiswick clo Croy
73 Z 11 Chiswick Common rd W4
22 E 10 Chiswick ct Pinn
74 B 12 Chiswick High rd W4
74 C 12 Chiswick High rd W4
74 C 13 Chiswick la NW4
74 D 15 Chiswick la SW4
74 D 15 Chiswick mall W4
85 V 2 Chiswick quay W4
18 L 8 Chiswick rd N8
73 V 12 Chiswick rd W4
73 S 15 Chiswick village W4
132 C 20 Chitty st W1
55 V 5 Chittys la Dgnhm
88 H 13 Chivalry rd SW11
124 F 20 Chive clo CR0
20 E 13 Chivers rd E4
68 F 11 Choats Manor way Dgnhm
69 N 10 Choats rd Dgnhm
105 O 4 Chobham gdns SW19
51 W 15 Chobham rd E15
47 S 1 Cholmeley cres N6
47 S 1 Cholmeley pk N6
116 A 16 Cholmley rd Surb
62 F 5 Cholmondeley av NW10
84 F 13 Cholmondeley wlk Rich
143 Y 13 Choppins ct E1
91 X 5 Choumert gro SE15
91 V 6 Choumert rd SE15
91 X 5 Choumert sq SE15
64 D 15 Chrisp st E14
64 E 18 Chrisp st E14
85 S 12 Christ Church rd SW14
24 B 12 Christchurch av Harrow
42 L 19 Christchurch av Wemb
23 Z 12 Christchurch av Harrow
15 P 19 Christchurch av N12
128 J 3 Christchurch av NW6
45 U 19 Christchurch av NW6
101 X 13 Christchurch av Tedd
106 G 19 Christchurch clo SW19
23 Z 12 Christchurch gdns Harrow
42 K 19 Christchurch grn Wemb
46 F 10 Christchurch hill NW3
4 F 10 Christchurch la Barnt
4 F 10 Christchurch pas Barnt
46 F 10 Christchurch pas NW3
154 C 16 Christchurch pk Sutton
106 G 19 Christchurch rd SW19
114 L 8 Christchurch rd Sidcp
125 O 2 Christchurch rd Becknhm
54 A 5 Christchurch rd Ilf
29 Z 19 Christchurch rd N8
117 N 16 Christchurch rd Surb
108 E 2 Christchurch rd SW2
63 O 4 Christchurch sq E9
147 N 13 Christchurch st SW3
147 O 13 Christchurch ter SW3
76 M 14 Christchurch way SE10
108 G 18 Christian fields SW16
143 U 7 Christian st E1
37 R 20 Christie gdns Rom
50 H 19 Christie rd E9
134 J 17 Christina st EC2
71 Y 8 Christopher av W7
96 K 15 Christopher clo Sidcp
55 V 14 Christopher gdns Dgnhm
132 G 13 Christopher pl NW1
134 G 19 Christopher st EC2
149 U 19 Chryssel rd SW9
75 V 17 Chubworthy st SE14
54 H 13 Chudleigh cres Ilf

154 D 4 Chudleigh gdns Sutton
128 E 1 Chudleigh rd NW6
92 M 14 Chudleigh rd SE4
93 N 13 Chudleigh rd SE4
83 V 17 Chudleigh rd Twick
63 T 17 Chudleigh rd E5
109 Z 12 Chulsa rd SE26
150 H 14 Chumleigh st SE5
116 M 10 Chumleigh Surb
109 P 8 Church appr SE21
125 O 1 Church av Becknhm
20 K 18 Church av E4
58 D 1 Church av Nthlt
47 T 18 Church av NW1
22 D 19 Church av Pinn
70 D 8 Church av S'hall
115 P 11 Church av Sidcp
85 Y 9 Church av SW14
12 J 18 Church clo Edg
15 X 11 Church clo N20
137 W 16 Church clo W8
63 S 1 Church cres E9
29 R 13 Church cres N10
15 X 11 Church cres N20
27 V 5 Church cres N3
141 T 7 Church ct WC2
22 G 18 Church end Harrow
31 R 7 Church dri NW9
33 R 14 Church end E17
26 K 11 Church end NW4
141 X 7 Church entry EC4
153 T 13 Church Farm la Sutton
87 S 6 Church ga SW6
72 G 6 Church gdns W5
41 Y 12 Church gdns Wemb
113 E 2 Church gro Kingst
93 S 12 Church gro SE13
155 N 10 Church hill Carsh
156 B 20 Church hill Crsh
99 P 11 Church hill Drtfrd
33 P 13 Church hill E17
41 T 3 Church hill Harrow
17 R 2 Church hill N21
16 A 5 Church Hill rd Barnt
5 W 20 Church Hill rd Barnt
15 X 1 Church Hill rd Barnt
33 S 12 Church Hill rd E17
116 J 12 Church Hill rd Surb
153 S 10 Church Hill rd Sutton
78 H 9 Church hill SW19
105 U 12 Church hill SW19
127 R 18 Church la Brom
77 R 11 Church la Chisl
56 J 20 Church la Dgnhm
52 A 3 Church la E11
51 Z 4 Church la E11
33 T 13 Church la E17
8 B 12 Church la Enf
23 V 6 Church la Harrow
31 S 4 Church la N17
25 X 18 Church la N17
28 G 9 Church la N2
30 C 13 Church la N8
18 H 8 Church la N9
44 B 18 Church la NW9
43 W 4 Church la NW9
22 C 11 Church la Pinn
107 O 12 Church la SW17
119 X 2 Church la SW19
101 W 13 Church la Tedd
72 F 5 Church la W5
155 X 6 Church la W8
149 U 20 Church Manor est SW9
79 Z 12 Church Manor way SE2
81 Z 8 Church Manor way Erith
44 G 18 Church Mead rd NW10
28 F 17 Church mt N2
116 J 12 Church pas Surb
120 J 6 Church pl Mitch
140 D 11 Church pl SW1
72 G 6 Church pl W5
156 L 2 Church pth Croy
33 R 14 Church pth E17
120 J 8 Church pth Mitch
15 P 13 Church pth N12
31 R 3 Church pth N17
44 B 20 Church pth NW10
39 P 14 Church pth Rom
70 E 7 Church pth S'hall
85 Y 7 Church pth SW14
119 W 2 Church pth SW19
71 S 2 Church pth W4
73 W 8 Church pth W4
126 E 3 Church rd Brom

125 Y 5 Church rd Brom
21 V 5 Church rd Buck Hl
98 A 9 Church rd Bxly Hth
156 K 4 Church rd Croy
156 K 7 Church rd Croy
159 N 10 Church rd Croy
51 N 3 Church rd E10
53 W 14 Church rd E12
32 G 8 Church rd E17
9 S 18 Church rd Enf
81 Y 13 Church rd Erith
70 F 19 Church rd Hounsl
36 G 19 Church rd Ilf
71 S 20 Church rd Islwth
116 M 3 Church rd Kingst
117 N 3 Church rd Kingst
120 G 4 Church rd Mitch
31 U 3 Church rd N17
29 O 18 Church rd N6
58 B 4 Church rd Nthlt
44 C 18 Church rd NW10
26 M 12 Church rd NW4
84 K 12 Church rd Rich
102 M 10 Church rd Rich
70 E 8 Church rd S'hall
109 S 20 Church rd SE19
115 O 11 Church rd Sidcp
115 V 13 Church rd Sidcp
11 P 16 Church rd Stanm
153 S 13 Church rd Sutton
86 F 3 Church rd SW13
105 R 13 Church rd SW19
101 U 11 Church rd Tedd
73 V 4 Church rd W3
59 T 19 Church rd W7
71 V 2 Church rd W7
155 W 5 Church rd Wallgtn
97 P 4 Church rd Welling
118 C 18 Church rd Worc Pk
110 F 2 Church rd SE23
114 C 20 Church row Chisl
46 C 13 Church row NW3
145 X 19 Church row NW9
156 K 4 Church row Croy
56 H 19 Church st Dgnhm
65 N 3 Church st E15
78 L 4 Church st E16
152 F 19 Church st Epsom
84 A 7 Church st Islwth
116 H 3 Church st Kingst
18 C 6 Church st N9
130 H 20 Church st NW8
76 G 17 Church st SE10
154 B 11 Church st Sutton
101 Z 1 Church st Twick
83 Z 20 Church st Twick
130 G 20 Church st W2
74 C 16 Church st W4
65 N 3 Church Street north E15
83 O 11 Church Stretton rd Hounsl
26 L 11 Church ter NW4
84 H 13 Church ter Rich
93 Y 9 Church ter SE13
89 Y 4 Church ter SW8
28 L 9 Church vale N2
110 E 4 Church vale SE23
12 D 19 Church way Edg
15 V 10 Church way N20
72 E 16 Church wlk Brentf
49 P 13 Church wlk N16
45 W 9 Church wlk NW2
26 M 11 Church wlk NW4
43 X 7 Church wlk NW9
84 H 12 Church wlk Rich
86 F 3 Church wlk SW13
86 K 13 Church wlk SW14
121 V 3 Church wlk SW16
118 M 5 Church wlk SW20
8 D 10 Churchbury clo Enf
8 C 12 Churchbury la Enf
8 D 8 Churchbury rd Enf
94 M 17 Churchbury rd SE9
95 N 19 Churchbury rd SE9
89 P 19 Churchcroft clo SW12
112 A 9 Churchdown Brom
111 Z 9 Churchdown Brom
15 S 18 Churchfield av N12
22 M 13 Churchfield clo Harrow
97 N 8 Churchfield rd Welling
72 C 3 Churchfield rd W13
73 V 3 Churchfield rd W3
71 S 5 Churchfield rd W7
100 F 6 Churchfields av Felt
34 F 4 Churchfields E18
124 H 2 Churchfields rd Becknhm

24 A 19	Churchill av Harrow
148 A 12	Churchill Garden's est SW1
148 B 12	Churchill Gardens rd SW1
147 Z 12	Churchill gdns SW1
61 R 18	Churchill gdns W3
23 U 13	Churchill pl Harrow
65 Y 17	Churchill rd E16
12 A 20	Churchill rd Edg
44 J 18	Churchill rd NW2
47 T 11	Churchill rd NW5
156 M 17	Churchill rd S Croy
20 B 12	Churchill ter E4
50 D 14	Churchill wlk E9
110 A 9	Churchley rd SE26
5 W 20	Churchmead clo Barnt
107 W 20	Churchmore rd SW16
101 P 3	Churchview rd Twick
132 F 12	Churchway NW1
50 B 15	Churchwell pth E9
149 X 5	Churchyard row SE11
65 V 3	Churston av E13
119 R 12	Churston dri Mrdn
16 H 20	Churston gdns N11
148 B 7	Churton pl SW1
148 B 8	Churton st SW1
114 K 6	Chyngton clo Sidcp
110 G 3	Cibber rd SE23
88 C 15	Cicada rd SW18
91 X 3	Cicely rd SE15
112 A 10	Cinderford way Brom
60 M 10	Cinema pde W5
75 O 3	Cinnamon st E1
23 Z 13	Cinnamon st E1
109 V 16	Cintra pk SE19
119 Y 5	Circle gdns SW19
44 C 10	Circle the NW2
12 L 18	Circle the NW7
31 V 9	Circular rd N17
78 H 16	Circular way SE18
139 N 1	Circus ms W1
160 G 2	Circus pl EC2
130 G 10	Circus rd NW8
76 G 19	Circus st SE10
129 X 20	Cirencester st W2
31 P 16	Cissbury rd N15
14 K 15	Cissbury Ring north N12
14 K 16	Cissbury Ring south N12
133 Y 10	City Garden row N1
134 C 12	City rd EC1
133 Y 11	City rd EC1
36 C 12	Civic way Ilf
147 O 4	Clabon ms SW1
75 R 6	Clack st SE16
32 H 18	Clacton rd E17
66 A 9	Clacton rd E6
31 U 9	Clacton rd N17
27 Z 5	Claigmar gdns N3
15 P 12	Claire ct N12
22 E 2	Claire ct Pinn
76 B 8	Claire pl E14
82 A 2	Clairvale rd Hounsl
107 T 11	Clairview rd SW16
71 U 2	Clairville gdns W7
10 G 18	Clamp hill Stanm
87 Z 5	Clancarty rd SW6
152 E 14	Clandon clo Epsom
73 U 4	Clandon clo W3
27 Y 11	Clandon gdns N2
54 H 7	Clandon rd Ilf
93 O 3	Clandon st SE8
137 V 10	Clanricarde gdns W2
89 R 11	Clapham comm SW4
89 N 11	Clapham Common West side SW4
89 P 10	Clapham Common North side SW4
89 U 12	Clapham Common South side SW4
89 X 11	Clapham cres SW4
89 X 9	Clapham High st SW4
89 X 8	Clapham Manor st SW4
89 X 10	Clapham Park rd SW4
90 C 2	Clapham rd SW9
149 R 18	Clapham rd SW9
89 Y 8	Clapham rd SW9
67 O 10	Claps Gate la Bark
49 W 2	Clapton comm E5
50 G 12	Clapton Park est E5
50 B 14	Clapton pas E5
50 B 14	Clapton sq E5

49 X 3	Clapton ter N16
49 X 11	Clapton way E5
78 J 10	Clara pl SE18
28 C 9	Clare clo N2
95 Y 20	Clare corner SE9
54 L 19	Clare gdns Bark
52 E 13	Clare gdns E7
11 R 17	Clare gdns Stanm
136 M 6	Clare gdns W11
75 O 10	Clare Hall pl SE16
134 B 1	Clare la N1
85 Y 14	Clare Lawn av SW14
141 O 6	Clare mkt WC2
33 Y 19	Clare rd E11
41 R 18	Clare rd Grnfd
82 C 9	Clare rd Hounsl
44 G 19	Clare rd NW10
92 K 3	Clare rd SE14
63 N 7	Clare st E2
135 X 9	Clare st E2
97 Y 1	Clare way Bxly Hth
135 V 10	Claredale st E2
151 Y 4	Clarehall pl SE16
118 H 10	Claremont av New Mald
24 K 16	Claremont av Harrow
78 K 3	Claremont clo E16
133 T 11	Claremont clo N1
99 R 10	Claremont cres Drtfd
54 G 7	Claremont gdns Ilf
116 J 10	Claremont gdns Surb
21 Y 18	Claremont gro Wdfd Grn
27 T 5	Claremont pk N3
5 T 2	Claremont rd Barnt
127 S 10	Claremont rd Brom
123 Y 10	Claremont rd Croy
51 W 9	Claremont rd E11
32 J 8	Claremont rd E17
52 K 15	Claremont rd E7
23 U 8	Claremont rd Harrow
39 V 19	Claremont rd Hornch
29 U 20	Claremont rd N6
45 N 2	Claremont rd NW2
118 H 11	Claremont rd Surb
101 W 11	Claremont rd Tedd
84 C 17	Claremont rd Twick
59 Y 14	Claremont rd W13
129 N 10	Claremont rd W9
133 S 10	Claremont sq N1
78 K 4	Claremont st E16
18 J 18	Claremont st N18
76 E 18	Claremont st SE10
45 N 3	Claremont way NW2
117 Y 3	Clarence av New Mald
127 R 8	Clarence av Brom
35 V 18	Clarence av Ilf
89 Y 14	Clarence av SW4
10 G 3	Clarence clo Bushey
115 P 8	Clarence cres Sidcp
89 Y 16	Clarence cres SW4
131 P 16	Clarence ga NW1
131 Z 14	Clarence gdns NW1
86 E 15	Clarence la SW15
50 A 14	Clarence ms E5
132 J 9	Clarence pas NW1
50 A 14	Clarence pl E5
127 P 7	Clarence rd Brom
97 X 9	Clarence rd Bxly Hth
123 O 16	Clarence rd Croy
53 N 14	Clarence rd E12
64 M 13	Clarence rd E16
32 F 7	Clarence rd E17
50 A 12	Clarence rd E5
9 P 18	Clarence rd Enf
31 N 14	Clarence rd N15
30 A 2	Clarence rd N22
129 O 2	Clarence rd NW6
85 O 3	Clarence rd Rich
113 R 5	Clarence rd SE9
115 P 8	Clarence rd Sidcp
153 Z 10	Clarence rd Sutton
106 A 15	Clarence rd SW19
105 Z 15	Clarence rd SW19
101 X 16	Clarence rd Tedd
73 P 14	Clarence rd W4
155 S 12	Clarence rd Wallgtn
116 H 3	Clarence st Kingst
84 J 10	Clarence st Rich
82 J 10	Clarence ter Hounsl
47 R 20	Clarence ter NW1
138 K 8	Clarendon clo W2
101 P 7	Clarendon cres Twick
136 L 11	Clarendon cross W11
86 M 9	Clarendon dri SW15

87 N 10	Clarendon dri SW15
42 H 11	Clarendon gdns Wemb
26 H 9	Clarendon gdns NW4
53 V 2	Clarendon gdns Ilf
130 C 18	Clarendon gdns W9
121 N 5	Clarendon gro Mitch
138 K 8	Clarendon ms W2
138 K 8	Clarendon pl W2
156 K 2	Clarendon rd Croy
51 X 2	Clarendon rd E11
33 R 18	Clarendon rd E17
34 E 10	Clarendon rd E18
23 T 19	Clarendon rd Harrow
30 X 14	Clarendon rd N15
18 K 18	Clarendon rd N18
30 C 9	Clarendon rd N22
30 D 11	Clarendon rd N8
106 H 18	Clarendon rd SW19
136 K 8	Clarendon rd W11
137 N 13	Clarendon rd W11
60 J 10	Clarendon rd W5
155 U 13	Clarendon rd Wallgtn
93 V 9	Clarendon ri SE13
148 A 8	Clarendon st SW1
147 Y 10	Clarendon st SW1
130 D 17	Clarendon ter W9
17 Z 1	Clarendon way N21
110 K 4	Clarens st SE6
123 S 7	Claret gdns SE25
146 D 7	Clareville gro SW7
146 D 7	Clareville st SW7
139 X 12	Clarges ms W1
139 Y 13	Clarges st W1
90 H 4	Claribel rd SW9
156 A 20	Clarice way SM6
110 D 19	Claridge rd Dgnhm
37 U 20	Clarina st E9
135 N 4	Clarissa rd Rom
99 W 2	Clarissa st E8
63 O 16	Clark clo Erith
143 Z 3	Clark st E1
70 A 20	Clark st E1
139 V 1	Clark way Hounsl
153 P 2	Clarke's pl W1
10 B 3	Clarke av Worc Pk
75 O 6	Clarks mead Bushey
143 Z 18	Clarks orchard SE16
142 J 4	Clarks pl EC3
54 F 7	Clarks rd Ilf
65 O 16	Clarkson rd E2
135 W 12	Clarkson st E2
67 P 6	Clarksons the Bark
99 R 11	Claston clo Drtfd
51 U 5	Claude rd E10
65 U 4	Claude rd E13
91 Z 7	Claude rd SE15
76 A 10	Claude st E14
105 R 2	Claudia pl SW19
65 Y 7	Claughton rd E13
60 A 5	Clausen way Grnfd
59 Z 5	Clausen wy Grnfd
40 L 14	Clauson av Grnfd
75 O 3	Clave st E1
143 Z 13	Clave st E1
90 E 19	Claverdale rd SW2
144 A 14	Clavering av SW13
74 K 16	Clavering av SW13
101 X 9	Clavering clo Twick
53 N 6	Clavering rd E12
27 Z 4	Claverley gro N3
148 C 12	Claverton st SW1
144 H 11	Claverton way E9
121 T 4	Clay av Mitch
8 E 3	Clay hill Enf
10 F 3	Clay la Bushey
12 B 7	Clay la Edg
139 R 2	Clay st W1
112 M 9	Claybridge rd SE12
144 G 13	Claybrook rd W6
35 R 10	Claybury bdwy Ilf
35 V 1	Claybury Hall Wdfd Grn
35 R 2	Claybury rd Wdfd Grn
156 B 9	Claydon dri CR0
114 B 5	Clayfarm rd SE9
57 V 13	Claygate clo Hornch
159 W 15	Claygate cres Croy
72 A 7	Claygate rd W13
35 T 8	Clayhall av Ilf
113 N 9	Clayhill cres SE9
149 R 16	Claylands pl SW8
119 X 17	Claymore clo Sutton
64 G 6	Claypole rd E15
72 J 13	Clayponds av Brentf
72 H 11	Clayponds gdns W5
72 K 14	Clayponds la Brentf

51 S 16	Clays la clo E15
51 T 14	Clays la E15
42 K 20	Clayton av Wemb
72 G 13	Clayton cres Brentf
26 B 3	Clayton field NW9
83 T 8	Clayton rd Islwth
56 K 4	Clayton rd Rom
91 Y 2	Clayton rd SE15
149 T 13	Clayton st SE11
58 B 14	Clayton ter Hay
97 P 15	Clayworth clo Sidcp
95 Z 3	Cleanthus clo SE18
96 A 2	Cleanthus rd SE18
95 Z 2	Cleanthus rd SE18
63 R 17	Clearbrook way E1
129 Y 19	Clearwell dri W9
116 G 12	Cleaveland rd Surb
149 U 10	Cleaver sq SE11
149 U 10	Cleaver st SE11
123 Z 14	Cleaverholme clo SE25
110 B 1	Cleeve hill SE23
65 T 6	Clegg st E13
143 Y 13	Clegg st E1
145 O 15	Clem Attlee ct SW6
62 F 20	Clematis st W12
63 Y 16	Clemence st E14
128 E 2	Clement clo NW6
124 F 4	Clement rd Becknhm
105 S 13	Clement rd SW19
55 T 18	Clementhorpe rd Dgnhm
50 K 5	Clementina rd E10
72 A 6	Clementine clo W13
65 T 19	Clements av E16
141 P 6	Clements Inn pass WC2
100 G 0	Clements la EC3
72 G 13	Clements pl Brentf
66 E 2	Clements rd E6
54 A 9	Clements rd Ilf
53 Z 9	Clements rd Ilf
151 V 3	Clements rd SE16
79 P 11	Clendon way SE18
79 R 10	Clendon way SE18
153 X 3	Clensham la Sutton
139 O 5	Clenston ms W1
49 N 18	Clephane rd N1
134 G 16	Clere pl EC2
134 G 17	Clere st EC2
133 V 17	Clerkenwell clo EC1
133 V 17	Clerkenwell grn EC1
133 W 17	Clerkenwell rd EC1
63 P 2	Clermont rd E9
46 A 20	Cleve rd NW6
45 Z 20	Cleve rd NW6
115 W 7	Cleve rd Sidcp
117 P 3	Clevedon rd Kingst
110 E 20	Clevedon rd SE20
84 G 15	Clevedon rd Twick
100 E 17	Cleveland av Hampt
119 U 3	Cleveland av SW20
74 C 11	Cleveland av W4
86 C 5	Cleveland gdns SW13
30 L 17	Cleveland gdns N4
45 P 6	Cleveland gdns NW2
138 B 6	Cleveland gdns W2
152 C 2	Cleveland gdns Worc
63 P 12	Cleveland gro E1
132 B 19	Cleveland ms W1
33 N 13	Cleveland Park av E17
33 N 13	Cleveland Park cres E17
60 A 14	Cleveland Park W13
140 D 13	Cleveland pl SW1
118 A 8	Cleveland rd New Mald
152 C 3	Cleveland rd Worc Pk
34 F 10	Cleveland rd E18
54 A 11	Cleveland rd Ilf
83 Y 10	Cleveland rd Islwth
134 F 2	Cleveland rd N1
86 D 5	Cleveland rd SW13
60 B 15	Cleveland rd W13
59 Y 15	Cleveland rd W13
73 W 9	Cleveland rd W4
96 L 5	Cleveland rd Welling
119 R 17	Cleveland ri Mrdn
140 B 15	Cleveland row SW1
138 B 7	Cleveland sq W2
132 A 19	Cleveland st W1
131 Z 18	Cleveland st W1
138 C 4	Cleveland ter W2
63 P 12	Cleveland way E1
78 B 10	Cleveley clo SE7
60 K 7	Cleveley cres W5
50 A 8	Cleveleys rd E5

152 J 19 Cleves av Epsom
66 A 4 Cleves av E6
102 D 7 Cleves rd Rich
100 F 18 Cleves way Hampt
36 C 2 Cleves wlk Ilf
23 P 5 Clewer cres Harrow
72 G 16 Clifden rd Brentf
50 D 14 Clifden rd E5
101 W 1 Clifden rd Twick
83 X 20 Clifden rd Twick
47 Y 17 Cliff rd NW1
93 P 4 Cliff ter SW4
47 Z 17 Cliff vlls NW1
65 P 13 Cliff wlk E16
157 O 11 Cliffe rd S Croy
113 T 15 Clifford av Chisl
35 Z 6 Clifford av Ilf
85 U 6 Clifford av SW14
155 U 8 Clifford av Wallgtn
58 B 5 Clifford clo Nthlt
90 H 11 Clifford dri SW9
128 C 9 Clifford gdns NW10
62 M 7 Clifford gdns NW10
110 C 18 Clifford gro SE20
5 O 12 Clifford rd Barnt
65 O 13 Clifford rd E16
33 U 8 Clifford rd E17
102 H 4 Clifford rd Rich
123 W 9 Clifford rd SE25
19 R 1 Clifford rd W9
60 F 3 Clifford rd Wemb
40 A 9 Clifford st W1
44 D 12 Clifford way NW1
93 O 9 Clifford way SE13
32 G 12 Clifton av E17
27 V 4 Clifton av N3
24 C 7 Clifton av Stanm
74 E 4 Clifton av W12
43 N 17 Clifton av Wemb
151 Z 18 Clifton cres SE15
6 M 15 Clifton gdns Enf
31 W 18 Clifton gdns N15
27 X 18 Clifton gdns NW11
73 Y 12 Clifton gdns W4
130 B 18 Clifton gdns W9
49 X 17 Clifton gro E8
130 C 5 Clifton hill NW8
129 Y 8 Clifton hill NW8
119 N 3 Clifton Park av SW20
138 H 7 Clifton pl W2
53 O 18 Clifton rd E12
65 N 13 Clifton rd E16
59 O 11 Clifton rd Grnfd
24 L 15 Clifton rd Harrow
39 V 19 Clifton rd Hornch
36 E 20 Clifton rd Ilf
83 S 4 Clifton rd Islwth
117 O 1 Clifton rd Kingst
103 O 19 Clifton rd Kingst
29 W 5 Clifton rd N22
28 D 4 Clifton rd N3
29 X 18 Clifton rd N8
62 F 7 Clifton rd NW10
70 C 10 Clifton rd S'hall
123 S 10 Clifton rd SE25
114 H 9 Clifton rd Sidcp
105 O 15 Clifton rd SW19
101 U 10 Clifton rd Tedd
130 D 17 Clifton rd W9
155 T 11 Clifton rd Wallgtn
97 S 7 Clifton rd Welling
75 W 19 Clifton ri SE14
134 H 19 Clifton st EC2
48 F 6 Clifton ter N4
130 A 20 Clifton vlls W9
75 Z 20 Clifton way SE15
151 Z 20 Clifton way SE15
60 K 3 Clifton way Wemb
16 H 19 Cline rd N11
134 J 6 Clinger ct N1
142 D 12 Clink st SE1
96 M 9 Clinton av Welling
63 V 9 Clinton rd E3
52 F 13 Clinton rd E7
31 N 14 Clinton rd N15
93 U 11 Clipper wy SE13
82 G 8 Clipstone rd Hounsl
132 A 20 Clipstone st W1
131 Z 20 Clipstone st W1
28 M 10 Clissold clo N2
49 N 11 Clissold cres N16
49 O 9 Clissold est N16
49 N 8 Clissold pk N16
49 O 9 Clissold rd N16
40 G 5 Clitheroe av Harrow
90 A 6 Clitheroe rd SW9
71 X 7 Clitherow av W7
72 C 13 Clitherow rd Brentf
45 N 5 Clitterhouse cres NW2

45 N 5 Clitterhouse rd NW2
99 T 17 Clive av Drtfrd
18 J 19 Clive av N18
109 O 8 Clive pass SE21
81 P 12 Clive rd Blvdr
8 J 14 Clive rd Enf
39 Y 17 Clive rd Rom
109 O 8 Clive rd SE21
106 J 15 Clive rd SW19
101 X 8 Clive rd Twick
8 J 15 Clive way Enf
15 P 14 Cliveden clo N12
147 S 6 Cliveden pl SW1
105 U 20 Cliveden rd SW19
60 A 13 Clivedon ct W13
20 L 17 Clivedon rd E4
160 D 8 Cloak la EC4
124 H 5 Clock House rd Becknhm
149 Y 6 Clock pl SE17
134 C 6 Clock Tower ms N1
83 X 8 Clock Tower rd Islwth
67 O 2 Clockhouse av Bark
105 N 5 Clockhouse clo SW19
38 H 2 Clockhouse la Rom
12 J 16 Cloister gdns Edg
123 Z 14 Cloister gdns SE25
45 U 8 Cloister rd NW2
61 V 15 Cloister rd W3
127 T 12 Cloisters av Brom
49 R 12 Clonbrock rd N16
87 R 3 Cloncurry st SW6
145 P 20 Clonmel rd SW6
87 W 1 Clonmel rd SW6
101 P 10 Clonmel rd NW6
31 P 11 Clonmell rd N17
105 W 2 Clonmore st SW18
41 R 5 Clonnel clo Harrow
45 X 11 Clorane gdns NW3
6 A 18 Close the Barnt
124 H 9 Close the Becknhm
98 C 17 Close the Bxly
154 K 18 Close the Carsh
33 V 3 Close the E4
23 N 8 Close the Harrow
83 P 3 Close the Islwth
120 K 10 Close the Mitch
29 S 8 Close the N10
16 K 8 Close the N14
14 H 7 Close the N20
117 X 4 Close the New Mald
85 S 7 Close the Rich
37 X 17 Close the Rom
115 R 11 Close the Sidcp
119 V 17 Close the Sutton
42 J 18 Close the Wemb
43 W 10 Close the Wemb
141 Y 1 Cloth ct EC1
141 Y 2 Cloth fair EC1
142 A 1 Cloth st EC1
160 A 1 Cloth st EC1
142 L 4 Clothier st E1
107 R 4 Cloudesdale rd SW17
133 T 6 Cloudesley pl N1
98 C 2 Cloudesley rd Bxly Hth
99 T 2 Cloudesley rd Erith
133 T 5 Cloudesley rd N1
133 T 4 Cloudesley sq N1
133 T 5 Cloudesley st N1
157 N 4 Clouston clo Wallgtn
52 F 16 Clova rd E7
26 C 12 Clovelly av NW9
18 D 3 Clovelly gdns Enf
38 H 5 Clovelly gdns Rom
80 K 17 Clovelly rd Bxly Hth
29 Y 12 Clovelly rd N8
73 X 7 Clovelly rd W4
72 E 6 Clovelly rd W5
40 D 8 Clovelly way Harrow
51 X 8 Clover clo E11
147 O 13 Clover ms SW3
96 J 16 Cloverdale gdns Sidcp
110 L 6 Clowders rd SE6
154 D 11 Clowser clo SM1
11 V 20 Cloyster wood Edg
126 G 17 Club Gardens rd Brom
135 N 16 Club row E2
70 D 14 Clunbury av S'hall
145 S 8 Cluny ms SW5
150 J 1 Cluny pl SE1
64 E 15 Clutton st E14
8 H 13 Clydach rd Enf
31 S 12 Clyde cir N15
51 P 2 Clyde pl E10
157 U 2 Clyde rd Croy
123 U 20 Clyde rd Croy

77 T 2 Clyde rd E16
31 T 12 Clyde rd N15
29 X 4 Clyde rd N22
153 Y 10 Clyde rd Sutton
155 V 13 Clyde rd Wallgtn
75 Z 17 Clyde st SE8
110 D 4 Clyde ter SE23
110 D 5 Clyde vale SE23
39 P 4 Clyde way Rom
24 G 9 Clydesdale av Stanm
9 S 16 Clydesdale Enf
85 S 10 Clydesdale gdns Rich
57 T 2 Clydesdale rd Hornch
137 P 5 Clydesdale rd W11
89 W 3 Clyston st SW8
86 M 12 Coalecroft rd SW15
69 R 7 Coaley row Dgnhm
135 U 8 Coate st E2
127 X 4 Coates Hill rd Brom
11 T 2 Coates rd Borehm Wd
72 J 15 Coates wlk Brentf
142 M 3 Cobb st E1
95 R 8 Cobbett rd SE9
100 J 1 Cobbett rd Twick
149 O 20 Cobbett st SW8
35 O 15 Cobbetts av Ilf
52 C 9 Cobbold rd E11
60 M 1 Cobbold rd NW10
74 C 6 Cobbold rd W12
141 X 7 Cobbs clo EC4
82 E 12 Cobbs rd Hounsl
52 A 8 Cobden rd E11
123 Y 12 Cobden rd SE25
18 F 10 Cobham av New Mald
127 P 16 Cobham clo Brom
88 K 15 Cobham clo SW11
155 Z 15 Cobham clo Wallgtn
97 X 12 Cobham pl Bxly Hth
33 V 5 Cobham rd E17
54 H 8 Cobham rd Ilf
117 P 2 Cobham rd Kingst
30 J 9 Cobham rd N22
112 M 10 Cobland rd SE12
63 V 8 Coborn rd E3
63 V 8 Coborn st E3
63 V 9 Coborn st E3
151 N 11 Cobourg rd SE5
132 C 14 Cobourg st NW1
148 C 4 Coburg clo SW1
30 D 9 Coburg rd N22
108 E 2 Coburgh st SW12
105 U 18 Cochrane rd SW19
130 H 10 Cochrane st NW8
142 L 3 Cock hill E1
141 X 3 Cock la EC1
6 A 14 Cockfosters pde Barnt
6 A 13 Cockfosters rd Barnt
5 X 4 Cockfosters rd Barnt
140 F 19 Cockpit steps SW1
133 O 19 Cockpit yd WC1
118 C 9 Cocks cres
140 G 13 Cockspur ct SW1
140 H 13 Cockspur st SW1
135 P 18 Code st E1
48 L 7 Codicote terr N4
143 U 13 Codling clo E1
42 F 12 Codling way Wemb
92 J 18 Codrington hill SE23
137 N 7 Codrington ms W11
155 Z 17 Cody clo Harrow
64 L 12 Cody rd Wallgtn
43 T 9 Cofers crcl Wemb
32 G 3 Cogan av E17
141 T 13 Coin st SE1
47 P 17 Coity rd NW5
143 T 4 Coke st E1
129 V 4 Colas ms NW6
146 A 7 Colbeck ms SW7
41 N 1 Colbeck rd Harrow
49 T 2 Colberg pl N16
152 M 3 Colborne way Worc Pk
153 N 2 Colborne way Worc Pk
154 F 6 Coldblow way Sutton
109 T 13 Colby rd SE19
53 U 10 Colchester av E12
51 T 1 Colchester rd E10
33 N 20 Colchester rd E17
25 W 2 Colchester rd Edg
143 P 5 Colchester st E1
75 T 17 Cold Blow la SE14
120 M 7 Cold blows Mitch
76 H 4 Cold harbour E14
133 S 17 Coldbath sq EC1

71 Y 3 Coldershaw rd W13
29 N 7 Coldfall av N10
30 H 6 Coldham ct Enf
9 V 1 Coldham gdns Enf
90 H 9 Coldharbour la SW9
156 F 11 Coldharbour rd Croy
156 G 11 Coldharbour way Croy
42 F 13 Colding way Wemb
87 V 16 Coldstream gdns SW18
80 D 3 Cole clo SE18
83 Y 15 Cole Park gdns Twick
83 X 15 Cole Park rd Twick
83 Y 18 Cole Park rd Twick
83 Y 17 Cole rd Twick
142 D 19 Cole st SE1
48 J 19 Colebeck ms N1
145 Z 7 Colebeck ms SW5
63 R 11 Colebert av E1
87 P 17 Colebrook clo SW15
122 A 1 Colebrook rd Brom
126 A 4 Colebrook ri Brom
16 F 17 Colebrook way N11
60 A 17 Colebrooke av W13
34 K 20 Colebrooke dri E11
133 X 7 Colebrooke row N1
150 G 19 Coleby pth SE5
24 D 4 Coledale dri Stanm
88 C 12 Colegrave rd SW18
51 W 13 Colegrave rd E15
151 R 16 Colegrove rd SE15
145 Y 12 Coleherne ms SW10
145 X 11 Coleherne rd SW10
87 S 3 Colehill gdns SW6
87 S 3 Colehill la SW6
134 B 4 Coleman fields N1
81 R 10 Coleman rd Blvdr
56 A 19 Coleman rd Dgnhm
55 Z 19 Coleman rd Dgnhm
150 H 17 Coleman st EC2
150 K 18 Coleman st EC2
160 E 4 Coleman st EC2
142 E 5 Coleman st EC2
160 E 3 Coleman Street bldgs EC2
113 X 7 Colemans heath SE9
50 D 11 Colenso rd E5
54 G 4 Colenso rd Ilf
96 D 12 Colepits Wood rd SE9
30 F 10 Coleraine rd N8
77 N 2 Coleraine rd SE3
53 R 17 Coleridge av E12
154 K 8 Coleridge av Sutton
89 T 4 Coleridge clo SW8
130 B 2 Coleridge gdns NW6
29 Z 18 Coleridge la N8
124 C 16 Coleridge rd Croy
32 L 12 Coleridge rd E17
15 P 17 Coleridge rd N12
48 F 8 Coleridge rd N4
29 X 19 Coleridge rd N8
39 Y 3 Coleridge rd Rom
27 X 14 Coleridge wlk NW11
40 K 7 Coles cres Harrow
44 H 5 Coles Green NW2
10 A 5 Coles grn Bushey
124 K 5 Colesburg rd Becknhm
101 U 15 Coleshill rd Tedd
88 K 4 Colestown st SW11
144 H 7 Colet gdns W14
133 P 17 Coley st WC1
110 G 1 Colfe rd SE23
158 K 4 Colin clo Croy
26 B 14 Colin clo NW9
26 E 15 Colin cres NW9
26 E 16 Colin dri NW9
26 E 15 Colin gdns NW9
26 A 13 Colin Park rd NW9
44 F 17 Colin rd NW10
30 J 14 Colina ms N15
30 J 15 Colina rd N15
25 Z 11 Colindale av NW9
26 H 14 Colindeep gdns NW4
26 F 13 Colindeep la NW9
86 L 10 Colinette rd SW15
55 R 6 Colinton rd Ilf
87 Y 18 Coliston rd SW18
106 H 3 Collamore av SW18
22 L 17 Collapit clo Harrow
76 G 16 College appr SE10
23 T 4 College av Harrow
50 C 14 College clo E9
23 U 2 College clo Harrow
46 F 19 College cres NW3
133 V 1 College cross N1

118 E 12	College gdns New Mald
20 D 4	College gdns E4
35 R 15	College gdns Ilf
18 H 16	College gdns N18
91 S 20	College gdns SE21
106 H 4	College gdns SE17
109 R 18	College gdns SE19
132 D 5	College gro NW1
160 D 8	College hill EC4
23 U 3	College Hill rd Harrow
23 V 4	College Hill rd Harrow
47 S 12	College la NW5
88 B 14	College ms SW18
18 F 20	College Park rd N17
33 Z 12	College pl E17
132 C 4	College pl NW1
126 E 1	College pl Brom
112 F 18	College rd Brom
157 O 4	College rd Croy
33 T 17	College rd E17
8 B 8	College rd Enf
23 T 3	College rd Harrow
23 U 19	College rd Harrow
83 V 3	College rd Islwth
18 F 20	College rd N17
17 U 8	College rd N21
128 B 8	College rd NW10
62 M 6	College rd NW10
109 S 1	College rd SE21
91 S 20	College rd SE21
106 G 16	College rd SW19
60 A 18	College rd W13
42 H 5	College rd Wemb
126 F 2	College slip Brom
160 D 9	College st EC4
63 X 8	College ter E3
27 W 6	College ter N3
113 O 3	College view SE9
50 D 18	Collent st E9
31 U 16	Colless rd N15
151 U 2	Collett rd SE16
70 K 4	Collett wy S'hall
25 P 7	Collier dri Edg
38 H 3	Collier Row la Rom
38 C 4	Collier Row rd Rom
133 N 9	Colliers st N1
122 G 10	Colliers Water la Thntn Hth
106 G 16	Colliers Wood High st SW19
74 J 2	Collinbourne rd W12
81 V 17	Collindale av Erith
97 O 20	Collindale av Sidcp
145 Z 7	Collingham gdns SW5
145 Y 6	Collingham pl SW5
110 C 9	Collingtree rd SE26
29 O 11	Collingwood av N10
117 V 18	Collingwood av Surb
82 N 18	Collingwood clo Twick
153 W 5	Collingwood rd Sutton
33 N 18	Collingwood rd E17
120 G 5	Collingwood rd Mitch
31 S 12	Collingwood rd N15
63 N 12	Collingwood st E1
135 X 17	Collingwood st E1
24 K 7	Collins av Stanm
48 M 11	Collins rd N5
94 B 6	Collins st SE3
133 X 5	Collins yd N1
142 A 19	Collinson st SE1
9 P 12	Collinwood av Enf
35 U 15	Collinwood gdns Ilf
92 C 1	Colls rd SE15
156 A 8	Collyer av Croy
91 V 2	Collyer pl SE15
156 A 8	Collyer rd CR0
156 A 8	Collyer rd Croy
65 Y 15	Colman rd E16
63 T 11	Colman clo E1
23 P 3	Colmer pl Harrow
108 B 19	Colmore rd SW16
9 R 14	Colmore rd Enf
149 W 2	Colnbrook st SE1
50 H 13	Colne rd E5
18 A 3	Colne rd N21
101 U 2	Colne rd Twick
65 S 10	Colne st E13
29 P 2	Colney Hatch la N10
15 Y 18	Colney Hatch la N11
16 A 20	Colney Hatch rd N11
88 G 10	Cologne rd SW11
77 N 14	Colomb st SE10
54 B 2	Colombo rd Ilf
141 W 15	Colombo st SE1
7 V 10	Colonels wlk Enf
83 N 15	Colonial av Twick
132 K 18	Colonnade WC1
131 Y 15	Colosseum ter NW1
157 R 2	Colson rd Croy
107 V 10	Colsterworth rd N15
31 V 12	Colson way SW16
154 X 8	Colston av Carsh
154 L 9	Colston ct Carsh
53 N 18	Colston rd E7
85 W 10	Colston rd SW14
80 C 13	Coltness cres SE2
30 M 10	Colton gdns N17
23 U 14	Colton rd Harrow
118 E 18	Columbia av Worc Pk
25 S 4	Columbia av Edg
65 R 13	Columbia rd E3
135 P 12	Columbia rd E2
68 D 15	Columbine av E6
156 J 16	Columbine av S Croy
93 T 5	Columbine way SE13
101 T 2	Colus all Twick
49 U 16	Colvestone cres E8
137 P 6	Colville gdns W11
137 R 6	Colville ms W11
140 D 2	Colville pl W1
51 V 9	Colville rd E11
32 J 8	Colville rd E11
18 L 4	Colville rd N9
137 P 5	Colville rd W11
137 R 7	Colville rd W11
73 U 8	Colville rd W3
137 O 6	Colville sq W11
137 O 5	Colville Square ms W11
137 P 6	Colville ter W11
34 J 13	Colvin gdns E11
20 H 11	Colvin gdns E4
36 B 3	Colvin gdns Ilf
66 D 2	Colvin rd E6
122 F 12	Colvin rd Thntn Hth
91 U 14	Colwell rd SE22
47 X 1	Colwick clo N6
144 E 14	Colwith rd W6
106 G 18	Colwood gdns SW19
150 B 8	Colworth gro SE17
123 X 20	Colworth rd Croy
34 A 20	Colworth rd E11
33 Z 19	Colworth rd E11
59 X 6	Colwyn av Grnfd
82 M 3	Colwyn cres Hounsl
44 K 9	Colwyn rd NW2
113 Z 4	Colyer clo SE9
98 M 1	Colyers la Erith
98 L 1	Colyers la Erith
99 S 1	Colyers la Erith
99 P 1	Colyers wlk Erith
97 V 1	Colyton clo Welling
42 D 17	Colyton rd Wemb
92 A 14	Colyton rd SE22
18 H 17	Colyton way N18
77 P 19	Combe av SE3
77 P 19	Combe ms SE3
103 V 17	Combe Wood Golf course Kingst
77 S 14	Combedale rd SE10
87 T 20	Combemartin rd SW18
44 H 8	Comber clo NW2
150 B 20	Comber gro SE5
90 C 7	Combermere rd SW9
50 A 6	Comberton rd E5
79 X 20	Combeside SE18
38 C 19	Combewood dri Rom
80 A 9	Combwell cres SE2
33 T 15	Comely Bank rd E17
144 M 10	Comeragh ms W14
144 L 11	Comeragh rd W14
145 N 10	Comeragh rd W14
92 K 11	Comerford rd SE4
76 A 20	Comet st SE8
72 C 18	Commerce rd Brentf
30 D 4	Commerce rd N22
63 O 17	Commercial rd E1
143 U 5	Commercial rd E1
18 F 19	Commercial rd N18
143 O 2	Commercial st E1
150 M 20	Commercial way SE15
151 T 18	Commercial way SE15
61 U 7	Commercial way NW10
77 N 13	Commerell st SE10
143 P 11	Commodity quay E1
63 V 13	Commodore st E1
10 D 11	Common rd Stanm
86 H 7	Common rd SW13
102 F 7	Common the Rich
10 H 9	Common the Stanm
72 K 2	Common the W5
86 M 6	Commondale SW15
106 H 13	Commonfield la SW17
121 P 7	Commonside east Mitch
121 N 8	Commonside west Mitch
137 S 20	Commonwealth institute W8
62 K 20	Commonwealth av W12
31 X 1	Commonwealth rd N17
80 E 13	Commonwealth way SE2
51 X 16	Community rd E15
59 P 4	Community rd Grnfd
38 M 15	Como rd Rom
110 H 5	Como rd SE23
39 N 14	Como st Rom
84 H 15	Compass hill Rich
46 B 19	Compayne gdns NW6
66 A 6	Compton av E6
48 J 19	Compton av N1
46 J 1	Compton av N6
131 Z 14	Compton clo NW1
59 Y 17	Compton clo W13
31 N 2	Compton cres N17
58 A 1	Compton cres Nthlt
73 V 17	Compton cres W4
132 K 15	Compton pl WC1
157 Z 1	Compton rd Croy
123 Z 20	Compton rd Croy
48 K 19	Compton rd N1
17 V 5	Compton rd N21
128 G 13	Compton rd NW10
105 V 14	Compton rd SW19
22 D 16	Compton ri Pinn
133 X 16	Compton st EC1
48 H 19	Compton ter N1
7 V 4	Comreddy clo Enf
150 H 6	Comus pl SE17
47 X 9	Comus rd SE17
88 J 11	Comyn rd SW11
65 O 14	Comyns clo E16
69 P 1	Comyns rd Dgnhm
10 A 6	Comyns the Bushey
90 B 10	Concanon rd SW2
141 P 14	Concert Hall appr SE1
82 J 6	Concord clo Hounsl
9 O 18	Concord rd Enf
61 S 12	Concord rd W3
89 W 2	Condell rd SW8
63 V 17	Conder st E14
90 L 7	Conderton rd SE5
57 X 20	Condor wlk Hornch
78 M 20	Condover cres SE18
4 D 20	Conduct rd Barnt
140 K 8	Conduit ct WC2
9 V 20	Conduit la Enf
19 U 2	Conduit la N9
157 X 12	Conduit la S Croy
138 F 7	Conduit ms W2
138 F 6	Conduit pas W2
138 G 6	Conduit pl W2
78 M 13	Conduit rd SE18
79 N 13	Conduit rd SE18
140 A 8	Conduit st W1
139 Z 9	Conduit st W1
43 V 20	Conduit way NW10
48 J 11	Conewood st N5
108 M 1	Coney av Islwth
20 M 7	Coney Burrows E4
40 A 18	Coneygrove pth Nthlt
80 G 10	Conference rd SE2
79 N 13	Congleton gro SE18
79 T 13	Congo rd SE18
80 F 11	Congress rd SE2
95 S 8	Congreve rd SE9
150 J 7	Congreve st SE17
7 Y 9	Conical corner Enf
8 D 20	Conifer gdns Enf
108 B 8	Conifer gdns SW16
102 C 18	Conifers clo Tedd
87 X 4	Coniger rd SW6
74 H 4	Coningham ms W12
74 J 6	Coningham rd W12
72 F 6	Coningsby cotts W5
20 D 18	Coningsby gdns E4
30 H 20	Coningsby rd N4
156 K 19	Coningsby rd S Croy
72 F 6	Coningsby rd W5
93 T 5	Conington rd SE13
6 H 17	Conisbee ct N14
111 U 7	Conisborough cres SE6
17 Z 12	Coniscliffe rd N13
67 U 2	Coniston av Bark
60 B 8	Coniston av Grnfd
96 G 8	Coniston av Welling
67 U 2	Coniston av Bark
98 K 3	Coniston clo Bxly Hth
119 N 13	Coniston clo Mrdn
15 S 11	Coniston clo N20
85 U 1	Coniston clo W4
42 E 3	Coniston gdns Wemb
154 F 14	Coniston gdns Sutton
35 R 12	Coniston gdns Ilf
19 P 6	Coniston gdns N9
25 Y 16	Coniston gdns NW9
112 A 17	Coniston rd Brom
111 Y 15	Coniston rd Brom
98 K 3	Coniston rd Bxly Hth
123 X 17	Coniston rd Croy
29 S 7	Coniston rd N10
18 J 20	Coniston rd N17
82 L 17	Coniston rd Twick
57 V 15	Coniston way Hornch
48 A 20	Conistone way N7
128 L 17	Conlan st W10
44 C 19	Conley rd NW10
77 N 13	Conley st SE10
16 A 5	Connaught av Barnt
20 J 2	Connaught av E4
8 F 9	Connaught av Enf
82 C 12	Connaught av Hounsl
85 V 9	Connaught av SW14
50 G 6	Connaught clo E10
8 F 10	Connaught clo Enf
154 F 3	Connaught clo Sutton
138 L 7	Connaught clo W2
27 Z 13	Connaught dri NW11
29 T 15	Connaught gdns N10
17 W 15	Connaught gdns N13
139 N 7	Connaught ms W2
139 N 7	Connaught pl W2
118 B 8	Connaught rd New Mald
23 W 5	Connaught rd Harrow
4 D 20	Connaught rd Barnt
51 Y 4	Connaught rd E11
66 A 20	Connaught rd E16
78 B 3	Connaught rd E16
65 Z 20	Connaught rd E16
33 N 16	Connaught rd E17
20 L 4	Connaught rd E4
54 D 8	Connaught rd Ilf
48 F 1	Connaught rd N4
62 B 5	Connaught rd NW10
84 L 13	Connaught rd Rich
154 G 4	Connaught rd Sutton
101 S 12	Connaught rd Tedd
72 A 1	Connaught rd W13
138 M 7	Connaught sq W2
139 N 6	Connaught sq W2
78 L 14	Connaught st SE18
138 M 6	Connaught st W2
17 X 14	Connaught way N13
60 N 11	Connell cres W5
61 N 11	Connell cres W5
20 K 10	Connington cres E4
9 S 2	Connop rd Enf
56 C 11	Connor rd Dgnhm
63 S 3	Connor st E9
71 S 2	Conolly rd W7
119 N 19	Conrad dri Worc Pk
141 U 16	Cons st SE1
118 G 9	Consfield av New Mald
83 S 14	Consort ms Islwth
92 A 7	Consort rd SE15
91 Z 5	Consort rd SE15
91 Z 5	Consort rd SE15
80 O 13	Constable clo Hounsl
28 B 19	Constable rd NW11
31 X 15	Constable cres N15
28 B 19	Constable gdns Edg
126 C 19	Constance cres Brom
122 J 16	Constance rd Croy
18 D 1	Constance rd Enf
154 E 9	Constance rd Sutton
82 L 19	Constance rd Twick
78 C 3	Constance st E16
46 L 13	Constantine rd NW3
139 Y 17	Constitution hill SW1
95 W 2	Constitution ri SE18
150 C 7	Content st SE17
72 D 11	Convent gdns W5
108 L 16	Convent hill SE19
108 L 16	Convent hill SE19
10 L 19	Conway clo Stanm

59 V 4	Conway cres Grnfd	
37 S 19	Conway cres Rom	
154 A 14	Conway dri Sutton	
153 Z 15	Conway dri Sutton	
8 D 3	Conway gdns Enf	
121 Z 9	Conway gdns Mitch	
42 D 2	Conway gdns Wemb	
61 Z 14	Conway gro W3	
82 F 18	Conway rd Hounsl	
17 O 10	Conway rd N14	
30 K 15	Conway rd N15	
44 L 8	Conway rd NW2	
79 U 12	Conway rd SE18	
105 N 20	Conway rd SW20	
132 A 18	Conway st W1	
46 K 20	Conybeare NW3	
20 M 19	Conyers clo Wdfd Grn	
107 W 12	Conyers rd SW16	
112 H 18	Cooden clo Brom	
153 S 13	Cookes la Sutton	
80 C 7	Cookhill rd SE2	
7 X 2	Cooks Hole rd Enf	
64 E 6	Cooks rd E15	
149 V 14	Cooks rd SE17	
44 B 3	Cool Oak la NW9	
65 U 19	Coolfin rd E16	
20 J 16	Coolgardie av E4	
29 X 18	Coolhurst rd N8	
129 O 15	Coomassie rd W9	
157 T 9	Coombe av Croy	
104 A 20	Coombe bank New Mald	
24 M 9	Coombe clo Edg	
82 H 12	Coombe clo Hounsl	
17 V 6	Coombe corner N21	
100 D 16	Coombe cres Hampt	
103 Y 18	Coombe end Kingst	
118 B 12	Coombe Field clo New Mald	
118 C 8	Coombe gdns New Mald	
118 G 2	Coombe gdns SW20	
104 C 18	Coombe Hill glade SW20	
103 Y 14	Coombe hill Kingst	
104 A 18	Coombe Hill rd Kingst	
103 Z 20	Coombe Ho chase Kingst	
158 B 12	Coombe la Croy	
117 U 1	Coombe la Kingst	
118 H 1	Coombe la SW20	
104 C 19	Coombe Lane west Kingst	
103 Y 19	Coombe Lane west Kingst	
127 S 7	Coombe lea Brom	
77 Y 16	Coombe lodge SE7	
103 X 18	Coombe neville Kingst	
157 X 8	Coombe pk Croy	
103 X 13	Coombe pk Kingst	
118 A 3	Coombe rd New Mald	
10 B 1	Coombe rd Bushey	
157 W 10	Coombe rd Croy	
100 D 16	Coombe rd Hampt	
117 P 1	Coombe rd Kingst	
30 G 7	Coombe rd N22	
43 Y 8	Coombe rd NW10	
109 Z 9	Coombe rd SE26	
72 B 8	Coombe rd W13	
74 B 14	Coombe rd W4	
103 V 20	Coombe ri Kingst	
103 V 13	Coombe ridings Kingst	
153 Z 5	Coombe wlk Sutton	
103 W 13	Coombe Wood rd Kingst	
5 Z 9	Coombehurst clo Barnt	
120 B 13	Coombemere rd Mrdn	
121 W 16	Coomber way Croy	
69 P 3	Coombes rd Dgnhm	
38 C 20	Coombewood dri Rom	
133 Y 10	Cooms st N1	
25 U 5	Cooms wlk Edg	
32 G 4	Coopar av E17	
141 U 20	Cooper clo SE1	
154 M 5	Cooper cres Carsh	
156 H 9	Cooper rd Croy	
44 F 16	Cooper rd NW10	
65 P 16	Cooper rd SE12	
142 M 8	Cooper's row EC3	
63 P 12	Coopers clo E1	
51 S 3	Coopers la E10	
132 G 9	Coopers la NW1	
112 G 4	Coopers la SE12	
151 P 10	Coopers rd SE1	
34 L 3	Coopersale clo Wdfd Grn	
50 G 15	Coopersale rd E9	
56 B 9	Coote gdns Dgnhm	
98 A 2	Coote rd Bxly Hth	
56 B 9	Coote rd Dgnhm	
145 U 2	Cope pl W8	
75 T 10	Cope st SE16	
33 S 17	Copeland rd E17	
91 Y 5	Copeland rd SE15	
56 A 1	Copen rd Dgnhm	
63 Y 17	Copenhagen pl E14	
132 L 5	Copenhagen st N1	
133 S 6	Copenhagen st N1	
110 M 18	Copers Cope rd Becknhm	
111 O 20	Copers Cope rd Becknhm	
134 A 3	Copford wlk N1	
133 Z 4	Copford wlk N1	
25 T 3	Copinger wlk Edg	
42 F 16	Copland av Wemb	
42 E 15	Copland clo Wemb	
42 J 17	Copland rd Wemb	
91 U 9	Copleston rd SE15	
149 Z 15	Copley clo SE17	
59 W 12	Copley clo W7	
127 N 1	Copley Dene Brom	
108 C 15	Copley pk SW16	
11 T 15	Copley rd Stanm	
63 T 15	Copley st E1	
94 C 10	Coppelia rd SE3	
35 V 4	Copper Beech clo Ilf	
44 L 9	Copper Mead clo NW2	
106 C 10	Copper Mill la SW17	
76 D 17	Copperas st SE8	
46 F 16	Copperbeech clo NW3	
18 E 15	Copperfield ms N18	
63 W 13	Copperfield rd E3	
68 G 18	Copperfield rd SE28	
142 A 16	Copperfield st SE1	
141 Z 16	Copperfield st SE1	
114 D 14	Copperfield way Chisl	
22 E 12	Copperfield way Pinn	
32 D 18	Coppermill la E17	
28 M 2	Coppets rd N10	
28 K 1	Coppetts clo N12	
29 N 4	Coppetts rd N10	
118 M 6	Coppice clo SW20	
86 H 17	Coppice dri SW15	
7 W 13	Coppice the Enf	
34 C 11	Coppice way E18	
14 L 10	Coppice wlk N20	
16 D 14	Coppies gro N11	
157 S 8	Copping clo Croy	
159 S 15	Coppins the Croy	
10 G 20	Coppins the Stanm	
88 H 6	Coppock clo SW11	
159 S 6	Copse av W Wckm	
116 G 19	Copse Glade Surb	
154 B 16	Copse Hill Sutton	
104 E 20	Copse hill SW20	
21 P 6	Copse the E4	
158 G 18	Copse view S Croy	
80 K 10	Coptefield dri Blvdr	
160 G 3	Copthall av EC2	
160 F 4	Copthall ct EC2	
26 G 1	Copthall dri NW7	
13 U 20	Copthall gdns NW7	
26 G 1	Copthall gdns NW7	
101 X 1	Copthall gdns Twick	
89 X 20	Copthorne av SW12	
140 J 2	Coptic st WC1	
15 V 14	Copwood clo N12	
37 U 11	Coral clo Rom	
141 T 18	Coral st SE1	
80 G 7	Coralline wlk SE2	
132 J 17	Coram st WC1	
19 S 2	Coran clo N9	
82 H 8	Corban rd Hounsl	
5 T 5	Corbar clo Barnt	
155 O 2	Corbet clo Wallgtn	
135 O 19	Corbet pl E1	
34 K 18	Corbett rd E11	
33 V 10	Corbett rd E17	
75 P 12	Corbetts la SE16	
75 P 12	Corbetts pas SE16	
52 A 1	Corbicum E11	
105 P 16	Corbiere ct SW19	
74 A 2	Corbins la Harrow	
63 N 5	Corbridge cres E2	
135 X 7	Corbridge cres E2	
7 O 14	Corby cres Enf	
61 X 7	Corby rd NW10	
114 H 1	Corbylands rd Sidcp	
96 H 20	Corbylands rd Sidcp	
48 A 5	Corbyn st N4	
64 D 17	Cordelia st E14	
64 E 16	Cording st E14	
63 U 8	Cordova rd E3	
76 B 7	Cordwain E14	
93 Y 12	Cordwell rd SE13	
95 P 3	Corelli rd SE3	
40 F 12	Corfe av Harrow	
63 N 10	Corfield st E2	
135 X 15	Corfton rd W5	
60 J 16	Corfton rd W5	
42 L 13	Corinium clo Wemb	
47 W 12	Corinne rd N19	
143 V 13	Cork sq E1	
140 A 10	Cork st W1	
140 A 10	Cork Street ms W1	
116 H 17	Corkran rd Surb	
159 X 5	Corkscrew hill W Wckm	
90 H 3	Cormont rd SE5	
57 X 20	Cormorant wlk Hornch	
24 H 1	Cornbury rd Edg	
48 D 19	Cornelia st N7	
115 Z 14	Cornell clo Sidcp	
94 D 7	Corner grn SE3	
26 D 4	Corner mead NW9	
74 B 18	Corney rd W4	
124 F 20	Cornflower la CR0	
91 Z 15	Cornflower ter SE22	
126 E 13	Cornford clo Brom	
107 T 3	Cornford gro SW12	
142 G 6	Cornhill EC3	
160 G 7	Cornhill EC3	
110 A 20	Cornish gro SE20	
93 T 8	Cornmill la SE13	
55 W 3	Cornshaw rd Dgnhm	
50 B 10	Cornthwaite rd E5	
63 O 9	Cornwall av E2	
30 B 5	Cornwall av N22	
27 Z 2	Cornwall av N3	
58 G 15	Cornwall av S'hall	
96 J 9	Cornwall av Welling	
54 L 19	Cornwall clo Bark	
136 L 7	Cornwall cres W11	
115 T 18	Cornwall dri Orp	
145 Y 3	Cornwall Gardens wlk SW7	
44 K 19	Cornwall gdns NW10	
146 A 3	Cornwall gdns SW7	
145 Z 3	Cornwall gdns SW7	
74 B 15	Cornwall gro W4	
146 A 3	Cornwall Mews south SW7	
145 X 2	Cornwall Mews west SW7	
156 H 14	Cornwall rd Croy	
22 M 17	Cornwall rd Harrow	
31 O 16	Cornwall rd N15	
18 K 15	Cornwall rd N18	
48 F 2	Cornwall rd N4	
22 E 3	Cornwall rd Pinn	
141 T 14	Cornwall rd SE1	
153 W 19	Cornwall rd Sutton	
83 Z 20	Cornwall rd Twick	
63 N 19	Cornwall st E1	
143 X 8	Cornwall st E1	
143 Y 8	Cornwall st E1	
131 S 18	Cornwall ter NW1	
19 N 8	Cornwallis av N9	
19 O 8	Cornwallis av N9	
114 D 5	Cornwallis av SE9	
19 O 8	Cornwallis gro N9	
55 X 13	Cornwallis rd Dgnhm	
32 G 14	Cornwallis rd E17	
48 A 7	Cornwallis rd N19	
47 Z 6	Cornwallis rd N19	
95 U 7	Cornwallis wlk SE9	
28 F 14	Cornwood clo N2	
63 P 17	Cornwood dri E1	
55 S 16	Cornworthy rd Dgnhm	
94 F 19	Corona rd SE12	
49 T 11	Coronation av N16	
97 W 15	Coronation clo Bxly	
36 C 13	Coronation clo Ilf	
57 Y 14	Coronation dri Hornch	
65 Z 10	Coronation rd E13	
61 O 9	Coronation rd NW10	
82 G 20	Coronation wlk Twick	
134 J 13	Coronet st N1	
82 A 10	Corporation av Hounsl	
133 U 16	Corporation row EC1	
64 M 7	Corporation st E15	
65 P 6	Corporation st E15	
90 A 11	Corrance rd SW2	
16 L 13	Corri av N14	
45 Z 2	Corrina ct NW11	
46 A 1	Corringham ct NW11	
46 A 1	Corringham rd NW11	
43 P 7	Corringham rd Wemb	
45 X 1	Corringham rd NW11	
46 A 1	Corringway NW11	
45 Z 2	Corringway NW11	
60 M 16	Corringway W5	
61 O 11	Corringway W5	
107 U 15	Corsehill st SW16	
134 G 13	Corsham st N1	
48 J 17	Corsica st N5	
87 W 5	Cortayne rd SW6	
86 L 15	Cortis rd SW15	
86 K 15	Cortis ter SW15	
89 V 1	Corunna rd SW8	
89 U 1	Corunna ter SW8	
90 L 13	Cosbycote av SE24	
155 X 15	Cosdach av Wallgtn	
156 H 10	Cosedge cres Croy	
132 L 20	Cosmo pl WC1	
74 D 7	Cosmur clo W12	
149 S 2	Cosser st SE1	
91 W 6	Costa st SE15	
59 R 8	Costons av Grnfd	
59 O 8	Costons la Grnfd	
130 L 20	Cosway st NW1	
64 B 16	Cotall st E14	
106 M 9	Coteford st SW17	
107 N 10	Coteford st SW17	
157 S 6	Cotelands Croy	
50 C 9	Cotesbach rd E5	
57 S 13	Cotesmore gdns Dgnhm	
122 M 8	Cotford rd Thntn Hth	
150 C 7	Cotham st SE17	
90 C 20	Cotherstone rd SW2	
115 W 3	Cotleigh av Bxly	
45 Y 20	Cotleigh rd NW6	
39 N 18	Cotleigh rd Rom	
28 C 18	Cotman clo NW11	
87 O 15	Cotman clo SW15	
25 O 7	Cotman gdns Edg	
97 O 6	Coton rd Welling	
117 X 12	Cotsford av New Mald	
99 P 4	Cotswold clo Bxly Hth	
103 U 16	Cotswold clo Kingst	
66 B 8	Cotswold gdns E6	
36 E 20	Cotswold gdns Ilf	
45 P 6	Cotswold gdns NW2	
7 P 13	Cotswold grn Enf	
100 G 14	Cotswold rd Hampt	
108 K 8	Cotswold st SE27	
7 P 12	Cotswold way Enf	
127 S 19	Cottage av Brom	
150 H 18	Cottage grn SE5	
116 G 15	Cottage gro Surb	
90 A 8	Cottage gro SW9	
89 Z 8	Cottage gro SW9	
146 J 2	Cottage pl SW3	
64 E 19	Cottage st E14	
115 U 2	Cottagefield clo Sidcp	
104 G 20	Cottenham dri SW20	
104 G 20	Cottenham Park rd SW20	
104 K 18	Cottenham pl SW20	
32 M 12	Cottenham rd E17	
116 L 20	Cotterill rd Surb	
75 V 18	Cottesbrook st SE14	
63 Y 12	Cottesford rd E3	
35 V 7	Cottesmore av Ilf	
146 A 1	Cottesmore gdns W8	
145 Z 1	Cottesmore gdns W8	
110 E 19	Cottingham rd SE20	
143 S 18	Cottingham rd SW8	
100 A 8	Cottington clo SE11	
149 V 9	Cottington st SE11	
61 Y 16	Cotton av W3	
11 W 9	Cotton hill Brom	
64 F 19	Cotton st E14	
134 M 12	Cotton's gdns E2	
39 N 16	Cottons app Rom	
142 H 13	Cottons la SE1	
43 X 19	Couch rd NW10	
35 T 7	Couchmore av Ilf	
92 J 8	Coulgate st SE4	
147 O 8	Coulson st SW3	
58 B 11	Coulter clo Grnfd	
144 A 2	Coulter rd W6	
74 K 8	Coulter rd W6	
150 A 20	Councillor st SE5	
142 E 15	Counter ct SE1	
142 H 13	Counter st SE1	
47 V 14	Countess rd NW5	
18 G 1	Countisbury av Enf	

100 B 9	Country way Felt
15 O 1	County ga Barnt
114 C 6	County ga SE9
67 V 6	County gdns Bark
90 L 1	County gro SE5
141 N 18	County Hall the SE1
66 L 15	County rd E6
122 J 4	County rd Thntn Hth
150 C 3	County st SE1
150 D 3	County st SE1
79 O 14	Coupland pla SW14
30 F 10	Courcy rd N8
89 Y 3	Courland gro SW8
89 Y 3	Courland st SW8
113 X 7	Course the SE9
81 N 13	Court av Blvdr
100 J 6	Court Clo av Twick
24 H 12	Court clo Harrow
155 X 17	Court clo Wallgtn
125 R 3	Court Downs rd Becknhm
156 D 7	Court dri Croy
11 X 14	Court dri Stanm
154 J 8	Court dri Sutton
58 G 1	Court Farm la Nthlt
58 H 1	Court Farm rd Nthlt
113 O 6	Court Farm rd SE9
14 M 18	Court House gdns N3
91 T 17	Court La gdns SE21
91 V 18	Court la SE21
58 E 8	Court mead Nthlt
70 E 13	Court rd S'hall
123 V 5	Court rd SE25
113 S 3	Court rd SE9
95 U 17	Court rd SE9
126 F 3	Court st Brom
10 A 13	Court the Ruislip
36 C 11	Court way Ilf
26 B 12	Court way NW9
83 W 18	Court way Twick
61 W 14	Court way W3
21 Y 16	Court way Wdfd Grn
95 S 17	Court yd SE9
95 T 16	Court yd SE9
47 Z 4	Courtauld rd N19
22 L 2	Courtenay av Harrow
23 N 6	Courtenay av Harrow
46 H 1	Courtenay av N6
28 H 20	Courtenay av N6
23 N 7	Courtenay av Harrow
23 N 6	Courtenay gdns Har
32 J 15	Courtenay pl E17
153 N 5	Courtenay rd Worc Pk
52 C 9	Courtenay rd E11
32 G 14	Courtenay rd E17
110 G 16	Courtenay rd SE20
149 S 10	Courtenay sq SE11
149 S 10	Courtenay st SE11
23 W 17	Courtfield av Harrow
23 X 16	Courtfield cres Harrow
145 Y 6	Courtfield gdns SW5
145 Z 6	Courtfield gdns SW5
59 Z 17	Courtfield gdns W13
146 A 6	Courtfield rd SW7
159 Y 5	Courtfield ri W Wckm
93 U 12	Courthill rd SE13
99 P 5	Courthope rd Grnfd
47 N 13	Courthope rd NW3
105 R 13	Courthope rd SW19
105 T 17	Courthope vla SE19
14 M 17	Courthouse rd N12
126 A 20	Courtland av Brom
21 P 8	Courtland av E4
53 U 6	Courtland av Ilf
12 M 9	Courtland av NW7
13 N 9	Courtland av NW7
108 D 18	Courtland av SW16
68 K 19	Courtland av SE28
66 D 2	Courtland av NW11
E 16	Courtlands av Hampt
85 T 3	Courtlands av Rich
94 G 12	Courtlands av SE12
152 C 14	Courtlands dri Epsom
117 P 16	Courtlands rd Surb
117 P 17	Courtlands rd Surb
85 P 12	Courtlands Rich
60 D 15	Courtlands dri Erith
98 H 2	Courtleet dri Erith
5 T 3	Courtleigh av Barnt
27 T 14	Courtleigh gdns NW11
30 M 2	Courtman rd N17
90 M 16	Courtmead clo SE24
137 S 5	Courtnell st W2
109 R 16	Courtney clo SE19
154 M 18	Courtney cres Carsh
156 G 5	Courtney pl Croy
156 F 5	Courtney rd Croy
48 F 14	Courtney rd N7
106 J 18	Courtney rd SW19
92 H 15	Courtrai rd SE23
29 X 19	Courtside N8
158 M 20	Courtswood la Croy
160 D 10	Cousin la EC4
77 W 18	Couthurst rd SE3
85 U 11	Coval gdns SW14
85 T 10	Coval la SW14
85 U 10	Coval rd SW14
140 L 8	Covent gdn WC2
137 N 6	Covent gdns W11
66 F 18	Coventry clo E6
129 V 7	Coventry clo NW6
63 N 12	Coventry rd E1
135 Y 15	Coventry rd E1
135 Y 17	Coventry rd E1
54 B 3	Coventry rd Ilf
53 Y 5	Coventry rd Ilf
123 X 8	Coventry rd SE25
140 E 10	Coventry st W1
124 J 18	Coverack clo Croy
16 F 1	Coverack clo N14
6 F 20	Coverack clo N14
11 P 15	Coverdale clo Stanm
157 U 6	Coverdale gdn Croy
45 R 19	Coverdale rd NW2
136 A 16	Coverdale rd W12
74 L 4	Coverdale rd W12
67 R 6	Coverdales the Bark
135 T 20	Coverley clo E1
5 S 7	Covert way Barnt
106 J 11	Coverton rd SW17
108 J 19	Covington gdns SW16
108 E 16	Covington way SW16
108 J 18	Covington way SW16
59 P 7	Cow la Grnfd
66 F 16	Cowan clo E6
150 J 13	Cowan st SE5
25 N 13	Cowbridge rd Harrow
133 X 20	Cowcross st EC1
111 O 9	Cowden st SE6
133 N 3	Cowdenbeath pth N1
57 V 13	Cowdray way Hornch
8 D 9	Cowdrey clo Eng
99 Z 20	Cowdrey ct Drtfd
106 B 14	Cowdrey rd SW19
50 K 17	Cowdry rd E9
41 O 8	Cowen av Harrow
59 S 8	Cowgate rd Grnfd
106 M 9	Cowick rd SW17
107 N 10	Cowick rd SW17
40 C 19	Cowings mead Nthlt
9 R 13	Cowland av Enf
116 K 1	Cowleaze rd Kingst
51 Z 9	Cowley la E11
34 G 15	Cowley rd E11
53 U 2	Cowley rd Ilf
39 Z 1	Cowley rd Rom
86 A 7	Cowley rd SW14
90 F 2	Cowley rd SW14
149 U 20	Cowley rd SW14
74 C 4	Cowley rd W3
148 J 1	Cowley st SW1
66 C 1	Cowper av E6
154 G 9	Cowper av Sutton
127 O 10	Cowper clo Brom
97 O 12	Cowper vla Welling
155 V 14	Cowper gdns Wallgtn
6 F 19	Cowper gdns N14
81 P 11	Cowper rd Blvdr
127 N 10	Cowper rd Brom
102 M 12	Cowper rd Kingst
16 E 5	Cowper rd N14
49 R 13	Cowper rd N18
18 J 18	Cowper rd N18
106 O 15	Cowper rd SW19
73 X 2	Cowper rd W3
59 V 19	Cowper rd W7
134 G 15	Cowper st EC2
136 F 2	Cowper ter W10
34 H 8	Cowslip rd E18
89 Y 1	Cowthorpe rd SW8
141 Z 3	Cox's ct EC1
78 A 13	Coxmount rd SE7
109 Y 2	Coxs wlk SE21
79 T 13	Coxwell rd SE18
111 W 18	Crab hill Becknhm
37 W 12	Crabtree av Rom
60 L 5	Crabtree av Wemb
51 S 15	Crabtree ct E15
144 F 17	Crabtree la SW6
81 W 7	Crabtree Manor way Blvdr
81 X 4	Crabtree Manorway north Blvdr
8 G 13	Craddock rd Enf
47 O 19	Craddock st NW5
114 D 2	Cradley rd E6
34 C 7	Craig gdns E18
18 M 15	Craig Park rd N18
102 E 9	Craig rd Rich
57 U 1	Craigdale rd Hornch
39 U 20	Craigdale rd Hornch
158 A 1	Craigen av Croy
124 A 20	Craigen av Croy
77 U 18	Craigerne rd SE3
95 X 3	Craigholm SE18
61 O 2	Craigmuir pk Wemb
90 E 18	Craignair rd SW2
122 D 2	Craignish av SW16
140 J 13	Craigs ct SW1
95 T 11	Craigton rd SE9
11 U 17	Craigwell clo Stanm
11 T 16	Craigwell dri Stanm
150 F 6	Crail row SE17
139 U 2	Cramer st W1
110 B 16	Crampton rd SE20
149 Z 8	Crampton st SE17
58 A 6	Cranberry clo Nthlt
135 T 18	Cranberry st E1
70 H 11	Cranborne av S'hall
67 S 3	Cranborne rd Bark
140 H 9	Cranbourn all WC2
140 H 9	Cranbourne all WC2
34 H 13	Cranbourne av E11
122 A 7	Cranbourne clo SW16
27 U 16	Cranbourne gdns NW11
36 D 10	Cranbourne gdns Ilf
51 U 12	Cranbourne rd E15
29 T 8	Cranbourne rd N10
126 E 15	Cranbrook clo Brom
82 K 20	Cranbrook dri Twick
63 S 7	Cranbrook est E2
32 K 15	Cranbrook ms E17
30 E 6	Cranbrook pk N22
98 C 1	Cranbrook rd Bxly Hth
122 M 2	Cranbrook rd Thntn Hth
5 V 20	Cranbrook rd Barnt
82 C 10	Cranbrook rd Hounsl
35 X 17	Cranbrook rd Ilf
53 X 6	Cranbrook rd Ilf
95 N 7	Cranbrook rd SE8
93 O 2	Cranbrook rd SE8
105 S 18	Cranbrook rd SW19
74 B 13	Cranbrook rd W4
35 U 19	Cranbrook rise Ilf
63 T 7	Cranbrook st E2
88 A 5	Cranbury rd SW6
83 Y 13	Crane av Islwth
61 X 20	Crane av W3
56 F 19	Crane clo Dgnhm
141 U 5	Crane ct EC4
48 G 18	Crane gro N7
75 S 12	Crane mead SE16
100 J 4	Crane Park rd Twick
100 G 4	Crane pk Twick
101 T 1	Crane rd Twick
76 J 15	Crane st SE10
83 O 17	Crane way Twick
101 O 3	Cranebrook Twick
83 W 19	Craneford clo Twick
83 U 19	Craneford way Twick
116 K 10	Cranes dri Surb
116 K 10	Cranes Park av Surb
116 L 10	Cranes Park cres Surb
116 K 11	Cranes pk Surb
70 F 13	Craneswater pk S'hall
26 A 3	Cranfield dri NW9
155 O 19	Cranfield rd Carsh
92 M 7	Cranfield rd SE4
108 L 8	Cranfield vlls SE27
17 O 16	Cranford av N13
104 H 19	Cranford clo SW20
63 T 19	Cranford cotts E1
70 B 19	Cranford la Hounsl
63 T 19	Cranford st E1
39 Z 18	Cranham rd Hornch
44 M 15	Cranhurst rd NW2
98 F 15	Cranleigh clo Bxly
123 Z 2	Cranleigh clo SE20
154 A 3	Cranleigh gdns Sutton
24 J 16	Cranleigh gdns Harrow
103 N 15	Cranleigh gdns Kingst
54 E 19	Cranleigh gdns Bark
7 T 17	Cranleigh gdns N21
58 D 17	Cranleigh gdns S'hall
123 S 5	Cranleigh gdns SE25
30 L 14	Cranleigh rd N15
119 X 6	Cranleigh rd SW19
132 C 9	Cranleigh st NW1
54 C 1	Cranley dri Ilf
36 C 20	Cranley dri Ilf
155 U 15	Cranley gdns Wallgtn
29 S 14	Cranley gdns N10
29 V 14	Cranley gdns N10
17 R 10	Cranley gdns N13
146 D 9	Cranley gdns SW7
146 D 9	Cranley ms SW7
146 F 7	Cranley pl SW7
65 V 14	Cranley rd E13
36 B 20	Cranley rd Ilf
89 Y 7	Cranmar ct SW4
72 B 8	Cranmer av W13
119 R 14	Cranmer clo Mrdn
24 E 1	Cranmer clo Stanm
100 K 11	Cranmer ct Hampt
120 L 9	Cranmer Farm clo Mitch
56 K 13	Cranmer gdns Dgnhm
156 K 5	Cranmer rd Croy
52 J 11	Cranmer rd E7
12 E 10	Cranmer rd Edg
100 L 11	Cranmer rd Hampt
102 K 13	Cranmer rd Kingst
12 N 10	Cranmer rd Mitch
149 W 8	Cranmer rd SW9
106 G 11	Cranmer ter SW17
71 N 19	Cranmore av Islwth
112 B 7	Cranmore rd Brom
113 V 11	Cranmore rd Chisl
29 V 12	Cranmore way N10
82 B 5	Cranston clo Hounsl
20 D 18	Cranston gdns E4
110 H 2	Cranston rd SE23
75 O 13	Cranswick rd SE16
151 Y 10	Cranswick rd SE16
111 S 4	Crantock rd SE6
18 A 1	Cranwich av N21
49 R 1	Cranwich rd N16
134 F 14	Cranwood st EC1
20 J 6	Cranworth cres E4
90 E 2	Cranworth gdns SW9
90 D 18	Craster rd SW2
94 H 14	Crathie rd SE12
93 T 7	Crathorn st SE13
58 E 16	Craven av S'hall
74 A 4	Craven av W5
67 U 7	Craven gdns Bark
36 D 7	Craven gdns Ilf
106 A 13	Craven gdns SW19
105 Z 13	Craven gdns SW19
138 C 9	Craven Hill gdns W2
138 C 8	Craven Hill ms W2
138 D 8	Craven hill W2
62 A 2	Craven Park ms NW10
31 V 19	Craven Park rd N15
62 C 4	Craven Park rd NW10
140 K 12	Craven pas WC2
123 Z 20	Craven rd Croy
102 M 20	Craven rd Kingst
103 N 20	Craven rd Kingst
61 Z 3	Craven rd NW10
138 D 7	Craven rd W2
O 20	Craven rd W5
140 K 12	Craven st WC2
138 D 8	Craven ter W2
49 W 1	Craven wlk E5
31 Y 20	Craven wlk N16
42 G 15	Crawford av Wemb
83 T 4	Crawford clo Islwth
17 W 10	Crawford gdns N13
58 F 8	Crawford gdns Nthlt
139 O 1	Crawford ms W1
133 T 17	Crawford pas EC1
138 L 3	Crawford pl W1
90 M 3	Crawford rd SE5
139 N 2	Crawford st W1
51 S 4	Crawley rd E10
18 E 3	Crawley rd Enf
30 L 7	Crawley rd N22
91 V 11	Crawthew gro SE22
99 X 12	Cray clo Drtfrd
81 S 17	Cray rd Blvdr
115 T 16	Cray rd Sidcp
115 P 10	Craybrooke rd Sidcp
114 B 5	Craybury end SE9
99 U 1	Craydene rd Erith
99 R 12	Crayford High st Drtfrd

47 Z 12 Crayford rd N7
99 S 12 Crayford way Drtfrd
99 V 7 Crayhill sq Drtfrd
21 P 17 Crealock gro
Wdfd Grn
88 B 17 Crealock st SW18
150 K 3 Creasy est SE1
91 Y 16 Crebor st SE22
107 U 16 Credenhall st SW16
151 V 17 Credenhall way SE15
46 A 15 Crediton hill NW6
65 T 17 Crediton rd E16
128 E 6 Crediton rd NW10
65 X 7 Credon rd E13
75 N 14 Credon rd SE16
151 Y 10 Credon rd SE16
39 R 3 Cree way Rom
142 L 6 Creechurch la EC3
142 L 6 Creechurch pl EC3
141 Y 6 Creed la EC4
67 X 9 Creek rd Bark
76 D 17 Creek rd SE8
76 C 17 Creekside SE8
110 M 3 Creeland gro SE6
144 J 16 Crefeld clo W6
61 R 20 Crefeld rd W3
144 J 15 Crefield clo W6
66 A 7 Creighton av E6
29 N 8 Creighton av N10
28 J 9 Creighton av N2
31 S 1 Creighton av N17
128 H 8 Creighton rd NW6
72 F 9 Creighton rd W5
134 M 10 Cremer st E2
146 G 16 Cremorne est SW10
146 D 20 Cremorne gdns SW10
146 E 19 Cremorne rd SW10
57 T 7 Crescent av Hornch
5 T 4 Crescent east Barnt
105 Y 7 Crescent gdns SW19
120 H 10 Crescent gro Mitch
89 V 11 Crescent gro SW4
89 X 13 Crescent la SW4
146 L 5 Crescent pl SW3
125 S 3 Crescent rd Becknhm
112 F 19 Crescent rd Brom
56 G 10 Crescent rd Dgnhm
51 P 5 Crescent rd E10
65 T 3 Crescent rd E13
34 K 6 Crescent rd E18
21 N 3 Crescent rd E4
65 Y 3 Crescent rd E6
7 W 13 Crescent rd Enf
103 R 17 Crescent rd Kingst
16 A 15 Crescent rd N11
30 H 11 Crescent rd N15
29 Y 4 Crescent rd N22
27 V 4 Crescent rd N3
29 Y 19 Crescent rd N8
18 K 5 Crescent rd N9
78 M 13 Crescent rd SE18
114 M 7 Crescent rd Sidcp
79 N 12 Crescent rd SW20
5 V 17 Crescent ri Barnt
29 X 3 Crescent ri N22
134 A 17 Crescent row EC1
87 R 12 Crescent stables
SW15
125 O 1 Crescent the
Becknhm
117 X 4 Crescent the
New Mald
125 Z 14 Crescent the
W Wckm
5 N 10 Crescent the Barnt
97 U 18 Crescent the Bxly
123 O 13 Crescent the Croy
32 J 17 Crescent the E17
143 N 9 Crescent the EC3
41 P 5 Crescent the Harrow
35 W 18 Crescent the Ilf
16 A 15 Crescent the N11
31 T 17 Crescent the N15
44 K 9 Crescent the NW2
70 D 5 Crescent the S'hall
114 L 10 Crescent the Sidcp
116 H 13 Crescent the Surb
154 F 9 Crescent the SW13
86 F 4 Crescent the SW19
105 Y 8 Crescent the SW19
42 A 7 Crescent the Wemb
15 V 19 Crescent way N12
93 N 8 Crescent way SE4
108 E 17 Crescent way SW16
109 W 7 Crescent west Barnt
109 W 7 Crescent Wood rd
SE26
88 A 2 Cresford rd SW6
26 J 18 Crespigny rd NW4
58 F 11 Cressage clo S'hall

50 D 18 Cresset rd E9
89 W 9 Cresset st SW4
47 P 14 Cressfield clo NW5
47 W 3 Cressida rd N19
90 G 19 Cressingham Gardens
est SW2
154 C 7 Cressingham gro
Sutton
93 U 7 Cressingham rd
SE13
12 L 20 Cressingham rd Edg
25 Y 2 Cressingham rd Edg
49 S 13 Cressington clo N16
146 B 9 Cresswell gdns SW5
94 C 7 Cresswell pk SE3
146 C 10 Cresswell pl SW10
123 O 7 Cresswell rd SE25
84 F 16 Cresswell rd Twick
17 T 2 Cresswell way N21
63 R 13 Cressy ct E1
63 R 14 Cressy pl E1
46 L 13 Cressy rd NW3
9 P 4 Crest dri Enf
126 B 18 Crest rd Brom
44 G 7 Crest rd NW2
157 Z 16 Crest rd S Croy
17 T 13 Crest the N13
27 O 14 Crest the NW4
117 R 13 Crest the Surb
17 V 10 Crestbrook av N13
132 K 12 Crestfield st WC1
153 P 2 Creston way
Worc Pk
86 H 15 Crestway SW15
100 A 8 Creswell clo Felt
61 S 19 Creswick rd W3
27 W 13 Creswick wlk NW11
78 K 9 Creton st SE18
149 S 19 Crewdson rd SW9
62 D 8 Crewe pl NW10
76 A 10 Crews st E14
45 W 8 Crewys rd NW2
92 A 5 Crewys rd SE15
155 X 9 Crichton av Wallgtn
154 L 16 Crichton rd Carsh
120 L 8 Cricket grn Mitch
127 Z 1 Cricket Ground rd
Chisl
7 Z 9 Cricketers Arms rd
Enf
149 X 7 Cricketers ct SE11
50 A 12 Cricketfield rd E5
108 B 4 Cricklade av SW2
45 O 12 Cricklewood bdwy
NW2
45 T 10 Cricklewood la NW2
65 O 4 Cridland st E15
88 E 16 Crieff rd SW18
102 D 19 Crieff rd Tedd
107 Y 2 Criffel av SW2
150 L 3 Crimscott st SE1
150 L 4 Crimscott st SE1
148 F 20 Crimsworth rd SW8
132 L 7 Crinan st N1
148 C 17 Cringle st SW8
16 E 20 Crinkwell rd B11
144 C 11 Crisp rd W6
74 M 15 Crisp rd W6
100 B 9 Crispen rd Felt
155 Z 4 Crispin clo Wallgtn
155 Y 4 Crispin cres Wallgtn
12 J 20 Crispin rd Edg
142 M 1 Crispin st E1
87 V 6 Cristowe rd SW6
47 X 7 Criterion ms N19
106 L 5 Crockerton rd SW17
113 X 10 Crockham way SE9
4 J 19 Crocus field Barnt
62 D 18 Crocus wlk W12
159 V 1 Croft av W Wckm
81 O 14 Croft clo Blvdr
113 U 11 Croft clo Chisl
12 M 11 Croft clo NW7
71 X 5 Croft gdns W7
21 V 18 Croft Lodge clo
Wdfd Grn
112 G 16 Croft rd Brom
9 V 7 Croft rd Enf
154 H 10 Croft rd Sutton
108 G 19 Croft rd SW16
106 D 19 Croft rd SW19
76 V 12 Croft st SE8
4 D 14 Croft the Barnt
70 C 18 Croft the Hounsl
62 D 5 Croft the NW10
22 F 20 Croft the Pinn
60 J 14 Croft the W5
42 C 14 Croft the Wemb
102 B 8 Croft way Rich
114 G 7 Croft way Sidcp

47 S 8 Croftdown rd NW5
83 R 13 Crofters clo Islwth
158 L 19 Crofters mead Croy
132 E 3 Crofters way NW1
158 L 19 Crofton av Bxly
92 K 16 Crofton Pk rd SE4
65 V 10 Crofton rd E13
91 T 2 Crofton rd SE5
84 M 10 Crofton ter Rich
5 N 19 Crofton way Barnt
7 T 8 Crofton way Enf
23 Y 17 Crofts rd Harrow
143 R 10 Crofts st E1
45 Y 12 Croftway NW3
47 P 19 Crogsland rd NW1
157 R 15 Croham clo S Croy
157 V 17 Croham hurst Croy
157 T 13 Croham Manor rd
S Croy
157 R 16 Croham mt S Croy
157 T 11 Croham Park av
S Croy
158 C 17 Croham Valley rd
S Croy
157 W 14 Croham Valley rd
S Croy
157 Y 16 Croham Valley rd
S Croy
122 B 2 Croindene rd SW16
47 Y 2 Cromartie rd N19
157 T 16 Crombie clo Ilf
114 F 1 Crombie rd Sidcp
92 B 20 Crombie rd Sidcp
77 R 13 Crome st SE10
5 P 13 Cromer rd Barnt
33 W 20 Cromer rd E10
31 X 6 Cromer rd N17
38 K 18 Cromer rd Rom
37 Z 18 Cromer rd Rom
123 Z 6 Cromer rd SE25
107 O 15 Cromer rd SW17
21 T 14 Cromer rd Wdfd Grn
132 K 14 Cromer st WC1
87 U 17 Cromer Villas rd
SW18
87 X 13 Cromford rd SW18
117 Z 1 Cromford way
New Mald
127 Z 2 Cromlix clo BR7
130 E 19 Crompton st W2
118 C 10 Cromwell av
New Mald
126 G 8 Cromwell av Brom
47 T 2 Cromwell av N6
74 J 12 Cromwell av W6
126 H 9 Cromwell clo Brom
28 F 13 Cromwell clo N2
145 S 5 Cromwell cres SW5
146 H 4 Cromwell gdns SW7
136 D 20 Cromwell gro W6
146 F 5 Cromwell ms SW7
47 T 3 Cromwell pl N6
85 W 7 Cromwell pl SW14
146 G 4 Cromwell pl SW7
124 K 5 Cromwell rd
Becknhm
123 N 17 Cromwell rd Croy
33 T 16 Cromwell rd E17
52 K 20 Cromwell rd E7
82 H 13 Cromwell rd Hounsl
116 K 2 Cromwell rd Kingst
29 P 1 Cromwell rd N10
28 C 6 Cromwell rd N3
106 A 12 Cromwell rd SW19
105 Z 12 Cromwell rd SW19
145 X 5 Cromwell rd SW5
146 C 5 Cromwell rd SW7
102 A 15 Cromwell rd Tedd
101 Z 15 Cromwell rd Tedd
60 J 6 Cromwell rd Wemb
152 A 6 Cromwell rd Worc Pk
82 H 10 Cromwell st Hounsl
87 Y 2 Crondace rd SW6
134 J 10 Crondall st N1
97 X 9 Crook log Bxly Hth
75 U 12 Crooke rd SE8
104 M 15 Crooked billet SW19
27 S 10 Crooked usage N3
52 B 7 Crookes clo E11
87 V 3 Crookham rd SW6
95 Y 7 Crookston rd SE9
76 H 19 Crooms Hill gro
SE10
76 J 20 Crooms hill SE10
134 E 10 Cropley st N1
56 E 14 Croppath rd Dgnhm
100 B 8 Crosby clo Felt
69 U 5 Crosby rd Dgnhm
52 E 17 Crosby rd E7
142 F 18 Crosby row SE1

142 J 5 Crosby sq EC3
23 H 2 Cross av
Worc Pk
101 W 3 Cross Deep gdns
Twick
101 X 4 Cross deep Twick
12 B 11 Cross Ga Edg
160 A 3 Cross Key sq EC1
139 U 2 Cross Keys clo W1
160 F 3 Cross Keys ct EC2
98 C 18 Cross la Bxly
142 K 10 Cross la EC3
30 B 12 Cross la N8
82 K 11 Cross Lances rd
Hounsl
123 P 20 Cross rd Croy
20 L 5 Cross rd E4
8 F 15 Cross rd Enf
100 B 10 Cross rd Felt
40 J 9 Cross rd Harrow
23 P 14 Cross rd Harrow
23 Y 8 Cross rd Harrow
103 N 18 Cross rd Kingst
16 F 15 Cross rd N11
38 F 12 Cross rd Rom
55 T 2 Cross rd Rom
91 T 4 Cross rd SE5
115 P 11 Cross rd Sidcp
154 G 10 Cross rd Sutton
105 Y 18 Cross rd SW19
101 N 13 Cross st Hampt
133 Y 3 Cross st N1
18 J 16 Cross st N18
18 K 16 Cross st N18
86 C 6 Cross st SW13
55 T 10 Cross way Dgnhm
23 U 6 Cross Way the
Harrow
21 Y 14 Cross way Wdfd Grn
95 P 6 Crossbrook rd SE3
30 L 11 Crossfield rd N17
46 G 19 Crossfield rd NW3
76 B 18 Crossfield st SE8
90 B 4 Crossford st SW9
42 B 18 Crossgate Grnfd
122 H 14 Crossland rd
Thntn Hth
70 E 14 Crosslands av S'hall
72 M 3 Crosslands av W5
73 N 3 Crosslands av W5
48 F 18 Crossley st N7
58 J 8 Crossmead av Grnfd
113 U 2 Crossmead SE9
67 V 10 Crossness rd Bark
91 O 11 Crossthwaite av SE5
142 M 8 Crosswall EC3
143 N 7 Crosswall EC3
18 D 2 Crossway Enf
47 T 15 Crossway N16
15 U 19 Crossway N16
26 D 14 Crossway NW9
26 E 14 Crossway NW9
80 G 1 Crossway SE28
68 H 20 Crossway SE28
118 M 9 Crossway SW20
30 K 3 Crossway the N22
113 O 4 Crossway the SE9
59 Y 11 Crossway the W13
17 Y 1 Crossway N21
125 N 9 Crossways rd
Becknhm
121 S 5 Crossways rd Mitch
39 Z 11 Crossways Rom
158 K 16 Crossways S Croy
154 F 18 Crossways Sutton
70 E 20 Crossways the
Hounsl
43 R 7 Crossways the
Wemb
135 U 3 Croston st E8
68 D 7 Crouch av Bark
111 P 16 Crouch clo Becknhm
113 X 7 Crouch croft SE9
29 Z 19 Crouch End hill N8
29 Y 18 Crouch Hall rd N8
48 A 1 Crouch hill N4
109 V 8 Crouchman clo SE26
56 H 1 Crow la Rom
107 P 13 Crowborough rd
SW17
80 H 1 Crowden way SE28
143 W 9 Crowder st E1
90 G 5 Crowhurst clo SW9
16 M 3 Crowland gdns N14
123 N 9 Crowland rd
Thntn Hth
31 V 16 Crowland rd N15
49 N 20 Crowland ter N1
120 B 13 Crowland wlk Mrdn
38 H 18 Crowlands av Rom

156 H 11	Crowley cres Croy
64 A 3	Crown clo E3
13 S 7	Crown clo NW7
160 C 6	Crown ct EC2
94 G 16	Crown ct SE12
140 M 7	Crown ct WC2
108 L 14	Crown dale SE19
156 L 4	Crown hill Croy
62 D 4	Crown Hill rd NW10
127 O 13	Crown la Brom
119 Z 7	Crown la Mrdn
16 H 5	Crown la N14
108 G 14	Crown la SW16
108 G 13	Crown Lane gdns SW16
127 O 13	Crown Lane spur Brom
141 T 8	Crown Office row EC4
140 C 14	Crown pas SW1
47 T 17	Crown pl NW5
8 M 14	Crown rd Enf
36 D 13	Crown rd Ilf
119 Z 8	Crown rd Mrdn
29 P 2	Crown rd N10
117 X 1	Crown rd New Mald
154 A 8	Crown rd Sutton
153 Z 9	Crown rd Sutton
84 C 17	Crown rd Twick
56 J 19	Crown st Dgnhm
41 S 4	Crown st Harrow
150 B 18	Crown st SE5
73 T 3	Crown st W3
84 M 9	Crown ter Rich
43 O 8	Crown wlk Wemb
95 Z 4	Crown Woods la SE18
96 F 12	Crown Woods way SE9
132 B 8	Crowndale rd NW1
36 F 17	Crownfield av Ilf
51 W 13	Crownfield rd E15
35 R 3	Crownhill rd Wdfd Grn
38 H 13	Crownmead way Rom
90 E 13	Crownstone rd SW2
71 V 17	Crowntree clo Islwth
96 A 5	Crownwoods la SE9
64 L 8	Crows rd E15
24 F 6	Crowshott av Stanm
72 K 12	Crowther av Brentf
123 X 10	Crowther rd SE25
25 O 9	Croxden clo Edg
120 C 14	Croxden wlk Mrdn
30 K 3	Croxford gdns N22
56 M 4	Croxford way Rom
129 R 13	Croxley rd W9
90 L 19	Croxted clo SE21
109 N 2	Croxted rd SE21
90 L 18	Croxted rd SE24
58 O 9	Croyde av Grnfd
96 E 18	Croyde clo Sidcp
122 H 19	Croydon gro Croy
124 L 6	Croydon rd Becknhm
156 B 8	Croydon rd Croy
65 R 12	Croydon rd E13
121 T 11	Croydon rd Mitch
110 D 20	Croydon rd SE20
123 Z 4	Croydon rd SE20
155 V 7	Croydon rd Wallgtn
18 J 5	Croyland rd N9
116 J 18	Croylands dri Surb
129 P 16	Croyton pth W9
50 G 16	Crozier ter E9
142 K 17	Crucifix la SE1
133 Y 6	Cruden st N1
52 B 14	Cruikshank rd E15
133 R 11	Cruikshank st WC1
26 B 16	Crummock gdns NW9
80 F 11	Crumpsall st SE2
25 R 17	Crundale av NW9
157 O 15	Crunden rd S Croy
157 S 6	Crusader gdn Croy
106 M 18	Crusoe rd Mitch
142 L 8	Crutched friars EC3
112 A 4	Crutchley rd SE6
109 U 12	Crystal ct SE19
109 V 13	Crystal Palace pde SE19
109 Y 12	Crystal Palace pk SE26
91 W 10	Crystal Palace rd SE22
109 W 16	Crystal Palace Station SE19
109 O 15	Crystal ter SE19
55 T 4	Crystal way Dgnhm
23 W 15	Crystal way Harrow
9 O 9	Cuba dri Enf
76 A 4	Cuba st E14
156 E 11	Cubitt st Croy
133 O 14	Cubitt st WC1
89 V 7	Cubitt ter SW4
59 U 13	Cuckoo av W7
59 S 13	Cuckoo dene W7
19 P 2	Cuckoo Hall la N9
59 T 19	Cuckoo la W7
152 D 7	Cudas clo Epsom
152 D 6	Cuddington av Worc Pk
93 T 18	Cudham st SE6
63 N 11	Cudworth st E1
135 X 16	Cudworth st E1
95 P 17	Cuff cres SE9
147 O 7	Culford gdns SW3
49 R 19	Culford ms N1
49 R 18	Culford rd N1
134 J 2	Culford rd N1
49 R 18	Culford rd N1
7 N 13	Culgaith gdns Enf
61 W 12	Cullen way NW10
75 O 7	Culling rd SE16
143 Z 20	Culling rd SE16
23 X 13	Cullington clo Harrow
44 H 15	Cullingworth rd NW10
7 V 9	Culloden clo Enf
64 H 17	Culloden st E14
142 J 7	Cullum st EC3
156 K 18	Culmington rd S Croy
72 D 3	Culmington rd W13
107 R 1	Culmore cross SW12
75 O 20	Culmore rd SE15
151 Z 19	Culmore rd SE15
89 O 13	Culmstock rd SW11
133 S 7	Culpepper st N1
30 L 14	Culross clo N15
139 S 9	Culross st W1
24 F 8	Culver gro Stanm
108 C 8	Culverhouse gdns SW16
11 N 14	Culverlands clo Stanm
93 R 20	Culverley rd SE6
111 U 1	Culverley rd SE6
154 L 2	Culvers av Carsh
155 N 1	Culvers av Carsh
154 L 3	Culvers way Carsh
89 O 5	Culvert pl SW11
31 R 16	Culvert rd N15
89 N 4	Culvert rd SW11
126 C 13	Culvestone clo Brom
130 K 10	Culworth st NW8
96 K 10	Cumberland av Welling
61 T 9	Cumberland av NW10
84 B 15	Cumberland clo Twick
105 N 18	Cumberland clo SW20
49 U 18	Cumberland clo E8
144 M 5	Cumberland cres W14
80 M 20	Cumberland dri Hth Hth
133 R 12	Cumberland gdns WC1
27 R 4	Cumberland gdns NW4
139 N 5	Cumberland mans W1
131 Z 12	Cumberland mkt NW1
73 W 1	Cumberland pk W3
61 X 20	Cumberland pk W3
131 X 12	Cumberland pl NW1
86 E 1	Cumberland rd SW13
22 K 15	Cumberland rd Harrow
24 N 11	Cumberland rd Stanm
126 C 8	Cumberland rd Brom
125 Z 8	Cumberland rd Brom
53 N 14	Cumberland rd E12
65 V 11	Cumberland rd E13
32 H 7	Cumberland rd E17
30 D 6	Cumberland rd N22
19 P 7	Cumberland rd N9
73 O 20	Cumberland rd Rich
124 A 13	Cumberland rd SE25
61 W 20	Cumberland rd W3
71 W 6	Cumberland rd W7
148 A 11	Cumberland st SW1
147 Y 10	Cumberland st SW1
131 W 10	Cumberland ter NW1
131 X 10	Cumberland Terrace ms NW1
123 W 7	Cumberlow av SE25
31 P 5	Cumberton rd N17
99 R 4	Cumbrian av Bxly Hth
45 R 7	Cumbrian gdns NW2
133 O 9	Cumming st N1
152 H 15	Cumnor gdns Epsom
154 E 13	Cumnor rd Sutton
65 X 18	Cunard rd NW10
150 H 14	Cunard st SE5
65 X 18	Cundy rd E16
147 V 7	Cundy st SW1
152 F 8	Cunliffe rd Worc Pk
107 V 14	Cunliffe st SW16
159 S 3	Cunningham clo W Wckm
23 P 15	Cunningham pk Harrow
130 F 16	Cunningham pl NW8
31 W 13	Cunningham rd N15
73 W 10	Cunnington st W4
89 R 1	Cupar rd SW11
112 G 12	Cupola clo Brom
148 G 8	Cureton st SW1
68 H 20	Curlew clo SE28
143 O 16	Curlew st SE1
107 U 5	Curlverden rd SW12
108 L 11	Curnicks la SE27
96 L 14	Curran av Sidcp
155 P 6	Curran av Wallgtn
41 P 18	Currey rd Grnfd
74 A 4	Curricle st W3
105 V 10	Currie Hill clo SW19
14 C 19	Curry ri NW7
141 S 4	Cursitor st EC4
134 K 14	Curtain rd EC2
6 L 15	Curthwaite gdns Enf
108 E 9	Curtis Field rd SW16
82 D 20	Curtis rd Hounsl
150 M 4	Curtis st SE1
151 N 5	Curtis way SE1
68 E 20	Curtis way SE28
62 F 20	Curve the W12
52 G 12	Curwen av E7
74 F 6	Curwen rd W12
9 U 17	Curzon av Enf
23 Y 5	Curzon av Stanm
67 X 8	Curzon cres Bark
62 C 1	Curzon cres NW10
44 C 20	Curzon cres NW10
139 V 14	Curzon pl W1
29 S 7	Curzon rd N10
122 E 14	Curzon rd Thntn Hth
60 B 12	Curzon rd W5
139 W 13	Curzon st W1
101 V 8	Cusack clo Twick
81 Z 13	Cusfield rd Erith
141 U 17	Cut the SE1
90 M 5	Cutcombe rd SE5
156 J 3	Cuthbert rd Croy
33 V 11	Cuthbert rd E17
18 K 15	Cuthbert rd N18
130 F 20	Cuthbert st W2
142 L 4	Cutler st E1
102 D 3	Cutthroat all Rich
97 X 12	Cuxton clo Bxly Hth
135 O 16	Cygnet st E2
100 A 10	Cygnets the Felt
133 P 9	Cynthia st N1
83 N 18	Cypress av Twick
132 C 19	Cypress pl W1
23 P 7	Cypress st Harrow
123 T 3	Cypress rd SE25
27 U 7	Cyprus av N3
27 T 6	Cyprus gdns N3
63 P 7	Cyprus pl E6
66 K 19	Cyprus pl E6
27 V 8	Cyprus rd N3
18 G 7	Cyprus rd N9
63 R 7	Cyprus rd E2
91 V 14	Cyrena rd SE22
98 A 5	Cyril rd Bxly Hth
133 X 15	Cyrus st EC1
75 Z 16	Czar st SE8

D

140 D 6	D'arblay st W1
24 H 14	D'arcy dri Harrow
69 P 2	D'arcy gdns Dgnhm
24 J 13	D'arcy gdns Harrow
153 O 8	D'arcy rd Sutton
147 S 5	D'Oyley st SW1
40 G 15	Dabbs Hill la Grnfd
93 T 2	Dabia la SE10
75 Z 15	Dacca st SE8
64 A 2	Dace rd E3
35 X 7	Dacre av Ilf
58 L 5	Dacre clo Grnfd
93 Z 10	Dacre gdn SE13
94 A 10	Dacre pk SE13
93 Z 7	Dacre pk SE13
122 A 17	Dacre rd Croy
52 B 3	Dacre rd E11
65 U 4	Dacre rd E13
140 F 20	Dacre st SW1
110 E 7	Dacres rd SE23
70 D 14	Dade way S'hall
124 G 19	Daffodil clo CR0
74 E 1	Daffodil st W12
62 E 20	Daffodil st W12
107 N 7	Dafforne rd SW17
56 C 20	Dagenham av Dgnhm
68 L 4	Dagenham av Dgnhm
68 M 3	Dagenham av Dgnhm
69 N 1	Dagenham av Dgnhm
56 J 11	Dagenham rd Dgnhm
50 M 3	Dagenham rd E10
57 N 8	Dagenham rd Rom
42 L 13	Dagmar av Wemb
43 N 13	Dagmar av Wemb
128 E 10	Dagenham gdns NW10
132 X 2	Dagmar pas N1
56 L 19	Dagmar rd Dgnhm
103 O 19	Dagmar rd Kingst
13 O 14	Dagmar rd N221
29 Y 4	Dagmar rd N22
48 F 1	Dagmar rd N4
70 C 9	Dagmar rd S'hall
123 R 10	Dagmar rd SE25
91 R 3	Dagmar rd SE5
133 X 3	Dagmar ter N1
123 P 13	Dagnall pk SE25
123 R 11	Dagnall rd SE25
89 N 3	Dagnall st SW11
89 T 17	Dagnan rd SW12
112 E 8	Dagonet gdns Brom
112 E 7	Dagonet rd Brom
121 X 9	Dahlia rd Mitch
80 D 12	Dahlia rd SE2
107 U 15	Dahomey rd SW16
156 A 15	Daimler way Wallgtn
53 V 10	Daines clo E12
111 W 12	Dainford clo Brom
112 K 19	Dainton clo Brom
23 Z 13	Daintry clo Harrow
50 L 17	Dairsie rd SE9
95 Y 7	Dairsie rd SE9
105 R 9	Dairy wlk SW19
124 F 20	Daisy clo CR0
87 Y 7	Daisy la SW6
34 H 8	Daisy rd E18
90 F 13	Dalberg rd SW2
80 J 9	Dalberg way SE2
88 C 11	Dalby rd SW18
81 N 18	Dalby st NW5
82 A 5	Dalcross rd Hounsl
24 M 6	Dale av Edg
25 N 7	Dale av Edg
82 C 7	Dale av Hounsl
5 N 20	Dale clo Barnt
99 U 14	Dale clo Drtfrd
94 D 8	Dale clo SE3
99 U 17	Dale end Drtfrd
21 V 13	Dale gdns Wdfd Grn
16 F 12	Dale Green rd N11
154 M 3	Dale Park av Carsh
155 N 3	Dale Park av Carsh
109 N 20	Dale Park rd SE19
99 U 16	Dale rd Drtfrd
65 N 14	Dale rd E16
58 K 15	Dale rd Grnfd
47 O 15	Dale rd NW5
78 M 17	Dale st SE17
149 Z 16	Dale st SE5
153 V 9	Dale rd Sutton
136 L 6	Dale row W11
74 A 14	Dale st W4
20 H 9	Dale View av E4
20 G 8	Dale View cres E4
20 H 9	Dale View gdns E4
106 K 4	Dalebury rd SW17
46 F 17	Daleham gdns NW3
46 F 17	Daleham ms NW3
107 S 12	Daleside rd SW16

99 V 4 Daleview Erith
31 S 19 Daleview rd N15
152 K 2 Dalewood gdns Worc Pk
50 F 17 Daley st E9
136 A 1 Dalgarno gdns W10
128 C 20 Dalgarno gdns W10
62 L 14 Dalgarno gdns W10
128 D 19 Dalgarno way W10
62 M 12 Dalgarno way W10
63 X 17 Dalgleish st E14
63 W 5 Daling way E3
11 W 17 Dalkeith gro Stanm
54 C 10 Dalkeith rd Ilf
90 M 20 Dalkeith rd SE21
44 H 1 Dallas rd NW4
110 A 8 Dallas rd SE26
109 Z 8 Dallas rd SE26
153 T 14 Dallas rd Sutton
60 M 14 Dallas rd W5
97 X 10 Dallin rd Bxly Hth
78 M 18 Dallin rd SE18
79 N 18 Dallin rd SE18
74 J 8 Dalling rd W6
94 B 17 Dallinger rd SE12
133 X 16 Dallington st EC1
92 F20 Dalmain rd SE23
123 W 17 Dalmally rd Croy
47 Z 14 Dalmeny av N7
122 F 4 Dalmeny av SW16
42 E 17 Dalmeny clo Wemb
83 P 9 Dalmeny cres Hounsl
5 S 20 Dalmeny rd Barnt
98 G 2 Dalmeny rd Bxly Hth
155 P 17 Dalmeny rd Carsh
47 X 10 Dalmeny rd N7
152 K 5 Dalmeny rd Worc Pk
108 M 3 Dalmore rd SE21
92 J 12 Dalrymple rd SE4
24 J 6 Dalston gdns Stanm
50 A 15 Dalston la E8
49 V 18 Dalston la E8
120 H 3 Dalton av Mitch
99 U 6 Dalton clo Drtfrd
108 K 5 Dalton st SE27
91 S 1 Dalwood st SE27
150 L 20 Dalwood st SE5
90 C 8 Dalyell rd SW9
146 C 19 Damer ter SW10
52 F 12 Dames rd E7
63 N 17 Damien st E1
143 Y 4 Damien st E1
115 R 7 Damon clo Sidcp
70 H 9 Damsonwood clo S'hall
108 B 19 Danbrook rd SW16
37 V 10 Danbury clo Rom
155 S 8 Danbury ms Wallgtn
133 Y 8 Danbury st N1
21 Y 20 Danbury way Wdfd Grn
91 U 7 Danby st SE15
85 P 7 Dancer rd Rich
87 V 3 Dancer rd SW6
94 G 8 Dando cres SE3
98 E 19 Dane clo Bxly
63 X 6 Dane pl E3
54 A 16 Dane rd Ilf
19 P 13 Dane rd N18
58 C 20 Dane rd S'hall
106 D 20 Dane rd SW19
72 D 2 Dane rd W13
86 B 16 Danebury av SW15
159 U 14 Danebury Croy
111 S 5 Daneby rd SE6
91 N 13 Danecroft rd SE24
35 S 17 Danehurst gdns Ilf
87 S 1 Danehurst st SW6
5 Z 20 Daneland Barnt
40 K 15 Danemead gro Nthlt
87 N 7 Danemere st SW15
23 S 11 Danes ga Harrow
38 K 20 Danes rd Rom
94 F 20 Danescombe SE12
154 D 3 Danescourt cres Sutton
157 V 5 Danescourt gdns Croy
27 R 16 Danescroft av NW4
27 R 16 Danescroft gdns NW4
50 H 18 Danesdale rd E9
111 T 7 Daneswood av SE6
42 F 18 Danethorpe rd Wemb
56 D 8 Danette gdns Dgnhm
91 N 3 Daneville rd SE5
34 E 19 Dangan rd E11
64 E 14 Daniel Bolt clo E14
106 J 15 Daniel clo SW17

150 M 16 Daniel gdns SE15
151 O 17 Daniel gdns SE15
26 J 20 Daniel pl NW4
61 O 20 Daniel rd W5
92 C 8 Daniels rd SE15
140 F 9 Dansey pl W1
97 O 9 Dansington rd Welling
97 O 9 Danson cres Welling
97 P 10 Danson la Welling
97 V 9 Danson mead Welling
97 U 15 Danson rd Bxly
97 V 12 Danson rd Bxly Hth
149 Y 12 Danson rd SE17
149 X 6 Dante pl SE11
149 X 6 Dante rd SE11
146 L 9 Danube st SW3
29 W 12 Danvers rd N8
146 H 15 Danvers st SW3
20 G 10 Daphne gdns E4
88 B 17 Daphne st SW18
155 V 8 Darcy av Wallgtn
121 Z 3 Darcy rd SW16
55 Z 10 Dare gdns Dgnhm
85 P 7 Darell rd Rich
49 V 2 Darenth rd N16
97 O 2 Darenth rd Welling
92 K 13 Darfield rd SE4
87 O 8 Darfur st SW15
109 V 17 Dargate clo SE19
88 G 8 Darien rd SW11
145 R 20 Darlan rd SW6
105 R 18 Darlaston rd SW19
124 H 16 Darley clo Croy
117 Y 3 Darley dri New Mald
18 G 4 Darley rd N9
93 O 7 Darling rd SE4
63 N 13 Darling row E1
135 Y 19 Darling row E1
108 K 12 Darlington rd SE27
88 L 15 Darly clo SW11
50 B 19 Darnley rd E9
32 G 4 Darnley rd Wdfd Grn
136 J 13 Darnley ter W11
91 X 13 Darrell rd SE22
89 Z 1 Darsley dri SW8
129 N 12 Dart st W10
19 R 1 Dartford av N9
99 Y 15 Dartford rd Drtfrd
150 B 13 Dartford st SE17
137 S 4 Dartmouth clo W2
93 V 3 Dartmouth gro SE10
93 V 3 Dartmouth hill SE10
47 T 9 Dartmouth Park av NW5
47 T 5 Dartmouth Park hill NW5
47 S 10 Dartmouth Park rd NW5
110 D 4 Dartmouth pl SE23
74 B 18 Dartmouth pl W4
126 F 17 Dartmouth rd Brom
65 S 17 Dartmouth rd E16
45 O 17 Dartmouth rd NW4
26 G 19 Dartmouth rd NW4
110 C 5 Dartmouth rd SE23
93 V 3 Dartmouth row SE10
140 F 19 Dartmouth st SW1
123 U 17 Dartnell rd Croy
49 V 10 Darville rd N16
66 J 7 Darwell clo E6
58 L 17 Darwin dri S'hall
30 J 7 Darwin rd N22
72 F 12 Darwin rd W5
96 L 8 Darwin rd Welling
150 G 5 Darwin st SE17
59 T 6 Daryngton dri Grnfd
98 E 14 Dashwood clo Bxly Hth
30 C 19 Dashwood rd N8
108 K 12 Dassett rd SE27
91 O 2 Datchelor pl SE5
110 L 6 Datchet rd SE6
150 D 10 Date st SE17
50 H 12 Daubeney rd N16
30 L 2 Daubeney rd N17
88 C 15 Dault rd SW18
156 J 7 Davenant rd Croy
47 Z 7 Davenant rd N19
143 T 2 Davenant st E1
93 T 16 Davenport rd SE6
115 Y 4 Davenport rd Sidcp
23 W 1 Daventer dri Stanm
33 O 17 Daventry av E17
130 K 20 Daventry st NW1
77 O 12 Davern clo SE10
48 E 19 Davey clo N7
151 O 15 Davey st SE15
59 T 8 David av Grnfd

131 S 20 David ms W1
55 X 6 David rd Dgnhm
51 Y 16 David st E15
141 X 19 Davidge st SE1
110 C 2 Davids rd SE23
36 G 1 Davids way Ilf
148 J 18 Davidson gdns SW8
123 U 15 Davidson rd Croy
52 A 5 Davies la E11
139 W 8 Davies ms W9
139 W 9 Davies st W1
55 R 16 Davington gdns Dgnhm
55 R 15 Davington rd Dgnhm
74 D 4 Davis rd W3
65 W 7 Davis st E13
74 G 6 Davisville rd W12
83 X 11 Dawes av Islwth
144 K 17 Dawes rd SW6
145 P 18 Dawes rd SW6
150 F 18 Dawes st SE17
150 G 9 Dawes st SE17
60 A 7 Dawlish av Grnfd
16 M 14 Dawlish av N13
17 N 15 Dawlish av N13
106 A 4 Dawlish av SW18
54 H 12 Dawlish dri Ilf
22 B 17 Dawlish dri Pinn
51 T 5 Dawlish rd E10
31 W 9 Dawlish rd N17
45 P 17 Dawlish rd NW2
82 B 7 Dawn clo Hounsl
106 E 4 Dawnay gdns SW18
106 E 3 Dawnay rd SW18
44 E 7 Dawpool rd NW2
13 T 16 Daws la NW7
67 W 2 Dawson av Bark
67 Y 2 Dawson av Bark
67 Y 2 Dawson gdns Bark
137 U 9 Dawson pl W2
45 N 13 Dawson rd Kingst
117 N 6 Dawson rd Surb
135 O 9 Dawson st E2
120 A 4 Daybrook rd SW19
86 G 9 Daylesford av SW15
96 G 20 Days la Sidcp
108 C 2 Daybrook rd SW2
92 C 1 Dayton gro SE15
134 K 4 De Beauvoir cres N1
134 J 2 De Beauvoir rd N1
49 R 20 De Beauvoir rd N1
134 K 1 De Beauvoir sq N1
49 S 20 De Beauvoir sq N1
6 D 20 De Bohun av N14
91 O 4 De Crespigny pk SE5
110 H 8 De Frene rd SE26
156 B 16 De Havilland rd Croy
25 S 8 De Havilland rd Edg
149 W 11 De Laune st SE17
80 E 10 De Lucy st SE2
107 Z 5 De Montford rd SW16
88 B 7 De Morgan rd SW6
31 O 4 De Quincey rd N17
53 T 5 De Vere gdns W8
138 A 19 De Vere gdns W8
138 A 20 De Vere ms W8
139 V 2 De Walden st W1
116 M 1 Deacon rd Kingst
44 G 16 Deacon rd NW2
150 B 4 Deacon st SE17
100 G 11 Deacons way Hampt
107 O 15 Deal rd SW17
135 S 19 Deal st E1
86 L 10 Dealtry rd SW15
148 J 4 Dean Bradley st SW1
50 D 14 Dean clo E9
42 C 9 Dean ct Wemb
24 K 8 Dean dri Stanm
140 F 20 Dean Farrar st SW1
33 W 12 Dean gdns E17
157 O 9 Dean rd Croy
100 F 13 Dean rd Hampt
82 L 14 Dean rd Hounsl
44 M 17 Dean rd NW2
148 J 4 Dean Ryle st SW1
52 E 14 Dean st E7
140 F 7 Dean st W1
148 J 3 Dean Stanley st SW1
148 J 3 Dean Trench st SW1
12 K 20 Dean wlk Edg
70 L 4 Dean wy S'hall
141 Y 7 Dean's ct EC4
140 H 20 Dean's yd SW1
63 O 17 Deancross st E1
143 Z 6 Deancross st E1
139 U 13 Deanery ms W1
52 A 19 Deanery rd E15
51 Z 18 Deanery rd E15

139 U 13 Deanery st W1
85 T 10 Deanhill rd SW14
85 U 10 Deanhill rd SW14
150 F 8 Deans bldgs SE17
157 U 5 Deans clo Croy
12 H 20 Deans clo Edg
73 T 16 Deans clo W4
12 K 16 Deans dri Edg
12 H 18 Deans la Edg
73 T 16 Deans la W4
139 X 4 Deans ms W1
148 E 8 Deans pl SW1
154 A 6 Deans rd Sutton
153 Z 7 Deans rd Sutton
71 W 4 Deans rd W7
12 G 17 Deans way Edg
25 U 1 Deansbrook clo Edg
25 S 2 Deansbrook rd Edg
12 H 20 Deansbrook rd Edg
13 N 20 Deansbrook rd Edg
43 W 5 Deanscroft av W5
28 G 13 Deansway N2
18 C 10 Deansway N9
120 J 5 Dearn gdns Mitch
10 L 17 Dearne clo Stanm
64 H 3 Deason st E15
57 Z 18 Debden wlk Hornch
75 P 12 Debnams rd SE16
83 S 1 Deborah clo Islwth
81 Z 16 Debrabant clo Erith
106 D 17 Deburgh rd SW19
150 J 1 Decima st SE1
27 U 14 Decoy av NW11
85 N 9 Dee rd Rich
64 J 16 Dee st E14
39 P 3 Dee way Rom
89 X 2 Deeley rd SW8
61 O 17 Deena clo W3
126 C 10 Deepdale av Brom
105 R 10 Deepdale SW19
157 V 7 Deepdene av Croy
34 F 13 Deepdene clo E11
7 W 20 Deepdene ct N21
90 C 18 Deepdene gdns SW2
91 N 9 Deepdene rd SE5
97 O 6 Deepdene rd Welling
54 S 8 Deepwell clo Islwth
59 R 8 Deepwood la Grnfd
103 R 18 Deer Park clo Kingst
120 C 3 Deer Park rd SW19
108 H 1 Deerbrook rd SE24
90 L 9 Deerdale rd SE24
88 N 2 Deere av Rainhm
45 P 19 Deerhurst rd NW2
108 C 13 Deerhurst rd SW16
106 F 7 Deeside rd SW17
155 Z 16 Defiant way Wallgtn
31 B 20 Defoe av Rich
106 J 15 Defoe clo SW17
49 S 8 Defoe rd N16
113 Y 12 Degema rd Chisl
44 F 2 Dehar cres NW9
91 S 16 Dekker rd SE21
118 L 20 Delacombe av Worc Pk
77 V 20 Delacourt rd SE3
77 X 13 Delafield rd SE7
75 O 13 Delaford rd SE16
151 Y 10 Delaford st SW6
145 N 16 Delaford st SW6
124 C 15 Delamere cres Croy
12 K 18 Delamere gdns NW7
119 P 1 Delamere rd SW20
72 L 4 Delamere rd W5
138 A 1 Delamere ter W2
129 Y 20 Delamere ter W2
131 X 6 Delancey st NW1
129 W 16 Delaware rd W9
91 N 16 Delawyk cres SE24
91 S 12 Delft way SE22
18 G 1 Delhi rd Enf
132 L 5 Delhi st N1
88 B 18 Delia st SW18
64 L 3 Dell E15
155 W 7 Dell clo Wallgtn
21 U 11 Dell clo Wdfd Grn
152 F 12 Dell la Epsom
9 P 2 Dell rd Enf
152 G 12 Dell rd Epsom
72 E 16 Dell the Brentf
109 U 19 Dell the SE19
79 Z 14 Dell the SE2
21 U 11 Dell the Wdfd Grn
42 C 14 Dell the Wemb
60 C 17 Dell way W13
118 B 4 Dell wlk New Mald
148 B 7 Dell's ms SW1
111 U 20 Dellfield clo Becknhm
4 C 16 Dellors clo Barnt

54 D 1	Dellow clo
36 D 20	Dellow clo Ilf
63 N 20	Dellow st E1
143 Y 8	Dellow st E1
35 X 11	Dellwood gdns Ilf
90 D 10	Delmare clo SW19
94 J 4	Delme cres SE3
157 V 5	Delmey clo Croy
93 N 2	Deloraine st SE8
144 H 15	Delorme st W6
152 C 5	Delta clo Worc Pk
152 C 5	Delta rd Worc Pk
135 S 12	Delta st E2
81 Y 13	Deluci rd Erith
56 J 12	Delversmead Dgnhm
149 Y 10	Delverton rd SE17
87 X 3	Delvino rd SW6
155 W 7	Demesne rd Wallgtn
43 V 9	Demeta clo Wemb
116 E 19	Dempster clo Surb
88 C 12	Dempster rd SW18
125 X 7	Den clo Beckhm
125 X 7	Den rd Brom
115 S 8	Denberry dri Sidcp
113 T 15	Denbigh clo Chisl
62 A 1	Denbigh clo NW10
44 A 20	Denbigh clo NW10
58 F 17	Denbigh clo S'hall
153 V 10	Denbigh clo Sutton
137 R 8	Denbigh clo W11
85 N 14	Denbigh gdns Rich
148 B 9	Denbigh pl SW1
66 B 10	Denbigh rd E6
82 L 4	Denbigh rd Hounsl
58 F 17	Denbigh rd S'hall
137 R 8	Denbigh rd W11
60 C 19	Denbigh rd W13
148 C 10	Denbigh st SW1
137 R 8	Denbigh ter W11
127 U 3	Denbridge rd Brom
82 E 7	Dene av Hounsl
97 S 19	Dene av Sidcp
126 C 20	Dene clo Brom
92 H 9	Dene clo SE4
152 D 2	Dene clo Worc Pk
11 S 16	Dene gdns Stanm
16 A 7	Dene rd N11
158 E 7	Dene the Croy
60 A 14	Dene the W13
42 J 12	Dene the Wemb
5 S 17	Dene wood Barnt
26 M 19	Denehurst gdns NW4
83 R 19	Denehurst gdns Twick
21 U 13	Denehurst gdns Wdfd Grn
85 R 10	Denehurst gdns Rich
73 S 3	Denehurst gdns W3
28 M 20	Denewood rd N6
120 L 9	Denham clo Mitch
97 T 8	Denham clo Welling
36 A 18	Denham dri Ilf
15 Y 10	Denham rd N20
77 R 13	Denham st SE10
67 W 3	Denham way Bark
57 U 18	Denholme wlk Rainhm
129 R 12	Denhome rd W9
28 C 11	Denison clo N2
106 F 16	Denison rd SW19
60 E 11	Denison rd W5
115 Y 3	Deniston av Bxly
17 S 4	Denleigh gdns N21
27 Z 15	Denman dri NW11
27 Z 14	Denman Drive north NW11
27 Z 15	Denman Drive south NW11
91 U 3	Denman rd SE15
140 E 9	Denman st W1
105 S 17	Denmark av SW19
119 Y 13	Denmark ct Mrdn
155 N 5	Denmark gdns Carsh
133 S 7	Denmark gro N1
26 E 11	Denmark Hill dri NW9
91 O 8	Denmark hill SE5
140 G 5	Denmark pl WC2
126 H 2	Denmark rd Brom
155 N 6	Denmark rd Carsh
60 C 20	Denmark rd Grnfd
116 J 6	Denmark rd Kingst
30 E 12	Denmark rd N8
129 R 9	Denmark rd NW6
123 Y 11	Denmark rd SE25
90 L 4	Denmark rd SE5
105 R 16	Denmark rd SW19
101 R 6	Denmark rd Twick
51 Y 10	Denmark st E11
65 U 13	Denmark st E13
31 Y 3	Denmark st N17
140 H 5	Denmark st WC2
108 L 10	Denmark wlk SE27
122 H 19	Denmead rd Croy
116 L 20	Dennan rd Surb
135 P 5	Denne ter E8
20 B 8	Denne rd E4
122 G 18	Dennett rd Croy
92 D 3	Dennetts dri SE14
92 E 4	Dennetts gro SE14
156 G 10	Denning av Croy
100 E 14	Denning clo Hampt
130 D 14	Denning clo NW8
46 G 12	Denning rd NW3
45 Y 16	Dennington Park rd NW6
42 L 14	Dennis av Wemb
11 R 15	Dennis gdns Stanm
11 O 12	Dennis la Stanm
119 S 1	Dennis Park cres SW2
60 A 5	Dennis rd Grnfd
107 N 20	Dennis Reeve clo Mitch
66 D 16	Denny clo E6
149 U 8	Denny cres SE11
55 S 20	Denny gdns Dgnhm
18 M 5	Denny rd N9
149 T 8	Denny st SE11
64 M 2	Densham rd E15
65 N 3	Densham rd E15
110 H 20	Densole clo Becknhm
19 P 10	Densworth dro N9
99 S 19	Denton rd Drtfrd
18 F 14	Denton rd N18
30 E 17	Denton rd N8
61 W 2	Denton rd NW10
84 G 17	Denton rd Twick
80 F 19	Denton rd Welling
88 B 15	Denton st SW18
50 F 9	Denton way E5
88 L 17	Dents rd SW11
99 X 19	Denver rd Drtfrd
49 R 1	Denver rd N16
146 M 6	Denyer st SW3
44 E 16	Denzil rd NW10
87 U 9	Deodar rd SW15
54 C 1	Depot cotts Ilf
83 P 7	Depot rd Hounsl
150 E 16	Depot st SE5
93 O 1	Deptford bdwy SE8
93 O 1	Deptford br SE8
76 B 17	Deptford Church st SE
76 B 12	Deptford Ferry rd E14
76 B 16	Deptford grn SE8
76 A 18	Deptford High st SE8
75 Y 12	Deptford strand SE8
23 P 5	Derby av Harrow
15 P 17	Derby av N12
38 J 19	Derby av Rom
140 K 17	Derby ga SW1
110 B 4	Derby Hill cres SE23
110 C 4	Derby hill SE23
156 J 1	Derby rd Croy
34 B 4	Derby rd E18
52 M 20	Derby rd E7
53 N 19	Derby rd E7
63 S 3	Derby rd E9
49 Y 19	Derby rd Enf
58 K 2	Derby rd Grnfd
82 K 10	Derby rd Hounsl
30 K 13	Derby rd N15
19 O 16	Derby rd N18
117 O 18	Derby rd Surb
85 T 10	Derby rd SW14
105 Y 18	Derby rd SW19
139 V 14	Derby st W1
135 U 14	Derbyshire st E2
134 K 15	Dereham pl EC2
54 L 16	Dereham rd Bark
155 S 7	Derek av Wallgtn
43 S 20	Derek av Wemb
156 L 9	Dericote st E8
156 M 9	Dering rd Croy
139 X 6	Dering st W1
106 M 8	Derinton rd SW17
107 N 10	Derinton rd SW17
93 W 12	Dermody gdns SE13
93 W 12	Dermody rd SE13
108 H 1	Deronda rd SE24
154 M 12	Deroy clo Carsh
77 X 10	Derrick gdns SE7
124 L 8	Derrick rd Becknhm
155 Z 4	Derry av Wallgtn
137 X 19	Derry st W8
53 V 13	Dersingham av E12
53 V 14	Dersingham av E12
53 V 16	Dersingham av E12
45 T 9	Dersingham rd NW2
15 Y 5	Derwent av Barnt
18 A 17	Derwent av N18
12 L 18	Derwent av N9
26 A 16	Derwent av NW9
30 M 3	Derwent av SW15
103 Z 9	Derwent av SW15
98 D 5	Derwent cres Bxly Hth
15 S 11	Derwent cres N20
24 E 7	Derwent cres Stanm
35 R 13	Derwent gdns Ilf
42 E 2	Derwent gdns Wemb
91 T 10	Derwent gro SE22
119 N 12	Derwent rd N13
17 P 11	Derwent rd N13
58 F 16	Derwent rd S'hall
123 Y 3	Derwent rd SE20
82 L 16	Derwent rd Twick
72 C 8	Derwent rd W5
26 A 17	Derwent ri NW9
76 M 12	Derwent st SE10
57 Y 15	Derwent way Hornch
155 S 17	Derwent wlk Wallgtn
73 V 2	Derwentwater rd W3
129 X 20	Desborough st W2
91 S 16	Desenfans rd SE21
65 N 12	Desford rd E16
75 W 17	Desmond st SE14
47 U 4	Despard rd N19
112 E 12	Detling rd Brom
66 L 19	Devalls clo E6
155 N 5	Devana end Carsh
65 O 1	Devana rd E13
104 M 20	Devas rd SW20
105 N 20	Devas rd SW20
64 F 1	Devas st E3
80 B 6	Devenish rd SE2
91 S 12	Deventer cres SE22
150 E 3	Deverell st SE1
141 R 7	Devereux ct WC2
88 M 16	Devereux rd SW11
39 P 4	Deveron way Rom
134 F 5	Devizes st N1
101 O 1	Devon av Twick
21 V 7	Devon clo Buck Hl
60 E 3	Devon clo Grnfd
31 W 9	Devon clo N17
60 E 3	Devon cres Grnfd
30 K 18	Devon gdns N4
67 U 3	Devon rd Bark
153 S 19	Devon rd Sutton
28 G 14	Devon ri N2
78 N 17	Devon st SE15
151 X 15	Devon st SE15
70 E 19	Devon way Hounsl
83 Z 19	Devoncroft gdns Twick
17 Y 19	Devonhurst pl W4
133 X 7	Devonia rd N1
35 T 19	Devonport gdns Ilf
74 K 4	Devonport rd W12
63 R 18	Devonport st E1
64 C 11	Devons est E3
154 C 17	Devonshire av Sutton
52 A 13	Devonshire clo E15
100 B 8	Devonshire clo Felt
17 Y 19	Devonshire clo N13
27 P 1	Devonshire clo NW7
17 Y 19	Devonshire cres NW7
76 D 20	Devonshire dri SE10
93 S 1	Devonshire dri Sutton
17 Z 2	Devonshire gdns N21
17 Z 20	Devonshire gdns N17
73 U 20	Devonshire gdns W4
75 N 17	Devonshire gro SE15
151 Y 16	Devonshire gro SE15
17 Y 19	Devonshire Hill la N17
18 A 20	Devonshire Hill la N17
31 O 1	Devonshire Hill la N17
131 V 19	Devonshire Mews west W1
131 W 20	Devonshire Mews south W1
131 X 20	Devonshire Mews north W1
74 A 13	Devonshire ms W4
45 X 9	Devonshire pl NW2
131 V 19	Devonshire pl W1
131 V 19	Devonshire Place ms W1
23 O 18	Devonshire rd Harrow
155 O 7	Devonshire rd Wallgtn
97 Z 10	Devonshire rd Bxly Hth
123 N 16	Devonshire rd Croy
65 W 17	Devonshire rd E16
33 O 18	Devonshire rd E17
36 G 20	Devonshire rd Ilf
17 Z 20	Devonshire rd N17
19 P 6	Devonshire rd N9
27 O 2	Devonshire rd NW7
22 D 3	Devonshire rd Pinn
58 G 13	Devonshire rd S'hall
110 D 2	Devonshire rd SE23
92 M 19	Devonshire rd SE23
113 P 4	Devonshire rd SE9
154 D 16	Devonshire rd SW19
106 L 16	Devonshire rd SW19
74 A 13	Devonshire rd W4
72 D 8	Devonshire rd W5
142 K 3	Devonshire row EC2
131 Y 19	Devonshire Row ms W1
126 J 8	Devonshire sq Brom
142 L 3	Devonshire sq EC2
131 X 19	Devonshire st W1
74 A 15	Devonshire st W4
138 C 7	Devonshire ter W2
158 K 2	Devonshire way Croy
159 N 1	Devonshire way Croy
91 X 8	Dewar st SE15
66 C 15	Dewberry gdns E6
56 J 18	Dewey rd Dgnhm
133 S 7	Dewey rd N1
106 M 12	Dewey st SW17
144 F 2	Dewhurst rd W14
22 C 19	Dewsbury clo Pinn
152 F 4	Dewsbury gdns Worc Pk
44 G 15	Dewsbury rd NW10
4 B 19	Dexter rd Barnt
90 G 12	Dexter rd SE24
31 N 4	Deyncourt rd N17
34 L 14	Deynecourt gdns E11
140 E 5	Diadem ct W1
55 T 4	Diamond clo Dgnhm
40 A 13	Diamond rd Pinn
150 L 19	Diamond st SE15
93 V 1	Diamond ter SE10
34 H 6	Diana clo E18
131 Z 17	Diana pl NW1
32 M 9	Diana rd E17
80 C 13	Dianthus clo SE2
57 Y 12	Diban av Hornch
133 Z 3	Dibden st N1
153 Y 4	Dibdin clo Sutton
153 Y 4	Dibdin rd Sutton
44 L 13	Dicey av NW2
28 D 5	Dickens av N3
102 J 3	Dickens clo Rich
114 C 14	Dickens clo Chisl
18 E 16	Dickens la N18
66 B 6	Dickens rd E6
150 C 1	Dickens sq SE1
89 T 4	Dickens st SW8
30 B 20	Dickenson rd N8
123 X 14	Dickensons la SE25
123 X 15	Dickensons pl SE25
117 V 4	Dickenson way New Mald
117 V 2	Dickerage rd Kingst
95 R 8	Dickson rd SE9
66 G 4	Didsbury clo E6
48 K 7	Digby cres N4
69 R 2	Digby gdns Dgnhm
157 V 4	Digby pl Croy
67 W 1	Digby rd Bark
50 F 16	Digby rd E9
63 R 9	Digby st E2
63 S 15	Diggon st E1
88 C 12	Dighton rd SW18
133 S 6	Dignum st N1
48 G 18	Digswell st N7
112 H 6	Dilhorne clo SE12
147 P 14	Dilke st SW3
48 D 13	Dillon pl N7
110 A 7	Dillwyn clo SE26
110 J 8	Dillwyn clo SE26
104 H 1	Dilton gdns SW15
41 R 15	Dimmock dri Grnfd
60 C 20	Dimond clo E7
18 J 1	Dimsdale dri Enf
43 W 4	Dimsdale dri NW9
65 S 5	Dimsdale wlk E13
64 B 20	Dingle gdns E14
107 X 5	Dingley la SW16
134 B 13	Dingley pl EC1
134 B 13	Dingley rd EC1
156 M 3	Dingwall av Croy

157 N 3	Dingwall av Croy
27 X 19	Dingwall gdns NW11
154 M 19	Dingwall rd Carsh
157 O 2	Dingwall rd Croy
88 C 19	Dingwall rd SW18
135 V 9	Dinmont st E2
5 O 18	Dinsdale gdns Barnt
123 T 10	Dinsdale gdns SE25
77 O 15	Dinsdale rd SE3
89 S 18	Dinsmore rd SW12
103 N 17	Dinton rd Kingst
106 G 14	Dinton rd SW19
65 O 3	Dirleton rd E15
144 L 15	Disbrowe rd W6
143 W 11	Discovery wlk E1
26 A 4	Dishforth la NW9
142 C 17	Disney pl SE1
142 C 17	Disney st SE1
9 S 6	Dison clo Enf
80 E 3	Disraeli rd SE28
52 F 17	Disraeli rd E7
61 X 6	Disraeli rd NW10
87 R 11	Disraeli rd SW15
72 F 3	Disraeli rd W5
135 O 11	Diss st E2
142 A 8	Distaff la EC4
160 A 8	Distaff la EC4
144 E 11	Distillery la W6
144 D 12	Distillery rd W6
149 S 7	Distin st SE11
42 B 16	District rd Wemb
93 R 2	Ditch all SE10
64 G 20	Ditchburn st E14
113 R 10	Dittisham rd SE9
116 F 20	Ditton Grange clo Surb
116 F 20	Ditton Grange dri Surb
116 C 20	Ditton Hill rd Surb
110 A 20	Ditton pl SE20
97 Y 13	Ditton rd Bxly Hth
70 E 13	Ditton rd S'hall
116 K 20	Ditton rd Surb
116 A 15	Ditton reach Surb
159 R 1	Dixon pl W Wckm
92 X 1	Dixon rd SE14
123 T 6	Dixon rd SE25
143 W 19	Dixons all SE16
23 Z 7	Dobbin clo Harrow
95 U 13	Dobell rd SE9
128 A 1	Dobree av NW10
62 K 1	Dobree av NW10
46 F 20	Dobson clo NW6
160 C 9	Doby ct EC4
75 U 5	Dock Hill av SE16
72 H 18	Dock rd Brentf
77 P 1	Dock rd E16
65 P 20	Dock rd E16
143 S 9	Dock st E1
143 P 18	Dockhead SE1
78 J 3	Dockland st E16
151 S 2	Dockley rd SE16
110 C 12	Doctors clo SE26
49 R 17	Docwras bldgs N1
64 A 17	Dod st E14
63 Z 17	Dod st E14
108 H 8	Dodbrooke rd SE27
149 X 12	Doddington gro SE17
149 W 13	Doddington pl SE17
141 V 20	Dodson st SE1
106 C 19	Doel clo SW19
141 P 1	Dog and Duck yd WC1
91 S 8	Dog Kennel hill SE22
44 B 13	Dog la NW10
93 O 19	Dogget rd SE6
5 W 19	Doggets clo Barnt
65 T 11	Doherty rd E13
141 X 14	Dolben st SE1
87 V 6	Dolby rd SW6
26 M 1	Dole st NW7
149 P 11	Dolland st SE11
27 V 4	Dollis av N3
4 E 20	Dollis Brook wlk Barnt
44 L 8	Dollis Hill av NW2
44 H 10	Dollis Hill la NW2
27 V 3	Dollis pk N3
27 T 3	Dollis rd NW7
4 H 18	Dollis Valley way Barnt
73 Y 12	Dolman rd W4
90 B 9	Dolman st SW4
39 S 14	Dolphin appr Rom
116 G 13	Dolphin clo Surb
64 C 20	Dolphin la E14
58 F 5	Dolphin rd Nthlt
148 D 12	Dolphin sq SW1
133 N 20	Dombey st WC1
109 V 9	Dome Hill pk SE26
91 P 9	Domett clo SE5
134 A 17	Domingo st EC1
123 U 16	Dominion rd Croy
70 C 7	Dominion rd S'hall
142 G 1	Dominion st EC2
160 G 1	Dominion st EC2
114 A 7	Domonic dri SE9
113 Z 8	Domville clo SE9
15 T 8	Domville clo N20
150 M 11	Domville gro SE5
91 O 1	Don Phelan clo SE5
39 P 3	Don way Rom
37 T 16	Donald dri Rom
122 E 16	Donald rd Croy
65 V 4	Donald rd E13
129 P 6	Donaldson rd NW6
78 L 20	Donaldson rd SE18
95 X 2	Donaldson rd SE18
40 E 17	Doncaster dri Nthlt
40 D 15	Doncaster gdns Nthlt
30 L 19	Doncaster gdns N4
18 M 3	Doncaster rd N9
133 R 9	Donegal st N1
87 P 3	Doneraile st SW6
65 V 9	Dongola rd E13
31 R 11	Dongola rd E17
65 U 9	Dongola Road west E13
36 C 15	Donington av Ilf
91 Y 17	Donkey all SE22
8 K 8	Donkey la Enf
121 T 8	Donne pl Mitch
146 L 5	Donne pl SW3
55 T 6	Donne rd Dgnhm
24 K 1	Donnefield av Edg
128 A 3	Donnington rd NW10
24 G 18	Donnington rd Harrow
152 H 3	Donnington rd Worc Pk
62 K 2	Donnington rd NW10
107 W 18	Donnybrook rd SW16
29 T 8	Donovan av N10
141 S 13	Doon st SE1
101 X 14	Doone clo Tedd
105 X 10	Dora rd SW19
63 Y 16	Dora st E14
154 M 11	Doral way Carsh
79 U 19	Doran gro SE18
64 H 1	Doran wlk E15
22 L 20	Dorchester av Harrow
97 X 19	Dorchester av Bxly
17 Y 13	Dorchester av N13
40 L 14	Dorchester clo Nthlt
16 F 2	Dorchester ct N14
90 M 12	Dorchester ct SE24
27 Y 12	Dorchester gdns NW11
20 B 14	Dorchester gdns E4
74 B 15	Dorchester gro W4
152 L 1	Dorchester rd Worc Pk
153 N 1	Dorchester rd Worc Pk
120 B 17	Dorchester rd Mrdn
40 L 14	Dorchester rd Nthlt
90 L 12	Dorchester rd SE24
24 M 18	Dorchester way Harrow
25 N 17	Dorchester way Harrow
97 Y 4	Dorcis av Bxly Hth
74 B 4	Dordrecht rd W3
53 W 15	Dore av E12
120 B 16	Dore gdns Mrdn
43 Y 3	Doreen av NW9
87 W 4	Doria rd SW6
57 X 5	Dorian rd Hornch
57 X 5	Dorian rd Hornch
125 S 1	Doric ct Becknhm
132 F 13	Doric way NW1
119 P 3	Dorien rd SW20
98 J 2	Doris av Erith
52 F 20	Doris rd E7
153 O 2	Dorking clo Worc Pk
75 Y 16	Dorking clo SE8
88 H 17	Dorlcote rd SW18
130 E 4	Dorman way NW8
87 Z 12	Dormay st SW18
4 B 18	Dormer clo Barnt
52 B 17	Dormer clo E15
58 G 17	Dormers av S'hall
58 L 18	Dormers ri S'hall
58 J 19	Dormers Wells la S'hall
70 K 1	Dormers Wells la S'hall
77 U 19	Dornberg rd SE3
77 U 19	Dornbergh clo SE3
87 T 4	Dorncliffe rd SW6
45 W 16	Dornfell st NW6
157 P 12	Dornton rd S Croy
107 T 4	Dornton rd SW12
60 L 1	Dorothy av Wemb
98 G 10	Dorothy Evans clo Bxly Hth
55 S 13	Dorothy gdns Dgnhm
88 L 8	Dorothy rd SW11
141 T 1	Dorrington st EC1
18 F 15	Dorrit ms N18
114 C 15	Dorrit way Chisl
43 Y 3	Dors clo NW9
39 O 10	Dorset av Rom
70 G 10	Dorset av S'hall
96 K 10	Dorset av Welling
141 V 7	Dorset bldgs EC4
131 O 19	Dorset clo NW1
12 A 20	Dorset dri Edg
11 Z 20	Dorset dri Edg
122 B 8	Dorset gdns Mitch
147 W 1	Dorset ms SW1
51 W 17	Dorset pl E15
148 F 9	Dorset pl SW1
124 E 6	Dorset rd Becknhm
52 M 20	Dorset rd E7
65 Z 1	Dorset rd E7
23 O 18	Dorset rd Harrow
120 K 3	Dorset rd Mitch
31 P 13	Dorset rd N15
30 A 6	Dorset rd N22
113 P 4	Dorset rd SE9
120 A 3	Dorset rd SW19
105 X 20	Dorset rd SW19
119 Z 2	Dorset rd SW19
148 M 18	Dorset rd SW8
149 P 19	Dorset rd SW8
72 F 7	Dorset rd W5
141 V 7	Dorset rd EC4
131 O 18	Dorset sq NW1
148 M 18	Dorset st Sch SW8
139 S 1	Dorset st W1
70 E 20	Dorset way Hounsl
101 O 1	Dorset way Twick
74 H 9	Dorville cres W6
94 D 14	Dorville rd SE12
79 P 19	Dothill rd SE18
133 N 17	Doughty ms WC1
133 O 17	Doughty st WC1
118 K 9	Douglas av New Mald
32 M 5	Douglas av E17
33 N 4	Douglas av E17
42 K 19	Douglas av Wemb
156 A 14	Douglas clo Croy
10 M 17	Douglas clo Stanm
159 N 5	Douglas dri Croy
102 G 1	Douglas ho Rich
76 G 12	Douglas pl E14
148 F 8	Douglas pth SW1
65 T 14	Douglas rd E16
20 M 4	Douglas rd E4
21 N 4	Douglas rd E4
39 U 19	Douglas rd Hornch
82 L 8	Douglas rd Hounsl
57 U 19	Douglas rd Hounsl
37 N 19	Douglas rd Ilf
117 T 5	Douglas rd Kingst
48 L 19	Douglas rd N1
30 G 4	Douglas rd N22
129 P 3	Douglas rd NW6
117 N 19	Douglas rd Surb
97 R 2	Douglas rd Welling
119 Y 14	Douglas sq Mrdn
148 F 7	Douglas st SW1
75 Z 19	Douglas way SE8
106 A 2	Dounesford gdns SW18
105 Z 2	Dounesforth gdns SW18
137 Z 20	Douro pl W8
64 A 5	Dout st E3
143 V 13	Douthwaite sq E1
66 C 15	Dove appr E6
58 A 10	Dove clo Nthlt
20 A 8	Dove House gdns E4
146 B 8	Dove ms SW5
22 F 2	Dove pk Pinn
49 O 18	Dove rd N1
135 T 7	Dove row E2
57 Y 19	Dove wlk Hornch
35 X 6	Dovedale av Ilf
97 N 3	Dovedale clo Welling
24 E 18	Dovedale rd Harrow
92 A 15	Dovedale rd SE22
106 M 19	Dovedale ri Mitch
67 R 6	Dovehouse mead Bark
146 J 11	Dovehouse st SW3
38 J 8	Dover clo Rom
154 B 6	Dover Court la Sutton
86 H 10	Dover House rd SW15
86 K 16	Dover Park dri SW15
52 K 6	Dover rd E12
19 P 9	Dover rd N9
37 Z 19	Dover rd Rom
109 O 15	Dover rd SE19
140 A 12	Dover st W1
139 Z 11	Dover st W1
122 G 10	Dovercourt av Thntn Hth
11 W 16	Dovercourt gdns Stanm
91 T 15	Dovercourt rd SE22
90 B 17	Doverfield rd SW2
17 W 14	Doveridge gdns N13
157 P 12	Doveton st S Croy
63 P 12	Doveton st E1
112 A 2	Dowanhill rd SE6
111 X 2	Dowanhill rd SE6
86 D 11	Dowdeswell clo SW15
10 L 18	Dowding pl Stanm
155 T 19	Dower av Wallgtn
160 D 9	Dowgate hill EC4
129 N 11	Dowland st W10
150 J 18	Dowlas st SE5
106 B 19	Dowman clo SW19
116 G 1	Down Hall rd Kingst
144 A 8	Down pl W6
74 K 12	Down pl W6
102 B 16	Down rd Tedd
139 X 15	Down st W1
26 M 8	Downage NW4
99 O 4	Downbank av Bxly Hth
111 Y 8	Downderry rd Brom
80 F 18	Downe clo Welling
89 V 9	Downe's cutts SW4
84 B 15	Downes clo Twick
17 T 5	Downes ct N21
129 W 18	Downfield clo W9
118 E 20	Downfield Worc Pk
38 F 2	Downham rd Rom
134 E 2	Downham rd N1
112 A 11	Downham way Brom
111 Y 11	Downham way Brom
31 O 10	Downhills av N17
30 L 11	Downhills Park rd N17
31 O 11	Downhills Park rd N17
30 M 9	Downhills way N17
12 L 17	Downhurst av NW7
23 O 10	Downing clo Harrow
59 S 4	Downing dri Grnfd
56 C 20	Downing rd Dgnhm
69 O 1	Downing rd Dgnhm
140 J 16	Downing st SW1
15 R 4	Downland clo N20
128 M 11	Downland st W10
53 S 18	Downleys clo SE9
95 S 8	Downman rd SE9
133 T 4	Downrey st N1
113 T 13	Downs av Chisl
22 D 20	Downs av Pinn
125 W 1	Downs Bridge rd Becknhm
49 Y 10	Downs est E5
111 W 20	Downs hill Becknhm
125 X 1	Downs hill Becknhm
50 A 13	Downs Park rd E5
49 X 14	Downs Park rd E8
125 R 2	Downs rd Becknhm
49 Y 12	Downs rd E5
8 F 15	Downs rd Enf
108 L 20	Downs rd Thntn Hth
105 O 19	Downs The SW20
83 X 1	Downs view Islwth
51 V 12	Downsell rd E15
31 V 8	Downsett rd N17
32 J 19	Downsfield rd E17
38 J 19	Downshall av Ilf
46 G 13	Downshire hill NW3
106 D 16	Downside clo SW19
46 K 16	Downside cres NW3
59 Y 12	Downside cres W13
154 N 14	Downside rd Sutton
101 V 6	Downside Twick
108 K 19	Downsview gdns SE19
108 L 17	Downsview rd SE19
154 C 18	Downsway the Sutton
108 B 3	Downton av SW2

75 W 5 Downtown rd SE16
28 H 1 Downway N12
91 P 10 Dowson clo SE5
142 B 16 Doyce st SE1
99 R 2 Doyle clo Erith
128 A 8 Doyle gdns NW10
62 H 3 Doyle gdns NW10
123 X 9 Doyle rd SE25
47 T 7 Doynton st N19
107 S 8 Dr Johnson av SW17
150 A 13 Draco st SE17
120 G 7 Dragmire la Mitch
75 X 14 Dragoon rd SE8
61 X 11 Dragor rd NW10
122 D 17 Drake rd Croy
121 N 13 Drake rd Croy
40 F 6 Drake rd Harrow
93 O 8 Drake rd SE4
8 B 6 Drake st Enf
92 F 6 Drakefell rd SE14
107 O 6 Drakefield rd SW17
48 H 12 Drakeley ct N5
66 H 5 Drakes wlk E6
107 X 18 Drakewood rd SW16
81 P 11 Draper clo Blvdr
51 V 13 Drapers rd E15
7 V 8 Drapers rd Enf
151 T 4 Drappers rd SE16
76 K 4 Drawdock rd SE10
79 W 13 Drawell clo SE18
104 F 18 Drax av SW20
105 T 14 Draxmont appr SW19
34 G 19 Draycot rd E11
24 B 18 Draycott av Harrow
146 K 6 Draycott av SW3
147 N 7 Draycott av SW3
24 C 18 Draycott clo Harrow
87 V 4 Draycott ms SW6
87 V 4 Draycott ms SW6
147 N 7 Draycott pl SW3
147 O 6 Draycott ter SW3
129 P 16 Drayford clo W9
137 V 18 Drayson ms W8
59 Z 20 Drayton av W13
59 V 19 Drayton Bridge rd W7
17 W 2 Drayton gdns N21
146 B 9 Drayton gdns SW10
59 Z 19 Drayton gdns W13
72 B 1 Drayton Green rd W13
59 Z 19 Drayton grn W13
59 Z 19 Drayton gro W13
48 G 15 Drayton pk N5
156 K 2 Drayton rd Croy
51 X 3 Drayton rd E11
31 S 8 Drayton rd N17
62 E 3 Drayton rd NW10
60 A 19 Drayton rd W13
24 C 17 Drayton way Harrow
77 O 9 Dreadnought st SE10
47 X 2 Dresden rd N19
93 O 14 Dressington av SE4
14 D 19 Drew av NW7
41 W 17 Drew gdns Grnfd
78 D 3 Drew rd E16
108 A 5 Drewstead rd SW16
107 X 4 Drewstead rd SW16
63 W 5 Driffield rd E3
107 P 20 Driftway the Mitch
40 K 6 Drinkwater rd Harrow
54 L 20 Drive the Bark
4 F 12 Drive the Barnt
5 P 20 Drive the Barnt
125 N 2 Drive the Becknhm
21 Y 3 Drive the Buck Hl
97 W 18 Drive the Bxly
114 J 19 Drive the Chisl
33 S 11 Drive the E17
34 E 9 Drive the E18
20 K 3 Drive the E4
12 E 15 Drive the Edg
8 C 7 Drive the Enf
152 C 14 Drive the Epsom
81 V 18 Drive the Erith
40 H 2 Drive the Harrow
22 H 20 Drive the Harrow
35 R 18 Drive the Ilf
53 T 2 Drive the Ilf
83 P 4 Drive the Islwth
103 V 19 Drive the Kingst
120 E 11 Drive the Mrdn
16 H 20 Drive the N11
14 L 20 Drive the N3
28 L 14 Drive the N6
27 S 20 Drive the NW11
45 T 1 Drive the NW11
38 L 3 Drive the Rom
39 N 2 Drive the Rom
115 R 9 Drive the Sidcp
116 J 18 Drive the Surb
122 C 6 Drive the SW16
104 M 18 Drive the SW20
123 N 8 Drive the Thntn Hth
125 W 18 Drive the W Wkhm
61 X 17 Drive the W3
155 X 20 Drive the Wallgtn
43 V 8 Drive the Wemb
109 X 8 Droitwich clo SE26
23 V 1 Dromey gdns Harrow
87 S 16 Dromore rd SW15
55 T 14 Dronfield gdns Dgnhm
128 J 14 Droop st W10
128 M 15 Droop st W10
75 N 18 Drover la SE15
151 Y 17 Drover la SE15
157 N 12 Drovers rd S Croy
91 T 16 Druce rd SE21
142 L 16 Druid st SE1
143 O 19 Druid st SE1
125 Y 8 Druids way Brom
143 P 5 Drum st E1
152 A 3 Drumaline ridge Worc Pk
38 M 14 Drummond av Rom
99 R 2 Drummond clo Erith
132 E 12 Drummond cres NW1
23 W 2 Drummond dri Stanm
148 F 10 Drummond ga SW1
148 F 10 Drummond ga SW1
156 L 2 Drummond rd Croy
34 K 18 Drummond rd E11
38 L 13 Drummond rd Rom
151 W 1 Drummond rd SE16
143 W 20 Drummond rd SE16
132 C 14 Drummond st NW1
21 W 8 Drummonds the Buck Hl
156 F 3 Drury cres CRO
140 L 5 Drury la WC2
41 N 2 Drury rd Harrow
23 N 20 Drury rd Harrow
43 X 15 Drury way NW10
87 O 8 Dryad st SW15
25 R 10 Dryburgh gdns NW9
86 M 9 Dryburgh rd SW15
59 V 18 Dryden av W7
149 V 6 Dryden ct SE11
8 F 19 Dryden rd Enf
23 W 6 Dryden rd Harrow
106 C 14 Dryden rd SW19
96 K 1 Dryden rd Welling
140 L 6 Dryden rd WC2
43 V 18 Dryfield clo NW10
12 J 19 Dryfield rd Edg
76 A 16 Dryfield wlk SE8
81 O 16 Dryhill rd Blvdr
30 B 18 Drylands rd N8
20 E 1 Drysdale av E4
93 T 3 Drysdale rd SE13
134 L 13 Drysdale st N1
71 T 4 Du Burstow ter W7
136 A 5 Du Cane rd W12
62 E 18 Du Cane rd W12
1 U 18 Du Cros dri Stanm
74 A 4 Du Cros rd W3
135 P 14 Ducal st E2
135 P 14 Ducat st E2
139 X 2 Duchess ms W1
137 T 18 Duchess of Bedford's wlk W8
139 Y 2 Duchess st W1
5 U 2 Duchy rd Barnt
141 T 12 Duchy st SE1
90 B 10 Ducie st SW4
140 D 7 Duck la W1
30 H 18 Duckett rd N4
63 U 13 Duckett st E1
99 T 13 Ducketts rd Drtfrd
39 P 14 Duckling Stool ct Rom
84 D 13 Ducks wlk Twick
44 E 14 Dudden Hill la NW10
113 N 9 Duddington clo SE9
24 D 10 Dudley av Harrow
119 S 18 Dudley dri Mrdn
41 O 5 Dudley gdns Harrow
72 C 5 Dudley gdns W13
33 O 9 Dudley rd E17
40 M 6 Dudley rd Harrow
41 N 5 Dudley rd Harrow
35 Z 11 Dudley rd Ilf
118 L 5 Dudley rd Kingst
28 A 8 Dudley rd N3
129 N 8 Dudley rd NW6
85 O 6 Dudley rd Rich
70 A 7 Dudley rd S'hall
105 Y 15 Dudley rd SW19
138 F 2 Dudley st W1
50 C 6 Duddington rd E5
146 H 9 Dudmaston ms SW3
99 X 14 Dudsbury rd Drtfrd
115 S 14 Dudsbury rd Sidcp
64 C 18 Duff st E14
134 D 17 Dufferin av EC1
134 D 18 Dufferin st EC1
23 W 16 Duffield clo Harrow
88 K 7 Duffield st SW11
140 C 7 Dufours pl W1
76 C 18 Dugald st SE8
94 A 2 Duke Humphrey rd SE3
93 Z 2 Duke Humphrey rd SE3
83 R 16 Duke of Cambridge clo Twick
154 F 4 Duke of Edinburgh rd Sutton
139 V 17 Duke of Wellington pl SW1
140 D 12 Duke of York st SW1
36 E 13 Duke rd Ilf
73 Z 13 Duke rd W4
84 H 12 Duke st Rich
154 E 8 Duke st Sutton
140 C 12 Duke st SW1
139 U 7 Duke st W1
142 G 13 Duke Street hill SE1
142 M 6 Duke's gil EC3
11 Z 18 Dukes av Edg
22 F 20 Dukes av Harrow
20 T 12 Dukes av Harrow
82 A 10 Dukes av Hounsl
102 D 10 Dukes av Kingst
102 G 11 Dukes av Kingst
29 U 9 Dukes av N10
28 A 4 Dukes av N3
27 Z 4 Dukes av N3
118 C 7 Dukes av New Mald
58 C 1 Dukes av Nthlt
73 Z 15 Dukes av W4
100 D 11 Dukes clo Hampt
66 K 3 Dukes ct E6
137 V 17 Dukes Head yd N6
29 T 10 Dukes ms N10
139 U 4 Dukes ms W1
98 K 20 Dukes orchard Bxly
66 J 3 Dukes rd E6
61 P 12 Dukes rd W3
132 G 14 Dukes rd WC1
110 F 10 Dukesthorpe rd SE26
48 E 5 Dulas st N4
136 J 8 Dulford st W11
88 M 14 Dulka rd SW11
114 D 4 Dulverton rd SE9
109 T 1 Dulwich comm SE21
91 U 19 Dulwich pk SE21
90 G 14 Dulwich rd SE24
91 P 15 Dulwich village SE21
109 S 11 Dulwich Wood av SE19
109 T 11 Dulwich Wood pk SE19
90 B 17 Dumbarton rd SW2
117 T 2 Dumbleton clo Kingst
95 V 9 Dumbreck rd SE9
49 T 8 Dumont N16
131 T 1 Dumpton pl NW1
124 J 8 Dunbar av Becknhm
56 E 10 Dunbar av Dgnhm
122 F 5 Dunbar av SW16
56 F 15 Dunbar gdns Dgnhm
52 G 18 Dunbar rd E7
30 H 5 Dunbar rd N22
117 W 8 Dunbar rd New Mald
108 L 7 Dunbar st SE27
95 S 6 Dunblane rd SE9
46 M 14 Dunboyne rd NW3
135 V 16 Dunbridge st E2
5 P 15 Duncan clo Barnt
62 A 17 Duncan gro W3
135 V 4 Duncan rd E8
84 L 10 Duncan rd Rich
133 V 8 Duncan st N1
133 W 9 Duncan st N1
140 J 11 Duncannon st WC2
63 N 18 Dunch st E1
143 Y 7 Dunch st E1
92 J 18 Duncombe hill SE23
47 X 4 Duncombe rd N19
93 Y 16 Duncrievie rd SE13
79 U 20 Duncroft SE18
92 G 8 Dundalk rd SE4
92 C 4 Dundas rd SE15
65 V 7 Dundee rd E13
124 A 12 Dundee rd SE25
143 X 15 Dundee st E1
152 K 9 Dundela gdns Worc Pk
128 F 6 Dundonald rd NW10
105 U 19 Dundonald rd SW19
51 S 9 Dunedin rd E10
54 C 3 Dunedin rd Ilf
108 K 7 Dunelm gro SE27
63 S 17 Dunelm st E1
111 S 11 Dunfield gdns SE6
111 S 11 Dunfield rd SE6
48 D 13 Dunford rd N7
86 F 9 Dungarvan av SW15
122 F 13 Dunheved clo Thntn Hth
122 F 14 Dunheved Rd west Thntn Hth
122 F 13 Dunheved Road north Thntn Hth
122 G 14 Dunheved Road south Thntn Hth
18 G 10 Dunholme grn N9
18 G 12 Dunholme la N9
18 G 12 Dunholme rd N9
143 S 1 Dunk st E1
55 S 6 Dunkeld rd Dgnhm
123 O 8 Dunkeld rd SE25
113 O 8 Dunkery rd SE9
108 L 9 Dunkirk st SE27
82 F 19 Dunlace rd E5
159 W 14 Dunleary clo Hounsl
31 O 10 Dunloe av N17
134 M 9 Dunloe st E2
135 P 9 Dunloe st E2
151 P 3 Dunlop pl SE16
128 K 5 Dunmore rd NW6
119 N 1 Dunmore rd SW20
105 O 20 Dunmore rd SW20
100 A 8 Dunmow clo Felt
37 S 15 Dunmow clo Rom
51 X 13 Dunmow rd E15
51 X 13 Dunmow rd E15
134 A 3 Dunmow wlk N1
26 C 3 Dunn mead NW9
49 U 14 Dunn st E8
57 U 14 Dunningford clo Hornch
66 E 17 Dunnock rd E6
47 V 14 Dunollie rd NW5
92 D 18 Dunoon rd SE23
7 U 8 Dunraven dri Enf
74 H 2 Dunraven rd W12
139 S 8 Dunraven st W1
144 E 3 Dunsany rd W14
159 T 17 Dunsfold way Croy
49 T 3 Dunsmure rd N16
35 Y 8 Dunspring la Ilf
131 V 20 Dunstable ms W1
84 K 11 Dunstable rd Rich
104 L 16 Dunstall rd SW20
45 V 5 Dunstan rd NW11
97 Z 15 Dunstans gro SE22
91 Y 17 Dunstans rd SE22
119 P 19 Dunster av Mrdn
4 D 15 Dunster clo Barnt
38 J 7 Dunster clo Rom
142 K 8 Dunster ct EC3
43 W 4 Dunster dri NW9
129 P 1 Dunster gdns NW6
40 B 9 Dunster way Harrow
20 C 0 Dunstor clo N2
135 N 5 Dunston rd E8
89 P 6 Dunston rd SW11
134 M 4 Dunston st E8
39 O 13 Dunton rd Rom
150 M 8 Dunton rd SE1
151 O 5 Dunton rd SE1
106 A 1 Duntshill rd SW18
95 V 11 Dunvegan rd SE9
98 B 2 Dunwich rd Bxly Hth
139 R 18 Duplex ride SW1
119 P 3 Dupont rd SW20
63 X 16 Dupont st E14
156 J 8 Duppas av Croy
156 K 7 Duppas Hill la Croy
156 G 7 Duppas Hill rd Croy
156 J 7 Duppas Hill ter Croy
156 H 7 Duppas rd Croy
77 U 13 Durand clo Carsh
120 L 20 Durand clo Carsh
154 M 1 Durand clo Carsh
90 O 2 Durand gdns SW9
61 U 1 Durand way NW10
135 S 11 Durant st E2
9 S 13 Durants Park av Enf

9 R 11 Durants pk Enf
9 R 14 Durants rd Enf
69 Y 1 Durban gdns Dgnhm
124 L 4 Durban rd Becknhm
64 M 8 Durban rd E15
32 K 4 Durban rd E17
54 G 3 Durban rd Ilf
18 F 20 Durban rd N17
108 M 9 Durban rd SE27
109 N 9 Durban rd SE27
58 F 17 Durban rd S'hall
55 W 14 Durell gdns Dgnhm
55 V 14 Durell rd Dgnhm
104 H 1 Durford cres SW15
126 C 9 Durham av Brom
70 F 15 Durham av Hounsl
140 L 11 Durham House st WC2
147 O 11 Durham pl SW3
126 C 6 Durham rd Brom
56 J 15 Durham rd Dgnhm
53 N 13 Durham rd E12
65 O 12 Durham rd E16
22 L 16 Durham rd Harrow
28 L 11 Durham rd N2
48 D 7 Durham rd N7
11 J 8 Durham rd N9
115 P 12 Durham rd Sidcp
104 K 20 Durham rd SW20
118 L 2 Durham rd SW20
72 G 9 Durham rd W5
79 R 14 Durham rd SE18
63 U 15 Durham row E1
149 O 12 Durham st SE11
137 W 4 Durham ter W2
111 R 17 Durlden clo Becknhm
22 B 19 Durley av Pinn
49 R 1 Durley rd N16
49 X 7 Durlston rd E5
102 J 15 Durlston rd Kingst
31 T 17 Durnford st N15
109 P 13 Durning rd SE19
105 Y 4 Durnsford av SW19
29 Y 1 Durnsford rd N11
87 U 3 Durrell rd SW6
104 M 19 Durrington av SW20
104 M 20 Durrington Park rd SW20
50 G 13 Dursington rd E5
94 K 4 Dursley clo SE3
95 N 2 Dursley gdns SE3
94 K 4 Dursley rd SE3
95 N 2 Dursley rd SE3
143 V 1 Durward st E1
135 W 20 Durward st E1
139 R 1 Durweston ms W1
139 P 1 Durweston st W1
4 H 7 Dury rd Barnt
87 Y 14 Dutch yd SW18
76 H 1 Duthie st E14
93 U 1 Dutton st SE10
57 Z 19 Duxford clo Hornch
64 B 4 Dye House la E3
141 T 3 Dyers bldgs EC1
51 Y 5 Dyers Hall rd E11
86 K 9 Dyers la SW15
39 X 3 Dyers way Rom
126 B 5 Dykes way Brom
81 S 8 Dylan rd Blvdr
91 P 10 Dylways SE5
35 W 9 Dymchurch clo Ilf
105 P 5 Dymes pth SW19
88 A 7 Dymock st SW6
39 T 20 Dymoke rd Hornch
129 N 1 Dyne rd NW6
112 L 8 Dyneley rd SE12
49 S 10 Dynevor rd N16
84 K 13 Dynevor rd Rich
45 Y 20 Dynham rd NW6
140 H 3 Dyott st WC1
102 E 11 Dysart av Kingst
134 H 19 Dysart st EC2
34 A 19 Dyson rd E11
52 C 18 Dyson rd E15
19 N 17 Dysons rd N18

E

48 L 1 Eade rd N4
30 M 20 Eade rd N4
31 O 20 Eade rd N4
28 G 11 Eagans clo N2
37 Y 19 Eagle av Rom
9 R 15 Eagle clo Enf
57 X 18 Eagle clo Hornch

57 X 19 Eagle clo Hornch
133 X 20 Eagle ct EC1
109 O 16 Eagle hill SE19
34 E 14 Eagle la E11
72 D 11 Eagle Park gdns W5
140 D 11 Eagle pl SW1
42 H 20 Eagle rd Wemb
141 O 2 Eagle st WC1
34 H 2 Eagle ter Wdfd Grn
134 D 7 Eagle Wharf rd N1
96 A 1 Eaglesfield rd SE18
78 M 20 Eaglesfield rd SE18
95 Z 3 Eaglesfield rd SE18
94 M 11 Ealdham sq SE9
72 G 2 Ealing grn W5
58 G 2 Ealing rd Brentf
42 J 17 Ealing rd Wemb
60 J 5 Ealing rd Wemb
60 L 18 Ealing village W5
130 L 9 Eamont st NW8
99 T 10 Eardemont clo Drtfrd
145 U 11 Eardley cres SW5
81 S 13 Eardley rd Blvdr
107 X 17 Eardley rd SW16
151 N 9 Earl cotts SE1
151 N 9 Earl rd SE1
85 W 9 Earl rd SW14
79 S 12 Earl st SE18
134 H 20 Earl st EC2
87 N 9 Earldom rd SW15
102 K 17 Earle gdns Kingst
52 F 15 Earlham gro E7
30 D 3 Earlham gro N22
140 J 6 Earlham st WC2
145 T 10 Earls Court Exhibition bldg SW5
145 X 7 Earls Court gdns SW5
145 T 2 Earls Court rd W8
145 W 10 Earls Court sq SW5
23 T 12 Earls cres Harrow
145 T 3 Earls ter W8
145 T 3 Earls wlk W8
132 M 3 Earlsferry way N1
106 C 1 Earlsfield rd SW18
88 D 19 Earlsfield rd SW18
95 U 10 Earlshall rd SE9
40 F 13 Earlsmead Harrow
31 U 15 Earlsmead rd N15
128 A 11 Earlsmead rd NW10
62 L 8 Earlsmead rd NW10
89 O 7 Earlsthorpe ms SW12
110 E 11 Earlsthorpe rd SE26
133 W 13 Earlstoke st EC1
63 N 3 Earlston gro E9
135 Y 5 Earlston gro E9
122 G 12 Earlswood av Thntn Hth
35 W 12 Earlswood gdns Ilf
77 N 15 Earlswood st SE10
131 X 3 Early ms NW1
140 H 4 Earnshaw st WC2
144 M 5 Earsby st W14
120 A 14 Easby cres Mrdn
55 S 16 Easebourne rd Dgnhm
57 X 15 Easedale dri Hornch
139 V 4 Easleys ms W1
62 B 20 East Acton la W3
73 Z 3 East Acton la W3
63 S 17 East Arbour st E1
53 R 20 East av E12
33 R 14 East av E17
58 D 20 East av S'hall
156 C 11 East av Wallgtn
5 V 18 East Barnet rd Barnt
73 Y 2 East Churchfield rd W3
6 C 14 East clo Barnt
59 O 6 East clo Grnfd
61 O 12 East clo W5
8 G 17 East cres Enf
16 A 12 East cres N11
42 E 8 East ct Wemb
154 K 19 East dri Carsh
91 R 14 East Dulwich gro SE22
91 V 9 East Dulwich rd SE22
28 E 11 East End rd N2
27 Y 8 East End rd N3
22 C 9 East End way Pinn
69 V 6 East entrance Dgnhm
76 E 9 East Ferry rd E14
106 J 15 East gdns SW17
22 C 10 East glade Pinn
66 H 14 East Ham Manor way E6
141 U 5 East Harding st EC4
46 G 10 East Heath rd NW3

88 B 13 East hill SW18
43 P 5 East hill SW18
98 L 1 East holme Erith
64 J 20 East India Dock Wall rd E14
64 K 18 East India Dock rd E14
116 G 5 East la Kingst
143 S 20 East la SE16
42 D 10 East la Wemb
127 S 3 East Mead clo Brom
109 N 4 East Mearn rd SE21
143 O 9 East minster E1
143 X 1 East Mount st E1
108 L 9 East pl SE27
141 X 1 East Poultry av EC1
16 B 4 East rd Barnt
65 R 3 East rd E15
25 U 4 East rd Edgw
9 R 3 East rd Enf
102 K 20 East rd Kingst
134 F 12 East rd N1
57 N 2 East rd Rom
37 X 14 East rd Rom
106 E 15 East rd SW19
97 P 4 East rd Welling
98 F 15 East Rochester way Bxly Hth
98 K 18 East Rochester way Bxly Hth
97 T 15 East Rochester way Sidcup
34 D 17 East row E11
128 L 17 East row W10
85 Y 10 East Sheen av SW14
143 R 11 East Smithfield E1
67 O 2 East st Bark
67 P 1 East st Bark
72 D 19 East st Brentf
126 F 2 East st Brom
37 X 16 East st Bxly Hth
150 C 10 East st SE17
150 G 8 East st SE17
150 K 7 East st SE17
151 N 19 East Surrey gro SE15
143 P 6 East Tenter st E1
4 H 10 East view Barnt
20 G 15 East view E4
158 J 4 East way Croy
34 H 15 East Way E11
16 B 4 East wlk Barnt
97 Z 20 East woodside Bxly
101 N 13 Eastbank rd Hampt
61 Y 18 Eastbourne av W3
85 V 8 Eastbourne gdns SW14
138 D 5 Eastbourne ms W2
72 F 14 Eastbourne rd Brentf
66 K 8 Eastbourne rd E6
100 A 3 Eastbourne rd Felt
31 S 19 Eastbourne rd N15
107 P 16 Eastbourne rd SW17
73 X 16 Eastbourne rd W4
138 D 5 Eastbourne ter W2
19 O 10 Eastbournia av N9
56 K 12 Eastbrook av Dgnhm
19 P 3 Eastbrook av N9
57 P 8 Eastbrook dri Rom
94 J 1 Eastbrook rd SE3
67 V 3 Eastbury av Bark
8 F 6 Eastbury av Enf
74 B 14 Eastbury gro W4
66 K 14 Eastbury rd E6
102 J 19 Eastbury rd Kingst
38 M 18 Eastbury rd Nthwd
67 X 3 Eastbury sq Bark
140 C 4 Eastcastle st W1
142 H 9 Eastcheap EC3
160 H 9 Eastcheap EC3
77 V 15 Eastcombe av SE7
41 Z 16 Eastcote av Grnfd
40 L 8 Eastcote av Harrow
40 E 11 Eastcote la Harrow
40 E 17 Eastcote la Nthlt
58 G 1 Eastcote la Nthlt
40 G 18 Eastcote Lane north Grnfd
41 N 10 Eastcote rd Harrow
22 B 14 Eastcote rd Pinn
96 F 6 Eastcote rd Welling
90 B 5 Eastcote st SW9
152 B 17 Eastcroft rd Epsom
50 L 16 Eastcross E9
93 X 11 Eastdown pk SE13
34 K 17 Eastern av E11
36 F 18 Eastern av Ilf
35 T 18 Eastern av Ilf

40 A 1 Eastern av Pinn
37 T 13 Eastern av Rom
38 J 13 Eastern Avenue east Rom
39 V 5 Eastern Avenue east Rom
38 M 10 Eastern Avenue west Rom
37 Y 14 Eastern Avenue west Rom
65 V 6 Eastern rd E13
33 V 15 Eastern rd E17
28 M 12 Eastern rd N2
30 A 4 Eastern rd N22
39 T 16 Eastern rd Rom
93 O 11 Eastern rd SE4
81 P 4 Eastern way Blvdr
80 L 3 Eastern way SE2
36 B 19 Easternville gdns Ilf
56 D 13 Eastfield gdns Dgnhm
56 C 13 Eastfield rd Dgnhm
33 O 12 Eastfield rd E17
9 S 3 Eastfield rd Enf
30 A 11 Eastfield rd N8
121 P 3 Eastfield rd Mitch
61 V 14 Eastfields rd W3
68 J 19 Eastgate clo SE28
28 B 14 Eastholm NW11
90 K 6 Eastlake rd SE5
91 U 17 Eastlands cres SE21
40 K 8 Eastleigh av Harrow
44 B 10 Eastleigh clo NW2
154 A 17 Eastleigh clo Sutton
98 L 7 Eastleigh rd Bxly Hth
86 G 19 Eastleigh wlk SW15
58 K 9 Eastmead av Grnfd
108 M 4 Eastmearn rd SE21
78 A 9 Eastmoor pl SE7
78 A 10 Eastmoor st SE7
122 H 19 Eastney rd Croy
76 K 15 Eastney st SE10
114 C 2 Eastnor rd SE9
133 S 15 Eaton st WC1
126 D 15 Eastry av Brom
81 S 18 Eastry rd Erith
27 U 14 Eastside rd NW11
79 V 19 Eastview av SE18
27 U 17 Eastville av NW11
126 E 17 Eastway Brom
51 N 14 Eastway E9
119 R 10 Eastway Mrdn
155 U 9 Eastway Wallgtn
110 H 19 Eastwell clo Becknhm
34 G 8 Eastwood clo E18
34 F 6 Eastwood rd E18
34 G 7 Eastwood rd E18
55 N 2 Eastwood rd Ilf
37 N 20 Eastwood rd Ilf
29 O 8 Eastwood rd N10
107 U 16 Eastwood st SW16
33 W 16 Eatington rd E10
11 O 13 Eaton clo Stanm
147 T 6 Eaton clo SW1
103 R 18 Eaton dri Kingst
38 F 3 Eaton dri Rom
90 H 11 Eaton dri SW9
147 V 3 Eaton ga SW1
55 Y 20 Eaton gdns Dgnhm
47 Y 9 Eaton gro N19
147 Y 2 Eaton la SW1
147 U 3 Eaton Mews north SW1
147 V 4 Eaton Mews south SW1
147 U 5 Eaton Mews west SW1
17 U 9 Eaton pk rd N13
147 U 3 Eaton pl SW1
8 E 13 Eaton rd Enf
83 R 11 Eaton rd Hounsl
26 M 15 Eaton rd NW4
115 W 5 Eaton rd Sidcp
154 E 14 Eaton rd Sutton
90 H 12 Eaton rd SW9
34 L 14 Eaton rd E11
60 F 17 Eaton rd N5
147 W 2 Eaton row SW1
147 U 3 Eaton sq SW1
147 S 5 Eaton ter SW1
147 S 5 Eaton ter SW1
147 T 5 Eaton Terrace ms SW1
20 A 8 Eatons mead E4
106 M 4 Eatonville rd SW17
107 N 4 Eatonville rd SW17
107 N 4 Eatonville vlls SW17
149 O 15 Ebbisham drive SE11
152 M 2 Ebbisham rd Worc Pk
45 R 13 Ebbsfleet rd NW2

94 H 9	Ebdon way SE3
134 E 13	Ebenezer st N1
121 U 1	Ebenezer wlk SW16
150 L 15	Ebley clo SE15
88 B 12	Ebner st SW18
134 M 16	Ebor st E2
24 F 19	Ebrington rd Harrow
92 G 19	Ebsworth st SE23
48 B 10	Ebourne rd N7
147 W 9	Ebury br SW1
147 V 11	Ebury Bridge rd SW1
147 W 4	Ebury Mews east SW1
147 W 5	Ebury ms SW1
147 V 7	Ebury sq SW1
147 V 6	Ebury st SW1
88 L 9	Eccles rd SW11
17 S 16	Ecclesbourne clo N13
17 S 16	Ecclesbourne gdns N13
122 L 11	Ecclesbourne rd Thntn Hth
134 B 2	Ecclesbourne rd N1
147 Y 5	Eccleston br SW1
5 Y 15	Eccleston clo Barnt
37 O 20	Eccleston cres Rom
55 P 1	Eccleston cres Rom
147 V 2	Eccleston ms SW1
147 W 6	Eccleston pl SW1
71 X 2	Eccleston rd W13
147 Z 7	Eccleston sq SW1
147 Z 7	Eccleston Square ms SW1
147 X 5	Eccleston st SW1
42 K 15	Ecclestone ms Wemb
43 N 15	Ecclestone pl Wemb
20 D 6	Echo Heights E4
105 P 10	Eckersley st E1
133 R 7	Eckford st N1
75 S 19	Eckington gdns SE16
88 A 10	Eckstein rd SW11
65 U 14	Eclipse rd E13
111 Y 5	Ector rd SE6
129 U 18	Edbrooke rd W9
87 W 4	Eddiscombe rd SW6
38 G 19	Eddy clo Rom
92 J 14	Eddystone rd SE4
100 E 8	Ede clo Hounsl
60 F 4	Eden clo Wemb
33 S 15	Eden gro E17
48 D 15	Eden gro N7
124 K 8	Eden Park av Becknhm
125 O 11	Eden Park av Becknhm
125 T 13	Eden pk Becknhm
124 G 8	Eden rd Becknhm
157 G 8	Eden rd Croy
33 S 15	Eden rd E17
108 K 11	Eden rd SE27
116 J 9	Eden st Kingst
124 M 12	Eden way Becknhm
125 O 14	Eden way Becknhm
63 T 1	Edenbridge rd E9
18 E 1	Edenbridge rd Enf
107 T 15	Edencourt rd SW16
99 O 4	Edendale rd Bxly Hth
152 E 4	Enfield gdns Worc Pk
87 U 7	Edenhurst av SW6
74 B 19	Edensor gdns W4
74 A 19	Edensor rd W4
107 P 18	Edenvale rd Mitch
88 C 6	Edenvale st SW6
133 Z 4	Eder wlk N1
122 E 5	Ederline av SW16
64 B 9	Edgar av SW6
64 D 9	Edgar rd E3
82 E 18	Edgar rd Hounsl
37 V 20	Edgar rd Rom
157 O 20	Edgar rd S Croy
87 S 2	Edgarley ter SW6
27 X 11	Edge Hill av N3
78 M 16	Edge hill SE18
105 O 17	Edge hill SW19
108 J 13	Edge Point clo SE27
137 U 14	Edge st W8
113 N 19	Edgeborough way Chisl
114 A 10	Edgebury Chisl
113 Z 10	Edgebury Chisl
114 B 9	Edgebury wlk Chisl
103 X 18	Edgecombe clo Kingst
158 E 18	Edgecoombe S Croy
31 R 15	Edgecot gro N15
73 U 4	Edgecote W3
54 L 20	Edgefield av Bark
56 E 12	Edgehill gdns Dgnhm
114 B 9	Edgehill rd Chisl
121 R 1	Edgehill rd Mitch
156 H 20	Edgehill rd S Croy
60 C 15	Edgehill rd W13
88 A 11	Edgel st SW18
89 X 8	Edgeley la SW4
89 X 8	Edgeley st SW4
124 G 19	Edgewood grn Croy
26 G 15	Edgeworth av NW4
26 F 15	Edgeworth clo NW4
26 G 15	Edgeworth cres NW4
5 X 13	Edgeworth rd Barnt
94 L 10	Edgeworth rd SE9
95 N 11	Edgeworth rd SE9
107 W 16	Edgington rd SW16
12 C 20	Edgware High st Edg
12 A 18	Edgware rd Edg
44 K 5	Edgware rd NW2
26 C 17	Edgware rd NW2
25 W 9	Edgware rd NW9
130 F 19	Edgware rd W2
138 K 3	Edgware rd W2
139 N 6	Edgware rd W2
12 B 12	Edgware way Edg
11 U 4	Edgware way Edg
12 C 16	Edgwarebury gdns Edg
11 X 3	Edgwarebury house Borhm Wd
11 Y 3	Edgwarebury la Borhm Wd
12 B 12	Edgwarebury la Edg.
12 B 8	Edgwarebury la Edg
12 C 14	Edgwarebury la Edg
12 A 10	Edgwarebury pk Edg
65 V 7	Edinburgh rd E13
32 M 16	Edinburgh rd E17
18 L 15	Edinburgh rd N18
154 E 4	Edinburgh rd Sutton
71 V 5	Edinburgh rd W7
9 P 10	Edington rd Enf
80 D 7	Edington rd SE2
131 U 2	Edis st NW1
57 T 4	Edison av Hornch
57 S 4	Edison clo Hornch
58 K 17	Edison dri S'hall
79 X 20	Edison gdns SE18
126 D 3	Edison rd Brom
29 Z 19	Edison rd N8
79 Y 20	Edison rd SE18
96 K 2	Edison rd Welling
117 S 16	Edith gdns Surb
146 B 15	Edith gro SW10
51 X 14	Edith rd E15
66 A 1	Edith rd E6
29 Y 2	Edith rd N11
37 V 20	Edith rd Rom
123 P 12	Edith rd SE25
106 B 15	Edith rd SW19
144 J 6	Edith rd W14
145 N 8	Edith rd W14
113 R 7	Edith st E25
146 B 17	Edith ter SW10
145 O 8	Edith vlls W14
90 B 7	Edithna st SW9
120 J 5	Edmund rd Mitch
97 O 6	Edmund rd Welling
150 F 18	Edmund st SE5
28 H 14	Edmunds wlk N2
119 O 3	Edna rd SW20
88 J 3	Edna st SW11
75 S 18	Edric rd SE14
12 G 20	Edrick rd Edg
12 G 20	Edrick wlk Edg
157 N 7	Edridge rd Croy
20 C 18	Edward av E4
120 F 11	Edward av Mrdn
101 N 13	Edward clo Hampt
18 H 3	Edward clo N9
5 T 16	Edward gro Barnt
131 Y 11	Edward ms NW1
75 Z 17	Edward pl SE8
5 T 16	Edward rd Barnt
112 J 17	Edward rd Brom
114 A 13	Edward rd Chisl
123 T 16	Edward rd Croy
32 G 16	Edward rd E17
101 N 12	Edward rd Hampt
23 N 11	Edward rd Harrow
37 X 18	Edward rd Rom
110 F 16	Edward rd SE20
133 N 6	Edward sq N1
65 S 13	Edward st E16
76 A 17	Edward st SE8
75 Z 17	Edward st SE8
65 O 1	Edward Temme av E15
145 R 3	Edwardes sq W8
153 O 3	Edwards clo Worc Pk
48 H 19	Edwards cotts N1
49 P 8	Edwards la N16
139 T 6	Edwards ms W1
81 R 9	Edwards rd Blvdr
133 N 6	Edwards sq N1
66 K 8	Edwin av E6
81 O 17	Edwin av Bxly Hth
12 K 20	Edwin rd Edg
101 U 1	Edwin rd Twick
65 S 15	Edwin st E16
50 K 12	Edwin's mead N7
35 P 16	Edwina gdns Ilf
145 U 19	Edwy clo Barnt
145 U 19	Effie pl SW6
145 U 19	Effie rd SW6
154 B 17	Effingham clo Sutton
122 D 17	Effingham rd Croy
30 H 14	Effingham rd N8
94 B 13	Effingham rd SE12
116 C 18	Effingham rd Surb
106 J 12	Effort st SW17
90 G 13	Effra pde SW2
106 B 14	Effra rd SW19
105 Z 14	Effra rd SW19
90 E 13	Effra rd SW2
151 W 10	Egan way SE16
131 T 3	Egbert pl NW1
131 T 2	Egbert st NW1
146 L 4	Egerton cres SW3
76 E 20	Egerton dri SE10
93 S 1	Egerton dri SE10
54 K 10	Egerton gdns Ilf
146 L 3	Egerton Gdns ms SW3
128 C 5	Egerton gdns NW10
26 K 13	Egerton gdns NW10
146 K 4	Egerton gdns SW3
60 B 17	Egerton gdns W13
146 L 3	Egerton nl SW3
31 U 20	Egerton rd N16
118 E 8	Egerton rd New Mald
123 R 7	Egerton rd SE25
83 U 17	Egerton rd Twick
60 L 1	Egerton rd Wemb
146 K 3	Egerton ter SW3
153 P 3	Egham clo Sutton
153 R 4	Egham cres Sutton
65 W 14	Egham rd E13
88 C 14	Eglantine rd SW18
120 A 15	Egleston rd Mrdn
20 K 2	Eglington rd E4
78 M 19	Eglinton hill SE18
78 K 17	Eglinton rd SE18
86 L 8	Egliston ms SW15
86 L 8	Egliston rd SW15
117 O 20	Egmont av Surb
118 E 7	Egmont rd New Mald
117 O 20	Egmont rd Surb
154 C 18	Egmont rd Sutton
75 T 20	Egmont st SE14
108 G 7	Egremont rd SE27
53 U 11	Eighth av E12
123 P 12	Eileen rd SE25
66 D 14	Eisenhower dri E6
47 N 14	Elaine gro NW5
90 J 5	Elam clo SE5
90 J 5	Elam st SE5
156 H 5	Eland rd Croy
89 N 7	Eland rd SW11
150 C 5	Elba pl SE17
88 C 4	Elbe st SW6
121 W 15	Elberon av Croy
123 X 11	Elborough rd SE25
105 X 2	Elborough st SW18
57 T 19	Elbury dri E16
146 L 19	Elcho st SW11
151 V 18	Elcot av SE15
30 A 17	Elder av N8
108 M 13	Elder rd SE27
134 M 19	Elder st E1
72 K 7	Elderberry rd W5
50 D 12	Elderfield rd E5
34 H 15	Elderfield wlk E11
125 P 13	Elderslie clo Becknhm
95 X 14	Elderslie rd SE9
110 H 10	Elderton rd SE26
121 U 1	Eldertree pl Mitch
121 T 2	Eldertree way Mitch
158 D 2	Eldon av Hounsl
70 G 19	Eldon av Hounsl
46 G 14	Eldon gro NW3
123 Z 8	Eldon pk SE25
32 L 14	Eldon rd E17
30 K 5	Eldon rd N22
19 O 7	Eldon rd N9
146 A 2	Eldon rd W8
145 Z 2	Eldon rd W8
160 G 1	Eldon st EC2
142 H 1	Eldon st EC2
61 S 7	Eldon way NW10
67 U 3	Eldred rd Bark
14 B 15	Eleanor cres NW7
4 B 18	Eleanor gdns Barnt
56 A 8	Eleanor gdns Dgnhm
86 C 8	Eleanor gro SW13
52 D 19	Eleanor rd E15
49 Z 18	Eleanor rd E8
17 N 20	Eleanor rd N11
64 X 9	Eleanor st E3
64 B 10	Eleanor st E3
90 E 10	Electric av SW9
116 F 15	Electric pde Surb
149 Y 3	Elephant and Castle SE1
75 O 5	Elephant la SE16
143 Z 17	Elephant la SE16
150 A 4	Elephant rd SE17
72 D 6	Elers rd W13
19 R 16	Eley rd N18
63 R 19	Elf row E1
101 V 13	Elfin gro Tedd
90 M 13	Elfindale rd SE24
91 N 14	Elfindale rd SE24
94 J 9	Elford clo SE3
48 G 12	Elfort rd N5
111 O 9	Elfrida cres SE6
59 T 13	Elfwine rd W7
117 R 19	Elgar av Surb
122 A 5	Elgar av SW16
72 K 5	Elgar av W5
11 S 2	Elgar clo Borehm Wd
75 W 7	Elgar st SE16
24 A 8	Elgin av Harrow
130 A 12	Elgin av W9
129 J 17	Elgin av W9
136 L 8	Elgin cres W11
137 N 7	Elgin cres W11
129 Z 12	Elgin Mews north W9
130 A 13	Elgin Mews south W9
136 M 5	Elgin ms W11
157 V 2	Elgin rd Croy
123 V 20	Elgin rd Croy
54 J 1	Elgin rd Ilf
29 V 7	Elgin rd N22
154 D 6	Elgin rd Sutton
155 U 13	Elgin rd Wallgtn
113 N 19	Elham clo Chisl
133 W 10	Elia st N1
149 S 16	Elias pl SE11
95 V 10	Elibank rd SE9
65 P 10	Elim way E13
110 A 3	Eliot bank SE23
40 J 6	Eliot dri Harrow
86 F 11	Eliot gdns SW15
93 V 5	Eliot hill SE13
93 V 5	Eliot pk SE13
93 Y 5	Eliot pl SE3
55 W 13	Eliot rd Dgnhm
93 X 10	Eliot vale SE3
7 X 10	Elizabeth av Enf
54 E 6	Elizabeth av Ilf
134 D 2	Elizabeth av N1
147 X 7	Elizabeth br SW1
4 B 12	Elizabeth clo Barnt
64 D 17	Elizabeth clo E14
38 G 5	Elizabeth clo Rom
130 D 17	Elizabeth clo W9
31 R 12	Elizabeth Clyde clo N15
85 O 2	Elizabeth cotts Rich
11 T 18	Elizabeth gdns Stanm
74 D 4	Elizabeth gdns W3
46 L 18	Elizabeth ms NW3
31 P 12	Elizabeth rd N15
66 A 2	Elizabeth rd E6
31 S 16	Elizabeth rd N15
19 O 3	Elizabeth ride N9
147 W 6	Elizabeth st SW1
95 U 15	Elizabeth ter SE9
109 U 18	Elizabeth wy SE19
65 U 12	Elkington rd E13
39 P 7	Elkins the Rom
129 O 20	Elkstone rd W10
30 B 20	Ella rd N8
144 F 15	Ellaline rd W6
19 N 15	Ellanby cres N18
92 C 11	Elland rd SE15
22 A 16	Ellement clo Pinn
127 O 6	Ellen clo Brom
19 P 10	Ellen ct N9
143 T 7	Ellen st E1
86 F 10	Ellenborough pl SW15
115 V 13	Ellenborough rd Sidcp
30 K 5	Ellenborough rd N22
157 T 20	Ellenbridge way S Croy
101 V 14	Elleray rd Tedd
87 P 2	Ellerby st SW6

46 D 14 Ellerdale clo NW3	27 O 17 Elm Park gdns NW4	23 X 15 Elmgrove gdns Harrow
46 D 14 Ellerdale rd NW3	146 F 11 Elm Park gdns SW10	72 K 4 Elmgrove rd W5
93 R 9 Ellerdale st SE13	146 F 12 Elm Park la SW3	107 R 19 Elmhurst av Mitch
83 O 11 Ellerdine rd Hounsl	146 D 14 Elm Park mans SW10	28 F 11 Elmhurst av N2
84 J 15 Ellerker gdns Rich	50 J 4 Elm Park rd E10	80 M 17 Elmhurst Blvdr
62 H 2 Ellerslie gdns NW10	17 X 4 Elm Park rd N21	81 N 17 Elmhurst Blvdr
74 J 2 Ellerslie rd W12	27 W 2 Elm Park rd N3	34 F 6 Elmhurst dri E18
89 Z 12 Ellerslie sq SW4	123 T 6 Elm Park rd SE25	52 H 20 Elmhurst rd E7
68 E 1 Ellerton gdns Dgnhm	146 E 14 Elm Park rd SW3	31 T 7 Elmhurst rd N17
68 F 2 Ellerton rd Dgnhm	11 P 17 Elm pk Stanm	113 P 6 Elmhurst rd SE9
116 M 20 Ellerton rd Surb	90 C 17 Elm pk SW2	89 X 7 Elmhurst st SW4
86 F 2 Ellerton rd SW13	90 E 18 Elm pk SW2	98 F 17 Elmington clo Bxly
88 F 20 Ellerton rd SW13	146 F 10 Elm pl SW7	150 E 20 Elmington rd SE5
106 G 1 Ellerton rd SW18	4 G 14 Elm rd Barnt	150 H 20 Elmington rd SE5
104 G 17 Ellerton rd SW20	124 L 2 Elm rd Becknhm	93 S 8 Elmira st SE13
109 O 18 Ellery rd SE19	51 W 8 Elm rd E11	113 U 15 Elmlee clo Chisl
92 A 6 Ellery st SE15	33 V 16 Elm rd E17	66 E 15 Elmley clo E6
125 X 4 Ellesmere av Becknhm	52 D 18 Elm rd E7	79 S 12 Elmley st SE18
12 K 10 Ellesmere av NW7	152 E 15 Elm rd Epsom	51 V 10 Elmore rd E11
34 D 16 Ellesmere clo E11	99 W 1 Elm rd Erith	9 S 4 Elmore rd Enf
35 R 17 Ellesmere gdns Ilf	116 L 1 Elm rd Kingst	49 N 20 Elmore st N1
4 G 16 Ellesmere gro Barnt	102 M 19 Elm rd Kingst	29 T 9 Elms av N10
63 V 5 Ellesmere rd E3	103 O 18 Elm rd Kingst	27 O 17 Elms av NW4
58 M 12 Ellesmere rd Grnfd	30 J 5 Elm rd N22	89 X 14 Elms cres SW4
44 G 15 Ellesmere rd NW10	117 Y 4 Elm rd New Mald	41 X 13 Elms ct Wemb
84 D 15 Ellesmere rd Twick	38 G 7 Elm rd Rom	56 A 11 Elms gdns Dgnhm
77 T 2 Ellesmere rd W4	114 M 2 Elm rd Sidcp	41 X 13 Elms gdns Wemb
73 X 15 Ellesmere rd W4	85 W 9 Elm rd SW14	41 Z 10 Elms la Harrow
64 C 17 Ellesmere st E14	123 N 10 Elm rd Thntn Hth	41 Z 12 Elms la Wemb
50 A 19 Ellingfort rd E8	121 P 20 Elm rd Wallgtn	138 E 9 Elms ms W2
51 X 13 Ellingham rd E15	42 K 15 Elm rd Wemb	41 Y 12 Elms Park av Wemb
74 G 5 Ellingham rd W12	119 V 16 Elm Road west Sutton	10 G 20 Elms rd Harrow
82 L 5 Ellington rd Hounsl	46 E 10 Elm row NW3	23 S 2 Elms rd Harrow
29 S 13 Ellington rd N10	133 P 17 Elm st WC1	89 U 13 Elms rd SW4
48 F 18 Ellington st N7	23 R 3 Elm ter Harrow	86 D 8 Elms the SW13
51 Z 20 Elliot clo E15	45 X 9 Elm ter NW2	7 Z 20 Elmscott gdns N21
43 O 9 Elliot clo Wemb	95 W 15 Elm ter SE9	112 A 12 Elmscott rd Brom
126 M 9 Elliot rd Brom	11 P 17 Elm ter Stanm	32 L 13 Elmsdale rd E17
127 N 9 Elliot rd Brom	58 F 7 Elm Tree clo Nthlt	86 H 13 Elmshare rd SW15
26 K 19 Elliot rd NW4	130 F 12 Elm Tree rd NW8	28 F 12 Elmshurst cres N2
130 L 1 Elliot sq NW3	130 F 13 Elm Tree rd NW8	159 S 14 Elmside Croy
39 Y 4 Elliott gdns Rom	16 B 20 Elm way N11	43 O 9 Elmside rd Wemb
122 K 9 Elliott rd Thntn Hth	44 A 10 Elm way NW10	24 C 13 Elmsleigh av Harrow
10 M 18 Elliott rd Stanm	152 M 4 Elm way Worc Pk	101 R 4 Elmsleigh rd Twick
149 W 20 Elliott rd SW9	45 Z 8 Elm wlk NW3	113 V 12 Elmstead av Chisl
74 A 11 Elliott rd W4	39 W 9 Elm wlk Rom	42 K 5 Elmstead av Wemb
149 X 4 Elliotts row SE11	118 M 8 Elm wlk SW20	43 N 7 Elmstead av Wemb
59 W 14 Ellis ct W7	119 O 9 Elm wlk SW20	152 B 12 Elmstead clo Epsom
59 W 14 Ellis ct W7	31 P 14 Elmar rd N15	14 K 8 Elmstead clo N20
77 X 16 Ellis ms SE7	4 A 15 Elmbank av Brentf	80 F 17 Elmstead cres Bxly Hth
120 M 14 Ellis rd Mitch	17 O 2 Elmbank gdns N14	152 F 5 Elmstead gdns Worc Pk
147 R 4 Ellis st SW1	59 S 13 Elmbank way W7	113 T 14 Elmstead glade Chisl
77 Y 15 Elliscombe rd SE7	81 U 12 Elmbourne dri Blvdr	113 U 10 Elmstead la Chisl
86 F 17 Ellisfield dri SW15	107 R 17 Elmbourne rd SW17	99 P 1 Elmstead rd Erith
70 D 10 Ellison gdns S'hall	117 W 16 Elmbridge av Surb	54 J 7 Elmstead rd Ilf
114 F 2 Ellison rd Sidcp	37 P 1 Elmbridge rd Ilf	87 W 1 Elmstone rd SW6
86 E 5 Ellison rd SW13	95 S 10 Elmbrook gdns SE9	82 K 4 Elmsworth av Hounsl
108 A 19 Ellison rd SW16	153 V 8 Elmbrook rd Sutton	101 U 11 Elmtree rd Tedd
107 Y 18 Ellison rd SW16	108 K 3 Elmcourt rd SE27	24 A 18 Elmwood av Harrow
39 Y 4 Ellmore clo Rom	34 H 14 Elmcroft av E11	17 O 15 Elmwood av N13
107 Y 13 Ellora rd SW16	9 N 20 Elmcroft av Enf	152 G 16 Elmwood clo Epsom
63 N 9 Ellsworth st E2	45 W 1 Elmcroft av NW11	155 R 4 Elmwood clo Wallgtn
135 X 12 Ellsworth st E2	96 L 17 Elmcroft av Sidcp	25 W 13 Elmwood cres NW9
72 L 4 Elm av W5	34 J 13 Elmcroft clo E11	97 Y 18 Elmwood dri Bxly
86 C 5 Elm Bank gdns SW13	60 G 16 Elmcroft clo Wemb	152 G 16 Elmwood ct Wemb
120 L 20 Elm clo Carsh	22 H 11 Elmcroft cres Harrow	59 T 18 Elmwood gdns W7
34 J 18 Elm clo E11	45 R 1 Elmcroft cres NW11	122 J 17 Elmwood rd Croy
22 J 19 Elm clo Harrow	25 P 14 Elmcroft gdns NW9	120 M 6 Elmwood rd Mitch
27 O 17 Elm clo NW4	50 C 11 Elmcroft st E5	91 O 14 Elmwood rd SE24
38 G 6 Elm clo Rom	17 R 17 Elmdale rd N13	73 V 16 Elmwood rd W4
157 P 14 Elm clo S Croy	124 K 13 Elmdene clo Becknhm	109 N 4 Elmworth gro SE21
117 W 17 Elm clo Surb	78 M 15 Elmdene rd SE18	109 N 5 Elmworth gro SE21
118 M 8 Elm clo SW20	117 X 20 Elmdene rd Surb	129 Y 18 Elnathan ms W9
100 K 5 Elm clo Twick	82 A 4 Elmdon rd Hounsl	32 L 7 Elphinstone rd E17
116 K 1 Elm cres Kingst	7 P 11 Elmer clo Enf	48 J 11 Elphinstone st N5
72 K 4 Elm cres W5	25 R 1 Elmer gdns Edg	49 X 18 Elrington rd E8
22 J 18 Elm dri Harrow	83 R 8 Elmer gdns Islwth	97 R 4 Elsa rd Welling
8 A 2 Elm gdns Enf	93 U 19 Elmer rd SE6	63 U 15 Elsa st E1
121 X 6 Elm gdns Mitch	124 H 8 Elmer Side rd Becknhm	50 D 18 Elsdale st E9
28 E 10 Elm gdns N2	124 D 5 Elmers End rd Becknhm	31 U 6 Elsden rd N17
62 A 17 Elm grn W3	123 Y 16 Elmers rd SE25	53 V 16 Elsenham rd E12
81 Z 18 Elm gro Erith	120 O 1 Elmfield av Mitch	105 V 2 Elsenham st SW18
40 G 2 Elm gro Harrow	30 A 16 Elmfield av N8	52 A 11 Elsham rd E11
116 L 1 Elm gro Kingst	101 X 12 Elmfield av Tedd	51 Z 11 Elsham rd E11
30 B 19 Elm gro N8	126 F 5 Elmfield pk Brom	136 K 19 Elsham rd W14
45 R 12 Elm gro NW2	126 G 5 Elmfield rd Brom	91 U 10 Elsie rd SE22
91 W 4 Elm gro SE15	32 E 17 Elmfield rd E17	17 Z 3 Elsiedene rd N21
154 B 9 Elm gro Sutton	20 J 7 Elmfield rd E4	92 M 13 Elsiemaud rd SE4
105 S 18 Elm gro SW19	28 F 9 Elmfield rd N2	110 J 2 Elsinore rd SE23
21 R 17 Elm gro Wdfd Grn	70 C 8 Elmfield rd S'hall	88 M 7 Elsley rd SW11
155 P 6 Elm Grove pde Wallgtn	107 P 3 Elmfield rd SW17	89 N 7 Elsley rd SW11
124 A 18 Elm Grove rd Croy	157 U 19 Elmfield way S Croy	82 D 8 Elsma ter Hounsl
86 G 4 Elm Grove rd SW13	12 J 15 Elmgate gdns Edg	88 M 9 Elspeth rd SW11
34 J 18 Elm Hall gdns E11	23 X 16 Elmgrove cres Harrow	42 J 15 Elspeth rd Wemb
110 M 3 Elm la SE6		119 Y 12 Elsrick av Mrdn
57 Y 12 Elm Park av Hornch		124 H 17 Elstan way Croy
31 W 18 Elm Park av N15		
150 G 8 Elsted st SE17		
95 V 13 Elstow clo SE9		
68 L 2 Elstow gdns Dgnhm		
68 L 3 Elstow rd Dgnhm		
80 M 10 Elstree gdns Blvdr		
81 N 10 Elstree gdns Blvdr		
54 B 15 Elstree gdns Ilf		
19 N 7 Elstree gdns N9		
112 A 17 Elstree hill Brom		
111 Z 17 Elstree hill Brom		
11 T 2 Elstree Hill south Borhm Wd		
11 S 5 Elstree rd Borhm Wd		
10 E 3 Elstree rd Bushey		
93 R 6 Elswick rd SE13		
88 C 3 Elswick st SW6		
130 J 4 Elsworthy rd NW3		
130 L 1 Elsworthy rd NW3		
130 L 3 Elsworthy ter NW3		
88 F 12 Elsynge rd SW18		
95 V 4 Eltham comm SE18		
94 L 12 Eltham Green rd SE9		
94 M 13 Eltham grn SE9		
95 T 14 Eltham High st SE9		
95 N 14 Eltham hill SE9		
95 S 18 Eltham pal SE9		
94 L 16 Eltham Palace rd SE9		
95 N 16 Eltham Palace rd SE9		
95 X 11 Eltham Park gdns SE9		
96 A 11 Eltham pk SE9		
94 F 12 Eltham st SE12		
150 E 8 Eltham st SE17		
87 Y 2 Elthiron rd SW6		
71 X 6 Elthorne av W7		
71 X 6 Elthorne Park rd W7		
25 Y 20 Elthorne rd NW9		
25 Y 19 Elthorne way NW9		
93 Y 16 Elthruda rd SE13		
53 V 12 Eltisley rd Ilf		
4 J 17 Elton av Barnt		
41 V 18 Elton av Grnfd		
42 C 14 Elton av Wemb		
102 E 19 Elton clo Kingst		
49 R 14 Elton pl N16		
103 O 20 Elton rd Kingst		
88 D 10 Eltringham st SW18		
146 C 2 Elvaston ms SW7		
146 C 2 Elvaston pl SW7		
61 P 5 Elveden pl NW10		
61 P 6 Elveden rd NW10		
17 N 18 Elverson rd N13		
93 R 5 Elverson rd SE13		
148 E 4 Elverton st SW1		
126 C 11 Elvington grn Brom		
26 A 4 Elvington la NW9		
44 L 16 Elvino rd SE26		
44 L 16 Elvis rd NW2		
125 U 8 Elwill way Becknhm		
135 R 12 Elwin st E2		
48 J 10 Elwood st N5		
94 F 19 Elwyn gdns SE12		
9 T 5 Ely clo Erith		
118 E 2 Ely clo New Mald		
56 L 9 Ely gdns Dgnhm		
35 R 20 Ely gdns Ilf		
141 U 2 Ely pl EC1		
123 O 11 Ely rd Croy		
33 U 20 Ely rd E10		
30 F 19 Elyne rd N4		
155 T 18 Elystan clo Wallgtn		
146 M 8 Elystan pl SW3		
147 N 8 Elystan st SW3		
146 K 7 Elystan st SW3		
133 S 5 Elystan wk N1		
61 W 18 Emanuel av W3		
143 V 19 Emba st SE16		
147 S 13 Embankment gdns SW3		
140 L 13 Embankment pl WC2		
87 O 6 Embankment the SW15		
101 Z 1 Embankment the Twick		
93 R 10 Embleton rd SE13		
100 E 13 Embleton wlk Hampt		
10 L 14 Embry clo Stanm		
10 M 18 Embry dri Stanm		
10 L 15 Embry way Stanm		
88 B 2 Emden st SW6		
66 C 18 Emerald clo E16		
56 D 5 Emerald gdns Dgnhm		
133 O 19 Emerald st WC1		
24 M 20 Emerson gdns Harrow		
35 W 20 Emerson rd Ilf		
53 X 1 Emerson rd Ilf		
142 A 12 Emerson st SE1		
148 C 3 Emery Hill st SW1		

141 T 20	Emery st SE1
81 Y 18	Emes rd Erith
48 G 13	Emily pl N7
65 P 18	Emily st E16
74 C 6	Emlyn gdns W12
74 B 6	Emlyn rd W12
65 P 8	Emma rd E13
135 V 8	Emma st E2
107 V 2	Emmanuel rd SW12
75 Z 1	Emmett st E14
36 C 16	Emmott av Ilf
63 V 12	Emmott clo E1
28 C 19	Emmott rd NW11
146 A 4	Emperors ga SW7
145 Z 4	Emperors ga SW7
18 A 19	Empire av N18
17 Y 18	Empire av N18
60 E 3	Empire rd Grnfd
43 O 11	Empire way Wemb
76 J 11	Empire Wharf rd E14
34 C 2	Empress av Wfdf Grn
52 M 7	Empress av E12
53 N 7	Empress av E12
33 P 2	Empress av E4
53 V 7	Empress av Ilf
113 Y 14	Empress dri Chisl
145 U 12	Empress pl SW5
150 B 13	Empress st SE17
64 F 12	Empson st E3
19 O 5	Emsworth clo N9
36 A 7	Emsworth rd Ilf
108 C 4	Emsworth st SW2
93 R 5	Ena rd SW8
122 A 5	Ena rd SW16
121 Z 6	Ena rd SW16
128 L 15	Enbrook st W10
68 A 7	Endeavour way Bark
121 X 16	Endeavour way Croy
106 A 9	Endeavour way SW19
140 J 5	Endell st WC2
76 L 13	Enderby st SE10
23 S 6	Enderley rd Harrow
26 G 14	Endersleigh gdns NW4
20 F 8	Endlebury rd E4
89 O 17	Endlesham rd SW12
53 U 5	Endsleigh gdns Ilf
116 E 16	Endsleigh gdns Surb
132 F 15	Endsleigh gdns WC1
132 F 16	Endsleigh pl WC1
70 D 10	Endsleigh rd S'hall
71 Y 1	Endsleigh rd W13
132 F 15	Endsleigh st WC1
46 E 7	Endway NW3
117 R 17	Endway Surb
92 J 6	Endwell rd SE4
48 G 2	Endymion rd N4
30 J 20	Endymion rd N4
90 C 16	Endymion rd SW2
6 M 12	Enfield cres Enf
72 F 13	Enfield rd Brentf
6 L 12	Enfield rd Enf
7 O 12	Enfield rd Enf
134 L 1	Enfield rd N1
73 S 6	Enfield rd W3
72 F 13	Enfield Road east Brentf
139 N 1	Enford st W1
157 T 6	Engadine clo Croy
105 W 2	Engadine st SW18
93 T 10	Engate st SE13
14 A 19	Engel pk NW7
78 J 16	Engineer clo SE18
43 R 12	Engineers way Wemb
46 L 18	Englands la NW3
122 K 15	Englefield clo Croy
7 T 10	Englefield clo Enf
49 N 19	Englefield rd N1
93 T 20	Engleheart rd SE6
89 T 15	Englewood rd SW12
142 J 13	English grounds SE1
142 J 13	English Grounds SE1
63 Y 12	English st E3
151 P 1	Enid st SE16
48 R 11	Enkel st N7
123 Y 11	Enmore av SE25
85 Z 13	Enmore gdns SW14
58 H 10	Enmore rd S'hall
123 Y 11	Enmore rd SE25
87 N 12	Enmore rd SW6
57 V 15	Ennerdale av Hornch
24 D 9	Ennerdale av Stanm
26 A 16	Ennerdale dri NW9
25 Z 16	Ennerdale dri NW9
42 E 4	Ennerdale gdns Wemb
98 E 2	Ennerdale rd Bxly Hth
85 N 3	Ennerdale rd Rich
93 W 14	Ennersdale rd SE13
48 F 4	Ennis rd N4
79 R 16	Ennis rd SE18
41 U 16	Ennismore av Grnfd
74 C 11	Ennismore av W4
138 H 20	Ennismore Gardens ms SW7
146 J 1	Ennismore Gardens ms SW7
146 J 1	Ennismore gdns SW7
138 K 20	Ennismore gdns SW7
146 J 1	Ennismore ms SW7
138 K 20	Ennismore ms SW7
146 K 1	Ennismore st SW7
146 J 1	Ennismore ter SW7
152 L 8	Ennor ct Worc Pk
17 X 10	Ensign dri N13
143 T 9	Ensign st E1
95 W 17	Enslin rd SE9
146 E 9	Ensor ms SW7
9 V 11	Enstone rd Enf
156 E 1	Enterprise clo CR0
87 Z 11	Enterprise way SW18
63 O 10	Entick st E2
145 S 17	Epirus ms SW6
145 S 17	Epirus rd SW6
38 H 11	Epping clo Rom
21 U 3	Epping forest Buck Hl
21 U 8	Epping New rd Buck Hl
48 F 19	Epping rd E4
87 W 2	Epple rd SW6
98 H 9	Epsom clo Bxly Hth
40 F 16	Epsom clo Nthlt
156 G 7	Epsom rd Croy
33 U 19	Epsom rd E10
36 K 20	Epsom rd Ilf
119 W 14	Epsom rd Mrdn
80 C 3	Epstein rd SE28
72 A 20	Epworth rd Brentf
134 G 17	Epworth st EC2
148 H 6	Erasmus st SW1
62 D 18	Erconwald st W12
129 T 2	Eresby pl NW6
125 P 19	Eresby rd W Wkhm
52 E 12	Eric clo E7
52 E 13	Eric rd E7
44 C 18	Eric rd NW10
55 X 1	Eric rd Rom
63 X 11	Eric st E3
159 P 7	Erica gdns Croy
62 H 20	Erica st W12
87 X 13	Ericcson clo SW18
73 Y 8	Eridge rd W4
79 T 17	Erindale SE18
79 T 17	Erindale ter SE18
38 J 3	Erith cres Rom
81 O 3	Erith marshes Blvdr
81 U 13	Erith rd Blvdr
98 G 8	Erith rd Bxly Hth
98 J 3	Erith rd Erith
92 F 2	Erlanger rd SE14
71 Y 7	Erlesmere gdns W13
31 T 17	Ermine rd N15
93 R 10	Ermine rd SE13
8 J 16	Ermine side Enf
114 C 4	Ermington rd SE9
66 D 5	Ernald av E6
83 W 17	Erncroft way Twick
108 K 9	Ernest av SE27
125 N 11	Ernest clo Becknhm
73 T 17	Ernest gdns W4
124 M 11	Ernest gro Becknhm
125 N 11	Ernest gro Becknhm
65 O 13	Ernest rd E16
117 S 4	Ernest rd Kingst
117 S 3	Ernest sq Kingst
63 U 13	Ernest st E1
104 L 17	Ernle rd SW20
87 T 13	Ernshaw pla SW15
86 M 7	Erpingham rd SW15
119 Y 3	Erridge rd S19
129 R 17	Errington rd W9
118 G 10	Errol gdns New Mald
134 D 18	Errol st EC1
39 T 13	Erroll rd Rom
154 H 6	Erskine clo Sutton
31 Z 13	Erskine cres N15
27 Y 15	Erskine hill NW11
131 R 1	Erskine ms NW3
32 L 12	Erskine rd E17
131 R 1	Erskine rd NW3
154 G 7	Erskine rd Sutton
78 E 13	Erwood rd SE7
108 G 13	Esam way SW16
113 R 10	Escott gdns SE9
78 H 11	Escreet gro SE18
129 U 14	Esendine rd W9
38 K 18	Esher av Rom
153 R 6	Esher av Sutton
115 Y 2	Esher clo Bxly
105 O 3	Esher gdns SW19
121 N 5	Esher ms Mitch
54 H 9	Esher rd Ilf
65 U 12	Esk rd E13
39 O 3	Esk way Rom
58 E 2	Eskdale av Nthlt
42 G 7	Eskdale clo Wemb
98 D 4	Eskdale rd Bxly Hth
109 P 18	Eskmont ridge SE19
44 F 1	Esmar cres NW9
151 T 8	Esmeralda rd SE1
129 R 17	Esmond rd NW6
73 Z 10	Esmond rd W4
87 T 11	Esmond st SW15
88 A 18	Esparto st SW18
81 R 13	Essenden rd Blvdr
157 R 17	Essenden rd S Croy
83 T 8	Essex av Islwth
32 G 12	Essex clo E17
119 N 16	Essex clo Mrdn
38 G 12	Essex clo Rom
86 D 4	Essex ct SW13
141 S 7	Essex ct WC2
30 K 18	Essex gdns N4
109 P 15	Essex gro SE19
74 B 4	Essex Park ms W3
15 N 20	Essex pk N3
73 X 12	Essex pl W4
66 J 15	Essex rd Bark
33 V 19	Essex rd Dgnhm
52 E 16	Essex rd E10
52 C 12	Essex rd E12
32 H 18	Essex rd E17
34 J 7	Essex rd E18
20 M 5	Essex rd E4
8 B 15	Essex rd Enf
49 N 18	Essex rd N1
133 Y 4	Essex rd N1
44 C 19	Essex rd NW10
38 H 12	Essex rd Rom
55 S 2	Essex rd Rom
61 U 19	Essex rd W3
73 X 11	Essex rd W4
51 X 1	Essex Road south E11
52 E 14	Essex st E7
141 R 8	Essex st WC2
137 U 19	Essex vlls W8
63 V 13	Essian st E1
25 N 9	Essoldo way NW9
50 M 4	Estate way E10
124 A 14	Estcourt rd SE25
145 N 17	Estcourt rd SW6
88 J 7	Este rd SW11
118 K 9	Estella av New Mald
47 N 13	Estelle rd NW3
148 F 6	Esterbrooke st SW1
17 U 2	Esther clo N21
33 Z 20	Esther rd E11
107 X 15	Estreham rd SW16
63 O 20	Estridge clo Hounsl
106 M 10	Eswyn rd SW17
107 N 12	Eswyn rd SW17
28 B 1	Etchingham Park rd N3
51 U 12	Etchingham rd E15
115 P 12	Etfield gro Sidcp
65 V 19	Ethel rd E16
150 B 7	Ethel st SE17
126 E 5	Ethelbert clo Brom
35 V 17	Ethelbert gdns Ilf
126 E 5	Ethelbert rd Brom
81 W 19	Ethelbert rd Erith
105 P 20	Ethelbert rd SW20
107 T 2	Ethelbert st SW12
88 K 1	Ethelburga st SW11
146 L 20	Ethelburga st SW11
74 J 3	Ethelden rd W12
29 U 13	Etheldene av N10
30 L 14	Etherley rd N15
91 W 17	Etherow st SE22
108 E 10	Etherstone grn SW16
108 E 10	Etherstone rd SW16
151 V 15	Ethnard rd SE15
97 Z 8	Ethronvi rd Bxly Hth
51 N 6	Etloe rd E10
70 F 16	Eton av Hounsl
15 R 20	Eton av N12
117 V 10	Eton av New Mald
46 H 19	Eton av NW3
42 E 13	Eton av Wemb
47 N 19	Eton College rd NW3
42 E 12	Eton ct Wemb
25 R 12	Eton gro NW9
93 Z 8	Eton gro SE13
54 D 13	Eton rd Ilf
46 M 19	Eton rd NW3
84 J 12	Eton st Rich
46 M 19	Eton vlls NW3
50 H 11	Etropol rd E5
75 X 15	Etta st SE8
64 H 16	Ettrick st E14
116 M 14	Etwell pl Surb
75 R 12	Eugenia rd SE16
117 O 4	Eureka rd Kingst
134 B 14	Europa pl EC1
78 F 8	Europe rd SE18
66 E 8	Eustace rd E6
55 X 1	Eustace rd Rom
145 T 16	Eustace rd Rom
122 E 20	Euston rd Croy
156 G 1	Euston rd Croy
132 E 15	Euston rd NW1
132 E 14	Euston sq NW1
132 D 14	Euston st NW1
132 D 13	Euston sta NW1
37 U 20	Eva rd Rom
90 G 4	Evandale rd SW9
47 T 13	Evangelist rd NW5
100 G 5	Evans gro Felt
112 A 5	Evans rd SE6
33 U 2	Evanston av E4
35 P 18	Evanston gdns Ilf
51 Z 12	Eve rd E11
65 N 6	Eve rd E15
93 Z 11	Eve rd Islwth
31 T 9	Eve rd N17
92 C 6	Evelina rd SE15
110 O 19	Evelina rd SE20
120 L 2	Eveline rd Mitch
25 X 12	Evelyn av NW9
82 J 18	Evelyn clo Twick
134 E 10	Evelyn ct N1
22 A 2	Evelyn dri Pinn
84 L 9	Evelyn gdns Rich
146 E 10	Evelyn gdns SW7
58 E 18	Evelyn gro S'hall
73 N 3	Evelyn gro W5
5 Z 15	Evelyn rd Barnt
77 V 2	Evelyn rd E16
33 U 14	Evelyn rd E17
102 E 6	Evelyn rd Rich
84 K 8	Evelyn rd Rich
106 A 14	Evelyn rd SW19
73 X 9	Evelyn rd W4
75 W 13	Evelyn st SE8
84 J 8	Evelyn ter Rich
155 X 7	Evelyn way Wallgtn
134 E 10	Evelyn wlk N1
140 E 4	Evelyn yd W1
111 V 19	Evening hill Becknhm
87 S 14	Evenwood clo SW15
16 G 19	Everard av Brom
42 H 11	Everard way Wemb
74 F 18	Everdon rd SW13
64 F 14	Everest pla E14
95 S 13	Everest rd SE9
81 O 15	Everett wk Blvdr
26 D 5	Everglade strand NW9
133 P 5	Everilda st N1
49 U 11	Evering rd N16
28 M 7	Everington rd N10
29 N 6	Everington rd N10
144 H 15	Everington st W6
48 E 5	Everitt rd NW10
13 N 20	Eversfield gdns NW7
84 M 4	Eversfield rd Rich
85 N 4	Eversfield rd Rich
132 C 10	Eversholt st NW1
48 C 4	Evershot rd N4
5 R 18	Eversleigh rd Barnt
66 B 3	Eversleigh rd E6
27 W 2	Eversleigh rd N3
89 O 5	Eversleigh rd SW11
99 P 5	Eversley av Bxly Hth
43 P 7	Eversley av Wemb
7 P 19	Eversley clo N21
83 R 2	Eversley cres Islwth
7 S 19	Eversley cres N21
99 R 5	Eversley cross Bxly Hth
7 R 19	Eversley mt N21
17 R 1	Eversley Park rd N21
7 R 20	Eversley Park rd N21
104 J 14	Eversley pk SW19
109 O 17	Eversley rd SE19
77 V 16	Eversley rd SE7
116 M 10	Eversley rd Surb
117 N 10	Eversley rd Surb
158 M 6	Eversley way Croy
91 U 8	Everthorpe rd SE15

24 L 10 Everton dri Stanm
123 W 19 Everton rd Croy
33 P 7 Evesham av E17
58 K 5 Evesham clo Grnfd
153 W 16 Evesham clo Sutton
120 A 14 Evesham grn Mrdn
65 O 2 Evesham rd E5
120 A 15 Evesham rd Mrdn
16 J 18 Evesham rd N11
136 G 11 Evesham st W11
35 X 11 Evesham way Ilf
89 P 6 Evesham wlk SW11
21 X 18 Ewanrigg ter
        Wdfd Grn
30 E 5 Ewart gro N22
92 F 20 Ewart rd SE23
48 A 18 Ewe clo N7
152 G 18 Ewell By-pass
        Epsom
152 B 12 Ewell Court av Epsom
152 G 16 Ewell Park way Epsom
116 A 18 Ewell rd Surb
117 P 20 Ewell rd Surb
153 P 15 Ewell rd Sutton
35 S 8 Ewellhurst rd Ilf
110 D 1 Ewelme rd SE23
90 F 20 Ewen cres SW2
141 Z 15 Ewer st SE1
157 U 20 Ewhurst av S Croy
153 N 20 Ewhurst clo Sutton
92 M 16 Ewhurst rd SE4
93 N 16 Ewhurst rd SE4
110 M 4 Exbury rd SE6
93 U 5 Excelsior gdns SE13
117 O 4 Excelsior rd Kings
142 L 4 Exchange bldgs E1
140 L 10 Exchange ct WC2
134 A 14 Exchange st EC1
39 P 16 Exchange st Rom
66 F 17 Exeter clo E6
53 S 2 Exeter gdns Ilf
123 T 17 Exeter rd Dgnhm
56 H 19 Exeter rd Dgnhm
65 T 16 Exeter rd E16
33 N 15 Exeter rd E17
9 T 12 Exeter rd Enf
100 E 7 Exeter rd Felt
40 C 6 Exeter rd Harrow
16 E 3 Exeter rd N14
19 O 9 Exeter rd N9
45 S 17 Exeter rd NW2
151 N 20 Exeter rd SE15
91 U 1 Exeter rd SE5
96 K 4 Exeter rd Welling
140 M 9 Exeter st WC2
141 N 9 Exeter st WC2
75 X 20 Exeter way SE14
112 H 2 Exford gdns SE12
112 H 2 Exford rd SE12
136 B 10 Exhibition clo W12
62 M 20 Exhibition clo W12
138 G 19 Exhibition rd SW7
146 G 2 Exhibition rd SW7
128 H 20 Exmoor st W10
133 T 16 Exmouth mkt EC1
126 G 7 Exmouth rd Brom
32 L 16 Exmouth rd E17
80 E 20 Exmouth rd Welling
63 P 17 Exmouth st E1
65 O 12 Exning rd E16
150 J 8 Exon st SE17
61 X 2 Exton cres NW10
55 U 14 Exton gdns Dgnhm
141 T 15 Exton st SE1
124 F 20 Eyebright clo CR0
57 W 11 Eyhurst av Hornch
44 H 6 Eyhurst clo NW2
108 M 11 Eylewood rd SE27
91 V 17 Eynella rd SE22
136 B 4 Eynham rd W10
62 M 17 Eynham rd W12
115 V 2 Eynsford cres Bxly
54 J 7 Eynsford rd Ilf
80 F 6 Eynsham dri SE2
115 S 13 Eynswood dri Sidcp
14 E 14 Eyot gdns W6
133 S 18 Eyre Street hill EC1
90 G 2 Eythorne rd SW9
135 P 11 Ezra st E2

F

26 G 16 Faber gdns NW4
145 P 17 Fabian rd SW6
66 F 12 Fabian st E6
156 H 2 Factory la Croy
31 V 8 Factory la N17
76 F 13 Factory pl E14
78 E 4 Factory rd E16
108 A 16 Factory sq SW16
71 T 3 Factory yd W7
126 F 13 Fair acres Brom
142 M 16 Fair st SE1
143 N 19 Fair st SE1
118 A 6 Fairacre New Mald
117 Z 7 Fairacre New Mald
158 L 19 Fairacres Croy
86 F 11 Fairacres SW15
90 H 2 Fairbairn grn SW9
31 W 11 Fairbanks rd N17
31 R 10 Fairbourne rd N17
47 Y 7 Fairbridge rd N19
17 T 18 Fairbrook clo N13
17 T 18 Fairbrook rd N13
94 H 13 Fairby rd SE12
134 L 17 Fairchild st EC2
143 T 6 Fairclough st E1
54 C 18 Faircross av Bark
38 L 2 Faircross av Rom
86 K 9 Fairdale gdns SW15
152 J 20 Fairfax av Epsom
94 M 3 Fairfax gdns SE3
130 C 1 Fairfax rd NW6
30 H 14 Fairfax rd N8
130 C 1 Fairfax rd NW6
46 E 20 Fairfax rd NW6
102 C 18 Fairfax rd Tedd
101 Z 16 Fairfax rd Tedd
74 B 9 Fairfax rd W4
12 E 20 Fairfield av Edg
25 S 1 Fairfield av Edg
26 L 20 Fairfield av NW4
100 L 1 Fairfield av Twick
9 U 16 Fairfield clo Enf
57 W 6 Fairfield clo Hornch
15 S 14 Fairfield clo N12
96 K 15 Fairfield clo Sidcp
12 E 20 Fairfield cres Edg
157 R 5 Fairfield Croy
60 E 4 Fairfield dri Grnfd
23 N 10 Fairfield dri Harrow
88 B 13 Fairfield dri SW18
116 K 3 Fairfield east Kingst
30 B 17 Fairfield gdns N8
71 Y 10 Fairfield gdns W7
78 A 15 Fairfield gdns SE7
116 K 3 Fairfield north Kingst
116 K 6 Fairfield pl Kingst
157 R 5 Fairfield pth Croy
125 O 2 Fairfield rd Beckhm
112 E 18 Fairfield rd Brom
98 B 5 Fairfield rd Bxly Hth
32 J 8 Fairfield rd E17
64 B 7 Fairfield rd E3
54 A 17 Fairfield rd Ilf
116 J 4 Fairfield rd Kingst
18 K 15 Fairfield rd N18
30 B 17 Fairfield rd N8
58 E 16 Fairfield rd S'hall
21 S 19 Fairfield rd Wdfd Grn
116 K 5 Fairfield south Kingst
88 A 11 Fairfield st SW18
4 L 17 Fairfield way Barnt
152 J 20 Fairfield way Epsom
116 K 4 Fairfield west Kingst
25 W 15 Fairfields clo NW9
25 W 14 Fairfields cres NW9
82 M 8 Fairfields rd Hounsl
64 B 11 Fairfoot rd E3
98 M 2 Fairford av Bxly Hth
99 N 2 Fairford av Bxly Hth
124 G 13 Fairford clo Becknhm
152 E 5 Fairford gdns
        Worc Pk
5 Y 10 Fairgreen Barnt
5 Z 11 Fairgreen ct Barnt
5 Y 11 Fairgreen east Barnt
124 E 16 Fairhaven av Croy
130 C 2 Fairhazel gdns NW6
46 C 20 Fairhazel gdns NW6
39 V 14 Fairholme av Rom
27 T 12 Fairholme clo N3
27 U 12 Fairholme gdns N3
122 G 17 Fairholme rd Croy
23 V 17 Fairholme rd Harrow
35 V 20 Fairholme rd Ilf
153 V 13 Fairholme rd Sutton
145 N 11 Fairholme rd W14
49 P 3 Fairholt clo N16
49 P 3 Fairholt rd N16
146 L 1 Fairholt st SW7
52 C 19 Fairland rd E15
122 D 10 Fairlands av
        Thntn Hth

21 U 7 Fairlands av
        Buck Hl
153 Z 2 Fairlands av Sutton
97 W 5 Fairlawn av Bxly Hth
28 K 12 Fairlawn av N2
73 W 11 Fairlawn av W4
100 E 9 Fairlawn clo Felt
103 U 15 Fairlawn clo Kingst
6 J 20 Fairlawn clo N14
34 F 2 Fairlawn dri
        Wdfd Grn
70 F 1 Fairlawn gdns S'hall
73 W 10 Fairlawn gro Bxly
110 J 12 Fairlawn pk SE26
105 V 19 Fairlawn rd SW19
77 X 18 Fairlawn SE7
87 R 13 Fairlawns SW15
84 F 17 Fairlawns Twick
60 F 13 Fairlea pl W5
92 D 19 Fairlie gdns SE23
21 T 20 Fairlight av
        Wdfd Grn
20 J 8 Fairlight av E4
62 B 6 Fairlight av NW10
152 L 8 Fairlight clo
        Worc Pk
20 J 8 Fairlight clo E4
106 H 10 Fairlight rd SW17
57 Z 19 Fairlop clo Hornch
36 C 2 Fairlop gdns Ilf
130 H 14 Fairlop pl NW8
36 H 7 Fairlop plain Ilf
51 X 2 Fairlop rd E11
36 B 8 Fairlop rd Ilf
127 U 10 Fairmead Brom
117 Z 7 Fairmead clo
        New Mald
127 U 10 Fairmead clo Brom
12 H 11 Fairmead cres Edg
35 P 16 Fairmead gdns Ilf
122 E 18 Fairmead rd Croy
47 Z 9 Fairmead rd N19
117 T 20 Fairmead Surb
107 X 12 Fairmile av SW16
90 D 15 Fairmount rd SW2
96 D 13 Fairoak dri SE9
39 O 8 Fairoak gdns Rom
10 E 8 Fairseat clo Bushey
134 A 3 Fairstead wlk N1
77 T 13 Fairthorn rd SE7
42 G 17 Fairview av Wemb
32 H 5 Fairview clo E17
40 G 3 Fairview cres Harrow
34 J 4 Fairview gdns
        Wdfd Grn
90 C 18 Fairview pl SW2
7 T 6 Fairview rd Enf
31 V 18 Fairview rd N15
154 H 12 Fairview rd Sutton
122 B 1 Fairview SW16
12 C 14 Fairview way Edg
97 N 10 Fairwater av Welling
25 T 10 Fairway av NW9
97 Z 13 Fairway Bxly Hth
124 H 13 Fairway clo Croy
46 C 1 Fairway clo NW11
58 M 2 Fairway dri Grnfd
54 B 15 Fairway gdns Ilf
118 L 6 Fairway SW20
117 Z 1 Fairway the
        New Mald
5 O 19 Fairway the Barnt
127 T 11 Fairway the Brom
103 Z 20 Fairway the Kingst
18 A 11 Fairway the N13
17 Z 10 Fairway the N13
6 F 19 Fairway the N14
41 N 17 Fairway the Nthlt
12 L 9 Fairway the NW7
62 B 17 Fairway the W3
42 C 5 Fairway the Wemb
21 Z 16 Fairway Wdfd Grn
24 J 7 Fairways Stanm
102 G 16 Fairways Tedd
45 N 11 Fairweather clo N15
31 X 19 Fairweather rd N16
110 H 8 Fairwyn rd SE26
127 R 7 Falcon av Brom
9 T 18 Falcon cres Enf
88 J 7 Falcon gro SW11
88 L 8 Falcon la SW11
9 S 18 Falcon rd Enf
100 F 17 Falcon rd Hampt
88 J 7 Falcon rd SW11
65 R 11 Falcon st E13
88 K 8 Falcon ter SW11
76 D 10 Falcon way E14
24 K 18 Falcon way Harrow
57 X 20 Falcon way Hornch
140 G 5 Falconberg ct W1

140 F 5 Falconberg ms W1
129 P 11 Falconer ms W9
96 H 6 Falconwood av
        Welling
96 J 10 Falconwood pde
        Welling
158 M 18 Falconwood rd Croy
159 N 17 Falconwood rd Croy
154 A 11 Falcourt clo Sutton
134 L 10 Falkirk st N1
16 D 13 Falkland av N11
27 Y 3 Falkland av N3
123 S 4 Falkland Park av SE25
4 E 10 Falkland rd Barnt
30 H 14 Falkland rd N8
47 V 14 Falkland rd NW5
53 X 11 Fallaize av Ilf
27 Y 13 Falloden way NW11
15 R 20 Fallow Court av N12
10 L 12 Fallowfield ct Stanm
10 K 12 Fallowfield Stanm
107 T 17 Fallsbrook rd SW16
33 P 10 Falmer rd E17
8 F 14 Falmer rd Enf
31 N 15 Falmer rd N15
20 L 17 Falmouth av E4
30 C 2 Falmouth clo N22
35 N 2 Falmouth gdns
        Wdfd Grn
35 P 16 Falmouth gdns Ilf
150 B 3 Falmouth rd SE1
150 E 1 Falmouth rd SE1
51 Y 16 Falmouth st E15
56 D 3 Fambridge rd Dgnhm
110 L 10 Fambridge rd SE26
145 P 12 Fane st W14
134 A 19 Fann st EC1
134 J 11 Fanshaw st N1
54 C 18 Fanshawe av Bark
56 A 15 Fanshawe cres
        Dgnhm
102 D 10 Fanshawe rd Rich
86 M 7 Fanthorpe st SW15
115 S 5 Faraday av Sidcp
48 D 19 Faraday clo N7
52 B 19 Faraday rd E15
58 K 18 Faraday rd S'hall
78 B 9 Faraday rd SE18
106 A 14 Faraday rd SW19
105 Z 14 Faraday rd SW19
128 L 20 Faraday rd W10
61 W 18 Faraday rd W3
96 M 7 Faraday rd Well
97 N 8 Faraday rd Welling
140 E 5 Fareham st W1
120 G 2 Farewell pl Mitch
127 X 16 Faringdon av Brom
64 M 1 Faringford rd E15
95 N 1 Farjeon rd SE3
126 D 16 Farleigh av Brom
49 U 12 Farleigh pl N16
49 V 12 Farleigh rd N16
54 J 4 Farley dri Ilf
123 X 9 Farley pl SE25
157 Z 18 Farley rd S Croy
93 T 17 Farley rd SE6
86 H 19 Farlington pl SW15
87 N 8 Farlow rd SW15
88 B 20 Farlton rd SW18
22 G 20 Farm av Harrow
45 T 10 Farm av NW2
108 A 9 Farm av SW16
42 E 18 Farm av Wemb
21 Y 12 Farm clo Buck Hl
69 W 1 Farm clo Dgnhm
58 K 19 Farm clo S'hall
154 H 16 Farm clo Sutton
158 M 2 Farm dri Croy
159 N 2 Farm dri Croy
158 M 3 Farm la Croy
6 C 20 Farm la N14
145 V 16 Farm la SW6
99 X 11 Farm pl Drtfrd
137 S 13 Farm pl W8
12 G 17 Farm rd Edg
22 A 12 Farm rd Mrdn
17 X 5 Farm rd N21
154 G 16 Farm rd Sutton
139 W 11 Farm st W1
98 G 16 Farm vale Bxly
21 Y 13 Farm way Buck Hl
152 M 5 Farm way Worc Pk
153 N 4 Farm way Worc Pk
27 X 17 Farm wlk NW11
112 F 1 Farmcote rd SE12
124 J 16 Farmdale rd Carsh
77 T 14 Farmdale rd SE10
51 R 3 Farmer rd E10
137 T 13 Farmer st W8

149 Y 19	Farmers rd SE5
14 L 14	Farmfield rd N12
112 A 13	Farmfield rd Brom
111 Y 12	Farmfield rd Brom
107 V 19	Farmhouse rd SW16
50 M 1	Farmilo rd E17
33 N 20	Farmilo rd E17
154 H 5	Farmington av Sutton
113 Y 19	Farmland wlk Chisl
7 T 6	Farmlands Enf
40 G 19	Farmlands the Nthlt
16 G 2	Farmleigh N14
23 R 6	Farmstead rd Harrow
111 S 9	Farmstead rd SE6
55 T 11	Farmway Dgnhm
112 A 20	Farnaby rd Brom
126 B 1	Farnaby rd Brom
111 Y 19	Farnaby rd Brom
94 M 11	Farnaby rd SE9
33 R 10	Farnan av E17
108 A 12	Farnan rd SW16
158 H 17	Farnborough av S Croy
32 G 11	Farnborough av E17
43 T 8	Farnborough clo Wemb
158 H 18	Farnborough cres S Croy
143 U 18	Farncombe st SE16
17 X 9	Farndale av N13
59 N 8	Farndale cres Grnfd
145 X 9	Farnell ms SW5
83 R 8	Farnell rd Islwth
15 R 2	Farnham clo N20
118 J 4	Farnham gdns New Mald
141 Y 14	Farnham pl SE1
30 M 20	Farnham rd Ilf
9? U 4	Farnham rd Welling
149 P 12	Farnham royal SE11
31 Y 2	Farningham rd N17
20 L 2	Farnley rd E4
123 P 9	Farnley rd SE25
144 H 2	Faroe rd W14
7 S 5	Farorna wlk Enf
109 U 14	Farquhar rd SE19
105 V 7	Farquhar rd SW19
122 L 19	Farquharson rd Croy
67 Z 6	Farr av Bark
8 B 7	Farr rd Enf
55 Z 1	Farrance rd Rom
37 Z 20	Farrance rd Rom
64 A 17	Farrance st E14
30 J 6	Farrant av N22
110 G 4	Farrer rd SE23
24 J 14	Farrer rd Harrow
29 X 13	Farrer rd N8
58 H 5	Farrier rd Nthlt
47 U 20	Farrier st NW1
133 U 17	Farringdon la EC1
133 U 18	Farringdon rd EC1
141 W 5	Farringdon st EC4
75 V 3	Farrins rents SE16
75 V 7	Farrow clo SE16
143 Y 12	Farthing fields E1
21 N 10	Farthings clo E4
115 S 9	Farwell rd Sidcp
112 E 20	Farwig la Brom
143 O 2	Fashion st E1
127 N 8	Fashoda rd Brom
49 X 17	Fassett rd E8
116 J 8	Fassett rd Kingst
49 X 17	Fassett sq E8
73 V 17	Fauconberg rd W4
92 D 1	Faulkner st SE14
37 S 20	Fauna clo Rom
149 X 11	Faunce st SE17
87 Y 2	Faure st SW8
21 O 6	Faversham av Enf
8 B 19	Faversham av Enf
124 M 3	Faversham rd Becknhm
120 B 14	Faversham rd Mrdn
92 M 21	Faversham rd SE6
88 G 6	Fawcett clo SW11
49 Y 3	Fawcett est E5
156 K 6	Fawcett rd Croy
62 C 2	Fawcett rd NW10
146 A 14	Fawcett st SW10
87 V 11	Fawe Park rd SW15
64 D 15	Fawe st E14
31 Y 12	Fawley rd N17
46 A 16	Fawley rd NW6
45 Z 16	Fawley rd NW6
65 X 6	Fawn rd E13
90 K 12	Fawnbrake av SE24
61 Y 1	Fawood av NW10
98 E 13	Faygate cres Bxly Hth
108 C 4	Faygate rd SW2
107 V 12	Fayland av SW16
77 S 12	Fearon st SE10
158 L 17	Featherbed la Croy
159 N 20	Featherbed la Croy
76 K 16	Feathers pl SE10
110 B 4	Featherstone av SE23
70 A 8	Featherstone rd S'hall
13 X 20	Featherstone rd NW7
134 E 16	Featherstone st EC1
70 C 7	Featherstone ter S'hall
90 H 6	Featley rd SW9
60 E 5	Federal rd Grnfd
80 F 12	Federation rd SE2
24 A 5	Felbridge av Stanm
23 Z 5	Felbridge av Stanm
154 C 19	Felbridge clo Sutton
108 F 9	Felbridge clo SW16
54 L 5	Felbrigge rd Ilf
93 R 16	Felday rd SE13
87 U 2	Felden st SW6
49 X 3	Feldman clo N16
22 C 3	Feldon clo Pinn
74 J 11	Felgate ms W6
113 Y 5	Felhampton rd SE9
56 J 12	Felhurst rd Dgnhm
30 A 17	Felix av N8
71 X 1	Felix rd W13
59 Z 20	Felix rd W13
63 N 6	Felix st E2
135 X 9	Felix st E2
31 U 10	Felixstowe rd N17
18 L 12	Felixstowe rd N9
62 K 8	Felixstowe rd NW10
80 E 9	Felixstowe rd SE2
156 M 5	Fell rd Croy
91 V 13	Fellbrigg rd SE22
135 Y 18	Fellbrigg st E1
102 B 8	Fellbrook Rich
154 J 4	Fellowes rd Carsh
46 K 19	Fellows rd NW3
77 T 12	Felltram way SE7
89 Z 11	Felmersham clo SW4
124 C 4	Felmingham rd SE20
56 G 10	Fels clo Dgnhm
56 L 10	Fels Farm av Dgnhm
90 B 17	Felsberg rd SW2
87 R 9	Felsham rd SW15
79 Y 14	Felspar clo SE18
35 V 6	Felstead av Ilf
76 F 14	Felstead gdns E14
34 G 20	Felstead rd E11
65 Z 18	Felstead rd E16
38 K 1	Felstead rd Rom
50 M 18	Felstead st E9
121 N 3	Feltham rd Mitch
127 Z 15	Felton clo Brom
67 W 5	Felton gdns Bark
114 K 11	Felton lea Sidcp
67 V 5	Felton rd Bark
72 C 5	Felton rd W13
134 G 5	Felton st N1
142 K 7	Fen ct EC3
96 J 14	Fen gro Sidcp
65 P 19	Fen st E16
36 D 3	Fencepiece rd Ilf
142 J 7	Fenchurch av EC3
142 L 7	Fenchurch bldgs EC3
142 L 8	Fenchurch pl EC3
142 J 8	Fenchurch st EC3
142 M 8	Fenchurch Street sta EC3
150 L 2	Fendall st SE1
65 R 18	Fendt clo E16
80 H 9	Fendyke rd Blvdr
145 R 6	Fendyke rd W14
32 A 4	Fenman ct N17
112 E 15	Fenn clo Brom
50 D 15	Fenn st E9
124 F 19	Fennel clo CRO
78 K 17	Fennel st SE18
152 C 20	Fennells mead Epsom
15 T 18	Fenstanton av N12
149 R 18	Fentiman rd SW8
113 T 12	Fenton clo Chisl
90 C 5	Fenton clo SW9
30 M 1	Fenton rd N17
143 X 5	Fenton st E1
65 U 8	Fentons av E13
78 J 17	Fenwick clo SE18
91 X 8	Fenwick gro SE15
89 Z 8	Fenwick pl SW9
91 X 8	Fenwick rd SE15
47 N 20	Ferdinand pl NW1
47 P 20	Ferdinand st NW1
48 J 16	Fergus rd N5
117 N 11	Ferguson av Surb
48 D 1	Ferme Park rd N4
30 B 16	Ferme Park rd N8
110 K 2	Fermor rd SE23
58 K 13	Fermoy rd Grnfd
129 P 18	Fermoy rd W9
121 Y 8	Fern av Mitch
60 B 14	Fern dene W13
70 D 15	Fern la Hounsl
64 B 12	Fern st E3
41 V 14	Fernbank av Wemb
96 H 14	Fernbrook av Sidcp
40 J 2	Fernbrook dri Harrow
94 A 15	Fernbrook rd SE13
92 B 16	Fernbrook rd SE13
49 W 14	Ferncliffe rd E8
15 Y 18	Ferncroft av N12
45 Z 11	Ferncroft av NW3
33 W 15	Ferndale av E17
82 C 8	Ferndale av Hounsl
126 L 4	Ferndale Brom
52 B 6	Ferndale rd E11
52 J 20	Ferndale rd E7
31 V 17	Ferndale rd N15
38 L 7	Ferndale rd Rom
124 A 12	Ferndale rd SE25
89 Z 9	Ferndale rd SW4
90 D 9	Ferndale rd SW9
66 L 19	Ferndale st E6
23 V 13	Ferndale ter Harrow
38 F 19	Ferndene way Rom
90 M 10	Ferndene rd SE24
91 N 8	Ferndene rd SE24
22 A 2	Ferndown clo Pinn
154 F 14	Ferndown clo Sutton
95 N 19	Ferndown rd SE9
16 B 4	Ferney rd Barnt
35 P 16	Fernhall dri Ilf
122 L 7	Fernham rd Thntn Hth
129 P 11	Fernhead rd W9
33 X 8	Fernhill ct E17
102 H 13	Fernhill gdns Kingst
78 G 3	Fernhill st E16
92 F 13	Fernholme rd SE15
12 B 18	Fernhurst gdns Edg
123 Z 19	Fernhurst rd Croy
87 T 1	Fernhurst rd SW6
121 D 2	Fernlea av Mitch
107 T 2	Fernlea rd Mitch
156 E 8	Fernleigh clo Croy
22 L 6	Fernleigh ct Harrow
42 J 6	Fernleigh ct Wemb
17 U 7	Fernleigh rd N21
52 B 18	Ferns rd E15
133 S 13	Fernsbury st WC1
146 B 16	Fernshaw rd SW10
12 L 10	Fernside av NW7
21 U 4	Fernside Buck Hl
45 Y 6	Fernside NW3
27 P 7	Fernside NW4
89 N 19	Fernside rd SW12
107 V 15	Fernthorpe rd SW16
49 O 14	Fernsteer rd N5
53 V 12	Fernways Ilf
107 Y 10	Fernwood av SW16
42 C 17	Fernwood av Wemb
126 K 2	Fernwood clo Brom
15 Z 10	Fernwood cres N20
158 J 19	Fernwood Croy
78 A 10	Ferranti clo SE18
70 H 16	Ferrard clo Hounsl
155 X 8	Ferrers av Walgtn
107 Y 13	Ferrers rd SW16
30 C 14	Ferrestone rd N8
88 B 11	Ferrier st SW18
41 N 4	Ferring clo Harrow
109 S 6	Ferrings SE21
158 L 6	Ferris av Croy
91 X 11	Ferris rd SE22
49 Z 10	Ferron rd E5
6 A 3	Ferry hill Barnt
72 J 18	Ferry la Brentf
31 Y 12	Ferry la N17
73 N 17	Ferry la Rich
74 E 17	Ferry la SW13
78 K 8	Ferry pl SE 18
116 A 16	Ferry rd SW13
86 G 1	Ferry rd SW13
102 A 12	Ferry rd Tedd
76 F 13	Ferry st E14
58 K 7	Ferrymead av Grnfd
58 H 7	Ferrymead dri Grnfd
59 O 6	Ferrymead gdns Grnfd
102 B 7	Ferrymoor Rich
87 O 7	Festing rd SW15
115 V 3	Festival clo Bxly
154 M 9	Festival wlk Carsh
141 T 4	Fetter la EC4
126 L 4	Field clo Brom
21 Y 11	Field clo Buck Hl
20 C 19	Field clo E4
141 R 1	Field ct WC1
40 A 19	Field end Ruis
40 C 14	Field End rd Ruis
101 W 10	Field end Tedd
72 D 19	Field la Brentf
101 Y 13	Field la Tedd
26 C 3	Field mead NW9
133 U 10	Field pl EC1
118 C 14	Field pl New Mald
33 N 14	Field rd E17
52 E 14	Field rd E7
31 P 10	Field rd N17
144 L 13	Field rd W6
133 N 11	Field st WC1
159 S 15	Field way Croy
159 T 13	Field way Croy
61 W 1	Field way NW10
58 K 4	Field wy Grnfd
107 W 20	Fieldend rd SW16
68 G 20	Fieldfare rd SE28
120 K 4	Fieldgate st E1
143 T 3	Fieldgate st E1
107 W 2	Fieldhouse rd SW12
101 N 6	Fielding av Twick
136 H 20	Fielding rd W14
74 A 7	Fielding rd W4
73 Z 8	Fielding rd W4
150 B 13	Fielding st SE17
110 C 1	Fieldings the SE23
37 V 15	Fields Park cres Rom
153 S 11	Fieldsend rd Sutton
111 X 13	Fieldside rd Brom
106 F 2	Fieldview SW18
48 G 16	Fieldway cres N5
66 C 11	Fieldway Dgnhm
88 T 4	Fiennes clo Dgnhm
65 S 15	Fife rd E16
116 H 3	Fife rd Kingst
30 K 3	Fife rd N22
85 W 14	Fife rd SW14
133 O 7	Fife ter N1
110 E 6	Fifield pth SE23
53 T 12	Fifth av E12
128 K 15	Fifth av W10
101 P 6	Fifth Cross rd Twick
43 S 12	Fifth way Wemb
107 O 18	Figgs rd Mitch
49 W 5	Filey av N16
154 D 16	Filey clo Sutton
8 F 8	Fillebrook av Enf
52 A 1	Fillebrook rd E11
51 Y 3	Fillebrook rd E11
145 N 19	Filmer rd SW6
88 T 1	Filmer rd SW6
81 W 13	Filston rd Erith
145 X 12	Finborough rd SW10
106 M 16	Finborough rd SW17
109 N 11	Finch av SE27
43 X 17	Finch clo NW10
160 G 6	Finch la EC3
76 A 18	Finch st SE8
80 A 8	Finchale rd SE2
34 M 1	Finchingfield av Wdfd Grn
15 N 20	Finchley ct N3
27 O 12	Finchley la NW4
15 S 12	Finchley pk N12
130 E 8	Finchley pl NW8
27 W 15	Finchley rd NW11
45 X 4	Finchley rd NW3
46 D 18	Finchley rd NW3
130 F 3	Finchley rd NW8
14 K 20	Finchley way N3
27 Y 1	Finchley way N3
141 P 19	Finck st SE1
52 K 16	Finden rd E7
64 G 16	Findhorn st E14
40 K 10	Findon clo Harrow
87 X 16	Findon clo SW18
18 L 5	Findon rd N9
74 G 4	Findon rd W12
77 P 13	Fingal st SE10
92 G 8	Finland rd SE4
75 W 8	Finland st SE16
87 P 2	Finlay st SW6
63 N 11	Finnis st E2
135 X 15	Finnis st E2
56 A 20	Finnymore rd Dgnhm
55 Z 20	Finnymore rd Dgnhm
142 H 1	Finsbury av EC2
160 H 1	Finsbury av EC2
142 G 2	Finsbury cir EC2
160 G 2	Finsbury cir EC2
30 B 3	Finsbury cotts N22
134 J 19	Finsbury est EC1
142 K 1	Finsbury mkt EC2
30 K 20	Finsbury Park av N4
48 H 7	Finsbury Park rd N4

134 F 20 Finsbury pavement EC2
48 J 3 Finsbury pk N4
30 B 3 Finsbury rd N22
134 G 20 Finsbury sq EC2
134 E 20 Finsbury st EC2
90 M 9 Finsen rd SE5
136 F 4 Finstock rd W10
57 W 17 Finucane gdns Rainhm
10 B 7 Finucane ri Bushey
118 E 13 Fir gro New Mald
100 A 13 Fir rd Felt
119 U 20 Fir st Sutton
109 Z 8 Fir st SE26
39 O 9 Fir Tree clo Rom
159 O 7 Fir Tree gdns Croy
155 N 18 Fir Tree gro Carsh
82 C 11 Fir Tree rd Hounsl
56 K 10 Fir Tree wlk Dgnhm
8 C 11 Fir Tree wlk Enf
75 W 3 Fir Trees clo SE16
66 B 14 Firbank clo E16
92 B 4 Firbank rd SE15
41 S 9 Fircroft gdns Harrow
106 M 6 Fircroft rd SW17
116 K 15 Firebell all surb
46 B 10 Firecrest dri NW3
155 Z 16 Firefly clo Wallgtn
111 O 7 Firhill rd SE6
29 P 12 Firs av N10
16 A 19 Firs av N11
85 W 11 Firs av SW14
29 P 12 Firs clo N10
92 G 20 Firs clo SE23
17 Y 3 Firs la N21
18 B 6 Firs Park av N21
18 A 6 Firs Park gdns N21
15 U 6 Firs the N20
60 F 15 Firs the W5
21 S 15 Firs wlk Wdfd Grn
158 F 1 Firsby av Croy
49 W 3 Firsby rd N16
17 Y 10 Firscroft N13
69 V 5 First av Dgnhm
53 R 13 First av E12
65 T 10 First av E13
33 P 14 First av E17
8 G 18 First av Enf
152 A 19 First av Epsom
19 P 15 First av N18
27 N 13 First av NW4
37 V 14 First av Rom
86 A 7 First av W10
129 N 16 First av W3
74 D 2 First av W3
74 D 3 First av W3
80 G 19 First av Welling
42 H 6 First av Wemb
101 S 3 First Cross rd Twick
146 M 4 First st SW3
118 L 4 Firstway SW20
152 C 11 Firswood av Epsom
152 C 12 Firswood av Epsom
87 S 3 Firth gdns SW6
121 N 2 Firtree av Mitch
152 E 10 Firtree clo Epsom
142 G 10 Fish Street hill EC3
160 G 10 Fish Street hill EC3
123 U 20 Fisher clo Croy
58 G 8 Fisher clo Grnfd
23 X 6 Fisher rd Harrow
65 R 14 Fisher st E16
140 M 2 Fisher st WC1
81 X 3 Fisher's way Blvdr
102 C 11 Fishermans clo Rich
75 U 5 Fishermans dri SE16
92 E 1 Fishers ct SE14
73 Z 12 Fishers la W4
130 F 17 Fisherton st NW8
160 F 10 Fishmongers Hall st EC4
106 K 8 Fishponds rd SW17
100 M 13 Fitz Wygram clo Hampt
27 V 10 Fitzalan rd N3
149 S 5 Fitzalan st SE11
103 Z 19 Fitzgeorge av Kingst
144 L 7 Fitzgeorge av W14
86 B 9 Fitzgerald av SW14
34 F 17 Fitzgerald rd E11
85 Y 7 Fitzgerald rd SW14
139 T 4 Fitzhardinge st W1
88 H 16 Fitzhugh gro SW18
157 Z 4 Fitzjames av Croy
144 M 6 Fitzjames av W14
4 H 14 Fitzjohn av Barnt
46 F 17 Fitzjohn's av NW3
139 X 12 Fitzmaurice pl W1
62 D 17 Fitzneal st W12

132 B 18 Fitzroy ct W1
109 S 18 Fitzroy gdns SE19
132 A 19 Fitzroy ms W1
46 M 5 Fitzroy pk N6
47 N 3 Fitzroy pk N6
131 T 2 Fitzroy rd NW1
132 A 18 Fitzroy sq W1
132 B 19 Fitzroy st W1
55 T 15 Fitzstephen rd Dghnm
47 V 3 Fitzwarren gdns N19
84 M 6 Fitzwilliam av Rich
89 V 7 Fitzwilliam rd SW4
26 C 6 Five acre NW9
56 A 11 Five Elms rd Dgnhm
149 W 4 Fives ct SE11
90 G 5 Fiveways rd SW9
31 O 19 Fladbury rd N15
34 A 18 Fladgate rd E11
124 F 19 Flag clo CR0
23 Z 18 Flambard rd Harrow
63 V 17 Flamborough st E14
57 W 19 Flamingo Hornch
68 G 1 Flamstead gdns Dgnhm
68 F 2 Flamstead rd Dgnhm
55 T 20 Flamstead rd Dgnhm
78 C 14 Flamstead rd SE7
43 P 19 Flamsted av Wemb
74 E 8 Flanchford rd W12
106 L 17 Flanders cres SW17
66 G 7 Flanders rd E6
74 C 10 Flanders rd W4
50 E 17 Flanders way E9
143 R 9 Flank st E1
46 E 12 Flask wlk NW3
119 Z 16 Flaxley rd Mrdn
140 E 6 Flaxman ct W1
90 L 5 Flaxman rd SE5
132 H 14 Flaxman ter WC1
96 F 1 Flaxton rd SE18
79 U 19 Flaxton rd SE18
10 J 16 Flecker clo Stanm
116 D 19 Fleece rd Surb
48 A 17 Fleece wlk N7
32 L 6 Fleeming clo E17
32 M 7 Fleeming rd E17
141 X 5 Fleet la EC4
46 K 14 Fleet rd NW3
133 O 14 Fleet sq WC1
141 T 6 Fleet st EC4
135 S 18 Fleet Street hill E1
66 B 14 Fleetwood clo E16
117 T 6 Fleetwood rd New Mald
44 H 15 Fleetwood rd NW10
117 T 6 Fleetwood sq New Mald
49 S 7 Fleetwood st N16
156 F 11 Fleming ct Croy
106 L 18 Fleming mead Mitch
58 M 17 Fleming rd S'hall
149 X 13 Fleming rd SE17
83 V 9 Fleming way Islwrth
68 K 20 Fleming way SE28
50 K 3 Flempton rd E10
126 J 9 Fletcher clo Brom
53 U 1 Fletcher la E10
73 W 7 Fletcher rd W4
143 T 8 Fletcher st E1
50 C 10 Fletching rd E5
77 Z 16 Fletching rd SE7
29 Z 1 Fletton rd N11
134 M 19 Fleur De Lis st E1
87 P 20 Fleur gates SW19
31 R 4 Flexmere rd N17
111 Z 13 Flimwell clo Brom
150 G 8 Flint st SE17
95 P 6 Flintmill st SE9
150 X 9 Flinton st SE17
140 H 5 Flitcroft st WC2
143 S 19 Flockton st SE16
90 K 1 Flodden rd SE5
146 L 11 Flood st SW3
146 K 12 Flood wlk SW3
64 C 17 Flora clo E14
37 S 19 Flora gdns Rom
74 H 10 Flora gdns W6
81 P 14 Flora st Blvdr
140 L 7 Floral st WC2
7 Y 11 Florence av Enf
120 D 12 Florence av Mrdn
92 M 1 Florence cotts SE14
7 Y 10 Florence dri Enf
73 V 17 Florence gdns W4
124 G 4 Florence rd Becknhm
126 F 1 Florence rd Brom
65 R 7 Florence rd E13
65 Z 3 Florence rd E6
103 N 19 Florence rd Kingst

48 E 2 Florence rd N4
157 N 20 Florence rd S Croy
70 A 9 Florence rd S'hall
92 M 2 Florence rd SE14
80 G 10 Florence rd SE2
106 A 15 Florence rd SW19
73 X 7 Florence rd W4
72 J 1 Florence rd W5
60 J 20 Florence rd W5
65 P 12 Florence st E16
133 X 2 Florence st N1
26 L 12 Florence st NW4
92 M 1 Florence ter SE14
154 F 7 Florian av Sutton
87 U 10 Florian rd SW15
10 C 7 Florida clo Bushey
122 H 1 Florida rd Thntn Hth
108 J 20 Florida rd Thntn Hth
135 T 13 Florida st E2
24 C 4 Floriston clo Stanm
24 C 4 Floriston gdns Stanm
105 S 1 Floss st SW15
86 M 6 Floss st SW15
111 V 12 Flower House clo SE6
111 V 11 Flower House est SE6
13 R 18 Flower la NW7
107 O 4 Flowers ms SW17
77 Y 13 Floyd rd SE7
93 Z 10 Fludyer st SE13
151 V 10 Folair SE16
140 B 1 Foley st W1
134 M 20 Folgate sq E1
134 L 20 Folgate st E1
62 C 18 Foliot st W12
33 R 13 Folkestone rd E17
66 K 7 Folkestone rd E6
18 K 14 Folkestone rd N18
26 A 5 Folkingham la NW9
14 H 17 Folkington corner N12
64 F 18 Follett st E14
5 T 11 Folly ho Barnt
76 H 6 Folly wall E14
32 J 3 Folly la E17
108 C 17 Fontaine rd SW16
89 P 9 Fontarabia rd SW11
57 R 20 Fontayne av Rainhm
39 P 9 Fontayne av Rom
107 U 4 Fontenoy rd SW12
34 M 6 Fonteyne gdns Ilf
48 E 6 Fonthill rd N4
86 F 20 Fontley way SW15
28 D 7 Fonts hill N2
23 T 1 Fontwell clo Harrow
40 H 17 Fontwell clo Nthlt
127 V 12 Fontwell dri Brom
41 V 3 Football la Harrow
115 V 15 Foots Cray High st Sidcp
115 U 3 Foots Cray la Sidcp
115 U 9 Foots Cray pl Sidcp
114 B 4 Foots Cray rd SE9
95 X 15 Foots Cray rd SE9
143 T 8 Forbes st E1
49 X 4 Forburg rd N16
122 J 13 Ford clo Thntn Hth
41 P 1 Ford clo Harrow
21 V 20 Ford end Wdfd Grn
56 C 20 Ford rd Dgnhm
69 P 1 Ford rd Dgnhm
69 S 1 Ford rd Dgnhm
63 X 6 Ford rd E3
68 N 16 Ford sq E1
143 Y 3 Ford sq E1
63 X 5 Ford st
65 P 17 Ford st E16
126 K 5 Forde av Brom
93 W 20 Fordel rd SE6
5 V 12 Fordham clo Barnt
5 W 13 Fordham rd Barnt
143 V 3 Fordham st E1
73 O 1 Fordhook av W5
129 R 14 Fordingley rd W9
28 M 14 Fordington rd N6
111 O 3 Fordmill rd SE6
17 X 5 Fords gro N21
65 T 17 Fords Park rd E16
45 S 13 Fordwych rd NW2
93 U 16 Fordyce rd SE13
56 A 5 Fordyke rd Dgnhm
142 D 2 Fore st EC2
160 D 2 Fore st EC2
18 J 13 Fore st N18
18 J 17 Fore st N18
160 E 2 Fore Street av EC2
90 J 5 Foreign st SE5
27 R 5 Foreland ct NW4
79 S 10 Foreland st SE18

144 D 7 Foreman ct W6
75 Y 12 Foreshore SE8
34 D 1 Forest appr Wdfd Grn
20 M 2 Forest appr E4
127 W 1 Forest clo BR7
34 D 16 Forest clo E11
21 U 12 Forest clo Wdfd Grn
34 A 13 Forest ct E11
21 P 6 Forest ct E4
53 O 10 Forest dri E12
33 X 20 Forest Drive east E11
51 V 1 Forest Drive west E11
21 Z 12 Forest edge Buck HI
26 A 14 Forest ga NW9
31 U 7 Forest gdns N17
34 A 18 Forest glade E11
33 Z 18 Forest glade E11
20 M 7 Forest glade E4
49 U 19 Forest gro E8
92 B 16 Forest Hill rd SE22
35 W 1 Forest ho Wdfd Grn
52 D 15 Forest la E15
51 S 16 Forest la E15
51 Z 16 Forest la E15
33 X 2 Forest Mount rd Wdfd Grn
51 V 1 Forest rd E11
33 X 20 Forest rd E11
32 C 13 Forest rd E17
33 O 10 Forest rd E17
52 F 11 Forest rd E7
49 T 19 Forest rd E8
99 W 2 Forest rd Erith
36 H 4 Forest rd Ilf
19 N 5 Forest rd N9
73 P 19 Forest rd Rich
38 H 11 Forest rd Rom
119 X 18 Forest rd Sutton
21 S 11 Forest rd Wdfd Grn
33 Y 11 Forest ri E17
33 Z 13 Forest ri E17
125 O 5 Forest ridge Becknhm
21 X 5 Forest side Buck HI
21 O 3 Forest side E4
52 G 11 Forest side E7
118 D 19 Forest side Worc Pk
52 F 15 Forest st E7
34 A 13 Forest the E11
33 X 16 Forest View av E10
52 C 1 Forest view E11
20 K 1 Forest view E4
53 P 12 Forest View rd E12
33 U 4 Forest View rd E17
96 E 20 Forest way Sidcp
21 U 12 Forest way Wdfd Grn
21 W 13 Forest way Wdfd Grn
16 K 13 Forestdale N14
92 A 9 Forester rd SE15
155 X 16 Foresters clo Wallgtn
98 F 10 Foresters cres Bxly Hth
33 X 14 Foresters dri E17
156 A 20 Foresters dri Wallgtn
155 Y 17 Foresters dri Wallgtn
110 B 4 Forestholme clo SE23
30 H 4 Forfar rd N22
89 P 1 Forfar rd SW11
100 B 13 Forge la Felt
153 S 16 Forge la Sutton
40 C 20 Forlong pth Nthlt
24 D 10 Formby av Stanm
130 A 18 Formosa st W9
129 Z 18 Formosa st W9
65 P 6 Formunt clo E16
10 J 18 Fornums acre Stanm
27 X 19 Forres gdns NW11
122 C 7 Forrest gdns SW16
110 D 10 Forrester pth SE26
139 N 5 Forset st W1
126 E 6 Forstall clo Brom
111 W 7 Forster Memorial pk SE6
124 H 6 Forster rd Bcknhm
122 L 15 Forster rd Croy
31 U 9 Forster rd N17
89 Z 18 Forster rd SW2
134 C 8 Forston st N1
123 S 1 Forsyte cres SE19
149 X 14 Forsyth gdns SE17
58 H 2 Fort rd Nthlt
151 R 7 Fort rd SE1
142 L 1 Fort st E1
77 V 3 Fort st E16
54 L 11 Fortescue gdns Ilf
63 N 1 Fortescue av E8
101 N 6 Fortescue av Twick

25 X 2 Fortescue rd Edg
106 G 19 Fortescue rd SW19
47 U 14 Fortess gro NW5
47 U 12 Fortess rd NW5
47 T 14 Fortess wlk NW5
89 O 9 Forthbridge rd SW11
65 Y 18 Fortis clo E16
29 N 12 Fortis Green av N2
29 P 11 Fortis Green rd N10
28 K 12 Fortis grn N2
29 P 11 Fortismere av N10
47 Z 7 Fortnam rd N19
89 Z 20 Fortrose gdns SW2
48 D 18 Fortuna clo N7
62 C 1 Fortune Gate rd NW10
45 Y 14 Fortune Green rd NW6
11 V 1 Fortune la Borhm Wd
134 B 19 Fortune st EC1
62 F 9 Fortune way NW10
40 C 19 Fortunes mead Nthlt
65 R 15 Forty Acre la E16
42 M 9 Forty av Wemb
43 O 8 Forty av Wemb
43 N 8 Forty clo Wemb
8 H 2 Forty hill Enf
43 T 8 Forty la Wemb
12 C 20 Forum way Edg
12 D 19 Forumside Edg
120 M 11 Forval clo Mitch
23 X 12 Forward dri Harrow
137 Z 10 Fosbury ms W2
129 V 19 Foscote ms W9
26 J 19 Foscote rd NW4
87 V 5 Foskett rd SW6
156 F 12 Foss av Croy
106 E 10 Foss rd SW17
77 W 14 Fossdene rd SE7
59 Z 14 Fosse way W13
93 P 9 Fossil rd SE13
80 J 10 Fossington rd Blvdr
55 U 5 Fossway Dgnhm
34 H 5 Foster clo E18
160 B 4 Foster la EC2
65 S 11 Foster rd E13
32 H 18 Foster rd E17
62 A 19 Foster rd W3
73 Y 14 Foster rd W4
26 M 14 Foster st NW4
113 T 12 Fosters clo Chisl
65 S 5 Fothergill clo E13
8 F 13 Fotheringham rd Enf
140 B 7 Foubert's pl W1
49 U 11 Foulden rd N16
146 G 9 Foulis ter SW7
107 N 8 Foulser rd SW17
123 N 7 Foulsham rd Thntn Hth
108 L 17 Founders gdns SE19
75 U 3 Foundry clo SE16
148 H 19 Fount st SW8
141 S 8 Fountain ct EC4
109 V 11 Fountain dri SE19
122 K 4 Fountain rd Thntn Hth
106 H 10 Fountain rd SW12
100 F 6 Fountains av Felt
100 F 5 Fountains clo Felt
16 M 2 Fountains cres N14
17 N 1 Fountains cres N14
31 X 14 Fountayne rd N15
49 W 7 Fountayne rd N16
153 V 2 Four season cres Sutton
10 C 2 Four tubs Bushey
20 L 6 Fouracre E4
9 V 7 Fouracres Enf
12 J 19 Fourland wlk Edg
143 O 1 Fournier st E1
53 S 12 Fourth av E12
56 M 5 Fourth av Rom
57 N 5 Fourth av Rom
128 L 15 Fourth av W10
101 P 4 Fourth Cross rd Twick
43 U 13 Fourth way Wemb
35 O 15 Fowey av Ilf
88 G 8 Fowler clo SW11
52 E 12 Fowler rd E7
121 P 2 Fowler rd Mitch
133 Y 2 Fowler rd N1
115 X 13 Fowlers clo Sidcp
60 G 11 Fowlers wlk W5
88 K 7 Fownes st W11
133 Y 20 Fox And Knot st EC1
63 R 11 Fox clo E1
65 S 16 Fox clo E16
141 S 1 Fox ct EC1
109 U 19 Fox Hill gdns SE19

109 V 19 Fox Hill SE19
97 X 6 Fox Hollow dri Bxly Hth
81 V 12 Fox House rd Blvdr
17 O 8 Fox la N13
60 J 12 Fox la W5
65 O 16 Fox st E16
120 H 4 Fox's pth Mitch
92 K 8 Foxberry rd SE4
93 N 14 Foxborough gdns SE4
107 R 4 Foxbourne rd SW17
114 F 16 Foxbury av Chisl
112 G 16 Foxbury clo Brom
112 G 16 Foxbury rd Brom
159 T 14 Foxcombe Croy
86 G 20 Foxcombe rd SW15
96 A 2 Foxcroft rd SE18
95 Z 2 Foxcroft rd SE18
158 C 20 Foxearth rd S Croy
158 C 19 Foxearth spur S Croy
125 X 6 Foxes dale Brom
94 D 8 Foxes dale SE3
62 D 19 Foxglove st W12
111 S 18 Foxgrove av Becknhm
17 N 12 Foxgrove N14
17 N 12 Foxgrove N14
111 U 19 Foxgrove rd Becknhm
47 X 9 Foxham rd N19
95 P 12 Foxhole rd SE9
61 V 1 Foxlands av Dgnhm
56 K 13 Foxlands rd Dgnhm
49 W 15 Foxley clo E8
149 V 18 Foxley rd SW9
122 H 8 Foxley rd Thntn Hth
88 L 3 Foxmore st SW11
92 H 7 Foxwell st SE4
94 B 10 Foxwood rd SE3
31 Y 4 Foyle rd N17
77 O 17 Foyle rd SE3
14 K 12 Framfield clo N12
107 O 19 Framfield rd Mitch
48 J 14 Framfield rd N5
59 V 17 Framfield rd W7
113 S 10 Framlingham cres SE9
153 X 15 Frampton clo Sutton
50 C 20 Frampton Park rd E9
82 B 12 Frampton rd Hounsl
130 H 17 Frampton st NW8
93 O 13 Francemary rd SE4
20 C 18 Frances rd E4
78 G 12 Frances st SE18
106 D 7 Franche Court rd SW17
98 F 4 Francis av Bxly Hth
23 Y 15 Francis av Harrow
54 E 6 Francis av Ilf
89 P 3 Frances Chichester way SW11
105 U 16 Francis gro SW19
122 J 16 Francis rd Croy
51 T 4 Francis rd E10
60 C 4 Francis rd Grnfd
23 Z 15 Francis rd Harrow
82 A 6 Francis rd Hounsl
54 E 6 Francis rd Ilf
28 M 12 Francis rd N2
155 V 14 Francis rd Wallgtn
51 Y 16 Francis st E15
54 D 6 Francis st Ilf
148 B 4 Francis st SW1
47 V 19 Francis ter N19
148 H 11 Francis wharf SW1
106 M 12 Franciscan rd SW17
107 O 10 Franciscan rd SW17
12 C 10 Francklyn gdns Edg
39 W 17 Francombe gdns Rom
89 W 14 Franconia rd SW4
91 S 20 Frank Dixon clo SE21
109 T 1 Frank Dixon way SE21
91 T 20 Frank Dixon way SE21
65 T 12 Frank st E13
90 M 13 Frankfurt rd SE24
91 N 13 Frankfurt rd SE24
76 B 19 Frankham st SE8
21 Y 17 Frankland clo Wdfd Grn
20 A 15 Frankland rd E4
15 R 2 Franklin clo N20
121 V 8 Franklin cres Mitch
40 M 6 Franklin ms Harrow
95 R 8 Franklin pas SE9

97 Z 2 Franklin rd Bxly Hth
117 P 5 Franklin rd Kingst
110 D 20 Franklin rd SE20
145 R 12 Franklin sq SW5
64 E 9 Franklin st E3
31 N 15 Franklin st N15
147 R 10 Franklins row SW3
57 N 18 Franklyn clo Dgnhm
117 O 5 Franklyn clo Kingst
44 D 19 Franklyn rd NW10
117 W 9 Franks av New Mald
127 Z 13 Frankswood av Brom
13 N 17 Frankton rd SE15
17 Z 14 Franlaw cres N13
57 V 4 Franmil rd Hornch
110 A 7 Fransfield gro SE26
110 C 19 Frant clo SE20
122 H 11 Frant rd Thntn Hth
66 D 19 Fraser clo E6
33 T 17 Fraser rd E9
60 D 4 Fraser rd Grnfd
18 L 11 Fraser rd N9
74 A 14 Fraser st W4
81 Z 14 Frason rd Erith
21 U 18 Frating cres Wdfd Grn
141 T 19 Frazier st SE1
151 S 1 Frean st SE16
33 S 18 Frederic ms SW1
32 H 17 Frederic st E17
20 K 2 Frederica rd E4
48 B 20 Frederica st N7
153 V 10 Frederick clo Sutton
133 N 7 Frederick clo W2
9 P 9 Frederick cres Enf
149 W 20 Frederick cres SW9
153 U 10 Frederick gdns Sutton
78 M 13 Frederick pl SE18
79 N 13 Frederick pl SE18
149 Y 12 Frederick rd
153 V 10 Frederick rd Sutton
133 O 13 Frederick st WC1
134 M 2 Frederick ter E8
160 D 6 Frederick's pl EC2
15 R 14 Fredericks pl N12
57 V 18 Freeborne gdns Rainhm
88 M 5 Freedom st SW11
48 B 15 Freegrove rd N7
27 R 7 Freeland pk NW4
60 M 20 Freeland rd W5
158 F 18 Freelands av S Croy
112 J 20 Freelands gro Brom
126 J 1 Freelands rd Brom
112 J 20 Freelands rd Brom
133 N 2 Freeling st N1
40 B 20 Freeman clo Nthlt
120 E 11 Freeman rd Mrdn
9 T 16 Freemantle av Enf
81 T 1 Freemantle st Blvdr
150 K 8 Freemantle st SE17
123 R 18 Freemasons rd Croy
65 U 15 Freemasons rd E16
109 R 19 Freethorpe clo SE19
89 P 9 Freke rd SW11
36 B 8 Fremantle rd Ilf
63 O 3 Fremont st E9
135 Z 4 Fremont st E9
134 L 14 French pl E1
92 G 10 Frendsbury rd SE4
159 U 17 Frensham dri Croy
104 F 5 Frensham dri SW15
114 E 5 Frensham rd SE9
151 T 15 Frensham st SE15
88 K 5 Frere st SW11
66 M 4 Fresh Wharf rd Bark
67 N 5 Fresh Wharf rd Bark
16 F 1 Freshfield dr N14
124 L 19 Freshfields Croy
106 D 6 Freshford st SW18
107 P 14 Freshwater clo SW17
55 W 3 Freshwater rd Dgnhm
37 S 14 Freshwell av Rom
155 T 19 Freshwood way Wallgtn
6 A 16 Freston gdns Barnt
27 V 7 Freston pk N3
136 F 9 Freston rd W11
98 A 12 Freta rd Bxly Hth
66 H 19 Frewin rd SW18
141 X 7 Friar st EC4
15 W 12 Friars av N20
15 X 12 Friars av N20
104 D 6 Friars av SW15
61 Y 18 Friars gdns W3
84 F 13 Friars la Rich
76 G 9 Friars mead E14

95 W 14 Friars ms SE9
141 X 19 Friars pl SE1
62 A 20 Friars Place la W3
61 Z 19 Friars Place la W3
66 B 4 Friars rd E6
84 K 16 Friars Stile rd Rich
61 Y 19 Friars way W3
23 U 3 Friars wlk Harrow
16 D 2 Friars wlk N14
16 D 4 Friars wlk N14
80 K 14 Friars wlk SE2
158 J 19 Friarswood S Croy
15 X 15 Friary clo N12
140 C 15 Friary st SW1
21 S 14 Friary la Wdfd Grn
15 W 14 Friary pk N12
15 W 13 Friary rd N12
151 U 18 Friary rd SE15
61 X 17 Friary rd W3
15 V 14 Friary way N12
20 L 8 Friday hill E4
20 M 11 Friday Hill east E4
20 L 9 Friday Hill west E4
81 Z 13 Friday rd Erith
106 L 19 Friday rd Mitch
142 A 7 Friday st EC4
47 U 16 Frideswide pl NW5
133 W 12 Friend st EC1
93 N 4 Friendly St ms SE8
93 N 4 Friendly st SE8
157 O 6 Friends rd Croy
15 S 9 Friern Barnet la N20
16 C 17 Friern Barnet rd N11
18 T 10 Friern ct N20
15 R 3 Friern Mount dri N20
15 S 16 Friern pk N12
91 W 18 Friern rd SE22
15 S 14 Friern Watch av N12
156 B 11 Frimley av Wallgtn
159 V 16 Frimley clo Croy
105 T 5 Frimley clo SW19
159 V 17 Frimley cres Croy
115 T 13 Frimley ct Sidcp
120 J 6 Frimley gdns Mitch
54 H 10 Frimley rd Ilf
33 X 2 Frimley way E1
66 B 9 Frinton rd E6
31 T 19 Frinton rd N15
38 D 1 Frinton rd Rom
115 Z 4 Frinton rd Sidcp
107 P 16 Frinton rd SW17
88 A 6 Friston st SW6
87 Z 6 Friston st SW6
27 T 2 Frith ct NW7
14 F 19 Frith la NW7
27 T 1 Frith la NW7
156 L 3 Frith rd Croy
51 W 11 Frith rd E11
140 F 7 Frith st W1
118 A 14 Fritham clo New Mald
136 B 13 Frithville gdns W12
74 L 3 Frithville gdns W12
56 G 9 Frizlands la Dgnhm
66 H 15 Frobisher rd E6
30 G 13 Frobisher rd N8
91 V 11 Frobisher rd SE22
153 R 7 Frogmore clo Sutton
70 F 12 Frogmore ct S'hall
153 R 7 Frogmore gdns Sutton
87 Y 12 Frogmore SW18
23 V 14 Frognal av Harrow
115 O 15 Frognal av Sidcp
46 C 14 Frognal clo NW3
46 D 17 Frognal ct NW3
46 C 15 Frognal gdns NW3
46 B 14 Frognal la NW3
46 C 12 Frognal NW3
115 O 15 Frognal pl Sidcp
46 C 11 Frognal ri NW3
46 C 13 Frognal way NW3
95 P 12 Froissart rd SE9
30 H 10 Frome rd N22
134 A 7 Frome st N1
133 Z 7 Frome st N1
153 S 11 Fromondes rd Sutton
89 T 5 Froude st SW8
66 A 2 Fry rd E6
62 E 2 Fry rd NW10
31 O 3 Fryatt rd N17
64 M 18 Fryatt st E14
133 U 8 Frye's bldgs N1
25 P 18 Fryent clo NW9
26 A 19 Fryent cres NW9
26 B 19 Fryent fields NW9
26 A 19 Fryent gro NW9
25 P 17 Fryent way NW9

```
43 S 2    Fryent way NW9
142 M 2   Frying Pan all E1
157 Z 3   Fryston av Croy
80 C 13   Fuchsia st SE2
26 A 4    Fulbeck dri NW9
22 M 8    Fulbeck way Harrow
33 T 4    Fulbourne rd E17
47 V 11   Fulbrook rd N19
75 N 6    Fulford st SE16
143 Y 18  Fulford st SE16
145 T 18  Fulham bdwy SW6
87 T 5    Fulham High st SW6
144 H 18  Fulham Palace rd SW6
87 R 3    Fulham Palace rd SW6
144 E 11  Fulham Palace rd W6
87 P 5    Fulham Palace rd SW6
87 U 5    Fulham Park gdns SW6
87 U 4    Fulham Park rd SW6
146 G 9   Fulham rd SW3
145 T 19  Fulham rd SW6
87 U 3    Fulham rd SW6
118 D 19  Fullbrooks av Worc Pk
55 S 11   Fuller rd Dgnhm
135 S 16  Fuller st E2
26 L 12   Fuller st NW4
34 C 3    Fullers av Wdfd Grn
38 J 3    Fullers clo Rom
38 J 2    Fullers la Rom
34 B 3    Fullers rd E18
159 O 9   Fullers wood Croy
154 H 18  Fullerton rd Carsh
123 U 17  Fullerton rd SE5
88 C 13   Fullerton rd SW18
35 W 4    Fullwell av Ilf
35 B 6    Fullwell av Ilf
100 K 8   Fullwell pk Twick
134 G 11  Fullwoods ms N1
57 X 19   Fulmar rd Hornch
88 B 2    Fulmead st SW6
100 C 14  Fulmer clo Hampt
66 A 16   Fulmer rd E16
72 A 9    Fulmer way W13
33 W 16   Fulready rd E10
82 D 10   Fulstone clo Hounsl
94 E 5    Fulthorp rd SE3
138 A 9   Fulton ms W2
43 R 11   Fulton rd Wemb
100 L 4   Fulwell Park av Twick
101 N 4   Fulwell Park av Twick
101 P 10  Fulwell rd Tedd
60 L 5    Fulwood av Wemb
83 X 16   Fulwood gdns Twick
141 R 2   Fulwood wlk WC1
105 R 1   Fulwood wlk SW19
22 H 1    Furham fields Pinn
151 T 20  Furley rd SE15
121 P 18  Furlong clo Mitch
48 F 18   Furlong rd N7
40 C 19   Furlongs wlk Grnfd
88 A 18   Furmage st SW18
108 K 12  Furneaux av SE27
99 T 7    Furner clo Drtfrd
40 L 3    Furness rd Harrow
120 B 15  Furness rd Mrdn
62 G 7    Furness rd NW10
88 B 4    Furness rd SW6
57 V 15   Furness way Hornch
141 T 3   Furnival st EC4
50 D 15   Furrow la E9
14 L 19   Fursby av N3
26 D 8    Further acre NW9
112 A 1   Further Green rd SE6
94 A 20   Further Green rd SE6
37 Z 7    Furze Farm clo Rom
122 M 5   Furze rd Thntn Hth
64 B 14   Furze st E3
107 S 12  Furzedown dri SW17
107 T 11  Furzedown rd SW17
113 Z 14  Furzefield clo Chisl
77 V 18   Furzefield rd SE3
126 F 3   Fyfe way Brom
125 Y 8   Fyfield clo BR2
33 W 11   Fyfield rd E17
8 C 12    Fyfield rd Enf
90 G 7    Fyfield rd SW9
34 L 1    Fyfield rd Wdfd Grn
148 F 5   Fynes st SW1
```

G

```
99 W 13   Gable clo Dartford
22 G 3    Gable clo Pinn

100 A 9   Gabriel clo Felt
38 K 1    Gabriel clo Rom
92 G 18   Gabriel st SE23
42 M 9    Gabrielle clo Wemb
43 N 9    Gabrielle clo Wemb
43 O 18   Gaddesden av Wemb
79 T 5    Gadwall way SE18
65 N 14   Gage rd E16
132 M 20  Gage st WC1
133 S 4   Gainford st N1
41 U 15   Gainsboro gdns Grnfd
97 X 9    Gainsboro sq Bxly Hth
55 P 11   Gainsborough Dgnhm
53 W 14   Gainsborough av E12
111 N 16  Gainsborough clo Becknhm
15 N 17   Gainsborough ct N12
46 G 11   Gainsborough gdns NW3
25 O 7    Gainsborough gdns Edg
83 P 13   Gainsborough gdns Islwth
45 U 1    Gainsborough gdns NW11
85 N 6    Gainsborough rd Rich
15 O 16   Gainsborough rd N12
117 Y 15  Gainsborough rd New Mald
52 A 1    Gainsborough rd E11
64 M 10   Gainsborough rd E15
65 N 10   Gainsborough rd E15
74 C 10   Gainsborough rd W4
32 K 13   Gainsford rd E17
143 O 17  Gainsford st SE1
122 K 13  Gairgreen Thntn Hth
91 S 4    Gairloch rd SE5
47 U 17   Gaisford st NW5
114 B 2   Gaitskell rd SE9
112 G 8   Galahad rd Brom
74 F 20   Galata rd SW13
91 Z 7    Galatea sq SE15
76 F 7    Galbraith st E14
5 P 12    Galdana av Barnt
100 C 14  Gale clo Hampt
120 F 6   Gale clo Mitch
68 H 4    Gale st Dgnhm
55 V 20   Gale st Dgnhm
64 B 14   Gale st E3
33 X 2    Galeborough av Wdfd Grn
140 K 2   Galen pl WC1
74 K 11   Galena rd W6
63 N 10   Gales gdns E2
135 Y 14  Gales gdns E8
35 S 1    Gales way Wdfd Grn
88 D 17   Galesbury rd SW18
105 R 1   Galgate clo SW19
15 Y 6    Gallants Farm rd Barnt
58 A 7    Gallery gdns Nrthlt
109 P 2   Gallery rd SE21
91 R 20   Gallery rd SE21
75 N 12   Galley Wall rd SE16
151 W 6   Galley Wall rd SE16
48 J 16   Gallia rd N5
9 N 20    Galliard av Enf
18 K 4    Galliard rd N9
18 L 1    Galliard rd N9
67 Z 10   Gallions clo Bark
77 W 11   Gallions rd SE7
77 Y 12   Gallon clo SE7
158 B 16  Gallop the S Croy
154 F 19  Gallop the Sutton
79 U 12   Gallosson rd SE18
74 G 2    Galloway rd W12
7 R 20    Gallus clo N21
94 G 8    Gallus sq SE3
122 B 10  Galpin's rd Thntn Hth
37 P 20   Galsworthy av Rom
103 S 19  Galsworthy rd Kingst
45 T 12   Galsworthy rd NW2
128 K 15  Galton st W10
6 A 14    Galva clo Barnt
87 W 13   Galveston rd SW15
134 C 14  Galway st EC1
89 T 5    Gambetta st SW8
141 X 15  Gambia st SE1
106 H 11  Gambole rd SW17
87 O 9    Gamlen rd SW15
153 W 13  Gander Green la Sutton
156 B 16  Gane clo Croy
140 B 7   Ganton st W1

35 V 15   Gantshill cres Ilford
106 A 11  Gap rd SW19
105 Z 11  Gap rd SW19
61 O 17   Garage rd
139 U 1   Garbutt pl W1
133 Y 12  Gard st EC1
98 D 6    Garden av Bxly Hth
107 R 19  Garden av Mitch
12 C 19   Garden city Edg
19 Z 17   Garden clo E4
100 F 13  Garden clo Hampt
58 B 3    Garden clo Nthlt
112 H 6   Garden clo SE12
86 K 20   Garden clo SW15
90 D 7    Garden clo SW9
156 A 11  Garden clo Wallgtn
14 M 15   Garden ct N12
112 J 15  Garden la Brom
108 B 1   Garden la SW2
137 U 10  Garden ms W2
112 J 17  Garden rd Brom
130 E 11  Garden rd NW8
85 P 9    Garden rd Rich
124 C 1   Garden rd SE20
149 X 2   Garden row SE1
63 T 15   Garden st E1
148 E 9   Garden ter SW1
43 X 17   Garden way NW10
134 J 15  Garden wlk EC2
122 J 19  Gardeners rd Croy
63 U 7    Gardeners rd E3
18 E 1    Gardenia rd Enf
125 V 2   Gardens the Becknhm
22 M 18   Gardens the Harrow
23 N 18   Gardens the Harrow
22 E 18   Gardens the Pinn
91 X 10   Gardens the SE22
44 M 14   Gardnor av NW2
34 H 18   Gardner clo E11
100 F 4   Gardner gro Felt
65 U 12   Gardner rd E13
46 F 12   Gardnor rd NW3
119 Z 16  Garendon gdns Mrdn
120 A 18  Garendon rd Mrdn
119 Z 16  Garendon rd Mrdn
153 N 2   Gareth clo Worc pk
112 F 9   Gareth gro Brom
65 P 13   Garfield rd E4
20 L 4    Garfield rd E4
9 R 16    Garfield rd Enf
89 P 8    Garfield rd SW11
106 D 14  Garfield rd SW19
83 Z 20   Garfield rd Twick
64 A 20   Garford st E14
68 H 20   Garganey st SE28
79 U 11   Garibaldi st SE18
79 T 19   Garland rd SE18
24 J 4    Garland st Stanm
160 B 8   Garlick hill EC4
142 C 9   Garlick hill EC4
110 J 6   Garlie's rd SE23
45 U 18   Garlinge rd NW2
32 B 2    Garman rd N17
133 T 13  Garnault ms EC1
133 U 14  Garnault pl EC1
8 H 4     Garnault rd Enf
33 T 4    Garner rd E17
143 Z 10  Garner st E1
135 U 9   Garner st E2
44 A 18   Garnet rd NW10
123 N 9   Garnet rd Thntn Hth
75 O 1    Garnet st E1
63 O 20   Garnet st E1
66 E 15   Garnet wlk E6
95 V 8    Garnett clo SE9
46 L 14   Garnett rd NW3
32 G 4    Garnett way E17
49 U 7    Garnham st N16
151 O 17  Garnies clo SE15
107 X 8   Garrads rd SW16
98 F 8    Garrard clo Bxly Hth
113 Z 10  Garrard clo Chisl
156 A 7   Garrard clo Wallgtn
106 G 9   Garratt la SW17
88 B 18   Garratt la SW18
12 D 20   Garratt rd Edgw
25 R 1    Garratt rd Edgw
106 J 11  Garratt ter SW17
134 B 17  Garrett st EC1
10 B 2    Garretts rd Bushey
27 U 19   Garrick av NW11
84 F 12   Garrick cl Rich
88 E 11   Garrick clo SW18
157 R 3   Garrick cres Croy
27 N 9    Garrick dri NW4
79 R 9    Garrick dri SE18
27 O 8    Garrick pk NW4
58 L 12   Garrick rd Grnfd
26 E 18   Garrick rd NW9
85 R 6    Garrick rd Rich

140 J 9   Garrick st WC2
27 O 12   Garrick way NW4
140 J 9   Garrick yd WC2
78 J 20   Garrison clo SE18
39 R 3    Garry clo Rom
39 O 2    Garry way Rom
100 K 16  Garside clo Hampt
79 R 9    Garside clo SE18
102 L 12  Garth clo Kingst
100 L 14  Garth Hampt
102 L 13  Garth Kingstn
119 O 18  Garth rd Mrdn
45 U 8    Garth rd NW2
73 X 15   Garth rd W4
25 N 18   Garth the Harrow
15 V 20   Garth way N12
92 F 18   Garthorne rd SE23
102 K 11  Garthside Rich
105 V 2   Gartmoor gdns SW19
54 L 5    Gartmore rd Ilf
88 B 16   Garton pl SW18
88 E 8    Gartons way SW11
144 K 14  Garvan clo W6
65 W 17   Garvary rd E16
137 W 7   Garway rd W2
34 A 2    Gascoigne gdns Wdfd Grn
135 N 12  Gascoigne pl E2
67 R 6    Gascoigne rd Bark
159 N 20  Gascoigne rd Croy
129 T 1   Gascony av NW6
99 U 6    Gascoyne dri Drtfrd
50 G 19   Gascoyne rd E9
14 B 1    Gaselee st E14
149 R 12  Gasholder pl SE11
25 V 6    Gaskarth rd Edg
89 T 17   Gaskarth rd SW12
28 M 18   Gaskell rd N6
89 Z 5    Gaskell st SW4
133 X 4   Gaskin st N1
106 M 10  Gassiot rd SW17
107 N 11  Gassiot rd SW17
154 G 5   Gassiot way Sutton
144 H 13  Gastein rd W6
84 L 7    Gaston Bell clo Rich
63 N 11   Gaston pl E2
121 O 5   Gaston rd Mitch
75 N 8    Gataker st SE16
151 X 2   Gataker st SE16
47 Y 10   Gatcombe rd N19
138 L 19  Gate ms SW7
18 K 14   Gate rd N18
141 N 3   Gate st WC2
130 J 17  Gateforth st NW8
103 W 19  Gatehouse clo Kingst
90 D 8    Gateley rd SW9
134 J 16  Gatesborough st EC2
106 L 7   Gateside rd SW17
109 S 16  Gatestone rd SE19
62 E 10   Gateway NW10
150 C 13  Gateway SE17
100 G 5   Gatfield gro Felt
63 T 7    Gathorne rd E2
30 F 6    Gathorne rd N22
147 W 11  Gatliff rd SW1
80 A 14   Gatling rd SE2
79 Z 13   Gatling rd SE2
91 U 1    Gatonby st SE15
154 C 19  Gatton clo Sutton
106 K 9   Gatton rd SW17
17 V 1    Gatward clo N21
18 F 8    Gatward grn N9
87 V 19   Gatwick rd SW18
89 X 6    Gauden clo SW4
89 X 7    Gauden rd SW4
149 Z 1   Gaunt st SE1
40 B 20   Gauntlet clo Nthlt
42 A 14   Gauntlett ct Wemb
41 Z 14   Gauntlett rd Wemb
154 G 12  Gauntlett rd Sutton
92 C 4    Gautrey rd SE15
150 G 6   Gavel st SE17
76 A 9    Gaverick st E14
94 H 19   Gavestone cres SE12
94 G 18   Gavestone rd SE12
79 U 11   Gavin st SE18
120 G 12  Gavina clo Mrdn
63 P 8    Gawber st E2
52 A 15   Gawsworth clo E15
44 K 14   Gay clo NW2
56 J 13   Gay gdns Dgnhm
64 H 6    Gay rd E15
26 A 5    Gaydon clo NW9
148 J 2   Gayfere st SW1
74 F 10   Gayford rd W12
49 X 20   Gayhurst rd E8
40 E 15   Gaylor rd Nthlt
```

35 R 1	Gaynes Hill rd Wdfd Grn	
154 M 17	Gaynesford rd Carsh	
110 F 4	Gaynesford rd SE23	
35 W 17	Gaysham av Ilf	
35 Y 11	Gaysham hall Ilf	
46 F 12	Gayton cres NW3	
23 W 19	Gayton rd Harrow	
46 F 12	Gayton rd NW3	
88 M 16	Gayville rd SW11	
108 E 1	Gaywood clo SW2	
33 O 10	Gaywood rd E17	
149 X 2	Gaywood st SE1	
149 W 11	Gaza st SE17	
36 A 12	Geariesville gdns Ilf	
44 H 14	Geary rd NW10	
48 D 15	Geary st N7	
30 M 4	Gedeney rd N17	
31 N 3	Gedeney rd N17	
143 O 20	Gedling pl SE1	
134 A 16	Gee st EC1	
133 Z 16	Gee st EC1	
65 P 3	Geere rd E15	
139 V 6	Gees ct W1	
113 S 6	Gefferys homes SE9	
134 M 9	Geffrye museum E2	
134 M 9	Geffrye st E2	
151 W 19	Geldart rd SE15	
49 Y 7	Geldeston rd E5	
92 D 4	Gellatly rd SE14	
38 G 2	Gelsthorpe rd Rom	
78 L 10	General Gordon pl SE18	
93 X 1	General Wolfe rd SE10	
78 M 17	Genesta rd SE18	
79 N 17	Genesta rd SE18	
90 G 10	Geneva dri SW9	
37 Y 16	Geneva gdns Rom	
116 K 8	Geneva rd Kingst	
122 L 10	Geneva rd Thntn Hth	
20 C 15	Genever clo E4	
19 N 18	Genista rd N18	
86 M 13	Genoa av SW15	
124 B 1	Genoa rd SE20	
8 C 13	Genotin rd Enf	
87 N 14	Genova av SW15	
7 Z 12	Gentlemans row Enf	
65 T 10	Gentry gdns E13	
90 L 5	Geoffrey clo SE5	
92 K 7	Geoffrey rd SE4	
146 G 3	Geological museum SW7	
22 F 10	Georg V av Pinn	
29 O 3	George cres N10	
140 L 11	George ct WC2	
142 F 15	George Inn yd SE1	
126 H 19	George la Brom	
34 G 8	George la E18	
93 S 16	George la SE13	
20 B 19	George rd E4	
103 X 18	George rd Kingst	
118 E 10	George rd New Mald	
143 S 19	George row SE16	
54 B 20	George st Bark	
67 N 1	George st Bark	
156 M 4	George st Croy	
157 O 3	George st Croy	
65 O 18	George st E16	
82 E 4	George st Hounsl	
84 H 12	George st Rich	
39 T 19	George st Rom	
70 B 11	George st S'hall	
154 A 10	George st Sutton	
139 T 2	George st W1	
71 U 3	George st W7	
22 G 11	George V clo Pinn	
60 B 3	George V way Grnfd	
87 S 18	George Wyver clo SW19	
139 V 8	George yd W1	
48 E 15	George's rd N7	
76 H 20	Georgette pl SE10	
35 Z 12	Georgeville gdns Ilf	
122 J 2	Georgia rd Thntn Hth	
126 H 19	Georgian clo Brom	
10 K 20	Georgian clo Stanm	
43 R 17	Georgian ct Wemb	
41 S 7	Georgian way Harrow	
132 B 3	Georgiana st NW1	
135 O 12	Georgina gdns E2	
112 G 9	Gerald rd Brom	
147 V 6	Gerald ms SW1	
56 A 5	Gerald rd Dgnhm	
65 O 12	Gerald rd E16	
147 U 6	Gerald st SW1	
149 U 2	Geraldine Mary Harmsworth pk SE11	
88 C 14	Geraldine rd SW18	
73 P 16	Geraldine rd W4	
149 V 2	Geraldine st SE1	
82 G 19	Gerard av Hounsl	
23 Z 18	Gerard rd Harrow	
86 D 2	Gerard rd SW13	
114 A 4	Gerda rd SE9	
64 M 9	Germander way E15	
63 V 7	Gernon rd E3	
44 K 5	Geron way NW2	
140 G 8	Gerrard pl W1	
133 X 8	Gerrard rd N1	
140 G 8	Gerrard st W1	
6 H 15	Gerrards clo N14	
141 U 20	Gerridge st SE1	
81 S 9	Gerrard rd Belv	
146 D 15	Gertrude st SW10	
43 W 9	Gervase clo Wemb	
25 X 5	Gervase rd Edgw	
75 N 18	Gervase st SE15	
151 Y 17	Gervase st SE15	
111 O 4	Ghent st SE8	
10 B 7	Giant Tree hill Bushey	
64 H 1	Gibbins rd E15	
102 K 19	Gibbon rd Kingst	
92 D 5	Gibbon rd SE15	
62 A 19	Gibbon rd W3	
61 Z 19	Gibbon rd W3	
86 H 12	Gibbon wlk SW15	
43 Z 19	Gibbons rd NW10	
109 O 13	Gibbs av SE19	
109 P 13	Gibbs clo SE19	
145 P 9	Gibbs Green est W14	
12 K 14	Gibbs grn Edg	
19 P 14	Gibbs rd N18	
109 O 13	Gibbs sq SE19	
63 H 11	Gibson clo E1	
49 U 7	Gibson gdns N16	
55 T 3	Gibson rd Dgnhm	
133 V 4	Gibson sq N1	
76 L 14	Gibson st SE10	
108 H 15	Gibson's hill SW16	
144 K 9	Giddon rd N14	
39 V 9	Gidea rd Rom	
39 V 8	Gidea park Rom	
81 U 10	Gideon clo Blvdr	
89 O 7	Gideon rd SW11	
39 V 10	Gides av Rom	
47 W 6	Giesbach rd N19	
18 D 18	Giffard rd N18	
76 B 19	Giffin st SE8	
59 S 14	Gifford gdns W7	
132 L 2	Gifford st N1	
133 N 1	Gifford st N1	
65 N 3	Gift la E15	
25 W 4	Gilbert gro Edg	
140 J 2	Gilbert pl WC1	
81 R 9	Gilbert rd Belv	
112 E 18	Gilbert rd Brom	
39 T 13	Gilbert rd Rom	
149 V 6	Gilbert rd SE11	
106 C 17	Gilbert rd SW19	
51 Y 13	Gilbert st E15	
139 V 7	Gilbert st W1	
106 J 11	Gilbey rd SW17	
79 X 17	Gilbourne rd SE18	
9 V 16	Gilda av Enf	
49 Y 5	Gilda cres N16	
139 Z 2	Gildea st W1	
47 O 16	Gilden cres NW5	
78 J 16	Gildersome st SE18	
109 T 11	Giles coppice SE19	
91 R 15	Gilkes cres SE21	
91 R 16	Gilkes pl SE21	
65 S 19	Gill av E16	
63 Z 19	Gill st E14	
57 X 18	Gillam way Rainham	
10 A 7	Gillan grn Bushey	
64 G 12	Gillender st E3	
48 G 10	Gillespie rd N5	
66 D 6	Gillett av E6	
123 N 9	Gillett rd Thntn Hth	
49 S 16	Gillett st N16	
119 V 19	Gillian Park rd Sutton	
93 P 12	Gillian st SE13	
47 R 15	Gillies st NW5	
147 Z 5	Gillingham ms SW1	
45 S 10	Gillingham rd NW2	
147 Z 4	Gillingham row SW1	
148 A 5	Gillingham st SW1	
147 Z 5	Gillingham st SW1	
65 O 3	Gillman rd E15	
15 Y 5	Gillum clo Barnt	
93 W 10	Gilmore rd SE13	
85 Z 10	Gilpin av SW14	
18 H 17	Gilpin cres N18	
82 K 17	Gilpin cres Twick	
50 H 12	Gilpin rd E5	
57 T 19	Gilroy clo Rainhm	
123 O 9	Gilsland rd Thntn Hth	
88 B 4	Gilstead rd SW6	
146 C 12	Gilston rd SW10	
111 Z 6	Gilton rd SE6	
141 X 3	Giltspur st EC1	
109 S 15	Gipsy hill SE19	
86 H 9	Gipsy la SW15	
108 M 10	Gipsy rd SE27	
109 O 11	Gipsy rd SE27	
80 H 20	Gipsy rd Welling	
97 W 1	Gipsy rd Welling	
108 M 11	Gipsy Road gdns SE27	
146 C 16	Giralda clo E16	
64 C 17	Giraud st E14	
144 H 4	Girdlers rd W14	
47 U 7	Girdlestone wlk N19	
87 T 18	Girdwood rd SW18	
145 R 19	Gironde st SW8	
25 R 11	Girton av NW9	
40 M 19	Girton clo Nthlt	
159 N 4	Girton gdns Croy	
40 M 18	Girton rd Grnfd	
41 N 17	Girton rd Grnfd	
110 F 12	Girton st SE26	
30 C 13	Gisburn rd N8	
65 P 7	Given Wilson wlk E13	
53 O 11	Gladding rd E12	
124 H 16	Glade gdns Croy	
70 J 6	Glade S'hall	
127 O 4	Glade the Brom	
124 H 15	Glade the Croy	
7 T 10	Glade the Enf	
152 H 12	Glade the Epsom	
35 T 5	Glade the Ilf	
17 O 1	Glade the N21	
77 X 19	Glade the SE7	
153 T 19	Glade the Sutton	
159 T 6	Glade the W Wkhm	
21 U 12	Glade the Wdfd Grn	
124 F 17	Gladeside Croy	
17 P 1	Gladeside N21	
31 V 17	Gladesmore rd N15	
81 U 10	Gladeswood rd Blvdr	
92 J 18	Gladiator st SE23	
49 U 11	Glading ter N16	
4 G 10	Gladsmuir rd Barnt	
47 V 4	Gladsmuir rd N19	
53 R 19	Gladstone av E12	
30 J 6	Gladstone av N22	
83 R 19	Gladstone av Twick	
73 X 9	Gladstone clo W4	
44 L 10	Gladstone Park gdn est NW2	
44 L 9	Gladstone Park gdns NW2	
44 G 12	Gladstone park NW2	
4 C 14	Gladstone pl Barnt	
21 X 5	Gladstone rd Buck HI	
123 P 17	Gladstone rd Croy	
117 R 6	Gladstone rd Kingst	
70 B 7	Gladstone rd S'hall	
105 X 18	Gladstone rd SW19	
149 W 1	Gladstone st SE1	
89 T 1	Gladstone ter SW8	
23 V 10	Gladstone way Harrow	
112 G 15	Gladwell rd Brom	
30 C 19	Gladwell rd N8	
87 O 7	Gladwyn rd SW15	
45 Y 19	Gladys rd NW6	
63 R 20	Glamis pl E1	
75 R 1	Glamis rd E1	
63 R 18	Glamis rd E1	
40 M 19	Glamis way Nthlt	
122 A 7	Glamorgan clo Mitch	
102 E 19	Glamorgan rd Kingst	
124 M 8	Glanfield rd Becknhm	
129 T 4	Glengall pass NW6	
97 Z 7	Glengall rd Bxly Hth	
151 P 12	Glengall rd SE15	
21 U 19	Glengall rd Wdfd Grn	
11 U 13	Glanleam rd Stanm	
52 H 17	Glanparke rd E7	
126 J 7	Glanville rd Brom	
90 A 14	Glanville rd SW2	
100 E 2	Glasbrook av Twick	
95 O 17	Glasbrook rd SE9	
49 T 2	Glaserton rd N16	
106 M 15	Glasford st SW17	
65 U 6	Glasgow rd E13	
18 L 15	Glasgow rd N18	
63 S 19	Glass House fields E1	
63 N 10	Glass st E2	
135 Y 15	Glass st E2	
141 Y 18	Glasshill st SE1	
140 C 10	Glasshouse st W1	
148 M 9	Glasshouse wlk SE11	
149 N 9	Glasshouse wlk SE11	
29 W 17	Glasslyn rd N8	
126 D 5	Glassmill la Brom	
119 Z 16	Glastonbury rd Mrdn	
45 W 16	Glastonbury st NW6	
64 C 13	Glaucus st E3	
101 U 17	Glazbrook rd Tedd	
109 O 3	Glazebrook clo SE21	
144 L 9	Glazebury rd W14	
7 W 11	Glebe av Enf	
21 S 20	Glebe av Wdfd Grn	
24 K 11	Glebe av Harrow	
120 H 4	Glebe av Mitch	
24 J 10	Glebe av Harrow	
27 N 12	Glebe cres NW4	
120 L 5	Glebe ct Mitch	
11 P 16	Glebe ct Stanm	
118 B 16	Glebe gdns New Mald	
109 T 10	Glebe Hyrst SE19	
24 J 12	Glebe la Harrow	
146 J 13	Glebe la Carsh	
120 K 6	Glebe pth Mitch	
112 F 20	Glebe rd Brom	
154 M 13	Glebe rd Carsh	
154 M 14	Glebe rd Carsh	
56 H 19	Glebe rd Dgnhm	
49 U 20	Glebe rd E8	
28 E 5	Glebe rd N3	
30 C 14	Glebe rd N8	
44 E 18	Glebe rd NW10	
11 R 16	Glebe rd Stanm	
11 R 17	Glebe rd Stanm	
153 C 10	Glebe rd Sutton	
86 F 4	Glebe rd SW13	
83 W 16	Glebe side Twick	
120 K 6	Glebe sq Mitch	
73 Z 13	Glebe st W4	
64 C 8	Glebe ter E3	
94 A 7	Glebe the SE3	
93 Z 7	Glebe the SE3	
118 D 19	Glebe the Worc Pk	
100 G 7	Glebe way Felt	
159 Y 3	Glebe way W Wkhm	
21 Y 17	Glebe way Wdfd Grn	
34 E 8	Glebelands av E18	
54 E 1	Glebelands av Ilf	
36 F 19	Glebelands clo	
109 T 11	Glebelands clo SE19	
91 S 7	Glebelands clo SE5	
99 T 10	Glebelands Drtfrd	
146 A 8	Glebelands rd W14	
144 L 11	Gledstanes rd W14	
10 B 7	Gleed av Bushey	
87 O 9	Glegg pl SW15	
105 P 4	Glen Albyn rd SW19	
21 V 20	Glen cres Wdfd Grn	
155 S 18	Glen End rd Carsh	
156 G 7	Glen gdns Croy	
107 Y 11	Glen ms SW16	
65 X 11	Glen rd E13	
21 V 19	Glen rd Wdfd Grn	
125 Z 3	Glen the Brom	
158 G 4	Glen the Croy	
7 W 14	Glen the Enf	
22 C 20	Glen the Pinn	
70 F 13	Glen the S'hall	
42 H 12	Glen the Wemb	
83 R 12	Glen wlk Islwth	
154 D 7	Glena mt SM1	
76 H 12	Glenaffric av E14	
24 K 12	Glenalmond rd Harrow	
78 C 10	Glenalvon way SE18	
50 C 13	Glenarm rd E5	
52 A 20	Glenavon rd E15	
95 Y 8	Glenbarr clo SE9	
112 A 13	Glenbow rd Brom	
111 Z 14	Glenbow rd Brom	
7 P 13	Glenbrook north Enf	
45 X 16	Glenbrook rd NW6	
7 R 13	Glenbrook south Enf	
116 J 15	Glenbuck rd Surb	
106 M 6	Glenburnie rd SW17	
60 C 13	Glencairn dri W5	
108 B 18	Glencairn rd SW16	
66 B 14	Glencairne clo E16	
66 B 14	Glencairne clo E16	
54 F 2	Glencoe av Ilf	
56 E 11	Glencoe dri Dgnhm	
58 A 14	Glencoe rd	
58 B 11	Glencoe rd Dgnhm	
12 B 15	Glendale av Edg	
30 E 2	Glendale av N22	
55 S 1	Glendale av Rom	
95 X 8	Glendale clo SE9	

105 V 12 Glendale dri SW19
42 J 5 Glendale gdns Wemb
81 Y 10 Glendale rd Erith
80 J 1 Glendale way SE28
90 C 9 Glendall st SW9
87 P 7 Glendarvon st SW15
31 Z 5 Glendish rd N17
12 M 14 Glendor gdns NW7
146 F 6 Glendower pl SW7
20 K 5 Glendower rd E4
85 Y 8 Glendower rd SW14
79 Z 14 Glendown rd SE2
62 B 20 Glendun rd W3
107 V 12 Gleneagle rd SW16
11 O 20 Gleneagles Stanm
107 Z 10 Gleneldon ms SW16
108 B 10 Gleneldon rd SW16
90 A 12 Glenelg rd SW2
95 Y 13 Glenesk rd SE9
93 W 20 Glenfarg rd SE6
107 V 1 Glenfield rd SW12
72 B 5 Glenfield rd W13
72 A 4 Glenfield ter W13
149 Y 18 Glenfinlas way SE5
77 P 13 Glenforth st SE10
76 A 8 Glengall causeway E14
76 F 8 Glengall gro E14
12 F 10 Glengall rd Edg
129 T 4 Glengall rd NW6
151 P 13 Glengall ter SE15
76 G 12 Glengarnock av E14
91 U 12 Glengarry rd SE22
35 Z 16 Glenham dri Ilf
95 Y 8 Glenhead clo SE9
27 Y 7 Glenhill clo N3
95 W 12 Glenhouse rd SE9
47 P 12 Glenhurst av NW5
72 E 15 Glenhurst av Brentf
15 U 15 Glenhurst rd N12
108 M 18 Glenhurst ri SE19
46 J 17 Glenilla rd NW3
107 Y 19 Glenister Park rd SW16
77 P 13 Glenister rd SE10
78 K 4 Glenister st E16
95 X 11 Glenlea rd SE9
9 R 9 Glenloch rd Enf
46 J 16 Glenloch rd NW3
77 T 18 Glenluce rd SE3
95 X 12 Glenlyon rd SE9
13 T 20 Glenmere av NW7
100 F 12 Glenmill Hampt
100 F 12 Glenmill Hampt
46 J 17 Glenmore rd NW3
79 X 20 Glenmore rd SE18
96 K 2 Glenmore rd Welling
68 A 8 Glenmore way Bark
154 D 7 Glenn mt Sutton
108 F 7 Glennie rd SE27
54 B 18 Glenny rd Bark
88 C 5 Glenrosa st SW6
136 B 4 Glenroy st W12
62 M 16 Glenroy st W12
92 L 8 Glensdale rd SE4
95 X 12 Glenshiel rd SE9
108 F 7 Glentanner way SW17
74 J 16 Glentham gdns SW13
74 J 16 Glentham rd SW13
124 B 19 Glenthorne av Croy
119 X 19 Glenthorne clo Sutton
119 X 19 Glenthorne gdns Sutton
35 Y 11 Glenthorne gdns Ilf
32 H 15 Glenthorne rd E17
116 L 8 Glenthorne rd Kingst
16 B 16 Glenthorne rd N11
144 A 6 Glenthorne rd W6
74 K 11 Glenthorne rd W6
119 P 12 Glenthorpe rd Mrdn
39 P 1 Glenton clo Rom
93 Y 10 Glenton rd SE13
39 P 2 Glenton way Rom
131 P 18 Glentworth st NW1
95 X 13 Glenure rd SE9
127 O 4 Glenview rd Brom
80 K 16 Glenview SE2
8 A 4 Glenville av Enf
75 Z 20 Glenville gro SE8
87 Z 19 Glenville ms SW18
103 O 20 Glenville rd Kingst
44 A 3 Glenwood av NW9
42 Z 3 Glenwood av NW9
23 W 16 Glenwood clo Harrow
39 V 14 Glenwood dri Rom

35 V 15 Glenwood gdns Ilf
43 V 4 Glenwood gro NW9
152 C 13 Glenwood rd Epsom
83 P 8 Glenwood rd Hounsl
30 K 15 Glenwood rd N15
13 O 10 Glenwood rd N15
110 M 1 Glenwood rd SE6
111 N 1 Glenwood rd SE6
124 F 15 Glenwood way Croy
76 H 11 Glenworth av E14
64 E 8 Glergion way E3
80 L 8 Glimpsing grn Blvdr
64 E 7 Global aptr E3
64 U 8 Globe la SE18
75 V 3 Globe Pond rd SE16
52 B 15 Globe rd E15
63 P 7 Globe rd E2
39 V 19 Globe rd Hornch
57 W 1 Globe rd Hornch
21 Z 18 Globe rd Wdfd Grn
142 D 20 Globe st SE1
63 P 8 Globe ter E2
139 X 7 Globe yd W1
157 P 19 Glossop rd S Croy
118 B 9 Gloster rd New Mald
96 K 11 Gloucester av Welling
131 T 2 Gloucester av NW1
114 J 5 Gloucester av Sidcp
76 G 19 Gloucester cir SE10
43 X 20 Gloucester clo NW10
131 X 4 Gloucester cres NW1
73 O 20 Gloucester ct Rich
48 K 6 Gloucester dri N4
27 Y 13 Gloucester dri NW11
131 W 7 Gloucester ga NW1
131 W 7 Gloucester Gate ms NW1
154 B 1 Gloucester gdns Sutton
6 C 15 Gloucester gdns Barnt
27 U 20 Gloucester gdns NW11
53 S 1 Gloucester gdns Ilf
25 X 5 Gloucester gdns Edg
138 C 6 Gloucester Mews west W2
138 D 6 Gloucester ms W2
131 O 18 Gloucester pl NW1
139 R 2 Gloucester pl W1
139 P 2 Gloucester Place ms W1
99 Z 18 Gloucester rd Dartfd
5 O 17 Gloucester rd Barnt
5 R 18 Gloucester rd Barnt
81 O 13 Gloucester rd Blvdr
123 P 18 Gloucester rd Croy
51 N 2 Gloucester rd E10
34 J 16 Gloucester rd E11
53 T 11 Gloucester rd E12
32 F 7 Gloucester rd E17
7 Z 3 Gloucester rd Enf
100 L 17 Gloucester rd Hampt
22 K 16 Gloucester rd Harrow
82 A 11 Gloucester rd Hounsl
117 R 4 Gloucester rd Kingst
31 P 11 Gloucester rd N17
18 G 17 Gloucester rd N18
73 P 19 Gloucester rd Rich
39 S 19 Gloucester rd Rom
146 C 8 Gloucester rd Wdfd
101 S 13 Gloucester rd Tedd
101 N 1 Gloucester rd Twick
73 X 4 Gloucester rd W3
72 E 7 Gloucester rd W5
138 H 7 Gloucester sq W2
148 B 8 Gloucester st SW1
138 C 6 Gloucester ter W2
133 U 14 Gloucester way EC1
137 U 16 Gloucester wlk W8
22 A 18 Glover rd Pinn
89 N 8 Glycena rd SW11
5 T 14 Glyn av Barnt
152 F 20 Glyn clo Epsom
123 P 2 Glyn clo SE25
115 R 11 Glyn dri Sidcp
50 F 11 Glyn rd E5
9 P 14 Glyn rd Enf
153 O 4 Glyn rd Worc Pk
149 N 11 Glyn st SE11
146 M 3 Glynde ms SW3
97 X 8 Glynde rd Bxly Hth
92 M 15 Glynde st SE4
79 R 12 Glyndon rd SE18
62 B 1 Glynfield rd NW10
110 C 5 Glynwood dri SE26
8 H 3 Goat la Enf

121 N 15 Goat rd Mitch
143 N 16 Goat st SE1
145 P 19 Goater's all SW6
38 M 1 Gobions av Rom
39 N 2 Gobions av Rom
156 B 10 Godalming av Wallgtn
64 C 16 Godalming rd E14
64 M 10 Godbold rd E15
124 G 9 Goddard rd Becknhm
58 A 3 Godfrey av Twick
83 R 18 Godfrey av Twick
78 E 12 Godfrey hill SE18
78 F 12 Godfrey rd SE18
64 G 4 Godfrey st E15
146 L 9 Godfrey st SW3
82 D 19 Godfrey way Hounsl
148 M 11 Godley rd SW18
106 F 2 Godley rd SW18
141 Z 7 Godliman st EC4
91 Z 6 Godman rd SE15
74 J 4 Godolphin rd W12
58 B 3 Godrey av Grnfd
80 C 3 Godric cres Croy
156 F 6 Godson rd Croy
133 S 9 Godson st N1
154 E 7 Godstone rd Sutton
84 A 17 Godstone rd Twick
80 E 6 Godstone rd SE2
126 L 7 Godwin rd Brom
52 J 12 Godwin rd E7
93 Y 3 Goffers rd SE3
155 Y 8 Goidel clo Wallgtn
129 N 19 Golborne gdns W10
136 L 1 Golborne ms W10
136 L 1 Golborne rd W10
128 M 20 Golborne rd W10
12 L 19 Gold hill Edg
12 L 20 Gold la Edg
4 C 18 Golda clo Barnt
26 A 2 Goldbeaters gro Edg
12 M 19 Goldbeaters gro Edg
13 N 20 Goldbeaters gro Edg
119 Y 16 Goldcliff clo Mrdn
66 B 15 Goldcrest clo E16
68 G 19 Goldcrest clo SE28
159 X 18 Goldcrest way Croy
84 G 13 Golden ct Rich
134 B 17 Golden la EC1
71 T 1 Golden mnr W7
59 T 20 Golden mnr W7
140 C 9 Golden sq W1
12 F 15 Golders clo Edg
45 U 1 Golders gdns NW11
45 W 2 Golders Green cres NW11
27 T 18 Golders Green rd NW11
45 V 1 Golders Green rd NW11
46 A 5 Golders Hill pk NW3
45 Z 6 Golders Hill pk NW3
27 R 19 Golders Manor dri NW11
45 Z 5 Golders Park clo NW11
27 O 15 Golders ri NW4
45 W 2 Golders way NW11
79 T 7 Goldfinch rd SE28
74 K 6 Goldhawk ms W12
136 B 19 Goldhawk rd W12
74 G 8 Goldhawk rd W12
34 M 2 Goldhaze clo Ilf
130 B 1 Goldhurst ter NW6
46 D 20 Goldhurst ter NW6
129 Y 2 Goldhurst ter NW6
127 N 13 Goldie st SE5
143 U 7 Golding st E1
132 E 7 Goldington cres NW1
132 F 8 Goldington st NW1
135 R 16 Goldman clo E2
129 T 18 Goldney rd W9
143 U 5 Goldney ter E1
148 G 20 Goldsboro' rd SW8
20 F 8 Goldsborough cres E4
89 Y 1 Goldsborough rd SW8
9 V 10 Goldsdown clo Enf
9 U 9 Goldsdown rd Enf
79 V 14 Goldsmid st SE18
79 V 14 Goldsmidt st SE18
53 R 17 Goldsmith av E12
26 B 17 Goldsmith av NW9
56 E 2 Goldsmith av Rom
61 X 20 Goldsmith av W3

40 J 5 Goldsmith clo Harrow
73 Z 1 Goldsmith clo W3
25 V 13 Goldsmith la NW9
51 P 4 Goldsmith rd E10
32 G 8 Goldsmith rd E17
15 Z 16 Goldsmith rd N11
91 X 1 Goldsmith rd SE15
73 X 1 Goldsmith rd W3
135 T 9 Goldsmith's row E2
135 U 7 Goldsmith's sq E2
75 R 12 Goldsworthy gdns SE16
122 D 8 Goldwell rd Thntn Hth
92 C 2 Goldwin clo SE14
24 C 2 Golf clo Stanm
103 Z 18 Golf Club dri Kingst
127 X 7 Golf rd Brom
60 M 17 Golf rd W5
101 S 7 Golf side Twick
54 F 10 Golfe rd Ilf
118 A 3 Golfside clo New Mald
156 A 16 Goliath clo Wallgt
77 Y 15 Gollogly ter SE7
101 Y 14 Gomer gdns Tedd
101 Y 14 Gomer pl Tedd
55 N 8 Gomm rd SE16
156 A 10 Gomshall av Wallgtn
45 V 14 Gondar gdns NW6
76 C 17 Gonson st SE8
105 S 5 Gonston clo SW19
40 L 19 Gonville cres Nrthlt
87 T 7 Gonville st SW6
51 V 10 Goodall rd E11
41 T 9 Gooden ct Harrow
105 U 18 Goodenough rd SW19
140 C 1 Goodge pl W1
140 D 1 Goodge st W1
62 C 9 Goodhall st NW10
125 Y 14 Goodhart way W Wkhm
47 Z 16 Goodlinge rd N7
107 Y 3 Goodman cres SW2
51 U 2 Goodman rd E10
143 R 6 Goodman st E1
143 O 8 Goodman's yd E1
143 S 5 Goodmans stile E1
55 N 3 Goodmayes av Ilf
55 N 6 Goodmayes la Ilf
55 O 4 Goodmayes rd Ilf
91 V 15 Goodrich rd SE22
132 J 8 Goods way NW1
62 B 1 Goodson rd NW10
64 J 17 Goodway gdns E14
115 W 6 Goodwin dri Sidcp
156 J 13 Goodwin gdns Croy
156 H 12 Goodwin rd Croy
19 S 7 Goodwin rd N9
74 H 5 Goodwin rd W12
48 F 7 Goodwin st N4
140 J 9 Goodwins ct WC2
9 P 1 Goodwood av Enf
119 Y 9 Goodwood clo Mrdn
40 G 18 Goodwood rd Nrthlt
75 V 20 Goodwood rd SE14
13 P 16 Goodwyn av NW7
29 R 5 Goodwyns vale N10
150 D 16 Goodyear pl SE5
27 O 16 Goodyers gdns NW4
79 R 8 Goosander way SE28
133 U 11 Goose rd EC1
24 H 15 Gooseacre la Harrow
66 K 9 Gooseley la E6
66 L 11 Gooseley la E6
160 E 9 Gophir la EC4
134 G 6 Gopsall st N1
20 L 18 Gordon av E4
57 T 6 Gordon av Hrnch
10 K 20 Gordon av Stanm
11 O 19 Gordon av Stanm
86 A 10 Gordon av SW14
84 A 13 Gordon av Twick
83 Z 13 Gordon av Twick
97 R 2 Gordon av Welling
123 T 19 Gordon cres Croy
62 L 17 Gordon ct W12
90 J 5 Gordon gro SE5
7 Y 6 Gordon hill Enf
47 P 12 Gordon House rd NW5
137 V 17 Gordon pl W8
67 U 4 Gordon rd Bark
124 L 7 Gordon rd Becknhm
81 X 10 Gordon rd Blvdr
154 L 14 Gordon rd Carsh
34 E 19 Gordon rd E11
53 W 10 Gordon rd E12
51 U 13 Gordon rd E15
34 H 5 Gordon rd E18

21 N 4	Gordon rd E4
8 A 8	Gordon rd Enf
23 T 10	Gordon rd Harrow
82 M 9	Gordon rd Hounsl
116 M 2	Gordon rd Kingst
117 N 1	Gordon rd Kingst
117 N 19	Gordon rd Kingst
54 E 9	Gordon rd Ilf
29 X 1	Gordon rd N11
27 V 2	Gordon rd N3
19 N 8	Gordon rd N9
85 O 6	Gordon rd Rich
38 A 19	Gordon rd Rom
70 C 11	Gordon rd S'hall
92 A 7	Gordon rd SE15
91 Z 3	Gordon rd SE15
96 H 13	Gordon rd Sidcp
73 U 16	Gordon rd W4
60 D 19	Gordon rd W5
132 F 17	Gordon sq WC1
65 T 10	Gordon st E13
132 E 16	Gordon st WC1
4 J 14	Gordon way Barnt
93 N 13	Gordonbrock rd SE4
105 Z 4	Gordondale rd SW19
25 P 16	Gore ct NW9
63 R 4	Gore rd E9
118 M 3	Gore rd SW20
146 C 1	Gore st SW7
129 U 8	Gorefield pla NW6
69 P 4	Goresbrook rd Dgnhm
136 J 11	Gorham pl W11
38 J 5	Goring clo Rom
55 T 13	Goring rd Dgnhm
57 N 19	Goring rd Dgnhm
16 M 19	Goring rd N11
17 N 19	Goring rd N11
142 L 5	Goring st EC3
59 N 7	Goring way Grnfd
31 O 15	Gorleston rd N15
144 M 6	Gorleston st W14
78 G 11	Gorman rd SE18
107 P 19	Gorringe Park av Mitch
103 V 14	Gorscombe clo Kingst
159 P 6	Gorse rd Croy
107 P 13	Gorse ri SW17
57 P 4	Gorse way Rom
61 X 11	Gorst rd NW10
88 L 17	Gorst rd SW11
135 N 11	Gorsuch pl E2
89 N 20	Gosberton rd SW12
56 E 5	Gosfield rd Dgnhm
139 Z 1	Gosfield st W1
35 T 15	Gosford gdns Ilf
140 G 5	Goslett yd WC2
58 G 8	Gosling clo Grnfd
90 F 2	Gosling way SW9
149 T 20	Gosling way SW9
30 L 3	Gospatrick rd N17
31 N 4	Gosport rd E17
32 L 16	Gosport rd E17
79 S 14	Gossage rd SE18
135 P 13	Gosset st E2
127 X 3	Gosshill rd Chisl
75 W 15	Gosterwood st SE8
100 J 1	Gostling rd Twick
122 F 7	Goston gdns Thntn Hth
133 X 14	Goswell pl EC1
133 Y 15	Goswell rd EC1
101 R 4	Gothic rd Twick
112 B 12	Goudhurst rd Brom
52 B 13	Gough rd E15
8 L 9	Gough rd Enf
141 U 5	Gough sq EC4
133 P 16	Gough st WC1
101 T 1	Gould rd Twick
50 A 16	Gould ter E8
143 O 4	Goulston st E1
50 A 13	Goulton rd E5
31 S 17	Gourley pl N15
31 S 17	Gourley st N15
95 W 13	Gourock rd SE9
65 N 1	Govier clo E15
87 S 2	Gowan av SW6
44 J 19	Gowan rd NW10
132 E 16	Gower ct WC1
140 F 1	Gower ms WC1
52 G 18	Gower rd E7
71 W 17	Gower rd Isl
132 C 15	Gower st WC1
132 C 15	Gower st WC1
143 S 5	Gower's wlk E1
124 L 4	Gowland pl Becknhm
91 W 8	Gowlett rd SE5
89 O 8	Gowrie rd SW11
98 C 4	Grace av Bxly Hth
113 N 8	Grace clo SE9
110 D 10	Grace pth SE26
122 L 15	Grace rd Croy
64 H 1	Grace rd E15
64 E 9	Grace st E3
143 T 9	Grace's all E1
91 P 3	Grace's ms SE5
91 R 3	Grace's st SE5
142 H 8	Gracechurch st EC3
160 H 8	Gracechurch st EC3
107 T 12	Gracedale rd SW16
108 A 8	Gracefield gdns SW16
109 W 11	Gradient the SE26
8 C 9	Graeme rd Enf
85 T 9	Graemesdyke av SW14
100 C 1	Grafton clo Hounsl
59 Y 17	Grafton clo W13
152 B 5	Grafton clo Worc Pk
47 S 18	Grafton cres NW1
55 Z 6	Grafton gdns Dgnhm
30 K 18	Grafton gdns N4
132 B 18	Grafton ms W1
152 B 4	Grafton Park rd Worc Pk
132 F 13	Grafton pl NW1
156 G 1	Grafton rd Croy
55 Z 6	Grafton rd Dgnhm
7 P 11	Grafton rd Enf
23 O 17	Grafton rd Harrow
118 B 7	Grafton rd New Mald
47 S 17	Grafton rd NW5
61 V 19	Grafton rd W3
152 A 5	Grafton rd Worc Pk
89 V 8	Grafton sq SW4
139 Z 10	Grafton st W1
47 N 16	Grafton ter NW5
132 B 18	Grafton way W1
47 T 18	Grafton yd NW5
121 O 1	Graham av Mitch
72 B 7	Graham av W13
158 M 2	Graham clo Croy
159 N 3	Graham clo Croy
40 D 15	Graham ct Nthlt
116 J 19	Graham gdns Surb
74 J 9	Graham mans W6
98 C 10	Graham rd Bxly Hth
65 S 10	Graham rd E13
49 X 18	Graham rd E8
100 F 9	Graham rd Hampt
23 T 9	Graham rd Harrow
121 N 1	Graham rd Mitch
30 J 11	Graham rd N15
26 H 19	Graham rd NW4
105 W 19	Graham rd SW19
73 X 7	Graham rd W4
133 Z 10	Graham st N1
147 T 7	Graham ter SW1
26 D 8	Grahame Park way NW9
13 P 20	Grahame Park way NW7
40 M 16	Grainger clo Nthlt
83 W 5	Grainger rd Islwth
30 L 5	Grainger rd N22
51 Y 7	Gramer clo E11
45 S 4	Grampian gdns NW2
106 L 12	Granada st SW17
86 K 14	Granard av SW15
88 M 18	Granard rd SW12
132 E 5	Granary way NW1
149 N 7	Granby bldgs SE11
95 U 6	Granby rd SE9
135 R 15	Granby st E2
132 A 10	Granby ter NW1
141 X 1	Grand av EC1
29 P 12	Grand av N10
117 U 16	Grand av Surb
43 P 16	Grand av Wemb
78 J 13	Grand Depot rd SE18
118 M 3	Grand dri SW20
119 O 12	Grand dri SW20
87 S 12	Grand Parade ms SW15
63 V 11	Grand wlk E1
122 A 3	Granden rd SW16
152 M 4	Grandison rd Worc Pk
88 M 12	Grandison rd SW11
89 N 13	Grandison rd SW11
88 H 2	Granfield st SW11
15 Y 4	Grange av Barnt
15 P 17	Grange av N12
14 D 4	Grange av N20
53 W 13	Grange av SE25
24 C 7	Grange av Stanm
101 U 3	Grange av Twick
34 D 1	Grange av Wdfd Grn
21 S 20	Grange av Wdfd Grn
118 F 11	Grange clo New Mald
12 J 17	Grange clo Edg
70 D 15	Grange clo Hounsl
114 M 6	Grange clo Sidcp
34 E 1	Grange clo Wdfd Grn
68 G 19	Grange cres SE28
141 P 6	Grange ct WC2
113 S 15	Grange dri Chisl
41 N 6	Grange Farm clo Harrow
16 L 6	Grange gdns N14
46 B 10	Grange gdns NW3
22 C 12	Grange gdns Pinn
123 R 3	Grange gdns SE25
48 K 18	Grange gro N1
12 J 16	Grange hill Edg
123 R 2	Grange hill SE25
109 V 4	Grange la SE21
7 X 20	Grange Park av N21
17 Y 1	Grange Park av N21
123 N 7	Grange Park rd Thntn Hth
51 P 4	Grange Park rd E10
72 K 3	Grange pk W5
151 R 3	Grange pl SE16
129 T 2	Grange pl NW6
51 O 4	Grange rd E10
65 R 10	Grange rd E13
32 H 17	Grange rd E17
12 M 20	Grange rd Edg
41 P 7	Grange rd Harrow
23 Y 17	Grange rd Harrow
54 A 11	Grange rd Ilf
116 J 6	Grange rd Kingst
18 K 20	Grange rd N17
29 N 19	Grange rd N6
44 K 19	Grange rd NW10
156 M 20	Grange rd S'hall
70 B 4	Grange rd SE1
150 L 2	Grange rd SE1
123 P 5	Grange rd SE25
154 A 16	Grange rd Sutton
153 Z 16	Grange rd Sutton
86 F 3	Grange rd SW13
73 T 13	Grange rd W4
72 G 2	Grange rd W5
134 G 6	Grange st N1
158 L 3	Grange the Croy
15 S 5	Grange the N20
150 M 1	Grange the SE1
105 P 14	Grange the SW19
61 O 1	Grange the Wemb
154 B 16	Grange vale Sutton
15 S 5	Grange View rd N20
21 Y 14	Grange way Wdfd Grn
150 L 2	Grange wlk SE1
151 N 1	Grange wlk SE1
151 N 2	Grange yd SE1
123 R 3	Grangecliffe gdns SE25
49 R 3	Grangecourt rd N16
95 V 8	Grangehill rd SE9
110 O 5	Grangemill rd SE6
110 O 5	Grangemill way SE6
39 W 19	Granger way Rom
35 R 15	Grangeway gdns Ilf
15 O 13	Grangeway N12
129 S 1	Grangeway NW6
7 X 19	Grangeway the N21
98 A 20	Grangewood Bxly
110 M 15	Grangewood la Becknhm
66 B 3	Grangewood st E6
65 Z 3	Grangewood st E6
18 H 9	Granham gdns N9
79 Y 13	Granite st SE18
51 Z 7	Granleigh rd E11
50 A 20	Gransden av E8
74 O 6	Gransden rd W12
16 G 3	Grant clo N14
123 V 20	Grant pl Croy
123 U 20	Grant rd Croy
23 U 9	Grant rd Harrow
88 G 9	Grant rd SW11
65 S 10	Grant st E13
133 S 8	Grant st N1
71 Y 18	Grant way Islwth
133 Y 7	Grantbridge st N1
41 W 9	Grantchester clo Harrow
11 W 10	Grantham clo Edg
38 A 20	Grantham gdns Rom
139 W 15	Grantham pl W1
53 W 11	Grantham rd E12
90 A 5	Grantham rd SW9
74 A 18	Grantham rd W4
63 T 10	Grantley st E1
33 X 5	Grantock rd E17
55 N 5	Granton rd Ilf
115 T 15	Granton rd Sidcp
107 V 19	Granton rd W9
27 N 1	Grants clo NW7
129 X 14	Grantully rd W9
82 G 14	Grantham av Hounsl
19 P 11	Granville av N9
108 C 19	Granville gdns SW16
73 O 2	Granville gdns W5
93 V 8	Granville gro SE13
45 T 10	Granville ms NW2
93 U 6	Granville pk SE13
139 S 7	Granville pl W1
4 B 13	Granville rd Barnt
33 R 17	Granville rd E17
34 J 8	Granville rd E18
53 Y 5	Granville rd Ilf
28 D 1	Granville rd N12
30 J 5	Granville rd N22
17 O 18	Granville rd N22
30 D 20	Granville rd N4
45 V 7	Granville rd NW2
129 T 10	Granville rd NW6
115 O 9	Granville rd Sidcp
87 X 18	Granville rd SW18
105 Y 18	Granville rd SW19
97 U 8	Granville rd Welling
133 R 13	Granville sq WC1
133 P 13	Granville st WC1
140 J 4	Grape st WC1
80 A 18	Grasdene rd SE18
82 J 16	Grasmere av Hounsl
104 A 9	Grasmere av SW15
103 Z 10	Grasmere av SW15
119 Y 6	Grasmere av SW19
61 X 19	Grasmere av W3
42 J 4	Grasmere av Wemb
20 Z 0	Grasmere gdns Harrow
35 S 14	Grasmere gdns Ilf
112 B 19	Grasmere rd Brom
98 K 4	Grasmere rd Bxly Hth
29 S 6	Grasmere rd N10
18 J 20	Grasmere rd N17
124 A 13	Grasmere rd SE25
108 B 11	Grasmere rd SW16
65 S 6	Grasmere rd E13
27 V 5	Grass pk N3
155 U 8	Grass way Wallgtn
115 N 11	Grassington rd Sidcp
110 B 3	Grassmount SE23
4 M 19	Grasvenor av Barnt
144 K 2	Gratton rd W14
45 O 10	Gratton ter NW2
98 G 13	Gravel hill Bxly Hth
98 G 15	Gravel hill clo Bxly Hth
158 H 14	Gravel hill Croy
27 W 7	Gravel hill N3
142 M 4	Gravel la E1
101 S 2	Gravel rd Twick
114 B 8	Gravelwood clo Chisl
106 J 10	Graveney rd SW17
74 G 1	Gravesend rd W12
52 G 6	Gray av Dgnhm
57 V 16	Gray gdns Rom
141 V 16	Gray st SE1
141 P 1	Gray's inn pl WC1
130 O 16	Gray's inn rd WC1
141 R 1	Gray's inn sq WC1
66 C 16	Grayford clo E6
117 Y 9	Grayham cres New Mald
117 X 9	Grayham rd New Mald
127 O 2	Grayland clo Brom
49 P 6	Grayling rd N16
107 X 18	Greyscroft rd SW16
89 N 6	Grayscroft rd SW11
118 J 4	Grayswood gdns New Mald
28 D 1	Graywood ct N12
49 O 7	Grazebrook rd N16
98 K 12	Grazeley clo Bxly Hth
10 R 11	Grazeley rd SE19
160 E 4	Great Bell all EC2
109 V 8	Great Brownings SE21
15 O 5	Great Bushey dri N20
8 L 5	Great Cambridge rd Enf
31 N 3	Great Cambridge rd N17
18 B 11	Great Cambridge rd N9
140 A 5	Great Castle st W1
139 Z 5	Great Castle st W1
131 N 20	Great Central st NW1
44 A 15	Great Central way NW10
43 X 14	Great Central way NW10

140 E 5 Great Chapel st W1
100 H 6 Great Chertsy rd Felt
85 X 2 Great Chertsy rd W4
144 G 8 Great Church la W6
148 J 1 Great College st SW1
57 P 7 Great Cullings Ro
139 O 6 Great Cumberland ms W1
139 P 6 Great Cumberland pl W1
150 F 2 Great Dover st SE1
51 X 18 Great Eastern rd E15
51 X 20 Great Eastern rd E15
134 J 15 Great Eastern st EC2
126 L 8 Great Elms rd Brom
26 D 7 Great Field strand NW9
39 Z 18 Great Gardens rd Rom
140 H 18 Great George st SW1
142 A 13 Great Guilford st SE1
113 W 8 Great Harry dri SE9
133 O 19 Great James st WC1
140 B 6 Great Marlborough st W1
142 G 15 Great Maze pond SE1
140 H 8 Great Newport st WC2
4 H 8 Great North rd Barnt
28 E 3 Great North rd N12
74 J 14 Great North rd W6
26 L 6 Great North way NW4
27 P 9 Great North way NW4
132 M 19 Great Ormond st WC1
133 N 19 Great Ormond st WC1
133 P 12 Great Percy st WC1
148 G 2 Great Peter st SW1
148 J 2 Great Peter st SW1
140 A 4 Great Portland st W1
139 Z 2 Great Portland st W1
140 D 8 Great Pulteney st W1
140 M 5 Great Queen st WC2
140 J 2 Great Russell st WC1
140 J 14 Great Scotland yd SW1
140 G 20 Great Smith st SW1
148 H 1 Great Smith st SW1
91 R 14 Great Spilmans SE22
142 J 5 Great St Helen's EC3
160 C 8 Great St Thomas apostle EC4
142 A 19 Great Suffolk st SE1
141 Y 15 Great Suffolk st SE1
133 Y 17 Great Sutton st EC1
160 F 4 Great Swan all EC2
140 A 2 Great Titchfield st W1
131 Z 19 Great Titchfield st W1
142 J 9 Great Tower st EC3
160 C 8 Great Trinity la EC4
141 O 3 Great Turnstile WC1
72 B 17 Great West rd Brentf
82 E 3 Great West rd Hounsl
71 U 19 Great West rd Islwth
74 J 13 Great West rd W4
73 T 15 Great West rd W4
144 A 9 Great West rd W6
137 S 2 Great Western rd W9
129 R 19 Great Western rd W9
160 H 3 Great Winchester st EC2
140 E 9 Great Windmill st W1
59 V 13 Greatdown rd W7
66 G 11 Greatfield av E6
93 O 11 Greatfield clo SE4
67 T 4 Greatfields rd Bark
143 S 2 Greatorex st E1
113 V 17 Greatwood Chisl
106 H 10 Greaves pl SW17
108 K 15 Grecian cres SE19
140 G 7 Greek st W1
4 J 3 Green Acre la Barnt
141 X 4 Green Arbour ct EC4
12 M 12 Green av NW7
13 N 12 Green av NW7
72 C 8 Green av W13
75 N 3 Green bank E1
143 U 14 Green bank E1
143 Y 14 Green bank E1
15 O 13 Green bank N12
125 Z 5 Green clo Brom
154 M 3 Green clo Carsh
100 C 12 Green clo Hampt
28 C 20 Green clo NW11
25 W 17 Green clo NW19
158 A 1 Green Court av Croy
158 A 1 Green Court gdns Croy
91 R 11 Green dri SE22

72 K 14 Green Dragon la Brentf
7 T 19 Green Dragon la N21
17 X 1 Green Dragon la N21
143 R 2 Green Dragon yd E1
70 J 2 Green dri S'hall
17 X 8 Green end N21
78 G 14 Green hill SE18
141 X 1 Green Hills rents EC1
151 V 15 Green Hundred rd SE15
114 A 14 Green la Chisl
56 B 6 Green la Dgnhm
12 A 14 Green la Edg
11 Z 12 Green la Edg
100 A 12 Green la Felt
122 K 2 Green La gdns Thntn Hth
54 D 8 Green la Ilf
55 T 5 Green la Ilf
120 B 17 Green la Mrdn
119 X 14 Green la Mrdn
117 W 11 Green la New Mald
27 P 16 Green la NW4
110 E 18 Green la SE20
113 X 4 Green la SE9
95 Y 19 Green la SE9
11 O 16 Green la Stanm
108 F 19 Green la SW16
122 J 2 Green la Thntn Hth
71 T 4 Green la W7
118 H 19 Green la Worc Pk
152 B 18 Green lanes Epsom
49 N 12 Green lanes N16
17 X 4 Green lanes N21
48 L 4 Green lanes N4
30 H 16 Green lanes N8
71 Z 1 Green Man gdns W13
71 Z 1 Green Man la W13
72 A 1 Green Man pas W13
17 W 2 Green Moor link N21
139 Y 16 Green pk SW1
99 S 12 Green pl Drtfrd
32 J 9 Green Pond rd E17
6 E 18 Green rd N14
15 S 10 Green rd N20
65 X 2 Green st E13
52 K 20 Green st E7
9 P 9 Green st Enf
139 S 8 Green st W1
126 E 18 Green the Brom
98 D 3 Green the Bxly Hth
158 M 19 Green the Croy
34 H 19 Green the E11
52 A 18 Green the E15
70 F 17 Green the Hounsl
119 R 9 Green the Mrdn
119 S 9 Green the Mrdn
117 X 5 Green the N Mald
16 K 10 Green the N14
16 L 10 Green the N14
17 V 4 Green the N21
18 K 9 Green the N9
115 R 18 Green the Orp
84 G 12 Green the Rich
70 C 8 Green the S'hall
154 A 6 Green the Sutton
105 O 13 Green the SW19
101 T 2 Green the Twick
62 B 17 Green the W3
21 T 16 Green the Wdfd Grn
96 J 11 Green the Welling
41 Z 6 Green the Wemb
97 W 13 Green vale Bxly Hth
60 M 16 Green vale W5
24 F 1 Green verges Stanm
127 S 14 Green way Brom
95 N 13 Green way SE9
B2 D 9 Green Way the Hounsl
21 Y 15 Green way Wdfd Grn
99 T 11 Green wlk Drtfrd
20 H 4 Green wlk E4
27 P 14 Green wlk NW4
158 K 15 Green wlk S Croy
70 G 14 Green wlk S'hall
150 H 2 Green wlk SE1
154 K 1 Green Wrythe cres Carsh
120 H 17 Green Wrythe la Carsh
154 K 2 Green Wrythe la Carsh
140 D 8 Green's ct W1
78 L 10 Green's end SE18
16 L 11 Greenacre wlk N14
10 D 8 Greenacres Bushey
157 U 6 Greenacres Croy
11 N 20 Greenacres dri Stanm
27 U 8 Greenacres N3

95 W 16 Greenacres SE9
46 B 13 Greenaway gdns NW3
41 Y 15 Greenbank av Wemb
27 S 13 Greenbank cres NW4
78 B 19 Greenbay rd SE7
130 K 10 Greenberry rd NW8
5 S 6 Greenbrook av Barnt
148 C 4 Greencoat pl SW1
148 D 3 Greencoat pl SW1
148 D 3 Greencoat row SW1
25 R 5 Greencourt av Edg
66 C 16 Greencroft clo E6
46 D 19 Greencroft gdns NW6
129 Y 1 Greencroft gdns NW6
8 E 11 Greencroft gdns Enf
82 D 2 Greencroft rd Hounsl
74 A 6 Greenend rd W4
76 M 7 Greenfell st SE10
77 N 8 Greenfell st SE10
117 T 15 Greenfield av Surb
68 H 3 Greenfield gdns Dgnhm
45 T 9 Greenfield gdns NW2
68 G 3 Greenfield rd Dgnhm
143 U 4 Greenfield rd E1
31 S 15 Greenfield rd N15
22 J 10 Greenfield way Harrow
58 H 18 Greenfields S'hall
70 E 1 Greenford av S'hall
58 E 20 Greenford av S'hall
59 T 14 Greenford av W7
58 M 8 Greenford gdns Grnfd
59 N 8 Greenford gdns Grnfd
41 T 17 Greenford grn Grnfd
59 O 10 Greenford rd Grnfd
41 T 17 Greenford rd Grnfd
71 N 1 Greenford rd S'hall
154 A 9 Greenford rd Sutton
42 A 17 Greengate Grnfd
65 V 8 Greengate st E13
28 D 14 Greenhalgh wlk N2
141 T 20 Greenham clo SE1
29 P 6 Greenheys dri E18
34 C 9 Greenheys dri E18
21 X 4 Greenhill Buck Hl
58 E 6 Greenhill gdns Nthlt
53 P 14 Greenhill gro E12
5 O 18 Greenhill pk Barnt
58 E 7 Greenhill ter Grnfd
78 G 13 Greenhill ter SE18
23 U 18 Greenhill way Harrow
43 T 6 Greenhill way Wemb
43 U 6 Greenhill Wemb
141 X 1 Greenhills rents EC1
49 O 19 Greenhills Ter N1
96 F 18 Greenholic clo Sidcp
95 Y 13 Greenholm rd SE9
108 G 12 Greenhurst rd SE27
80 F 11 Greening st SE2
58 U 14 Greenland ms SE16
131 Z 4 Greenland av NW1
75 U 10 Greenland quay SE16
4 A 19 Greenland rd Barnt
132 A 3 Greenland rd NW1
131 Z 4 Greenland rd NW1
131 Z 4 Greenland rd NW1
118 E 16 Greenlaw gdns New Mald
78 H 9 Greenlaw st SE18
32 M 11 Greenleaf rd E17
33 N 11 Greenleaf rd E17
65 Y 4 Greenleaf rd E6
35 Z 10 Greenleafe dri Ilf
134 A 2 Greenman st N1
133 Z 3 Greenman st N1
105 O 8 Greenoak way SW19
107 X 20 Greenock rd SW16
73 U 9 Greenock rd W3
55 T 5 Greenside Dgnhm
122 G 16 Greenside rd Croy
74 G 7 Greenside rd W12
74 A 6 Greenside rd W4
84 H 12 Greenside Rich
34 K 1 Greenstead av Wdfd Grn
21 Z 20 Greenstead av Wdfd Grn
21 Y 19 Greenstead clo Wdfd Grn

86 H 14 Greenstead gdns SW15
21 Y 19 Greenstead gdns Wdfd Grn
34 E 18 Greenstone ms E11
95 U 11 Greenvale rd SE9
124 J 13 Greenview av Becknhm
124 H 15 Greenview av Croy
33 W 12 Greenway av E17
113 X 11 Greenway Chisl
14 L 9 Greenway clo N20
48 M 7 Greenway clo N4
25 X 9 Greenway clo NW9
55 U 5 Greenway Dgnhm
58 J 8 Greenway gdns Grnfd
23 U 6 Greenway gdns Harrow
158 K 6 Greenway gdns Croy
25 X 8 Greenway gdns NW9
24 K 16 Greenway Harrow
16 M 9 Greenway N14
17 N 7 Greenway N14
14 L 7 Greenway N20
15 N 8 Greenway N20
118 M 8 Greenway SW20
23 U 6 Greenway the Harrow
25 Y 8 Greenway the NW9
22 E 19 Greenway the Pinn
155 U 9 Greenway Wallgtn
125 O 4 Greenways Becknhm
16 C 20 Greenways clo N11
131 Z 18 Greenwell st W1
76 G 16 Greenwich Church st SE10
66 D 15 Greenwich cres E6
76 F 19 Greenwich High rd SE10
76 L 18 Greenwich pk SE10
93 S 2 Greenwich South st SE10
56 H 11 Greenwood av Dgnhm
9 U 7 Greenwood av Enf
10 E 4 Greenwood clo Bushey
119 S 9 Greenwood clo Mrdn
115 O 4 Greenwood clo Sidcp
20 H 16 Greenwood dri E4
17 V 10 Greenwood gdns N13
36 C 3 Greenwood gdns Ilf
100 L 12 Greenwood la Hampt
104 B 17 Greenwood pk Kingst
47 T 14 Greenwood pl NW5
122 K 16 Greenwood rd Croy
65 R 5 Greenwood rd E13
49 X 16 Greenwood rd E8
83 U 7 Greenwood rd Islwth
121 X 7 Greenwood rd Mitch
61 Y 4 Greenwood ter NW10
23 O 4 Greer rd Harrow
141 V 16 Greet st SE1
77 T 20 Gregor ms SE3
95 O 19 Gregory cres SE9
137 W 18 Gregory pl W8
65 X 19 Gregory rd E16
37 U 12 Gregory rd Rom
70 H 8 Gregory rd S'hall
30 A 15 Greig clo N8
149 Y 13 Greig ter SE17
85 N 11 Grena gdns Rich
85 N 11 Grena rd Rich
123 O 18 Grenaby av Croy
123 O 18 Grenaby rd Croy
77 Z 20 Grenada rd SE7
63 Z 20 Grenade st E14
78 H 4 Grenadier st E16
43 P 7 Grendon gdns Wemb
130 K 17 Grendon st NW8
57 T 4 Grenfell av Hornch
141 T 20 Grenfell gdns Harrow
107 N 17 Grenfell rd Mitch
136 H 9 Grenfell rd W11
154 E 3 Grennell clo Sutton
154 E 4 Grennell rd Sutton
17 S 18 Grenoble gdns N13
117 V 20 Grenville clo Surb
34 K 3 Grenville gdns Wdfd Grn
100 J 12 Grenville ms Hampt
146 B 6 Grenville ms SW7
12 K 16 Grenville pl NW7
146 A 4 Grenville pl SW7
159 V 20 Grenville rd Croy

48 A 4	Grenville rd N19	
132 L 18	Grenville st WC1	
15 Y 13	Gresham av N20	
98 A 16	Gresham clo Bxly	
7 Y 12	Gresham clo Enf	
37 R 18	Gresham dri Rom	
45 T 3	Gresham gdns NW11	
124 G 3	Gresham rd Becknhm	
65 W 18	Gresham rd E16	
66 G 7	Gresham rd E6	
12 A 20	Gresham rd Edg	
100 G 15	Gresham rd Hampt	
83 N 2	Gresham rd Hounsl	
43 Z 16	Gresham rd NW10	
123 W 10	Gresham rd SE25	
90 G 8	Gresham rd SW9	
160 C 4	Gresham st EC2	
142 C 5	Gresham st EC2	
31 N 14	Gresley clo N15	
47 W 2	Gresley rd N19	
140 E 3	Gresse st W1	
87 V 17	Gressenhall rd SW18	
115 O 7	Greswell clo Sidcp	
87 O 2	Greswell st SW6	
31 T 3	Greton rd N17	
84 A 18	Greville clo Twick	
129 W 6	Greville ms NW6	
129 Y 8	Greville rd NW6	
33 U 13	Greville rd E17	
129 Z 8	Greville rd NW6	
85 N 15	Greville rd Rich	
141 T 1	Greville st EC1	
28 C 18	Grey clo NW11	
135 O 19	Grey Eagle st E1	
148 E 3	Greycoat pl SW1	
148 E 3	Greycoat st SW1	
111 O 12	Greycott rd Becknhm	
11 P 15	Greyfell clo Stanm	
26 H 11	Greyhound hill NW4	
107 Z 16	Greyhound la SW16	
31 T 10	Greyhound rd N17	
128 A 12	Greyhound rd NW10	
62 L 8	Greyhound rd NW10	
154 C 11	Greyhound rd Sutton	
144 G 14	Greyhound rd W6	
144 J 13	Greyhound rd W6	
107 V 20	Greyhound ter SW16	
99 P 15	Greyhound way Drtfrd	
92 C 18	Greystead rd SE23	
22 H 10	Greystoke av Pinn	
6 L 14	Greystoke gdns Enf	
60 L 12	Greystoke gdns W5	
60 H 9	Greystoke Park ter W5	
141 T 4	Greystoke pl EC4	
24 D 19	Greystone gdns Harrow	
36 C 6	Greystoke gdns Ilf	
107 T 15	Greyswood st SW16	
92 G 16	Grierson rd SE23	
44 K 16	Griffin clo NW10	
79 T 9	Griffin Manor way SE28	
31 R 8	Griffin rd N17	
79 T 11	Griffin rd SE18	
152 K 4	Griffiths clo Worc Pk	
105 Z 17	Griffiths rd SW19	
150 L 1	Grigg's pl SE1	
54 B 7	Griggs app Ilf	
33 V 19	Griggs rd E10	
135 P 17	Grimsby st E2	
22 D 2	Grimsdyke rd Pinn	
87 V 6	Grimston rd SW6	
157 Y 6	Grimwade av Crny	
92 H 6	Grimwade cres SE15	
83 X 17	Grimwood rd Twick	
141 S 19	Grindal st SE1	
76 A 17	Grinling pl SE8	
75 Z 17	Grinling pl SE8	
75 W 14	Grinstead rd SE8	
129 T 16	Grittledon rd W9	
43 T 19	Grittleton av Wemb	
110 A 4	Grizedale ter SE23	
160 E 6	Grocers Hall ct EC2	
160 E 5	Grocers Hall gdns EC2	
88 F 19	Groom cres SW18	
139 V 20	Groom pl SW1	
65 Y 15	Groombridge clo E16	
97 O 13	Groombridge clo Welling	
63 T 1	Groombridge rd E9	
107 O 9	Groomfield clo SW17	
155 O 13	Grosvenor rd SE18	
22 L 19	Grosvenor av Harrow	
48 L 17	Grosvenor av N5	
49 N 16	Grosvenor av N5	
84 J 13	Grosvenor av Rich	
86 A 8	Grosvenor av SW14	
147 S 5	Grosvenor cotts SW1	
139 T 18	Grosvenor Cres ms SW1	
25 R 13	Grosvenor cres NW9	
139 T 19	Grosvenor cres SW1	
16 H 1	Grosvenor ct N14	
147 X 1	Grosvenor Gardens ms north SW1	
147 X 2	Grosvenor Gardens ms north SW1	
147 X 3	Grosvenor Gardens ms south SW1	
86 A 9	Grosvenor gdns SW14	
102 H 14	Grosvenor gdns Kingst	
45 N 16	Grosvenor gdns NW2	
155 U 16	Grosvenor gdns Wallgtn	
27 U 17	Grosvenor gdns NW1	
21 U 20	Grosvenor gdns Wdfd Grn	
66 A 8	Grosvenor gdns E6	
29 U 11	Grosvenor gdns NW2	
6 K 15	Grosvenor gdns N14	
147 X 2	Grosvenor gdns SW1	
105 S 14	Grosvenor hill SW19	
139 X 9	Grosvenor hill W1	
33 P 16	Grosvenor Park rd E17	
150 A 16	Grosvenor pk SE5	
149 Z 17	Grosvenor pk SE5	
139 W 19	Grosvenor rd W1	
159 S 1	Grosvenor rd W Wkhm	
97 X 13	Grosvenor rd Bxly Hth	
81 R 15	Grosvenor rd Blvdr	
72 H 17	Grosvenor rd Brentf	
56 C 3	Grosvenor rd Dgnhm	
51 U 3	Grosvenor rd E10	
34 G 17	Grosvenor rd E11	
66 B 3	Grosvenor rd E6	
52 H 19	Grosvenor rd E7	
82 E 8	Grosvenor rd Hounsl	
54 A 9	Grosvenor rd Ilf	
29 S 5	Grosvenor rd N10	
27 W 1	Grosvenor rd N3	
19 N 5	Grosvenor rd N9	
84 K 13	Grosvenor rd Rich	
57 N 3	Grosvenor rd Rom	
70 E 7	Grosvenor rd S'hall	
123 W 8	Grosvenor rd SE25	
147 Y 13	Grosvenor rd SW1	
87 Y 20	Grosvenor rd Twick	
73 T 14	Grosvenor rd W4	
71 X 3	Grosvenor rd W7	
155 S 12	Grosvenor rd Wallgtn	
33 S 16	Grosvenor Rise east E17	
139 V 9	Grosvenor sq W1	
139 W 9	Grosvenor st W1	
150 B 15	Grosvenor ter SE17	
149 Z 16	Grosvenor ter SE17	
76 J 12	Grosvenor Wharf rd E14	
93 Z 5	Grotes pl SE3	
106 B 3	Groton rd SW18	
139 U 1	Grotto pas W1	
101 W 4	Grotto rd Twick	
29 U 8	Grove av N10	
27 Y 2	Grove av N3	
22 B 14	Grove av Pinn	
153 Y 14	Grove av Sutton	
101 W 1	Grove av Twick	
59 U 17	Grove av W7	
100 B 11	Grove clo Felt	
116 L 9	Grove clo Kingst	
92 G 20	Grove clo SE23	
146 L 12	Grove cotts SW3	
34 D 7	Grove cres E18	
100 B 10	Grove cres Felt	
116 J 7	Grove cres Kingst	
25 X 13	Grove cres NW9	
91 R 5	Grove cres SE5	
51 Y 18	Grove Crescent rd E15	
34 A 7	Grove end E18	
130 F 14	Grove End rd NW8	
56 K 10	Grove gdns Dgnhm	
9 T 4	Grove gdns Enf	
26 F 14	Grove gdns NW4	
130 K 14	Grove gdns NW8	
101 Z 10	Grove gdns Tedd	
51 U 9	Grove Green rd E11	
34 B 7	Grove hill E18	
41 U 2	Grove hill Harrow	
41 U 1	Grove Hill rd Harrow	
91 S 7	Grove Hill rd SE5	
86 E 15	Grove ho SW15	
30 A 14	Grove House rd N8	
116 K 8	Grove la Kingst	
91 N 2	Grove la SE5	
95 T 15	Grove Market pl SE9	
144 B 2	Grove ms W6	
74 L 8	Grove ms W6	
33 P 2	Grove Park av E4	
73 V 19	Grove Park bri W4	
73 U 19	Grove Park gdns W4	
31 S 13	Grove Park rd N15	
112 M 6	Grove Park rd SE9	
113 N 5	Grove Park rd SE9	
73 T 19	Grove Park rd W4	
73 T 18	Grove Park ter W4	
101 Y 11	Grove pass Tedd	
116 J 10	Grove path Surb	
34 G 17	Grove pk E11	
25 W 12	Grove pk NW9	
91 S 6	Grove pk SE5	
85 V 1	Grove pk W4	
67 O 2	Grove pl Bark	
46 F 11	Grove pl NW3	
73 V 3	Grove pl W3	
72 H 1	Grove pl W5	
5 V 12	Grove rd Barnt	
81 P 16	Grove rd Blvdr	
72 F 14	Grove rd Brentf	
98 K 11	Grove rd Bxly Hth	
52 B 2	Grove rd E11	
33 P 17	Grove rd E17	
34 C 6	Grove rd E18	
63 V 7	Grove rd E3	
20 F 13	Grove rd E4	
12 B 18	Grove rd Frdg	
82 G 10	Grove rd Hounsl	
83 U 3	Grove rd Islwrth	
121 P 4	Grove rd Mitch	
16 F 15	Grove rd N11	
15 T 18	Grove rd N12	
31 P 16	Grove rd N15	
44 L 17	Grove rd NW2	
22 O 15	Grove rd Pinn	
84 M 16	Grove rd Rich	
85 N 15	Grove rd Rich	
55 S 1	Grove rd Rom	
37 S 19	Grove rd Rom	
116 G 11	Grove rd Surb	
154 B 13	Grove rd Sutton	
153 Y 14	Grove rd Sutton	
86 D 4	Grove rd SW13	
106 D 18	Grove rd SW19	
122 E 10	Grove rd Thntn Hth	
101 R 8	Grove rd Twick	
73 W 3	Grove rd W3	
72 H 1	Grove rd W5	
9 R 1	Grove road west Enfield	
18 H 18	Grove st N18	
75 X 10	Grove st SE8	
47 R 11	Grove ter NW5	
101 Y 10	Grove ter Tedd	
97 W 10	Grove the Bxly Hth	
51 Y 18	Grove the E15	
12 F 13	Grove the Edg	
7 T 9	Grove the Enf	
58 M 17	Grove the Grnfd	
83 T 3	Grove the Islwrth	
17 T 13	Grove the N13	
27 X 3	Grove the N3	
48 D 1	Grove the N4	
30 C 19	Grove the N6	
45 T 1	Grove the NW11	
25 Y 16	Grove the NW9	
101 Y 11	Grove the Tedd	
159 T 6	Grove the W Wkhm	
72 G 2	Grove the W5	
113 W 14	Grove vale Chisl	
91 T 9	Grove vale SE22	
64 E 19	Grove vlls E14	
16 J 1	Grovebury ct N14	
80 D 6	Grovebury rd SE2	
47 X 5	Grovedale rd N19	
108 D 18	Groveland av SW16	
160 C 6	Groveland ct EC4	
124 L 6	Groveland rd Becknhm	
91 R 5	Grovelands clo SE5	
16 J 4	Grovelands clo N14	
17 P 4	Grovelands pk N21	
17 R 12	Grovelands rd N13	
31 X 18	Grovelands rd N15	
115 P 19	Grovelands rd Orp	
117 X 11	Grovelands way New Mald	
61 R 15	Groveside clo W3	
20 M 9	Groveside rd E4	
21 O 10	Groveside rd E4	
55 V 11	Groveway SW9	
90 E 3	Groveway SW9	
43 U 15	Groveway Wemb	
85 O 3	Grovewood rd Rich	
91 U 2	Grummant rd SE15	
64 D 18	Grundy st E14	
28 A 1	Gruneisen rd N3	
90 K 13	Gubyon av SE24	
63 Y 8	Guerin sq E3	
90 L 18	Guernsey gro SE24	
51 W 5	Guernsey rd E11	
112 G 1	Guibal rd SE12	
94 G 20	Guibal rd SE12	
78 B 15	Guild rd SE7	
108 A 17	Guildersfield rd SW16	
107 Z 18	Guildersfield rd SW16	
116 M 11	Guildford av Surb	
93 S 1	Guildford gro SE10	
133 N 18	Guildford pl WC1	
123 O 14	Guildford rd Croy	
33 V 4	Guildford rd E17	
66 F 18	Guildford rd E6	
54 J 8	Guildford rd Ilf	
90 A 1	Guildford rd SW8	
132 K 19	Guildford st WC1	
133 O 17	Guildford st WC1	
115 L 15	Guildford vlls Surb	
156 B 10	Guildford way Wallgtn	
100 D 4	Guildhall bldgs EC2	
142 C 4	Guildhall EC2	
148 A 6	Guildhouse st SW1	
15 N 12	Guildown av N12	
32 K 5	Guilds way E17	
63 V 1	Guinness clo E9	
150 K 5	Guinness sq SE1	
87 W 4	Guion rd SW6	
156 A 17	Gull clo Wallgtn	
57 X 19	Gull way Hornch	
58 D 3	Gulliver clo Nthlt	
114 G 5	Gulliver rd Sidcp	
75 X 8	Gulliver st SE16	
72 D 11	Gumleigh rd W5	
83 X 7	Gumley gdns Islwrth	
142 M 1	Gun st E1	
126 L 7	Gundulph rd Brom	
63 X 3	Gunmakers la E3	
78 K 14	Gunner st SW18	
20 F 10	Gunners gro E4	
106 G 3	Gunners rd SW18	
73 P 9	Gunnersbury av W3	
72 M 2	Gunnersbury av W3	
73 P 6	Gunnersbury cres W3	
73 N 7	Gunnersbury dri W5	
73 P 6	Gunnersbury gdns W3	
73 R 6	Gunnersbury la W3	
72 K 9	Gunnersbury pk W3	
79 U 10	Gunning st SE18	
49 S 11	Gunstor rd N16	
25 X 4	Gunter gro Edg	
146 B 16	Gunter gro SW10	
144 L 8	Gunterstone rd W14	
145 N 8	Gunterstone rd W14	
143 P 3	Gunthorpe st E1	
50 A 0	Gunton rd E5	
107 P 16	Gunton rd SW17	
75 T 4	Gunwhale clo SE16	
77 U 14	Gurdon rd SE7	
59 X 11	Gurnell gro W13	
52 A 14	Gurney clo E15	
122 D 20	Gurney cres Croy	
28 E 14	Gurney dri N2	
155 N 7	Gurney rd Carsh	
52 A 14	Gurney rd E15	
51 Z 14	Gurney rd E15	
146 J 9	Guthrie st SW3	
160 B 5	Gutter la EC2	
155 Y 6	Guy rd Wallgtn	
142 G 17	Guy st SE1	
121 P 2	Guyatt gdns Mitch	
93 T 13	Guyscliffe rd SE13	
87 P 9	Gwalior rd SW15	
87 O 12	Gwendolen av SW15	
87 O 13	Gwendolen clo SW15	
65 V 3	Gwendoline av E13	
144 M 9	Gwendwr rd W14	
145 N 8	Gwendwr rd W14	
97 O 14	Gwillim clo Sidcp	
124 F 7	Gwydor rd Becknhm	
126 D 5	Gwydyr rd Brom	

124 E 16 Gwynne av Croy
133 P 14 Gwynne pl WC1
88 G 4 Gwynne rd SW11
148 M 10 Gye st SE11
91 P 11 Gylcote clo SE5
24 E 4 Gyles pk Stanm
54 L 10 Gyllyngdune gdns IIf

H

78 H 16 Ha-Ha rd SE18
144 F 3 Haarlem rd W14
134 G 12 Haberdasher st N1
155 O 2 Hackbridge grn Wallgtn
155 N 2 Hackbridge Park gdns Carsh
155 P 1 Hackbridge rd Wallgtn
90 E 2 Hackford rd SW9
149 R 20 Hackford rd SW9
111 O 15 Hackington cres Becknhm
50 A 19 Hackney gro E8
135 T 9 Hackney rd E2
106 C 16 Hacombe rd SW19
41 R 17 Hadden way Grnfd
79 U 9 Hadden way SE28
111 X 9 Haddington rd Brom
76 F 17 Haddo st SE10
118 C 11 Haddon clo New Mald
8 K 20 Haddon clo Enf
96 M 18 Haddon gro Sidcp
154 A 9 Haddon rd Sutton
63 P 11 Hadleigh clo E1
18 M 2 Hadleigh rd N9
19 N 2 Hadleigh rd N9
63 P 10 Hadleigh rd N9
7 U 19 Hadley clo N21
4 K 9 Hadley Common Barnt
5 N 9 Hadley Common Barnt
5 O 10 Hadley Common Barnt
70 D 14 Hadley gdns S'hall
73 Y 13 Hadley gdns W4
4 H 9 Hadley Green rd Barnt
4 G 8 Hadley Green west Barnt
4 G 10 Hadley gro Barnt
4 H 6 Hadley highstone Barnt
4 J 8 Hadley ho Barnt
6 D 3 Hadley rd Barnt
5 O 10 Hadley rd Barnt
81 O 9 Hadley rd Blvdr
7 R 4 Hadley rd Enf
121 X 9 Hadley rd Mitch
4 G 11 Hadley ridge Barnt
47 S 18 Hadley st NW1
7 T 20 Hadley way N21
109 W 17 Hadlow pl SE19
115 O 10 Hadlow rd Sidcp
80 G 19 Hadlow rd Welling
156 B 15 Hadrian clo Wall
76 M 14 Hadrian st SE10
8 H 16 Hadrians ride Enf
74 F 5 Hadyn Park rd W12
88 K 11 Hafer rd SW11
112 A 2 Hafton rd SE6
84 A 19 Haggard rd Twick
135 N 2 Haggerston rd E8
135 U 14 Hague st E2
11 R 17 Haig st Stanm
65 Y 8 Haig Road east E13
65 X 8 Haig Road west E13
36 A 13 Haigville gdns Ilf
106 C 15 Hailes clo SW19
81 S 6 Hailey rd Blvdr
8 H 20 Haileybury av Enf
108 C 5 Hailsham av SW2
116 H 17 Hailsham clo Surb
23 S 10 Hailsham dri Harrow
107 P 16 Hailsham rd SW17
18 A 15 Hailsham ter N13
95 O 12 Haimo rd SE9
33 X 14 Hainault ct E17
38 A 17 Hainault gdns Pinn
37 T 11 Hainault ho Rom
33 Z 20 Hainault rd E11
38 B 18 Hainault rd Rom

38 L 10 Hainault rd Rom
54 A 7 Hainault st Ilf
114 A 2 Hainault st SE9
92 G 10 Hainsford clo SE4
108 H 8 Hainthorpe rd SE27
20 B 14 Hal la E4
56 B 11 Halbutt gdns Dgnhm
56 B 11 Halbutt st Dgnhm
134 J 6 Halcomb st N1
98 G 12 Halcot av Bxly Hth
63 O 16 Halcrow st E1
20 G 20 Haldan rd E4
33 V 1 Haldan rd E4
29 R 1 Haldane clo N10
88 A 20 Haldane pl SW18
66 D 8 Haldane rd E6
68 J 20 Haldane rd SE28
145 R 17 Haldane rd SW6
58 M 18 Haldane rd S'hall
87 W 15 Haldon rd SW18
20 G 10 Hale clo E4
12 J 16 Hale clo Edg
12 J 19 Hale clo NW7
33 W 8 Hale End rd E17
20 J 19 Hale End rd E4
33 V 8 Hale End rd Wdfd Grn
31 X 11 Hale gdns N17
73 P 2 Hale gdns W3
12 M 16 Hale Grove gdns NW7
13 N 17 Hale Grove gdns NW7
12 E 15 Hale la Edg
12 L 16 Hale la NW7
13 O 17 Hale la NW7
66 D 12 Hale rd E6
31 X 11 Hale rd N17
64 D 19 Hale st E14
33 W 2 Hale the E4
31 X 11 Hale the N17
59 U 15 Hale wlk W7
31 Z 6 Halefield rd N17
76 A 20 Hales st SE8
120 A 19 Halesowen rd Mrdn
119 Z 18 Halesowen rd Mrdn
93 P 7 Halesworth rd SE13
26 M 18 Haley rd NW4
72 F 17 Half acre Brentf
71 S 2 Half Acre rd W7
142 A 2 Half Moon ct EC1
90 L 15 Half Moon la SE24
91 N 15 Half Moon la SE24
143 O 5 Half Moon pass E1
139 Y 14 Half Moon st W1
133 R 6 Halfmoon cres N1
33 W 16 Halford rd E10
84 J 13 Halford rd Rich
145 T 15 Halford rd SW6
96 F 20 Halfway st Sidcp
114 J 2 Halfway st Sidcp
83 Z 12 Haliburton rd Twick
49 O 17 Haliday wlk N1
50 C 14 Halidon clo E9
8 A 8 Halifax rd Enf
58 L 3 Halifax rd Grnfd
110 A 8 Halifax st SE26
80 L 10 Halifield dri Blvdr
156 L 16 Haling gro S Croy
156 K 13 Haling Park gdns S Croy
156 M 14 Haling Park rd S Croy
157 N 14 Haling Park rd S Croy
157 O 13 Haling rd S Croy
139 S 20 Halkin ms SW1
147 S 1 Halkin pl SW1
139 U 19 Halkin st SW1
110 B 11 Hall dri SE26
59 U 16 Hall dri E7
11 N 12 Hall Farm clo Stanm
83 R 18 Hall Farm dri Twick
130 E 13 Hall ga NW8
19 Z 14 Hall gdns E4
19 Y 14 Hall la E4
26 G 7 Hall la NW4
130 F 19 Hall pl W2
98 L 14 Hall Place cres Bxly
51 X 12 Hall rd E15
66 G 3 Hall rd E6
83 R 12 Hall rd Islwth
130 C 14 Hall rd NW8
37 U 18 Hall rd Rom
155 T 18 Hall rd Wallgtn
133 X 11 Hall st EC1
15 P 16 Hall st N12
94 E 8 Hall the SE3
113 N 4 Hall view SE9
113 T 13 Hallam clo Chisl
22 C 2 Hallam gdns Pinn
131 Y 20 Hallam ms W1
30 J 14 Hallam rd N5
131 Y 19 Hallam st W1

139 Z 1 Hallam st W1
49 P 17 Hallday wlk N1
93 X 10 Halley gdns SE13
63 W 14 Halley pl E14
52 K 18 Halley rd E7
53 P 16 Halley rd E7
63 V 15 Halley st E14
134 D 1 Halliford st N1
90 B 15 Halliwell rd SW2
29 O 4 Hallswick rd N10
154 A 5 Hallmead rd Sutton
153 Z 5 Hallmead rd Sutton
155 Z 7 Hallowell av Croy
121 O 5 Hallowell clo Mitch
8 G 4 Hallside rd Enf
65 O 17 Hallsville rd E16
27 V 15 Hallswelle rd NW11
95 X 17 Halons rd SE9
150 H 7 Halpin pl SE17
94 M 6 Halsbrook rd SE3
95 P 11 Halsbrook rd SE3
11 O 15 Halsbury clo Stanm
41 O 13 Halsbury Rd east Nthlt
74 H 3 Halsbury rd W12
40 L 14 Halsbury Rd west Nthlt
147 N 6 Halsey st SW3
54 K 16 Halsham cres Bark
90 K 2 Halsmere rd SE5
18 A 5 Halstead gdns N21
34 G 15 Halstead rd E11
8 E 14 Halstead rd Enf
99 P 1 Halstead rd Erith
18 A 5 Halstead rd N21
128 F 13 Halstow rd NW10
77 R 15 Halstow rd SE10
81 V 10 Halt Robin la Blvdr
81 T 10 Halt Robin rd Blvdr
133 Y 3 Halton Cross st N1
48 J 20 Halton rd N1
133 Y 2 Halton rd N1
102 D 6 Ham clo Rich
102 H 9 Ham Farm rd Rich
102 H 8 Ham Gate av Rich
102 C 2 Ham House Rich
52 E 20 Ham Park rd E7
110 A 20 Ham pl SE20
102 M 11 Ham ridings Rich
102 C 3 Ham st Rich
72 E 20 Ham the Brentf
122 J 15 Ham view Croy
140 D 9 Ham wd W1
89 V 14 Hambalt rd SW4
88 B 7 Hamble st SW6
123 U 6 Hambledon gdns SE25
87 V 19 Hambledon rd SW18
96 F 19 Hambledown rd Sidcp
126 F 19 Hambro av Brom
107 Y 13 Hambro rd SW16
123 Z 6 Hambrook rd SE25
70 B 2 Hambrough rd S'hall
56 G 9 Hamden cres Dgnhm
64 G 18 Hamelin st E14
66 J 10 Hameway E6
52 C 17 Hamfrith rd E15
36 B 14 Hamilton av Ilf
18 K 2 Hamilton av N9
38 M 8 Hamilton av Rom
39 N 8 Hamilton av Rom
153 S 1 Hamilton av Sutton
5 X 14 Hamilton clo Barnt
31 W 11 Hamilton clo N17
130 E 15 Hamilton clo NW8
75 W 6 Hamilton clo SE16
40 F 9 Hamilton cres Harrow
82 K 14 Hamilton cres Hounsl
17 U 14 Hamilton cres N13
60 L 20 Hamilton ct W5
130 D 11 Hamilton gdns NW8
48 J 13 Hamilton la N5
139 V 16 Hamilton ms W1
84 H 13 Hamilton Park west N5
48 J 13 Hamilton pk N5
139 V 16 Hamilton pl W1
123 N 5 Hamilton rd Thntn Hth
5 X 14 Hamilton rd Barnt
72 G 16 Hamilton rd Brentf
97 Z 4 Hamilton rd Bxly Hth
65 N 10 Hamilton rd E15
32 J 9 Hamilton rd E17
23 U 15 Hamilton rd Harrow
53 Z 12 Hamilton rd Ilf
28 D 10 Hamilton rd N2
18 J 3 Hamilton rd N9
44 G 14 Hamilton rd NW10

45 R 1 Hamilton rd NW11
39 Y 16 Hamilton rd Rom
70 E 2 Hamilton rd S'hall
109 O 9 Hamilton rd SE27
114 M 9 Hamilton rd Sidcp
106 B 18 Hamilton rd SW19
101 U 1 Hamilton rd Twick
74 A 7 Hamilton rd W4
60 L 19 Hamilton rd W5
130 B 12 Hamilton rd NW8
129 Z 9 Hamilton rd NW8
155 X 19 Hamilton way Wallgtn
14 K 20 Hamilton way N3
94 D 12 Hamlea clo SE12
38 D 2 Hamlet clo Rom
74 F 11 Hamlet gdns W6
38 C 2 Hamlet rd Rom
109 W 18 Hamlet rd SE19
91 R 7 Hamlet the SE5
63 Y 11 Hamlets way E3
109 R 19 Hamlyn gdns SE19
112 E 20 Hammerfield dri
13 U 14 Hammers la NW7
144 D 7 Hammersmith bdwy W6
144 A 11 Hammersmith br W6
74 K 15 Hammersmith br W6
144 B 10 Hammersmith Bridge rd W6
74 L 13 Hammersmith Bridge rd W6
144 D 9 Hammersmith flyover W6
74 M 13 Hammersmith flyover W6
136 A 20 Hammersmith gro W6
144 C 5 Hammersmith gro W6
74 L 7 Hammersmith gro W6
144 H 6 Hammersmith rd W6
74 E 14 Hammersmith ter W6
143 N 9 Hammett st EC3
121 R 4 Hammond av Mitch
4 F 18 Hammond clo Barnt
41 R 14 Hammond clo Grnfd
9 N 10 Hammond rd Enf
70 D 9 Hammond rd S'hall
47 U 17 Hammond st NW5
68 D 20 Hammond way SE28
10 C 6 Hamonde clo Edg
124 K 4 Hampden av Becknhm
132 G 9 Hampden clo NW1
139 O 6 Hampden Gurney st W1
31 W 5 Hampden la N17
124 J 4 Hampden rd Becknhm
23 O 5 Hampden rd Harrow
117 R 5 Hampden rd Kingst
29 P 1 Hampden rd N10
31 X 4 Hampden rd N17
47 Y 8 Hampden rd N19
30 G 13 Hampden rd N8
38 H 2 Hampden rd Rom
16 E 6 Hampden way N14
18 M 17 Hampshire clo N18
30 D 1 Hampshire rd N22
47 X 16 Hampshire st NW5
90 C 1 Hampson way SW8
80 B 3 Hampstead clo SE28
27 X 19 Hampstead gdns NW11
46 J 14 Hampstead grn NW3
46 D 11 Hampstead gro NW3
46 F 13 Hampstead heath NW3
46 H 13 Hampstead High st NW3
46 H 13 Hampstead Hill gdns NW3
46 K 2 Hampstead la N6
47 N 2 Hampstead la N6
132 B 11 Hampstead rd NW1
46 E 10 Hampstead sq NW3
46 C 4 Hampstead way NW11
27 X 16 Hampstead way NW11
129 T 13 Hampton clo NW6
104 L 18 Hampton clo SW20
116 C 8 Hampton Court pk Kingst
48 H 18 Hampton la Felt
100 C 10 Hampton la Felt
122 M 14 Hampton rd Croy
51 X 5 Hampton rd E11

20 A 16 Hampton rd E4
19 X 16 Hampton rd E4
52 G 15 Hampton rd E7
54 B 13 Hampton rd Ilf
101 R 13 Hampton rd Tedd
101 R 6 Hampton rd Twick
152 H 3 Hampton rd Worc Pk
24 K 19 Hampton ri Harrow
100 G 9 Hampton Road east Felt
100 C 6 Hampton Road west Felt
149 Z 6 Hampton st SE17
114 L 5 Hamshades clo Sidcp
77 U 3 Hanameel st E16
134 B 5 Hanbury ms N1
31 Y 7 Hanbury rd Carsh
73 T 7 Hanbury rd W3
135 S 20 Hanbury st E1
64 F 9 Hancock rd E3
109 O 16 Hancock rd SE19
141 P 2 Hand ct WC1
122 H 19 Handcroft rd Croy
11 Z 19 Handel clo Edg
132 K 16 Handel st WC1
25 O 1 Handel way Edg
94 C 14 Handen rd SE12
149 S 18 Handforth rd SW9
63 R 2 Handley rd E9
65 T 17 Hands wlk E16
153 P 1 Handside clo Worc Pk
20 J 19 Handsworth av E4
31 P 11 Handsworth rd N17
67 N 5 Handtrough way Bark
105 V 1 Hanford clo SW10
104 M 14 Hanford row SW19
61 O 11 Hanger grn W5
60 K 12 Hanger Hill pk W5
60 L 14 Hanger la W5
60 M 17 Hanger Vale la W5
61 O 15 Hanger Vale la W5
61 O 16 Hanger View way W3
141 V 6 Hanging Sword all EC4
142 F 19 Hankey pl SE1
13 N 10 Hankins la NW7
48 A 5 Hanley rd N4
43 W 13 Hannah clo NW10
144 L 18 Hannell rd SW6
108 K 8 Hannen rd SE27
63 R 14 Hannibal rd E1
156 C 13 Hannibal way Croy
50 L 17 Hannington point E9
89 S 8 Hannington rd SW4
73 O 19 Hanover clo Rich
153 T 8 Hanover clo Sutton
130 M 13 Hanover ga NW1
36 B 2 Hanover gdns Ilf
149 S 16 Hanover gdns SE11
91 X 3 Hanover pk SE15
140 L 7 Hanover pl WC2
31 V 13 Hanover rd N15
128 C 3 Hanover rd NW10
62 M 2 Hanover rd NW10
106 E 17 Hanover rd SW19
139 Y 7 Hanover sq W1
156 J 6 Hanover st Croy
139 Z 7 Hanover st W1
131 N 14 Hanover ter NW1
131 N 15 Hanover Terrace ms NW1
97 X 9 Hanover way Bxly Hth
133 Z 8 Hanover yd N1
139 O 20 Hans cres SW1
147 O 2 Hans pl SW1
147 N 1 Hans rd SW3
147 P 2 Hans st SW1
136 J 18 Hansard ms W14
7 U 7 Hansart way Enf
10 J 17 Hanselin clo Stanm
25 X 4 Hanshaw dri Edgw
91 V 13 Hansler rd SE22
97 Y 12 Hanson rd Bxly Hth
89 S 19 Hanson cl SW12
93 X 7 Hanson gdns S'hall
140 A 1 Hanson st W1
132 A 20 Hanson st W1
140 F 3 Hanway pl W1
59 T 16 Hanway rd W7
140 F 4 Hanway st W1
100 J 14 Hanworth rd Hampt
82 H 14 Hanworth rd Hounsl
82 K 10 Hanworth ter Hounsl
41 P 15 Hapgood clo Har
143 T 9 Harads pl E1
46 E 20 Harben rd NW6
65 P 3 Harberson rd E15

89 R 20 Harberson rd SW12
47 V 4 Harberton rd N19
19 U 17 Harbet rd E4
138 H 2 Harbet rd W2
98 F 18 Harbex clo Bxly
76 D 12 Harbinger rd E14
87 X 1 Harbledown rd SW6
91 O 4 Harbord clo SE5
87 P 1 Harbord st SW6
96 J 18 Harborough av Sidcp
108 D 9 Harborough rd SW16
88 D 2 Harbour av SW10
90 L 7 Harbour rd SE5
86 F 18 Harbridge av SW15
154 H 17 Harbut rd Carsh
88 F 11 Harbut rd SW11
49 R 10 Harcombe rd N16
53 T 14 Harcourt av E12
12 G 11 Harcourt av Edg
97 T 18 Harcourt av Sidcp
155 T 9 Harcourt av Wallgtn
97 Z 9 Harcourt Bxly Hth
83 Z 6 Harcourt clo Islwth
155 T 8 Harcourt field Wallgtn
122 D 14 Harcourt rd Thntn Hth
65 O 6 Harcourt rd E15
29 W 4 Harcourt rd N22
92 J 9 Harcourt rd SE4
105 Y 19 Harcourt rd SW19
155 S 8 Harcourt rd Wallgtn
138 M 2 Harcourt st W1
146 A 12 Harcourt ter SW10
145 Z 11 Harcourt ter SW10
150 G 7 Hardcourts clo W Wkhm
108 G 2 Hardel ri SW2
78 D 10 Harden st SE18
78 A 9 Hardens manorway SE7
91 Z 3 Harders rd SE15
92 A 2 Harders Road ms SE15
90 K 8 Hardess st SE24
43 W 15 Hardie clo NW10
56 K 10 Hardie rd Dgnhm
98 A 4 Harding rd Bxly Hth
18 D 18 Harding rd N18
128 C 6 Hardinge rd NW10
62 L 4 Hardinge rd NW10
63 R 19 Hardinge st E1
108 E 16 Hardings la SE20
116 K 2 Hardman rd Kingst
77 U 13 Hardman rd SE7
11 R 16 Hardwick clo Stanm
133 T 13 Hardwick st EC1
82 H 2 Hardwicke av Hounsl
60 B 14 Hardwicke grn W13
17 N 18 Hardwicke rd N13
102 C 9 Hardwicke rd Rich
73 X 11 Hardwicke rd W4
87 Z 14 Hardwicks way SW18
142 J 17 Hardwidge st SE1
77 R 17 Hardy rd SE3
106 B 18 Hardy rd SW19
7 U 6 Hardy way Enf
94 A 4 Hare and Billet rd SE3
93 X 4 Hare and Billet rd SE3
141 G 7 Hare ct EC4
39 Y 12 Hare Hall la Rom
135 S 17 Hare marsh E2
63 N 5 Hare row E2
135 X 7 Hare row E2
78 J 9 Hare st SE18
134 L 9 Hare wlk N1
58 B 11 Harecastle clo Grnfd
48 L 17 Harecourt rd N1
90 M 11 Haredale rd SE24
92 D 18 Haredon clo SE23
29 X 15 Harefield av N8
153 R 20 Harefield av Sutton
7 U 5 Harefield clo Enf
92 K 7 Harefield ms SE4
92 L 8 Harefield rd SE4
93 N 8 Harefield rd SE4
115 W 6 Harefield rd Sidcp
108 D 18 Harefield rd SW16
56 F 19 Haresfield rd Dgnhm
58 D 1 Harewood av Nthlt
130 M 17 Harewood av NW1
131 N 20 Harewood av NW1
58 D 1 Harewood clo Nthlt
35 T 7 Harewood dri Ilf
139 Y 6 Harewood pl W1

71 V 20 Harewood rd Islwth
83 W 1 Harewood rd Islwth
157 S 14 Harewood rd S Croy
106 K 16 Harewood rd SW19
130 M 20 Harewood row NW1
70 F 11 Harewood ter S'hall
91 R 7 Harfield gdns SE5
22 E 1 Harford clo E4
20 E 2 Harford rd E4
63 U 12 Harford rd E16
28 G 14 Harford wlk N2
24 K 19 Hargood clo Harrow
94 L 4 Hargood rd SE3
47 U 8 Hargrave pk N19
47 X 16 Hargrave pl N7
47 W 7 Hargrave rd N19
90 B 8 Hargwyne st SW9
30 D 13 Haringey gro N8
30 A 19 Haringey pk N8
30 A 14 Haringey rd N8
23 V 6 Harkett clo Harrow
157 W 5 Harland av Croy
114 E 6 Harland av Sidcp
94 E 20 Harland rd SE12
112 F 1 Harland rd SE12
17 O 11 Harlech rd N14
71 Z 17 Harlequin av Brentf
102 A 17 Harlequin rd Tedd
92 F 10 Harlescott rd SE15
62 D 3 Harlesden gdns NW10
62 H 2 Harlesden rd NW10
44 J 20 Harlesden rd NW10
42 G 17 Harley clo Wemb
23 R 13 Harley cres Harrow
146 C 11 Harley gdns SW10
63 Z 9 Harley grn E3
139 W 2 Harley pl W1
23 R 12 Harley rd Harrow
62 B 6 Harley rd NW6
130 H 2 Harley rd NW3
131 W 19 Harley st W1
139 X 2 Harley st W1
112 K 20 Harleyford Brom
149 O 13 Harleyford rd SE11
149 S 15 Harleyford rd SE11
98 A 7 Harlington rd Bxly Hth
18 A 10 Harman av Wdfd Grn
21 O 20 Harman av Wdfd Grn
20 K 14 Harman clo E4
45 T 11 Harman clo NW2
45 T 11 Harman dri NW2
96 K 16 Harman dri Sidcup
8 G 16 Harman rd Enf
155 Z 19 Harmony clo SM6
47 R 20 Harmood pl NW1
47 R 20 Harmood st NW1
149 W 12 Harmsworth st SE17
14 J 6 Harmsworth way N20
79 Z 6 Harness rd SE28
81 O 14 Harold av Belvdr
149 R 12 Harold pl SE11
51 Z 4 Harold rd E11
65 X 3 Harold rd E13
20 F 12 Harold rd E4
31 V 14 Harold rd N15
30 C 14 Harold rd N8
61 X 8 Harold rd NW10
109 R 16 Harold rd SE19
154 F 9 Harold rd Sutton
34 G 4 Harold rd Wdfd Grn
32 G 16 Haroldstone rd F17
141 V 4 Harp all EC4
43 Y 7 Harp Island clo NW10
142 K 10 Harp la EC3
59 V 12 Harp rd W7
52 K 6 Harpenden rd E12
108 H 5 Harpenden rd SE27
66 G 18 Harper rd E6
142 B 20 Harper rd SE1
150 C 1 Harper rd SE1
63 S 10 Harpley sq E1
54 B 19 Harpour rd Bark
89 O 3 Harpsden st SW11
133 N 20 Harpur st WC1
94 L 2 Harraden rd SE3
64 J 20 Harrap st E14
57 Y 19 Harrier clo Hornch
79 T 6 Harrier ms SE28
135 R 4 Harriet clo E8
157 X 2 Harriet gdns Croy
139 R 20 Harriet st SW1
10 C 3 Harriet way Bushey
139 R 19 Harriet wlk SW1
84 X 20 Harriets clo W5
30 J 14 Harringay gdns N15
30 G 12 Harringay pass N8

30 J 13 Harringay rd N15
30 J 14 Harringay rd N15
155 Z 3 Harrington clo Wallgtn
146 A 7 Harrington gdns SW7
50 B 4 Harrington hill E5
52 A 4 Harrington rd E11
124 B 8 Harrington rd SE25
123 Y 9 Harrington rd SE25
146 E 6 Harrington rd SW7
132 B 9 Harrington sq NW1
132 A 12 Harrington st NW1
18 B 12 Harrington ter N18
78 B 8 Harrington way SE18
77 O 12 Harriott clo SE10
7 V 6 Harris clo Enf
82 G 2 Harris clo Hounsl
98 A 2 Harris rd Bxly Hth
56 B 15 Harris rd Dgnhm
50 L 1 Harris st E17
150 G 19 Harris st SE5
56 F 19 Harrison rd Dgnhm
132 M 14 Harrison st WC1
156 J 5 Harrison's ri Croy
55 R 15 Harrold rd Dgnhm
18 H 1 Harrow av Enf
39 Z 3 Harrow cres Rom
57 Z 3 Harrow dri Hornch
18 G 4 Harrow dri N9
51 Z 9 Harrow grn E11
64 F 20 Harrow la E14
80 F 2 Harrow Lodge park Hornch
57 Y 7 Harrow Lodge park Hornch
90 F 7 Harrow Manor way SE2
41 U 6 Harrow pk Harrow
142 M 3 Harrow pl E1
67 V 3 Harrow rd Bark
154 J 12 Harrow rd Carsh
52 D 9 Harrow rd E11
66 D 2 Harrow rd E6
54 C 14 Harrow rd Ilf
128 D 14 Harrow rd NW10
62 J 8 Harrow rd NW10
138 B 2 Harrow rd W2
129 O 17 Harrow rd W9
43 P 17 Harrow rd Wemb
41 X 12 Harrow rd Wemb
23 R 14 Harrow view Harrow
60 C 12 Harrow view rd W5
10 D 18 Harrow Weald pk Harrow
88 F 5 Harroway rd SW11
138 M 4 Harrowby st W1
139 N 4 Harrowby st W1
42 F 14 Harrowden rd Wemb
101 Z 17 Harrowdene gdns Tedd
42 G 10 Harrowdene rd Wemb
12 D 10 Harrowes meade Edg
41 U 10 Harrowfields gdns Harrow
50 G 19 Harrowgate rd E9
58 G 14 Hart gro S'hall
73 O 2 Hart gro W5
142 L 8 Hart st EC3
141 S 1 Hart yd EC1
82 F 5 Harte rd Hounsl
105 V 17 Hartfield cres SW19
110 B 20 Hartfield gro SE20
105 W 18 Hartfield rd SW19
64 B 7 Hartfield ter E3
24 A 10 Hartford av Harrow
23 Z 10 Hartford av Harrow
98 F 17 Hartford rd Bxly
27 H 14 Hartford wlk N2
83 X 1 Hartham clo Islwth
48 A 15 Hartham clo N7
83 X 2 Hartham rd Islwth
31 U 6 Hartham rd N17
48 A 15 Hartham rd N7
113 P 8 Harting rd SE9
41 T 12 Hartington clo Harrow
65 V 17 Hartington rd E16
32 H 19 Hartington rd E17
70 B 7 Hartington rd S'hall
148 J 20 Hartington rd SW8
89 Z 1 Hartington rd SW8
84 B 17 Hartington rd Twick
72 B 1 Hartington rd W13
73 U 20 Hartington rd W4
85 W 3 Hartington rd W4
145 R 17 Hartismere rd SW6
50 G 18 Hartlake rd E9

212 Har–Haz

12 C 9 Hartland clo Edg
12 B 9 Hartland dri Edg
52 B 20 Hartland rd E15
65 O 1 Hartland rd E15
100 K 10 Hartland rd Hampt
57 W 8 Hartland rd Hornch
83 Z 6 Hartland rd Islwth
119 Z 18 Hartland rd Mrdn
15 Z 17 Hartland rd N11
47 R 20 Hartland rd NW1
129 O 7 Hartland rd NW6
47 S 19 Hartland st NW1
158 H 2 Hartland way Croy
158 H 4 Hartland way Croy
119 W 16 Hartland way Mrdn
66 D 4 Hartley av E6
13 R 17 Hartley av NW7
127 V 4 Hartley clo Brom
13 R 17 Hartley clo NW7
122 K 16 Hartley rd Croy
52 C 3 Hartley rd E11
80 F 18 Hartley rd Welling
63 S 8 Hartley st E2
78 A 2 Hartman rd E16
48 D 15 Hartnoll st N7
113 N 20 Harton clo Chisl
19 N 9 Harton rd N9
93 N 1 Harton st SE8
53 Z 18 Harts la Bark
92 G 1 Harts la SE14
9 O 15 Harts way Enf
10 B 8 Hartsbourne av Bushey
10 D 8 Hartsbourne rd Bushey
66 J 11 Hartshorn gdns E6
80 H 4 Hartslock dri SE2
113 T 3 Hartsmead rd SE9
74 C 7 Hartswood rd W12
79 V 11 Hartville rd SE18
20 F 19 Hartwell dri E4
49 U 17 Hartwell st E8
73 U 15 Harvard hill W4
73 V 15 Harvard la W4
83 T 3 Harvard rd Islwth
93 V 14 Harvard rd SE13
73 T 14 Harvard rd W4
80 J 14 Harvel cres SE2
83 R 12 Harvesters clo Islwth
77 Z 13 Harvey gdns SE7
52 B 3 Harvey rd E11
82 F 19 Harvey rd Hounsl
54 A 16 Harvey rd Ilf
53 Z 16 Harvey rd Ilf
30 C 15 Harvey rd N8
91 N 1 Harvey rd SE5
134 G 5 Harvey st N1
57 P 6 Harvey's la Rom
115 X 13 Harvill rd Sidcp
128 H 11 Harvist rd NW6
129 N 9 Harvist rd NW6
28 L 12 Harwell pas N2
126 G 3 Harwood av Brom
120 J 6 Harwood av Mitch
145 V 19 Harwood rd SW6
88 A 1 Harwood ter SW6
17 U 2 Harwoods yd N21
18 F 8 Haselbury rd N9
89 Z 10 Haselrigge rd SW4
110 K 10 Haseltine rd SE26
55 W 13 Haskard rd Dgnhm
146 M 4 Hasker st SW3
119 T 19 Haslam av Sutton
48 G 20 Haslam clo N1
15 Z 6 Haslemere av Barnt
120 F 3 Haslemere av Mitch
27 O 18 Haslemere av NW4
106 A 3 Haslemere av SW18
72 A 8 Haslemere av W13
71 Z 9 Haslemere Av W13
156 A 12 Haslemere clo Wallgtn
100 F 12 Haslemere clo Hampt
27 U 11 Haslemere gdns N3
98 C 5 Haslemere rd Bxly Hth
122 H 11 Haslemere rd Thntn Hth
54 K 6 Haslemere rd Ilf
17 V 7 Haslemere rd N21
29 Z 20 Haslemere rd N8
68 F 19 Hasler clo SE28
7 W 13 Haslewood dri Enf
5 O 19 Hasluck gdns Barnt
77 V 18 Hassendean rd SE3
50 G 17 Hassett rd E9
110 A 6 Hassocks clo SE26
121 X 1 Hassocks rd SW16
45 O 11 Hassop rd NW2
113 P 9 Hassop wlk SE9
78 B 13 Hasted rd SE7
36 B 14 Hastings av Ilf
5 R 14 Hastings clo Barnt
151 S 19 Hastings clo SE15
123 U 19 Hastings rd Croy
16 J 17 Hastings rd N11
31 O 9 Hastings rd N17
39 Y 17 Hastings rd Rom
60 B 20 Hastings rd W13
132 J 14 Hastings st WC1
58 A 11 Hastoe clo Grnfd
37 Z 13 Hatch gro Rom
20 K 13 Hatch la E4
122 A 3 Hatch rd SW16
9 S 7 Hatch the Enf
92 D 1 Hatcham gdns SE15
92 F 1 Hatcham Park rd SE14
75 P 16 Hatcham rd SE15
75 P 16 Hatcham rd SE16
47 Z 6 Hatchard rd N19
26 H 11 Hatchcroft NW4
94 B 8 Hatcliffe clo SE3
77 O 13 Hatcliffe st SE10
35 Z 9 Hatfield clo Ilf
120 E 9 Hatfield clo Mitch
75 R 19 Hatfield clo SE14
119 X 12 Hatfield mead Mrdn
68 M 1 Hatfield rd Dgnhm
55 Z 20 Hatfield rd Dgnhm
52 A 14 Hatfield rd E15
71 Y 3 Hatfield rd W13
73 Z 5 Hatfield rd W4
141 U 12 Hatfields SE1
10 K 17 Hathaway clo Stanm
53 U 17 Hathaway cres E12
37 V 15 Hathaway gdns Rom
59 Y 14 Hathaway gdns W13
122 K 18 Hathaway rd Croy
119 Y 9 Hatherleigh clo Mrdn
115 O 6 Hatherley cres Sidcp
66 B 8 Hatherley gdns E6
137 X 5 Hatherley gro W2
32 M 13 Hatherley rd E17
33 N 12 Hatherley rd E17
85 N 3 Hatherley rd Rich
115 O 8 Hatherley rd Sidcp
148 D 6 Hatherley st SW1
113 W 10 Hathern gdns SE9
100 D 18 Hatherop rd Hampt
92 D 6 Hathway st SE15
36 B 13 Hatley av Ilf
15 Y 15 Hatley clo N11
48 E 7 Hatley rd N4
120 L 17 Hatropp av SW4
88 L 15 Hatston clo SW11
81 O 11 Hattersfield clo Blvdr
79 S 19 Hatton clo SE18
133 T 20 Hatton gdn EC1
141 U 1 Hatton gdn EC1
120 M 11 Hatton gdns Mitch
122 G 19 Hatton rd Croy
130 G 19 Hatton row NW8
130 G 18 Hatton st NW8
133 T 19 Hatton wall EC1
139 X 7 Haunch of Venison rd W1
39 R 17 Havana cl Rom
105 Z 4 Havana rd SW19
76 B 5 Havannah st E14
33 U 11 Havant rd E17
57 V 13 Havard wlk Hornch
23 U 19 Havelock pl Harrow
81 O 12 Havelock rd Blvdr
126 L 8 Havelock rd Brom
157 V 2 Havelock rd Croy
99 Y 18 Havelock rd Drtfd
23 T 10 Havelock rd Harrow
31 Y 7 Havelock rd N17
70 D 8 Havelock rd S'hall
106 C 12 Havelock rd SW19
54 A 8 Havelock st Ilf
132 M 4 Havelock st N1
89 T 1 Havelock ter SW8
147 Z 20 Havelock ter SW8
110 C 2 Havelock wlk SE23
105 O 6 Haven clo SW19
60 G 18 Haven grn W5
60 J 17 Haven la W5
60 G 19 Haven pl W5
131 Y 1 Haven st NW1
85 S 7 Haven the Rich
7 T 10 Havenhurst ri Enf
43 U 8 Havenwood Wemb
73 P 19 Haverfield gdns Rich
63 U 8 Haverfield rd E3
25 N 5 Haverford way Edg
20 H 6 Haverhill rd E4
107 V 2 Haverhill rd SW12
39 P 11 Havering dri Rom
37 W 14 Havering gdns Rom
38 M 9 Havering rd Rom
39 N 3 Havering rd Rom
63 S 18 Havering st E1
68 D 8 Havering way Bark
84 H 17 Haversham clo Twick
46 K 17 Haverstock hill NW3
47 N 15 Haverstock rd NW5
133 Y 10 Haverstock st N1
150 J 20 Havil st SE5
150 L 14 Havil st SE5
91 S 1 Havil st SE5
90 L 18 Hawarden gro SE24
44 G 10 Hawarden hill NW2
32 F 13 Hawarden rd E17
51 W 3 Hawbridge rd E11
125 V 19 Hawes la W Wkhm
159 X 1 Hawes la W Wkhm
112 H 20 Hawes rd Brom
18 L 19 Hawes rd N18
133 X 2 Hawes st N1
64 B 14 Hawgood st E3
30 K 9 Hawke Park rd N22
109 P 14 Hawke rd SE19
156 B 16 Hawker clo Croy
76 J 20 Hawkes ms SE10
116 L 4 Hawkes pass Kingst
106 L 20 Hawkes rd Mitch
86 J 13 Hawkesbury rd SW15
110 K 5 Hawkesfield rd SE23
101 X 8 Hawkesley clo Twick
107 Y 19 Hawkhurst rd SW16
159 S 2 Hawkhurst way W Wkhm
117 X 11 Hawkhurst way New Mald
102 B 15 Hawkins clo Tedd
41 P 1 Hawkins cres Harrow
37 T 19 Hawkridge clo Rom
116 M 3 Hawks rd Kingst
117 N 4 Hawks rd Kingst
125 T 14 Hawksbrook la Becknhm
112 A 18 Hawkshead clo Brom
44 D 20 Hawkshead rd NW10
74 A 7 Hawkshead rd W4
92 E 13 Hawkslade rd SE15
49 P 8 Hawksley ct N16
49 P 9 Hawksley rd N16
66 C 17 Hawksmoor clo E6
143 W 8 Hawksmoor ms E1
144 H 15 Hawksmoor st W6
20 F 3 Hawksmouth E4
75 R 10 Hawkstone rd SE16
50 A 3 Hawkwood mt E5
40 A 1 Hawlands dri Pinn
100 E 15 Hawley clo Hampt
131 Y 1 Hawley cres NW1
108 K 5 Hawley gdns SE27
47 S 20 Hawley rd NW1
47 S 20 Hawley st NW1
93 R 17 Hawstead rd SE6
122 H 1 Hawthorn av Thntn Hth
155 P 16 Hawthorn av Carsh
17 O 16 Hawthorn av N13
100 F 13 Hawthorn clo Hampt
22 G 19 Hawthorn dri Harrow
72 H 8 Hawthorn gdns W5
8 C 4 Hawthorn gro Enf
110 A 19 Hawthorn gro SE20
72 C 20 Hawthorn hatch Brentf
27 S 5 Hawthorn ms NW7
72 B 20 Hawthorn rd Brentf
21 Z 14 Hawthorn rd Buck Hl
98 B 12 Hawthorn rd Bxly Hth
18 F 18 Hawthorn rd N18
29 Y 11 Hawthorn rd N8
44 H 19 Hawthorn rd NW10
154 H 12 Hawthorn rd Sutton
155 T 15 Hawthorn rd Wallgtn
18 F 9 Hawthorn way N9
120 G 3 Hawthorne av Mitch
127 T 7 Hawthorne clo Brom
49 R 17 Hawthorne clo N1
154 C 3 Hawthorne clo Sutton
58 C 4 Hawthorne Farm av Nthlt
25 W 20 Hawthorne gro NW9
127 U 6 Hawthorne rd Brom
33 O 10 Hawthorne rd E17
21 S 10 Hawthorns Buck Hl
130 K 1 Hawtrey rd NW3
112 H 20 Haxted rd Brom
65 N 1 Hay clo E15
64 E 16 Hay Currie st E14
139 Z 11 Hay hill W1
25 X 13 Hay la NW9
139 W 11 Hay's ms W1
57 U 4 Hayburn way Hornch
62 H 4 Haycroft gdns NW10
90 B 13 Haycroft rd SW2
65 S 14 Hayday rd E16
38 K 7 Hayden way Rom
137 N 5 Hayden's pl W11
40 G 17 Haydock av Nthlt
40 G 17 Haydock grn Nthlt
25 W 14 Haydon clo NW9
106 A 12 Haydon Park rd SW19
105 Z 12 Haydon Park rd SW19
55 V 7 Haydon rd Dgnhm
143 O 7 Haydon wlk EC3
106 B 13 Haydon's rd SW19
125 Y 13 Hayes chase W Wkhm
27 V 15 Hayes cres NW11
153 P 7 Hayes cres Sutton
126 A 20 Hayes hill Brom
126 B 20 Hayes Hill rd Brom
125 Z 20 Hayes hill W Wkhm
125 U 7 Hayes la Becknhm
126 G 14 Hayes la Brom
126 A 20 Hayes mead Brom
125 Z 20 Hayes Mead rd W Wkhm
130 M 19 Hayes pl NW1
126 F 10 Hayes rd Brom
126 G 20 Hayes st Brom
125 U 8 Hayes way Becknhm
153 P 20 Hayes wlk Sutton
126 H 20 Hayes Wood av Brom
126 D 12 Hayesford Park dri Brom
63 S 14 Hayfield pass E1
63 R 13 Hayfield yd E1
105 P 13 Haygarth pl SW19
25 X 14 Hayland clo NW9
149 X 3 Hayles st SE11
133 X 2 Hayman st N1
140 F 11 Haymarket SW1
152 G 5 Haymer gdn Worc Pk
151 S 15 Haymerle rd SE15
124 L 2 Hayne rd Becknhm
141 Z 1 Hayne st EC1
133 Z 20 Hayne st EC1
94 A 8 Haynes clo SE3
109 S 16 Haynes la SE19
42 K 20 Haynes rd Wemb
119 T 5 Haynt wlk SW20
142 H 13 Hays la SE1
123 Y 4 Haysleigh gdns SE20
39 O 13 Haysoms clo Rom
90 C 12 Hayter rd SW2
141 P 13 Hayward Art gallery SE1
98 M 13 Hayward clo Bxly Hth
106 B 20 Hayward clo SW19
86 M 16 Hayward gdns SW15
87 N 16 Hayward gdns SW15
15 P 8 Hayward rd N20
133 W 17 Hayward's pl EC1
26 A 5 Haywood av NW9
127 N 8 Haywood rd Brom
72 B 18 Hazel clo Brentf
57 Y 11 Hazel clo Hornch
121 Z 9 Hazel clo Mitch
18 A 11 Hazel clo N13
91 Y 5 Hazel clo SE15
83 O 18 Hazel clo Twick
99 X 2 Hazel dri Erith
12 E 13 Hazel gdns Edg
18 J 1 Hazel gro Enf
37 X 9 Hazel gro Rom
110 G 11 Hazel gro SE26
60 K 5 Hazel gro Wemb
102 J 4 Hazel la Rich
99 X 2 Hazel rd Erith
128 B 12 Hazel rd NW10
62 L 8 Hazel rd NW10
19 X 19 Hazel way E4
127 X 15 Hazel wlk Brom
112 A 4 Hazelbank rd SE6
111 Z 4 Hazelbank rd SE6
89 T 16 Hazelbourne rd SW12
36 F 1 Hazelbrouck gdns Ilf
18 F 12 Hazelbury grn N9
18 F 12 Hazelbury la N9
61 Z 1 Hazeldean rd NW10
55 P 6 Hazeldene rd Ilf
97 T 5 Hazeldene rd Welling
92 J 13 Hazeldon rd SE4
125 V 1 Hazelhurst Becknhm
106 E 9 Hazelhurst rd SW17

38 G 3	Hazell cres Rom	
58 F 6	Hazelmere clo Grnfd	
58 F 5	Hazelmere rd Nthlt	
129 S 6	Hazelmere rd NW6	
126 E 14	Hazelmere way Brom	
58 F 5	Hazelmere wlk Nthlt	
58 B 9	Hazeltree la Nthlt	
47 X 2	Hazelville rd N19	
120 B 9	Hazelwood av Mrdn	
72 K 5	Hazelwood clo W5	
17 T 13	Hazelwood cres N13	
116 J 14	Hazelwood ct Surb	
17 T 13	Hazelwood la N13	
32 H 16	Hazelwood rd E17	
8 J 19	Hazelwood rd Enf	
88 A 4	Hazlebury rd SW6	
157 R 4	Hazledean rd Croy	
73 V 16	Hazledene rd W4	
118 H 19	Hazlemere gdns Worc Pk	
87 N 12	Hazlewell rd SW15	
128 M 17	Hazlewood cres W10	
129 N 17	Hazlewood cres W10	
144 K 2	Hazlitt ms W14	
144 K 3	Hazlitt rd W14	
122 D 8	Headcorn rd Thntn Hth	
112 D 12	Headcorn rd Brom	
31 U 2	Headcorn rd N17	
139 V 19	Headfort pl SW1	
106 E 2	Headington rd SW18	
89 X 17	Headlam rd SW4	
63 N 12	Headlam st E1	
35 Y 17	Headley appr Ilf	
156 D 10	Headley av Wallgtn	
159 J 16	Headley dri Croy	
36 A 18	Headley dri Ilf	
35 Y 17	Headley dri Ilf	
92 A 6	Headley st SE15	
23 P 11	Headstone dri Harrow	
23 O 12	Headstone gdns Harrow	
22 L 8	Headstone la Harrow	
22 M 11	Headstone mnr Harrow	
23 S 18	Headstone rd Harrow	
152 D 20	Headway the Epsom	
93 N 2	Heald st SE14	
47 S 18	Healey st NW1	
134 K 18	Hearn st EC2	
73 P 15	Hearne rd W4	
150 G 8	Hearns bldgs SE17	
89 O 20	Hearnville rd SW12	
80 J 17	Heath av Bxly Hth	
46 C 8	Heath brow NW3	
46 A 2	Heath clo NW3	
39 W 10	Heath clo Rom	
61 O 12	Heath clo W5	
45 Z 13	Heath dri NW3	
39 W 9	Heath dri Rom	
154 C 19	Heath dri Sutton	
118 M 8	Heath dri SW20	
119 N 8	Heath dri SW20	
101 V 2	Heath gdns Twick	
110 B 18	Heath gro SE20	
46 J 13	Heath Hurst rd NW3	
93 Y 6	Heath la SE3	
105 O 6	Heath mead SW19	
39 X 15	Heath Park rd Rom	
99 T 17	Heath rd Drtfrd	
23 N 20	Heath rd Harrow	
82 L 11	Heath rd Hounsl	
83 P 10	Heath rd Hounsl	
55 Y 1	Heath rd Romford	
89 R 7	Heath rd SW8	
89 T 6	Heath rd SW8	
122 M 5	Heath rd Thntn Hth	
101 W 2	Heath rd Twick	
126 D 14	Heath ri Brom	
87 R 16	Heath ri SW15	
46 H 11	Heath side NW3	
46 D 10	Heath st NW3	
28 D 12	Heath View clo N2	
28 E 12	Heath view N2	
79 W 15	Heath vlls SE8	
98 L 2	Heath way Erith	
21 Z 15	Heath way Wdfd Grn	
83 V 19	Heatham pk Twick	
10 G 8	Heathbourne rd Stanm	
99 Y 20	Heathclose av Drtfrd	
99 W 20	Heathclose rd Drtfrd	
35 U 7	Heathcote av Ilf	
20 F 9	Heathcote gro E4	
84 C 14	Heathcote rd Twick	
133 N 15	Heathcote st WC1	
46 B 3	Heathcroft NW11	
61 N 12	Heathcroft W5	
82 B 8	Heathdale av Hounsl	
81 U 12	Heathdene dri Blvdr	
155 T 16	Heathdene rd Wallgtn	
81 V 12	Heathdene rd Blvdr	
108 C 18	Heathdene rd SW16	
39 O 7	Heather av Rom	
66 L 18	Heather clo E6	
100 F 20	Heather clo Hampt	
39 N 5	Heather clo Rom	
99 V 19	Heather dri Drtfrd	
39 O 7	Heather dri Rom	
27 S 19	Heather gdns NW11	
39 O 6	Heather gdns Rom	
153 X 14	Heather gdns Sutton	
39 N 7	Heather glen Rom	
61 R 2	Heather Park dri Wemb	
44 D 7	Heather rd NW2	
112 F 2	Heather rd SE12	
39 N 6	Heather way Rom	
158 F 18	Heather way S Croy	
10 J 20	Heather way Stanm	
12 E 16	Heather wlk Edg	
127 Y 3	Heatherbank BR7	
95 V 5	Heatherbank SE9	
103 R 17	Heatherdale clo Kingst	
120 H 10	Heatherdene clo Mitch	
35 S 9	Heatherley dri Ilf	
108 D 19	Heatherset gdns SW16	
115 V 6	Heatherside rd Sidcp	
52 K 7	Heatherwood clo E12	
88 G 17	Heathfield ave SW18	
114 C 16	Heathfield Chisl	
66 A 14	Heathfield clo E16	
73 X 13	Heathfield ct W4	
20 G 10	Heathfield E4	
88 F 15	Heathfield gdns SW18	
27 P 20	Heathfield gdns NW11	
73 V 14	Heathfield gdns W4	
114 B 17	Heathfield la Chisl	
83 V 17	Heathfield north Twick	
44 M 19	Heathfield pk NW2	
98 A 11	Heathfield rd Bxly Hth	
112 D 18	Heathfield rd Brom	
157 N 9	Heathfield rd Croy	
88 F 16	Heathfield rd SW18	
73 S 6	Heathfield rd W3	
158 D 14	Heathfield S Croy	
83 V 18	Heathfield south Twick	
88 F 18	Heathfield sq SW18	
79 W 16	Heathfield ter SE18	
73 W 13	Heathfield ter W4	
158 G 18	Heathfield vale S Croy	
28 A 19	Heathgate NW11	
157 R 19	Heathhurst rd S Croy	
49 P 3	Heathland rd N16	
99 Y 17	Heathlands ri Drtfrd	
94 B 10	Heathlee rd SE3	
114 C 15	Heathley end Chisl	
87 W 3	Heathmans rd SW6	
98 A 4	Heathside av Bxly Hth	
97 Z 3	Heathside av Bxly Hth	
87 F 19	Heathside Hounsl	
62 H 18	Heathstam rd W12	
99 S 17	Heathview av Drtfrd	
99 X 20	Heathview cres Drtfrd	
80 H 16	Heathview dri SE2	
86 L 19	Heathview gdns SW15	
122 F 8	Heathview rd Thntn Hth	
48 A 2	Heathville rd N19	
88 M 8	Heathwall st SW11	
158 M 5	Heathway Croy	
56 C 12	Heathway Dgnhm	
69 R 2	Heathway Dgnhm	
77 S 20	Heathway SE3	
78 D 13	Heathwood gdns SE7	
99 O 20	Heathwood lodge Bxly	
39 Y 2	Heaton av Rom	
39 U 6	Heaton Grange rd Rom	
51 V 15	Heaton pl E15	
107 O 17	Heaton rd Mitch	
91 Y 6	Heaton rd SE15	
88 G 6	Heaver clo SW11	
79 R 15	Heavitree clo SE18	
79 S 14	Heavitree rd SE18	
106 K 7	Hebdon rd SW17	
45 O 14	Heber rd NW2	
91 V 15	Heber rd SE22	
144 A 2	Hebron rd W6	
74 L 9	Hebron rd W6	
32 H 6	Heckham clo E17	
145 T 19	Heckfield pl SW6	
63 T 19	Heckford st E1	
79 U 12	Hector st SE18	
83 Y 9	Heddon clo Islwth	
6 A 15	Heddon Court av Bark	
5 Z 16	Heddon rd Barnt	
140 B 10	Heddon st W1	
7 W 6	Hedge hill Enf	
17 V 11	Hedge la N13	
35 T 13	Hedgeley Ilf	
55 W 20	Hedgeman's rd Dgnhm	
56 C 17	Hedgemans rd Dgnhm	
55 Y 19	Hedgemans way Dgnhm	
58 M 7	Hedgerly gdns Grnfd	
50 H 18	Hedgers gro E9	
35 V 14	Hedgewood gdns Ilf	
94 B 12	Hedgley st SE12	
134 A 1	Hadingham clo N1	
55 P 16	Hedingham rd Dgnhm	
115 R 17	Hedley clo Sidcp	
49 O 14	Hedley rw N5	
8 A 8	Heene rd Enf	
66 C 2	Heigham rd E6	
156 J 10	Heighton gdns Croy	
41 Y 15	Heights av Grnfd	
104 J 19	Heights clo SW20	
40 F 15	Heights clo SW20	
77 Z 15	Heights the SE7	
89 Y 16	Helby rd SW4	
94 C 19	Helder gro SE12	
157 O 13	Helder st S Croy	
83 R 9	Helenam clo Islwth	
28 C 10	Helen clo N2	
78 M 11	Helen st SE18	
156 C 16	Helena clo Croy	
60 G 14	Helena ct W5	
65 R 7	Helena rd E13	
33 N 17	Helena rd E17	
44 J 14	Helena rd NW10	
60 H 14	Helena rd W5	
5 U 2	Helens clo Barnt	
45 X 4	Helenslea av NW11	
90 D 15	Helix gdns SW2	
90 E 16	Helix rd SW2	
143 U 14	Hellings st E1	
105 V 12	Helme clo SW19	
134 B 15	Helmet row EC1	
58 A 11	Helmsdale clo Grnfd	
39 R 2	Helmsdale rd Rom	
39 R 1	Helmsdale rd Rom	
107 W 19	Helmsdale rd SW16	
135 X 2	Helmsley pl E8	
22 E 3	Helston clo Pinn	
77 O 13	Helvelius clo SE10	
110 L 5	Helvetia st SE8	
148 H 18	Hemans st SW8	
90 A 7	Hemberton rd SW9	
41 P 14	Hemery clo Grnfd	
25 S 1	Heming rd Edg	
153 N 8	Hemingford rd Sutton	
133 P 2	Hemingford rd	
15 Y 16	Hemington av N11	
86 E 3	Hemitage the SW13	
62 E 20	Hemlock rd W12	
100 G 20	Hemming clo Hampt	
135 U 17	Hemming st E1	
150 F 6	Hemp wlk SE17	
21 S 8	Hempstead clo Buck Hl	
33 X 9	Hempstead rd E17	
63 N 2	Hemsley st E8	
45 Y 20	Hemstal rd NW6	
26 A 5	Hemswell dri NW9	
134 J 7	Hemsworth st N1	
146 L 10	Hemus pl SW3	
62 D 19	Henchman st W12	
26 H 10	Hendale av NW4	
43 V 17	Henderson clo NW10	
130 F 16	Henderson dri NW8	
123 N 13	Henderson rd Croy	
52 K 17	Henderson rd E7	
18 M 4	Henderson rd N9	
88 H 18	Henderson rd SW18	
106 K 4	Hendham rd SW17	
27 V 16	Hendon av N3	
27 U 9	Hendon av N3	
27 V 17	Hendon Park row NW11	
13 S 7	Hendon pk NW7	
18 K 7	Hendon rd N9	
45 T 6	Hendon way NW2	
26 L 18	Hendon way NW4	
13 T 4	Hendon Wood la NW7	
150 K 7	Hendre rd SE1	
41 P 15	Hendren clo Grnfd	
88 M 18	Hendrick av SW12	
142 L 5	Heneage la EC3	
143 P 1	Heneage st E1	
98 E 15	Henfield clo Bxly	
47 W 5	Henfield clo N19	
119 V 1	Henfield rd SW19	
105 V 20	Henfield rd SW19	
120 F 9	Hengelo gdns Mitch	
81 X 18	Hengist rd Erith	
94 J 18	Hengist rd SE12	
125 Y 9	Hengist way Brom	
92 E 17	Hengrave rd SE23	
146 E 13	Heniker ms SW3	
153 R 5	Henley av Sutton	
59 O 6	Henley clo Grnfd	
83 V 3	Henley clo Islwth	
16 G 3	Henley ct N14	
104 C 18	Henley dri Kingst	
37 Y 15	Henley gdns Rom	
78 H 5	Henley rd E16	
54 B 13	Henley rd Ilf	
18 D 13	Henley rd N18	
128 D 3	Henley rd W10	
83 O 4	Henley st SW11	
110 E 7	Hennel clo SE23	
66 C 8	Henniker gdns E6	
146 E 13	Henniker ms SW3	
51 Y 15	Henniker rd E15	
88 H 3	Henning st SW11	
31 P 3	Henningham rd N17	
139 W 5	Henrietta pl W1	
51 V 15	Henrietta st E15	
140 K 9	Henrietta st WC2	
143 T 6	Henriques st E1	
113 N 8	Henry Cooper way SE9	
14 D 17	Henry Darlot dri NW7	
87 O 8	Henry Jackson rd SW18	
5 T 17	Henry rd Barnt	
66 E 6	Henry rd E6	
48 K 5	Henry rd N4	
112 J 20	Henry st Brom	
21 P 16	Henrys av Wdfd Grn	
36 D 2	Henrys wlk Ilf	
92 M 13	Henryson rd SE4	
36 D 3	Henryson rd SE4	
110 A 9	Hensford gdns SE26	
49 P 18	Henshall st N1	
150 E 5	Henshaw st SE17	
55 X 9	Henshawe rd Dgnhm	
91 Y 13	Henslowe rd SE22	
44 L 14	Henson av NW2	
24 G 11	Henson pth Harrow	
130 J 7	Henstridge pl NW8	
146 L 20	Henty clo SW11	
86 J 14	Henty wlk SW15	
126 J 1	Henville rd Brom	
95 P 8	Henwick rd SE9	
76 P 0	Henwood rd SE16	
84 A 4	Hepple clo Islwth	
86 K 16	Hepplestone clo SW15	
51 N 19	Hepscott rd E9	
55 N 15	Hepworth gdns Bark	
108 B 19	Hepworth rd SW16	
155 Z 17	Heracles clo Wallgtn	
63 O 10	Herald st E2	
135 Y 15	Herald st E2	
133 T 18	Herbal hill EC1	
133 U 18	Herbal pl EC1	
147 O 1	Herbert cres SW1	
128 A 8	Herbert gdns NW10	
62 J 5	Herbert gdns NW10	
55 W 1	Herbert gdns Rom	
73 T 17	Herbert gdns W4	
127 P 11	Herbert rd Brom	
98 A 5	Herbert rd Bxly Hth	
97 Z 4	Herbert rd Bxly Hth	
53 R 14	Herbert rd E12	
32 L 20	Herbert rd E17	
116 L 7	Herbert rd Kingst	
54 G 6	Herbert rd Ilf	
16 M 20	Herbert rd N11	
31 V 15	Herbert rd N15	
18 M 8	Herbert rd N9	

26 E 19	Herbert rd NW9
70 E 2	Herbert rd S'hall
78 J 19	Herbert rd SE18
105 W 18	Herbert rd SW19
90 A 7	Herbert rd SW9
65 T 8	Herbert st E13
47 O 17	Herbert st NW5
78 L 18	Herbert ter SE18
132 J 17	Herbrand st WC1
48 B 10	Hercules rd N7
149 R 1	Hercules rd SE1
48 A 10	Hercules st N7
15 Y 6	Hereford av Barnt
35 S 20	Hereford gdns Ilf
22 B 15	Hereford gdns Pinn
137 V 6	Hereford gdns Twick
34 J 15	Hereford ms W2
137 V 5	Hereford rd E11
61 U 19	Hereford rd W2
72 K 9	Hereford rd W3
151 R 16	Hereford retreat SE15
146 C 7	Hereford sq SW7
135 T 15	Hereford st E2
35 S 12	Herent dri Ilf
17 U 17	Hereward gdns N13
106 K 8	Hereward rd SW17
41 T 8	Herga ct Harrow
23 V 12	Herga rd Harrow
20 A 9	Heriot av E4
47 N 14	Heriot pl NW5
26 M 15	Heriot rd NW4
27 N 15	Heriot rd NW4
19 W 16	Heriot way E4
10 L 13	Heriots clo Stanm
41 W 9	Heritage view Harrow
106 K 8	Herlwyn gdns SW17
133 R 9	Hermes st N1
155 Y 15	Hermes way Wallgtn
30 A 15	Hermiston av N8
129 W 5	Hermit pl NW6
65 P 13	Hermit rd E16
133 W 12	Hermit st EC1
34 C 13	Hermitage clo E18
7 W 9	Hermitage clo Enf
34 E 13	Hermitage ct E18
45 X 9	Hermitage ct NW2
108 M 16	Hermitage gdns SE19
45 Y 9	Hermitage gdns NW2
123 X 16	Hermitage la Croy
18 B 17	Hermitage la N18
45 X 9	Hermitage la NW2
108 C 19	Hermitage la SW16
30 K 20	Hermitage rd N4
31 N 18	Hermitage rd N4
108 M 16	Hermitage rd SE19
109 N 16	Hermitage rd SE19
138 F 2	Hermitage st W2
138 F 2	Hermitage st W2
84 J 14	Hermitage the Rich
143 T 14	Hermitage wall E1
23 Z 5	Hermitage way Stanm
34 C 12	Hermitage wlk E18
34 F 14	Hermon hill E11
88 C 14	Herndon rd SW18
43 Y 16	Herne clo NW10
90 L 9	Herne Hill rd SE24
90 L 14	Herne hill SE24
18 K 14	Herne ms N18
90 J 14	Herne pl SE24
32 K 7	Heron clo E17
44 B 19	Heron clo NW10
114 H 8	Heron cres Sidcp
126 L 10	Heron ct Brom
84 G 14	Heron ct Rich
57 Y 19	Heron Flight av Hornch
81 P 12	Heron hill Belvdr
53 Y 7	Heron ms Ilf
157 T 1	Heron rd Croy
90 K 10	Heron rd SE24
84 A 11	Heron rd Twick
83 Z 11	Heron rd Twick
21 Y 15	Heron way Wdfd Grn
106 H 1	Herondale av SW18
8 F 9	Herongate clo Enf
52 L 7	Herongate rd E12
21 T 4	Herons clo Buck Hl
12 C 17	Herons ga Edg
5 X 15	Herons ri Barnt
60 D 16	Heronsforde W13
11 W 16	Heronslea dri Stanm
48 L 9	Herrick rd N5
148 H 7	Herrick st SW1
128 M 11	Herries st W10
150 L 14	Herring st SE5
77 Y 9	Herringham rd SE7
62 H 3	Hersant clo NW10
92 G 19	Herschell rd SE23
86 G 19	Hersham clo SW15
9 P 9	Hertford rd Enf
86 A 11	Hertford av SW14
85 Z 12	Hertford av SW14
5 T 11	Hertford clo Barnt
132 B 19	Hertford pl W1
53 X 20	Hertford rd Bark
5 S 11	Hertford rd Barnt
66 L 1	Hertford rd E6
36 G 18	Hertford rd Ilf
49 T 20	Hertford rd N1
28 J 10	Hertford rd N2
18 L 8	Hertford rd N9
139 V 14	Hertford st W1
121 Z 10	Hertford way Mitch
81 S 14	Hertford wk Blvdr
48 C 11	Hertslet rd N7
27 Y 4	Hervey clo N3
32 J 12	Hervey Park rd E17
94 G 2	Hervey rd SE3
27 Y 5	Hervey wlk N3
136 J 10	Hesketh pl W11
52 E 11	Hesketh rd E7
107 N 2	Heslop rd SW12
145 Y 8	Hesper ms SW5
76 D 11	Hesperus cres E14
72 A 5	Hessel rd W13
71 Z 6	Hessel rd W13
143 V 5	Hessel st E1
18 J 17	Hester rd N18
146 K 18	Hester rd SW11
87 T 3	Hestercombe av SW6
70 C 18	Heston av Hounsl
70 D 17	Heston Grange la Hounsl
70 G 15	Heston rd Hounsl
70 H 19	Heston rd Hounsl
92 M 2	Heston st SE8
93 N 2	Heston st SE8
89 Z 11	Hetherington rd SW4
109 T 18	Hetley gdns SE19
74 J 4	Hetley rd W12
74 L 11	Hetton st W6
113 X 10	Hever croft SE9
127 W 4	Hever gdns Brom
79 U 11	Heverham rd SE18
98 E 3	Heversham rd Bxly Hth
128 H 20	Hewer st W10
11 O 13	Hewett clo Stanm
55 V 13	Hewett rd Dgnhm
134 K 17	Hewett st EC2
18 D 14	Hewish rd N18
30 H 8	Hewitt av N22
30 H 16	Hewitt rd N8
63 W 6	Hewitt rd E3
47 N 4	Hexagon the N6
111 Z 6	Hexal rd SE6
71 Z 19	Hexham gdns Islwth
5 O 14	Hexham rd Barnt
119 Z 18	Hexham rd Mrdn
108 L 4	Hexham rd SE27
32 A 2	Heybourne rd N17
108 B 17	Heybridge av SW16
36 E 9	Heybridge dri Ilf
50 K 3	Heybridge way E17
119 W 7	Heyford av Mrdn
119 V 6	Heyford av SW20
148 M 17	Heyford av SW8
120 K 2	Heyford rd Mitch
148 L 17	Heyford ter SW8
150 A 6	Heygate st SE17
63 Y 8	Heylyn sq E3
55 T 12	Heynes rd Dgnhm
31 P19	Heysham rd N15
105 W 3	Heythorp st SW18
26 A 4	Heywood av NW9
52 B 14	Heyworth rd E5
49 Z 11	Heyworth rd E5
50 L 2	Hibbert rd E17
23 W 7	Hibbert rd Harrow
88 E 9	Hibbert st SW11
82 H 12	Hibernia gdns Hounsl
82 H 12	Hibernia rd Hounsl
92 E 12	Hichisson rd SE15
77 Z 12	Hickin clo SE7
76 F 7	Hickin st E14
53 Z 14	Hickling rd Ilf
20 G 18	Hickman av E4
66 A 15	Hickman clo E16
55 T 1	Hickman rd Rom
89 W 8	Hickmore wlk SW4
59 S 8	Hicks av Grnfd
88 H 7	Hicks clo SW11
75 V 13	Hicks st SE8
118 J 5	Hidcote gdns New Mald
148 E 6	Hide pl SW1
23 P 13	Hide rd Harrow
48 E 17	Hide st N7
157 T 16	High beech S Croy
115 Z 12	High beeches Sidcp
125 R 17	High Broom cres W Wkhm
31 V 11	High Cross rd N17
86 H 20	High Cross way SW15
117 W 1	High dri New Mald
21 R 17	High Elms Wdfd Grn
95 F 1	High gro SE18
79 S 20	High gro SE18
50 B 3	High Hill ferry E5
140 K 4	High Holborn WC1
141 P 2	High Holborn WC1
59 R 17	High la W7
109 X 10	High Level dri SE26
62 M 14	High Lever rd W10
23 U 15	High mead Harrow
159 Y 3	High mead W Wkhm
25 X 16	High Meadow cres NW9
26 G 18	High mt NW4
7 R 4	High oaks Enf
85 P 3	High Park av Rich
85 P 3	High Park rd Rich
113 Z 7	High point SE9
106 B 20	High pth SW19
10 C 5	High rd Bushey
34 E 7	High rd E18
28 H 9	High Rd east Finchley
28 G 7	High Rd Finchley N12
23 S 3	High rd Harrow
54 B 8	High rd Ilf
53 Y 9	High rd Ilf
33 R 19	High Rd Leyton E10
51 S 5	High Rd Leyton E10
51 U 13	High Rd Leyton E15
52 A 4	High Rd Leytonstone E11
51 Y 11	High rd Leytonstone E11
16 E 16	High rd N11
28 E 1	High rd N12
31 V 4	High rd N17
15 R 11	High rd N20 N12
30 D 6	High rd N22
44 J 18	High rd NW10
55 P 2	High rd Rom
37 X 20	High rd Rom
21 R 20	High rd Wdfd Grn
42 L 15	High rd Wemb
36 C 9	High st Barkingside Ilf
4 G 12	High st Barnt
125 N 2	High st Becknhm
126 D 2	High st Brom
155 O 9	High st Carsh
114 A 16	High st Chisl
156 M 5	High st Croy
159 S 1	High st Croy
34 F 16	High st E11
65 T 7	High st E13
64 G 4	High st E15
51 X 20	High st E15
33 N 13	High st E17
12 C 20	High st Edg
9 P 7	High st Enf
101 N 15	High st Hampt
41 T 4	High st Harrow
23 T 7	High st Harrow
82 L 8	High st Hounsl
116 E 2	High st Kingst
116 G 5	High st Kingst
16 K 7	High st N14
30 C 13	High st N8
118 C 9	High st New Mald
62 F 6	High st NW10
13 X 15	High st NW7
22 B 11	High st Pinn
39 O 16	High st Rom
70 G 2	High st S'hall
110 D 17	High st SE20
113 V 8	High st SE25
115 O 10	High st Sutton
154 B 9	High st Sutton
153 T 14	High st Sutton
105 O 13	High st SW19
87 U 7	High st W6
101 X 13	High st Tedd
122 M 8	High st Thntn Hth
123 O 8	High st Thntn Hth
82 M 18	High st Twick
183 W 18	High st Twick
73 U 3	High st W3
60 G 20	High st W5
42 M 13	High st Wemb
43 N 13	High st Wemb
53 P 14	High street north E12
66 E 2	High street north E6
66 F 5	High street south E6
112 G 19	High Tor clo Brom
59 S 20	High Tree ct W7
5 X 16	High trees Barnt
124 J 19	High trees Croy
108 A 19	High trees SW2
90 F 19	High trees SW2
105 P 1	High trees SW2
123 T 3	High View clo SE19
57 S 11	High View gdns N3
34 A 9	High View rd E18
109 P 16	High View rd SE19
115 R 9	High View rd Sidcp
40 E 3	High worple Harrow
32 J 10	Higham Hill rd E17
32 H 9	Higham pl E17
31 O 9	Higham rd N17
21 S 20	Higham rd Wdfd Grn
32 J 10	Higham st E17
20 C 19	Higham Station av E4
20 F 18	Highams pk E4
21 N 16	Highams pk E4
80 B 20	Highbanks clo Welling
123 W 19	Highbarrow rd Croy
66 M 4	Highbridge rd Bark
76 K 14	Highbridge SE10
94 M 7	Highbrook rd SE3
95 N 7	Highbrook rd SE3
122 H 3	Highbury av Thntn Hth
159 S 3	Highbury clo W Wkhm
117 W 10	Highbury clo New Mald
48 H 17	Highbury cres N5
54 G 6	Highbury gdns Ilf
48 K 13	Highbury grange N5
48 K 16	Highbury gro N5
48 G 11	Highbury hill N5
48 G 17	Highbury ms N5
48 M16	Highbury New pk N5
48 K 11	Highbury pk N5
48 H 17	Highbury pl N5
48 K 10	Highbury quadrant N5
105 T 12	Highbury rd SW19
48 G 19	Highbury Station rd N1
48 H 15	Highbury Ter ms N5
48 J 15	Highbury ter N5
117 Y 7	Highclere rd New Mald
110 H 10	Highclere st SE26
86 E 16	Highcliffe dri SW15
35 R 16	Highcliffe gdns Ilf
113 P 2	Highcombe clo SE9
77 W 16	Highcombe SE7
61 O 1	Highcroft av Wemb
27 V 18	Highcroft rd NW1
25 Z 15	Highcroft NW9
48 A 2	Highcroft rd N19
122 B 8	Highdaun dri Mitch
86 J 15	Highdown rd SW15
152 C 2	Highdown Worc Pk
81 W 17	Highfield av Erith
41 U 15	Highfield av Grnfd
27 S 19	Highfield av NW11
25 W 15	Highfield av NW11
22 O 16	Highfield av Pinn
42 L 8	Highfield av Wemb
25 W 15	Highfield clo NW9
116 E 20	Highfield clo Surb
159 T 4	Highfield dri W Wkhm
126 A 8	Highfield dri Brom
152 D 14	Highfield dri Epsom
27 S 19	Highfield gdns NW11
109 P 19	Highfield hill SE19
35 R 3	Highfield rd Wdfd Grn
127 T 10	Highfield rd Brom
98 C 14	Highfield rd Bxly Hth
83 U 1	Highfield rd Islwth
17 W 7	Highfield rd N21
27 T 18	Highfield rd NW11
117 U 17	Highfield rd Surb
154 J 10	Highfield rd Sutton
61 U 13	Highfield rd W3
29 S 20	Highgate av N6
47 O 2	Highgate clo N6
47 R 3	Highgate High st N6
47 U 5	Highgate hill N19

47 S 13 Highgate rd NW5
47 O 6 Highgate West hill N6
47 O 7 Highgate West hill N6
55 S 14 Highgrove rd Dgnhm
56 K 9 Highland av Dgnhm
59 T 16 Highland av W7
155 T 9 Highland cotts Wallgtn
111 R 13 Highland croft Becknhm
26 B 1 Highland rd Brom
112 B 19 Highland rd Brom
98 E 12 Highland rd Bxly Hth
109 R 15 Highland rd SE19
61 V 20 Highlands av W3
82 K 3 Highlands clo Hounsl
53 T 2 Highlands gdns Ilf
86 L 20 Highlands heath SW15
4 M 16 Highlands rd Barnt
25 T 6 Highlands the Edg
26 B 3 Highlea clo NW9
136 C 1 Highlever rd W10
42 M 20 Highmead cres Wemb
79 X 20 Highmead SE18
77 N 18 Highmore rd SE3
91 W 3 Highshore rd SE15
18 L 11 Highstone av E11
156 C 11 Highview av Wallgtn
12 G 14 Highview gdns Edg
16 H 17 Highview gdns N11
12 M 11 Highview NW7
59 Z 16 Highview rd W13
63 S 20 Highway the E1
143 W 10 Highway the E1
23 X 1 Highway the Stanm
154 D 20 Highway the Sutton
31 T 16 Highweek rd N15
15 R 13 Highwood av N12
35 U 14 Highwood gdns Ilf
12 M 15 Highwood gro NW7
13 S 10 Highwood hill NW7
13 R 9 Highwood ho NW7
47 Z 10 Highwood rd N19
16 L 17 Highworth rd N11
121 N 5 Hilary av Mitch
98 H 2 Hilary clo Bxly Hth
145 X 18 Hilary clo SW6
62 D 20 Hilary rd W12
153 P 6 Hilbert rd E16
65 N 12 Hilda rd E16
66 A 1 Hilda rd E6
112 B 14 Hildenborough gdns Brom
125 Y 3 Hildenlea pl BR2
107 R 1 Hildreth st SW12
145 U 14 Hildyard rd SW6
128 B 11 Hiley rd NW10
62 L 8 Hiley rd NW10
130 O 2 Hilgrove rd NW6
24 E 8 Hiliary gdns Stanm
127 P 1 Hill brow Brom
113 O 20 Hill brow Chisl
99 U 17 Hill brow Drtfrd
113 Y 12 Hill clo Chisl
41 T 11 Hill clo Harrow
27 Z 18 Hill clo NW11
44 J 10 Hill clo NW2
11 N 13 Hill clo Stanm
23 Y 16 Hill cres Harrow
15 N 7 Hill cres N20
117 O 10 Hill cres Surb
153 N 3 Hill cres Worc Pk
27 S 11 Hill Crest gdns N3
97 O 19 Hill crest Sidcp
40 H 15 Hill ct Grnfd
43 U 4 Hill dri NW9
136 E 1 Hill Farm rd W10
128 E 20 Hill Farm rd W10
39 P 9 Hill gro Rom
23 W 1 Hill House av Stanm
17 T 2 Hill House clo N3
108 D 13 Hill House rd SW16
108 D 13 Hill pth SW16
154 K 14 Hill rd Carsh
23 Y 16 Hill rd Harrow
107 T 19 Hill rd Mitch
29 N 6 Hill rd N10
130 D 10 Hill rd NW8
22 A 17 Hill rd Pinn
154 A 11 Hill rd Sutton
42 A 8 Hill rd Wemb
9 N 20 Hill ri Enf
59 O 2 Hill ri Grnfd
19 N 1 Hill ri N9
28 B 14 Hill ri NW11
84 H 14 Hill ri Rich

110 A 2 Hill ri SE23
84 H 14 Hill st Rich
139 V 12 Hill st W1
28 B 13 Hill top NW11
119 T 18 Hill top Sutton
35 T 18 Hill View cres Ilf
96 G 4 Hill View dri Welling
25 Y 15 Hill View gdns NW9
14 B 14 Hill View rd NW7
22 D 1 Hill View rd Pinn
83 Y 16 Hill View rd Twick
70 H 7 Hillary rd S'hall
70 H 8 Hillary rd S'hall
75 O 18 Hillbeck cl SE15
151 Z 16 Hillbeck clo SE15
59 P 3 Hillbeck way Grnfd
106 C 19 Hillborough clo SW19
135 O 3 Hillborough ct E8
107 O 9 Hillbrook rd SW17
118 E 7 Hillbrow New Mald
111 Z 16 Hillbrow rd Brom
24 C 16 Hillbury av Harrow
107 T 6 Hillbury rd SW17
108 E 18 Hillcote av SW16
15 N 18 Hillcourt av N12
91 Z 17 Hillcourt rd SE22
12 E 14 Hillcrest av Edg
27 U 14 Hillcrest av NW11
124 K 13 Hillcrest clo Becknhm
109 X 11 Hillcrest clo SE26
44 F 10 Hillcrest gdns NW2
17 U 2 Hillcrest N21
29 P 20 Hillcrest N6
112 C 11 Hillcrest rd Brom
99 S 18 Hillcrest rd Drtfrd
33 Y 7 Hillcrest rd E17
34 D 7 Hillcrest rd E18
57 V 1 Hillcrest rd Hornch
39 Y 20 Hillcrest rd Hornch
73 R 3 Hillcrest rd W3
60 L 13 Hillcrest rd W5
124 K 14 Hillcrest view Becknhm
22 E 20 Hillcroft av Pinn
60 H 16 Hillcroft cres W5
42 M 12 Hillcroft cres Wemb
43 N 12 Hillcroft cres Wemb
66 L 14 Hillcroft rd E6
154 G 13 Hillcroome rd Sutton
119 S 11 Hillcross av Mrdn
153 V 9 Hilldale rd Sutton
126 B 19 Hilldown rd Brom
108 B 17 Hilldown rd SW16
47 Y 15 Hilldrop cres N7
47 Y 15 Hilldrop la N7
112 G 15 Hilldrop rd Brom
47 Z 14 Hilldrop rd N7
95 Y 3 Hillend SE18
12 A 16 Hillerdon av Edg
86 F 4 Hillersdon av SW13
150 F 6 Hillery clo SE17
120 H 13 Hillfield av Mrdn
30 B 13 Hillfield av N8
26 B 15 Hillfield av NW9
42 M 20 Hillfield clo Harrow
23 N 13 Hillfield clo Harrow
46 J 16 Hillfield ct NW3
29 S 12 Hillfield Park ms N10
29 S 12 Hillfield pk N10
17 S 9 Hillfield pk N21
100 D 10 Hillfield rd Hampt
45 X 14 Hillfield rd NW6
38 K 5 Hillfoot av Rom
38 J 5 Hillfoot rd Rom
137 T 13 Hillgate pl W8
137 T 13 Hillgate st W8
75 O 2 Hilliards ct E1
143 Z 13 Hilliards ct E1
5 N 20 Hillier clo Barnt
156 G 11 Hillier gdns Croy
89 N 16 Hillier rd SW11
155 Z 6 Hilliers la Wallgtn
98 L 8 Hillingdon rd Bxly Hth
150 A 14 Hillingdon st SE17
149 X 16 Hillingdon st SE5
35 O 7 Hillington gdns Wdfd Grn
50 A 18 Hillman st E8
48 A 14 Hillmarton rd N7
90 H 10 Hillmead dri SW9
110 G 12 Hillmore gro SE26
78 E 13 Hillreach SE18
140 B 6 Hills pl W1
21 V 6 Hills rd Buck Hl
91 S 13 Hillsboro rd SE22
15 Z 18 Hillside av N11

21 X 18 Hillside av Wdfd Grn
21 Z 18 Hillside av Wdfd Grn
42 L 12 Hillside av Wemb
5 S 17 Hillside Barnt
119 S 8 Hillside clo Mrdn
129 Y 9 Hillside clo NW6
21 Y 17 Hillside clo Wdfd Grn
8 B 2 Hillside cres Enf
40 M 5 Hillside cres Harrow
12 B 18 Hillside dri Edg
31 U 20 Hillside est N15
4 E 14 Hillside gdns Barnt
33 X 9 Hillside gdns E17
12 A 14 Hillside gdns Edg
42 K 1 Hillside gdns Harrow
42 K 1 Hillside gdns N11
155 V 17 Hillside gdns Wallgtn
16 K 3 Hillside gro N14
26 F 1 Hillside gro NW7
61 W 2 Hillside NW10
25 X 14 Hillside NW9
156 J 8 Hillside rd Croy
99 V 15 Hillside rd Drtfrd
31 T 19 Hillside rd N15
58 G 11 Hillside rd S'hall
117 O 10 Hillside rd Surb
153 V 16 Hillside rd Sutton
108 F 3 Hillside rd SW2
60 J 15 Hillside rd W5
105 P 16 Hillside SW19
137 N 18 Hillsleigh rd W8
50 E 8 Hillstowe st E5
26 J 6 Hilltop gdns NW4
45 Y 19 Hilltop rd NW6
10 L 11 Hilltop way Stanm
24 J 16 Hillview av Harrow
22 H 11 Hillview gdns Harrow
27 P 12 Hillview gdns NW4
113 X 11 Hillview rd Chisl
154 E 4 Hillview rd Sutton
104 J 19 Hillview SW20
47 P 7 Hillway N6
44 A 2 Hillway NW9
90 F 19 Hillworth rd SW2
93 N 9 Hilly Fields cres SE4
7 X 1 Hilly Fields pk Enf
90 E 3 Hillyard st SW9
32 G 8 Hillyfield E17
50 C 11 Hilsea st E5
15 U 18 Hilton av N12
91 S 11 Hilversum cres SE22
106 K 14 Himley rd SW17
156 C 14 Hinchcliffe clo Croy
91 W 9 Hinckley rd SE15
81 Z 18 Hind cres Erith
141 U 5 Hind ct EC4
64 B 17 Hind gro E14
139 V 4 Hinde ms W1
139 U 4 Hinde st W1
23 R 17 Hindes rd Harrow
49 S 3 Hindhead clo N16
58 B 3 Hindhead gdns Nthlt
156 A 10 Hindhead way Croy
91 X 13 Hindmans rd SE22
69 P 10 Hindmans way Dgnhm
143 U 8 Hindmarsh clo E1
50 A 14 Hindrey rd E5
110 D 3 Hindsley pl SE23
156 B 17 Hinkler clo Croy
24 G 11 Hinkler rd Harrow
80 H 7 Hinksey pth SE2
79 P 18 Hinstock rd SE18
82 A 10 Hinton av Hounsl
113 R 2 Hinton clo SE9
18 D 14 Hinton rd N18
90 K 9 Hinton rd SE24
55 V 14 Hinton rd Wallgtn
136 L 11 Hippodrome ms W11
136 L 11 Hippodrome pl W11
77 W 3 Hiroshima wlk SE7
50 K 3 Hitcham rd E17
63 W 6 Hitchin sq E3
93 V 14 Hither Green la SE13
55 Y 7 Hitherfield rd Dgnhm
108 E 5 Hitherfield rd SW16
23 O 4 Hitherwell dri Harrow
109 U 10 Hitherwood dri SE19
10 D 8 Hive clo Bushey
10 E 9 Hive rd Bushey
107 X 5 Hoadly rd SW16
15 W 8 Hobart clo N20
123 N 6 Hobart gdns Thntn Hth
84 M 18 Hobart pl Rich
147 W 2 Hobart pl SW1
55 X 12 Hobart rd Dgnhm

36 C 8 Hobart rd Ilf
152 J 5 Hobart rd Worc Pk
59 R 16 Hobbayne rd W7
66 J 14 Hobbes wlk SW15
28 E 10 Hobbs grn N2
109 N 11 Hobbs rd SE27
64 C 16 Hobday st E14
114 H 15 Hoblands end Chisl
135 R 20 Hobsons pl E1
146 D 15 Hobury st SW10
135 N 14 Hocker st E2
75 X 10 Hockett clo SE8
66 D 6 Hockley av E6
45 U 10 Hocroft av NW2
59 W 6 Hodder dri Grnfd
81 S 14 Hoddesdon rd Blvdr
45 W 3 Hodford rd NW11
68 K 20 Hodgkin clo SE28
75 R 10 Hodnet gro SE16
40 E 9 Hodson clo Nthlt
8 L 4 Hoe la Enf
9 P 3 Hoe la Enf
33 O 12 Hoe st E17
144 V 17 Hofland rd W14
38 B 2 Hog Hill rd Rom
138 E 1 Hogan ms W2
49 X 6 Hogan way E5
66 A 14 Hogarth clo E16
60 L 14 Hogarth clo W5
122 M 17 Hogarth cres Croy
120 F 1 Hogarth cres SW19
147 X 7 Hogarth ct EC3
70 H 20 Hogarth gdns Hounsl
27 W 13 Hogarth hill NW11
74 A 16 Hogarth la W4
25 O 6 Hogarth rd Edg
145 W 7 Hogarth rd SW6
18 E 8 Hoggin rd N9
96 J 16 Holbeach gdns Sidcp
93 R 18 Holbeach rd SE6
151 U 19 Holbeck row SE15
147 S 8 Holbein ms SW1
147 S 9 Holbein pl SW1
62 J 8 Holberton gdns NW10
141 S 2 Holborn bldgs EC4
141 T 2 Holborn EC1
65 V 13 Holborn rd E13
141 U 3 Holborn viaduct EC1
8 J 4 Holbrook clo Enf
47 T 5 Holbrook clo N19
114 G 19 Holbrook la Chisl
65 O 5 Holbrook rd E15
127 U 13 Holbrook way Brom
48 A 11 Holbrooke ct N7
84 H 14 Holbrooke pla Rich
94 K 3 Holburne clo SE3
94 M 3 Holburne rd SE3
94 K 4 Holburne rd SE3
94 L 3 Holburne rd SE3
95 P 3 Holburne rd SE3
13 T 11 Holcombe dale NW7
13 T 11 Holcombe hill NW7
53 W 2 Holcombe rd Ilf
31 W 9 Holcombe rd N17
74 K 12 Holcombe st W6
80 M 10 Holcote clo Blvdr
63 R 1 Holcroft rd E9
15 N 15 Holden av N12
43 W 4 Holden av NW9
15 N 13 Holden rd N12
89 O 6 Holden st SW11
92 J 13 Holdenby rd SE4
20 C 2 Holdenhurst av N12
107 N 5 Holderness rd SW17
108 K 13 Holderness way SE27
27 P 9 Holders Hill av NW4
27 S 3 Holders Hill circus NW7
27 P 8 Holders Hill crs NW4
27 R 9 Holders Hill dri NW4
27 R 8 Holders Hill gdns NW4
27 S 4 Holders Hill rd NW7
133 P 12 Holford pl WC1
46 E 9 Holford rd NW3
133 R 11 Holford st WC1
88 F 8 Holgate av SW11
56 D 17 Holgate gdns Dgnhm
56 D 16 Holgate rd Dgnhm
153 X 19 Holland av Sutton
104 E 20 Holland av SW20
15 T 1 Holland clo Barnt
10 M 16 Holland clo Stanm
144 L 1 Holland gdns W14
149 V 19 Holland gro SW9
145 O 2 Holland ms W14

36 J 18	Holland Pk av Ilf
136 J 16	Holland Pk av W11
137 O 14	Holland Pk av W11
136 L 16	Holland Pk gdns W14
137 N 15	Holland Pk ms W11
145 P 2	Holland Pk rd W14
136 M 15	Holland pk W11
137 N 15	Holland pk W11
137 P 17	Holland pl W8
37 W 17	Holland pl W8
65 N 8	Holland rd E15
66 J 2	Holland rd E6
30 A 14	Holland rd N8
62 H 5	Holland rd NW10
123 Y 10	Holland rd SE25
136 K 19	Holland rd W14
145 N 2	Holland rd W14
42 F 19	Holland rd Wemb
137 U 18	Holland st W8
136 L 19	Holland Vlls rd W14
47 X 5	Holland wlk N19
10 M 16	Holland wlk Stanm
137 R 16	Holland wlk W8
152 D 1	Hollands the Worc Pk
118 E 20	Hollands the Worc Pk
49 U 9	Hollar rd N16
140 D 5	Holles st W1
139 Y 5	Holles st W1
15 Y 19	Hollickwood av N12
56 G 20	Hollidge way Dgnhm
114 J 2	Hollies av Sidcp
100 H 13	Hollies clo Hampt
101 V 3	Hollies clo Twick
13 X 15	Hollies end NW7
72 D 11	Hollies rd W5
16 T 6	Hollies the N20
114 L 1	Hollies the Sidcp
89 P 17	Hollies way SW12
112 F 20	Holligrave rd Brom
98 B 1	Hollingbourne av Bxly Hth
60 A 15	Hollingbourne gdns W13
90 L 14	Hollingbourne rd SE24
158 A 14	Hollingsworth rd Croy
48 E 17	Hollingsworth st N7
118 E 15	Hollington cres New Mald
66 F 9	Hollington rd E6
31 X 6	Hollington rd N17
127 Z 16	Hollingworth rd Brom
108 H 16	Hollman gdns SW16
21 R 13	Hollow the Wdfd Grn
51 Y 9	Holloway rd E11
66 H 9	Holloway rd E6
47 X 7	Holloway rd N19
48 C 13	Holloway Rd N7
82 L 7	Holloway st Hounsl
40 A 19	Hollowfield wlk Nthlt
73 N 15	Hollows the Brentf
24 K 9	Holly av Stanm
114 D 19	Holly Brake clo Chisl
46 D 11	Holly Bush hill NW3
100 G 18	Holly Bush la Hampt
46 D 12	Holly Bush vale NW3
100 B 12	Holly clo Felt
44 A 20	Holly clo NW10
33 X 1	Holly cres Becknhm
20 E 2	Holly dri E4
43 W 1	Holly gro NE9
91 W 4	Holly gro SE15
7 P 19	Holly hill N21
46 D 12	Holly hill NW3
81 X 13	Holly Hill rd Blvdr
44 A 19	Holly la NW10
47 O 5	Holly Lodge gdns N6
47 P 5	Holly Lodge gdns N6
146 D 11	Holly ms SW7
27 X 10	Holly Park gdns N3
16 B 15	Holly Park rd N11
71 V 1	Holly Park rd W7
27 W 10	Holly pk N3
48 B 2	Holly pk N4
34 D 20	Holly pl E11
100 M 14	Holly rd Hampt
82 L 9	Holly rd Hounsl
101 X 1	Holly rd Twick
135 O 1	Holly st E8
15 R 9	Holly ter N20
121 X 7	Holly way Mitch
8 A 11	Holly wlk Enf
46 D 12	Holly wlk NW3
100 G 13	Hollybank clo Hampt
34 D 16	Hollybush clo E11
23 U 3	Hollybush clo Harrow
63 N 8	Hollybush gdns E2
135 Y 12	Hollybush gdns E2
34 D 16	Hollybush hill E11
63 N 8	Hollybush pl E2
135 Y 12	Hollybush pl E2
102 L 13	Hollybush rd Kingst
65 W 8	Hollybush st E13
45 Y 10	Hollycroft av NW3
42 M 8	Hollycroft av Wemb
92 B 4	Hollydale rd SE15
51 X 9	Hollydown way E11
70 A 13	Hollyfarm rd S'hall
15 Z 18	Hollyfield av N11
116 M 19	Hollyfield rd Surb
117 N 17	Hollyfield rd Surb
10 D 3	Hollygrove Bushey
93 V 12	Hollyhouse ter SE13
154 L 7	Hollymead Carsh
93 U 2	Hollymount clo SE10
96 L 18	Hollyoak Wood pk Sidcp
105 P 1	Hollytree clo SW19
146 B 13	Hollywood ms SW10
19 W 16	Hollywood rd E4
146 B 13	Hollywood rd SW10
33 X 1	Hollywood Way Wdfd Grn
94 F 6	Holm wlk SE3
152 F 19	Holman ct Epsom
88 F 5	Holman rd SW11
9 T 14	Holmbridge gdns Enf
27 R 14	Holmbrook dri NW4
158 L 18	Holmbury gro Croy
50 A 3	Holmbury view E5
87 S 16	Holmbush rd SW15
48 L 16	Holmcote gdns N5
127 U 13	Holmcroft way Brom
27 R 15	Holmdale gdns NW4
114 B 13	Holmdale rd Chisl
45 Y 15	Holmdale rd NW6
31 T 19	Holmdale ter N15
22 J 11	Holmdene av Harrow
13 U 19	Holmdene av NW7
90 M 13	Holmdene av SE24
91 N 14	Holmdene av SE24
125 T 4	Holmdene clo Becknhm
94 C 16	Holme Lacey rd SE12
66 E 3	Holme rd E6
10 J 19	Holme way Stanm
145 Z 19	Holmead rd SW6
10 E 8	Holmebury clo Bushey
32 K 10	Holmes av E17
14 E 17	Holmes av NW7
146 C 13	Holmes av SW10
47 T 16	Holmes rd NW5
106 E 18	Holmes rd SW19
101 W 4	Holmes rd Twick
141 T 17	Holmes ter SE1
10 E 8	Holmesbury clo Bushey
85 U 9	Holmesdale av SW14
123 U 7	Holmesdale clo SE26
34 E 16	Holmesdale ct E18
97 W 4	Holmesdale rd Bxly Hth
17 N 6	Holmesdale rd Brom
29 T 20	Holmesdale rd N6
85 N 2	Holmesdale rd Rich
123 U 7	Holmesdale rd SE25
102 D 16	Holmesdale rd Tedd
92 H 15	Holmesley rd SE23
90 C 19	Holmewood gdns SW2
123 S 7	Holmewood rd SE25
90 B 20	Holmewood rd SW2
27 P 15	Holmfield av NW4
81 V 13	Holmhurst rd Blvdr
49 T 3	Holmleigh rd N16
135 S 8	Holms st E2
99 R 7	Holmsdale gro Bxly Hth
110 J 9	Holmshaw clo SE26
89 P 16	Holmside rd SW12
118 C 16	Holmsley clo New Mald
25 V 8	Holmstall av Edg
40 K 18	Holmwood clo Nthlt
22 M 9	Holmwood clo Harrow
153 P 18	Holmwood clo Sutton
155 R 14	Holmwood gdns Wallgtn
27 Y 8	Holmwood gdns N3
12 L 17	Holmwood gro NW7
54 H 8	Holmwood rd Ilf
153 N 19	Holmwood rd Sutton
119 W 15	Holne cha Mrdn
28 E 18	Holne chase N2
52 B 19	Holness rd E15
86 M 12	Holroyd rd SW15
80 K 8	Holstein way Blvdr
54 A 8	Holstock rd Ilf
22 M 15	Holsworth clo Harrow
133 R 18	Holsworthy sq WC1
29 O 14	Holt clo N10
68 F 20	Holt clo SE28
51 S 14	Holt ct E15
78 D 3	Holt rd E16
42 C 9	Holt rd Wemb
155 U 7	Holt the Wallgtn
63 S 11	Holton st E1
7 Z 7	Holtwhites av Enf
7 V 6	Holtwhites hill Enf
22 A 14	Holwell pl Pinn
89 X 11	Holwood pl SW4
126 G 4	Holwood rd Brom
86 G 19	Holybourne av SW15
64 C 10	Holyhead clo E3
149 W 6	Holyoak rd SE11
28 C 12	Holyoake wlk N2
60 E 11	Holyoake wlk W5
144 E 18	Holyport rd SW6
40 C 13	Holyrood av Harrow
25 T 8	Holyrood gdns Edg
5 T 20	Holyrood rd Barnt
142 J 16	Holyrood st SE1
134 L 17	Holywell la EC2
134 J 18	Holywell row EC2
154 L 3	Home clo Carsh
58 E 8	Home clo Nthlt
56 K 10	Home gdns Dgnhm
24 F 3	Home mead Stanm
105 V 9	Home Park rd SW19
24 F 3	Home Park wlk Kingst
88 J 4	Home st SW11
30 K 4	Homecroft rd SE26
110 D 12	Homecroft rd SE26
59 V 17	Homefarm rd W7
74 C 12	Homefield rd W4
36 G 17	Homefield av Ilf
43 X 19	Homefield clo NW10
120 E 2	Homefield gdns Mitch
28 G 11	Homefield gdns N2
126 K 1	Homefield rd Brom
12 L 20	Homefield rd Edg
105 R 14	Homefield rd SW19
42 A 12	Homefield rd Wemb
134 K 10	Homefield st N1
109 R 19	Homelands dri SE19
92 F 12	Homeleigh rd SE15
127 U 11	Homemead rd Brom
121 W 14	Homemead rd Croy
98 J 3	Homer ct Bxly Hth
124 F 15	Homer rd Croy
50 J 18	Homer rd E9
138 M 2	Homer row W1
138 M 2	Homer st W1
117 R 3	Homersham rd Kingst
50 E 15	Homerton gro E9
50 F 16	Homerton High st E9
50 M 14	Homerton rd E9
50 D 15	Homerton row E9
50 D 15	Homerton ter E9
126 M 6	Homesdale rd Brom
27 Y 14	Homesfield NW11
92 C 14	Homestall rd SE22
6 D 17	Homestead paddock N14
56 B 8	Homestead rd Dgnhm
145 P 19	Homestead rd SW6
100 D 14	Homewood clo Hampt
114 H 16	Homewood cres Chisl
114 G 17	Homewood cres Chisl
44 E 10	Homstead pk NW2
134 A 17	Honduras st EC1
160 C 6	Honey la EC2
45 Z 15	Honeybourne rd NW6
89 U 18	Honeybrook rd SW12
115 Z 14	Honeyden rd Sidcp
25 N 13	Honeypot clo NW9
25 O 15	Honeypot la NW9
24 J 6	Honeypot la Stanm
31 V 7	Honeysett rd N17
124 F 19	Honeysuckle gdns CR0
88 L 16	Honeywell rd SW11
83 Z 10	Honeywood rd Islwth
62 D 7	Honeywood rd NW10
154 M 9	Honeywood wlk Carsh
24 C 3	Honister clo Stanm
24 C 3	Honister gdns Stanm
24 C 4	Honister pl Stanm
129 P 7	Honiton rd NW6
39 N 18	Honiton rd Rom
96 K 4	Honiton rd Welling
93 T 18	Honley rd SE6
92 D 17	Honor Oak pk SE23
104 E 18	Honor Oak rd SE23
92 C 19	Honor Oak rd SE23
92 C 17	Honor Oak ri SE23
16 F 1	Hood av N14
6 F 20	Hood av N14
85 W 13	Hood av SW14
156 J 1	Hood clo Croy
104 E 18	Hood rd SW20
38 G 5	Hood wlk Rom
17 V 2	Hoodcote gdns N21
7 V 20	Hoodcote gdns N21
126 M 12	Hook Farm rd Brom
96 J 12	Hook la Welling
97 O 8	Hook la Welling
15 U 1	Hook the Barnt
12 J 20	Hook wlk Edg
32 F 11	Hookers rd E17
22 J 14	Hooking grn Harrow
56 L 9	Hooks Hall dri Dgnhm
45 W 1	Hoop la NW11
27 X 20	Hoop la NW11
65 T 18	Hooper rd E16
143 S 7	Hooper st E1
140 J 10	Hop gdns WC2
112 H 6	Hope clo SE12
21 Z 17	Hope clo Wdfd Grn
112 D 19	Hope pk Brom
88 E 9	Hope st SW11
143 U 5	Hope Walk gdns E1
77 V 17	Hopedale rd SE7
128 M 7	Hopefield av NW6
143 P 2	Hopetown st E1
143 R 2	Hopetown st E1
150 F 19	Hopewell st SE5
136 C 15	Hopgood st W12
74 M 4	Hopgood st W12
140 D 7	Hopwood rd
17 U 5	Hoppers rd N21
20 M 8	Hoppett rd E4
118 B 5	Hoppingwood av New Mald
118 G 14	Hopton gdns New Mald
108 A 12	Hopton rd SW16
107 Z 12	Hopton rd SW16
141 X 12	Hopton st SE1
150 G 13	Hopwood rd SE17
56 L 4	Horace av Rom
52 H 12	Horace rd E7
36 B 9	Horace rd Ilf
116 L 7	Horace rd Kingst
135 P 10	Horatio st E2
156 C 12	Horatius wy Croy
137 S 11	Horbury cres W11
137 R 11	Horbury ms W11
146 D 15	Horbury st SW10
87 T 2	Horder rd SW6
77 W 11	Horizon way SE7
98 D 13	Horley clo Bxly Hth
113 P 9	Horley rd SE9
129 P 19	Hormead rd W9
73 U 2	Horn la W3
61 V 18	Horn la W3
21 T 20	Horn la Wdfd Grn
94 G 13	Horn Park clo SE12
94 F 13	Horn Park la SE12
149 S 5	Hornbeam clo SE11
72 C 18	Hornbeam cres Brentf
21 N 10	Hornbeam gro E4
98 J 4	Hornbeam la Bxly Hth
127 X 16	Hornbeam way Brom
41 P 7	Hornbuckle clo Harrow
46 G 20	Hornby clo NW3
94 F 18	Horncastle clo SE12
94 F 18	Horncastle rd SE12
57 Y 3	Hornchurch rd Hrnch
86 H 20	Horndean clo SW15
38 L 4	Horndon clo Rom
38 K 4	Horndon grn Rom
38 L 5	Horndon rd Rom
86 M 5	Horne way SW15
78 A 19	Hornfair rd SE7
77 Z 17	Hornfair rd SE7
57 R 2	Hornford way Rom

110 A 1	Horniman dri SE23
92 B 20	Horniman dri SE23
110 A 1	Horniman museum SE23
113 S 9	Horning clo SE9
36 D 12	Horns rd Ilf
47 U 3	Hornsey la N6
47 U 1	Hornsey Lane gdns N6
30 E 11	Hornsey Park rd N8
48 B 7	Hornsey rd N19
47 Z 2	Hornsey ri N19
47 Z 1	Hornsey Rise gdns N19
48 D 14	Hornsey st N7
75 R 17	Hornshay st SE15
137 V 19	Hornton pl W8
137 V 17	Hornton st W8
156 B 16	Horsa clo Croy
81 W 19	Horsa rd Erith
94 K 19	Horsa st SE12
140 F 8	Horse & Dolphin yd W1
116 H 2	Horse fair Kingst
140 K 15	Horse Guards av SW1
140 H 15	Horse Guards par SW1
140 H 16	Horse Guards rd SW1
104 M 3	Horse ride SW19
142 C 12	Horse Shoe all SE1
154 B 3	Horse Shoe grn Sutton
7 Z 11	Horse Shoe la Enf
139 X 7	Horse Shoe yd W1
133 X 4	Horse yd N1
25 Y 2	Horsecroft rd Edg
76 F 16	Horseferry pl SE10
148 F 4	Horseferry rd SW1
48 F 15	Horsell rd N5
143 N 16	Horselydown la SE1
41 U 14	Horsenden av Grnfd
41 V 15	Horsenden cres Grnfd
41 U 17	Horsenden Lane north Grnfd
59 Y 2	Horsenden Lane north Grnfd
59 Z 7	Horsenden Lane south Grnfd
58 G 4	Horseshoe cres Nthlt
14 B 4	Horseshoe la N20
95 P 12	Horsfeld gdns SE9
95 P 12	Horsfeld rd SE9
90 C 13	Horsford rd SW2
15 Y 17	Horsham av N12
98 C 14	Horsham rd Bxly Hth
44 J 6	Horshoe clo NW2
159 U 17	Horsley dri Croy
112 H 20	Horsley rd Brom
20 G 8	Horsley rd E4
150 D 13	Horsley st SE17
58 B 16	Horsman st SE5
92 L 15	Horsmonden rd SE4
146 A 17	Hortensia rd SW10
73 X 14	Horticultural pl W4
45 T 12	Horton av NW2
49 Z 18	Horton rd E8
20 H 7	Hortus rd E4
70 D 6	Hortus rd S'hall
107 N 3	Hosack rd SW17
112 E 3	Hoser av SE12
141 X 2	Hosier la EC1
65 Z 17	Hoskins clo E16
76 L 14	Hoskins st SE10
82 J 19	Hospital Bridge rd Twick
100 K 2	Hospital Bridge rd Twick
83 V 13	Hospital la Islwth
82 G 9	Hospital rd Hounsl
86 M 8	Hotham rd SW15
87 O 9	Hotham rd SW15
106 D 18	Hotham rd SW19
64 L 3	Hotham st E15
75 R 8	Hothfield pl SE16
58 G 5	Hotspur rd Nthlt
149 S 9	Hotspur st SE11
84 L 12	Houblon rd Rich
78 K 9	Hough st SE18
100 C 15	Houghton clo Hampt
31 T 14	Houghton rd N15
141 O 6	Houghton st WC2
156 H 12	Houlder cres Croy
142 L 4	Houndsditch EC3
13 R 1	Houndsfield rd N9
17 R 1	Hounsden rd N21
100 B 4	Hounslow av Felt
82 L 13	Hounslow av Hounsl
82 L 13	Hounslow gdns Hounsl
82 B 5	Hounslow heath Hounsl
82 K 9	Hounslow High st Hounsl
82 M 16	Hounslow rd Twick
140 K 20	Houses of Parliament SW1
150 F 20	Housman way SE5
110 K 6	Houston rd SE23
32 L 17	Hove av E17
154 B 1	Hove gdns Sutton
75 O 20	Hove st SE15
151 Z 19	Hove st SE15
45 R 14	Hoveden rd NW2
68 F 19	Hoveton rd SE28
135 N 7	How's st E2
97 U 20	Howard av Bxly
100 M 17	Howard clo Hampt
16 B 9	Howard clo N11
45 S 11	Howard clo NW2
61 S 16	Howard clo W3
125 U 2	Howard ct Becknhm
67 S 4	Howard rd Bark
112 E 19	Howard rd Brom
33 P 10	Howard rd E17
66 G 6	Howard rd E6
53 Z 12	Howard rd Ilf
83 V 7	Howard rd Islwth
31 S 18	Howard rd N15
49 R 13	Howard rd N16
118 C 7	Howard rd New Mald
60 S 13	Howard rd NW2
58 L 17	Howard rd S'hall
110 C 20	Howard rd SE20
123 Y 12	Howard rd SE25
116 L 15	Howard rd Surb
116 A 17	Howard rd Surb
91 X 20	Howard way SE22
28 E 13	Howard wlk N2
125 V 4	Howards Crest clo BR3
86 L 12	Howards la SW15
87 N 11	Howards la SW15
65 T 9	Howards rd E13
51 S 15	Howarth ct E15
80 B 13	Howarth rd SE2
11 U 20	Howberry clo Edg
24 H 1	Howberry rd Edg
11 V 19	Howberry rd Edg
123 N 2	Howberry rd Thntn Hth
99 V 5	Howbury la Erith
92 C 7	Howbury rd SE15
14 L 20	Howcroft cres N3
27 Y 1	Howcroft la Grnfd
59 R 9	Howcroft la Grnfd
80 J 1	Howden clo SE2
123 T 4	Howden rd SE25
91 W 7	Howden st SE15
38 F 6	Howe clo Rom
37 V 16	Howell clo Rom
149 Y 6	Howell wlk SE11
85 X 8	Howgate rd SW14
148 C 2	Howick pl SW1
146 K 19	Howie st SW11
46 K 17	Howitt rd NW3
132 C 20	Howland Ms east W1
132 B 20	Howland st W1
75 W 6	Howland way SE16
91 N 15	Howletts rd SE24
130 D 20	Howley pl W2
156 K 5	Howley rd Croy
74 G 18	Howsman rd SE1
92 J 10	Howson rd SE4
84 J 16	Howson ter Rich
10 B 6	Howton pl Bushey Watf
134 J 13	Hoxton sq N1
134 J 7	Hoxton st N1
121 U 6	Hoylake gdns Mitch
62 A 18	Hoylake rd W3
151 V 17	Hoyland clo SE15
106 J 11	Hoyle rd SW17
108 M 8	Hubbard rd SE27
64 L 4	Hubbard st E15
90 B 8	Hubert gro SW9
66 A 8	Hubert rd E6
63 Z 14	Huddart st E3
47 V 10	Huddleston rd N7
52 C 12	Huddlestone rd E7
44 J 18	Huddlestone rd NW2
79 O 13	Hudson pl SE18
98 A 5	Hudson rd Bxly Hth
102 L 20	Hudson rd Kingstn
147 Z 5	Hudson's pl SW1
160 B 8	Huggin hill EC4
147 Y 7	Hugh ms SW1
148 F 5	Hugh pl SW1
147 Y 6	Hugh st SW1
51 Y 14	Hughan rd E15
24 B 14	Hughenden av Harrow
118 H 16	Hughenden rd Worc Pk
51 U 11	Hughendon ter E15
122 L 16	Hughes wlk Croy
57 U 19	Hugo gdns Rainhm
47 V 12	Hugo rd N19
88 A 7	Hugo rd SW6
88 D 13	Huguenot pl SW18
88 D 14	Huguenot pl SW18
91 Z 7	Huguenot sq SE15
75 U 4	Hull clo SE16
37 Y 18	Hull rd Rom
134 A 13	Hull st EC1
134 E 2	Hullbridge ms N1
54 F 18	Hulse av Bark
38 H 4	Hulse av Rom
154 A 20	Hulverston clo Sutton
44 K 7	Humber rd NW2
77 O 16	Humber rd SE3
65 Y 10	Humberstone rd E13
144 L 15	Humbolt rd W6
71 V 6	Humes av W7
35 U 5	Humphrey clo Ilf
151 N 9	Humphrey st SE1
56 A 12	Humphries clo Dgnhm
26 C 7	Hundred acre NW9
20 F 4	Hungerdown E4
141 N 13	Hungerford foot br SE1
48 A 15	Hungerford rd N7
47 Z 16	Hungerford rd N7
143 X 6	Hungerford st E1
143 Y 5	Hungerford st E1
55 Z 18	Hunsdon clo Dgnhm
75 S 18	Hunsdon rd SE14
63 R 8	Hunslett st E2
120 A 19	Hunt rd Mrdn
70 G 8	Hunt rd S'hall
136 G 12	Hunt st W11
91 X 20	Hunt way SE22
150 G 3	Hunter clo SE1
54 A 15	Hunter rd Ilf
53 Z 16	Hunter rd Ilf
104 M 20	Hunter rd SW20
105 N 20	Hunter rd SW20
123 N 6	Hunter rd Thntn Hth
132 K 16	Hunter st WC1
65 S 5	Hunter wlk E13
107 O 2	Hunters clo SW17
24 E 13	Hunters gro Harrow
56 F 13	Hunters Hall rd Dgnhm
56 E 12	Hunters sq Dgnhm
157 T 9	Hunters way Croy
7 T 5	Hunters way Croy
122 A 8	Huntingdon clo Mitch
152 L 6	Huntingdon gdns Worc Pk
28 K 10	Huntingdon rd N2
19 R 7	Huntingdon rd N9
65 P 19	Huntingdon rd E16
133 O 1	Huntingdon st N1
158 M 16	Huntingfield Croy
86 H 13	Huntingfield rd SW15
51 S 19	Huntings rd Dgnhm
132 D 18	Huntley st WC1
118 F 3	Huntley way SW20
14 M 19	Huntly dri N3
123 S 7	Huntly rd SE25
135 R 19	Hunton st E1
94 F 5	Hunts clo SE3
140 H 10	Hunts ct WC2
64 F 7	Hunts la E15
113 T 20	Hunts Mead clo Chisl
9 T 11	Hunts Mead Enf
109 S 5	Hunts Slip rd SE21
37 P 1	Huntsman rd Ilf
150 H 8	Huntsman st SE17
88 D 12	Huntsmoor rd Epsom
106 E 7	Huntspill st SW17
131 O 18	Huntsworth ms NW1
58 K 15	Hurley rd Grnfd
87 V 7	Hurlingham gdns SW6
87 X 8	Hurlingham house SW6
87 V 19	Hurlingham pk SW6
81 P 20	Hurlingham rd Bxly Hth
87 U 6	Hurlingham rd SW6
48 J 10	Hurlock st N5
123 R 11	Hurlstone rd SE25
107 P 6	Huron rd SW17
93 Z 6	Hurren clo SE3
65 N 2	Hurry clo E15
20 B 11	Hurst av E4
29 W 19	Hurst av N6
126 C 20	Hurst clo Brom
20 A 12	Hurst clo E4
40 E 16	Hurst clo Northolt
28 A 18	Hurst clo NW11
80 H 14	Hurst la SE2
80 H 15	Hurst Pl est SE2
98 D 20	Hurst rd Bxly
115 Y 2	Hurst rd Bxly
157 O 10	Hurst rd Croy
33 R 10	Hurst rd E17
98 K 1	Hurst rd Erith
81 Y 20	Hurst rd Erith
17 U 6	Hurst rd N21
4 L 12	Hurst ri Bart
115 Z 2	Hurst springs Bxly
90 J 15	Hurst st SE24
157 S 15	Hurst View rd S Croy
157 S 15	Hurst way S Croy
54 F 18	Hurstbourne gdns Bark
110 J 2	Hurstbourne rd SE23
153 Z 2	Hurstcourt rd Sutton
126 C 20	Hurstdene av Brom
31 T 20	Hurstdene gdns N15
126 E 11	Hurstfield Brom
35 V 5	Hurstleigh gdns Ilf
12 F 12	Hurstmead ct Edg
99 R 3	Hurstwood av Bxly
115 Z 1	Hurstwood av Bxly
34 J 12	Hurstwood av E18
127 U 7	Hurstwood dri Brom
27 V 13	Hurstwood rd NW11
46 J 20	Huson clo NW3
126 E 20	Husseywell cres Brom
76 A 6	Hutchings st E14
28 B 14	Hutchings wlk NW11
64 G 1	Hutchins clo E15
42 H 10	Hutchinson ter Wemb
41 P 13	Hutton clo Grnfd
21 V 13	Hutton clo Wdfd Grn
23 N 2	Hutton gdns Harrow
15 P 18	Hutton gro N12
22 N 2	Hutton la Harrow
141 V 7	Hutton st EC4
23 N 1	Hutton wlk Harrow
92 M 13	Huxbear st SE4
51 T 8	Huxley clo E10
58 C 5	Huxley clo Nthlt
55 P 1	Huxley dri Rom
61 N 7	Huxley gdns NW10
18 A 16	Huxley pde N18
17 W 12	Huxley rd N13
51 U 7	Huxley rd E10
18 B 13	Huxley rd N18
96 L 9	Huxley rd Welling
18 A 18	Huxley st N18
128 K 14	Huxley st W10
104 G 1	Hyacinth rd SW15
4 H 12	Hyde clo Barnt
26 B 17	Hyde cres E13
88 J 1	Hyde la SW11
18 A 6	Hyde Park av N21
17 Z 7	Hyde Park av N21
139 V 17	Hyde Park corner W1
138 K 6	Hyde Park cres W2
138 C 19	Hyde Park ga SW7
138 J 8	Hyde Park Gardens ms W2
138 C 20	Hyde Park Gate ms SW7
17 Z 6	Hyde Park gdns N21
138 J 9	Hyde Park gdns W2
138 K 7	Hyde Park sq W2
138 K 7	Hyde Park Square ms W2
138 K 7	Hyde Park st W2
138 K 12	Hyde Park W2
139 O 14	Hyde Park W2
98 C 5	Hyde rd Bxly Hth
134 G 5	Hyde rd N1
84 L 12	Hyde rd Rich
26 B 15	Hyde the NW9
25 V 11	Hyde the NW9
76 H 20	Hyde vale SE10
93 W 2	Hyde vale SE10
119 Z 17	Hyde wlk Mrdn
18 B 6	Hydefield clo N21
18 E 7	Hydefield ct N9
48 J 19	Hydes pl N1
18 G 9	Hydeside gdns N9
18 G 9	Hydethorpe av N9
107 U 1	Hydethorpe rd SW12
89 V 20	Hydethorpe rd SW12

18 G 9 Hydeway N9
57 Z 2 Hyland clo Hrnch
57 Y 3 Hyland way Hrnch
33 Y 8 Hylands rd E17
79 X 10 Hylton st SE18
110 E 7 Hyndewood SE23
151 W 14 Hyndman st SE15
55 U 7 Hynton rd Dgnhm
156 K 10 Hyrstdene S Croy
75 N 12 Hyson rd SE16
80 M 20 Hythe av Bxly Hth
81 N 20 Hythe av Bxly Hth
18 L 14 Hythe clo N18
123 O 5 Hythe path Thntn Hth
62 G 11 Hythe rd NW10
123 O 5 Hythe rd Thntn Hth
12 M 2 Hyver hill NW7

I

9 S 7 Ian sq Enf
65 P 16 Ibbotson av E16
63 R 10 Ibbott st E1
155 Y 8 Iberian av Wallgtn
85 V 3 Ibis la W14
56 K 19 Ibscott clo Dgnhm
104 F 1 Ibsley gdns SW15
86 F 20 Ibsley gdns SW15
5 Y 15 Ibsley way Barnt
64 B 3 Iceland rd E3
49 Z 9 Ickburgh rd E5
113 R 10 Ickleton rd SE9
36 A 16 Icknield dri Ilf
35 Z 16 Icknield dri Ilf
32 J 12 Ickworth rd E17
3 O 14 Ida rd N15
64 F 18 Ida st E14
126 A 6 Iden clo Brom
107 O 14 Iddecombe rd SW17
118 E 18 Idmiston rd
    Worc Pk
52 B 14 Idmiston rd E15
108 L 5 Idmiston rd SE27
118 E 18 Idmiston sq
    Worc Pk
142 J 10 Idol la EC3
75 Z 19 Idonia st SE8
144 A 5 Iffley rd W6
74 L 10 Iffley rd W6
146 A 15 Ifield rd SW10
145 Y 13 Ifield rd SW10
81 S 19 Ightham rd Erith
128 H 13 Ilbert st W10
137 X 9 Ilchester gdns W2
137 P 20 Ilchester pl W14
55 T 15 Ilchester rd Dgnhm
109 O 5 Ildersley gro SE21
75 P 17 Ilderton rd SE15
75 O 13 Ilderton rd SE16
151 Y 9 Ilderton rd SE16
44 C 18 Ilex rd NW10
108 F 12 Ilex way SW16
53 X 9 Ilford hill Ilf
54 A 15 Ilford la Ilf
53 Y 10 Ilford la Ilf
55 P 1 Ilfracombe gdns Rom
112 B 7 Ilfracombe rd Brom
149 Y 8 Iliffe st SE17
149 Z 8 Iliffe St yd SE17
65 X 16 Ilkley rd E16
120 G 6 Illingworth clo Mitch
8 E 16 Illingworth way Enf
24 F 18 Ilmington rd Harrow
88 K 10 Ilminster gdns SW11
16 J 1 Imber clo N14
134 E 6 Imber st N1
22 G 19 Imperial clo Harrow
40 F 2 Imperial dri Harrow
22 H 19 Imperial dri Harrow
146 E 2 Imperial Institute rd
    SW7
66 A 7 Imperial ms E6
30 A 4 Imperial rd N22
88 C 2 Imperial rd SW6
64 F 10 Imperial st E3
149 U 3 Imperial War
    Museum SE11
114 C 8 Imperial way Chisl
156 E 15 Imperial way Croy
24 L 19 Imperial way Harrow
95 Y 19 Inca dri SE9
111 S 3 Inchmery rd SE6
159 R 8 Inchwood Croy
94 B 6 Independents rd SE3

30 D 18 Inderwick rd N8
76 C 6 Indescon ct E14
143 N 7 India st EC3
77 W 14 India way W12
77 Z 20 Indus rd SE7
65 T 13 Ingal rd E13
89 T 2 Ingate pl SW8
52 K 5 Ingatestone rd E12
34 G 2 Ingatestone rd Wdfd
    Grn
123 Y 10 Ingatestone SE25
89 R 5 Ingelow rd SW8
9 R 4 Ingersoll rd Enf
74 J 3 Ingersoll rd W12
140 D 7 Ingestre pl W1
52 F 12 Ingestre rd E7
47 T 11 Ingestre rd NW5
158 E 19 Ingham clo S Croy
45 X 13 Ingham rd NW6
158 D 19 Ingham rd S Croy
22 C 11 Ingle clo Pinn
133 S 12 Inglebert st EC1
90 E 4 Ingleborough st SW9
56 G 19 Ingleby clo Dgnhm
41 R 8 Ingleby dri Harrow
56 G 19 Ingleby rd Dgnhm
53 Z 4 Ingleby rd Ilf
48 A 9 Ingleby rd N7
113 X 13 Ingleby way Chisl
155 X 18 Ingleby way Wallgtn
79 T 13 Ingledew rd SE18
143 Y 13 Inglefield sq E1
35 T 17 Inglehurst gdns Ilf
107 N 17 Inglemere rd Mitch
110 E 6 Inglemere rd SE23
111 N 18 Ingleside clo
    Becknhm
77 R 17 Ingleside gro SE3
87 O 1 Inglethorpe st SW6
97 O 12 Ingleton av Welling
154 H 18 Ingleton rd Carsh
18 J 19 Ingleton rd N18
15 V 19 Ingleway N12
114 D 15 Inglewood Chisl
127 T 3 Inglewood Copse
    Brom
158 J 19 Inglewood Croy
98 M 9 Inglewood rd Bxly
    Hth
45 Y 16 Inglewood rd NW6
123 V 19 Inglis rd Croy
60 M 19 Inglis rd W5
16 N 20 Inglis rd W5
90 K 3 Inglis st SE5
46 D 1 Ingram av NW11
11 R 17 Ingram clo Stanm
28 K 13 Ingram rd N2
122 L 1 Ingram rd Thntn Hth
108 L 20 Ingram rd Thntn Hth
59 R 4 Ingram way Grnfd
39 O 13 Ingrave rd Rom
88 H 7 Ingrave st SW11
74 A 13 Ingress rd W4
78 C 18 Inigo Jones rd SE7
140 K 9 Inigo pl WC2
47 S 17 Inkerman rd NW5
20 F 16 Inks grn E4
62 A 2 Inman rd NW10
88 C 20 Inman rd SW18
21 T 15 Inmans row Wdfd
    Grn
131 S 13 Inner crcl NW1
105 O 1 Inner Pk rd SW19
141 T 7 Inner Temple la EC4
86 K 16 Innes gdns SW15
65 Y 7 Inniskilling rd E13
51 P 7 Inskip clo E10
55 W 5 Inskip rd Dgnhm
49 Z 16 Institute pl E8
156 B 15 Instone clo Croy
133 S 13 Insurance st WC1
79 S 15 Inveraray pl SE18
37 V 14 Inverclyde gdns Rom
152 F 6 Inveresk gdns
    Worc Pk
46 C 7 Inverforth clo NW3
16 F 18 Inverforth rd N11
77 W 14 Inverine rd SE7
79 O 11 Invermore pl SE18
8 F 6 Inverness av Enf
137 W 15 Inverness gdns W8
137 Z 9 Inverness ms W2
137 Z 9 Inverness pl W2
82 F 10 Inverness rd Hounsl
18 M 15 Inverness rd N18
70 C 11 Inverness rd S'hall
119 O 20 Inverness rd Worc Pk
131 X 3 Inverness st NW1
137 Z 9 Inverness ter W2
92 E 11 Inverton rd SE15

113 W 12 Invicta clo Chisl
58 D 9 Invicta gro Nthlt
77 T 18 Invicta rd SE3
150 G 12 Inville rd SE17
82 M 8 Inwood av Hounsl
83 N 8 Inwood av Hounsl
158 J 2 Inwood clo Croy
82 M 8 Inwood rd Hounsl
88 J 4 Inworth st SW11
134 A 4 Inworth wlk N1
93 N 17 Iona clo SE6
31 T 16 Ipplepen rd N15
107 R 16 Ipswich rd SW17
141 Y 8 Ireland yd EC4
47 Y 3 Irene rd SW6
47 Y 8 Ireton rd N19
98 A 15 Iris av Bxly
97 Z 15 Iris av Bxly
124 E 19 Iris clo CR0
116 L 19 Iris clo Surb
81 O 17 Iris cres Bxly
19 Y 20 Iris way E4
8 H 5 Irkdale av Enf
99 X 10 Iron Mill la Drtfd
99 T 11 Iron Mill pl Drtfd
88 A 15 Iron Mill pl SW11
88 B 16 Iron Mill rd SW18
160 D 6 Ironmonger la EC2
134 C 15 Ironmonger row EC1
76 C 11 Ironmongers pl E14
38 K 2 Irons way Rom
24 A 10 Irvine av Harrow
23 Z 10 Irvine av Harrow
15 W 9 Irvine clo N20
58 A 2 Irving av Nthlt
90 B 5 Irving gr SW9
144 H 1 Irving rd W14
140 H 10 Irving st WC2
26 E 17 Irving way NW9
79 V 18 Irwin av SE18
128 A 6 Irwin gdns NW10
62 L 4 Irwin gdns NW10
90 E 2 Isabel st SW9
50 C 16 Isabella rd E9
141 V 15 Isabella st SE1
76 G 10 Isambard ms E14
39 R 2 Isbell gdns Rom
91 S 13 Isel way SE22
121 Z 3 Isham rd SW16
86 L 9 Isis clo SW15
106 C 4 Isis st SW18
79 O 17 Isla rd SE18
106 L 18 Island rd Mitch
63 X 19 Island row E14
48 E 10 Isledon rd N7
127 Y 1 Islehurst clo Chisl
133 W 5 Islington grn N1
133 V 1 Islington High st N1
48 G 20 Islington Pk st N1
12 K 20 Islip gdns Edg
40 C 20 Islip gdns Nthlt
40 C 20 Islip Manor rd Nthlt
47 V 16 Islip st NW5
52 H 20 Ismailia rd E7
65 X 10 Isom clo E13
24 B 8 Ivanhoe dri Harrow
23 Z 9 Ivanhoe dri Harrow
91 T 7 Ivanhoe rd SE5
145 R 11 Ivatt pl SW6
51 O 6 Ive Farm clo E10
61 P 5 Iveagh av NW10
63 U 2 Iveagh clo E9
61 P 6 Iveagh clo NW10
97 T 5 Ivedon rd Welling
89 U 6 Iveley rd SW4
135 U 13 Ivemey st E2
4 M 18 Ivere dri Barnt
5 N 19 Ivere dri Barnt
97 X 12 Iverhurst clo Bxly
    Hth
137 V 20 Iverna ct W8
145 V 1 Iverna gdns W8
159 S 16 Ivers way Croy
45 V 19 Iverson rd NW6
39 U 14 Ives gdns Rom
64 L 14 Ives rd E16
146 L 6 Ives st SW3
92 C 18 Ivestor ter SE23
8 D 7 Ivinghoe clo Enf
10 B 2 Ivinghoe rd Bushey
    Watf
55 P 15 Ivinghoe rd Dgnhm
113 Z 1 Ivor gro SE9
131 O 17 Ivor pl NW1
47 U 20 Ivor st NW1
24 B 20 Ivorydown Brom
83 X 17 Ivy Bridge clo Twick
40 D 12 Ivy clo Harrow
73 U 10 Ivy cres W4
121 X 7 Ivy gdns Mitch

30 A 19 Ivy gdns N8
82 D 10 Ivy la Hounsl
116 L 15 Ivy rd Surb
65 T 17 Ivy rd E16
33 P 19 Ivy rd E17
82 L 11 Ivy rd Hounsl
16 J 3 Ivy rd N14
44 M 12 Ivy rd NW2
45 N 12 Ivy rd NW2
92 L 11 Ivy rd SE4
93 O 12 Ivy rd SE4
134 J 8 Ivy st N1
55 Y 18 Ivy wlk Dgnhm
140 M 10 Ivybridge la WC2
110 B 18 Ivychurch clo SE20
155 N 2 Ivydale rd Carsh
92 F 9 Ivydale rd SE15
108 C 8 Ivyday gro SW16
154 D 8 Ivydene clo Sutton
135 V 12 Ivydene rd E8
56 B 18 Ivyhouse rd Dgnhm
55 Y 18 Ivyhouse rd Dgnhm
108 F 8 Ivymount rd SE27
146 K 9 Ixworth pl SW3
98 A 12 Izane rd Bxly Hth

J

30 D 8 Jack Barnett way
    N22
53 W 13 Jack Cornwell st E12
21 R 14 Jacklin grn Wdfd Grn
44 A 10 Jackmans ms NW10
135 V 5 Jackman st E8
67 T 4 Jackson rd Bark
5 V 20 Jackson rd Barnt
127 T 20 Jackson rd Brom
48 E 13 Jackson rd N7
78 J 16 Jackson st SE18
70 M 4 Jackson way S'hall
29 R 20 Jacksons la N6
123 P 20 Jacksons pl Croy
143 R 17 Jacob st SE1
139 U 3 Jacobs Well ms W1
58 C 3 Jacqueline clo
    Nthlt
55 T 4 Jade clo Dgnhm
66 B 18 Jade clo E16
108 K 10 Jaffray pl SE27
126 M 9 Jaffray rd Brom
88 M 20 Jaggard way SW12
79 P 16 Jago clo SE18
143 P 19 Jamaica rd SE1
75 N 7 Jamaica rd SE16
143 X 20 Jamaica rd SE16
122 H 13 Jamaica rd Thntn
    Hth
63 R 16 Jamaica st E1
56 C 5 James av Dgnhm
44 M 14 James av NW2
65 T 6 James clo E13
39 W 15 James clo Rom
30 K 2 James gdns N22
33 X 20 James la E11
31 U 3 James pl N17
99 V 17 James rd Drtfd
67 O 1 James st Bark
8 H 16 James st Enf
83 O 8 James st Hounsl
139 V 6 James st W1
140 K 8 James st WC2
137 U 13 Jameson st W8
131 X 2 Jamestown rd NW1
143 W 5 Jane st E1
76 B 7 Janet st E14
143 U 19 Janeway st SE16
51 Z 14 Janson clo E15
44 A 8 Janson clo NW10
52 A 14 Janson rd E15
51 Z 13 Janson rd E15
31 S 11 Jansons rd N15
48 C 3 Japan cres N4
37 W 20 Japan rd Rom
150 K 13 Jardin st SE5
108 H 1 Jarrett clo SW2
120 A 12 Jarrow clo Mrdn
31 Z 12 Jarrow rd N15
37 U 18 Jarrow rd Rom
50 K 13 Jarrow way E9
4 C 18 Jarvis clo Barnt
157 O 14 Jarvis rd S Croy
91 T 11 Jarvis rd SE22
159 P 6 Jasmine gdns Croy
40 H 7 Jasmine gdns Harrow
110 A 20 Jasmine gro SE20

139 V 4 Jason ct W1
113 W 9 Jason wlk SE9
9 P 4 Jasper clo Enf
66 C 18 Jasper rd E16
109 U 13 Jasper rd SE19
58 A 10 Javelin way Grnfd
138 D 19 Jay ms SW7
90 B 16 Jebb av SW2
64 C 7 Jebb st E3
65 X 8 Jedburgh rd E13
89 P 10 Jedburgh st SW8
74 D 5 Jeddo rd W12
36 A 16 Jefferson clo Ilf
72 B 9 Jefferson clo W13
64 F 9 Jefferson est E3
9 X 14 Jeffreys rd Enf
90 A 5 Jeffreys rd SW4
89 Z 4 Jeffreys rd SW4
47 T 20 Jeffreys st NW1
9 X 12 Jeffreys way Enf
89 Z 3 Jeffreys wlk SW4
153 W 9 Jeffs rd Sutton
94 L 11 Jeken rd SE9
90 F 12 Jelf rd SW2
10 K 18 Jellicoe gdns Stanm
31 O 3 Jellicoe rd N17
67 O 8 Jenkins la Bark
65 W 12 Jenkins rd E13
74 H 17 Jenner pl SW13
49 W 9 Jenner rd N16
156 F 4 Jennett rd Croy
112 D 6 Jennifer rd Brom
91 V 15 Jennings rd SE22
4 A 12 Jennings way Barnt
81 Y 3 Jenningtree way Blvdr
109 T 18 Jenson way SE19
97 Y 3 Jenton av Bxly Hth
52 L 19 Jephson rd E7
91 O 3 Jephson st SE5
87 X 16 Jephtha rd SW18
120 L 9 Jeppos la Mitch
145 U 18 Jerdan pl SW6
64 C 18 Jeremiah st E14
19 O 13 Jeremys grn N18
140 B 12 Jermyn st SW1
35 Y 7 Jerningham av Ilf
92 H 2 Jerningham rd SE14
130 J 15 Jerome cres NW8
135 N 19 Jerome st E1
93 S 7 Jerrard st SE13
24 C 9 Jersey av Stanm
51 W 5 Jersey rd E11
65 X 15 Jersey rd E16
82 L 1 Jersey rd Hounsl
70 L 20 Jersey rd Hounsl
53 Z 13 Jersey rd Ilf
71 P 18 Jersey rd Islwth
107 R 16 Jersey rd SW17
71 Y 7 Jersey rd W7
135 X 13 Jersey st E2
133 W 18 Jerusalem pass EC1
108 F 14 Jerviston gdns SW16
43 O 17 Jesmond av Wemb
123 U 17 Jesmond rd Croy
11 Y 15 Jesmond way Stanm
49 Z 4 Jessam av E5
71 V 3 Jessamine rd W7
51 T 5 Jesse rd E10
88 E 15 Jessica rd SW18
90 K 11 Jessop rd SE24
121 V 15 Jessops way Mitch
79 O 10 Jessup clo SE18
58 A 9 Jetstar way Nthlt
112 J 2 Jevington way SE12
33 N 10 Jewel rd E17
142 M 7 Jewry st EC3
88 B 10 Jews row SW18
110 A 10 Jews wlk SE26
44 L 16 Jeymer av NW2
58 M 4 Jeymer dri Grnfd
59 N 3 Jeymer dri Grnfd
88 D 17 Jeypore rd SW18
100 H 18 Jillian clo Hampt
95 O 19 Joan cres SE9
55 Y 6 Joan gdns Dgnhm
55 Y 6 Joan rd Dgnhm
141 V 15 Joan st SE1
58 C 3 Joave clo Grnfd
84 K 8 Jocelyn rd Rich
141 P 1 Jockeys fields WC1
63 Z 2 Jodrell rd E3
141 S 18 Johanna st SE1
140 L 11 John Adam st WC2
16 K 6 John Bradshaw rd N14
67 V 2 John Burns dri Bark
49 S 15 John Campbell rd N16

141 V 8 John Carpenter st EC4
143 S 19 John Felton rd SE16
143 R 10 John Fisher st E1
148 G 8 John Islip st SW1
97 S 8 John Newton ct Welling
56 G 20 John Parker clo Dgnhm
93 S 2 John Penn st SE13
139 Z 5 John Prince's st W1
143 Y 11 John Rennie wlk E1
151 U 1 John Roll way SE16
150 B 14 John Ruskin st SE5
149 Y 17 John Ruskin st SE5
48 K 18 John Spencer sq N1
65 O 4 John st E15
8 G 16 John st Enf
82 C 4 John st Hounsl
123 Y 9 John st SE25
133 P 19 John st WC1
78 J 11 John Wilson st SE18
93 Y 9 John Woolley clo SE13
26 L 13 Johns av NW4
120 D 12 Johns la Mrdn
133 O 18 Johns ms WC1
143 Y 4 Johns pl E1
123 P 20 Johns ter Croy
135 T 3 Johnson clo E8
127 N 12 Johnson rd Brom
123 N 17 Johnson rd Croy
63 P 19 Johnson st E1
154 M 4 Johnsons clo Carsh
141 U 6 Johnsons ct EC4
140 D 12 Johnsons al SW1
61 S 11 Johnsons Way NW10
21 S 18 Johnston rd Wdfd Grn
66 H 10 Johnstone rd E6
45 O 10 Johnstone ter NW2
142 G 14 Joiner st SE1
58 B 13 Jolly's la Hayes
41 P 4 Jollys la Harrow
149 O 8 Jonathan st SE11
65 W 13 Jones Avenue rd E13
65 W 13 Jones rd E13
139 X 10 Jones st W1
121 T 8 Jonson clo Mitch
151 W 11 Jordan clo Harrow
87 P 11 Jordan ct SW15
60 D 2 Jordan rd Grnfd
83 U 3 Jordans clo Islwth
89 U 16 Joseph Powell clo SW12
63 Y 13 Joseph st E3
90 D 14 Josephine av SW2
64 F 16 Joshua st E14
88 M 5 Joubert st SW11
151 P 19 Jowett st SE15
18 H 17 Joyce av N18
90 F 16 Joyce wlk SW2
37 P 18 Joydon dri Rom
20 G 18 Jubilee av E4
38 H 17 Jubilee av Rom
83 O 20 Jubilee av Twick
25 Y 18 Jubilee clo NW9
38 H 16 Jubilee clo Rom
76 G 9 Jubilee cres E14
18 K 4 Jubilee cres N9
40 A 12 Jubilee dri Ruisl
50 H 15 Jubilo gdns S'hall
18 L 3 Jubilee pk N9
146 M 10 Jubilee pl SW3
60 A 2 Jubilee rd Grnfd
153 P 15 Jubilee rd Sutton
63 P 17 Jubilee st E1
120 B 1 Jubilee way Mitch
115 N 5 Jubilee way Sidcp
132 J 14 Judd st WC1
65 P 18 Jude st E16
46 C 9 Judges wlk NW3
88 K 1 Juer st SW11
146 L 19 Juer st SW11
68 J 5 Julia gdns Bark
47 O 14 Julia st NW5
61 U 20 Julian av W3
4 M 12 Julian clo Barnt
41 T 8 Julian hill Harrow
76 E 12 Julian pl E14
72 D 10 Julien rd W5
93 T 7 Junction appr SE13
138 K 4 Junction ms W2
138 H 4 Junction pl W2
65 V 6 Junction rd E13
23 S 19 Junction rd Harrow
31 X 9 Junction rd N17
31 N 19 Junction rd N19
18 K 6 Junction rd N9

39 T 14 Junction rd Rom
157 O 12 Junction rd S Croy
72 F 11 Junction rd W5
55 X 1 Junction Road west SE26
55 Z 1 Junction Road east Rom
53 X 11 Juniper rd Ilf
63 P 19 Juniper st E1
75 T 16 Juno way SE14
48 D 18 Jupiter way N7
64 J 1 Jupp rd E15
64 H 2 Jupp Road west E15
146 J 15 Justice wlk SW3
72 H 19 Justin clo Brent
33 N 1 Justin rd E4
9 W 10 Jute la Enf
65 T 12 Jutland rd E13
93 T 19 Jutland rd SE6
38 G 19 Jutsums la Rom
22 L 5 Juxon clo Harrow
149 P 5 Juxon st SE11

K

80 K 6 Kale rd Blvdr
88 G 6 Kambala rd SW11
110 L 11 Kangley Bridge rd SE26
59 R 5 Karoline gdns Grnfd
79 X 12 Kashgar rd SE18
78 A 18 Kashmir rd SE7
88 M 2 Kassala rd SW11
156 M 4 Katharine st Croy
157 N 4 Katharine st Croy
36 C 1 Katherine gdns Ilf
95 N 12 Katherine gdns SE9
66 C 3 Katherine rd E6
52 L 16 Katherine rd E7
83 Z 20 Katherine rd Twick
61 W 13 Kathleen av W3
60 K 1 Kathleen av Wemb
42 K 20 Kathleen av Wemb
88 L 8 Kathleen rd SW11
90 B 6 Kay rd SW9
64 K 1 Kay st E15
135 T 9 Kay st E2
97 R 2 Kay st Welling
154 H 15 Kayemoor rd Sutton
45 P 14 Kayes rd NW2
141 N 6 Kean st WC2
108 X 11 Keary rd SW15
58 J 15 Keat's way Grnfd
39 Y 2 Keats av Rom
46 H 12 Keats gro NW3
81 W 8 Keats rd Blvdr
96 J 1 Keats rd Welling
124 C 15 Keats way Croy
41 O 16 Keble clo Nthlt
118 E 20 Keble clo Worc Pk
106 D 9 Keble st SW17
126 F 17 Kechill gdns Brom
112 B 11 Keedonwood rd Brom
111 Z 11 Keedonwood rd Brom
75 U 4 Keel clo SE16
156 L 3 Keeley rd Croy
141 N 5 Keeley st WC2
94 M 13 Keeling rd SE9
156 M 8 Keen's rd Croy
48 J 18 Keens yd N1
102 M 17 Keep the Kingst
94 E 6 Keep the SE3
151 V 1 Keeton's rd SE16
87 R 19 Keevil dri SW19
48 A 14 Keighley clo N7
114 D 2 Keightley dri SE9
88 L 11 Keildon rd SW11
49 Z 4 Keir Hardie est E5
68 A 1 Keir Hardie way Bark
74 G 4 Keith gro W12
67 T 5 Keith rd Bark
32 L 6 Keith rd E17
95 P 6 Kelbrook rd SE3
114 A 8 Kelby path SE9
44 H 5 Kelceda clo NW2
50 M 20 Kelday rd E9
136 E 4 Kelfield gdns W10
141 Y 20 Kell st SE1
65 T 11 Kelland rd E13
94 M 5 Kellaway rd SE3
95 N 3 Kellaway rd SE3
93 Y 13 Kellerton rd SE13

90 F 11 Kellett rd SW2
122 H 16 Kelling gdns Croy
106 L 9 Kellino st SW17
79 X 8 Kellner rd SE28
14 D 18 Kelly rd NW7
47 T 18 Kelly st NW1
37 Y 17 Kelly way Rom
89 Y 5 Kelman clo SW4
91 X 10 Kelmore gro SE22
74 G 7 Kelmscot gdns W12
32 K 6 Kelmscott clo E17
88 K 14 Kelmscott rd SW11
48 K 12 Kelross rd N5
94 H 4 Kelsall clo SE3
125 N 7 Kelsey la Becknhm
125 R 5 Kelsey Pk av Becknhm
125 P 3 Kelsey Pk rd Becknhm
125 N 3 Kelsey sq Becknhm
135 V 15 Kelsey st E2
125 O 6 Kelsey way Becknhm
145 Y 2 Kelso pl W8
120 E 17 Kelso rd Carsh
36 A 6 Kelston rd Ilf
35 Z 7 Kelston rd Ilf
103 O 15 Kelvedon clo Kingst
145 P 20 Kelvedon rd SW6
17 R 18 Kelvin av N13
101 T 15 Kelvin av Tedd
10 F 20 Kelvin cres Harrow
84 C 15 Kelvin dri Twick
58 G 17 Kelvin gdns S'hall
110 A 7 Kelvin gro SE26
48 K 13 Kelvin rd N5
96 M 7 Kelvin rd Welling
124 J 16 Kelvington clo Croy
92 E 14 Kelvington rd SE15
156 G 5 Kemble rd Croy
31 W 6 Kemble rd N17
110 G 2 Kemble rd SE23
141 N 6 Kemble st WC2
125 S 4 Kemerton rd Becknhm
123 U 17 Kemerton rd Becknhm
90 L 8 Kemerton rd SE5
50 H 16 Kemeys st E9
114 E 9 Kemnal manor Chisl
114 D 13 Kemnal rd Chisl
114 D 15 Kemnal Warren Chisl
122 K 15 Kemp clo Croy
55 W 4 Kemp rd Dgnhm
128 G 10 Kempe rd NW6
91 S 13 Kempis way SE22
46 G 12 Kemplay rd NW3
145 V 11 Kempsford gdns SW5
149 U 7 Kempsford rd SE11
108 A 17 Kempshott rd SW16
107 Z 17 Kempshott rd SW16
145 W 20 Kempson rd SW6
87 Z 1 Kempson rd SW6
78 J 17 Kempt st SE18
75 X 11 Kempthorne rd SE8
40 H 16 Kempton av Northolt
81 X 16 Kempton clo Erith
100 B 20 Kempton pk Felt
66 F 3 Kempton rd E6
124 K 14 Kempton wlk Croy
97 Z 17 Kemsing clo Bxly
122 M 9 Kemsing clo Thntn Hth
77 S 14 Kemsing rd SE10
90 L 4 Kenbury st SE5
148 K 20 Kenchester clo SW8
81 P 6 Kencot way Blvdr
67 U 2 Kendal av Bark
18 B 14 Kendal av N18
61 S 14 Kendal av W3
21 R 9 Kendal clo Wdfd Grn
57 V 15 Kendal croft Hornch
18 B 14 Kendal gdns N18
18 A 14 Kendal gdns N18
44 H 13 Kendal rd NW10
138 M 6 Kendal st W2
111 Z 13 Kendale rd Brom
124 H 3 Kendall av Becknhm
157 O 20 Kendall av S Croy
154 D 2 Kendall gdns Sutton
139 S 3 Kendall pl W1
124 H 3 Kendall rd Becknhm
83 X 5 Kendall rd Islwth
75 R 20 Kender st SE14
89 Y 9 Kendoa rd SW4
34 J 17 Kendon clo E11
120 A 4 Kendor gdns SW19
156 J 16 Kendra Hall rd S Croy
83 S 17 Kendrey gdns Twick

146 F 6 Kendrick ms SW7
146 F 6 Kendrick pl SW7
41 Y 9 Kenelm clo Harrow
4 O 17 Kenerne dri Barnt
89 T 18 Keniford rd SW12
40 D 12 Kenilworth av Harrow
33 P 9 Kenilworth av E17
105 X 11 Kenilworth av SW19
8 E 6 Kenilworth cres Enf
58 F 10 Kenilworth gdns S'hall
54 K 6 Kenilworth gdns Ilf
95 Y 4 Kenilworth gdns SE18
63 V 6 Kenilworth rd E3
12 G 12 Kenilworth rd Edg
152 F 12 Kenilworth rd Epsom
129 R 3 Kenilworth rd NW6
110 E 20 Kenilworth rd SE20
72 J 3 Kenilworth rd W5
26 A 6 Kenley av NW9
98 F 19 Kenley clo Bxly
122 H 9 Kenley gdns Thntn Hth
117 U 3 Kenley rd Kingst
120 A 6 Kenley rd SW19
119 X 4 Kenley rd SW19
84 A 16 Kenley rd Twick
153 N 9 Kenley wlk Sutton
136 K 12 Kenley wlk W11
106 G 13 Kenlor rd SW17
106 M 19 Kenmare dri Mitch
17 Y 14 Kenmare gdns N13
122 E 14 Kenmare rd Thntn Hth
61 O 2 Kenmere gdns Wemb
97 T 4 Kenmere rd Welling
62 J 8 Kenmont gdns NW10
24 A 7 Kenmore av Harrow
23 Z 13 Kenmore av Harrow
23 Z 8 Kenmore av Harrow
25 T 7 Kenmore av Harrow
24 G 12 Kenmore rd Harrow
50 A 16 Kenmore rd E8
64 H 1 Kennard rd E15
15 Z 17 Kennard rd N11
78 F 3 Kennard st E16
89 N 3 Kennard st SW11
9 R 19 Kennedy av Enf
65 T 7 Kennedy clo E13
59 V 12 Kennedy path W7
67 U 4 Kennedy rd Bark
59 U 13 Kennedy rd W7
88 F 9 Kennet clo SW11
99 X 8 Kennet rd Drtfrd
83 V 7 Kennet rd Islwth
129 P 17 Kennet rd W9
143 U 12 Kennet st E1
160 B 9 Kennet Wharf la EC4
53 X 12 Kenneth av Ilf
44 L 15 Kenneth cres NW2
10 K 19 Kenneth rd Stanm
55 X 1 Kenneth rd Rom
75 R 5 Kenning st SE16
134 H 4 Kenning ter N1
49 Y 10 Kenninghall rd E5
19 O 16 Kenninghall rd N18
149 V 10 Kennings way SE11
149 O 12 Kennington gro SE11
149 V 8 Kennington la SE11
149 P 15 Kennington oval SE11
149 U 15 Kennington park SE11
149 W 14 Kennington Pk gdns SE11
149 V 13 Kennington Pk pl SE11
149 V 11 Kennington Pk rd SE11
149 T 11 Kennington rd SE11
14 E 18 Kenny rd NW7
139 S 1 Kenrick pl W1
128 J 16 Kensal rd W10
129 N 17 Kensal rd W10
53 R 19 Kensington av E12
122 F 1 Kensington av Thntn Hth
137 W 18 Kensington Ch st W8
137 V 14 Kensington Ch st W8
137 W 18 Kensington Ch wlk W8
137 Z 20 Kensington Ct pl W8
137 Z 19 Kensington ct W8
35 O 6 Kensington dri Wdfd Grn
138 B 20 Kensington ga W8

53 T 5 Kensington gdns Ilf
137 X 7 Kensington Gdns sq W2
138 F 19 Kensington gore SW7
145 R 2 Kensington High st W8
137 W 19 Kensington High st W8
137 V 13 Kensington mall W8
137 W 12 Kensington Pal gdns W8
137 Y 15 Kensington Palace London museum W8
137 P 10 Kensington Pk gdns W11
137 N 6 Kensington Pk ms W11
137 O 7 Kensington Pk rd W11
137 T 14 Kensington pl W8
58 G 5 Kensington rd Nthlt
38 L 18 Kensington rd Rom
138 D 19 Kensington rd SW7
137 X 20 Kensington sq W8
157 O 17 Kensington ter S Croy
69 T 6 Kent av Dgnhm
60 A 13 Kent av W13
56 L 11 Kent av Welling
122 A 8 Kent clo Mitch
6 C 15 Kent dri Barnt
101 S 13 Kent dri Tedd
158 M 14 Kent Gate way Croy
159 O 12 Kent Gate way Croy
60 B 13 Kent gdns W13
110 J 14 Kent House la Becknhm
110 F 19 Kent House rd Becknhm
131 N 15 Kent pas NW1
56 H 15 Kent rd Dgnhm
116 G 5 Kent rd Kingst
18 A 3 Kent rd N21
73 P 19 Kent rd Rich
125 S 20 Kent rd W Wckm
73 V 8 Kent rd W4
65 X 10 Kent st E13
135 P 7 Kent st E2
130 M 14 Kent ter NW1
54 H 7 Kent View gdns Ilf
138 L 19 Kent yd SW7
58 B 4 Kentford way Nthlt
142 E 16 Kentish bldgs SE1
81 S 11 Kentish rd Blvdr
47 T 18 Kentish Town rd NW5
131 Z 2 Kentish Town rd NW1
79 V 11 Kentmere rd SE18
23 V 20 Kenton av Harrow
58 H 20 Kenton av S'hall
24 D 15 Kenton gdns Harrow
24 C 16 Kenton la Harrow
10 H 19 Kenton la Harrow
23 X 5 Kenton la Harrow
24 F 14 Kenton Pk av Harrow
24 F 15 Kenton Pk clo Harrow
24 E 14 Kenton Pk cres Harrow
24 E 14 Kenton Pk rd Harrow
50 E 18 Kenton rd E9
24 C 17 Kenton rd Harrow
23 Y 19 Kenton rd Harrow
132 K 16 Kenton st WC1
74 G 19 Kentwode grn SW13
15 S 20 Kenver av N12
94 L 13 Kenward rd SE9
145 W 7 Kenway Rd SW5
38 J 7 Kenway Rom
43 W 8 Kenway Wemb
6 L 17 Kenwood av Enf
92 D 1 Kenwood av SE14
46 F 3 Kenwood clo NW3
125 U 6 Kenwood dri Becknhm
35 W 14 Kenwood gdns Ilf
46 J 3 Kenwood ho NW3
28 M 17 Kenwood rd N6
18 K 6 Kenwood rd N9
50 H 15 Kenworthy rd E9
44 C 8 Kenwyn dri NW2
118 M 1 Kenwyn rd SW20
89 Y 9 Kenwyn rd SW4
77 Z 20 Kenya rd SE7
24 D 17 Kenyngton pl Harrow
144 G 20 Kenyon st SW6

87 O 1 Kenyon st SW6
52 A 17 Keough rd E15
90 A 10 Kepler rd SW4
55 X 12 Keppel rd Dgnhm
66 E 1 Keppel rd E6
142 A 15 Keppel row SE1
132 G 20 Keppel st WC1
135 R 16 Kerbela st E2
64 D 18 Kerbey st E14
91 O 3 Kerfield pl SE5
72 H 3 Kerrison pl W5
64 J 3 Kerrison rd E15
88 J 7 Kerrison rd SW11
72 H 4 Kerrison rd W5
11 T 13 Kerry av Stanm
65 U 18 Kerry clo E16
11 T 14 Kerry ct Stanm
113 P 9 Kersey gdns SE9
87 P 16 Kersfield rd SW15
88 E 16 Kershaw clo SW18
56 F 9 Kershaw rd Dgnhm
88 L 3 Kersley ms SW11
49 T 9 Kersley rd N16
88 L 3 Kersley st SW11
31 R 17 Kerswell cl N15
48 B 20 Kerwick clo N7
128 G 9 Keslake rd NW6
31 Z 14 Kessock clo N15
97 U 16 Kestlake rd Bxly
18 C 12 Keston clo N18
80 E 19 Keston clo Welling
31 O 12 Keston rd N17
91 W 8 Keston rd SE15
122 E 13 Keston rd Thntn Hth
66 D 16 Kestrel av E6
90 L 13 Kestrel av SE24
57 X 20 Kestrel clo Hornch
159 X 18 Kestrel way Croy
103 Z 13 Keswick av Kingst
104 A 13 Keswick av SW15
119 X 4 Keswick av SW19
154 D 8 Keswick clo Sutton
35 P 14 Keswick gdns
85 S 13 Keswick gdns Ilf
42 J 14 Keswick gdns Wemb
72 J 4 Keswick ms W5
98 D 3 Keswick rd Bxly Hth
87 T 15 Keswick rd SW15
82 M 17 Keswick rd Twick
159 Z 1 Keswick rd W Wckm
9 S 1 Kettering rd Enf
107 U 16 Kettering st SW16
50 K 4 Kettlebaston rd E10
31 N 6 Kevelioc rd N17
73 O 16 Kew Bridge Brentf
73 O 15 Kew Bridge ct W4
72 L 16 Kew Bridge rd Brentf
153 U 5 Kew cres Sutton
84 J 9 Kew Foot rd Rich
72 L 20 Kew Gardens Brentf
85 O 1 Kew Gardens rd Rich
73 N 18 Kew grn Rich
85 S 3 Kew Meadows pth Rich
84 C 7 Kew Observatory Rich
72 L 18 Kew Palace Brentf
73 N 17 Kew rd Rich
85 N 2 Kew rd Rich
63 O 12 Key clo E1
135 Z 19 Key clo E1
141 Y 20 Key North st SE1
108 D 5 Keymer rd SW2
29 N 12 Keynes clo N2
21 N 14 Keynsham av Wdfd Grn
95 P 13 Keynsham gdns SE9
119 Z 19 Keynsham rd Mrdn
95 P 13 Keynsham rd SE9
151 O 4 Keyse rd SE1
132 M 10 Keystone cres N1
149 Y 1 Keyworth st SE1
75 U 14 Kezia st SE8
106 J 10 Khama rd SW17
65 V 10 Khartoum rd E13
54 A 15 Khartoum rd Ilf
53 Z 15 Khartoum rd Ilf
106 G 10 Khartoum rd SW17
88 J 6 Khyber rd SW11
149 O 19 Kibworth st SW8
94 F 3 Kidbrooke gdns SE3
94 F 2 Kidbrooke gdns SE3
95 R 10 Kidbrooke la SE9
94 H 3 Kidbrooke Pk clo SE3
94 G 2 Kidbrooke Pk rd SE3
78 D 13 Kidd pl SE7
122 K 18 Kidderminster rd Croy
45 Y 12 Kidderpore av NW3

45 Z 12 Kidderpore gdns NW3
129 T 3 Kilburn High rd NW6
45 V 20 Kilburn High rd NW6
128 K 11 Kilburn la W10
129 O 10 Kilburn la W9
129 V 12 Kilburn Pk rd NW6
129 V 5 Kilburn pl NW6
129 X 7 Kilburn priory NW6
129 T 5 Kilburn sq NW6
129 W 5 Kilburn vale est NW6
137 V 5 Kildare gdns W2
65 T 14 Kildare rd E16
137 V 4 Kildare ter W2
90 A 13 Kildoran rd SW2
55 N 5 Kildowan rd Ilf
92 H 15 Kilgour rd SE23
88 C 5 Kilkie st SW6
88 D 16 Killarney rd SW18
111 X 1 Killarn rd SE6
152 L 9 Killester gdns Worc Pk
133 N 10 Killick st N1
108 A 2 Killieser av SW2
107 Z 3 Killieser av SW2
65 R 17 Killip clo E16
41 O 13 Killowen av Northolt
50 E 19 Killowen rd E9
89 W 5 Killyon rd SW8
144 M 20 Kilmaine rd SW6
144 A 5 Kilmarsh rd W6
74 L 10 Kilmarsh rd W6
122 E 6 Kilmartin av SW16
55 O 7 Kilmartin rd Ilf
57 Y 16 Kilmartin way Hornch
74 F 17 Kilmington rd SW13
84 A 11 Kilmorey gdns Twick
84 B 11 Kilmorey rd Twick
110 H 2 Kilmorie rd SE23
47 P 13 Kiln pl NW5
64 A 15 Kilner st E14
128 L 13 Kilravock st W10
8 C 3 Kilvington dri Enf
87 S 2 Kimbell gdns SW6
88 A 19 Kimber rd SW18
66 C 6 Kimberley av Ilf
54 F 2 Kimberley av Ilf
38 J 19 Kimberley av Rom
92 B 6 Kimberley av SE15
115 X 5 Kimberley av SE15
8 G 13 Kimberley gdns Enf
30 J 17 Kimberley gdns N4
124 G 4 Kimberley rd Becknhm
122 K 13 Kimberley rd Croy
51 X 6 Kimberley rd E11
65 O 12 Kimberley rd E16
32 K 4 Kimberley rd E17
20 M 5 Kimberley rd E4
21 N 6 Kimberley rd E4
31 X 9 Kimberley rd N17
19 N 19 Kimberley rd N18
128 M 3 Kimberley rd NW6
90 B 6 Kimberley rd SW9
20 M 5 Kimberley way E4
21 N 5 Kimberley way E4
10 A 2 Kimble cres Bushey Watf
106 G 14 Kimble rd SW19
94 C 17 Kimbolton clo SE12
113 R 9 Kimm gdns SE9
113 R 10 Kimmeridge rd SE9
91 O 1 Kimpton rd SE5
153 V 3 Kimpton rd Sutton
75 S 4 Kinburn st SE16
151 V 20 Kincaid rd SE15
42 L 1 Kinch gro Harrow
80 H 1 Kinder clo SE2
143 W 6 Kinder st E1
55 O 4 Kinfauns rd Ilf
108 G 4 Kinfauns rd SW2
111 O 10 King Alfred av SE6
150 C 9 King And Queen st SE17
140 J 17 King Charles st SW1
105 S 2 King Charles wlk SW19
117 N 16 King Charles' cres Surb
116 M 13 King Charles' rd Surb
63 O 20 King David la E1
4 M 14 King Edward rd Barnt
5 N 15 King Edward rd Barnt
51 T 4 King Edward rd E10
32 G 11 King Edward rd E17
39 T 17 King Edward rd Rom

141 Z 4 King Edward st EC1
149 T 1 King Edward wlk SE1
73 P 3 King Edward's gdns W3
102 C 15 King Edward's gro Tedd
67 S 5 King Edward's rd Bark
9 U 14 King Edward's rd Enf
63 O 2 King Edwards rd E9
135 Y 3 King Edwards rd E9
18 M 2 King Edwards rd N9
19 N 3 King Edwards rd N9
156 H 10 King Edwards Croy
66 A 18 King George av E16
65 Z 17 King George av E16
38 K 11 King George clo Rom
152 B 7 King George Field Auriol pk Epsom
87 Z 20 King George pk SW18
76 H 20 King George st SE10
121 N 8 King George VI av Mitch
131 P 2 King George's ms NW1
131 P 2 King George's ter NW1
58 E 14 King Georges dri S'hall
80 M 18 King Harold's way Bxly Hth
49 S 15 King Henry st N16
159 V 18 King Henry's dri Croy
117 T 5 King Henry's rd Kingst
130 K 1 King Henry's rd NW3
131 O 1 King Henry's rd NW3
49 R 17 King Henry's wlk N1
141 Y 19 King James st SE1
134 L 16 King John ct EC2
63 T 15 King John st E1
95 P 19 King John's wlk SE9
133 Z 13 King sq EC1
65 S 12 King st E13
142 C 5 King st EC2
160 D 5 King st EC2
31 U 3 King st N17
28 G 8 King st N2
84 G 13 King st Rich
70 C 9 King st S'hall
140 C 14 King st SW1
101 Y 1 King st Twick
73 U 3 King st W3
144 B 7 King st W6
74 F 12 King st W6
140 K 9 King st WC2
75 N 5 King Stairs clo SE16
142 F 7 King William st EC4
160 F 8 King William st EC4
76 H 16 King William wlk SE10
160 F 5 King's Arms yd EC2
58 L 16 King's av Grnfd
29 P 10 King's av N10
17 V 5 King's av N21
89 Z 14 King's av SW4
60 H 16 King's av W5
21 W 18 King's av Wdfd Grn
141 Y 17 King's Bench st SE1
99 O 11 King's clo Drtfd
46 H 20 King's College rd NW3
48 L 8 King's cres N4
92 A 1 King's gro SE15
151 Y 20 King's gro SE15
142 F 15 King's Head yd SE1
79 X 17 King's highway SE18
50 K 13 King's Mead way E9
95 S 15 King's orchard SE9
51 Y 1 King's rd E11
18 L 15 King's rd N17
116 D 20 King's rd Surb
147 T 4 King's rd SW1
85 Z 9 King's rd SW14
105 Y 14 King's rd SW19
146 J 12 King's rd SW3
145 Z 20 King's rd SW6
101 P 12 King's rd Tedd
60 G 15 King's rd W5
148 B 4 King's Scholars' pas SW1
132 A 6 King's ter NW1
57 V 20 Kingaby gdns Rainham
45 Y 17 Kingdon rd NW6
60 G 11 Kingfield rd W5
76 G 11 Kingfield st E14
68 H 20 Kingfisher clo SE28

102 C 9 Kingfisher dri Rich
66 E 15 Kingfisher st E6
88 C 18 Kingham clo SW18
141 Z 2 Kinghorn st EC1
150 J 11 Kinglake st SE17
150 L 9 Kinglake st SE17
140 B 8 Kingly ct W1
141 X 3 Kingly st W1
143 S 2 Kings Arms ct E1
112 B 16 Kings av Brom
21 Z 7 Kings av Buck Hl
154 K 18 Kings av Carsh
89 Z 17 Kings Av clo SW4
89 Y 13 Kings Av gdns SW4
82 L 2 Kings av Hounsl
118 C 8 Kings av New Mald
38 C 18 Kings av Rom
141 T 8 Kings Bench wlk EC4
51 R 2 Kings clo E10
27 R 13 Kings clo NW4
133 O 12 Kings Cross rd WC1
132 K 9 Kings Cross station N1
65 W 4 Kings ct E13
12 A 15 Kings dri Edg
11 Z 14 Kings dri Edg
117 P 15 Kings dri Surb
43 S 5 Kings dri Wemb
43 S 7 Kings dri Wemb
85 O 11 Kings Farm av Rich
54 D 4 Kings gdns Ilf
129 V 2 Kings gdns NW6
39 V 17 Kings gro Rom
110 F 18 Kings Hall rd SE20
160 H 10 Kings Head ct EC3
20 F 3 Kings Head hill E4
154 G 12 Kings la Sutton
86 K 12 Kings lawn clo SW15
89 Z 13 Kings ms SW4
133 P 19 Kings ms WC1
116 G 4 Kings pas Kingst
21 Z 8 Kings pl Buck Hl
142 B 20 Kings pl SE1
73 V 12 Kings pl W4
54 A 20 Kings rd Bark
4 A 13 Kings rd Barnt
20 J 5 Kings rd E4
65 Y 3 Kings rd E6
40 E 9 Kings rd Harrow
102 J 19 Kings rd Kingst
103 O 17 Kings rd Kingst
121 P 5 Kings rd Mitch
31 U 3 Kings rd N17
30 D 4 Kings rd N22
44 J 20 Kings rd N10
84 M 12 Kings rd Rich
39 V 17 Kings rd Rom
123 V 6 Kings rd SE25
84 C 17 Kings rd Twick
85 P 12 Kings Ride ga Rich
156 D 11 Kings way Croy
23 T 12 Kings way Harrow
21 Y 16 Kings way Wdfd Grn
102 H 19 Kings wlk Kingst
112 F 3 Kingsand rd SE12
58 A 11 Kingsash dri Grnfd
73 N 5 Kingsbridge av W3
58 E 15 Kingsbridge cres S'hall
67 T 7 Kingsbridge rd Berk
119 P 17 Kingsbridge rd Mrdn
70 D 17 Kingsbridge rd S'hall
136 D 3 Kingsbridge rd W10
49 S 17 Kingsbury rd N1
26 B 17 Kingsbury rd NW9
25 U 15 Kingsbury rd NW9
49 S 17 Kingsbury ter N1
86 F 17 Kingsclere clo SW15
105 V 3 Kingscliffe gdns SW19
123 Z 18 Kingscote rd Croy
117 Y 7 Kingscote rd New Mald
73 X 10 Kingscote rd W4
141 W 8 Kingscote st EC4
107 Z 7 Kingscourt rd SW16
45 U 17 Kingscroft rd NW2
136 H 15 Kingsdale gdns W11
79 X 17 Kingsdale rd SE18
110 F 19 Kingsdale rd SE20
156 K 20 Kingsdown av S Croy
72 C 5 Kingsdown av W13
62 B 18 Kingsdown av W3
136 J 7 Kingsdown clo W11
52 A 10 Kingsdown rd E11
48 A 7 Kingsdown rd N19
47 Z 8 Kingsdown rd N19
153 S 11 Kingsdown rd Sutton

126 E 15 Kingsdown way Brom
116 L 18 Kingsdowne rd Surb
104 D 1 Kingsfarm lodge SW15
22 L 14 Kingsfield av Harrow
23 N 15 Kingsfield av Harrow
41 S 2 Kingsfield rd Harrow
41 R 2 Kingsfield ter Harrow
156 B 17 Kingsford av Croy
46 M 15 Kingsford st NW5
27 Y 10 Kingsgate av N3
97 Y 1 Kingsgate clo Bxly Hth
129 T 2 Kingsgate pl NW6
129 U 2 Kingsgate rd NW6
45 X 20 Kingsgate rd NW6
43 U 8 Kingsgate Wemb
95 O 18 Kingsground SE9
24 B 13 Kingshill av Harrow
118 H 16 Kingshill av Worc Pk
24 B 11 Kingshill dri Harrow
63 P 1 Kingshold rd E9
95 P 9 Kingsholme gdns SE9
94 F 19 Kingshurst rd SE12
49 T 17 Kingsland High st E8
49 T 17 Kingsland pass E8
65 V 9 Kingsland rd E13
134 L 6 Kingsland rd E2
49 T 19 Kingsland rd E8
83 N 4 Kingsley av Hounsl
58 G 20 Kingsley av S'hall
154 G 8 Kingsley av Sutton
59 Y 16 Kingsley av W13
56 G 12 Kingsley clo Dgnhm
29 C 15 Kingsley ala N2
152 E 1 Kingsley dri Worc Pk
20 B 15 Kingsley gdns E4
145 Z 2 Kingsley ms W8
47 R 2 Kingsley pl N6
122 F 19 Kingsley rd Croy
33 U 8 Kingsley rd E17
52 F 20 Kingsley rd E7
40 M 11 Kingsley rd Harrow
41 N 10 Kingsley rd Harrow
82 L 4 Kingsley rd Hounsl
83 N 6 Kingsley rd Hounsl
36 C 4 Kingsley rd Ilf
17 U 13 Kingsley rd N13
129 P 3 Kingsley rd NW6
22 E 14 Kingsley rd Pinn
106 B 12 Kingsley rd SW19
88 M 7 Kingsley st SW11
89 N 6 Kingsley st SW11
28 C 15 Kingsley way N2
113 U 7 Kingsley Wood dri SE9
123 R 1 Kingslyn cres SE19
78 G 9 Kingsman pk SE18
78 G 9 Kingsman st SE18
152 J 4 Kingsmead av Worc Pk
121 V 5 Kingsmead av Mitch
18 M 6 Kingsmead av N9
43 Y 1 Kingsmead av N9
39 S 18 Kingsmead av Rom
4 L 14 Kingsmead Barnt
114 M 5 Kingsmead clo Sidcp
40 E 20 Kingsmead dri Nthlt
108 F 5 Kingsmead dri SW2
43 U 5 Kingsmere pk NW9
105 R 3 Kingsmere rd SW19
56 B 16 Kingsmill gdns Dgnhm
56 B 16 Kingsmill rd Dgnhm
130 G 9 Kingsmill ter NW8
103 T 16 Kingsnympton pk Kingst
34 D 9 Kingspark ct E18
110 E 10 Kingsthorpe rd SE26
153 T 5 Kingston av Sutton
116 F 3 Kingston br Kingst
118 B 12 Kingston By-pass New Mald
104 B 15 Kingston By-pass SW20
58 E 2 Kingston clo Northolt
37 Y 9 Kingston clo Rom
102 A 15 Kingston clo Tedd
124 L 1 Kingston cres Becknhm
103 P 17 Kingston gate Kingst
116 H 5 Kingston Hall rd Kingst
37 Z 9 Kingston Hill av Rom
103 S 18 Kingston hill Kingst
103 W 10 Kingston Hill place Rich

102 A 15 Kingston la Tedd
101 Z 13 Kingston la Tedd
5 U 17 Kingston rd Barnt
152 C 12 Kingston rd Epsom
152 E 17 Kingston rd Epsom
54 B 12 Kingston rd Ilf
18 L 8 Kingston rd N9
117 V 7 Kingston rd New Mald
39 U 13 Kingston rd Rom
70 D 7 Kingston rd S'hall
104 J 2 Kingston rd SW15
86 M 20 Kingston rd SW15
105 V 19 Kingston rd SW19
119 P 2 Kingston rd SW20
102 B 15 Kingston rd Tedd
104 A 8 Kingston vale SW15
103 Y 9 Kingston vale SW15
131 S 4 Kingston rd NW1
158 D 20 Kingsway av S Croy
22 M 14 Kingsway cres Harrow
9 N 15 Kingsway Enf
140 M 4 Kingsway Hall WC2
15 R 18 Kingsway N12
118 L 10 Kingsway New Mald
153 S 15 Kingsway rd Sutton
85 U 8 Kingsway SW14
141 N 5 Kingsway WC2
42 K 12 Kingsway Wemb
47 S 9 Kingsway Wemb
82 D 4 Kingswood av Hounsl
122 G 13 Kingswood av Thntn Hth
81 O 10 Kingswood av Blvdr
125 Y 0 Kingswood av Brom
100 K 15 Kingswood av Hampt
128 L 7 Kingswood av NW6
118 D 15 Kingswood clo New Mald
15 R 1 Kingswood clo N20
116 K 16 Kingswood clo Surb
148 L 19 Kingswood clo SW8
109 T 10 Kingswood dri SE19
27 U 6 Kingswood pk N3
93 Z 9 Kingswood pl SE13
126 A 5 Kingswood rd Brom
125 Y 6 Kingswood rd Brom
54 M 3 Kingswood rd Ilf
55 N 1 Kingswood rd Ilf
110 B 16 Kingswood rd SE20
105 W 19 Kingswood rd SW19
90 A 18 Kingswood rd SW2
89 Z 17 Kingswood rd SW2
73 V 9 Kingswood rd W4
156 A 10 Kingswood way Croy
124 H 10 Kingsworthy clo BR3
43 Y 20 Kingthorpe rd NW10
143 T 1 Kingward st E1
5 U 3 Kingwell rd Barnt
144 L 20 Kingwood rd SW6
96 B 1 Kinlet td SE18
44 A 1 Kinloch dri NW9
43 Z 1 Kinloch dri NW9
48 D 10 Kinloch st N7
27 U 11 Kinloss gdns N3
120 D 18 Kinloss rd Carsh
112 C 16 Kinnaird av Brom
73 U 20 Kinnaird av W4
112 D 16 Kinnaird clo Brom
74 C 5 Kinnear rd W12
139 R 18 Kinnerton Place north SW1
139 R 19 Kinnerton Place south SW1
139 S 20 Kinnerton st SW1
139 S 19 Kinnerton st SW1
144 L 14 Kinnoul rd W6
152 F 4 Kinross av Worc Pk
24 L 16 Kinross clo Harrow
142 L 19 Kinross st SE1
91 X 8 Kinsale rd SE15
151 N 4 Kintore st SE1
122 D 4 Kintyre clo SW16
78 C 14 Kinveachy gdns SE7
110 D 9 Kinver rd SE26
10 H 18 Kipling pl Stanm
97 Z 1 Kipling rd Bxly Hth
142 G 18 Kipling st SE1
36 S 1 Kipling ter N21N9
113 O 1 Kippington dri SE9
152 D 12 Kirby clo Epsom
142 J 17 Kirby gro SE1
141 U 1 Kirby st EC1
133 U 20 Kirby st EC1
72 A 1 Kirchen rd W13
79 O 16 Kirk la SE18
32 M 18 Kirk rd E17
52 A 2 Kirkdale rd E11

110 B 9 Kirkdale SE26
66 E 16 Kirkham rd E6
79 V 18 Kirkham st SE18
35 W 7 Kirkland av Ilf
96 G 15 Kirkland clo Sidcp
55 T 16 Kirklees rd Dgnhm
122 E 10 Kirklees rd Thntn Hth
105 Z 19 Kirkley rd SE19
157 S 20 Kirkly clo S Croy
140 E 1 Kirkman pl W1
64 H 17 Kirkmichael rd E14
63 X 15 Kirks pl E3
77 S 17 Kirkside rd SE3
31 O 12 Kirkstall av N17
107 Z 1 Kirkstall gdns SW2
108 A 1 Kirkstall rd SW2
107 Z 1 Kirkstall rd SW2
119 Z 19 Kirksted rd Mrdn
112 A 17 Kirkstone way Brom
31 R 14 Kirkton rd N15
63 R 8 Kirkwall pl E2
47 O 19 Kirkwood pl NW1
92 A 3 Kirkwood rd SE15
72 A 1 Kirn rd W13
148 B 17 Kirtling st SW8
73 Y 12 Kirton clo W4
135 P 13 Kirton gdns E2
65 X 5 Kirton rd E13
25 W 2 Kirton wlk Edg
149 Z 18 Kirwyn way SE5
64 B 8 Kitcat ter E3
58 J 17 Kitchener rd Dgnhm
33 R 4 Kitchener rd E17
52 H 18 Kitchener rd E7
31 P 10 Kitchener rd N17
28 H 11 Kitchener rd N2
123 N 5 Kitchener rd Thntn Hth
123 U 1 Kitley gdns SE19
150 D 17 Kitson rd SE5
86 F 3 Kitson rd SW13
92 F 6 Kitto rd SE14
4 H 5 Kitts End rd Barnt
47 Z 7 Kiver rd N19
89 U 15 Klea av SW4
110 A 4 Knapdale clo SE23
111 P 5 Knapmill rd SE6
111 P 5 Knapmill way SE6
44 B 17 Knapp clo NW10
64 B 12 Knapp rd E3
145 X 6 Knaresborough pl SW5
61 Z 3 Knatchbull rd NW10
90 J 3 Knatchbull rd SE5
33 O 4 Knebworth av E17
49 R 11 Knebworth rd N16
80 G 11 Knee Hill cres SE2
80 G 13 Knee hill SE2
83 P 15 Kneller gdns Islwth
83 R 16 Kneller hall Twick
117 Z 17 Kneller rd New Mald
92 J 10 Kneller rd SE4
82 M 16 Kneller rd Twick
83 O 16 Kneller rd Twick
72 L 7 Knight's av W5
143 V 15 Knights st E1
49 Z 6 Knightland rd E5
38 M 18 Knighton clo Rom
156 J 17 Knighton clo S Croy
21 V 13 Knighton dri Wdfd Grn
21 U 13 Knighton dri Wdfd Grn
21 V 9 Knighton la Buck Hl
110 G 12 Knighton Pk rd SE26
52 F 11 Knighton rd E7
38 L 18 Knighton rd Rom
141 Z 8 Knightrider st EC4
70 A 14 Knights arbour S'hall
108 J 12 Knights hill SE27
108 K 9 Knights hill sq SE27
18 K 10 Knights la N9
116 J 5 Knights pk Kingst
77 T 4 Knights rd E16
11 S 13 Knights rd Stanm
149 W 7 Knights wlk SE11
39 N 16 Knightsbridge grn Rom
139 N 19 Knightsbridge grn SW7
138 L 18 Knightsbridge SW7
139 O 18 Knightsbridge SW7
12 G 8 Knightswood clo Edg
118 B 14 Knightwood cres New Mald
145 T 15 Knivett rd SW6
64 D 2 Knobs Hill rd E15
95 N 12 Knockholt rd SE9
99 X 19 Knole clo Drtfrd
113 W 10 Knole the SE9

16 C 3 Knoll dri N14
98 D 17 Knoll rd Bxly
115 R 12 Knoll rd Sidcp
88 C 14 Knoll rd SW18
125 R 1 Knoll the Becknhm
60 C 15 Knoll W13
117 X 20 Knollmead Surb
152 J 4 Knolls clo Worc Pk
108 G 6 Knolly's Clo SW16
108 E 6 Knolly's rd SW16
63 S 8 Knottisford st E2
33 T 18 Knotts Green rd E10
81 N 18 Knowle av Bxly Hth
90 E 7 Knowle clo SW9
101 T 2 Knowle rd Twick
93 W 13 Knowles Hill cres SE13
126 D 12 Knowlton grn Brom
70 J 3 Knowsley av S'hall
88 L 6 Knowsley rd SW11
52 D 18 Knox rd E7
139 O 1 Knox st W1
75 V 17 Knoyle st SE14
106 B 12 Kohat rd SW19
76 M 13 Kossuth st SE10
145 V 11 Kramer Mews SW5
108 D 19 Kuala gdns SW16
52 F 14 Kuhn way E7
45 Y 19 Kylemore rd NW6
23 T 19 Kymberley rd Harrow
39 T 20 Kyme rd Hornch
24 D 5 Kynance gdns Stanm
146 A 2 Kynance mans SW7
146 A 2 Kynance ms SW7
146 A 1 Kynance pl SW7
49 T 9 Kynaston av N16
122 L 11 Kynaston av Thntn Hth
23 R 1 Kynaston clo Harrow
122 M 11 Kynaston cres Thntn Hth
112 G 12 Kynaston rd Brom
8 B 7 Kynaston rd Enf
49 S 9 Kynaston rd N16
122 M 10 Kynaston rd Thntn Hth
23 R 1 Kynaston wood Harrow
19 R 15 Kynoch rd N18
89 O 14 Kyrle rd SW11
49 V 4 Kyverdale rd N16

57 U 9 Laburnum av Hornch
31 O 1 Laburnum av N17
18 F 9 Laburnum av N9
154 H 6 Laburnum av Sutton
19 Y 19 Laburnum clo E4
16 C 20 Laburnum clo N11
151 Z 20 Laburnum clo SE15
11 P 15 Laburnum ct Stanm
121 P 4 Laburnum est Mitch
17 Y 7 Laburnum gdns N21
82 F 11 Laburnum gro Hounsl
17 Y 7 Laburnum gro N21
117 X 4 Laburnum gro New Mald
25 W 20 Laburnum gro NW9
58 F 12 Laburnum gro S'hall
121 P 4 Laburnum gro Mitch
106 E 18 Laburnum rd SW19
134 M 6 Laburnum st E2
135 N 6 Laburnum st E2
127 Y 16 Laburnum way Brom
11 Y 13 Lacey dri Edg
134 G 20 Lackington st EC2
106 C 16 Lacock clo SW19
91 W 11 Lacon rd SE22
87 R 9 Lacy rd SW15
108 K 11 Ladas rd SE27
136 L 6 Ladbroke cres W11
137 O 9 Ladbroke gdns W11
128 H 15 Ladbroke gro W10
136 K 3 Ladbroke gro W10
137 P 13 Ladbroke gro W11
8 H 19 Ladbroke gro Enf
137 O 13 Ladbroke rd W11
137 P 10 Ladbroke Sq gdns W11
137 R 11 Ladbroke sq W11
137 R 12 Ladbroke ter W11

137 R 12 Ladbroke wlk W11
22 D 17 Ladbrook clo Pinn
123 P 8 Ladbrook rd SE25
115 X 8 Ladbrooke cres Sidcp
103 U 13 Ladderstile ride Kingst
16 G 17 Ladderswood way N11
152 C 1 Lady hay Worc Pk
70 E 1 Lady Margaret rd S'hall
58 E 17 Lady Margaret rd S'hall
47 V 13 Lady Margaret rd NW5
47 T 13 Lady Somerset rd NW5
93 P 8 Ladycroft rd SE13
24 G 6 Ladycroft wlk Stanm
158 G 20 Ladygrove S Croy
66 C 6 Ladysmith av E6
54 F 2 Ladysmith av Ilf
65 O 10 Ladysmith rd E16
8 F 12 Ladysmith rd Enf
23 T 8 Ladysmith rd Harrow
31 W 8 Ladysmith rd N17
19 N 18 Ladysmith rd N18
95 X 17 Ladysmith rd SE9
93 S 12 Ladywell rd SE13
65 P 4 Ladywell st E15
143 N 17 Lafone st SE1
75 U 3 Lagado ms SE16
123 P 15 Lahore rd Croy
120 K 2 Laings av Mitch
82 K 3 Lainlock pl Hounsl
87 X 19 Lainson st SW18
90 L 20 Lairdale clo SE21
48 B 17 Lairs clo N7
89 S 20 Laitwood rd SW12
107 T 1 Laitwood rd SW12
112 F 15 Lake av Brom
56 D 15 Lake gdns Dgnhm
26 B 8 Lake gdns Rich
155 R 7 Lake gdns Wallgtn
52 E 7 Lake House rd E11
158 L 1 Lake rd Croy
37 W 13 Lake rd Rom
105 U 13 Lake rd SW19
39 T 9 Lake rise Rom
10 B 9 Lake the Bushey Watf
11 Z 17 Lake view Edg
97 O 10 Lake View rd Welling
79 V 15 Lakedale rd SE18
30 J 9 Lakefield rd N22
122 J 12 Lakehall gdns Thntn Hth
122 J 12 Lakehall rd Thntn Hth
152 A 12 Lakehurst rd Epsom
10 C 19 Lakeland clo Harrow
6 J 17 Lakenheath N14
6 K 20 Lakenheath N14
87 U 15 Laker pl SW15
35 N 13 Lakeside av Ilf
123 W 3 Lakeside clo SE25
97 U 14 Lakeside clo Sidcp
6 A 18 Lakeside cres Barnt
48 K 6 Lakeside ct N4
6 K 13 Lakeside Enf
17 P 12 Lakeside rd N13
144 F 1 Lakeside rd W14
136 G 20 Lakeside rd W14
60 D 15 Lakeside W13
155 S 7 Lakeside Wallgtn
43 R 13 Lakeside way Wemb
108 H 12 Lakeview rd SE27
12 K 10 Laleham av NW7
93 T 18 Laleham rd SE6
87 S 3 Lalor st SW6
63 N 1 Lamb la E8
135 X 1 Lamb la E8
134 M 20 Lamb st E1
135 N 20 Lamb st E1
142 J 19 Lamb wlk SE1
113 X 9 Lambarde av SE9
56 A 4 Lamberhurst rd Dgnhm
108 F 11 Lamberhurst rd SE27
85 S 8 Lambert av Rich
65 V 17 Lambert rd E16
15 S 17 Lambert rd N12
90 C 14 Lambert rd SW2
133 R 2 Lambert st N1
15 S 17 Lambert way N12
123 P 20 Lamberts pl Croy
116 L 12 Lamberts rd Surb
148 L 4 Lambeth br SW1
149 N 5 Lambeth High st SE1

160 A 8 Lambeth hill EC4
149 O 7 Lambeth ms SE11
149 N 2 Lambeth Palace rd SE1
141 O 20 Lambeth Palace rd SE1
149 O 3 Lambeth palace SE1
148 M 3 Lambeth Pier SW1
122 G 18 Lambeth rd Croy
149 P 3 Lambeth rd SE1
143 S 6 Lambeth st E1
149 O 7 Lambeth wlk SE11
47 O 14 Lamble st NW5
55 R 18 Lambley rd Dgnhm
46 K 18 Lambolle pl NW3
46 J 18 Lambolle rd NW3
117 T 2 Lambourn clo W7
71 U 8 Lambourn clo W7
89 T 7 Lambourn rd SW4
105 V 9 Lambourne av SW19
67 X 1 Lambourne gdns Bark
20 B 8 Lambourne gdns E4
8 G 9 Lambourne gdns Enf
94 H 1 Lambourne pla SE3
67 W 2 Lambourne rd Bark
51 V 2 Lambourne rd E11
54 H 6 Lambourne rd Ilf
87 R 2 Lambrook ter SW6
134 D 18 Lambs bldgs EC1
18 J 8 Lambs clo N9
141 N 1 Lambs Conduit pas WC1
133 N 19 Lambs Conduit st WC1
133 X 6 Lambs ms N1
35 N 7 Lambs ms Wdfd Grn
72 M 15 Lambs pas Brentf
134 D 19 Lambs pas EC1
18 C 8 Lambs ter N9
7 Z 9 Lambs wlk Enf
112 M 8 Lambscroft av SE9
113 N 7 Lambscroft av SE9
137 S 8 Lambton Pl W11
48 A 4 Lambton rd N19
118 L 2 Lambton rd SW20
104 L 20 Lambton rd SW20
112 C 9 Lamerock rd Brom
36 A 6 Lamerton rd Ilf
76 B 17 Lamerton st SE8
31 P 1 Lamford clo N17
74 J 10 Lamington st W6
149 X 4 Lamlash st SE11
121 O 3 Lammas av Mitch
121 O 4 Lammas av Mitch
109 Z 5 Lammas grn SE26
72 E 4 Lammas Pk gdns W5
72 F 4 Lammas Pk rd W5
50 H 5 Lammas rd E10
63 U 1 Lammas rd E9
102 D 11 Lammas rd Rich
89 T 19 Lammermoor rd SW12
146 E 15 Lamont Rd pas SW10
146 E 15 Lamont rd SW10
114 K 3 Lamorbey clo Sidcp
115 P 1 Lamorbey park Bxly
24 G 6 Lamorna gro Stanm
49 U 4 Lampard gro N16
144 K 15 Lampeter sq W6
94 B 12 Lampmead rd SE12
82 J 3 Lampton av Hounsl
78 G 10 Lampton clo SE18
105 O 10 Lampton Ho clo SW19
82 G 5 Lampton park Hounsl
82 J 6 Lampton Park rd Hounsl
82 J 5 Lampton rd Hounsl
25 Z 5 Lanacre av Edg
26 B 6 Lanacre av NW9
144 F 15 Lanarch rd W6
60 E 14 Lanark clo W5
130 D 17 Lanark pl W9
130 B 14 Lanark rd W9
129 Z 12 Lanark rd W9
92 F 11 Lanbury rd SE15
34 G 12 Lancashire av E18
139 Y 8 Lancashire ct W1
67 V 2 Lancaster av Bark
5 T 3 Lancaster av Barnt
112 A 9 Lancaster av Mitch
122 A 9 Lancaster av Mitch
108 K 4 Lancaster av SE27
105 R 12 Lancaster av SW19
155 Z 2 Lancaster clo Wallgtn
126 B 10 Lancaster clo Brom
102 H 12 Lancaster clo Kingst

145 S 20 Lancaster ct SW6
76 G 3 Lancaster dri E14
57 Z 16 Lancaster dri Hornch
46 H 18 Lancaster dri NW3
138 C 10 Lancaster ga W2
102 H 13 Lancaster gdns Kingst
105 S 11 Lancaster gdns SW19
72 C 4 Lancaster gdns W13
46 H 18 Lancaster gro NW3
138 D 9 Lancaster ms W2
84 J 14 Lancaster pk Rich
105 R 12 Lancaster pl SW19
83 Z 17 Lancaster pl Twick
141 N 9 Lancaster pl WC2
5 T 17 Lancaster rd Barnt
32 F 8 Lancaster rd E 17
52 A 7 Lancaster rd E11
52 F 20 Lancaster rd E7
65 U 1 Lancaster rd E7
8 C 6 Lancaster rd Enf
22 H 17 Lancaster rd Harrow
16 L 18 Lancaster rd N11
18 G 17 Lancaster rd N18
48 F 2 Lancaster rd N4
40 M 17 Lancaster rd Nthlt
44 F 14 Lancaster rd NW10
58 B 20 Lancaster rd S'hall
123 V 5 Lancaster rd SE25
105 R 12 Lancaster rd SW19
136 L 5 Lancaster rd W11
137 O 4 Lancaster rd W11
138 F 8 Lancaster ter W2
41 N 2 Lance rd Harrow
129 O 14 Lancefield st W10
49 T 8 Lancell st N16
42 G 12 Lancelot av Wemb
42 G 13 Lancelot cres Wemb
16 B 3 Lancelot gdns Barnt
139 N 19 Lancelot pl SW7
36 G 1 Lancelot rd Ilf
97 O 9 Lancelot rd Welling
42 H 15 Lancelot rd Wemb
78 B 10 Lancey clo SE7
29 N 15 Lanchester rd N6
18 H 5 Lancing gdns N9
122 D 16 Lancing rd Croy
36 E 19 Lancing rd Ilf
72 A 1 Lancing rd W13
132 F 13 Lancing st NW1
91 V 15 Landcroft rd SE22
91 V 16 Landells rd SE22
49 X 11 Landford st E6
49 X 14 Landford clo
86 M 9 Landford rd SW15
105 X 11 Landgrove rd SW19
75 T 15 Landmann way SE14
147 O 1 Landon pl SW3
76 G 2 Landons clo E14
90 A 7 Landor rd SW9
74 F 6 Landor wlk W12
7 V 19 Landra gdns N21
87 U 4 Landridge rd SW6
30 B 18 Landrock rd N8
34 H 2 Landscape rd Wdfd Grn
53 V 15 Landseer av E12
25 R 7 Landseer clo Edg
120 E 1 Landseer clo SW19
117 Z 16 Landseer rd New Mald
8 J 18 Landseer rd Enf
48 A 8 Landseer rd N19
153 X 14 Landseer rd Sutton
14 E 17 Lane appr NW7
44 J 10 Lane clo NW2
98 F 8 Lane end Bxly Hth
10 F 4 Lane gdns Bushey
130 A 10 Lane the NW8
94 F 7 Lane the SE3
108 G 3 Lanercost clo SW2
16 M 1 Lanercost gdns N14
108 G 3 Lanercost rd SW2
56 C 2 Laneside av Dgnhm
114 A 12 Laneside Chisl
12 H 17 Laneside Edg
86 J 14 Laneway SW15
63 V 7 Lanfranc rd E3
141 T 20 Lanfranc st SE1
145 O 11 Lanfrey pl W14
63 P 11 Lang st E1
47 P 7 Langbourne av N6
95 O 6 Langbrook rd SE3
120 M 5 Langdale av Mitch
98 E 1 Langdale cres Bxly Hth
57 W 15 Langdale gdns Hornch
60 C 8 Langdale gdns Grnfd

122 F 9 Langdale rd Thntn Hth
76 F 20 Langdale rd SE10
143 V 7 Langdale st E1
66 K 5 Langdon cres E6
62 A 3 Langdon ct NW10
43 U 3 Langdon dri NW9
47 U 1 Langdon Park rd N6
85 V 7 Langdon pl SW14
66 J 4 Langdon rd E6
120 C 12 Langdon rd Mrdn
114 K 12 Langdon shaw Sidcp
49 W 14 Langford clo E8
130 D 9 Langford clo NW8
5 Z 13 Langford cres Barnt
91 R 7 Langford grn SE5
130 D 9 Langford pl NW8
115 N 7 Langford pl Sidcp
21 Z 20 Langford rd Wdfd Grn
88 B 3 Langford rd SW6
37 P 18 Langham dri Rom
42 D 7 Langham gdns Wemb
25 V 1 Langham gdns Edg
7 U 17 Langham gdns N21
102 E 9 Langham gdns Rich
60 B 20 Langham gdns W13
102 F 9 Langham House clo Rich
30 H 11 Langham pde N15
139 Z 3 Langham pl W1
12 H 20 Langham rd Edg
30 M 12 Langham rd N15
119 N 1 Langham rd SW20
102 A 14 Langham rd Tedd
139 Z 2 Langham st W1
18 G 19 Langhedge clo N18
18 H 18 Langhedge la N18
89 Y 19 Langholm clo SW12
10 A 4 Langholme Bushey
56 D 19 Langhorne rd Dgnhm
24 H 8 Langland Crescent east Stanm
24 H 8 Langland Crescent west Stanm
158 L 2 Langland gdns Croy
46 B 14 Langland gdns NW3
128 E 11 Langler rd NW10
116 H 20 Langley av Surb
153 O 2 Langley av Worc Pk
68 H 2 Langley cres Dgnhm
34 K 20 Langley cres E11
12 J 12 Langley cres Edg
125 S 9 Langley ct Becknhm
140 K 7 Langley ct WC2
34 J 19 Langley dri E11
73 T 4 Langley dri W3
126 L 9 Langley gdns Brom
127 Z 14 Langley gdns Brom
68 H 2 Langley gdns Dgnhm
118 A 3 Langley gro New Mald
117 Z 3 Langley gro New Mald
148 M 14 Langley la SW8
154 E 15 Langley Park rd Sutton
13 O 18 Langley pk NW7
124 G 9 Langley rd Becknhm
83 W 3 Langley rd Islwth
158 E 20 Langley rd S Croy
116 K 17 Langley rd Surb
119 W 1 Langley rd SW19
105 X 20 Langley rd W Wckm
80 F 18 Langley rd Welling
140 K 7 Langley st WC2
126 A 17 Langley way W Wckm
125 Y 18 Langley way W Wckm
10 D 4 Langmead dri Bushey
108 K 9 Langmead SE27
106 L 5 Langroyd rd SW17
86 F 10 Langside av SW15
16 L 11 Langside cres N14
160 F 3 Langthorn ct EC2
51 V 10 Langthorne rd E11
144 G 20 Langthorne st SW6
66 K 9 Langton av E6
15 S 3 Langton av N20
133 O 15 Langton clo WC1
22 M 3 Langton rd Harrow
23 N 2 Langton rd Harrow
44 M 10 Langton rd NW2
90 K 1 Langton rd SW9
149 Y 20 Langton rd SW9
91 Z 18 Langton ri SE22
92 A 18 Langton ri SE23
128 D 16 Langton st SW10
157 T 7 Langton way Croy

94 D 1 Langton way SE3
77 U 20 Langton way SE3
58 A 5 Langtry rd Nthlt
129 Y 5 Langtry rd NW8
130 A 4 Langtry wlk NW8
102 E 16 Langwood chase Tedd
129 U 16 Lanhill rd W9
93 V 15 Lanier rd SE13
28 G 6 Lankaster gdns N2
22 F 18 Lankers dri Harrow
125 T 1 Lankton clo Becknhm
114 A 1 Lannoy rd SE9
64 L 16 Lanrick rd E14
80 J 8 Lanridge rd SE2
68 A 1 Lansbury av Bark
18 C 18 Lansbury av N18
37 Z 16 Lansbury av Rom
9 T 7 Lansbury rd Enf
18 C 18 Lansbury way N18
64 H 17 Lansby gdns E14
121 O 3 Landsell rd Mitch
52 L 19 Lansdown rd E7
115 P 7 Lansdown rd Sidcp
80 H 19 Lansdowne av Welling
105 N 18 Lansdowne clo SW20
101 V 1 Lansdowne clo Twick
137 N 10 Lansdowne cres W11
152 F 2 Lansdowne ct Worc Pk
135 V 3 Lansdowne dri E8
49 X 19 Lansdowne dri E8
90 A 1 Lansdowne gdns SW8
148 K 20 Lansdowne gdns SW8
44 B 14 Lansdowne gro NW10
108 J 6 Lansdowne hill SE27
78 A 15 Lansdowne la SE7
77 Z 15 Lansdowne la SE7
137 N 14 Lansdowne ms W11
150 G 1 Lansdowne pl SE1
109 T 17 Lansdowne pl SE19
82 K 7 Lansdowne rd Hounsl
112 G 18 Lansdowne rd Brom
157 N 2 Lansdowne rd Croy
123 O 20 Lansdowne rd Croy
52 B 7 Lansdowne rd E11
33 N 17 Lansdowne rd E17
34 E 10 Lansdowne rd E18
20 A 9 Lansdowne rd E4
54 K 2 Lansdowne rd Ilf
29 V 8 Lansdowne rd N10
31 W 5 Lansdowne rd N17
27 X 1 Lansdowne rd N3
11 S 20 Lansdowne rd Stanm
105 N 17 Lansdowne rd SW20
136 M 9 Lansdowne rd W11
137 N 12 Lansdowne rd W11
136 M 10 Lansdowne rd W11
139 Y 12 Lansdowne row W1
132 M 17 Lansdowne ter W11
89 Z 2 Lansdowne way SW8
90 A 2 Lansdowne way SW8
137 O 12 Lansdowne wlk W11
18 J 13 Lensfield av Wick
142 A 18 Lant st SE1
86 G 10 Lantern clo SW15
42 G 15 Lantern clo Wemb
76 C 7 Lanterns ct E14
92 B 5 Lanvanor rd SE15
109 Y 3 Lapswood wlk SE26
24 D 19 Lapstone gdns Harrow
93 V 16 Lara clo SE13
107 U 19 Larbert rd SW16
74 A 3 Larch av W3
16 A 20 Larch clo N11
107 R 3 Larch clo SW12
45 N 12 Larch rd NW2
159 P 6 Larch Tree way Croy
127 W 16 Larch way Brom
85 X 10 Larches av SW14
17 Y 10 Larches the N13
114 A 5 Larchwood rd SE9
113 Z 4 Larchwood rd SE9
150 C 7 Larcom st SE17
74 B 4 Larden rd W3
63 O 4 Lark row E2
135 Z 6 Lark row E2
110 H 10 Larkbere rd SE26
10 A 5 Larken dri Bushey

24 C 10 Larkfield av Harrow
84 K 10 Larkfield rd Rich
114 K 8 Larkfield rd Sidcp
89 X 5 Larkhall la SW4
89 V 6 Larkhall ri SW4
9 N 7 Larkshall rd E4
20 H 14 Larkshall cres E4
20 J 10 Larkshall rd E4
66 D 14 Larkspur clo E6
31 O 3 Larkspur clo N17
20 C 15 Larkswood rd E4
25 Z 14 Larkway clo NW9
86 L 13 Larpent av SW15
41 P 15 Larwood clo Grnfd
41 R 1 Lascelles av Harrow
51 X 8 Lascelles clo E11
17 R 20 Lascotts rd N22
95 S 13 Lassa rd SE9
76 L 14 Lassell st SE10
34 J 5 Latchett rd E18
62 H 8 Latchford gdns NW10
102 K 11 Latchmere clo Rich
88 L 6 Latchmere gro SW11
102 L 14 Latchmere la Kingst
88 K 5 Latchmere pas SW11
102 K 17 Latchmere rd Kingst
103 N 15 Latchmere rd Kingst
88 L 8 Latchmere rd SW11
88 L 4 Latchmere st SW11
72 G 17 Lateward rd Brentf
83 X 17 Latham clo Twick
98 F 13 Latham rd Bxly Hth
83 X 18 Latham rd Twick
156 C 1 Latham's way Croy
18 J 2 Lathkill clo Enf
66 E 16 Lathom clo E6
66 E 1 Lathom rd E6
66 G 4 Latimer av E6
152 K 8 Latimer clo Worc Pk
136 C 4 Latimer pl W10
5 N 10 Latimer rd Barnt
156 J 5 Latimer rd Croy
52 J 11 Latimer rd E7
31 S 18 Latimer rd N15
106 A 16 Latimer rd SW19
101 V 12 Latimer rd Tedd
136 D 5 Latimer rd W10
62 M 15 Latimer rd W10
63 T 15 Latimer st E1
151 R 15 Latona rd SE15
18 G 5 Latymer rd N9
18 C 9 Latymer way N9
156 L 7 Laud st Croy
149 N 10 Laud st Croy
102 G 6 Lauderdale dri Rich
130 A 15 Lauderdale rd W9
129 X 15 Lauderdale rd W9
58 A 4 Laughton rd Nthlt
112 G 10 Launcelot rd Brom
141 S 18 Launcelot st SE1
60 C 2 Launceston gdns Grnfd

146 A 2 Launceston pl W8
60 C 3 Launceston rd Grnfd
76 F 7 Launch st E14
144 K 15 Laundry rd W6
34 K 15 Laura clo E11
8 D 17 Laura clo Enf
50 B 12 Laura rd E3
29 N 12 Lauradale rd N2
101 V 1 Laura rd Twick
115 N 7 Laurel clo Sidcp
159 O 6 Laurel cres Croy
57 P 5 Laurel cres Rom
17 S 2 Laurel rd E12
20 D 2 Laurel gdns E4
82 A 11 Laurel gdns Hounsl
71 T 2 Laurel gdns NW7
71 T 2 Laurel gdns W7
110 B 18 Laurel gro SE20
110 G 11 Laurel gro SE26
86 F 5 Laurel rd SW13
104 H 20 Laurel rd SW20
101 P 13 Laurel rd Tedd
49 V 18 Laurel st E8
15 N 11 Laurel way N17
34 C 12 Laurel way E18
14 L 10 Laurel way N20
8 A 6 Laurelbank rd Enf
23 V 2 Laurels the Harrow
160 F 9 Laurence Poutney la EC4
160 F 8 Laurence Poutney hill EC4
92 J 1 Laurie gro SE14
59 T 14 Laurie rd W7
39 R 14 Laurie wlk Rom

123 U 16 Laurier rd Croy
47 S 10 Laurier rd NW5
11 P 19 Laurimel clo Stanm
63 S 1 Lauriston rd E9
105 O 15 Lauriston rd SW19
30 G 13 Lausanne rd N8
92 D 4 Lausanne rd SE15
49 O 13 Lavell st N16
120 J 1 Lavender av Mitch
43 V 3 Lavender av NW9
153 N 5 Lavender av Worc Pk
155 P 9 Lavender clo Carsh
88 M 9 Lavender gdns SW11
7 X 4 Lavender gdns Enf
49 W 20 Lavender gro E8
120 K 1 Lavender gro Mitch
7 T 5 Lavender hill Enf
88 L 9 Lavender hill SW11
89 O 8 Lavender hill SW11
155 P 10 Lavender rd Carsh
122 B 14 Lavender rd Croy
8 C 5 Lavender rd Enf
75 W 2 Lavender rd SE16
154 F 7 Lavender rd Sutton
88 G 7 Lavender rd SW11
51 Z 18 Lavender st E15
88 L 10 Lavender sweep SW11
155 X 14 Lavender vale Wallgtn
124 F 15 Lavender way Croy
88 L 10 Lavender wlk SW11
108 L 4 Lavengro rd SE27
105 X 2 Lavenham rd SW18
98 F 5 Lavernock rd Bxly Hth
49 T 9 Lavers rd N16
86 F 19 Laverstoke gdns SW15
145 Y 8 Laverton ms SW5
145 Y 7 Laverton pl SW5
113 S 5 Lavidge rd SE9
132 M 8 Lavina gro N1
156 C 7 Lavington rd Croy
72 C 3 Lavington rd W13
141 Z 14 Lavington st SE1
150 G 1 Law st SE1
156 K 8 Lawdons gdns Croy
155 Z 19 Lawford clo Wallgtn
134 J 2 Lawford rd N1
47 V 18 Lawford rd NW5
73 W 18 Lawford rd W4
132 B 2 Lawfords wharf NW1
16 E 3 Lawley rd N14
50 D 12 Lawley st E5
112 H 16 Lawn clo Brom
18 H 3 Lawn clo N9
118 A 4 Lawn clo New Mald
85 N 4 Lawn cres Rich
37 Y 11 Lawn Farm gro Rom
71 T 2 Lawn gdns W7
148 M 14 Lawn la SW8
149 N 15 Lawn la SW8
110 M 18 Lawn rd Becknhm
47 R 1 Lawn rd N6
46 L 15 Lawn rd NW3
94 B 7 Lawn ter SE3
70 H 13 Lawn the S'hall
22 A 6 Lawn vale Pinn
20 C 16 Lawns the E4
22 K 1 Lawns the Pinn
123 O 1 Lawns the SE3
94 B 7 Lawns the SE3
115 S 9 Lawns the Sidcp
153 T 17 Lawns the Sutton
38 L 2 Lawns way Rom
94 B 11 Lawnside SE3
118 A 17 Lawrence av New Mald
117 Z 15 Lawrence av New Mald
53 V 14 Lawrence av E12
32 G 4 Lawrence av N13
17 V 15 Lawrence av N13
13 P 13 Lawrence av NW7
15 U 10 Lawrence bldgs N16
Lawrence Campe clo N20
31 R 12 Lawrence clo N15
56 G 9 Lawrence cres Dgnhm
25 P 8 Lawrence cres Edg
13 O 15 Lawrence ct NW7
13 S 10 Lawrence gdns NW7
20 B 7 Lawrence hill E4
160 C 5 Lawrence la EC2
132 L 4 Lawrence pl N1
65 V 3 Lawrence rd E13
64 A 8 Lawrence rd E3

66 C 2 Lawrence rd E6
100 E 18 Lawrence rd Hampt
31 R 13 Lawrence rd N15
18 M 14 Lawrence rd N18
102 E 9 Lawrence rd Rich
39 Y 17 Lawrence rd Rom
123 V 9 Lawrence rd SE25
72 F 10 Lawrence rd W5
65 P 16 Lawrence st E16
13 S 12 Lawrence st NW7
146 J 15 Lawrence st SW3
60 A 4 Lawrence way Grnfd
119 X 13 Lawrence Weaver clo Mrdn
31 S 13 Lawrence yd N15
110 B 11 Lawrie Park av SE26
110 A 13 Lawrie Park cres SE26
110 B 12 Lawrie Park gdns SE26
110 B 14 Lawrie Park rd SE26
105 O 8 Lawson clo SW19
9 O 8 Lawson rd Enf
58 G 12 Lawson rd S'hall
65 Z 16 Lawsons clo E16
5 T 12 Lawton rd Barnt
51 T 4 Lawton rd E10
63 W 10 Lawton rd E3
149 Y 18 Laxley clo SE5
131 Z 16 Laxton pl NW1
8 H 5 Layard rd Enf
123 O 3 Layard rd Thntn Hth
151 X 4 Layard sq SE16
48 G 19 Laycock st N1
61 P 20 Layer gdns W3
44 K 1 Layfield clo NW4
44 J 1 Layfield cres NW4
44 K 2 Layfield rd NW4
159 Z 11 Layhams rd W Wckhm
81 O 9 Laymarsh clo Blvdr
40 A 19 Laymead clo Nthlt
133 S 18 Laystall st EC1
156 H 11 Layton cres Croy
72 G 14 Layton rd Brentf
82 L 10 Layton rd Hounsl
133 U 7 Layton rd N1
112 H 6 Le May av SE12
50 E 6 Lea Bridge rd E10
33 T 18 Lea Bridge rd E10
33 X 15 Lea Bridge rd E11
42 L 14 Lea gdns Wemb
51 O 3 Lea Hall rd E10
125 O 2 Lea rd Becknhm
8 A 6 Lea rd Enf
70 B 11 Lea rd S'hall
98 M 11 Lea vale Bxly Hth
20 B 1 Lea Valley rd E4
9 Y 19 Lea Valley rd Enf
41 T 10 Leabank clo Harrow
31 Y 17 Leabank view N15
31 W 20 Leabourne rd N16
96 K 13 Leachcroft av Sidcp
88 M 19 Leacroft av SW12
20 A 9 Leadale av E4
31 X 18 Leadale rd N15
160 H 7 Leaden Hall av EC3
142 J 6 Leadenhall mkt EC3
142 J 7 Leadenhall pl EC3
142 K 6 Leadenhall st EC3
53 X 16 Leadane av E12
43 V 9 Leadings the Wemb
108 F 11 Leaf gro SE27
108 H 16 Leafield clo SW16
153 X 3 Leafield rd Sutton
119 W 5 Leafield rd SW20
112 L 8 Leafy Oak rd SE12
157 T 3 Leafy way Croy
50 D 9 Leagrave st E5
94 A 15 Leahurst rd SE13
93 X 13 Leahurst rd SE13
141 R 18 Leake st SE1
31 U 17 Lealand rd N15
112 K 12 Leamington av Brom
33 O 17 Leamington av E17
119 U 8 Leamington av Mrdn
83 O 12 Leamington clo Hounsl
112 K 11 Leamington clo Brom
53 S 15 Leamington clo E12
40 C 10 Leamington cres Harrow
54 K 7 Leamington gdns Ilf
61 X 16 Leamington pk W3
137 R 3 Leamington Road vlls W11
144 A 7 Leamore st W6
74 L 11 Leamore st W6
66 C 16 Leamouth gdns E6
64 K 18 Leamouth rd E14
58 G 6 Leander rd Nthlt
90 E 16 Leander rd SW2

122 D 8 Leander rd Thntn Hth
66 J 19 Learoyd gdns E6
113 W 7 Leas dale SE9
114 L 15 Leas grn Chisl
29 O 11 Leaside av N10
50 B 5 Leaside rd E5
51 O 3 Leasowes rd E10
81 P 7 Leather Bottle grn Blvdr
121 O 4 Leather clo Mitch
64 M 4 Leather gdns E15
133 T 19 Leather la EC1
141 T 2 Leather la EC1
63 T 10 Leatherdale st E1
49 T 3 Leatherhead clo N16
142 H 18 Leathermarket st SE1
40 L 10 Leathsail rd Harrow
88 M 11 Leathwaite rd SW11
93 R 5 Leathwell rd SE8
125 O 9 Leaveland clo Becknhm
59 S 7 Leaver gdns Grnfd
10 M 19 Leavesden rd Stanm
11 N 20 Leavesden rd Stanm
50 G 5 Leaway E10
87 X 14 Lebanon gdns SW18
84 B 20 Lebanon pk Twick
157 T 2 Lebanon rd Croy
87 X 14 Lebanon rd SW18
94 G 9 Lebrun sq SE3
34 M 7 Lechmere appr Wdfd Grn
34 M 7 Lechmere av Wdfd Grn
44 K 18 Lechmere rd NW2
106 E 2 Leckford rd SW18
80 L 17 Leckwith av Bxly Hth
146 F 10 Lecky st SW7
86 D 9 Leconfield av SW13
49 N 13 Leconfield rd N5
9 S 4 Leda av Enf
137 T 7 Ledbury ms N W11
137 S 8 Ledbury ms W W11
157 N 9 Ledbury pl Croy
157 N 9 Ledbury rd Croy
137 S 7 Ledbury rd W11
151 U 17 Ledbury st SE15
109 W 16 Ledrington rd SE19
42 M 2 Ledway dri Wemb
43 N 1 Ledway dri Wemb
37 X 19 Lee av Rom
94 A 10 Lee Church st SE13
32 E 6 Lee clo E17
50 L 14 Lee Conservancy rd E9
93 V 9 Lee High rd SE13
19 V 12 Lee Parkway N9
94 B 10 Lee pk SE3
8 K 20 Lee rd Enf
60 D 3 Lee rd Grnfd
120 B 1 Lee rd Mitch
27 R 2 Lee rd NW7
94 C 11 Lee rd SE3
134 M 3 Lee st E8
135 N 3 Lee st E8
94 A 8 Lee ter SE3
93 Z 8 Lee ter SE3
7 W 6 Lee view Enf
155 P 6 Leechcroft rd Wallgtn
4 E 14 Leecroft rd Barnt
48 D 4 Leeds pla N4
54 F 4 Leeds rd Ilf
18 J 17 Leeds st N18
133 N 12 Leeke st WC1
71 Z 2 Leeland rd W13
72 A 2 Leeland ter W13
44 C 12 Leeland way NW10
27 O 13 Leemount clo NW4
139 T 8 Lees pl W1
158 L 3 Lees the Croy
4 F 19 Leeside Barnt
27 U 18 Leeside cres NW11
19 P 20 Leeside rd N17
90 G 12 Leeson rd SE24
105 U 14 Leeward gdns SW19
22 C 2 Leeway clo Pinn
75 Y 13 Leeway SE8
63 Z 4 Lefevre wk E3
74 H 6 Leffern rd W12
74 C 5 Lefroy rd W12
48 J 11 Legard rd N5
94 M 13 Legatt rd SE9
95 N 13 Legatt rd SE9
64 G 6 Leggatt rd E15
93 T 12 Legge st SE13
62 F 5 Leghorn rd NW10
79 T 14 Leghorn rd SE18
119 Y 14 Legion ct Mrdn
59 O 4 Legion rd Grnfd

56 L 5 Legon av Rom
140 G 9 Leicester ct WC2
152 M 7 Leicester ct Worc Pk
36 J 20 Leicester gdns Ilf
140 G 9 Leicester pl WC2
5 R 14 Leicester rd Barnt
123 S 18 Leicester rd Croy
34 J 16 Leicester rd E11
28 K 11 Leicester rd N2
43 Z 20 Leicester rd NW10
140 G 10 Leicester sq WC2
140 F 9 Leicester st WC2
35 N 13 Leigh av Ilf
117 X 8 Leigh clo New Mald
159 T 16 Leigh cres Croy
41 S 5 Leigh ct Harrow
128 C 9 Leigh gdns NW10
62 M 6 Leigh gdns NW10
142 A 17 Leigh Hunt st SE1
108 C 8 Leigh Orchard clo SW16
141 T 1 Leigh pl EC1
97 O 4 Leigh pl Welling
51 V 2 Leigh rd E10
53 V 19 Leigh rd E6
83 P 10 Leigh rd Hounsl
48 J 13 Leigh rd N5
132 J 15 Leigh st WC1
108 A 7 Leigham av SW16
108 B 5 Leigham Court rd SW16
71 U 19 Leigham dri Islwth
108 E 6 Leigham vale SW16
53 W 16 Leighton av E12
22 B 10 Leighton av Pinn
25 R 7 Leighton clo Edg
47 W 14 Leighton cres NW5
128 C 7 Leighton gdns NW10
62 L 5 Leighton gdns NW10
47 W 14 Leighton gro NW5
8 H 18 Leighton rd Enf
23 O 7 Leighton rd Harrow
47 V 15 Leighton rd NW5
72 A 5 Leighton rd W13
71 Z 5 Leighton rd W13
122 H 20 Leighton st Croy
85 V 9 Leinster av SW14
138 B 7 Leinster gdns W2
138 B 10 Leinster ms W2
138 A 7 Leinster pl W2
29 T 13 Leinster rd N10
129 T 12 Leinster rd NW6
137 W 7 Leinster sq W2
138 B 10 Leinster ter W2
43 Y 4 Leith clo NW9
30 H 4 Leith rd N22
129 U 4 Leith rd NW6
108 C 9 Leithcote gdns SW16
135 S 5 Lelitia clo E8
143 R 7 Leman st E1
11 R 17 Lemark clo Stanm
76 M 15 Lemmon rd SE10
52 A 2 Lemna rd E11
96 A 15 Lemonwell ct SE9
31 Y 17 Lemsford clo N15
88 B 16 Lemuel st SW18
144 D 2 Lena gdns W6
74 M 9 Lena gdns W6
89 Y 8 Lendal ter SW4
117 P 20 Lenelby rd Surb
81 O 17 Lenham rd Bxly Hth
94 B 11 Lenham rd SE12
154 B 10 Lenham rd Sutton
123 O 4 Lenham rd Thntn Hth
110 K 17 Lennard rd Becknhm
127 U 20 Lennard rd Brom
122 K 19 Lennard rd Croy
44 M 16 Lennon rd NW2
159 N 4 Lennox clo Rom
147 N 4 Lennox Gardens ms SW1
156 K 9 Lennox gdns Croy
53 S 4 Lennox gdns Ilf
44 D 13 Lennox gdns NW10
147 N 4 Lennox gdns SW1
32 M 19 Lennox rd E17
48 E 7 Lennox rd N4
97 Y 11 Lenor clo Bxly Hth
65 X 1 Lens rd E7
80 G 7 Lensbury way SE2
146 B 5 Lenthall pl SW7
49 W 20 Lenthall rd E8
77 P 13 Lenthorpe rd SE10
112 C 7 Lentmead rd Brom
79 R 10 Lenton st SE18
151 U 10 Lenville way SE16
75 O 19 Leo st SE15
151 Z 17 Leo st SE15

133 Y 18 Leo yd EC1
111 P 12 Leof cres SE6
120 D 13 Leominster rd Mrdn
120 C 13 Leominster wlk Mrdn
120 D 12 Leonard av Mrdn
56 M 4 Leonard av Rom
20 B 19 Leonard rd E4
52 E 13 Leonard rd E7
18 J 12 Leonard rd N9
107 U 20 Leonard rd SW16
78 D 3 Leonard st E16
134 F 16 Leonard st EC2
151 T 19 Leontine clo SE15
105 W 12 Leopold av SW19
33 O 16 Leopold rd E17
19 N 18 Leopold rd N18
28 G 9 Leopold rd N2
62 B 1 Leopold rd NW10
105 X 12 Leopold rd SW19
72 M 2 Leopold rd W5
73 N 2 Leopold rd W5
63 Z 14 Leopold st E3
149 N 10 Leopold wlk SE11
89 X 13 Leppoc rd SW4
150 J 3 Leroy st SE1
110 J 7 Lescombe clo SE23
110 J 7 Lescombe rd SE23
98 G 18 Lesley clo Bxly
153 Y 15 Leslie gdns Sutton
123 S 20 Leslie Park rd Croy
51 V 12 Leslie rd E11
65 V 18 Leslie rd E16
28 G 10 Leslie rd N2
80 K 10 Lesnes Abbey remains Blvdr
80 L 12 Lesnes Abbey pk SE2
81 Z 16 Lesney pk Erith
89 I 14 Lessar av SW4
92 G 17 Lessing st SE23
106 M 8 Lessingham av SW17
107 N 10 Lessingham av SW17
35 U 9 Lessingham av Ilf
38 K 19 Lessington av Rom
80 J 18 Lessness av Bxly Hth
81 P 12 Lessness pk Blvdr
81 R 15 Lessness rd Blvdr
120 E 13 Lessness rd Mrdn
65 N 11 Lester av E15
49 U 10 Leswin pl N16
49 U 9 Leswin rd N16
62 H 8 Letchford ms NW10
22 K 4 Letchford ter Har
126 F 11 Letchworth clo Brom
126 F 12 Letchworth dri Brom
106 L 9 Letchworth st SW17
93 T 3 Lethbridge rd SE10
64 J 2 Lett rd E15
145 N 19 Letterstone rd SW6
87 V 3 Lettice st SW6
91 R 4 Lettsom st SE5
65 S 6 Lettsom wlk E13
32 H 16 Leucha rd E17
105 R 2 Levanna clo SW19
90 A 4 Levehurst way SW4
64 J 16 Leven rd E14
110 K 4 Levendale rd SE23
134 A 14 Lever st EC1
133 Y 14 Lever st EC1
146 M 6 Leverett st SW3
113 W 9 Leverholme gdns SE9
107 V 16 Leverson st SW16
47 U 15 Leverton pl NW5
47 U 14 Leverton st NW5
54 H 18 Levett rd Bark
54 K 11 Levett rd Ilf
68 K 6 Levine gdns Bark
47 W 5 Levison way N19
40 H 18 Lewes clo Nthlt
127 N 3 Lewes rd Brom
15 W 18 Lewes rd N12
105 O 2 Leweston clo SW19
49 U 2 Lewgars av NW9
25 W 18 Lewgars av NW9
97 Z 11 Lewin rd Bxly Hth
85 Z 9 Lewin rd SW14
107 Z 14 Lewin rd SW16
33 O 4 Lewis av E17
43 X 16 Lewis cres NW10
28 G 6 Lewis gdns N2
93 U 9 Lewis gro SE13
120 J 3 Lewis rd Mitch
84 H 13 Lewis rd S'hall
70 C 5 Lewis rd Sidcp
115 T 7 Lewis rd Sutton
154 B 7 Lewis rd Sutton
97 U 8 Lewis rd Welling

47 T 19 Lewis st NW1
93 T 12 Lewisham High st SE13
93 U 6 Lewisham hill SE13
93 T 14 Lewisham pk SE13
93 T 3 Lewisham rd SE13
140 G 19 Lewisham st SW1
92 L 2 Lewisham way SE13
93 O 5 Lewisham way SE4
37 P 18 Lexden dri Rom
121 W 8 Lexden rd Mitch
73 T 2 Lexden rd W3
145 Y 4 Lexham Gdns ms W8
145 X 4 Lexham gdns W8
145 V 4 Lexham ms W8
145 Y 3 Lexham wlk W8
140 D 8 Lexington st W1
4 C 15 Lexington way Barnt
89 Z 20 Lexton gdns SW12
54 C 5 Ley st Ilf
36 D 20 Ley st Ilf
53 Y 8 Ley st Ilf
72 D 5 Leyborne av W13
85 O 1 Leyborne pk Rich
126 E 13 Leybourne clo Brom
52 C 4 Leybourne rd E11
52 O 15 Leybourne rd NW9
94 E 13 Leybridge ct SE12
33 T 13 Leyburn clo E17
157 S 3 Leyburn gdns Croy
18 K 19 Leyburn gro N18
18 L 19 Leyburn rd N18
99 X 2 Leycroft gdns Erith
142 M 3 Leyden st E1
143 N 3 Leyden st E1
75 T 3 Leydon clo SE16
66 A 19 Leyes rd E10
65 Z 19 Leyes rd E16
152 C 1 Leyfield Worc Pk
9 V 8 Leyland av Enf
21 Y 17 Leyland gdns Wdfd Grn
94 D 13 Leyland rd SE12
75 T 19 Leylang rd SE14
69 Y 2 Leys av Dgnhm
23 R 14 Leys clo Harrow
6 B 16 Leys gdns Barnt
9 V 5 Leys Road east Enf
9 V 5 Leys Road west Enf
24 L 18 Leys the Harrow
28 D 13 Leys the N2
98 K 11 Leysdown av Bxly Hth
113 S 4 Leysdown rd SE9
74 H 7 Leysfield rd W12
52 C 3 Leyspring rd E11
36 G 14 Leyswood dri Ilf
73 V 6 Leythe rd W3
51 O 5 Leyton Grange est
33 T 20 Leyton Green rd E10
51 U 8 Leyton Park rd E10
51 V 14 Leyton rd E15
106 E 18 Leyton rd SW19
51 Y 14 Leytonstone rd E15
64 M 5 Leywick st E15
75 W 17 Liardet st SE14
48 J 17 Liberia rd N5
120 E 1 Liberty av Mitch
106 F 20 Liberty av Mitch
90 D 1 Liberty st SW9
149 R 20 Liberty st SW9
39 R 15 Liberty the Rom
65 S 5 Libra rd E3
63 Y 4 Libra rd E3
141 X 19 Library st SE1
84 J 11 Lichfield gdns Rich
28 A 7 Lichfield gro N3
27 X 5 Lichfield gro N3
55 S 10 Lichfield rd Dgnhm
63 W 9 Lichfield rd E3
66 B 10 Lichfield rd E6
18 J 8 Lichfield rd N9
45 S 12 Lichfield rd NW2
85 N 2 Lichfield rd Rich
21 N 14 Lichfield rd Wdfd Grn
14 E 18 Lidbury rd NW7
24 H 11 Liddell clo Harrow
128 C 7 Liddell gdns NW10
62 M 5 Liddell gdns NW10
24 H 16 Lidding rd Harrow
65 P 3 Liddington rd E15
126 M 6 Liddon rd Brom
127 N 6 Liddon rd Brom
65 U 10 Liddon rd E13
49 O 13 Lidfield rd N16
106 E 3 Lidiard rd SW18
132 B 10 Lidlington pl NW1
47 V 5 Lidyard rd N19

79 T 13 Liffler rd SE18
87 P 10 Lifford st SW15
17 U 12 Lightcliffe rd N13
30 B 14 Lightfoot rd N8
60 L 2 Lightley clo Wemb
19 Y 19 Lilac clo E4
159 O 5 Lilac gdns Croy
57 O 4 Lilac gdns Rom
72 G 8 Lilac gdns W5
62 F 19 Lilac st W12
95 R 14 Lilburne gdns SE9
95 S 13 Lilburne rd SE9
43 V 17 Lilburne wlk NW10
59 U 15 Lile cres W7
130 K 17 Lilestone st NW8
90 J 4 Lilford rd SE5
34 J 4 Lilian gdns Wdfd Grn
107 U 20 Lilian rd SW16
55 T 16 Lillechurch rd Dgnhm
120 F 14 Lilleshall rd Mrdn
12 M 15 Lilley la NW7
73 O 7 Lillian av W3
41 P 15 Lillian Board way Grnfd
74 H 16 Lillian rd SW13
145 V 13 Lillie Bridge ms SW6
144 H 16 Lillie rd SW6
145 P 14 Lillie rd SW6
145 U 13 Lillie rd SW6
89 T 7 Lillieshall rd SW4
148 D 8 Lillington Garden est SW1
58 D 3 Lilliput av Nthlt
57 N 1 Lilliput rd Rom
144 J 8 Lily clo W14
60 E 7 Lily gdns Wemb
33 P 20 Lily rd E17
87 V 1 Lilyville rd SW6
56 B 2 Limbourne av Dgnhm
88 K 11 Limburg rd SW11
154 L 1 Lime clo Carsh
143 U 13 Lime clo E1
38 J 14 Lime clo Rom
137 V 11 Lime ct W8
14 G 4 Lime gro N20
117 Z 6 Lime gro New Mald
96 L 15 Lime gro Sidcp
83 X 16 Lime gro Twick
136 B 16 Lime gro W12
74 L 4 Lime gro W12
81 N 7 Lime rd Blvdr
81 N 7 Lime row Blvdr
32 H 13 Lime st E17
142 J 7 Lime st EC3
59 T 20 Lime ter W7
110 A 20 Lime av SE20
108 D 2 Lime Tree clo SW2
159 N 5 Lime Tree gro Croy
158 L 6 Lime Tree gro Hounsl
82 K 1 Lime Tree rd Hounsl
70 K 20 Lime Tree rd Hounsl
10 F 6 Lime Tree wlk Bushey
7 X 3 Lime Tree wlk Enf
76 E 6 Limeharbour E14
63 Z 20 Limehouse causeway E14
89 U 19 Limerick clo SW12
154 I 1 Limes av Carsh
156 E 6 Limes av Croy
34 J 14 Limes av E11
15 R 12 Limes av N12
27 T 20 Limes av NW11
110 A 19 Limes av SE20
86 L 5 Limes av SW13
16 G 16 Limes av the N11
86 A 7 Limes Field rd SW14
87 Y 17 Limes gdns SW18
93 U 10 Limes gro SE13
11 N 9 Limes ho Stanm
125 S 3 Limes rd Becknhm
123 N 16 Limes rd Croy
92 B 9 Limes wlk SE15
72 H 7 Limes wlk W5
25 V 8 Limesdale gdns Edg
92 E 10 Limesford rd SE15
146 D 14 Limerston rd SW9
121 S 1 Limetree pl Mitch
60 C 16 Limewood clo W13
81 Y 19 Limewood rd Erith
122 D 12 Limpsfield av Thntn Hth
105 P 3 Limpsfield av SW19
151 T 18 Limpston Garden est SE15
44 K 18 Linacre rd NW2
75 X 11 Linberry wk SE8
94 D 19 Linchmere rd SE12
16 G 9 Lincoln av N14
57 O 4 Lincoln av Rom

105 O 7 Lincoln av SW19
100 M 3 Lincoln av Twick
101 N 2 Lincoln av Twick
99 T 5 Lincoln clo Erith
58 M 3 Lincoln clo Grnfd
59 N 3 Lincoln clo Grnfd
22 E 16 Lincoln clo Harrow
8 F 17 Lincoln cres Enf
49 P 2 Lincoln ct N16
53 S 1 Lincoln gdns Ilf
129 N 3 Lincoln ms NW6
65 U 13 Lincoln rd E13
34 D 6 Lincoln rd E18
53 N 19 Lincoln rd E7
8 L 17 Lincoln rd Enf
9 P 18 Lincoln rd Enf
99 U 4 Lincoln rd Enf
100 D 7 Lincoln rd Felt
22 F 16 Lincoln rd Harrow
122 A 10 Lincoln rd Mitch
28 K 11 Lincoln rd N2
117 V 6 Lincoln rd New Mald
123 Z 7 Lincoln rd SE25
115 R 12 Lincoln rd Sidcp
42 G 18 Lincoln rd Wemb
118 H 19 Lincoln rd Worc Pk
51 Y 8 Lincoln st E11
147 O 8 Lincoln st SW3
8 M 16 Lincoln way Enf
141 O 5 Lincolns Inn fields WC2
13 S 9 Lincolns the NW7
112 C 7 Lincombe rd Brom
154 E 11 Lind st SE8
93 P 4 Lind st SE8
7 O 15 Lindal cres Enf
02 L 14 Lindal rd SE4
155 Z 18 Lindbergh rd Wallgtn
8 K 6 Linden av Enf
82 K 12 Linden av Hounsl
128 E 11 Linden av NW10
122 H 8 Linden av Thntn Hth
42 M 14 Linden av Wemb
43 N 14 Linden av Wemb
6 G 19 Linden clo N14
11 N 16 Linden clo Stanm
21 U 18 Linden cres Wdfd Grn
41 V 17 Linden cres Grnfd
117 N 4 Linden cres Kingst
74 L 2 Linden ct W12
127 Y 3 Linden field BR7
8 K 5 Linden gdns Enf
137 V 11 Linden gdns W2
73 Z 13 Linden gdns W4
118 A 6 Linden gro New Mald
92 A 8 Linden gro SE15
110 D 16 Linden gro SE20
101 V 1 Linden gro Tedd
42 L 14 Linden lawns Wemb
28 E 17 Linden lee N2
159 X 2 Linden lees Wkhm
137 U 11 Linden rd W2
100 G 20 Linden rd Hampt
29 T 13 Linden rd N10
16 A 8 Linden rd N11
30 L 13 Linden rd N15
39 O 14 Linden st Rom
16 H 1 Linden way N14
6 H 20 Linden way N14
159 U 13 Lindens the Croy
15 T 16 Lindens the N12
85 V 1 Lindens the W4
46 C 15 Lindfield gdns NW3
123 V 15 Lindfield rd Croy
60 D 11 Lindfield rd W5
64 B 17 Lindfield st E14
55 T 9 Lindisfarne rd Dgnhm
104 G 19 Lindisfarne rd SW20
50 K 13 Lindisfarne way E9
51 T 6 Lindley rd E10
63 O 14 Lindley st E1
143 Z 1 Lindley st E1
92 D 5 Lindo st SE15
88 L 12 Lindore rd SW11
120 C 18 Lindores rd Carsh
88 C 4 Lindrop st SW6
24 M 16 Lindsay dri Harrow
100 L 10 Lindsay rd Hampt
152 K 2 Lindsay rd Worc Pk
67 O 4 Lindsell rd Bark
93 S 1 Lindsell st SE10
15 O 20 Lindsey clo Brom
92 P 7 Lindsey clo SE15
122 A 7 Lindsey clo Mitch
55 S 11 Lindsey gdns Dgnhm
141 Y 1 Lindsey st EC1
102 C 18 Lindum rd Tedd

108 H 13 Lindway SE27
33 V 11 Linford E17
89 U 2 Linford st SW8
65 T 14 Ling rd E16
81 Y 17 Ling rd Erith
93 V 11 Lingards rd SE13
114 L 3 Lingey clo Sidcp
116 K 9 Lingfield av Kingst
8 D 19 Lingfield clo Enf
96 E 10 Lingfield cres SE9
19 N 2 Lingfield gdns N9
105 P 14 Lingfield rd SW19
152 M 6 Lingfield rd Worc Pk
90 B 5 Lingham st SW9
4 C 16 Lingholm way Barnt
21 U 9 Lingrove gdns Buck Hl
109 O 3 Lings coppice SE21
106 K 6 Lingwell rd SW17
71 T 18 Lingwood gdns Islwth
49 Y 1 Lingwood rd E5
31 X 20 Lingwood rd N16
131 N 18 Linhope st NW1
156 A 13 Link la Wallgtn
155 Y 13 Link la Wallgtn
69 T 7 Link rd Dgnhm
16 B 13 Link rd N11
155 O 1 Link rd Wallgtn
50 D 16 Link st E9
9 V 5 Link the Enf
40 D 16 Link the Nthlt
61 S 16 Link the W3
42 D 4 Link the Wemb
127 R 16 Link way Brom
126 E 14 Linkfield Brom
83 Y 5 Linkfield rd Islwth
26 B 3 Linklea clo NW9
119 Y 8 Links av Mrdn
39 Z 6 Links av Rom
14 M 6 Links dri N20
108 E 18 Links gdns SW16
44 C 8 Links rd NW2
107 R 17 Links rd SW17
125 V 20 Links rd W Wkhm
61 P 16 Links rd W3
21 S 16 Links rd Wdfd Grn
7 S 12 Links side Enf
7 R 11 Linkside gdns Enf
14 J 18 Linkside N12
118 B 4 Linkside New Mald
27 O 8 Linksway NW4
55 U 11 Linkway Dgnhm
102 B 5 Linkway Rich
118 K 7 Linkway SW20
4 M 20 Linkway the Barnt
154 E 20 Linkway the Sutton
38 J 9 Linley cres Rom
31 S 6 Linley rd N17
27 Z 19 Linnell clo NW11
27 Z 20 Linnell dri NW11
18 K 15 Linnell rd N18
91 S 3 Linnell rd SE5
68 G 20 Linnet clo SE28
89 N 18 Linnet ms SW12
20 H 13 Linnett clo E4
90 A 11 Linom rd SW4
50 C 13 Linscott rd E5
151 S 5 Linsey st SE16
151 T 3 Linsey st SE16
45 X 19 Linstead st NW6
87 S 18 Linstead way SW18
42 F 17 Linthorpe av Wemb
5 W 12 Linthorpe rd Barnt
49 T 1 Linthorpe rd N16
97 O 3 Linton clo Well
39 O 7 Linton ct Rom
66 D 16 Linton gdns E6
158 H 20 Linton glade CRO
108 L 11 Linton gro SE27
54 B 20 Linton rd Bark
67 O 1 Linton rd Bark
134 C 5 Linton st N1
87 W 5 Linver rd SW6
66 F 15 Linwood clo E6
29 Z 13 Linzee rd N8
101 V 2 Lion av Twick
84 M 6 Lion Gate gdns Rich
85 N 5 Lion gdns Rich
98 A 10 Lion rd Bxly Hth
122 L 13 Lion rd Croy
66 G 15 Lion rd E6

18 K 9 Lion rd N9
101 V 1 Lion rd Twick
72 F 18 Lion way Brentf
84 A 8 Lion Wharf rd Islwth
95 O 13 Lionel gdns SE9
128 J 9 Lionel ms W10
128 K 20 Lionel ms W10
72 M 14 Lionel rd Brentf
73 O 14 Lionel rd Brentf
95 O 13 Lionel rd SE9
112 M 8 Lions clo SE9
113 N 8 Lionsdale clo SE9
92 B 19 Liphook cres SE23
68 F 19 Lipton clo SE28
63 T 18 Lipton st E1
100 M 5 Lisbon av Twick
101 N 4 Lisbon av Twick
46 M 13 Lisburne rd NW3
91 V 1 Lisford st SE15
145 N 6 Lisgar ter W14
114 C 16 Liskeard clo Chisl
94 F 2 Liskeard gdns SE3
140 G 9 Lisle st W2
83 X 5 Lismore clo Islwth
31 O 11 Lismore rd N17
157 R 5 Lismore rd S Croy
47 P 12 Lissenden gdns NW5
130 G 15 Lisson gro NW8
130 K 20 Lisson st NW1
18 A 16 Lister gdns N18
17 Z 16 Lister gdns N18
52 A 5 Lister rd E11
31 W 5 Liston rd N17
89 V 8 Liston rd SW4
34 L 2 Liston way Wdfd Grn
56 E 8 Listowel rd Dgnhm
149 X 20 Listowel clo SW9
149 X 20 Listowel st SW9
49 T 6 Listria pk N16
44 G 19 Litchfield gdns NW10
51 Z 18 Litchfield av E15
119 V 16 Litchfield av Mrdn
154 B 9 Litchfield rd Sutton
140 H 8 Litchfield st WC2
28 C 16 Litchfield way NW11
46 C 17 Lithos rd NW3
75 O 10 Litlington st SE16
151 Y 5 Litlington st SE16
125 P 7 Little acre Bcknhm
131 Z 14 Little Albany st NW1
140 A 6 Little Argyll st W1
114 H 5 Little birches Sidcp
146 A 11 Little Boltons the SW10
145 Z 10 Little Boltons the SW5
109 S 8 Little bournes SE21
142 A 3 Little Britain EC1
160 A 3 Little Britain EC1
141 Y 2 Little Britain EC1
18 C 4 Little Bury st N9
10 C 1 Little Bushey la Bushey
15 P 12 Little cedars N12
139 W 20 Little Chester st SW1
148 J 2 Little College st SW1
87 R 18 Little Cote clo SW19
159 Z 3 Little ct W Wkhm
107 T 3 Little dimocks SW12
142 C 16 Little Dorrit st SE1
72 F 9 Little Ealing la W5
131 Y 12 Little Edward st NW1
141 R 8 Little Essex st WC2
141 R 8 Little Essex st WC2
20 M 9 Little Friday hill E4
35 Z 14 Little Gearies Ilf
140 J 19 Little George st SW1
47 S 12 Little Green st NW5
5 X 20 Little gro Barnt
37 O 13 Little Heath lodge Rom
98 A 1 Little Heath rd Bxly Hth
81 P 20 Little Heath rd Bxly Hth
157 Z 17 Little Heath rd S Croy
37 P 14 Little Heath Rom
78 D 14 Little Heath SE7
53 U 12 Little Ilford la E12
59 V 16 Little John rd W7
140 B 7 Little Marlborough st W1
22 C 7 Little Moss la Pinn
141 V 5 Little New st EC4
140 G 9 Little Newport st WC2
22 A 7 Little Orchard clo Pinn
100 A 4 Little Park dri Felt

8 A 12 Little Park gdns Enf
21 Z 5 Little Plucketts way Buck Hl
140 A 4 Little Portland st W1
10 D 2 Little Potters Bushey
101 V 15 Little Queens rd Tedd
127 P 2 Little Redlands Brom
140 J 2 Little Russell st WC1
140 H 19 Little Sanctuary SW1
148 H 2 Little Smith st SW1
143 N 6 Little Somerset st E1
140 B 15 Little St James st SW1
85 W 8 Little St Leonards SW14
26 D 7 Little strand NW9
140 A 3 Little Titchfield st W1
160 B 8 Little Trinity la EC4
141 N 3 Little turnstile WC1
38 B 1 Little Venice W2
89 X 8 Littlebury rd SW4
87 P 15 Littlecombe clo SW15
77 W 16 Littlecombe SE7
22 C 3 Littlecote pl Pinn
95 V 7 Littlecroft SE9
80 A 17 Littledale SE2
47 V 11 Littlefield clo N19
25 U 1 Littlefield rd Edg
158 A 20 Littleheath rd S Croy
113 U 7 Littlemede SE9
54 E 10 Littlemoor rd Ilf
80 A 7 Littlemoor rd SE2
106 E 20 Littlers clo SW19
111 O 16 Littlestone clo Bcknhm
21 O 6 Littleton av E4
41 W 7 Littleton cres Harrow
41 X 8 Littleton rd Harrow
106 E 5 Littleton st SW18
72 B 9 Littlewood clo W13
93 V 15 Littlewood rd SE13
135 O 2 Livermere rd E8
150 C 11 Liverpool gro SE17
122 M 7 Liverpool rd Thntn Hth
33 V 17 Liverpool rd E10
65 N 13 Liverpool rd E16
103 R 17 Liverpool rd Kingst
133 U 2 Liverpool rd N1
48 F 17 Liverpool rd N7
72 H 5 Liverpool rd W5
142 J 2 Liverpool st EC2
142 K 2 Liverpool Street sta EC2
151 T 14 Livesey pl SE15
76 F 14 Livingstone pl E14
82 M 9 Livingstone rd Hounsl
123 N 4 Livingstone rd Thntn Hth
83 N 9 Livingstone rd Hounsl
64 H 4 Livingstone rd E15
33 R 18 Livingstone rd E17
17 N 18 Livingstone rd N13
58 A 20 Livingstone rd S'hall
88 G 8 Livingstone rd SW11
66 L 18 Livingstone rd E6
140 D 7 Livonia st W1
134 C 15 Lizard st EC1
77 V 19 Lizban st SE3
45 W 8 Llanelly rd NW2
78 K 18 Llanover rd SE18
42 G 10 Llanover rd Wemb
120 F 13 Llanthony rd Mrdn
45 W 7 Llanvanor rd NW2
143 T 18 Llewellyn st SE16
122 B 1 Lloyd av SW16
133 S 12 Lloyd Baker st WC1
157 V 8 Lloyd Park av Croy
157 V 8 Lloyd pk Croy
33 N 7 Lloyd rd E17
56 C 19 Lloyd rd Dgnhm
32 F 13 Lloyd rd E17
66 F 4 Lloyd rd E6
153 N 4 Lloyd rd Worc Pk
133 R 13 Lloyd sq WC1
133 S 12 Lloyd st WC1
142 L 7 Lloyds av EC3
94 A 5 Lloyds pl SE3
133 V 13 Lloyds row EC1
124 K 11 Lloyds way Bcknhm
93 P 6 Loampit hills SE13
93 S 7 Loampit vale SE13
89 Z 15 Loats rd SW4
66 D 14 Lobelia clo E6

59 P 10 Locarno rd Grnfd
73 V 3 Locarno rd W3
93 Z 11 Lochaber st SE13
144 E 13 Lochaline st W6
58 B 12 Lochan clo Grnfd
89 R 19 Lochinvar st SW12
64 G 14 Lock chase SE3
94 A 8 Lock rd Rich
102 E 9 Lock rd Rich
57 U 19 Locke clo Rainhm
23 U 9 Locket rd Harrow
9 X 8 Lockfield av Enf
48 C 18 Lockhart clo N7
63 Z 12 Lockhart st E3
50 F 12 Lockhurst st E5
89 T 1 Lockington rd SW8
31 Y 18 Lockmead rd N15
93 V 7 Lockmead rd SE13
81 V 17 Lockmere clo Erith
121 N 2 Locks la Mitch
63 Y 15 Locksley st E14
102 B 10 Locksmead rd Rich
110 G 10 Lockwood clo SE26
54 C 8 Lockwood rd Ilf
151 W 2 Lockwood sq SE16
32 E 9 Lockwood way E17
39 R 16 Lockwood wlk Rom
142 F 18 Lockyer st SE1
50 B 20 Loddiges rd E9
156 E 6 Lodge av Croy
68 B 4 Lodge av Dgnhm
55 P 13 Lodge av Dgnhm
24 J 14 Lodge av Harrow
39 U 12 Lodge av Rom
85 Z 8 Lodge av SW14
12 A 18 Lodge clo Edg
84 A 1 Lodge clo Islwth
18 A 17 Lodge clo N18
154 B 10 Lodge clo Sutton
155 O 1 Lodge clo Wallgtn
6 K 13 Lodge cres Enf
17 T 14 Lodge dri N13
124 M 12 Lodge gdns Bcknhm
35 S 12 Lodge hill Ilf
80 E 18 Lodge hill Welling
97 V 14 Lodge la Bxly
159 P 15 Lodge la N12
15 P 15 Lodge la N12
38 D 3 Lodge la Rom
112 K 17 Lodge rd Brom
122 K 17 Lodge rd Croy
122 L 17 Lodge rd Croy
26 M 12 Lodge rd NW4
130 H 15 Lodge rd NW8
155 R 10 Lodge rd Wallgtn
21 P 20 Lodge vlls Wdfd Grn
40 L 6 Lodgehill Park clo Harrow
26 A 15 Lodore gdns NW9
64 F 18 Lodore st E14
143 U 18 Loftie st SE16
133 S 1 Lofting rd N1
74 K 3 Loftus rd W12
9 T 7 Logan clo Enf
145 T 5 Logan ms W8
145 T 5 Logan pl W8
18 O 9 Logan rd N9
82 D 9 Logan rd Wemb
113 R 19 Logs hill Chisl
127 S 1 Logs hill Chisl
113 R 20 Logs Hill clo Chisl
149 S 7 Lollard st SE11
141 Y 16 Loman st SE1
159 U 16 Lomas clo CRO
135 U 19 Lomas st E1
9 R 7 Lombard av Enf
54 G 5 Lombard av Ilf
160 H 8 Lombard ct EC3
141 U 7 Lombard la EC4
16 F 16 Lombard rd N11
120 B 2 Lombard rd SW19
142 G 7 Lombard st EC3
160 G 7 Lombard st EC3
77 V 10 Lombard way SE7
137 Y 10 Lombardy pl W2
31 S 14 Lomond clo N15
43 N 20 Lomond clo Wemb
150 D 19 Lomond gro SE5
150 L 13 Loncroft rd SE5
49 R 11 Londesborough rd N16
142 F 12 London Br EC4
142 H 14 London Bridge station SE1
142 F 14 London Bridge st SE1

135 W 2 London Fields East side E8
49 Y 20 London Fields West side E8
112 F 17 London la Brom
50 A 20 London la E8
138 G 5 London ms W2
137 Z 15 London museum W8
66 M 2 London rd Bark
67 O 1 London rd Bark
112 C 19 London rd Brom
99 P 13 London rd Drtfrd
65 R 7 London rd E13
152 K 11 London rd Epsom
41 T 7 London rd Harrow
84 A 1 London rd Islwth
83 X 2 London rd Islwth
117 N 2 London rd Kingst
120 K 8 London rd Mitch
107 N 19 London rd Mitch
121 P 17 London rd Mitch
119 X 11 London rd Mrdn
38 D 19 London rd Rom
149 X 2 London rd SE1
110 B 2 London rd SE23
11 U 14 London rd Stanm
153 O 4 London rd Sutton
122 D 4 London rd SW16
83 Y 17 London rd Twick
155 S 3 London rd Wallgtn
42 M 17 London rd Wemb
142 K 8 London st EC3
138 G 6 London st W2
160 C 3 London wall EC2
142 G 3 London wall EC2
160 G 3 London wall EC2
155 P 14 Long Acre pl Carsh
140 L 6 Long acre WC2
20 M 6 Long Deacon rd E4
58 L 4 Long dri Grnfd
40 A 10 Long dri Pinn
62 B 16 Long dri W3
22 L 5 Long elmes Harrow
23 R 4 Long elmes Harrow
26 C 4 Long field NW9
80 K 20 Long la Bxly Hth
97 Z 1 Long la Bxly Hth
124 B 14 Long la Croy
141 Y 1 Long la EC1
28 D 8 Long la N2
27 Z 3 Long la N3
142 D 18 Long la SE1
20 E 19 Long leys E4
66 A 16 Long Mark rd E16
26 D 5 Long mead NW9
47 X 16 Long meadow NW5
114 G 2 Long Meadow rd Sidcp
94 A 2 Long Pond rd SE3
93 Z 3 Long Pond rd SE3
89 U 10 Long rd SW4
134 M 11 Long st E2
64 J 8 Long wlk E15
117 W 5 Long wlk New Mald
150 L 1 Long wlk SE1
78 L 16 Long wlk SE18
86 C 6 Long wlk SW13
133 N 18 Long yd WC1
33 W 4 Longacre rd E17
89 N 9 Longbeach rd SW11
45 V 8 Longberrys NW2
55 P 12 Longbridge rd Dgnhm
54 G 16 Longbridge rd Bark
93 T 12 Longbridge way SE13
113 V 7 Longcroft SE9
24 H 1 Longcrofte rd Edg
111 O 9 Longdown rd SE6
32 L 20 Longfellow rd E17
33 N 18 Longfellow rd E17
63 V 10 Longfellow rd E3
152 H 1 Longfellow rd Worc Pk
32 G 14 Longfield av E17
9 R 2 Longfield av Enf
57 T 1 Longfield av Hornch
26 G 3 Longfield av NW7
60 E 20 Longfield av W5
155 P 1 Longfield av Wallgtn
121 P 20 Longfield av Wallgtn
42 J 5 Longfield av Wemb
112 D 20 Longfield av Brom
110 C 6 Longfield cres SE26
85 S 13 Longfield dri SW14
60 F 19 Longfield rd W5
87 X 19 Longfield st SW18
60 E 18 Longfield wlk W5
70 J 1 Longford av S'hall

58 J 20 Longford av S'hall
100 G 10 Longford clo Hampt
31 R 18 Longford clo N15
154 D 4 Longford gdns Sutton
100 J 2 Longford rd Twick
131 Z 16 Longford st NW1
37 W 12 Longhayes av Rom
124 D 12 Longheath gdns Croy
89 O 4 Longhedge st SW11
111 X 6 Longhill rd SE6
124 B 14 Longhurst rd Croy
94 A 14 Longhurst rd SE13
93 Z 14 Longhurst rd SE13
151 S 10 Longhurst ct SE1
15 N 9 Longland dri N20
115 N 5 Longlands la Sidcp
114 G 6 Longlands Park cres Sidcp
114 J 6 Longlands rd Sidcp
8 F 19 Longleat rd Enf
80 E 16 Longleigh la SE2
61 N 4 Longley av Wemb
122 H 18 Longley rd Croy
23 P 14 Longley rd Harrow
106 J 14 Longley rd SW17
151 S 6 Longley st SE1
45 N 10 Longley way NW2
127 Y 3 Longmead BR7
45 X 4 Longmead dri Sidcp
106 L 11 Longmead rd SW17
5 S 17 Longmore av Barnt
148 B 7 Longmore st SW1
63 U 10 Longnor rd E1
67 X 12 Longreach rd Bark
58 L 18 Longridge la S'hall
145 T 7 Longridge rd SW5
140 G 11 Longs ct WC2
20 K 11 Longshaw rd E4
75 Y 11 Longshore SE8
87 Z 17 Longstaff cres SW18
87 Z 17 Longstaff rd SW18
62 F 4 Longstone av NW10
107 S 13 Longstone rd SW17
121 W 3 Longthornton rd SW16
109 Y 10 Longton av SE26
110 A 9 Longton gro SE26
109 Z 10 Longton gro SE26
38 L 5 Longview way Rom
149 X 5 Longville rd SE11
86 H 17 Longwood dri SW15
35 U 14 Longwood gdns Ilf
68 K 19 Longworth clo SE28
9 O 2 Loning the Enf
26 B 12 Loning the Enf
66 G 11 Lonsdale av E6
38 J 18 Lonsdale av Rom
42 L 16 Lonsdale av Wemb
66 D 11 Lonsdale clo E6
22 C 3 Lonsdale clo Pinn
35 Y 18 Lonsdale cres Ilf
6 K 14 Lonsdale dri Enf
7 O 14 Lonsdale dri Enf
122 C 8 Lonsdale gdns Thntn Hth
85 O 2 Lonsdale ms Rich
133 U 2 Lonsdale pl N1
98 B 6 Lonsdale rd Bxly Hth
34 D 20 Lonsdale rd E11
129 O 6 Lonsdale rd NW6
123 Z 8 Lonsdale rd SE25
86 D 3 Lonsdale rd SW13
74 F 18 Lonsdale rd SW13
137 R 7 Lonsdale rd W11
74 C 10 Lonsdale rd W4
133 T 2 Lonsdale sq N1
31 T 11 Lonsbert rd N15
36 A 9 Looe gdns Ilf
114 A 16 Loop rd Chisl
18 D 13 Lopen rd N18
9 P 17 Loraine clo Enf
48 D 12 Loraine rd N7
73 S 17 Loraine rd W4
35 V 10 Lord av Ilf
103 X 20 Lord Chancellor wlk Kingst
35 S 12 Lord gdns Ilf
129 Y 20 Lord Hills rd W2
148 J 2 Lord North st SW1
145 X 19 Lord Robert's ms SW6
78 K 15 Lord Robert's ter SE18
78 E 3 Lord st E16
78 F 9 Lord Warwick st SE18
135 P 13 Lorden wlk E2
100 C 5 Lords clo Felt
108 M 2 Lords clo SE21

130 G 13 Lords Cricket ground NW8
49 P 7 Lordship gro N16
31 O 6 Lordship la N17
30 G 6 Lordship la N22
91 V 15 Lordship la SE22
48 M 7 Lordship pk N16
49 O 6 Lordship pk N16
146 K 15 Lordship pl SW3
49 O 4 Lordship rd N16
40 B 20 Lordship rd Nthlt
49 P 8 Lordship ter N16
31 S 6 Lordsmead rd N17
133 O 11 Lorenzo st WC1
24 J 13 Loretto gdns Harrow
15 N 13 Lorian clo N12
83 V 4 Loring rd Islwth
15 V 8 Loring rd N20
144 D 2 Loris rd W6
90 E 4 Lorn rd SW9
124 F 17 Lorne av Croy
130 L 15 Lorne clo NW8
124 G 16 Lorne gdns Croy
34 K 14 Lorne gdns E11
136 J 17 Lorne gdns W11
33 N 17 Lorne rd E17
52 K 11 Lorne rd E7
23 V 8 Lorne rd Harrow
48 D 3 Lorne rd N4
84 L 13 Lorne rd Rich
23 T 2 Lorraine pk Harrow
149 Y 14 Lorrimore rd SE17
149 Z 13 Lorrimore sq SE17
151 U 10 Losberne way SE16
72 F 7 Lothair rd W5
30 J 20 Lothair Road north N4
30 H 20 Lothair Road south N4
88 H 8 Lothair st SW11
142 F 5 Lothbury EC2
160 F 5 Lothbury EC2
149 Y 20 Lothian ms SW9
90 J 1 Lothian rd SW9
149 Y 20 Lothian rd SW9
128 L 13 Lothrop st W10
146 A 19 Lots rd SW10
106 M 14 Loubet st SW17
130 D 5 Loudon rd NW8
36 A 15 Loudoun av Ilf
35 Z 14 Loudoun av Ilf
48 D 16 Lough rd N7
90 J 9 Loughborough pk SW9
90 F 4 Loughborough rd SW9
90 H 6 Loughborough rd SW9
149 R 10 Loughborough st SE11
63 S 13 Louisa st E1
52 A 17 Louise rd E15
107 O 6 Louisville rd SW17
68 G 11 Louvaine rd SW11
44 D 11 Lovat la EC3
142 H 10 Lovat la EC3
160 H 10 Lovat la EC3
12 E 18 Lovatt clo Edg
98 C 17 Love la Bxly
160 C 4 Love la EC2
120 K 4 Love la Mitch
120 A 16 Love la Mrdn
119 Z 17 Love la Mrdn
31 U 2 Love la N17
22 A 10 Love la Pinn
78 K 11 Love la SE18
124 A 7 Love la SE25
153 T 13 Love la Sutton
153 U 12 Love la Sutton
91 N 4 Love wlk SE5
72 B 4 Loveday rd W13
151 T 12 Lovegrove st SE1
116 K 2 Lovekyn clo Kingst
96 M 5 Lovel av Well
97 N 4 Lovel av Welling
127 X 15 Lovelace av Brom
54 M 14 Lovelace gdns Bark
116 F 17 Lovelace gdns Surb
95 T 8 Lovelace grn SE9
15 W 2 Lovelace rd Barnt
108 L 2 Lovelace rd SE21
116 H 17 Lovelace rd Surb
75 R 16 Lovelinch st SE15
75 V 7 Lovell pl SE16
102 D 7 Lovell rd Rich
72 E 18 Lovell rd S'hall
57 V 17 Lovell wlk Rainhm
45 V 18 Loveridge rd NW6
27 X 1 Lovers wlk N3
14 H 19 Lovers wlk NW7
120 E 17 Lovett dri Carsh
43 W 15 Lovett way NW10

109 V 7 Low Cross Wood la SE21
20 B 3 Low Hall clo E4
53 Z 14 Lowbrook rd Ilf
19 N 5 Lowden rd N9
58 B 19 Lowden rd S'hall
90 K 11 Lowden rd SE24
65 T 15 Lowe av E16
63 W 17 Lowell st E14
123 W 20 Lower Addiscombe rd Croy
147 W 2 Lower Belgrave st SW1
71 T 4 Lower Boston rd W7
69 R 3 Lower Broad st Dgnhm
113 U 20 Lower Camden Chisl
127 V 1 Lower Camden Chisl
156 J 13 Lower Church st Croy
50 B 12 Lower Clapton rd E5
86 K 8 Lower Common south SW15
156 L 7 Lower Coombe st Croy
105 P 20 Lower Downs rd SW20
119 R 1 Lower Downs rd SW20
18 K 13 Lower Fore st N9
127 T 20 Lower Gravel rd Brom
120 K 7 Lower Green west Mitch
147 Y 1 Lower Grosvenor pl SW1
19 W 15 Lower Hall la E4
102 G 14 Lower Ham rd Kingst
116 H 1 Lower Ham rd Kingst
96 A 7 Lower Jackwood clo SE9
140 C 9 Lower James st W1
140 C 9 Lower John st W1
6 L 16 Lower Kenwood av N14
16 H 18 Lower Maidstone rd N11
144 B 11 Lower Mall W6
74 K 14 Lower Mall W6
69 Y 7 Lower Mardyke av Rainhm
116 M 8 Lower Marsh la Kingst
117 R 9 Lower Marsh la Kingst
141 R 19 Lower Marsh SE1
130 K 1 Lower Merton ri NW3
119 P 14 Lower Morden la Mrdn
84 J 10 Lower Mortlake rd Rich
81 T 9 Lower Park rd Blvdr
16 G 18 Lower Park rd N11
81 U 9 Lower rd Blvdr
32 J 10 Lower rd Erith
41 P 4 Lower rd Harrow
92 Z 6 Lower rd Rainhm
75 R 8 Lower rd SE16
154 E 9 Lower rd Sutton
140 E 12 Lower Regent st W1
86 L 7 Lower Richmond rd SW15
87 O 7 Lower Richmond rd SW15
85 S 7 Lower Richmond rd SW14
147 R 8 Lower Sloane st SW1
85 U 1 Lower Staithe W4
99 P 16 Lower Station rd Drtfd
26 D 8 Lower Strand NW9
102 F 19 Lower Teddington rd Kingst
116 F 2 Lower Teddington rd Kingst
40 C 9 Lower ter NW3
142 G 10 Lower Thames st EC3
160 G 10 Lower Thames st EC3
10 B 1 Lower tub Watford
42 G 6 Loweswater clo Wemb
45 X 19 Lowfield rd NW6
61 V 17 Lowfield rd W3
32 J 19 Lowhall la E17
23 T 14 Lowick rd Harrow
38 H 17 Lowlands gdns Rom
23 S 20 Lowlands rd Harrow
48 D 13 Lowman rd N7
147 U 2 Lowndes clo SW1
140 B 7 Lowndes ct W1
147 T 2 Lowndes ct W1
139 R 19 Lowndes sq SW1
147 S 1 Lowndes st SW1
126 F 4 Lownds av Brom
63 O 20 Lowood st E1
143 Y 9 Lowood st E1
38 F 4 Lowshoe la Rom
90 M 4 Lowth rd SE5
6 M 12 Lowther dri Enf
7 N 13 Lowther dri Enf
92 J 19 Lowther hill SE23
32 G 8 Lowther rd E17

103 N 19 Lowther rd Kingst
48 E 16 Lowther rd N7
24 M 10 Lowther rd Stanm
86 E 2 Lowther rd SW13
74 E 20 Lowther rd SW13
66 B 7 Loxford av E6
54 G 13 Loxford la Ilf
54 A 18 Loxford rd Bark
54 B 17 Loxford ter Ilf
33 P 1 Loxham rd E4
132 L 13 Loxham st WC1
110 F 12 Loxley clo SE26
100 E 10 Loxley rd Hampt
88 H 20 Loxley rd SW18
110 G 2 Loxton rd SE23
31 S 11 Loxwood rd N17
113 U 19 Lubbock rd Chisl
75 R 20 Lubbock st SE14
88 K 7 Lubeck st SW11
146 K 6 Lucan pl SW3
4 F 11 Lucan rd Barnt
65 W 3 Lucas av E13
40 G 6 Lucas av Harrow
110 D 16 Lucas rd SE20
93 N 3 Lucas st SE8
17 N 12 Lucerne clo N13
33 X 14 Lucerne gro E17
137 V 13 Lucerne ms W8
48 J 12 Lucerne rd N5
122 K 10 Lucerne rd Thntn Hth
151 T 4 Lucey rd SE16
107 O 10 Lucien rd SW19
105 Z 4 Lucien rd SW18
94 C 17 Lucorn clo SE12
21 Y 4 Luctons av Buck Hl
61 V 13 Lucy cres W3
56 A 10 Lucy gdns Dgnhm
81 S 18 Luddesdon rd Erith
26 A 7 Ludford clo NW9
141 X 7 Ludgate broadway EC4
141 W 6 Ludgate cir EC4
141 X 6 Ludgate hill EC4
141 Y 7 Ludgate sq EC4
40 F 12 Ludlow clo Harrow
60 E 11 Ludlow rd W5
28 C 13 Ludlow way N2
86 C 10 Ludovick wlk SW15
75 V 19 Ludwick ms SE14
75 V 18 Ludwick rd SE14
80 D 8 Luffield rd SE2
112 J 6 Luffman rd SE12
92 A 4 Lugard rd SE15
134 H 17 Luke st EC2
20 J 12 Lukin cres E4
63 P 18 Lukin st E1
115 P 17 Lullingstone clo Orp
115 O 18 Lullingstone cres Orp
81 O 15 Lullingstone rd Blvdr
112 A 18 Lullingston garth Brom
14 G 17 Lullington garth N12
68 L 1 Lullington rd Dgnhm
55 Y 20 Lullington rd Dgnhm
109 X 18 Lullington rd SE20
47 T 6 Lulot gdns N19
70 L 20 Lulworth av Hounsl
42 D 1 Lulworth av Wemb
40 C 9 Lulworth clo Harrow
22 A 20 Lulworth dri Pinn
40 C 8 Lulworth gdns Harrow
92 A 5 Lulworth rd SE15
113 P 5 Lulworth rd SE9
96 K 6 Lulworth rd Welling
81 T 15 Lumen clo Blvdr
140 L 9 Lumley ct WC2
153 S 12 Lumley gdns Sutton
153 S 12 Lumley rd Sutton
139 U 7 Lumley st W1
123 N 6 Luna rd Thntn Hth
109 R 15 Lunham rd SE19
124 E 19 Lupin clo CR0
108 H 3 Lupin clo SW2
112 H 8 Lupton clo SE12
47 U 13 Lupton st NW5
148 A 11 Lupus st SW1
147 Z 11 Lupus st SW1
76 J 12 Luralda gdns E14
144 H 13 Lurgan av W6
89 R 1 Lurline gdns SW11
148 J 17 Luscombe way SW8
62 J 6 Lushington rd NW10
111 P 11 Lushington rd SE6
12 H 9 Luther clo Edg
101 V 12 Luther rd Tedd
90 C 18 Lutheran pl SW2
76 H 20 Luton pl SE10
32 K 10 Luton rd E17
115 T 6 Luton rd Sidcp
130 H 18 Luton st NW8

86 L 13 Luttrell av SW15
110 K 4 Lutwyche rd SE6
131 T 19 Luxborough st W1
144 E 5 Luxemburg gdns W6
113 R 2 Luxfield rd SE9
75 S 11 Luxford st SE16
92 L 3 Luxmore st SE4
90 K 6 Luxor st SE5
63 W 7 Lyal rd E3
109 T 8 Lyall av SE21
147 T 2 Lyall ms SW1
147 S 3 Lyall ms W SW1
147 S 3 Lyall st SW1
124 K 18 Lyconby gdns Croy
114 J 8 Lydd clo Sidcp
81 O 18 Lydd rd Bxly Hth
96 G 16 Lydden ct SE6
88 A 19 Lydden gro SW18
88 A 20 Lydden rd SW18
53 T 20 Lydeard rd E6
31 P 16 Lydford rd N15
45 O 17 Lydford rd NW2
129 R 15 Lydford rd W9
108 D 5 Lydhurst av SW2
150 L 17 Lydney clo SE15
105 T 3 Lydney clo SW19
89 U 8 Lydon rd SW4
113 X 11 Lydstep rd Chisl
88 H 20 Lyford rd SW18
106 J 1 Lyford rd SW18
147 X 3 Lygon pl SW1
90 A 17 Lyham clo SW2
90 A 15 Lyham rd SW2
89 Z 13 Lyham rd SW2
94 F 11 Lyme Farm rd SE12
50 B 19 Lyme gro E9
97 S 2 Lyme rd Welling
132 A 2 Lyme st NW1
132 B 2 Lyme ter NW1
109 U 12 Lymer av SE19
153 Y 3 Lymescote gdns Sutton
114 K 9 Lyminge clo Sidcp
106 J 2 Lyminge gdns SW18
30 H 8 Lymington av N22
121 W 3 Lymington clo SW16
152 D 10 Lymington gdns Epsom
55 W 3 Lymington rd Dgnhm
46 B 16 Lymington rd NW6
45 Z 17 Lymington rd NW6
17 V 14 Lynbridge gdns N13
150 K 17 Lynbrook clo SE15
75 Z 15 Lynch wlk SE8
89 R 9 Lyncott cres SW4
22 A 16 Lyncroft av Pinn
152 E 20 Lyncroft gdns Epsom
83 N 12 Lyncroft gdns Hounsl
45 Z 14 Lyncroft gdns NW6
72 D 4 Lyncroft gdns W13
45 W 10 Lyndale av NW2
77 O 17 Lyndale clo SE10
45 W 11 Lyndale NW2
15 Y 18 Lyndhurst av NW7
13 O 20 Lyndhurst av NW7
70 K 3 Lyndhurst av S'hall
117 U 19 Lyndhurst av Surb
121 Y 4 Lyndhurst av Twick
100 G 2 Lyndhurst av Twick
100 H 2 Lyndhurst av Twick
98 H 7 Lyndhurst clo Bxly Hth
157 U 6 Lyndhurst clo Croy
43 Z 8 Lyndhurst clo NW10
118 C 16 Lyndhurst dri New Mald
51 V 1 Lyndhurst dri E10
54 G 17 Lyndhurst gdns Bark
8 D 15 Lyndhurst gdns Enf
36 E 19 Lyndhurst gdns Ilf
27 U 4 Lyndhurst gdns N3
46 G 15 Lyndhurst gdns NW3
91 T 4 Lyndhurst gro SE15
122 F 9 Lyndhurst rd Thntn Hth
98 H 7 Lyndhurst rd Bxly Hth
33 U 1 Lyndhurst rd E4
58 K 10 Lyndhurst rd Grnfd
18 K 14 Lyndhurst rd N18
17 S 20 Lyndhurst rd N18
46 G 14 Lyndhurst rd NW3
91 U 3 Lyndhurst sq SE15
46 F 14 Lyndhurst ter NW3
91 U 2 Lyndhurst way SE15
96 K 13 Lyndon av Sidcp
155 P 6 Lyndon av Wallgtn
81 S 9 Lyndon rd Blvdr
108 H 13 Lyndway SE27
32 K 5 Lyne cres E17
55 X 5 Lynett rd Dgnhm

89 T 15 Lynette av SW4
25 V 3 Lynford clo Edg
12 E 12 Lynford gdns Edg
54 L 7 Lynford gdns Ilf
18 F 4 Lynford ter N9
97 R 5 Lynmere rd Welling
18 H 1 Lynmouth av Enf
119 O 15 Lynmouth av Mrdn
60 C 2 Lynmouth gdns Grnfd
32 H 18 Lynmouth rd E17
60 C 3 Lynmouth rd Grnfd
49 U 4 Lynmouth rd N16
28 M 12 Lynmouth rd N2
23 P 9 Lynn clo Harrow
51 Z 8 Lynn rd E11
54 D 1 Lynn rd Ilf
89 T 17 Lynn rd SW12
8 A 6 Lynn st Enf
44 A 19 Lynne way NW10
156 H 19 Lynscott way CR2
126 K 3 Lynstead clo Brom
98 F 12 Lynsted clo Bxly Hth
95 O 9 Lynsted gdns SE9
15 T 13 Lynton av N12
26 C 12 Lynton av NW9
38 F 5 Lynton av Rom
59 Y 17 Lynton av W13
83 W 10 Lynton clo Islwth
35 Z 19 Lynton cres Ilf
18 E 4 Lynton gdns Enf
158 H 20 Lynton glade S Croy
14 M 9 Lynton mead N20
122 F 15 Lynton rd Croy
51 X 12 Lynton rd E11
20 D 15 Lynton rd E4
40 C 8 Lynton rd Harrow
29 Z 16 Lynton rd N8
117 Y 11 Lynton rd New Mald
129 P 7 Lynton rd NW6
151 X 8 Lynton rd SE1
61 T 18 Lynton rd W3
34 K 4 Lynwood clo E18
40 B 9 Lynwood clo Harrow
152 G 3 Lynwood dri Worc Pk
38 H 1 Lynwood gdns Croy
156 D 8 Lynwood gdns Croy
58 E 16 Lynwood gdns S'hall
17 T 4 Lynwood gro N21
106 M 8 Lynwood rd SW17
60 H 10 Lynwood rd W5
24 F 5 Lyon meade Stanm
42 J 18 Lyon Park av Wemb
61 N 1 Lyon Park av Wemb
23 V 19 Lyon rd Harrow
57 T 1 Lyon rd Rom
120 D 1 Lyon rd SW19
59 T 3 Lyon way Grnfd
130 F 17 Lyons pl NW8
5 R 19 Lyonsdown av Barnt
5 R 16 Lyonsdown rd Barnt
58 L 11 Lyric dri Grnfd
86 D 3 Lyric rd SW13
47 W 4 Lysander gro N19
144 G 18 Lysia st SW6
89 R 17 Lysias rd SW12
86 H 12 Lysons wlk SW15
112 G 17 Lytchett rd Brom
9 O 6 Lytchett way Enf
157 T 17 Lytchgate clo S Croy
91 T 13 Lytcott gro SE22
60 L 8 Lytham gro W5
150 E 12 Lytham st SE17
130 K 1 Lyttelton clo NW3
28 F 15 Lyttelton rd N2
30 F 11 Lyttelton rd N8
51 S 9 Lyttleton rd E10
9 X 3 Lytton av Enf
17 V 8 Lytton av N13
28 F 17 Lytton clo N2
58 E 1 Lytton clo Nthlt
155 X 7 Lytton gdns Wallgtn
87 S 16 Lytton gro SW15
5 R 14 Lytton rd Barnt
33 Z 20 Lytton rd E11
22 B 3 Lytton rd Pinn
39 Z 17 Lytton rd Rom
77 V 18 Lyveden rd SE3
106 K 15 Lyveden rd SW17

M

109 V 18 Maberley cres SE19
124 F 6 Maberley rd Becknhm

109 V 19 Maberley rd SE19
132 H 14 Mabledon pl WC1
144 K 18 Mablethorpe rd SW6
50 J 15 Mabley st E9
78 B 16 Macarthur ter SE7
66 C 6 Macaulay rd E6
89 T 9 Macaulay rd SW4
89 T 9 Macaulay sq SW4
80 F 2 Macaulay way SE2
78 K 9 Macbeth st W6
74 K 12 Macbeth st W6
124 B 12 Macclesfield rd SE25
140 F 9 Macclesfield st W1
56 J 10 Macdonald av Dgnhm
33 V 7 Macdonald rd E17
52 E 13 Macdonald rd E7
16 A 17 Macdonald rd N11
47 V 6 Macdonald rd N19
89 P 1 Macduff rd SW11
136 C 13 Macfarlane pl W12
74 M 2 Macfarlane rd W12
136 C 14 Macfarlane rd W12
74 M 3 Macfarlane rd W12
131 U 18 Macfarren pl NW1
66 A 14 Macgregor rd E16
62 Z 14 Macgregor rd E16
92 C 7 Machell rd SE15
89 S 7 Mackay rd SW4
130 L 9 Mackennal st NW8
124 D 4 Mackenzie rd Becknhm
48 C 17 Mackenzie rd N7
46 L 13 Mackeson rd NW3
90 E 19 Mackie rd SW2
50 F 16 Mackintosh la E9
140 L 4 Macklin st WC2
151 T 5 Macks rd SE16
132 A 11 Mackworth st NW1
50 H 12 Maclaren st E5
92 H 16 Maclean rd SE23
50 D 12 Macleod st SE17
144 K 3 Maclise rd W14
79 S 17 Macoma rd SE18
79 S 16 Macoma ter SE18
76 E 11 Macquarie way E14
48 B 11 Macready pl N7
129 R 12 Macroom rd W9
131 S 19 Madame Tussauds NW8
64 C 13 Maddams st E3
101 W 16 Maddison clo Tedd
149 Y 15 Maddock way SE17
115 X 14 Maddocks clo Sidcp
140 A 7 Maddox st W1
139 Y 8 Maddox st W1
112 A 20 Madeira av Brom
111 Z 17 Madeira av Brom
21 X 18 Madeira gro Wdfd Grn
51 Y 5 Madeira rd E11
120 M 8 Madeira rd Mitch
121 N 8 Madeira rd Mitch
17 W 12 Madeira rd N13
108 B 11 Madeira rd SW16
60 L 18 Madeley rd W5
109 X 19 Madeline rd SE20
80 G 19 Madison cres Welling
126 D 7 Madison gdns Brom
80 G 19 Madison gdns Welling
48 F 17 Madras pl N7
53 Y 13 Madras rd Ilf
86 G 1 Madrid rd SW13
74 G 20 Madrid rd SW13
150 L 8 Madron st SE17
72 H 16 Mafeking av Brentf
66 C 6 Mafeking av E6
54 F 2 Mafeking av Ilf
65 S 11 Mafeking rd E16
8 G 13 Mafeking rd Enf
31 X 8 Mafeking rd N17
47 T 6 Magdala av N19
157 O 16 Magdala rd Croy
83 Z 8 Magdala rd Islwth
143 P 8 Magdalen pas E1
106 C 3 Magdalen rd SW18
88 G 19 Magdalen rd SW18
142 K 15 Magdalen st SE1
66 J 11 Magdalene gdns E6
149 T 14 Magee st SE11
10 G 3 Magnaville rd Bushey
103 U 16 Magnolia clo Kingst
24 M 20 Magnolia ct Harrow
73 S 17 Magnolia rd W4
141 U 8 Magpie all EC4
127 S 16 Magpie Hall clo Brom

127 T 15 Magpie Hall la Brom
10 F 7 Magpie Hall rd Bushey
102 E 10 Maguire dri Rich
143 P 16 Maguire st SE1
75 V 3 Mahogany clo SE16
84 F 12 Maid of Honour row Rich
20 D 3 Maida av E9
130 E 19 Maida av W2
81 S 8 Maida rd Blvdr
99 X 14 Maida Vale rd Drtfrd
130 C 14 Maida vale W9
20 D 3 Maida way E4
97 Z 20 Maiden Erlegh av Bxly
99 W 10 Maiden la Drtfrd
140 L 9 Maiden la WC2
132 L 7 Maiden Lane br N1
52 A 20 Maiden rd E15
93 U 2 Maidenstone hill SE10
38 K 7 Maidstone av Rom
142 D 15 Maidstone bldgs SE1
16 K 18 Maidstone rd N11
115 W 15 Maidstone rd Sidcp
135 T 8 Maidstone st E2
134 L 11 Mail Coach yd E2
8 J 17 Main av Enf
71 P 17 Main dri W7
39 X 10 Main rd Rom
114 J 8 Main rd Sidcp
100 A 12 Main st Felt
113 X 11 Mainridge rd Chisl
151 T 16 Maisemore st SE15
82 D 8 Maitland clo Hounsl
47 N 18 Maitland Park rd NW3
47 N 17 Maitland Park vlls NW3
52 B 19 Maitland rd E15
110 E 15 Maitland rd SE26
50 H 10 Maiwand rd E5
79 S 13 Majendie rd SE18
51 V 14 Major rd E15
151 U 1 Major rd SE16
143 U 20 Major rd SE16
47 O 7 Makepeace av N6
58 C 4 Makepeace rd Nthlt
146 L 7 Makins st SW3
76 B 6 Malabar st E14
64 C 19 Malam gdns E14
57 X 17 Malan sq Rainhm
86 L 10 Malbrook rd SW15
26 F 17 Malcolm cres NW4
11 S 17 Malcolm ct Stanm
60 M 11 Malcolm ct W5
63 O 10 Malcolm pl E2
63 O 11 Malcolm rd E1
110 B 17 Malcolm rd SE20
123 X 15 Malcolm rd SE25
105 T 16 Malcolm rd SW19
44 E 14 Malcolm way E11
41 S 17 Malden av Grnfd
124 A 7 Malden av SE25
123 Z 7 Malden av SE25
47 P 19 Malden cres NW1
118 J 7 Malden ct New Mald
118 F 19 Malden Green av Worc Pk
118 D 8 Malden Hill gdns New Mald
118 C 7 Malden hill New Mald
152 A 1 Malden la Worc Pk
118 D 14 Malden pk New Mald
47 N 15 Malden pl NW5
118 C 13 Malden rd New Mald
47 O 16 Malden rd NW5
38 J 20 Malden rd Rom
153 N 7 Malden rd Sutton
117 Y 15 Malden way New Mald
91 R 7 Maldon clo SE5
18 H 10 Maldon rd N9
56 J 1 Maldon rd Rom
61 W 20 Maldon rd W3
155 T 10 Maldon rd Wallgtn
21 Y 20 Maldon wlk Wdfd Grn
132 E 18 Malet pl WC1
132 F 19 Malet st WC1
108 K 3 Maley av SE27
34 D 9 Malford gro E18
91 T 7 Malfort rd SE5
110 F 1 Malham rd SE23
25 Z 6 Malington way NW9
74 K 13 Mall rd W6
56 D 19 Mall the Dgnhm
24 M 20 Mall the Harrow
16 L 10 Mall the N14

17 O 9 Mall the N14
116 F 13 Mall the Surb
140 D 15 Mall the SW1
85 V 13 Mall the SW14
60 H 20 Mall the W5
90 G 7 Mallams ms SW9
15 U 1 Mallard clo Barnt
101 Y 7 Mallard pl Twick
43 V 2 Mallard way NW9
34 J 2 Mallards rd Wdfd Grn
40 E 15 Mallet rd Nthlt
93 X 16 Mallet rd SE13
124 B 14 Malling clo Croy
120 C 13 Malling gdns Mrdn
126 C 16 Malling way Brom
88 K 12 Mallinson rd SW11
155 Y 4 Mallinson rd Wallgtn
146 G 13 Mallord st SW3
92 H 9 Mallory clo SE4
16 B 3 Mallory gdns Barnt
130 L 17 Mallory st NW8
124 E 20 Mallow clo CR0
27 T 2 Mallow mead NW7
134 E 15 Mallow st EC1
125 V 10 Malmains clo Becknhm
125 V 9 Malmains way Becknhm
65 N 15 Malmesbury rd E16
34 C 5 Malmesbury rd E18
64 A 7 Malmesbury rd E3
63 Y 8 Malmesbury rd E3
120 C 16 Malmesbury rd Mrdn
65 O 14 Malmesbury ter E16
55 V 19 Malpas rd Dgnhm
92 L 3 Malpas rd SE4
161 G 10 Malt st E1
51 N 2 Malta rd E10
133 X 15 Malta st EC1
151 N 1 Maltby st SE1
143 N 19 Maltby st SE1
88 B 2 Maltings pl SW6
136 K 4 Malton ms W10
136 J 4 Malton rd W10
79 V 17 Malton st SE18
141 P 8 Maltravers st WC2
88 A 14 Malva clo SW18
80 L 20 Malvern av E4
33 W 1 Malvern av E4
42 V 6 Malvern av Harrow
121 V 6 Malvern clo Mitch
116 X 20 Malvern clo Surb
137 N 1 Malvern clo W10
111 T 20 Malvern ct Becknhm
21 X 15 Malvern dri Wdfd Grn
54 K 13 Malvern dri Ilf
24 L 12 Malvern gdns Harrow
45 S 6 Malvern gdns NW2
129 P 11 Malvern gdns W9
129 T 14 Malvern ms NW6
129 R 11 Malvern pl W9
52 B 6 Malvern rd E11
52 C 6 Malvern rd E6
135 S 1 Malvern rd E8
49 W 20 Malvern rd E8
100 H 19 Malvern rd Hampt
39 V 20 Malvern rd Hornch
31 W 9 Malvern rd N17
30 E 10 Malvern rd N8
129 S 12 Malvern rd NW6
122 F 10 Malvern rd Thntn Hth
133 S 3 Malvern ter N1
18 H 6 Malvern ter N9
60 B 14 Malvern way W13
89 R 17 Malwood rd SW12
93 P 13 Malyons ter SE13
140 C 11 Man in Moon pas W1
76 G 3 Managers st E14
91 Z 6 Manaton clo SE15
58 G 16 Manaton cres S'hall
51 Z 17 Manbey gro E15
51 Z 17 Manbey Park rd E15
51 Z 18 Manbey rd E15
52 A 18 Manbey st E15
51 Z 18 Manbey st E15
66 H 9 Manborough av E6
128 K 18 Manchester dri W10
76 F 12 Manchester gro E14
139 T 3 Manchester ms W1
122 M 6 Manchester rd Thntn Hth
76 G 6 Manchester rd E14
31 P 19 Manchester rd N15
139 U 4 Manchester sq W1
139 T 2 Manchester st W1
56 G 13 Manchester way Dgnhm

89 P 14 Manchuria rd SW11
142 F 20 Manciple st SE1
89 U 14 Mandala rd SW4
43 W 20 Mandela clo NW10
132 C 5 Mandela st NW1
149 T 20 Mandela st SW9
150 L 6 Mandela way SE1
77 R 20 Mandeville clo SE3
139 U 4 Mandeville pl W1
83 X 4 Mandeville rd Islwth
16 F 9 Mandeville rd N14
58 D 2 Mandeville rd Nthlt
40 H 19 Mandeville rd Nthlt
50 G 10 Mandeville st E5
106 M 6 Mandrake rd SW17
90 A 13 Mandrell rd SW2
140 G 6 Manette st W1
87 V 13 Manfred rd SW15
80 K 8 Mangold way Blvdr
76 B 5 Manilla st E14
80 A 8 Manister rd SE2
88 K 6 Manlays yd SW11
131 T 3 Manley st NW1
37 P 20 Mannin rd Rom
42 H 1 Manning gdns Harrow
56 E 20 Manning rd Dgnhm
32 G 14 Manning rd E17
143 R 5 Manningtree st E1
30 J 10 Mannock rd N22
83 W 12 Manns clo Islwth
12 C 19 Manns rd Edg
100 M 5 Manoel rd Twick
74 B 13 Manor all W4
58 D 1 Manor av Nthlt
92 M 4 Manor av SE4
94 F 10 Manor brook SE3
4 F 13 Manor clo Barnt
57 O 19 Manor clo Dgnhm
99 O 10 Manor clo Drtfrd
25 R 14 Manor clo NW9
39 V 16 Manor clo Rom
68 G 19 Manor clo SE28
118 C 20 Manor clo Worc Pk
28 C 8 Manor Cotts appr N2
90 K 19 Manor cotts SE24
71 S 1 Manor Court rd W7
59 T 20 Manor Court rd W7
117 O 14 Manor cres Surb
16 L 8 Manor ct N14
152 B 14 Manor dri Epsom
16 F 4 Manor dri N14
15 Y 11 Manor dri N20
12 L 16 Manor dri NW7
117 O 15 Manor dri Surb
43 N 11 Manor dri Wemb
118 A 19 Manor Drive north Worc Pk
117 Y 16 Manor Drive north Surb
152 B 1 Manor Drive the Worc Pk
118 B 20 Manor Drive the Worc Pk
152 E 1 Manor Drive the Worc Pk
20 M 10 Manor Farm dri E4
21 N 9 Manor Farm dri E4
122 F 2 Manor Farm rd SW16
60 F 5 Manor Farm rd Wemb
87 O 15 Manor fields SW15
40 B 20 Manor gate Nthlt
100 L 18 Manor gdns Hampt
48 A 9 Manor gdns N7
85 O 10 Manor gdns Rich
157 U 14 Manor gdns S Croy
119 V 2 Manor gdns SW20
73 R 10 Manor gdns W3
125 R 3 Manor gro Becknhm
85 O 9 Manor gro Rich
85 R 9 Manor gro Rich
75 O 17 Manor gro SE15
27 O 7 Manor Hall av NW4
27 O 8 Manor Hall dri NW4
51 P 3 Manor Hall gdns E10
99 P 9 Manor ho Bxly Hth
128 H 1 Manor House dri NW6
45 P 20 Manor House dri NW6
84 A 7 Manor House way Islwth
94 B 18 Manor la SE12
93 Z 12 Manor la SE12
154 B 10 Manor la Sutton
93 Z 12 Manor Lane ter SE13
92 M 4 Manor ms SE4
110 C 1 Manor mt SE23

125 R 20 Manor Park clo W Wkhm
14 P 4 Manor Park cres Edg
22 J 10 Manor Park dri Harrow
12 C 18 Manor Park gdns Edg
114 D 20 Manor Park rd Chisl
53 O 13 Manor Park rd E12
28 E 10 Manor Park rd N2
62 C 4 Manor Park rd NW10
125 R 20 Manor Park rd W Wkhm
154 C 11 Manor Park rd Sutton
53 R 10 Manor pk E12
118 E 17 Manor pk New Mald
85 O 10 Manor pk Rich
93 Y 11 Manor pk SE13
121 V 7 Manor pl Mitch
150 A 9 Manor pl SE17
149 Y 10 Manor pl SE17
154 B 9 Manor pl Sutton
54 L 19 Manor rd Bark
4 F 14 Manor rd Barnt
125 P 2 Manor rd Becknhm
98 H 20 Manor rd Bxly
56 L 19 Manor rd Dgnhm
57 N 19 Manor rd Dgnhm
99 P 9 Manor rd Drtfrd
51 O 2 Manor rd E10
65 N 5 Manor rd E15
32 H 6 Manor rd E17
8 A 9 Manor rd Enf
23 Y 17 Manor rd Harrow
21 X 1 Manor rd Lghtn
121 U 7 Manor rd Mitch
49 P 5 Manor rd N17
31 Y 3 Manor rd N17
17 O 20 Manor rd N22
85 O 9 Manor rd Rich
37 U 19 Manor rd Rom
39 W 17 Manor rd Rom
119 U 3 Manor rd SE25
114 L 6 Manor rd Sidcp
153 U 18 Manor rd Sutton
123 W 8 Manor rd SW20
101 Z 11 Manor rd Tedd
101 O 4 Manor rd Twick
159 R 1 Manor rd W Wkhm
60 A 20 Manor rd W13
59 Z 20 Manor rd W13
155 S 9 Manor rd Wallgtn
155 R 8 Manor Road north Wallgtn
55 V 7 Manor sq Dgnhm
24 B 8 Manor vale Brentf
28 A 8 Manor view N3
21 Z 16 Manor way Wdfd Grn
125 P 5 Manor way Becknhm
127 S 18 Manor way Brom
98 D 20 Manor way Bxly
98 L 8 Manor way Bxly Hth
78 M 2 Manor way E16
20 J 13 Manor way E4
18 D 1 Manor way Enf
22 K 13 Manor way Harrow
121 U 7 Manor way Mitch
26 A 12 Manor way NW9
157 T 14 Manor way S Croy
94 C 10 Manor way SE3
155 T 8 Manor Way the Wallgtn
118 C 20 Manor way Worc Pk
08 H 19 Manordene rd SE28
117 P 1 Manorgate rd Kingst
4 F 15 Manorside Barnt
80 G 10 Manorside clo SE2
86 F 19 Manresa ho SW15
146 J 11 Manresa rd SW3
107 P 13 Mansard beeches SW17
49 V 11 Manse rd N16
33 N 4 Mansel gro E17
105 T 15 Mansel rd SW19
58 L 13 Mansell rd Grnfd
73 Y 4 Mansell rd W3
143 O 7 Mansell st E1
6 B 18 Mansfield av Barnt
31 O 13 Mansfield av N15
20 C 5 Mansfield hill E4
139 X 2 Mansfield ms W1
20 B 6 Mansfield pk E4
34 H 19 Mansfield rd E11
32 L 13 Mansfield rd E17
53 X 6 Mansfield rd Ilf
46 M 14 Mansfield rd NW3
47 O 13 Mansfield rd NW3
157 O 15 Mansfield rd S Croy
61 T 12 Mansfield rd W3
139 X 2 Mansfield st W1

135 U 10 Mansford st E2
107 O 20 Manship rd Mitch
46 B 9 Mansion gdns NW3
160 F 7 Mansion House pl EC4
142 E 6 Mansion House st EC2
146 D 6 Manson ms SW7
146 E 7 Manson pl SW7
55 U 1 Mansted gdns Rom
70 G 11 Manston av S'hall
124 C 1 Manston clo SE26
57 Z 19 Manston way Hornch
45 S 14 Manstone rd NW2
133 T 7 Mantell st N1
79 P 13 Manthorpe rd SE18
107 P 10 Mantilla rd SW17
92 J 8 Mantle rd SE4
71 X 6 Manton av W7
80 A 11 Manton rd SE2
79 Z 11 Manton rd SE2
88 G 7 Mantua clo SW11
63 P 10 Mantus clo E1
63 P 10 Mantus rd E1
15 P 7 Manus way N20
107 R 5 Manville gdns SW17
107 R 5 Manville rd SW17
92 L 15 Manwood rd SE4
107 T 3 Many gates SW12
45 S 17 Mapesbury rd NW2
19 Y 19 Maple av E4
40 L 8 Maple av Harrow
74 B 3 Maple av W3
57 Y 10 Maple clo Hornch
121 S 1 Maple clo Mitch
31 Y 19 Maple clo N16
89 Y 15 Maple clo SW4
97 N 15 Maple cres Sidcp
118 A 6 Maple ct New Mald
114 C 14 Maple Dene Chisl
26 A 2 Maple gdns Edg
72 B 18 Maple gro Brentf
43 V 1 Maple gro NW9
58 F 13 Maple gro S'hall
72 H 7 Maple gro W5
63 N 14 Maple pl E1
132 B 19 Maple pl W1
34 A 19 Maple rd E11
110 C 18 Maple rd SE20
116 F 15 Maple rd Surb
38 K 14 Maple st Rom
132 C 19 Maple st W1
66 C 16 Maplecroft clo E6
157 Y 4 Mapledale av Croy
49 W 20 Mapledene rd E8
35 Z 11 Mapleleafe gdns Ilf
68 D 4 Maplestead rd Dgnhm
90 C 19 Maplestead rd SW2
122 G 9 Maplethorpe rd Thntn Hth
126 D 13 Mapleton clo Brom
88 A 16 Mapleton cr SW18
9 O 3 Mapleton cres Enf
9 N 10 Mapleton rd Enf
87 Z 16 Mapleton rd SW18
7 R 18 Maplin clo N21
65 U 17 Maplin rd E16
33 Z 1 Mapperley dri Wdfd Grn
80 J 7 Maran way Blvdr
129 O 12 Marban rd W9
73 S 3 Marble clo W3
84 B 18 Marble Hill clo Twick
84 A 19 Marble Hill gdns Twick
84 B 19 Marble Hill pk Twick
112 K 6 Marbrook ct SE12
48 C 9 Marcellus rd N7
83 X 18 March rd Twick
51 Y 8 Marchant rd E11
145 R 13 Marchbank rd SW5
155 V 17 Marchmont rd Wallgtn
84 M 14 Marchmont rd Rich
85 N 14 Marchmont rd Rich
132 K 17 Marchmont st WC1
150 K 20 Marchwood clo SE5
60 F 16 Marchwood cres W5
150 M 7 Marcia rd SE1
144 A 3 Marco rd W6
74 L 9 Marco rd W6
49 Z 16 Marcon pl E8
58 K 18 Marconi way S'hall
65 N 4 Marcus ct E15
99 W 19 Marcus rd Drtfd
65 O 3 Marcus st E15
88 B 15 Marcus st SE18

25 Z 17 Mardale dri NW9
74 L 6 Mardale st W12
124 E 12 Mardell rd Croy
126 D 15 Marden av Brom
98 L 13 Marden cres Bxly
122 D 14 Marden cres Croy
122 D 15 Marden rd Croy
31 R 9 Marden rd N17
39 S 18 Marden rd Rom
75 O 8 Marden sq SE16
72 A 6 Marder rd W13
71 Z 6 Marder rd W13
50 A 18 Mare st E8
63 N 4 Mare st E8
135 Y 2 Mare st E8
114 F 6 Marechal Niel av Sidcp
157 S 4 Maresfield Croy
46 E 18 Maresfield gdns NW3
67 M 1 Marg Bonfield av Bark
20 E 1 Margaret av E4
39 Y 16 Margaret clo Rom
140 A 4 Margaret ct W1
49 U 5 Margaret gdns N16
5 V 14 Margaret rd Barnt
97 W 15 Margaret rd Bxly
49 U 5 Margaret rd N16
39 Y 16 Margaret rd Rom
140 A 4 Margaret st W1
139 Z 4 Margaret st W1
35 P 17 Margaret way Ilf
146 L 13 Margaretta ter SW3
52 L 5 Margaretting rd E12
90 A 13 Margate rd SW2
52 E 18 Margate Park rd E7
55 X 8 Margery rd Dgnhm
133 R 15 Margery st WC1
105 P 11 Margin dri SW19
144 H 10 Margravine gdns W6
144 H 12 Margravine rd W6
120 C 14 Marham gdns SW18
106 H 3 Marham gdns SW18
63 S 13 Maria ter E1
117 Z 11 Maria Theresa clo New Mald
153 Z 11 Marian st Sutton
135 V 7 Marian pl E2
107 V 20 Marian rd SW16
135 V 7 Marian sq E2
135 W 8 Marian st E2
62 D 1 Marian way NW10
23 P 4 Maricas av Harrow
156 B 18 Mariette way SM6
143 V 19 Marigold st SE16
19 Y 20 Marigold way E4
118 J 13 Marina av New Mald
126 D 6 Marina clo Brom
96 H 4 Marina dri Welling
38 J 17 Marina gdns Rom
102 F 17 Marina way Tedd
78 G 11 Marine dri SE18
151 R 1 Marine st SE16
88 B 4 Marinefield rd SW6
102 C 8 Mariner gdns Rich
53 V 12 Mariner rd E12
36 D 1 Marion clo Ilf
21 N 15 Marion gro Wdfd Grn
13 T 16 Marion rd NW7
123 N 11 Marion rd Thntn Hth
93 W 9 Marischal rd SE13
63 Y 12 Maritime st E3
107 O 3 Marius pass SW17
107 O 3 Marius rd SW17
89 N 10 Marjorie gro SW11
20 E 1 Mark av E4
70 J 2 Mark clo Bxly Hth
70 J 2 Mark clo S'hall
142 K 8 Mark la EC3
30 K 6 Mark rd N22
51 Y 20 Mark st E15
134 H 16 Mark st EC2
140 A 5 Market ct W1
78 K 9 Market hill SE18
25 V 6 Market la Edg
39 P 14 Market link Rom
139 W 14 Market ms W1
91 X 6 Market pl SE15
72 F 18 Market pl Brentf
116 G 4 Market pl Kingst
28 H 11 Market pl N2
28 B 14 Market pl NW11
39 R 14 Market pl Rom
140 A 5 Market pl W1
73 U 3 Market pl W3
48 A 18 Market rd N7
47 Z 19 Market rd N7
85 P 8 Market rd Rich

126 E 3 Market sq Brom
64 E 18 Market sq E14
18 L 9 Market sq N9
66 G 6 Market st E6
78 K 11 Market st SE18
64 E 18 Market way E14
42 J 16 Market way Wemb
20 D 1 Markfield gdns E4
31 X 14 Markfield rd N15
147 N 9 Markham sq SW3
146 M 9 Markham st SW3
100 E 19 Markhole clo Hampt
32 J 18 Markhouse av E17
32 K 18 Markhouse rd E17
50 M 1 Markhouse rd E17
50 K 1 Markmanor av E17
38 A 12 Marks hall Rom
38 L 16 Marks rd Rom
85 R 7 Marksbury av Rich
109 Z 9 Markwell clo SE26
55 R 16 Markyate rd Dgnhm
88 B 11 Marl st SW18
35 S 10 Marlands rd Ilf
35 T 9 Marlands rd Ilf
135 S 5 Marlborough av E8
12 F 11 Marlborough av Edg
16 G 10 Marlborough av N14
146 L 5 Marlborough bldgs SW3
106 H 16 Marlborough clo SW19
15 Z 12 Marlborough clo N20
149 Z 7 Marlborough clo SE17
73 Z 9 Marlborough cres W4
140 B 7 Marlborough ct W1
35 R 10 Marlborough dri Ilf
15 Z 11 Marlborough gdns N20
151 S 12 Marlborough gro SE1
130 D 6 Marlborough hill NW8
23 U 13 Marlborough hill Harrow
140 D 15 Marlborough ho SW1
77 Y 18 Marlborough la SE7
97 N 20 Marlborough Park av Sidcp
130 B 9 Marlborough pl NW8
72 A 20 Marlborough rd Brentf
100 H 15 Marlborough rd Hampt
106 H 16 Marlborough rd SW19
126 L 9 Marlborough rd Brom
156 M 16 Marlborough rd S Croy
55 T 14 Marlborough rd Dgnhm
97 W 7 Marlborough rd Bxly Hth
153 Y 4 Marlborough rd Sutton
52 A 13 Marlborough rd E15
34 G 9 Marlborough rd E18
20 C 19 Marlborough rd E4
52 K 19 Marlborough rd E7
48 A 6 Marlborough rd N19
47 Y 7 Marlborough rd N19
30 B 1 Marlborough rd N22
17 O 20 Marlborough rd N22
18 H 7 Marlborough rd N9
84 L 16 Marlborough rd Rich
38 H 13 Marlborough rd Rom
140 D 15 Marlborough rd SW1
73 U 13 Marlborough rd W4
72 H 5 Marlborough rd W5
146 K 8 Marlborough rd SW3
110 K 2 Marler rd SE23
80 J 17 Marley av Bxly Hth
58 G 7 Marley clo Grnfd
100 G 16 Marlingdene clo Hampt
42 F 12 Marloes clo Wemb
145 W 4 Marloes rd W8
124 A 5 Marlow clo SE20
83 V 15 Marlow cres Twick
26 C 11 Marlow ct NW9
153 P 4 Marlow dri Sutton
66 F 9 Marlow rd E6
70 E 8 Marlow rd S'hall
124 B 4 Marlow rd SE20
75 T 5 Marlow way SE16
114 D 17 Marlowe clo Chisl
36 C 5 Marlowe clo Ilf
95 X 15 Marlowe gdns SE9
33 U 12 Marlowe rd E17

121 U 8 Marlowe sq Mitch
156 B 2 Marlowe way CRO
99 N 11 Marlowes the Drtfrd
130 F 4 Marlowes the NW8
131 V 18 Marlyebone rd NW1
131 N 19 Marlyebone sta NW1
79 X 10 Marmadon rd SE18
20 A 13 Marmion av E4
19 Y 13 Marmion av E4
20 A 13 Marmion clo E4
89 P 8 Marmion ms SW11
89 N 8 Marmion rd SW11
151 U 20 Marmont st SE15
91 Y 1 Marmont rd SE15
92 C 15 Marmora rd SE22
16 D 13 Marne av N11
96 M 8 Marne av Welling
128 L 12 Marne st W10
89 O 10 Marney rd SW11
45 S 11 Marnham av NW2
58 K 6 Marnham cres Grnfd
58 K 8 Marnham cres Grnfd
92 K 14 Marnock rd SE4
63 V 15 Maroon st E14
48 M 20 Marquess rd N1
49 N 18 Marquess rd N1
61 O 1 Marquis clo Wemb
17 R 20 Marquis rd N22
48 E 3 Marquis rd N4
47 Z 19 Marquis rd NW1
86 H 9 Marrick clo SW15
9 X 3 Marrilyne av Enf
4 D 12 Marriott Barnt
64 L 2 Marriott rd E15
28 M 5 Marriott rd N10
29 N 5 Marriott rd N4
48 C 5 Marriott rd N4
26 D 19 Marriotts clo NW9
105 S 10 Marryat pl SW19
105 P 12 Marryat rd SW19
93 S 10 Marsala rd SE13
18 M 8 Marsden rd N9
91 V 8 Marsden st SE15
47 O 18 Marsden st NW1
121 N 2 Marsh av Mitch
13 R 11 Marsh clo NW7
26 D 19 Marsh clo NW9
101 U 1 Marsh Farm rd Twick
83 V 20 Marsh Farm rd Twick
69 R 4 Marsh Green rd Dgnhm
50 H 15 Marsh hill E9
51 N 5 Marsh la E10
32 A 4 Marsh la N17
12 M 12 Marsh la NW7
13 O 11 Marsh la NW7
11 S 18 Marsh la NW7
24 G 1 Marsh la Stanm
22 C 14 Marsh rd Pinn
60 H 8 Marsh rd W5
76 C 11 Marsh st E14
76 B 4 Marsh wall E14
41 O 1 Marsh clo Harrow
82 E 12 Marshall clo Hounsl
149 X 2 Marshall gdns SE1
31 P 4 Marshall rd N17
140 C 7 Marshall st W1
39 P 9 Marshalls dri Rom
78 E 10 Marshalls gro SE18
38 M 14 Marshalls rd Rom
154 B 8 Marshalls rd Sutton
142 C 17 Marshalsea rd SE1
113 Y 12 Marsham clo Chisl
148 H 3 Marsham st SW1
95 N 7 Marshbrook clo SE3
76 G 8 Marshfield st E14
64 D 3 Marshgate la E15
51 R 20 Marshgate la E15
149 Z 11 Marsland clo SE17
149 Y 11 Marsland clo SE17
56 D 8 Marston av Dgnhm
56 D 8 Marston clo Dgnhm
46 D 20 Marston clo NW6
35 R 6 Marston rd Ilf
102 B 13 Marston rd Tedd
108 K 18 Marsworth av SE19
22 A 3 Marsworth av Pinn
140 L 8 Mart st WC2
14 B 16 Martaban rd N16
109 N 7 Martell rd SE21
50 A 19 Martello st E8
33 P 6 Marten rd E17
98 J 10 Martens av Bxly Hth
98 J 11 Martens av Bxly Hth
98 J 11 Martens clo Bxly Hth
98 J 9 Martens Grove pk Bxly Hth
52 B 17 Martha rd E15
63 O 18 Martha st E1

143 Z 7 Martha st E1
68 J 20 Martham clo SE28
23 R 8 Marthorne cres Harrow
95 U 8 Martin Bowes rd SE9
156 E 1 Martin cres Croy
98 B 13 Martin dene Bxly Hth
40 E 15 Martin dr Nthlt
55 U 13 Martin gdns Dgnhm
119 X 7 Martin gro Mrdn
142 F 9 Martin la EC4
160 F 9 Martin la EC4
55 V 13 Martin rd Dgnhm
98 B 13 Martin ri Bxly Hth
119 T 7 Martin way Mrdn
119 R 4 Martin way SW20
82 B 7 Martindale rd SW12
85 V 12 Martindale SW14
48 H 13 Martineau rd N5
63 P 19 Martineau st E1
102 G 7 Martingale clo Rich
159 Y 1 Martins clo Croy
4 M 13 Martins mt Barnt
126 A 3 Martins rd Brom
29 N 4 Martins wlk N10
140 L 7 Martlett ct WC2
35 Z 16 Martley dri Ilf
23 Z 13 Martock clo Harrow
111 O 7 Marton clo SE6
112 J 5 Marvels clo SE12
112 K 5 Marvels la SE12
122 M 11 Marvels la Thntn Hth
145 O 20 Marville rd SW6
97 P 8 Marwood clo Welling
151 U 10 Marwood way SE16
104 A 8 Mary Adelaide clo SW15
76 B 18 Mary Ann bldgs SE8
24 M 12 Mary clo Stanm
91 O 1 Mary Datchelor clo SE5
41 P 14 Mary Peters dr Grnfd
136 J 10 Mary pl W11
65 P 15 Mary st E16
134 B 5 Mary st N1
131 Z 6 Mary ter NW1
40 J 6 Maryatt av Harrow
78 F 10 Marybank SE18
51 Z 15 Maryland pk E15
51 X 16 Maryland rd E15
122 J 1 Maryland rd Thntn Hth
108 K 20 Maryland rd Thntn Hth
17 S 20 Maryland rd N22
52 A 15 Maryland sq E15
51 Y 16 Maryland st E15
134 A 3 Maryland wlk N1
129 V 18 Marylands rd W9
139 U 1 Marylebone High st W1
131 U 20 Marylebone High st W1
139 V 5 Marylebone la W1
139 V 2 Marylebone ms W1
139 X 1 Marylebone ms W1
140 B 4 Marylebone pas W1
139 U 2 Marylebone st W1
149 R 8 Marylee way
78 D 11 Maryon gro SE18
46 J 13 Maryon ms NW3
78 D 12 Maryon rd SE7
83 Y 19 Marys ter Twick
136 J 20 Masbro rd W14
77 X 17 Mascalls rd SE7
87 R 9 Mascotte rd SW15
44 K 10 Mascotts clo NW2
6 G 19 Masefield av N14
58 H 19 Masefield av S'hall
10 J 17 Masefield av Stanm
99 U 3 Masefield clo Erith
120 F 5 Masefield clo Mitch
6 G 18 Masefield cres NW4
66 J 11 Masefield gdns E6
100 F 9 Masefield rd Hampt
62 A 17 Mashie rd W3
38 M 5 Mashiters hill Rom
39 R 9 Mashiters wlk Rom
108 G 2 Maskall clo SW2
106 C 8 Maskell rd SW17
88 K 1 Maskelyn clo SW11
98 F 8 Mason clo Bxly Hth
65 S 19 Mason clo E16
43 O 7 Mason ct Wemb
21 N 14 Mason rd Wdfd Grn
150 H 5 Mason st SE17
139 Z 7 Masons Arm ms W1
157 N 7 Masons av Croy

160 D 4 Masons av EC2
23 V 12 Masons av Harrow
61 P 12 Masons Green la W3
126 G 7 Masons hill Brom
78 M 12 Masons hill SE18
106 L 20 Masons pl Mitch
140 C 12 Masons yd SW1
16 E 15 Massey clo N11
35 Z 8 Massford ct Ilf
49 X 18 Massie rd E8
150 J 6 Massinger st SE17
63 S 11 Massingham st E1
76 B 11 Mast House ter E14
95 R 1 Master Gunner pl SE18
78 D 20 Master Gunners pl SE7
63 U 14 Masters st E1
76 C 5 Mastmaker st E14
82 M 12 Maswell Park cres Hounsl
82 L 12 Maswell Park rd Hounsl
52 A 9 Matcham rd E11
78 J 20 Matchless dri SE18
126 D 13 Matfield clo Brom
81 S 16 Matfield rd Blvdr
91 U 11 Matham gro SE22
145 O 6 Matheson rd W14
66 K 7 Mathews av E6
52 C 19 Mathews Park av E15
133 O 4 Matilda st N1
90 M 11 Matlock clo SE24
153 T 9 Matlock cres Sutton
153 T 9 Matlock cres Sutton
153 T 8 Matlock pl Sutton
33 U 18 Matlock rd E10
00 U 10 Matlock st E14
117 Y 1 Matlock way New Mald
89 V 5 Matrimony pl SW4
140 G 19 Matthew Parker st SW1
41 R 15 Matthews rd Grnfd
88 L 5 Matthews st SW11
49 R 14 Mathias rd N16
30 H 17 Mattison rd N4
72 E 2 Mattock la W13
67 X 6 Maud gdns Bark
82 D 13 Maud gdns E13
51 U 10 Maud rd E10
65 R 5 Maud rd E13
32 H 15 Maude rd E17
91 R 3 Maude rd SE5
32 H 14 Maude ter E17
143 R 13 Maudlins grn E1
95 U 7 Maudslay rd SE9
71 T 3 Maudsville cotts W7
90 A 13 Mauleverer rd SW2
71 V 4 Maunder rd W7
148 E 4 Maunsel st SW1
30 K 8 Maurice av N22
14 C 18 Maurice Brown clo NW7
62 J 18 Maurice st W12
28 C 14 Maurice wlk NW11
77 N 12 Mauritius rd SE10
49 W 8 Maury rd N16
113 P 19 Mavelstone clo Chisl
113 P 20 Mavelstone rd Chisl
64 A 4 Maverton rd E3
152 B 11 Mavis av Epsom
152 B 10 Mavis clo Epsom
151 P 10 Mawbey pl SE1
161 P 11 Mawbey rd SE1
148 K 20 Mawbey st SW8
38 G 9 Mawney clo Rom
38 K 10 Mawney pk Rom
38 J 7 Mawney rd Rom
39 N 15 Mawney rd Rom
119 T 4 Mawson clo SW20
74 C 15 Mawson la W4
55 Y 14 Maxey rd Dgnhm
79 O 10 Maxey rd SE18
136 H 5 Maxilla gdns W10
7 T 18 Maxim rd N21
41 S 1 Maxted pk Harrow
91 W 7 Maxted st SE15
145 Y 19 Maxwell rd NW6
96 M 9 Maxwell rd Welling
12 L 15 Maxwelton clo NW7
60 E 7 May gdns Wemb
99 X 9 May Place av Drtfrd
78 M 17 May Place la SE18
65 U 6 May rd E13
20 A 19 May rd E4
101 T 1 May st Twick
145 N 12 May st W14
10 K 20 May Tree la Stanm
108 F 4 May Tree wlk SW12

65 U 5 May wlk E13
28 D 13 Maya rd N2
90 H 12 Mayall rd SE24
57 Z 15 Maybank av Hornch
41 Y 14 Maybank av Wemb
34 J 6 Maybank rd E18
34 K 5 Maybank rd E18
116 M 17 Mayberry pl Surb
110 A 13 Maybourne clo SE26
127 Z 12 Maybury rd Bark
44 J 19 Maybury gdns NW10
68 A 6 Maybury rd Bark
67 Y 6 Maybury rd Bark
65 X 13 Maybury rd E13
106 H 13 Maybury st SW17
24 G 3 Maychurch clo Stanm
119 W 8 Maycross av Mrdn
95 R 4 Mayday gdns SE3
122 H 15 Mayday rd Thntn Hth
95 O 13 Mayerne rd SE9
30 D 8 Mayes rd N22
30 E 9 Mayes rd N22
67 X 4 Mayesbrook rd Bark
55 O 9 Mayesbrook rd Ilf
37 U 20 Mayesford rd Rom
112 L 9 Mayeswood rd SE12
97 X 3 Mayfair av Bxly Hth
53 U 7 Mayfair av Ilf
37 X 19 Mayfair av Rom
82 M 19 Mayfair av Twick
118 F 19 Mayfair av Worc Pk
111 R 20 Mayfair ct Becknhm
34 F 1 Mayfair gdns Wdfd Grn
18 A 20 Mayfair gdns N17
17 T 20 Mayfair gdns N10
139 Z 12 Mayfair pl W1
16 K 3 Mayfair ter N14
21 S 20 Mayfield av Wdfd Grn
32 G 7 Mayfield av E17
24 B 17 Mayfield av Harrow
15 S 13 Mayfield av N12
16 J 8 Mayfield av N14
72 B 6 Mayfield av W13
74 B 11 Mayfield av W4
98 B 9 Mayfield Bxly Hth
49 U 19 Mayfield clo E8
89 Y 12 Mayfield clo SW4
122 C 10 Mayfield cres Thntn Hth
8 M 19 Mayfield cres Enf
22 E 12 Mayfield dri Pinn
27 P 18 Mayfield gdns NW4
59 S 15 Mayfield gdns W7
122 C 10 Mayfield rd Thntn Hth
81 X 10 Mayfield rd Blvdr
127 R 11 Mayfield rd Brom
55 S 5 Mayfield rd Dgnhm
65 P 13 Mayfield rd E13
20 J 7 Mayfield rd E4
135 N 1 Mayfield rd Enf
9 T 9 Mayfield rd Enf
30 D 18 Mayfield rd N8
157 P 18 Mayfield rd S Croy
154 F 14 Mayfield rd Sutton
105 W 20 Mayfield rd SW19
61 S 19 Mayfield rd W3
43 O 6 Mayfields clo Wemb
43 O 7 Mayfields Wemb
90 A 6 Mayflower rd GW0
75 O 6 Mayflower st SE16
143 Z 18 Mayflower st SE16
124 F 7 Mayford clo BR3
88 M 20 Mayford clo SW12
88 M 19 Mayford rd SW12
89 N 18 Mayford rd SW12
133 R 7 Maygood st N1
57 U 2 Maygreen cres Hornch
45 V 18 Maygrove rd NW6
20 A 10 Mayhew clo E4
4 E 19 Mayhill rd Barnt
77 V 17 Mayhill rd SE7
57 Z 13 Maylands av Hornch
115 W 7 Maylands dri Sidcp
151 R 15 Maymerle rd SE15
33 T 15 Maynard rd E17
123 N 12 Mayo rd Croy
44 B 19 Mayo rd NW10
50 C 12 Mayola rd E5
110 E 9 Mayow pk SE26
110 F 11 Mayow rd SE26
99 X 10 Mayplace av Bxly Hth
98 G 9 Mayplace clo Bxly Hth
99 N 9 Mayplace rd Bxly Hth

99 J 9 Mayplace rd east Bxly Hth
98 F 10 Mayplace rd west Bxly Hth
36 D 1 Maypole cres Ilf
140 J 10 Mays ct WC2
126 A 6 Mays Hill rd Brom
125 Z 4 Mays Hill rd Brom
4 G 18 Mays la Barnt
13 X 2 Mays la Barnt
20 H 8 Mays la E4
101 P 11 Mays rd Tedd
88 F 9 Maysoule rd SW11
56 L 17 Mayswood gdns Dgnhm
48 C 10 Mayton st N7
12 G 10 Maytree clo Edg
58 C 10 Maytree ct Nthlt
51 Y 7 Mayville rd E11
51 Z 8 Mayville rd E11
53 Y 14 Mayville rd Ilf
111 R 18 Maywood clo Becknhm
76 L 15 Maze hill SE10
77 O 19 Maze hill SE10
94 C 1 Maze hill SE3
73 P 19 Maze rd Rich
129 U 2 Mazenod av NW6
7 W 8 McAdam dri SE1
89 Z 4 McAll clo SW4
149 S 1 McAuley clo SE1
78 C 14 McCall cres SE7
46 G 17 McCrone ms SW3
63 Y 5 McCullum rd E3
68 H 7 McDermott clo SW11
91 W 6 McDermott rd SE15
90 L 2 McDowall st SE5
65 R 15 McDowall clo E16
64 L 3 McEwen way E15
52 C 17 McGrath rd E15
137 P 3 McGregor rd W11
156 A 15 McIntosh clo Croy
39 P 10 McIntosh clo Rom
39 P 10 McIntosh rd Rom
104 L 17 McKay rd SW20
10 B 8 McKellar clo Bushey
91 Y 2 McKerrel rd SE15
80 C 12 McLeod rd SE2
146 A 4 McLeods ms SW7
145 Z 4 McLeods ms SW7
76 B 16 McMillan st SE8
23 R 5 Mead clo Harrow
39 V 6 Mead clo E4
20 H 13 Mead cres E4
154 H 7 Mead cres Sutton
25 X 16 Mead ct NW9
37 X 9 Mead gro Rom
122 K 20 Mead pl Croy
50 D 18 Mead pl E9
43 X 17 Mead plat NW10
114 B 15 Mead rd Chisl
12 B 20 Mead rd Edg
102 E 8 Mead rd Rich
149 T 1 Mead row SE1
125 U 2 Mead the Becknhm
125 W 20 Mead the W Wkhm
60 A 14 Mead the W13
155 Y 13 Mead the Wallgtn
126 E 14 Mead way Brom
158 J 2 Mead way Croy
21 Y 15 Mead way Wdfd Grn
149 V 14 Meadcroft rd SE11
73 P 16 Meade clo W4
28 U 7 Meade the N2
12 E 7 Meadfield Edg
107 V 19 Meadfoot rd SW16
102 F 4 Meadlands dri Rich
124 F 14 Meadow av Croy
17 P 1 Meadow bank N21
94 D 8 Meadow bank SE3
116 L 13 Meadow bank Surb
43 N 19 Meadow clo Barnt
113 Z 12 Meadow clo Chisl
20 D 6 Meadow clo E4
9 U 4 Meadow clo Enf
82 G 17 Meadow clo Hounsl
58 H 5 Meadow clo Northolt
102 J 2 Meadow clo Rich
111 O 12 Meadow clo SE6
154 B 2 Meadow clo Sutton
118 M 9 Meadow clo SW20
119 N 9 Meadow clo SW20
29 R 9 Meadow dri N10
26 L 8 Meadow dri NW4
43 X 19 Meadow garth NW10
12 G 18 Meadow gdns Edg
118 A 14 Meadow hill New Mald
149 O 16 Meadow ms SW8

148 M 18 Meadow pl SW8
67 Z 2 Meadow rd Bark
126 A 2 Meadow rd Brom
56 A 18 Meadow rd Dgnhm
100 B 3 Meadow rd Felt
22 A 14 Meadow rd Pinn
56 K 2 Meadow rd Rom
70 F 1 Meadow rd S'hall
58 F 20 Meadow rd S'hall
154 H 9 Meadow rd Sutton
106 D 19 Meadow rd SW19
149 O 15 Meadow rd SW8
150 A 3 Meadow row SE1
114 B 15 Meadow the Chisl
122 H 12 Meadow View rd Thntn Hth
25 Z 15 Meadow way NW9
23 T 5 Meadow Way the Harrow
42 H 12 Meadow way Wemb
70 B 18 Meadow waye Hounsl
56 A 17 Meadow wlk Dgnhm
34 E 12 Meadow wlk E18
152 D 17 Meadow wlk Epsom
155 R 5 Meadow wlk Wallgtn
144 E 19 Meadowbank clo SW6
131 O 2 Meadowbank NW3
43 X 1 Meadowbank rd NW9
94 D 11 Meadowcourt rd SE3
127 U 7 Meadowcroft Brom
17 U 9 Meadowcroft rd N13
153 S 20 Meadowside rd Sutton
94 L 11 Meadowside SE9
111 O 12 Meadowview clo SE6
152 B 19 Meadowview rd Epsom
98 A 17 Meadowview rd Bxly
110 M 11 Meadowview rd SE6
111 N 11 Meadowview rd SE6
97 P 17 Meadowview Sidcp
54 H 1 Meads la Ilf
9 V 6 Meads rd Enf
30 H 9 Meads rd N22
12 M 19 Meads the Edg
153 R 5 Meads the Sutton
123 V 16 Meadvale rd Croy
60 C 11 Meadvale rd W5
4 K 14 Meadway Barnt
125 U 1 Meadway Becknhm
21 Z 6 Meadway Buck Hl
4 K 13 Meadway clo Barnt
28 B 19 Meadway clo NW11
102 C 10 Meadway clo Rich
27 Z 19 Meadway ga NW11
54 J 11 Meadway Ilf
16 L 8 Meadway N14
17 N 8 Meadway N14
28 B 18 Meadway NW11
27 Z 19 Meadway NW11
39 V 7 Meadway Rom
118 M 9 Meadway SW20
119 N 8 Meadway SW20
93 Y 6 Meadway the SE3
83 P 20 Meadway Twick
110 A 18 Meaford way SE20
53 R 13 Meanley rd E12
140 E 7 Meard st W1
65 O 6 Meath rd E15
54 C 9 Meath rd Ilf
89 R 1 Meath st SW11
133 N 17 Mecklenburg pl WC1
133 N 16 Mecklenburg sq WC1
133 N 15 Mecklenburg st WC1
132 E 8 Medburn st NW1
133 U 10 Medcalf pl N1
9 Z 1 Medcalf rd Enf
85 U 10 Medcroft gdns SW14
94 F 7 Medebourne clo SE3
17 V 19 Medesenge wy N13
86 H 18 Medfield st SW15
43 Y 13 Medhurst rd E3
63 V 8 Medhurst rd E3
50 C 14 Median rd E5
48 E 9 Medina gro N7
48 E 9 Medina rd N7
121 O 19 Medland clo Mitch
58 A 6 Medlar clo Nthlt
150 B 20 Medlar st SE5
90 M 1 Medlar st SE5
45 Y 18 Medlar rd NW6
115 R 8 Medomsley clo Sidcp
38 M 13 Medora rd Rom

90 E 18 Medora rd SW2
93 R 16 Medusa rd SE6
124 C 14 Medway clo Croy
54 C 16 Medway clo Ilf
59 W 6 Medway dri Grnfd
41 Y 13 Medway gdns Wemb
59 W 7 Medway pde Grnfd
99 W 9 Medway rd Drtfrd
63 W 7 Medway rd E3
148 F 3 Medway st SW1
90 B 10 Medwin st SW4
94 L 8 Meerbrook rd SE3
65 O 1 Meeson rd E15
50 H 13 Meeson st E5
75 N 2 Meeting House all E1
143 X 13 Meeting House all E1
75 N 20 Meeting House la SE15
151 W 20 Meeting House la SE15
91 Z 1 Meeting House la SE15
50 C 16 Mehetabel rd E9
113 T 13 Melanda clo Chisl
97 Y 1 Melanie clo Bxly Hth
93 S 3 Melba way SE13
17 R 18 Melbourne av N13
22 K 9 Melbourne av Pinn
71 Z 2 Melbourne av W13
155 U 11 Melbourne clo Wallgtn
109 Y 18 Melbourne ct SE20
37 Y 14 Melbourne gdns Rom
91 T 10 Melbourne gro SE22
90 G 3 Melbourne ms SW9
141 O 7 Melbourne pl WC2
155 T 12 Melbourne rd Wallgtn
51 P 1 Melbourne rd E10
32 J 12 Melbourne rd E17
66 G 5 Melbourne rd E6
54 A 4 Melbourne rd Ilf
53 Z 4 Melbourne rd Ilf
105 Z 20 Melbourne rd SW19
102 F 15 Melbourne rd Tedd
90 F 3 Melbourne sq SW9
8 H 20 Melbourne way Enf
70 J 9 Melbury av S'hall
113 S 15 Melbury clo Chisl
145 R 1 Melbury ct W8
150 J 20 Melbury dri SE5
104 J 20 Melbury gdns SW20
25 N 16 Melbury rd Harrow
145 O 1 Melbury rd W14
130 M 19 Melbury ter NW1
131 N 19 Melcombe st NW1
131 P 19 Melcombe st NW1
88 A 2 Meldon clo SW6
55 O 8 Meldrum rd Ilf
111 T 11 Melfield gdns SE6
54 J 17 Melford rd Bark
51 Z 7 Melford rd E11
32 K 14 Melford rd E17
66 G 10 Melford rd E6
54 E 8 Melford rd Ilf
91 Y 20 Melford rd SE22
122 J 7 Melfort av Thntn Hth
122 K 7 Melfort rd Thntn Hth
48 G 16 Melgund rd N5
130 E 14 Melina pl NW8
74 H 6 Melina rd W12
142 H 16 Melior pl SE1
142 H 16 Melior st SE1
111 Y 5 Melior st SE1
76 M 15 Mell st SE10
155 Z 4 Meller clo Wallgtn
79 V 17 Melling st SE18
67 X 4 Mellish ct Bark
106 L 13 Mellison rd SW17
62 D 15 Mellitus st W12
35 U 9 Mellows rd Ilf
155 X 11 Mellows rd Wallgtn
113 S 10 Mells cres SE9
88 D 14 Melody rd SW18
137 W 16 Melon pl W8
91 W 1 Melon rd SE15
58 L 6 Melrose av Mitch
107 R 18 Melrose av Mitch
30 J 4 Melrose av N22
44 M 15 Melrose av NW2
45 N 15 Melrose av NW2
122 E 5 Melrose av SW16
105 X 6 Melrose av SW19
82 L 19 Melrose av Twick
58 K 6 Melrose clo Grnfd
70 H 1 Melrose dri S'hall
25 T 9 Melrose gdns Edg
117 Y 7 Melrose gdns New Mald
144 D 1 Melrose gdns W6

22 F 13 Melrose rd Pinn
86 D 3 Melrose rd SW13
87 U 17 Melrose rd SW18
119 Y 2 Melrose rd SW19
73 U 8 Melrose rd W3
136 D 20 Melrose ter W6
74 M 7 Melrose ter W6
120 C 14 Melsa rd Mord
151 X 11 Meltham way SE16
95 P 2 Melthorpe gdns SE3
57 T 1 Melton gdns Rom
132 D 15 Melton st NW1
41 V 16 Melville av Grnfd
157 V 12 Melville av S Croy
17 U 17 Melville av SW20
32 L 12 Melville rd E17
61 Y 1 Melville rd NW10
38 G 3 Melville rd Rom
115 T 5 Melville rd Sidcp
86 F 2 Melville rd SW13
134 A 2 Melville st N1
110 B 20 Melvin rd SE20
47 W 13 Melyn clo N7
134 A 17 Memel st EC1
64 M 8 Memorial av E15
65 N 9 Memorial av E15
70 E 17 Memorial clo Hounsl
105 R 5 Mendip clo SW19
28 G 20 Mendip cres SW11
45 R 8 Mendip dri NW2
99 P 3 Mendip rd Bxly Hth
57 W 2 Mendip rd Hornch
36 G 16 Mendip rd Ilf
88 D 8 Mendip rd SW11
145 N 16 Mendora rd SW6
45 T 13 Menelik rd NW2
109 N 18 Menlo gdns SE19
24 E 18 Mentmore clo Harrow
50 A 20 Mentmore ter E8
73 V 5 Meon rd W3
121 U 2 Meopham rd Mitch
23 N 2 Mepham cres Harrow
23 N 2 Mepham gdns Harrow
141 R 16 Mepham st SE1
98 F 9 Mera dri Bxly Hth
93 X 9 Mercator rd SE13
140 J 6 Mercer st WC2
63 N 12 Merceron st E1
135 X 18 Merceron st E1
77 P 12 Mercers clo SE10
47 Y 10 Mercers rd N19
63 Z 10 Merchant st E3
111 V 3 Merchiston rd SE6
114 C 2 Merchland rd SE9
93 V 9 Mercia gro SE13
87 S 13 Mercier rd SW15
39 S 14 Mercury gdns Rom
72 F 15 Mercury rd Brentf
75 S 15 Mercury way SE14
93 R 12 Mercy ter SE13
87 R 18 Mere clo SW19
124 F 18 Mere end Croy
156 D 10 Merebank la Croy
45 N 14 Meredith av NW2
65 T 10 Meredith st E13
133 V 14 Meredith st EC1
86 G 4 Meredyth rd SW13
92 H 9 Meretone clo SE4
120 D 14 Merevale cres Mrdn
101 S 1 Mereway rd Twick
127 V 3 Merewood clo Brom
98 J 4 Merewood rd Bxly Hth
126 C 12 Mereworth clo Brom
79 O 20 Mereworth dri SE18
113 O 19 Meriden clo Chisl
36 B 4 Meriden clo Ilf
78 A 18 Meridian rd SE7
18 F 19 Meridian wlk N17
94 L 10 Merifield rd SE9
97 O 15 Merino pl Sidcp
41 O 2 Merivale rd Harrow
87 T 10 Merivale rd SW15
127 T 1 Merlewood dri Chisl
113 T 20 Merlewood dri Chisl
43 W 3 Merley ct NW9
157 S 7 Merlin clo Croy
25 N 4 Merlin cres Edgw
112 E 8 Merlin gdns Brom
124 M 10 Merlin gro Becknhm
125 N 10 Merlin gro Becknhm
36 A 1 Merlin gro Ilf
52 M 7 Merlin rd E12
96 M 9 Merlin rd Well
97 O 10 Merlin rd Welling
133 T 14 Merlin st WC1
40 F 9 Merlins av Harrow

142 E 16 Mermaid ct SE1
70 E 9 Merrick rd S'hall
150 D 1 Merrick sq SE1
7 V 19 Merridene N21
69 P 5 Merrielands cres Dgnhm
118 M 20 Merrilands rd Worc Pk
96 G 20 Merrilees rd Sidcp
94 M 1 Merriman rd SE3
95 N 1 Merriman rd SE3
145 U 13 Merrington rd SW6
11 T 15 Merrion av Stanm
92 L 13 Merritt rd SE4
35 O 13 Merrivale av Ilf
6 K 18 Merrivale N14
153 O 19 Merrow rd Sutton
150 D 12 Merrow st SE17
150 F 11 Merrow st SE17
159 V 14 Merrow way Croy
150 G 10 Merrow wd SE17
127 S 1 Merrydown way Chisl
11 T 18 Merryfield gdns Stanm
94 D 5 Merryfield SE3
20 D 3 Merryfild clo E4
7 N 15 Merryhills dri Enf
32 L 9 Mersey rd E17
25 R 16 Mersham dri NW9
110 A 20 Mersham pl SE20
123 N 4 Mersham rd Thntn Hth
55 Z 1 Merten rd Rom
74 K 17 Merthyr ter SW13
41 N 15 Merton av Nthlt
74 C 11 Merton av W4
127 Z 11 Merton gdns Brom
105 T 20 Merton Hall gdns SW20
105 T 20 Merton Hall rd SW19
119 U 1 Merton Hall rd SW19
106 D 19 Merton High st SW19
47 N 6 Merton la N6
119 P 4 Merton mans SW20
67 Y 1 Merton pk Bark
33 T 17 Merton rd E17
8 A 4 Merton rd Enf
41 N 4 Merton rd Harrow
36 K 20 Merton rd Ilf
123 W 11 Merton rd SE25
87 Y 18 Merton rd SW18
106 A 18 Merton rd SW19
46 J 19 Merton ri NW3
92 F 12 Merttins rd SE15
90 F 12 Mervan rd SW2
114 C 6 Mervyn av SE9
91 V 13 Mervyn rd W13
61 X 18 Messaline av W3
94 L 12 Messent rd SE9
95 W 15 Messeter pl SE9
129 U 1 Messina av NW6
89 P 10 Meteor st SW11
156 A 16 Meteor way Wallgtn
155 Z 17 Meteor way Wallgtn
26 A 6 Metheringham way NW9
149 U 11 Methley st SE11
25 O 2 Methuen clo Edg
29 T 9 Methuen pk N10
81 Y 10 Methuen rd Blvdr
98 B 11 Methuen rd Bxly Hth
25 O 3 Methuen rd Edg
136 F 1 Methwold rd W10
128 F 20 Methwold rd W10
143 S 12 Mews st E1
35 O 16 Mews the Ilf
134 C 4 Mews the N1
39 P 14 Mews the Rom
115 O 9 Mews the Sidcp
87 W 13 Mexfield rd SW15
8 K 3 Meyer gro Enf
81 Y 16 Meyer rd Erith
141 V 14 Meymott st SE1
50 E 20 Meynell cres E9
50 E 20 Meynell gdns E9
50 F 20 Meynell rd E9
39 Z 1 Meynell rd Rom
44 F 17 Meyrick rd NW10
88 H 8 Meyrick rd SW11
13 O 17 M1 Motorway NW7
72 B 14 M4 motorway Brentf
70 G 15 M4 motorway Hounsl
110 J 8 Miall wlk SE26
134 C 11 Micawber st N1
71 X 3 Michael Gaynor clo W7
52 A 4 Michael rd E11

123 R 7 Michael rd SE25
88 B 1 Michael rd SW6
94 C 15 Micheldever rd SE12
101 X 6 Michelham gdns Twick
84 J 9 Michels row Rich
53 S 12 Michigan av E12
14 J 13 Mickleham down N12
153 R 13 Mickleham gdns Sutton
159 X 15 Mickleham way Croy
145 U 15 Micklethwaite rd SW6
12 L 11 Middle dene NW7
130 F 3 Middle Field NW8
29 Z 17 Middle la N8
101 V 14 Middle la Tedd
94 M 15 Middle Park av SE9
95 O 18 Middle Park av SE9
113 S 1 Middle Park av SE9
41 P 5 Middle path Harrow
5 V 19 Middle rd Barnt
65 S 8 Middle rd E13
41 P 6 Middle rd Harrow
121 W 3 Middle rd SW16
128 K 17 Middle row W10
156 L 4 Middle st Croy
141 Z 1 Middle st EC1
141 S 7 Middle Temple la EC4
121 X 4 Middle way SW16
23 U 7 Middle Way the Harrow
35 Z 20 Middlefield gdns Ilf
60 A 14 Middlefield W13
158 H 20 Middlefields Croy
18 K 19 Middleham gdns N18
18 K 19 Middleham rd N18
18 K 18 Middlesborough rd N18
74 E 12 Middlesex ct W4
141 Z 2 Middlesex pas EC1
122 A 10 Middlesex rd Mitch
142 M 3 Middlesex st E1
143 N 5 Middlesex st E1
50 D 6 Middlesex wharf E5
20 A 11 Middleton av E4
59 S 5 Middleton av Grnfd
115 S 14 Middleton av Sidcp
140 A 2 Middleton bldgs W1
19 Z 12 Middleton clo E4
75 I 5 Middleton clo SE16
36 A 20 Middleton gdns Ilf
35 Z 19 Middleton gdns Ilf
47 Z 15 Middleton gro N7
134 M 1 Middleton rd E8
135 O 1 Middleton rd E8
120 B 14 Middleton rd Mrdn
120 J 17 Middleton rd Mrdn
119 Z 15 Middleton rd Mrdn
45 X 1 Middleton rd NW11
63 N 8 Middleton st E2
135 W 11 Middleton st E2
93 X 9 Middleton way SE13
28 B 17 Middleway NW11
98 K 7 Midfield av Bxly Hth
115 R 20 Midfield way Orp
132 C 18 Midford pl W1
28 A 13 Midholm clo NW11
28 A 14 Midholm NW11
158 J 4 Midholm rd Croy
43 R 5 Midholm Wemb
132 L 13 Midhope st WC1
122 G 16 Midhurst av Croy
29 N 11 Midhurst av N10
57 U 13 Midhurst clo Hornch
98 D 15 Midhurst hill Bxly Hth
72 A 8 Midhurst rd W13
71 Z 6 Midhurst rd W13
76 G 14 Midland pl E14
51 U 3 Midland rd E10
132 H 12 Midland rd NW1
62 B 12 Midland ter NW10
45 O 10 Midland ter NW2
117 V 5 Midleton rd New Mald
63 X 13 Midlothian rd E3
107 V 1 Midmoor rd SW12
105 R 19 Midmoor rd SW19
44 B 12 Midstrath rd NW10
82 D 11 Midsummer av Hounsl
119 V 17 Midway Sutton
44 H 9 Midwood clo NW2
66 K 2 Miers clo E6
35 O 14 Mighell av Ilf
146 C 12 Milborne gro SW10

50 D 19 Milborne st E9
94 A 18 Milborough cres SE12
141 X 19 Milcote st SE1
91 U 16 Mild rd SE22
50 B 11 Mildenhall rd E5
49 O 16 Mildmay av N1
49 O 16 Mildmay gro N1
49 P 15 Mildmay pk N1
54 A 10 Mildmay rd Ilf
53 Z 10 Mildmay rd Ilf
49 P 15 Mildmay rd N1
38 K 15 Mildmay rd Rom
49 P 17 Mildmay st N1
40 L 16 Mildred av Nthlt
63 T 12 Mile End pl E1
63 O 13 Mile End rd E1
32 F 6 Mile End the E17
121 U 19 Mile rd Wallgtn
160 F 10 Miles la EC4
130 J 20 Miles pl NW1
116 M 9 Miles pl Surb
120 H 5 Miles rd N8
30 B 11 Miles rd N8
148 K 15 Miles st SW8
15 X 9 Miles way N20
13 Y 17 Milespit hill NW7
154 E 15 Milestone clo Sutton
109 U 16 Milestone rd SE19
62 G 20 Milfoil st W12
80 M 16 Milford clo SE2
25 P 3 Milford gdns Edg
42 G 14 Milford gdns Wemb
154 C 7 Milford gro Sutton
141 R 7 Milford la WC2
141 S 8 Milford la WC2
70 H 1 Milford rd S'hall
58 H 20 Milford rd S'hall
72 A 3 Milford rd W13
143 S 3 Milfred st E1
112 H 14 Milk st Brom
78 L 4 Milk st E16
160 B 5 Milk st EC2
75 P 1 Milk yd E1
34 J 1 Milkwell gdns Wdfd Grn
90 K 11 Milkwood rd SE24
155 O 3 Mill clo Carsh
4 H 7 Mill corner Barnt
82 C 20 Mill Farm cres Hounsl
100 C 1 Mill Farm clo Twick
110 A 8 Mill gdns SE26
121 O 16 Mill Green rd Mitch
13 R 16 Mill Hill clr NW7
14 D 20 Mill Hill East sta NW7
73 U 4 Mill Hill gro W3
13 T 17 Mill Hill pk NW7
86 G 6 Mill Hill rd SW13
73 S 4 Mill Hill rd W3
73 T 4 Mill Hill ter W3
121 U 11 Mill ho Mitch
155 N 8 Mill la Carsh
156 E 5 Mill la Croy
152 E 18 Mill la Epsom
45 T 16 Mill la NW6
37 Y 19 Mill la Rom
78 K 14 Mill la SE18
21 R 17 Mill la Wdfd Grn
31 Z 11 Mill Mead rd N17
113 Y 20 Mill pl Chisl
99 X 11 Mill pl Drtfrd
63 X 18 Mill pl E14
116 K 5 Mill pl Kingst
83 Y 5 Mill Plat av Islwth
84 A 6 Mill Plat Islwth
83 Z 6 Mill Plat Islwth
77 W 3 Mill rd E16
81 X 20 Mill rd Erith
53 W 9 Mill rd Ilf
106 E 19 Mill rd SW19
101 O 4 Mill rd Twick
12 B 17 Mill ridge Edg
134 L 5 Mill row N1
87 N 1 Mill Shot clo SW6
116 K 5 Mill st Kingst
143 P 18 Mill st SE1
139 Z 8 Mill st W1
126 D 4 Mill vale Brom
158 E 5 Mill View gdns Croy
143 S 8 Mill yd E1
53 X 16 Millais av E12
25 P 7 Millais gdns Edg
51 V 12 Millais rd E11
78 H 8 Millais rd Enf
117 Z 16 Millais rd New Mald
49 S 15 Millard clo N16
56 D 18 Millard ter Dgnhm
148 K 7 Millbank SW1
94 E 14 Millbank way SE12

100 C 9 Millbourne rd Felt
96 F 10 Millbrook av Welling
38 A 17 Millbrook gdns Rom
39 S 6 Millbrook gdns Rom
18 L 6 Millbrook rd N9
90 H 8 Millbrook rd SW9
122 E 20 Miller rd Croy
106 G 15 Miller rd SW19
132 A 7 Miller st NW1
49 U 13 Millers av E8
49 U 14 Millers ter E8
136 E 18 Millers way W12
58 L 8 Millet rd Grnfd
32 J 5 Millfield av E17
47 N 8 Millfield la N6
47 O 7 Millfield pl N6
25 W 7 Millfield rd Edg
82 C 20 Millfield rd Hounsl
50 F 10 Millfields rd E5
89 N 3 Millgrove st SW11
76 D 6 Millharbour E14
37 R 18 Millhaven clo Rom
108 K 11 Millhouse pl SE27
50 M 3 Millicent rd E10
25 Y 1 Milling rd Edg
133 N 17 Millman ms WC1
133 N 18 Millman st WC1
92 J 6 Millmark gro SE14
9 Y 8 Millmarsh la Enf
64 F 16 Mills gro E14
27 O 11 Mills gro NW4
154 M 2 Millside Carsh
84 A 6 Millside clo Islwth
143 N 19 Millstream rd SE1
76 B 8 Millwall Dock rd E14
63 N 15 Millward st E1
41 N 10 Millway gdns Nhlt
13 N 14 Millway NW7
82 M 13 Millwood rd Hounsl
83 N 13 Millwood rd Hounsl
136 J 2 Millwood st W10
128 J 8 Milman rd NW6
146 G 16 Milman st SW10
22 G 1 Milne field Pinn
95 R 13 Milne gdns SE9
83 P 18 Milner dri Twick
133 V 3 Milner pl N1
64 M 9 Milner rd E15
116 G 7 Milner rd Kingst
120 F 11 Milner rd Mrdn
106 A 19 Milner rd SW19
123 N 5 Milner rd Thntn Hth
133 V 2 Milner sq N1
147 N 5 Milner st SW3
73 N 6 Milnthorpe rd W4
144 J 1 Milson rd W14
4 J 15 Milton av Barnt
123 P 18 Milton av Croy
66 B 1 Milton av E6
57 U 6 Milton av Hornch
47 U 1 Milton av N6
61 X 4 Milton av NW10
25 U 11 Milton av NW9
154 H 8 Milton av Sutton
28 D 17 Milton clo N2
22 A 3 Milton clo Pinn
154 G 6 Milton clo Sutton
75 X 18 Milton Court rd SE14
36 A 20 Milton cres Ilf
134 D 20 Milton ct EC2
16 J 16 Milton gro N11
49 P 13 Milton gro N16
47 U 1 Milton pk N6
48 E 15 Milton pl N7
81 R 11 Milton rd Blvdr
123 P 18 Milton rd Croy
33 O 12 Milton rd E17
100 H 19 Milton rd Hampt
23 U 19 Milton rd Harrow
107 P 18 Milton rd Mitch
30 J 12 Milton rd N15
47 U 1 Milton rd N6
13 T 15 Milton rd NW7
39 V 18 Milton rd NW9
90 H 14 Milton rd SE24
153 X 7 Milton rd Sutton
85 X 9 Milton rd SW14
106 C 15 Milton rd SW19
73 X 2 Milton rd W3
59 W 20 Milton rd W7
155 W 14 Milton rd Wallgtn
96 J 1 Milton rd Welling
65 T 5 Milton st EC2
134 D 20 Milton st EC2
54 K 6 Milverton gdns Ilf
128 D 1 Milverton rd NW6
45 N 20 Milverton rd NW6
149 U 11 Milverton way SE11

113 X 9 Milverton way SE9
143 X 1 Milward st E1
87 V 2 Mimosa st SW6
150 M 9 Mina rd SE17
105 Z 20 Mina rd SW19
93 Y 19 Minard rd SE6
111 Z 3 Minard rd SE6
16 J 11 Minchenden cres N14
142 K 8 Mincing la EC3
109 Z 20 Minden rd SE20
153 U 3 Minden rd SM3
40 G 9 Minehead rd Harrow
108 C 13 Minehead rd SW16
147 U 6 Minera ms SW1
79 T 12 Mineral st SE18
114 G 9 Minerva clo Sidcp
61 X 10 Minerva rd E4
116 L 3 Minerva rd Kingst
61 X 10 Minerva rd NW10
135 W 9 Minerva st E2
62 A 5 Minet av NW10
62 A 5 Minet gdns NW10
90 J 5 Minet rd SW9
136 E 19 Minford gdns W14
64 A 20 Ming st E14
117 N 10 Minniedale rd Surb
116 M 11 Minniedale Surb
143 N 8 Minories EC3
89 W 3 Minshull st SW8
89 X 3 Minshull st SW8
63 T 2 Minson rd E9
86 D 17 Minstead gdns SW15
118 A 15 Minstead way New Maln
153 Y 4 Minster av Sutton
60 L 13 Minster cri W5
157 S 7 Minster dri Croy
112 H 17 Minster rd Brom
45 T 15 Minster rd NW2
30 A 14 Minster wlk N8
155 R 9 Mint rd SE1
142 B 17 Mint st E1
156 M 5 Mint wlk Croy
157 N 5 Mint wlk Croy
17 W 11 Mintern clo N13
134 G 8 Mintern st N1
70 H 10 Minterne av S'hall
25 O 17 Minterne rd Harrow
135 W 12 Minto pl E2
145 P 17 Mirabel rd SW6
44 A 19 Miranda rd N19
78 A 10 Mirfield st SE7
79 U 13 Miriam rd SE18
112 M 7 Mirror pth SE9
Missenden gdns Mrdn
32 K 15 Mission gro E17
91 X 1 Mission pl SE15
124 E 20 Mistletoe clo CR0
121 T 15 Mitcham comm Mitch
107 U 14 Mitcham la SW16
120 L 9 Mitcham pk Mitch
122 C 16 Mitcham rd Croy
66 E 9 Mitcham rd E6
36 L 20 Mitcham rd Ilf
106 L 12 Mitcham rd SW17
80 F 13 Mitchell clo SE2
17 X 15 Mitchell rd N13
134 B 15 Mitchell st EC1
43 V 18 Mitchell way NW10
43 V 18 Mitchellbrook way NW10
49 O 19 Mitchison rd N1
31 W 9 Mitchley rd N17
48 B 7 Mitford rd N19
154 E 16 Mitre clo Sutton
160 B 5 Mitre ct EC2
64 M 5 Mitre rd E15
141 U 17 Mitre rd SE1
142 M 6 Mitre sq EC3
142 L 6 Mitre st EC3
63 Y 19 Mitre the E14
62 L 14 Mitre way NW10
27 Z 10 Moat cres N3
65 Y 8 Moat dri E13
23 O 13 Moat dri Harrow
40 F 19 Moat Farm rd Nthlt
99 X 3 Moat la Erith
90 D 7 Moat pl SW9
61 T 16 Moat pl W3
9 R 13 Moat side Enf
118 A 1 Moat the New Mald
47 N 18 Modbury gdns NW5
47 O 17 Modbury st NW5
87 P 9 Model pl SW15
85 W 9 Model cotts SW14
72 B 4 Model cotts W13

113 R 6	Model Farm clo SE9
141 W 5	Modern ct EC4
23 X 16	Moelyn ms Harrow
120 G 7	Moffat gdns Mitch
17 N 18	Moffat rd N13
106 K 9	Moffat rd SW17
122 M 4	Moffat rd Thntn Hth
123 N 3	Moffat rd Thntn Hth
83 X 12	Mogden la Islwth
6 C 20	Mohan clo N14
76 A 7	Moiety rd E14
157 W 20	Moir clo S Croy
31 R 7	Moira clo N17
95 U 9	Moira rd SE9
75 S 12	Moland mead SE16
114 B 7	Molescroft SE9
153 S 4	Molesey dri Sutton
87 Y 3	Molesford rd SW6
93 T 9	Molesworth st SE13
9 W 8	Mollison av Enf
9 X 5	Mollison av Enf
156 B 14	Mollison dri Wallgtn
155 Y 17	Mollison dri Wallgtn
24 M 9	Mollison way Edg
25 O 8	Mollison way Edg
89 U 19	Molly Huggins clo SW12
138 M 3	Molyneux st W1
92 D 4	Mona SE15
65 P 15	Mona st E16
81 S 9	Monarch rd Blvdr
8 B 9	Monastery gdns Enf
148 G 3	Monck st SW1
91 R 9	Monclar rd SE5
138 H 20	Moncorvo clo SW7
66 D 17	Moncrieff clo E6
91 X 4	Moncrieff st SE15
53 P 17	Monega rd E12
52 K 18	Monega rd E7
64 A 1	Monier rd E3
110 L 19	Monivea rd Becknhm
65 R 19	Monk dri E16
78 J 10	Monk st SE18
6 D 20	Monkfrith av N14
16 D 2	Monkfrith clo N14
16 D 2	Monkfrith way N14
21 V 18	Monkhams av Wdfd Grn
21 V 17	Monkhams dri Wdfd Grn
21 T 15	Monkhams la Wdfd Grn
21 X 11	Monkhams la Buck Hl
119 T 8	Monkleigh rd Mrdn
15 S 1	Monks av Barnt
5 S 20	Monks av Barnt
7 X 9	Monks clo Enf
80 H 10	Monks clo SE2
61 P 16	Monks dri W3
125 P 16	Monks Orchard rd Becknhm
43 T 19	Monks Park gdns Wemb
43 U 16	Monks Park Wemb
7 X 8	Monks rd Enf
125 O 13	Monks way Becknhm
154 B 4	Monksdene gdns Sutton
29 P 4	Monkswell ct N10
35 W 11	Monkswood gdns Ilf
96 L 4	Monkton rd Welling
149 U 5	Monkton st SE11
27 V 13	Monkville av NW11
160 B 2	Monkwell sq EC2
34 H 11	Monmouth av E18
102 F 19	Monmouth av Kingst
97 N 9	Monmouth clo Welling
122 B 8	Monmouth clo Mitch
137 W 6	Monmouth pl W2
56 B 15	Monmouth rd Dgnhm
66 F 10	Monmouth rd E6
18 M 8	Monmouth rd N9
19 P 9	Monmouth rd N9
137 W 7	Monmouth rd W2
140 J 8	Monmouth st WC2
47 V 10	Monnery rd N19
151 T 6	Monnow rd SE1
32 M 4	Monoux gro E17
23 S 1	Monro gdns Harrow
8 M 7	Monroe cres Enf
85 T 13	Monroe dri SW14
127 R 14	Mons way Croy
94 B 5	Monsell rd N4
62 H 6	Monson rd NW10
75 S 20	Monson rd SE14
10 G 2	Montacute rd Bushey
159 T 20	Montacute rd Croy
120 E 15	Montacute rd Mrdn
92 L 18	Montacute rd SE6
19 N 15	Montagu cres N18
155 V 9	Montagu gdns Wallgtn
19 N 14	Montagu gdns N18
139 R 2	Montagu mans W1
139 P 2	Montagu Mews north W1
139 P 5	Montagu Mews south W1
139 P 4	Montagu Mews west W1
140 H 1	Montagu pl W1
139 P 2	Montagu pl W1
31 W 12	Montagu rd N15
19 O 12	Montagu rd N18
139 R 2	Montagu row W1
139 P 3	Montagu sq W1
139 P 4	Montagu st W1
92 M 10	Montague av SE4
93 N 10	Montague av SE4
71 V 3	Montague av W7
142 E 13	Montague clo SE1
61 P 19	Montague gdns W3
64 F 20	Montague pl E14
132 H 20	Montague pl WC1
122 J 19	Montague rd Croy
52 B 8	Montague rd E11
49 W 15	Montague rd E8
82 K 7	Montague rd Hounsl
30 C 16	Montague rd N8
26 G 19	Montague rd NW4
84 K 15	Montague rd S'hall
70 B 10	Montague rd S'hall
105 Z 18	Montague rd SW19
60 B 17	Montague rd W13
71 V 4	Montague rd W7
75 P 20	Montague sq SE14
140 J 1	Montague st WC1
70 A 9	Montague waye S'hall
21 O 14	Montalt rd Wdfd Grn
21 O 16	Montalt rd Wdfd Grn
107 O 8	Montana rd SW17
105 N 20	Montana rd SW20
113 Z 7	Montbelle rd SE9
126 F 15	Montcalm clo Brom
78 A 18	Montcalm rd SE7
54 C 18	Monteagle av Bark
89 S 5	Montefiore st SW8
63 Y 3	Montefiore rd E3
118 A 9	Montem rd New Mald
117 Z 8	Montem rd New Mald
92 K 19	Montem rd SE23
48 C 15	Montem st N4
29 W 17	Montenotte rd N8
149 S 12	Montford pl SE11
87 R 20	Montfort pl SW19
122 B 9	Montgomery clo Mitch
96 J 15	Montgomery clo Sidcp
12 A 20	Montgomery rd Edg
73 V 10	Montgomery rd W4
88 M 16	Montholme rd SW11
143 R 2	Monthope st E1
86 L 12	Montolieu gdns SW15
97 W 19	Montpelier av Bxly
60 E 15	Montpelier av W5
66 B 8	Montpelier gdns E6
55 T 1	Montpelier gdns Rom
47 V 14	Montpelier gro NW5
138 M 20	Montpelier ms SW7
138 L 20	Montpelier pl SW7
28 C 6	Montpelier rd N3
92 A 1	Montpelier rd SE15
151 X 20	Montpelier rd SE15
154 E 8	Montpelier rd Sutton
60 G 15	Montpelier rd W5
45 S 1	Montpelier ri NW11
42 F 5	Montpelier ri Wemb
84 D 19	Montpelier row Twick
94 C 4	Montpelier row SE3
138 L 20	Montpelier sq SW7
138 M 20	Montpelier st SW7
94 B 5	Montpelier vale SE3
45 S 1	Montpelier way NW11
138 L 20	Montpelier wlk SW7
110 C 16	Montrave rd SE20
141 O 8	Montreal pl WC2
54 A 2	Montreal rd Ilf
90 A 20	Montreal rd SW2
25 W 7	Montrose av Edg
128 M 7	Montrose av NW6
97 O 18	Montrose av Sidcp
82 L 20	Montrose av Twick
96 G 8	Montrose av Welling
21 S 13	Montrose clo Wdfd Grn
96 J 7	Montrose clo Welling
28 C 1	Montrose cres N12
15 O 20	Montrose cres N12
42 J 17	Montrose cres N12
138 H 20	Montrose ct SW7
154 B 4	Montrose gdns Sutton
120 M 5	Montrose gdns Mitch
139 U 19	Montrose gdns Sutton
23 V 8	Montrose rd Harrow
110 E 2	Montrose rd SW23
33 X 2	Montserrat av Wdfd Grn
33 X 2	Montserrat av Wdfd Grn
87 S 10	Montserrat rd SW15
142 H 10	Monument st EC3
160 H 10	Monument st EC3
31 V 11	Monument way N17
75 P 1	Monza st E1
75 R 7	Mookdee st SE16
63 T 10	Moody st E1
4 H 12	Moon la Barnt
133 V 4	Moon st N1
94 F 11	Moons ct SE12
25 O 17	Moor ct NW9
142 D 1	Moor la EC2
160 D 2	Moor la EC2
134 E 20	Moor la EC2
142 F 2	Moor pl EC2
160 F 2	Moor pl EC2
140 G 7	Moor st W1
107 Z 6	Moorcroft rd SW16
22 A 16	Moorcroft way Pinn
78 L 20	Moordown SE18
95 Y 2	Moordown SE18
121 S 4	Moore clo Mitch
85 W 8	Moore clo SW14
156 A 18	Moore clo Wallgtn
145 V 20	Moore Park rd SW6
108 K 14	Moore rd SE19
147 O 5	Moore st SW3
52 G 13	Moore wlk E7
31 U 9	Moorefield rd N17
77 R 6	Moorehead way SE3
112 D 19	Moorend rd Brom
65 O 4	Moorey clo E15
60 H 11	Moorfield av W5
9 O 7	Moorfield rd Enf
142 E 2	Moorfields EC2
160 E 2	Moorfields EC2
160 E 4	Moorgate EC2
142 F 2	Moorgate EC2
24 H 10	Moorhouse rd Harrow
137 T 5	Moorhouse rd W2
100 E 13	Moorland clo Hampt
38 H 3	Moorland clo Rom
24 K 14	Moorland rd Harrow
90 H 10	Moorland rd SW9
13 X 20	Moorlands av NW7
152 B 11	Moormead dri Epsom
83 Z 16	Moormead rd Twick
112 A 7	Moorside rd Brom
44 M 11	Mora rd NW2
45 N 11	Mora rd NW2
134 C 13	Mora st EC1
30 C 4	Morant pl N22
64 B 19	Morant st E14
90 E 1	Morat st SW9
149 P 20	Morat st SW9
146 G 16	Moravian pl SW10
63 P 8	Moravian st E2
39 O 3	Moray clo Rom
48 D 6	Moray ms N4
48 E 5	Moray rd N4
39 O 3	Moray way Rom
61 Z 4	Mordant rd NW10
68 M 1	Mordaunt gdns Dgnhm
90 C 8	Mordaunt st SW9
93 U 3	Morden clo SE13
119 Z 9	Morden ct Mrdn
41 X 15	Morden gdns Grnfd
120 G 9	Morden gdns Mrdn
120 C 7	Morden hall Mrdn
120 D 6	Morden Hall pk Mrdn
120 B 7	Morden Hall rd Mrdn
93 U 4	Morden hill SE13
93 U 3	Morden la SE13
119 U 13	Morden pk Mrdn
36 K 20	Morden rd Ilf
120 A 3	Morden rd Mitch
38 A 20	Morden rd Rom
37 Z 20	Morden rd Rom
94 E 4	Morden rd SE3
94 F 5	Morden rd SE3
106 A 20	Morden rd SW19
94 E 5	Morden Road ms SE3
93 S 3	Morden st SE13
119 X 18	Morden way Sutton
76 M 9	Morden Wharf rd SE10
65 P 17	More clo E14
144 J 7	More clo W14
57 Z 16	Morecambe clo Hornch
11 V 14	Morecambe gdns Stanm
150 C 8	Morecambe st SE17
18 A 13	Morecambe ter N18
103 T 17	Morecoombe clo Kingst
18 J 15	Moree way N18
99 Z 14	Moreland av Drtfrd
46 B 4	Moreland clo NW11
133 V 12	Moreland st EC1
20 E 10	Moreland way E4
5 R 11	Morell clo Barnt
88 L 18	Morella rd SW12
110 M 10	Moremead rd SE6
111 O 10	Moremead rd SE6
93 R 18	Morena st SE6
117 T 17	Moresby av Surb
50 A 4	Moresby rd E5
49 Z 5	Moresby rd E5
83 S 1	Moreton av Islwth
50 B 5	Moreton clo E5
31 O 18	Moreton clo N15
13 Z 20	Moreton clo NW7
148 C 9	Moreton pl SW1
31 P 18	Moreton rd N15
157 P 12	Moreton rd S Croy
152 H 3	Moreton rd Worc Pk
148 D 10	Moreton st SW1
148 C 9	Moreton ter SW1
33 Y 13	Morgan av E17
69 R 1	Morgan clo Dgnhm
112 E 19	Morgan rd Brom
48 F 16	Morgan rd N7
137 N 1	Morgan rd W10
65 P 14	Morgan st E16
63 W 9	Morgan st E3
142 J 14	Morgans la SE1
146 J 19	Morgans wlk SW11
88 A 12	Morie st SW18
50 L 4	Morieux rd E10
107 P 10	Morning rd SW17
109 R 6	Morkyns wlk SE21
123 S 19	Morland av Croy
61 Y 1	Morland gdns Dgnhm
70 L 3	Morland gdns S'hall
133 U 1	Morland ms N1
123 U 18	Morland rd Croy
69 T 2	Morland rd Dgnhm
32 G 17	Morland rd E17
53 Y 6	Morland rd Ilf
110 F 16	Morland rd SE20
154 D 12	Morland rd Sutton
33 W 2	Morley av E4
18 K 14	Morley av N18
30 J 6	Morley av N22
24 F 9	Morley Cres east Stanm
12 G 9	Morley cres Edg
24 E 9	Morley cres Stanm
24 E 10	Morley Cres west Stanm
8 B 4	Morley hill Enf
67 S 4	Morley rd Bark
51 U 5	Morley rd E10
65 P 6	Morley rd E15
37 Y 17	Morley rd Rom
93 U 11	Morley rd SE13
119 V 20	Morley rd Sutton
84 F 16	Morley rd Twick
141 U 19	Morley st SE1
90 M 3	Morna rd SE5
50 B 17	Morning la E9
152 L 3	Morningside rd Worc Pk
126 M 7	Mornington av Brom
35 V 20	Mornington av Ilf
145 O 8	Mornington av W14
21 S 13	Mornington clo Wdfd Grn
132 A 8	Mornington cres NW1
64 A 9	Mornington gro E3
90 K 1	Mornington ms SE5
132 A 9	Mornington pl NW1
131 Z 9	Mornington pl NW1
21 S 13	Mornington rd Wdfd Grn

52 B 2 Mornington rd E11
20 J 2 Mornington rd E4
58 K 12 Mornington rd Grnfd
75 Z 20 Mornington rd SE8
131 Y 8 Mornington st NW1
131 Y 7 Mornington ter NW1
102 E 9 Mornington wlk Rich
142 J 19 Morocco st SE1
63 S 4 Morpeth gro E9
63 S 4 Morpeth rd E9
63 S 9 Morpeth st E2
148 B 3 Morpeth ter SW1
54 K 9 Morrab gdns Ilf
53 T 15 Morris av E12
87 X 17 Morris gdns SW18
48 F 6 Morris pl N4
56 C 7 Morris rd Dgnhm
64 D 15 Morris rd E14
51 Y 12 Morris rd E15
83 V 7 Morris rd Islwth
39 Z 1 Morris rd Rom
63 N 18 Morris st E1
143 Y 7 Morris st E1
90 A 19 Morrish rd SW2
31 S 10 Morrison av N17
68 K 6 Morrison rd Bark
89 O 6 Morrison st SW11
65 R 10 Morse clo E13
129 W 14 Morshead rd W9
113 T 10 Morston gdns SE9
89 X 16 Morten clo SW4
31 O 4 Morteyne rd N17
64 L 4 Mortham st E15
107 X 3 Mortimer clo SW16
129 Y 6 Mortimer cres NW6
132 D 18 Mortimer mkt WC1
129 X 6 Mortimer pl NW6
66 F 9 Mortimer rd E6
81 Z 17 Mortimer rd Erith
120 L 2 Mortimer rd Mitch
134 K 2 Mortimer rd N1
49 S 20 Mortimer rd N1
128 D 12 Mortimer rd NW10
60 C 17 Mortimer rd W13
136 H 11 Mortimer sq W11
140 B 3 Mortimer st W1
139 Z 3 Mortimer st W1
47 R 12 Mortimer ter NW5
156 B 5 Mortlake clo Croy
85 Y 6 Mortlake High st SW14
65 W 16 Mortlake rd E16
54 D 13 Mortlake rd Ilf
73 O 19 Mortlake rd Rich
85 S 3 Mortlake rd Rich
91 Z 2 Mortlock clo SE15
16 J 13 Morton cres N14
155 V 10 Morton gdns Wallgtn
145 X 7 Morton ms SW5
149 S 2 Morton pl SE1
65 O 2 Morton rd E15
120 F 12 Morton rd Mrdn
134 D 2 Morton rd N1
16 H 12 Morton way N14
90 F 14 Morval rd SW2
81 O 11 Morvale clo Blvdr
106 L 7 Morven rd SW17
64 A 6 Morville st E3
140 F 2 Morwell st WC1
137 X 8 Moscow pl W2
137 W 9 Moscow rd W2
30 H 6 Moselle av N22
30 B 11 Moselle clo N8
31 V 2 Moselle pl N17
31 V 2 Moselle st N17
154 H 10 Moss clo Carsh
143 U 1 Moss clo E1
22 D 8 Moss clo Pinn
158 E 17 Moss gdn S Croy
15 O 19 Moss Hall cres N12
15 N 19 Moss Hall gro N12
22 C 8 Moss la Pinn
39 V 18 Moss la Rom
56 F 20 Moss rd Dgnhm
15 N 19 Mossborough clo N12
88 K 9 Mossbury rd SW11
81 T 12 Mossdown clo Blvdr
35 Z 8 Mossford ct Ilf
36 A 9 Mossford grn Ilf
36 B 5 Mossford la Ilf
63 X 12 Mossford st E3
151 Z 6 Mossington rd SE16
127 O 12 Mosslea rd Brom
110 C 16 Mosslea rd SE20
146 L 6 Mossop st SW3
119 V 7 Mossville gdns Mrdn
42 M 19 Mostyn av Wemb
43 N 14 Mostyn av Wemb

128 F 11 Mostyn gdns NW10
63 Z 7 Mostyn gro E3
26 A 3 Mostyn rd Edg
25 Z 2 Mostyn rd Edg
119 W 1 Mostyn rd SW19
90 F 5 Mostyn rd SW9
127 R 15 Mosul way Brom
139 S 20 Mostyn st SW1
13 R 7 Mote end NW7
118 G 13 Motspur pk New Mald
113 O 2 Mottingham gdns SE9
112 K 2 Mottingham hall SE9
94 K 19 Mottingham la SE9
112 L 1 Mottingham la SE9
113 N 2 Mottingham la SE9
19 S 1 Mottingham rd N9
113 S 6 Mottingham rd SE9
80 A 10 Mottisfont rd SE2
79 Z 9 Mottisfont rd SE2
63 R 2 Moulins rd E9
82 D 4 Moulton av Hounsl
113 V 8 Mound the SE9
31 X 19 Moundfield rd N16
91 X 19 Mount Adon pk SE22
86 E 19 Mount Angelus rd SW15
84 K 13 Mount Ararat rd Rich
110 A 6 Mount Ash rd SE26
109 Z 7 Mount Ash rd SE26
20 C 12 Mount av E4
58 G 18 Mount av S'hall
60 H 13 Mount av W5
6 B 15 Mount clo Barnt
113 P 20 Mount clo Chisl
155 P 19 Mount clo Wallgtn
159 Z 2 Mount ct W Wkhm
115 X 15 Mount Culver av Sidcp
97 Y 13 Mount dri Bxly Hth
22 E 15 Mount dri Harrow
43 V 7 Mount dri Wemb
108 C 6 Mount Earl gdns SW16
20 D 6 Mount Echo av E4
20 E 4 Mount Echo dri E4
107 Y 7 Mount Ephraim la SW16
107 Y 6 Mount Ephraim rd SW16
109 Z 6 Mount gdns SE26
12 K 12 Mount gro Edg
48 K 9 Mount Grove rd N5
49 L 7 Mount ho Barnt
133 Z 14 Mount mills EC1
63 T 16 Mount Morres rd E1
108 C 6 Mount Nod rd SW16
41 S 7 Mount Park av Harrow
156 J 20 Mount Park av S Croy
60 G 18 Mount Park cres W5
41 R 9 Mount Park rd Harrow
60 G 15 Mount Park rd W5
155 P 18 Mount pk Wallgtn
60 K 2 Mount pleasant Wemb
61 N 2 Mount pleasant Wemb
6 A 14 Mount pleasant Barnt
5 Y 14 Mount pleasant Barnt
48 C 2 Mount Pleasant cres N4
50 B 6 Mount Pleasant hill E5
50 A 4 Mount Pleasant la E5
128 C 2 Mount Pleasant rd NW10
60 E 13 Mount Pleasant rd W5
32 H 7 Mount Pleasant rd E17
31 R 7 Mount Pleasant rd N17
93 T 15 Mount Pleasant rd SE13
117 X 5 Mount Pleasant rd New Mald
48 C 1 Mount Pleasant vlls N4
133 N 17 Mount pleasant WC1
133 R 18 Mount pleasant WC1
98 K 14 Mount Pleasant wlk Bxly
5 W 16 Mount rd Barnt
97 X 13 Mount rd Bxly Hth
56 C 3 Mount rd Dgnhm
99 U 15 Mount rd Drtfrd
100 B 6 Mount rd Felt
53 Z 16 Mount rd Ilf

120 G 2 Mount rd Mitch
117 X 6 Mount rd New Mald
44 L 9 Mount rd NW2
26 G 20 Mount rd NW4
109 P 16 Mount rd SE19
105 Z 4 Mount rd SW19
139 W 10 Mount row W1
139 W 10 Mount row W1
24 F 20 Mount Stewart av Harrow
143 V 2 Mount ter E1
15 R 8 Mount the N20
118 E 7 Mount the New Mald
46 D 10 Mount the NW3
43 U 7 Mount the Wemb
152 K 9 Mount the Worc Pk
7 R 3 Mount view Enf
12 L 11 Mount view NW7
20 J 3 Mount View rd E4
48 B 1 Mount View rd N4
30 E 19 Mount View rd N4
25 Y 14 Mount View rd NW9
108 J 7 Mount vlls SE27
155 P 20 Mount way Wallgtn
109 W 8 Mountacre clo SE26
109 S 13 Mountbatten clo SE18
79 U 17 Mountbatten clo SE18
88 C 20 Mountbatten ms SW18
23 Y 6 Mountbatten rd Stanm
116 J 16 Mountcombe clo Surb
66 H 8 Mountfield rd E6
63 N 3 Mountfield rd N3
60 H 18 Mountfield rd W5
143 E 1 Mountford st E1
133 R 1 Mountfort ter N1
126 C 18 Mountthurst rd Brom
80 D 5 Mountjoy clo SE2
93 W 4 Mounts Pond rd SE3
93 W 15 Mountsfield ct SE13
23 X 4 Mountside Stanm
30 H 13 Mountview ct N15
67 T 4 Movers la Bark
47 Y 5 Mowatt clo N19
5 P 16 Mowbray rd Barnt
12 D 13 Mowbray rd Edg
45 T 19 Mowbray rd NW6
102 D 7 Mowbray rd SE19
109 V 19 Mowbray rd SE19
38 K 6 Mowbrays clo Rom
38 K 7 Mowbrays rd Rom
63 O 5 Mowlem st E2
135 Y 7 Mowlem st E2
52 J 8 Mowll st SW9
65 P 7 Moxon clo E13
4 H 13 Moxon st Barnt
139 T 2 Moxon st W1
135 T 7 Moye clo E2
144 M 15 Moyers rd E10
74 F 2 Moylan rd W6
76 Moyne pl NW10
107 U 14 Moyser rd SW16
129 O 14 Mozart st W10
120 E 14 Muchelney rd Mrdn
77 S 8 Mudlarks way SE7
56 G 12 Muggeridge rd Dgnhm
49 Y 11 Muir rd E5
78 F 3 Muir st E16
85 X 10 Muirdown av SW14
62 C 18 Muirfield W3
111 V 2 Muirkirk rd SE6
5 U 14 Mulberry clo Barnt
20 C 8 Mulberry clo E4
58 B 5 Mulberry clo Nthlt
46 F 14 Mulberry clo NW3
26 M 12 Mulberry clo NW4
107 U 10 Mulberry clo SE7
72 C 19 Mulberry cres Brentf
54 K 19 Mulberry ct Bark
157 V 1 Mulberry la Croy
155 U 13 Mulberry ms Wallgtn
74 E 14 Mulberry pl W6
143 S 3 Mulberry st E1
81 Y 5 Mulberry way Blvdr
34 H 8 Mulberry way E18
36 C 13 Mulberry way Ilf
146 G 12 Mulberry wlk SW3
157 O 7 Mulgrave rd Croy
41 X 8 Mulgrave rd Harrow
44 E 13 Mulgrave rd NW10
154 B 14 Mulgrave rd Sutton
153 V 16 Mulgrave rd Sutton
145 O 14 Mulgrave rd W14
60 H 10 Mulgrave rd W5
121 T 3 Mulholland clo Mitch
89 Y 17 Muller rd SW4
85 Y 7 Mullins pth SW14

22 J 3 Mullion clo Harrow
130 J 18 Mulready st NW8
74 A 5 Multi way W3
88 G 20 Multon rd SW18
142 G 18 Mulvaney way SE1
160 C 5 Mumford ct EC2
90 J 14 Mumford rd SE24
89 N 12 Muncaster clo SW11
145 P 11 Mund st W14
92 B 15 Mundania rd SE22
65 S 19 Munday rd E16
144 K 6 Munden st W14
50 C 6 Mundford rd E5
54 E 4 Mundon gdns Ilf
10 A 8 Mungo Park clo Bushy
57 W 17 Mungo Park rd Rainhm
83 P 14 Munnings gdns Islwth
128 M 20 Munro ms W10
82 C 12 Munster av Hounsl
17 X 13 Munster gdns N13
144 K 18 Munster rd SW6
87 U 3 Munster rd SW6
102 C 16 Munster rd Tedd
131 Z 15 Munster sq NW1
150 D 5 Munton rd SE17
115 X 1 Murchison av Bxly
97 Y 20 Murchison av Bxly
51 U 5 Murchison rd E10
65 R 16 Murdock clo E16
63 W 13 Murdock cottages E3
105 R 4 Murfett clo SW19
133 P 7 Muriel st N1
93 Y 11 Murillo rd SE13
141 S 19 Murphy st SE1
126 J 3 Murray av Brom
82 K 14 Murray av Hounsl
134 E 10 Murray gro N1
47 X 19 Murray ms NW1
102 C 4 Murray rd Rich
105 P 15 Murray rd SW19
72 D 12 Murray rd W5
65 U 19 Murray sq E16
47 W 19 Murray st NW1
144 L 14 Musard rd W6
63 P 17 Musbury st E1
154 J 3 Muschamp rd Carsh
91 V 8 Muschamp rd SE15
142 L 9 Muscovy st EC3
140 J 2 Museum st WC1
5 R 6 Musgrave clo Barnt
145 V 20 Musgrave cres SW6
87 Z 1 Musgrave cres SW6
83 V 1 Musgrave rd Islwth
92 G 3 Musgrove st SE14
58 S 8 Musjid clo SW11
49 Z 6 Muston rd E5
29 R 6 Muswell av N10
29 S 8 Muswell av N10
29 R 11 Muswell Hill bdwy N10
29 U 11 Muswell hill N10
29 T 12 Muswell Hill pl N10
29 R 16 Muswell Hill rd N10
29 S 9 Muswell ms N10
29 T 9 Muswell rd N10
129 V 3 Mutrix rd NW6
117 V 4 Muybridge rd New Mald
90 J 1 Myatt rd SW9
77 S 18 Mycenae rd SE3
17 X 2 Myrddelton gdns N21
133 T 12 Myddelton pas EC1
15 V 8 Myddelton pk N20
30 B 11 Myddelton rd N8
133 T 11 Myddelton sq EC1
133 U 14 Myddelton st EC1
8 F 4 Myddleton av Enf
8 G 5 Myddleton clo Enf
30 A 1 Myddleton ms N22
30 A 1 Myddleton rd N22
30 B 12 Myddleton rd N8
110 A 9 Mylis clo SE26
80 A 11 Mylne st EC1
143 U 4 Myrdle st E1
93 V 8 Myron pl SE13
16 A 5 Myrtle clo Barnt
99 R 1 Myrtle clo Erith
71 T 2 Myrtle gdns W7
8 C 4 Myrtle gro Enf
117 W 4 Myrtle gro New Mald
159 P 5 Myrtle rd Croy
32 J 19 Myrtle rd E17
66 E 4 Myrtle rd E6
100 M 16 Myrtle rd Hampt
82 M 6 Myrtle rd Hounsl
53 Z 7 Myrtle rd Ilf
17 Z 11 Myrtle rd N13

154 D 10 Myrtle rd Sutton
73 W 2 Myrtle rd W3
134 J 10 Myrtle st N1
80 A 13 Myrtledene rd SE2
88 M 9 Mysore rd SW11
89 N 9 Mysore rd SW11
109 N 7 Myton rd SE21

N

77 Y 15 Nadine st SE7
77 X 8 Nagasaki way SE7
33 X 9 Nagle clo E17
134 B 17 Nags Head ct EC1
97 P 7 Nags Head la Welling
64 G 15 Nairn st E14
91 P 12 Nairne gro SE24
122 C 8 Namton dri Thntn Hth
13 S 8 Nan Clarks la NW7
64 B 19 Nankin st E14
89 P 9 Nansen rd SW11
15 O 14 Nansen village N12
45 V 6 Nant rd NW2
63 O 8 Nant st E2
88 D 11 Nantes clo SW18
87 V 7 Napier av SW6
75 Y 18 Napier clo SE8
145 N 1 Napier clo W14
134 C 9 Napier gro N1
145 O 2 Napier pl W14
81 P 12 Napier rd Blvdr
126 J 8 Napier rd Brom
52 A 9 Napier rd E11
51 Z 11 Napier rd E11
65 N 6 Napier rd E15
66 H 4 Napier rd E6
9 U 17 Napier rd Enf
83 Y 11 Napier rd Islwth
31 S 11 Napier rd N17
62 K 8 Napier rd NW10
157 O 16 Napier rd S Croy
123 Z 10 Napier rd SE25
145 N 2 Napier rd W14
42 H 17 Napier rd Wemb
75 Y 19 Napier st SE8
133 V 3 Napier ter N1
84 B 18 Napoleon rd Twick
89 U 14 Narbonne av SW4
87 Z 6 Narborough st SW6
45 X 16 Narcissus rd NW6
11 R 18 Naresby fold Stanm
49 X 8 Narford rd E5
63 V 20 Narrow st E14
73 U 2 Narrow st W3
127 R 14 Narrow way Brom
136 B 5 Nascot st W12
62 M 17 Nascot st W12
83 U 2 Naseby clo Islwth
46 E 19 Naseby clo NW6
56 E 10 Naseby rd Dgnhm
35 T 5 Naseby rd Ilf
109 O 15 Naseby rd SE19
161 P 21 Nash grn Brom
19 P 8 Nash rd N9
37 U 11 Nash rd Rom
92 G 12 Nash rd SE4
74 J 8 Nasmyth st W6
86 D 3 Nassau rd SW13
140 B 2 Nassau st W1
46 L 12 Nassington rd NW3
53 Y 13 Natal rd Ilf
16 M 17 Natal rd N11
107 Y 13 Natal rd SW16
123 N 6 Natal rd Thntn Hth
80 A 5 Nathan way SE28
79 V 9 Nathan way SE28
42 E 6 Nathans rd Wemb
20 G 4 Nation way E4
141 P 13 National Film theatre SE1
140 H 11 National Gallery WC2
76 J 17 National Maritime Museum SE10
140 H 11 National Portrait Gallery WC2
141 R 13 National Theatre SE1
146 F 3 Natural History museum SW7
64 H 20 Naval row E14
49 Y 17 Navarino gro E8
49 Y 16 Navarino rd E8

66 E 5 Navarre rd E6
134 M 15 Navarre st E2
34 K 3 Navestock cres Wdfd Grn
89 X 7 Navy st SW4
9 T 18 Naylor gro Enf
9 T 18 Naylor gro Enf
15 P 8 Naylor rd N20
151 W 18 Naylor rd SE15
134 M 11 Nazrul st E2
58 F 10 Neal av S'hall
140 J 6 Neal st WC2
140 J 6 Neal's yd WC2
90 B 7 Nealden st SW9
28 D 12 Neale clo N2
98 J 1 Neals yd Erith
26 C 6 Near acre NW9
88 B 14 Neasden clo NW10
44 B 11 Neasden la NW10
44 B 15 Neasden la NW10
44 C 17 Neasden la NW10
43 Y 9 Neasden la NW10
55 P 16 Neasham rd Dgnhm
150 K 14 Neate st SE5
151 O 14 Neate st SE5
120 C 15 Neath gdns Mrdn
148 A 4 Neathouse pl SW1
66 C 16 Neatscourt rd E6
142 D 19 Nebraska st SE1
151 O 1 Neckinger SE16
93 S 4 Nectarine way SE13
137 T 6 Needham rd W11
45 P 10 Needham ter NW2
75 S 6 Needleman st SE16
26 J 16 Neeld cres NW4
43 P 16 Neeld cres Wemb
93 P 19 Nelgarde rd SE6
144 F 14 Nella rd W6
75 O 11 Nelldale rd SE16
151 Z 6 Nelldale rd SE16
38 G 6 Nelson clo Rom
82 G 15 Nelson gdns Hounsl
106 C 20 Nelson Grove rd SW19
29 N 8 Nelson Mandela clo N10
133 X 10 Nelson pl N1
115 N 10 Nelson pl Sidcp
73 T 3 Nelson pl W3
81 O 12 Nelson rd Blvdr
126 M 9 Nelson rd Brom
34 G 13 Nelson rd E11
20 C 20 Nelson rd E4
9 T 19 Nelson rd Enf
41 R 3 Nelson rd Harrow
82 G 16 Nelson rd Hounslow
31 S 12 Nelson rd N15
30 C 18 Nelson rd N8
19 N 9 Nelson rd N9
118 A 11 Nelson rd New Mald
117 Z 12 Nelson rd New Mald
76 H 17 Nelson rd SE10
115 N 10 Nelson rd Sidcp
11 R 18 Nelson rd Stanm
83 N 17 Nelson rd Twick
141 X 16 Nelson sq SE1
63 N 16 Nelson st E1
143 W 4 Nelson st E1
65 O 19 Nelson st E16
65 P 19 Nelson st E16
66 K 4 Nelson st E6
133 X 10 Nelson ter N1
89 X 10 Nelsons row SW4
61 V 20 Nemoure rd W3
100 E 5 Nene gdns Felt
88 J 6 Nepaul rd SW11
86 G 17 Nepean st SW15
23 P 19 Neptune rd Harrow
75 P 7 Neptune st SE16
93 Z 6 Nesbit clo SE3
95 N 10 Nesbit rd SE9
143 S 12 Nesham st E1
151 S 2 Neston st SE16
21 O 18 Nesta rd Wdfd Grn
75 R 4 Neston st SE16
7 W 19 Nestor av N21
27 Y 1 Nether clo N3
14 G 20 Nether Court Golf course N3
15 P 17 Nether st N12
14 L 20 Nether st N3
27 X 4 Nether st N3
74 D 12 Netheravon rd W4
74 D 15 Netheravon rd W4
71 V 2 Netheravon rd W7
72 F 9 Netherbury rd W5
6 M 14 Netherby gdns Enf
92 C 18 Netherby rd SE23
40 L 18 Nethercourt av N3

54 E 19 Netherfield gdns Bark
15 O 16 Netherfield rd N12
107 O 7 Netherfield rd SW17
89 V 6 Netherford rd SW4
46 E 15 Netherhall gdns NW3
46 D 16 Netherhall way NW3
15 V 2 Netherland rd N20
5 T 19 Netherlands rd Barnt
47 T 4 Netherleigh clo N6
39 S 7 Netherpark dri Rom
146 C 15 Netherton gro SW10
48 A 14 Netherton rd N15
83 Z 13 Netherton rd Twick
136 F 20 Netherwood pl W14
136 F 20 Netherwood rd W14
45 V 19 Netherwood st NW6
159 V 16 Netley clo Croy
153 P 11 Netley clo Sutton
120 C 16 Netley gdns Mrdn
72 J 13 Netley rd Brentf
32 L 15 Netley rd E17
36 E 16 Netley rd Ilf
120 C 16 Netley rd Mrdn
132 A 14 Netley st NW1
154 A 20 Nettlecombe clo Sutton
43 P 17 Nettleden av Wemb
108 J 8 Nettlefold pl SE27
92 G 1 Nettleton rd SE14
107 Y 19 Nettlewood rd SW16
110 K 4 Neuchatel rd SE6
76 H 18 Nevada st SE10
145 T 7 Nevern pl SW5
145 T 7 Nevern rd SW5
145 T 7 Nevern sq SW5
49 S 9 Nevill rd N16
103 Z 20 Neville av Kinst
52 C 9 Neville clo E11
82 J 3 Neville clo Hounsl
132 G 9 Neville clo NW1
129 R 10 Neville clo NW6
114 L 9 Neville clo Sidcp
73 W 4 Neville clo W3
28 D 19 Neville dri N2
91 X 1 Neville dri SE15
55 V 8 Neville gdns Dgnhm
87 Z 15 Neville Gill clo SW18
30 D 4 Neville pl N22
123 P 7 Neville rd Croy
55 V 8 Neville rd Dgnhm
65 T 2 Neville rd E7
36 C 4 Neville rd Ilf
117 R 3 Neville rd Kingst
129 S 9 Neville rd NW6
120 C 5 Neville rd Rich
60 F 10 Neville rd W5
146 F 9 Neville st SW7
146 F 9 Neville ter SW7
120 J 18 Neville wlk Carsh
20 F 6 Nevin dri E4
39 R 1 Nevis clo Rom
107 N 3 Nevis rd SW17
65 U 12 New Barn st E13
121 X 10 New Barns av Mitch
139 Y 7 New Bond st W1
139 Z 10 New Bond st W1
81 Y 10 New br Erith
26 M 15 New Brent st NW4
27 N 14 New Brent st NW4
141 W 7 New Bridge st EC4
160 H 3 New Broad st EC2
60 F 20 New broadway W5
140 A 9 New Burlington ms W1
140 A 8 New Burlington pl W1
140 A 9 New Burlington st W1
76 B 20 New Butt la SE8
139 X 1 New Cavendish st W1
142 A 6 New Change EC4
160 A 6 New Change EC4
150 D 18 New Church rd SE5
150 E 16 New Church rd SE5
65 Y 8 New City rd E13
100 B 12 New clo Felt
120 D 4 New clo SW19
140 H 5 New Compton st WC2
148 D 20 New Covent Garden market SW8
140 G 10 New Coventry st W1
92 G 18 New Cross rd SE14
75 P 19 New Cross rd SE14
141 R 8 New ct WC2
46 E 11 New End NW3
46 F 11 New End sq NW3

126 E 8 New Farm av Brom
141 U 3 New Fetter la EC4
142 H 11 New Fresh wharf EC3
143 N 4 New Goulston st E1
70 F 18 New Heston rd Hounsl
120 C 17 New House wlk Mrdn
134 L 15 New Inn sq EC2
134 K 15 New Inn st EC2
134 K 16 New Inn yd EC2
150 D 4 New Kent rd SE1
76 A 16 New King st SE8
87 W 4 New Kings rd SW6
142 L 8 New London st EC3
77 Z 9 New Lydenberg st SE7
64 K 2 New Mount st E15
134 J 17 New North pl EC2
36 D 1 New North rd Ilf
134 F 9 New North rd N1
132 M 20 New North st WC1
28 E 8 New Oak rd N2
47 Y 1 New Orleans wlk N19
140 H 4 New Oxford st WC1
140 K 19 New Palace yd SW1
18 A 12 New Park av N13
17 Z 12 New Park av N13
40 A 19 New Park clo Nthlt
107 Y 1 New Park rd SW2
89 Z 20 New Park rd SW2
151 W 1 New Place sq SE16
65 O 4 New Plaistow rd E15
139 R 6 New Quebec st W1
72 H 15 New rd Brentf
69 U 6 New rd Dgnhm
143 V 4 New rd E1
20 F 13 New rd E4
20 J 12 New rd E4
100 B 11 New rd Felt
82 K 11 New rd Hounsl
54 H 6 New rd Ilf
103 P 17 New rd Kingst
121 O 19 New rd Mitch
31 U 3 New rd N17
30 L 5 New rd N22
29 Z 16 New rd N8
18 K 10 New rd N9
27 R 1 New rd NW7
13 S 2 New rd NW7
102 E 8 New rd Rich
80 J 13 New rd SE2
97 P 6 New rd Welling
41 V 12 New rd Wemb
17 V 12 New River cres N13
48 L 18 New River wlk N1
140 J 9 New row WC2
128 F 1 New Scotland yard SW1
148 M 11 New Spring Gardens wlk SE11
141 R 5 New sq WC2
142 K 3 New st EC2
141 U 4 New St Sq EC4
112 H 13 New Street hill Brom
28 F 9 New Trinity rd N2
76 H 7 New Union clo E14
142 E 1 New Union st EC2
160 E 1 New Union st EC2
34 O 18 New Wanstead E11
26 C 14 New Way rd NW9
132 M 8 New Wharf rd N1
61 Y 9 Newark cres NW10
157 O 14 Newark rd S Croy
63 O 15 Newark st E1
143 W 2 Newark st E1
26 H 11 Newark way NW4
99 T 1 Newbery rd Erith
153 O 10 Newbolt av Sutton
10 H 18 Newbolt rd Stanm
117 Y 9 Newborough grn New Mald
73 V 2 Newburgh rd W3
140 B 7 Newburgh st W1
149 P 9 Newburn st SE11
9 X 2 Newbury av Enf
40 O 17 Newbury clo Nthlt
152 D 8 Newbury gdns Epsom
126 E 7 Newbury rd Brom
20 H 20 Newbury rd E4
36 G 19 Newbury rd Ilf
141 Z 1 Newbury st EC1
40 C 17 Newbury way Nthlt
8 F 9 Newby clo Enf
64 F 19 Newby pl E14
89 T 6 Newby st SW8
141 W 4 Newcastle clo EC4
138 H 1 Newcastle pl W2
133 U 16 Newcastle row EC1

108 B 8	Newcombe gdns SW16	
61 N 2	Newcombe pk Wemb	
13 O 16	Newcombe pk NW7	
137 U 13	Newcombe st W8	
52 B 9	Newcomen rd E11	
88 F 7	Newcomen rd SW11	
142 E 16	Newcomen st SE1	
130 K 10	Newcourt st NW8	
18 L 9	Newdale clo N9	
63 Y 19	Newell st E14	
120 L 19	Newent clo Carsh	
150 J 16	Newent clo SE15	
100 G 20	Newfield clo Hampt	
100 H 19	Newfield clo Hampt	
44 H 9	Newfield ri NW2	
24 M 4	Newgate gdns Edg	
100 C 6	Newgate clo Felt	
122 M 19	Newgate Croy	
20 M 12	Newgate st E4	
21 N 11	Newgate st E4	
141 X 4	Newgate st EC1	
67 S 7	Newham way Bark	
65 Y 14	Newham way E16	
66 F 13	Newham way E6	
142 L 20	Newhams row SE1	
95 N 9	Newhaven gdns SE9	
123 P 11	Newhaven rd SE25	
37 W 10	Newhouse av Rom	
118 B 18	Newhouse clo New Mald	
98 G 15	Newick clo Bxly	
50 B 10	Newick rd E5	
113 O 18	Newing grn Chisl	
48 C 8	Newington Barrow way N7	
149 Y 6	Newington butts SE11	
149 Z 2	Newington causeway SE1	
149 Y 8	Newington cres SE17	
49 O 16	Newington Green rd N1	
49 O 14	Newington grn N16	
43 P 7	Newland ct Wemb	
8 M 6	Newland dri Enf	
71 Y 6	Newland gdns W13	
30 A 10	Newland rd N8	
78 E 3	Newland st E1	
11 X 10	Newlands clo Edg	
70 B 13	Newlands clo S'hall	
42 E 17	Newlands clo Wemb	
110 D 13	Newlands pk SE26	
4 B 16	Newlands pl Barnt	
21 R 9	Newlands rd Wdfd Grn	
122 B 3	Newlands rd SW16	
155 X 17	Newlands the Wallgtn	
158 K 19	Newlands wood Croy	
66 H 17	Newling clo E6	
40 C 2	Newlyn gdns Harrow	
4 G 15	Newlyn rd Barnt	
31 U 6	Newlyn rd N17	
44 L 4	Newlyn rd N2	
96 K 5	Newlyn rd Welling	
140 D 3	Newman av W1	
126 G 2	Newman rd Brom	
122 C 18	Newman rd Croy	
65 U 10	Newman rd E13	
32 G 14	Newman rd E17	
140 C 2	Newman st W1	
160 H 6	Newmans ct EC4	
141 P 3	Newmans row WC2	
5 S 7	Newmans way Barnt	
40 K 16	Newmarket av Nthlt	
95 O 18	Newmarket grn SE9	
120 D 15	Newminster rd Mrdn	
122 L 3	Newnham clo Thntn Hth	
40 M 16	Newnham clo Nthlt	
41 N 17	Newnham clo Nthlt	
30 E 4	Newnham rd N22	
149 R 1	Newnham ter SE1	
141 R 20	Newnham ter SE1	
24 L 14	Newnham way Harrow	
127 V 6	Newnhams clo Brom	
49 O 1	Newnton clo N4	
65 W 12	Newport av E13	
140 G 8	Newport ct WC2	
140 G 8	Newport pl WC2	
51 V 6	Newport rd E10	
32 J 14	Newport rd E17	
88 H 1	Newport rd SW13	
149 O 6	Newport st SE11	
40 C 7	Newquay cres Harrow	
111 S 4	Newquay rd SE6	
83 Z 12	Newry rd Twick	
31 O 15	Newsam av N15	
94 B 18	Newstead rd SE12	
105 R 8	Newstead way SW19	
120 D 17	Newstead wlk Carsh	
29 R 3	Newton av N10	
73 V 6	Newton av W3	
74 A 10	Newton gro W4	
40 H 7	Newton pk Harrow	
51 Y 14	Newton rd E15	
23 T 6	Newton rd Harrow	
83 V 4	Newton rd Islwth	
31 W 14	Newton rd N15	
44 M 11	Newton rd NW2	
105 U 18	Newton rd SW19	
137 W 5	Newton rd W2	
96 M 8	Newton rd Welling	
60 M 1	Newton rd Wemb	
89 S 2	Newton st SW11	
140 M 4	Newton st WC2	
17 Z 16	Newton way N18	
25 T 4	Newton wlk Edg	
87 Z 14	Newtons yd SW18	
72 C 10	Niagra av W5	
23 T 15	Nibthwaite rd Harrow	
16 J 4	Nichol clo N14	
112 G 17	Nichol la Brom	
58 L 5	Nicholas clo Grnfd	
72 F 4	Nicholas gdns W5	
160 G 8	Nicholas la EC4	
156 B 8	Nicholas rd Croy	
56 B 8	Nicholas rd Dgnhm	
63 R 12	Nicholas st E1	
82 G 11	Nicholas rd Hounsl	
135 S 7	Nicholl st E2	
60 J 14	Nicholls grn N5	
123 V 20	Nicholson rd Croy	
141 X 14	Nicholson st SE1	
84 C 15	Nicol clo Twick	
23 R 7	Nicola clo Harrow	
156 L 14	Nicola clo S Croy	
26 K 26	Nicoll pl NW4	
62 B 4	Nicoll rd NW10	
10 A 7	Nicolson dri Bushey	
88 H 18	Nicosia rd SW18	
110 G 8	Niederwald rd SE26	
58 B 4	Nigel clo Nthlt	
53 Y 12	Nigel ms Ilf	
74 J 12	Nigel Playfair av W6	
52 M 15	Nigel rd E7	
91 X 7	Nigel rd SE15	
77 Z 19	Nigeria st SE7	
20 L 15	Nightingale av E4	
155 N 3	Nightingale clo Carsh	
20 L 13	Nightingale clo E4	
73 V 18	Nightingale clo W4	
93 X 13	Nightingale gro SE13	
126 L 4	Nightingale la Brom	
127 N 5	Nightingale la Brom	
34 G 15	Nightingale la E11	
46 J 3	Nightingale la N6	
29 Z 13	Nightingale la N8	
84 K 18	Nightingale la Rich	
88 L 19	Nightingale la SW12	
89 O 17	Nightingale la SW12	
78 K 15	Nightingale pl SE18	
155 N 4	Nightingale rd Carsh	
49 Y 9	Nightingale rd E5	
100 H 15	Nightingale rd Hampt	
30 C 3	Nightingale rd N22	
19 S 6	Nightingale rd N9	
62 E 7	Nightingale rd NW10	
71 V 2	Nightingale rd W7	
89 O 18	Nightingale rd SW12	
78 K 16	Nightingale vale SE18	
66 E 14	Nightingale way E6	
89 R 15	Nightingale wlk SW4	
65 X 7	Nile rd E13	
134 D 12	Nile st N1	
151 O 12	Nile ter SE15	
91 S 12	Nimegen way SE22	
10 D 4	Nimmo dri Bushey	
107 T 12	Nimrod rd SW16	
53 R 15	Nine Acres clo E12	
148 H 15	Nine Elms la SW8	
78 M 18	Nithdale rd SE18	
79 N 18	Nithdale rd SE18	
4 B 19	Niton clo Barnt	
85 P 8	Niton rd Rich	
144 F 18	Niton st SW6	
19 R 15	Nobel rd N18	
160 A 4	Noble st EC2	
30 F 8	Noel Park rd N22	
66 C 12	Noel rd E6	
133 X 8	Noel rd N1	
61 P 17	Noel rd W3	
55 T 11	Noel sq Dgnhm	
140 C 6	Noel st W1	
49 Y 11	Nolan way E5	
25 N 6	Nolton pla Edg	
152 L 15	Nonsuch pk Epsom Sutton	
153 N 13	Nonsuch pk Epsom Sutton	
153 O 19	Nonsuch wlk Sutton	
153 P 20	Nonsuch wlk Sutton	
27 P 13	Nora gdns NW4	
41 T 3	Nora ter Harrow	
117 R 3	Norbiton av Kingst	
117 U 5	Norbiton Comm rd Kingst	
63 X 17	Norbiton rd E14	
62 D 19	Norbroke st W12	
136 J 2	Norburn st W10	
83 P 11	Norbury av Hounsl	
108 C 20	Norbury av SW16	
122 E 1	Norbury clo SW16	
108 H 19	Norbury clo SW16	
122 C 4	Norbury Court rd SW16	
121 Z 4	Norbury Court rd SW16	
122 C 1	Norbury cres SW16	
121 Z 5	Norbury cross SW16	
37 V 16	Norbury gdns Rom	
13 O 10	Norbury gro NW7	
108 J 17	Norbury hill SW16	
20 A 15	Norbury rd E4	
122 M 4	Norbury rd Thntn Hth	
123 N 4	Norbury rd Thntn Hth	
122 A 5	Norbury ri SW16	
121 Z 5	Norbury ri SW16	
24 D 17	Norcombe gdns	
49 X 8	Norcott rd N16	
91 W 17	Norcroft gdns SE22	
101 T 1	Norcutt rd Twick	
17 X 20	Norfolk av N13	
31 V 18	Norfolk av N15	
6 B 14	Norfolk clo Barnt	
17 X 19	Norfolk clo N13	
28 H 10	Norfolk clo N2	
84 B 15	Norfolk clo Twick	
96 H 18	Norfolk cres Sidcp	
138 L 5	Norfolk cres W2	
98 B 1	Norfolk gdns Bxly Hth	
107 Y 6	Norfolk House rd SW16	
138 H 5	Norfolk pl W2	
96 M 4	Norfolk pl Welling	
67 U 2	Norfolk rd Bark	
4 M 12	Norfolk rd Barnt	
56 H 15	Norfolk rd Dgnhm	
32 G 7	Norfolk rd E17	
66 H 3	Norfolk rd E6	
9 O 18	Norfolk rd Enf	
22 L 16	Norfolk rd Harrow	
54 H 1	Norfolk rd Ilf	
44 B 20	Norfolk rd NW10	
130 J 5	Norfolk rd NW8	
38 L 18	Norfolk rd Rom	
106 J 16	Norfolk rd SW19	
122 M 6	Norfolk rd Thntn Hth	
149 O 4	Norfolk row SE11	
138 G 5	Norfolk sq W2	
138 G 6	Norfolk Square ms W2	
52 F 14	Norfolk st E7	
144 K 12	Norfolk ter W6	
89 P 20	Norgrove st SW12	
123 U 5	Norhyrst av SE25	
136 L 14	Norland pl W11	
136 H 15	Norland rd W11	
136 L 14	Norland sq W11	
127 Z 1	Norlands cres BR7	
104 H 2	Norley vale SW15	
51 V 4	Norlington rd E10	
100 C 4	Norman av Felt	
30 K 4	Norman av N22	
58 C 19	Norman av S'hall	
84 C 18	Norman av Twick	
38 J 6	Norman clo Rom	
63 X 7	Norman gro E3	
100 E 4	Norman ho Felt	
126 J 14	Norman pk Brom	
81 T 7	Norman rd Blvdr	
51 Y 7	Norman rd E11	
66 H 11	Norman rd E6	
57 X 1	Norman rd Hornch	
54 A 16	Norman rd Ilf	
53 Z 16	Norman rd Ilf	
31 V 15	Norman rd N15	
76 E 17	Norman rd SE10	
153 X 11	Norman rd Sutton	
106 D 17	Norman rd SW19	
122 J 11	Norman rd Thntn Hth	
134 B 15	Norman st EC1	
16 M 9	Norman way N14	
61 T 16	Norman way W3	
87 U 13	Normanby clo SW15	
44 E 13	Normanby rd NW10	
144 M 13	Normand ms W14	
145 N 15	Normand gdn W14	
145 N 13	Normand rd W14	
4 H 14	Normandy av Barnt	
90 F 2	Normandy rd SW9	
65 U 18	Normandy ter E16	
99 P 2	Normandy way Erith	
97 W 3	Normanhurst av Bxly Hth	
83 Z 13	Normanhurst dri Twick	
108 D 3	Normanhurst rd SW2	
43 X 18	Normans clo NW10	
43 X 18	Normans mead NW10	
102 E 18	Normansfield av	
20 F 13	Normanshire av E4	
20 C 14	Normanshire dri E4	
105 X 5	Normanton av SW19	
20 M 10	Normanton pk E4	
21 N 9	Normanton rd E4	
157 R 13	Normanton rd S Croy	
110 G 5	Normanton st SE23	
108 F 11	Normington clo SW16	
28 F 17	Norrice lea N2	
140 E 11	Norris st SW1	
99 U 6	Norris way Drtfd	
87 P 11	Norroy rd SW15	
5 Z 15	Norrys clo Barnt	
5 Y 15	Norrys rd Barnt	
58 L 4	Norseman way Grnfd	
104 F 4	Norstead pl SW15	
32 G 18	North Access rd E17	
26 B 6	North acre NW9	
61 Y 8	North Acton rd NW10	
139 T 8	North Audley st W1	
155 N 16	North av Carsh	
22 L 18	North av Harrow	
132 M 9	North av N1	
18 L 13	North av N18	
85 O 3	North av Rich	
58 F 20	North av S'hall	
60 B 15	North av W13	
130 J 14	North Bank NW8	
51 X 10	North Birkbeck rd E11	
44 D 6	North Circular rd NW2	
18 F 15	North Circular rd N18	
60 L 8	North Circular rd Wemb	
45 N 1	North Circular rd NW2	
53 R 17	North Circular rd E12	
61 R 3	North Circular rd NW10	
53 S 5	North Circular rd Ilf	
17 V 16	North Circular rd N13	
43 W 18	North Circular rd NW10	
19 V 17	North Circular rd E4	
66 G 10	North Circular rd E6	
28 C 8	North Circular rd N2	
27 A 11	North Circular rd N2	
97 W 10	North clo Bxly Hth	
69 S 4	North clo Dgnhm	
119 S 8	North clo Mrdn	
60 L 20	North Common rd W5	
32 L 6	North Countess rd E17	
115 Y 15	North Cray rd Sidcp	
27 V 9	North cres N3	
132 E 20	North cres WC1	
36 A 14	North Cross rd Ilf	
91 V 12	North Cross rd SE22	
132 C 20	North ct W1	
82 J 3	North dene Hounsl	
12 L 10	North dene NW7	
159 S 20	North Downs cres Croy	
83 O 6	North dri Hounsl	
107 V 9	North dri SW16	
46 D 6	North End av NW3	
21 Y 3	North end Buck Hl	
145 N 7	North End cres W14	
156 L 3	North end Croy	
46 C 5	North end NW3	
45 Z 4	North End rd NW11	
46 B 4	North End rd NW3	

144 L 5 North End rd SW6
145 R 13 North End rd W14
43 R 10 North End rd Wemb
46 C 7 North End way NW3
74 E 13 North Eyot gdns W6
106 G 17 North gdns SW19
98 B 20 North Glade the Bxly
132 B 14 North Gower st NW1
31 O 16 North gro N15
47 O 2 North gro N6
29 N 17 North Hill av N6
29 O 19 North hill N6
70 A 13 North Hyde la S'hall
101 V 14 North la Tedd
87 P 14 North Lodge clo SW15
133 P 18 North ms WC1
87 Y 12 North pas SW18
95 U 17 North pk SE9
106 L 17 North pl Mitch
136 B 3 North Pole rd W10
62 L 15 North Pole rd W10
81 U 6 North rd Blvdr
72 L 16 North rd Brentf
112 H 20 North rd Brom
99 U 17 North rd Drtfrd
25 T 3 North rd Edg
54 G 7 North rd Ilf
47 P 1 North rd N6
48 B 16 North rd N7
47 Z 17 North rd N7
18 M 4 North rd N7
85 O 8 North rd Rich
37 X 16 North rd Rom
58 F 20 North rd S'hall
70 G 1 North rd S'hall
79 W 9 North rd SE18
116 G 14 North rd Surb
106 D 15 North rd SW19
125 S 20 North rd W Wkhm
72 G 9 North rd W5
139 T 7 North row W1
93 V 4 North several SE3
153 W 5 North Spur rd Sutton
27 Z 17 North sq NW11
54 A 20 North st Bark
67 N 1 North st Bark
126 E 2 North st Brom
98 E 9 North st Bxly Hth
154 M 8 North st Carsh
155 N 9 North st Carsh
65 U 6 North st E13
83 Y 6 North st Islwth
27 N 15 North st NW4
39 O 13 North st Rom
89 U 6 North st SW4
143 P 6 North Tenter st E1
146 J 4 North ter SW3
35 N 7 North View dri Wdfd Grn
29 Y 11 North View rd N8
104 L 12 North view SW19
60 D 11 North view W5
47 Y 18 North vlls NW1
19 S 8 North way N9
25 S 10 North way NW9
138 F 3 North Wharf rd W2
159 U 13 North wlk Croy
78 A 4 North Woolwich rd E16
77 S 3 North Woolwich rd E16
86 A 7 North Worple way SW14
85 Z 7 North Worple way SW14
98 J 6 Northall rd Bxly Hth
49 N 16 Northampton gro N1
49 N 16 Northampton pk N1
157 X 2 Northampton rd Croy
133 T 16 Northampton rd EC1
9 X 15 Northampton rd Enf
133 T 16 Northampton row EC1
133 X 13 Northampton sq EC1
48 L 20 Northampton st N1
107 Z 16 Northanger rd SW16
33 T 7 Northbank rd E17
122 C 4 Northborough rd SW16
121 Y 5 Northborough rd SW16
126 F 16 Northbourne Brom
89 Y 12 Northbourne rd SW4
4 F 20 Northbrook rd Barnt
123 N 12 Northbrook rd Croy
53 V 7 Northbrook rd Ilf
30 B 1 Northbrook rd N22
93 Y 12 Northbrook rd SE13
133 X 17 Northburgh st EC1

43 O 18 Northchurch rd Wemb
49 N 20 Northchurch rd N1
134 J 1 Northchurch ter N1
152 B 6 Northcliffe clo Worc Pk
14 H 5 Northcliffe dr N20
58 C 20 Northcote av S'hall
70 D 1 Northcote av S'hall
117 S 16 Northcote av Surb
83 Y 12 Northcote av Twick
60 J 20 Northcote av W5
117 X 7 Northcote rd New Mald
123 P 14 Northcote rd Croy
32 J 14 Northcote rd E17
62 B 1 Northcote rd NW10
114 H 10 Northcote rd Sidcp
88 K 12 Northcote rd SW11
84 A 12 Northcote rd Twick
83 Z 12 Northcote rd Twick
30 A 4 Northcott av N22
152 A 17 Northcroft rd Epsom
72 B 7 Northcroft rd W13
31 U 19 Northdene gdns N15
36 G 15 Northdown gdns Ilf
97 P 5 Northdown rd Welling
57 Y 2 Northdown rd Hornch
132 M 10 Northdown st N1
99 S 2 Northend rd Erith
18 F 9 Northern av N9
65 W 5 Northern rd E13
119 T 10 Northernhay wlk Mrdn
63 W 20 Northey st E14
72 B 3 Northfield av W13
153 S 9 Northfield cres Sutton
56 B 12 Northfield gdns Dgnhm
5 W 12 Northfield rd Barnt
56 B 12 Northfield rd Dgnhm
53 V 20 Northfield rd E6
9 P 19 Northfield rd Enf
49 T 1 Northfield rd N16
72 A 5 Northfield rd W13
61 U 14 Northfields rd W3
87 X 11 Northfields SW18
14 K 12 Northiam N12
14 M 12 Northiam N12
63 O 4 Northiam st E8
135 Y 6 Northiam st E9
133 P 19 Northington st WC1
90 L 6 Northlands st SE5
12 K 14 Northolm Edg
25 P 4 Northolme gdns Edg
48 K 11 Northolme rd N5
41 W 15 Northolt gdns Grnfd
40 K 12 Northolt rd Harrow
41 O 7 Northolt rd Harrow
112 C 7 Northover Brom
134 H 6 Northport st N1
108 G 4 Northstead rd SW2
18 H 10 Northumberland gdns N9
121 Y 11 Northumberland gdns Mitch
142 M 7 Northumberland all EC3
96 G 9 Northumberland av Welling
140 K 13 Northumberland av WC2
52 L 4 Northumberland av E12
9 N 5 Northumberland av Enf
83 V 1 Northumberland av Islwth
71 X 20 Northumberland av Islwth
98 K 1 Northumberland clo Erith
31 Z 2 Northumberland gro N17
81 X 19 Northumberland pk Erith
31 Y 1 Northumberland pk N17
84 G 16 Northumberland pl Rich
137 U 5 Northumberland pl W2
22 H 16 Northumberland rd Harrow
51 N 1 Northumberland rd E17

15 P 1 Northumberland rd Barnt
66 E 16 Northumberland rd E6
140 J 12 Northumberland st WC2
99 N 2 Northumberland way Erith
64 B 17 Northumbria st E14
44 C 13 Northview cres NW10
12 L 12 Northway cir NW7
12 M 13 Northway cres NW7
119 T 8 Northway Mrdn
28 A 17 Northway NW11
28 B 15 Northway NW11
16 G 19 Northway NW11
123 U 15 Northway rd Croy
90 L 8 Northway rd SE5
155 V 8 Northway Wallgtn
24 A 20 Northwick av Harrow
23 Z 19 Northwick av Harrow
24 D 18 Northwick cir Harrow
130 F 17 Northwick clo NW8
42 B 2 Northwick pk Harrow
23 X 18 Northwick Park rd Harrow
60 H 4 Northwick rd Wemb
130 E 17 Northwick ter NW8
41 W 1 Northwick wlk Harrow
49 Y 7 Northwold rd E5
49 U 7 Northwold rd N16
57 X 12 Northwood av Hornch
15 T 16 Northwood gdns N12
41 W 15 Northwood gdns Grnfd
35 W 12 Northwood gdns Ilf
81 N 7 Northwood pl Blvdr
122 L 3 Northwood rd Thntn Hth
123 N 1 Northwood rd Thntn Hth
155 O 14 Northwood rd Carsh
47 T 1 Northwood rd N6
110 K 2 Northwood rd SE23
117 T 16 Norton av Surb
20 B 15 Norton clo E4
8 M 9 Norton clo Enf
134 L 19 Norton folgate E1
122 A 3 Norton gdns SW16
57 N 18 Norton rd Dgnhm
50 M 3 Norton rd E10
42 G 18 Norton rd Wemb
75 W 8 Norway ga SE16
63 X 18 Norway pl E14
76 E 16 Norway st SE10
122 M 7 Norwich rd Thntn Hth
69 S 7 Norwich rd Dgnhm
52 E 16 Norwich rd E7
58 L 3 Norwich rd Grnfd
141 T 3 Norwich st EC4
25 W 2 Norwich wlk Edg
57 P 3 Norwood av Rom
60 M 5 Norwood av Wemb
70 F 12 Norwood clo S'hall
22 G 18 Norwood dri Harrow
70 D 10 Norwood gdns S'hall
70 H 12 Norwood Grn rd S'hall
108 K 8 Norwood High st SE27
108 M 12 Norwood Park rd SE27
109 N 12 Norwood Park rd SE27
70 G 12 Norwood rd S'hall
108 J 7 Norwood rd SE27
150 E 18 Notley st SE5
123 Z 10 Notson rd SE25
137 T 12 Notting Hill ga W11
65 Y 16 Nottingham av E16
140 K 6 Nottingham ct WC2
131 T 19 Nottingham pl W1
156 L 10 Nottingham rd S Croy
156 L 11 Nottingham rd S Croy
33 U 18 Nottingham rd E10
83 V 4 Nottingham rd Islwth
106 L 2 Nottingham rd SW17
131 T 20 Nottingham st W1
119 S 18 Nova ms Sutton
122 K 18 Nova rd Croy
114 B 2 Novar rd SE9
87 X 2 Novello st SW6
74 G 17 Nowell rd SW13
22 E 12 Nower hill Pinn

106 M 6 Noyna rd SW17
93 P 8 Nuding clo SE13
48 A 4 Nugent rd N19
123 T 6 Nugent rd SE25
130 C 11 Nugent ter NW8
22 C 4 Nugents pk Pinn
160 E 3 Nun ct EC2
68 K 1 Nuneaton rd Dgnhm
91 Y 8 Nunhead cres SE15
92 A 7 Nunhead grn SE15
92 B 8 Nunhead gro SE15
92 A 8 Nunhead la SE15
113 R 7 Nunnington clo SE9
7 Z 8 Nunns rd Enf
4 A 19 Nupton dri Barnt
15 W 20 Nursery app N12
98 C 7 Nursery av Bxly Hth
158 E 3 Nursery av Croy
28 C 7 Nursery av N3
158 E 4 Nursery clo Croy
9 T 5 Nursery clo Enf
100 E 11 Nursery clo Hampt
37 W 19 Nursery clo Rom
87 O 11 Nursery clo SW15
21 U 16 Nursery clo Wdfd Grn
9 T 6 Nursery gdns Enf
52 G 17 Nursery la E7
136 B 2 Nursery la W10
62 M 14 Nursery la W10
120 J 7 Nursery rd Mitch
120 A 1 Nursery rd Mrdn
16 H 3 Nursery rd N14
28 G 5 Nursery rd N2
154 D 9 Nursery rd Sutton
105 R 19 Nursery rd SW19
90 D 9 Nursery rd SW9
123 O 9 Nursery rd Thntn Hth
150 D 8 Nursery row SE17
31 U 3 Nursery st N17
89 S 7 Nursery st SW8
26 L 10 Nursery wlk NW4
39 N 20 Nursery wlk Rom
81 T 20 Nurstead rd Erith
128 K 12 Nutbourne st W10
91 W 8 Nutbrook st SE15
69 P 3 Nutbrowne rd Dgnhm
151 V 18 Nutcroft rd SE16
18 J 19 Nutfield clo N18
54 L 7 Nutfield gdns Ilf
51 U 12 Nutfield rd E15
44 F 9 Nutfield rd NW2
91 V 11 Nutfield rd SE22
139 N 4 Nutfield rd Thntn Hth
79 T 6 Nutford pl W1
108 D 3 Nuthatch gdns SE28
46 E 17 Nuthurst av SW2
11 U 8 Nutter la NW3
151 P 18 Nutt st SE15
134 L 7 Nuttall st N1
34 K 16 Nutter la E11
81 R 14 Nuxley rd Blvdr
79 T 18 Nyanza st SE18
85 P 4 Nylands av Rich
118 J 5 Nymans gdns SW20
75 V 18 Nynehead st SE14
110 K 5 Nyon gro SE6
47 Z 4 Nyton clo N19

O

63 P 14 O'Leary sq E1
142 C 15 O'meara st SE1
63 Y 3 O'Shea gro E3
159 P 1 Oak av Croy
7 P 3 Oak av Enf
100 C 14 Oak av Hampt
70 A 20 Oak av Hounsl
29 S 2 Oak av N10
31 P 1 Oak av N17
29 Z 14 Oak av N8
159 V 13 Oak bank Croy
99 S 11 Oak clo Drtfrd
16 D 3 Oak clo N14
154 D 4 Oak clo Sutton
62 C 17 Oak common W3
112 A 2 Oak Cottage clo SE6
65 N 15 Oak cres E16
39 Y 19 Oak Dene clo Rom
60 A 14 Oak dene W13
159 O 1 Oak gdns Croy
25 U 7 Oak gdns Edg
45 R 12 Oak gro NW2

159 V 1	Oak gro W Wkhm
124 C 2	Oak Grove rd SE20
34 H 19	Oak Hall rd E11
33 X 2	Oak Hill clo Wdfd Grn
33 Y 1	Oak Hill cres Wdfd Grn
34 A 3	Oak Hill gdns Wdfd Grn
46 C 12	Oak Hill Park ms NW3
116 K 16	Oak Hill Surb
46 B 11	Oak Hill way NW3
34 A 2	Oak hill Wdfd Grn
33 X 1	Oak hill Wdfd Grn
33 Z 1	Oak hill Wdfd Grn
63 X 19	Oak la E14
16 L 19	Oak la N11
28 F 7	Oak la N2
28 F 7	Oak la N2
83 U 9	Oak la Twick
83 Z 19	Oak la Twick
21 R 13	Oak la Wdfd Grn
11 S 15	Oak Lodge clo Stanm
125 S 18	Oak Lodge dri W Wkhm
103 O 3	Oak lodge Rich
87 P 20	Oak Park gdns SW19
81 X 20	Oak rd Erith
99 X 3	Oak rd Erith
117 X 3	Oak rd New Mald
121 U 3	Oak row Mitch
38 J 14	Oak st Rom
72 H 1	Oak st W5
24 C 3	Oak Tree clo Stanm
60 E 18	Oak Tree clo W13
25 X 16	Oak Tree dell NW9
15 O 6	Oak Tree dri N20
112 J 11	Oak Tree gdns Brom
130 J 14	Oak Tree rd NW8
47 O 13	Oak village NW5
124 G 13	Oak way Croy
16 D 2	Oak way N14
74 A 2	Oak way W3
90 L 10	Oakbank gro SE24
112 H 9	Oakbrook clo SE12
88 A 5	Oakbury rd SW6
104 A 19	Oakcombe clo New Mald
93 W 5	Oakcroft rd SE13
24 K 15	Oakdale av Harrow
125 T 2	Oakdale Becknhm
20 G 15	Oakdale ct E4
16 G 4	Oakdale N14
51 W 7	Oakdale rd E11
34 J 8	Oakdale rd E18
52 J 20	Oakdale rd E7
30 M 18	Oakdale rd N4
31 N 18	Oakdale rd N4
92 D 7	Oakdale rd SE15
108 B 12	Oakdale rd SW16
149 U 6	Oakden st SE11
113 V 11	Oakdene av Chisl
81 X 17	Oakdene av Erith
22 E 1	Oakdene clo Pinn
117 V 19	Oakdene dri Surb
27 W 1	Oakdene pk N3
116 K 17	Oakenshaw clo Surb
66 H 18	Oakes clo E6
47 P 6	Oakeshott av N6
30 F 20	Oakfield rd N4
24 B 10	Oakfield av Harrow
118 D 12	Oakfield clo New Mald
27 P 20	Oakfield ct NW11
20 C 10	Oakfield E4
125 P 13	Oakfield gdns Becknhm
120 K 20	Oakfield gdns Carsh
59 P 10	Oakfield gdns Grnfd
18 C 14	Oakfield gdns N18
109 T 12	Oakfield gdns SE19
122 L 20	Oakfield rd Croy
32 J 7	Oakfield rd E17
66 C 4	Oakfield rd E6
54 A 9	Oakfield rd Ilf
17 N 9	Oakfield rd N14
28 A 5	Oakfield rd N3
48 G 1	Oakfield rd N4
110 B 17	Oakfield rd SE20
105 R 6	Oakfield rd SW19
27 T 17	Oakfields rd NW11
47 U 12	Oakford rd NW5
34 J 18	Oakhall ct E11
27 P 3	Oakham dri Brom
46 A 12	Oakhall av NW3
22 A 7	Oakhill av Pinn
116 K 16	Oakhill cres Surb
116 L 17	Oakhill dri Surb
16 B 1	Oakhill gro Surb
116 J 15	Oakhill gro Surb
15 Z 2	Oakhill pk Barnt
87 X 12	Oakhill pl SW15
116 J 15	Oakhill rd Bcknhm
125 T 4	Oakhill rd Bcknhm
116 K 16	Oakhill rd Surb
154 B 6	Oakhill rd Sutton
87 X 12	Oakhill rd SW15
122 B 2	Oakhill rd SW16
98 E 12	Oakhouse rd Bxly Hth
15 V 2	Oakhurst av Barnt
80 L 20	Oakhurst av Bxly Hth
33 Z 12	Oakhurst clo E17
21 P 5	Oakhurst clo E4
80 M 20	Oakhurst gdns Bxly Hth
33 Z 13	Oakhurst gdns E17
21 P 5	Oakhurst gdns E4
91 X 10	Oakhurst gro SE22
40 G 2	Oakington av Harrow
42 M 9	Oakington av Wemb
43 O 9	Oakington av Wemb
43 P 15	Oakington Manor dri Wemb
129 U 17	Oakington rd W9
30 A 20	Oakington way N8
152 A 13	Oakland way Epsom
122 F 8	Oaklands av Thntn Hth
159 T 5	Oaklands av W Wkhm
98 C 13	Oaklands clo Bxly Hth
9 N 20	Oaklands av Enf
71 W 16	Oaklands av Islwth
20 O 12	Oaklands av N9
96 K 18	Oaklands av Sidcp
42 F 16	Oaklands ct Wemb
74 H 3	Oaklands gro W12
17 P 8	Oaklands N21
54 C 7	Oaklands Park av Ilf
112 B 17	Oaklands rd Brom
98 B 12	Oaklands rd Bxly Hth
14 G 2	Oaklands rd N20
45 O 13	Oaklands rd NW2
85 X 8	Oaklands rd SW14
71 W 5	Oaklands rd W7
82 M 19	Oaklands Twick
155 W 16	Oaklands way SM6
116 H 6	Oaklea pas Kingst
35 Y 10	Oakleafe gdns Ilf
25 T 5	Oakleigh av Edg
15 V 7	Oakleigh av N20
16 A 11	Oakleigh clo N20
15 X 10	Oakleigh cres N20
25 V 8	Oakleigh ct Edg
12 A 15	Oakleigh gdns Edg
15 S 5	Oakleigh gdns N20
127 X 2	Oakleigh Park av Chisl
15 U 5	Oakleigh Park north N20
15 V 4	Oakleigh Park south N20
15 V 2	Oakleigh pk Barnt
16 A 11	Oakleigh Road north N20
15 U 7	Oakleigh Road north N20
16 C 13	Oakleigh Road south N11
121 S 1	Oakleigh way Mitch
54 L 20	Oakley av Bark
156 B 8	Oakley av Croy
61 P 19	Oakley av W5
66 E 17	Oakley clo E6
83 R 2	Oakley clo Islwth
53 S 19	Oakley clo W7
133 X 10	Oakley cres N1
114 E 3	Oakley dri Sidcp
30 C 15	Oakley gdns N8
146 L 13	Oakley gdns SW3
127 O 18	Oakley ho Brom
97 S 19	Oakley pk Sidcp
151 N 11	Oakley pl SE1
127 P 20	Oakley rd Brom
23 S 17	Oakley rd Harrow
49 O 20	Oakley rd N1
124 A 11	Oakley rd SE25
123 Z 12	Oakley rd SE25
132 C 8	Oakley sq NW1
146 K 14	Oakley st SW3
144 J 14	Oakley wk W6
126 F 15	Oakmead av Brom
12 K 13	Oakmead gdns Edg
121 X 14	Oakmead rd Mitch
107 R 2	Oakmead rd SW12
80 A 16	Oakmere rd SE2
111 X 11	Oakridge rd Brom
100 A 4	Oaks av Felt
38 L 8	Oaks av Rom
109 R 11	Oaks av SE19
152 L 8	Oaks av Worc Pk
20 M 8	Oaks gro E4
158 D 4	Oaks la Croy
36 G 14	Oaks la Ilf
158 C 8	Oaks rd Croy
157 Z 10	Oaks rd Croy
15 P 14	Oaks the N12
79 O 15	Oaks the SE18
154 M 17	Oaks way Carsh
155 N 17	Oaks way Carsh
109 Z 8	Oaksford av SE26
111 Y 9	Oakshade rd Brom
88 B 19	Oakshaw rd SW18
17 S 15	Oakthorpe rd N13
17 U 10	Oaktree av N13
124 K 19	Oakview gro Croy
111 R 12	Oakview rd SE6
125 W 4	Oakway Brom
97 Z 16	Oakway clo Bxly
118 M 9	Oakway SW20
119 N 9	Oakway SW20
95 Y 15	Oakways SE9
125 U 3	Oakwood av Becknhm
126 H 7	Oakwood av Brom
120 G 3	Oakwood av Mitch
70 H 1	Oakwood av S'hall
58 H 20	Oakwood av S'hall
113 V 16	Oakwood clo Chisl
6 J 20	Oakwood clo N14
42 A 18	Oakwood cres Grnfd
41 Z 17	Oakwood cres Grnfd
7 O 18	Oakwood cres N21
145 O 1	Oakwood ct W14
98 L 9	Oakwood dri Bxly Hth
12 G 18	Oakwood dri Edg
109 P 15	Oakwood dri SE19
54 K 7	Oakwood gdns Ilf
137 O 20	Oakwood la W14
16 M 1	Oakwood Park rd N14
17 N 1	Oakwood Park rd N14
122 F 15	Oakwood pl Croy
122 F 15	Oakwood rd Croy
28 A 15	Oakwood rd NW11
27 Z 14	Oakwood rd NW11
104 H 20	Oakwood rd SW20
16 L 1	Oakwood view N14
155 T 19	Oakwood Wallgtn
136 E 1	Oakworth rd W10
160 B 3	Oat la EC2
125 X 5	Oates clo BR2
32 H 9	Oatland ri E17
9 P 7	Oatlands rd Enf
65 Z 10	Oban rd E13
123 O 8	Oban rd SE25
64 K 16	Oban st E14
88 G 10	Oberstein rd SW11
90 K 14	Oborne clo SE24
137 U 17	Observatory gdns W8
85 V 11	Observatory rd SW14
95 Z 1	Occupation la SE18
72 G 11	Occupation la W5
150 A 9	Occupation rd SE17
72 A 10	Occupation rd W13
72 B 4	Occupation rd W13
63 U 14	Ocean st E1
49 O 19	Ockendon rd N1
115 O 18	Ockham dri Orp
122 C 17	Ockley rd Croy
107 Z 8	Ockley rd SW16
120 H 11	Octavia clo Mrdn
83 V 6	Octavia rd Islwth
76 A 19	Octavia st SE8
88 J 3	Octavia st SW11
80 E 1	Octavia way SE28
52 E 14	Odessa rd E7
62 H 7	Odessa rd NW10
75 X 7	Odessa st SE16
88 M 5	Odger st SW11
50 K 13	Offa's mead E9
113 U 9	Offenham rd SE9
89 V 8	Offerton rd SW4
14 H 16	Offham slope N12
149 S 18	Offley rd SW9
48 D 20	Offord rd N1
78 F 12	Ogilby st SE18
91 V 8	Oglander rd SE15
140 A 1	Ogle st W1
56 D 9	Oglethorpe rd Dgnhm
65 P 13	Ohio rd E13
44 C 20	Oldfield rd NW10
107 O 11	Okeburn rd SW17
15 T 15	Okehampton clo N12
80 H 20	Okehampton cres Welling
97 S 1	Okehampton cres Welling
128 E 6	Okehampton rd NW10
136 K 19	Olaf st W11
141 X 5	Old bailey EC4
153 S 16	Old Barn clo Sutton
98 L 9	Old Barn way Bxly Hth
139 T 18	Old Barrack yd SW1
65 N 4	Old Barrowfield E15
135 T 12	Old Bethnal Green rd E2
141 R 4	Old bldgs WC2
140 A 12	Old Bond st W1
46 F 13	Old Brewery ms NW3
58 H 4	Old Bridge clo Nthlt
116 F 2	Old Bridge st Kingst
142 H 3	Old Broad st EC2
160 H 3	Old Broad st EC2
111 X 12	Old Bromley rd Brom
146 B 9	Old Brompton rd SW5
140 A 10	Old Burlington st W1
143 O 4	Old Castle st E1
139 X 5	Old Cavendish st W1
160 A 7	Old Change ct EC4
43 X 7	Old Church la NW9
24 E 1	Old Church la Stanm
11 P 19	Old Church la Stanm
11 T 20	Old Church la Stanm
63 T 17	Old Church rd E1
20 B 11	Old Church rd E4
146 J 15	Old Church st SW3
140 E 8	Old Compton st W1
70 G 17	Old Cote dri Hounsl
137 X 17	Old Court pl W8
84 K 8	Old Deer Park gdns Rich
84 F 7	Old Deer pk Rich
89 S 20	Old Devonshire rd SW12
73 P 17	Old Dock clo Rich
77 U 19	Old Dover rd SE3
82 E 2	Old Farm av N14
114 E 2	Old Farm av Sidcp
82 E 9	Old Farm clo Hounsl
100 G 15	Old Farm rd Hampt
28 G 4	Old Farm rd N2
114 L 3	Old Farm Rd west Sidcp
114 M 3	Old Farm Road east Sidcp
4 G 7	Old Fold clo Barnt
4 G 7	Old Fold la Barnt
4 A 12	Old Fold view Barnt
135 Z 11	Old Ford rd E2
63 U 5	Old Ford rd E3
10 M 13	Old Forge clo Stanm
8 G 4	Old Forge rd Enf
10 M 14	Old Forge Stanm
115 R 11	Old Forge way Sidcp
132 L 20	Old Gloucester st WC1
140 M 1	Old Gloucester st WC1
22 B 5	Old Hall clo Pinn
22 B 5	Old Hall dri Pinn
113 Y 20	Old Hill Chisl
105 S 12	Old House clo SW19
151 R 1	Old Jamaica rd SE16
91 Z 8	Old James st SE15
142 D 6	Old Jewry EC2
160 D 6	Old Jewry EC2
150 K 7	Old Kent rd SE1
75 O 18	Old Kent rd SE15
151 X 16	Old Kent rd SE15
25 T 16	Old Kenton la NW9
10 M 16	Old Lodge way Stanm
83 O 15	Old Manor dri Islwth
98 M 7	Old Manor way Bxly Hth
145 W 8	Old Manor yd SW5
138 L 2	Old Marylebone rd NW1
34 K 9	Old Mill ct E18
79 S 16	Old Mill rd SE18
141 T 7	Old Mitre ct EC4
143 R 2	Old Montague st E1
135 U 20	Old Montague st E1
23 S 17	Old ms Harrow
134 M 15	Old Nichol st E2
135 N 15	Old Nichol st E2
141 N 1	Old North st WC1

62 C 11 Old Oak Comm la NW10
62 C 18 Old Oak Comm la W3
62 C 9 Old Oak la NW10
62 D 20 Old Oak rd W3
74 E 3 Old Oak rd W3
46 L 12 Old Orchard the NW3
84 E 12 Old Palace la Rich
156 K 4 Old Palace rd Croy
84 F 12 Old Palace yd Rich
149 O 5 Old Paradise st SE11
7 Z 12 Old Park av Enf
89 P 16 Old Park av SW12
7 Y 15 Old Park gro Enf
139 W 16 Old Park la W1
70 F 20 Old Park ms Hounsl
7 W 12 Old Park rd Enf
17 R 12 Old Park rd N13
80 A 14 Old Park rd SE2
7 X 18 Old Park ridings N21
7 V 14 Old Park Road south Enf
7 U 11 Old Park view Enf
114 G 17 Old Perry st Chisl
148 F 1 Old Pye st SW1
139 R 7 Old Quebec st W1
140 G 19 Old Queen st SW1
98 M 12 Old rd Drtfrd
9 P 6 Old rd Enf
93 Z 11 Old rd SE13
12 C 18 Old Rectory gdns Edg
10 C 14 Old Redding Harrow
152 C 19 Old Schools la Epsom
141 W 5 Old Seacoal la EC4
148 L 18 Old South Lambeth rd SW8
141 R 4 Old sq WC2
65 W 7 Old st E13
134 J 14 Old st EC1
127 W 1 Old Station hill Chisl
154 L 9 Old Swan yd Carsh
156 K 5 Old Town Croy
89 U 9 Old Town SW4
76 K 15 Old Woolwich rd SE10
88 B 12 Old York rd SW18
12 M 19 Oldberry rd Edg
42 D 9 Oldborough rd Wemb
131 T 19 Oldbury pl W1
8 L 9 Oldbury rd Enf
57 P 1 Oldchurch pk Rom
39 O 20 Oldchurch rd Rom
39 P 20 Oldchurch ri Rom
127 V 9 Oldfield clo Brom
41 T 17 Oldfield clo Grnfd
10 L 15 Oldfield clo Grnfd
59 P 4 Oldfield Farm gdns Grnfd
75 T 11 Oldfield gro SE16
59 P 5 Oldfield la Grnfd
41 R 19 Oldfield Lane north Grnfd
47 V 2 Oldfield ms N6
127 U 8 Oldfield rd Brom
98 A 5 Oldfield rd Bxly Hth
97 Z 5 Oldfield rd Bxly Hth
49 S 9 Oldfield rd N16
88 A 11 Oldfield rd SW18
105 S 14 Oldfield rd SW19
74 D 5 Oldfield rd W12
41 O 17 Oldfields cir Grnfd
153 X 3 Oldfields rd Sutton
73 V 4 Oldhams ter W3
49 X 3 Oldhill st N16
89 R 18 Oldridge rd SW12
111 W 10 Oldstead rd Brom
63 S 15 Oley pl E1
63 W 7 Olga st E3
76 H 9 Oliffe st E14
31 U 19 Olinda rd N16
128 K 11 Oliphant st W10
65 Z 9 Olive rd E13
44 L 12 Olive rd NW2
45 N 12 Olive rd NW2
106 D 18 Olive rd SW19
72 G 9 Olive rd W5
39 N 15 Olive st Rom
123 U 7 Oliver av SE25
51 P 7 Oliver clo E10
66 E 16 Oliver gdns E6
123 V 8 Oliver gro SE25
51 P 7 Oliver rd E10
33 V 14 Oliver rd E17
117 W 3 Oliver rd New Mald
154 E 9 Oliver rd Sutton
73 R 16 Olivers clo W4

134 F 17 Olivers yd EC2
87 P 9 Olivette st SW15
63 Z 2 Ollerton grn E3
16 K 17 Ollerton rd N11
74 F 3 Ollgar clo W12
151 R 13 Olmar st SE1
150 A 14 Olney rd SE17
149 Z 14 Olney rd SE17
97 X 14 Olron cres Bxly Hth
79 P 18 Olven rd SE18
120 G 14 Olveston wlk Carsh
97 O 3 Olyffe av Welling
111 T 20 Olyffe dri Beckmhm
144 M 3 Olympia av W14
144 L 4 Olympia W14
137 Z 9 Olympia yd W2
58 M 4 Olympic way Grnfd
43 P 10 Olympic way Wemb
44 K 13 Oman av NW2
132 M 10 Omega pl N1
92 G 3 Ommaney rd SE14
91 V 9 Ondine rd SE15
92 D 17 One Tree clo SE23
75 V 8 Onega ga SE16
37 T 14 Ongar clo Rom
145 T 13 Ongar rd SW6
33 O 20 Onra rd E17
84 K 14 Onslow av Rich
20 H 9 Onslow clo E4
127 Z 1 Onslow cres BR7
115 V 5 Onslow dri Sidcp
34 J 10 Onslow gdns E18
29'S 15 Onslow gdns N10
7 U 17 Onslow gdns N21
146 E 8 Onslow gdns SW7
155 U 16 Onslow gdns Wllgtn
146 F 7 Onslow Mews east SW7
146 E 8 Onslow Mews west SW7
122 F 19 Onslow rd Croy
118 F 8 Onslow rd New Mald
84 K 14 Onslow rd Rich
146 G 6 Onslow sq SW7
133 U 19 Onslow st EC1
149 Y 2 Ontario st SE1
66 B 18 Opal clo E16
53 Z 8 Opal ms Ilf
149 V 9 Opal st SE17
80 C 12 Openshaw rd SE2
106 E 2 Openview SW18
91 W 3 Ophir ter SE15
131 O 2 Oppidans ms NW3
131 O 1 Oppidans rd NW3
143 U 14 Orange ct E1
25 V 1 Orange Hill rd Edg
75 P 9 Orange st SE16
140 F 11 Orange st WC2
140 G 6 Orange yd W1
95 U 14 Orangery la SE9
150 E 8 Orb st SE17
144 M 19 Orbain rd SW6
88 H 3 Orbel st SW11
118 C 5 Orchard av New Mald
80 M 16 Orchard av Blvdr
81 N 16 Orchard av Blvdr
158 H 1 Orchard av Croy
124 J 18 Orchard av Croy
124 J 20 Orchard av Croy
99 Y 20 Orchard av Drtfrd
70 C 20 Orchard av Hounsl
121 O 19 Orchard av Mitch
16 H 1 Orchard av N14
15 U 8 Orchard av N20
27 X 10 Orchard av N3
70 D 2 Orchard av S'hall
10 C 5 Orchard clo Bushey
97 Y 2 Orchard clo Bxly Hth
11 Y 18 Orchard clo Edg
41 N 17 Orchard clo Nthlt
44 F 10 Orchard clo NW2
92 C 17 Orchard clo SE23
116 B 19 Orchard clo Surb
118 L 8 Orchard clo SW20
60 K 2 Orchard clo Wemb
12 H 17 Orchard cres Edg
8 G 6 Orchard cres Enf
152 E 1 Orchard ct Worc Pk
11 Z 15 Orchard dri Edg
93 Y 4 Orchard dri SE3
93 S 4 Orchard est SE13
42 C 18 Orchard ga Grnfd
26 A 12 Orchard ga NW9
153 X 20 Orchard gdns Sutton
124 J 17 Orchard gro Croy
25 R 5 Orchard gro Edg
25 N 15 Orchard gro Harrow
155 N 10 Orchard hill Carsh
99 O 12 Orchard hill Drtfrd

93 S 3 Orchard hill SE13
104 K 20 Orchard la SW20
21 X 13 Orchard la Wdfd Grn
109 X 20 Orchard lodge SE20
134 G 2 Orchard ms N1
64 M 19 Orchard pl E14
31 U 3 Orchard pl N17
4 G 14 Orchard rd Barnt
81 R 12 Orchard rd Blvdr
72 E 16 Orchard rd Brentf
112 M 20 Orchard rd Brom
69 T 3 Orchard rd Dgnhm
8 R 18 Orchard rd Enf
100 F 17 Orchard rd Hampt
82 F 12 Orchard rd Hounsl
116 J 5 Orchard rd Kingst
121 O 19 Orchard rd Mitch
29 T 20 Orchard rd N6
85 P 9 Orchard rd Rich
38 G 6 Orchard rd Rom
93 Y 4 Orchard rd SE3
114 J 9 Orchard rd Sidcp
153 Y 10 Orchard rd Sutton
84 A 14 Orchard rd Twick
83 Z 14 Orchard rd Twick
97 R 6 Orchard rd Welling
124 K 19 Orchard ri Croy
103 V 20 Orchard ri Kingst
85 S 11 Orchard ri Rich
96 J 13 Orchard Rise east Sidcp
96 G 13 Orchard Rise west Sidcp
32 H 12 Orchard st E17
139 T 6 Orchard st W1
8 A 19 Orchard the Enf
83 O 5 Orchard the Hounsl
152 D 16 Orchard the KT17
27 X 16 Orchard the NW11
93 X 4 Orchard the SE3
73 Z 10 Orchard the W4
124 J 16 Orchard way Croy
8 D 11 Orchard way Enf
154 G 8 Orchard way Sutton
9 O 9 Orchardleigh av Enf
8 B 19 Orchardmede Enf
130 F 18 Orchardson st NW8
66 D 14 Orchid clo E6
16 G 3 Orchid rd N14
62 G 20 Orchid st W12
133 N 19 Orde Hali st WC1
63 Z 7 Ordell rd E3
76 M 5 Ordnance cres SE10
130 G 6 Ordnance hill NW8
130 H 8 Ordnance ms NW8
65 O 14 Ordnance rd E16
78 J 18 Ordnance rd SE18
53 S 11 Oregon av E12
101 V 5 Orford gdns Twick
34 G 10 Orford rd E17
33 P 16 Orford rd E17
20 G 9 Organ la E4
121 X 7 Oriel clo Mitch
35 T 11 Oriel gdns Ilf
46 E 13 Oriel pl NW3
50 G 17 Oriel rd E9
40 K 19 Oriel way Nthlt
149 W 4 Orient st SE11
50 F 9 Orient way E5
78 A 3 Oriental rd E16
80 D 1 Oriole way SE28
68 D 20 Oriole way SE28
72 C 9 Orion pk W13
79 U 13 Orissa rd SE18
89 N 3 Orkney st SW11
89 U 9 Orlando rd SW4
109 P 17 Orleans rd SE19
84 C 19 Orleans rd Twick
48 G 18 Orleston ms N7
48 G 18 Orleston rd N7
41 S 11 Orley Farm rd Harrow
76 L 14 Orlop st SE10
109 Y 11 Ormanton rd SE26
137 Y 10 Orme Court ms W2
137 Y 9 Orme ct W2
137 X 10 Orme la W2
117 T 3 Orme rd Kingst
137 X 10 Orme sq W2
102 J 7 Ormeley lodge Rich
89 S 20 Ormeley rd SW12
121 P 2 Ormerod gdns Mitch
59 N 7 Ormesby gdns Grnfd
24 M 17 Ormesby way Harrow
74 H 3 Ormiston gro W12
77 S 14 Ormiston rd SE10
100 K 20 Ormond av Hampt
132 M 20 Ormond clo WC1
100 K 20 Ormond cres Hampt
100 L 19 Ormond cres Hampt

100 L 18 Ormond dri Hampt
132 M 18 Ormond ms WC1
48 A 4 Ormond rd N19
84 H 14 Ormond rd Rich
140 C 12 Ormond rd SW1
147 O 11 Ormonde ga SW3
85 U 9 Ormonde rd SW14
21 Y 5 Ormonde rise Buck Hl
131 O 6 Ormonde ter NW8
135 N 8 Ormsby st E2
46 H 15 Ornan rd NW3
49 S 11 Orpen wlk N16
91 N 3 Orpheus st SE5
18 D 12 Orpington gdns N18
17 V 6 Orpington rd N21
100 D 14 Orpwood clo Hampt
138 A 4 Orsett ms W2
137 Z 4 Orsett ms W2
149 P 9 Orsett st SE11
138 A 4 Orsett ter W2
137 Z 4 Orsett ter W2
34 K 3 Orsett ter Wdfd Grn
134 L 5 Orsman rd N1
143 T 14 Orton st E1
88 G 4 Orville rd SW11
65 X 5 Orville rd E13
49 W 5 Osbaldeston rd N16
148 E 7 Osbert st SW1
94 E 13 Osberton rd SE12
135 S 5 Osborn clo E8
92 J 20 Osborn la SE23
143 P 3 Osborn st E1
94 C 11 Osborn ter SE3
124 J 9 Osborne clo Becknhm
39 Z 19 Osborne clo Hornch
154 F 12 Osborne clo Sutton
60 K 14 Osborne ct W5
27 O 2 Osborne gdns NW7
122 L 3 Osborne gdns Thntn Hth
32 L 14 Osborne gro E17
81 O 15 Osborne rd Blvdr
21 V 6 Osborne rd Buck Hl
56 C 14 Osborne rd Dgnhm
51 S 8 Osborne rd E10
52 G 15 Osborne rd E7
50 M 17 Osborne rd E9
9 V 9 Osborne rd Enf
39 Y 18 Osborne rd Hornch
82 E 9 Osborne rd Hounsl
102 K 17 Osborne rd Kingst
17 U 11 Osborne rd N13
48 E 4 Osborne rd N4
44 K 17 Osborne rd NW2
58 M 17 Osborne rd S'hall
122 L 3 Osborne rd Thntn Hth
73 S 7 Osborne rd W3
56 B 13 Osborne rd Dgnhm
93 N 3 Oscar st SE8
47 W 17 Oseney cres NW5
16 E 4 Osidge la N14
63 R 12 Osier st E1
51 P 8 Osier way E10
120 K 11 Osier way Mitch
87 Y 11 Osiers rd SW18
111 S 12 Oslac rd SE6
31 P 18 Oslo av N15
18 K 12 Osman rd N9
41 O 7 Osmond clo Harrow
155 V 10 Osmond gdns Wllgtn
62 E 16 Osmond st W12
131 Z 16 Osnaburgh st NW1
131 Z 17 Osnaburgh ter NW1
120 G 14 Osney wlk Carsh
66 C 15 Osprey clo E6
96 F 17 Ospringe ct SE9
47 U 13 Ospringe rd NW5
134 J 9 Osric pth N1
48 C 1 Ossian rd N4
139 T 1 Ossington bldgs W1
137 W 11 Ossington st W2
151 R 12 Ossory rd SE1
32 F 11 Ossulston st NW1
28 D 11 Ossulton way N2
90 D 18 Ostade rd SW2
145 Z 3 Osten ms SW7
71 P 19 Osterley av Islwth
83 U 1 Osterley cres Islwth
122 L 2 Osterley gdns Thntn Hth
70 K 13 Osterley la S'hall
71 O 15 Osterley Park ho Islwth
70 D 7 Osterley Park rd S'hall
71 U 6 Osterley Park View rd W7
70 M 10 Osterley pk S'hall

83 S 1 Osterley av Islwth
71 S 20 Osterley rd Islwth
49 R 11 Osterley rd N16
70 C 2 Oswald rd S'hall
50 J 12 Oswald's mead E9
158 M 20 Osward Croy
18 L 8 Osward pla N9
106 M 3 Osward rd SW17
149 X 4 Oswin st SE11
91 S 4 Oswyth rd SE5
127 X 6 Otford clo Brom
98 G 16 Otford clo Bxly
92 K 16 Otford cres SE4
149 W 9 Othello clo SE11
64 F 9 Otis st E3
35 Z 18 Otley appr Ilf
36 A 17 Otley dri Ilf
35 Z 17 Otley dri Ilf
65 X 16 Otley rd E16
50 E 8 Otley ter E5
69 Z 1 Ottawa gdns Dgnhm
59 N 12 Ottaway st E5
156 K 2 Otter rd Grnfd
20 K 11 Otterbourne rd Croy
71 Y 19 Otterbourne rd E4
Otterburn gdns Islwth
107 N 15 Otterburn st SW17
111 N 9 Otterden st SE6
149 W 14 Otto st SE17
54 K 16 Oulton cres Bark
31 P 15 Oulton rd N15
10 B 1 Oundle av Bushey
106 M 1 Ouseley rd SW12
130 M 11 Outer circle NW1 NW8
131 W 10 Outer circle NW1 NW8
44 D 20 Outgate rd NW10
157 W 2 Outram rd Croy
66 C 3 Outram rd E6
29 X 5 Outram rd N22
132 L 4 Outram st N1
142 K 4 Outwich st EC3
149 R 14 Oval Cricket ground SE11
157 S 1 Oval rd Croy
131 X 5 Oval rd NW1
69 V 4 Oval Road north Dgnhm
69 U 6 Oval Road south Dgnhm
135 W 8 Oval the E2
97 N 18 Oval the Sidcp
149 P 12 Oval way SE11
111 O 13 Overbrae Becknhm
25 O 1 Overbrook wlk Edg
125 T 5 Overbury av Becknhm
125 U 4 Overbury av Becknhm
31 O 19 Overbury rd N15
50 G 11 Overbury st E5
93 P 8 Overcliff rd SE13
97 P 14 Overcourt clo Sidcp
117 X 3 Overdale av New Mald
72 D 8 Overdale rd W5
111 P 9 Overdown rd SE6
91 X 19 Overhill rd SE22
125 V 12 Overhill way Becknhm
49 X 2 Overlea rd E5
96 E 19 Overmead Sidcp
125 O 10 Overstand clo Becknhm
124 K 16 Overstone gdns Croy
144 B 5 Overstone rd W6
74 L 10 Overstone rd W6
83 U 3 Overton clo Islwth
43 V 18 Overton clo NW10
52 F 2 Overton dri E11
55 U 2 Overton dri Rom
50 J 3 Overton rd E10
6 M 18 Overton rd N14
7 N 17 Overton rd N14
80 H 8 Overton rd SE2
153 Y 17 Overton rd Sutton
90 G 6 Overton rd SW9
156 L 4 Overtons yd Croy
40 D 5 Ovesdon av Harrow
146 L 2 Ovington gdns SW3
146 M 2 Ovington ms SW3
146 M 2 Ovington sq SW3
146 M 4 Ovington st SW3
147 N 5 Ovington st SW3
80 F 3 Owen clo SE28
17 Y 15 Owen rd N13
133 V 11 Owen st EC1
92 V 11 Owen st EC1

43 V 16 Owen way NW10
80 D 11 Owenite st SE2
133 W 11 Owens ct EC1
133 V 11 Owens row EC1
92 J 20 Owens way SE23
150 G 20 Owgan pl SE5
152 G 20 Ox la Epsom
87 T 4 Oxberry av SW6
140 F 10 Oxendon st SW1
91 U 8 Oxenford st SE15
42 L 2 Oxenpark av Wemb
75 W 13 Oxestalls rd SE8
70 F 15 Oxford av Hounsl
119 S 2 Oxford av SW20
140 A 6 Oxford cir W1
140 A 6 Oxford Circus av W1
121 U 7 Oxford clo Mitch
18 M 7 Oxford clo N9
117 Y 14 Oxford cres New Mald
15 S 7 Oxford gdns N20
18 A 2 Oxford gdns N21
136 J 4 Oxford gdns W4
73 R 15 Oxford gdns W4
154 J 11 Oxford rd Carsh
51 X 18 Oxford rd E15
9 N 18 Oxford rd Enf
23 O 18 Oxford rd Harrow
23 V 11 Oxford rd Harrow
54 C 14 Oxford rd Ilf
48 F 4 Oxford rd N4
19 N 8 Oxford rd N9
129 W 7 Oxford rd NW6
109 O 15 Oxford rd SE19
115 R 13 Oxford rd Sidcp
87 S 12 Oxford rd SW15
101 R 12 Oxford rd Tedd
77 H 1 Oxford rd W5
60 H 20 Oxford rd W5
155 U 12 Oxford rd Wallgtn
21 Z 16 Oxford Road W4
73 T 13 Oxford Road north W4
73 S 14 Oxford Road south W4
138 L 6 Oxford sq W2
54 A 19 Oxford st Bark
140 E 4 Oxford st W1
139 T 7 Oxford st W1
70 E 3 Oxford wlk S'hall
44 L 7 Oxgate gdns NW2
44 J 6 Oxgate la NW2
127 X 13 Oxhawth cres Brom
96 E 6 Oxleas clo Welling
40 F 4 Oxleay av Harrow
118 A 11 Oxleigh clo New Mald
44 L 9 Oxleys rd NW2
124 E 20 Oxlip clo CR0
56 D 12 Oxlow la Dgnhm
56 G 12 Oxlow la Dgnhm
120 F 6 Oxted clo Mitch
121 X 2 Oxtoby way SW16
32 F 14 Oyster ter E17

P

143 Y 7 Pace pl E1
65 T 17 Pacific rd E16
134 A 6 Packington sq N1
133 Y 4 Packington st N1
96 F 14 Packmores rd SE9
135 P 14 Padbury ct E2
74 H 8 Paddenswick rd W6
138 G 1 Paddington grn W2
139 S 1 Paddington st W1
138 F 6 Paddington station W2
152 A 1 Paddock clo KT4
58 H 5 Paddock clo Nthlt
110 E 9 Paddock clo SE26
94 G 6 Paddock clo SE3
109 T 15 Paddock gdns SE19
97 Z 11 Paddock rd Bxly Hth
44 G 8 Paddock rd NW2
40 A 9 Paddock rd Ruis
114 F 19 Paddock way Chisl
40 K 12 Paddocks clo Harrow
5 Z 13 Paddocks the Barnt
43 T 7 Paddocks the Wemb
90 K 7 Padfield rd SE5
30 V 12 Padnall rd Rom
7 W 7 Padstow rd Enf
110 C 20 Padua rd SE20
100 B 14 Page clo Hampt
24 M 20 Page clo Harrow

156 G 10 Page cres Croy
31 W 15 Page Green rd N15
31 U 16 Page Green ter N15
127 P 5 Page Heath la Brom
127 N 6 Page Heath vlls Brom
26 G 3 Page st NW7
13 V 20 Page st NW7
148 G 5 Page's yd W4
74 C 16 Page's yd W4
157 S 5 Pageant wlk Croy
123 Y 17 Pagehurst rd Croy
29 P 7 Pages hill N10
29 R 8 Pages la N10
150 L 3 Pages wlk SE1
154 G 6 Paget av Sutton
101 O 10 Paget clo Hampt
127 Z 1 Paget gdns BR7
83 S 9 Paget la Islwth
53 Y 14 Paget rd Ilf
49 P 4 Paget rd N16
78 K 18 Paget ri SE18
133 W 12 Paget st EC1
78 L 18 Paget ter SE18
75 X 19 Pagnell st SE14
84 M 8 Pagoda av Rich
93 X 6 Pagoda gdns SE3
31 S 19 Paignton rd N15
22 C 10 Paines clo Pinn
22 B 10 Paines la Pinn
121 T 4 Paines clo Mitch
49 S 8 Painsthorpe rd N16
36 L 9 Painters la Ilf
37 O 9 Painters rd Ilf
120 F 19 Paisley rd Carsh
30 J 4 Paisley rd N22
48 C 10 Pakeman st N7
107 O 2 Pakenham clo SW12
133 P 15 Pakenham st WC1
137 Z 17 Palace av W8
29 U 9 Palace Ct gdns N10
24 J 18 Palace ct Harrow
137 W 10 Palace ct W8
138 B 19 Palace ga W8
29 Z 6 Palace Gates rd N22
137 W 12 Palace Gdns ms W8
137 W 14 Palace Gdns ter W8
158 M 17 Palace grn Croy
137 Y 17 Palace gro Brom
109 U 18 Palace gro Brom
147 U 7 Palace ms SW1
126 G 1 Palace rd Brom
116 G 10 Palace rd Kingst
29 Z 2 Palace rd N11
29 Y 15 Palace rd N8
40 A 11 Palace rd Pinn
109 V 17 Palace rd SE19
108 D 2 Palace rd SW2
109 U 17 Palace sq SE19
148 B 2 Palace st SW1
126 J 6 Palace view Brom
158 L 7 Palace view Croy
20 E 16 Palace view rd E4
112 F 3 Palace view SE12
51 N 3 Palamos rd E10
49 T 12 Palatine av N16
62 H 7 Palermo rd NW10
120 F 1 Palestine gro SW19
85 Z 12 Palewell Comm dri SW14
85 Y 10 Palewell pk SW14
149 R 17 Palfrey pl SW8
58 G 20 Palgrave av S'hall
74 D 8 Palgrave rd W12
135 O 14 Palissy st E2
140 G 13 Pall Mall east SW1
140 C 14 Pall Mall pl SW1
140 E 14 Pall Mall SW1
95 P 1 Pallett way SE18
144 K 10 Palliser rd W14
130 G 16 Pallitt dri NW8
115 W 15 Palm av Sidcp
72 J 7 Palm gro W5
38 L 16 Palm rd Rom
98 E 6 Palmar rd Bxly Hth
98 D 6 Palmar rd Bxly Hth
97 W 7 Palmeira rd Bxly Hth
152 M 9 Palmer av Sutton
153 N 10 Palmer av Sutton
82 F 2 Palmer clo Hounsl
116 J 5 Palmer cres Kingst
4 B 18 Palmer gdns Barnt
48 F 16 Palmer pl N7
65 W 13 Palmer rd E13
140 D 20 Palmer st SW1
148 E 1 Palmer st SW1
8 O 6 Palmers la Enf
63 U 8 Palmers rd E2
16 G 17 Palmers rd N11
85 W 8 Palmers rd SW14

122 C 3 Palmers rd SW16
17 R 17 Palmerston cres N13
105 Y 18 Palmerston gro SW19
23 U 11 Palmerston rd Harrow
21 X 7 Palmerston rd Buck Hl
155 N 7 Palmerston rd Carsh
32 K 14 Palmerston rd E17
52 H 17 Palmerston rd E7
30 C 2 Palmerston rd N22
17 P 18 Palmerston rd N22
45 W 20 Palmerston rd NW6
79 P 17 Palmerston rd SE18
154 E 10 Palmerston rd Sutton
85 V 11 Palmerston rd SW14
105 Y 17 Palmerston rd SW19
123 N 11 Palmerston rd Thntn Hth
83 U 16 Palmerston rd Twick
73 U 7 Palmerston rd W3
136 F 6 Pamber st W10
156 K 17 Pampisford rd S Croy
160 D 7 Pancras la EC4
132 E 7 Pancras rd NW1
45 X 16 Pandora rd NW6
35 W 18 Panfield ms Ilf
80 B 6 Panfield rd SE2
136 D 1 Pangbourne av W10
11 X 15 Pangbourne dri Stanm
5 S 18 Pank av Barnt
104 K 20 Panmuir rd SW20
48 J 12 Panmure clo W5
110 A 7 Panmure rd SE20
109 Z 7 Panmure rd SE26
58 L 19 Pannard pl S'hall
62 G 20 Pansy gdns W12
127 R 6 Pantiles the Brom
10 D 4 Pantiles the Bushey Watf
81 O 20 Pantiles the Bxly Hth
27 W 14 Pantiles the NW11
140 G 10 Panton st WC2
141 T 8 Paper bldg EC4
94 E 6 Papillons wk SE3
94 G 5 Papillons wk SE3
48 D 16 Papworth gdns N7
90 G 19 Papworth way SE24
108 H 3 Parade ms SW2
99 S 13 Parade the Drtfrd
16 K 5 Parade the N14
147 S 16 Parade the SW11
90 A 4 Paradise rd SW4
63 N 9 Paradise row E2
143 Y 19 Paradise st SE16
147 P 13 Paradise wlk SW3
116 M 14 Paragon gro Surb
94 C 4 Paragon pl SE3
50 B 18 Paragon rd E9
94 D 4 Paragon the SE3
92 H 16 Parbury rd SE23
122 K 6 Parchmore rd Thntn Hth
122 K 3 Parchmore way Thntn Hth
133 Y 16 Pardon st EC1
150 F 1 Pardoner st SE1
142 G 20 Pardoner st SE1
143 U 4 Parfett st E1
144 E 13 Parfrey st W6
35 Y 17 Parham dri Ilf
29 U 8 Parham way N10
141 U 19 Paris gdn SE1
96 G 15 Parish Gate dri Sidcp
110 E 17 Parish la SE20
75 O 9 Park appr SE16
97 P 9 Park appr Welling
54 D 18 Park av Bark
112 F 16 Park av Brom
155 O 13 Park av Carsh
51 Z 18 Park av E15
66 J 4 Park av E6
152 H 15 Park Av east Epsom
8 E 20 Park av Enf
82 K 15 Park av Hounsl
53 X 5 Park av Ilf
107 S 18 Park av Mitch
17 U 12 Park av N13
18 J 14 Park av N18
30 C 5 Park av N22
28 C 4 Park av N3
29 X 13 Park Av north NW10
44 K 15 Park Av north NW10
61 N 8 Park av NW10
46 A 4 Park av NW2
44 L 18 Park av NW2
70 E 4 Park av S'hall
29 W 14 Park Av south N8

85 Z 11 Park av SW14
159 U 3 Park av W Wkhm
21 V 16 Park av Wdfd Grn
60 L 7 Park av Wemb
152 F 15 Park Av west Epsom
32 A 2 Park Avenue rd N17
39 T 6 Park blvd Rom
42 M 12 Park chase Wemb
43 N 11 Park chase Wemb
155 N 13 Park clo Carsh
23 T 3 Park clo Harrow
83 N 13 Park clo Hounsl
61 N 7 Park clo NW10
44 H 10 Park clo NW2
8 B 16 Park cres Enf
81 Y 17 Park cres Erith
23 T 4 Park cres Harrow
39 V 20 Park cres Hornch
131 Y 18 Park Cres Mews east W1
131 W 19 Park Cres Mews west W1
28 C 3 Park cres N3
83 R 20 Park cres Twick
131 X 18 Park cres W1
25 W 4 Park croft Edg
116 D 1 Park ct Kingst
117 Z 9 Park ct New Mald
42 L 14 Park ct Wemb
56 L 10 Park dri Dgnhm
10 D 20 Park dri Harrow
22 F 20 Park dri Harrow
17 Y 1 Park dri N21
7 Y 20 Park dri N21
45 Z 5 Park dri NW11
39 P 12 Park dri Rom
78 D 15 Park dri SE7
85 Z 11 Park dri SE14
73 P 8 Park dri W3
78 D 15 Park Drive clo SE7
112 C 20 Park end Brom
46 K 12 Park end NW3
39 R 13 Park End rd Rom
28 D 11 Park Farm clo N2
127 O 1 Park Farm rd Brom
102 L 17 Park Farm rd Kingst
28 G 10 Park ga N2
17 O 3 Park ga N21
60 F 14 Park ga W5
103 T 14 Park Gate clo Kingst
81 Y 11 Park gdns Erith
103 O 14 Park gdns Kingst
25 U 11 Park gdns NW9
126 H 1 Park gro Brom
98 J 11 Park gro Bxly Hth
65 S 3 Park gro E15
12 A 16 Park gro Edg
29 Y 2 Park gro N11
51 Z 7 Park Grove rd E11
28 K 12 Park Hall rd N2
109 N 6 Park Hall rd SE21
127 T 9 Park hill Brom
154 L 13 Park hill Carsh
154 K 12 Park Hill clo Carsh
125 Y 3 Park Hill rd Brom
157 R 8 Park Hill rd Croy
114 G 6 Park Hill rd Sidcp
155 S 16 Park Hill rd Wallgtn
157 T 4 Park hill ri Croy
84 M 16 Park hill Rich
110 B 3 Park hill SE23
89 Y 12 Park hill SW4
60 H 15 Park hill W5
84 D 14 Park House gdns Twick
155 P 9 Park la Carsh
64 H 2 Park la E15
40 J 9 Park la Harrow
39 U 19 Park la Hornch
57 V 2 Park la Hornch
57 Y 17 Park la Hornch
32 A 3 Park la N17
31 W 3 Park la N17
18 H 12 Park la N9
84 G 11 Park la Rich
37 V 19 Park la Sutton
153 R 14 Park la Sutton
101 W 15 Park la Tedd
42 L 14 Park la Wemb
31 X 3 Park Lane clo N17
42 L 13 Park lawns Wemb
40 K 10 Park mead Harrow
97 T 15 Park mead Sidcp
62 E 5 Park pde NW10
100 M 15 Park pl Hampt
140 B 14 Park pl SW1
73 R 9 Park pl W3
72 H 3 Park pl W5
42 M 13 Park pl Wemb
43 N 13 Park pl Wemb
130 D 20 Park Place vlls W2

4 H 13 Park rd Barnt
5 X 15 Park rd Barnt
110 M 17 Park rd Becknhm
111 O 19 Park rd Becknhm
126 G 2 Park rd Brom
114 A 14 Park rd Chisl
51 O 4 Park rd E10
52 J 5 Park rd E15
65 R 3 Park rd E15
32 L 16 Park rd E17
65 Y 3 Park rd E6
103 N 12 Park Rd east Kingst
73 U 5 Park Rd east W3
100 L 11 Park rd Hampt
82 L 13 Park rd Hounsl
83 N 13 Park rd Hounsl
54 D 9 Park rd Ilf
84 A 4 Park rd Islwth
116 D 1 Park rd Kingst
103 O 15 Park rd Kingst
29 Z 2 Park rd N11
16 K 4 Park rd N14
30 J 14 Park rd N15
18 J 13 Park rd N18
28 H 10 Park rd N2
28 H 11 Park rd N2
29 X 15 Park rd N8
117 Z 10 Park rd New Mald
73 U 6 Park Rd north W3
131 O 17 Park rd NW1
62 A 3 Park rd NW10
26 K 20 Park rd NW4
130 L 13 Park rd NW8
43 Y 1 Park rd NW9
84 M 15 Park rd Rich
123 T 9 Park rd SE25
117 N 13 Park rd Surb
153 S 13 Park rd SW19
106 H 15 Park rd SW19
90 B 18 Park rd SW2
101 W 15 Park rd Tedd
84 E 14 Park rd Twick
73 Y 16 Park rd W4
59 X 19 Park rd W7
155 R 3 Park rd Wallgtn
155 T 10 Park rd Wallgtn
42 K 18 Park rd Wemb
103 N 12 Park Rd west Kingst
23 T 5 Park ri Harrow
92 J 20 Park ri SE23
30 E 10 Park ridings N8
110 J 1 Park Rise rd SE23
76 J 15 Park row SE10
61 S 8 Park royal NW10
61 W 11 Park Royal rd NW10
131 X 17 Park Square east NW1
131 W 17 Park Square ms NW1
131 W 17 Park Square west NW1
156 M 4 Park st Croy
157 N 4 Park st Croy
142 B 12 Park st SE1
101 U 14 Park st Tedd
139 S 7 Park st W1
139 T 11 Park st W1
9 V 4 Park ter Enf
152 F 1 Park ter Worc Pk
155 N 12 Park the Carsh
29 P 20 Park the N6
46 A 4 Park the NW11
109 T 18 Park the SE19
110 B 3 Park the SE23
114 M 11 Park the Sidcp
72 G 4 Park the W5
16 E 14 Park View cres N11
67 U 7 Park View gdns Bark
35 T 13 Park View gdns Ilf
30 G 4 Park View gdns N22
27 O 17 Park View gdns NW4
17 P 2 Park view N21
118 E 7 Park view New Mald
22 F 3 Park view Pinn
31 X 10 Park View rd N17
28 B 4 Park View rd N3
44 E 12 Park View rd NW10
70 G 1 Park View rd S'hall
60 K 15 Park View rd W5
97 U 8 Park view rd Welling
61 W 14 Park view rd W3
43 U 14 Park view Wemb
131 Y 9 Park Village east NW1
131 X 8 Park Village west NW1
76 L 17 Park vista SE10
37 W 19 Park vlls Rom
77 T 19 Park vlls SE3
25 T 6 Park way Edg
7 S 10 Park way Enf
15 Y 14 Park way N20
27 T 16 Park way NW11

21 Z 16 Park way Wdfd Grn
138 L 5 Park West pl W2
29 P 20 Park wlk N6
146 D 13 Park wlk SW10
16 A 12 Park wood N20
98 B 20 Park Wood rd Bxly
94 B 18 Parkcroft rd SE12
79 U 14 Parkdale rd SE18
74 E 20 Parke rd SW13
86 F 1 Parke rd SW13
156 M 8 Parker rd Croy
78 C 3 Parker st WC2
140 M 4 Parker st WC2
143 R 19 Parkers row SE1
22 M 7 Parkfield av Harrow
23 N 8 Parkfield av Harrow
58 B 6 Parkfield av Nthlt
86 A 10 Parkfield av SW14
12 E 20 Parkfield clo Edg
58 C 5 Parkfield clo Nthlt
22 M 8 Parkfield cres Harrow
40 B 8 Parkfield cres Ruis
58 A 7 Parkfield dri Nthlt
22 L 10 Parkfield gdns Harrow
41 N 9 Parkfield rd Harrow
58 B 5 Parkfield rd Nthlt
44 H 20 Parkfield rd NW10
92 K 1 Parkfield rd SE14
133 U 8 Parkfield st N1
127 V 13 Parkfield way Brom
44 A 3 Parkfields av NW9
43 Z 3 Parkfields av NW9
118 J 1 Parkfields av SW20
124 L 20 Parkfields Croy
103 N 13 Parkfields rd Kingst
86 M 11 Parkfields SW15
5 P 5 Parkgate av Barnt
5 P 7 Parkgate cres Barnt
85 X 14 Parkgate gdns SW14
102 M 8 Parkgate ho Rich
146 K 20 Parkgate rd SW11
155 S 11 Parkgate rd Wallgtn
94 D 9 Parkgate SE3
106 M 6 Parkhall rd SE27
88 H 2 Parkham st SW11
88 B 19 Parkhill rd Bxly
98 D 19 Parkhill rd Bxly
20 H 4 Parkhill rd E4
46 M 17 Parkhill rd NW3
46 M 16 Parkhill wlk NW3
49 W 18 Parkholme rd E8
150 G 17 Parkhouse st SE5
98 D 19 Parkhurst gdns Bxly
98 E 18 Parkhurst rd Bxly
53 W 14 Parkhurst rd E12
16 C 15 Parkhurst rd N11
32 J 14 Parkhurst rd N17
31 W 7 Parkhurst rd N17
30 D 1 Parkhurst rd N22
17 R 20 Parkhurst rd N22
48 A 12 Parkhurst rd N7
154 F 7 Parkhurst rd Sutton
39 S 9 Parkland av Rom
105 P 1 Parkland gdns SW19
34 G 2 Parkland rd Wdfd Grn
30 D 7 Parkland rd N22
29 X 20 Parkland wlk N6
27 S 11 Parklands dri N3
107 T 12 Parklands rd SW16
116 M 13 Parklands Surb
152 B 4 Parklands way Worc Pk
26 B 4 Parklea clo NW9
120 A 2 Parkleigh rd SW19
102 G 10 Parkleys Rich
13 R 18 Parkmead gdns NW7
86 J 16 Parkmead SW15
21 S 15 Parkmore clo Wdfd Grn
8 A 2 Parknook gdns Enf
84 H 10 Parkshot Rich
127 R 9 Parkside av Brom
99 S 6 Parkside av Bxly Hth
39 O 9 Parkside av Rom
105 O 11 Parkside av SW19
21 V 7 Parkside Buck Hl
117 V 15 Parkside cres Surb
99 O 5 Parkside cres Bxly Hth
12 B 12 Parkside dri Edg
16 A 4 Parkside gdns Barnt
105 O 10 Parkside gdns SW19
101 O 13 Parkside Hampt
6 G 2 Parkside ho Barnt
28 A 3 Parkside N3
44 H 11 Parkside NW2
26 E 1 Parkside NW7

13 T 19 Parkside NW7
81 W 10 Parkside rd Blvdr
82 J 12 Parkside rd Hounsl
115 R 6 Parkside Sidcp
89 N 2 Parkside st SW11
153 S 14 Parkside Sutton
105 N 9 Parkside SW19
18 A 13 Parkside ter N13
22 M 13 Parkside way Harrow
23 N 12 Parkside way Harrow
86 H 13 Parkstead rd SW15
18 F 18 Parkstone av N18
33 U 10 Parkstone rd E17
91 Y 5 Parkstone rd SE15
22 K 19 Parkthorne clo Harrow
22 J 19 Parkthorne dri Harrow
89 X 19 Parkthorne rd SW12
123 Y 19 Parkview rd Croy
113 Y 3 Parkview rd SE9
145 O 19 Parkville rd SW6
110 H 9 Parkway Becknhm
80 L 7 Parkway Belvdr
159 T 20 Parkway Croy
54 K 10 Parkway Ilf
16 M 7 Parkway N14
131 X 5 Parkway NW1
39 T 7 Parkway Rom
119 O 9 Parkway SW20
83 W 1 Parkwood rd Islwth
105 W 13 Parkwood rd SW19
46 L 11 Parliament hill NW3
140 J 19 Parliament sq SW1
140 J 18 Parliament st SW1
88 L 10 Parma cres SW11
135 Y 8 Parmiter pl E2
63 O 6 Parmiter st E2
135 Y 9 Parmiter st E2
12 G 12 Parnell clo Edg
63 Y 2 Parnell rd E3
63 X 17 Parnham st E14
47 W 4 Parolles rd N19
81 R 9 Paroma rd Blvdr
66 A 4 Parr rd E6
24 H 4 Parr st Stanm
134 D 7 Parr st N1
157 O 19 Parrs clo S Croy
66 G 19 Parry av E6
152 H 15 Parry clo Epsom
79 N 10 Parry pl SE18
123 R 7 Parry st SE25
148 K 14 Parry st SW8
45 Y 14 Parsifal rd NW6
56 B 16 Parsloes av Dgnhm
55 X 14 Parsloes av Dgnhm
55 X 17 Parsloes pk Dgnhm
26 M 12 Parson st NW4
27 O 9 Parson st NW4
8 A 10 Parsonage gdns Enf
8 A 9 Parsonage la Enf
81 T 17 Parsonage Manor way Blvdr
76 G 12 Parsonage st E14
12 B 10 Parsons cres Edg
87 W 2 Parsons Green la SW6
87 X 3 Parsons grn SW6
12 C 10 Parsons gro Edg
78 H 9 Parsons hill SE18
122 J 20 Parsons mead Croy
156 K 1 Parsons mead Croy
65 X 7 Parsons rd E13
87 Y 2 Parthenia rd SW6
14 C 16 Partingdale la NW7
47 Y 3 Partington clo N19
66 A 16 Partridge clo E16
113 V 6 Partridge grn SE9
100 G 15 Partridge rd Hampt
114 G 8 Partridge rd Sidcp
66 E 14 Partridge sq E6
30 B 4 Partridge way N22
89 X 1 Parvin st SW8
148 H 18 Pascal st SW8
93 X 13 Pascoe rd SE13
149 Z 11 Pasley rd SE17
32 J 10 Pasquier rd E17
95 U 15 Passey pl SE9
64 E 14 Passfield dri E14
16 K 20 Passmore gdns N11
147 T 8 Passmore st SW1
141 Y 5 Paternoster sq EC4
18 A 17 Pasteur gdns N18
17 X 17 Pasteur gdns N18
94 J 19 Paston cres SE12
149 Y 4 Pastor st SE11
42 B 10 Pasture clo Wemb
56 A 14 Pasture rd Dgnhm
112 B 1 Pasture rd SE6
42 A 8 Pasture rd Wemb
14 H 5 Pastures the N20

154 C 18 Patcham ct Sutton
89 S 1 Patcham ter SW8
145 T 2 Pater st W8
160 A 5 Paternoster row EC4
106 A 20 Path the SW19
107 Y 15 Pathfield rd SW16
88 J 6 Patience rd SW11
89 X 15 Patio clo SW4
89 V 1 Patmore st SW8
90 H 1 Patmos rd SW9
149 W 20 Patmos rd SW9
64 B 8 Paton clo E3
134 A 14 Paton st EC1
80 C 20 Patricia ct SE2
88 H 4 Patrick pass SW11
65 Z 9 Patrick rd E13
63 O 7 Patriot sq E2
135 Y 10 Patriot sq E2
93 R 17 Patrol pl SE6
47 V 18 Patshull pl NW5
47 U 18 Patshull rd NW5
84 H 14 Patten all Rich
88 J 19 Patten rd SW18
110 M 2 Pattenden rd SE6
112 B 16 Patterdale clo Brom
75 P 18 Patterdale rd SE15
109 U 17 Patterson ct SE19
109 U 16 Patterson rd SE19
45 X 10 Pattison rd NW2
64 L 2 Paul clo E15
157 U 4 Paul gdns Croy
64 L 2 Paul st E15
134 H 18 Paul st EC2
90 K 4 Paulet rd SE5
24 G 12 Paulhan rd Harrow
17 T 2 Paulin dri N21
100 M 1 Pauline cres Twick
83 N 20 Pauline cres Twick
146 H 14 Paultons sq SW3
146 H 15 Paultons st SW3
47 V 5 Pauntley st N19
146 J 19 Paveley dri SW11
130 L 15 Paveley st NW8
89 V 10 Pavement the SW4
56 G 18 Pavet clo Dgnhm
53 U 1 Pavilion rd Ilf
139 P 20 Pavilion rd SW1
147 P 4 Pavilion st SW1
147 P 3 Pavilion st SW1
25 U 2 Pavilion way Edg
110 C 19 Pawleyne clo SE20
65 U 2 Pawsey clo E13
122 L 13 Pawsons rd Croy
42 A 17 Paxford rd Wemb
85 N 4 Paxton clo Rich
109 P 10 Paxton pl SE27
112 F 18 Paxton rd Brom
31 W 2 Paxton rd N17
74 A 17 Paxton rd W4
64 D 7 Payne rd E3
76 A 18 Payne st SE8
75 Z 18 Payne st SE8
144 K 14 Paynes wlk W6
85 Y 9 Paynesfield av SW14
10 G 3 Paynesfield rd Bushey
147 X 10 Peabody av SW1
147 Y 12 Peabody clo SW1
31 R 5 Peabody est N17
90 K 19 Peabody est SW24
148 F 11 Peabody est SW1
128 C 19 Peabody est W10
90 K 20 Peabody Hill est SE24
43 T 8 Peace gro Wemb
135 T 17 Peace st E1
78 K 16 Peace st SE18
153 R 17 Peaches clo Sutton
77 P 16 Peachum rd SE3
149 Y 8 Peacock st SE17
149 Z 8 Peacock yd SE17
110 C 10 Peak Hill av SE26
110 D 10 Peak Hill gdns SE26
110 C 10 Peak Hill south SE26
110 C 8 Peak the SE26
35 O 14 Peaketon av Ilf
59 Y 10 Peal gdns W13
122 C 14 Peall rd Croy
25 Y 14 Pear clo NW9
141 T 17 Pear gdns SE1
99 N 2 Pear Tree clo Erith
133 U 17 Pear Tree ct EC1
55 P 13 Pear Tree gdns Dgnhm
134 A 15 Pear Tree st EC1
133 Z 15 Pear Tree st EC1
110 C 2 Pearcefield av SE23
51 W 7 Pearcroft rd E11
89 T 6 Peardon st SW8

24 H 6 Peareswood gdns Stanm
110 G 6 Pearfield rd SE23
66 J 17 Pearl clo E6
33 N 10 Pearl rd E17
75 O 1 Pearl st E1
75 O 2 Pearl st E1
141 T 19 Pearman st SE1
83 O 7 Pears rd Hounsl
88 B 3 Pearscroft ct SW6
88 A 3 Pearscroft rd SW6
134 M 8 Pearson st E2
88 B 3 Pearson st E2
120 K 4 Peartree clo Mitch
38 G 7 Peartree gdns Rom
8 E 12 Peartree rd Enf
63 R 8 Peary pl E2
41 Y 6 Pebworth rd Harrow
109 X 6 Peckarmans wood SE26
48 K 13 Peckett sq N5
90 F 6 Peckford pl SW9
150 K 18 Peckham gro SE15
91 V 2 Peckham High st SE15
151 R 19 Peckham Hill st SE15
91 X 1 Peckham Hill st SE15
151 U 14 Peckham Park rd SE15
91 S 2 Peckham rd SE5
92 B 11 Peckham Rye east SE15
92 A 12 Peckham Rye pk SE22
91 Y 9 Peckham rye SE15
47 V 16 Peckwater st NW5
48 B 17 Pedlars wlk N7
55 T 4 Pedley rd Dgnhm
135 R 18 Pedley st E1
50 G 11 Pedro st E5
151 Z 7 Pedworth rd SE16
105 P 12 Peek cres SW19
35 R 8 Peel dri Ilf
63 O 7 Peel gro E2
63 Z 10 Peel gro E2
35 P 8 Peel dri Ilf
129 S 10 Peel Precinct ct NW6
34 B 5 Peel rd E18
23 U 10 Peel rd Harrow
42 F 9 Peel rd Wemb
137 U 14 Peel st W8
134 E 14 Peerless st EC1
19 P 12 Pegamoid rd N18
149 S 13 Pegasus pl SE11
156 F 15 Pegasus rd Croy
112 G 3 Pegley gdns SE12
79 U 18 Pegwell st SE18
64 B 18 Pekin st E14
85 N 12 Peldon ct Rich
84 M 12 Peldon pas Rich
84 M 12 Peldon pas Rich
67 W 4 Pelham av Bark
91 S 6 Pelham clo SE5
146 J 7 Pelham cres SW7
146 J 6 Pelham pl SW7
124 D 3 Pelham rd Becknhm
98 F 8 Pelham rd Bxly Hth
34 G 10 Pelham rd E18
54 F 8 Pelham rd Ilf
31 U 13 Pelham rd N15
30 F 8 Pelham rd N22
106 A 17 Pelham rd SW19
105 Y 18 Pelham rd SW19
146 J 6 Pelham st SW7
160 B 13 Pelier st SE17
111 Y 5 Pelinore rd SE6
144 M 16 Pellant rd SW6
30 E 5 Pellatt gro N22
91 V 14 Pellatt rd SE22
49 S 14 Pellerin rd N16
64 A 17 Pelling st E14
17 S 11 Pellipar clo N13
78 F 13 Pellipar gdns SE18
65 T 4 Pelly rd E13
65 T 6 Pelly rd E13
135 N 12 Pelter st E2
76 M 13 Pelton rd SE10
32 G 11 Pembar av E17
128 F 13 Pember rd NW10
39 Z 10 Pemberton av Rom
37 Y 16 Pemberton gdns Rom
47 W 8 Pemberton gdns N19
47 X 8 Pemberton gdns N19
30 H 17 Pemberton rd N4
141 U 5 Pemberton row EC4
100 D 1 Pembridge av Twick
137 S 9 Pembridge cres W11
137 U 11 Pembridge gdns W2

137 S 9 Pembridge ms W11
137 U 8 Pembridge pl W2
137 T 10 Pembridge rd W11
137 U 9 Pembridge sq W2
137 T 8 Pembridge vlls W11
9 N 7 Pembroke av Harrow
24 A 9 Pembroke av Harrow
23 Z 9 Pembroke av Harrow
117 T 11 Pembroke av Surb
121 O 4 Pembroke clo Mitch
139 U 18 Pembroke clo SW1
145 S 4 Pembroke Gardens clo W8
56 G 10 Pembroke gdns Dgnhm
145 S 5 Pembroke gdns W8
102 L 3 Pembroke lodge Rich
145 T 3 Pembroke ms W8
25 P 3 Pembroke pl Edg
83 S 4 Pembroke pl Islwth
145 T 2 Pembroke pl W8
126 M 4 Pembroke rd Brom
127 N 4 Pembroke rd Brom
33 R 15 Pembroke rd E17
81 Y 12 Pembroke rd Erith
58 L 10 Pembroke rd Grnfd
54 K 2 Pembroke rd Ilf
29 P 3 Pembroke rd N10
18 A 12 Pembroke rd N13
17 Z 12 Pembroke rd N13
31 V 15 Pembroke rd N15
30 A 12 Pembroke rd N8
123 R 9 Pembroke rd SE25
145 R 6 Pembroke rd W14
42 H 10 Pembroke rd Wemb
145 T 4 Pembroke sq W8
132 M 3 Pembroke st N1
145 R 3 Pembroke studios W8
84 F 11 Pembroke vlls Rich
145 T 4 Pembroke vlls W8
145 T 4 Pembroke wlk W8
118 G 18 Pembury av Worc Pk
126 D 17 Pembury clo Brom
115 Y 5 Pembury cres Sidcp
50 A 13 Pembury est E5
80 M 18 Pembury rd Bxly Hth
81 N 17 Pembury rd Bxly Hth
49 Z 14 Pembury rd E5
31 U 6 Pembury rd N17
123 Y 9 Pembury rd SE25
122 G 17 Pemdevon rd Croy
63 R 11 Pemell clo E1
134 F 4 Penally pl N1
75 O 2 Penang st E1
143 Y 12 Penang st E1
75 O 16 Penarth st SE15
111 V 3 Penberth rd SE6
70 D 12 Penbury rd S'hall
151 V 15 Pencraig way SE15
50 H 12 Penda rd E5
81 W 18 Penda rd Erith
50 K 12 Penda's mead E9
104 L 20 Pendarves rd SW20
31 O 10 Pendennis rd N17
95 N 8 Pendennis rd SW16
76 C 18 Pender st SE8
82 H 12 Penderel rd Hounsl
111 V 4 Penderry ri SE6
47 Z 12 Penderyn way N7
107 T 13 Pendle rd SW16
33 P 17 Pendlestone rd E17
112 D 7 Pendragon rd Brom
92 G 6 Pendrell rd SE4
79 T 17 Pendrell st SE18
111 R 1 Penerley rd SE6
111 T 2 Penerley rd SE6
115 W 2 Penfold la Bxly
115 W 4 Penfold la Bxly
130 H 19 Penfold pl NW8
19 S 5 Penfold rd N9
95 N 8 Penford gdns SE9
90 J 4 Penford st SE5
97 W 14 Pengarth rd Bxly
110 D 17 Penge la SE20
65 X 3 Penge rd E13
123 X 6 Penge rd SE25
77 Z 10 Penhall rd SE7
97 U 18 Penhill rd Bxly
36 A 2 Penhurst rd Ilf
59 S 8 Penifather la Grnfd
108 A 17 Penistone rd SW16
41 P 9 Penketh dri Harrow
80 B 8 Penmont rd SE2
58 M 7 Penn clo Grnfd
24 C 14 Penn clo Harrow
127 Z 2 Penn gdns BR7
38 E 1 Penn gdns Rom
48 A 14 Penn rd N7
134 G 5 Penn st N1

145 X 4 Pennant ms W8
32 L 7 Pennant ter E17
136 C 16 Pennard rd W12
74 M 5 Pennard rd W12
105 S 5 Penner clo SW19
63 O 4 Pennethorne clo E9
151 V 20 Pennethorne rd SE15
45 S 5 Pennine dri NW2
99 P 3 Pennine way Bxly Hth
143 V 11 Pennington st E1
61 T 8 Pennyroad E8
158 G 19 Pennycroft S Croy
64 A 20 Pennyfields E14
66 K 18 Pennyroyal av E6
50 A 17 Penpoll rd E8
97 R 9 Penpool la Welling
32 M 6 Penrhyn av E17
33 O 4 Penrhyn av E17
33 P 4 Penrhyn cres E17
85 W 10 Penrhyn cres SW14
33 N 5 Penrhyn gro E17
116 H 8 Penrhyn rd Kingst
107 U 14 Penrith st SW16
87 T 14 Penrith rd SW15
57 X 16 Penrith cres Hornch
31 O 15 Penrith rd N15
117 Z 9 Penrith rd New Mald
122 M 2 Penrith rd Thntn Hth
150 A 11 Penrose gro SE17
150 A 10 Penrose st SE17
150 A 12 Penrose st SE17
150 L 8 Penry st SE1
132 E 8 Penryn st NW1
99 V 4 Pensbury pl SW8
89 V 4 Pensbury st SW8
85 H 4 Pensford av Rich
35 Z 15 Penshore clo
97 O 15 Penshurst av Sidcp
12 F 16 Penshurst gdns Edg
126 C 12 Penshurst grn Brom
98 B 1 Penshurst rd Bxly Hth
122 H 11 Penshurst rd Thntn Hth
63 T 2 Penshurst rd E9
31 U 2 Penshurst rd N17
153 Y 18 Penshurst way Sutton
33 W 5 Pentire rd E17
45 S 8 Pentland clo NW11
88 B 15 Pentland gdns SW18
80 C 16 Pentland st SW18
121 R 6 Pentlands clo Mitch
86 M 6 Pentlow st SW15
20 H 5 Pentney rd E4
107 U 1 Pentney rd SW12
105 R 19 Pentney rd SW12
133 S 9 Penton gro N1
150 A 10 Penton pl SE17
149 X 8 Penton pl SE17
133 P 11 Penton ri WC1
133 S 9 Penton st N1
133 R 10 Pentonville rd N1
8 K 4 Pentrich av Enf
150 M 20 Pentridge st SE15
18 B 16 Pentyre av N18
71 N 20 Penwerris av Islwth
106 A 3 Penwith rd SW18
105 Z 3 Penwith rd SW18
107 T 15 Penwortham rd SW16
25 R 3 Penylan pl Edg
145 V 9 Penywern rd SW5
136 L 12 Penzance pl W11
136 L 13 Penzance st W11
62 F 19 Peony gdns W12
128 H 9 Peploe rd NW6
142 A 16 Pepper st E1
4 B 17 Pepys cres Barnt
92 F 2 Pepys rd SE14
104 L 19 Pepys rd SW20
118 M 1 Pepys rd SW20
142 L 9 Pepys st EC3
46 H 15 Perceval av NW3
49 U 13 Perch st E8
31 V 1 Percival ct N17
37 U 18 Percival gdns Rom
8 H 14 Percival rd Enf
85 V 12 Percival rd SW14
133 W 15 Percival st EC1
80 G 10 Percival st SE2
133 P 12 Percy cir WC1
9 T 7 Percy gdns Enf
117 Z 19 Percy gdns Worc Pk
140 E 3 Percy ms W1
98 A 6 Percy rd Bxly Hth
97 Z 6 Percy rd Bxly Hth
33 Z 20 Percy rd E11
65 N 14 Percy rd E16

100 G 17 Percy rd Hampt
36 M 20 Percy rd Ilf
37 N 20 Percy rd Ilf
83 Z 9 Percy rd Islwth
121 O 17 Percy rd Mitch
15 R 16 Percy rd N21
17 Z 3 Percy rd N21
38 J 9 Percy rd Rom
124 E 1 Percy rd SE20
123 V 11 Percy rd SE25
100 K 3 Percy rd Twick
82 M 20 Percy rd Twick
74 G 6 Percy rd W12
140 E 2 Percy st W1
100 M 1 Percy way Twick
133 P 13 Percy yd WC1
104 M 17 Peregrine way SW19
57 X 19 Peregrine wlk Hornch
144 M 12 Perham rd W14
145 N 12 Perham rd W14
66 E 15 Peridot st E6
109 N 1 Perifield SE21
60 E 5 Perimeade rd Grnfd
95 N 11 Periton rd SE9
60 A 11 Perivale gdns W13
59 Y 8 Perivale la Grnfd
59 T 10 Perivale pk Grnfd
42 A 14 Perkins clo Wemb
36 E 16 Perkins rd Ilf
148 F 2 Perkins rents SW1
93 Y 6 Perks clo SE3
96 F 17 Perpins rd SE9
108 H 2 Perran rd SW2
72 J 15 Perran wlk Brentf
47 S 18 Perren st NW5
74 J 9 Perrers rd W6
42 A 12 Perrin rd Wemb
46 E 13 Perrins la NW3
46 D 13 Perrins wlk NW3
61 Y 17 Perry av W3
69 Z 6 Perry clo Rainhm
31 R 18 Perry ct N15
18 C 10 Perry gdns N9
110 L 5 Perry hill SE6
118 C 19 Perry how Worc Pk
7 W 7 Perry mead Enf
110 J 8 Perry rd SE23
114 K 15 Perry st Chisl
114 H 16 Perry Street gdns Chisl
114 H 17 Perry Street shaw Chisl
110 D 3 Perry vale SE23
26 E 20 Perryfield way NW9
102 B 5 Perryfield way Rich
36 D 17 Perrymans Farm rd Ilf
87 Z 4 Perrymead st SW6
73 Y 1 Perryn rd W3
61 Z 19 Perryn rd W3
140 E 4 Perrys pl W1
111 Z 5 Persant rd SE6
149 U 20 Perseverance pl SW9
35 Z 15 Pershore clo Ilf
120 G 14 Pershore gro Carsh
29 R 1 Pert clo N10
43 Z 2 Perth av NW9
118 F 3 Perth clo SW20
67 T 5 Perth rd Bark
125 U 3 Perth rd Becknhm
50 K 4 Perth rd E10
65 V 8 Perth rd E13
36 A 20 Perth rd Ilf
54 B 1 Perth rd Ilf
35 X 18 Perth rd Ilf
30 H 5 Perth rd N22
48 F 4 Perth rd N4
63 R 16 Perth st E1
54 C 2 Perth ter Ilf
40 E 5 Perwell av Harrow
44 J 20 Peter av NW10
62 J 1 Peter av NW10
140 E 7 Peter st W1
77 N 10 Peterboat clo SE10
87 X 4 Peterborough ms SW6
120 H 13 Peterborough rd Carsh
41 U 3 Peterborough rd Harrow
87 X 4 Peterborough rd SW6
33 W 18 Peterborough rd E10
88 A 2 Peterborough vlls SW6
88 D 10 Petergate SW11
11 U 18 Peters clo Stanm
141 Z 7 Peters hill EC4
133 X 20 Peters la EC1

109 Z 9 Peters pth SE26
17 Y 17 Petersfield clo N18
73 W 5 Petersfield rd W3
86 J 20 Petersfield ri SW15
102 H 3 Petersham clo Rich
153 W 12 Petersham clo Sutton
146 B 1 Petersham la SW7
102 G 1 Petersham lodge Rich
146 B 2 Petersham ms SW7
102 L 2 Petersham pk Rich
146 B 2 Petersham rd SW7
102 H 3 Petersham rd Rich
84 J 16 Petersham rd Rich
80 D 7 Peterstone rd SE2
105 T 3 Peterstow clo SW19
49 N 13 Petherton rd N5
144 E 16 Petley rd W6
131 Y 17 Peto pl NW1
65 O 19 Peto st E16
45 T 17 Petrie clo NW2
78 D 10 Pett st SE18
142 M 4 Petticoat la E1
39 R 6 Pettits blvd Rom
39 P 7 Pettits clo Rom
39 P 7 Pettits la Rom
39 N 4 Pettits Lane north Rom
56 D 16 Pettits pl Dgnhm
56 D 15 Pettits rd Dgnhm
39 N 16 Pettley gdns Rom
79 R 9 Pettman cres SE28
42 E 14 Petts Grove av Wemb
40 K 16 Petts hill Nthlt
140 D 20 Petty France SW1
40 E 20 Petworth clo Nthlt
154 B 5 Petworth clo Sutton
118 J 5 Petworth gdn New Mald
98 D 14 Petworth rd Bxly Hth
15 X 17 Petworth rd N12
88 K 2 Petworth st SW11
57 U 13 Petworth way Hornch
146 J 15 Petyt pl SW3
146 M 7 Petyward SW3
8 C 8 Pevensey av Enf
16 K 17 Pevensey av N11
52 D 12 Pevensey rd E7
100 B 2 Pevensey rd Felt
106 G 10 Pevensey rd SW17
101 R 12 Peveril dri Tedd
19 Z 17 Pewsy clo E4
76 G 19 Peyton pl SE10
150 E 13 Phelp st SE17
146 L 14 Phene st SW3
141 S 9 Philbeach gdns SW5
143 T 7 Philchurch pl E1
57 N 4 Philip av Rom
57 N 4 Philip clo Rom
158 K 2 Philip gdns Croy
31 U 11 Philip la N15
91 Y 7 Philip st SE15
65 R 12 Philip st E13
95 U 16 Philipot pth SE9
95 N 12 Philippa gdns SE9
128 B 4 Phillimore gdns NW10
62 L 3 Phillimore gdns W10
137 S 19 Phillimore gdns W8
137 T 19 Phillimore pl W8
137 T 20 Phillimore wlk W8
134 L 6 Phillipp st N1
99 Y 15 Phillips gdns Drtfrd
126 F 4 Phillips way Brom
142 H 9 Philpot la EC3
160 H 9 Philpot la EC3
143 X 4 Philpot st E1
105 O 2 Philsdon clo SW19
95 R 7 Phineas Pett rd SE9
134 J 17 Phipp st EC2
120 E 1 Phipps Bridge rd SW19
120 E 4 Phipps Bridge rd SW19
8 A 2 Phipps Hatch la Enf
7 Z 2 Phipps Hatch la Enf
147 X 4 Phipps ms SW1
120 F 1 Phipps ter SW19
93 O 13 Phoebeth rd SE4
133 R 16 Phoenix clo E8
132 E 11 Phoenix rd NW1
132 G 10 Phoenix rd NW1
110 C 16 Phoenix rd SE20
140 H 6 Phoenix st WC2
118 K 10 Phyllis av New Mald
81 U 7 Picardy Manorway Blvdr
81 S 13 Picardy rd Blvdr

81 S 9 Picardy st Blvdr
140 B 12 Piccadilly arc SW1
140 E 10 Piccadilly cir W1
140 C 11 Piccadilly pl W1
140 B 12 Piccadilly W1
139 Y 14 Piccadilly W1
133 Z 12 Pickard st EC1
66 K 7 Pickering av E6
137 Y 5 Pickering ms W2
133 Z 3 Pickering st N1
10 D 5 Pickets clo Bushey
89 R 18 Pickets st SW12
24 F 5 Pickett croft Stanm
19 U 8 Picketts Lock la N9
97 Y 5 Pickford clo Bxly Hth
97 Z 2 Pickford la Bxly Hth
97 Y 9 Pickford rd Bxly Hth
126 B 17 Pickhurst grn Brom
126 A 13 Pickhurst la W Wkhm
125 Z 12 Pickhurst la W Wkhm
126 B 17 Pickhurst mead Brom
126 B 13 Pickhurst pk Brom
126 A 18 Pickhurst ri W Wkhm
125 V 19 Pickhurst ri W Wkhm
142 L 14 Pickle Herring st SE1
148 L 20 Pickwick clo SW18
18 E 15 Pickwick ms N18
41 T 1 Pickwick pl Harrow
91 R 18 Pickwick rd SE21
142 B 18 Pickwick st SE1
114 C 15 Pickwick way Chisl
139 U 6 Picton pl W1
150 F 19 Picton st SE5
79 T 14 Piedmont rd SE18
78 J 4 Pier pde E16
78 J 4 Pier rd E16
76 H 10 Pier st E14
88 B 10 Pier ter SW18
79 R 7 Pier way SE18
91 Z 13 Piermont grn SE22
91 Z 13 Piermont rd SE22
61 T 19 Pierrepoint rd W3
133 W 7 Pierrepont row N1
100 G 11 Pigeon la Hampt
64 A 17 Piggot st E14
112 G 13 Pike clo Brom
58 B 12 Pikestone clo Grnfd
108 L 8 Pilgrim hill SE27
141 W 6 Pilgrim st EC4
43 T 4 Pilgrim's way Wemb
142 F 19 Pilgrimage st SE1
41 N 16 Pilgrims clo Nthlt
46 G 13 Pilgrims la NW3
5 X 17 Pilgrims ri Barnt
47 X 3 Pilgrims way N19
91 Z 5 Pilgrims way S Croy
115 S 17 Pilkington rd SE15
150 C 9 Pilton pl SE17
148 E 13 Pimlico gdns SW1
147 U 8 Pimlico gdns SW1
5 V 14 Pimlico rd SW1
20 K 8 Pimms Brook dri Barnt
95 O 11 Pimp Hall pk E4
143 T 8 Pin st SE9
98 E 11 Pinchin st E1
106 B 20 Pincott rd Bxly Hth
134 K 20 Pincott rd SW19
129 Z 17 Pindar st EC2
125 R 19 Pindock ms W9
16 H 3 Pine av W Wkhm
11 N 12 Pine clo N14
158 F 9 Pine clo Surb
117 R 14 Pine coombe Croy
14 K 5 Pine gdns Surb
48 B 7 Pine gro N20
105 U 13 Pine gro N4
16 A 8 Pine gro SW19
45 N 12 Pine rd N11
155 O 19 Pine rd NW2
133 T 16 Pine ridge Carsh
127 R 3 Pine st EC1
129 Z 17 Pines rd Brom
114 H 2 Pinewood av Sidcp
158 H 6 Pinewood clo Croy
60 E 17 Pinewood gro W13
126 F 8 Pinewood rd Brom
80 H 16 Pinewood rd SE2
108 A 9 Pinfold rd SW16
16 F 19 Pinkham way N11
21 Z 11 Pinley gdns Dgnhm
98 H 11 Pinnacle hill Bxly Hth
95 O 12 Pinnell rd SE9

22 G 13 Pinner ct Pinn
22 B 15 Pinner gro Pinn
22 L 9 Pinner Park av Harrow
23 N 8 Pinner Park av Harrow
23 O 9 Pinner Park gdns Harrow
22 F 6 Pinner pk Pinn
22 J 14 Pinner rd Harrow
23 O 19 Pinner rd Harrow
23 N 17 Pinner view Harrow
66 D 15 Pintail rd E6
34 J 1 Pintail rd Wdfd Grn
94 G 10 Pinto way SE3
48 C 17 Piper clo N7
117 O 5 Piper rd Kingst
11 W 11 Pipers Green la Edg
25 W 17 Pipers grn NW9
120 H 14 Pipewell rd Carsh
124 K 19 Pippin clo Croy
124 C 4 Piquet rd SE20
159 V 14 Pirbright cres Croy
87 X 20 Pirbright rd SW18
77 V 3 Pirie st E16
38 E 12 Pitcairn clo Rom
106 M 17 Pitcairn rd Mitch
89 S 6 Pitcairn st SW8
64 L 2 Pitchford st E15
134 H 14 Pitfield st N1
9 P 5 Pitfield way Enf
43 V 18 Pitfield way NW10
43 W 17 Pitfield way NW10
94 F 17 Pitfold clo SE12
94 E 17 Pitfold rd SE12
156 J 2 Pitlake Croy
150 A 18 Pitman st SE5
63 T 18 Pitsea pl E1
63 T 18 Pitsea st E1
60 D 12 Pitshanger la W5
60 B 9 Pitshanger pk Grnfd
106 A 10 Pitt cres SW19
105 Z 10 Pitt cres SW19
41 N 7 Pitt rd Harrow
122 M 12 Pitt rd Thntn Hth
137 V 17 Pitt st W8
142 K 14 Pitt st W8
139 V 14 Pitts Head ms W1
126 E 18 Pittsmead av Brom
123 X 5 Pittville gdns SE25
63 Y 17 Pixley st E14
158 H 20 Pixton way Croy
142 F 18 Plaistow gro Brom
112 G 18 Plaistow gro Brom
65 O 4 Plaistow gro E15
112 G 18 Plaistow la Brom
126 M 2 Plaistow la Brom
65 U 5 Plaistow Park rd E13
65 R 6 Plaistow rd E15
109 Z 8 Plane st SE26
55 W 2 Plantagenet gdns Rom
55 X 2 Plantagenet pl Rom
5 P 14 Plantagenet rd Barnt
99 V 1 Plantation rd Erith
94 F 5 Plantation the SE3
66 A 1 Plashet gro E6
53 O 20 Plashet gro E6
65 X 2 Plashet gro E6
65 U 2 Plashet rd E13
93 S 19 Plassy rd SE6
134 G 17 Platina st EC2
90 A 11 Plato rd SW2
132 F 9 Platt st NW1
87 R 8 Platt the SW15
45 Y 11 Platts la NW3
9 R 7 Platts rd Enf
110 G 20 Plawsfield rd Becknhm
126 L 2 Plaxtol clo Brom
77 T 14 Plaxtol pl SE10
81 T 18 Plaxtol rd Erith
144 E 12 Playfair st W6
38 J 4 Playfield av Rom
91 T 13 Playfield cres SE22
25 W 6 Playfield rd Edg
48 E 6 Playford rd N4
48 F 8 Playford rd N4
111 O 8 Playgreen way SE6
124 G 4 Playground clo Becknhm
141 X 8 Playhouse yd EC4
86 J 12 Pleasance the SW15
86 J 11 Pleasance the SW15
158 L 5 Pleasant gro Croy
133 Z 2 Pleasant pl N1
131 Z 5 Pleasant row NW1
60 F 5 Pleasant way Wemb
20 B 8 Pleasaunce E4
132 B 6 Plender pl NW1

132 B 6	Plender st NW1
47 W 13	Pleshey rd N7
156 A 18	Plesman way SM6
31 S 18	Plevna clo N15
31 S 17	Plevna cres N15
18 L 10	Plevna rd N9
76 F 7	Plevna st E14
66 K 19	Plevna st E6
109 V 17	Pleydell av SE19
74 E 10	Pleydell av W6
141 U 6	Pleydell ct EC4
141 U 6	Pleydell st EC4
48 G 8	Plimsoll rd N4
160 G 8	Plough ct EC3
91 W 17	Plough la SE22
106 B 11	Plough la SW19
156 A 12	Plough la Wallgtn
156 B 20	Plough la Wallgtn
155 Z 8	Plough la Wallgtn
155 Z 10	Plough Lane clo Wallgtn
141 T 4	Plough pl EC4
88 G 10	Plough rd SW11
88 G 10	Plough ter SW11
75 W 10	Plough way SE16
134 K 18	Plough yd EC2
132 E 3	Ploughmans clo NW1
83 R 13	Ploughmans end Islwth
55 U 3	Plowman rd Dgnhm
70 B 9	Pluckington pl S'hall
72 H 12	Plum garth Brentf
79 O 18	Plum la SE18
93 T 2	Plumb st SE10
133 U 15	Plumbers pl EC1
143 T 3	Plumbers row E1
120 L 2	Plummer la Mitch
89 X 18	Plummer rd SW4
40 G 17	Plumpton clo Nthlt
154 J 5	Plumpton way Carsh
78 L 15	Plumstead Common rd SE18
79 P 16	Plumstead Common rd SE18
79 W 12	Plumstead High st SE18
79 O 10	Plumstead rd SE18
155 X 16	Plumtree clo SM6
141 V 3	Plumtree ct EC4
112 J 20	Plymouth rd Brom
65 S 16	Plymouth rd E16
76 J 10	Plymouth wharf E14
129 N 2	Plympton av NW6
80 L 10	Plympton clo Blvdr
130 K 18	Plympton pl NW8
129 O 1	Plympton rd NW6
130 K 18	Plympton st NW8
80 F 20	Plymstock rd Welling
26 A 7	Pocklington clo NW9
141 X 17	Pocock st SE1
88 C 11	Podmore rd SW18
49 N 14	Poets rd N5
23 U 14	Poets way Harrow
93 U 2	Point clo SE10
93 V 2	Point hill SE10
87 X 11	Point pleasant SW18
28 D 6	Pointalls clo N3
140 C 5	Poland st W1
20 F 3	Pole Hill rd E4
94 L 6	Polebrook rd SE3
110 L 4	Polecroft la SE6
118 J 4	Polesden gdns New Mald
68 K 1	Polesworth rd Dgnhm
55 X 20	Polesworth rd Dgnhm
65 S 19	Pollard clo E16
48 D 14	Pollard clo N7
120 G 12	Pollard rd Mrdn
15 W 9	Pollard rd N20
135 U 13	Pollard row E2
135 U 13	Pollard st E2
122 B 6	Pollards cres SW16
122 C 5	Pollards Hill east SW16
122 C 5	Pollards Hill north SW16
122 C 7	Pollards Hill south SW16
122 B 6	Pollards Hill west SW16
122 A 5	Pollards Wood rd SW16
139 Z 7	Pollen st W1
130 G 16	Pollitt dri NW8
92 L 19	Polsted rd SE6
79 R 10	Polthorne gro SE18
108 A 13	Polworth rd SW16
132 D 11	Polygon rd NW1
89 U 9	Polygon the SW4
78 K 11	Polytechnic st SE18
143 O 4	Pomell way E1
75 P 26	Pomeroy sq SE14
92 C 2	Pomeroy st SE14
90 K 7	Pomfret rd SE5
94 D 5	Pond clo SE3
91 P 15	Pond mead SE21
146 J 8	Pond pl SW3
64 L 6	Pond rd E15
94 D 5	Pond rd SE3
47 P 3	Pond sq N6
46 H 14	Pond st NW3
102 D 16	Pond way Tedd
48 C 20	Ponder st N7
126 A 20	Pondfield rd Brom
56 G 14	Pondfield rd Dgnhm
153 R 12	Pondhill gdns Sutton
143 V 7	Ponler st E1
62 J 8	Ponsard rd NW10
50 D 16	Ponsford st E9
148 H 9	Ponsonby pl SW1
86 J 19	Ponsonby rd SW15
148 H 9	Ponsonby ter SW1
147 R 2	Pont st SW1
147 N 2	Pont Street ms SW3
112 D 12	Pontefract rd Brom
148 F 16	Ponton rd SW8
141 V 17	Pontypool pl SE1
41 P 2	Pool rd Harrow
82 B 4	Poole Court rd Hounsl
50 E 19	Poole rd E9
134 E 6	Poole st N1
68 M 5	Pooles la Dgnhm
146 B 20	Pooles la SW10
48 E 8	Pooles pk N4
75 T 5	Poolmans st SE16
26 B 12	Poolsford rd NW9
63 P 19	Poonah st E1
127 N 12	Pope rd Brom
142 M 19	Pope st SE1
160 F 7	Pope's Head all EC3
101 U 3	Popes av Twick
27 Y 3	Popes dri N3
158 L 4	Popes gro Croy
101 V 4	Popes gro Twick
72 G 9	Popes la W5
90 F 9	Popes st SW9
100 D 8	Popham clo Felt
134 A 3	Popham rd N1
134 A 4	Popham st N1
133 Y 4	Popham st N1
120 M 1	Poplar av Mitch
70 K 8	Poplar Bath st E14
105 Y 11	Poplar ct SW19
117 Z 4	Poplar gdns New Mald
16 A 20	Poplar gro N11
117 Z 6	Poplar gro New Mald
136 D 20	Poplar gro W6
43 X 9	Poplar gro Wembl
64 D 20	Poplar High st E14
81 V 10	Poplar mt Blvdr
80 G 2	Poplar pl SE2
137 Y 9	Poplar pl W2
119 Y 6	Poplar rd S SW19
90 K 9	Poplar rd SE24
119 U 20	Poplar rd Sutton
38 K 13	Poplar st Rom
36 C 13	Poplar way Ilf
156 L 1	Poplar wlk Croy
90 L 10	Poplar wlk SE24
44 M 19	Poplars av NW2
33 R 18	Poplars rd E17
141 V 5	Poppins ct EC4
34 A 20	Poppleton rd E11
15 Y 11	Porch way N20
91 N 10	Porchester clo SE5
137 Z 4	Porchester ms W2
138 L 6	Porchester pl W2
117 T 4	Porchester rd Kingst
137 Y 5	Porchester rd W2
137 Y 4	Porchester sq W2
138 K 4	Porchester st W2
138 B 10	Porchester ter W2
137 Z 3	Porchester Terrace north W2
113 S 4	Porcupine clo SE9
90 D 11	Porden rd SW2
41 N 3	Porlock av Harrow
18 F 3	Porlock rd Enf
142 F 18	Porlock st SE1
113 V 20	Porrington clo Chisl
108 G 6	Portal clo SE27
8 B 11	Portcullis Lodge rd Enf
63 S 10	Portelet rd E1
144 J 2	Porten rd W14
66 H 18	Porter rd E6
131 R 20	Porter st W1
55 V 14	Porters av Dgnhm
138 E 1	Porteus rd W2
129 P 15	Portgate clo W9
110 J 10	Porthcawe rd SE26
97 N 9	Porthkerry av Welling
63 Y 13	Portia way E3
87 U 14	Portinscale rd SW15
118 E 16	Portland av New Mald
49 U 2	Portland av N16
97 O 17	Portland av Sidcp
58 L 13	Portland cres Grnfd
113 P 4	Portland cres SE9
24 C 5	Portland cres Stanm
24 J 8	Portland cres Stanm
30 K 19	Portland gdns N4
37 X 15	Portland gdns Rom
90 B 1	Portland gro SW8
140 C 7	Portland ms W1
139 Y 1	Portland pl W1
131 Y 19	Portland pl W1
112 L 11	Portland rd Brom
116 K 7	Portland rd Kingst
120 J 3	Portland rd Mitch
31 T 13	Portland rd N15
70 O 7	Portland rd S'hall
123 X 9	Portland rd SE25
113 R 4	Portland rd SE9
136 M 12	Portland rd W11
48 K 4	Portland ri N4
48 K 4	Portland Rise est N4
143 W 13	Portland sq E1
150 E 11	Portland st SE17
84 G 11	Portland ter Rich
85 Y 9	Portman av SW14
139 S 4	Portman clo W1
63 R 9	Portman pl E2
117 N 4	Portman rd Kingst
139 S 6	Portman sq W1
139 R 6	Portman st W1
80 H 4	Portmeadow wlk SE2
129 O 11	Portnall rd W9
39 N 7	Portnoi clo Rom
137 T 10	Portobello ms W11
136 M 2	Portobello rd W10
128 K 19	Portobello rd W11
137 T 10	Portobello rd W11
133 S 20	Portpool la EC1
30 C 3	Portree clo N22
27 V 19	Portree st E14
138 M 6	Portsea ms W2
138 M 6	Portsea pl W2
89 V 4	Portslade rd SW8
116 F 12	Portsmouth rd Surb & Kingst
86 L 19	Portsmouth rd SW15
141 O 5	Portsmouth st WC2
143 O 8	Portsoken st E1
86 D 17	Portswood pl SW15
100 M 4	Portugal gdns Twick
141 P 5	Portugal st WC2
65 O 2	Portway E15
152 G 20	Portway Epsom
31 S 4	Pospect pl N17
52 G 16	Post Office appr E7
148 F 16	Post Office way SW8
7 U 10	Postern grn Enf
150 G 2	Potier st SE1
63 N 10	Pott st E2
135 X 14	Pott st E2
121 T 4	Potter clo Mitch
87 P 19	Potterne clo SW19
142 L 15	Potters fields SE1
117 W 9	Potters gro New Mald
4 M 14	Potters la Barnt
107 W 14	Potters la SW16
5 O 13	Potters rd Barnt
136 L 12	Pottery la W11
72 K 16	Pottery rd Brentf
143 V 18	Pottery st SE16
101 X 2	Pouletts gdns Twick
66 G 5	Poulett rd E6
120 J 13	Poulter pk Carsh
154 H 5	Poulton av Sutton
142 D 6	Poultry EC2
160 D 6	Poultry EC2
116 D 19	Pound clo Surb
44 F 18	Pound la NW10
78 A 12	Pound Park rd SE7
95 V 15	Pound pl SE9
154 L 11	Pound st Carsh
89 O 7	Pountney rd SW11
82 E 20	Powder Mill la Twick
100 G 1	Powder Mill la Twick
11 Z 18	Powell clo Edg
155 Z 16	Powell clo Wallgtn
56 D 12	Powell gdns Dgnhm
21 Z 3	Powell rd Buck Hl
50 A 11	Powell rd E5
74 B 17	Powells wlk W4
73 B 12	Power rd W4
84 G 18	Powers ct Twick
50 D 11	Powerscroft rd E5
115 T 17	Powerscroft rd Sidcp
45 U 2	Powis gdns NW11
137 P 5	Powis gdns SW11
136 R 5	Powis ms W11
132 L 19	Powis pl WC1
64 D 9	Powis rd E3
137 R 6	Powis sq W11
64 L 9	Powis st E15
78 J 9	Powis st SE18
137 R 5	Powis ter W11
47 R 19	Powlett pl NW1
82 L 10	Pownall gdns Hounsl
135 R 5	Pownall rd E8
82 L 10	Pownall rd Hounsl
12 L 12	Powster rd Brom
80 K 18	Powys clo Bxly Hth
16 M 14	Powys la N13
17 N 14	Powys la N13
16 M 13	Powys la N14
89 V 18	Poynders gdns SW4
89 W 18	Poynders rd SW4
47 U 9	Poynings rd N19
14 K 17	Poynings way N12
114 F 20	Poyntell cres Chisl
9 J 19	Poynter rd Enf
31 Z 6	Poynton rd N17
88 L 6	Poyntz rd SW11
63 N 7	Poyser st E2
135 Y 1	Poyser st E2
138 G 5	Praed ms W2
138 F 6	Praed st W2
65 X 8	Pragel st E13
112 G 3	Pragneil rd SE12
90 A 14	Prague pl SW2
48 G 8	Prah rd N4
89 R 4	Prairie st SW8
132 A 5	Pratt ms NW1
132 C 3	Pratt st NW1
149 O 4	Pratt wlk SE11
45 P 3	Prayle gro NW2
74 D 11	Prebend gdns W4
134 B 5	Prebend st N1
87 R 10	Premier pl SW15
94 A 17	Prendergast rd SE3
107 Z 9	Prentis rd SW16
78 A 12	Prentiss ct SE7
118 B 10	Presburg rd New Mald
25 N 5	Prescelly pl Edg
143 O 8	Prescot st E1
127 Y 15	Prescott av Brom
108 A 17	Prescott clo SW16
89 X 9	Prescott pl SW4
143 W 12	Presidents dri E1
43 Z 9	Press rd NW10
64 H 20	Prestage st E14
64 J 20	Prestage st E14
52 L 20	Prestbury rd E7
113 T 9	Prestbury sq SE9
88 J 9	Prested rd SW11
20 J 20	Preston av E4
150 J 6	Preston clo SE1
101 S 5	Preston clo Twick
97 W 3	Preston dri Bxly Hth
34 K 16	Preston dri E11
152 C 13	Preston dri Epsom
9 X 1	Preston gdns Enf
35 S 19	Preston gdns Ilf
44 C 18	Preston gdns NW10
42 K 1	Preston hill Harrow
24 M 18	Preston hill Harrow
44 H 18	Preston pl NW2
82 L 13	Preston pl Rich
34 A 20	Preston rd E11
64 G 20	Preston rd E15
20 J 20	Preston rd E4
42 K 2	Preston rd Harrow
108 J 15	Preston rd SE19
104 E 18	Preston rd SW20
42 J 3	Preston wave Harrow
76 G 3	Prestons rd E14
70 B 14	Prestwick clo S'hall
24 B 13	Prestwood av Harrow
24 C 13	Prestwood clo Harrow
122 L 16	Prestwood gdns Croy
32 G 12	Pretoria av E17

246   Pre–Pyr

31 U 1 Pretoria clo N17
20 H 6 Pretoria cres E4
51 W 4 Pretoria rd E11
52 O 11 Pretoria rd E16
20 H 5 Pretoria rd N17
53 Y 14 Pretoria rd Ilf
31 U 1 Pretoria rd N17
38 J 14 Pretoria rd SW16
107 T 14 Pretoria rd SW16
18 G 18 Pretoria Road north N18
6 B 7 Prevost rd N11
14 E 18 Price clo NW7
106 L 8 Price clo SW17
156 J 10 Price rd Croy
100 D 15 Price way Hampt
141 Y 14 Prices st SE1
133 O 4 Prices yd N1
5 O 19 Pricklers hill Barnt
61 Z 20 Prideaux pl W3
133 R 12 Prideaux rd WC1
90 A 7 Prideaux rd SW9
123 N 9 Pridham Road east Thntn Hth
110 J 7 Priestfield rd SE23
114 K 7 Priestlands Park rd Sidcp
31 V 20 Priestley clo N16
37 P 19 Priestley gdns Rom
121 P 2 Priestley rd Mitch
32 E 10 Priestley way E17
44 G 3 Priestley way NW2
39 N 8 Priests av Rom
86 C 9 Priests br SW14
149 T 17 Prima rd SW9
8 C 5 Primrose av Enf
37 P 20 Primrose av Rom
55 R 1 Primrose av Rom
34 H 7 Primrose clo E18
40 D 11 Primrose clo Harrow
46 K 17 Primrose gdns NW3
141 V 7 Primrose Hill rd EC4
46 L 19 Primrose Hill rd NW3
131 N 1 Primrose Hill rd NW3
131 S 3 Primrose Hill studios NW1
124 D 20 Primrose la Croy
51 P 4 Primrose rd E10
34 G 7 Primrose rd E18
134 K 20 Primrose st EC2
60 F 6 Primrose way Wemb
62 F 18 Primula st W12
130 K 11 Prince Albert rd NW1
131 P 6 Prince Albert rd NW1
46 E 13 Prince Arthur ms NW3
46 E 14 Prince Arthur rd NW3
94 B 3 Prince Charles rd SE3
155 S 4 Prince Charles way Wallgtn
138 E 20 Prince Consort rd SW7
66 A 17 Prince Edward cres E16
50 M 17 Prince Edward rd E9
6 J 16 Prince George Av N14
7 N 18 Prince George av N14
49 S 13 Prince George rd N16
119 N 3 Prince Georges av SW20
106 G 20 Prince Georges rd SW19
78 B 19 Prince Henry rd SE7
114 A 17 Prince Imperial rd Chisl
113 Z 19 Prince Imperial rd Chisl
78 H 20 Prince Imperial way SE18
95 R 13 Prince John rd SE9
26 K 12 Prince of Wales clo NW4
88 K 2 Prince of Wales dri SW11
89 O 1 Prince of Wales dri SW8
147 W 20 Prince of Wales dri SW8
147 Y 20 Prince of Wales dri SW11
94 C 3 Prince of Wales rd SE3

154 G 3 Prince of Wales rd Sutton
47 S 18 Prince of Wales rd NW5
65 Y 18 Prince of Wales rd E16
74 A 13 Prince of Wales ter W4
137 Z 19 Prince of Wales ter W8
123 R 10 Prince rd SE25
65 X 12 Prince Regent la E13
82 L 7 Prince Regent rd Hounsl
95 T 8 Prince Rupert rd SE9
76 A 16 Prince st SE8
75 Z 16 Prince st SE8
160 E 5 Prince's st EC2
136 L 13 Princedale rd W11
135 P 20 Princelet st E1
140 C 12 Princes arc SW1
154 K 18 Princes av Carsh
58 L 16 Princes av Grnfd
29 R 11 Princes av N10
17 V 17 Princes av N13
29 Y 4 Princes av N22
27 Z 4 Princes av N3
25 P 13 Princes av NW9
73 R 7 Princes av W3
21 X 14 Princes av Wdfd Grn
12 B 16 Princes clo Edg
25 P 13 Princes clo Sidcp
115 V 7 Princes clo Sidcp
101 P 10 Princes clo Tedd
42 K 14 Princes ct Wemb
138 G 19 Princes ga SW7
138 X 19 Princes ga SW7
146 H 2 Princes Gate ms SW7
146 H 1 Princes gdns SW7
138 H 20 Princes gdns SW7
61 R 14 Princes gdns W3
60 D 13 Princes gdns W5
29 R 11 Princes la N10
137 W 9 Princes ms W2
27 T 17 Princes Park av NW11
140 C 13 Princes pl SW1
136 L 13 Princes pl W11
127 T 19 Princes plain Brom
21 Y 8 Princes rd Buck Hl
36 D 13 Princes rd Ilf
103 P 19 Princes rd Kingst
19 P 13 Princes rd N18
84 M 12 Princes rd Rich
85 N 1 Princes rd Rich
39 V 18 Princes rd Rom
110 F 16 Princes rd SE20
85 Z 8 Princes rd SW14
105 X 15 Princes rd SW19
101 P 11 Princes rd Tedd
72 C 2 Princes rd W13
93 U 5 Princes ri SE13
99 X 17 Princes Road north Drtfrd
137 W 8 Princes sq W2
98 A 9 Princes st Bxly Hth
142 E 5 Princes st EC2
18 E 20 Princes st N17
84 J 11 Princes st Rich
154 F 8 Princes st Sutton
139 Z 6 Princes st W1
65 W 4 Princes st E13
21 Y 8 Princes way Buck Hl
156 D 12 Princes way Croy
40 B 12 Princes way Ruis
105 S 2 Princes way SW19
42 L 6 Princess av Wemb
49 S 13 Princess May rd N16
46 G 16 Princess ms NW3
122 M 14 Princess rd Croy
123 N 13 Princess rd Croy
131 U 3 Princess rd NW1
129 U 9 Princess rd NW6
149 Y 3 Princess st SE1
110 F 10 Princethorpe rd SE26
141 N 1 Princeton st WC1
107 U 10 Pringle gdns SW16
141 U 4 Printers st EC4
141 X 8 Printing House sq EC4
77 X 14 Priolo rd SE7
154 H 15 Prior av Sutton
48 K 19 Prior Bolton st N1
53 X 9 Prior rd Ilf
76 G 20 Prior st SE10
150 G 3 Prioress st SE1
32 J 8 Priors croft E17
40 B 19 Priors field Nthlt
8 D 6 Priors mead Enf

33 O 15 Priory av E17
20 B 11 Priory av E4
19 Z 11 Priory av E4
29 Y 13 Priory av N8
153 P 8 Priory av Sutton
74 B 9 Priory av W4
41 X 12 Priory av Wemb
124 J 7 Priory clo Becknhm
127 U 2 Priory clo Chisl
34 E 4 Priory clo E18
19 Z 11 Priory clo E4
100 F 19 Priory clo Hampt
6 F 17 Priory clo N14
14 G 3 Priory clo N20
27 V 5 Priory clo N3
41 W 12 Priory clo Wemb
109 N 18 Priory cres SE19
153 P 8 Priory cres Sutton
41 Y 10 Priory cres Wemb
32 K 8 Priory ct E17
89 Z 2 Priory ct SW8
80 J 14 Priory dri SE2
10 H 10 Priory dri Stanm
10 J 10 Priory dri Stanm
100 E 19 Priory gdns Hampt
29 S 18 Priory gdns N6
86 C 8 Priory gdns SW13
74 A 10 Priory gdns W4
60 K 8 Priory gdns W5
41 Y 10 Priory gdns Wemb
89 Z 3 Priory gdns SW8
41 Y 11 Priory hill Wemb
86 D 10 Priory la SW15
89 Z 2 Priory ms SW8
129 P 4 Priory Park rd NW6
41 X 12 Priory Park rd Wemb
94 C 9 Priory pk SE3
54 E 20 Priory rd Barnt
122 F 17 Priory rd Croy
66 A 5 Priory rd E6
100 E 19 Priory rd Hampt
83 O 13 Priory rd Hounsl
29 X 13 Priory rd N8
46 A 19 Priory rd NW6
129 X 1 Priory rd NW6
73 P 18 Priory rd Rich
153 P 9 Priory rd Sutton
106 F 18 Priory rd SW19
73 X 9 Priory rd W4
64 B 8 Priory st E3
129 X 4 Priory ter NW6
94 C 9 Priory the SE3
10 E 3 Priory view Bushey
22 K 12 Priory way Harrow
146 C 11 Priory wlk SW10
135 V 8 Pritchards rd E2
151 T 2 Priter rd SE16
151 T 3 Priter way SE16
8 C 17 Private rd Enf
90 G 12 Probert st SW2
108 H 4 Probyn rd SW2
141 N 2 Procter st WC1
156 D 3 Progress way Croy
8 L 19 Progress way Enf
30 F 4 Progress way N22
74 A 20 Promenade Approach rd W4
86 C 2 Promenade the W4
81 S 12 Prospect clo Blvdr
82 F 3 Prospect clo Hounsl
87 X 11 Prospect cottages SE18
83 N 16 Prospect cres Twick
33 S 12 Prospect hill E17
126 H 7 Prospect pl Brom
75 P 2 Prospect pl E1
28 H 12 Prospect pl N2
38 K 8 Prospect pl Rom
116 C 15 Prospect pl Surb
21 Z 18 Prospect rd Wdfd Grn
4 M 15 Prospect rd Barnt
5 N 14 Prospect rd Barnt
45 W 9 Prospect rd NW2
109 Z 9 Prospect rd SE26
28 H 11 Prospect ring N2
75 N 7 Prospect st SE16
143 X 20 Prospect st SE16
78 D 11 Prospect vale SE18
63 T 8 Prospect wlk E2
47 W 4 Prospero rd N19
26 K 15 Prothero gdns NW4
145 N 17 Prothero rd SW6
44 C 13 Prout gro NW10
50 A 9 Prout rd E5
134 A 8 Provence st N1
134 A 8 Provence st N1
139 U 8 Providence ct W1
133 V 5 Providence pl N1
38 B 6 Providence pl Rom

46 M 19 Provost rd NW3
134 E 12 Provost st N1
10 A 8 Prowse av Bushey
132 A 1 Prowse pl NW1
47 U 20 Prowse pl NW1
16 J 9 Pruden clo N14
160 D 5 Prudent pas EC2
75 O 2 Prusom st E1
143 Z 12 Prusom st E1
142 H 10 Pudding la EC3
160 H 10 Pudding la EC3
64 E 4 Pudding Mill la E15
141 X 9 Puddle dock EC4
87 V 19 Pulborough rd SW18
31 P 18 Pulford rd N15
28 E 12 Pulham av N2
4 E 10 Puller rd Barnt
66 E 8 Pulleyns av E6
86 M 15 Pullman gdns SW15
90 C 9 Pulross rd SW9
63 Y 4 Pulteney clo E3
34 G 10 Pulteney rd E18
133 R 5 Pulteney ter N1
145 T 19 Pulton pl SW6
135 O 20 Puma ct E1
72 H 18 Pump all Brentf
58 H 6 Pump clo Nthlt
141 S 7 Pump ct EC4
156 K 7 Pump Pail north Croy
156 L 7 Pump Pail south Croy
74 B 18 Pumping Station rd W4
63 N 8 Pundersons gdns E2
135 X 12 Pundersons gdns E2
118 E 15 Purbeck av New Mald
45 R 6 Purbeck dri NW2
57 X 2 Purbeck rd Hornch
142 M 20 Purbrook st SE1
144 J 17 Purcell cres SW6
58 K 13 Purcell rd Grnfd
134 J 9 Purcell st N1
12 B 15 Purcells av Edg
132 G 9 Purchese st NW1
64 C 11 Purdy st E3
56 B 4 Purland clo Dgnhm
79 Z 6 Purland st SE28
45 S 8 Purley av NW2
35 X 8 Purley clo Ilf
48 H 20 Purley pl N1
18 C 11 Purley rd N9
157 N 18 Purley rd S Croy
122 D 19 Purley way Croy
156 E 4 Purley way Croy
94 M 9 Purneys rd SE9
95 N 10 Purneys rd SE9
79 X 13 Purrett rd SE18
87 W 2 Pursers Cross rd SW6
26 K 1 Pursley rd NW7
128 C 10 Purves rd NW10
62 M 7 Purves rd NW10
87 S 8 Putney br SW6
87 S 7 Putney Bridge app SW6
87 U 10 Putney Bridge rd SW15
86 L 7 Putney comm SW15
87 P 17 Putney Heath la SW15
86 L 17 Putney heath SW15
87 N 16 Putney heath SW15
104 M 3 Putney heath SW19
87 R 11 Putney High st SW15
87 P 14 Putney hill SW15
86 G 10 Putney Park av SW15
86 J 10 Putney Park la SW15
14 J 14 Pyecombe corner N12
153 Z 6 Pylbrook rd Sutton
5 U 17 Pym clo Barnt
109 N 1 Pymers mead SE21
16 B 4 Pymes brook Barnt
17 O 17 Pymes clo N13
18 H 12 Pymmes Gardens north N9
18 H 12 Pymmes Gardens south N9
5 W 14 Pymmes gdns Barnt
16 F 12 Pymmes Green rd N11
18 G 13 Pymmes pk N18
17 O 18 Pymmes rd N13
80 B 9 Pynham clo SE2
11 O 16 Pynnicles clo Stanm
49 N 15 Pyrland rd N5
85 N 16 Pyrland rd Rich
108 H 7 Pyrmont gro SE27
54 B 8 Pyrmont rd Ilf
73 P 15 Pyrmont rd W4

108 M 16 Pytchley cres SE19
91 T 8 Pytchley rd SE22

Q

39 R 15 Quadrant arc Rom
47 N 16 Quadrant gro NW5
122 J 8 Quadrant rd Thntn Hth
84 H 11 Quadrant rd Rich
80 K 20 Quadrant the Bxly Hth
84 J 11 Quadrant the Rich
154 C 13 Quadrant the Sutton
105 S 20 Quadrant the SW20
94 E 10 Quaggy wlk SE3
43 Y 10 Quainton st NW10
71 X 19 Quaker la Islwth
83 Z 1 Quaker la Islwth
70 H 7 Quaker rd S'hall
135 N 18 Quaker st E1
26 C 5 Quakers course NW9
8 A 20 Quakers wlk Enf
141 S 4 Quality ct WC2
45 O 7 Quantock gdns NW2
99 R 3 Quantock rd Bxly Hth
130 U 11 Quarr rd Barnt
87 Y 4 Quarrendon st SW6
153 U 13 Quarry Park rd Sutton
88 E 15 Quarry rd SW18
153 U 13 Quarry ri Sutton
94 E 10 Quarry wlk SE3
51 P 12 Quarter Mile la E10
139 P 6 Quebec ms W1
54 A 1 Quebec rd Ilf
36 B 19 Quebec rd Ilf
75 U 7 Quebec way SE16
110 D 17 Queen Adelaide rd SE20
97 X 8 Queen Ann ga Bxly Hth
126 D 7 Queen Anne av Brom
120 K 6 Queen Anne gdns Mitch
139 Y 3 Queen Anne ms W1
50 F 19 Queen Anne rd E9
139 X 3 Queen Anne st W1
31 T 15 Queen Annes av N15
101 R 7 Queen Annes clo Twick
140 F 19 Queen Annes ga SW1
74 A 8 Queen Annes gdns W4
8 E 20 Queen Annes gdns Enf
72 J 6 Queen Annes gdns W5
74 A 9 Queen Annes gro W4
72 K 5 Queen Annes gro W5
18 C 2 Queen Annes gro Enf
8 F 19 Queen Annes pl Enf
74 L 14 Queen Caroline st W6
144 C 10 Queen Caroline st W6
119 Y 9 Queen Elizabeth gdns Mrdn
141 P 13 Queen Elizabeth hall SE1
32 H 10 Queen Elizabeth rd E17
116 L 3 Queen Elizabeth rd Kingst
142 M 16 Queen Elizabeth st SE1
143 O 17 Queen Elizabeth st SE1
49 N 6 Queen Elizabeths clo N16
16 M 6 Queen Elizabeths dri N14
17 N 4 Queen Elizabeths dri N14
159 W 20 Queen Elizabeths dri Croy
49 N 4 Queen Elizabeths wlk N16
155 Y 8 Queen Elizabeths wlk Wallgtn
49 R 16 Queen Margarets gro N1
119 O 12 Queen Mary av Mrdn

108 K 14 Queen Mary rd SE19
154 L 17 Queen Marys av Carsh
131 S 15 Queen Marys gdns NW1
132 K 19 Queen sq WC1
132 K 19 Queen Square pl WC1
98 A 9 Queen st Bxly Hth
156 L 7 Queen st Croy
160 C 7 Queen st EC4
142 C 9 Queen st EC4
139 X 13 Queen st Mayfair W1
39 O 17 Queen st Rom
142 C 10 Queen Street pl EC4
160 C 10 Queen Street pl EC4
42 G 20 Queen Victoria st Wemb
160 A 8 Queen Victoria st EC4
142 B 8 Queen Victoria st EC4
141 Y 8 Queen Victoria st EC4
144 M 13 Queen's Club gdns W14
145 N 13 Queen's Club gdns W14
144 L 12 Queen's Club the W14
35 X 12 Queenborough gdns Ilf
158 A 20 Queenhill rd S Croy
160 B 9 Queenhithe EC4
153 R 16 Queens acre Sutton
58 M 16 Queens av Grnfd
59 N 16 Queens av Grnfd
29 R 10 Queens av N10
15 U 9 Queens av N20
17 X 6 Queens av N21
28 D 4 Queens av N3
24 D 9 Queens av Stanm
21 W 16 Queens av Wdfd Grn
147 X 20 Queens cir SW11
12 C 17 Queens clo Edg
155 S 10 Queens clo Wallgtn
84 G 4 Queens cott Rich
47 O 18 Queens cres NW5
85 N 13 Queens cres Rich
110 B 3 Queens ct SE23
51 O 1 Queens dri N4
48 J 6 Queens dri E10
117 R 15 Queens dri Surb
61 O 17 Queens dri W3
60 M 18 Queens dri W5
146 G 10 Queens Elm pde SW3
146 G 11 Queens Elm sq SW3
138 D 20 Queens Gate SW7
146 D 3 Queens Gate SW7
139 Z 19 Queens Gallery SW1
146 B 3 Queens Gate gdns SW7
146 B 1 Queens Gate ms SW7
138 C 20 Queens Gate ms SW7
146 D 3 Queens Gate ms SW7
146 D 4 Queens Gate Place Ms SW7
146 C 1 Queens Gate ter SW7
69 Z 7 Queens gdns Rainhm
82 B 2 Queens gdns Hounsl
27 N 16 Queens gdns NW4
138 B 8 Queens gdns W2
60 E 13 Queens gdns W5
130 F 7 Queens gro NW8
20 K 5 Queens Grove rd E4
133 Y 5 Queens Head st N1
142 E 15 Queens Head yd SE1
76 L 17 Queens la SE10
29 S 10 Queens la N10
126 B 4 Queens Mead rd Brom
137 Y 8 Queens ms W2
15 Z 18 Queens Parade clo N11
128 K 7 Queens pk NW6
119 Z 8 Queens pl Mrdn
54 A 20 Queens rd Bark
4 C 13 Queens rd Barnt
124 J 3 Queens rd Becknhm
78 K 9 Queens rd Brom
21 W 7 Queens rd Buck Hl
114 A 15 Queens rd Chisl
122 K 14 Queens rd Croy
51 Y 2 Queens rd E11
65 V 5 Queens rd E13
32 L 19 Queens rd E17
33 N 17 Queens rd E17
8 E 13 Queens rd Enf
100 K 10 Queens rd Hampt

82 J 7 Queens rd Hounsl
103 R 19 Queens rd Kingst
119 Z 8 Queens rd Mrdn
28 D 5 Queens rd N11
28 D 5 Queens rd N3
18 M 9 Queens rd N9
118 E 10 Queens rd New Mald
26 M 17 Queens rd NW4
27 N 16 Queens rd NW4
84 L 17 Queens rd Rich
85 N 12 Queens rd Rich
85 N 14 Queens rd Rich
70 A 7 Queens rd S'hall
92 C 2 Queens rd SE14
147 V 18 Queens rd SW11
85 Z 8 Queens rd SW14
106 B 13 Queens rd SW19
120 E 4 Queens rd SW19
105 Z 14 Queens rd SW19
101 W 16 Queens rd Tedd
83 X 20 Queens rd Twick
101 Y 1 Queens rd Twick
60 J 16 Queens rd W5
155 S 10 Queens rd Wallgtn
97 P 3 Queens rd Welling
84 M 15 Queens ri Rich
86 G 9 Queens ride SW13
65 U 5 Queens Road west E13
150 D 13 Queens row SE17
83 Z 8 Queens sq Islwth
18 E 20 Queens st N17
55 W 4 Queens ter E13
83 Z 1 Queens ter Islwth
130 F 7 Queens ter NW8
27 N 15 Queens way NW4
20 J 4 Queens wlk E4
22 S 12 Queens wlk Harrow
43 W 6 Queens wlk NW9
60 D 14 Queens wlk W5
146 E 5 Queensberry Mews west SW7
146 E 5 Queensberry pl SW7
146 F 5 Queensberry way SW7
138 A 8 Queensborough pas W2
138 A 10 Queensborough ter W2
83 T 14 Queensbridge pk Islwth
135 P 3 Queensbridge rd E8
49 V 18 Queensbridge rd E8
24 M 12 Queensbury pk Harrow
60 M 6 Queensbury rd Wemb
61 O 5 Queensbury rd Wemb
43 X 2 Queensbury rd NW9
134 C 2 Queensbury rd N1
25 N 10 Queensbury Station pde Edg
42 K 12 Queenscourt Wemb
95 P 15 Queenscroft rd SE9
136 H 13 Queensdale cres W11
136 J 14 Queensdale pl W11
136 H 15 Queensdale rd W11
136 K 14 Queensdale wlk W11
49 Z 12 Queensdown rd E5
129 T 2 Queensgate pl NW6
106 A 20 Queensland av SW19
17 Z 18 Queensland av N18
48 G 13 Queensland pl N7
48 F 13 Queensland rd N7
153 N 20 Queensmead Sutton
105 O 5 Queensmead clo SW19
105 O 5 Queensmere rd SW19
144 G 19 Queensmill rd SW6
110 E 10 Queensthorpe rd SE26
89 R 6 Queenstown rd SW8
147 W 17 Queenstown rd SW8
89 X 19 Queensville rd SW12
156 C 13 Queensway Croy
156 E 12 Queensway Croy
9 P 16 Queensway Enf
137 Y 6 Queensway W2
15 W 12 Queenswell av N20
82 E 4 Queenswood av Hounsl
122 G 12 Queenswood av Thntn Hth
100 K 15 Queenswood av Hampt

155 X 9 Queenswood av Wallgtn
33 U 6 Queenswood av E17
52 G 5 Queenswood gdns E11
27 T 6 Queenswood pk N3
110 G 8 Queenswood rd SE23
96 K 15 Queenswood rd Sidcp
29 T 17 Queenswood rd N10
48 C 14 Quemerford rd N7
94 A 8 Quentin rd SE13
112 E 15 Quernmore clo Brom
112 E 15 Quernmore rd Brom
30 F 19 Quernmore rd N4
88 C 5 Quernn st SW6
94 N 6 Quex ms NW6
129 V 3 Quex rd NW6
133 X 5 Quick pl N1
74 A 14 Quick rd W4
133 X 9 Quick st N1
106 C 17 Quicks rd SW19
46 K 20 Quickswood NW3
130 M 1 Quickswood NW3
87 P 10 Quill la SW15
142 B 17 Quilp st SE1
135 R 12 Quilter st E2
4 A 18 Quinta dri Barnt
119 U 1 Quinton av SW20
125 V 6 Quinton clo Becknhm
155 R 8 Quinton clo Wallgtn
106 C 5 Quinton st SW18
64 J 20 Quixley st E14
91 T 9 Quorn rd SE22

R

137 V 12 Rabbit row W8
53 R 11 Rabbits rd E12
40 B 16 Rabournmead dri Nthlt
117 Z 8 Raby rd New Mald
63 V 17 Raby la E14
145 S 15 Racton rd SW6
72 E 10 Radbourne av W5
33 W 9 Radbourne cres E17
107 W 1 Radbourne rd SW12
89 W 19 Radbourne rd SW12
8 A 5 Radcliffe av Enf
62 F 5 Radcliffe av NW10
154 J 18 Radcliffe gdns Carsh
157 V 3 Radcliffe rd Croy
23 Y 8 Radcliffe rd Harrow
17 W 4 Radcliffe rd N21
87 P 15 Radcliffe rd SE1
137 N 2 Raddington rd W10
96 F 18 Radfield way Sidcp
93 V 15 Radford rd SE13
67 X 9 Radford way Bark
87 V 1 Radipole rd SW6
65 R 18 Radland rd E16
110 B 5 Radlett av SE26
52 D 17 Radlett clo E7
130 K 5 Radlett pl NW8
54 L 13 Radley av Ilf
24 L 14 Radley gdns Harrow
34 E 8 Radley la E18
145 V 4 Radley ms W8
31 T 7 Radley rd N17
50 C 6 Radley sq E5
56 G 18 Radleys mead Dgnhm
51 N 4 Radlix rd E10
23 S 15 Radnor av Harrow
97 R 13 Radnor av Welling
114 H 16 Radnor clo Chisl
122 A 10 Radnor clo Mitch
35 T 17 Radnor cres Ilf
8 E 5 Radnor gdns Enf
101 V 3 Radnor gdns Twick
138 H 6 Radnor ms W2
138 J 6 Radnor pl W2
23 T 16 Radnor rd Harrow
128 L 5 Radnor rd NW6
151 S 17 Radnor rd SE15
101 W 2 Radnor rd Twick
134 C 14 Radnor st EC1
148 K 17 Radnor ter SW8
145 O 4 Radnor ter W14
61 S 10 Radnor way NW10
124 K 16 Radnor wlk Croy

146 M 11	Radnor wlk SW3	
147 N 13	Radnor wlk SW3	
151 T 13	Radsley st SE1	
24 A 11	Radstock av Harrow	
23 Z 11	Radstock av Harrow	
146 K 19	Radstock st SW11	
99 Z 14	Raeburn av Drtfrd	
117 S 19	Raeburn av Surb	
102 F 19	Raeburn clo Kingst	
28 C 19	Raeburn clo NW11	
25 O 6	Raeburn rd Edg	
96 J 16	Raeburn rd Sidcp	
90 B 11	Raeburn st SW2	
126 G 4	Rafford way Brom	
113 X 20	Raggleswood Chisl	
156 K 10	Raglan ct S Croy	
81 O 12	Raglan rd Blvdr	
126 M 9	Raglan rd Brom	
33 V 15	Raglan rd E17	
18 F 2	Raglan rd Enf	
47 T 17	Raglan st NW5	
40 K 13	Raglan ter Harrow	
41 N 18	Raglan way Northolt	
73 U 4	Ragley clo W3	
38 F 5	Raider clo Rom	
47 U 14	Railey ms NW5	
84 A 10	Railshead rd Twick	
90 G 12	Railton rd SE24	
23 V 13	Railway appr Harrow	
30 G 19	Railway appr N8	
142 F 14	Railway appr SE1	
83 Y 20	Railway appr Twick	
155 S 12	Railway appr Wallgtn	
75 P 5	Railway av SE16	
136 L 5	Railway ms W10	
101 X 15	Railway pas Tedd	
81 T 8	Railway pl Blvdr	
142 L 8	Railway pl EC3	
105 V 16	Railway pl SW19	
101 V 11	Railway rd Tedd	
86 B 7	Railway side SW13	
132 L 9	Railway st N1	
55 T 2	Railway st Rom	
33 V 5	Railway ter E17	
93 R 13	Railway ter SE13	
43 V 16	Rainborough clo NW10	
150 J 17	Rainborn st SE5	
75 N 2	Raine st E1	
143 Y 12	Raine st E1	
96 F 15	Rainham clo SE9	
88 K 15	Rainham clo SW11	
128 D 13	Rainham rd NW10	
57 T 18	Rainham rd Rainhm	
56 H 9	Rainham Road north Dgnhm	
56 K 19	Rainham Road south Dgnhm	
64 C 9	Rainhall way E3	
75 V 12	Rainsborough av SE8	
11 P 15	Rainsford clo Stanm	
61 S 7	Rainsford rd NW10	
138 J 4	Rainsford st W2	
57 U 4	Rainsford way Hornch	
77 U 13	Rainton rd SE7	
144 E 16	Rainville rd W6	
16 K 12	Raith av N14	
76 H 2	Raleana rd E14	
101 U 16	Raleigh av Tedd	
155 X 8	Raleigh av Wallgtn	
26 L 15	Raleigh clo NW4	
155 T 15	Raleigh ct Wallgtn	
15 X 10	Raleigh dri N20	
117 V 20	Raleigh dri Surb	
120 L 4	Raleigh dri Mitch	
8 B 15	Raleigh rd Enf	
30 G 13	Raleigh rd N8	
85 N 8	Raleigh rd Rich	
70 B 12	Raleigh rd S'hall	
110 E 18	Raleigh rd SE20	
133 Z 6	Raleigh st N1	
16 L 14	Raleigh way N14	
150 C 2	Ralph st SE1	
147 O 11	Ralston st SW3	
50 C 17	Ram pl E9	
41 T 7	Rama ct Harrow	
77 U 12	Ramac way SE7	
107 U 10	Ramber clo SW16	
90 A 15	Ramillies clo SW2	
140 B 5	Ramillies pl W1	
13 O 9	Ramillies rd NW7	
97 P 16	Ramillies rd Sidcp	
73 Y 9	Ramillies rd W4	
140 B 6	Ramillies st W1	
148 F 9	Rampayne st SW1	
20 A 10	Rampton clo E4	
37 Z 12	Rams gro Rom	
41 O 15	Ramsay clo Grnfd	
52 C 11	Ramsay rd E7	
73 V 7	Ramsay rd W3	
18 C 4	Ramscroft clo N9	
107 R 13	Ramsdale rd SW17	
38 F 3	Ramsden dri Rom	
81 Z 20	Ramsden rd Erith	
15 Z 16	Ramsden rd N11	
89 P 20	Ramsden rd SW12	
122 E 13	Ramsey rd NW9	
26 D 9	Ramsey rd Thntn Hth	
135 T 16	Ramsey st E2	
16 H 4	Ramsey way N14	
49 V 17	Ramsgate st E8	
36 K 14	Ramsgill appr Ilf	
36 K 14	Ramsgill dri Ilf	
58 A 12	Ramulis dri Hay	
95 P 9	Rancliffe gdns SE9	
66 E 7	Rancliffe rd E6	
44 C 8	Randall av NW2	
81 Y 17	Randall clo Erith	
88 J 2	Randall clo SW11	
76 F 18	Randall pl SE10	
39 T 18	Randall rd Rom	
149 N 8	Randall rd SE11	
149 N 8	Randall row SE11	
64 L 13	Randall st E16	
132 L 3	Randell's rd N1	
102 E 9	Randle rd Rich	
111 R 7	Randlesdown rd SE6	
65 Z 17	Randolph appr E 16	
130 C 17	Randolph av W9	
129 Z 12	Randolph av W9	
98 J 7	Randolph clo Bxly Hth	
103 W 13	Randolph clo Kingst	
130 B 17	Randolph cres W9	
129 X 10	Randolph gdns NW6	
130 C 18	Randolph ms W9	
33 S 15	Randolph rd E17	
70 D 5	Randolph rd S'hall	
130 C 18	Randolph rd W9	
132 B 1	Randolph st NW1	
22 K 7	Randon clo Harrow	
86 G 5	Ranelagh av SW13	
87 U 7	Ranelagh av SW6	
12 B 13	Ranelagh clo Edg	
12 B 13	Ranelagh dri Edg	
84 C 12	Ranelagh dri Twick	
34 K 15	Ranelagh gdns E11	
53 U 3	Ranelagh gdns Ilf	
87 U 8	Ranelagh gdns SW6	
73 U 18	Ranelagh gdns W4	
147 V 9	Ranelagh gro SW1	
118 A 10	Ranelagh pl New Mald	
51 Z 11	Ranelagh rd E11	
65 O 6	Ranelagh rd E15	
66 J 4	Ranelagh rd E6	
31 T 10	Ranelagh rd N17	
30 C 6	Ranelagh rd N22	
62 D 7	Ranelagh rd NW10	
70 A 1	Ranelagh rd S'hall	
148 C 11	Ranelagh rd SW1	
72 G 5	Ranelagh rd W5	
42 H 17	Ranelagh rd Wemb	
153 Z 2	Ranfurly rd Sutton	
112 C 13	Rangefield rd Brom	
111 Z 11	Rangefield rd Brom	
31 V 16	Rangemoor rd N15	
21 R 2	Rangers rd E4	
93 W 1	Rangers sq SE10	
142 M 7	Rangoon st EC3	
26 B 10	Rankin clo NW9	
81 P 19	Ranleigh gdns Bxly Hth	
89 T 20	Ranmere st SW12	
23 R 14	Ranmoor clo Harrow	
23 S 13	Ranmoor gdns Harrow	
157 V 7	Ranmore av Croy	
153 O 20	Ranmore rd Sutton	
144 D 13	Rannoch rd W6	
144 E 16	Rannoch rd W6	
44 A 1	Rannock av NW9	
77 Y 12	Ransom rd SE7	
130 K 20	Ranston st NW1	
45 V 11	Ranulf rd NW2	
63 X 4	Ranwell clo E3	
99 S 4	Ranworth clo Erith	
19 O 10	Ranworth rd N9	
39 S 9	Raphael av Rom	
39 T 8	Raphael pk Rom	
139 N 19	Raphael st SW7	
15 S 9	Rasper rd N20	
107 X 3	Rastell av SW2	
134 C 14	Ratcliff gro EC1	
52 K 16	Ratcliff rd E7	
63 T 18	Ratcliffe Cross st E1	
63 U 18	Ratcliffe la E1	
63 T 19	Ratcliffe orchard E1	
63 N 20	Ratcliffe st E1	
140 E 3	Rathbone pl W1	
65 O 16	Rathbone st E16	
140 D 2	Rathbone st W1	
30 D 15	Rathcoole av N8	
30 D 15	Rathcoole gdns N8	
110 M 2	Rathfern rd SE6	
72 C 4	Rathgar av W13	
27 V 6	Rathgar clo N3	
90 J 7	Rathgar rd SW9	
89 X 16	Rathmell dri SW4	
77 V 13	Rathmore rd SE7	
90 F 12	Rattray rd SW2	
91 X 3	Raul rd SE15	
47 U 13	Raveley st NW5	
34 K 6	Raven ct E18	
63 N 14	Raven row E1	
143 X 1	Raven row E1	
89 R 2	Ravenet st SW11	
106 M 8	Ravenfield rd SW17	
65 Y 6	Ravenhill rd E13	
87 P 12	Ravenna rd SW15	
58 L 8	Ravenor Park rd Grnfd	
59 N 9	Ravenor Park rd Grnfd	
58 M 9	Ravenor pk Grnfd	
126 C 5	Ravens clo Brom	
8 D 5	Ravens clo Enf	
94 E 12	Ravens way SE12	
111 X 19	Ravensbourne av Brom	
125 Y 1	Ravensbourne av Brom	
60 A 15	Ravensbourne gdns W13	
36 A 5	Ravensbourne gdns Ilf	
35 X 4	Ravensbourne gdns Ilf	
92 M 18	Ravensbourne Park cres SE6	
93 N 18	Ravensbourne rd SE6	
84 D 14	Ravensbourne rd Twick	
126 E 6	Ravensbourne rd Brom	
92 K 20	Ravensbourne rd SE6	
99 V 7	Ravensbury av Drtfrd	
120 D 11	Ravensbury av Mordn	
121 N 4	Ravensbury clo Mitch	
120 F 9	Ravensbury gro Mitch	
120 F 9	Ravensbury la Mitch	
120 F 8	Ravensbury pth Mitch	
106 A 3	Ravensbury rd SW18	
105 Z 3	Ravensbury rd SW18	
111 Z 10	Ravenscar rd Brom	
74 G 11	Ravenscourt av W6	
74 F 10	Ravenscourt gdns W6	
74 G 11	Ravenscourt pk W6	
74 H 11	Ravenscourt pl W6	
74 H 12	Ravenscourt rd W6	
74 F 9	Ravenscourt sq W6	
16 G 14	Ravenscraig rd N11	
42 L 3	Ravenscroft av Wemb	
45 V 1	Ravenscroft av NW11	
27 W 20	Ravenscroft av NW11	
65 S 14	Ravenscroft clo E16	
4 D 12	Ravenscroft Park rd Barnt	
4 D 13	Ravenscroft pk Barnt	
124 F 1	Ravenscroft rd Becknhm	
65 T 14	Ravenscroft rd E16	
73 W 11	Ravenscroft rd W4	
135 P 10	Ravenscroft st E2	
15 S 14	Ravensdale av N12	
109 P 19	Ravensdale gdns SE19	
82 B 7	Ravensdale rd Hounsl	
31 V 20	Ravensdale rd N16	
149 U 11	Ravensdon st SE11	
55 X 12	Ravensfield clo Dgnhm	
152 B 10	Ravensfield gdns Epsom	
45 W 17	Ravenshaw st NW6	
127 Y 2	Ravenshill Chisl	
26 L 12	Ravenshurst av NW4	
88 M 19	Ravenslea rd SW12	
111 X 18	Ravensmead rd Brom	
74 D 12	Ravensmeade way W4	
30 E 11	Ravenstone rd N8	
26 E 19	Ravenstone rd NW9	
107 R 12	Ravenstone st SW12	
125 T 20	Ravenswood av W Wkhm	
115 Z 1	Ravenswood Bxly	
156 J 6	Ravenswood clo Croy	
40 D 7	Ravenswood cres Harrow	
125 T 19	Ravenswood cres W Wkhm	
103 U 16	Ravenswood ct Kingst	
83 T 1	Ravenswood gdns Islwth	
89 S 19	Ravenswood rd SW12	
156 J 6	Ravenswood rd Croy	
33 T 14	Ravenswood rd E17	
62 K 8	Ravensworth rd NW10	
113 T 8	Ravensworth rd SE9	
149 P 5	Ravent rd SE11	
51 Y 6	Ravey st EC2	
79 U 17	Ravine gro SE18	
147 N 6	Rawlings st SW3	
27 S 9	Rawlins clo N3	
158 K 16	Rawlins clo S Croy	
31 V 11	Rawlinson ter N17	
120 G 10	Rawnsley av Mrdn	
89 R 3	Rawson st SW11	
65 S 6	Rawstone wlk E13	
133 W 12	Rawstorne pl EC1	
133 W 12	Rawstorne st EC1	
68 A 6	Ray gdns Bark	
11 P 16	Ray gdns Stanm	
21 Z 18	Ray Lodge rd Wdfd Grn	
133 U 18	Ray st EC1	
4 M 18	Raydean rd Barnt	
47 S 7	Raydon st N19	
55 Z 14	Raydons gdns Dgnhm	
56 A 14	Raydons rd Dgnhm	
55 Y 15	Raydons rd Dgnhm	
127 P 14	Rayfield clo Brom	
94 C 19	Rayford av SE12	
95 Z 2	Rayleas clo SE18	
117 O 3	Rayleigh clo N13	
117 O 3	Rayleigh ct Kingst	
34 L 1	Rayleigh rd Wdfd Grn	
21 X 20	Rayleigh rd Wdfd Grn	
18 A 10	Rayleigh rd N13	
17 Z 10	Rayleigh rd N13	
105 U 20	Rayleigh rd SW19	
53 Y 14	Rayleigh ri S Croy	
122 G 11	Raymead av Thntn Hth	
27 N 11	Raymead NW4	
79 T 19	Raymere gdns SE18	
34 B 9	Raymond av E18	
71 Z 8	Raymond av W13	
110 C 11	Raymond clo SE26	
124 H 10	Raymond rd Becknhm	
65 X 2	Raymond rd E13	
54 D 2	Raymond rd Ilf	
105 T 15	Raymond rd SW19	
75 O 11	Raymouth rd SE16	
151 Y 6	Raymouth rd SE16	
34 C 12	Rayne ct E18	
40 F 4	Rayners la Harrow	
22 F 20	Rayners la Pinn	
87 R 13	Rayners rd SW15	
52 L 1	Raynes av E11	
18 K 18	Raynham av N18	
18 K 16	Raynham rd N18	
74 J 10	Raynham rd W6	
18 K 17	Raynham ter N18	
70 D 3	Raynor clo S'hall	
134 C 3	Raynor pl N1	
42 G 14	Raynors clo Wemb	
40 B 3	Raynton clo Harrow	
19 P 15	Rays av N18	
19 P 15	Rays rd N18	
89 T 1	Raywood st SW8	
132 C 2	Reachview clo NW1	
50 A 18	Reading la E8	
49 Z 19	Reading la E8	
40 L 14	Reading rd Nthlt	
154 D 12	Reading rd Sutton	
14 D 16	Reading way NW7	
132 E 3	Reapers clo NW1	
83 R 13	Reapers way Islwth	
75 N 3	Reardon pth E1	

143 X 15 Reardon pth E1
75 N 2 Reardon st E1
143 X 13 Reardon st E1
75 R 19 Reaston st SE14
75 P 9 Rebecca ter SE16
73 Z 14 Reckitt rd W4
75 O 15 Record st SE15
106 J 12 Recovery st SW17
38 L 17 Recreation av Rom
126 B 3 Recreation rd Brom
70 A 10 Recreation rd S'hall
110 E 9 Recreation rd SE26
121 Y 8 Recreation way Mitch
134 A 5 Rector st N1
99 R 11 Rectory clo Drtfrd
20 B 10 Rectory clo E4
27 W 6 Rectory clo N3
115 R 10 Rectory clo Sidcp
11 O 17 Rectory clo Stanm
116 C 20 Rectory clo Surb
118 M 4 Rectory clo SW20
34 K 18 Rectory cres E11
77 X 18 Rectory Field cres SE7
58 F 2 Rectory gdns Grnfrd
30 A 12 Rectory gdns N8
89 V 7 Rectory gdns SW4
124 M 1 Rectory grn Becknhm
156 J 4 Rectory gro Croy
100 F 12 Rectory gro Hampt
89 V 7 Rectory gro SW4
12 C 17 Rectory la Edg
115 R 11 Rectory la Sidcp
115 U 11 Rectory la Sidcp
11 O 17 Rectory la Stanm
116 C 20 Rectory la Surb
107 P 13 Rectory la SW17
155 V 7 Rectory la Wallgtn
58 D 8 Rectory Park av Nthlt
58 B 7 Rectory pk Nthlt
78 J 11 Rectory pl SE18
124 M 2 Rectory rd Becknhm
111 O 20 Rectory rd Becknhm
56 F 20 Rectory rd Dgnhm
53 U 16 Rectory rd E12
33 R 12 Rectory rd E17
49 V 9 Rectory rd N16
70 E 9 Rectory rd S'hall
153 Z 7 Rectory rd Sutton
86 G 4 Rectory rd SW13
73 U 2 Rectory rd W3
63 I 14 Rectory sq E1
18 K 14 Reculver ms N18
75 S 13 Reculver rd SE16
78 F 11 Red Barracks st SE18
113 Y 13 Red Hill Chisl
97 Y 11 Red House la Bxly Hth
121 X 13 Red House rd Croy
81 R 17 Red Leaf clo Blvdr
141 U 5 Red Lion ct EC4
28 F 8 Red Lion hill N2
78 J 20 Red Lion la SE18
95 W 1 Red Lion la SE18
95 W 2 Red Lion pl SE18
117 O 20 Red Lion rd Surb
150 D 14 Red Lion row SE17
141 N 2 Red Lion sq WC1
84 H 13 Red Lion st Rich
141 O 2 Red Lion st WC1
139 W 13 Red Lion yd W1
125 V 17 Red Lodge rd W Wkhm
139 T 8 Red pl W1
91 N 11 Red Post hill SE24
137 Y 6 Redan pl W2
144 G 1 Redan st W14
90 K 5 Redan ter SE5
146 H 15 Redanchor clo SW3
110 C 6 Redberry gro SE26
27 Z 4 Redbourne av N3
150 K 20 Redbridge gdns SE5
35 N 18 Redbridge Lane east Ilf
34 L 18 Redbridge Lane west E11
147 N 12 Redburn st SW3
40 K 16 Redcar clo Nthlt
150 A 19 Redcar st SE5
63 P 20 Redcastle clo E1
135 N 16 Redchurch st E2
145 W 10 Redcliffe clo SW5
53 V 3 Redcliffe gdns Ilf
146 B 14 Redcliffe gdns SW10
145 Y 10 Redcliffe gdns SW10
145 Z 12 Redcliffe ms SW10
146 B 15 Redcliffe pl SW10
146 C 13 Redcliffe rd SW10

145 Z 11 Redcliffe sq SW10
145 Z 13 Redcliffe st SW10
119 X 12 Redclose av Mrdn
65 Y 4 Redclyffe rd E6
58 M 18 Redcroft rd S'hall
142 C 15 Redcross way SE1
142 D 14 Redcross wlk SE1
13 S 12 Reddings clo NW7
13 S 11 Reddings the NW7
157 R 20 Reddington clo S Croy
151 R 16 Reddins rd SE15
110 G 18 Reddons rd Becknhm
137 V 8 Rede pl W2
71 X 19 Redesdale gdns Islwth
146 M 12 Redesdale st SW3
82 G 19 Redfern av Hounsl
62 B 1 Redfern rd NW10
93 U 18 Redfern rd SE6
145 V 6 Redfield la SW5
122 D 9 Redford av Thntn Hth
155 Z 14 Redford av Wallgtn
133 Z 4 Redford wlk N1
87 R 15 Redgate ter SW15
87 P 9 Redgrave rd SW15
25 U 8 Redhill dri Edg
131 Y 11 Redhill st NW1
46 B 11 Redington gdns NW3
46 A 10 Redington rd NW3
9 V 4 Redlands rd Enf
90 B 19 Redlands way SW2
151 U 10 Redlaw way SE16
83 W 9 Redlees pk Islwth
83 Y 11 Redless clo Islwth
63 P 14 Redmans rd E1
143 S 14 Redmead la E1
143 U 13 Redmead la E1
74 J 10 Redmore rd W6
80 K 7 Redpoll way Blvdr
38 J 7 Redriff rd Rom
75 U 8 Redriff rd SE16
65 R 5 Redriffe rd E13
30 C 2 Redruth clo N22
63 S 3 Redruth rd E9
66 D 14 Redstart clo E6
29 W 12 Redston rd N8
30 F 7 Redvers rd N22
134 L 11 Redvers st E2
50 G 13 Redwald rd E5
83 O 19 Redway dri Twick
79 S 6 Redwing gdn SE28
16 L 3 Redwood clo N14
75 W 4 Redwood clo SE16
104 F 2 Redwood SW15
146 E 6 Reece ms SW7
65 S 16 Reed clo E16
94 F 13 Reed clo SE12
47 U 19 Reed pl NW1
39 U 7 Reed Pond wlk Rom
31 V 9 Reed rd N17
56 G 16 Reede gdns Dgnhm
56 D 17 Reede rd Dgnhm
56 J 16 Reede rd Dgnhm
56 G 17 Reede way Dgnhm
31 Z 12 Reedham clo N15
91 W 6 Reedham st SE15
49 P 12 Reedholm vlls N16
149 T 7 Reedworth st SE11
11 U 13 Reenglass rd Stanm
123 U 14 Rees gdns Croy
134 D 5 Rees st N1
53 W 17 Reesland clo E12
26 B 18 Reets Farm clo NW9
43 X 1 Reeves av NW9
156 K 4 Reeves corner Croy
139 U 10 Reeves ms W1
64 D 10 Reeves rd E3
78 L 17 Reeves rd SE18
31 V 7 Reform row N17
88 M 5 Reform st SW11
143 U 1 Regal clo E1
60 H 16 Regal clo W5
155 S 5 Regal cres Wallgtn
18 H 16 Regal ct N18
131 V 5 Regal la NW1
24 K 19 Regal way Harrow
134 J 9 Regan way N1
39 R 18 Regarth av Rom
100 E 11 Regency clo Hampt
60 K 18 Regency clo W5
83 T 14 Regency ms Islwth
148 F 4 Regency pl SW1
148 F 8 Regency st SW1
124 L 15 Regency wlk Croy
97 X 9 Regency w Bxly Hth
24 J 19 Regent clo Harrow
15 R 17 Regent clo N12
140 C 9 Regent pl W1

90 J 14 Regent rd SE24
117 O 12 Regent rd Surb
81 U 11 Regent sq Blvdr
64 C 9 Regent sq E3
132 L 14 Regent sq WC1
128 G 14 Regent st NW10
140 B 10 Regent st W1
139 Z 4 Regent st W1
73 P 15 Regent st W4
131 T 8 Regent's Park Zoological gdns NW1
47 O 20 Regent's Park rd NW1
131 U 4 Regent's Park rd NW1
131 W 4 Regent's Park ter NW1
17 S 17 Regents av N13
157 S 13 Regents clo S Croy
11 X 14 Regents ct Edg
130 D 9 Regents ms NW8
27 V 11 Regents Park rd N3
94 E 4 Regents pl SE3
4 B 11 Regina clo Barnt
48 D 4 Regina rd N4
70 B 10 Regina rd S'hall
123 Y 6 Regina rd SE25
71 Z 3 Regina rd W13
72 A 3 Regina ter W13
52 D 19 Reginald rd E7
76 B 20 Reginald rd SE8
47 S 15 Regis rd NW5
132 C 15 Regnart bldgs NW1
79 U 10 Reidhaven rd SE18
120 B 19 Reigate av Sutton
112 D 6 Reigate rd Brom
54 J 8 Reigate rd Ilf
156 B 10 Reigate way Wallgtn
49 Y 8 Reighton rd E5
136 D 12 Relay rd W12
91 X 7 Relf rd SE15
154 G 10 Relko gdn Sutton
146 L 1 Relton ms SW7
76 H 9 Rembrandt clo E14
147 S 8 Rembrandt clo SW1
25 P 6 Rembrandt rd Edg
93 Y 11 Rembrandt rd SE13
66 C 16 Remington rd E6
31 P 18 Remington rd N15
133 Y 10 Remington st N1
141 N 4 Remnant st WC2
64 A 1 Remus rd E3
49 Y 10 Rendlesham rd E5
7 X 4 Rendlesham rd Enf
75 R 7 Renforth st SE16
66 H 19 Renfrew clo E6
82 A 5 Renfrew clo Hounsl
82 A 4 Renfrew rd Hounsl
103 U 17 Renfrew rd Kingst
149 W 6 Renfrew rd SE11
106 M 15 Renmuir st SW17
32 J 11 Renness rd E17
96 F 13 Rennets clo SE9
96 E 14 Rennets Wood rd SE9
141 V 12 Rennie st SE1
156 J 1 Renown clo Croy
38 F 4 Renown clo Rom
32 F 17 Rensburg rd E17
81 P 16 Renshaw clo Blvdr
26 M 19 Renters av NW4
27 N 19 Renters av NW4
68 E 10 Renwick rd Bark
150 H 3 Rephidim st SE1
105 W 1 Replingham rd SW18
78 G 15 Repository rd SE18
39 W 11 Repton av Rom
42 D 13 Repton av Wemb
154 H 12 Repton clo Carsh
111 S 20 Repton ct Becknhm
35 U 4 Repton ct Ilf
39 W 12 Repton dri Rom
39 W 11 Repton gdns Rom
35 U 4 Repton gro Ilf
25 N 14 Repton rd Harrow
144 M 20 Repton rd SW6
63 V 16 Repton st E14
38 F 4 Repulse clo Rom
6 G 16 Reservoir rd N14
92 H 5 Reservoir rd SE4
77 N 16 Restell clo SE3
155 P 2 Restmor way Wallgtn
138 B 20 Reston pl SW7
96 G 16 Restons cres SE9
82 H 13 Restormel clo Hounsl
47 T 6 Retcar clo N6
134 L 11 Retford st E2
20 D 9 Retingham way E4

24 F 16 Retreat clo Harrow
50 D 18 Retreat pl E9
84 G 13 Retreat rd Rich
123 N 8 Retreat the Thntn Hth
40 J 2 Retreat the Harrow
25 X 15 Retreat the NW9
92 B 3 Retreat the SE15
116 M 15 Retreat the Surb
117 N 15 Retreat the Surb
86 B 8 Retreat the SW14
152 K 4 Retreat the Worc Pk
86 L 10 Rettiward clo SW15
75 W 6 Reveley clo SE16
117 U 2 Revell rd Kingst
153 U 13 Revell rd Sutton
79 X 17 Revell ri SE18
92 H 9 Revelon rd SE4
105 X 4 Revelstoke rd SW18
114 B 2 Reventlow rd SE9
151 R 6 Reverdy rd SE1
40 K 9 Reverend clo Harrow
120 H 15 Revesby rd Carsh
69 T 4 Review rd Dgnhm
44 E 6 Review rd NW2
146 A 19 Rewell st SW6
120 F 15 Rewley rd Carsh
38 J 3 Rex clo Rom
139 U 11 Rex pl W1
34 K 17 Reydon av E11
127 V 5 Reynard clo Brom
109 T 18 Reynard dri SE19
30 M 2 Reynardson rd N17
31 N 2 Reynardson rd N17
53 X 15 Reynolds av E12
55 T 1 Reynolds av Rom
37 U 19 Reynolds av Rom
155 N 1 Reynolds clo Carsh
121 N 20 Reynolds clo Carsh
46 A 2 Reynolds clo NW11
52 C 9 Reynolds ct E11
25 O 9 Reynolds dri Edg
84 M 17 Reynolds pl Rich
77 W 19 Reynolds pl SE3
117 Z 17 Reynolds rd New Mald
92 D 12 Reynolds rd SE15
73 W 7 Reynolds rd W4
157 S 8 Reynolds way Croy
133 Z 7 Rheidol ms N1
133 Z 7 Rheidol ter N1
156 A 19 Rheingold way SM6
31 V 6 Rheola clo N17
135 O 15 Rhode st E2
29 T 5 Rhodes av N22
119 V 14 Rhodes Moorhouse ct Mrdn
48 D 16 Rhodes st N7
51 X 6 Rhodesia rd E11
63 X 15 Rhodeswell rd E14
63 X 17 Rhodeswell rd E14
63 X 9 Rhondda gro E3
59 X 6 Rhyl rd Grnfd
47 P 17 Rhyl st NW5
29 Y 1 Rhys av N11
121 P 2 Rialto rd Mitch
21 Z 17 Ribalta clo Wdfd Grn
40 L 18 Ribblesdale av Grnfd
30 C 14 Ribblesdale rd N8
107 S 14 Ribblesdale rd SW16
59 W 8 Ribchester av Nthlt
64 C 18 Ricardo st E14
105 W 12 Ricards rd SW19
03 Z 19 Rich st E14
73 U 3 Richard cotts W3
143 W 7 Richard st E1
146 M 5 Richard's pl SW3
38 L 17 Richards av Rom
23 Y 16 Richards clo Harrow
33 O 11 Richards pl E17
64 M 6 Richardson rd E15
132 A 19 Richardson's ms W1
45 R 13 Richborough rd NW2
149 P 18 Richbourne ter SW8
53 A 8 Riches rd Ilf
10 B 3 Richfield rd Bushey
10 B 4 Richfield rd Bushey
65 P 3 Richford st E14
144 B 1 Richford st W6
136 B 19 Richford st W6
74 L 7 Richford st W6
152 H 9 Richlands av Epsom
20 J 15 Richmond av E4
133 O 3 Richmond av N1
44 L 19 Richmond av NW10
119 U 2 Richmond av Mrdn
140 E 6 Richmond bldgs W1
84 G 14 Richmond br Rich
32 M 19 Richmond clo E17

250   Ric–Roc

20 K 16 Richmond cres E4
18 K 5 Richmond cres N9
10 H 20 Richmond gdns Harrow
23 V 1 Richmond gdns Harrow
26 H 15 Richmond gdns NW4
156 B 6 Richmond grn Croy
133 X 1 Richmond gro N1
116 L 15 Richmond gro Surb
84 J 15 Richmond Hill ct Rich
84 K 17 Richmond hill Rich
140 E 7 Richmond ms W1
102 K 19 Richmond Park rd Kingst
85 X 10 Richmond Park rd SW14
85 T 17 Richmond pk Rich
79 O 11 Richmond pl SE18
122 J 7 Richmond rd Thntn Hth
5 P 17 Richmond rd Barnt
5 R 17 Richmond rd Barnt
51 V 6 Richmond rd E11
20 K 5 Richmond rd E4
52 J 15 Richmond rd E7
50 A 19 Richmond rd E8
49 U 20 Richmond rd E8
54 B 9 Richmond rd Enf
83 Z 8 Richmond rd Islwth
102 J 19 Richmond rd Kingst
17 N 20 Richmond rd N11
31 R 19 Richmond rd N15
28 D 8 Richmond rd N2
118 J 1 Richmond rd SW20
84 D 19 Richmond rd Twick
72 J 4 Richmond rd W5
65 U 7 Richmond st E13
140 K 16 Richmond ter SW1
140 K 17 Richmond Terrace ms SW1
52 E 6 Richmond way E11
136 G 19 Richmond way W14
94 F 9 Richmond gdns SE3
145 U 13 Rickett st SW6
63 P 10 Rickman st E1
48 A 7 Rickthorne rd N19
95 R 10 Rickyard pth SE9
41 V 14 Ridding la Grnfd
112 L 7 Riddons rd SE12
72 C 13 Ride the Brentf
9 R 13 Ride the Enf
78 F 12 Rideout st SE18
96 G 15 Rider clo Sidcp
64 C 7 Ridgdale st E3
99 T 16 Ridge av Drtfrd
18 A 2 Ridge av N21
17 Y 2 Ridge av N21
27 P 8 Ridge clo NW4
25 Z 13 Ridge clo NW9
7 R 5 Ridge crest Enf
45 T 3 Ridge hill NW11
107 S 17 Ridge rd Mitch
18 A 4 Ridge rd N21
30 E 19 Ridge rd N8
45 W 9 Ridge rd NW2
153 U 1 Ridge rd Sutton
119 V 20 Ridge rd Sutton
98 B 18 Ridge the Bxly
117 O 12 Ridge the Surb
83 P 18 Ridge the Twick
99 T 16 Ridge way Drtfrd
100 A 7 Ridge way Felt
21 Z 15 Ridge way Wdfd Grn
94 L 9 Ridgebrook rd SE3
94 M 8 Ridgebrook rd SE3
158 G 1 Ridgemount av Croy
109 Z 17 Ridgemount clo SE20
132 E 19 Ridgemount gdns WC1
7 U 10 Ridgemount gdns Enf
4 C 20 Ridgeview clo Barnt
15 P 10 Ridgeview rd N20
5 Y 20 Ridgeway av Barnt
112 H 10 Ridgeway dri Brom
96 J 13 Ridgeway east Sidcp
35 R 14 Ridgeway gdns Ilf
17 N 8 Ridgeway N14
20 D 8 Ridgeway pk E4
71 T 20 Ridgeway rd Islwth
83 U 1 Ridgeway rd Islwth
71 T 18 Ridgeway Road north Islwth
156 C 7 Ridgeway the Croy
7 T 6 Ridgeway the Enf
24 D 20 Ridgeway the Harrow
22 J 19 Ridgeway the Harrow
40 K 2 Ridgeway the Harrow
15 Y 14 Ridgeway the N11

28 A 3 Ridgeway the N3
45 V 3 Ridgeway the NW11
14 B 16 Ridgeway the NW7
13 U 11 Ridgeway the NW7
13 V 13 Ridgeway the NW7
25 Z 14 Ridgeway the NW9
39 V 13 Ridgeway the Rom
11 R 19 Ridgeway the Stanm
73 P 7 Ridgeway the W3
96 H 12 Ridgeway west Sidcp
69 V 3 Ridgewell clo Dgnhm
12 J 14 Ridgmont gdns Edg
88 B 14 Ridgmount rd SW18
132 F 20 Ridgmount st WC1
105 O 17 Ridgway gdns SW19
105 S 16 Ridgway pl SW19
90 J 8 Ridgway rd SW9
105 N 17 Ridgway SW19
154 G 14 Ridgway the Sutton
65 Z 14 Ridgwell rd E16
140 A 2 Riding House st W1
45 V 2 Riding the NW11
7 X 15 Ridings av N21
117 R 11 Ridings the Surb
45 V 2 Ridings the Surb
60 M 11 Ridings the W5
61 N 12 Ridings the W5
8 F 4 Ridler rd Enf
72 B 8 Ridley av W13
39 Z 4 Ridley clo Rom
126 D 6 Ridley rd Brom
52 K 11 Ridley rd E7
49 U 16 Ridley rd E8
62 H 5 Ridley rd NW10
106 A 17 Ridley rd SW19
97 O 2 Ridley rd Welling
96 D 14 Riefield rd SE9
158 C 14 Riesco dri Croy
44 L 15 Riffel rd NW2
149 U 13 Rifle ct SE11
136 H 12 Rifle pl W11
64 D 15 Rifle st E14
87 U 5 Rigault rd SW6
156 F 4 Rigby clo Croy
53 X 7 Rigby ms Ilf
64 C 18 Rigden st E14
62 H 8 Rigeley rd NW10
50 G 4 Rigg appr E10
107 W 11 Riggindale rd SW16
9 R 4 Riley rd Enf
142 M 19 Riley rd SE1
146 F 16 Riley st SW10
89 R 19 Rinaldo rd SW12
112 J 17 Ring clo Brom
48 F 16 Ringcroft st N7
126 F 6 Ringer's rd Brom
87 X 15 Ringford rd SW18
87 T 3 Ringmer av SW6
48 A 7 Ringmer gdn N19
8 B 18 Ringmer pl N21
127 T 11 Ringmer way Brom
92 B 19 Ringmore rd SE23
30 D 7 Ringslade rd N22
93 S 18 Ringstead rd SE6
154 G 10 Ringstead rd Sutton
16 G 19 Ringway N11
70 B 14 Ringway S'hall
122 B 16 Ringwood av Croy
28 M 9 Ringwood av N2
104 G 3 Ringwood gdns SW15
32 K 18 Ringwood rd E17
100 H 10 Ringwood way Hampt
17 V 4 Ringwood way N21
127 T 11 Ripley clo BR1
159 U 15 Ripley clo Croy
154 C 8 Ripley gdns Sutton
85 Z 7 Ripley gdns SW14
81 P 10 Ripley rd Blvdr
65 Y 17 Ripley rd E16
7 Y 4 Ripley rd Enf
100 G 18 Ripley rd Hampt
54 J 8 Ripley rd Ilf
40 J 16 Ripon clo Nthlt
35 P 20 Ripon gdns Ilf
31 O 12 Ripon rd N17
19 N 3 Ripon rd N9
78 L 17 Ripon rd SE18
97 N 3 Rippersley rd Welling
68 C 4 Ripple rd Bark
67 P 2 Ripple rd Bark
69 N 5 Ripple rd Dgnhm
133 R 2 Ripplevale gro N1
79 X 13 Rippolson rd SE18
64 A 1 Rippoth rd E3
118 H 17 Risborough dri Worc Pk
141 Z 16 Risborough st SE1
75 P 7 Risdon st SE16

39 S 5 Rise Park blvd Rom
39 P 7 Rise Park pl Rom
39 S 2 Rise pk Rom
99 U 11 Rise the Drtfrd
34 D 15 Rise the E11
12 E 15 Rise the Edg
41 Y 15 Rise the Grnfd
17 T 14 Rise the N13
43 Z 11 Rise the NW10
13 S 20 Rise the NW7
158 C 20 Rise the S Croy
97 T 19 Rise the Sidcp
39 U 1 Risebridge chase Rom
39 U 6 Risebridge rd Rom
98 J 6 Risedale rd Bxly Hth
92 H 17 Riseldine rd SE23
141 Y 1 Rising Sun ct EC1
133 R 8 Risinghill st N1
23 T 6 Risingholme clo Harrow
23 T 6 Risingholme rd Harrow
33 X 13 Risings the E17
30 M 5 Risley av N17
31 O 5 Risley av N17
148 M 16 Rita rd SW8
149 N 17 Rita rd SW8
30 L 16 Ritches rd N15
124 A 15 Ritchie rd Croy
133 T 7 Ritchie st N1
32 H 12 Ritchings av E17
107 P 4 Ritherdon rd SW17
62 G 7 Ritson rd E8
78 J 17 River st SE18
50 C 18 Rivaz pl E9
34 B 13 Rivenhall gdns E18
17 V 9 River av N13
17 Y 3 River bank N21
76 K 6 River bank SE10
76 L 11 River bank SE10
76 H 7 River Barge clo E14
34 L 18 River clo E11
8 C 12 River front Enf
155 O 5 River gdns Carsh
124 M 1 River Grove pk Becknhm
102 H 1 River la Rich
84 H 20 River la Rich
100 J 6 River Meads av Felt
111 X 17 River Park gdns Brom
30 D 7 River Park rd N22
133 Z 1 River pl N1
68 B 14 River rd Bark
102 E 14 River reach Tedd
133 T 12 River st EC1
144 B 11 River ter W6
74 L 15 River ter W6
74 K 16 River View gdns SW13
101 W 5 River View gdns Twick
152 A 11 River way Epsom
77 O 7 River way SE10
100 J 5 River way Twick
67 Y 14 River yd Bark
74 H 12 Rivercourt rd W6
84 E 14 Riverdale gdns Twick
98 A 17 Riverdale rd Bxly
97 Z 17 Riverdale rd Bxly
81 W 14 Riverdale rd Erith
79 W 13 Riverdale rd SE18
79 W 14 Riverdale rd SE18
100 C 9 Riverdale rd Twick
84 E 15 Riverdale rd Twick
12 J 12 Riverdene Edg
53 X 10 Riverdene rd Ilf
32 E 7 Riverhead clo E17
152 A 19 Riverholme dri Epsom
102 C 14 Rivermead clo Tedd
48 K 10 Riversdale rd N5
38 F 2 Riversdale rd Rom
8 E 11 Riversfield rd Enf
116 Q 8 Riverside clo Kingst
59 U 12 Riverside clo W7
155 R 6 Riverside clo Wallgtn
120 J 11 Riverside dri Mitch
102 C 4 Riverside dri Rich
86 B 1 Riverside dri W4
73 Z 20 Riverside dri W4
8 A 10 Riverside gdns Enf
74 J 12 Riverside gdns W6
60 E 6 Riverside gdns Wemb
44 J 1 Riverside NW4
64 H 7 Riverside rd E15
31 Y 18 Riverside rd N15
115 Z 5 Riverside rd Sidcp
106 D 8 Riverside rd SW17
77 V 8 Riverside SE7

102 A 1 Riverside Twick
97 W 19 Riverside wlk Bxly Hth
83 U 7 Riverside wlk Islwth
141 N 17 Riverside wlk SE1
144 A 14 Riverview gdns SW13
73 T 18 Riverview gro W4
111 N 3 Riverview pk SE6
73 T 18 Riverview rd W4
17 U 14 Riverway N13
35 N 6 Rivington av Wdfd Grn
26 C 3 Rivington cres NW9
134 K 14 Rivington pl EC2
134 L 14 Rivington st EC2
135 T 4 Rivington wlk E8
30 K 2 Rivulet rd N17
31 N 2 Rivulet rd N17
53 R 15 Rixsen rd E12
64 B 1 Roach rd E3
51 O 20 Roach rd E3
48 B 6 Roads pl N4
76 F 18 Roan st SE10
10 M 19 Robb rd Stanm
139 T 4 Robert Adam st W1
130 D 18 Robert clo W9
75 U 19 Robert Lowe clo SE14
156 M 5 Robert st Croy
78 K 4 Robert st E16
132 A 13 Robert st NW1
131 Y 13 Robert st NW1
79 R 11 Robert st SE18
147 W 12 Robert st WC2
72 G 7 Robert's all W5
133 U 16 Robert's pl EC1
135 T 13 Robert st E22
126 L 1 Roberton dri Brom
39 Z 4 Roberts clo Rom
153 P 16 Roberts clo Sutton
147 T 2 Roberts ms SW1
81 T 14 Roberts rd Blvdr
33 R 4 Roberts rd E17
14 D 18 Roberts rd NW7
120 E 18 Robertsbridge rd Carsh
89 S 6 Robertson st SW8
38 M 1 Robin clo Rom
160 C 5 Robin ct EC2
72 D 17 Robin gro Brentf
25 O 19 Robin gro Harrow
47 O 6 Robin gro N6
113 R 14 Robin Hill dri Chisl
121 V 7 Robin Hood clo Mitch
23 V 3 Robin Hood dri Harrow
97 Z 12 Robin Hood la Bxly Hth
64 G 19 Robin Hood la E14
121 W 7 Robin Hood la Mitch
153 Y 11 Robin Hood la Sutton
104 A 11 Robin Hood la SW15
104 C 11 Robin Hood rd SW15 SW19
104 A 8 Robin Hood way SW15
41 X 17 Robin Hood way Grnfd
97 X 10 Robina clo Bxly Hth
125 V 2 Robins ct Becknhm
112 K 7 Robins ct SE12
56 D 11 Robinson rd Dgnhm
63 P 6 Robinson rd E2
106 K 16 Robinson rd SW17
147 N 13 Robinson st SW3
59 Z 15 Robinsons clo W13
103 Y 9 Robinwood pl SW15
90 E 4 Robsart st SW9
62 H 1 Robson av NW10
66 D 17 Robson clo E6
7 V 9 Robson clo Enf
108 K 7 Robson rd SE27
25 N 6 Roch av Edg
51 N 1 Rochdale rd E17
80 B 13 Rochdale rd SE2
75 Z 18 Rochdale way SE8
122 B 1 Roche dri W16
120 F 15 Roche wlk Carsh
88 E 11 Rochelle clo SW11
135 N 14 Rochelle st E2
126 J 4 Rochester av Brom
65 X 4 Rochester av E13
8 F 7 Rochester clo Enf
94 K 7 Rochester clo SE3
97 P 15 Rochester clo Sidcp
108 B 19 Rochester clo SW16

Ref	Name
98 F 15	Rochester dri Bxly Hth
157 T 5	Rochester gdns Croy
53 T 2	Rochester gdns Ilf
47 V 19	Rochester ms NW1
47 U 19	Rochester pl NW1
155 N 8	Rochester rd Carsh
47 U 19	Rochester rd NW1
148 C 5	Rochester row SW1
47 W 20	Rochester sq NW1
148 E 4	Rochester st SW1
47 U 19	Rochester ter NW1
99 O 19	Rochester way Bxly
96 C 9	Rochester Way east SE9
94 H 2	Rochester way SE3
94 K 6	Rochester way SE3
95 V 8	Rochester way SE9
37 T 14	Rochford av Rom
66 A 6	Rochford clo E6
57 Y 19	Rochford clo Hornch
121 Z 15	Rochford way Croy
85 Z 8	Rock av SW14
56 G 15	Rock gdns Dgnhm
109 U 10	Rock hill SE26
48 G 7	Rock st N4
110 E 2	Rockbourne rd SE23
92 A 17	Rockell's pl SE22
60 A 7	Rockford av Grnfd
45 O 13	Rockhall rd NW2
108 F 10	Rockhampton clo SE27
108 F 9	Rockhampton rd SE27
157 R 14	Rockhampton rd S Croy
39 Z 20	Rockingham av Hornch
86 D 11	Rockingham clo SW15
150 B 2	Rockingham st SE1
24 C 8	Rocklands dri Stanm
136 F 18	Rockley rd W14
79 Y 13	Rockmount rd SE18
86 G 8	Rocks la SW13
59 S 2	Rockware av Grnfd
109 T 11	Rockwell gdns SE19
56 G 15	Rockwell rd Dgnhm
136 C 17	Rockwood pl W12
133 Y 9	Rocliffe st N1
94 C 7	Rocque la SE3
45 W 4	Rodborough rd NW1
123 R 15	Roden gdns SE25
48 C 11	Roden st N7
53 X 9	Roden way Ilf
89 Y 14	Rodenhurst rd SW4
46 M 13	Roderick rd NW3
66 M 1	Roding av Bark
34 M 13	Roding la South Ilf
35 N 12	Roding la South Ilf
35 N 14	Roding la South Ilf
35 O 8	Roding Lane north Wdfd Grn
50 G 13	Roding rd E5
66 L 14	Roding rd E6
21 Y 19	Rodings the Wdfd Grn
139 R 2	Rodmarton st W1
14 H 15	Rodmell slope N12
77 O 14	Rodmere st SE10
90 A 20	Rodmill la SW2
118 A 10	Rodney clo New Mald
32 J 7	Rodney pl E17
150 C 5	Rodney pl SE17
106 C 20	Rodney pl SW19
34 G 13	Rodney rd E11
120 H 5	Rodney rd Mitch
118 A 10	Rodney rd New Mald
150 D 6	Rodney rd SE17
150 F 7	Rodney rd SE17
82 G 17	Rodney rd Twick
133 P 8	Rodney st N1
78 L 8	Rodney st SE18
112 H 19	Rodway rd Brom
86 G 18	Rodway rd SW15
12 B 19	Rodwell pl Edg
91 V 14	Rodwell rd SE22
25 V 12	Roe end NW9
25 T 12	Roe la NW9
156 B 14	Roe way Wallgtn
78 J 4	Roebourne way E16
18 H 20	Roebuck clo N17
21 Y 4	Roebuck la Buck Hl
9 O 4	Roedean av Enf
9 O 4	Roedean clo Enf
86 A 14	Roedean cres SW15
86 G 11	Roehampton clo SW15
114 C 16	Roehampton dri Chisl
86 B 15	Roehampton ga SW15
86 H 18	Roehampton High st SW15
86 F 11	Roehampton la SW15
104 K 1	Roehampton la SW15
104 C 6	Roehampton vale SW15
76 F 6	Roffey st E14
133 O 18	Roger st WC1
56 F 15	Rogers gdns Dgnhm
56 F 17	Rogers rd Dgnhm
65 R 18	Rogers rd E16
106 H 9	Rogers rd SW17
110 E 1	Rojack rd SE23
34 F 4	Rokeby gdns Wdfd Grn
92 L 3	Rokeby rd SE4
64 L 3	Rokeby st E15
96 F 4	Rokesby clo Welling
42 F 16	Rokesby pl Wemb
30 A 15	Rokesly av N8
146 C 9	Roland gdns SW7
63 S 13	Roland ms E1
33 W 14	Roland rd E17
150 F 12	Roland way SE17
146 C 9	Roland way SW7
37 X 12	Roles gro Rom
5 X 16	Rolfe clo Barnt
35 W 16	Roll gdns Ilf
68 F 19	Rollesby way SE28
127 Z 15	Rolleston av Brom
127 Z 10	Rolleston clo Orp
157 O 17	Rolleston rd S Croy
75 R 16	Rollins st SE15
82 H 13	Rollit cres Hounsl
48 E 14	Rollit st N7
141 S 5	Rolls bldgs EC4
20 C 18	Rolls Park av E4
20 O 17	Rolls Park rd E4
141 S 4	Rolls pas EC4
151 R 9	Rolls rd SE1
90 L 13	Rollscourt av SE24
75 X 16	Rolt st SE8
113 O 18	Rolvenden gdns Chisl
57 S 2	Rom cres Rom
32 J 10	Roma rd E17
86 H 20	Roma Road clo SW15
73 T 6	Roman clo W3
63 U 7	Roman rd E3
66 E 12	Roman rd E6
39 X 2	Roman rd Ilf
53 Z 17	Roman rd Ilf
29 R 2	Roman rd N10
74 C 10	Roman rd W4
109 P 14	Roman ri SE19
156 J 2	Roman way Croy
99 R 14	Roman way Drtfrd
8 H 16	Roman way Enf
48 C 18	Roman way N7
126 A 10	Romanhurst av Brom
125 Z 9	Romanhurst av Brom
125 Y 9	Romanhurst gdns Brom
32 G 4	Romany gdns E17
119 X 18	Romany gdns Sutton
107 O 7	Romberg rd SW17
93 T 13	Romborough gdns SE13
94 K 11	Romero sq SE9
108 D 7	Romeyn rd SW16
53 U 11	Romford rd E12
51 Z 19	Romford rd E15
52 K 16	Romford rd E7
37 Z 1	Romford rd Rom
143 U 3	Romford st E1
48 H 8	Romilly rd N4
140 G 7	Romilly st W1
109 N 8	Rommany rd SE27
40 J 1	Romney clo Harrow
31 Z 4	Romney clo N17
46 B 4	Romney clo NW11
113 O 18	Romney dri Chisl
22 H 20	Romney dri Harrow
40 J 1	Romney dri Harrow
98 C 1	Romney gdns Bxly Hth
117 Y 15	Romney rd New Mald
76 J 17	Romney rd SE10
148 H 3	Romney st SW1
108 H 1	Romola rd SE24
68 J 2	Romsey gdns Dgnhm
68 J 3	Romsey rd Dgnhm
71 Y 1	Romsey rd W13
47 N 13	Rona rd NW3
65 N 10	Ronald av E15
124 M 10	Ronald clo Becknhm
63 R 18	Ronald st E1
112 F 20	Ronalds rd Brom
48 G 15	Ronalds rd N5
96 J 15	Ronaldstone rd Sidcp
45 S 14	Rondu rd NW2
94 D 20	Ronver rd SE12
142 J 9	Rood la EC3
57 X 20	Rook clo Hornch
57 Y 20	Rook clo Hornch
17 W 8	Rookby ct N21
77 O 13	Rookel way SE10
26 D 15	Rookery clo NW9
69 V 1	Rookery cres Dgnhm
126 L 14	Rookery la Brom
127 N 14	Rookery la Brom
89 U 11	Rookery rd SW4
26 C 16	Rookery way NW9
29 U 12	Rookfield av N10
29 U 12	Rookfield clo N10
106 L 13	Rookstone rd SW17
118 F 9	Rookwood av New Mald
155 X 8	Rookwood av Wallgtn
21 O 7	Rookwood gdns E4
31 W 20	Rookwood rd N16
57 O 19	Roosevelt way Dgnhm
75 W 9	Rope st SE16
78 L 8	Rope Yard rails SE18
75 V 7	Ropemaker rd SE16
142 F 1	Ropemaker st EC2
160 F 1	Ropemakers fields E14
142 L 1	Roper la SE1
95 V 14	Roper st SE9
121 P 2	Roper way Mitch
20 G 17	Ropers av E4
146 J 16	Ropers gdns SW3
63 Y 12	Ropery st E3
135 R 10	Ropley st E2
48 K 12	Rosa Alba ms N5
144 L 19	Rosaline rd SW6
109 Z 8	Rosamond st SE26
82 B 5	Rosary clo Hounsl
146 C 8	Rosary gdns SW7
145 O 19	Rosaville rd SW6
134 C 18	Roscoe st EC1
25 T 3	Roscott clo Edg
140 C 13	Rose & Crown yd SW1
142 B 12	Rose all SE1
34 J 7	Rose av E18
120 M 1	Rose av Mitch
106 M 20	Rose av Mitch
120 D 11	Rose av Mrdn
32 L 11	Rose Bank gro E17
109 Z 17	Rose Bank st SE20
144 E 19	Rose Bank SW6
25 O 13	Rose Bates dri NW9
119 N 20	Rose end Worc Pk
58 H 11	Rose gdns S'hall
72 H 8	Rose gdns W5
25 X 12	Rose glen NW9
57 P 4	Rose glen Rom
154 B 2	Rose hill Sutton
120 B 20	Rose hill Sutton
37 Z 12	Rose la Rom
10 A 6	Rose lawn Bushey
140 J 8	Rose st WC2
117 T 10	Rose wlk Surb
159 W 2	Rose wlk W Wkhm
60 A 13	Roseacre clo W13
97 S 9	Roseacre rd Welling
41 V 13	Rosebank av Wemb
63 X 7	Rosebank gdns E3
33 P 19	Rosebank rd E17
71 U 6	Rosebank rd W7
33 O 14	Rosebank vlls E17
61 X 16	Rosebank way W3
30 J 18	Roseberry gdns N4
49 U 19	Roseberry pl E8
49 U 19	Roseberry pl E8
151 W 7	Roseberry rd SE16
118 C 5	Rosebery av New Mald
122 M 3	Rosebery av Thntn Hth
53 H 18	Rosebery av EC1
133 T 14	Rosebery av EC1
40 C 11	Rosebery av Harrow
31 Z 7	Rosebery av N17
96 H 18	Rosebery av Sidcp
119 O 15	Rosebery av Mrdn
30 A 16	Rosebery gdns N8
59 Z 17	Rosebery gdns W13
29 U 6	Rosebery ms N10
83 O 13	Rosebery rd Hounsl
117 S 4	Rosebery rd Kingst
29 U 7	Rosebery rd N10
18 K 10	Rosebery rd N9
153 V 14	Rosebery rd Sutton
90 A 16	Rosebery rd SW2
89 Z 16	Rosebery rd SW2
117 R 4	Rosebery sq Kingst
83 R 19	Rosebine av Twick
88 B 6	Rosebery rd SW6
122 C 15	Rosecourt rd Croy
45 Z 10	Rosecroft av NW3
83 R 20	Rosecroft gdns Twick
44 G 10	Rosecroft gdns NW2
58 H 12	Rosecroft rd S'hall
80 C 8	Rosedale clo SE2
11 O 20	Rosedale clo Stanm
71 V 6	Rosedale clo W7
68 C 1	Rosedale gdns Dgnhm
68 C 1	Rosedale rd Dgnhm
52 L 16	Rosedale rd E7
152 G 10	Rosedale rd Epsom
84 J 9	Rosedale rd Rich
38 L 10	Rosedale rd Rom
122 B 17	Rosedene av Croy
58 H 8	Rosedene av Grnfd
119 Y 12	Rosedene av Mrdn
108 D 7	Rosedene av SW16
35 X 12	Rosedene gdns Ilf
128 H 3	Rosedene NW6
51 R 7	Rosedene ter E10
144 F 14	Rosedew rd W6
64 A 19	Rosefield gdns E14
11 Y 18	Rosegarden clo Edg
137 U 7	Roseheart ms W11
37 W 10	Rosehatch av Rom
82 E 12	Rosehill rd Hounsl
120 C 19	Rosehill av Sutton
41 W 15	Rosehill gdns Grnfd
154 C 1	Rosehill gdns Sutton
154 C 1	Rosehill Park west Sutton
154 A 1	Rosehill pk Sutton
88 C 15	Rosehill rd SW18
31 O 2	Rosedale clo N17
48 J 13	Roseleigh av N5
84 F 17	Roselieu clo Twick
8 D 5	Rosemary av Enf
82 A 6	Rosemary av Hounsl
28 B 8	Rosemary av N3
18 M 6	Rosemary av N9
19 N 7	Rosemary av N9
39 T 10	Rosemary dri Ilf
35 O 16	Rosemary dri Ilf
56 B 4	Rosemary gdns Dgnhm
85 W 7	Rosemary la SW14
151 O 18	Rosemary rd SE15
106 B 8	Rosemary rd SW17
96 L 2	Rosemary rd Welling
134 F 3	Rosemary st N1
121 V 4	Rosemead av Mitch
42 L 16	Rosemead av Wemb
15 R 19	Rosemont av N12
117 V 6	Rosemont New Mald
46 C 17	Rosemont rd NW3
84 L 16	Rosemont rd Rich
61 S 20	Rosemont rd W3
73 T 1	Rosemont rd W3
60 L 20	Rosemoor rd Wemb
147 N 6	Rosemoor st SW3
127 U 8	Rosemount dri Brom
59 Z 16	Rosemount rd W13
12 F 11	Rosen's wlk Edg
88 K 2	Rosenau cres SW11
88 K 1	Rosenau rd SW11
90 K 19	Rosendale rd SE21
108 M 1	Rosendale rd SE21
17 V 5	Roseneath av N21
89 O 15	Roseneath rd SW11
8 C 14	Roseneath wlk Enf
93 S 17	Rosenthal rd SE6
92 E 13	Rosenthorpe rd SE15
76 G 6	Roserton st E14
124 E 14	Rosery the Croy
34 C 1	Roses the Wdfd Grn
148 K 18	Rosetta st SW8
112 L 9	Roseveare rd SE12
82 G 13	Roseville av Hounsl
118 M 1	Rosevine rd SW20
94 E 14	Roseway SE12
91 P 17	Roseway SE21
41 Y 17	Rosewood av Grnfd
57 X 15	Rosewood av Hornch
115 S 6	Rosewood clo Sidcp

155 U 13 Rosewood gdns Wallgtn
154 E 2 Rosewood gro Sutton
64 H 1 Rosher clo E15
50 E 16 Rosina st E9
87 O 7 Roskell rd SW15
73 T 8 Roslin rd W3
112 F 14 Roslin way Brom
120 F 3 Roslyn clo Mitch
39 S 7 Roslyn gdns Rom
31 P 15 Roslyn rd N15
136 M 9 Rosmead rd W11
133 V 15 Rosoman pl EC1
133 T 16 Rosoman st EC1
56 A 5 Ross av Dgnhm
14 E 17 Ross av NW7
23 N 1 Ross clo Harrow
155 T 12 Ross pde Wallgtn
99 V 17 Ross rd Drtfrd
123 S 4 Ross rd SE25
100 L 2 Ross rd Twick
155 V 12 Ross rd Wallgtn
95 R 7 Ross way SE9
39 W 19 Rossall clo Hornch
60 M 9 Rossall cres NW10
9 O 20 Rossdale dri Enf
19 O 2 Rossdale dri N9
43 U 4 Rossdale dri NW9
87 N 9 Rossdale rd SW15
154 K 9 Rossdale Sutton
94 G 1 Rosse ms SE3
132 D 2 Rossendale way NW1
82 H 12 Rossindel rd Hounsl
49 Y 6 Rossington st E5
107 T 1 Rossiter rd SW12
98 F 13 Rossland clo Bxly Hth
15 W 1 Rosslyn av Barnt
56 D 2 Rosslyn av Dgnhm
21 O 8 Rosslyn av E4
86 C 8 Rosslyn av SW13
23 W 14 Rosslyn cres Harrow
42 J 11 Rosslyn cres Wemb
23 W 14 Rosslyn Crescent south Harrow
46 H 14 Rosslyn hill NW3
46 G 14 Rosslyn Park ms NW3
54 F 20 Rosslyn rd Bark
67 S 1 Rosslyn rd Bark
33 U 14 Rosslyn rd E17
84 D 16 Rosslyn rd Twick
130 L 17 Rossmore rd NW1
131 N 16 Rossmore rd NW1
155 T 13 Rosswood gdns SM6
106 G 10 Rostella rd SW17
31 V 19 Rostrevor av N15
70 C 14 Rostrevor gdns S'hall
105 X 13 Rostrevor rd SW19
87 U 2 Rostrevor rd SW6
141 X 20 Rotary st SE1
71 Z 20 Rothbury gdns Islwth
50 M 20 Rothbury rd E9
31 Y 3 Rothbury wlk N17
155 P 10 Rotherfield rd Carsh
9 T 1 Rotherfield rd Enf
134 B 1 Rotherfield st N1
107 Y 16 Rotherhill av SW16
75 R 11 Rotherhithe New rd SE16
151 V 11 Rotherhithe New rd SE16
75 S 10 Rotherhithe Old rd SE16
75 T 2 Rotherhithe st SE16
143 X 18 Rotherhithe st SE16
75 S 1 Rotherhithe tunnel E1
156 E 12 Rothermere rd Croy
61 O 13 Rotherwick hill W5
45 X 2 Rotherwick rd NW11
87 O 7 Rotherwick rd SW15
133 X 4 Rothery st N1
41 O 18 Rothesay av Grnfd
85 S 9 Rothesay av Rich
119 T 2 Rothesay av SW20
123 P 9 Rothesay rd SE25
52 L 19 Rothsay rd E7
150 H 2 Rothsay st SE1
73 V 9 Rothschild rd W4
108 K 10 Rothschild st SE27
68 G 2 Rothwell gdns Dgnhm
68 G 3 Rothwell rd Dgnhm
131 R 3 Rothwell st NW1
76 H 8 Rotherdam dri E14
78 E 14 Rotunda clo SE18
151 S 5 Rouel rd SE16

119 X 15 Rougemont av Mrdn
124 G 17 Round gro Croy
110 B 6 Round hill SE26
127 Y 3 Round wood BR7
110 E 5 Roundhay clo SE23
7 R 3 Roundhedge way Enf
7 P 15 Roundhill dri Enf
112 D 6 Roundtable rd Brom
42 A 15 Roundtree rd Wemb
30 M 4 Roundway N17
31 O 3 Roundway N17
35 T 6 Roundway rd Ilf
62 F 2 Roundwood pk NW10
44 C 19 Roundwood rd NW10
64 B 11 Rounton rd E3
108 D 1 Roupell rd SW2
90 E 20 Roupell rd SW2
141 U 15 Roupell st SE1
132 B 1 Rousden st NW1
109 S 9 Rouse gdns SE21
88 J 19 Routh rd SW18
151 R 3 Rovel rd SE16
144 K 19 Rowallan rd SW6
19 Z 19 Rowan av E4
118 A 4 Rowan clo New Mald
121 V 1 Rowan clo SW16
72 L 6 Rowan clo W5
41 Z 10 Rowan clo Wemb
121 V 1 Rowan clo SW16
26 F 11 Rowan dri NW9
157 V 4 Rowan gdn Croy
72 B 20 Rowan rd Brentf
98 A 8 Rowan rd Bxly Hth
97 Z 8 Rowan rd Bxly Hth
121 V 2 Rowan rd SW16
144 F 6 Rowan rd W6
144 F 6 Rowan ter W6
37 U 11 Rowan way Rom
28 E 17 Rowan wlk N2
17 X 11 Rowans the N13
18 B 4 Rowantree clo N21
7 W 9 Rowantree rd Enf
18 B 4 Rowantree rd N21
15 N 5 Rowben clo N20
151 O 10 Rowcross pl SE1
151 O 9 Rowcross st SE1
58 H 2 Rowdell rd Nthlt
110 K 20 Rowden rd Becknhm
20 C 20 Rowden rd E4
89 N 4 Rowditch la SW11
44 K 20 Rowdon av NW10
159 Z 20 Rowdown cres Croy
69 O 1 Rowdowns rd Dgnhm
67 Z 7 Rowe gdns Bark
40 G 9 Rowe way Harrow
88 J 5 Rowena cres SW11
107 O 2 Rowfant rd SW17
50 A 12 Rowhill rd E5
129 Y 20 Rowington clo W2
24 E 11 Rowland av Harrow
65 O 12 Rowland ct E16
18 A 20 Rowland Hill av N17
46 J 14 Rowland Hill st NW3
106 A 20 Rowland way SW19
22 J 1 Rowlands av Pinn
29 O 19 Rowlands clo N6
26 F 2 Rowlands clo NW7
56 B 8 Rowlands rd Dgnhm
97 P 19 Rowley av Sidcp
61 N 1 Rowley clo Wemb
43 N 20 Rowley clo Wemb
48 K 1 Rowley gdns N4
30 L 16 Rowley rd N15
130 A 4 Rowley way NW8
129 Z 4 Rowley way NW8
117 O 5 Rowlls rd Kingst
55 S 18 Rowney gdns Dgnhm
55 R 18 Rowney rd Dgnhm
101 S 1 Rowntree rd Twick
64 G 2 Rowse clo E15
26 L 9 Rowsley av NW4
47 Z 16 Rowstock gdns N7
79 P 18 Rowton rd SE18
41 S 1 Rowton st SE18
71 W 19 Roxborough av Harrow
40 A 19 Roxborough av Islwth
23 S 20 Roxborough Nthlt
41 T 2 Roxborough pk Harrow
40 A 19 Roxborough pk Harrow
40 A 4 Roxbourne clo Nthlt
108 H 11 Roxbourne pk Nthlt
145 V 13 Roxburgh rd SE27
    Roxby pl SW6

40 L 7 Roxeth Green av Harrow
40 L 12 Roxeth gro Harrow
41 R 6 Roxeth hill Harrow
93 S 16 Roxley rd SE13
159 N 12 Roxton gdns Croy
68 B 7 Roxwell rd Bark
74 G 5 Roxwell rd W12
34 M 1 Roxwell way Wdfd Grn
37 S 20 Roxy av Rom
36 J 14 Roxy gro Hampt
100 K 14 Roy gro Hampt
140 B 11 Royal Academy W1
138 E 20 Royal Albert hall SW7
81 U 12 Royal Alfred home Blvdr
140 A 11 Royal arc W1
147 O 9 Royal av SW3
152 B 3 Royal av Worc Pk
84 K 5 Royal Botanic Gardens Rich
108 H 7 Royal cir SE27
152 A 3 Royal clo Worc Pk
132 C 3 Royal College st NW1
47 U 20 Royal College st NW1
136 H 15 Royal Cres ms W11
40 A 11 Royal cres Ruis
136 J 15 Royal cres W11
43 O 13 Royal ct Wemb
160 F 6 Royal Exchange bldgs EC2
141 O 14 Royal Festival Hall SE1
76 F 20 Royal hill SE10
76 G 19 Royal hill SE10
147 P 12 Royal Hospital rd SW3
78 F 14 Royal Military repository SE18
143 P 9 Royal Mint E1
143 P 9 Royal Mint st E1
76 H 16 Royal Naval College SE10
92 A 16 Royal Oak pl SE22
98 C 12 Royal Oak rd Bxly Hth
49 Y 18 Royal Oak rd E8
140 F 13 Royal Opera arc SW1
114 C 19 Royal pde Chisl
94 B 5 Royal pde SE3
60 K 10 Royal pde W5
76 G 20 Royal rd E16
65 Z 18 Royal rd E16
149 W 14 Royal rd SE17
115 W 6 Royal rd Sidcp
101 R 11 Royal rd Tedd
141 P 20 Royal rd SE1
63 T 6 Royal Victor pl E3
155 S 4 Royal wlk Wallgtn
67 X 7 Roycraft av Bark
67 X 6 Roycraft clo Bark
67 Y 6 Roycraft gdns Bark
34 H 5 Roycroft clo E18
108 F 2 Roycroft clo SW2
79 U 14 Roydene rd SE18
39 Y 17 Royle clo Rom
59 Y 12 Royle cres W13
20 C 17 Royston av E4
154 G 5 Royston av Sutton
155 Y 8 Royston av Wallgtn
35 N 19 Royston gdns Ilf
154 F 5 Royston pk Sutton
99 S 16 Royston rd Drtfrd
84 L 14 Royston rd Rich
124 F 1 Royston rd SE20
110 F 20 Royston rd SE20
63 R 8 Royston st E2
117 S 11 Roystons the Surb
89 U 6 Rozel rd SW4
110 M 5 Rubens st SE6
9 Y 11 Ruberoid rd Enf
33 O 10 Ruby rd E17
151 W 15 Ruby st SE15
151 W 13 Ruby triangle SE15
51 S 10 Ruckholt clo E10
51 P 12 Ruckholt rd E10
62 E 6 Rucklidge av NW10
46 F 12 Rudall cres NW3
79 N 11 Rudd st SE18
75 W 19 Ruddigore rd SE14
98 H 8 Rudland rd Bxly Hth
89 U 17 Rudloe rd SW12
65 R 7 Rudolph rd E13
12 H 18 Rudyard gro NW7

157 Z 15 Ruffetts clo S Croy
158 A 16 Ruffetts the S Croy
23 Z 19 Rufford clo Harrow
132 K 3 Rufford st N1
40 A 10 Rufus clo Ruis
134 J 14 Rufus st EC1
41 S 17 Rugby av Grnfd
18 G 5 Rugby av N9
42 C 14 Rugby av Wemb
23 S 14 Rugby clo Harrow
55 S 19 Rugby gdns Dgnhm
153 P 20 Rugby la Sutton
55 P 19 Rugby rd Dgnhm
25 S 12 Rugby rd NW9
83 U 15 Rugby rd Twick
73 Z 6 Rugby rd W4
133 N 19 Rugby st WC1
58 K 11 Ruislip clo Grnfd
59 P 11 Ruislip rd East Grnfd
58 L 11 Ruislip rd Grnfd
58 B 8 Ruislip rd Nthlt
106 M 9 Ruislip rd SW17
75 O 2 Rum clo E1
143 Z 10 Rum clo E1
145 Y 19 Rumbold rd SW6
100 E 15 Rumsey clo Hampt
90 D 7 Rumsley rd SW9
43 Y 6 Runbury cir NW9
136 J 9 Runcorn pl W11
26 J 17 Rundell cres NW4
41 T 10 Runnelfield Harrow
141 W 14 Running Horse yd SE1
82 L 17 Runnymede clo Twick
107 Z 20 Runnymede cres SW16
82 K 17 Runnymede gdns Twick
59 T 6 Runnymede gdns Grnfd
82 L 16 Runnymede rd Twick
106 P 20 Runnymede SW19
75 P 6 Rupack st SE16
42 K 16 Rupert av Wemb
140 F 9 Rupert ct W1
90 J 6 Rupert gdns SW9
47 Y 8 Rupert rd N19
129 R 10 Rupert rd NW6
74 B 9 Rupert rd W4
140 E 8 Rupert st W1
107 T 17 Rural way SW16
65 P 17 Ruscoe rd E16
152 F 1 Rush ct Worc Pk
56 L 3 Rush Green gdns Rom
56 K 4 Rush Green rd Rom
78 H 12 Rush Grove st SE18
89 P 8 Rush Hill rd SW11
88 N 17 Rusham rd SW12
89 N 17 Rusham rd SW12
32 M 6 Rushbrook cres E17
114 A 5 Rushbrook rd SE9
33 R 1 Rushcroft dri E4
33 R 1 Rushcroft rd E4
90 F 11 Rushcroft rd SW2
109 P 18 Rushden clo SE19
35 X 10 Rushden gdns Ilf
14 A 18 Rushden gdns NW7
15 X 3 Rushdene av Barnt
80 G 9 Rushdene SE2
120 G 19 Rushen wlk Carsh
116 A 19 Rushett clo Surb
116 A 18 Rushett rd Surb
117 X 10 Rushey clo New Mald
93 S 18 Rushey grn SE6
7 P 15 Rushey hill Enf
93 O 14 Rushey mead SE13
93 O 14 Rushey mead SE4
92 M 16 Rushford rd SE4
26 D 13 Rushgrove av NW9
157 U 8 Rushmead clo Croy
12 G 7 Rushmead clo Edg
102 B 8 Rushmead Rich
127 R 7 Rushmere clo Brom
50 E 12 Rushmore cres E5
50 C 12 Rushmore rd E5
56 E 9 Rusholme av Dgnhm
109 T 12 Rusholme gro SE19
87 R 17 Rusholme rd SW15
24 A 19 Rushout av Harrow
134 F 8 Rushton st N1
26 G 11 Rushworth av NW4
26 G 12 Rushworth gdns NW4
141 Y 18 Rushworth st SE1
53 T 17 Ruskin av E12
73 R 20 Ruskin av Rich
96 M 6 Ruskin av Welling

97 N 6 Ruskin av Welling
28 A 18 Ruskin clo NW11
97 N 6 Ruskin dri Welling
152 L 2 Ruskin dri Worc Pk
24 M 15 Ruskin gdns Harrow
25 N 13 Ruskin gdns Harrow
39 Y 4 Ruskin gdns Rom
60 F 11 Ruskin gdns W5
97 N 6 Ruskin gro Welling
81 R 11 Ruskin rd Blvdr
155 O 11 Ruskin rd Carsh
156 K 2 Ruskin rd Croy
83 V 8 Ruskin rd Islwth
31 U 4 Ruskin rd N17
58 A 20 Ruskin rd S'hall
120 F 1 Ruskin way SW18
127 T 13 Ruskin wlk Brom
18 J 8 Ruskin wlk N9
90 L 14 Ruskin wlk SE24
23 T 14 Rusland Park rd
44 M 10 Rusper clo NW2
11 S 14 Rusper clo Stanm
55 U 18 Rusper rd Dgnhm
30 L 9 Rusper rd N22
30 H 8 Russell av N22
125 S 5 Russell clo Becknhm
98 D 10 Russell clo Bxly Hth
99 W 9 Russell clo Drtfrd
61 V 1 Russell clo NW10
77 W 19 Russell clo SE7
140 B 15 Russell ct SW1
130 K 20 Russell Gardens ms W14
15 X 8 Russell gdns N20
27 T 19 Russell gdns NW11
102 C 4 Russell gdns Rich
144 L 1 Russell gdns Wemb
13 N 14 Russell gro NW7
16 A 6 Russell la N20
15 X 8 Russell la N20
23 V 3 Russell mead Harrow
148 F 9 Russell pl SW1
21 X 6 Russell rd Buck Hl
21 Y 5 Russell rd Buck Hl
33 R 20 Russell rd E10
65 U 17 Russell rd E16
32 K 11 Russell rd E17
19 X 14 Russell rd E4
8 G 3 Russell rd Enf
120 K 6 Russell rd Mitch
17 O 18 Russell rd N13
31 R 16 Russell rd N15
15 X 7 Russell rd N20
41 N 13 Russell rd Nthlt
26 E 19 Russell rd NW9
105 X 17 Russell rd SW19
83 V 17 Russell rd Twick
144 M 2 Russell rd W14
132 J 19 Russell sq WC1
140 M 8 Russell sq WC2
153 Z 11 Russell way SM1
108 C 12 Russells footpath
48 C 14 Russet cres N7
20 J 13 Russets clo E4
160 C 5 Russett ct EC2
75 W 4 Russia Dock rd SE16
63 O 6 Russia la E2
135 Z 8 Russia la E2
160 C 5 Russia row EC2
75 U 9 Russia wlk SE16
150 D 17 Russ sq SE5
73 Y 8 Rusthall av W4
124 C 13 Rusthall clo Croy
107 T 17 Rustic av SW16
42 F 11 Rustic pl Wemb
119 V 16 Rustington wlk Mrdn
117 S 17 Ruston av Surb
136 K 5 Ruston ms W11
63 Z 3 Ruston st E3
108 A 12 Rutford rd SW16
24 M 11 Ruth clo Harrow
154 F 13 Rutherford clo Sutton
148 F 4 Rutherford st SW1
10 D 5 Rutherford way Bushey
43 R 11 Rutherford way Wemb
79 Z 15 Rutherglen rd SE2
152 G 14 Rutherwyke clo Epsom
26 A 18 Ruthin clo NW9
77 T 16 Ruthin rd SE3
63 T 3 Ruthven st E9
97 N 18 Rutland av Sidcp
115 W 3 Rutland clo Bxly
85 U 7 Rutland clo SW14

106 H 16 Rutland clo SW19
119 W 15 Rutland dri Mrdn
81 U 14 Rutland ga Blvdr
126 D 9 Rutland ga Brom
138 K 19 Rutland gdns Harrow
138 L 19 Rutland Gardens ms SW7
138 K 20 Rutland Gate ms SW7
157 T 9 Rutland gdns Croy
55 S 14 Rutland gdns Dgnhm
30 J 18 Rutland gdns N4
138 L 19 Rutland gdns SW7
59 Y 15 Rutland gdns W13
144 A 10 Rutland gro W6
74 K 14 Rutland gro W6
146 K 1 Rutland Mews south SW7
146 K 1 Rutland Mews west SW7
45 N 18 Rutland pk NW2
110 M 5 Rutland pk SE6
34 J 14 Rutland rd E11
33 O 18 Rutland rd E17
53 N 20 Rutland rd E7
63 S 3 Rutland rd E9
9 N 18 Rutland rd Enf
23 N 18 Rutland rd Harrow
54 A 11 Rutland rd Ilf
53 Z 11 Rutland rd Ilf
58 G 14 Rutland rd S'hall
106 J 16 Rutland rd SW19
101 P 4 Rutland rd Twick
146 K 1 Rutland st SW7
110 M 4 Rutland wlk SE6
105 Y 20 Rutlish rd SW19
120 E 9 Rutter gdns Mitch
88 E 1 Rutts ter SE14
10 D 5 Rutts the Bushey
87 P 7 Ruvigny gdns SW15
115 X 15 Ruxley clo Sidcp
115 X 16 Ruxley corner Sidcp
94 J 10 Ryan clo SE9
91 W 18 Rycott pth SE22
94 C 4 Ryculff sq SE3
27 R 5 Rydal clo NW4
60 C 7 Rydal cres Grnfd
98 H 3 Rydal dri Bxly Hth
82 K 16 Rydal gdns Hounsl
26 B 15 Rydal gdns N15
104 A 12 Rydal gdns SW15
42 E 3 Rydal gdns Wemb
107 X 11 Rydal rd SW16
9 R 19 Rydal way Enf
84 F 15 Ryde pl Twick
112 H 13 Ryder clo Brom
140 B 13 Ryder ct SW1
66 K 17 Ryder gdns E6
57 U 18 Ryder gdns Rainhm
140 C 13 Ryder st SW1
140 C 12 Ryder yd SW1
130 A 8 Ryders ter NW8
107 T 3 Rydevale rd SW12
134 C 4 Rydon st N1
95 P 7 Rydons clo SE9
48 B 20 Rydston clo N7
98 G 15 Rye clo Bxly
92 B 11 Rye Hill pk SE15
91 X 4 Rye la SE15
92 E 12 Rye rd SE15
16 J 2 Rye the N14
12 A 19 Rye way Edg
87 P 14 Rye wlk SW15
109 S 1 Ryecotes mead SE21
35 Z 7 Ryecroft av Ilf
100 L 2 Ryecroft av Twick
82 L 20 Ryecroft av Twick
93 V 13 Ryecroft rd SE13
108 G 15 Ryecroft rd SW16
31 V 10 Ryecroft rd SW6
91 Z 16 Ryedale SE22
108 M 15 Ryefield rd SE19
105 X 6 Ryfold rd SW19
16 F 13 Ryhope rd N11
47 S 17 Ryland rd NW5
44 G 9 Rylandes rd NW2
94 J 16 Rylands cres SE12
74 D 7 Rylett cres W12
74 F 8 Rylett rd W12
18 A 11 Rylston rd N13
145 O 16 Rylston rd SW6
123 T 17 Rymer rd Croy
88 B 12 Rymer rd SW18
90 J 15 Rymer st SE24
78 J 4 Rymill st E16
139 O 20 Rysbrack st SW3

S

65 O 18 Sabbarton st E16
88 M 7 Sabine rd SW11
89 N 7 Sabine rd SW8
48 J 20 Sable st N1
50 A 6 Sach rd E5
126 E 19 Sackville av Brom
41 P 10 Sackville clo Harrow
53 T 3 Sackville gdns Ilf
153 X 17 Sackville rd Sutton
140 B 11 Sackville st W1
14 K 16 Saddlescombe way N12
120 L 3 Sadler clo Mitch
30 G 9 Sadlings the N22
112 H 4 Sadstone rd SE12
27 V 17 Saffron clo NW11
133 U 19 Saffron hill EC1
141 V 1 Saffron hill EC1
38 L 7 Saffron rd Rom
133 U 19 Saffron st EC1
66 A 18 Saigasso clo E16
149 P 4 Sail st SE11
107 P 4 Sainfoin rd SW17
109 R 12 Sainsbury rd SE19
97 O 3 St Abb's St Welling
103 N 16 St Agathas clo Kingst
63 P 4 St Agnes clo E3
149 V 15 St Agnes pl SE11
72 C 6 St Aidan's rd W13
91 Z 14 St Aidans rd SE22
66 J 9 St Alban's av E6
101 Z 12 St Alban's gdns Tedd
120 K 10 St Alban's gro Carsh
140 A 1 St Alban's gro W8
145 Z 1 St Alban's gro W8
133 V 5 St Alban's pl N1
54 K 2 St Alban's rd Ilf
62 A 3 St Alban's rd NW10
47 P 9 St Alban's rd NW5
144 K 12 St Alban's ter W6
73 Y 10 St Albans av W4
34 E 3 St Albans cres Wdfd Grn
30 F 6 St Albans cres N22
45 Y 4 St Albans la NW11
138 H 1 St Albans ms W2
34 D 3 St Albans rd Wdfd Grn
4 C 4 St Albans rd Barnt
102 K 16 St Albans rd Kingst
153 U 9 St Albans rd Sutton
140 F 12 St Albans st SW1
76 G 17 St Alfege pas SE10
78 B 15 St Alfege rd SE7
142 C 2 St Alphage gdn EC2
160 C 2 St Alphage gdn EC2
25 W 7 St Alphage rd Edgw
19 O 3 St Alphage rd N9
89 W 11 St Alphonsus rd SW4
111 O 9 St Amund's clo SE6
141 V 3 St Andrew st EC4
41 Y 12 St Andrew's av Wemb
24 E 7 St Andrew's clo Stanm
44 J 10 St Andrew's clo NW2
41 Y 11 St Andrew's clo Wemb
15 P 13 St Andrew's clo N12
49 O 4 St Andrew's gro N16
49 R 3 St Andrew's ms N16
131 X 16 St Andrew's pl NW1
44 J 19 St Andrew's rd NW10
27 W 19 St Andrew's rd NW11
154 K 4 St Andrew's rd Carsh
156 L 8 St Andrew's rd E11
65 V 10 St Andrew's rd E13
32 G 9 St Andrew's rd E17
8 C 12 St Andrew's rd Enf
53 U 1 St Andrew's rd Ilf
19 P 4 St Andrew's rd N9
43 X 5 St Andrew's rd NW9
116 G 14 St Andrew's rd W3
62 B 18 St Andrew's rd W3
116 F 14 St Andrew's sq Surb
106 C 3 St Andrews ct SE16
24 E 5 St Andrews dri Stanm
141 Y 7 St Andrews hill EC4
33 Z 19 St Andrews rd E11
63 N 4 St Andrews rd E2
39 O 18 St Andrews rd Rom

115 X 7 St Andrews rd Sidcp
144 M 12 St Andrews rd W14
71 S 5 St Andrews rd W7
136 J 6 St Andrews sq W11
31 P 18 St Ann's clo N15
88 C 15 St Ann's cres SW18
47 O 16 St Ann's gdns NW5
88 C 17 St Ann's hill SW18
88 C 17 St Ann's Park of SW18
23 U 18 St Ann's rd Harrow
30 J 16 St Ann's rd N15
18 G 7 St Ann's rd N9
86 D 3 St Ann's rd SW13
136 H 13 St Ann's rd W11
67 R 4 St Ann's st Bark
148 G 1 St Ann's st SW1
130 G 8 St Ann's ter NW8
156 K 14 St Ann's way Croy
63 Z 18 St Anne st E14
42 H 15 St Anne's rd Wemb
63 Z 18 St Anne's row E14
47 P 8 St Annes clo N6
140 E 6 St Annes ct W1
60 L 8 St Anne gdns Wemb
63 Y 19 St Annes pas E14
51 V 5 St Annes rd E11
148 G 2 St Anns la SW1
86 C 7 St Anns pas SW13
30 B 13 St Anns rd N8
136 J 14 St Anns vlls W11
130 V 7 St Anselm's pl W1
34 K 1 St Anthony's av Wdfd Grn
143 S 13 St Anthony's clo E1
106 J 4 St Anthony's clo SW17
65 U 7 St Anthony's rd E7
157 T 5 St Arvan's clo Croy
92 F 7 St Asaph rd SE4
82 G 14 St Aubyn's av Hounsl
105 U 12 St Aubyn's av SW19
109 T 16 St Aubyn's rd SE19
98 F 4 St Audrey av Bxly Hth
42 K 9 St Augustine's av Wemb
156 L 15 St Augustine's av S Croy
127 R 12 St Augustine's av Brom
60 L 7 St Augustine's av W5
81 P 9 Saint Augustine's rd Blvdr
47 Y 19 St Augustine's rd NW1
24 M 8 St Austell clo Edg
93 V 4 St Austell rd SE13
67 S 2 St Awdry's rd Bark
67 P 1 St Awdrys wlk Bark
125 T 3 St Barnabas clo Becknhm
154 F 10 St Barnabas rd Sutton
34 J 2 St Barnabas rd Wdfd Grn
21 X 20 St Barnabas rd Mitch
33 N 18 St Barnabas rd E17
107 P 18 St Barnabas rd Mitch
147 V 10 St Barnabas vlls SW8
90 A 1 St Barnabas vlls SW8
66 F 5 St Bartholomews rd E6
133 Z 19 St Barts Medical School EC1
107 P 13 St Benedicts clo SW17
106 J 4 St Benet clo SW17
120 C 18 St Benet's gro Carsh
66 B 4 St Bernard's rd E6
109 O 9 St Bernards clo SE27
157 S 7 St Bernards Croy
126 G 3 St Blaise av Brom
143 N 5 St Botolph St EC3
24 M 5 St Bride's av Edg
141 W 7 St Bride's pas EC4
141 V 5 St Bride's st EC4
106 J 4 St Catherines clo SW17
92 F 6 St Catherines dri SE14
20 B 9 St Catherines rd E4
132 M 11 St Chad's pl WC1
37 X 20 St Chad's rd Rom
132 L 12 St Chad's st WC1
55 Y 1 St Chads gdns Rom
37 W 18 St Chads pk Rom
136 K 2 St Charles pl W10

136 H 2 St Charles sq W10
128 J 20 St Charles sq W10
139 V 5 St Christopher's pl W1
83 S 2 St Christophers clo Islwth
152 J 7 St Clair dri Worc Pk
65 V 8 St Clair rd E13
35 T 7 St Claire clo Ilf
157 S 3 St Clairs rd Croy
143 N 7 St Clare st EC3
48 E 19 St Clement St N7
160 G 8 St Clement's ct EC3
141 P 6 St Clement's la WC2
109 N 8 St Cloud rd SE27
58 F 16 St Crispin's clo S'hall
133 U 20 St Cross st EC1
45 U 17 St Cuthbert's rd NW2
22 F 1 St Cuthberts gdns Pinn
106 L 10 St Cyprians's st SW17
125 S 18 St David's clo W Wkhm
43 V 10 St David's clo Wemb
24 M 4 St David's dri Edg
26 J 20 St David's pl NW4
109 N 9 St Denis rd SE27
87 W 3 St Dionis rd SW6
92 K 3 St Donatts rd SE14
61 Y 19 St Dunstan's gdns W3
153 T 11 St Dunstan's hill Sutton
125 T 13 St Dunstan's la Becknhm
123 V 8 St Dunstan's rd SE25
52 K 16 St Dunstan's rd E7
144 F 12 St Dunstan's rd W6
71 T 6 St Dunstan's rd W7
61 Y 18 St Dunstans av W3
141 L 16 St Dunstans ct EC4
142 J 10 St Dunstans hill EC3
18 J 3 St Edmund's rd N9
130 M 7 St Edmund's ter NW8
131 N 5 St Edmund's ter NW8
106 J 4 St Edmunds clo SW17
131 N 6 St Edmunds clo NW8
80 J 5 St Edmunds clo Blvdr
24 A 4 St Edmunds dri Stanm
23 Z 4 St Edmunds dri Stanm
82 K 19 St Edmunds la Twick
35 V 19 St Edmunds rd Ilf
39 O 15 St Edward's way Rom
27 X 19 St Edwards clo NW11
20 F 5 St Egberts way E4
74 E 5 St Elmo rd W12
75 U 5 St Elmos rd SE16
67 R 2 St Erkenwald rd Bark
140 E 20 St Ermins hill SW1
129 N 20 St Ervan's rd W10
137 O 1 St Ervan's rd W10
108 J 2 St Faith's rd SE21
7 Z 4 St Faiths clo Enf
93 V 20 St Fillans rd SE6
52 G 5 St Gabriel's clo E11
45 P 15 St Gabriel's rd NW2
139 Z 8 St George st W1
52 J 20 St George's av E7
47 X 11 St George's av N7
25 W 12 St George's av NW9
70 E 1 St George's av S'hall
141 W 20 St George's cir SE1
27 U 19 St George's clo NW11
148 B 9 St George's dri SW1
147 Y 7 St George's dri SW1
131 P 2 St George's ms NW1
125 P 1 St George's rd Becknhm
155 R 11 St George's rd Wallgtn
105 U 16 St George's rd SW19
27 V 18 St George's rd NW11
127 T 6 St George's rd Brom
51 U 8 St George's rd E10
52 H 19 St George's rd E7

100 A 10 St George's rd Felt
53 T 1 St George's rd Ilf
103 O 19 St George's rd Kingst
121 S 6 St George's rd Mitch
18 L 10 St George's rd N9
149 X 3 St George's rd SE1
115 X 14 St George's rd Sidcp
84 B 13 St George's rd Twick
73 Z 6 St George's rd W4
71 W 3 St George's rd W7
127 S 2 St George's Road west Brom
52 J 20 St George's sq E7
28 D 10 St George's sq SW1
148 E 11 St George's sq SW1
148 E 11 St George's Square ms SW1
150 K 15 St George's way SE15
151 O 15 St George's way SE15
148 F 13 St George's wharf SW1
156 M 4 St George's wlk Croy
138 L 7 St Georges fields W2
72 F 5 St Georges av W5
41 Z 10 St Georges clo Wemb
66 F 11 St Georges ct E6
106 F 6 St Georges gro SW17
160 H 9 St Georges la EC3
56 A 12 St Georges rd Dgnhm
55 Y 14 St Georges rd Dgnhm
8 G 3 St Georges rd Enf
17 P 9 St Georges rd N13
85 N 9 St Georges rd Rich
131 P 2 St Georges ter NW1
94 E 2 St German's pl SE3
92 J 20 St Germans rd SE23
56 H 19 St Giles av Dgnhm
56 H 19 St Giles clo Dgnhm
140 H 5 St Giles High st WC2
140 H 6 St Giles pas WC2
150 H 20 St Giles rd SE5
91 R 1 St Giles rd SE5
109 N 10 St Gothard rd SE27
109 O 9 St Gothard rd SE27
122 D 1 St Helen's cres SW16
136 G 4 St Helen's gdns W10
142 J 5 St Helen's pl EC3
122 D 2 St Helen's rd SW16
75 R 12 St Helena rd SE16
133 S 13 St Helena st WC1
35 U 19 St Helens rd Ilf
80 J 5 St Helens rd SE2
72 C 2 St Helens rd W13
72 C 13 St Helier av Mrdn
82 G 14 St Heliers av Hounsl
33 T 19 St Heliers rd E10
128 H 3 St Hildas clo NW6
74 H 16 St Hildas rd SW13
109 Z 19 St Hugh's rd SE20
39 V 12 St Ivians dri Rom
124 J 6 St James av Becknhm
71 Y 3 St James av W13
118 C 12 St James clo New Mald
106 L 3 St James clo SW17
90 G 7 St James cres SW9
136 J 13 St James gdns W11
88 M 4 St James gro SW11
140 E 11 St James mkt SW1
140 F 18 St James rd E15
107 P 19 St James rd Mitch
18 M 9 St James rd N9
115 Z 12 St James way Sidcp
60 J 1 St James' gdns Wemb
52 C 15 St James' rd E15
116 H 13 St James' rd Surb
92 J 2 St James' SE14
63 R 6 St James' s av E2
100 M 13 St James's av Hampt
15 N 11 St James's av N20
15 W 11 St James's av N20
153 X 10 St James's av Sutton
15 W 12 St James's clo N20
79 O 13 St James's clo SE18
84 J 12 St James's cott Rich
106 L 2 St James's dri SW17
29 S 12 St James's la N10
76 G 10 St James's ms E14
140 B 15 St James's pal SW1

122 L 17 St James's pk Croy
140 B 14 St James's pl SW1
154 K 5 St James's rd Carsh
123 O 19 St James's rd Croy
100 L 12 St James's rd Hampt
116 H 4 St James's rd Kingst
151 U 11 St James's rd SE1
151 T 1 St James's rd SE16
153 Y 13 St James's rd Sutton
140 D 13 St James's sq SW1
140 B 13 St James's st SW1
144 C 11 St James's st W6
74 M 14 St James's st W6
131 N 7 St James's ter NW8
131 N 6 St James's Terrace ms NW8
133 V 17 St James's wlk EC1
18 H 7 St Joans rd N9
133 W 15 St John St EC1
15 Z 18 St John's av N11
62 D 3 St John's av NW10
50 C 15 St John's av Surb E9
42 K 15 St John's clo Wemb
90 F 7 St John's cres SW9
83 V 5 St John's ct Islwth
110 C 18 St John's cts SE27
148 H 4 St John's gdns SW1
136 M 11 St John's gdns W11
137 N 11 St John's gdns W11
47 W 8 St John's gro N19
84 J 9 St John's gro Rich
88 F 11 St John's Hill gro SW11
88 G 11 St John's hill SW11
133 X 19 St John's la EC1
133 W 19 St John's pl EC1
133 X 19 St John's pth EC1
117 V 7 St John's rd New Mald
67 U 5 St John's rd Bark
154 K 5 St John's rd Carsh
156 J 5 St John's rd Croy
65 S 17 St John's rd E16
33 T 9 St John's rd E17
20 E 13 St John's rd E4
66 E 4 St John's rd E6
100 C 10 St John's rd Felt
23 V 18 St John's rd Harrow
54 G 1 St John's rd Ilf
36 H 20 St John's rd Ilf
83 W 5 St John's rd Islwth
116 E 2 St John's rd Kingst
31 R 19 St John's rd N15
84 K 10 St John's rd Rich
110 C 16 St John's rd SE20
115 P 10 St John's rd Sidcp
153 Z 3 St John's rd Sutton
88 K 10 St John's rd SW11
105 R 16 St John's rd SW11
97 P 8 St John's rd Welling
42 H 13 St John's rd Wemb
133 W 18 St John's sq EC1
8 B 1 St John's ter Enf
79 R 15 St John's ter SE18
128 H 15 St John's ter W10
93 O 4 St John's vale SE8
47 X 6 St John's vils N19
47 X 4 St John's way N19
130 G 7 St John's Wood barrack NW8
130 K 11 St John's Wood High st NW8
130 G 3 St John's Wood pk NW8
130 J 8 St John's Wood ter NW8
87 P 13 St Johns av SW15
21 X 5 St Johns ct Buck Hl
106 A 1 St Johns dri SW8
137 S 7 St Johns ms W11
77 S 20 St Johns pk SE3
27 W 19 St Johns rd NW11
70 B 8 St Johns rd S'hall
52 J 17 St Johns ter E7
130 G 14 St Johns Wood rd NW8
19 O 5 St Joseph rd N9
70 D 3 St Joseph's dri S'hall
89 S 1 St Joseph's st SW8
93 X 6 St Joseph's vale SE3
49 S 16 St Jude st N16
63 N 7 St Jude's rd E2
135 X 11 St Judes rd E2
108 F 11 St Julian's clo SW16
108 H 9 St Julian's Farm rd SE27
129 S 3 St Julians rd NW6
143 O 12 St Katharine's way E1

131 W 8 St Katherine's precinct NW1
80 J 5 St Katherines rd SE2
113 S 10 St Keverne rd SE9
71 Z 4 St Kilda rd W13
23 S 18 St Kilda's rd Harrow
49 O 4 St Kilda's rd N16
128 J 6 St Laurence's clo NW6
24 M 1 St Lawrence clo Edg
76 H 1 St Lawrence st E14
136 L 2 St Lawrence ter W10
90 G 4 St Lawrence way SW9
97 O 8 St Leonard's clo Welling
61 Z 11 St Leonard's rd NW10
64 G 18 St Leonard's rd E14
116 F 12 St Leonard's rd Surb
60 C 19 St Leonard's rd W13
108 C 18 St Leonard's wlk SW16
24 C 15 St Leonards av Harrow
20 L 18 St Leonards av E4
82 A 1 St Leonards gdns Hounsl
54 B 16 St Leonards gdns Ilf
85 U 8 St Leonards rd SW14
156 H 6 St Leonards rd Croy
47 P 18 St Leonards sq NW5
147 P 10 St Leonards ter SW3
147 O 11 St Leonards ter SW3
146 M 14 St Loo av SW3
109 N 10 St Louis rd SE27
31 T 9 St Loy's rd N17
58 Z 18 St Luke's av Enf
53 Z 15 St Luke's av Ilf
89 X 10 St Luke's av W4
102 L 20 St Luke's pas Kingst
65 P 17 St Luke's sq E16
146 K 9 St Luke's st SW3
129 O 11 St Luke's yd W9
124 A 14 St Lukes clo SE25
137 P 4 St Lukes ms W11
137 P 3 St Lukes rd W11
19 O 9 St Malo av N9
140 K 19 St Margaret st SW1
114 E 6 St Margaret's av Sidcp
40 M 8 St Margaret's av Harrow
153 S 5 St Margaret's av Sutton
30 J 13 St Margaret's av N15
15 R 6 St Margaret's av N20
86 K 13 St Margaret's cres SW15
84 B 12 St Margaret's dri Twick
84 A 15 St Margaret's gro Twick
79 O 15 St Margaret's gro SE18
83 Z 15 St Margaret's pas Twick
93 Z 9 St Margaret's pas SE13
128 A 11 St Margaret's rd NW10
84 A 13 St Margaret's rd Twick
124 F 9 St Margaret's rd Becknhm
62 L 8 St Margaret's rd NW10
52 L 7 St Margaret's rd E12
12 E 17 St Margaret's rd Edg
31 S 9 St Margaret's rd N17
92 L 11 St Margaret's rd SE4
79 P 14 St Margaret's ter SE18
67 R 3 St Margarets Bark
143 P 7 St Mark st E1
5 N 13 St Mark's clo Barnt
131 U 4 St Mark's cres NW1
63 Y 1 St Mark's ga E9
116 K 13 St Mark's hill Surb
136 L 6 St Mark's pl W11
8 H 19 St Mark's rd E9
121 N 4 St Mark's rd Mitch
123 Y 9 St Mark's rd SE25
102 B 17 St Mark's rd Tedd
128 F 20 St Mark's rd W10
136 G 2 St Mark's rd W11

71 T 5 St Mark's rd W7
49 V 15 St Mark's ri E8
131 T 5 St Mark's sq NW1
105 V 15 St Marks pl SW19
126 G 7 St Marks rd Brom
72 K 3 St Marks rd W5
66 A 7 St Martin's av E6
80 J 5 St Martin's clo Blvdr
8 M 5 St Martin's clo NW1
132 A 4 St Martin's clo NW1
140 H 9 St Martin's ct WC2
140 J 9 St Martin's la WC2
142 A 4 St Martin's le Grand EC1
140 H 11 St Martin's pl WC2
18 M 8 St Martin's rd N9
90 C 4 St Martin's rd SW9
140 G 11 St Martin's st WC2
106 C 8 St Martins la SW17
160 A 4 St Martins le Grand EC1
145 P 3 St Mary Abbot's pl W8
145 P 2 St Mary Abbots ter W14
142 J 10 St Mary at hill EC3
155 R 6 St Mary av Wallgtn
142 K 4 St Mary Axe EC3
143 Z 18 St Mary Church st SE16
18 C 9 St Mary grn N2
33 P 14 St Mary rd E17
78 H 10 St Mary rd SE18
63 T 16 St Mary's appr E12
126 A 7 St Mary's av Brom
125 Z 6 St Mary's av Brom
27 U 7 St Mary's av N3
70 K 11 St Mary's av S'hall
101 W 15 St Mary's av SW6
152 F 17 St Mary's clo Epsom
71 R 19 St Mary's cres Islwth
48 K 19 St Mary's gro N1
85 N 11 St Mary's gro Rich
86 J 8 St Mary's gro SW13
73 T 17 St Mary's gro W4
130 E 20 St Mary's mans W2
133 X 4 St Mary's pth N1
15 Y 3 St Mary's rd Barnt
51 U 8 St Mary's rd E10
54 D 8 St Mary's rd Ilf
30 B 14 St Mary's rd N8
19 O 5 St Mary's rd N9
62 C 2 St Mary's rd NW10
27 S 20 St Mary's rd NW11
92 C 5 St Mary's rd SE15
123 R 7 St Mary's rd SE25
116 E 18 St Mary's rd Surb
105 U 13 St Mary's rd SW19
72 G 5 St Mary's rd W5
152 C 3 St Mary's rd Worc Pk
138 F 1 St Mary's sq W2
75 P 5 St Marychurch st SE16
34 H 20 St Marys av E11
67 S 5 St Marys Bark
31 W 6 St Marys clo N17
26 J 11 St Marys cres NW4
66 G 10 St Marys ct E6
72 F 5 St Marys ct W5
149 U 5 St Marys gdns SE11
129 X 2 St Marys ms NW6
138 E 1 St Marys ter W2
149 U 5 St Marys wlk SE11
148 F 2 St Matthew st SW1
116 K 19 St Matthew's av Surb
127 U 6 St Matthew's dri Brom
90 E 13 St Matthew's rd SW2
135 S 15 St Matthew's row E2
72 K 3 St Matthews rd W5
26 D 15 St Matthias clo NW9
87 V 2 St Maur rd SW6
79 S 18 St Merryn clo SE18
111 N 16 St Merryn ct Becknhm
15 V 16 St Michael clo N12
43 R 17 St Michael's av Wemb
19 P 3 St Michael's av N9
127 P 6 St Michael's clo Brom
93 Z 9 St Michael's clo SE13
22 C 18 St Michael's cres Pinn
136 K 1 St Michael's gdns W10

97 P 8 St Michael's rd Welling
155 U 12 St Michael's rd Wallgtn
156 M 1 St Michael's rd Croy
122 M 20 St Michael's rd NW2
44 L 12 St Michael's rd NW2
90 C 4 St Michael's rd SW9
138 J 3 St Michaels st W2
30 B 6 St Michaels ter N22
160 E 6 St Mildred's ct EC2
94 C 19 St Mildred's rd SE12
57 X 11 St Nicholas av Hornch
107 O 13 St Nicholas glebe SW17
127 S 1 St Nicholas la Chisl
154 B 11 St Nicholas rd Sutton
79 Y 12 St Nicholas rd SE18
92 M 3 St Nicholas st SE8
154 A 10 St Nicholas way Sutton
92 J 8 St Norbert grn SE4
92 H 10 St Norbert gro SE4
92 G 12 St Norbert rd SE4
144 M 20 St Olaf's rd SW6
66 J 3 St Olave's rd E6
121 W 3 St Olave's wlk SW16
149 O 11 St Oswald's pl SE11
108 H 20 St Oswald's rd SW16
148 H 7 St Oswulf st SW1
132 J 11 St Pancras sta NW1
132 E 6 St Pancras way NW1
47 V 20 St Pancras way NW1
134 C 4 St Paul st N1
24 M 15 St Paul's av Harrow
44 M 17 St Paul's av NW2
75 U 2 St Paul's av SE16
141 Z 6 St Paul's Cathedal EC4
141 Z 6 St Paul's Church yd EC4
49 N 17 St Paul's pl N1
122 M 7 St Paul's rd Thntn Hth
67 P 3 St Paul's rd Bark
72 G 17 St Paul's rd Brentf
81 W 19 St Paul's rd Erith
48 L 17 St Paul's rd N1
49 N 18 St Paul's rd N1
84 M 8 St Paul's rd Rich
72 D 1 St Paul's rd W5
126 D 3 St Paul's sq Brom
149 Y 12 St Paul's ter SE17
64 A 14 St Paul's way E14
28 A 3 St Paul's way N3
160 A 7 St Pauls Churchyard EC4
120 H 19 St Pauls clo Carsh
82 C 6 St Pauls clo Hounsl
78 A 15 St Pauls clo SE7
114 E 20 St Pauls Cray rd Chisl
47 Y 19 St Pauls cres NW1
51 X 16 St Pauls dri E15
31 Y 3 St Pauls rd N17
63 Z 15 St Pauls way E3
160 H 7 St Peter's all EC3
33 Y 12 St Peter's av E17
18 L 14 St Peter's av N18
114 E 19 St Peter's clo Chisl
135 U 11 St Peter's clo N6
36 J 13 St Peter's clo Ilf
106 J 4 St Peter's clo SW17
27 N 15 St Peter's ct NW4
108 F 8 St Peter's gdns SE27
74 F 12 St Peter's gro W6
157 O 9 St Peter's rd Croy
117 O 4 St Peter's rd Kingst
19 O 6 St Peter's rd N9
58 G 15 St Peter's rd S'hall
84 C 12 St Peter's rd Twick
74 G 13 St Peter's rd W6
135 T 10 St Peter's sq E2
74 F 12 St Peter's sq W6
133 X 6 St Peter's st N1
157 O 12 St Peter's st S Croy
60 H 14 St Peter's way W5
10 C 5 St Peters clo Bushey
94 D 12 St Peters clo SE3
145 N 20 St Peters ter SW6
74 F 12 St Peters vills W6
137 X 9 St Petersburgh ms W2
137 X 10 St Petersburgh pl W2
49 W 19 St Philip's rd E8

116 G 14 St Philip's rd Surb
89 S 6 St Philips st SW8
134 C 5 St Philips way N1
152 J 2 St Phillip's av Worc Pk
96 L 8 St Quentin rd Welling
136 C 2 St Quintin av W10
65 V 8 St Quintin rd E13
43 X 16 St Raphaels way NW10
29 S 6 St Regis clo N10
5 U 4 St Ronans clo Barnt
34 E 2 St Ronans cres Wdfd Grn
89 U 5 St Rule st SW8
122 K 16 St Saviour's rd Croy
90 C 14 St Saviours rd SW2
47 O 18 St Silas pl NW5
87 N 13 St Simons av SW15
60 A 16 St Stephen's av W13
58 F 16 St Stephen's clo S'hall
137 V 4 St Stephen's cres W2
84 D 17 St Stephen's gdns Twick
137 U 3 St Stephen's gdns W2
137 U 3 St Stephen's ms W2
84 E 17 St Stephen's pas Twick
4 B 17 St Stephen's rd Barnt
82 H 14 St Stephen's rd Hounsl
33 S 16 St Stephen's rd E17
63 X 4 St Stephen's rd E3
9 S 1 St Stephen's rd Enf
60 C 16 St Stephen's rd W13
160 E 7 St Stephen's row EC4
33 T 17 St Stephens av E17
74 K 6 St Stephens av W12
130 K 5 St Stephens clo NW8
33 S 16 St Stephens clo E17
122 E 6 St Stephens cres Thntn Hth
87 V 12 St Stephens gdns SW15
93 U 7 St Stephens gro SE13
65 Y 1 St Stephens gro E6
149 N 20 St Stephens ter SW8
160 F 8 St Swithin's la EC4
93 W 14 St Swithun's rd SE13
98 D 19 St Thomas dr Bxly
22 C 5 St Thomas dri Pinn
54 B 17 St Thomas gdns Ilf
81 W 6 St Thomas rd Blvdr
65 S 17 St Thomas rd E16
16 L 3 St Thomas rd N14
73 U 18 St Thomas rd W4
142 F 14 St Thomas rd SE1
145 P 17 St Thomas' way SW6
47 O 17 St Thomas's gdns NW5
50 B 20 St Thomas's pl E9
62 B 3 St Thomas's rd NW10
48 G 9 St Thomas's rd E10
50 B 20 St Thomas's sq E9
22 A 17 St Ursula gro Pinn
58 H 16 St Ursula rd S'hall
82 M 17 St Vincent rd Twick
139 U 2 St Vincent st W1
5 V 17 St Wilfreds clo Barnt
102 C 14 St Winifred's rd Tedd
53 U 15 St Winifride's av E12
52 M 14 Saints dri E7
149 N 7 Salamanca pl SE1
148 N 7 Salamanca st SE1 & SE11
11 N 19 Salamond clo Stanm
119 P 19 Salcombe dri Mrdn
38 C 20 Salcombe dri Rom
13 Z 20 Salcombe gdns NW7
50 M 1 Salcombe rd E17
49 T 14 Salcombe rd N16
156 B 7 Salcott rd Croy
88 L 13 Salcott rd SW11
138 J 3 Sale pl W2
24 K 16 Salehurst clo Harrow
92 L 16 Salehurst rd SE4
156 K 6 Salem pl Croy
137 Y 8 Salem rd W2

107 X 2 Salford rd SW2
67 S 1 Salisbury av Bark
27 U 3 Salisbury av N3
153 U 15 Salisbury av Sutton
152 C 5 Salisbury clo Worc Pk
150 E 6 Salisbury clo SE17
141 V 6 Salisbury ct EC4
105 T 18 Salisbury gdns SW19
145 O 18 Salisbury ms SW6
131 P 20 Salisbury pl W1
117 Y 5 Salisbury rd New Mald
4 E 12 Salisbury rd Barnt
127 P 12 Salisbury rd Brom
98 E 20 Salisbury rd Bxly
154 M 13 Salisbury rd Carsh
56 H 19 Salisbury rd Dgnhm
51 V 7 Salisbury rd E10
53 O 14 Salisbury rd E12
72 B 6 Salisbury rd E13
33 U 16 Salisbury rd E17
20 C 11 Salisbury rd E4
52 E 18 Salisbury rd E7
9 Z 1 Salisbury rd Enf
23 R 16 Salisbury rd Harrow
54 H 6 Salisbury rd Ilf
30 G 6 Salisbury rd N22
30 K 17 Salisbury rd N4
18 J 10 Salisbury rd N9
84 K 10 Salisbury rd Rich
33 E 10 Salisbury rd Rom
70 D 11 Salisbury rd S'hall
123 Y 16 Salisbury rd SE25
105 S 18 Salisbury rd SW19
152 C 5 Salisbury rd Worc Pk
150 E 6 Salisbury row SE17
141 V 6 Salisbury sq EC4
130 H 18 Salisbury st NW8
73 W 4 Salisbury st W3
63 V 12 Salisbury wlk N19
65 R 7 Salmen rd E13
63 U 17 Salmon la E14
63 X 17 Salmon la E14
81 T 14 Salmon rd Blvdr
43 U 3 Salmon st NW9
25 V 20 Salmon st NW9
18 K 5 Salmons rd N9
65 X 14 Salomons rd E13
32 F 18 Salop rd E17
153 U 19 Saltash clo Sutton
36 D 1 Saltash rd Ilf
97 U 2 Saltash rd Welling
74 A 6 Saltcoats rd W4
43 S 4 Saltcroft clo Wemb
75 U 3 Salter rd SE16
82 Z 20 Salter st E14
62 G 11 Salter st NW10
109 N 13 Salter's rd SE19
33 X 13 Salter's rd E17
107 P 14 Salterford rd SW17
48 B 10 Salterton rd N7
90 F 11 Saltoun rd SW2
31 V 12 Saltram clo N15
129 R 12 Saltram cres W9
64 B 19 Saltwell st E14
128 M 4 Salusbury rd NW6
129 N 8 Salusbury rd NW6
106 K 12 Salvador pl SW17
59 Z 4 Salvia gdns Grnfd
87 O 8 Salvin rd SW15
51 Y 19 Salway clo Wdfd Grn
51 X 19 Salway rd E15
77 Z 13 Sam Bartram clo SE7
130 H 18 Samford st NW8
93 O 19 Samos clo SE3
124 A 3 Samos rd SE20
4 C 18 Sampson av Barnt
80 J 10 Sampson clo Blvdr
143 U 14 Sampson st E1
65 X 7 Samson st E13
135 R 5 Samuel clo E8
108 E 9 Samuel Johnson clo SW16
78 K 10 Samuel st SE18
44 K 11 Sancroft clo NW2
23 X 8 Sancroft rd Harrow
149 P 8 Sancroft st SE11
142 B 18 Sanctuary st SE1
97 V 17 Sanctuary the Bxly
88 B 1 Sand's End la SW6
18 K 18 Sandal rd N18
117 Z 10 Sandal rd New Mald
64 L 3 Sandal st E15
49 O 10 Sandale clo N16
60 K 11 Sandall clo W5
47 W 18 Sandall rd NW5

60 J 11 Sandall rd W5
63 V 12 Sandalwood clo E1
119 Z 4 Sandbourne av SW19
92 H 4 Sandbourne rd SE4
12 M 18 Sandbrook clo NW7
49 R 10 Sandbrook rd N16
95 R 8 Sandby grn SE9
81 Z 12 Sandcliff rd Erith
141 T 16 Sandell st SE1
26 M 1 Sanders la NW7
27 O 1 Sanders la NW7
47 Z 5 Sanders way N19
47 R 14 Sanderson clo NW5
59 Z 4 Sanderson cres Grnfd
45 S 8 Sanderstead av NW2
89 V 18 Sanderstead rd SW12
157 O 18 Sanderstead rd S Croy
50 J 3 Sanderstead rd E10
42 A 15 Sanderton rd Wemb
122 K 6 Sandfield gdns Thntn Hth
122 K 6 Sandfield rd Thntn Hth
30 L 3 Sandford av N22
66 F 11 Sandford clo E6
49 R 3 Sandford ct N16
126 F 8 Sandford rd Brom
97 Z 9 Sandford rd Bxly Hth
66 F 9 Sandford rd E6
146 A 20 Sandford rd SW6
150 F 9 Sandford row SE17
75 U 17 Sandford wlk SE14
80 F 18 Sandgate rd Welling
151 V 13 Sandgate st SE15
155 Y 7 Sandhills Wallgtn
22 L 19 Sandhurst av Harrow
117 S 17 Sandhurst av Surb
25 O 10 Sandhurst clo NW9
157 T 18 Sandhurst clo S Croy
54 L 13 Sandhurst dri Ilf
97 V 14 Sandhurst rd Bxly
9 R 20 Sandhurst rd Enf
19 S 1 Sandhurst rd N9
25 P 11 Sandhurst rd NW9
111 X 1 Sandhurst rd SE6
114 M 7 Sandhurst rd Sidcp
157 T 18 Sandhurst way S Croy
153 U 3 Sandiford rd Sutton
157 X 3 Sandilands Croy
88 A 3 Sandilands rd SW6
91 W 6 Sandison st SE15
141 O 2 Sandland st WC1
113 V 7 Sandling ri SE9
30 G 9 Sandlings the N22
90 A 10 Sandmere rd SW4
89 Z 9 Sandmere rd SW4
56 J 18 Sandown av Dgnhm
155 N 19 Sandown dri Carsh
124 A 11 Sandown rd SE25
123 Z 11 Sandown rd SE25
40 C 17 Sandown way Nthlt
111 Y 13 Sandpit rd Brom
158 F 7 Sandpits rd Croy
102 H 3 Sandpits rd Rich
82 K 14 Sandra clo Hounsl
23 U 12 Sandridge clo Harrow
119 T 2 Sandringham av SW20
8 E 8 Sandringham clo Enf
36 C 10 Sandringham clo Ilf
40 H 8 Sandringham cres Harrow
96 H 4 Sandringham dri Welling
30 B 19 Sandringham gdns N8
36 C 10 Sandringham gdns Ilf
15 T 19 Sandringham gdns N12
112 F 13 Sandringham rd Brom
40 H 20 Sandringham rd Nthlt
152 H 5 Sandringham rd Worc Pk
44 J 17 Sandringham rd NW2
45 S 2 Sandringham rd NW11
54 L 16 Sandringham rd Bark
122 M 12 Sandringham rd Croy
33 X 19 Sandringham rd E10
52 K 16 Sandringham rd E7
49 X 15 Sandringham rd E8
30 L 9 Sandringham rd N22

158 F 8 Sandrock pl Croy
93 P 7 Sandrock rd SE13
78 C 10 Sands st SE18
47 T 7 Sandstone pl N19
77 V 16 Sandtoft rd SE7
45 Y 17 Sandwell cres NW6
132 J 14 Sandwich st WC1
78 L 15 Sandy Hill rd SE18
78 L 13 Sandy Hill rd SE18
155 V 19 Sandy Hill rd Wallgtn
121 P 1 Sandy la Mitch
155 Z 11 Sandy la North Wallgtn
115 X 18 Sandy la Orp
102 E 5 Sandy la Rich
155 X 13 Sandy la South Wallgtn
153 T 18 Sandy la Sutton
102 A 19 Sandy la Tedd
101 Y 17 Sandy la Tedd
46 B 6 Sandy rd NW3
113 V 15 Sandy ridge Chisl
158 K 5 Sandy way Croy
84 C 17 Sandycombe rd Twick
85 O 8 Sandycombe rd Rich
79 Z 16 Sandycroft SE2
53 Y 13 Sandyhill rd Ilf
11 T 17 Sandymount av Stanm
142 L 1 Sandys row E1
49 U 8 Sanford la N16
75 U 16 Sanford st SE14
49 V 8 Sanford ter N16
123 T 8 Sangley rd SE25
93 R 20 Sangley rd SE6
111 U 1 Sangley rd SE6
88 G 11 Sangora rd SW11
133 V 16 Sans wlk EC1
52 B 7 Sansom rd E11
52 B 8 Sansom rd E11
150 F 20 Sansom st SE5
91 P 1 Sansom st SE5
66 A 17 Santana clo E16
90 B 10 Santley st SW4
87 X 13 Santos rd SW18
10 E 17 Santway the Stanm
66 H 17 Sapphire clo E6
75 W 12 Sapphire rd SE8
64 B 18 Saracen st E14
142 M 7 Saracen's Head yd EC3
134 K 12 Sarah st N1
50 C 11 Saratoga rd E5
141 O 5 Sardinia st WC2
23 O 7 Sarita clo Harrow
105 R 5 Sarjant clo SW19
70 H 20 Sark clo Hounsl
65 V 16 Sark wlk E16
8 A 13 Sarnesfield rd Enf
45 V 14 Sarre rd NW2
82 F 4 Sarsen av Hounsl
106 M 2 Sarsfeld rd SW12
107 N 2 Sarsfeld rd SW12
60 C 5 Sarsfeld rd Grnfd
26 D 4 Satchell mead NW9
135 R 14 Satchwell rd E2
135 R 14 Satchwell st E2
92 E 11 Sator rd SE15
24 A 9 Sauls Green E11
100 L 13 Saunders clo Hampt
76 J 12 Saunders Ness rd E14
79 X 13 Saunders rd SE18
68 D 20 Saunders way SE28
42 B 15 Saunderton gdns Wemb
57 V 7 Saunton rd Hornch
66 H 18 Savage gdns E6
142 M 9 Savage gdns EC3
18 K 1 Savernake rd N9
47 N 12 Savernake rd NW3
118 B 12 Savile clo New Mald
157 V 3 Savile gdns Croy
140 A 10 Savile row W1
118 H 5 Savile gdns New Mald
21 R 18 Savill row Wdfd Grn
78 D 3 Saville rd E16
38 B 20 Saville rd Rom
101 V 2 Saville rd Twick
73 X 8 Saville rd W4
9 S 10 Saville row Enf
140 A 10 Saville row W1
105 R 17 Savona clo SW19
148 A 19 Savona st SW8
140 M 9 Savoy bldgs WC2
12 B 16 Savoy clo Edg
141 N 10 Savoy hill WC2
140 M 11 Savoy pl WC2

141 N 11 Savoy pl WC2
141 N 10 Savoy row WC2
141 N 10 Savoy st WC2
141 N 10 Savoy steps WC2
140 M 10 Savoy way WC2
105 R 4 Sawkin clo SW19
74 F 2 Sawley rd W12
120 H 17 Sawtry clo Carsh
142 A 17 Sawyer st SE1
141 Z 16 Sawyer st SE1
56 J 18 Sawyers clo Dgnhm
59 Y 18 Sawyers lawn W13
90 A 17 Saxby rd SW2
67 V 5 Saxham rd Berk
20 L 11 Saxlingham rd E4
115 T 14 Saxon and Mallard wlk Sidcp
100 G 6 Saxon av Felt
61 T 15 Saxon dri W3
58 C 20 Saxon gdns S'hall
100 E 4 Saxon ho Felt
112 D 18 Saxon rd Brom
63 X 7 Saxon rd E3
66 F 12 Saxon rd E6
54 A 17 Saxon rd Ilf
53 Z 17 Saxon rd Ilf
30 J 4 Saxon rd N22
70 C 1 Saxon rd S'hall
123 O 12 Saxon rd SE25
43 U 9 Saxon rd Wemb
6 J 19 Saxon way N14
120 F 6 Saxonbury clo Mitch
116 E 20 Saxonbury gdns Surb
93 X 9 Saxton clo SE13
150 A 4 Sayer st SE17
84 M 18 Sayers wlk Rich
75 Z 15 Sayes Court st SE8
114 L 16 Scadbury pk Chisl
140 D 1 Scala st W1
31 W 10 Scales rd N17
136 G 5 Scamps ms W10
143 W 14 Scandrett st E1
48 G 3 Scarborough rd N4
19 P 2 Scarborough rd N9
143 P 7 Scarborough st E1
156 L 5 Scarbrook rd Croy
42 H 18 Scarle rd Wemb
111 Y 6 Scarlet rd SE6
95 O 7 Scarsbrook rd SE3
145 X 1 Scarsdale pl W8
40 M 11 Scarsdale rd Harrow
145 U 3 Scarsdale vlls W8
86 F 7 Scarth rd SW13
75 V 13 Scawen rd SE8
135 P 9 Scawfell st E2
14 K 14 Scaynes link N12
63 P 9 Sceptre rd E2
20 J 6 Scholar's rd E4
107 U 2 Scholar's rd SW12
47 Y 6 Scholefield rd N19
63 S 19 School House la E1
116 D 1 School la Kingst
22 B 12 School la Pinn
97 S 7 School la Welling
70 F 1 School pass S'hall
63 N 12 School pl E1
100 M 14 School Rd av Hampt
114 C 19 School rd Chisl
69 T 3 School rd Dgnhm
53 T 13 School rd E12
100 M 14 School rd Hampt
83 N 8 School rd Hounsl
116 E 1 School rd Kingst
31 P 19 School rd N15
61 Z 12 School rd NW10
15 U 19 School way N12
63 W 7 Schoolbell ms E3
102 C 19 Schoolhouse la Tedd
76 G 13 Schooner st E14
87 V 13 Schubert rd SW15
146 G 2 Science museum SW7
135 O 17 Sclater st E1
49 V 12 Scoble pl N16
108 G 1 Scoles cres SW2
141 X 15 Scoresby st SE1
59 Y 6 Scorton av Grnfd
22 A 2 Scot gro Pinn
60 A 13 Scotch comm W13
59 Z 13 Scotch comm W13
34 J 1 Scoter clo Wdfd Grn
9 T 17 Scotland Green rd Enf
9 U 15 Scotland Green Road north Enf
31 V 7 Scotland grn N17
140 K 14 Scotland pl SW1
21 Y 6 Scotland rd Buck Hl

153 T 15 Scotsdale clo Sutton
94 J 15 Scotsdale rd SE12
133 V 16 Scotswood st EC1
31 Y 1 Scotswood wlk N17
122 B 1 Scott clo SW16
99 T 2 Scott cres Erith
40 J 5 Scott cres Harrow
130 E 14 Scott Ellis gdns NW8
143 T 20 Scott Lidgett cres SE16
51 T 5 Scott's rd E10
136 A 18 Scott's rd W12
74 K 6 Scott's rd W12
55 W 3 Scotts la Dgnhm
125 Y 3 Scotts av Brom
100 K 17 Scotts dri Hampt
125 W 7 Scotts la Brom
112 E 19 Scotts rd Brom
65 R 17 Scoulding rd E16
64 H 20 Scouler st E14
64 J 20 Scouler st E14
54 D 8 Scout la SW4
12 M 13 Scout way NW7
53 Z 10 Scrafton rd Ilf
68 J 5 Scrattons ter Bark
135 P 3 Scriven st E8
33 R 17 Scrooby st SE6
62 H 10 Scrubs la NW10
89 X 19 Scrutton clo SW12
134 J 17 Scrutton st EC2
25 U 12 Scudamore la NW9
92 B 14 Scutari rd SE22
91 Y 7 Scylla rd SE15
159 Z 3 Seabrook dri W Wkhm
56 E 2 Seabrook gdns Rom
59 V 5 Seabrook rd Dgnhm
141 X 5 Seacoal la EC4
80 H 5 Seacourt rd SE2
16 K 15 Seafield rd N11
33 R 11 Seaford rd E17
8 F 14 Seaford rd Enf
31 P 14 Seaford rd N15
72 A 3 Seaford rd W13
132 M 14 Seaford st WC1
118 K 9 Seaforth av New Mald
39 R 1 Seaforth clo Rom
48 L 15 Seaforth cres N5
152 D 9 Seaforth gdns Epsom
17 S 4 Seaforth gdns N21
21 Y 17 Seaforth gdns Wdfd Grn
63 Y 14 Seager pl E3
145 U 3 Seagrave rd SW6
34 F 20 Seagry rd E11
49 V 13 Seal st E8
48 D 4 Searle pl N4
146 L 20 Searles clo SW11
150 F 4 Searles rd SE1
150 E 18 Sears st SE5
54 J 14 Seaton av Ilf
65 T 13 Seaton clo E13
86 K 20 Seaton clo SW15
83 P 16 Seaton clo Twick
99 W 19 Seaton rd Drtfrd
120 J 4 Seaton rd Mitch
83 O 16 Seaton rd Twick
96 H 2 Seaton rd Welling
60 J 5 Seaton rd Wemb
18 L 17 Seaton st N18
133 X 14 Sebastian st EC1
18 K 12 Sebastopol rd N9
133 X 1 Sebbon st N1
52 L 13 Sebert rd E7
135 U 9 Sebright pas E2
4 D 10 Sebright rd Barnt
22 M 6 Secker cres Harrow
141 S 15 Secker st SE1
69 V 5 Second av Dgnhm
53 S 14 Second av E12
65 T 9 Second av E13
33 P 15 Second av E17
8 G 17 Second av E17
19 P 13 Second av N18
27 O 12 Second av NW4
37 T 15 Second av Rom
86 A 6 Second av SW14
129 N 15 Second av W10
74 D 3 Second av W3
42 G 6 Second av Wemb
101 S 3 Second Cross rd Twick
43 T 13 Second way Wemb
150 H 9 Sedan way SE17
51 T 6 Sedcote rd Enf
147 S 6 Sedding st SW1
120 G 12 Seddon rd Mrdn
133 O 14 Seddon st WC1
95 O 6 Sedgebrook rd SE3
```
```

24 E 16 Sedgecombe av Harrow
74 E 2 Sedgeford rd W12
111 R 12 Sedgehill rd SE6
28 D 10 Sedgemere av N2
80 G 9 Sedgemere rd SE2
56 E 11 Sedgemoor dri Dgnhm
150 J 20 Sedgemoor pl SE5
112 B 2 Sedgeway SE6
126 C 16 Sedgewood clo Brom
51 T 7 Sedgwick rd E10
50 F 16 Sedgwick st E9
87 W 15 Sedleigh rd SW18
145 S 14 Sedlescombe rd SW6
139 X 7 Sedley pl W1
109 T 9 Seeley dri SE21
44 F 2 Seelig av NW9
107 N 14 Seely rd SW17
142 L 9 Seething la EC3
116 E 15 Seething Wells la Surb
23 R 5 Sefton av Harrow
12 K 18 Sefton av NW7
157 Y 1 Sefton rd Croy
123 Y 20 Sefton rd Croy
86 M 6 Sefton st SW15
92 H 20 Segal clo SE23
133 W 16 Sekforde st EC1
44 D 15 Selbie av NW10
115 Y 1 Selborne av Bxly
53 W 11 Selborne av E12
59 Y 5 Selborne gdns Grnfd
26 G 13 Selborne gdns NW4
118 A 3 Selborne rd New Mald
167 T 7 Selborne rd Croy
32 M 15 Selborne rd E17
33 O 14 Selborne rd E17
53 W 8 Selborne rd IIf
16 M 10 Selborne rd N14
17 O 10 Selborne rd N14
30 C 5 Selborne rd N22
115 R 10 Selborne rd Sidcp
113 W 14 Selby clo Chisl
66 D 16 Selby clo E6
58 H 12 Selby gdns S'hall
120 K 16 Selby grn Carsh
120 J 16 Selby rd Carsh
52 A 10 Selby rd E11
51 Z 10 Selby rd E11
65 V 14 Selby rd E13
18 D 20 Selby rd N17
31 R 1 Selby rd N17
123 Y 3 Selby rd SE20
60 C 12 Selby rd W5
135 U 18 Selby st E1
92 D 5 Selden rd SE15
123 R 14 Selhurst New rd SE25
123 R 15 Selhurst pl SE25
18 C 11 Selhurst rd N9
123 S 11 Selhurst rd SE25
56 A 2 Selina la Dgnhm
99 S 2 Selkirk dri Erith
106 K 10 Selkirk rd SW17
100 M 3 Selkirk rd Twick
101 N 2 Selkirk rd Twick
27 X 3 Sellers Hall clo N3
106 K 13 Sellincourt rd SW17
110 M 19 Sellindge clo Becknhm
149 O 7 Sellon ms SE11
62 E 4 Sellons av NW10
4 C 17 Sellwood dr Barnt
132 C 5 Selous st NW1
157 O 13 Selsdon av S Croy
38 J 4 Selsdon clo Rom
116 K 12 Selsdon clo Surb
158 G 19 Selsdon Park rd S Croy
34 E 20 Selsdon rd E11
65 Y 6 Selsdon rd E13
65 Y 4 Selsdon rd E6
44 F 8 Selsdon rd NW2
157 O 12 Selsdon rd S Croy
108 H 8 Selsdon rd SE27
49 T 15 Selsea pl N16
97 V 2 Selsey cres Welling
49 T 15 Selsey pl N16
64 A 15 Selsey st E14
12 K 14 Selvage la NW7
146 E 9 Selwood pl SW7
124 A 20 Selwood rd Croy
157 Z 1 Selwood rd Croy
119 V 19 Selwood rd Sutton
146 F 10 Selwood ter SW7
34 E 17 Selworthy clo E11
110 K 7 Selworthy rd SE6

20 H 19 Selwyn av E4
36 J 18 Selwyn av IIf
84 L 8 Selwyn av Rich
82 B 9 Selwyn clo Hounsl
97 O 9 Selwyn cres Welling
25 R 3 Selwyn ct Edg
65 U 4 Selwyn rd E13
63 X 7 Selwyn rd E3
117 Y 11 Selwyn rd New Mald
43 Z 20 Selwyn rd NW10
147 W 7 Semley pl SW1
122 C 2 Semley rd SW16
92 D 6 Senate st SE5
90 A 10 Seneca rd SW4
122 L 9 Seneca rd Thntn Hth
121 P 20 Senga rd Wallgtn
153 N 6 Senhouse rd Sutton
129 Y 20 Senior st W2
112 H 2 Senlac rd SE12
18 F 2 Sennen rd Enf
113 R 7 Sennen wlk SE9
63 S 17 Senrab st E1
27 N 14 Sentinel sq NW4
11 P 19 September way Stanm
10 B 6 Sequoia clo Bushey
51 V 2 Serbin clo E10
141 P 5 Serle st WC2
141 Z 7 Sermon la EC4
113 N 19 Serviden dri Chisl
151 N 5 Setchell rd SE1
150 M 5 Setchell way SE1
75 R 6 Seth st SE16
68 G 1 Seton gdns Dgnhm
65 R 7 Settle rd E13
143 U 4 Settles st E1
87 Z 6 Settrington rd SW6
36 L 19 Seven Kings pk IIf
56 J 6 Seven Kings rd IIf
31 P 18 Seven Sisters rd N15
48 J 5 Seven Sisters rd N4
48 D 9 Seven Sisters rd N7
63 N 20 Seven Star all E1
98 H 11 Sevenoaks clo Bxly Hth
92 K 15 Sevenoaks rd SE4
115 S 19 Sevenoaks way Sidcp
53 U 12 Seventh av E12
39 Z 9 Severn av Rom
8 L 2 Severn dri Enf
44 C 15 Severn way NW10
88 J 10 Severus rd SW11
139 P 18 Seville st SW1
26 H 19 Sevington rd NW4
129 W 18 Sevington st W9
124 F 3 Seward rd Becknhm
71 Y 5 Seward rd W7
134 A 14 Seward st EC1
133 Z 15 Seward st EC1
63 R 5 Sewardstone rd E2
20 C 1 Sewardstone rd E4
50 E 11 Sewdley st E5
80 B 6 Sewell rd SE2
65 T 9 Sewell st E13
76 J 10 Sextant av E14
39 O 10 Seymer rd Rom
152 K 20 Seymour av Epsom
119 P 17 Seymour av Mrdn
31 W 7 Seymour av N17
21 P 8 Seymour ct E4
44 H 7 Seymour ct NW2
127 U 20 Seymour dri BR2
53 T 4 Seymour gdns IIf
117 N 12 Seymour gdns Surb
84 A 19 Seymour gdns Twick
139 N 3 Seymour hall W1
139 T 5 Seymour ms W1
123 Z 9 Seymour pl SE25
139 N 4 Seymour pl W1
155 O 11 Seymour rd Carsh
50 L 4 Seymour rd E10
20 D 4 Seymour rd E4
66 A 5 Seymour rd E6
101 N 11 Seymour rd Hampt
116 F 1 Seymour rd Kingst
102 F 20 Seymour rd Kingst
121 O 18 Seymour rd Mitch
28 B 2 Seymour rd N3
30 H 16 Seymour rd N8
19 N 9 Seymour rd N9
87 W 17 Seymour rd SW18
105 P 5 Seymour rd SW19
73 W 9 Seymour rd W4
139 R 6 Seymour st W1
123 Z 1 Seymour ter SE20
123 Z 1 Seymour ter SE20
146 C 13 Seymour wlk SW10
76 H 11 Seyssel st E14
73 Z 1 Shaa rd W3

101 U 10 Shacklegate la Tedd
58 F 20 Shackleton rd S'hall
49 V 13 Shacklewell grn E8
49 V 13 Shacklewell la E8
49 U 12 Shacklewell rd N16
49 U 13 Shacklewell row E8
135 P 15 Shacklewell st E2
143 P 18 Shad Thames SE1
152 D 3 Shadbolt clo Worc Pk
58 E 7 Shadwell dri Nthlt
63 O 19 Shadwell pl E1
143 Z 7 Shadwell pl E1
10 A 2 Shadybush clo
101 Z 17 Shaef way Tedd
56 J 17 Shafter rd Dgnhm
24 H 19 Shaftesbury av Harrow
42 J 1 Shaftesbury av Harrow
40 M 3 Shaftesbury av Harrow
41 O 6 Shaftesbury av Harrow
5 P 13 Shaftesbury av Barnt
9 S 9 Shaftesbury av Enf
70 H 9 Shaftesbury av S'hall
140 E 10 Shaftesbury av W1
145 U 4 Shaftesbury ms W8
124 M 4 Shaftesbury rd Becknhm
120 H 16 Shaftesbury rd Carsh
51 O 5 Shaftesbury rd E10
33 R 17 Shaftesbury rd E17
20 K 5 Shaftesbury rd E4
52 M 20 Shaftesbury rd E7
65 X 1 Shaftesbury rd E7
73 R 17 Shaftesbury rd N18
48 A 3 Shaftesbury rd N19
84 J 9 Shaftesbury rd Rich
39 U 17 Shaftesbury rd Rom
134 D 9 Shaftesbury rd N1
101 S 7 Shaftesbury way Twick
67 O 5 Shaftesburys the Bark
147 O 3 Shafto ms SW1
63 T 3 Shafton pl E9
61 X 3 Shakespeare av NW10
16 H 16 Shakespeare av N11
25 O 20 Shakespeare clo Harrow
53 T 19 Shakespeare cres E12
61 Y 3 Shakespeare cres NW10
25 O 20 Shakespeare ct Harrow
25 N 20 Shakespeare dri Harrow
28 M 13 Shakespeare gdns N2
90 J 10 Shakespeare rd SE24
97 Y 2 Shakespeare rd Bxly Hth
32 G 8 Shakespeare rd E17
13 T 14 Shakespeare rd NW7
39 U 18 Shakespeare rd Rom
73 W 1 Shakespeare rd W3
59 W 19 Shakespeare rd W7
49 R 12 Shakespeare wlk N16
146 D 16 Shalcomb st SW10
119 S 11 Shaldon dri Mrdn
24 M 7 Shaldon rd Edg
136 F 8 Shallfleet dri W10
61 U 19 Shalimar gdns W3
61 U 19 Shalimar rd W3
113 Y 9 Shallons rd SE9
116 L 15 Shalston vlls Surb
85 T 7 Shalstone rd SW14
122 C 13 Shamrock rd Croy
89 W 7 Shamrock st SW4
16 E 5 Shamrock way N14
142 K 16 Shand st SE1
89 V 15 Shandon rd SW4
63 T 13 Shandy st E1
31 X 13 Shanklin rd N15
29 Y 17 Shanklin rd N8
70 A 14 Shannon clo S'hall
90 D 10 Shannon gro SW9
130 L 8 Shannon pl NW8
120 L 19 Shap cres Carsh
135 N 8 Shap st E2
151 U 14 Shard's sq SE15
90 K 13 Shardcroft av SE24
92 K 3 Shardeloes rd SE14
114 M 10 Sharman st Sidcp
64 C 15 Sharman st E14

97 T 8 Sharnbrooke clo Welling
116 E 19 Sharon clo Surb
63 P 3 Sharon gdns E9
9 V 8 Sharon rd Enf
73 Y 13 Sharon rd W4
131 R 2 Sharpleshall st NW1
75 P 16 Sharratt st SE15
149 W 11 Sharsted st SE17
140 F 10 Shaver's pl SW1
68 L 6 Shaw av Bark
10 D 8 Shaw clo Bushey
80 E 3 Shaw clo SE28
68 L 6 Shaw gdns Bark
112 B 8 Shaw rd Brom
9 S 6 Shaw rd Enf
32 J 5 Shaw sq E17
155 Z 15 Shaw way Wallgtn
94 M 13 Shawbrooke rd SE9
95 N 11 Shawbrooke rd SE9
91 V 12 Shawbury rd SE22
127 O 2 Shawfield pk Brom
146 M 11 Shawfield st SW3
86 H 19 Shawford ct SW15
159 V 20 Shaxton cres Croy
48 A 17 Shearling way N7
94 B 9 Shearman rd SE3
99 V 7 Shearwood cres Drtfrd
26 B 13 Sheaveshill av NW9
135 P 18 Sheba st E1
85 R 12 Sheen Common dri Rich
85 R 10 Sheen Court rd Rich
85 V 10 Sheen Gate gdns SW14
133 R 4 Sheen gro N1
85 W 7 Sheen la SW14
84 L 11 Sheen pk Rich
84 K 12 Sheen rd Rich
85 P 12 Sheen rd Rich
156 C 10 Sheen way Wallgtn
85 V 13 Sheen wood SW14
84 M 9 Sheendale rd Rich
110 A 11 Sheenewood SE26
135 W 5 Sheep la E8
88 M 5 Sheepcote la SW11
89 N 5 Sheepcote la SW11
23 W 18 Sheepcote rd Harrow
37 X 13 Sheepcotes rd Rom
118 A 18 Sheephouse way New Mald
117 Z 18 Sheephouse way New Mald
66 A 14 Sheerwater rd E16
63 Z 8 Sheffield sq E3
141 O 6 Sheffield st WC2
137 U 15 Sheffield ter W8
38 G 1 Sheila clo Rom
38 G 1 Sheila rd Rom
22 D 11 Shelbourne clo Pinn
31 Z 6 Shelbourne rd N17
48 D 12 Shelbourne rd N7
115 N 9 Shelbury clo Sidcp
92 B 14 Shelbury rd SE22
35 Y 7 Sheldon av IIf
46 K 1 Sheldon av N6
28 M 17 Sheldon av N6
98 B 3 Sheldon rd Bxly Hth
55 Y 20 Sheldon rd Dgnhm
18 F 14 Sheldon rd N18
45 P 13 Sheldon rd NW2
156 L 6 Sheldon st Croy
137 S 17 Sheldrake pl W8
120 F 2 Sheldrick clo Mitch
127 R 14 Sheldwick ter BR2
49 O 10 Shelford pl N16
4 A 20 Shelford rd Barnt
109 T 19 Shelford ri SE19
88 L 12 Shelgate rd SW11
127 S 15 Shell clo Brom
93 P 7 Shell rd SE13
53 T 18 Shelley av E12
59 P 8 Shelley av Grnfd
57 U 6 Shelley av Hornch
12 B 15 Shelley clo Edg
59 P 9 Shelley clo Grnfd
58 F 18 Shelley cres S'hall
96 J 2 Shelley dri SE18
42 D 8 Shelley gdns Wemb
50 A 14 Shellness rd E5
88 M 6 Shellwood rd SW11
64 A 14 Shelmerdine clo E3
105 Y 19 Shelton rd SW19
140 J 7 Shelton st WC2
34 G 2 Shenfield st Wdfd Grn
34 G 2 Shenfield rd Wdfd Grn
134 K 10 Shenfield st N1

82 B 2	Shenley rd Hounsl
91 S 2	Shenley rd SE5
98 L 11	Shenstone clo Bxly Hth
36 L 15	Shenstone gdns Ifl
36 L 15	Shenstone gdns Ilf
139 X 13	Shepherd mkt W1
139 X 14	Shepherd st W1
29 T 19	Shepherd's clo N6
99 Y 19	Shepherd's la Drtfrd
46 F 14	Shepherd's wlk NW3
134 D 12	Shepherdess wlk N1
134 B 8	Shepherdess wlk N1
136 G 18	Shepherds Bush shopping centre W12
136 E 17	Shepherds Bush comm W12
136 F 17	Shepherds Bush grn W12
136 C 16	Shepherds Bush mkt W12
74 M 5	Shepherds Bush mkt W12
136 G 16	Shepherds Bush pl W12
144 D 5	Shepherds Bush rd W6
136 E 19	Shepherds Bush rd W6
37 V 15	Shepherds clo Rom
114 E 18	Shepherds grn Chisl
29 S 19	Shepherds hill N6
50 E 16	Shepherds la E9
139 T 8	Shepherds pl W1
40 C 19	Shepherds pth Nthlt
158 E 17	Shepherds way S Croy
155 O 4	Shepley clo Carsh
9 N 4	Sheppard clo Enf
116 J 10	Sheppard clo Surb
65 P 12	Sheppard st E16
134 C 3	Shepperton rd N1
55 U 20	Sheppey gdns Dgnhm
55 P 20	Sheppey rd Dgnhm
66 K 19	Shepstone st E6
95 S 12	Sherard rd SE9
140 D 6	Sheraton st W1
70 G 10	Sherborne av S'hall
120 H 17	Sherborne cres Carsh
60 B 15	Sherborne gdns W13
25 P 10	Sherborne gdns NW9
160 F 8	Sherborne la EC4
153 X 1	Sherborne rd Sutton
134 E 3	Sherborne st N1
31 T 18	Sherboro rd N15
17 W 3	Sherbrook gdns N21
98 D 9	Sherbrooke clo Bxly Hth
66 H 16	Sherbrooke gdns E6
144 L 19	Sherbrooke rd SW6
35 Y 16	Shere rd Ilf
20 L 17	Sheredan rd E4
86 C 16	Sherfield gdns SW15
24 F 19	Sheridan gdns Harrow
81 R 10	Sheridan rd Blvdr
97 Z 7	Sheridan rd Bxly Hth
53 T 16	Sheridan rd E12
52 D 10	Sheridan rd E7
102 D 8	Sheridan rd Rich
119 W 1	Sheridan rd SW19
63 O 18	Sheridan st E1
143 Z 6	Sheridan st E1
143 Z 7	Sheridan st E1
154 L 12	Sheridan wlk Carsh
27 X 18	Sheridan wlk NW11
127 Z 2	Sheriden cres BR7
53 U 12	Sheringham av E12
6 K 18	Sheringham av N14
100 F 2	Sheringham av Twick
54 L 16	Sheringham dri Bark
48 E 17	Sheringham rd N7
124 B 5	Sheringham rd SE20
22 H 1	Sherington av Pinn
77 V 17	Sherington rd SE7
101 X 1	Sherland rd Twick
83 X 20	Sherland rd Twick
147 X 9	Sherland st SW1
126 G 1	Sherman rd Brom
64 F 8	Sherman st E17
33 T 13	Shernhall st E17
53 O 16	Sherrard rd E12
52 K 17	Sherrard rd E7
4 M 19	Sherrards way Barnt
44 J 15	Sherrick Green rd NW10
45 Y 19	Sherriff rd NW6
31 X 7	Sherringham av N17
38 L 19	Sherringham av Rom
26 H 12	Sherrock gdns NW4
92 F 3	Sherwell st SE14
34 H 11	Sherwood av E18
41 U 16	Sherwood av Grnfd
108 A 20	Sherwood av SW16
107 Y 19	Sherwood av SW16
97 T 17	Sherwood clo Bxly
86 K 8	Sherwood clo SW15
72 A 3	Sherwood clo W13
54 E 20	Sherwood gdns Bark
97 S 16	Sherwood Park av Sidcp
121 V 8	Sherwood Park rd Mitch
153 Y 12	Sherwood Park rd Sutton
123 Z 18	Sherwood rd Croy
100 M 11	Sherwood rd Hampt
40 M 8	Sherwood rd Harrow
41 N 8	Sherwood rd Harrow
36 D 14	Sherwood rd Ilf
26 M 10	Sherwood rd NW4
27 N 9	Sherwood rd NW4
105 V 19	Sherwood rd SW19
96 G 6	Sherwood rd Welling
15 S 10	Sherwood st N20
140 D 9	Sherwood st W1
15 T 10	Sherwood ter N20
159 T 2	Sherwood way W Wkhm
63 Y 6	Shetland rd E3
72 A 16	Shield dri Brentf
71 Z 17	Shield dri Brentf
80 E 11	Shieldhall st SE2
138 M 1	Shillibeer pl W1
133 X 2	Shillingford st N1
17 X 16	Shillitoe rd N13
136 B 5	Shinfield st W12
62 M 17	Shinfield st W12
110 F 6	Shinford pth SE23
81 R 18	Shinglewell rd Erith
78 M 8	Ship & Half Moon pas SE18
142 H 17	Ship & Mermaid row SE1
85 W 6	Ship la SW14
93 N 2	Ship st SE8
160 H 7	Ship Tavern pas EC3
107 S 1	Shipka rd SW12
65 X 18	Shipman rd E16
110 G 4	Shipman rd SE23
55 V 9	Shipton clo Dgnhm
135 R 11	Shipton st E2
75 W 6	Shipwright rd SE16
142 H 14	Shipwright yd SE1
92 D 20	Shirburn clo SE23
64 C 19	Shirbutt st E14
95 O 6	Shirebrook rd SE3
27 P 18	Shirehall clo NW4
27 P 18	Shirehall gdns NW4
27 P 17	Shirehall la NW4
27 O 19	Shirehall pk NW4
102 J 10	Shires the Rich
129 R 15	Shirland ms W9
129 P 14	Shirland rd W9
97 V 20	Shirley av Bxly
158 C 1	Shirley av Croy
154 H 8	Shirley av Sutton
153 U 20	Shirley av Sutton
158 F 5	Shirley Church rd Croy
159 N 9	Shirley Church rd CR0
33 S 14	Shirley clo Hounsl
82 M 14	Shirley clo Hounsl
124 G 10	Shirley cres Becknhm
82 L 14	Shirley dri Hounsl
54 G 17	Shirley gdns Bark
71 X 2	Shirley gdns W7
19 S 3	Shirley gro N9
89 P 7	Shirley gro SW11
158 C 2	Shirley Hills rd Croy
77 Y 18	Shirley House dri SE7
158 E 1	Shirley Oaks rd CR0
124 B 19	Shirley Park rd Croy
158 C 2	Shirley rd Croy
52 A 20	Shirley rd E15
7 Y 12	Shirley rd Enf
114 H 7	Shirley rd Sidcp
73 Z 7	Shirley rd W4
155 U 19	Shirley rd Wallgtn
65 P 17	Shirley st E16
133 P 4	Shirley st N1
158 L 4	Shirley way Croy
159 N 3	Shirley way Croy
46 M 12	Shirlock rd NW3
47 N 13	Shirlock rd NW3
31 O 5	Shobden rd N17
141 V 6	Shoe la EC4
53 U 20	Shoebury rd E6
45 T 17	Shoot Up hill NW2
24 E 12	Shooters av Harrow
95 S 2	Shooters Hill rd SE18
94 A 2	Shooters Hill rd SE3
77 Y 20	Shooters Hill rd SE3
96 C 4	Shooters hill SE18
7 V 5	Shooters rd Enf
100 C 14	Shore clo Hampt
100 F 4	Shore gro Felt
63 P 1	Shore pl E9
63 P 1	Shore rd E9
120 E 1	Shore st SW19
134 M 15	Shoreditch High st EC2
115 W 2	Shoreham clo Bxly
124 C 13	Shoreham clo Croy
88 A 13	Shoreham clo SW18
126 D 15	Shoreham way Brom
150 M 10	Shorncliffe rd SE1
93 U 20	Shorndean st SE6
97 R 15	Shorne clo Sidcp
127 W 5	Shornefield clo Brom
80 E 12	Shornells way SE2
145 R 18	Shorrold's rd SW6
14 J 12	Short ga N12
82 H 3	Short hedges Hounsl
51 V 6	Short rd E11
64 J 2	Short rd E15
74 A 16	Short rd W4
67 P 3	Short st Bark
141 V 16	Short st SE1
64 G 8	Short wall E15
15 X 19	Short way N12
95 P 8	Short way SE9
83 N 19	Short way Twick
152 E 16	Shortcroft rd Epsom
56 B 17	Shortcrofts rd Dgnhm
143 O 9	Shorter st E1
18 C 12	Shortlands clo N18
126 A 2	Shortlands gdns Brom
125 X 5	Shortlands gro Brom
125 Y 5	Shortlands rd Brom
51 R 1	Shortlands rd E10
102 M 19	Shortlands rd Kingst
103 O 18	Shortlands rd Kingst
144 G 8	Shortlands W6
25 U 13	Shorts croft NW9
140 J 6	Shorts gdns WC2
154 K 10	Shorts rd Carsh
155 S 14	Shotfield Wallgtn
87 X 1	Shottendane rd SW6
113 R 6	Shottery clo SE9
86 A 10	Shottfield av SW14
139 N 3	Shouldham st W1
95 T 8	Shrapnel rd SE9
24 K 14	Shrewsbury av Harrow
85 X 11	Shrewsbury av SW14
61 Z 3	Shrewsbury cres NW10
95 Z 3	Shrewsbury la SE18
137 T 3	Shrewsbury ms W2
79 R 20	Shrewsbury pk SE18
124 J 6	Shrewsbury rd Becknhm
120 K 18	Shrewsbury rd Carsh
53 N 16	Shrewsbury rd E7
53 N 20	Shrewsbury rd E7
16 J 18	Shrewsbury rd N11
137 T 5	Shrewsbury rd W2
106 M 16	Shrewton rd SW17
112 B 8	Shroffold rd Brom
111 Z 9	Shroffold rd Brom
122 A 9	Shropshire clo Mitch
132 D 19	Shropshire pl W1
30 C 1	Shropshire rd N22
130 L 19	Shroton st NW1
34 F 7	Shrubberies the E18
17 W 3	Shrubbery gdns N21
18 J 12	Shrubbery rd N9
70 F 1	Shrubbery rd S'hall
108 A 10	Shrubbery rd SE9
152 L 6	Shrubland gro Worc Pk
33 P 20	Shrubland rd E10
33 N 16	Shrubland rd E17
135 R 2	Shrubland rd E8
159 O 7	Shrublands clo N20
15 U 7	Shrublands clo N20
5 U 20	Shurland av Barnt
15 V 1	Shurland av Barnt
151 P 18	Shurland gdns SE15
96 K 19	Shuttle clo Sidcp
99 V 8	Shuttle rd Drtfrd
135 R 18	Shuttle st E1
98 B 18	Shuttlemead Bxly
88 H 4	Shuttleworth rd SW11
89 X 6	Sibella rd SW4
97 Y 13	Sibley clo Bxly Hth
53 R 20	Sibley gro E12
120 L 3	Sibthorp rd Mitch
94 J 18	Sibthorpe rd SE12
120 J 17	Sibton rd Carsh
140 L 2	Sicilian av WC1
48 M 20	Sickert ct N1
69 W 10	Sickle corner Dgnhm
87 S 1	Sidbury st SW6
114 J 12	Sidcup By-pass rd Sidcp
115 U 17	Sidcup By-pass rd Sidcp
114 M 9	Sidcup High st Sidcp
115 T 14	Sidcup Hill gdns Sidcp
115 R 12	Sidcup hill Sidcp
94 J 14	Sidcup rd SE12
114 C 6	Sidcup rd SE9
113 X 4	Sidcup rd SE9
131 P 18	Siddons la NW1
156 G 4	Siddons rd Croy
31 X 5	Siddons rd N17
110 G 5	Siddons rd SE23
32 K 16	Side rd E17
114 E 1	Sidewood rd SE9
149 R 2	Sidford pl SE1
51 T 8	Sidings the E11
83 T 4	Sidmouth av Islwth
51 T 8	Sidmouth rd E10
128 B 1	Sidmouth rd NW10
62 M 1	Sidmouth rd NW10
45 N 19	Sidmouth rd NW2
91 V 1	Sidmouth rd SE15
80 F 20	Sidmouth rd Welling
132 M 15	Sidmouth st WC1
17 R 18	Sidney av N13
129 W 1	Sidney Boyd ct NW6
72 F 16	Sidney gdns Brentf
133 W 11	Sidney gro EC1
124 H 2	Sidney rd Becknhm
52 E 10	Sidney rd E7
23 O 11	Sidney rd Harrow
123 W 11	Sidney rd SE25
90 D 5	Sidney rd SW9
83 Z 16	Sidney rd Twick
63 O 16	Sidney sq E1
143 Z 3	Sidney sq E1
143 O 17	Sidney st E1
143 Z 1	Sidney st E1
135 Z 20	Sidney st E1
63 P 15	Sidney Street est E1
63 N 1	Sidworth st E8
135 X 2	Sidworth st E8
77 T 17	Siebert rd SE3
78 B 9	Siemens rd SE18
49 Y 15	Sigdon rd E8
136 H 7	Silchester rd W10
98 F 3	Silecroft rd Bxly Hth
141 Y 19	Silex st SE1
94 E 14	Silk clo SE12
93 T 5	Silk Mills pth SE13
160 D 1	Silk st EC2
160 D 1	Silk st EC2
26 C 15	Silkfield rd NW9
25 X 6	Silkstream rd Edg
30 D 9	Silsoe rd N8
20 A 19	Silver Birch av E4
19 Y 19	Silver Birch av E4
16 B 20	Silver Birch clo N11
23 P 2	Silver clo Harrow
73 T 12	Silver cres W4
159 X 2	Silver la W Wkhm
140 C 8	Silver pl W1
63 E 12	Silver rd W12
81 V 16	Silver Spring clo Erith
8 C 12	Silver st Enf
18 C 15	Silver st N18
38 F 11	Silver way Rom
75 X 3	Silver wlk SE16
5 W 15	Silvercliffe gdns Barnt
36 J 17	Silverdale av E4
40 E 16	Silverdale clo Nthlt
153 U 8	Silverdale clo Sutton
71 U 2	Silverdale clo W7
57 X 16	Silverdale dri Hornch
7 O 15	Silverdale Enf
98 G 6	Silverdale rd Bxly Hth
156 J 4	Silverdale rd Croy

20 K 19	Silverdale rd E4	
110 D 9	Silverdale SE26	
83 Y 6	Silverhall st Islwth	
42 J 2	Silverholme Harrow	
78 G 3	Silverland st E16	
122 C 9	Silverleigh rd Thntn Hth	
93 P 17	Silvermere rd SE6	
40 L 18	Silverst clo Grnfd	
11 S 19	Silverston clo Stanm	
11 S 19	Silverston way Stanm	
20 C 7	Silverthorne gdns E4	
89 T 5	Silverthorn rd SW8	
144 F 16	Silverton rd W6	
78 B 3	Silverton By-pass E16	
65 O 18	Silvertown way E16	
77 S 3	Silvertown way E16	
59 R 8	Silvertree la Grnfd	
91 V 14	Silvester st SE22	
142 D 18	Silvester st SE1	
75 R 12	Silwood st SE16	
94 B 10	Sim's wlk SE3	
75 V 18	Simla clo SE14	
15 X 7	Simmons clo N20	
20 K 9	Simmons la E4	
78 L 13	Simmons rd SE18	
15 W 7	Simmons way N20	
154 J 3	Simms clo Carsh	
94 H 18	Simnel st SE12	
137 S 9	Simon clo W11	
51 O 6	Simonds rd E10	
127 P 1	Simone clo Brom	
51 X 16	Simons wlk E15	
82 E 17	Simpson rd Hounsl	
57 U 19	Simpson rd Rainhm	
102 C 9	Simpson rd Rich	
88 H 5	Simpson st SW11	
126 F 7	Simpson's rd Brom	
64 E 20	Simpsons rd E14	
87 Y 14	Simrose ct SW18	
39 T 14	Sims clo Rom	
136 H 19	Sinclair gdns W14	
27 R 18	Sinclair gro W11	
19 X 17	Sinclair rd E4	
19 X 18	Sinclair rd E4	
23 J 19	Sinclair rd W14	
144 K 1	Sinclair rd W14	
60 A 5	Sindall rd Grnfd	
71 Z 1	Singapore rd W13	
134 G 15	Singer st EC2	
122 K 16	Singleton clo Croy	
106 L 16	Singleton clo SW17	
5b C 16	Singleton rd Dgnhm	
14 L 15	Singleton scarp N12	
32 F 4	Sinnott rd E17	
84 A 20	Sion rd Twick	
74 C 2	Sir Alexander clo W3	
74 D 2	Sir Alexander rd W3	
30 K 8	Sirdar rd N22	
136 J 11	Sirdar rd W11	
160 D 7	Sise la EC4	
87 V 15	Sisley rd Bark	
87 V 15	Sispara gdns SW18	
123 Y 17	Sissinghurst rd Croy	
89 N 8	Sisters av SW11	
107 T 1	Sistova rd SW12	
18 B 1	Sittingbourne av Enf	
8 C 20	Sittingbourne rd SE15	
10 H 17	Sitwell gro Stanm	
56 H 20	Siviter way Dgnhm	
126 J 7	Siward rd Brom	
31 O 5	Siward rd N17	
106 C 7	Siward rd SW17	
53 U 14	Sixth av W10	
128 J 15	Sixth av W10	
100 M 6	Sixth Cross rd Twick	
101 O 8	Sixth Cross rd Twick	
45 S 14	Skardu rd NW2	
87 T 19	Skeena hill SW18	
66 F 3	Skeffington rd E6	
106 B 4	Skelbrook st SW18	
87 V 11	Skelgill rd SW15	
65 O 1	Skelly rd E15	
52 G 19	Skelton rd E7	
51 S 1	Skeltons la E10	
144 D 15	Skelwith rd W6	
75 S 13	Sketchley gdns SE16	
8 H 12	Sketty rd Enf	
64 L 3	Skiers st E15	
90 G 20	Skiffington clo SW2	
142 A 12	Skin Market pl SE1	
147 T 7	Skinner pl SW1	
134 C 1	Skinner st EC1	
160 C 8	Skinners la EC4	
82 J 1	Skinners la Hounsl	
66 H 10	Skipsey av E6	
149 Y 2	Skipton st SE1	
63 R 3	Skipworth rd E9	
33 W 3	Sky Peals rd Wdfd Grn	
99 U 1	Slade gdns Erith	
99 V 1	Slade Green rd Erith	
79 U 16	Slade the SE18	
150 C 19	Slade wlk SE5	
95 O 7	Sladebrook rd SE3	
79 V 14	Sladedale rd SE18	
7 T 11	Slades clo Enf	
114 B 9	Slades dri Chisl	
7 S 10	Slades gdns Enf	
7 U 11	Slades hill Enf	
7 T 11	Slades ri Enf	
93 P 12	Slagrove pl SE13	
146 C 16	Slaidburn st SW10	
93 U 11	Slaithwaite rd SE13	
48 E 14	Slaney pl N7	
148 B 18	Sleaford st SW8	
140 J 8	Slingsby pl WC2	
151 X 1	Slippers pl SE16	
146 K 6	Sloane av SW3	
147 R 9	Sloane Court east SW3	
147 R 9	Sloane Court west SW3	
147 S 7	Sloane gdns SW1	
147 R 7	Sloane sq SW1	
139 P 19	Sloane st SW1	
147 R 4	Sloane st SW1	
147 R 5	Sloane ter SW1	
124 K 14	Sloane wlk Croy	
80 F 1	Slocum clo SE28	
25 V 17	Slough la NW9	
143 W 5	Sly st E1	
143 W 6	Sly st E1	
83 W 4	Smallberry av Islwth	
138 E 7	Smallbrook ms W2	
49 I 18	Smalley clo N16	
106 F 10	Smallwood rd SW17	
88 C 12	Smardale rd SW18	
81 R 12	Smarden clo Blvdr	
113 T 8	Smarden gro SE9	
39 Z 4	Smart clo Rom	
63 T 8	Smart st E2	
140 L 4	Smarts pl WC2	
87 X 19	Smeaton rd SW18	
143 V 13	Smeaton st E1	
89 Y 4	Smedley st SW8 & SW4	
64 A 1	Smeed rd E3	
72 K 17	Smith hill Brentf	
148 J 3	Smith st SW1	
116 M 15	Smith st Surb	
147 N 10	Smith st SW3	
147 N 11	Smith ter SW3	
141 X 3	Smithfield st EC1	
51 T 14	Smithies ct E15	
80 C 11	Smithies rd SE2	
30 J 4	Smithson rd N17	
105 S 3	Smithwood clo SW19	
63 P 15	Smith's st E1	
122 M 15	Smock wlk Croy	
88 A 10	Smugglers way SW18	
150 L 9	Smyrk's rd SE17	
129 U 2	Smyrna rd N16	
64 E 20	Smythe st E14	
6 G 11	Snakes la Barnt	
21 S 17	Snakes la Wdfd Grn	
21 T 18	Snakes la Wdfd Grn	
11 V 14	Snaresbrook dri Stanm	
34 E 12	Snaresbrook hall E18	
34 C 14	Snaresbrook rd E11	
33 Z 14	Snaresbrook rd E11	
136 C 3	Snarsgate st W10	
62 M 18	Snarsgate st W10	
27 U 20	Sneath av NW11	
18 H 18	Snells pk N18	
44 M 13	Sneyd rd NW2	
141 W 3	Snow hill EC1	
88 B 5	Snowbury rd SW6	
26 A 18	Snowden dri NW9	
134 J 19	Snowden st EC2	
142 G 17	Snowsfields SE1	
53 N 15	Snowshill rd E12	
53 P 14	Snowshill rd E12	
91 U 8	Soames st SE15	
118 A 1	Soames wlk New Mald	
141 O 4	Soane Museum WC2	
126 G 15	Socket la Brom	
67 Z 6	Soho sq W1	
140 E 5	Soho st W1	
45 X 15	Solent rd NW6	
133 S 12	Soley ms WC1	
86 L 14	Solna av SW15	
18 A 13	Solna rd N21	
92 A 10	Solomon's pass SE15	
90 A 10	Solon New rd SW4	
90 A 11	Solon rd SW2	
82 C 7	Solway rd Hounsl	
30 H 4	Solway rd N22	
91 X 10	Solway rd SE22	
5 U 19	Somaford gro Barnt	
45 U 14	Somali rd NW2	
54 D 20	Somerby rd Bark	
5 X 11	Somercoates clo Barnt	
101 U 12	Somerset rd Tedd	
48 J 7	Somerfield rd N4	
49 U 13	Somerford gro N16	
31 Y 2	Somerford gro N17	
135 X 17	Somerford gro N17	
75 W 6	Somerford way SE16	
97 O 18	Somerhill av Sidcp	
97 R 4	Somerhill rd Welling	
90 G 10	Somerleyton rd SW9	
132 F 9	Somers clo NW1	
138 J 6	Somers cres W2	
90 C 17	Somers rd E17	
32 L 14	Somers rd E17	
90 C 17	Somers rd SW2	
35 T 15	Somersby gdns Ilf	
118 J 3	Somerset av SW20	
96 L 11	Somerset av Welling	
118 B 13	Somerset clo New Mald	
34 G 4	Somerset clo E18	
122 D 6	Somerset gdns SW16	
47 R 1	Somerset gdns N6	
92 P 6	Somerset gdns SE13	
101 T 12	Somerset gdns Tedd	
141 O 9	Somerset Ho WC2	
5 O 16	Somerset rd Barnt	
5 R 16	Somerset rd Barnt	
72 F 17	Somerset rd Brentf	
99 Z 17	Somerset rd Drtfrd	
33 O 17	Somerset rd E17	
22 M 17	Somerset rd Harrow	
117 N 4	Somerset rd Kingst	
31 V 11	Somerset rd N17	
18 G 16	Somerset rd N18	
26 L 13	Somerset rd NW4	
58 H 15	Somerset rd S'hall	
105 O 8	Somerset rd SW19	
72 C 3	Somerset rd W13	
73 X 7	Somerset rd W4	
137 N 19	Somerset sq W14	
70 A 18	Somerset waye Hounsl	
97 Z 5	Somersham rd Bxly Hth	
85 S 8	Somerton av Rich	
45 S 9	Somerton rd NW2	
92 A 10	Somerton rd SE15	
112 H 5	Somertrees av SE12	
40 J 14	Somervell rd Harrow	
37 U 15	Somerville rd Rom	
110 F 7	Somerville rd SE20	
48 D 8	Sonderburg rd N7	
150 F 13	Sondes st SE17	
23 V 20	Sonia ct Harrow	
70 G 20	Sonia gdns Hounsl	
15 P 14	Sonia gdns N12	
44 D 12	Sonia gdns NW10	
123 X 15	Sonning rd SE25	
48 C 18	Sophia clo N7	
51 P 2	Sophia rd E10	
65 V 16	Sophia rd E16	
64 C 16	Sophia st E14	
80 B 3	Sorrel clo SE18	
39 S 10	Sorrel wlk Rom	
00 D 14	Sorrell gdns E6	
154 A 6	Sorrento rd Sutton	
153 Z 6	Sorrento rd Sutton	
48 K 11	Sotheby rd N5	
135 T 4	Sotheran clo E8	
145 Z 20	Sotheron rd SW6	
88 M 3	Soudan rd SW11	
144 H 4	Souldern rd W14	
32 H 19	South Access rd E17	
26 C 8	South acre NW9	
136 A 10	South Africa rd W12	
74 J 1	South Africa rd W12	
62 L 20	South Africa rd W12	
139 V 12	South Audley st W1	
155 N 17	South av Carsh	
20 E 1	South av E4	
85 O 4	South av Rich	
58 D 20	South av S'hall	
58 D 20	South Avenue gdns S'hall	
116 K 14	South bank Surb	
116 K 10	South bank ter Surb	
51 X 10	South Birkbeck st E11	
74 F 14	South Black Lion la W6	
146 A 10	South Bolton gdns SW5	
17 R 16	South Church ct N13	
4 H 12	South clo Barnt	
97 W 11	South clo Bxly Hth	
69 S 5	South clo Dgnhm	
119 X 14	South clo Mrdn	
29 R 17	South clo N6	
40 E 2	South clo Pinn	
100 H 6	South clo Twick	
32 K 10	South Countess rd E17	
140 F 1	South cres WC1	
36 A 15	South Cross rd Ilf	
109 O 6	South Croxted rd SE21	
12 L 12	South dene NW7	
153 S 20	South dri Sutton	
72 G 9	South Ealing rd W5	
18 G 11	South Eastern av N9	
147 V 6	South Eaton pl SW1	
125 R 16	South Eden Park rd Becknhm	
145 S 3	South Edwardes sq W8	
46 J 13	South End clo NW3	
156 M 8	South end Croy	
46 K 14	South End grn NW3	
57 Z 14	South End rd Hornch	
46 J 12	South End rd NW3	
145 Y 1	South End row W8	
145 X 1	South end W8	
52 K 19	South Esk rd E7	
106 G 18	South gdns SW19	
32 K 16	South gro E17	
31 P 16	South gro N15	
47 P 4	South gro N6	
41 O 10	South Hill av Harrow	
113 S 16	South hill Chisl	
41 T 12	South Hill gro Harrow	
46 K 11	South Hill Park gdns NW3	
46 K 12	South Hill pk NW3	
126 A 9	South Hill rd Brom	
125 Z 8	South Hill rd Brom	
113 T 19	South Hill rd Chisl	
143 S 19	South Island pl SW9	
116 G 6	South la Kingst	
118 B 17	South la New Mald	
117 Z 15	South la New Mald	
149 O 19	South Lambeth est SW8	
148 L 13	South Lambeth pl SE1	
148 L 17	South Lambeth rd SW8	
117 X 9	South Lane new New Mald	
122 A 8	South Lodge av Mitch	
121 Z 8	South Lodge av Mitch	
6 K 13	South Lodge cres Enf	
6 J 14	South Lodge dri N14	
7 N 17	South Lodge dri N14	
26 D 5	South mead NW9	
139 W 7	South Molton la W1	
139 W 7	South Molton pas W1	
65 T 16	South Molton rd E16	
139 W 7	South Molton st W1	
123 T 4	South Norwood hill SE25	
108 D 9	South Oak rd SW16	
76 K 19	South observatory	
54 F 9	South Park cres Ilf	
94 A 20	South Park cres SE6	
112 B 1	South Park cres SE6	
54 G 9	South Park dri Ilf	
117 V 10	South Park gro New Mald	
157 P 10	South Park Hill rd S Croy	
54 F 9	South Park rd Ilf	
106 A 16	South Park rd SW19	
105 X 16	South Park rd SW19	
54 F 11	South Park ter Ilf	
146 G 10	South pde SW3	
73 Y 10	South pde W4	
160 F 1	South pl EC2	
142 G 1	South pl EC2	
116 L 16	South pl Surb	
142 F 2	South Place ms EC2	
160 G 1	South Place ms EC2	
25 U 4	South rd Edg	
100 A 14	South rd Felt	
100 D 16	South rd Hampt	
18 L 5	South rd N9	
37 X 18	South rd Rom	

70 E 4 South rd S'hall
110 E 4 South rd SE23
106 D 16 South rd SW19
101 R 8 South rd Twick
72 G 10 South rd W5
154 K 19 South ri Carsh
94 C 4 South row SE3
75 X 8 South Sea st SE16
74 O 9 South side W6
27 Z 18 South sq NW11
141 R 1 South sq WC1
126 F 2 South st Brom
9 S 18 South st Enf
69 Y 7 South st Rainhm
39 P 15 South st Rom
139 T 12 South st W1
143 P 7 South Tenter st E1
116 K 13 South ter Surb
146 J 5 South ter SW7
41 U 12 South vale Harrow
109 R 16 South vale SE19
126 J 3 South view Brom
98 B 17 South View clo Bxly
35 Y 18 South View cres Ilf
34 J 11 South view dri E18
99 O 13 South view Drtfrd
29 Z 11 South View rd N8
47 Y 18 South vlls NW1
158 K 5 South way Croy
22 H 14 South way Harrow
14 M 7 South way N20
19 R 8 South way N9
43 P 14 South way Wemb
84 A 16 South Western rd Twick
83 Z 15 South Western rd Twick
138 G 4 South Wharf rd W2
159 Z 5 South wlk W Wkhm
86 A 8 South Worple av SW14
86 A 8 South Worple way SW14
85 Y 8 South Worple way SW14
142 E 19 Southall pl SE1
89 S 2 Southalm st SW11
128 M 19 Southam st W10
141 R 3 Southampton bldgs WC2
121 Z 11 Southampton gdns Mitch
140 L 2 Southampton pl WC1
46 M 14 Southampton rd NW5
132 K 19 Southampton row WC1
140 L 9 Southampton st WC2
150 G 18 Southampton way SE5
150 K 19 Southampton way SE5
91 T 1 Southampton way SE5
114 A 8 Southbank Chisl
116 A 17 Southbank Surb
116 G 19 Southborough clo Surb
127 S 12 Southborough la Brom
116 J 20 Southborough rd Surb
127 S 12 Southborough rd Brom
63 S 2 Southborough rd E9
25 W 8 Southbourne av NW9
126 F 18 Southbourne Brom
22 B 20 Southbourne clo Pinn
27 S 13 Southbourne cres NW4
94 H 12 Southbourne gdns SE12
54 B 16 Southbourne gdns Ilf
156 K 7 Southbridge pl Croy
156 M 8 Southbridge rd Croy
70 D 6 Southbridge way S'hall
94 C 15 Southbrook rd SE12
122 A 1 Southbrook rd SW16
136 A 19 Southbrook st W12
8 K 15 Southbury av Enf
8 G 13 Southbury rd Enf
66 G 7 Southchurch rd E6
35 V 14 Southcombe st W14
117 S 18 Southcote av Surb
32 F 15 Southcote rd E17
47 V 12 Southcote rd N19
124 B 13 Southcote rd SE25

96 H 7 Southcroft av Welling
159 U 3 Southcroft av W Wkhm
107 N 14 Southcroft rd SW17
105 U 3 Southdean gdns SW19
16 F 12 Southdene ct N11
71 X 9 Southdown av W7
40 L 5 Southdown cres Harrow
36 G 15 Southdown cres Ilf
105 O 19 Southdown dri SW20
57 X 2 Southdown rd Hornch
155 O 19 Southdown rd Carsh
105 R 20 Southdown rd SW20
95 Y 15 Southend clo SE9
95 Y 15 Southend cres SE9
110 K 9 Southend la SE6 & SE26
111 O 10 Southend la SE6 & SE26
35 N 8 Southend rd Wdfd Grn
111 P 17 Southend rd Becknhm
33 X 5 Southend rd E17
34 F 6 Southend rd E18
53 U 19 Southend rd E6
77 T 16 Southern appr SE10
123 V 6 Southern av SE25
63 Y 10 Southern gro E3
65 W 6 Southern rd E13
28 L 13 Southern rd N2
128 K 18 Southern row W10
133 N 9 Southern st N1
38 F 19 Southern way Rom
144 B 5 Southerton rd W6
74 L 10 Southerton rd W6
31 S 15 Southey rd N15
105 Z 17 Southey rd SW19
90 E 1 Southey rd SW9
110 D 18 Southey st SE20
4 B 20 Southfield Barnt
71 W 5 Southfield cotts W7
101 V 8 Southfield gdns Twick
22 J 14 Southfield pk Harrow
9 P 19 Southfield rd Enf
74 A 7 Southfield rd W4
73 X 6 Southfield rd W4
26 H 9 Southfields NW4
87 X 16 Southfields rd SW18
134 G 1 Southgate gro N1
134 G 2 Southgate rd N1
49 P 18 Southgate rd N1
79 Z 18 Southland rd SE18
83 P 13 Southland way Hounsl
127 R 7 Southlands gro Brom
126 M 10 Southlands rd Brom
127 P 8 Southlands rd Brom
153 X 6 Southly clo Sutton
152 C 16 Southmead rd Epsom
87 S 20 Southmead rd SW19
42 L 15 Southmeadows Wemb
113 V 8 Southold ri SE9
112 F 14 Southover Brom
14 K 11 Southover N12
14 L 14 Southover N12
79 S 11 Southport rd SE18
116 J 9 Southsea rd Kingst
105 O 14 Southside comm SW19
96 F 18 Southspring Sidcp
94 A 6 Southvale rd SE3
44 D 14 Southview av NW10
155 V 17 Southview gdns Wallgtn
111 X 9 Southview rd Brom
89 Y 2 Southville SW8
142 C 11 Southwark br SE1
142 B 16 Southwark Bridge rd SE1
142 A 14 Southwark gro SE1
151 T 5 Southwark Park rd SE16
151 X 2 Southwark Park rd SE16
143 X 20 Southwark Park rd SE16
127 U 7 Southwark pl Brom
142 C 14 Southwark rd SE1
63 Y 17 Southwater clo E14
126 E 18 Southway Brom
74 L 6 Southway clo W12
14 L 9 Southway N20

28 B 17 Southway NW11
119 N 10 Southway SW20
155 V 9 Southway Wallgtn
40 J 17 Southwell av Nthlt
146 B 4 Southwell gdns SW7
51 Z 7 Southwell Grove rd E11
122 F 15 Southwell rd Croy
24 H 18 Southwell rd Croy
90 L 7 Southwell rd SE5
51 X 3 Southwest rd E11
138 J 5 Southwick ms W2
138 J 7 Southwick pl W2
138 J 5 Southwick st W2
55 N 15 Southwold dri Bark
98 G 17 Southwold rd Bxly
50 A 7 Southwold rd E5
103 W 20 Southwood av Kingst
29 R 20 Southwood av N6
153 P 1 Southwood clo Worc Pk
127 V 9 Southwood clo Brom
117 W 17 Southwood dri Surb
35 Z 14 Southwood gdns Ilf
47 P 2 Southwood la N6
29 P 20 Southwood la N6
47 R 1 Southwood Lawn rd N6
47 R 1 Southwood pk N6
80 D 3 Southwood rd SE28
114 A 3 Southwood rd SE9
113 Y 4 Southwood rd SE9
60 D 15 Sovereign clo W5
95 T 14 Sowerby clo SE9
57 U 17 Sowrey av Rainhm
123 R 2 Spa clo SE25
109 O 19 Spa hill SE19
151 O 2 Spa rd SE16
151 S 2 Spa rd SE16
133 T 15 Spafield st EC1
107 S 13 Spalding rd SW17
64 B 12 Spanby rd E3
46 E 3 Spaniards clo NW11
46 F 4 Spaniards end NW3
46 E 6 Spaniards rd NW3
139 U 3 Spanish pl W1
88 E 12 Spanish rd SW18
23 T 13 Sparkbridge rd Harrow
152 H 9 Sparrow Farm rd E1
56 G 8 Sparrow grn Dgnhm
96 B 20 Sparrows la SE9
114 C 1 Sparrows la SE9
10 A 4 Sparrows way Bushey
67 V 4 Sparsholt rd Bark
48 B 3 Sparsholt rd N19
93 T 3 Sparta st SE10
145 V 7 Spear ms SW5
78 K 17 Spearman st SE1
36 K 14 Spearpoint gdns Ilf
48 A 4 Spears rd N19
70 B 20 Speart la Hounsl
68 B 10 Speedwell clo NW3
76 A 20 Speedwell st SE8
132 K 14 Speedy pl WC1
113 U 8 Speke hill SE9
123 N 3 Speke rd Thntn Hth
126 D 13 Speldhurst clo Brom
63 S 2 Speldhurst rd E9
73 Z 7 Speldhurst rd W4
143 R 1 Spelman st E1
135 R 20 Spelman st E1
17 R 19 Spencer av N13
21 Y 17 Spencer clo Wdfd Grn
123 P 17 Spencer clo Croy
61 N 7 Spencer clo NW10
28 D 19 Spencer dri N2
95 T 13 Spencer gdns SE9
105 T 17 Spencer Hill rd SW19
105 S 17 Spencer hill SW19
144 K 14 Spencer ms W6
88 F 13 Spencer pk SW18
112 B 18 Spencer rd Brom
33 U 6 Spencer rd E17
66 B 3 Spencer rd E6
23 U 8 Spencer rd Harrow
54 L 4 Spencer rd Ilf
83 O 3 Spencer rd Islwth
121 N 18 Spencer rd Mitch
121 P 6 Spencer rd Mitch
16 D 14 Spencer rd N11
31 X 5 Spencer rd N17
30 C 16 Spencer rd N8
157 S 11 Spencer rd S Croy
88 G 12 Spencer rd SW18
118 K 1 Spencer rd SW20

101 T 5 Spencer rd Twick
73 V 2 Spencer rd W3
73 V 20 Spencer rd W4
42 C 6 Spencer rd Wemb
47 T 11 Spencer ri NW5
133 X 13 Spencer st EC1
87 O 10 Spencer wlk SW15
49 R 13 Spenser gro N16
90 G 14 Spenser rd SE24
148 C 1 Spenser st SW1
49 P 9 Spensley wlk N16
79 X 13 Speranza st SE18
31 T 9 Sperling rd N17
63 V 20 Spert st E14
6 G 20 Spey side N14
64 F 15 Spey st E14
39 P 2 Spey way Rom
62 G 6 Spezia rd NW10
157 N 9 Spice's yd CRO
90 J 5 Spicer clo SE5
118 E 13 Spiers clo New Mald
31 N 5 Spigurnell rd N17
58 C 18 Spikes Br rd S'hall
26 A 7 Spilsby clo NW9
79 V 14 Spindel st SE18
157 R 8 Spindlewood gdns Croy
76 D 11 Spindrift av E14
79 Y 14 Spinel clo SE18
40 D 4 Spinnells rd Harrow
118 A 11 Spinney clo New Mald
56 A 14 Spinney gdns Dgnhm
127 S 3 Spinney oak Brom
5 O 10 Spinney the Barnt
17 S 2 Spinney the N21
115 Y 12 Spinney the Sidcp
11 X 14 Spinney the Stanm
152 M 9 Spinney the Sutton
107 V 6 Spinney the SW16
41 X 10 Spinney the Wemb
127 T 3 Spinneys the Brom
143 U 12 Spirit Quay E1
134 L 20 Spital sq E1
135 R 19 Spital st E1
134 M 20 Spitalfields mkt E1
31 W 13 Spondon rd N15
155 Y 10 Spooner wlk Wallgtn
93 U 20 Sportsbank st SE6
30 L 3 Spottons gro N17
159 O 11 Spout hill Croy
34 F 18 Spratt Hall rd E11
83 R 14 Spray la Islwth
78 M 10 Spray st SE18
79 N 10 Spray st SE18
147 N 8 Sprimont pl SW3
17 P 1 Spring bank N21
60 G 19 Spring Bridge rd W5
153 S 12 Spring Close la Sutton
7 S 3 Spring Court rd Enf
34 J 1 Spring gdns Wdfd Grn
57 Y 13 Spring gdns Hrnch
48 L 16 Spring gdns N5
38 J 17 Spring gdns Rom
140 H 13 Spring gdns Wallgtn
155 U 11 Spring gdns Wallgtn
148 M 11 Spring Gdns wlk SE11
73 O 15 Spring gro W4
82 M 2 Spring Grove cres Hounsl
82 L 3 Spring Grove rd Hounsl
83 N 3 Spring Grove rd Hounsl
84 M 12 Spring Grove rd Rich
85 N 13 Spring Grove rd Rich
49 X 2 Spring hill E5
50 A 2 Spring la E5
124 A 15 Spring la SE25
123 Z 14 Spring la SE25
11 N 13 Spring lake Stanm
139 R 1 Spring ms W1
158 G 4 Spring Park av Croy
158 F 3 Spring Park rd Croy
159 T 7 Spring pk Croy
47 R 16 Spring rd NW5
152 D 20 Spring st Epsom
138 F 7 Spring st W2
98 H 10 Spring vale Bxly Hth
144 G 2 Spring vale ter W14
25 P 1 Spring Villa rd Edg
75 N 20 Springall st SE15
151 X 19 Springall st SE15
93 Z 17 Springbank rd SE13

111 U 20	Springbourne ct Becknhm
28 L 12	Springcroft av N2
49 N 12	Springdale rd N16
100 K 14	Springfield av Hampt
29 V 11	Springfield av N10
119 U 5	Springfield av SW20
10 C 4	Springfield Bushey
10 L 11	Springfield clo Stanm
14 M 16	Springfield clo N12
36 B 17	Springfield dri Ilf
50 A 3	Springfield E5
49 Y 4	Springfield E5
34 L 2	Springfield gdns Wdfd Grn
159 T 2	Springfield gdns W Wkhm
127 U 9	Springfield gdns Brom
25 Z 16	Springfield gdns NW9
50 A 4	Springfield gdns E5
77 Y 17	Springfield gro SE7
129 W 6	Springfield la NW6
26 A 15	Springfield mt NW9
49 Z 2	Springfield pk E5
98 G 10	Springfield rd Bxly Hth
122 L 1	Springfield rd Thntn Hth
108 L 20	Springfield rd Thntn Hth
97 P 7	Springfield rd Welling
155 S 11	Springfield rd Wallgtn
127 U 9	Springfield rd Brom
65 N 8	Springfield rd E15
32 K 19	Springfield rd E17
20 L 4	Springfield rd E4
53 U 19	Springfield rd E6
116 K 7	Springfield rd Kingst
16 G 17	Springfield rd N11
31 X 12	Springfield rd N15
130 A 6	Springfield rd NW8
110 B 14	Springfield rd SE26
105 W 13	Springfield rd SW19
101 Y 13	Springfield rd Tedd
82 H 20	Springfield rd Twick
71 T 2	Springfield rd W7
109 Z 8	Springfield ri SE26
129 W 5	Springfield wlk NW6
91 P 8	Springhill clo SE5
158 L 8	Springhurst clo CR0
125 V 5	Springpark dri Becknhm
48 M 3	Springpark dri N4
56 Z 15	Springpond rd Dgnhm
93 W 16	Springrice rd SE13
72 H 13	Springvale av Brentf
95 W 2	Springwater clo SE18
62 E 4	Springwell av NW10
108 D 10	Springwell clo SW16
70 A 20	Springwell rd Hounsl
108 E 11	Springwell rd SW16
12 F 7	Springwood cres Edg
39 V 16	Springwood way Rom
52 F 16	Sprowston ms E7
52 F 16	Sprowston rd E7
33 T 9	Spruce Hills rd E17
158 F 8	Sprucedale gdn Croy
155 Z 20	Sprucedale gdns Wallgtn
92 H 6	Sprules rd SE4
67 O 8	Spur rd Bark
67 O 9	Spur rd Bark
11 Y 12	Spur rd Edg
71 Z 20	Spur rd Islwth
31 O 13	Spur rd N15
140 B 19	Spur rd SW1
109 O 19	Spurgeon av SE19
109 O 19	Spurgeon rd SE19
150 E 1	Spurgeon st SE1
56 C 17	Spurling rd Dgnhm
91 V 10	Spurling rd SE22
49 Z 16	Spurstowe rd E8
49 Y 16	Spurstowe ter E8
155 N 10	Square the Carsh
53 W 1	Square the Ilf
21 R 17	Square the Wdfd Grn
106 E 7	Squarey st SW17
28 E 4	Squire's la N3
46 F 10	Squires mt NW3
113 S 18	Squires Wood cres Chisl
15 P 13	Squirrels clo N12
152 E 2	Squirrels grn Worc Pk
39 Y 11	Squirrels Heath av Rom
22 E 11	Squirrels the Pinn
135 T 13	Squirries st E2
132 E 15	Sta fore ct NW1
58 G 5	Stable clo Nthlt
28 G 4	Stable wk N2
140 B 16	Stable Yard rd SW1
140 B 16	Stable yd SW1
21 Y 2	Stables the Buck Hl
149 S 10	Stables way SE11
19 P 14	Stacey av N18
33 W 17	Stacey clo E10
140 H 6	Stacey st WC2
139 P 20	Stackhouse st SW3
78 F 18	Stadium rd SE18
146 D 19	Stadium st SW10
99 R 14	Stadium way Drtfrd
43 P 13	Stadium way Wemb
50 G 3	Staffa rd E10
6 G 16	Stafford clo N14
129 T 13	Stafford clo NW6
153 T 13	Stafford clo Sutton
156 D 10	Stafford gdns Croy
84 L 18	Stafford pl Rich
140 A 20	Stafford pl SW1
117 V 6	Stafford rd New Mald
156 E 10	Stafford rd Croy & Wallgtn
63 Y 7	Stafford rd E3
52 M 19	Stafford rd E7
23 N 3	Stafford rd Harrow
129 T 11	Stafford rd NW6
114 H 3	Stafford rd Sidcp
156 B 12	Stafford rd Wallgtn
155 U 14	Stafford rd Wallgtn
140 A 12	Stafford st W1
137 T 19	Stafford ter W8
91 Y 1	Staffordshire st SE15
25 U 7	Stag clo Edg
21 V 7	Stag la Buck Hl
25 V 10	Stag la NW9
104 E 5	Stag la SW15
148 A 1	Stag pl SW1
71 V 18	Stags way Islwth
121 S 5	Stainbank rd Mitch
31 V 12	Stainby rd N15
142 G 15	Stainer st SE1
153 P 3	Staines av Sutton
82 E 10	Staines rd Hounsl
54 D 14	Staines rd Ilf
100 H 7	Staines rd Twick
101 O 4	Staines rd Twick
115 V 15	Staines wlk Sidcp
33 P 13	Stainforth rd E17
54 F 1	Stainforth rd Ilf
36 F 20	Stainforth rd N17
160 B 4	Staining la EC2
114 E 20	Stainmore clo Chisl
63 R 7	Stainsbury st E2
64 A 16	Stainsby pl E14
64 A 17	Stainsby rd E14
9 R 5	Stainton rd Enf
93 W 18	Stainton rd SE6
130 L 20	Stalbridge st NW1
75 N 9	Stalham st SE16
151 Y 3	Stalham st SE16
109 S 19	Stambourne way SE19
159 V 4	Stambourne way W Wkhm
148 M 18	Stamford bldgs SW8
145 Y 18	Stamford Bridge stadium SW6
74 E 10	Stamford Brook av W6
74 E 9	Stamford Brook gdns W6
74 E 9	Stamford Brook rd W6
23 T 1	Stamford clo Harrow
31 X 14	Stamford clo N15
70 H 1	Stamford clo S'hall
126 D 10	Stamford dri Brom
49 W 3	Stamford Green east N16
49 W 4	Stamford Green west N16
49 U 4	Stamford hill N16
68 C 2	Stamford rd Dgnhm
55 U 20	Stamford rd Dgnhm
66 C 3	Stamford rd E6
31 W 14	Stamford rd N15
141 T 13	Stamford st SE1
135 O 11	Stamp pl E2
49 S 1	Stanard clo N16
100 E 14	Stanborough clo Hampt
83 R 7	Stanborough rd Hounsl
87 N 8	Stanbridge rd SW15
80 C 6	Stanbrook rd SE2
92 B 4	Stanbury rd SE15
26 A 15	Stancroft NW9
81 R 14	Standard rd Blvdr
97 Z 10	Standard rd Bxly Hth
9 W 1	Standard rd Enf
82 C 7	Standard rd Hounsl
61 X 10	Standard rd NW10
87 X 20	Standen rd SW18
74 G 12	Standish rd W6
106 B 19	Stane clo SW19
107 Z 11	Stane pas SW16
56 F 17	Stanfield gdns Dgnhm
56 F 15	Stanfield rd Dgnhm
63 W 7	Stanfield rd E3
100 E 15	Stanford clo Hampt
38 G 18	Stanford clo Rom
150 J 7	Stanford pl SE17
16 A 16	Stanford rd N11
122 B 2	Stanford rd SW16
121 Z 2	Stanford rd SW16
145 Y 2	Stanford rd W8
148 E 6	Stanford st SW1
121 X 3	Stanford way SW16
123 X 10	Stanger rd SE25
99 X 11	Stanham pl Drtfrd
126 E 20	Stanhope av Harrow
23 P 5	Stanhope av Harrow
27 W 10	Stanhope av N3
139 U 13	Stanhope ga W1
56 A 8	Stanhope gdns Dgnhm
53 T 3	Stanhope gdns Ilf
30 K 18	Stanhope gdns N4
29 U 19	Stanhope gdns N6
13 R 17	Stanhope gdns SW7
146 D 6	Stanhope gdns SW7
124 L 10	Stanhope gro Becknhm
146 D 5	Stanhope Mews east SW7
146 C 6	Stanhope Mews south SW7
146 C 5	Stanhope Mews west SW7
59 N 10	Stanhope Park rd Grnfd
139 N 7	Stanhope pl W2
4 B 19	Stanhope rd Barnt
98 A 4	Stanhope rd Bxly Hth
97 Z 4	Stanhope rd Bxly Hth
155 O 17	Stanhope rd Carsh
157 R 7	Stanhope rd Croy
56 A 8	Stanhope rd Dgnhm
33 R 16	Stanhope rd E17
59 N 13	Stanhope rd Grnfd
15 S 16	Stanhope rd N12
47 V 1	Stanhope rd N6
29 V 20	Stanhope rd N6
114 M 8	Stanhope rd Sidcp
139 W 15	Stanhope row W1
132 A 12	Stanhope ter W2
138 G 8	Stanhope ter W2
145 R 11	Stanier clo W14
74 L 3	Stanlake ms W12
136 A 14	Stanlake rd W12
74 K 2	Stanlake rd W12
136 A 15	Stanlake vils W12
74 L 3	Stanlake vils W12
67 X 8	Stanley av Bark
125 U 5	Stanley av Becknhm
56 C 3	Stanley av Dgnhm
58 M 3	Stanley av Grnfd
59 N 3	Stanley av Grnfd
118 F 11	Stanley av New Mald
39 W 14	Stanley av Rom
60 K 1	Stanley av Wemb
39 X 12	Stanley clo Rom
149 N 16	Stanley clo SW8
60 K 1	Stanley clo Wemb
137 O 9	Stanley cres W11
101 T 11	Stanley Gardens rd Tedd
45 N 16	Stanley gdns NW2
107 N 16	Stanley gdns SW17
137 P 9	Stanley gdns W11
74 A 5	Stanley gdns W3
155 U 15	Stanley gdns Wallgtn
122 F 15	Stanley gro Croy
89 R 5	Stanley gro SW8
60 M 2	Stanley Park dri Wemb
155 S 14	Stanley Park rd Wallgtn
154 M 16	Stanley Park rd Carsh
132 J 9	Stanley pas NW1
126 K 8	Stanley rd Brom
155 O 18	Stanley rd Carsh
122 G 15	Stanley rd Croy
33 R 19	Stanley rd E10
53 R 16	Stanley rd E12
64 H 4	Stanley rd E15
34 C 5	Stanley rd E18
20 K 4	Stanley rd E4
8 F 13	Stanley rd Enf
40 M 7	Stanley rd Harrow
41 N 8	Stanley rd Harrow
82 M 9	Stanley rd Hounsl
83 N 9	Stanley rd Hounsl
54 D 8	Stanley rd Ilf
119 Y 8	Stanley rd Mrdn
29 R 2	Stanley rd N10
16 L 17	Stanley rd N11
30 K 13	Stanley rd N15
28 G 12	Stanley rd N2
18 F 7	Stanley rd N9
58 A 20	Stanley rd S'hall
115 O 8	Stanley rd Sidcp
154 A 16	Stanley rd Sutton
153 Z 16	Stanley rd Sutton
85 T 10	Stanley rd SW14
105 Y 16	Stanley rd SW19
101 U 13	Stanley rd Tedd
73 U 8	Stanley rd W3
43 N 17	Stanley rd Wemb
155 N 19	Stanley sq Carsh
66 L 19	Stanley st E6
75 Y 19	Stanley st SE8
48 A 8	Stanley ter N4
83 R 3	Stanleycroft clo Islwth
99 K 4	Stanmer st SW11
154 D 6	Stanmore gdns Sutton
85 N 8	Stanmore gdns Rich
10 L 11	Stanmore hill Stanm
11 O 14	Stanmore hill Stanm
131 Y 4	Stanmore pl NW1
81 Y 10	Stanmore rd Blvdr
52 C 4	Stanmore rd E11
30 K 12	Stanmore rd N15
84 M 7	Stanmore rd Rich
133 N 3	Stanmore st N1
125 P 2	Stanmore ter Becknhm
66 K 17	Stannard cres E6
49 W 17	Stannard rd E8
149 U 12	Stannary pl SE11
149 U 13	Stannary st SE11
90 D 7	Stansfield rd SW9
56 E 9	Stansgate rd Dgnhm
56 C 13	Stanstead clo Brom
153 Z 13	Stanstead manor Sutton
34 H 15	Stanstead rd E11
110 J 1	Stanstead rd SE23
57 T 19	Stansted clo Hornch
115 V 2	Stansted cres Bxly
150 K 20	Stanswood gdns SE5
108 A 11	Stanthorpe rd SW16
107 Z 11	Stanthorpe rd SW16
101 T 14	Stanton av Tedd
153 O 1	Stanton clo Worc Pk
122 L 18	Stanton clo Croy
86 D 4	Stanton clo SW13
119 O 1	Stanton clo SW20
91 W 1	Stanton clo SE15
110 K 9	Stanton way SE20
12 G 17	Stanway gdns Edg
73 P 1	Stanway gdns W3
134 K 9	Stanway st N1
145 O 7	Stanwick rd W14
42 A 9	Stapenhill rd Wemb
22 A 1	Staple Field clo Pinn
41 S 3	Staple Inn bldgs WC1
141 S 3	Staple Inn WC1
142 G 13	Staple st SE1
108 A 1	Staplefield clo SW16
36 H 17	Staplefield av Ilf
117 P 5	Staplefield clo Kingst
87 R 20	Stapleford clo SW19
42 G 20	Stapleford rd Wemb
68 D 8	Stapleford way Bark
154 J 17	Staplehurst rd Carsh
93 Y 14	Staplehurst rd SE13
57 W 19	Stapleton cres Rainhm
156 F 10	Stapleton gdns Croy
48 D 3	Stapleton Hall rd N4
30 E 20	Stapleton Hall rd N4
107 N 2	Stapleton rd SW17
81 R 14	Stapley rd Blvdr
4 F 12	Stapylton rd Barnt

84 L 20 Star & Garter hill Rich
63 N20 Star & Garter rd E1
142 K 8 Star all EC3
99 O 12 Star hill Drtfrd
64 M 12 Star la E16
65 N 13 Star la E16
83 P 5 Star rd Islwth
145 O 12 Star rd W14
65 P 13 Star st E16
138 J 4 Star st W2
141 S 5 Star yd WC2
76 C 8 Starboard way E14
36 E 7 Starch House la Ilf
132 C 14 Starcross st NW1
74 G 6 Starfield rd W12
151 X 10 Starkleigh way SE16
21 U 6 Starling clo Buck Hl
79 S 6 Starling la SE18
101 W 1 Staten gdns Twick
83 W 20 Statham gdns Twick
49 N 11 Statham gro N16
18 D 15 Statham gro N16
98 F 20 Station appr Bxly
98 J 5 Station appr Bxly Hth
113 R 16 Station appr Chisl
127 W 2 Station appr Chisl
99 S 14 Station appr Drtfrd
152 F 11 Station appr Epsom
100 H 20 Station appr Hampt
23 U 20 Station appr Harrow
117 R 2 Station appr Kingst
16 D 16 Station appr N11
22 B 12 Station appr Pinn
73 Y 20 Station Appr rd W4
85 O 1 Station appr Rich
99 S 12 Station appr SE9
113 T 1 Station appr SE9
153 T 16 Station appr Sutton
107 Y 12 Station appr SW16
87 U 6 Station appr SW6
97 O 5 Station appr Welling
42 C 17 Station appr Wemb
118 C 6 Station av New Mald
152 C 19 Station av Epsom
85 O 3 Station av Rich
90 K 7 Station av SW9
100 K 20 Station clo Hampt
20 C 10 Station clo N3
31 N 14 Station cres N15
7 S 15 Station cres SE3
42 B 17 Station cres Wemb
73 W 20 Station gdns W4
42 J 17 Station gro W4
57 X 13 Station pde Hornch
44 M 17 Station pde NW2
45 N 17 Station pde NW2
25 N 10 Station pde NW9
85 O 2 Station pde Rich
48 G 7 Station pl N4
81 T 9 Station rd Blvdr
126 A 3 Station rd Brom
98 A 6 Station rd Bxly Hth
97 Z 6 Station rd Bxly Hth
155 N 7 Station rd Carsh
122 L 20 Station rd Croy
157 P 3 Station rd Croy
99 T 15 Station rd Drtfrd
51 V 10 Station rd E10
53 O 13 Station rd E12
51 W 18 Station rd E15
32 J 17 Station rd E17
20 K 3 Station rd E4
52 F 13 Station rd E7
12 D 18 Station rd Edg
100 H 20 Station rd Hampt
22 K 15 Station rd Harrow
23 V 19 Station rd Harrow
82 K 12 Station rd Hounsl
117 P 1 Station rd Kingst
36 F 11 Station rd Ilf
53 Z 8 Station rd Ilf
16 E 17 Station rd N11
31 Y 11 Station rd N17
47 V 10 Station rd N19
17 W 5 Station rd N21
30 A 1 Station rd N22
30 D 7 Station rd N22
28 A 7 Station rd N3
27 Y 5 Station rd N3
118 J 12 Station rd New Mald
26 G 18 Station rd NW4
13 P 18 Station rd NW7
55 W 1 Station rd Rom
110 C 15 Station rd SE25
123 V 9 Station rd SE25
115 N 8 Station rd Sidcp
86 D 9 Station rd SW13
86 F 7 Station rd SW13

106 F 20 Station rd SW19
101 X 14 Station rd Tedd
83 W 20 Station rd Twick
159 U 1 Station rd W Wkhm
125 U 20 Station rd W Wkhm
60 M 18 Station rd W5
61 N 17 Station rd W5
71 T 2 Station rd W7
108 J 3 Station ri SE27
81 U 8 Station Road north Blvdr
51 W 20 Station st E15
78 L 4 Station st E16
128 E 9 Station ter NW10
90 M 2 Station ter SE5
59 P 2 Station view Grnfd
153 S 15 Station way Sutton
83 X 19 Station yd Twick
141 Y 6 Stationers Hall ct EC4
102 L 17 Staunton rd Kingst
75 Y 17 Staunton st SE8
75 V 3 Stave yard rd SE16
48 B 14 Staveley clo N7
92 A 1 Staveley clo SE15
85 Z 1 Staveley gdns W4
73 W 18 Staveley rd W4
44 M 19 Staverton rd NW2
120 C 18 Stavordale rd Carsh
48 G 13 Stavordale rd N5
63 S 12 Stayners rd E1
153 X 4 Stayton rd Sutton
150 D 7 Stead st SE17
135 N 4 Stean st E8
108 A 6 Steatham st SW16
68 B 6 Stebbing way Bark
76 H 10 Stebondale st E14
140 J 3 Stedham pl WC1
149 Z 7 Steedman st SE17
28 M 6 Steeds rd N10
46 M 18 Steel's rd NW3
51 Z 12 Steele rd E11
83 Y 11 Steele rd Islwth
31 T 9 Steele rd N17
61 W 7 Steele rd NW10
73 X 8 Steele rd W4
46 M 18 Steeles ms NW3
63 R 18 Steels la E1
31 S 12 Steen way SE22
107 Y 8 Steep hill SW16
105 T 11 Steeple clo SW19
87 T 6 Steeple clo SW6
17 Y 17 Steeplestone clo N18
106 C 5 Steerforth st SW18
120 K 1 Steers mead Mitch
106 L 20 Steers mead Mitch
75 W 6 Steers way SE16
107 N 14 Stella rd SW17
49 W 11 Stellman clo E5
124 A 4 Stembridge rd SE20
135 U 4 Stephan clo E8
57 V 17 Stephen av Rainhm
140 E 3 Stephen ms W1
98 X 9 Stephen rd Bxly Hth
140 E 3 Stephen st W1
88 B 6 Stephendale rd SW6
65 O 4 Stephens rd E15
59 W 16 Stephenson rd W7
62 C 8 Stephenson st NW10
64 M 15 Stephenson st E16
132 C 15 Stephensons way NW1
63 T 19 Stepney causeway E1
63 S 13 Stepney grn E1
63 U 16 Stepney High st E1
63 R 15 Stepney way E1
143 W 2 Stepney way E1
12 A 13 Sterling av Edg
11 Z 13 Sterling av Edg
8 A 5 Sterling rd Enf
138 L 20 Sterling st SW7
18 C 15 Sterling way N18
144 E 2 Sterndale rd W14
136 F 16 Sterne st SE15
91 Y 6 Sternhall la SE15
108 A 4 Sternhold av SW2
107 Y 3 Sternhold av SW2
56 D 14 Sterry cres Dgnhm
152 A 8 Sterry dri Epsom
56 E 17 Sterry gdns Dgnhm
67 X 4 Sterry rd Bark
56 D 12 Sterry rd Dgnhm
142 E 19 Sterry st SE1
92 J 20 Steucers la SE23
97 U 5 Stevedale rd Welling
53 V 18 Stevenage rd E6
144 E 20 Stevenage rd SW6

87 O 3 Stevenage rd SW6
50 D 17 Stevens av E9
100 D 14 Stevens clo Hampt
10 B 6 Stevens grn Bushey
55 R 9 Stevens rd Dgnhm
142 L 20 Stevens st SE1
74 E 1 Stevenson rd W12
142 L 1 Steward st E1
134 M 20 Steward st E1
39 R 16 Steward clo Hampt
100 C 15 Stewart clo Hampt
25 W 19 Stewart clo NW9
51 V 13 Stewart rd E15
76 H 6 Stewart st E14
146 J 9 Stewart's gro SW3
147 Z 20 Stewart's la SW8
148 A 20 Stewart's rd SW8
89 W 3 Stewart's rd SW8
17 X 17 Stewartsby clo N18
73 T 2 Steyne rd W3
113 T 10 Steyning gro SE9
14 K 17 Steynings way N12
115 X 3 Steynton av Bxly
81 S 10 Stickland rd Blvdr
58 K 10 Stickleton clo Grnfd
73 P 14 Stile Hall gdns W4
42 B 11 Stilecroft gdns Wemb
127 U 13 Stiles clo Brom
74 G 18 Stillingfleet rd SW13
148 C 4 Stillington st SW1
92 K 17 Stillness rd SE23
61 X 1 Stilton cres NW10
58 B 11 Stipularis dri Grnfd
65 V 7 Stirling rd E13
32 G 9 Stirling rd E17
23 V 9 Stirling rd Harrow
31 X 5 Stirling rd N17
30 H 4 Stirling rd N22
90 A 6 Stirling rd SW9
82 H 20 Stirling rd Twick
73 T 8 Stirling rd W3
32 G 9 Stirling Road pth E17
122 A 18 Stirling way Croy
117 T 14 Stirling wlk Surb
40 E 10 Stiven cres Harrow
48 C 14 Stock Orchard cres N7
48 C 15 Stock Orchard st N7
65 T 8 Stock st E13
124 B 14 Stockbury rd Croy
56 B 6 Stockdale rd Dgnhm
59 X 9 Stockdove way Grnfd
87 Z 3 Stockenchurch st SW6
108 D 6 Stockfield rd SW16
87 N 6 Stockhurst clo SW15
9 X 10 Stockingswater la Enf
38 M 19 Stockland rd Rom
107 X 20 Stockport rd SW16
33 V 11 Stocksfield rd E17
30 L 3 Stockton gdns N17
12 M 10 Stockton gdns NW7
13 N 10 Stockton gdns NW7
30 L 3 Stockton rd N17
18 L 18 Stockton rd N18
90 D 8 Stockwell av SW9
90 C 3 Stockwell gdns SW9
90 C 6 Stockwell grn SW9
90 C 5 Stockwell la SW9
90 C 6 Stockwell ms SW9
90 D 4 Stockwell Park cres SW9
90 D 4 Stockwell Park rd SW9
90 E 7 Stockwell Park wlk SW9
90 C 5 Stockwell rd SW9
76 H 18 Stockwell st SE10
90 B 2 Stockwell ter SW9
124 B 1 Stodart rd SE20
110 B 20 Stodart rd SE20
87 S 20 Stoford clo SW19
49 U 9 Stoke Newington High st N16
49 V 8 Stoke Newington comm N16
49 O 9 Stoke Newington Church st N16
49 T 13 Stoke Newington rd N16
62 D 9 Stoke pl NW10
103 V 18 Stoke rd Kingst
124 G 15 Stokes rd Croy
66 C 11 Stokes rd E6
62 E 17 Stokesley st W12
55 R 14 Stonard rd Dgnhm
17 U 9 Stonard rd N13

92 H 16 Stondon pk SE23
141 R 3 Stone bldgs WC2
56 C 8 Stone clo Dgnhm
11 Y 14 Stone gro Edg
17 S 2 Stone Hall rd N21
142 K 3 Stone House ct EC3
125 P 8 Stone Park av Beckenhm
152 G 2 Stone pl Worc Pk
126 D 10 Stone rd Brom
156 E 12 Stone st Croy
61 Y 1 Stonebridge pk NW10
31 T 16 Stonebridge rd N15
43 T 18 Stonebridge way Wemb
119 S 20 Stonecroft clo Sutton
81 X 20 Stonecroft rd Erith
122 A 16 Stonecroft way Croy
141 V 4 Stonecutter st EC4
98 E 8 Stonefield clo Bxly Hth
40 A 14 Stonefield clo Ruislip
133 T 4 Stonefield st N1
40 B 14 Stonefield way Ruislip
78 B 19 Stonefield way SE7
11 Y 16 Stonegrove gdns Edg
35 R 19 Stonehall av Ilf
16 J 18 Stoneham rd N11
85 Y 13 Stonehill clo SW14
85 X 13 Stonehill rd SW14
75 R 14 Stonehill rd W4
109 T 6 Stonehills ct SE21
9 R 16 Stonehorse rd Enf
152 G 7 Stoneleigh av Worc Pk
9 N 5 Stoneleigh av Enf
152 E 10 Stoneleigh cres Epsom
124 G 13 Stoneleigh Park av Croy
152 F 10 Stoneleigh Park rd Epsom
136 H 10 Stoneleigh pl W11
120 H 16 Stoneleigh rd Carsh
35 S 11 Stoneleigh rd Ilf
31 V 9 Stoneleigh rd N17
88 M 15 Stoneleigh st W11
48 D 5 Stoneset st N4
142 A 19 Stones End st SE1
95 Y 4 Stonells rd SW18
142 M 4 Stoney la E1
109 T 17 Stoney la SE19
142 D 13 Stoney st SE1
94 C 18 Stoneycroft clo SE12
32 H 13 Stoneydown av E17
32 G 13 Stoneydown E17
12 J 14 Stoneyfields gdns Edg
12 J 13 Stoneyfields la Edg
89 W 9 Stonhouse st SW4
145 P 7 Stonor rd W14
65 T 3 Stopford rd E13
149 Z 11 Stopford rd SE17
78 H 5 Store rd E16
51 Y 16 Store st E15
140 H 19 Store st WC1
76 J 11 Storers quay E14
32 L 14 Storey rd E17
29 N 18 Storey rd N6
78 K 4 Storey st E16
140 H 19 Storeys ga SW1
91 R 7 Stories rd SE5
52 D 19 Stork rd E7
151 U 3 Stork's rd SE16
26 A 2 Storksmead rd Edg
46 L 1 Stormont rd N6
28 L 20 Stormont rd N6
89 O 10 Stormont rd SW11
123 U 19 Storrington rd Croy
133 N 3 Story st N1
63 P 12 Stothard st E1
153 R 10 Stoughton av Sutton
104 G 1 Stoughton clo SW15
70 H 9 Stour av S'hall
56 F 7 Stour rd Dgnhm
99 V 8 Stour rd Drtfd
64 A 2 Stour rd E3
139 N 5 Stourcliffe st W1
87 R 19 Stourhead clo SW19
118 H 5 Stourhead gdns New Mald
100 D 9 Stourton av Felt
32 J 3 Stove st E17
76 C 16 Stowage the SE8
18 H 6 Stowe gdns N9
31 S 11 Stowe pl N15
74 J 6 Stowe rd W12

23 P 5 Stoxmead Harrow
52 F 13 Stracey rd E7
61 Z 3 Stracey rd NW10
104 M 16 Strachan pl SW19
35 S 9 Stradbroke gro Ilf
48 L 13 Stradbroke rd N5
90 L 16 Stradella rd SE24
35 X 7 Strafford av Ilf
4 E 11 Strafford rd Barnt
82 F 8 Strafford rd Hounsl
84 A 19 Strafford rd Twick
83 Z 18 Strafford rd Twick
73 U 6 Strafford rd W3
76 B 5 Strafford st E14
63 W 8 Strahan rd E3
70 A 6 Straight the S'hall
76 G 18 Straightsmouth SE10
66 G 19 Strait rd E6
92 A 11 Straker's rd SE15
91 Z 11 Straker's rd SE22
18 D 15 Strand pl N18
140 L 10 Strand WC2
141 P 8 Strand WC2
73 R 17 Strand-on-the-Green W4
79 V 13 Strandfield clo SE18
145 O 2 Strangways ter W14
132 M 3 Stranraer way N1
67 Z 2 Stratford clo Bark
56 J 20 Stratford clo Dgnhm
117 Y 8 Stratford ct New Mald
87 R 10 Stratford gro SW15
139 V 6 Stratford pl W1
122 G 8 Stratford rd Thntn Hth
65 S 5 Stratford rd E13
70 A 11 Stratford rd S'hall
145 V 4 Stratford rd W8
145 V 3 Stratford studios W8
47 W 20 Stratford vlls NW1
88 N 11 Strath ter SW11
87 U 16 Strathan clo SW18
94 H 15 Strathaven rd SE12
88 H 12 Strathblaine rd SW11
108 C 18 Strathbrook rd SW16
42 F 7 Strathcona rd Wemb
108 D 12 Strathdale SW16
106 F 8 Strathdon dri SW17
100 L 1 Strathearn av Twick
82 M 20 Strathearn av Twick
138 J 8 Strathearn pl W2
153 Y 10 Strathearn rd Sutton
105 Y 11 Strathearn rd SW19
94 E 1 Stratheden rd SE3
77 S 20 Stratheden rd SE3
54 F 18 Strathfield gdns Bark
90 A 12 Strathleven rd SW2
57 U 5 Strathmore gdns Hornch
25 S 7 Strathmore gdns Edg
28 A 6 Strathmore gdns N3
137 V 13 Strathmore gdns NW8
123 N 17 Strathmore rd Croy
105 S 9 Strathmore rd SW19
101 S 9 Strathmore rd Tedd
151 T 7 Strathnairn st SE1
46 H 19 Strathray gdns NW3
106 A 2 Strathville rd SW18
105 Z 2 Strathville rd SW18
122 E 6 Strathyre av SW16
8 C 2 Stratton av Enf
155 X 20 Stratton av Wallgtn
97 Z 7 Stratton clo Bxly Hth
11 Z 20 Stratton clo Edg
82 F 4 Stratton clo Hounsl
119 W 3 Stratton clo SW19
54 J 16 Stratton dri Bark
58 F 17 Stratton gdns S'hall
97 Z 8 Stratton rd Bxly Hth
119 X 3 Stratton rd SW19
139 Z 13 Stratton st W1
76 F 9 Strattondale st E14
73 Y 7 Strauss rd W4
101 V 8 Strawberry Hill clo Twick
101 V 6 Strawberry Hill rd Twick
101 V 6 Strawberry hill Twick
155 N 5 Strawberry la Carsh
101 X 6 Strawberry vale Twick
28 F 5 Strawberry vale N2
44 G 5 Streakes Field rd NW2
81 R 16 Stream way Blvdr
80 B 17 Streamdale SE2
126 F 8 Streamside clo Brom

66 F 4 Streatfield av E6
24 F 10 Streatfield rd Harrow
108 B 5 Streatham clo SW16
108 B 15 Streatham Common south SW16
108 C 14 Streatham Common north SW16
108 A 17 Streatham High rd SW16
107 Z 12 Streatham High rd SW16
108 B 2 Streatham hill SW2
90 A 20 Streatham pl SW2
107 P 19 Streatham rd Mitch
140 J 3 Streatham st WC1
107 W 18 Streatham vale SW16
107 O 5 Streathbourne rd SW17
46 E 12 Streatley pl NW3
129 P 1 Streatley rd NW6
94 G 7 Streetfield ms SE3
64 H 6 Streimer rd E15
62 A 19 Strelley way W3
123 S 17 Stretton rd Croy
102 C 5 Stretton rd Rich
88 F 19 Strickland row SW18
93 O 3 Strickland st SE8
65 P 7 Stride rd E13
29 P 1 Strode clo N10
52 F 12 Strode rd E7
31 S 9 Strode rd N17
44 H 19 Strode rd NW10
144 K 17 Strode rd SW6
53 O 17 Strone rd E12
52 K 13 Strone rd E7
95 T 13 Strongbow cres SE9
95 U 13 Strongbow rd SE9
40 H 3 Strongbridge clo Harrow
74 D 5 Stronsa rd W12
56 M 4 Strood av Rom
40 F 6 Stroud cres SW15
40 K 13 Strood field Nthlt
40 K 13 Strood ga Harrow
124 B 16 Stroud Green gdns Croy
48 D 3 Stroud Green rd N4
124 B 15 Stroud Green way Croy
124 B 16 Stroud Green way Croy
123 Y 15 Stroud rd SE25
105 X 6 Stroud rd SW19
118 C 18 Stroudes clo Worc Pk
64 D 9 Stroudley wlk E3
135 N 12 Strouts pl E2
148 E 3 Strutton ground SW1
142 M 2 Strype st E1
126 E 19 Stuart av Brom
40 D 10 Stuart av Harrow
44 G 2 Stuart av NW9
73 N 4 Stuart av W5
158 L 6 Stuart cres Croy
30 E 5 Stuart cres N22
97 T 7 Stuart Evans clo Welling
101 U 12 Stuart gro Tedd
106 L 20 Stuart pl Mitch
67 X 2 Stuart rd Bark
15 X 3 Stuart rd Barnt
23 W 10 Stuart rd Harrow
129 U 14 Stuart rd NW6
102 C 5 Stuart rd Rich
92 D 11 Stuart rd SE15
105 X 5 Stuart rd SW19
122 M 8 Stuart rd Thntn Hth
73 V 1 Stuart rd W3
97 R 1 Stuart rd Welling
120 F 1 Stubbs way SW19
70 M 20 Stucley rd Hounsl
131 Y 1 Stucley st NW1
133 W 4 Studd st N1
87 Y 5 Studdridge st SW6
45 Z 13 Studholme ct NW3
75 N 19 Studholme st SE15
151 X 18 Studholme st SE15
139 R 18 Studio pl SW1
114 L 7 Studland clo Sidcup
124 G 3 Studland rd Kingst
110 E 14 Studland rd SE26
59 S 16 Studland rd W7
74 J 11 Studland st W6
20 J 20 Studley av E4
33 W 1 Studley av E4
50 H 15 Studley clo E5
115 S 12 Studley ct Sidcp

35 O 18 Studley dri Ilf
71 U 6 Studley Grange dri W7
68 K 2 Studley rd Dgnhm
52 H 18 Studley rd E7
90 A 3 Studley rd SW4
90 A 4 Studley rd SW4
65 V 1 Stukeley rd E7
140 L 4 Stukeley st WC2
111 O 16 Stumps hill la Becknhm
92 A 6 Sturdy rd SE15
33 T 8 Sturge av E17
141 Z 17 Sturge st SE1
149 Z 11 Sturgeon rd SE17
114 E 16 Sturges field Chisl
44 H 1 Sturgess av NW4
26 K 20 Sturgess av NW4
48 C 14 Sturmer way N7
31 O 14 Sturrock clo N15
64 D 18 Sturry st E14
134 B 10 Sturt st N1
143 U 7 Stutfield st E1
90 J 7 Styles gdns SW9
125 U 10 Styles way Becknhm
90 C 12 Sudbourne rd SW2
102 H 7 Sudbrook gdns Rich
102 J 2 Sudbrook la Rich
102 J 6 Sudbrook pk Rich
89 O 17 Sudbrooke rd SW12
42 F 10 Sudbury av Wemb
41 X 9 Sudbury Court dri Harrow
41 X 10 Sudbury Court rd Harrow
112 E 13 Sudbury cres Brom
42 B 15 Sudbury cres Wemb
41 X 11 Sudbury croft Wemb
157 T 7 Sudbury gdns Croy
42 A 16 Sudbury Heights av Grnfd
41 Y 15 Sudbury Heights av Grnfd
41 X 10 Sudbury Hill clo Wemb
41 U 10 Sudbury hill Harrow
54 K 15 Sudbury rd Bark
133 X 9 Sudeley st N1
87 V 12 Sudlow rd SW18
142 A 18 Sudrey st SE1
59 W 6 Suez av Grnfd
9 W 13 Suez rd Enf
9 W 15 Suez rd Enf
20 E 13 Suffield rd E4
31 T 15 Suffield rd N15
124 B 5 Suffield rd SE20
51 O 2 Suffolk ct Ilf
36 H 18 Suffolk ct Ilf
160 E 9 Suffolk la EC4
32 J 13 Suffolk pk E17
140 F 12 Suffolk pl SW1
67 U 2 Suffolk rd Bark
56 J 15 Suffolk rd Dgnhm
65 R 10 Suffolk rd E13
9 N 18 Suffolk rd Enf
22 F 17 Suffolk rd Harrow
36 H 18 Suffolk rd Ilf
31 O 17 Suffolk rd N15
44 B 20 Suffolk rd NW10
123 V 7 Suffolk rd SE25
115 T 15 Suffolk rd Sidcup
74 F 20 Suffolk rd SW13
152 E 3 Suffolk rd Worc Pk
57 F 14 Suffolk st E7
140 F 12 Suffolk st SW1
64 F 6 Sugar House la E15
63 O 8 Sugar Loaf wlk E2
116 A 20 Sugden rd Surb
89 O 10 Sugden rd SW11
150 E 16 Sugden st SE5
67 Y 6 Sugden way Bark
144 C 1 Sulgrave rd W6
136 D 19 Sulgrave rd W6
74 M 8 Sulgrave rd W6
90 A 19 Sulina rd SW2
66 A 14 Sullivan av E16
88 H 7 Sullivan clo SW11
87 Y 6 Sullivan ct SW6
149 V 5 Sullivan rd SE11
87 Y 8 Sullivan rd SW6
11 S 1 Sullivan way Borhm Wd
34 G 14 Sultan rd E11
124 G 3 Sultan st Becknhm
150 A 18 Sultan st SE5
45 X 17 Sumatra rd NW6
127 X 3 Summer hill Chisl
113 Z 20 Summer hill Chisl
63 R 17 Summercourt rd E1
128 M 8 Summerfield av NW6

129 N 8 Summerfield av NW6
18 D 1 Summerfield gro Enf
60 B 12 Summerfield rd W5
94 D 20 Summerfield st SE12
31 P 13 Summerhill rd N15
82 B 1 Summerhouse av Hounsl
49 T 7 Summerhouse rd N16
29 S 11 Summerland gdns N10
73 V 1 Summerlands av W3
28 L 12 Summerlee av N2
28 L 13 Summerlee gdns N2
106 B 4 Summerley st SW18
153 Y 17 Summers clo Sutton
43 T 4 Summers clo Wemb
28 F 1 Summers la N12
15 X 19 Summers la N12
15 X 19 Summers row N12
133 T 18 Summers st EC1
29 R 17 Summersby rd N6
106 D 8 Summerstown SW17
68 K 18 Summerton way SE28
153 U 14 Summerville gdns Sutton
83 W 14 Summerwood rd Islwth
25 Y 15 Summit av NW9
25 P 2 Summit clo Edgw
16 G 8 Summit clo NW2
45 S 17 Summit clo NW2
25 Y 14 Summit clo NW9
35 O 6 Summit dri Wdfd Grn
33 T 13 Summit rd E17
59 H 1 Summit rd Nthlt
16 F 8 Summit way N14
109 T 19 Summit way SE19
91 V 1 Sumner av SE15
122 G 19 Sumner gdns Croy
146 G 7 Sumner pl SW7
146 G 6 Sumner Place ms SW7
122 H 19 Sumner rd Croy
41 N 1 Sumner rd Harrow
122 G 20 Sumner rd S Croy
151 O 15 Sumner rd SE15
91 V 1 Sumner rd SE15
142 A 13 Sumner st SE1
141 Z 13 Sumner st SE1
46 E 18 Sumpter clo NW3
84 H 10 Sun all Rich
160 H 6 Sun st EC2
77 V 20 Sun la SE3
145 O 12 Sun rd W14
134 H 20 Sun st EC2
142 J 1 Sun St pas EC2
134 J 20 Sun St pas EC2
61 X 12 Sunbeam rd NW10
89 P 15 Sunburgh rd SW12
12 L 15 Sunbury av NW7
85 Z 11 Sunbury av SW14
12 L 15 Sunbury gdns NW7
88 G 2 Sunbury la SW11
153 R 5 Sunbury rd Sutton
78 G 9 Sunbury st SE18
99 U 4 Suncourt Erith
110 B 7 Suncroft pl SE26
158 F 20 Sundale av S Croy
91 Y 19 Sunderland ct SE22
110 F 2 Sunderland rd SE23
72 G 8 Sunderland rd W5
137 W 5 Sunderland ter W2
53 N 5 Sunderland way E12
74 F 1 Sundew av W12
62 G 19 Sundew av W12
123 U 5 Sundial av SE25
77 X 14 Sundorne rd SE7
96 F 6 Sundridge av Welling
127 N 1 Sundridge av Brom
113 O 19 Sundridge av Chisl
113 N 17 Sundridge Park Chisl
113 O 15 Sundridge pk Chisl
123 W 19 Sundridge rd Croy
77 V 19 Sunfields pl SE3
156 A 18 Sunkist way SM6
97 Z 11 Sunland av Bxly Hth
60 K 3 Sunleigh rd Wemb
59 Y 4 Sunley gdns Grnfd
67 R 2 Sunningdale av Bark
100 B 4 Sunningdale av Felt
62 B 19 Sunningdale av W3
10 M 20 Sunningdale clo Stanm
25 U 17 Sunningdale gdns NW9
16 L 15 Sunningdale N14

153 V 8 Sunningdale rd Sutton
127 R 10 Sunningdale rd Brom
26 K 9 Sunningfields cres NW4
26 K 10 Sunningfields rd NW4
36 L 14 Sunninghill gdns Ilf
93 R 6 Sunninghill rd SE13
123 X 7 Sunny bank SE25
61 V 1 Sunny cres NW10
26 L 9 Sunny Gardens rd NW4
26 J 10 Sunny hill NW4
26 J 8 Sunny Hill pk NW4
157 O 13 Sunny Nook gdns S Croy
9 U 8 Sunny Road the Enf
25 Y 14 Sunny view NW9
28 J 1 Sunny way N12
82 K 5 Sunnycroft rd Hounsl
58 H 13 Sunnycroft rd S'hall
123 X 7 Sunnycroft rd SE25
94 H 12 Sunnydale rd SE12
20 L 16 Sunnydene av E4
42 E 20 Sunnydene gdns Wemb
110 G 10 Sunnyfield SE26
13 R 12 Sunnyfield NW7
108 A 9 Sunnyhill rd SW16
153 Y 5 Sunnyhurst clo Sutton
121 W 5 Sunnymead av Mitch
86 J 14 Sunnymead rd SW15
25 X 20 Sunnymead rd NW9
152 A 18 Sunnymede av Epsom
35 Z 13 Sunnymede dri Ilf
20 G 3 Sunnyside dri E4
51 N 3 Sunnyside rd E10
47 Y 1 Sunnyside rd N19
45 W 9 Sunnyside rd NW2
101 R 10 Sunnyside rd Tedd
72 F 4 Sunnyside rd W5
18 J 12 Sunnyside Road east N9
18 J 11 Sunnyside Road north N9
18 J 12 Sunnyside Road south N9
105 S 15 Sunnyside SW19
127 T 13 Sunray av Brom
91 O 11 Sunray av SE24
100 E 7 Sunrise clo Felt
20 E 4 Sunset av E4
21 R 14 Sunset av Wdfd Grn
123 T 3 Sunset gdns SE25
90 M 10 Sunset rd SE5
91 N 10 Sunset rd SE5
4 F 9 Sunset view Barnt
120 L 2 Sunshine way Mitch
91 Z 3 Sunwell clo SE15
116 H 9 Surbiton cres Surb
116 F 14 Surbiton ct Surb
116 H 10 Surbiton Hall clo Kingst
116 M 13 Surbiton Hill pk Surb
117 O 11 Surbiton Hill pk Surb
116 J 10 Surbiton Hill rd Kingst
116 M 12 Surbiton hill Surb
116 H 8 Surbiton rd Kingst
68 J 20 Surlingham clo SE28
116 A 16 Surr st N7
129 V 18 Surrendale pl W9
75 P 15 Surrey Canal rd SE14
91 U 1 Surrey gro SE17
154 G 4 Surrey gro Sutton
88 J 2 Surrey la SW11
109 P 10 Surrey ms SE27
110 A 1 Surrey mt SE23
75 S 7 Surrey Quays rd SE16
67 U 2 Surrey rd Bark
56 J 14 Surrey rd Dgnhm
22 M 17 Surrey rd Harrow
92 E 12 Surrey rd SE15
125 S 20 Surrey rd W Wkhm
141 X 17 Surrey row SE1
65 W 10 Surrey sq SE17
141 P 8 Surrey st WC2
75 T 4 Surrey Water rd SE16
109 O 16 Surridge gdns SE19
38 J 11 Susan clo Rom
94 J 5 Susan rd SE3
113 X 20 Susan wood Chisl
127 Y 1 Susan wood Chisl
64 E 18 Susannah st E14
83 S 8 Sussex av Islwth

35 T 17 Sussex clo Ilf
84 B 15 Sussex clo Twick
40 G 18 Sussex cres Nthlt
30 K 17 Sussex gdns N4
138 H 6 Sussex gdns W2
138 H 8 Sussex ms E W2
138 G 9 Sussex ms W W2
81 V 19 Sussex pl Erith
118 B 8 Sussex pl New Mald
130 M 16 Sussex pl NW1
138 H 7 Sussex pl W2
144 C 9 Sussex pl W6
74 L 13 Sussex pl W6
154 M 15 Sussex rd Carsh
66 J 5 Sussex rd E6
81 V 19 Sussex rd Erith
22 M 16 Sussex rd Harrow
23 N 17 Sussex rd Harrow
118 B 8 Sussex rd New Mald
157 P 13 Sussex rd S Croy
70 A 8 Sussex rd S'hall
115 R 13 Sussex rd Sidcup
125 S 20 Sussex rd W Wkhm
14 L 16 Sussex ring N12
138 G 8 Sussex sq W2
65 W 10 Sussex st E13
147 Z 10 Sussex st SW1
6 D 16 Sussex way Barnt
48 A 7 Sussex way N19
47 Z 5 Sussex way N7
28 B 16 Sutcliffe clo NW11
94 J 13 Sutcliffe pk SE9
79 V 17 Sutcliffe rd SE18
97 U 4 Sutcliffe rd Welling
96 L 12 Sutherland av Welling
60 A 18 Sutherland av W13
130 B 15 Sutherland av W9
129 V 19 Sutherland av W9
4 F 14 Sutherland ct Barnt
25 S 14 Sutherland ct NW9
86 B 9 Sutherland gdns SW14
118 J 19 Sutherland gdns Worc Pk
87 U 20 Sutherland gro SW18
101 U 12 Sutherland gro Tedd
137 T 5 Sutherland pl W2
81 S 7 Sutherland rd Blvdr
122 F 18 Sutherland rd Croy
32 G 9 Sutherland rd E17
63 Y 6 Sutherland rd E3
9 S 19 Sutherland rd Enf
31 X 3 Sutherland rd N17
18 L 5 Sutherland rd N9
58 E 17 Sutherland rd S'hall
59 Z 18 Sutherland rd W13
74 A 16 Sutherland rd W4
32 F 9 Sutherland Road pth E17
147 Y 9 Sutherland row SW1
150 A 12 Sutherland sq SE17
147 Z 11 Sutherland st SW1
150 B 12 Sutherland wlk SE17
77 Z 19 Sutlej rd SE7
48 B 19 Sutterton st N7
154 A 4 Sutton Common rd Sutton
119 U 18 Sutton Common rd Sutton
153 Y 2 Sutton Common rd Sutton
65 Y 9 Sutton Court rd E13
154 C 13 Sutton Court rd Sutton
73 V 17 Sutton Court rd W4
4 D 16 Sutton cres Barnt
154 C 15 Sutton ct Sutton
73 V 17 Sutton ct W4
82 J 3 Sutton dene Hounsl
128 B 19 Sutton est NW10
67 V 5 Sutton gdns Bark
123 V 12 Sutton gdns SE25
154 G 10 Sutton gro Sutton
70 G 20 Sutton Hall rd Hounsl
82 E 7 Sutton la Hounsl
73 W 13 Sutton la W4
73 U 16 Sutton Lane south W4
154 A 13 Sutton Park rd Sutton
50 C 15 Sutton pl E9
54 H 5 Sutton rd Bark
67 W 4 Sutton rd Bark
65 R 12 Sutton rd E13
32 F 6 Sutton rd E17
82 J 1 Sutton rd Hounsl
29 P 5 Sutton rd N10
140 F 5 Sutton row W1
82 E 2 Sutton sq Hounsl
63 O 18 Sutton st E1

82 F 1 Sutton way Hounsl
128 B 19 Sutton way W10
62 M 13 Sutton way W10
134 D 19 Suttons way EC1
106 D 3 Swaby rd SW18
30 J 1 Swaffham way N22
17 W 20 Swaffham way N22
88 B 19 Swaffield rd SW18
122 M 10 Swain rd Thntn Hth
47 R 4 Swain's la N6
106 M 17 Swain's rd SW17
74 C 4 Swainson rd W3
99 Z 15 Swaisland rd Drtfrd
99 T 13 Swaislands dri Drtfrd
5 W 8 Swale rd Drtfrd
111 P 9 Swallands rd SE6
92 E 2 Swallow clo SE14
58 F 5 Swallow dri Nthlt
139 Z 6 Swallow pas W1
66 E 14 Swallow st E6
140 C 11 Swallow st W1
57 X 19 Swallow wlk Hornch
158 G 20 Swallowdale S Croy
77 W 14 Swallowfield rd SE7
66 D 15 Swan appr E6
100 B 10 Swan clo Felt
99 T 19 Swan la Drtfrd
160 F 10 Swan la EC4
16 R 9 Swan la N20
150 P 3 Swan mead SE1
90 C 3 Swan ms SW9
86 E 4 Swan pl SW13
100 B 11 Swan rd Felt
58 K 17 Swan rd S'hall
75 R 5 Swan rd SE16
78 B 9 Swan rd SE18
84 A 7 Swan st Islwth
142 C 19 Swan st SE1
9 S 8 Swan way Enf
15 R 9 Swan way N20
142 F 11 Swan wharf EC4
39 R 15 Swan wlk Rom
147 O 14 Swan wlk SW3
48 H 19 Swan yd N1
33 U 2 Swanage rd E4
88 D 16 Swanage rd SW18
98 F 3 Swanbridge rd Bxly Hth
88 B 11 Swandon way SW18
135 O 15 Swanfield st E2
97 U 3 Swanley rd Welling
136 H 14 Swanscombe rd W11
74 B 13 Swanscombe rd W4
9 O 14 Swansea rd Enf
32 G 4 Swansland gdns E17
105 R 1 Swanton gdns SW19
81 T 19 Swanton rd Erith
86 D 18 Swanwick clo SW15
81 S 13 Swaton rd E3
81 S 17 Swaylands clo Blvdr
75 W 10 Sweden ga SE16
143 V 9 Swedenborg gdns E1
143 O 19 Sweeney cres SE1
18 G 12 Sweet Briar grn N9
18 F 11 Sweet Briar gro N9
18 F 14 Sweet Briar wlk N18
15 T 9 Sweets way N20
65 T 8 Swete st E13
94 G 5 Sweyn pl SE3
40 K 7 Swift clo Harrow
75 S 3 Swift clo SE16
70 F 7 Swift rd S'hall
87 U 2 Swift st SW6
112 A 15 Swiftsden way Brom
137 N 1 Swinbrook rd W10
124 C 16 Swinburn cres Croy
86 H 12 Swinburne rd SW15
42 H 18 Swinderby rd Wemb
54 H 6 Swindon clo Ilf
136 A 14 Swindon st W12
74 K 2 Swindon st W12
100 A 9 Swinfield clo Felt
90 H 7 Swinford gdns SW9
79 V 16 Swingate la SE18
50 J 16 Swinnerton st E9
43 T 5 Swinton clo Wemb
133 N 13 Swinton pl WC1
133 O 12 Swinton st WC1
113 V 9 Swithland gdns SE9
72 C 12 Swyncombe av W5
50 L 2 Sybourn st E17
96 L 15 Sycamore av Sidcp
72 G 8 Sycamore av W5
5 U 19 Sycamore clo Barnt
154 L 8 Sycamore clo Carsh
64 M 13 Sycamore clo E16
58 C 4 Sycamore clo Nthlt

120 G 4 Sycamore gdns Mitch
136 A 20 Sycamore gdns W6
74 K 7 Sycamore gdns W6
118 A 4 Sycamore gro New Mald
117 Z 5 Sycamore gro New Mald
43 W 1 Sycamore gro NW9
109 Y 20 Sycamore gro SE20
104 M 15 Sycamore rd SW19
134 A 17 Sycamore st EC1
122 E 10 Sycamore way Thntn Hth
110 A 12 Sydenham av SE26
109 Y 7 Sydenham hill SE26
110 C 7 Sydenham Park rd SE26
110 B 8 Sydenham pk SE26
108 J 6 Sydenham rd Croy
157 N 1 Sydenham rd Croy
123 P 15 Sydenham rd Croy
110 F 11 Sydenham rd SE26
110 A 2 Sydenham ri SE23
109 Z 3 Sydenham ri SE23
110 Z 3 Sydenham ri SE23
49 V 11 Sydner rd N16
146 H 8 Sydney gro NW4
26 L 16 Sydney gro NW4
146 H 7 Sydney ms SW3
146 H 7 Sydney pl SW3
97 X 10 Sydney rd Bxly Hth
8 B 14 Sydney rd Enf
36 B 8 Sydney rd Ilf
29 R 5 Sydney rd N10
30 F 12 Sydney rd N8
84 K 11 Sydney rd Rich
80 H 8 Sydney rd SE2
114 J 9 Sydney rd Sidcup
119 P 3 Sydney rd SW20
101 V 13 Sydney rd Tedd
84 A 16 Sydney rd Twick
72 A 5 Sydney rd W13
71 Z 3 Sydney rd W13
21 S 15 Sydney rd Wdfd Grn
146 J 8 Sydney st SW3
30 E 1 Sylvan av N22
27 Z 7 Sylvan av N3
13 P 18 Sylvan av NW7
38 C 18 Sylvan av Rom
116 F 19 Sylvan gdns Surb
75 N 17 Sylvan gro SE15
151 Y 16 Sylvan gro SE15
109 S 19 Sylvan hill SE19
34 E 15 Sylvan rd E11
33 N 15 Sylvan rd E17
52 G 17 Sylvan rd E7
109 U 20 Sylvan rd SE19
123 V 1 Sylvan rd SE19
55 P 11 Sylvan way Dgnhm
159 Z 8 Sylvan way W Wkhm
113 T 16 Sylvester pth E8
50 A 18 Sylvester pth E8
50 A 17 Sylvester rd E8
28 F 7 Sylvester rd N2
42 E 14 Sylvester rd Wemb
43 S 20 Sylvia gdns Wemb
147 P 6 Symons st SW3
71 Z 19 Syon Gate way Brentf

84 D 3 Syon ho Islwth
72 A 20 Syon la Brentf
71 V 16 Syon la Islwth
71 V 18 Syon Park gdns Islwth
84 D 2 Syon pk Islwth

T

142 D 18 Tabard st SE1
150 F 1 Tabard st SE1
65 T 12 Tabernacle av E13
134 G 18 Tabernacle st EC2
89 W 12 Tabler av SW4
47 Z 11 Tabley rd N7
153 T 15 Tabor gdns Sutton
105 U 17 Tabor gro SW19
74 K 9 Tabor rd W6
148 B 6 Tachbrook ms SW1
148 E 9 Tachbrook st SW1
93 N 6 Tack ms SE4
146 C 18 Tadema rd SW10
136 E 15 Tadmor st W12
118 D 10 Tadworth av New Mald

57 Y 13	Tadworth pde Hornch
44 G 7	Tadworth rd NW2
76 D 10	Taeping st E14
120 K 5	Taffy's how Mitch
64 F 8	Taft st E3
143 P 2	Tailworth st E1
123 R 16	Tait rd Croy
38 L 7	Takeley clo Rom
47 R 18	Talacre rd NW5
28 F 11	Talbot av N2
31 U 13	Talbot clo N15
26 G 16	Talbot cres NW4
54 M 7	Talbot gdns Ilf
94 A 3	Talbot pl SE3
93 Z 3	Talbot pl SE3
126 G 7	Talbot rd Brom
155 O 10	Talbot rd Carsh
56 B 19	Talbot rd Dgnhm
66 H 5	Talbot rd E6
52 E 12	Talbot rd E7
23 X 9	Talbot rd Harrow
83 Z 10	Talbot rd Islwth
31 V 13	Talbot rd N15
29 W 6	Talbot rd N22
29 O 19	Talbot rd N6
70 C 10	Talbot rd S'hall
123 O 9	Talbot rd Thntn Hth
101 U 1	Talbot rd Twick
83 U 20	Talbot rd Twick
137 P 6	Talbot rd W11
71 Y 2	Talbot rd W13
137 U 4	Talbot rd W2
42 G 17	Talbot rd Wemb
138 G 6	Talbot sq W2
142 F 15	Talbot yd SE1
91 U 2	Talfourd pl SE15
91 T 2	Talfourd rd SE15
144 J 9	Talgarth rd W14
109 W 9	Talisman sq SE16
42 L 9	Talisman way Wemb
126 C 10	Tall Elms clo Brom
23 U 3	Tallack clo Harrow
50 M 4	Tallack rd E10
77 W 16	Tallis gro SE7
141 U 8	Tallis st EC4
15 R 17	Tallyho corner N12
83 T 17	Talma gdns Twick
90 G 12	Talma rd SW2
92 C 20	Talmage clo SE23
11 T 18	Talman gro Stanm
64 E 10	Talwin st E3
21 W 19	Tamar sq Wdfd Grn
78 B 10	Tamar st SE7
31 W 10	Tamar way N17
62 E 20	Tamarisk sq W12
152 A 1	Tamesis gdns KT4
129 S 16	Tamplin ms W9
21 N 18	Tamworth av Wdfd Grn
121 R 4	Tamworth la Mitch
121 T 8	Tamworth Lodge est Mitch
121 S 7	Tamworth pk Mitch
145 T 14	Tamworth st SW6
121 T 8	Tamworth vlls Mitch
30 J 20	Tancred rd N4
44 C 11	Tanfield av NW2
156 L 8	Tanfield rd Croy
85 R 9	Tangier rd Rich
10 F 10	Tanglewood clo Stanm
158 D 5	Tanglewood clo Croy
86 E 17	Tangley gro SW15
100 E 12	Tangley Park rd Hampt
57 Z 19	Tangmere cres Hornch
26 B 7	Tangmere way NW9
132 L 13	Tankerton st WC1
107 Y 17	Tankerville rd SW16
44 K 7	Tankridge rd NW2
54 B 18	Tanner st SE1
142 K 18	Tanner st SE1
143 O 18	Tanner st SE1
18 E 15	Tanners End la N18
92 M 3	Tanners hill SE8
93 N 1	Tanners hill SE8
36 C 10	Tanners la Ilf
124 E 10	Tannery clo Becknhm
56 G 8	Tannery clo Dgnhm
48 G 10	Tannington ter N4
110 E 12	Tannsfeld rd SE26
147 Z 15	Tansley clo N7
141 T 18	Tanswell st SE1
66 K 18	Tansy clo E6
65 P 16	Tant av E16
89 N 20	Tantallon rd SW12
37 X 11	Tantony gro Rom
156 K 3	Tanworth pl Croy
156 K 3	Tanworth rd Croy
46 L 11	Tanza rd NW3
154 A 16	Tapestry clo Sutton
134 B 10	Taplow st N1
135 X 17	Tapp st E1
92 B 7	Tappesfield rd SE15
4 G 13	Tapster st Barnt
91 T 12	Tarbert rd SE22
18 L 20	Tariff rd N17
110 A 3	Tarleton gdns SE23
115 R 8	Tarling clo Sidcp
65 R 19	Tarling rd E16
28 E 6	Tarling rd N2
63 O 18	Tarling st E1
143 Y 6	Tarling st E1
7 O 16	Tarn bank Enf
95 U 20	Tarnwood pk SE9
107 X 8	Tarrington clo SW16
149 Y 10	Tarver rd SE17
76 E 18	Tarves way SE10
16 E 16	Tash pl N11
46 M 16	Tasker rd NW3
90 A 8	Tasman rd SW9
66 A 18	Tasman wk E16
17 Z 19	Tasmania ter N18
144 K 14	Tasso rd W6
43 X 19	Tatam rd E16
148 J 7	Tate gallery SW1
78 E 3	Tate rd E16
153 X 12	Tate rd Sutton
92 H 16	Tatnell rd SE23
95 R 12	Tattersall clo SE9
150 G 7	Tatum st SE17
82 M 4	Taunton av Hounsl
83 N 3	Taunton av Hounsl
118 J 3	Taunton av SW20
99 N 6	Taunton clo Bxly Hth
119 W 20	Taunton clo Sutton
7 T 11	Taunton dri Enf
131 O 18	Taunton ms NW1
131 N 17	Taunton pl NW1
58 K 2	Taunton rd Grnfd
94 C 13	Taunton rd SE12
24 K 8	Taunton way Stanm
24 K 9	Taunton way Stanm
48 K 13	Taverner sq N5
136 K 15	Taverners clo W11
32 G 11	Tavistock av E17
60 A 6	Tavistock av Grnfd
59 Z 7	Tavistock av Grnfd
49 T 15	Tavistock clo N16
122 A 9	Tavistock cres Mitch
121 Z 9	Tavistock cres Mitch
137 O 2	Tavistock cres W10
54 H 13	Tavistock gdns Ilf
123 N 18	Tavistock gro Croy
137 N 5	Tavistock ms W11
34 F 11	Tavistock pl E18
16 E 1	Tavistock pl N14
132 H 16	Tavistock pl WC1
126 D 8	Tavistock rd Brom
120 C 20	Tavistock rd Carsh
123 N 19	Tavistock rd Croy
52 B 19	Tavistock rd E15
34 E 11	Tavistock rd E18
52 B 11	Tavistock rd E7
25 O 5	Tavistock rd Edg
31 N 19	Tavistock rd N4
62 D 5	Tavistock rd NW10
137 O 3	Tavistock rd W11
97 T 2	Tavistock rd Welling
132 G 16	Tavistock sq WC1
140 M 9	Tavistock st WC2
141 N 7	Tavistock st WC2
47 Z 9	Tavistock ter N19
120 G 20	Tavistock wlk Carsh
75 T 10	Taviton st WC1
39 S 4	Tawny way SE16
83 U 16	Tayben av Twick
89 P 10	Taybridge rd SW11
64 F 17	Tayburn clo E14
85 S 4	Taylor av Rich
101 N 12	Taylor clo Hampt
31 X 1	Taylor clo N17
38 E 1	Taylor clo Rom
106 K 18	Taylor rd Mitch
155 R 11	Taylor rd Wallgtn
78 M 11	Taylor's la NW10
44 A 20	Taylor's la NW10
62 B 16	Taylors grn W3
4 G 6	Taylors la Barnt
109 Y 10	Taylors la SE26
110 B 3	Taymount ri SE23
58 E 9	Taywood rd Nthlt
75 V 4	Teak clo SE16
66 A 16	Teal clo E16
135 U 8	Teale st E2
124 D 20	Teasel clo CR0
64 M 8	Teasel way E15
31 T 3	Tebworth rd N17
158 E 18	Tedder rd S Croy
101 X 17	Teddington lodge Tedd
101 W 10	Teddington Park rd Tedd
101 W 11	Teddington pk Tedd
147 N 11	Tedworth gdns SW3
147 N 11	Tedworth sq SW3
62 A 17	Tee the W3
59 V 6	Tees av Grnfd
83 Z 2	Teesdale av Islwth
83 Z 2	Teesdale rd Islwth
34 B 20	Teesdale st E1
135 V 10	Teesdale yd E2
123 X 17	Teevan clo Croy
123 X 18	Teevan rd Croy
25 N 8	Teignmouth clo SE9
89 X 11	Teignmouth clo SW4
59 Y 7	Teignmouth gdns Grnfd
97 T 3	Teignmouth rd Welling
45 O 16	Teignmouth rd NW2
45 Z 9	Telegraph hill NW3
55 N 2	Telegraph ms Ilf
86 K 17	Telegraph rd SW15
160 F 4	Telegraph st EC2
94 J 9	Telemann sq SE9
145 R 14	Telephone pl W14
107 W 1	Telferscot rd SW12
108 A 2	Telford av SW2
107 Y 2	Telford av SW2
16 H 18	Telford rd N11
58 K 18	Telford rd S'hall
114 D 5	Telford rd SE9
128 K 20	Telford rd W10
62 A 15	Telford way W3
66 H 7	Telham rd E6
91 U 11	Tell gro SE22
95 P 1	Tellson av SE18
89 P 18	Temperley rd SW12
57 W 18	Tempest way Rainhm
45 U 17	Tempro ho NW2
100 G 17	Templar pl Hampt
90 J 3	Templar st SE5
27 W 19	Templars av NW11
27 X 8	Templars cres N3
30 B 19	Templars pth Harrow
158 L 4	Temple av Croy
56 D 3	Temple av Dgnhm
141 U 8	Temple av EC4
15 T 3	Temple av N20
27 V 8	Temple clo N3
79 P 7	Temple clo SE18
27 Y 16	Temple Fortune hill NW11
27 Y 18	Temple Fortune la NW11
55 V 9	Temple gdns Dgnhm
17 W 9	Temple gdns N21
27 V 18	Temple gdns NW11
7 W 10	Temple gro Enf
27 X 17	Temple gro NW11
141 U 7	Temple la EC4
11 N 20	Temple Mead clo Stanm
62 A 18	Temple Mead clo W3
51 R 13	Temple Mill la E15
51 P 13	Temple Mill rd E15
141 P 9	Temple pl WC2
66 C 3	Temple rd Croy
82 L 5	Temple rd Hounsl
30 C 13	Temple rd N8
44 M 11	Temple rd NW2
45 N 10	Temple rd NW2
85 N 6	Temple rd Rich
73 V 9	Temple rd W4
72 F 9	Temple rd W5
85 T 11	Temple Sheen SW14
85 U 12	Temple sheen SW14
135 V 9	Temple st E2
154 G 6	Temple way Sutton
63 O 3	Templecombe rd E9
135 Z 3	Templecombe rd E9
119 R 11	Templecombe way Mrdn
44 M 1	Templehof av NW4
59 W 14	Templeman rd W7
20 C 12	Templeton av E4
123 P 1	Templeton clo SE19
145 U 6	Templeton pl SW5
31 O 18	Templeton rd N15
46 B 10	Templewood av NW3
46 B 10	Templewood gdns NW3
60 B 14	Templewood W13
22 M 8	Temsford clo Harrow
89 Z 20	Tenbury ct SW2
24 B 8	Tenby av Harrow
31 V 13	Tenby clo N15
37 Y 19	Tenby clo Rom
40 G 18	Tenby gdns Nthlt
32 G 15	Tenby rd E17
25 N 6	Tenby rd Edgw
9 P 13	Tenby rd Enf
37 Y 19	Tenby rd Rom
97 V 1	Tenby rd Welling
143 W 13	Tench st E1
151 V 8	Tenda rd SE16
37 S 15	Tendring way Rom
107 X 2	Tenham av SW2
140 B 8	Tenison ct W1
141 R 14	Tenison way SE1
138 A 8	Tenniel clo Rom
142 E 17	Tennis st SE1
123 T 10	Tennison rd SE25
8 F 7	Tenniswood rd Enf
118 K 12	Tennyson av New Mald
52 F 1	Tennyson av E11
53 P 20	Tennyson av E12
25 V 11	Tennyson av NW9
101 W 2	Tennyson av Twick
96 J 2	Tennyson clo SE10
51 S 5	Tennyson rd E10
51 Z 19	Tennyson rd E15
32 L 18	Tennyson rd E17
82 M 3	Tennyson rd Hounsl
129 P 5	Tennyson rd NW6
13 T 15	Tennyson rd NW7
110 F 17	Tennyson rd SE20
106 C 14	Tennyson rd SW19
59 V 20	Tennyson rd W7
89 S 5	Tennyson rd SW8
57 U 6	Tennyson way Hornch
70 G 8	Tensing rd S'hall
135 V 17	Tent st E1
70 H 12	Tentelow la S'hall
143 N 2	Tenter ground E1
27 O 10	Tenterden clo NW4
27 P 11	Tenterden dri NW4
27 O 11	Tenterden gdns NW4
27 O 11	Tenterden gro NW4
123 Y 16	Tenterden rd Croy
56 B 5	Tenterden rd Dgnhm
31 T 2	Tenterden rd N17
139 Y 6	Tenterden st W1
91 R 13	Terborch way SE22
52 B 9	Terling clo E11
56 D 5	Terling rd Dgnhm
147 Z 4	Terminus pl SW1
86 C 4	Terrace gdns SW13
84 K 17	Terrace la Rich
65 U 4	Terrace rd E13
50 D 20	Terrace rd E9
21 S 18	Terrace the Wdfd Grn
129 S 3	Terrace the NW6
56 A 16	Terrace wlk Dgnhm
55 Z 16	Terrace wlk Dgnhm
147 P 16	Terrace wlk SW11
107 S 5	Terrapin rd SW17
133 W 2	Terretts pl N1
30 A 6	Terrick rd N22
62 K 18	Terrick st W12
22 D 10	Terrilands Pinn
30 L 14	Terront rd N15
75 V 11	Terry la SE8
59 T 20	Testwood clo W7
133 V 6	Tetbury pl N1
29 O 8	Tetherdown N10
151 U 10	Tetterby way SE16
126 E 4	Tetty way Brom
90 A 1	Teversham la SW8
97 R 1	Teviot rd Welling
64 F 13	Teviot st E14
22 C 17	Tewkesbury av Pinn
92 A 20	Tewkesbury av SE23
31 O 19	Tewkesbury clo N15
25 U 10	Tewkesbury gdns SE9
120 F 19	Tewkesbury rd Carsh
31 O 20	Tewkesbury rd N15
71 Y 1	Tewkesbury rd W13
16 H 18	Tewkesbury ter N11
79 V 13	Tewson rd SE18
8 B 20	Teynham av Enf
30 M 5	Teynton ter N17
31 X 8	Thackeray av N17
40 H 4	Thackeray clo Harrow

105 P 18 Thackeray clo SW19
55 O 2 Thackeray dri Rom
66 B 6 Thackeray rd E6
89 S 5 Thackeray rd SW8
137 Y 20 Thackeray st W8
109 Z 11 Thakeham clo SE26
28 E 8 Thakrah clo N2
76 K 16 Thalia clo SE10
75 T 5 Thame rd SE16
69 W 8 Thames av Dgnhm
59 V 6 Thames av Grnfd
88 E 1 Thames av SW10
85 W 5 Thames bank SW14
38 L 8 Thames Hill av Rom
75 Z 1 Thames pl E1
84 B 11 Thames promenade Twick
68 A 8 Thames rd Bark
67 W 9 Thames rd Bark
99 W 8 Thames rd Drtfrd
78 A 4 Thames rd E16
73 R 17 Thames rd W4
102 F 17 Thames side Kingst
116 G 2 Thames side Kingst
76 E 16 Thames st SE10
85 V 2 Thames Village W4
68 G 17 Thamesbank pl SE28
102 B 10 Thamesgate clo Rich
68 B 20 Thamesmere dri SE28
82 H 6 Thamesville clo Hounsl
48 D 9 Thame vlls N7
157 T 6 Thanescroft gdns Croy
156 M 3 Thanet pl Croy
157 N 7 Thanet pl Croy
98 E 19 Thanet rd Bxly
132 J 14 Thanet st WC1
155 X 11 Tharp rd Wallgtn
15 R 3 Thatcham gdns N20
83 R 13 Thatchers way Islwth
37 Y 12 Thatches gro Rom
141 U 3 Thavies in EC4
105 O 18 Thaxted clo SW20
114 B 5 Thaxted rd SE9
145 R 13 Thaxton rd SW6
139 U 4 Thayer st W1
124 J 1 Thayers Farm rd Becknhm
88 M 8 Theatre st SW11
133 V 4 Theberton st N1
141 T 14 Theed st SE1
95 P 2 Thelma gdns SE3
101 X 14 Thelma gro Tedd
22 L 5 Theobald cres Harrow
156 J 2 Theobald rd Croy
150 E 3 Theobald st SE1
133 O 20 Theobald's rd WC1
15 P 14 Theobalds av N12
93 V 15 Theodore rd SE13
122 A 15 Therapia la Croy
121 X 17 Therapia la Croy
92 C 15 Therapia rd SE22
74 G 12 Theresa rd W6
74 G 12 Theresa rd W6
76 E 11 Thermopylae ga E14
110 F 17 Thesiger rd SE20
148 A 19 Thessaly rd SW8
89 X 3 Thessally rd SW8
17 W 20 Thetford clo N13
68 K 2 Thetford gdns Dgnhm
118 A 12 Thetford rd New Mald
117 Z 13 Thetford rd New Mald
68 K 2 Thetford rd Dgnhm
21 X 19 Theydon gro Wdfd Grn
50 C 5 Theydon rd E5
50 L 1 Theydon st E17
154 E 8 Thicket cres Sutton
55 U 17 Thicket gro Dgnhm
109 X 17 Thicket gro SE20
110 A 16 Thicket rd SE20
109 Y 18 Thicket rd SE20
154 E 7 Thicket rd Sutton
69 V 5 Third av Dgnhm
53 S 13 Third av E12
65 T 9 Third av E13
33 P 15 Third av E17
8 G 17 Third av Enf
37 T 17 Third av Rom
128 M 15 Third av W10
74 C 3 Third av W3
42 G 6 Third av Wemb
101 S 4 Third Cross rd Twick
43 U 13 Third way Wemb
25 X 4 Thirleby rd SE18

148 C 3 Thirleby rd SW1
60 C 8 Thirlmere av Grnfd
42 E 4 Thirlmere gdns Wemb
98 K 3 Thirlmere rd Bxly Hth
29 T 5 Thirlmere rd N10
107 X 10 Thirlmere rd SW16
112 B 16 Thirlmere ri Brom
40 J 17 Thirsk clo Nthlt
107 P 17 Thirsk rd Mitch
123 P 8 Thirsk rd SE25
89 N 8 Thirsk rd SW11
146 C 9 Thistle gro SW5
80 F 7 Thistlebrook SE2
24 G 6 Thistlecroft gdns Stanm
40 C 10 Thistledown av Harrow
127 Y 3 Thistlemead BR7
50 B 10 Thistlewaite rd E5
48 D 7 Thistlewood clo N7
71 P 18 Thistleworth clo Islwth
41 W 11 Thomas à Beckett clo W11
88 G 9 Thomas Baines rd SW11
149 X 1 Thomas Doyle st SE1
93 P 19 Thomas la SE6
143 S 12 Thomas More st SE1
28 C 9 Thomas More way N3
64 A 15 Thomas rd E14
63 Z 16 Thomas rd E14
78 K 10 Thomas st SE18
85 S 6 Thompson av Rich
56 C 10 Thompson rd Dgnhm
91 V 16 Thompson rd SE22
150 A 17 Thompsons av SE5
156 F 1 Thomson cres Croy
122 F 19 Thomson cres Croy
23 U 9 Thomson rd Harrow
51 S 7 Thonrey sq SE1
134 B 11 Thoresby st N1
116 A 17 Thorkhill rd Surb
10 A 6 Thorn av Bushey
12 D 20 Thorn bank Edg
127 X 14 Thorn clo Brom
58 E 8 Thorn clo Nthlt
18 L 18 Thornaby gdns N18
71 P 20 Thornbury av Islwth
71 R 19 Thornbury rd Islwth
83 R 4 Thornbury rd Islwth
90 A 17 Thornbury rd SW2
89 Z 16 Thornbury rd SW2
47 U 4 Thornbury sq N19
50 C 10 Thornby rd E5
70 F 12 Thorncliffe rd S'hall
89 Z 17 Thorncliffe rd SW2
91 T 12 Thorncombe rd SE22
39 T 18 Thorncroft Hornch
153 Z 10 Thorncroft rd Sutton
148 J 19 Thorncroft st SW8
106 C 5 Thorndean st SW18
16 A 7 Thorndene av N11
146 B 18 Thorndike clo SW10
148 D 8 Thorndike st SW1
152 C 9 Thorndon gdns Epsom
51 Y 11 Thorne clo E11
65 R 17 Thorne clo E16
81 W 16 Thorne clo Erith
117 V 8 Thorne clo New Mald
86 B 6 Thorne pas SW13
117 V 8 Thorne rd New Mald
148 L 20 Thorne rd SW8
65 R 17 Thorne st E16
86 B 6 Thorne st SW13
156 H 12 Thorneloe gdns Croy
125 T 6 Thornes clo Becknhm
127 W 7 Thornet Wood rd Brom
73 T 12 Thorney Hedge rd W4
148 J 6 Thorney st SW1
27 S 3 Thornfield av NW7
136 A 17 Thornfield rd W12
74 K 5 Thornfield rd W12
93 U 14 Thornford rd SE13
129 V 17 Thorngate rd W9
65 W 3 Thorngrove rd E13
51 V 16 Thornham gro E15
132 H 19 Thornhaugh st WC1
79 V 19 Thornhill av SE18
133 O 7 Thornhill bri N1
133 N 7 Thornhill Bridge wharf N1
133 O 1 Thornhill cres N1
54 H 20 Thornhill gdns Bark
51 S 7 Thornhill gdns E10

116 A 19 Thornhill gdns Surb
133 R 2 Thornhill gro N1
122 M 17 Thornhill rd Croy
51 R 7 Thornhill rd E10
48 F 20 Thornhill rd N1
133 S 2 Thornhill rd N1
133 O 2 Thornhill sq N1
108 H 9 Thornlaw rd SE27
31 Z 1 Thornley clo N17
146 H 19 Thornley cres SW11
40 L 7 Thornley dri Harrow
76 L 13 Thornley pl SE10
111 U 3 Thornsbeach rd SE6
123 Z 4 Thornsett rd SE20
124 A 5 Thornsett rd SE20
123 Z 4 Thornsett rd SE20
106 B 3 Thornsett rd SW18
122 C 15 Thornton av Croy
107 Y 1 Thornton av SW2
74 B 11 Thornton av W4
125 O 3 Thornton dene Becknhm
107 X 1 Thornton gdns SW12
105 R 18 Thornton hill SW19
122 E 13 Thornton rd Thntn Hth
4 E 13 Thornton rd Barnt
81 T 9 Thornton rd Blvdr
112 F 12 Thornton rd Brom
120 J 18 Thornton rd Carsh
51 X 6 Thornton rd E11
53 Y 13 Thornton rd Ilf
89 W 19 Thornton rd SW12
85 X 9 Thornton rd SW14
105 P 17 Thornton rd SW19
122 F 11 Thornton row Thntn Hth
90 E 5 Thornton rd SW9
28 B 17 Thornton way NW11
56 M 5 Thorntons Farm av Rom
78 B 14 Thorntree rd SE7
93 N 3 Thornville st SE8
34 J 7 Thornwood clo E18
94 A 13 Thornwood rd SE13
93 Z 13 Thornwood rd SE13
52 A 16 Thorogood gdns E15
54 C 4 Thorold rd Ilf
53 Z 7 Thorold rd Ilf
30 B 2 Thorold rd N22
148 G 20 Thorparch rd SW8
89 Y 1 Thorparch rd SW8
32 L 6 Thorpe cres E17
33 V 6 Thorpe Hall rd E17
126 M 4 Thorpe ms W10
54 D 20 Thorpe rd Bark
33 T 7 Thorpe rd E17
66 F 4 Thorpe rd E6
52 C 11 Thorpe rd E7
102 K 18 Thorpe rd Kingst
31 T 19 Thorpe rd N15
74 G 3 Thorpebank rd W12
35 Y 12 Thorpedale gdns Ilf
48 B 5 Thorpedale rd N4
110 B 5 Thorpewood av SE26
109 R 11 Thorsden way SE19
45 R 10 Thorverton rd NW2
63 V 7 Thoydon rd E3
107 U 13 Thrale rd SW16
142 C 14 Thrale st SE1
143 O 2 Thrawl st E1
142 G 2 Threadneedle st EC2
160 G 6 Threadneedle st EC2
63 Y 19 Three Colt st E14
63 N 11 Three Colts la E2
135 Y 16 Three Colts la E2
98 H 6 Three corners Bxly Hth
121 N 6 Three Kings rd Mitch
139 W 8 Three Kings' yd W1
64 F 9 Three Mill la E3
143 N 17 Three Oak la SE1
142 E 16 Three Tuns ct SE1
136 J 9 Threshers pl W11
110 D 8 Thriffwood SE23
65 W 18 Throckmorten rd E16
160 G 4 Throgmorton av EC2
142 G 5 Throgmorton st EC2
80 E 8 Throwley clo SE2
154 B 12 Throwley rd Sutton
154 C 11 Throwley rd Sutton
154 B 8 Throwley way Sutton
121 T 3 Thrupp clo Mitch
149 Z 9 Thrush st SE17
111 R 12 Thurbarn rd SE6
151 S 1 Thurland rd SE16
108 G 9 Thurlby rd SE27

42 H 19 Thurlby rd Wemb
89 P 16 Thurleigh av SW12
88 L 17 Thurleigh rd SW12
89 O 16 Thurleigh rd SW12
119 R 11 Thurleston av Mrdn
54 K 14 Thurlestone av Ilf
15 Y 19 Thurlestone av N12
108 H 9 Thurlestone rd SE27
146 J 4 Thurloe clo SW7
39 S 19 Thurloe gdns Rom
146 J 4 Thurloe pl SW7
146 G 4 Thurloe Place ms SW7
146 H 5 Thurloe sq SW7
146 G 5 Thurloe st SW7
42 H 16 Thurlow gdns Wemb
108 K 2 Thurlow hill SE21
108 K 3 Thurlow Park rd SE21
46 G 14 Thurlow rd NW3
71 Y 6 Thurlow rd W7
150 H 10 Thurlow st SE17
47 N 17 Thurlow ter NW5
115 Y 14 Thursland rd Sidcup
159 W 16 Thursley cres Croy
105 P 5 Thursley gdns SW19
113 S 8 Thursley rd SE9
106 G 9 Thurso st SW17
58 F 18 Thurston rd S'hall
93 S 6 Thurston rd SE13
104 J 17 Thurston rd SW20
135 O 7 Thurtle rd E2
81 W 16 Thwaite clo Erith
15 O 19 Thyra gro N12
64 D 11 Tibbatt's rd E3
134 A 2 Tibberton sq N1
105 O 2 Tibbets clo SW19
87 O 17 Tibbets ride SW15
132 L 6 Tiber gdns N1
110 J 5 Ticehurst rd SE23
138 K 6 Tichbourne row W2
88 G 20 Tichwell rd SW18
80 E 5 Tickford clo SE2
65 R 20 Tidal Basin rd E16
157 T 5 Tidenham gdns Croy
86 L 15 Tideslye rd SW15
158 M 5 Tideswell rd Croy
87 N 12 Tideswell rd SW15
102 B 10 Tideway clo Rich
64 B 13 Tidey st E3
96 K 4 Tidford rd Welling
108 A 1 Tierney rd SW2
90 A 20 Tierney rd SW2
75 R 8 Tiger bay SE16
74 B 10 Tiger la Brom
49 Y 11 Tiger way E5
94 M 8 Tilbrook rd SE3
51 T 2 Tilbury rd E10
65 T 6 Tilbury rd E6
17 Y 16 Tile Kiln la N13
47 U 3 Tile Kiln la N6
153 R 11 Tilehurst rd Sutton
106 G 2 Tilehurst rd SW18
47 Z 20 Tileyard rd N1
159 U 18 Tilford av Croy
105 P 2 Tilford gdns SW19
50 A 13 Tilia rd E5
76 B 8 Tiller rd E14
43 V 19 Tillett clo NW10
135 T 12 Tillett way E2
45 N 1 Tilling rd NW2
27 W 11 Tillingbourne gdns N3
27 W 12 Tillingbourne way N3
14 M 13 Tillingham way N12
143 X 7 Tillman st E1
133 N 2 Tilloch st N1
22 K 3 Tillotson rd Harrow
53 W 1 Tillotson rd Ilf
18 F 7 Tillotson rd N9
63 S 15 Tillotson st E1
134 C 16 Tilney ct EC1
21 U 8 Tilney dri Buck Hl
49 O 18 Tilney gdns N1
56 B 19 Tilney rd Dgnhm
139 U 13 Tilney st W1
89 Z 18 Tilson gdns SW2
31 X 5 Tilson rd N17
144 M 15 Tilton st SW6
61 X 20 Tiltwood the W3
95 T 17 Tiltyard appr SE9
127 W 2 Timber clo Chisl
75 U 4 Timber pond rd SE16
134 A 17 Timber st EC1
152 A 8 Timbercroft Epsom
79 U 18 Timbercroft la SE18
27 R 7 Timberdene NW4
63 N 18 Timberland rd E1
143 Y 6 Timberland rd E1
89 Y 7 Timberslip dri SW4
155 Y 20 Timberslip dri SM6
31 Y 19 Timberwharf rd N16

127 X 2	Timer clo	BR7
154 B 11	Times sq	Sutton
63 X 14	Timothy rd	E3
86 G 20	Timsbury wlk	SW15
90 J 1	Tindal st	SW9
149 X 20	Tindal st	SW9
85 Z 7	Tinderbox all	SW14
63 R 14	Tinsley rd	E1
91 U 10	Tintagel cres	SE22
11 V 15	Tintagel dri	Stanm
25 T 10	Tintern av	NW9
87 R 14	Tintern clo	SW19
106 D 16	Tintern clo	SW19
17 N 2	Tintern gdns	N14
120 F 20	Tintern rd	Carsh
30 L 5	Tintern rd	N22
90 B 10	Tintern st	SW4
40 K 4	Tintern way	Harrow
65 T 13	Tinto rd	E16
148 M 8	Tinworth st	SE11
149 N 9	Tinworth st	SE11
7 Z 7	Tippetts clo	Enf
89 O 7	Tipthorpe rd	SW11
157 S 8	Tipton dri	Croy
35 X 9	Tiptree cres	Ilf
156 L 15	Tirlemont rd	S Croy
122 L 15	Tirrell rd	Croy
140 E 9	Tisbury ct	W1
121 Z 3	Tisbury rd	SW16
150 G 8	Tisdall pl	SE17
120 F 19	Titchfield rd	Carsh
9 U 1	Titchfield rd	Enf
130 M 7	Titchfield rd	NW8
131 N 7	Titchfield rd	NW8
120 G 18	Titchfield wlk	Carsh
147 P 13	Tite st	SW3
116 M 7	Tithe Barn clo	Kingst
26 F 4	Tithe clo	NW7
40 G 9	Tithe Farm av Harrow	
40 G 9	Tithe Farm clo Harrow	
26 G 3	Tithe wlk	NW7
10 E 3	Titian av	Bushey
20 B 16	Titley clo	E4
80 F 2	Titmuss av	SE28
35 W 9	Tiverton av	Ilf
114 B 1	Tiverton dri	SE9
96 B 20	Tiverton dri	SE9
24 M 9	Tiverton rd	Edg
82 L 4	Tiverton rd	Hounsl
31 O 18	Tiverton rd	N15
18 D 18	Tiverton rd	N18
128 H 6	Tiverton rd	NW10
60 K 5	Tiverton rd	Wemb
150 A 2	Tiverton rd	SE1
78 D 10	Tivoli gdns	SE18
82 B 11	Tivoli rd	Hounsl
29 X 16	Tivoli rd	N8
108 L 13	Tivoli rd	SE27
35 W 9	Tivoton rd	Ilf
143 W 11	Tobacco Wharf	E1
76 A 5	Tobago st	E14
46 K 19	Tobin clo	NW3
63 V 12	Toby la	E1
160 F 5	Tokenhouse yd	EC2
43 P 18	Tokyngton av	Wemb
88 G 14	Toland sq	SW15
42 K 2	Toley av	Wemb
36 D 9	Tollesbury gdns	Ilf
63 S 11	Tollet st	E1
109 T 5	Tollgate dri	SE21
129 W 8	Tollgate gdns	NW6
65 Y 15	Tollgate rd	E16
66 E 15	Tollgate rd	E6
66 F 14	Tollgate sq	E6
47 V 6	Tollhouse way	N19
48 D 5	Tollington pk	N4
48 C 6	Tollington pl	N4
48 C 12	Tollington rd	N7
48 A 9	Tollington way	N7
132 C 15	Tolmers sq	NW1
133 T 7	Tolpuddle st	N1
50 A 15	Tolsford rd	E5
93 Y 8	Tolson rd	Islwth
118 M 1	Tolverne rd	SW20
37 X 15	Tolworth gdns	Rom
117 W 17	Tolworth ri	Surb
117 U 19	Tolworth Rise north Surb	
117 V 19	Tolworth Rise south Surb	
95 S 10	Tom Coombs clo	SE9
79 R 9	Tom Cribb st	SE18
67 V 4	Tom Mann clo	Bark
64 B 9	Tomlin's gro	E3
101 Y 1	Tomlins all	Twick
67 O 4	Tomlins orchard	Bark
63 X 17	Tomlins ter	E14
135 P 14	Tomlinson clo	E2
73 T 13	Tomlinson clo	W4
133 X 14	Tompion st	EC1
36 C 5	Tomswood ct	Ilf
36 A 2	Tomswood hill	Ilf
36 C 5	Tomswood hill	Ilf
132 J 12	Tonbridge st	WC1
119 V 19	Tonfield rd	Sutton
125 O 12	Tonge clo	Becknhm
88 B 13	Tonsley hill	SW18
88 B 13	Tonsley pl	SW18
88 B 13	Tonsley rd	SW18
88 B 12	Tonsley st	SW18
121 O 3	Tonstall rd	Mitch
141 S 4	Took's ct	EC4
22 A 4	Tooke clo	Pinn
142 K 15	Tooley st	SE1
143 N 18	Tooley st	SE1
23 P 7	Toorack rd	Harrow
107 T 7	Tooting Bec comm SW16	
107 X 9	Tooting Bec gdns SW16	
107 R 8	Tooting Bec rd SW17	
106 J 12	Tooting gro	SW17
106 J 13	Tooting High st SW17	
126 A 10	Tootswood rd	Brom
125 Z 10	Tootswood rd	Brom
125 Y 11	Top pk	Becknhm
149 R 5	Topaz st	SE11
30 M 4	Topham sq	N17
133 S 17	Topham st	EC1
20 H 3	Tophouse ri	E4
84 M 8	Topiary sq	Rich
94 M 9	Topley st	SE9
44 I 7	Topp wlk	NW2
29 Z 15	Topsfield rd	NW2
107 N 8	Topsham rd	SW17
137 U 16	Tor gdns	W8
97 T 1	Tor rd	Welling
129 O 2	Torbay rd	NW6
24 L 2	Torbridge clo	Edg
97 Z 16	Torbrook clo	Bxly
110 C 4	Torcross dri	SE23
112 C 17	Tormead clo	Brom
79 U 15	Tormount rd	SE18
53 T 11	Toronto av	E12
51 X 12	Toronto rd	E11
54 A 3	Toronto rd	Ilf
35 P 13	Torquay gdns	Ilf
71 V 2	Torquay st	W2
110 F 18	Torr rd	SE20
120 H 19	Torre wlk	Carsh
52 B 18	Torrens rd	E15
90 C 13	Torrens rd	SW2
52 B 17	Torrens sq	E15
133 V 9	Torrens st	N1
47 X 17	Torriano av	NW5
47 Y 17	Torriano cotts	NW5
92 B 10	Torridge gdns	SE15
122 J 11	Torridge rd Thntn Hth	
93 Y 18	Torridon rd	SE6
111 Y 3	Torridon rd	SE6
15 U 16	Torrington av	N12
40 L 11	Torrington dri Harrow	
60 D 2	Torrington gdns Grnfd	
16 H 20	Torrington gdns N11	
9 W 16	Torrington gro N12	
15 S 15	Torrington pk N12	
143 V 14	Torrington pl	E1
132 D 19	Torrington pl	WC1
56 C 3	Torrington rd	Dnghm
34 F 10	Torrington rd	E18
60 D 3	Torrington rd	Grnfd
119 Y 16	Torrington way Mrdn	
23 U 14	Torver rd	Harrow
86 H 14	Torwood rd	SW15
140 G 20	Tothill st	SW1
16 E 2	Totnes rd	Welling
28 G 14	Totnes wlk	N2
17 V 18	Tottenhall rd	N13
132 C 18	Tottenham Court rd W1	
140 F 2	Tottenham Court rd W1	
31 U 13	Tottenham Green east N15	
30 C 15	Tottenham la	N8
140 C 1	Tottenham ms	W1
49 P 18	Tottenham rd	N1
140 C 1	Tottenham st	W1
106 M 11	Totterdown st	SW17
13 W 9	Totteridge comm N20	
14 K 7	Totteridge grn	N20
15 O 7	Totteridge la	N20
14 F 5	Totteridge village N20	
24 E 16	Totternhoe clo Harrow	
122 G 6	Totton rd Thntn Hth	
142 A 18	Toulmin st	SE1
150 A 18	Toulon st	SE5
150 E 9	Tounly st	SE17
145 R 17	Tournay rd	SW6
123 Y 3	Tovil clo	SE20
64 E 12	Towcester rd	E3
143 N 14	Tower br	E1
143 O 11	Tower Bridge appr E1	
150 J 3	Tower Bridge rd SE1	
142 M 18	Tower Bridge rd SE1	
109 Z 17	Tower clo	SE20
140 H 7	Tower ct	WC2
30 M 6	Tower Gardens rd N17	
31 O 6	Tower Gardens rd N17	
33 O 11	Tower Hamlets rd E17	
52 D 14	Tower Hamlets rd E7	
142 L 10	Tower hill	EC3
143 N 10	Tower hill	EC3
33 O 14	Tower ms	E17
142 M 11	Tower of London EC3	
142 L 10	Tower rd	Bxlvdr
81 X 12	Tower rd	Blvdr
98 F 10	Tower rd	Bxly Hth
44 G 20	Tower rd	NW10
101 W 6	Tower rd	Twick
84 J 7	Tower ri	Rich
140 H 7	Tower st	WC2
30 C 8	Tower ter	N22
131 H 19	Tower view	Croy
84 J 12	Towers pl	Rich
22 A 4	Towers rd	Pinn
58 H 10	Towers rd	S'hall
100 D 4	Towfield rd	Felt
31 U 12	Town Hall Approach rd N15	
73 X 13	Town Hall av	W4
88 M 8	Town Hall rd	SW11
72 H 18	Town mead	Brentfd
67 N 4	Town quay	Bark
18 M 8	Town rd	N9
19 O 11	Town rd	N9
48 M 3	Towncourt pth	N4
58 E 7	Towney mead	Nthlt
71 V 7	Townley ct	F15
52 C 19	Townley ct	F15
98 B 14	Townley rd	Bxly Hth
98 D 11	Townley rd	Bxly Hth
91 S 13	Townley rd	SE22
150 D 8	Townley st	SE17
85 T 4	Townmead rd	Rich
88 D 4	Townmead rd	SW6
16 L 13	Townsend av	N14
25 Y 18	Townsend la	NW9
43 Z 2	Townsend la	NW9
31 U 16	Townsend rd	N15
70 B 2	Townsend rd	S'hall
150 H 6	Townsend st	SE17
47 R 3	Townsend yd	N6
113 Z 13	Townshend rd	Chisl
130 L 8	Townshend rd	NW8
84 M 11	Townshend rd	Rich
85 N 10	Townshend ter	Rich
108 L 5	Towton rd	SE27
105 S 20	Toynbee rd	SW20
143 N 3	Toynbee st	E1
149 S 7	Tracey st	SE11
44 L 14	Tracy av	NW2
24 D 2	Tracy ct	Stanm
148 M 20	Tradescant rd	SW8
61 V 11	Trading Estate rd NW10	
18 D 20	Trafalgar av	N17
151 O 11	Trafalgar av	SE15
119 P 20	Trafalgar av	Worc Pk
63 T 13	Trafalgar gdns	E1
76 K 16	Trafalgar gdns	SE10
34 F 13	Trafalgar pl	E11
76 K 15	Trafalgar rd	SE10
106 C 17	Trafalgar rd	SW19
101 R 4	Trafalgar rd	Twick
140 H 12	Trafalgar sq	SW1
140 H 12	Trafalgar sq	WC2
150 F 10	Trafalgar st	SE17
156 E 3	Trafalgar way	CRO
51 S 16	Trafford clo	E15
122 D 11	Trafford rd	Thntn Hth
51 Y 20	Tramway av	E15
19 O 4	Tramway av	N9
121 N 12	Tramway pth	Mitch
50 F 15	Tranby pl	E9
46 K 13	Tranley ms	NW3
18 G 4	Tranmere rd	N9
106 D 4	Tranmere rd	SW18
82 L 19	Tranmere rd	Twick
94 A 5	Tranquil vale	SE3
138 K 2	Transept st	NW1
72 B 16	Transport av	Brentf
103 Z 19	Traps la	Kingst
118 A 1	Traps la	New Mald
48 E 9	Travers rd	N7
10 B 7	Treacy clo	Bushey
136 H 9	Treagold st	W11
135 W 9	Treadway st	E2
132 M 6	Treaty st	N1
139 X 14	Trebeck st	W1
145 U 9	Trebovir rd	SW5
63 Y 12	Treby st	E3
47 Y 13	Trecastle way	N7
64 A 5	Tredegar rd	E3
63 Z 6	Tredegar rd	E3
29 Y 3	Tredegar rd	N11
83 Y 6	Tredegar sq	E3
63 X 8	Tredegar ter	E3
135 U 3	Trederwen rd	E8
110 D 13	Tredown rd	SE26
127 P 9	Tredwell clo	Brom
108 H 10	Tredwell rd	SE27
102 H 1	Tree clo	Rich
65 Y 17	Tree rd	E16
147 R 16	Tree wlk	SW11
86 C 8	Treen av	SW13
81 N 13	Treetops clo	SE2
112 H 10	Treewall gdns	Brom
56 E 7	Trefgarne rd	Dgnhm
48 B 12	Trefil wlk	N7
88 D 14	Trefoil rd	SW18
30 A 20	Tregaron av	N8
89 P 10	Tregarvon rd	SW11
40 O 11	Tregenna av	Harrow
14 N 14	Tregenna clo	N14
50 M 20	Trego rd	E9
90 A 7	Tregothnan rd	SW9
146 A 12	Tregunter rd	SW10
36 E 1	Treharen rd	Ilf
85 Z 8	Treharne rd	SW14
107 P 8	Treherne ct	SW17
50 H 14	Trehurst st	E5
51 U 10	Trelawn rd	E10
90 F 13	Trelawn rd	SW2
36 E 1	Trelawney rd	Ilf
63 Z 8	Trellis sq	E3
109 O 16	Treloar gdns	SE19
89 Y 9	Tremadoc rd	SW4
93 O 6	Tremaine clo	SE4
124 A 4	Tremaine rd	SE20
47 U 8	Tremlett gro	N19
47 U 9	Tremlett ms	N19
54 L 9	Trenance gdns	Ilf
11 N 19	Trenchard clo	Stanm
119 Y 14	Trenchard ct	Mrdn
76 K 15	Trenchard st	SE10
148 K 16	Trenchold st	SW8
109 Z 18	Trenholme clo	SE20
109 Z 18	Trenholme rd	SE20
109 Z 18	Trenholme ter	SE20
62 K 9	Trenmar gdns	NW10
72 E 8	Trent av	W5
6 E 20	Trent gdns	N14
16 F 1	Trent gdns	N14
6 E 6	Trent pk	Barnt
21 V 6	Trent rd	Buck Hl
90 C 14	Trent rd	SW2
152 L 4	Trent way	Worc Pk
105 X 1	Trentham st	SW18
7 O 10	Trentwood side Enf	
88 B 18	Tresco clo	SE15
111 Z 16	Tresco clo	Brom
54 L 8	Tresco gdns	Ilf
92 B 9	Tresco rd	SE15
40 C 2	Trescoe gdns	Harrow
67 X 1	Tresham rd	Bark
93 O 8	Tressillian cres	SE4
92 M 9	Tressillian rd	SE4
93 O 6	Tressillian rd	SE4
58 A 13	Trestis clo	Hayes
68 M 3	Treswell rd	Dgnhm
69 N 3	Treswell rd	Dgnhm
13 P 12	Tretawn gdns	NW7
13 O 12	Tretawn pk	NW7
144 M 8	Trevanion rd	W14
41 O 2	Treve av	Harrow
24 H 20	Trevelyan cres Harrow	
42 J 1	Trevelyan cres Harrow	
128 C 5	Trevelyan gdns NW10	
62 M 4	Trevelyan gdns NW10	
52 B 13	Trevelyan rd	E15
106 J 14	Trevelyan rd	SW17
141 X 14	Treveris st	SE1

128 J 19	Treverton st W10	
86 J 18	Treville st SW15	
110 G 3	Treviso rd SE23	
76 B 15	Trevithick st SE8	
22 C 18	Trevone gdns Pinn	
5 U 18	Trevor clo Barnet	
126 D 18	Trevor clo Brom	
23 W 1	Trevor clo Harrow	
83 W 12	Trevor clo Islwth	
25 Y 4	Trevor gdns Edg	
138 M 20	Trevor pl SW7	
25 Y 4	Trevor rd Edg	
105 T 19	Trevor rd SW19	
34 G 1	Trevor rd Wdfd Grn	
138 M 20	Trevor sq SW7	
139 N 19	Trevor sq SW7	
138 M 19	Trevor st SW7	
33 W 4	Trevose rd E17	
118 M 1	Trewince rd SW20	
106 B 4	Trewint st SW18	
110 F 12	Trewsbury rd SE26	
58 A 13	Triandra way Hayes	
66 A 14	Triangle ct E16	
65 Z 15	Triangle ct E16	
89 X 10	Triangle pl SW4	
135 W 3	Triangle rd E8	
117 U 4	Triangle the New Mald	
63 N 2	Triangle the E8	
149 P 16	Trigon rd SW8	
110 G 3	Trilby rd SE23	
48 B 3	Trinder gdns N19	
4 A 17	Trinder rd Barnt	
48 B 3	Trinder rd N19	
58 E 16	Tring av S'hall	
73 N 3	Tring av W5	
43 P 18	Tring av Wemb	
36 D 17	Tring clo Ilf	
69 Z 1	Trinidad gdns Dgnhm	
63 Z 20	Trinidad st E14	
8 J 20	Trinity av Enf	
28 F 11	Trinity av N2	
74 K 17	Trinity Church rd SW13	
142 C 20	Trinity Church sq SE1	
52 A 6	Trinity clo E11	
82 B 9	Trinity clo Hounsl	
46 F 13	Trinity clo NW3	
157 T 19	Trinity clo S Croy	
93 W 11	Trinity clo SE13	
106 M 5	Trinity cres SW17	
107 N 5	Trinity cres SW17	
134 J 3	Trinity ct N1	
65 P 13	Trinity gdns E16	
90 C 10	Trinity gdns SW9	
93 T 2	Trinity gro SE10	
98 B 10	Trinity pl Bxly Hth	
36 A 9	Trinity rd Ilf	
28 F 9	Trinity rd N2	
30 A 2	Trinity rd N22	
85 N 9	Trinity rd Rich	
70 A 2	Trinity rd S'hall	
106 L 3	Trinity rd SW17	
107 N 6	Trinity rd SW17	
88 G 17	Trinity rd SW18	
105 Z 16	Trinity rd SW19	
90 H 20	Trinity ri SW2	
142 M 9	Trinity sq EC3	
65 R 16	Trinity st E16	
7 Y 8	Trinity st Enf	
142 C 20	Trinity st SE1	
62 C 20	Trinity way W3	
142 C 20	Trio pl SE1	
94 A 8	Tristan sq SE3	
33 X 9	Tristram clo E17	
112 D 9	Tristram rd Brom	
132 A 16	Triton sq NW1	
156 A 7	Tritton av Croydon	
109 O 7	Tritton rd SE21	
66 G 16	Triumph rd E6	
156 D 4	Trojan way Croydon	
81 R 17	Trosley rd Blvdr	
91 T 12	Trossachs rd SE22	
151 T 6	Trothy rd SE1	
29 N 2	Trott rd N10	
88 H 3	Trott st SW11	
77 W 13	Troughton rd SE7	
92 G 2	Troutbeck rd SE14	
89 U 16	Trouville rd SW4	
50 M 18	Trowbridge rd E9	
102 E 15	Trowlock av Tedd	
102 F 15	Trowlock way Tedd	
109 P 15	Troy rd SE19	
91 X 7	Troy town SE6	
66 G 18	Truesdale rd E6	
31 X 1	Trulock rd N17	
31 X 2	Trulock rd N17	
75 N 7	Truman st SE16	
49 T 14	Trumans rd N16	
122 K 10	Trumble gdns Thntn Hth	
160 C 5	Trump st EC2	
71 V 7	Trumpers way W7	
52 B 11	Trumpington rd E7	
142 A 17	Trundle st SE1	
10 E 5	Trundlers way Bushey	
75 U 14	Trundley's rd SE8	
53 R 2	Truro gdns Ilf	
32 L 14	Truro rd E17	
30 A 3	Truro rd N22	
47 O 19	Truro st NW5	
108 H 12	Truslove rd SE27	
144 B 2	Trussley rd W6	
74 L 8	Trussley rd W6	
57 V 2	Truston's gdns Hornch	
35 P 15	Tryfan clo Ilf	
147 N 9	Tryon st SW3	
79 R 17	Tuam rd SE18	
62 E 7	Tubbs rd NW10	
57 W 18	Tuck rd Rainhm	
86 E 18	Tuckton wlk SW15	
100 L 20	Tudinghall la Felt	
100 H 17	Tudor av Hampt	
39 W 11	Tudor av Rom	
152 L 9	Tudor av Worc Pk	
127 U 1	Tudor clo Chisl	
113 U 20	Tudor clo Chisl	
99 Y 16	Tudor clo Drtfrd	
46 J 16	Tudor clo NW3	
13 V 20	Tudor clo NW7	
43 W 6	Tudor clo NW9	
153 P 12	Tudor clo Sutton	
155 W 17	Tudor clo Wallgtn	
21 V 16	Tudor clo Wdfd Grn	
43 R 16	Tudor Court north Wemb	
43 R 17	Tudor Court south Wemb	
7 X 4	Tudor cres Enf	
32 K 20	Tudor ct E17	
102 H 11	Tudor dri Kingst	
103 N 14	Tudor dri Kingst	
119 T 17	Tudor dri Mrdn	
39 V 12	Tudor dri Rom	
43 W 7	Tudor gdns NW9	
39 W 12	Tudor gdns Rom	
86 C 8	Tudor gdns SW13	
101 W 1	Tudor gdns Twick	
159 T 6	Tudor gdns W Wkhm	
61 R 15	Tudor gdns W3	
63 O 1	Tudor gro E9	
135 Z 2	Tudor gro E9	
106 X 19	Tudor pl Mitch	
140 F 3	Tudor pl W1	
67 X 3	Tudor rd Bark	
4 M 11	Tudor rd Barnt	
5 N 11	Tudor rd Barnt	
125 S 6	Tudor rd Becknhm	
20 E 19	Tudor rd E4	
65 Z 4	Tudor rd E6	
63 O 2	Tudor rd E9	
135 Y 3	Tudor rd E9	
100 H 18	Tudor rd Hampt	
23 P 8	Tudor rd Harrow	
83 P 10	Tudor rd Hounsl	
103 P 18	Tudor rd Kingst	
19 O 4	Tudor rd N9	
58 B 20	Tudor rd S'hall	
109 U 18	Tudor rd SE19	
124 B 13	Tudor rd SE25	
141 U 8	Tudor st EC4	
16 K 5	Tudor way N14	
73 O 6	Tudor way W3	
11 P 17	Tudor Well clo Stanm	
97 Z 15	Tudor wlk Bxly	
94 K 9	Tudway rd SE3	
47 V 11	Tufnell Park rd N19	
48 A 11	Tufnell Park rd N7	
20 A 14	Tufton rd E4	
148 H 2	Tufton st SW1	
123 O 14	Tugela rd Croy	
110 M 4	Tugela st SE6	
135 S 9	Tuilerie st E2	
124 E 20	Tulip clo CR0	
125 U 6	Tulse clo Becknhm	
90 F 18	Tulse hill SW2	
108 G 1	Tulse hill SW2	
108 M 4	Tulsmere rd SE27	
18 D 12	Tuncombe rd N18	
136 A 14	Tunis rd W12	
74 L 3	Tunis rd W12	
62 B 2	Tunley rd NW10	
107 N 3	Tunley rd SW17	
65 X 10	Tunmarsh la E13	
63 T 19	Tunnel appr E14	
76 L 6	Tunnel appr SE10	
76 L 6	Tunnel av SE10	
77 O 11	Tunnel av SE10	
75 P 6	Tunnel entrance SE16	
29 V 2	Tunnel gdns N11	
157 T 1	Tunstall rd Croy	
90 D 10	Tunstall rd SW9	
81 N 9	Tunstock way Blvdr	
25 V 19	Tunworth clo Ruislip	
86 C 17	Tunworth cres SW15	
88 E 11	Tunworth clo SW18	
19 P 4	Turin rd N9	
135 S 14	Turin st E2	
109 R 19	Turkey oak clo SE19	
133 W 19	Turks Head yd EC1	
147 R 9	Turks row SW3	
48 C 5	Turle rd N4	
121 Z 2	Turle rd SW16	
48 C 5	Turlewray clo N4	
65 N 4	Turley clo E15	
141 W 4	Turnagain la EC4	
55 Y 5	Turnage rd Dgnhm	
89 S 8	Turnchapel ms SW4	
106 L 20	Turner av Mitch	
31 R 14	Turner av N15	
101 O 6	Turner av Twick	
28 A 19	Turner clo NW11	
33 T 11	Turner rd E17	
24 L 8	Turner rd Edg	
117 Y 16	Turner rd New Mald	
143 W 4	Turner st E1	
65 P 17	Turner st E16	
124 K 1	Turners Meadow way BR3	
63 Y 15	Turners rd E3	
156 F 3	Turners way CR0	
46 D 2	Turners wood NW11	
35 O 13	Turneville rd W14	
145 O 13	Turneville rd W14	
90 M 19	Turney rd SE21	
91 O 18	Turney rd SE21	
145 O 13	Turney rd W14	
74 A 11	Turnham Green ter W4	
92 H 12	Turnham rd SE4	
133 V 19	Turnmill st EC1	
75 Y 18	Turnpike clo SE8	
30 E 12	Turnpike la N8	
154 D 11	Turnpike la SM1	
157 S 4	Turnpike link Croy	
147 X 10	Turpentine la SW1	
38 E 1	Turpin av Rom	
47 X 5	Turpin way N19	
155 T 16	Turpin way Wallgtn	
127 P 16	Turpington clo Brom	
127 P 16	Turpington la Brom	
150 C 8	Tuscan rd SE17	
42 J 15	Turret gro SW4	
79 T 14	Turton rd Wemb	
76 M 15	Tuskar st SE10	
21 U 8	Tuttlebee la Buck Hl	
39 O 3	Tweed way Rom	
51 S 14	Tweedale ct E15	
120 F 19	Tweedale rd Carsh	
65 V 7	Tweedmouth rd E13	
126 F 2	Tweedy rd Brom	
141 R 8	Tweezer's all WC2	
64 F 11	Twelve Trees ct E14	
21 U 15	Twentyman clo Wdfd Grn	
84 D 13	Twickenham br Twick	
156 B 5	Twickenham clo Croy	
23 T 2	Twickenham gdns Harrow	
41 X 15	Twickenham gdns Grnfd	
83 X 12	Twickenham rd Islwth	
51 V 6	Twickenham rd E11	
84 E 12	Twickenham rd Rich	
101 Y 9	Twickenham rd Tedd	
88 A 18	Twilley st SW18	
14 M 13	Twineham grn N12	
101 O 6	Twining av Twick	
14 E 19	Twinn rd NW7	
47 S 11	Twisden rd NW5	
61 W 1	Twybridge way NW10	
43 W 20	Twybridge way NW10	
60 M 9	Twyford Abbey rd NW10	
28 L 11	Twyford av N2	
29 N 10	Twyford av N2	
73 P 1	Twyford av W3	
61 P 19	Twyford av W3	
73 R 2	Twyford cres W3	
141 N 4	Twyford pl WC2	
120 F 19	Twyford rd Carsh	
40 J 2	Twyford rd Harrow	
54 B 14	Twyford rd Ilf	
133 N 4	Twyford rd Ilf	
65 O 13	Tyas rd E16	
119 X 5	Tybenham rd SW19	
9 O 10	Tyberry rd Enf	
139 O 8	Tyburn way W1	
142 J 18	Tyers ga SE1	
149 O 8	Tyers st SE11	
149 O 10	Tyers ter SE11	
81 O 14	Tyeshurst clo SE2	
122 C 3	Tylecroft rd SW16	
121 Z 3	Tylecroft rd SW16	
54 B 14	Tylehurst gdns Ilf	
135 N 8	Tyler clo E2	
111 R 20	Tyler rd Becknhm	
77 N 14	Tyler St SE10	
24 L 19	Tylers ga Harrow	
109 U 12	Tylney av SE19	
127 N 3	Tylney rd Brom	
52 K 11	Tylney rd E7	
48 J 20	Tyndale ter N1	
51 T 7	Tyndall rd E10	
96 L 8	Tyndall rd Welling	
54 A 7	Tyne rd Ilf	
89 O 6	Tyneham rd SW11	
B L 3	Tynemouth dri Enf	
107 O 17	Tynemouth rd Mitch	
31 W 13	Tynemouth rd N15	
88 C 4	Tynemouth st SW6	
63 S 6	Type st E2	
87 Z 1	Tyrawley rd SW6	
41 T 12	Tyrell clo Harrow	
154 M 8	Tyrell ct Carsh	
91 X 11	Tyrell rd SE22	
114 J 11	Tyron way Sidcp	
66 H 7	Tyrone rd E6	
26 D 20	Tyrrel way NW9	
97 P 13	Tyrrell av Welling	
93 O 6	Tyrwhitt rd SE4	
133 T 15	Tysoe st EC1	
92 D 19	Tyson rd SE23	
49 U 17	Tyssen pas E8	
49 V 17	Tyssen st E8	
47 X 10	Tytherton rd N19	

U

64 E 14	Uamvar st E14	
107 P 19	Uckfield gro Mitch	
9 U 1	Uckfield rd Enf	
148 D 6	Udall st SW1	
101 Z 13	Udney Park rd Tedd	
62 H 3	Uffington rd NW10	
108 G 9	Uffington rd SE27	
22 L 3	Ufford clo Harrow	
22 L 2	Ufford rd Harrow	
141 W 17	Ufford st SE1	
49 P 20	Ufton gro N1	
134 H 2	Ufton rd N1	
49 R 20	Ufton rd N1	
107 V 10	Ullathorne rd SW16	
17 P 11	Ulleswater rd N13	
103 Y 10	Ullswater clo SW15	
104 A 10	Ullswater cres SW15	
103 Y 9	Ullswater cres SW15	
108 J 5	Ullswater rd SE27	
74 G 20	Ullswater rd SW13	
57 W 14	Ullswater way Hornch	
17 X 13	Ulster gdns N13	
48 C 12	Ulster ms N7	
131 W 18	Ulster pl NW1	
77 N 16	Ulundi rd SE3	
87 P 12	Ulva rd SW15	
91 W 13	Ulverscroft rd SE22	
33 X 7	Ulverston rd E17	
108 J 5	Ulverstone rd SE27	
45 W 14	Ulysses rd NW6	
143 V 5	Umberton st E1	
86 G 17	Undine st SW15	
30 H 19	Umfreville rd N4	
93 P 6	Undercliff rd SE13	
4 K 16	Underhill Barnt	
131 Z 5	Underhill pas NW1	
91 Z 19	Underhill st SE22	
131 Z 5	Underhill st NW1	
16 F 9	Underne av N14	
77 V 20	Underpass SE3	
142 J 6	Undershaft EC3	
112 B 8	Undershaw rd Brom	

159 U 12 Underwood Croy
135 S 19 Underwood rd E1
20 E 15 Underwood rd E4
34 M 2 Underwood rd Ilf
134 D 11 Underwood st N1
113 V 5 Underwood the SE9
76 E 10 Undine rd E14
76 E 10 Undine rd E14
106 L 12 Undine st SW17
59 R 9 Uneeda dri Grnfd
142 L 15 Unicorn pas SE1
63 W 12 Union dri E1
89 X 4 Union gro SW8
127 O 11 Union rd Brom
122 M 16 Union rd Croy
16 L 18 Union rd N11
58 H 5 Union rd Nthlt
89 X 4 Union rd SW8
42 J 18 Union rd Wemb
18 H 20 Union row N17
134 B 6 Union sq N1
4 F 13 Union st Barnt
64 H 4 Union st E15
116 H 4 Union st Kingst
142 A 15 Union st SE1
141 X 16 Union st SE1
134 M 11 Union wlk E2
78 A 8 Unity way SE18
26 C 2 University clo NW9
132 E 17 University college WC1
132 H 20 University of London WC1
106 G 15 University rd SW19
132 C 18 University st WC1
83 U 7 Unwin rd Islwth
151 R 16 Unwin rd SE15
138 D 7 Upbrook ms W2
146 C 19 Upcerne rd SW10
110 A 18 Upchurch clo SE20
12 H 15 Upcroft av Edg
158 A 3 Upfield Croy
157 Z 5 Upfield Croy
59 V 13 Upfield rd W7
53 Z 16 Uphall rd Ilf
74 B 11 Upham Park rd W4
13 O 15 Uphill dri NW7
25 W 16 Uphill dri NW9
13 P 13 Uphill gro NW7
13 O 14 Uphill rd NW7
98 B 8 Upland rd Bxly Hth
65 R 12 Upland rd E13
157 O 12 Upland rd S Croy
91 X 12 Upland rd SE22
91 X 18 Upland rd SE22
154 G 14 Upland rd Sutton
32 F 9 Uplands av E17
125 N 4 Uplands Becknhm
85 T 13 Uplands clo SW14
35 P 2 Uplands end Wdfd Grn
7 U 9 Uplands Park rd Enf
16 B 6 Uplands rd Barnt
30 E 17 Uplands rd N8
37 U 11 Uplands rd Rom
35 P 2 Uplands rd Wdfd Grn
7 T 16 Uplands way N21
54 L 20 Upney la Bark
67 Y 1 Upney la Bark
150 L 10 Upnor way SE17
36 C 18 Uppark dri Ilf
81 R 10 Upper Abbey rd Blvdr
136 J 17 Upper Addison gdns W14
147 V 1 Upper Belgrave st SW1
139 P 5 Upper Berkeley st W1
109 R 20 Upper Beulah hill SE19
116 G 16 Upper Brighton rd Surb
139 S 9 Upper Brook st W1
72 F 17 Upper butts Brentf
27 X 9 Upper Cavendish av N3
146 K 14 Upper Cheyne row SW3
50 A 8 Upper Clapton rd E5
49 Y 4 Upper Clapton rd E5
124 J 10 Upper Elmers end Becknhm
125 P 13 Upper Elmers End rd Becknhm
18 J 17 Upper Fore st N18
120 L 4 Upper green Mitch
139 T 10 Upper Grosvenor st W1
101 V 4 Upper Grotto rd Twick
141 S 13 Upper ground SE1
141 V 12 Upper ground SE1
81 O 16 Upper Grove rd Blvdr

123 T 9 Upper grove SE25
102 G 8 Upper Ham rd Rich
131 U 17 Upper Harley st NW1
22 D 1 Upper Hill view rd Pinn
81 V 13 Upper Holly Hill rd Blvdr
140 C 8 Upper James st W1
140 C 9 Upper John st W1
74 H 14 Upper Mall W6
141 P 20 Upper Marsh SE1
139 O 1 Upper Montagu st W1
153 T 16 Upper Mulgrave rd Sutton
64 B 15 Upper North st E14
81 U 12 Upper Park rd Blvdr
112 K 20 Upper Park rd Brom
103 O 16 Upper Park rd Kingst
16 G 17 Upper Park rd N11
46 L 17 Upper Park rd NW3
137 T 19 Upper Phillmore gdns W8
57 T 11 Upper Rainham rd Hornch
65 R 9 Upper rd E13
155 Z 11 Upper rd Wallgtn
86 G 9 Upper Richmond rd SW15
87 R 12 Upper Richmond rd SW15
85 T 10 Upper Richmond Road west SW14
157 T 17 Upper Selsdon rd S Croy
81 R 10 Upper Sheridan rd Blvdr
159 D 4 Upper Shirley rd Croy
140 J 8 Upper St Martins la WC2
48 H 19 Upper st N1
133 V 8 Upper st N1
133 W 2 Upper st N1
85 U 1 Upper Staithe W4
82 G 2 Upper Sutton la Hounsl
102 D 19 Upper Teddington rd Kingst
46 D 10 Upper ter NW3
142 B 9 Upper Thames st EC4
160 C 9 Upper Thames st EC4
160 F 10 Upper Thames st EC4
141 Z 8 Upper Thames st EC4
48 F 4 Upper Tollington pk N4
90 D 20 Upper Tulse hill SW2
106 M 4 Upper Tooting pk SW17
107 N 4 Upper Tooting pk SW17
106 L 9 Upper Tooting rd SW17
107 N 6 Upper Tooting rd SW17
58 J 12 Upper Town rd Grnfd
154 F 10 Upper Vernon rd Sutton
33 W 11 Upper Walthamstow rd E17
97 P 5 Upper Wickham la Welling
131 V 20 Upper Wimpole st W1
132 G 15 Upper Woburn pl WC1
114 M 12 Upperton rd Sidcp
65 Y 8 Upperton Road east E13
65 X 9 Upperton Road west E13
24 E 9 Uppingham av Stanm
17 S 19 Updsell av N13
90 K 3 Upstall st SE5
52 G 20 Upton av E7
98 B 15 Upton clo Bxly
153 Z 16 Upton dene Sutton
24 C 17 Upton gdns Harrow
52 F 19 Upton la E7
65 T 1 Upton la E7
52 J 20 Upton Park rd E7
65 V 1 Upton Park rd E7
98 A 13 Upton rd Bxly Hth
97 Y 10 Upton rd Bxly Hth
82 H 9 Upton rd Hounsl
18 L 16 Upton rd N18
79 P 17 Upton rd SE18
123 N 2 Upton rd Thntn Hth
15 V 20 Upway N12
94 D 16 Upwood rd SE12
122 A 1 Upwood rd SW16
150 B 16 Urlwin st SE5
105 T 1 Urmston dri SW19
88 J 3 Ursula st SW11

68 K 1 Urswick gdns Dgnhm
68 K 1 Urswick rd Dgnhm
50 C 15 Urswick rd E9
149 O 18 Usborne ms SW8
63 Z 5 Usher rd E3
65 P 20 Usk st E16
63 S 8 Usk st E2
56 E 9 Uvedale rd Dgnhm
8 B 17 Uvedale rd Enf
146 B 18 Uverdale rd SW10
100 L 13 Uxbridge rd Hampt
22 K 1 Uxbridge rd Harrow
23 O 1 Uxbridge rd Harrow
116 G 10 Uxbridge rd Kingst
70 K 2 Uxbridge rd S'hall
10 K 18 Uxbridge rd Stanm
11 O 17 Uxbridge rd Stanm
136 B 16 Uxbridge rd W12
74 G 3 Uxbridge rd W12
72 B 2 Uxbridge rd W13
60 K 20 Uxbridge rd W5
73 O 2 Uxbridge rd W5
137 S 13 Uxbridge st W8
42 K 4 Uxendon cres Wemb
42 M 3 Uxendon hill Wemb
43 N 2 Uxendon hill Wemb

V

125 Z 7 Valan leas Brom
21 O 6 Valance av E4
130 B 13 Vale clo W9
126 F 6 Vale cotts Brom
104 B 8 Vale cres SW15
22 A 15 Vale croft Pinn
4 K 16 Vale dri Barnt
91 T 9 Vale end SE22
30 L 20 Vale gro N4
73 Y 4 Vale gro W3
61 P 15 Vale la W3
127 V 2 Vale rd Brom
52 H 17 Vale rd E7
152 E 8 Vale rd Epsom
121 W 8 Vale rd Mitch
30 M 20 Vale rd N4
31 N 19 Vale rd N4
153 Z 8 Vale rd Sutton
152 E 5 Vale rd Worc Pk
45 V 4 Vale ri NW11
48 J 10 Vale row N5
132 J 1 Vale royal N7
158 G 3 Vale the Croy
70 B 17 Vale the Hounsl
29 O 4 Vale the N10
17 N 1 Vale the N14
16 L 3 Vale the N20
74 C 3 Vale the N3
45 T 6 Vale the NW11
146 G 14 Vale the SW3
74 C 3 Vale the W3
34 F 3 Vale the Wdfd Grn
55 W 3 Valence av Dgnhm
55 X 10 Valence cir Dgnhm
55 Y 8 Valence pk Dgnhm
56 A 9 Valence Wood rd Dgnhm
55 X 10 Valence Wood rd Dgnhm
11 S 14 Valencia rd Stanm
90 G 9 Valentia pl SW9
115 Y 2 Valentine av Bxly
110 E 5 Valentine ct SE23
141 V 18 Valentine pl SE1
50 E 19 Valentine rd E9
40 L 10 Valentine rd Harrow
141 W 18 Valentine row SE1
53 Y 4 Valentine's la Ilf
57 P 8 Valentine's way Rom
53 Y 2 Valentines pk Ilf
64 M 9 Valerian way E15
112 B 13 Valeswood rd Brom
65 R 5 Valetta gro E13
63 O 13 Valetta rd W3
50 B 18 Valette st E9
38 F 7 Valiant clo Rom
143 U 1 Vallance rd E1
135 U 14 Vallance rd E2
29 V 6 Vallance rd N22
33 U 12 Vallentin rd E17
15 U 14 Valley av N12
99 U 15 Valley clo Drtfrd
25 R 18 Valley dri NW9
7 T 9 Valley Fields cres Enf

106 G 17 Valley gdns SW19
42 L 20 Valley gdns Wemb
77 Y 13 Valley gro SE7
101 X 3 Valley ms Twick
81 X 11 Valley rd Blvdr
126 A 4 Valley rd Brom
99 U 15 Valley rd Drtfrd
115 R 20 Valley rd Orp
108 D 8 Valley rd SW6
20 B 5 Valley side E4
20 A 7 Valley Side parade E4
4 F 19 Valley view Barnt
158 C 2 Valley wlk Croy
108 D 11 Valleyfield rd SW16
62 H 8 Valliere rd NW10
114 G 2 Valliers Wood rd Sidcp
59 Y 13 Vallis way W13
90 M 3 Valmar rd SE5
91 N 3 Valmar rd SE5
106 M 12 Valnay st SW17
32 H 4 Valognes av E17
97 Y 15 Valonia gdns SW18
79 O 16 Vamberry rd SE18
117 Z 17 Van Dyck av New Mald
66 A 16 Vanbrugh clo E16
77 O 18 Vanbrugh fields SE3
77 O 17 Vanbrugh hill SE3
77 P 20 Vanbrugh Park rd SE3
77 O 18 Vanbrugh Park Road west SE3
77 P 19 Vanbrugh pk SE3
73 Z 8 Vanbrugh rd W4
94 C 1 Vanbrugh ter SE3
25 T 5 Vancouver rd Edg
102 E 11 Vancouver rd Kingst
110 K 3 Vancouver rd SE23
88 C 20 Vanderbilt rd SW18
65 U 18 Vandome clo E16
140 D 20 Vandon pas SW1
148 D 1 Vandon st SW1
87 P 17 Vandyke clo SW15
95 P 14 Vandyke cross SE9
24 M 19 Vane clo Harrow
46 F 14 Vane clo NW3
148 D 5 Vane st SW1
81 S 13 Vanessa clo Blvdr
38 E 8 Vanguard clo Rom
93 O 2 Vanguard st SE8
156 A 16 Vanguard way Wallgtn
112 E 8 Vanoc gdns Brom
52 D 12 Vansittart rd E7
75 W 18 Vansittart st SE14
145 U 18 Vanston pl SW6
106 M 13 Vant rd SW17
107 N 13 Vant rd SW17
75 O 15 Varcoe rd SE16
151 Z 12 Varcoe rd SE16
63 N 16 Varden st E1
143 W 3 Varden st E1
88 G 12 Vardens rd SW11
65 W 16 Varley rd E16
132 A 12 Varndell st NW1
31 P 19 Vartry rd N15
149 V 20 Vassall rd SW9
151 P 3 Vauban st SE16
26 G 16 Vaughan av NW4
74 E 10 Vaughan av W6
100 D 15 Vaughan clo Hampt
53 T 1 Vaughan gdns Ilf
52 C 19 Vaughan rd E15
23 H 20 Vaughan rd Harrow
90 L 6 Vaughan rd SE5
116 A 17 Vaughan rd Surb
96 L 5 Vaughan rd Welling
143 T 12 Vaughan way E1
76 A 19 Vaughan Williams clo SE8
148 J 10 Vauxhall br SW1 & SE11
148 C 6 Vauxhall Bridge rd SW1
156 M 15 Vauxhall gdns S Croy
148 M 13 Vauxhall gro SW8
149 N 13 Vauxhall gro SW8
148 M 15 Vauxhall pk SE11
149 P 8 Vauxhall st SE11
148 L 13 Vauxhall stn SE11
149 N 8 Vauxhall wlk SE11
63 O 13 Vawdrey clo E1
107 R 16 Vectis rd SW17
93 P 11 Veda rd SE13
10 A 3 Vega rd Bushey
91 S 12 Velde way SE22
130 H 19 Venables st NW8
74 G 12 Vencourt pl W6
30 J 20 Venetia rd N4
72 F 7 Venetia rd W5

90 M 5 Venetian rd SE5
89 W 9 Venn st SW4
110 D 14 Venner rd SE26
99 P 4 Venners clo Bxly Hth
24 C 6 Venner st
15 N 9 Ventnor dri N20
54 G 17 Ventnor gdns Bark
75 T 19 Ventnor rd SE14
154 B 17 Ventnor rd Sutton
97 Y 18 Venture clo Bxly
78 F 8 Venus rd SE18
7 U 18 Vera av N21
87 T 2 Vera rd SW6
74 F 14 Verbena gdns W6
112 A 2 Verdant la SE6
158 F 2 Verdayne av Croy
80 A 18 Verdun rd SE18
74 F 19 Verdun rd SW13
139 X 6 Vera st W1
145 N 12 Vereker rd W14
136 J 7 Verity clo W11
109 P 16 Vermont rd SE19
154 A 4 Vermont rd Sutton
88 B 16 Vermont rd SW18
55 Y 13 Verney gdns Dgnhm
55 Y 12 Verney rd Dgnhm
75 O 14 Verney rd SE16
151 V 12 Verney rd SE16
43 Y 10 Verney st NW10
151 V 11 Verney way SE16
79 O 16 Vernham rd SE18
53 T 13 Vernon av E12
119 O 3 Vernon av SW20
34 G 1 Vernon av Wdfd Grn
6 B 18 Vernon cres Barnt
24 A 4 Vernon ct Stanm
24 A 4 Vernon dri Stanm
23 Z 4 Vernon dri Stanm
144 L 6 Vernon ms W14
140 L 2 Vernon pl WC1
52 A 5 Vernon rd E11
51 Z 4 Vernon rd E11
51 Z 19 Vernon rd E15
32 L 14 Vernon rd E17
63 Z 6 Vernon rd E3
54 K 5 Vernon rd Ilf
30 Q 11 Vernon rd N8
154 E 10 Vernon rd Sutton
85 Y 8 Vernon rd SW14
41 P 16 Vernon ri Grnfd
133 P 12 Vernon ri WC1
133 O 11 Vernon sq WC1
144 L 6 Vernon st W14
97 Y 5 Veroan rd Bxly Hth
52 F 20 Verona rd E7
107 S 5 Veronica rd SW17
36 A 15 Veronique gdns Ilf
89 R 19 Verran rd SW12
109 X 19 Versailles rd SE20
58 J 11 Verulam av E17
133 S 20 Verulam rd Grnfd
22 M 8 Verwood rd Harrow
74 F 4 Vespan rd W12
92 J 5 Vesta rd SE4
110 G 4 Vestris rd SE23
91 R 2 Vestry ms SE5
33 R 14 Vestry rd E17
91 S 2 Vestry rd SE5
134 F 12 Vestry st N1
110 K 5 Vevey st SE6
56 D 9 Veysey gdns Dgnhm
141 V 2 Viaduct bldgs EC1
135 W 14 Viaduct pl E2
135 W 14 Viaduct st E2
34 G 8 Viaduct the E18
93 S 8 Vian st SE13
90 D 20 Vibart gdns SW2
132 L 4 Vibart wlk N1
135 Z 5 Vicar's clo E9
109 S 15 Vicar's Oak rd SE19
47 O 14 Vicar's rd NW5
77 T 20 Vicarage av SE3
81 X 16 Vicarage clo Erith
58 F 1 Vicarage clo Ruis
88 G 3 Vicarage cres SW11
67 R 2 Vicarage dri Bark
85 X 12 Vicarage dri SW14
70 C 20 Vicarage Farm rd Hounsl
82 C 3 Vicarage Farm rd Hounsl
137 W 16 Vicarage ga W8
120 J 7 Vicarage gdns Mitch
137 W 15 Vicarage gdns W8
91 P 1 Vicarage gro SE5
52 B 19 Vicarage la E15
65 O 2 Vicarage la E15
66 K 8 Vicarage la E6
152 G 19 Vicarage la Epsom

54 D 5 Vicarage la Ilf
79 P 14 Vicarage pk SE18
47 Z 1 Vicarage pth N8
35 S 2 Vicarage rd Wdfd Grn
156 G 4 Vicarage rd Croy
56 F 20 Vicarage rd Dgnhm
51 O 1 Vicarage rd E10
52 B 20 Vicarage rd E15
57 X 4 Vicarage rd Hornch
116 G 2 Vicarage rd Kingst
31 X 3 Vicarage rd N4
26 G 20 Vicarage rd NW4
153 Z 7 Vicarage rd Sutton
85 Y 12 Vicarage rd SW14
101 X 12 Vicarage rd Tedd
82 M 16 Vicarage rd Twick
101 T 4 Vicarage rd Twick
40 G 1 Vicarage way Harrow
43 Z 10 Vicarage way NW10
88 G 2 Vicarage wlk SW11
60 K 6 Vicars Br clo Wemb
65 S 3 Vicars clo E15
63 O 4 Vicars clo E9
8 F 10 Vicars clo Enf
93 P 9 Vicars hill SE13
17 U 3 Vicars Moor la N21
55 R 10 Vicars wlk Dgnhm
90 A 1 Viceroy rd SW8
148 J 7 Vickers Building SW1
42 L 20 Victor gro Wemb
23 O 11 Victor rd Harrow
62 K 7 Victor rd NW10
110 F 17 Victor rd SE20
101 T 11 Victor rd Tedd
18 C 10 Victor vlls N9
146 H 3 Victoria and Albert Museum SW7
5 U 15 Victoria av Barnt
66 A 3 Victoria av E6
142 K 2 Victoria av EC2
82 G 12 Victoria av Hounsl
27 W 5 Victoria av N3
116 F 16 Victoria av Surb
155 P 5 Victoria av Wallgtn
5 V 15 Victoria clo Barnt
85 O 3 Victoria cotts Rich
31 R 16 Victoria cres N15
109 R 14 Victoria cres SE19
105 W 17 Victoria cres SW19
43 P 17 Victoria ct Wemb
65 N 17 Victoria Dock rd E16
57 S 19 Victoria Dock rd E16
105 R 3 Victoria dri SW19
105 S 4 Victoria dri SW19
140 L 16 Victoria emb EC4 WC2 SW1
141 S 9 Victoria emb EC4 WC2 SW1
82 A 1 Victoria gdns Hounsl
137 S 12 Victoria gdns W11
15 T 15 Victoria gro N12
146 A 1 Victoria gro W8
137 V 10 Victoria Grove ms W2
4 H 14 Victoria la Barnt
129 S 4 Victoria ms NW6
63 W 2 Victoria park E9
83 P 3 Victoria Park rd E9
135 Y 5 Victoria Park rd E9
63 O 8 Victoria Park sq E2
135 Z 11 Victoria Park sq E2
84 H 13 Victoria pl Rich
54 A 18 Victoria rd Bark
53 Z 18 Victoria rd Bark
5 U 16 Victoria rd Barnt
127 P 12 Victoria rd Brom
98 D 12 Victoria rd Bxly Hth
113 X 12 Victoria rd Chisl
56 J 14 Victoria rd Dgnhm
51 Y 12 Victoria rd E11
65 S 7 Victoria rd E13
33 T 7 Victoria rd E17
34 H 8 Victoria rd E18
20 M 5 Victoria rd E4
21 N 4 Victoria rd E4
36 A 15 Victoria rd Ilf
117 N 3 Victoria rd Kingst
106 K 19 Victoria rd Mitch
31 W 14 Victoria rd N15
29 W 5 Victoria rd N22
48 E 3 Victoria rd N4
18 J 9 Victoria rd N9
62 A 11 Victoria rd NW10
27 N 13 Victoria rd NW4
129 O 8 Victoria rd NW6
129 T 4 Victoria rd NW6
13 R 15 Victoria rd NW7
39 S 18 Victoria rd Rom
40 B 13 Victoria rd Ruis

70 D 9 Victoria rd S'hall
114 M 8 Victoria rd Sidcp
116 G 15 Victoria rd Surb
154 F 12 Victoria rd Sutton
85 X 7 Victoria rd SW14
101 X 15 Victoria rd Tedd
84 A 18 Victoria rd Twick
61 Y 13 Victoria rd W3
60 C 14 Victoria rd W5
138 A 19 Victoria rd W8
89 S 10 Victoria ri SW4
147 Y 1 Victoria sq SW1
81 P 14 Victoria st Blvdr
51 Y 20 Victoria st E15
148 D 2 Victoria st SW1
140 G 20 Victoria st SW1
147 Y 5 Victoria sta SW1
41 S 4 Victoria ter Harrow
48 F 4 Victoria ter N4
148 K 1 Victoria Tower gdns SW1
85 N 9 Victoria vlls Rich
77 V 13 Victoria way SE7
49 T 10 Victorian gro N16
49 T 11 Victorian rd N16
100 D 15 Victors dri Hampt
120 D 11 Victory av Mrdn
150 D 5 Victory pl SE17
109 T 16 Victory pl SE19
106 C 18 Victory rd SW19
150 G 17 Victory sq SE5
38 F 7 Victory way Rom
75 W 6 Victory way SE16
93 O 2 Victory wlk SE8
23 P 12 View clo Harrow
28 M 20 View rd N6
29 N 19 View rd N6
81 N 13 View the SE2
42 J 2 Viewfield clo Harrow
97 T 20 Viewfield rd Sidcp
87 V 16 Viewfield rd SW18
79 W 14 Viewland rd SE18
7 U 19 Viga rd N21
109 X 9 Vigilant clo SE26
56 F 1 Vignoles rd E2
140 B 10 Vigo st W1
58 C 19 Viking rd S'hall
90 F 7 Villa rd SW9
150 F 10 Villa st SE17
150 G 12 Villa st SE17
80 A 18 Villacourt rd SE18
20 H 16 Village clo E4
99 U 11 Village Green rd Drtfrd
8 D 19 Village rd Enf
27 S 7 Village rd N3
153 X 19 Village row Sutton
78 A 16 Village the SE7
77 Z 16 Village the SE7
125 N 3 Village way Becknhm
40 F 1 Village way E Harrow
44 A 12 Village way NW10
43 Z 12 Village way NW10
40 D 1 Village way Pinn
91 O 15 Village way SE21
79 P 12 Village way SE18
116 L 11 Villiers av Surb
100 F 2 Villiers av Twick
51 O 6 Villiers clo E10
117 N 9 Villiers clo Surb
15 S 4 Villiers ct Surb
116 L 11 Villiers pth Surb
124 F 4 Villiers rd Becknhm
67 R 2 Villiers rd Islwth
116 M 6 Villiers rd Kingst
44 G 17 Villiers rd NW2
70 F 4 Villiers rd S'hall
140 K 12 Villiers st WC2
82 H 18 Vincam clo Twick
134 G 14 Vince st EC1
4 M 11 Vincent clo Barnt
126 J 10 Vincent clo Brom
75 V 6 Vincent clo SE16
114 G 2 Vincent clo Sidcp
44 E 10 Vincent gdns NW2
123 S 18 Vincent rd Croy
68 L 2 Vincent rd Dgnhm
20 K 20 Vincent rd E4
62 A 3 Vincent rd Islwth
117 P 5 Vincent rd Kingst
30 L 13 Vincent rd N15
30 F 7 Vincent rd N22
79 N 11 Vincent rd SE18
73 U 8 Vincent rd W3
61 N 1 Vincent rd Wemb
100 M 14 Vincent row Hampt
148 E 5 Vincent sq SW1
65 P 16 Vincent st E16
148 F 6 Vincent st SW1

133 X 9 Vincent ter N1
40 B 18 Vincents pth Nthlt
117 N 13 Vine clo Surb
154 C 5 Vine clo Sutton
143 U 2 Vine ct E1
143 U 2 Vine ct E1
24 K 17 Vine ct Harrow
54 B 15 Vine gdns Ilf
133 S 18 Vine hill EC1
142 L 15 Vine la SE1
82 J 10 Vine pl Hounsl
86 D 9 Vine rd SW13
143 N 7 Vine st EC3
38 L 14 Vine st Rom
140 C 11 Vine st W1
142 B 18 Vine syd SE1
33 T 13 Vinegar all E17
143 W 13 Vinegar st E1
13 X 16 Vines av N3
56 C 16 Vineries clo Dgnhm
8 E 11 Vineries the Enf
6 H 18 Vineries the N14
130 K 14 Vinery vlls NW8
28 A 5 Vines av N3
158 L 18 Viney bank Croy
93 S 8 Viney rd SE13
27 S 2 Vineyard av NW7
105 X 9 Vineyard Hill rd SW19
84 J 13 Vineyard pas Rich
85 X 7 Vineyard pth SW14
84 K 14 Vineyard the Rich
133 T 16 Vineyard wlk EC1
90 F 10 Vining st SW9
160 C 9 Vinters pl EC4
80 C 12 Viola av SE2
62 E 20 Viola sq W12
8 B 3 Violet av Enf
156 J 12 Violet gdns Croy
130 B 10 Violet hill NW8
156 J 9 Violet la Croy
33 P 19 Violet rd E17
34 H 7 Violet rd E18
64 C 12 Violet rd E3
139 N 1 Virgil pl W1
149 R 1 Virgil st SE1
34 M 14 Virginia gdns Ilf
108 J 20 Virginia rd Thtn Hth
143 T 10 Virginia st E1
90 D 16 Virginia wlk SW2
134 B 19 Viscount st EC1
9 T 9 Vista av Enf
35 O 16 Vista dri Ilf
95 P 19 Vista the SE9
24 J 19 Vista way Harrow
26 J 17 Vivian av NW4
43 S 17 Vivian av Wemb
43 O 15 Vivian gdns Wemb
63 V 6 Vivian rd E3
91 Z 7 Vivian sq SE15
28 G 15 Vivian way N2
84 F 17 Vivienne clo Twick
96 F 1 Voce rd SE18
79 T 20 Voce rd SE18
118 D 14 Voewood clo New Mald
89 X 8 Voltaire rd SW4
34 E 18 Voluntary pl E11
47 V 7 Vorley rd N19
108 B 16 Voss st SW16
135 U 14 Voss st E2
156 C 15 Vulcan clo Croy
7 U 9 Vulcan ga Enf
92 K 5 Vulcan rd SE4
92 L 4 Vulcan ter SE4
94 A 3 Vulcan way N7
98 H 8 Vyne the Bxly Hth
61 Z 20 Vyner rd W3
63 N 4 Vyner st E2
135 Y 7 Vyner st E2

W

150 D 7 Wadding st SE17
51 X 16 Waddington rd E15
51 X 17 Waddington rd E15
98 F 11 Waddington ter Bxly Hth
108 M 19 Waddington way SE19
109 N 20 Waddington way SE19
156 G 4 Waddon clo Croy

156 E 6 Waddon Coutt rd Croy
122 C 20 Waddon Marsh way Croy
156 D 1 Waddon Marsh way Croy
156 H 4 Waddon New rd Croy
156 F 7 Waddon Park av Croy
156 H 5 Waddon rd Croy
156 F 14 Waddon way Croy
65 Y 19 Wade rd E16
64 C 19 Wade's pl E14
17 T 3 Wades gro N21
7 T 19 Wades hill N21
17 U 3 Wades hill N21
63 O 5 Wadeson st E2
135 Y 7 Wadeson st E2
38 A 20 Wadeville av Rom
81 S 15 Wadeville clo Blvdr
33 S 3 Wadham av E17
41 P 17 Wadham gdns Grnfd
130 J 2 Wadham gdns NW3
33 T 3 Wadham rd E17
87 T 11 Wadham rd SW15
123 Z 3 Wadhurst clo SE20
89 U 1 Wadhurst rd SW8
73 Y 9 Wadhurst rd W4
33 Z 20 Wadley rd E11
60 D 6 Wadsworth clo Grnfd
74 J 9 Wadsworth mans W6
60 C 6 Wadsworth rd Grnfd
63 Y 13 Wager st E3
18 J 20 Waggon la N17
65 X 4 Waghorn rd E13
24 H 11 Waghorn rd Harrow
91 X 7 Waghorn st SE15
76 P 19 Wagner st SE16
5 W 1 Wagon la Barnt
38 K 8 Wainfleet av Rom
87 P 20 Wainford clo SW19
83 R 11 Wainwright rd Islwth
94 C 19 Waite Davies rd SE12
151 O 13 Waite st SE15
109 S 18 Wakefield gdns SE19
35 P 20 Wakefield gdns Ilf
16 L 17 Wakefield rd N11
31 U 15 Wakefield rd N15
84 H 13 Wakefield rd Rich
66 E 3 Wakefield st E6
18 K 17 Wakefield st N18
132 L 15 Wakefield st WC1
49 O 18 Wakeham st N1
22 E 11 Wakehams hill Pinn
88 K 13 Wakehurst rd SW11
89 N 12 Wakehurst rd SW11
64 M 6 Wakelin rd E15
59 W 15 Wakeling rd W7
63 U 18 Wakeling st E14
128 D 13 Wakeman rd NW10
25 Y 14 Wakemans Hill av NW9
54 B 19 Wakering rd Bark
66 G 18 Wakerley clo E6
133 X 11 Wakley st EC1
148 M 19 Walberswick st SW8
160 E 8 Walbrook EC4
143 W 7 Walburgh st E1
150 C 8 Walcorde av SE17
9 X 8 Walcot rd Enf
149 U 4 Walcot sq SE11
148 D 5 Walcott st SW1
109 H 7 Waldeck gro SE27
30 J 12 Waldeck rd N15
85 W 7 Waldeck rd SW14
60 C 18 Waldeck rd W13
73 P 15 Waldeck rd W4
101 V 9 Waldegrave gdns Twick
101 V 9 Waldegrave pk Twick
55 T 6 Waldegrave rd Dgnhm
127 S 10 Waldegrave rd Brom
30 G 10 Waldegrave rd N8
109 V 18 Waldegrave rd SE19
101 V 8 Waldegrave rd Twick
60 M 18 Waldegrave rd W5
157 U 7 Waldegrove Croy
87 T 3 Waldemar av SW6
72 D 4 Waldemar av W13
105 X 11 Waldemar rd SW19
113 U 10 Walden av Chisl
17 Z 13 Walden av N13
69 Z 7 Walden av Rainhm
81 O 13 Walden clo Blvdr
122 D 7 Walden gdns Thntn Hth
113 U 14 Walden rd Chisl

31 O 6 Walden rd N17
143 V 3 Walden st E1
36 H 1 Walden way Ilf
14 D 19 Walden way NW7
110 C 2 Waldenshaw rd SE23
106 K 18 Waldo pl Mitch
126 M 7 Waldo rd Brom
62 J 9 Waldo rd NW10
156 J 17 Waldorf clo S Croy
110 D 2 Waldram cres SE23
110 E 2 Waldram Park rd SE23
110 D 3 Waldram pl SE23
81 P 5 Waldrist way Blvdr
125 W 6 Waldron gdns Brom
146 H 14 Waldron ms SW3
41 S 4 Waldron st Harrow
106 D 5 Waldron sd SW18
156 K 9 Waldronhyrst Croy
156 K 9 Waldrons pth S Croy
156 K 8 Waldrons the Croy
10 J 17 Waleran clo Stanm
93 V 6 Walerand rd SE13
154 K 12 Wales av Carsh
61 Y 15 Wales Farm rd W3
63 U 14 Waley st E1
15 O 1 Walfield av N20
49 T 12 Walford rd N16
56 A 20 Walfrey gdns Dgnhm
145 X 19 Walham Green ct SW6
145 U 17 Walham gro SW6
145 T 16 Walham yd SW6
113 X 11 Walkden rd Chisl
99 S 7 Walker clo Drtfrd
79 O 10 Walker clo SE18
71 S 4 Walker clo W7
140 E 8 Walker's cr W1
87 R 9 Walkers pl SW15
108 M 2 Walkerscroft mead SE21
109 N 2 Walkerscroft mead SE21
99 Y 14 Walkley rd Drtfrd
28 G 9 Walks the N2
66 H 2 Wall End rd E6
64 J 20 Wall rd E14
49 P 19 Wall st N1
139 T 4 Wallace collection W2
154 L 11 Wallace cres Carsh
48 M 17 Wallace rd N1
92 H 6 Wallbutton rd SE4
45 P 3 Wallcote av NW2
39 Z 11 Wallenger av Rom
92 E 3 Waller rd SE14
74 E 1 Wallflower st W12
145 W 6 Wallgrave rd SW5
136 E 4 Wallingford av W10
36 L 20 Wallington rd Ilf
155 U 14 Wallington sq Wallgtn
88 F 8 Wallis clo SW11
50 M 19 Wallis rd E9
51 N 18 Wallis rd E9
58 K 17 Wallis rd S'hall
85 Z 10 Wallorton gdns SW14
51 X 2 Wallwood rd E11
63 Z 15 Wallwood st E14
45 R 15 Walm la NW2
38 H 8 Walmer clo Rom
71 Z 7 Walmer gdns W13
139 N 1 Walmer pl W1
136 K 9 Walmer rd W11
139 N 1 Walmer st W1
79 R 11 Walmer ter SE18
60 B 4 Walmgate rd Grnfd
14 K 18 Walmington fold N12
154 K 11 Walnut clo Carsh
36 C 12 Walnut clo Ilf
152 D 19 Walnut fields KT17
8 B 18 Walnut gro Enf
154 C 16 Walnut ms Sutton
120 J 4 Walnut Tree av Mitch
72 K 16 Walnut Tree clo Brentf
114 D 20 Walnut Tree clo Chisl
105 R 12 Walnut Tree cotts SW19
70 F 17 Walnut Tree rd Hounsl
72 F 4 Walnut Tree rd Brentf
55 X 7 Walnut Tree rd Dgnhm
77 N 15 Walnut Tree rd SE10
149 S 4 Walnut Tree wlk SE11
84 M 5 Walpole av Rich

72 D 4 Walpole clo W13
101 V 13 Walpole cres Tedd
101 U 6 Walpole gdns Twick
73 V 13 Walpole gdns W4
101 V 13 Walpole gdns W4
101 U 12 Walpole pl Tedd
127 N 11 Walpole rd Brom
157 N 2 Walpole rd Croy
32 J 12 Walpole rd E17
34 B 5 Walpole rd E18
65 Y 2 Walpole rd E6
30 M 7 Walpole rd N17
116 H 16 Walpole rd Surb
106 G 15 Walpole rd SW19
101 V 13 Walpole rd Tedd
101 T 4 Walpole rd Twick
147 O 9 Walpole st SW3
42 L 17 Walrond av Wemb
49 W 3 Walsham clo N16
68 J 20 Walsham clo SE28
92 E 4 Walsham rd SE14
152 C 10 Walsingham gdns Epsom
49 Y 10 Walsingham rd E5
8 B 16 Walsingham rd Enf
120 M 10 Walsingham rd Mitch
71 Y 2 Walsingham rd W13
116 J 1 Walter st Kingst
63 T 16 Walter ter E1
12 J 20 Walter wlk Edg
9 R 16 Walters rd Enf
123 S 10 Walters rd SE25
63 T 9 Walters st E2
92 E 17 Walters way SE23
126 E 2 Walters yd Brom
48 A 2 Waltersville rd N19
129 R 17 Walterton rd W9
75 R 19 Waltham av NW9
99 V 15 Waltham clo Drtfrd
25 P 9 Waltham dri Edg
33 N 3 Waltham Park way E17
120 G 19 Waltham rd Carsh
70 B 8 Waltham rd S'hall
105 S 14 Waltham ri SW19
20 B 5 Waltham way E4
19 Y 12 Waltham way E4
31 N 5 Waltheof av N17
31 N 4 Waltheof gdns N17
40 E 12 Walton av Harrow
118 D 10 Walton av New Mald
153 U 5 Walton av Sutton
23 R 12 Walton clo Harrow
44 K 7 Walton clo NW2
148 L 17 Walton clo SW8
40 E 12 Walton cres Harrow
23 R 13 Walton dri Harrow
61 T 15 Walton gdns W3
42 J 7 Walton gdns Wemb
159 U 17 Walton grn Croy
147 O 1 Walton pl SW3
53 W 12 Walton rd E12
53 W 13 Walton rd E12
65 X 6 Walton rd E13
23 R 12 Walton rd Harrow
31 V 14 Walton rd N15
38 C 2 Walton rd Rom
115 S 8 Walton rd Sidcp
146 L 5 Walton st Enf
147 N 3 Walton st SW3
148 K 17 Walton ter SW8
121 U 9 Walton way Mitch
61 T 15 Walton way W3
150 C 10 Walworth pl SE17
150 B 9 Walworth rd SE17
127 N 7 Walwyn av Brom
104 H 1 Wanborough dri SW15
104 H 1 Wanborough dri SW15
155 Z 6 Wandle bank Wallgtn
106 E 18 Wandle bank SW19
155 Z 6 Wandle Court gdns Wallgtn
156 A 5 Wandle rd Croy
156 L 6 Wandle rd Croy
120 E 10 Wandle rd Mrdn
106 K 3 Wandle rd SW17
155 R 3 Wandle rd Wallgtn
156 E 6 Wandle side Croy
155 R 5 Wandle side Wallgtn
120 L 11 Wandle way Mitch
106 A 1 Wandle way SW18
145 Z 18 Wandon rd SW6
88 A 5 Wandsworth Bridge rd SW6
88 G 15 Wandsworth common SW18
88 E 13 Wandsworth Common North side SW18

88 E 15 Wandsworth Common West side SW18
87 Y 14 Wandsworth High st SW18
87 V 10 Wandsworth pk SW15
87 Z 13 Wandsworth plain SW18
148 H 18 Wandsworth rd SW8
89 T 6 Wandsworth rd SW8
87 Z 15 Wandsworth stadium SW8
55 V 1 Wangey rd Rom
90 L 8 Wanless rd SE24
91 P 9 Wanley rd SE5
65 W 11 Wanlip rd E13
50 M 20 Wansbeck rd E9
145 W 18 Wansdown pl SW6
150 B 7 Wansey st SE17
34 K 4 Wansford rd Wdfd Grn
126 L 3 Wanstead clo Brom
52 K 2 Wanstead ho E11
35 S 19 Wanstead la Ilf
53 N 7 Wanstead Park av E12
52 M 5 Wanstead Park av E12
35 O 19 Wanstead Park rd Ilf
53 S 3 Wanstead Park rd Ilf
34 F 17 Wanstead pl E11
126 K 3 Wanstead rd Brom
98 L 20 Wansunt rd Bxly
94 B 13 Wantage rd SE12
56 G 12 Wantz rd Dgnhm
143 Z 14 Wapping Dock st E1
75 O 3 Wapping High st E1
143 T 14 Wapping High st E1
75 N 1 Wapping la E1
143 X 10 Wapping la E1
75 P 2 Wapping wall E1
104 C 19 Warbank la Kingst
74 K 4 Warberry rd N22
30 D 6 Warberry rd N22
103 U 14 Warboys app Kingst
20 H 17 Warboys cres E4
103 T 14 Warboys rd Kingst
10 B 19 Warburton clo Harrow
63 N 2 Warburton rd E8
135 X 3 Warburton rd Twick
100 J 1 Warburton rd Twick
33 S 8 Warburton ter E17
81 Z 7 Ward clo Enf
64 H 2 Ward rd E15
47 V 11 Ward rd N19
149 P 8 Ward st SE11
75 O 9 Wardale clo SE16
26 B 2 Wardell clo NW9
26 C 4 Wardell field NW9
40 E 4 Warden av Harrow
47 R 17 Warden rd NW5
142 A 15 Wardens gro SE1
50 F 5 Wardle st E9
88 A 19 Wardley st SW18
87 R 2 Wardo av SW6
75 R 12 Wardon st SE16
140 D 6 Wardour ms W1
140 E 7 Wardour st W1
141 Y 7 Wardrobe pl EC4
141 Y 7 Wardrobe ter EC4
54 F 1 Wards rd Ilf
82 J 10 Wareham clo Hounsl
35 Y 15 Waremead rd Ilf
100 L 20 Warfield rd Hampt
128 F 14 Warfield rd NW10
128 F 14 Warfield yd NW10
31 V 18 Wargrave av N15
40 M 10 Wargrave rd Harrow
23 W 8 Warham rd Harrow
30 H 16 Warham rd N4
156 M 10 Warham rd S Croy
149 X 18 Warham st SE5
115 R 7 Waring pk Sidcp
115 T 15 Waring rd Sidcp
108 L 9 Waring st SE27
71 Y 19 Warkworth gdns Islwth
31 P 3 Warkworth rd N17
79 T 20 Warland rd SE18
56 C 2 Warley av Dgnhm
35 X 4 Warley rd Ilf
19 P 8 Warley rd N9
34 H 2 Warley rd Wdfd Grn
63 S 9 Warley st E2
122 J 8 Warlingham rd Thntn Hth
129 R 16 Warlock rd W9
48 B 12 Warlters clo N7
48 B 12 Warlters rd N7
50 F 9 Warming clo E5

90 M 15	Warmington rd SE24
65 T 11	Warmington st E13
123 W 4	Warminster gdns SE25
123 W 5	Warminster rd SE25
123 X 3	Warminster sq SE25
121 T 2	Warminster way Mitch
24 H 11	Warneford rd Harrow
135 Y 4	Warneford st E9
153 S 2	Warner av Sutton
52 A 16	Warner clo E15
135 T 10	Warner pl E2
112 C 18	Warner rd Brom
32 H 13	Warner rd E17
29 X 13	Warner rd N8
90 M 2	Warner rd SE5
133 R 17	Warner st EC1
133 S 18	Warner yd EC1
21 S 16	Warners clo Wdfd Grn
154 M 16	Warnham Court rd Carsh
15 V 17	Warnham rd N12
74 A 4	Warple way W3
111 Z 17	Warren av Brom
51 V 8	Warren av E11
85 T 9	Warren av Rich
158 E 17	Warren av S Croy
98 E 12	Warren clo Bxly Hth
19 S 4	Warren clo N9
42 H 6	Warren clo Wemb
18 H 3	Warren cres N9
111 N 19	Warren ct Becknhm
103 X 17	Warren cutting Kingst
58 L 11	Warren dri Grnfd
57 X 10	Warren dri Hornch
117 S 20	Warren dri N Surb
117 U 20	Warren dri S Surb
52 K 1	Warren dri The E11
51 X 16	Warren gdns E15
103 W 15	Warren ho Kingst
78 L 8	Warren la SE18
78 M 9	Warren la SE18
10 K 9	Warren la Stanm
131 Z 18	Warren ms W1
154 H 12	Warren Park rd Sutton
103 X 16	Warren pk Kingst
21 P 3	Warren Pond rd E4
10 B 5	Warren rd Bushey
98 D 12	Warren rd Bxly Hth
123 T 19	Warren rd Edg
51 V 9	Warren rd E10
34 K 19	Warren rd E11
52 L 1	Warren rd E11
20 G 8	Warren rd E4
36 D 15	Warren rd Ilf
103 V 15	Warren rd Kingst
44 E 8	Warren rd NW2
115 T 8	Warren rd Sidcp
106 J 16	Warren rd SW19
83 O 17	Warren rd Twick
103 Y 20	Warren ri Kingst
132 B 17	Warren st W1
37 X 14	Warren ter Rom
154 H 20	Warren the Carsh
53 R 12	Warren the E12
70 D 20	Warren the Hounsl
14 E 18	Warren way NW7
77 Y 16	Warren wlk SE7
47 V 11	Warrender rd N19
12 F 6	Warrens Shawe la Edg
89 N 2	Warriner gdns SW11
130 A 17	Warrington cres W9
130 A 19	Warrington gdns W9
23 T 16	Warrington rd Harrow
55 X 7	Warrington rd Dgnhm
156 H 6	Warrington rd Croy
55 X 7	Warrington sq Dgnhm
149 Z 18	Warrior rd SE5
53 V 12	Warrior sq E12
78 C 8	Warspite rd SE18
64 G 3	Warton rd E15
12 G 11	Warwick av Edg
40 D 13	Warwick av Harrow
130 A 19	Warwick av W9
129 Y 17	Warwick av W9
5 V 16	Warwick clo Barnt
10 F 3	Warwick clo Bushey
100 M 18	Warwick clo Hampt
138 B 1	Warwick cres W2
141 R 2	Warwick ct WC1
72 K 3	Warwick dene W5
86 J 9	Warwick dri SW15
54 A 5	Warwick gdns Ilf
30 L 17	Warwick gdns N4
145 P 3	Warwick gdns W14
50 A 5	Warwick gro E5
49 Z 5	Warwick gro E5
116 L 16	Warwick gro Surb
140 F 13	Warwick House st SW1
141 Y 5	Warwick la EC4
129 Z 18	Warwick ms W5
72 G 4	Warwick pl W5
130 A 20	Warwick pl W9
147 Z 8	Warwick Place north SW1
122 E 7	Warwick rd Thntn Hth
117 U 5	Warwick rd New Mald
5 N 15	Warwick rd Barnt
34 J 15	Warwick rd E11
53 R 16	Warwick rd E12
52 O 18	Warwick rd E15
32 K 6	Warwick rd E17
20 A 16	Warwick rd E4
9 Z 1	Warwick rd Enf
16 L 17	Warwick rd N11
18 F 15	Warwick rd N18
70 E 8	Warwick rd S'hall
124 B 6	Warwick rd SE20
115 R 13	Warwick rd Sidcp
154 C 10	Warwick rd Sutton
145 T 8	Warwick rd SW5
102 D 20	Warwick rd Tedd
101 U 1	Warwick rd Twick
145 P 5	Warwick rd W14
72 G 4	Warwick rd W5
97 T 7	Warwick rd Welling
148 A 1	Warwick row SW1
147 Z 2	Warwick row SW1
141 Y 5	Warwick sq EC4
148 A 8	Warwick sq SW1
148 A 8	Warwick Square ms SW1
140 C 9	Warwick st W1
79 T 16	Warwick ter SE18
148 B 6	Warwick way SW1
147 X 9	Warwick way SW1
75 Z 18	Warwickshire pth SE8
53 S 11	Washington av E12
74 G 19	Washington rd SW13
152 J 1	Washington rd Worc Pk
34 C 7	Washington rd E18
65 Y 2	Washington rd E6
117 O 4	Washington rd Kingst
64 E 9	Washington st E3
110 G 1	Wastdale rd SE23
93 W 3	Wat Tyler rd SE10
73 P 17	Watcombe cotts Rich
124 A 10	Watcombe rd SE25
123 Z 11	Watcombe rd SE25
11 O 19	Water gdns Stanm
32 A 18	Water la E15
54 J 10	Water la Ilf
116 G 2	Water la Kingst
84 G 13	Water la Rich
101 Z 1	Water la Twick
18 D 17	Water mill la N18
100 G 5	Water Mill way Felt
61 N 4	Water rd Wemb
141 R 8	Water st WC2
157 P 8	Water Tower hill Croy
156 L 5	Water Works yd Croy
111 T 8	Waterbank rd SE6
26 B 8	Waterbeach dri NW9
55 T 18	Waterbeach rd Dgnhm
27 N 16	Waterbrook la NW4
80 A 17	Waterdale rd SE2
51 P 18	Waterden rd E15
155 Y 14	Waterer ri Wallgtn
16 G 10	Waterfall clo N14
16 F 14	Waterfall rd N11
106 H 15	Waterfall rd SW19
106 J 14	Waterfall ter SW17
80 C 2	Waterfield clo SE18
88 A 1	Waterford rd SW6
141 W 8	Watergate EC4
76 A 15	Watergate SE18
140 L 12	Watergate wlk WC2
20 L 13	Waterhall av E4
66 A 14	Waterhouse clo E16
46 G 14	Waterhouse clo NW3
144 H 8	Waterhouse clo W6
141 O 11	Waterloo br WC2
50 D 14	Waterloo clo E9
63 P 5	Waterloo gdns E2
39 O 18	Waterloo gdns Rom
129 R 1	Waterloo pas NW6
84 J 12	Waterloo pl Rich
140 F 13	Waterloo pl SW1
51 N 2	Waterloo rd E10
65 Y 2	Waterloo rd E6
52 D 14	Waterloo rd E7
36 B 7	Waterloo rd Ilf
44 G 5	Waterloo rd NW2
39 O 17	Waterloo rd Rom
141 U 18	Waterloo rd SE1
154 F 10	Waterloo rd Sutton
141 R 16	Waterloo sta SE1
133 W 2	Waterloo ter N1
47 U 4	Waterlow rd N19
87 R 9	Waterman st SW15
143 W 12	Waterman way E1
102 H 18	Watermans clo Kingst
120 M 15	Watermead la Carsh
111 T 9	Watermead rd SE6
102 C 8	Watermill clo Rich
56 E 16	Waters gdns Dgnhm
117 S 5	Waters rd Kingst
112 B 6	Waters rd SE6
111 Y 7	Waters rd SE6
117 S 5	Waters sq Kingst
24 H 2	Watersfield way Edg
124 M 1	Waterside Becknhm
58 F 7	Waterside rd S'hall
143 T 19	Waterside clo SE16
99 S 12	Waterside Drtfrd
131 U 3	Waterside pl NW1
70 G 7	Waterside rd S'hall
134 L 12	Waterson st N1
50 E 8	Waterworks la E5
90 B 15	Waterworks rd SW2
115 S 17	Watery la Sidcp
119 V 2	Watery la SW20
120 L 14	Wates way Mitch
30 M 5	Watevile rd N17
10 M 1	Watford By-pass Borhm Wd
11 P 3	Watford By-pass Borhm Wd
88 K 1	Watford clo SW11
65 T 15	Watford rd E16
41 Y 2	Watford rd Harrow
42 A 12	Watford rd Wemb
26 E 4	Watford way NW7
13 O 14	Watford way NW7
43 S 11	Watkin rd Wemb
48 C 17	Watkinson rd N7
26 A 1	Watling av Edg
25 U 6	Watling av SE9
160 B 7	Watling ct EC4
11 R 5	Watling Farm clo Borhm Wd
98 H 11	Watling st Bxly Hth
99 X 15	Watling st Drtfrd
142 B 7	Watling st EC4
160 B 7	Watling st EC4
110 H 12	Watlington gro SE26
143 Y 6	Watney mkt E1
143 R 18	Watney pas SE1
85 V 6	Watney rd SW14
63 N 18	Watney st E1
143 Y 8	Watney st E1
121 W 12	Watney's rd Mitch
53 W 20	Watson av E6
49 P 14	Watson av Sutton
49 P 14	Watson clo N16
106 K 16	Watson clo SW19
65 U 5	Watson st E13
49 P 14	Watson st N16
75 Z 20	Watson's st SE8
30 D 6	Watsons rd N22
44 F 6	Watsons yd NW2
30 K 11	Watt way E1
101 Y 12	Watt's la Tedd
50 C 9	Wattisfield rd E5
64 C 13	Watts grn E3
114 A 20	Watts la Chisl
113 Z 20	Watts la Chisl
75 N 3	Watts st E1
143 X 13	Watts st E1
17 V 15	Wauthier clo N13
129 W 2	Wavel ms NW6
96 J 15	Wavel rd Sidcp
73 Y 14	Wavendon av W4
92 A 10	Waveney av SE15
33 W 10	Waverley av E17
19 X 15	Waverley av E4
117 U 4	Waverley av Surb
154 B 4	Waverley av Sutton
82 E 20	Waverley av Twick
100 G 1	Waverley av Twick
43 N 16	Waverley av Wemb
127 N 12	Waverley clo Brom
34 K 6	Waverley clo E18
79 R 15	Waverley cres SE18
67 U 7	Waverley gdns Bark
66 E 16	Waverley gdns E6
36 D 8	Waverley gdns Ilf
61 N 7	Waverley gdns NW10
27 R 10	Waverley av No3
130 F 8	Waverley pl NW8
33 V 10	Waverley rd E17
34 K 6	Waverley rd E18
7 X 12	Waverley rd Enf
152 J 11	Waverley rd Epsom
40 C 4	Waverley rd Harrow
31 V 8	Waverley rd N17
31 Y 2	Waverley rd N17
29 Z 20	Waverley rd N8
58 H 19	Waverley rd S'hall
79 R 14	Waverley rd SE18
124 A 8	Waverley rd SE25
154 K 14	Waverley way Carsh
88 C 19	Waverton rd SW18
139 V 12	Waverton st W1
34 F 7	Wavertree rd E18
108 B 2	Wavertree rd SW2
58 G 17	Waxlow cres S'hall
61 X 6	Waxlow rd NW10
22 A 8	Waxwell clo Pinn
22 A 9	Waxwell la Pinn
141 P 20	Waxwell ter SE1
58 A 10	Wayfarer rd Nthlt
88 K 6	Wayford st SW11
49 X 15	Wayland av E8
108 J 6	Waylett pl SE27
42 F 11	Waylett pl Wemb
136 F 7	Wayneflete sq W10
158 J 7	Wayneflete av Croy
106 D 4	Wayneflete st SW18
10 C 1	Wayside av Bushey
6 J 19	Wayside clo N14
39 S 10	Wayside clo Rom
84 D 15	Wayside ct Twick
56 D 14	Wayside gdns Dgnhm
113 U 10	Wayside gdns SE9
113 T 10	Wayside gro SE9
45 T 4	Wayside NW11
85 W 12	Wayside SW14
23 S 5	Weald la Harrow
23 V 3	Weald ri Harrow
49 Y 6	Weald sq E5
113 U 15	Weald the Chisl
38 G 19	Weald way Rom
153 V 3	Wealdstone rd Sutton
20 K 10	Weale rd E4
135 W 13	Wear pl E2
8 C 6	Weardale gdns Enf
93 X 11	Weardale rd SE13
63 Z 14	Weatherley clo E3
135 S 18	Weaver st E1
108 K 10	Weaver wlk SE27
83 U 9	Weavers clo Islwrth
142 L 15	Weavers la SE1
132 E 2	Weavers way NW1
49 Y 2	Webb est E5
77 P 17	Webb rd SE3
150 J 3	Webb st SE1
141 V 19	Webber row SE1
141 X 18	Webber st SE1
88 L 12	Webbs rd SW11
88 M 14	Webbs rd SW11
72 G 3	Webster gdns W5
51 V 11	Webster rd E11
151 U 2	Webster rd SE16
67 T 4	Wedderburn rd Bark
46 G 15	Wedderburn rd NW3
108 L 16	Wedgewood way SE19
128 M 17	Wedlake st W10
35 W 4	Wedmore av Ilf
47 X 8	Wedmore gdns N19
47 Y 8	Wedmore ms N19
59 R 10	Wedmore rd Grnfd
47 Y 9	Wedmore st N19
45 X 13	Weech rd NW6
47 O 15	Weedington rd NW5
143 T 5	Wehill rd E1
94 F 12	Weigall rd SE12
139 V 7	Weighhouse st W1
124 A 3	Weighton ms SE20
23 R 4	Weighton rd Harrow
123 Y 2	Weighton rd SE20
154 G 11	Weihurst gdns Sutton
87 R 9	Weimar st SW15
18 B 19	Weir Hall av N18
18 A 15	Weir Hall gdns N18
31 P 1	Weir Hall rd N18
18 C 17	Weir Hall rd N18
89 V 19	Weir rd Bxly
89 V 19	Weir rd SW12
106 B 9	Weir rd SW19

132 G 13	Weir's pas NW1
15 Z 7	Weirdale av N20
15 Z 8	Weirdale av N20
87 P 8	Weiss rd SW15
112 G 10	Welbeck av Brom
115 N 2	Welbeck av Sidcp
118 C 11	Welbeck clo New Mald
152 F 17	Welbeck clo Epsom
15 T 15	Welbeck clo N12
5 V 19	Welbeck rd Barnt
120 H 20	Welbeck rd Carsh
86 A 8	Welbeck rd E6
40 K 3	Welbeck rd Harrow
154 G 2	Welbeck rd Sutton
139 W 5	Welbeck st W1
139 W 4	Welbeck way W1
90 K 3	Welby st SE5
16 F 17	Weld pl N11
105 T 10	Welford pl SW19
107 R 13	Welham rd SW17
154 H 1	Welhouse rd Carsh
4 A 16	Well appr Barnt
40 B 10	Well clo Ruis
34 K 19	Well Cottage clo E11
160 C 6	Well ct EC4
95 T 13	Well Hall rd SE9
85 V 12	Well la SW14
7 T 13	Well pass NW3
4 A 17	Well rd Barnt
46 G 10	Well rd NW3
51 Y 17	Well st E15
50 D 20	Well st E9
63 P 1	Well st E9
135 Z 1	Well st E9
46 G 10	Well wlk NW3
34 C 19	Wellacre rd Harrow
97 P 10	Wellan clo Welling
59 W 7	Welland gdns Grnfd
76 G 17	Welland st SE10
127 U 3	Wellclose clo Brom
143 T 8	Wellclose sq E1
143 T 10	Wellclose st E1
23 T 17	Welldon cres Harrow
124 A 17	Weller st SE1
132 J 10	Wellers ct NW1
74 H 8	Wellesley av W6
157 N 3	Wellesley Court rd Croy
101 S 5	Wellesley cres Twick
157 O 3	Wellesley gro Croy
156 M 2	Wellesley rd Croy
122 M 20	Wellesley rd Croy
157 N 3	Wellesley rd Croy
34 F 16	Wellesley rd E11
33 O 18	Wellesley rd E17
23 T 17	Wellesley rd Harrow
54 B 4	Wellesley rd Ilf
53 Y 6	Wellesley rd Ilf
30 F 7	Wellesley rd N22
47 O 14	Wellesley rd NW5
154 D 13	Wellesley rd Sutton
101 S 6	Wellesley rd Twick
73 P 14	Wellesley rd W4
63 R 16	Wellesley st E1
134 C 12	Wellesley ter N1
29 S 9	Wellfield av N10
108 B 10	Wellfield rd SW16
108 D 11	Wellfield wlk SW16
90 K 8	Wellfit rd SE24
42 A 18	Wellgarth gdns Grnfd
46 A 4	Wellgarth rd NW11
4 B 14	Wellhouse la Barnt
125 N 9	Wellhouse rd Becknhm
97 R 8	Welling High st Welling
96 D 7	Welling way SE9
152 M 6	Wellington av Worc Pk
20 C 9	Wellington av E4
82 G 13	Wellington av Hounsl
31 W 18	Wellington av N15
19 N 10	Wellington av Pinn
22 E 4	Wellington av Pinn
97 N 15	Wellington av Sidcp
147 V 11	Wellington bldgs SW1
69 X 1	Wellington clo Dgnhm
92 E 3	Wellington clo SE14
137 S 6	Wellington clo W11
117 W 7	Wellington cres New Mald
69 Y 1	Wellington dri Dgnhm
101 P 9	Wellington gdns Hampt
77 X 14	Wellington gdns SE7
77 X 15	Wellington ms SE7
130 H 12	Wellington pl NW8

23 T 9	Wellington rd Harrow
81 P 12	Wellington rd Blvdr
126 L 9	Wellington rd Brom
97 V 14	Wellington rd Bxly
122 J 17	Wellington rd Croy
50 H 3	Wellington rd E10
34 G 14	Wellington rd E11
32 J 12	Wellington rd E17
66 G 5	Wellington rd E6
52 D 14	Wellington rd E7
8 E 18	Wellington rd Enf
18 E 4	Wellington rd Enf
101 P 10	Wellington rd Hampt
128 G 14	Wellington rd NW10
130 G 10	Wellington rd NW8
22 D 4	Wellington rd Pinn
105 Z 5	Wellington rd SW19
72 D 9	Wellington rd W5
82 E 10	Wellington Road north Hounsl
82 G 14	Wellington Road south Hounsl
135 R 12	Wellington row E2
147 N 10	Wellington sq SW3
67 O 2	Wellington st Bark
64 L 14	Wellington st E16
78 K 11	Wellington st SE18
140 M 8	Wellington st WC2
141 N 8	Wellington st WC2
41 R 4	Wellington ter Harrow
143 W 12	Wellington ter E1
137 W 11	Wellington ter W2
64 A 10	Wellington way E3
93 Z 18	Wellmeadow rd SE13
71 Y 10	Wellmeadow rd W7
120 G 20	Wellow wlk Carsh
43 X 5	Wells dri NW9
56 G 16	Wells gdns Dgnhm
53 R 1	Wells gdns Ilf
57 U 18	Wells gdns Rainhm
62 B 13	Wells House rd NW10
140 B 3	Wells ms W1
110 A 8	Wells Park rd SE26
109 X 8	Wells Park rd SE26
127 U 3	Wells rd Brom
136 C 19	Wells rd W12
74 M 7	Wells rd W12
131 O 6	Wells ri NW8
133 O 14	Wells sq WC1
140 B 3	Wells st W1
48 F 6	Wells ter N4
16 L 4	Wells The N14
150 H 16	Wells way SE5
48 E 15	Wells yd N7
4 A 15	Wellside clo Barnt
85 V 12	Wellside gdns SW14
127 W 5	Wellsmoor gdns Brom
43 U 9	Wellsprings cres Wemb
19 R 4	Wellstead av N9
66 J 7	Wellstead rd E6
55 N 2	Wellwood rd Ilf
151 S 8	Welsford st SE1
65 R 10	Welsh clo E13
135 U 4	Welshpool st E8
74 G 13	Weltje rd W6
79 U 20	Welton rd SE18
63 P 0	Welwyn st E2
42 L 10	Wembley Hill rd Wemb
43 N 13	Wembley Hill rd Wemb
42 M 11	Wembley Park dri Wemb
43 O 10	Wembley Park dri Wemb
100 G 19	Wembley rd Hampt
43 U 17	Wembley way Wemb
24 E 3	Wemborough rd Stanm
47 U 1	Wembury rd N6
94 C 5	Wemyss rd SE3
41 S 8	Wendela ct Harrow
74 C 7	Wendell rd W12
154 F 1	Wendling rd Sutton
63 Z 3	Wendon st E3
118 E 14	Wendover dri New Mald
126 H 7	Wendover rd Brom
62 D 6	Wendover rd NW10
95 O 7	Wendover rd SE9
150 H 10	Wendover SE17
97 O 11	Wendover way Welling

150 J 12	Wendover wlk SE17
8 G 19	Wendy clo Enf
60 K 4	Wendy way Wemb
12 G 20	Wenlock rd Edg
134 B 10	Wenlock rd N1
134 D 10	Wenlock st N1
63 T 6	Wennington rd E3
34 D 1	Wensley av Wdfd Grn
18 M 19	Wensley rd N18
35 S 5	Wensleydale av Ilf
100 K 18	Wensleydale gdns Hampt
100 J 19	Wensleydale pass Hampt
100 J 17	Wensleydale rd Hampt
111 Y 4	Wentland clo SE6
111 Y 5	Wentland rd SE6
14 M 20	Wentworth av N3
27 Z 1	Wentworth av N3
119 W 17	Wentworth clo Mrdn
151 T 20	Wentworth cres SE15
99 V 17	Wentworth dri Drtfrd
17 V 12	Wentworth gdns N13
42 M 3	Wentworth hill Wemb
43 N 3	Wentworth hill Wemb
63 X 11	Wentworth ms E3
27 Z 2	Wentworth pk N3
4 D 11	Wentworth rd Brentf
122 F 18	Wentworth rd Croy
53 N 14	Wentworth rd E12
27 V 19	Wentworth rd NW11
143 P 3	wentworth st E1
22 A 13	Wentworth way Pinn
98 F 4	Wenvoe av Bxly Hth
79 P 15	Wernbrook st SE18
123 X 10	Werndee rd SE25
35 V 10	Werneth Hall rd Ilf
132 D 10	Werrington st NW1
87 R 11	Werter rd SW15
82 D 4	Wesley av Hounsl
61 X 8	Wesley av NW10
41 N 6	Wesley av NW10
48 D 8	Wesley clo N7
149 X 8	Wesley clo SE17
51 U 2	Wesley rd E10
61 X 3	Wesley rd NW10
139 V 1	Wesley st W1
47 R 12	Wesleyan pl NW5
119 Z 5	Wessex av SW19
36 H 18	Wessex clo Ilf
117 S 2	Wessex clo Kingst
99 S 3	Wessex dri Erith
22 B 2	Wessex dri Pinn
45 S 3	Wessex gdns NW11
53 R 7	Wessex la Grnfd
63 P 10	Wessex st E2
45 S 2	Wessex way NW11
63 R 17	West Arbour st E1
33 R 15	West av E17
14 L 19	West av N3
27 O 15	West av NW4
22 D 19	West av Pinn
58 D 19	West av S'hall
56 B 12	West av Wallgtn
33 P 14	West Avenue rd E17
66 M 3	West bank Bark
7 Y 10	West bank Enf
49 S 2	West bank N16
118 L 9	West Barnes la New Mald
30 G 9	West Beech rd N22
140 K 4	West Central st WC1
22 J 4	West chantry Harrow
6 B 14	West clo Barnt
59 N 6	West clo Grnfd
100 C 15	West clo Hampt
18 H 10	West clo N9
42 M 4	West clo Wemb
43 N 4	West clo Wemb
45 Y 15	West cotts NW6
145 T 6	West Cromwell rd SW5
72 A 17	West Cross way Brentf
71 Z 18	West Cross way Brentf
42 D 8	West ct Wemb
10 C 19	West dri Harrow
153 P 19	West dri Sutton
107 U 9	West dri SW16
10 C 20	West Drive gdns Harrow
147 S 4	West Eaton pl SW1
147 S 4	West Eaton Place ms SW1
62 A 1	West Ella rd NW10
33 V 16	West End rd E10

22 A 13	West End av Pinn
4 C 14	West End la Barnt
129 V 4	West End la NW6
45 Z 15	West End la NW6
45 Z 20	West End la NW6
22 A 15	West End la Pinn
70 B 2	West End rd S'hall
76 D 12	West Ferry rd E14
3 B 20	West gdns E1
106 J 15	West gdns SW17
30 K 13	West Green rd N15
31 P 14	West Green rd N15
21 Z 17	West gro Wdfd Grn
147 S 1	West Halkin st SW1
85 S 3	West Hall rd Rich
113 O 1	West Hallowes SE9
64 M 2	West Ham la E15
65 R 1	West Ham la E15
45 Z 19	West Hampstead ms NW6
141 T 5	West Harding st EC4
45 Y 5	West Heath av NW11
99 U 16	West Heath clo Drtfrd
45 Y 9	West Heath clo NW3
45 Y 4	West Heath dri NW11
45 Y 8	West Heath gdns NW3
99 U 16	West Heath rd Drtfrd
46 R 9	West Heath rd NW3
45 Y 7	West Heath rd NW3
80 H 17	West Heath rd SE2
44 H 3	West Hendon bdwy NW9 NW2
47 U 6	West hill N6
41 S 6	West hill Harrow
47 P 3	West hill N6
47 N 6	West Hill pk N6
87 W 16	West Hill rd SW18
157 S 19	West hill S Croy
87 S 17	West hill SW18
15 N 6	West Hill way N20
42 M 4	West hill Wemb
43 O 4	West hill Wemb
98 L 1	West Holme Erith
64 A 20	West India Dock rd E14
143 W 19	West la SE16
73 P 3	West Lodge av W3
137 V 12	West mall W8
152 B 14	West Mead Epsom
147 Z 8	West ms SW1
11 W 20	West oak Becknhm
85 R 2	West Park av Rich
37 X 16	West Park clo Rom
85 P 3	West Park rd Rich
113 R 2	West pk SE9
104 L 12	West pl SW19
141 W 2	West Poultry av EC1
62 F 17	West Quarters W12
16 B 5	West rd Barnt
65 R 3	West rd E15
103 W 20	West rd Kingst
18 M 20	West rd N17
31 Z 1	West rd N17
56 M 3	West rd Rom
37 X 17	West rd Rom
89 Z 12	West rd SW4
60 J 14	West rd W5
58 M 6	West Ridge gdns Grnfd
128 J 17	West row W10
84 L 10	West Sheen vale Rich
104 M 13	West Side comm SW19
105 N 15	West Side comm SW19
141 X 2	West Smithfield EC1
149 W 3	West sq SE11
126 E 2	West st Brom
98 A 9	West st Bxly Hth
154 L 9	West st Carsh
156 M 7	West st Croy
51 Z 8	West st E11
33 R 16	West st E17
63 N 7	West st E2
156 M 7	West st Harrow
154 A 11	West st Sutton
140 H 7	West st WC2
154 M 8	West Street la Carsh
85 T 12	West Temple sheen SW14
143 O 7	West st E1
18 D 3	West View cres N9
26 M 15	West view NW4
147 Z 8	West Warwick pl SW1
12 G 19	West way Edg

158 G 2 West Way gdns Croy
82 D 1 West way Hounsl
18 C 15 West way N18
43 Z 10 West way NW10
125 Y 15 West way W Wkhm
62 J 19 West way W12
16 B 4 West wlk Barnt
60 J 15 West wlk W5
97 Z 20 West Woodside Bxly
47 Y 3 Westacott clo N19
100 M 15 Westbank rd Hampt
11 U 15 Westbere dri Stanm
45 T 14 Westbere rd NW2
153 S 1 Westbourne av Sutton
61 X 18 Westbourne av W3
138 E 8 Westbourne cres W2
110 E 4 Westbourne dri SE23
137 X 4 Westbourne gdns W2
137 W 6 Westbourne gro W2
137 T 7 Westbourne Grove ms W11
137 X 5 Westbourne Grove ter W2
137 X 5 Westbourne Park ms W2
137 R 4 Westbourne Park rd W11
137 X 4 Westbourne Park rd W2
137 W 3 Westbourne Park vlls W2
19 N 11 Westbourne pl N9
80 K 19 Westbourne rd Bxly Hth
123 V 15 Westbourne rd Croy
48 D 17 Westbourne rd N7
110 E 14 Westbourne rd SE26
138 G 9 Westbourne st W2
138 A 1 Westbourne ter W2
138 A 3 Westbourne ter W2
138 C 5 Westbourne Terrace ms W2
138 A 1 Westbourne Terrace rd W2
88 H 2 Westbridge rd SW11
146 J 20 Westbridge rd SW11
100 E 17 Westbrook av Hampt
5 U 11 Westbrook clo Barnt
5 T 12 Westbrook cres Barnt
123 O 2 Westbrook rd Thntn Hth
70 E 19 Westbrook rd Hounsl
94 H 2 Westbrook rd SE3
5 T 11 Westbrook sq Barnt
97 T 6 Westbrooke cres Welling
97 T 7 Westbrooke rd Welling
114 F 5 Westbrooke rd Sidcp
30 H 10 Westbury av N22
30 L 6 Westbury av N22
58 G 12 Westbury av S'hall
42 K 20 Westbury av Wemb
14 L 18 Westbury gro N3
21 Y 7 Westbury la Buck Hl
72 G 15 Westbury pl Brentf
124 J 6 Westbury rd Becknhm
117 Z 11 Westbury rd New Mald
67 S 3 Westbury rd Bark
127 O 1 Westbury rd Brom
113 O 20 Westbury rd Brom
21 Y 6 Westbury rd Buck Hl
123 O 15 Westbury rd Croy
32 M 12 Westbury rd E17
33 N 13 Westbury rd E17
52 J 16 Westbury rd E7
100 A 2 Westbury rd Felt
53 V 7 Westbury rd Ilf
17 N 19 Westbury rd N11
14 M 17 Westbury rd N12
124 E 1 Westbury rd SE20
60 J 18 Westbury rd W5
42 K 20 Westbury rd Wemb
89 V 5 Westbury st SW8
52 J 17 Westbury ter E7
27 O 10 Westchester dri NW4
118 E 1 Westcombe av SW20
122 B 16 Westcombe av Croy
4 L 17 Westcombe dri Barnt
77 T 18 Westcombe hill SE3
77 T 14 Westcombe hill SE7

77 N 15 Westcombe Park rd SE10
77 R 18 Westcombe Park rd SE3
107 V 13 Westcote rd SW16
127 S 11 Westcott clo BR1
159 T 19 Westcott clo Croy
31 T 18 Westcott clo N15
59 U 16 Westcott cres W7
149 X 12 Westcott rd SE17
45 S 12 Westcroft clo NW2
119 U 8 Westcroft gdns Mrdn
155 P 8 Westcroft rd Carsh
74 F 11 Westcroft sq W6
45 S 12 Westcroft way NW2
112 K 2 Westdean av SE12
51 U 12 Westdown rd E15
93 N 18 Westdown rd SE6
77 S 14 Westerdale rd SE10
31 T 15 Westerfield rd N15
80 L 15 Westergate rd SE2
18 C 11 Westerham av N9
97 S 15 Westerham dri Sidcp
33 S 20 Westerham rd E10
110 L 11 Westerley cres SE26
73 O 17 Westerley warehouse Rich
56 L 17 Western av Dgnhm
57 N 17 Western av Dgnhm
58 F 3 Western av Grnfd
60 F 8 Western av Grnfd
59 S 7 Western av Grnfd
27 R 19 Western av NW11
62 B 19 Western av W3
61 U 13 Western av W3
60 F 8 Western av W5
137 S 1 Western Avenue extension W2
14 M 20 Western ct N3
61 O 19 Western gdns W5
89 O 18 Western la SW12
129 R 19 Western ms W9
4 M 17 Western pde Barnt
65 X 5 Western rd E13
33 U 16 Western rd E17
120 J 2 Western rd Mitch
28 L 12 Western rd N2
61 U 11 Western rd NW10
39 S 15 Western rd Rom
70 B 8 Western rd S'hall
153 X 12 Western rd Sutton
90 G 8 Western rd SW9
72 H 1 Western rd W5
60 H 20 Western rd W5
14 M 1 Western way Barnt
79 T 8 Western way SE18
36 B 20 Westernville gdns Ilf
72 A 4 Westfield clo Enf
153 U 8 Westfield clo Sutton
24 H 14 Westfield dri Harrow
24 G 13 Westfield gdns Harrow
24 G 13 Westfield la Harrow
22 E 1 Westfield pk Pinn
124 L 3 Westfield rd Becknhm
98 L 7 Westfield rd Bxly Hth
156 J 3 Westfield rd Croy
56 A 13 Westfield rd Dgnhm
120 K 4 Westfield rd Mitch
30 B 14 Westfield rd N8
12 M 11 Westfield rd NW7
116 F 13 Westfield rd Surb
153 U 8 Westfield rd Sutton
87 N 8 Westfield st SE18
86 C 7 Westfields av SW13
61 U 15 Westfields rd W3
86 D 7 Westfields SW13
125 S 2 Westgate rd Becknhm
111 T 19 Westgate rd Becknhm
124 A 9 Westgate rd SE25
123 Z 9 Westgate rd SE25
135 X 3 Westgate st E8
145 Y 12 Westgate ter SW10
60 K 9 Westgate W5
24 F 16 Westglade ct Harrow
33 V 11 Westgrove la SE10
149 Z 19 Westhall rd SE5
85 U 12 Westhay gdns SW14
28 A 14 Westholm NW11
94 G 17 Westhorne av SE12
95 P 11 Westhorne av SE9
27 N 11 Westhorpe gdns NW4
87 N 8 Westhorpe rd SW15

105 S 1 Westhouse clo SW19
114 A 12 Westhurst dri Chisl
17 T 11 Westlake clo N13
134 D 12 Westland pl N1
89 U 17 Westlands ter SW12
71 X 8 Westlea rd W7
86 L 14 Westleigh av SW15
87 O 15 Westleigh av SW15
127 R 2 Westleigh dri Brom
25 P 6 Westleigh gdns Edg
154 H 9 Westmead rd Sutton
86 J 17 Westmead SW15
12 K 10 Westmere dri NW7
148 B 3 Westminster Cathedral SW1
140 J 20 Westminster Abbey SW1
122 H 2 Westminster av Thntn Hth
140 L 18 Westminster br SW1
141 P 18 Westminster Bridge rd SE1
101 X 12 Westminster clo Tedd
36 E 8 Westminster clo Ilf
17 N 17 Westminster dri N13
67 U 7 Westminster gdns Bark
36 D 8 Westminster gdns Ilf
154 E 1 Westminster rd Sutton
19 N 6 Westminster rd N9
71 U 4 Westminster rd W7
111 U 18 Westmoat clo Becknhm
9 S 8 Westmoor gdns Enf
9 S 9 Westmoor rd Enf
78 A 10 Westmoor st SE7
96 H 9 Westmoreland av Welling
154 B 18 Westmoreland rd Sutton
147 Y 11 Westmoreland pl SW1
60 F 14 Westmoreland pl W5
126 B 10 Westmoreland rd Brom
86 F 2 Westmoreland rd SW13
25 N 11 Westmoreland rd NW9
139 V 1 Westmoreland st W1
147 V 10 Westmoreland ter SW1
121 Z 10 Westmoreland way Mitch
84 B 15 Westmorland clo Twick
53 N 4 Westmorland clo E12
22 L 16 Westmorland rd Harrow
33 O 19 Westmorland rd E17
95 W 10 Westmount rd SE9
19 N 10 Westoe rd N9
55 N 15 Weston dri Bark
24 C 5 Weston dri Stanm
83 R 3 Weston gdns Islwth
56 A 11 Weston grn Dgnhm
112 D 19 Weston gro Brom
30 C 17 Weston pk N8
112 D 19 Weston rd Brom
55 Z 11 Weston rd Dgnhm
8 C 8 Weston rd Enf
73 U 9 Weston rd W4
133 O 11 Weston ri WC1
142 H 17 Weston st SE1
135 Z 1 Weston wlk E9
45 Y 7 Westover hill NW3
88 E 17 Westover rd SW18
109 T 15 Westow hill SE19
109 T 17 Westow st SE19
6 F 15 Westpole av Barnt
63 T 17 Westport rd E1
65 V 13 Westport rd E13
54 K 19 Westrow dri Bark
54 M 14 Westrow dri Bark
54 L 9 Westrow gdns Ilf
87 N 15 Westrow rd SW15
26 H 6 Westside NW4
44 C 14 Westview clo NW10
35 N 6 Westview dri Wdfd Grn
74 G 6 Westville rd W12
20 A 18 Westward rd E4
19 X 18 Westward rd E4
24 K 19 Westward way Harrow

118 K 6 Westway clo SW20
118 L 9 Westway SW20
136 B 7 Westway W12
152 E 8 Westways Epsom
107 T 15 Westwell rd SW16
136 E 19 Westwick gdns W14
40 L 12 Westwood av Harrow
109 N 19 Westwood av SE19
127 P 5 Westwood clo BR1
86 D 8 Westwood gdns SW13
110 B 10 Westwood hill SE26
96 L 10 Westwood la Welling
97 N 13 Westwood la Welling
92 A 19 Westwood pk SE23
110 B 1 Westwood pk SE23
77 V 3 Westwood rd E16
54 L 4 Westwood rd Ilf
86 D 8 Westwood rd SW13
24 C 6 Wetheral dri Stanm
40 J 17 Wetherby clo Nthlt
146 A 8 Wetherby gdns SW5
145 Y 9 Wetherby ms SW5
146 B 7 Wetherby pl SW7
7 Z 4 Wetherby rd Enf
50 L 1 Wetherden st E17
63 T 3 Wetherell rd E9
29 P 4 Wetherill rd N10
88 L 19 Wexford rd SW12
106 C 6 Weybourne st SW18
122 G 10 Weybridge rd Thntn Hth
105 S 2 Weydown clo SW19
56 B 10 Weylond rd Dgnhm
94 M 2 Weyman rd SE3
18 B 20 Weymarks the N17
13 O 15 Weymouth av NW7
72 E 8 Weymouth av W5
153 Z 16 Weymouth ct Sutton
139 X 1 Weymouth ms W1
135 O 8 Weymouth pl E2
139 W 1 Weymouth st W1
131 X 20 Weymouth st W1
135 O 9 Weymouth ter E2
10 L 20 Weymouth wlk Stanm
48 F 7 Whadcoat st N4
38 A 18 Whalebone av Rom
160 F 4 Whalebone av EC2
38 A 18 Whalebone gro Rom
64 M 1 Whalebone la N13
38 A 7 Whalebone Lane north Rom
37 Y 3 Whalebone Lane north Rom
38 A 17 Whalebone Lane south Rom
56 B 3 Whalebone Lane south Dgnhm
101 Y 2 Wharf la Twick
135 U 7 Wharf pl E2
64 J 3 Wharf rd E15
9 V 19 Wharf rd Enf
9 W 18 Wharf rd Enf
134 A 9 Wharf rd N1
134 B 11 Wharf rd N1
132 G 4 Wharf rd NW1
64 L 15 Wharf rd E16
132 L 8 Wharfdale rd N1
122 D 7 Wharfedale gdns Thntn Hth
145 X 11 Wharfedale st SW10
71 P 2 Wharncliffe dri S'hall
123 R 4 Wharncliffe gdns SE25
123 R 4 Wharncliffe rd SE25
44 B 17 Wharton clo NW10
133 R 13 Wharton cotts WC1
126 H 1 Wharton rd Brom
133 P 13 Wharton st WC1
110 F 17 Whateley rd SE20
91 V 13 Whateley rd SE22
119 R 5 Whatley av SW20
92 G 19 Whatman rd SE23
9 U 7 Wheatfields Enf
124 A 6 Wheathill rd SE20
123 Z 5 Wheathill rd SE20
70 H 17 Wheatlands Hounsl
107 O 7 Wheatlands rd SW17
26 G 8 Wheatley clo NW4
18 C 9 Wheatley gdns N9
83 V 7 Wheatley rd Islwth
139 V 1 Wheatley st W1
40 C 16 Wheatsheaf clo Nthlt
144 E 18 Wheatsheaf la SW6
148 K 17 Wheatsheaf la SW8
39 T 18 Wheatsheaf rd Rom

145 R 20 Wheatsheaf ter SW6
56 K 9 Wheel Farm dri Dgnhm
132 K 4 Wheatley gdns N1
67 S 7 Wheelers cross Bark
153 X 5 Wheelers st Sutton
48 C 20 Wheelwright st N7
155 Y 5 Whelan way Wallgtn
135 N 18 Wheler st E1
74 A 7 Whellock rd W4
80 H 1 Whernside clo SE28
15 S 8 Whetstone clo N20
141 O 3 Whetstone pk WC2
94 L 4 Whetstone rd SE3
48 A 7 Whewell rd N19
132 K 13 Whidborne st WC1
68 G 19 Whimbrel clo SE2
107 X 11 Whinfell clo SW16
95 R 8 Whinyates rd SE9
33 W 15 Whipps cross E17
34 B 18 Whipps Cross rd E11
33 X 16 Whipps Cross rd E11
133 V 14 Whiskin st EC1
25 N 7 Whistler gdns Edg
48 H 14 Whistler st N5
146 H 20 Whistlers av SW11
134 M 7 Whiston rd E2
135 S 6 Whiston rd E2
31 W 4 Whitbread clo N17
92 K 11 Whitbread rd SE4
93 S 11 Whitburn rd SE13
61 S 8 Whitby av NW10
25 R 10 Whitby gdns NW9
154 F 1 Whitby gdns Sutton
40 M 10 Whitby rd Harrow
41 N 10 Whitby rd Harrow
70 F 11 Whitby rd SE18
133 N 10 Whitby st E1
75 V 17 Whitcher clo SE14
47 V 19 Whitcher pl NW1
24 M 2 Whitchurch av Edg
11 Z 19 Whitchurch clo Edg
11 Z 20 Whitchurch gdns Edg
12 B 20 Whitchurch la Edg
24 K 2 Whitchurch la Edg
136 G 9 Whitchurch rd W11
140 G 11 Whitcomb st WC2
26 C 7 White acre NW9
76 O 10 White Adder way E14
103 P 5 White Ash lodge Rich
133 T 19 White Boar yd EC1
143 S 4 White Church la E1
136 B 10 White City clo W12
62 L 20 White City clo W12
136 A 9 White City rd W12
62 K 19 White City rd W12
136 B 19 White City Stadium W10
133 T 7 White Conduit st N1
23 V 2 White Gate gdns Harrow
56 D 17 White gdns Dgnhm
142 J 3 White Hart ct EC2
31 S 1 White Hart la N17
30 J 2 White Hart la N22
44 D 18 White Hart la NW10
38 E 4 White Hart la Rom
86 B 6 White Hart la SW13
79 V 11 White Hart rd SE11
149 V 9 White Hart st SE11
142 F 15 White Hart yd SE1
113 V 10 White Horse hill Chisl
63 T 13 White Horse la E1
63 U 17 White Horse rd E1
66 G 8 White Horse rd E6
139 Y 14 White Horse st W1
160 D 3 White Horse yd EC2
11 S 14 White House dri Stanm
7 Z 5 White House dri Stanm
142 M 4 White Kennett st E1
160 H 6 White Lion ct EC2
141 Z 9 White Lion hill EC4
133 S 9 White Lion st N1
139 X 8 White Lion yd W1
154 E 15 White Lodge clo Sutton
28 H 19 White Lodge clo N2
103 Y 1 White lodge Rich
108 K 17 White lodge SE19
10 K 17 White orchards Stanm
14 G 3 White orchards N20
51 N 19 White Post la
75 P 19 White Post st SE15
52 A 20 White rd E15
143 N 2 White's row E1
89 Y 10 White's sq SW4
51 X 17 Whitear wlk E15
69 S 3 Whitebarn la Dgnhm
127 W 16 Whitebeam av Brom
143 R 3 Whitechapel High st E1
143 R 4 Whitechapel pas E1
143 U 2 Whitechapel rd E1
135 X 20 Whitechapel rd E1
58 L 18 Whitecote rd S'hall
125 W 8 Whitecroft clo Becknhm
125 V 9 Whitecroft way Becknhm
134 H 20 Whitecross pl EC2
134 C 17 Whitecross st EC1
134 C 17 Whitecross st EC2
45 N 2 Whitefield av NW2
87 T 17 Whitefield clo SW18
112 A 7 Whitefoot la Brom
112 B 7 Whitefoot ter Brom
23 S 8 Whitefriars av Harrow
23 S 7 Whitefriars dri Harrow
141 U 6 Whitefriars st EC4
140 K 14 Whitehall clo SW1
20 L 6 Whitehall gdns E4
140 K 15 Whitehall gdns SW1
73 R 3 Whitehall gdns W3
73 T 16 Whitehall gdns W4
21 U 8 Whitehall la Buck Hl
99 Y 3 Whitehall la Erith
73 T 16 Whitehall Park rd W4
47 V 3 Whitehall pk N19
140 K 13 Whitehall pl SW1
155 R 9 Whitehall pl Wallgtn
122 F 13 Whitehall rd Thntn Hth
21 P 7 Whitehall rd Wdfd Grn
127 O 10 Whitehall rd Brom
23 S 20 Whitehall rd Harrow
71 Y 7 Whitehall rd W7
31 U 2 Whitehall st N17
140 J 15 Whitehall SW1
126 F 3 Whitehart slip Brom
126 E 9 Whitehaven clo BR2
130 J 19 Whitehaven st NW8
88 B 19 Whitehead rd SW18
146 M 8 Whitehead's gro SW3
99 W 14 Whitehill rd Drtfrd
123 P 8 Whitehorse la SE25
122 M 17 Whitehorse rd Croy
123 N 13 Whitehorse rd Croy
16 L 9 Whitehouse ct N14
16 E 10 Whitehouse way N14
60 D 17 Whiteledges W13
65 P 7 Whitelegg rd E13
65 P 7 Whitelegg rd E13
109 P 12 Whiteley rd SE19
100 H 7 Whiteley's way Felt
145 P 8 Whiteleys cotts
125 V 3 Whiteoak dri Becknhm
59 R 8 Whiteoaks la Grnfd
93 O 8 Whitepost la SE13
36 G 17 Whites av Ilf
142 L 17 Whites grounds SE1
72 E 13 Whitestile rd Brentf
46 E 9 Whitestone la NW3
158 A 1 Whitethorn gdns Croy
8 A 16 Whitethorn gdns Enf
64 B 13 Whitethorn st E3
132 B 18 Whitfield pl W1
81 N 18 Whitfield rd Bxly Hth
65 Z 2 Whitfield rd E6
93 X 3 Whitfield rd SE3
132 B 18 Whitfield st W1
140 D 1 Whitfield st W1
120 L 6 Whitford gdns Mitch
156 L 11 Whitgift av S Croy
156 M 2 Whitgift sq Croy
156 L 5 Whitgift st Croy
149 N 6 Whitgift st SE11
67 N 1 Whiting av Bark
154 G 1 Whitland rd Carsh
31 T 7 Whitley rd N17
87 T 20 Whitlock dri SW19
63 V 10 Whitman rd E3
16 F 17 Whitmore clo N11
128 C 8 Whitmore gdns NW10
62 M 6 Whitmore gdns NW10
124 L 6 Whitmore rd Becknhm
40 M 2 Whitmore rd Harrow
41 N 2 Whitmore rd Harrow
87 O 14 Whitnell way SW15
35 N 12 Whitney av Ilf
51 P 1 Whitney rd E10
115 Y 16 Whitney wlk Sidcp
53 O 12 Whitta rd E12
65 Z 2 Whittaker rd E6
153 V 5 Whittaker rd Sutton
147 S 7 Whittaker st SW1
110 C 8 Whittall gdns SE26
87 V 2 Whittingstall rd SW6
142 J 7 Whittington av EC3
30 A 1 Whittington rd N22
17 O 20 Whittington rd N22
22 C 16 Whittington way Pinn
58 K 17 Whittle clo S'hall
155 N 17 Whittlebury clo Carsh
22 M 4 Whittlesea pth Harrow
23 N 3 Whittlesea rd Harrow
23 N 4 Whittlesea rd Harrow
141 T 15 Whittlesey st SE1
41 V 15 Whitton Avenue east Grnfd
41 P 16 Whitton Avenue west Nthlt
42 B 19 Whitton clo Grnfd
82 M 14 Whitton dene Hounsl
83 T 13 Whitton dene Islwth
41 Z 17 Whitton dri Grnfd
83 O 14 Whitton Manor rd Islwth
82 L 13 Whitton rd Hounsl
83 J 11 Whitton rd Twick
82 H 16 Whitton waye Hounsl
65 S 10 Whitwell rd E13
78 K 18 Whitworth rd SE18
123 U 8 Whitworth rd SE25
77 N 13 Whitworth st SE10
91 Y 8 Whorlton rd SE15
30 G 10 Whymark av N22
52 H 18 Whyteville rd E7
64 A 3 Wick la E3
50 E 18 Wick rd E9
89 P 5 Wick rd SW11
102 C 19 Wick rd Tedd
143 V 7 Wicker st E1
109 U 11 Wickers Oake SE19
89 P 7 Wickersley rd SW11
159 O 11 Wicket the Croy
63 O 11 Wickford st E1
135 Z 17 Wickford way E17
32 E 12 Wickford way E17
158 H 1 Wickham av Croy
152 M 10 Wickham av Sutton
153 O 11 Wickham av Sutton
126 A 16 Wickham chase W Wkhm
125 X 18 Wickham chase W Wkhm
118 C 13 Wickham clo New Mald
9 O 11 Wickham clo Enf
159 O 11 Wickham Court rd W Wkhm
159 V 2 Wickham cres W Wkhm
159 Y 9 Wickham ct W Wkhm
92 L 8 Wickham gdns SE4
80 B 18 Wickham la SE2
79 Z 14 Wickham la SE2
92 M 6 Wickham ms SE4
125 S 5 Wickham rd Becknhm
158 F 3 Wickham rd Croy
159 N 1 Wickham rd Croy
33 U 1 Wickham rd E4
23 R 8 Wickham rd Harrow
92 M 6 Wickham rd SE4
93 N 4 Wickham st SE11
149 O 9 Wickham st SE11
96 M 3 Wickham st Welling
97 O 1 Wickham st Welling
125 T 8 Wickham way Becknhm
27 T 9 Wickliffe av N3
43 R 6 Wickliffe gdns Wemb
132 M 12 Wicklow st WC1
133 N 12 Wicklow st WC1
113 N 8 Wicks clo SE9
90 K 6 Wickwood st SE5
48 C 13 Widdenham rd N7
40 B 7 Widdicombe av Harrow
64 L 1 Widdin st E15
121 X 6 Wide way Mitch
35 R 12 Widecombe gdns Ilf
113 S 7 Widecombe rd SE9
28 F 15 Widecombe way N2
142 L 2 Widegate st E1
129 V 15 Widley rd W9
127 O 4 Widmore Lodge rd Brom
126 K 2 Widmore rd Brom
127 O 3 Widmore rd Brom
79 S 7 Wigeon pth SE28
43 R 19 Wiggington av Wemb
102 C 4 Wiggins and Pointers cotts Rich
26 D 3 Wiggins mead NW9
30 G 17 Wightman rd N4
100 A 2 Wigley rd Felt
139 X 4 Wigmore pl W1
154 H 1 Wigmore rd Carsh
139 W 4 Wigmore st W1
154 G 2 Wigmore wlk Carsh
34 K 18 Wigram rd E11
33 V 9 Wigram sq E17
65 W 11 Wigston rd E13
24 J 5 Wigton gdns Stanm
149 T 11 Wigton pl SE11
32 L 5 Wigton rd E17
48 H 6 Wilberforce rd N4
26 F 18 Wilberforce rd NW9
105 O 15 Wilberforce way SW19
147 R 5 Wilbraham pl SW1
18 B 17 Wilbury way N18
137 P 12 Wilby ms W11
148 K 19 Wilcox clo SW8
153 Z 9 Wilcox rd Sutton
148 J 18 Wilcox rd SW8
101 R 9 Wilcox rd Tedd
140 M 5 Wild ct WC2
92 D 3 Wild Goose dri SE14
27 Z 20 Wild hatch NW11
140 M 6 Wild st WC2
150 H 1 Wild's rents SE1
11 U 20 Wildcroft gdns Edg
86 M 20 Wildcroft rd SW15
87 N 17 Wildcroft rd SW15
135 T 4 Wilde clo E8
113 Z 18 Wilderness rd Chisl
100 K 10 Wilderness the Hampt
49 T 2 Wilderton rd N16
93 R 18 Wildfell rd SE6
142 H 20 Wilds rents SE1
94 D 18 Wildwood clo SE12
46 C 5 Wildwood groo NW3
28 C 19 Wildwood rd NW11
46 C 2 Wildwood rd NW11
46 E 3 Wildwood ri NW11
8 A 12 Wilford cl Enf
148 B 1 Wilfred st SW1
61 V 13 Wilfrid gdns W3
17 V 18 Wilk pl N13
109 U 11 Wilkers oak SE19
143 O 1 Wilkes st E1
135 O 19 Wilkes st E1
135 O 20 Wilkes st E1
135 P 18 Wilkes st E1
91 X 20 Wilkie way SE22
47 R 17 Wilkin st NW5
65 Y 16 Wilkinson rd E16
149 N 20 Wilkinson st SW8
73 X 6 Wilkinson way W4
134 K 9 Wilks pl N1
95 N 10 Will Crooks gdns SE9
31 P 8 Willan rd N17
65 O 19 Willan wall E16
89 S 7 Willard st SW8
73 R 3 Willcott rd W3
6 P 20 Willenhall av Barnt
78 L 15 Willenhall rd SE18
114 K 2 Willersley av Sidcp
96 L 19 Willersley av Sidcp
114 K 1 Willersley clo Sidcp
47 S 17 Willes rd NW5
128 M 1 Willesden la NW6 & NW2
129 R 2 Willesden la NW6 & NW2
45 O 19 Willesden la NW6
151 X 11 Willett way SE16
122 F 11 Willett pl Thntn Hth
122 F 11 Willett rd Thntn Hth
113 X 5 William Barefoot dri SE9
109 Y 20 William Booth rd SE20

23 U 19 William Carey way Harrow
38 L 6 William clo Rom
86 K 12 William gdns SW15
140 J 11 William IV st WC2
65 Z 3 William Morley clo E6
32 K 10 William Morris clo E17
139 R 18 William ms SW1
132 A 15 William rd NW1
154 E 10 William rd Sutton
105 T 18 William rd SW19
54 A 20 William st Bark
154 L 5 William st Carsh
33 T 19 William st E10
15 R 15 William st N12
31 U 1 William st N17
139 R 18 William st SW1
32 K 5 Williams gro E17
30 F 5 Williams gro N22
120 D 12 Williams la Mrdn
85 V 6 Williams la SW14
70 B 12 Williams rd S'hall
156 F 13 Williams ter Croy
48 A 13 Williamson st N7
14 F 18 Williamson way NW7
27 Y 17 Willifield way NW11
21 Z 20 Willingale clo Wdfd Grn
30 J 8 Willingdon rd N22
47 W 15 Willingham clo NW5
47 V 15 Willingham Ter NW5
117 P 4 Willingham way Kingst
90 A 8 Willington rd SW9
154 H 14 Willis av Sutton
122 M 16 Willis rd Croy
65 P 5 Willis rd E15
81 Y 10 Willis rd Erith
64 E 17 Willis st E14
156 C 8 Willoughby av Croy
32 A 2 Willoughby la N17
19 N 20 Willoughby la N17
31 Z 1 Willoughby Park rd N17
103 N 20 Willoughby rd Kingst
30 G 12 Willoughby rd N8
46 F 12 Willoughby rd NW3
84 F 14 Willoughby rd Twick
140 H 2 Willoughby st WC1
97 N 15 Willow av Sidcp
86 E 6 Willow av SW13
102 B 6 Willow bank Rich
87 T 7 Willow bank SW6
48 L 19 Willow Bridge rd N1
72 E 17 Willow clo Brentf
127 U 13 Willow clo Brom
98 B 16 Willow clo Bxly Hth
57 Y 10 Willow clo Hornch
122 H 14 Willow clo Thntn Hth
49 U 6 Willow cotts N16
73 O 17 Willow cotts Rich
11 Y 13 Willow ct Edg
4 F 15 Willow dri Barnt
14 K 8 Willow end N20
116 J 19 Willow end Surb
82 G 3 Willow gdns Chisl
113 Z 15 Willow gro Chisl
65 S 5 Willow gro E13
152 M 7 Willow Hayne gdns Worc Pk
120 M 12 Willow la Mitch
157 T 7 Willow mt Croy
148 C 5 Willow pl SW1
8 E 9 Willow rd Enf
99 X 3 Willow rd Erith
117 U 8 Willow rd New Mald
46 G 11 Willow rd NW3
37 Y 18 Willow rd Rom
72 K 6 Willow rd W5
155 T 16 Willow rd Wallgtn
20 K 4 Willow st E4
134 H 15 Willow st EC2
38 L 14 Willow st Rom
113 X 15 Willow vale Chisl
74 G 3 Willow vale W12
120 F 1 Willow view SW19
28 A 3 Willow way N3
110 B 7 Willow way Twick
100 K 5 Willow way Twick
41 Z 10 Willow way Wemb
32 L 15 Willow wlk E17
30 J 12 Willow wlk N15
28 G 8 Willow wlk N2
7 P 20 Willow wlk N21
150 L 5 Willow wlk SE1
151 N 6 Willow wlk SE1
153 V 4 Willow wlk Sutton

123 R 14 Willow Wood cres SE25
70 G 9 Willowbrook rd S'hall
151 P 17 Willowbrook rd SE15
24 B 16 Willowcourt av Harrow
10 G 4 Willowdene Bushey
82 M 18 Willowdene clo Twick
60 F 13 Willowmead clo W5
120 A 12 Willows av Mrdn
106 B 1 Willowtree clo SW18
80 E 12 Willrose cres SE2
82 J 17 Wills cres Hounsl
13 V 16 Wills gro NW7
49 Y 20 Wilman gro E8
125 R 20 Wilmar gdns W Wkhm
103 O 13 Wilmer cres Kingst
134 K 6 Wilmer gdns N1
64 H 1 Wilmer Lea clo E15
49 T 7 Wilmer pl N16
16 L 15 Wilmer way N14
73 X 20 Wilmington av W4
54 E 19 Wilmington gdns Bark
54 G 20 Wilmington gdns Bark
133 S 15 Wilmington sq WC1
133 S 14 Wilmington st WC1
120 A 1 Wilmore end Mitch
28 E 7 Wilmot clo N2
151 S 20 Wilmot clo SE15
47 V 19 Wilmot pl NW1
71 U 4 Wilmot pl W7
154 L 11 Wilmot rd Carsh
99 Y 14 Wilmot rd Drtfrd
51 R 7 Wilmot rd E10
31 O 10 Wilmot rd N17
135 X 14 Wilmot st E2
28 G 11 Wilmott clo N2
78 M 11 Wilmount st SE18
88 B 20 Wilna rd SW18
88 C 19 Wilna rd SW18
136 J 12 Wilsham st W11
93 N 1 Wilshaw st SE14
23 U 1 Wilsmere dri Harrow
40 C 16 Wilsmere dri In Nthlt
106 K 20 Wilson av Mitch
42 M 1 Wilson dri Wemb
22 M 20 Wilson gdns Harrow
143 V 19 Wilson gro SE16
66 A 8 Wilson rd E6
65 Z 8 Wilson rd E6
22 M 20 Wilson rd Harrow
53 U 1 Wilson rd Ilf
91 P 3 Wilson rd SE5
65 R 5 Wilson st E13
33 T 15 Wilson st E17
142 G 1 Wilson st EC2
160 G 1 Wilson st EC2
134 G 19 Wilson st EC2
17 U 3 Wilson st N21
31 V 8 Wilsons av N1
56 H 20 Wilthorne gdns Dgnhm
74 B 14 Wilton av W4
139 S 19 Wilton cres SW1
105 V 20 Wilton cres SW19
38 L 2 Wilton dri Rom
118 D 13 Wilton gro New Mald
105 V 20 Wilton gro SW19
147 V 1 Wilton ms SW1
139 S 18 Wilton pl SW1
5 Y 13 Wilton rd Barnt
53 Y 11 Wilton rd Ilf
29 P 6 Wilton rd N10
80 G 10 Wilton rd SE2
148 A 6 Wilton rd SW1
147 Z 4 Wilton rd SW1
106 J 16 Wilton rd SW19
139 T 19 Wilton row SW1
134 E 4 Wilton sq N1
147 W 1 Wilton st SW1
139 T 20 Wilton ter SW1
134 D 4 Wilton vlls N1
50 A 18 Wilton way E8
49 Y 18 Wilton way E8
101 O 1 Wiltshire gdns Twick
122 G 7 Wiltshire rd Thntn Hth
90 G 4 Wiltshire rd SW9
90 G 7 Wiltshire rd SW9
58 A 11 Wiltstone clo Grnfd
118 B 15 Wilverley cres New Mald
90 C 18 Wimbart rd SW2
104 E 13 Wimbledon comm SW19

105 U 14 Wimbledon Hill rd SW19
105 T 4 Wimbledon Park rd SW18
87 X 17 Wimbledon Park rd SW18
105 O 3 Wimbledon Park side SW19
106 E 9 Wimbledon rd SW17
135 S 11 Wimbolt st E2
70 G 11 Wimborne av S'hall
94 C 13 Wimborne clo SE12
25 P 10 Wimborne dri NW9
22 A 20 Wimborne dri Pinn
60 B 15 Wimborne gdns W13
31 S 7 Wimborne rd N17
18 H 8 Wimborne rd N9
124 G 8 Wimborne way Becknhm
21 X 8 Wimbourne clo Buck Hl
134 E 8 Wimbourne st N1
117 O 4 Wimpole clo Kingst
139 W 1 Wimpole ms W1
139 W 2 Wimpole st W1
90 E 6 Winans wlk SW9
40 J 15 Wincanton cres Nthlt
35 Z 9 Wincanton gdns Ilf
87 V 18 Wincanton rd SW18
79 S 7 Winchat rd SE18
95 P 8 Winchcomb gdns SE9
120 G 18 Winchcombe rd Carsh
154 J 1 Winchcombe rd Carsh
81 N 20 Winchelsea av Bxly Hth
87 O 14 Winchelsea clo SW15
61 Z 3 Winchelsea rd NW10
52 D 11 Winchelsea rd E7
31 T 10 Winchelsea rd N17
157 U 14 Winchelsey ri Croy
87 V 1 Winchendon rd SW6
101 R 10 Winchendon rd Tedd
70 F 16 Winchester av Hounsl
128 M 2 Winchester av NW6
25 P 12 Winchester av NW9
103 T 17 Winchester clo Kingst
126 B 7 Winchester clo Brom
8 D 19 Winchester clo Enf
149 Y 7 Winchester clo SE17
46 G 20 Winchester ms NW3
126 B 7 Winchester pk Brom
49 U 16 Winchester pl E8
47 T 3 Winchester pl N6
24 L 12 Winchester rd Harrow
97 W 4 Winchester rd Bxly Hth
126 B 7 Winchester rd Brom
20 H 20 Winchester rd E4
33 V 2 Winchester rd E4
100 D 6 Winchester rd Felt
54 D 10 Winchester rd Ilf
47 T 2 Winchester rd N6
18 H 6 Winchester rd N9
46 G 20 Winchester rd NW3
130 H 1 Winchester rd NW3
84 A 16 Winchester rd Twick
142 E 12 Winchester sq SE1
148 A 10 Winchester st SW1
147 Y 9 Winchester st SW1
73 W 4 Winchester st W3
142 E 13 Winchester wlk SE1
24 E 17 Winchfield clo Harrow
110 J 11 Winchfield rd SE26
16 K 5 Winchmore Hill rd N14
17 P 2 Winchmore Hill rd N21
149 T 6 Wincott st SE11
96 E 10 Wincrofts dri SE9
155 O 17 Windborough rd Carsh
42 E 3 Windermere av Wemb
57 W 14 Windermere av Hornch
119 Z 6 Windermere av SW19
27 Y 9 Windermere av N3
128 M 6 Windermere av NW6

35 S 17 Windermere gdns Ilf
42 E 4 Windermere gro Wemb
104 A 11 Windermere rd SW15
98 J 4 Windermere rd Bxly Hth
121 W 2 Windermere rd SW16
159 Z 2 Windermere rd W Wkhm
123 U 19 Windermere rd Croy
29 S 5 Windermere rd N10
47 W 7 Windermere rd N19
58 F 13 Windermere rd S'hall
72 D 7 Windermere rd W5
88 H 4 Windermere rd SW11
110 D 10 Windfield clo SE26
85 N 7 Windham rd Rich
55 U 9 Winding way Dgnhm
41 S 11 Winding way Harrow
75 X 12 Windlass pl SE8
105 P 1 Windlesham gro SW19
110 C 4 Windley clo SE23
116 C 19 Windmill clo Surb
89 S 13 Windmill dri SW4
7 S 10 Windmill gdns Enf
7 X 11 Windmill hill Enf
46 C 10 Windmill hill NW3
10 E 5 Windmill la Bushey
51 X 17 Windmill la E15
59 N 13 Windmill la Grnfd
116 B 17 Windmill la Surb
122 L 17 Windmill rd Croy
100 L 13 Windmill rd Hampt
121 U 11 Windmill rd Mitch
18 C 12 Windmill rd N18
88 F 15 Windmill rd SW18
104 K 11 Windmill rd SW19
74 A 11 Windmill rd W4
72 D 10 Windmill rd W5
72 D 13 Windmill rd W5
149 S 11 Windmill row SE11
10 F 4 Windmill st Bushey
140 E 2 Windmill st W1
141 U 16 Windmill wlk SE1
25 Y 12 Windover av NW9
88 F 9 Windrush clo SW11
85 V 1 Windrush clo W4
110 F 6 Windrush la SE23
117 W 13 Windsor av New Mald
32 J 7 Windsor av E17
12 E 12 Windsor av Edg
153 T 6 Windsor av Sutton
120 D 1 Windsor av SW19
72 A 17 Windsor clo Brentf
40 H 11 Windsor clo Harrow
27 T 8 Windsor clo N3
40 G 11 Windsor cres Harrow
43 R 9 Windsor cres Wemb
16 G 3 Windsor ct N14
5 Y 19 Windsor dri Barnt
99 X 15 Windsor dri Drtfrd
108 L 10 Windsor gro SE27
148 C 4 Windsor pl SW1
122 K 4 Windsor rd Thntn Hth
4 D 19 Windsor rd Barnt
97 Y 11 Windsor rd Bxly Hth
55 Z 10 Windsor rd Dgnhm
51 R 7 Windsor rd E10
52 F 6 Windsor rd E11
20 D 13 Windsor rd E4
52 H 15 Windsor rd E7
23 O 5 Windsor rd Harrow
54 B 12 Windsor rd Ilf
102 K 18 Windsor rd Kingst
17 U 12 Windsor rd N13
31 X 7 Windsor rd N17
27 T 8 Windsor rd N3
48 A 10 Windsor rd N7
44 J 17 Windsor rd NW2
85 N 5 Windsor rd Rich
70 E 8 Windsor rd S'hall
115 S 16 Windsor rd Sidcp
101 R 11 Windsor rd Tedd
72 J 1 Windsor rd W5
60 J 20 Windsor rd W5
152 H 3 Windsor rd Worc Pk
133 Y 4 Windsor st N1
134 B 11 Windsor ter N1
144 J 5 Windsor way W6
91 P 5 Windsor wlk SE5
49 U 5 Windus rd N16
49 V 5 Windus wlk N16
127 R 1 Windy Ridge Brom
105 P 11 Windyridge clo SW19

75 O 1	Wine clo E1	
75 O 2	Wine clo E1	
143 Z 11	Wine clo E1	
141 V 5	Wine Office ct EC4	
93 U 1	Winforton st SE10	
88 C 20	Winfrith rd SW18	
121 Z 13	Wingate cres Croy	
53 Z 15	Wingate rd Ilf	
115 T 14	Wingate rd Sidcp	
74 H 8	Wingate rd W6	
51 Y 13	Wingfield rd E15	
33 R 15	Wingfield rd E17	
103 O 14	Wingfield rd Kingst	
91 W 7	Wingfield st SE15	
90 A 16	Wingford rd SW2	
90 L 8	Wingmore rd SE24	
144 E 15	Wingrave rd W6	
112 A 5	Wingrove rd SE6	
89 N 10	Winifred gro SW11	
56 A 5	Winifred rd Dgnhm	
99 Y 14	Winifred rd Drtfrd	
100 G 9	Winifred rd Hampt	
105 Y 20	Winifred rd SW19	
78 G 3	Winifred st E16	
18 G 3	Winifred ter N9	
65 U 8	Winkfield rd E13	
30 G 5	Winkfield rd N22	
25 N 15	Winkley clo Harrow	
111 Y 10	Winlaton rd Brom	
56 A 10	Winmill rd Dgnhm	
79 W 15	Winn Common rd SE18	
94 F 20	Winn rd SE12	
112 J 1	Winn rd SE12	
140 E 8	Winnett st W1	
40 B 18	Winnings wlk Nthlt	
28 F 18	Winnington clo N2	
9 O 1	Winnington rd Enf	
46 F 2	Winnington rd N2	
28 G 17	Winnington rd N2	
32 K 10	Winns av E17	
33 N 9	Winns av E17	
31 S 14	Winns ms N15	
33 N 9	Winns ter E17	
33 W 9	Winnsbeach E17	
60 F 12	Winscombe cres W5	
47 T 8	Winscombe st N19	
10 M 15	Winscombe way Stanm	
110 L 6	Winsford rd SE6	
18 A 16	Winsford ter N18	
89 O 13	Winsham gro SW11	
138 G 5	Winslade ms W2	
90 B 13	Winslade rd SW2	
93 R 19	Winslade way SW2	
138 F 4	Winsland st W2	
140 B 4	Winsley st W1	
20 M 9	Winslow gro E4	
144 E 12	Winslow rd W6	
100 A 7	Winslow way Felt	
66 J 15	Winsor ter E6	
88 G 8	Winstanley rd SW11	
56 K 14	Winstead gdns Dgnhm	
44 A 1	Winston av NW9	
10 H 20	Winston clo Harrow	
38 H 13	Winston clo Rom	
22 J 3	Winston ct Harrow	
49 O 12	Winston rd N16	
54 B 8	Winston way Ilf	
53 Z 9	Winston way Ilf	
73 X 10	Winston wlk W4	
66 E 4	Winter av E6	
122 F 8	Winterbourne rd Thntn Hth	
55 T 7	Winterbourne rd Dgnhm	
92 L 20	Winterbourne rd SE6	
90 L 16	Winterbrook rd SE24	
105 S 4	Winterfold clo SW19	
116 B 16	Winters rd Surb	
13 U 16	Winterstoke gdns NW7	
110 L 1	Winterstoke rd SE6	
146 O 13	Winterton pl SW10	
90 B 13	Winterwell rd SW2	
87 T 11	Winthorpe rd SW15	
135 W 20	Winthrop st E1	
29 V 2	Winton av N11	
19 S 3	Winton clo N9	
25 N 1	Winton gdns Edg	
65 X 19	Winton rd E16	
108 G 13	Winton way SW16	
123 P 11	Wisbeach rd Croy	
157 V 20	Wisborough rd S Croy	
56 H 5	Wisdons clo Rom	
13 U 18	Wise la NW7	
13 X 19	Wise la NW7	
64 J 3	Wise rd E15	
51 N 6	Wiseman rd E10	
106 K 1	Wiseton rd SW17	
95 N 3	W.shart rd SE3	
115 P 18	Wisley rd Orp	
89 N 14	Wisley rd SW11	
93 W 11	Wisteria rd SE13	
135 Y 15	Witan st E2	
56 F 15	Witham rd Dgnhm	
39 Y 15	Witham rd Dgnhm	
124 C 5	Witham rd SE20	
71 Z 1	Witham rd W13	
157 S 10	Witherby clo Croy	
151 X 10	Witherfield way SE16	
48 G 15	Witherington rd N5	
26 D 4	Withers mead NW9	
113 V 5	Witherston way SE9	
20 K 12	Withy Mead E4	
87 O 20	Withycombe rd SW19	
159 U 15	Witley cres Croy	
70 E 11	Witley gdns S'hall	
47 W 7	Witley rd N19	
110 F 6	Witney path SE23	
20 K 10	Wittenham way E4	
112 B 12	Wittersham rd Brom	
91 Z 6	Wivenhoe clo SE15	
68 C 6	Wivenhoe rd Bark	
110 D 14	Wiverton rd SE26	
68 J 3	Wix rd Dgnhm	
89 R 10	Wix's la SW4	
57 W 12	Woburn av Hornch	
106 D 16	Woburn clo SW19	
132 H 17	Woburn pl WC1	
154 J 1	Woburn rd Carsh	
122 M 20	Woburn rd Croy	
123 N 20	Woburn rd Croy	
102 O 10	Woburn sq WC1	
132 G 15	Woburn wlk WC1	
102 D 19	Woffington clo Kingst	
86 D 10	Woking clo SW15	
86 D 11	Woking clo SW15	
126 K 7	Woldham rd Brom	
70 F 10	Wolf br S'hall	
126 F 14	Wolfe clo Brom	
78 A 14	Wolfe cres SE7	
53 U 12	Wolferton rd E12	
52 B 18	Wolffe gdns E15	
108 J 9	Wollaston clo SE27	
93 Y 12	Wolfram rd SE13	
88 H 7	Wolftencroft clo SW11	
12 D 12	Wolmer clo Edg	
12 C 11	Wolmer gdns Edg	
105 X 4	Wolseley clo SW19	
73 T 15	Wolseley gdns W4	
52 H 20	Wolseley rd E7	
23 T 9	Wolseley rd Harrow	
121 O 17	Wolseley rd Mitch	
30 C 6	Wolseley rd N22	
29 X 17	Wolseley rd N8	
57 N 2	Wolseley rd Rom	
73 W 10	Wolseley rd W4	
143 R 18	Wolseley st SE1	
32 L 11	Wolsey av E17	
66 K 9	Wolsey av E6	
83 N 11	Wolsey clo Hounsl	
117 T 1	Wolsey clo Kingst	
103 T 20	Wolsey clo Kingst	
152 F 7	Wolsey clo Worc Pk	
159 U 19	Wolsey cres Croy	
119 T 16	Wolsey cres Mrdn	
102 J 14	Wolsey dri Kingst	
26 Z 1	Wolsey gro Edg	
47 U 16	Wolsey ms NW5	
9 N 9	Wolsey rd Enf	
100 L 14	Wolsey rd Hampt	
49 P 15	Wolsey rd N1	
63 O 15	Wolsey st E1	
143 Z 1	Wolsey st E1	
14 J 16	Wolsley clo Drtfrd	
14 J 16	Wolstonbury N12	
80 H 6	Wolvercote rd SE2	
117 R 1	Wolverton av Kingst	
103 R 20	Wolverton av Kingst	
73 N 1	Wolverton gdns W5	
144 E 6	Wolverton gdns W6	
24 C 1	Wolverton rd Stanm	
11 P 20	Wolverton rd Stanm	
6 J 17	Wolverton way N14	
30 G 2	Wolves la N22	
17 U 20	Wolves la N22	
30 B 19	Womersley rd N8	
153 O 19	Wonersh way Sutton	
104 B 20	Wonford clo New Mald	
107 N 3	Wonford way SW17	
135 S 16	Wood clo E2	
41 P 2	Wood clo Harrow	
43 Y 2	Wood clo NW9	
113 R 14	Wood dri Chisl	
40 L 12	Wood End av Harrow	
41 N 13	Wood End av Harrow	
41 O 14	Wood End clo Nthlt	
41 O 14	Wood End gdns Nthlt	
41 O 15	Wood End la Nthlt	
40 L 16	Wood End la Nthlt	
41 R 12	Wood End rd Harrow	
41 O 15	Wood End way Nthlt	
56 C 9	Wood la Dgnhm	
56 G 5	Wood la Dgnhm	
55 W 12	Wood la Dgnhm	
57 V 16	Wood la Hornch	
71 U 18	Wood la Islwth	
83 W 2	Wood la Islwth	
29 R 18	Wood la N6	
44 A 2	Wood la NW9	
43 Y 2	Wood la NW9	
10 M 12	Wood la Stanm	
11 S 7	Wood la Stanm	
136 C 10	Wood la W12	
62 L 17	Wood la W12	
74 M 2	Wood la W12	
21 O 15	Wood la Wdfd Grn	
113 P 18	Wood Lodge gdns Brom	
159 W 5	Wood Lodge la W Wkhm	
4 C 13	Wood st Barnt	
51 Y 10	Wood st E11	
65 V 19	Wood st E16	
33 V 12	Wood st E17	
33 W 14	Wood st E17	
160 B 5	Wood st EC2	
142 C 2	Wood st EC2	
116 H 2	Wood st Kingst	
121 N 17	Wood st Mitch	
74 A 14	Wood st W4	
92 A 18	Wood Vale est SE23	
29 U 16	Wood vale N10	
92 B 17	Wood vale SE23	
109 Z 1	Wood vale SE23	
91 Z 20	Wood vale SE23	
76 F 16	Wood wharf SE10	
150 K 2	Wood's pl SE1	
64 E 19	Woodall clo E14	
9 U 19	Woodall rd Enf	
112 C 7	Woodbank rd Brom	
110 G 14	Woodbastwick rd SE26	
22 M 13	Woodberry av Harrow	
23 N 13	Woodberry av Harrow	
17 U 8	Woodberry av N21	
29 R 9	Woodberry cres N10	
48 L 3	Woodberry down N4	
15 P 20	Woodberry gdns N12	
15 R 19	Woodberry gro N12	
48 L 2	Woodberry gro N4	
49 N 2	Woodberry gro N4	
2C	Woodberry way E4	
116 H 7	Woodberry way N12	
101 P 5	Woodbine clo Twick	
8 C 3	Woodbine gro Enf	
110 A 19	Woodbine gro SE20	
152 L 5	Woodbine la Worc Pk	
34 G 18	Woodbine pl E11	
96 G 20	Woodbine rd Sidcp	
50 C 17	Woodbine ter E9	
86 K 10	Woodborough rd SW15	
107 Z 7	Woodbourne av SW16	
155 T 17	Woodbourne gdns Wallgtn	
44 H 9	Woodbridge clo NW2	
48 D 7	Woodbridge clo N7	
35 S 2	Woodbridge ct Wdfd Grn	
54 K 16	Woodbridge rd Bark	
55 N 16	Woodbridge rd Bark	
133 V 16	Woodbridge st EC1	
80 A 17	Woodbrook rd SE2	
27 R 17	Woodburn clo NW4	
157 V 3	Woodbury clo Croy	
34 H 14	Woodbury clo E11	
60 B 12	Woodbury Park rd W13	
33 R 13	Woodbury rd E17	
106 K 12	Woodbury st SW17	
129 X 20	Woodchester sq W2	
114 G 8	Woodchurch clo Sidcp	
113 O 18	Woodchurch dri Chisl	
129 W 1	Woodchurch rd NW6	
127 X 2	Woodclyffe dri Chisl	
42 F 2	Woodcock Dell av Harrow	
24 E 16	Woodcock hill Harrow	
42 F 1	Woodcock hill Harrow	
24 G 17	Woodcock pk Harrow	
110 D 1	Woodcombe cres SE23	
122 J 9	Woodcote av Thntn Hth	
155 R 19	Woodcote av Wallgtn	
57 W 11	Woodcote av Hornch	
13 Z 18	Woodcote av NW7	
9 R 20	Woodcote clo Enf	
103 N 13	Woodcote clo Kingst	
155 U 20	Woodcote grn Wallgtn	
155 T 13	Woodcote ms Wallgtn	
156 A 20	Woodcote pl Wallgtn	
108 K 12	Woodcote pl SE27	
52 E 1	Woodcote rd E11	
155 T 15	Woodcote rd Wallgtn	
13 O 20	Woodcroft av NW7	
23 X 3	Woodcroft av Stanm	
41 Z 18	Woodcroft cres Grnfd	
17 S 6	Woodcroft N21	
122 H 13	Woodcroft rd Thntn Hth	
113 U 6	Woodcroft SE9	
21 U 5	Woodedge clo E4	
7 N 15	Woodend gdns Enf	
33 U 7	Woodend rd E17	
108 L 14	Woodend SE19	
154 C 3	Woodend Sutton	
155 R 19	Woodend the Wallgtn	
52 D 13	Wooder gdns E7	
4 J 16	Woodfall av Barnt	
99 S 10	Woodfall dri Drtfrd	
48 E 6	Woodfall rd N4	
147 O 10	Woodfall st SW3	
91 P 11	Woodfarrs SE5	
155 N 15	Woodfield av Carsh	
107 X 5	Woodfield av SW16	
60 E 12	Woodfield av Wemb	
42 D 10	Woodfield av Wemb	
108 L 17	Woodfield clo SE19	
60 F 12	Woodfield cres W5	
16 A 4	Woodfield dri Barnt	
39 X 13	Woodfield dri Rom	
118 D 11	Woodfield gdns New Mald	
107 Y 6	Woodfield gro SW16	
107 X 6	Woodfield la SW16	
44 B 4	Woodfield pk NW9	
129 S 19	Woodfield pl W9	
60 E 13	Woodfield rd W5	
129 R 20	Woodfield rd W9	
10 D 2	Woodfield ri Bushey	
16 J 20	Woodfield way N11	
29 W 1	Woodfield way N11	
35 S 13	Woodford av Ilf	
35 R 12	Woodford Bridge rd Ilf	
34 B 3	Woodford New rd Wdfd Grn	
33 Z 11	Woodford New rd E17	
42 H 4	Woodford pl Wemb	
34 D 13	Woodford rd E18	
34 E 9	Woodford rd E18	
52 G 11	Woodford rd E7	
74 M 7	Woodger rd W12	
136 C 19	Woodger rd W6	
66 D 16	Woodget clo E6	
24 F 15	Woodgrange av Harrow	
8 K 19	Woodgrange av Enf	
15 T 19	Woodgrange av N12	
73 O 2	Woodgrange av W5	
24 F 16	Woodgrange clo Harrow	
8 L 19	Woodgrange gdns Enf	
52 G 14	Woodgrange rd E7	
22 A 6	Woodhall av Pinn	
109 U 6	Woodhall av SE21	
22 A 4	Woodhall dri Pinn	
109 U 7	Woodhall dri SE21	
22 A 5	Woodhall gdns Pinn	
34 B 14	Woodham ct E18	
111 U 6	Woodham rd SE6	

66 C 16	Woodhatch clo E6
36 A 12	Woodhaven gdns Ilf
113 Y 16	Woodhayes Chisl
104 M 17	Woodhayes rd SW19
105 N 15	Woodhayes rd SW19
43 Z 17	Woodheyes rd NW10
24 G 19	Woodhill cres Harrow
78 E 12	Woodhill SE18
59 X 5	Woodhouse av Grnfd
59 W 4	Woodhouse clo Grnfd
53 P 19	Woodhouse gro E12
52 A 9	Woodhouse rd N12
15 T 18	Woodhouse rd N12
80 A 12	Woodhurst rd SE2
73 V 1	Woodhurst rd W3
95 V 16	Woodington clo SE9
63 W 13	Woodison st E3
127 T 2	Woodknoll dri Brom
41 Z 17	Woodland appr Grnfd
21 V 10	Woodland clo Wdfd Grn
152 B 15	Woodland clo Epsom
25 V 17	Woodland clo NW9
109 T 14	Woodland clo SE19
76 L 15	Woodland cres SE10
83 T 7	Woodland gdns Islwth
29 S 14	Woodland gdns N10
109 T 14	Woodland hill SE19
122 G 10	Woodland rd Thntn Hth
20 H 5	Woodland rd E4
16 E 16	Woodland rd N11
109 T 14	Woodland rd SE19
41 Z 18	Woodland ri Grnfd
29 S 14	Woodland ri N10
78 C 12	Woodland ter SE7
159 U 4	Woodland way W Wkhm
21 V 10	Woodland way Wdfd Grn
124 H 20	Woodland way Croy
107 P 18	Woodland way Mitch
119 V 9	Woodland way Mrdn
17 T 6	Woodland way N21
13 P 18	Woodland way NW7
80 H 12	Woodland way SE2
76 M 14	Woodland wlk SE10
28 C 4	Woodland's av N3
33 V 10	Woodland's rd E17
152 E 2	Woodland's av Worc Pk
96 H 20	Woodlands av Sidcp
117 X 2	Woodlands av New Mald
52 G 4	Woodlands av E11
37 Y 20	Woodlands av Rom
114 H 1	Woodlands av Sidcp
73 T 3	Woodlands av W3
27 S 16	Woodlands clo NW11
127 U 4	Woodlands clo Brom
10 H 19	Woodlands dri Stanm
83 U 5	Woodlands gro Islwth
22 F 14	Woodlands Harrow
15 R 19	Woodlands N12
27 S 17	Woodlands NW11
30 L 14	Woodlands Park rd N15
76 M 15	Woodlands Park rd SE10
98 A 7	Woodlands rd Bxly Hth
23 W 15	Woodlands rd Harrow
97 Z 7	Woodlands rd Bxly Hth
127 S 4	Woodlands rd Brom
51 Z 6	Woodlands rd E11
8 A 5	Woodlands rd Enf
54 A 10	Woodlands rd Ilf
83 S 7	Woodlands rd Islwth
19 P 6	Woodlands rd N9
39 T 11	Woodlands rd Rom
70 A 2	Woodlands rd S'hall
116 G 18	Woodlands rd Surb
86 D 8	Woodlands rd SW13
93 X 17	Woodlands rd SE13
119 N 9	Woodlands SW20
155 R 19	Woodlands the Wallgtn
83 U 6	Woodlands the Islwth
16 E 6	Woodlands the N14
93 X 18	Woodlands the SE13
108 M 18	Woodlands the SE19
87 U 12	Woodlands way SW15
87 V 14	Woodlawn clo SW15
100 J 3	Woodlawn cres Twick
100 A 4	Woodlawn dri Felt
144 F 19	Woodlawn rd SW6
87 O 1	Woodlawn rd SW6
87 P 2	Woodlawn rd SW6
126 A 12	Woodlea dri Brom
49 R 9	Woodlea rd N16
15 X 18	Woodleigh av N12
108 A 7	Woodleigh gdns SW16
78 K 4	Woodman st E16
136 A 2	Woodmans ms W10
62 K 15	Woodmans ms W10
155 U 20	Woodmansterne la Wallgtn
154 K 18	Woodmansterne rd Carsh
107 X 20	Woodmansterne rd SW16
124 D 18	Woodmere av Croy
124 G 17	Woodmere clo Croy
124 E 18	Woodmere gdns Croy
95 T 20	Woodmere SE9
125 W 11	Woodmere way Becknhm
107 T 11	Woodnook rd SW16
8 M 20	Woodpecker clo Enf
158 J 19	Woodpecker mt Croy
75 V 17	Woodpecker rd SE14
68 G 20	Woodpecker rd SE2
90 K 13	Woodquest av SE24
5 T 5	Woodride Barnt
22 E 4	Woodridings av Pinn
22 C 2	Woodridings clo Pinn
51 Y 1	Woodriffe rd E11
60 B 2	Woodrow clo Grnfd
78 F 12	Woodrow SE18
37 V 13	Woodrush way Rom
139 S 9	Woods ms W1
43 V 3	Woods rd SE15
135 R 20	Woodseer st E1
136 M 17	Woodsford sq W14
56 H 10	Woodshire rd Dgnhm
114 B 14	Woodside av Chisl
23 P 13	Woodside av N10
15 O 14	Woodside av N12
28 M 15	Woodside av N6
123 Y 14	Woodside av SE25
60 X 3	Woodside av Wemb
21 X 8	Woodside Buck Hl
99 O 9	Woodside clo Bxly Hth
11 N 16	Woodside clo Stanm
117 U 18	Woodside clo Surb
60 L 3	Woodside clo Wemb
123 Y 18	Woodside Court rd Croy
114 H 7	Woodside cres Sidcp
60 L 4	Woodside end Wemb
20 E 18	Woodside gdns E4
31 T 8	Woodside gdns N17
15 O 13	Woodside Grange rd N12
123 Y 14	Woodside grn SE25
123 Y 14	Woodside grn SW13
15 P 12	Woodside gro N12
97 X 15	Woodside la Bxly
15 P 11	Woodside la N12
27 Y 14	Woodside NW11
33 X 14	Woodside Park av E17
15 P 14	Woodside Park rd N12
123 Y 13	Woodside pk SE25
60 L 4	Woodside pl Wemb
118 A 4	Woodside rd New Mald
99 N 10	Woodside rd Bxly Hth
21 S 12	Woodside rd Wdfd Grn
117 Z 3	Woodside rd New Mald
127 R 11	Woodside rd Brom
65 X 12	Woodside rd E13
102 J 18	Woodside rd Kingst
30 E 2	Woodside rd N22
123 Z 15	Woodside rd SE25
114 H 7	Woodside rd Sidcp
154 C 6	Woodside rd Sutton
105 U 14	Woodside SW19
123 Z 14	Woodside view SE25
124 B 14	Woodside way Croy
121 T 1	Woodside way Mitch
47 S 10	Woodsome rd NW5
105 T 3	Woodspring rd SW19
11 Y 20	Woodstead gro Edg
83 Y 12	Woodstock av Islwth
45 T 1	Woodstock av NW11
58 F 9	Woodstock av S'hall
119 V 17	Woodstock av Sutton
71 Z 7	Woodstock av W13
24 L 9	Woodstock clo Stanm
98 B 20	Woodstock clo Bxly
8 M 19	Woodstock cres Enf
94 D 17	Woodstock ct SE12
54 M 6	Woodstock gdns Ilf
136 H 18	Woodstock gro W12
139 V 1	Woodstock ms W1
10 G 2	Woodstock rd Bushey
155 P 12	Woodstock rd Carsh
155 O 7	Woodstock rd Croy
33 W 7	Woodstock rd E17
52 K 20	Woodstock rd E7
48 G 5	Woodstock rd N4
45 W 3	Woodstock rd NW11
74 A 9	Woodstock rd W4
60 M 1	Woodstock rd Wemb
119 U 18	Woodstock ri Sutton
65 N 17	Woodstock st E16
139 X 7	Woodstock st W1
64 D 19	Woodstock ter E14
121 T 2	Woodstock way Mitch
152 H 11	Woodstone av Epsom
109 V 9	Woodsyse SE26
86 K 11	Woodthorpe rd SW15
123 U 5	Woodvale av SE25
20 G 13	Woodview av E4
94 E 13	Woodville clo SE12
101 X 10	Woodville clo Tedd
45 P 1	Woodville gdns NW11
35 Z 12	Woodville gdns Ilf
60 L 17	Woodville gdns W5
122 M 8	Woodville rd Thntn Hth
123 N 7	Woodville rd Thntn Hth
5 N 14	Woodville rd Barnt
52 C 3	Woodville rd E11
32 J 14	Woodville rd E17
34 H 8	Woodville rd E18
119 X 8	Woodville rd Mrdn
49 P 15	Woodville rd N16
45 R 1	Woodville rd NW11
129 R 8	Woodville rd NW6
102 C 6	Woodville rd Rich
60 H 18	Woodville rd W5
94 J 1	Woodville SE3
26 G 17	Woodward av NW4
55 S 20	Woodward gdns Dgnhm
68 C 1	Woodward rd Dgnhm
55 U 20	Woodward rd Dgnhm
91 T 16	Woodwarde rd SE22
83 O 16	Woodwards Foot path Twick
23 Z 17	Woodway cres Harrow
88 D 13	Woodwell st SW18
91 S 19	Woodyard la SE21
94 D 16	Woodyates rd SE12
104 K 16	Wool rd SW20
94 J 4	Woolacombe rd SE3
30 H 19	Woolaston rd N4
150 F 10	Wooler st SE17
80 D 3	Woolf clo SE28
44 F 2	Woolmead av NW9
18 L 18	Woolmer gdns N18
18 L 17	Woolmer rd N18
64 G 19	Woolmore st E14
88 A 7	Woolneigh st SW6
87 Z 7	Woolneigh st SW6
87 Z 7	Woolneigh st SW6
151 R 4	Woolstaplers way SE16
110 J 4	Woolstone rd SE23
63 G 19	Woolwich Church st SE18
78 G 18	Woolwich comm SE18
78 H 8	Woolwich High st E16
78 L 4	Woolwich manorway SE18
78 K 13	Woolwich New rd SE18
98 D 10	Woolwich rd Bxly Hth
98 E 6	Woolwich rd Bxly Hth
77 O 13	Woolwich rd SE10
80 K 15	Woolwich rd SE2
81 P 13	Woolwich rd SE7
78 B 10	Woolwich rd SE7
77 Y 12	Woolwich rd SE7
64 J 17	Wooster gdns E14
27 Y 6	Wootton gro N3
141 U 15	Wootton st SE1
124 B 3	Worbeck rd SE20
8 K 3	Worcester av Enf
31 W 1	Worcester av N17
158 M 3	Worcester clo Croy
159 N 3	Worcester clo Croy
121 R 5	Worcester clo Mitch
21 X 14	Worcester cres Wdfd Grn
13 O 10	Worcester cres NW7
152 C 5	Worcester gdns Worc Pk
41 O 18	Worcester gdns Grnfd
35 R 20	Worcester gdns Ilf
160 C 9	Worcester pl EC4
53 T 11	Worcester rd E12
32 F 6	Worcester rd E17
154 A 15	Worcester rd Sutton
153 Z 15	Worcester rd Sutton
105 V 13	Worcester rd SW19
59 P 7	Wordsworth av Grnfd
53 P 19	Wordsworth av E12
34 C 9	Wordsworth av E18
153 N 9	Wordsworth dri Sutton
30 H 13	Wordsworth pde N8
100 E 10	Wordsworth rd Hampt
155 W 15	Wordsworth rd Wallgtn
49 S 13	Wordsworth rd N16
96 H 2	Wordsworth rd SE18
110 E 18	Wordsworth rd SE20
27 X 14	Wordsworth wlk NW11
146 M 19	Worfield st SW11
149 N 9	Worgan st SE11
52 A 19	Worland rd E15
7 S 13	World's End la Enf
144 C 10	Worlidge st W6
74 L 13	Worlidge st W6
91 V 10	Worlingham rd SE22
74 G 3	Wormholt rd W12
142 H 3	Wormwood st EC2
128 K 18	Wornington rd W10
128 M 19	Wornington rd W10
137 N 1	Wornington rd W10
130 H 5	Woronzow rd NW8
83 Y 13	Worple av Islwth
105 S 18	Worple av SW19
40 E 3	Worple clo Harrow
83 Z 8	Worple rd Islwth
105 T 18	Worple rd SW19
118 M 2	Worple rd SW20
119 O 1	Worple rd SW20
105 U 16	Worple Road ms SW19
85 Y 7	Worple st SW14
40 E 4	Worple way Harrow
84 L 12	Worple way Rich
134 G 19	Worship st EC2
106 F 11	Worslade rd SW17
110 M 11	Worsley Bridge rd SE26
111 N 13	Worsley Bridge rd SE26
52 A 11	Worsley rd E11
51 Z 11	Worsley rd E11
89 V 12	Worsopp dri SW4
64 M 4	Worthing clo E15
70 D 17	Worthing rd Hounsl
116 M 20	Worthington rd Surb
122 E 16	Wortley rd Croy
66 A 1	Wortley rd E6
83 P 4	Worton gdns Islwth
83 R 9	Worton rd Islwth
83 P 5	Worton way Islwth
44 M 11	Wotton rd NW2
75 Z 17	Wotton rd SE8
65 O 17	Wouldham rd E16
52 A 10	Wragby rd E11
18 K 7	Wrampling pl N9

35 W 10 Wray av Ilf
48 B 6 Wray cres N4
153 U 19 Wray rd Sutton
153 P 7 Wrayfield rd Sutton
79 P 18 Wrekin rd SE18
44 M 13 Wren av NW2
70 F 10 Wren av S'hall
65 R 16 Wren clo E16
55 W 14 Wren gdns Dgnhm
57 S 5 Wren gdns Hornch
79 S 7 Wren pth SE28
55 W 14 Wren rd Dgnhm
91 N 2 Wren rd SE5
115 U 7 Wren rd Sidcp
133 O 16 Wren st WC1
128 F 7 Wrentham av NW10
111 Z 10 Wrenthorpe rd Brom
64 B 7 Wrexham rd E3
94 J 3 Wricklemarsh rd SE3
95 P 2 Wricklemarsh rd SE3
75 S 19 Wrigglesworth st
SE14
49 S 17 Wright rd N1
137 W 20 Wright's la W8
105 N 16 Wrights all SW19
93 W 11 Wrights clo SE13
145 W 1 Wrights la W8
63 X 5 Wrights rd E3
123 S 6 Wrights rd SE25
155 R 9 Wrights row Wallgtn
85 X 7 Wrights wlk SW14
4 E 9 Wrotham rd Barnt
132 C 1 Wrotham rd NW1
72 C 2 Wrotham rd W13
97 U 3 Wrotham rd Welling
62 H 6 Wrottesley rd NW10
79 N 16 Wrottesley rd SE18
89 N 15 Wroughton rd SW11
26 K 12 Wroughton ter NW4
55 U 17 Wroxall rd Dgnhm
29 W 2 Wroxham gdns N11
68 J 20 Wroxham rd SE15
92 B 5 Wroxton rd SE15
154 M 5 Wrythe Green rd
Carsh
154 L 5 Wrythe grn Carsh
120 C 19 Wrythe la Carsh
154 G 1 Wrythe la Carsh
62 D 16 Wulfstan st W12
60 K 2 Wyatt ct Wemb
108 B 3 Wyatt Park rd SW2
99 T 8 Wyatt rd Drtfrd
52 F 18 Wyatt rd E7
48 K 9 Wyatt rd N5
33 U 11 Wyatt's la E17
43 V 20 Wyborne way
NW10
4 H 11 Wyburn av Barnt
102 M 19 Wych Elm pas Kingst
157 N 18 Wyche gro S Croy
77 O 18 Wychelby clo SE3
5 N 19 Wycherley cres Barnt
122 K 6 Wychwood av
Thnt Hth
11 U 19 Wychwood av Edg
11 U 19 Wychwood clo Edg
47 W 1 Wychwood end N6
35 V 13 Wychwood gdns Ilf
133 W 14 Wyclif st EC1
96 K 3 Wycliffe clo Welling
89 P 5 Wycliffe rd SW11
106 B 16 Wycliffe rd SW19
45 X 6 Wycombe gdns
NW11
35 U 16 Wycombe rd Ilf
31 Y 5 Wycombe rd N17
61 R 2 Wycombe rd Wemb
123 Z 17 Wydehurst rd Croy
119 N 15 Wydell clo Mrdn
112 H 9 Wydeville Manor rd
SE12
88 G 7 Wye st SW11
36 A 5 Wyfields Ilf
35 Z 5 Wyfields Ilf
144 L 20 Wyfold rd SW6
87 S 1 Wyfold rd SW6
56 J 19 Wyhill wlk Dgnhm
71 W 17 Wyke clo Islwth
71 X 9 Wyke gdns W7
64 A 1 Wyke rd E3
119 N 2 Wyke rd SW20
55 U 17 Wykeham av Dgnhm
55 T 17 Wykeham grn
Dgnhm
42 M 3 Wykeham hill Wemb
43 N 3 Wykeham hill Wemb
24 A 12 Wykeham rd Harrow
26 L 16 Wykeham rd NW4
14 F 5 Wykeham ri N20
43 T 17 Wyld way Wemb

46 C 4 Wyldes clo NW11
18 G 8 Wyldfield gdns N9
92 H 17 Wyleu st SE23
70 H 8 Wylie rd S'hall
63 O 12 Wyllen clo E1
20 M 7 Wymead cres E4
129 V 14 Wymering rd W9
87 N 7 Wymond st SW15
114 J 1 Wyncham av Sidcp
96 J 20 Wyncham av Sidcp
23 U 2 Wynchgate Harrow
16 L 5 Wynchgate N14
17 N 4 Wynchgate N14
158 E 20 Wyncote way S Croy
127 U 7 Wyncroft clo Brom
25 R 17 Wyndale av NW9
77 V 15 Wyndcliff rd SE7
7 V 12 Wyndcroft clo Enf
153 X 17 Wyndham clo Sutton
82 F 15 Wyndham cres
Hounsl
47 U 10 Wyndham cres N19
139 O 2 Wyndham ms W1
139 O 2 Wyndham pl W1
15 Z 6 Wyndham rd Barnt
65 Z 1 Wyndham rd E6
103 N 17 Wyndham rd Kingst
150 B 19 Wyndham rd SE5
149 Z 19 Wyndham rd SE5
72 A 7 Wyndham rd W13
139 O 1 Wyndham st W1
91 O 13 Wyneham rd SE24
110 G 6 Wynell rd SE23
133 O 8 Wynford rd N1
133 R 8 Wynford rd N1
113 U 6 Wynford way SE9
34 H 4 Wynndale rd E18
90 E 6 Wynne rd SW9
96 L 13 Wynns av Sidcp
145 U 1 Wynnstay gdns W8
88 E 9 Wynter st SW11
123 T 10 Wynton gdns SE25
61 T 16 Wynton pl W3
149 R 10 Wynyard ter SE11
133 W 12 Wynyatt st EC1
12 F 11 Wyre gro Edg
59 W 8 Wyresdale Cres
Grnfd
139 O 5 Wythburn pl W1
95 Y 15 Wythens wlk SE9
56 F 10 Wythenshawe rd
Dgnhm
127 T 3 Wythes clo Brom
78 C 3 Wythes rd E16
95 T 15 Wythfield rd SE9
40 M 11 Wyvenhoe rd Harrow
148 J 17 Wyvil est SW8
148 K 16 Wyvil rd SW8
64 E 14 Wyvis st E14

118 B 19 Yew Tree clo
Worc Pk
17 T 4 Yew Tree clo N21
97 N 3 Yew Tree clo Welling
39 O 16 Yew Tree gdns Rom
37 Z 15 Yew Tree gdns Rom
62 F 20 Yew Tree rd W12
126 J 2 Yew Tree wlk BR1
82 E 13 Yew Tree wlk Hounsl
41 S 3 Yew wlk Harrow
112 A 16 Yewdale clo Brom
44 D 19 Yewfield rd NW10
124 K 5 Yewtree rd Becknhm
49 P 6 Yoakley rd N16
48 B 18 Yoke clo N7
95 R 13 Yolande gdns SE9
48 E 8 Yonge pk N4
150 B 9 York av Sidcp
114 J 4 York av Sidcp
24 B 6 York av Stanm
85 W 12 York av SW14
71 U 2 York av W7
140 L 11 York bldgs WC2
66 F 19 York clo E6
119 Z 9 York clo Mrdn
71 U 2 York clo W7
131 U 18 York ga N14
92 C 2 York ga NW1
108 J 5 York gro SE15
137 X 17 York hill SE27
53 X 8 York House pl W8
47 T 15 York ms Ilf
53 X 8 York ms NW5
88 E 7 York pl Ilf
71 T 2 York pl SW11
140 K 11 York pl W7
72 G 15 York pl WC2
122 F 16 York rd Brentf
51 T 9 York rd Croy
32 F 17 York rd E10
19 Z 18 York rd E17
52 E 19 York rd E4
82 K 8 York rd E7
53 X 8 York rd Hounsl
103 N 19 York rd Ilf
16 L 19 York rd Kingst
18 M 18 York rd N11
18 B 3 York rd N18
84 M 13 York rd N21
141 P 16 York rd Rich
153 X 16 York rd SE1
88 E 8 York rd Sutton
106 B 15 York rd SW11
101 T 10 York rd SW19
61 X 16 York rd Tedd
72 K 9 York rd W3
47 S 10 York rd W5
63 V 18 York rd NW5
67 N 4 York sq N1
121 O 18 York st Bark
83 Z 20 York st Mitch
139 R 1 York st Twick
7 Z 3 York st W1
98 J 1 York ter Enf
131 U 18 York ter Erith
131 T 18 York Terrace east
NW1
100 D 7 York Terrace west
NW1
132 K 4 York way Felt
15 Y 10 York way N1
47 Z 19 York way N20
96 J 8 York way N7
18 M 17 Yorkland av Welling
63 V 18 Yorkshire gdns N18
122 A 9 Yorkshire rd E14
121 Z 10 Yorkshire rd Mitch
135 R 9 Yorkshire rd Mitch
65 Y 16 Yorkton st E2
137 Y 19 Young rd E16
7 Z 6 Young st W8
36 D 17 Youngmans clo Enf
36 B 18 Youngs rd Ilf
36 B 18 Yoxley appr Ilf
89 S 18 Yoxley dri Ilf
44 A 19 Yukon rd SW12
Yuletide clo NW10

44 M 3 Zeland clo NW2
89 T 20 Zennor rd SW12
91 U 10 Zenoria st SE22
122 L 10 Zermatt rd Thntn Hth
64 F 14 Zetland st E14
90 A 5 Zimbabwe rd SW9
123 O 10 Zion pl Thntn Hth
123 O 10 Zion rd Thntn Hth
142 A 13 Zoar st SE1
47 Y 6 Zoffany st N19

Y

76 H 2 Yabsley st E14
151 R 5 Yalding rd SE16
57 V 13 Yale way Hornch
120 E 1 Yarborough rd
SW19
133 S 14 Yardley st WC1
31 Z 15 Yarmouth cres N15
139 X 14 Yarmouth pl W1
80 H 6 Yarnton way Belvdr
66 D 14 Yarrow cres E6
78 B 10 Yateley st SE18
40 B 5 Yeading av Harrow
22 G 16 Yeading wlk Harrow
134 E 1 Yeate st N1
29 N 19 Yeatman rd N6
93 V 6 Yeats clo SE13
144 E 10 Yeldham rd W6
88 G 5 Yelverton rd SW11
119 Y 15 Yenston clo Mrdn
64 C 14 Yeo st E3
40 C 20 Yeoman rd Nthlt
75 V 11 Yeoman st SE8
83 S 14 Yeomans ms Islwth
9 O 9 Yeomans way Enf
143 P 8 Yeomans yd E1
143 R 8 Yeomans yd E1
146 L 3 Yeomans' row SW3
47 Y 9 Yerbury rd N19
113 S 19 Yester dri Chisl
113 U 16 Yester pk Chisl
113 U 17 Yester rd Chisl
45 R 13 Yew gro NW2

Z

75 P 14 Zampa rd SE16
95 P 2 Zangwill rd SE3
63 V 5 Zealand rd E3

LONDON INFORMATION

CONTENTS

Drivers' Information 281
  Breakdown services 281
  24-Hour Garages 281
  Wheelclamped 281
Theatres, Cinemas, Shops 282
Theatres & Cinemas Map 283
Shopping Map 284
Public Transport 285–7
  London Transport 285
  British Rail 285–6

Thamesline Riverbus 286
Coaches 286
Airports 286
  Airport Bus Services 286–7
Exchange Facilities 287
Lost Credit Cards 287
Lost Property 287
Late Chemist 287–8
Late Post 288
24-Hour Casualty 288
Taxis 288

BREAKDOWN SERVICES

AA Breakdown Service
(0800) 887766 – freephone, for breakdown only. For information: 01-954 9599.
RAC Breakdown Service
(0923) 33555 (north of the Thames). 01-681 3611 (south of the Thames and Kent, Surrey, Sussex). *24hrs.*
Cavendish Motors   *45 U 20*
Cavendish Rd NW6. 01-459 0046. *Not 24hrs.*

24-HOUR GARAGES

Chiswick Flyover Service Station   *73 R 13*
1 Great West Rd W4. 01-994 1119.
Fina   *65 R 13*
95–99 Barking Rd, Barking E16. 01-476 6953.
Heron Service Station   *49 N 19*
316 Essex Rd N1. 01-226 5991.
Heron Station   *65 O 18*
51 Brunel St E16. 01-474 5746.
St Nicholas Filling Station   *148 D 7*
148 Vauxhall Bridge Rd SW1. 01-828 1371.
Sealand Garage   *146 L 7*
Sloane Ave SW3. 01-589 1226.

Star Service Station   *150 M 3*
Grange Rd SE1. 01-237 4171.
Star Service Station   *45 X 14*
63 Fortune Green Rd NW6. 01-453 2211.
Texaco Station   *149 T 6*
212 Kennington Rd SE11. 01-735 2191.

WHEELCLAMPED

How to get released
Take the label attached to your vehicle along with the fixed penalty notice to one of the police car pounds listed below. You will have to pay a fine before the clamp is removed. All major credit cards (A.Ax.Dc.V.) accepted. In an emergency contact the Metropolitan Police at the Bermondsey Communications Centre, 20 Maltby Street SE1. 01-252 2222.
Hyde Park Car Pound   *139 R 12*
NCP Park Lane Car Park, Marble Arch W1. *Open 24hrs Mon–Sun.*
Camden Town Car Pound   *131 W 4*
Oval Rd NW1. *Open 09.00–23.00 Mon–Sat, 09.00–17.00 Sun.*
Warwick Road Car Pound   *145 T 8*
245 Warwick Rd W14. *Open 08.00–24.00 Mon–Sat.*

THEATRES

Adelphi *836 7611*
Albery *867 1115*
Aldwych *836 6404*
Ambassadors *836 1171*
Apollo *437 2663*
Apollo Victoria *828 8665*
Arts *836 3334*
Astoria *434 0403*
Bloomsbury *387 9629*
Coliseum *836 3161*
Comedy *930 2578*
Criterion *867 1117*
Dominion *580 9562*
Donmar Warehouse
867 1111
Drury Lane, Theatre Royal
836 8108

Duchess (Players) *836 8243*
Duke of York's *836 5122*
Fortune *836 2238*
Garrick *379 6107*
Globe *437 3667*
Haymarket *930 9832*
Her Majesty's *839 2244*
ICA *930 3647*
Jeannetta Cochrane
242 7040
Lyric *437 3686*
Mayfair *629 3036*
Mermaid *236 5568*
National *928 2252*
New London *405 0072*
Old Vic *928 7616*
Palace *434 0909*
Palladium *437 7373*
Phoenix *836 2294*
Piccadilly *437 4506*

Playhouse *839 4401*
Prince Edward *734 8951*
Prince of Wales *839 5987*
Queen's *734 1166*
Royal Court *730 1745*
Royal Festival Hall
928 8800
Royal Opera House
240 1066
St Martin's *836 1443*
Savoy *836 8888*
Shaftesbury *379 5399*
Strand *836 2660*
Vaudeville *836 9987*
Victoria Palace *834 1317*
Westminster *834 0283*
Whitehall *867 1119*
Wigmore Hall *935 2141*
Wyndham's *867 1116*
Young Vic *928 6363*

CINEMAS

Cannon Haymarket
839 1527
Cannon Oxford St *636 0310*
Cannon Panton St *930 0631*
Cannon Piccadilly *437 3561*
Cannon Première *439 4470*
Cannon Shaftesbury Ave
836 8861

Cannon Tott Ct Rd
636 6148
Curzon Mayfair *499 3737*
Curzon Phoenix *240 9661*
Curzon West End *439 4805*
Empire 1, 2 & 3 *437 1234*
ICA *930 3647*
Lumière *836 0691*
Metro *437 0757*
Minema *235 4225*
Moulin *437 1653*

National Film Theatre
928 3232
Odeon Haymarket *839 7697*
Odeon Leicester Sq *930 6111*
Odeon Marble Arch
723 2011
Odeon West End *930 5252*
Plaza 1, 2, 3 & 4 *437 1234*
Prince Charles *437 8181*
Renoir *837 8402*
Warner West End *439 0791*

SHOPS

Aquascutum *734 6090*
Army & Navy *834 1234*
Asprey *493 6767*
Austin Reed *734 6789*
BHS (Oxford St) *629 2011*
C & A *629 7272*
Cartier *493 6962*
Christies *839 9060*
Conran Shop *589 7401*
Covent Garden Market
836 9137
Debenhams *580 3000*
Design Centre *839 8000*
Dickins & Jones *734 7070*
Fenwick *629 9161*
Fortnum & Mason *734 8040*
Foyles *437 5660*
General Trading Company
730 0411
Habitat (King's Rd)
351 1211

Habitat (Tott Ct Rd)
631 3880
Hamleys *734 3161*
Harrods *730 1234*
Harvey Nichols *235 5000*
Hatchard's *437 3924*
Heal's *636 1666*
HMV *631 3423*
House of Fraser (Ken High
St) *937 5432*
House of Fraser (Oxford St)
629 8800
Jaeger *734 8211*
John Lewis *629 7711*
Laura Ashley (Regent St)
437 9760
Laura Ashley (Sloane St)
235 9728
Liberty *734 1234*
Lillywhites *930 3181*
London Pavilion *437 1838*
Maples *387 7000*
Marks & Spencer (Marble
Arch) *935 7954*

Marks & Spencer (Oxford
St) *437 7722*
Marks & Spencer (Ken High
St) *938 3711*
Mothercare *629 6621*
Next (Ken High St)
937 0498
Next (Regent St) *434 2515*
Peter Jones *730 3434*
Plaza on Oxford St
436 4425
Reject Shop *352 2750*
Selfridges *629 1234*
Simpson *734 2002*
Sotheby's *493 8080*
Top Shop *636 7700*
Tower Records *439 2500*
Trocadero *439 1791*
Victoria Place Shopping
Centre *931 8811*
Virgin Megastore *631 1234*

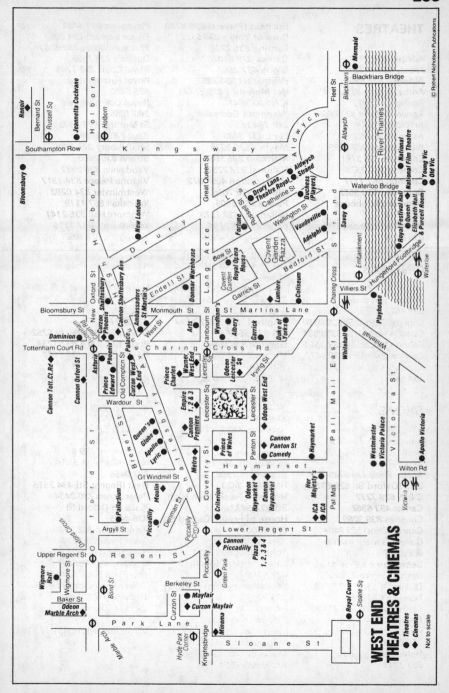

© Robert Nicholson Publications

WEST END THEATRES & CINEMAS

● Theatres
◆ Cinemas

Not to scale

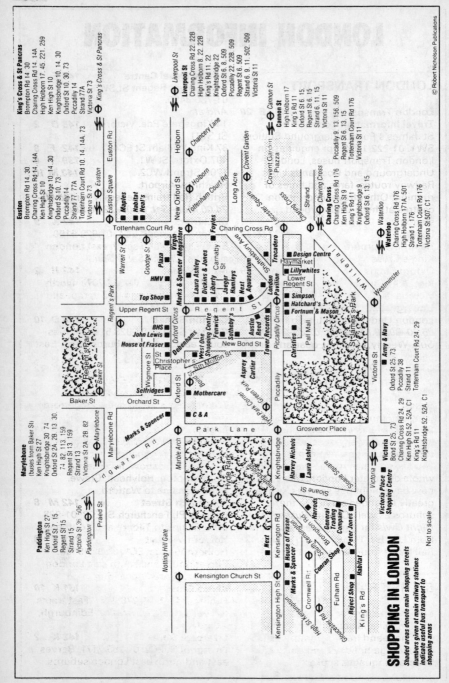

LONDON INFORMATION

LONDON TRANSPORT

London Transport   *140 E 20*
Travel Information Centre
St James's Park Underground Station
SW1. 01-222 1234. For enquiries on
London Transport buses, London
Underground and Docklands Light
Railway routes, fares and times of
running. Other travel information
centres at these Underground
stations:

Euston   *132 D 13*
Heathrow Airport
King's Cross   *132 K 10*
Oxford Circus   *139 Z 5*
Piccadilly Circus   *140 E 10*
Victoria   *147 Z 3*

Underground
London Underground tube trains run
*05.30–00.15 Mon–Sat, 07.30–23.30
Sun.* Weekly, monthly, quarterly or
annual Travelcards provide
considerable savings. Travelcards can
be used on both the Underground and
buses.

Buses
London Transport buses run *06.00–
24.00 Mon–Sat, 07.30–23.00 Sun.* They
tend to be slower, especially in the
rush hours, but more pleasant and
you see so much more. They cover the
whole of Greater London. Many routes
now have night bus services, with a
greatly extended service to the
suburbs as well. Consult *Buses for
Night Owls* for night buses, available
from London Transport and British
Rail travel information centres.

BRITISH RAIL

Booking centres for rail travel in
Britain, rail and sea journeys to the
Continent and Ireland, motorail and
rail package holidays and tours.
Several languages spoken.

British Travel Centre   *140 E 12*
4–12 Lower Regent St SW1.
01-730 3400.
And at:
14 Kingsgate Pde, Victoria   *148 D 2*
St SW1.
87 King William St EC4.   *142 F 8*
407 Oxford St W1.   *139 T 6*
170b Strand WC2.   *140 M 10*
Heathrow Airport.
British Rail trains generally run *06.00–
24.00 Mon–Sat, 07.00–22.30 Sun.*
Blackfriars   *141 X 9*
Queen Victoria St EC4. 01-928 5100.
Serves south and south east London
suburbs. *Closed Sat & Sun.*
Broad Street   *142 H 2*
Liverpool St EC2. 01-387 7070. North
London line to Richmond and peak
hour trains to Watford.
Cannon Street   *142 D 10*
Cannon St EC4. 01-928 5100. Serves
south east London suburbs, Kent, East
Sussex. *Closed Sat & Sun.*
Charing Cross   *140 K 12*
Strand WC2. 01-928 5100. Serves
south east London suburbs, Kent.
Trains from here go over Hungerford
Bridge.
Euston   *132 D 13*
Euston Rd NW1. 01-387 7070. Fast
trains to Birmingham, Manchester,
Liverpool, Glasgow, Inverness,
Northampton, Holyhead, Crewe.
Suburban line to Watford.
Fenchurch Street   *142 M 8*
Railway Pl, Fenchurch St EC3. 01-928
5100. Trains to Tilbury and Southend.
Holborn Viaduct   *141 U 3*
Holborn Viaduct EC1. 01-928 5100.
Serves south and south east London
suburbs. *Closed Sat & Sun.*
King's Cross   *131 K 10*
Euston Rd N1. 01-278 2477. Fast trains
to Leeds, York, Newcastle, Edinburgh,
Aberdeen.
Liverpool Street   *142 K 2*
Liverpool St EC2. 01-283 7171. Serves
east and north east London suburbs.

Fast trains to Cambridge, Colchester,
Norwich, Harwich Docks.

London Bridge   *142 H 14*
Borough High St SE1. 01-928 5100.
Serves south and south east London
suburbs, Kent, Sussex, East Surrey.

Marylebone   *131 N 19*
Boston Pl NW1. 01-387 7070.
Suburban lines to Amersham, High
Wycombe, Banbury, Aylesbury.

Moorgate   *142 E   1*
Moorgate EC2. 01-278 2477. Suburban
services to Welwyn Garden City,
Hertford.

Paddington   *138 E   5*
Praed St W2. 01-262 6767. Fast trains
to Bath, Bristol, Cardiff, Hereford,
Swansea, Reading, Swindon, Devon,
Cornwall.

St Pancras   *132 J 11*
Euston Rd NW1. Information 01-387
7070. Fast trains to Nottingham,
Leicester, Sheffield, Derby. Suburban
services to Luton, Bedford, St Albans.

Victoria   *147 Y   5*
Terminus Pl SW1. 01-928 5100. Serves
south and south east London suburbs,
Kent, Sussex, East Surrey. Fast trains
to Brighton. 'Gatwick Express' *every
15 mins from 05.30–22.00, every 30
mins from 22.00–24.00, every hour
from 24.00–05.30.*

Waterloo   *141 S 17*
York Rd SE1. Information 01-928 5100.
Serves south west London suburbs,
west Surrey, Hampshire, Dorset. Fast
trains to Portsmouth, Southampton,
Bournemouth. There is also a separate
station, Waterloo East, where all trains
from Charing Cross stop.

THAMESLINE RIVERBUS

Information 01-987 0311. Waterjet
propelled catamaran service between
Chelsea Harbour Pier and Greenland
Pier with seven stops in between,
including Charing Cross Pier, South
Bank Festival Pier, Swan Lane Pier for
the City, and London Bridge Pier for
Hay's Galleria. Boats run *Mon–Fri* at
15-minute intervals between *07.00–
10.00* and *16.00–19.00*; and at 30-

minute intervals between *10.00–16.00*
and *19.00–22.00*. On *Sat & Sun* boats
run every 30 minutes between *10.00–
18.00.*

COACHES

Green Line Coaches
Enquiries: 01-668 7261. These are
express buses run by the London
Country Bus company. Most run from
central London to outlying areas,
departing from Eccleston Bridge,
Victoria or Regent Street. There is a
special service, route 747, from
Gatwick to Heathrow and Luton
airports. Services generally run every
hour. Green Line can be used for
travel within central London but the
bus stops are quite far apart and the
fares are high for short journeys.

Victoria Coach Station   *147 Z   3*
164 Buckingham Palace Rd SW1.
01-730 0202. The main provincial
coach companies operate from here,
travelling all over Britain and the
Continent. Booking necessary.

AIRPORTS

London City Airport   *78 E   2*
Gate 20, King George V Dock,
Connaught Rd E16. 01-474 5555.

London Gatwick Airport
Horley, Surrey. (0293) 28822 or 01-668
4211.

London Heathrow Airport
Hounslow, Middx. 01-759 4321.

London Stansted Airport
Stansted, Essex. (0279) 502380.

Luton Airport
Luton, Beds. (0582) 405100.

Southend Airport
Southend-on-Sea, Essex. (0702)
340201.

AIRPORT BUS SERVICES

London Regional Transport
A1 Victoria – Marble Arch – Heathrow
A2 Euston – Earl's Court – Heathrow

Flightline
747 London – Gatwick, Heathrow
757 Victoria – Luton
767 Victoria – Heathrow
777 Victoria – Gatwick

EXCHANGE FACILITIES

Chequepoint Bureaux de Change
222 Earl's Court Rd SW5.   **145 W 7**
01-370 3238. *Open 7 days, 24hrs.*
47 Old Brompton Rd SW7.   **146 G 6**
01-584 7214. *Open 7 days 08.30–23.00.*
548 Oxford St W1   **139 R 7**
(Marble Arch). 01-723 2646. *Open 7 days, 24hrs.*
58 Queensway W2. 01-229   **137 Z 9**
4268. *Open 7 days, 24hrs.*
78 Strand WC2. 01-836 5292.   **140 K 11**
Open 7 days 08.30–24.00.

Eurochange Bureaux
Knightsbridge Underground   **139 P 18**
Station SW3. 01-589 1891.
Open 7 days 08.00–19.00.
Paddington Underground   **138 F 6**
Station, 179 Praed St W2.
01-258 0442. *Open 7 days 08.00–21.00.*
Tottenham Court Rd   **140 G 4**
Underground Station W1. 01-734 0279.
Open 7 days 08.00–22.00.

Thomas Cook
104 Kensington High St W8.   **137 V 20**
01-937 3673. *Open 09.00–17.30 Mon–Fri, 09.30–17.00 Sat.*
Marks & Spencer   **139 S 7**
(Marble Arch), 458 Oxford St W1.
01-935 7954. *Open 09.00–20.00 Mon–Fri, 09.00–18.00 Sat.*
Selfridges, 400 Oxford St   **139 U 6**
W1. 01-629 1234. *Open 09.30–18.00 Mon–Sat (to 20.00 Thur).*
Victoria Station SW1.   **147 Z 3**
01-828 4422. *Open 7 days 07.45–22.00.*

LOST OR STOLEN CREDIT CARDS

During office hours the loss or theft of a credit card can be reported to any branch of the credit card company.

Outside office hours contact the *24hr* number listed and confirm by letter within seven days.

Access/Mastercard/Eurocard
Joint Credit Card Company, Access House, 200 Priory Cres, Southend-on-Sea, Essex. (0702) 352211.

American Express
Lost and Stolen Dept, American Express Company, PO Box 68, Edward St, Brighton, East Sussex. (0273) 69355 or 01-222 9633 *(until 18.00).*

Barclaycard/Visa
Barclaycard Centre, Dept G, Northampton. (0604) 230230.

Diners Club
Diners Club House, Kingsmead, Farnborough, Hants. (0252) 513500.

LOST PROPERTY

British Rail
Contact the final destination of the train on which you were travelling. They will be able to tell you if your lost property has been recovered and where it has been taken to.

London Transport   **131 R 19**
Lost Property Office, 200 Baker St W1 (next to Baker Street Underground Station). Call in person, send someone with written authority or apply by letter. No telephone enquiries. *Open 09.30–17.30 Mon–Fri.*

Taxis   **133 S 9**
Apply to 15 Penton St N1 or nearest police station.

Lost anywhere else
Apply to the nearest police station.

LATE CHEMISTS

Bliss Chemist   **139 P 7**
5 Marble Arch W1. 01-723 6116. *Open 09.00–24.00 Mon–Sun.*
Also at 50–56 Willesden   **129 R 2**
Lane NW6. 01-624 8000. *Open 09.00–02.00 Mon–Sun.*

Boots   **140 D 10**
Piccadilly Circus W1. 01-734 6126. *Open 08.00–20.00 Mon–Sat.*

Underwoods　　　　　**140 F　9**
62 Shaftesbury Ave W1. 01-434 3647.
Open 09.00–23.00 Mon–Sat, 11.00–
22.00 Sun.

Warman Freed　　　　　**45 W　3**
45 Golders Green Rd NW11. 01-455
4351. *Open 08.00–24.00 daily*
throughout year.

LATE POST

Post Office　　　　　　**140 J　11**
St Martin's Pl, Trafalgar Sq WC2.
01-930 9580. *Open 08.00 (08.30 Fri)–*
20.00 Mon–Sat. Closed Sun.

24-HOUR CASUALTY

In an emergency dial 999 and ask for
an ambulance, or make your own way
to one of the casualty departments
listed below. If at all practicable,
contact your doctor as casualty
hospitals are for serious emergencies
only.

Barnet General Hospital　　**4 B　14**
Wellhouse Lane, Barnet, Herts. 01-440
5111.

Chase Farm Hospital　　　**7 T　4**
The Ridgeway, Enfield, Middx. 01-366
6600.

Ealing General Hospital　　**71 P　4**
Uxbridge Rd, Southall, Middx. 01-574
2444.

Greenwich District Hospital　**77 O　14**
Vanbrugh Hill SE10. 01-858 8141.

Guy's Hospital　　　　　**142 F　16**
St Thomas St SE1. 01-407 7600.

Hammersmith Hospital　　**62 H　17**
150 Du Cane Rd W12. 01-743 2030.

Hillingdon Hospital
Pield Heath Rd, Hillingdon, Middx.
(0895) 38282.

Kingston Hospital　　　　**103 R　20**
Galsworthy Rd, Kingston-upon-
Thames, Surrey. 01-546 7711.

Mayday Hospital　　　　**122 H　13**
Mayday Road, Thornton Heath,
Surrey. 01-684 6999.

New Charing Cross Hospital　144 F　12
Fulham Palace Rd W6. 01-748 2040.

Newham General Hospital　　**65 Y　11**
Glen Road E13. 01-476 1400.

Northwick Park Hospital　　**41 Y　1**
Watford Rd, Harrow, Middx. 01-864
5311.

Queen Mary's Hospital　　**86 G　16**
Roehampton Lane SW15. 01-789 6611.

Queen Mary's Hospital　　**115 N　14**
Frognal Ave, Sidcup, Kent. 01-302
2678.

Royal Free Hospital　　　**46 H　14**
Pond St NW3. 01-794 0500.

St Bartholomew's Hospital　**141 X　2**
West Smithfield EC1. 01-601 8888.

St George's Hospital　　　**106 G　12**
Blackshaw Rd SW17. 01-672 1255.

St Mary's Hospital　　　　**138 F　6**
Praed St W2. 01-725 6666.

St Stephen's Hospital　　**146 C　15**
369 Fulham Rd SW10. 01-352 8161.

St Thomas's Hospital　　　**141 N　20**
Lambeth Palace Rd SE1. 01-928 9292.

University College Hospital　**132 D　17**
Gower St WC1. 01-387 9300.

Westminster Hospital　　　**148 J　4**
Dean Ryle St, Horseferry Rd SW1.
01-828 9811.

Whipps Cross Hospital　　**33 X　17**
Whipps Cross Rd E11. 01-539 5522.

Medical Express　　　　**139 X　5**
Chapel Place, Oxford St W1. 01-499
1991. Emergency medical centre, no
appointment needed for minor
accident treatment. Not part of the
National Health Service – you will be
charged.

TAXIS

If you can't hail a black cab in the
street, or find one at a taxi rank
contact one of the following *24hr* taxi
services:

Computercab: 01-286 0286.
Datacab: 01-727 7200.
Dial A Cab: 01-253 5000.
Radio Taxicabs: 01-272 0272.

Lady Cabs　　　　　　**49 N　11**
150 Green Lanes N16. 01-254 3501.
Late night cabs for women, driven by
women. *Open to 24.30 Mon–Thur, to*
01.00 Fri, to 02.00 Sat, to 24.00 Sun.